FERHENGA BIRÛSKÎ
Kurmanji – English
Dictionary

Volume Two
M - Z

I dedicate this book to my dear friends
Birûsk Tugan and Zoya Nazari and Ramin, Zanyar and Luqman and to all our friends who left us too soon.
Ez vê pirtûkê dikim diyarî bo hevalên xwe
Birûsk Tûẍan û Zoya Nazarî û her wisa bo Ramîn, Zanyar û Luqman yên ku zû xatira xwe ji me xwest.

FERHENGA BIRÛSKÎ

Kurmanji - English
Dictionary
Volume Two
M-Z

Compiled by

Michael L. CHYET

LANGUAGE SERIES

TRANSNATIONAL PRESS LONDON
2020

FERHENGA BIRÛSKÎ

Kurmanji – English Dictionary

Volume Two M-Z

Compiled by Michael L. CHYET

[Language Series: 2]

First Published in 2020 by TRANSNATIONAL PRESS LONDON in the United Kingdom, 12 Ridgeway Gardens, London, N6 5XR, UK.

www.tplondon.com

ISBN: 978-1-912997-07-7 (paperback)

ISBN: 978-1-912997-08-4 (hardcover)

Cover Image and Design: Secor & Ahmad and Gizem Çakır

www.tplondon.com

M م

ma مـا *intrg. particle (signals questions)*: **•Lawo *ma* tu çi dikî, tu li ku yî, *ma* tu qet li me napirsî. *Ma* tu nabêjî ev diya min heye, tuneye, wele te em ji bîr ve kirin!** (LC, 39) Son, what are you up to, where are you, you never ask about us. Don't you ever say [=think] 'How's that mother of mine doing?' By God, you've forgotten all about us! **•*Ma* ez jê ditirsim?** (BX, 268) Am I supposed to be afraid of him? **•*Ma* kî naxwaze serbest û azad bijî?** (CT, 214) Who doesn't want to live free and liberated? **•"--*Ma* tiştekî weha tu çawa ji min dipêy? Ez naxwazim nînoga xortekî jî li kevirekî bikeve"** (HMp, 16 = Epl, 102) How can you expect such a thing from me? I don't want even the fingernail of a young man to fall on a rock [=to be hurt] **•*Ma* zinar ji cihê xwe radibe û tê bajêr?** (RD, 145) *[Since when]* do boulders get up from their places and come to town? {also: <ma> مـا (HH)} [BX/CT/A/IFb/B/HH/SK/GF/TF] <gelo; qey>

Macarî ماجارى *adj.* Hungarian. {also: Mecarî (Wkt)} {syn: Hungarî} Sor Meceřî مەجەڕى [ZF3/SS/CS//Wkt]

maç' I مـاچ *f./m.(SK)* **(-a/;-ê/).** kiss: **-maç' kirin/maçî kirin** (L) to kiss {syn: hatin řûyê fk-ê; paç' kirin; řamûsan}: **•Des[t] di sukirê werand ku *dê maçî ket*** (M-Ak #534, 242) He put his arm around 'her' neck, *intending to kiss* 'her' **•Ênîya hespê *maçî kir*** (L) He kissed the horse's forehead **•Hingo 'adet kirîye, kesê destê merĥemetê bi serê hingoda bînît dê leqekî li wî destî den, we kesê pîyê bi-gû di serê hingo bihusût mirç-mirç *dê* wî pê *maç ken*** (SK 57:661) If anyone lays a compassionate hand upon your head you have been accustomed to bite that hand, and if anyone wipes a dung-covered foot on your face then *you kiss* that foot noisily. {also: maçî (L); maç'û (Z-2); [maç مـاچ/macíp مـاچـپ] (JJ); <maç مـاچ /maçêk مـاچـيك> (HH)} {syn: paç' I; řamûsan} Cf. P māč kardan ماچ کردن; Sor maç kirdin ماچ کِردِن [L/K(s)/A/JB3/IFb/B/JJ/HH/SK/GF/TF]

maç II ماچ (Bw) = spades (in card games). See **maçe**.

maç' III مـاچ *f.* **(-a;-ê).** 1) {syn: destedû} handle of plow: **•Mêrik řabû *maç'a* cot girt** (HCK-5, #41, 227) The man took hold of the plow *handle*; 2) rudder, helm, steering wheel. {also: manc (GGC)} < Arm mač մաճ < P āmāj آمـاج = 'ploughshare' [HCK/K/B/Tsab/Nbh 124:32//GGC] <cot>

maça مـاچـا (IFb/HH) = spades *(in card games)*. See **maçe**.

maç•e ماچه *f.* **(;•ê).** spades *(suit in playing cards)*: **•sê *maçê*** (Bw) 3 *of spades*. {also: maç II (Bw); maça (IFb); <maça> مـاچـا (Hej)} {syn: qeremaç} cf. T maça = 'spades (in cards)' [Bw//Wn//IFb/Hej]

maçî ماچى (L) = kiss. See **maç' I**.

maç'û ماچوو (Z-2) = kiss. See **maç' I**.

Mad ماد (A/GF) = Mede. See **Med**.

madak ماداك (IF/HH) = female buffalo. See **medek**.

madam مـادام *conj.* as long as, so long as, since *(reason)*: **•*Madam* jin tabiê mêr e, lazim e go tuê me bi mêrê me re bişînî** (L) *Since* woman is the follower of man, you must send us with our men. Cf. P mādām مـادام --> T madem [ki] < Ar mā dāma ما دام = 'so long as it lasts' [L/K]

made ماده (XF/K) = appetite. See **me'de**.

madek مادەك (K/JJ) = female buffalo. See **medek**.

maf مـاف *m.* **(-ê;).** right *(as opposed to privilege or obligation)*: **•Elbet ne tenê *mafê* Kurdan, îro li vî welatî kî daxwaza *mafê* xwe dike, lazim e herkes bigihêje *mafê* xwe** (Nbh 129:4) Not only the Kurds, today in this country whoever seeks his *rights*, everyone should obtain his *rights*. {syn: destûr [2]; ĥed [2]; heq} Cf. P mu'āf مـعـاف & T muaf = 'exempt(ed), free, excused (from)', fr. Ar mu'āfá[n] معافى & mu'fá[n] معفى, Clq Iq Ar ma'fī مـعـفـي = 'exempt(ed), free, excused' & Clq Eg Ar mu'āf مـعـاف = 'exempted from military service' [Ber/A/JB3/IFb/ZF/Tsab]

mafdar مـافـدار *adj.* entitled (to): **•Tu ji vir heta mala xwedê *mafdar* î ku wisa bihizirî. Lê ev *mafdar-bûna* te nayê wê wateyî** [sic] **ku ev tiştên ku ez**

niha behsê dikim, ne rast bin (Mîr Qasimlo. Dilya & Zalar, 180) You are *entitled* from here until God's house [i.e., as much as you wish] to think that way. But this *entitledness* of yours does not mean that the things I am now discussing are not correct. *The use of this word as a translation of T haklı = 'right, correct' is best replaced by **Xebera te ye** or **Tu rast dibêjî**.* [M.Qasimlo/RZ/SS]

mafûr ماڤوور (Wkt) = carpet. See **mehfûr**.

mahfûr ماهفوور (IFb) = carpet. See **mehfûr**.

mahî ماهى (FS) = female pig. See **mahû**.

mahîv ماهيڤ (FS) = female pig. See **mahû**.

mahlû ماهلوو (Kmc-6/IFb) = wooden harrow. See **mehlî I**.

mahne ماهنه (A/IFb) = meaning; reason. See **me'na**.

mahu ماهو (A) = female pig. See **mahû**.

mahû ماهوو *f.* **(-ya;-yê).** sow, female pig. {also: mahî (FS); mahîv (FS-2); mahu (A); mawî (AA/AD/GF-2); mehû (GF); <mahû> ماهوو (HH)} {syn: beraza mê} **ma-**: [Pok. 3. mā- 694.] 'mother' (cf. P māda ماده = 'female') + **-hû**: [Pok. sū̆-s, suu̯-ós 1038.] 'pig, swine, sow: O Ir hū-: Mid P xūg (M3); P xūk خوک; *also* Lat sūs, suis & Gr hys ὗς, hyos ὑός; Eng sow & *with* ***no**-derivative* swine; Germ Schwein; Rus svin'ia свинья; = Sor malos مالۆس [Qrj/IFb/HH/ZF3//A//GF//FS//AA/AD]

mak ماک *f.* **(-a;-ê).** 1) {syn: dê I} mother, *particularly of animals*: •**Kar ku mezin dibin, *maka* wan şîret dike** (J) When the kids (=young goats) grow up, their *mother* advises them; **-zarê berê maka** (EP-7) nursing infants [lit. 'children in front of mothers']: •**Nezera *zar̄ê* wane *berê maka* usanin, be'rêda ç'e'vê masî dertîne** (EP-7) The looks of their *nursing children* are such [that] they make the eyes of fish in the sea come (=pop) out; 2) {syn: dêl I; mê} female *(of animals)*; mature female (A/IF); 3) source, origin (JJ). {also: mang; [mak] ماک (JJ); <mak> ماک (HH)} [Pok. 3. mā- 694. & māter- 700.] 'mother': Skt mātár-; Av & OP mātar- (Kent); Mid P mād/mādar (M3); P mādar مادر; Sor ma- ما = 'female, she-' & mak ماک = 'mother' [J/K/A/JB3/IF/B/JJ/HH] <dê I>

Makedonî ماکەدۆنی *adj.* Macedonian. {also: Masêdonî (BF)} [Wkt/ZF3//BF]

mak'er ماکەر *f.* **(-a;-ê).** she-ass, female donkey: •**Meselekî meşhûr e li- naw me Kurdan. Dibêjin ew kesê jinê dixazît *maker* e, ew kesê jinê didet nêreker e, belê paşî birinê şol ber-'eks e** (SK 42:411) It is a well-known proverb among us Kurds. They say that the person who asks for a woman is a *she-donkey* and the one who gives her is a he-ass, but after she has been taken the case is reversed. {also: manker (IFb-2); mêker (GF-2); [ma-ker] ماكر (JJ); <maker> ماكر (HH)} {syn: k'era mê; ≠k'erê nêr; ≠nêrek'er} <mak/mê = 'female' + k'er = 'donkey'; Sor maker ماکەر; Hau mahere *f.* (M4) [BX/K(s)/A/JB3/IFb/JJ/HH/SK/GF/TF] <k'er III; guhdirêj>

makîn•e ماكينه *f.* **(•a;).** machine: **-makîna cilşuştinê** (LC) washing machine, washer: •**Li vî welatê gawiran cilşuştin jî bi serê xwe derdekî giran e … Dermanê şuştinê û yê nermkirinê bigrin herin cilşoyê bavêjin *makîna cilşuştinê*, piştî saetekê derxin … paşê bavêjin *makîna zuhakirinê*, paşê derxin qat kin, dûz kin û bînin mal** (LC, 12) In this country of infidels, doing laundry is a big headache … Take the detergent and fabric softener and go to the laundromat, throw [the laundry] into *the washing machine*, take it out an hour later … then throw it in *the dryer*, then take it out, fold it, flatten it, and bring it home; **-makîna zuhakirinê** (LC) (clothes) dryer. < It macchina [LC/K/IFb/GF/TF/OK/AD]

mal I مال *f.* **(-a;-ê).** 1) {syn: xanî} home, house, household: •**Çû *mala* hakim** (L) He went to the king's *house*; **-li mal** = at home: •**Ezê *li mal* bim** (L) I'll be/stay *at home*; **-mal û ḧal** (Z-1) household responsibilities: •[After the death of Mem & Zin] **Destê P'erî-xatûnê ji *mal û ḧala* sar bûbû** (Z-1) Peri Khatun lost interest [lit. 'her hand got cold from'] her *household duties* •**Min *mal û ḧalê* xwe, bavê xwe t'erkandye** (EP-7) I have left my *home* and father (=family); **-mala cihûd** (Z-1) "dog house" [lit. 'Jew's house']: •**Memê, malxirab, min tu birî, ha birî,/ Min tu *mala cihûd* hasê kirî** (Z-1) Mem, you wretch, I've beaten you [at chess],/ I've chased you into the *Jew's house*; 2) {syn: k'ulfet; malbat} family: **-Xwedê mala te ava ke** = May God make your household/family prosper *[a common blessing]*; **-Xwedê mala te xerab ke** = May God ruin your household/family [a common curse]; 3) *[adv.]* home, homeward {also: malê}: •**Ez diçim *mal[ê]*** = I'm going *home* •**Tarî bû, em diçin *malê*** (AB) It's gotten dark, we are going *home*. {also: [mal] مال (JJ); <mal> مال (HH)} Sor mał ماڵ [BX/K/A/JB3/

IF/B/JJ/HH]

mal II مـــــال *m.* **(-ê; mêl, vî malî).** goods, property; money; cattle: **•Ezê vê qesrê û *malê* tê de timam teslîmê te bikim** (L) I will completely hand over to you this palace and *the property* in it; **-mal xwarin** (JR) to appropriate, get hold of money: **•Ew dixweze perê min bixwe** (K) He wants to appropriate my money **•[Meger Memedî ew mal û estir birine Tiflîsê û firotine û zaf diraf înaye û bi ĥîle ev şola digel min kirîye ku *ewî malî* bi tenê *bixwit*]** (JR) It turns out that Memed took the goods and mules to Tiflis and sold them, and brought back a lot of money, and by a ruse he did this thing to me, so that he *could have [lit. 'eat'] all the money* for himself. {also: [mal] مـــــال (JJ); <mal> مـال (HH)} {syn: eşya} < Ar māl مـال [BX/K/A/JB3/IF/B/JJ/HH] <sermaye>

malan مالان (Ad) = to sweep. See **maliştin**.

malava مـــالاڤـا *adj.* 1) {≠malxerab} happy, prosperous (K); one whose household prospers {related to the expression **Xwedê mala te ava ke** = May God make your household/family prosper} [Cf. Ar ʻammār عمّار]: **•*Malava*, tuê çî min bi xwî?** (J) *My dear man*, why do you want to [lit. 'will you'] eat me?; 2) bravo! (BX); Come on! (IF). < mal = 'house' + ava = 'built up' [BX/K/A/IF/ZF3]

malbat مالبات *f.* **(-a;-ê).** 1) {syn: k'ulfet; mal I} family, line, lineage: **•Di *malbata* me de, hetta di nav eşîra me de--yên ku bi destê hukmatê hatine kuştin û yên ku bi qotikê mirine ne tê de--kes bi ciwanî nemirîye** (LC, 10) In our *family*, even in our tribe--except for those who were killed by the [Turkish] government or who died from plague--no one has died in his youth **•Li gor *malbata* min, çêtir e ku mirov xwe Tirk bihesibîne** (Wlt 1:35, 16) According to my *family*, it is better that one consider oneself a Turk; 2) [*m.*] wealthy landlord (B). {also: Cf. [mal-bati] مـالـبـاتـى (JJ) = 'cousins, relatives who constitute an extended family'} [Ber/Wlt/K/A/JB3/IFb/B/GF/TF/RZ] <azbat>

maldar مـالـدار *adj.* 1) {syn: dewlemend; dewletî; heyî; xurt [4]} rich, wealthy; 2) [*m.*] rich person. {also: [mal-dar] مـــالـــدار (JJ); <maldar> مـــالـــدار (HH)} {maldarî} [HB/K/A/B/JJ/HH/FS]

maldarî مـــالـــدارى *f.* **(-ya;-yê).** wealth, riches. {syn: dewlemendî; malhebûn} [K/A/JB3/IF/B/ZF3] <maldar>

maldoxîn مـــالـــدۆخـــيـــن *f.* **(-a;-ê).** drawstring "canal," tunnel or seam for the drawstring at the waistline of a pair of shalvar. {syn: pizî I} [Bw/Hk/Kmc-#4763/ZF3/FS] <doxîn>

malhebûn مـالـهـهـبـوون *f.* **(;-ê).** wealth, riches, property. {also: mal û hebûn (Z-1)} {syn: dewlemendî; maldarî} [K/A/B/ZF3] <mal II>

malik مـــالـــك *f.* **(-a;-ê).** 1) stanza, strophe: **•*Malikek* ji dû-sê-çar r̄êzkan çêdibît** (Bw) *A stanza* is made up of two, three, or four lines; 2) square, box, cell *(fig. on a printed page, in an application, chessboard, & lit. in a honeycomb, etc.)*: **-malka r̄eş** (Btm) dark square (in chess); **-malka spî** (Btm) light square (in chess). <dim. of **mal I**. cf. range of meanings of Ar bayt = 'house, room, box, verse' [Bw/K(s)/IFb/GF/TF/OK/ZF/Btm] <nîvmalik; r̄êzik; sebeqe>

malim مـالـم *m.* **().** rabbi: **•Cû çûn, şîr dîtin** [sic]**, înane** [sic] **kinîştê nik *malim* Zexeriya** (SK 26:235) The Jews went, found the sword, and brought it to *Rabbi* Zachariah at the synagogue. {also: [mãlem (giú)] مـــعـــلـــم (JJ); <malim> مـــالـــم (Hej)} < Ar muʻallim معلّم = 'teacher'; Jewish NENA malim = 'Jewish religious functionary' (Garbell) & mu'allim = 'schoolmaster' (Brauer) [SK/JJ/Hej] <kinîşt I>

maliştin مـــالـشـتـن *vt.* **(-mal-).** 1) {syn: gêzî kirin; r̄êç kirin [r̄êç I]} to sweep; 2) to clean, wipe: **•Wextê mîr di keviya çemê mezin de hate kuştin Heyzebûn ewçend giriya bû ko jinmîr bi xwe hêstirên xwe *dimaliştin* û li ber dilê cêriyê dida** (Rnh 3:23, 5) When the emir was killed on the banks of the big river, Heyzebûn cried so much that the emir's wife herself *wiped away* her own tears and consoled the servant girl. {also: malan (Ad); malîn (K[s]/IF/A/M); maltin; maştin (M-2); miştin (-mal-) (K[s]/IF/A/JJ); [michtin] مشتن (JJ); <maliştin مـالـشـتـن/miştin مشتن (dimale) (دمـالـه)> (HH)} [Pok. mĕlĝ- (or meləĝ-?) 722.] 'to rub off, wipe': Skt mṛjáti etc. = 'wipes, rubs off, cleans'; O Ir *mṛd-/z- (Tsb 37): Av marəz-/mərəz- = 'to brush up against'; Mid P muštan/mālīdan (māl-) = 'to rub, sweep' (M3); Sor małîn مـاڵـيـن/maştin مـاشـتـن (Muk-2)/marîn مـاريـن (Arb); Hau małay (mał-) *vt.* = 'to rub' [JB3/HH//K(s)/A/IF/M//JJ//Ad] <gêzî>

malî I مـــــالـــــى *f.* **(-ya;).** bunches of branches tied together; **-malîya çolî** (Zeb) do. {also: mehlî II (FS)} [Zeb//FS] <çilo II>

malî II مالى (Kmc-16) = wooden harrow. See **mehlî** I.

malîfet مـــالــيــفــەت (L) = honor; courtesy; skill. See **me'rîfet**.

malîn مالين (K[s]/IF/A/M) = to sweep. See **malîştin**.

malmezin مـالـمـەزِن *f.* **().** noble or aristocratic family: **•mezinê malmezinan** (Ardû, 119) the head of the nobles. [Ardû/CS]

***malok** مـــالـــۆك *m.&f.* **().** one-year-old calf. {syn: k'endik; mozik I} [Krç] <golik>

Maltayî مالتايى *adj.* Maltese. [Wkt/BF/Wkp]

maltin مالتِن = to sweep. See **malîştin**.

mal û hebûn مـــال و هـــەبـــوون (Z-1) = wealth. See **malhebûn**.

malxerab مالخەراب (L/A/IF) = unlucky. See **malxirab**.

malxê مالخێ (B) = master of the house. See **malxwê**.

malxirab مالخِراب *adj.* unlucky, wretched, miserable; one whose house has been ruined {related to the expression **Xwedê mala te xirab ke** = May God ruin your household/family} [Cf. Ar yixrab baytak يـخـرب بـيـتـك]: **•Malxerabo!** (L) You wretch! [malheureux]; **-Malxerab bûn** (IF) To become extinct; **-malxerab kirin** (IF) to make extinct, extirpate. {also: malxerab (L/A/IF); malxirav (Z-1)} {syn: belengaz; bikul; dêran II; r̄eben I; şerpeze; xwelîser I; ≠malava} < mal = 'house' + xerab = 'bad, ruined' {malxirabî} [L/A/IF//K/B]

malxirabî مـــالـــخِـــرابـــى *f.* **(;-yê).** 1) unluckiness, misfortune; 2) ruin, destruction. [K/B] <malxirab>

malxirav مالخِراڤ (Z-1) = unlucky. See **malxirab**.

malxo مـــالـــخـــۆ (SK/JJ) = master of the house. See **malxwê**.

malxu مالخو (OK) = master of the house. See **malxwê**.

malxuê مـــالـــخـــوئـێ (B) = master of the house. See **malxwê**.

malxwe مالخوە (L) = master of the house. See **malxwê**.

malxwê مـــالـــخـــوێ *m.* **(malxweyê [L]/malxê [SK];).** head of the house, master of the house; lord, master, boss: **•Du malxwê di malekê da nabin** (IFb) Two masters in one house cannot be (~ Too many cooks spoil the broth) *[prv.]* **•Malxweyê me Om e, xwelî li serê me kom e** (L-I, #79, 200) Our master is Om, ashes are heaped on our head (=a bad chief is the cause of all misfortune) [prv.]. {also: malxê (B-2); malxo (SK); malxu (OK); malxuê (B-2); malxwe (L); [mal-kho] مـالـخـو (JJ)} {syn: sermiyan} {malxwêtî} [L//K/A/IFb/B/OK//JJ/SK] <mêr; şû; xwedî>

malxwêtî مـــالـــخـــوێـتـــى *f.* **(;-yê).** being master of the house. [K/A/B] <malxwê>

malzarok مالزارۆك *f.* **(;-ê).** uterus, womb: **•Çawa wê zarok çêbibe, malzarok tuneye?** (HYma 33) How will a child be born, [when] there is no womb? {also: malzarûk (Kmc)} mal + zaro[k] [HYma/CS//Kmc] <p'izdan>

malzarûk مالزارووك (Kmc) = uterus. See **malzarok**.

mam مـــام *m.* **(;-ê [B]).** 1) {syn: ap} paternal uncle, father's brother; 2) term of respect for an older man (IF). {also: [mam] مـــعـــم (JJ); <mam> مـــام (HH)} Sor mam مـام; Hau mamo *m.* (M4) [K/A/JB3/IFb/B/ JJ/HH/SK/JB1-A&S/GF/TF/Msr] <amojin; ap; jinap; met; pismam; qîzap; xal I>

mambiz مـامـبِـز *m.&f.* **(;-î/).** deer, gazelle: **•Gurg r̄abû, got e r̄îwî, "Simbêlêt min bel bûne?" R̄îwî got, "Wato bel bûne dê bêjî şaxêt mambizî ne"** (SK 6:68) The wolf got up and said to the fox, "Have my whiskers bristled?" The fox said, "They've bristled so much you'd think they were deer's antlers": **-mambiza mê** (OK) doe, female deer. {also: mamiz (K[s]/A/IFb-2/GF/OK-2)} {syn: ask; gak'ûvî; şivir; xezal I} Sor mamiz مامِز = 'gazelle' [SK/IFb/OK//K(s)/A/GF]

mamik مـــامِـــك *f.* **(-a;-ê).** riddle. {syn: apik (Kg); têderxistinok; tiştik (IFb)} cf. Ar mu'ammá معمّى = 'enigma, (literary) riddle' [K/JB3/IFb/GF/TF/OK/ZF]

mamir مـــامِـــر *f.* **(-a;).** hen, female chicken: **•Bes ev mamirka çendî ku yeksalane bûye jî, biaqiltirîn mamirk bûye** (M. Xalid Sadînî. Çîrokên gelêrî) But although this hen was only one year old, it was the smartest hen **•Carekê nivîştek ji kurka me re çêkir, bîst hêk di bin de bûn, çîçik hemû mamir derketin** (DBgb, 9) Once she made an amulet for our brooding hen, who had 20 eggs under her; the chicks all turned out to be hens. {also: mamirk (CS)} {syn: kurk II; mirîşk} < ma- = 'female' + mir (cf. mirîşk) = 'fowl, bird'; Sor mamir مامِر = 'hen' [DBgb/IFb/FJ/GF/AA//CS]

mamirk مامِرك (CS) = hen. See **mamir**.

mamiz مامِز (K[s]/A/IFb/GF/OK) = deer. See **mambiz**.

mamosta مـامـۆسـتـا *m.&f.* **(/-ya;).** teacher, professor: **•Mamostayên Kurd** (Ber) Kurdish teachers (=teachers who are Kurds). {also: mamoste (JB3)} {syn: dersdar; seyda} < imam = 'religious leader' [or perhaps mam = 'paternal uncle'] + ustād/hosta = 'master (e.g., of a profession)'; Sor mamosta مامۆستا/mamwesta ماموەستا {mamostatî; mamostayî} [K(s)/A/IF//JB3] <dibistan; seyda; xwendek'ar>

mamostatî ماموٚستاتی (K) = teaching. See **mamostayî.**

mamostayî ماموٚستایی *f.* **(;-yê).** teaching (as a profession), professorship. {also: mamostatî (K)} [IF//K] <mamosta>

mamoste ماموٚسته (JB3) = teacher. See **mamosta.**

mamûr مامورر (JB2) = civil servant. See **me'mûr.**

man مان *vi.* **(-mîn-/-mên-).** 1) to remain, stay: **•Qîzik ma cîê xweda** (J) The girl stayed in her place (or bed); **-li bendî *fk-ê* man** (L) to wait for: **•Ez mam li bendî den** (L) I waited for the cauldron [to appear]; 2) to be, become, get: **-'ecêb man** (K/HH)/**mayîn** (B/IF) [+ **ser**] to be[come] amazed, shocked (at): **•Gundî ew yeka ku bihîstin 'ecêv man** (Dz, 385) The villagers were shocked at what they heard; 3) to stay alive, survive: **-mirin û mayîn** (Wlt) life and death, dying and staying alive; 4) {syn: şibîn} to resemble, to look, sound, or smell like [Cf. mîna ...] (SW): **•Min di kitêba "Elf leyle û leyle - Hezar û şevekê" de çîrokeke piçûk dîtiye ko dimîne Mem û Zînê** (SW) In the book "1,001 Nights" I saw a little story that resembles [that of] Mem û Zîn; 5) [+ **ji**] to miss (a train, bus, etc.): **•Erê, piştî nîvsaeta din divê ez herim. An na ez ê ji balafirê bimînim** (KZ, 52) I must go in another half an hour; otherwise I will miss the plane **•Lê heta bajêr jî ez bi tirs bûm, tirsa ku ez ê ji refê hecacan bimînin. Li termînalê tirsa min hate serê min. Ez jê mam** (Lab, 77-78) But all the way to town I was afraid, afraid that I would miss the pilgrims' group. At the terminal my fear came true. I missed it. {also: mandin (BX); mayin (JB1-A-2/JB1-S); mayîn II (K/JB3/IFb-2/B); [màin] ماين (JJ); <man مان/ mayîn ماين (dimîne) (دمينه)> (HH)} [Pok. 5. men- 729.] = 'to remain': O Ir *man- (Tsb 42): Av man- (*pres.* mānaya-); OP ²man- (Kent); P māndan ماندن; Sor man مان (-mên-); SoK min-/mand-, etc. (Fat 356); Za mânännân (Hadank)/ mandene (Mal)/ manenã [mendiş] (Srk); Hau meney (men-) *vi.* (M4); cf. also Lat manere; Gr [peri]menō [περι]μένω [A/IFb/HH/SK/JB1-A/GF/TF//K/JB3/B/JJ//JB1-S] <neman>

mana مانی (K/GF) = meaning; reason. See **me'na.**

manat مانات *m.* **().** ruble (USSR): **•Min o Mîrza Ḧesen hizar o heşt-ṣed o çil manotê ûrosî teslîmi Mela 'Ebdullah kirin** (SK 54:614) Mirza Hasan and I gave one thousand eight hundred and forty roubles to Mullah Abdullah. {also: manot (SK); menat (SK-2)} [Z-922/K/B//SK] <kapêk; şeyî>

manc مانج (GGC) = handle of plow. See **maç' III.**

mandinماندِن (BX) = to remain. See **man.**

mandira ماندِرا (Nbh) = two-story house. See **mendele.**

mane مانه (B/IFb) = meaning; reason. See **me'na.**

manek مانەك (IF) = pedigreed horse. See **me'negî.**

manegî مانەگی (A/IFb/B) = pedigreed horse. See **me'negî.**

mang مانگ = mother; female. See **mak.**

manga مانگا (GF) = cow. See **mange.**

mang•e مانگه *f.* **(•a/•eya;•ê).** 1) {syn: ç'êlek} cow; 2) {syn: medek} female buffalo (JJ/B/HH). {also: manga (GF); [manghé/mangá مانگه/mangaié مانگایه] (JJ); <mang> مانگ (HH)} < man = 'female' + ga = 'bull, ox'; Cf. Southern Tati dialects (all *f.*): Chali & Takestani māgāva; Eshtehardi, Ebrahim-abadi & Sagz-abadi gowa; Xiaraji magowa = 'cow' (Yar-Shater); Sor manga مانگا; Za manga *f.* (Todd); Hau mangawe *f.* (M4) [Bg/Ad/Rh/BX/K/IFb/B/JJ//HH] <ga>

mangêr̄ مانگێڕ *f.* **(-a;-ê).** harrow: **-mangêr̄a dar** (B) wooden harrow {syn: mehlî I}; **-mangêr̄a ḧesin** (B) iron harrow. [Kmc-6/K/IFb/B/GF] <mehlî I>

manî مانی (L) = meaning; reason. See **me'na.**

manker مانکەر (IFb) = female donkey. See **mak'er.**

manot مانۆت (SK) = ruble. See **manat.**

maqes ماقەس (LC) = scissors. See **meqes.**

maqûl ماقوول *adj.* 1) honorable, noble, respectable, distinguished; respected, honored; 2) prudent, reasonable, sensible, wise (K/IFb); 3) *[m.]* elder, wiseman, notable: **•Wextê ko Smail Paşa zanî dîharîya maqûlêt Mizûrîyan kûr in, pîçek di dilê xo da sil bû** (SK 24:222,224) When Ismail Pasha learnt that the present of the Mizuri elders was kids [=young goats], he became a little annoyed in his heart. {also: [mâqoul] معقول (JJ); <maqûl> ماقول (HH)} < Ar ma'qūl معقول = 'reasonable' (√'-q-l عقل = 'to be smart or sensible') {maqûlî; maqûltî} [EP-7/K/IFb/B/JJ/HH/JB1-A/ SK/[TF]/GF/OK]

maqûlî ماقوولی *f.* **(;-yê).** politeness. {also: maqûltî (B-2)} [K/B/[TF]] <maqûl>

maqûltî ماقوولتی (B) = politeness. See **maqûlî.**

mar I مار *m.* **(-ê; mêr, vî marî).** snake: **•Eydî her̄o, serê sibehê lawik dihat cihê mêr û li bilûra xwe dixist** (Dz, #22, 389) So every day, in the morning the boy came to the snake's place and played on his flute **•Ser sîngê Dûmanlûê cîcîna xulexula**

cewikêd avê bû, êd ku mînanî mara jorda dişûlikîn (Ba2:1, 202) On the slope of [Mount] Dumanlu here and there was the babbling of brooks (of water), those which crept from above like snakes •**Wê jî hinek ji wî marî xwar** (HR 3:249) And she ate some of that snake. {also: mer I (F); me'r (B/MK/GF-2); [mar] مـــار (JJ); <mar> مـــار (HH)} Cf. Mid P mār; P mār مـــار; Sor mar مار; Za mar *m.* (Mal); Hau mar *m.* (M4) [K/A/JB3/IFb/JJ/HH/SK/GF/TF/OK//F//B/MK] <jehr; k'ufîn; vedan>

mar II مار (K/JJ/JR/Z-3) = wedding. See **mehir**.

maran مـــاران **().** 1) wooden wheel of plow or wagon; 2) bolt, large iron pin (JJ). {also: [maran] مـــــاران (JJ)} [Kmc/Nbh 124:32/JJ]

margesk مارگەسك (GF) = adder. See **margîsk**.

margîsk مــارگـيـسـك *m.* **().** 1) lizard; 2) adder, viper (JB3/IFb/GF); grass snake (JJ); 3) evil person, villain (IFb). {also: margesk (GF); me'rgîsk (B); [marghisk] مارگسك (JJ)} [Ba2/K/JB3/IFb/JJ/OK/ TF//B//GF]

marî مارى *f.* **(-ya;-yê).** female partridge: •**Kewên kûvî ku dengê marîyê bihîstin** [sic], **bi dilsafî tev hatin li dorê civîyan ... Lê marîya bêbext a ku ew dan kuştin hêj jî dixwend** (AB, 52) When the wild partridges heard the voice of the female partridge, they all naïvely came and gathered around ... But the treacherous female, which had gotten them killed, was still singing. {syn: mêkew} [BX/GF/AD/Kmc] <kew>

marîfet مـــاريـــفـــەت (IFb) = honor; courtesy; skill. See **me'rîfet**.

marîs ماريس (IFb) = pimp; atheist. See **me'rîs**.

marmarok مـــارمـــارۆك (A/IFb/GF/TF) = gecko lizard. See **marmaroşk I**.

marmaroşk I مـارمـارۆشـك *f.* **(-a;).** small lizard, wall gecko, zool. *Gekkonidae*. {also: marmarok (A/IFb/GF-2/TF); [mārejōk] مــــــارجــــــوك (JJ-Lx); <marmaroşk> مـارمـاروشـك (HH)} [Msr/HH/GF//A/IFb/TF//JJ] <kilîfe; mar I>

marmasik مارماسِك (OK) = eel. See **marmasî**.

marmasî مـــارمـــاســـى *m.* **().** 1) eel, zool. *Apodes*. {also: marmasik (OK-2); me'rme'sî (B); <marmasî> مـارمـاصـى (HH)} <mar = 'snake' + masî = fish: P mārmāhī مـارمـاهـى; Sor marmasî مـارمـاسـى; Za marmase *m.* (Mal) [Bw/Zx/K/A/IFb/GF/TF/OK// B//HH] <masî>

marpêç مـــارپـــێـــچ (IFb/GF/OK/Hej/AA) = tube of waterpipe; waterhose. See **marpîç**.

marpîç مارپيچ *m./f.(OK)* **(-ê/ ;).** 1) long, flexible tube of a nargileh [hookah, waterpipe]; 2) {syn: sonde} water hose: **-marpîçê avê** (Dh) do. {also: marpêç (IFb/GF/OK/AA); <marpêç> مـــارپـــێـــچ (Hej)} < P mārpīč مارپيچ = 'spiral, helix, e.g., spiral tube' --> T marpuç = 'tube of nargileh' [Dh/RZ//IFb/GF/OK/Hej/AA]

mart'ak مارتاك (B/HH) = roof beam. See **mertak**.

mas ماس (BK) = yoghurt. See **mast**.

mas•e مـــاســـە *f.* **(•a/•eya;•ê).** table: •**Di dersxanê da çend mase hene?** (DZK) How many tables (=desks) are there in the class(room)? •**Ger we maseyeke vala dît wê wextê hûnê xwe nêzî wê maseyê bikin, lê divê maseya ku we dît bi kêmanî çar kursî li dorê hebin** (LC, 33) If you find an empty table, then you will approach that table, but there must be at least four chairs around the table you found. < T masa; Za mase *m.* (Mal) [Ks/K/JB3/IFb/TF]

Masêdonî مـــاســـێـــدۆنـــى (BF) = Macedonian. See **Makedonî**.

masî مـــاســـى *m./f.(Hk/Zeb)* **(/-ya; /-yê).** 1) fish: •**Erê ew masîyêt tu dihînî d nêr in ya d mê ne?** (X. Salih. Hindek serhatiyên Kurdî, 55) Are those fish that you bring male or female?; **-me'sî girtin** (B) to catch fish; 2) Pisces (astr.). {also: mesî; me'sî (B); [masi] مـــاســـى (JJ); <masî> مـــاصـــى (HH)} [Pok. mad- 694.] = 'moist, wet' (according to this the fish is 'the wet one'): Skt matsya- *m.*; [Hindi/Urdu machhlī مچهلى]; Av masya-; Mid P māhīg (M3); P māhī مـاهـى; Sor masî مـاسـى; Za mase *m.* (Mal/Todd); Hau masawî *f.* (M4) [K/A/JB3/IFb/JJ/GF/TF/OK/ZF//B//HH] <masîgîr; t'ov̄an; xerz; types of fish: *birek; *bizîrî; *cur̄î; *dumbek; *dûşeṯîk; *ferx; gamasî; marmasî; *masîcuhî; *masîpank; *masîşînk; *masîzerk; *mêk; *naqor; *serceleb; *sergolik; *ser̄ing; *simbêlok; *şilavil; *tilpeḧnk; *xîzik; *ze'îmî>

masîgir مـــاســـيـــگـــر (IFb/GF/ZF) = fisherman. See **masîgîr**.

masîgîr ماسيگير *m.* **().** fisherman, angler: •**Masîgir jî her roj diçû ser rûbarî masî digirtin û her roj masîyek bo ḧakimî dibir û li cihê wê her roj zêrek werdigirt** (X.Salih. Hindek serhatiyên Kurdî, 54) And the fisherman went every day to the river and caught fish, and every day he would take a fish to the king, and in return for it every day he would get a gold coin. {also: masîgir (IFb/GF/ZF); masîvan (K-2/JB3/GF-2/TF); me'sîgir (B); [masighir] ماسی گیر (JJ)} {syn: t'ořvan} < masî = 'fish' + gîr- = 'catch': Cf. P māhīgīr ماهیگیر; Sor masîgir ماسیگِر/masîyewan ماسییەوان (K2) [K/A/JJ//IFb/GF/ZF//B//JB3/TF]

masîvan ماسیڤان (K/JB3/GF/TF) = fisherman. See **masîgîr**.

mast ماست *m.* **(-ê; mêst, vî mastî).** yoghurt. {also: mas (BK-2); [mast] ماست (JJ); <mast> ماست (HH)} {syn: qatix (Ag/Wn)} [Pok. maĝ- 696. & 2. māk- 698.] = 'to knead, fashion' *although Pok ascribes the yoghurt words to his* [Pok mad- 694] 'moist, wet' (>masî = 'fish), the idea of **kneading** is paralleled by Turkish yoğurt (<yoğurmak = 'to knead'): Mid P māst = 'curds, sour milk' (M3); P māst ماست; Sor mast ماست = 'curds, yoghurt'; Za mast *m.* = 'yoghurt' (Todd); cf. also Arm macun մածուն = 'yoghurt, fermented milk' [Ad/K/A/IF/B/JJ/HH/BK/Wn/Tkm/Hk/Dy/Rh] <dew I; doxeba; to I>

mastbir ماستبِر (A/IFb) = disease afflicting the hooves of sheep. See **mazber**.

masterk ماسترك (GF) = funnel. See **mastêrk**.

mastêrik ماستێرك (IFb) = funnel. See **mastêrk**.

mastêrk ماستێرك *f.* **(-a;-ê).** funnel. {also: masterk (GF); mastêrik (IFb)} {syn: gewrî [2]; kovik} [Qzl//IFb/GF]

masûle ماسووله (IFb) = spool. See **masûr**.

masûr ماسوور *m.* **(-ê;).** spool *(of thread)*; bobbin. {also: masûle (IFb); masûre (IFb-2); <masûr ماسور/masûlke ماسولکه /masołe ماسوڵه> (Hej)} Sor masûłe ماسووڵه = 'whistle, bobbin' [Krş/Mzg/Kmc-13/GF/Hej//IFb] <dezî; dirûtin>

masûre ماسووره (IFb) = spool. See **masûr**.

maş ماش *f.* **(-a;).** Indian pulse, green gram, mung bean, bot. *Phaseolus aureus, often fed to cattle*: **•Wekî maşa şevî lê hatî** (Bw) He was served musty, old food [last night's mung beans]. {also: maşik I (A/TF); [mach/māsh (Rh)] ماش (JJ); <maşik> ماشك (HH)} <Skt māṣa = 'Phaseolus radiatus' (Laufer, p.585); Mid P māš = 'vetch, pulse' (M3); Sor maş ماش; Hau maşe *m.* (M4) [SK/Bw/K/IFb/JJ/GF/OK//A/HH/TF] <kizin; şolik>

maşe ماشه (K/B/IFb/GF/HH/CS) = tongs, pincers. See **maşik II**.

maşik I ماشِك (A/TF/HH) = mung bean. See **maş**.

maşik II ماشِك *f.* **(-a;-ê).** fire tongs, pincers, pliers: **•Xemê bi maşika agir pêloxek girt danî ser girêka doxînê** (DBgb, 46) Kh. grabbed a firebrand with the fire tongs and placed it on the knot of the drawstring. {also: maşe (K-2/B/IFb/GF/CS); [machik] ماشك (JJ); <maşe> ماشه (HH)} {syn: p'elegirk} Cf. P māše ماشه = 'pincers, tongs' [DBgb/K/TF/JJ/Kmc/ZF//B/IFb/GF/HH/CS]

maşiq ماشِق (B) = in love; lover. See **maşoq**.

maşoq ماشۆق *adj.* 1) [+ ezafeh] in love [with]: **•Ëemû xortê yêrê bûbûn maşoqê wê** (Ba) All the local youths were in love with her **•Zelîxe bûbû maşoqa Ûsib** (Ba) Zelikha fell in love with Joseph; 2) beloved; lover (B). {also: maşiq (B)} < Ar maʿšūq معشوق [Ba/KJ//B]

maşot ماشۆت *f./m.* **(/-ê;-ê/).** little green worms that damage fruit and vegetables (Qzl); caterpillar, larva (TF). {also: <maşot> ماشۆت (Hej)} [Qzl/TF/Hej/Kmc] <kurm>

maştin ماشتِن (M) = to sweep. See **malîştin**.

mat I مات *f.* **().** marble, small glass ball that boys like to play with. {syn: dîndoq; t'ebel; x̄ar III} [Bw/FS]

mat II مات (K/IFb/SK) = silent. See **mit**.

ma tê kirin ما تێ كِرِن (AId) = to interfere; interference. See **maytêkirin**.

mawij ماوِژ (FS) = raisin(s). See **mewîj**.

mawî ماوی (AA/AD/GF) = female pig. See **mahû**.

max ماخ *m.* **().** 1) {syn: garîte; k'êran} beam, girder; cross-beam, transom (K/Hej): **•Bavekî pîr û keça xwe di binê maxên xaniyekî mezin de bi hev re dijîn** (Ardû, 71) An old father and his daughter live together under the beams of a large house; 2) the space between two beams in a ceiling (A/IFb). {also: max̄ (K); <max> ماخ (Hej)} T mağ = 'open space between two crosspieces [atma] in a ceiling, covered with wood or wooden beams [mertek]' (Kars: AC-1); cf. Arm mał մաղ = 'filter, sieve' [Ardû/A/IFb/GF/Hej//K] <mertak; řot>

maxwene ماخوەنە *conj.* as if: **•Maxwene ezê wê xwîna ku ji min rijiya ji bîr bikim?** (HYma 11) As if I can forget the blood which poured out of me? [HYma/TF] <qey; xwedêgiravî>

max̄ ماغ (K) = beam, girder. See **max**.

may مای *f.* **(-a;).** meddling, intereference {*only occurs in the following expressions*}: **•Maya te tê naçît** (Zeb) It's none of your business; **-may tê kirin** (Zeb/Dh) to interfere. See **maytêkirin**. [Zeb/Msl] <maytêker>

mayin ماین (JB1-A&S) = to remain. See **man**.

mayî مایی (TF/Alkan) = the rest of. See **mayîn I**.

mayîn I مایین *adj.* 1) the rest of: **•şixulêd mayîn** (K) the rest of the matters; 2) {syn: din I} other, different: •**cara mayn** (EP-7) once again, another time •**Derê mayîn veke** (K) Open the other door •**Tirşo, şîlan, cat'irî û p'incarêd mayîn** (L) Sorrel, dogrose, marjoram, and other greens. {also: mayî (TF/Alkan); mayn; [màï] مـــاى (JJ)} [Ba2/K/B//TF/Alkan//JJ]

mayîn II مـايـين (K/JB3/IFb/B/JJ/HH) = to remain. See **man**.

mayn ماين = other. See **mayîn I**.

maytêker مای تێ کەر *adj.* nosy, meddlesome. [Zeb/OK]

maytêkirin مای تێ کِرِن *vt.* **().** 1) to interfere, meddle: •**Tu mayê xwe di karê min da neke** (BF) Don't interfere in my affairs; Mind your own business •**Tu bes vê carê jî min xilas ke, ... ne beĥsê te bikem ne mayê xo di te bikem** (X. Saliĥ. Hindek serhatiyên Kurdî, 83) If you just let me go this time, ... I won't speak of you, nor will I meddle in your business; 2) [*f.* **().**] interference. {also: ma tê kirin (AId)} [Zeb/Dh/OK/BF//AId]

maz I مـاز *m.* **().** adult (or old) farm animal: three-year old ram (ZF3); four-year old billy goat (FS); five-year old ram (G/FD): •**Nêrîyê çar salî dibêjnê *maz*, û yê pênc dibêjnê qert** (FS) A four-year old billy goat they call '*maz*', and a five-year old they call 'qert'; -**çêleka maz** (ZF3) old cow. [FS/ZF3/G/FD] <nêrî I; beran; qert>

maz II ماز = oak tree. See **mazî**.

mazber مـــازبـــر **().** disease afflicting the hooves of sheep and goats; hoof and mouth disease? {also: mastbir (A/IFb); mazbir (IFb-2); mazîr (GF-2); <mazber> مـاظـبر (HH)} {syn: tebeq I} [Hej/GF//HH//IFb//A]

mazbir مـازبِـر (IFb) = disease afflicting the hooves of sheep. See **mazber**.

***mazelîlk** مازەلیلك *f.* **().** small lizard. [Haz] <mazîzerk>

mazin مازن (M-Ak/TF) = big, great. See **mezin**.

mazî مـــازى *f.* **().** 1) oak tree; Valonia oak [T palamut] (A); oak, bot. *Quercus* [T meşe ağacı] (IF) *{according to Talib Berzincî of Suleimaniyeh, Iraq,* ***gezo*** *(q.v.) accumulates on the branches of this tree overnight}*; 2) oak-gall (K/JJ/HH). {also: maz II; mazu; mazû; mezî; [mazi] مـــــــازى (JJ); <mazî> مــاظـــى (HH)} Cf. T mazı = 'gallnut'; Sor mazû مازوو = 'oak-gall' [K/A/IF/JJ//HH]

mazîr مــازيــر (GF) = disease afflicting the hooves of sheep. See **mazber**.

mazîzerk مــازيــزەرك *f.* **(-a;-ê).** type of lizard, *which traditionally it is forbidden to kill.* [Msr/ZF3] <mazelîlk; qumqumok>

mazmazk مـــازمـــازك, f. (B) = backbone, spine. See **mezmezk**.

maztir مازتِر (M-Ak) = bigger. See **mezintir**.

mazu مازو = oak tree. See **mazî**.

mazû مازوو = oak tree. See **mazî**.

mazûban مـــازووبـــان *m.&f.* **(-ê/ ; mazûbên/).** host (or hostess [f.]), one who looks after a guest: •**Di havînê de, bira mêvan çavê xwe pîs meke ji bo taştîyê, di zivistanê de, mazûban mêvanê xwe bira mede çavê xwe pîs bike ji bo taştîyê** (L-#152) In summer, may the guest not make trouble [lit. 'make his eyes dirty'] about meals, in the winter, may the host not force his guest to be difficult about meals *[prv.]*. {also: meĥsûban (Frq); mazûvan (IFb)} {syn: mêvandar} Mid P mēzdbān (M3); P mīzbān مـــيـــزبـــان = 'host' < mīz/mēz مـــيـــز = 'guest', cf. Av myazda, Pahl my'zd [mēzd] = 'sacrifice, offering meal' (Vahman) + bān = 'guard, protector' [Frq//K/L//IFb] <mêvan>

mazûvan مازووڤان (IFb) = host. See **mazûban**.

me مـه *prn.* us; we *(as the logical subject of past tense transitive verbs)*; our {oblique case of **em**}: •**Ew me dibîne** = He sees us •**Me ew dît** = We saw him/her/it •**mala me** = our house. {also: [mé] مـه (JJ); <me[h]> مه (HH)} Cf. P mā ما; Sor ême ئێمە & -man مان; Za ma [BX/K/A/JB3/IF/B/JJ/HH] <em>

meaş مەئاش/**me'aş** مەعاش [JB1-A/OK] *m./f.(B)* **(-ê/ ; /-ê).** wages, salary, earnings: •**[Eger dixwazî ez wan biqewrînim û ewan maşêd wan ĥemû bidime te]** (JR) If you want, I'll chase them away and give you all their possessions •**Ma hek'e ez nehat'ibama da çi l min key? An da me'aşê min biŕî, da min j nik xo key derê, an da min kujî** (JB1-A #135) If I hadn't come, what would you have done to me? You would either have cut off my wages, or kicked me out, or killed me •**Perên ku didane me ne pir bin jî, dîsa jî ji meaşên hemû karmend û karkerên wan zêdetir bûn** (AW72B3) Even if the money they gave us was not a lot, it was still more than the wages of all their workers. {also: miaş (B); [mâch] معاش (JJ); <maş> مــاش (HH)} Ar ma'āš مــعــاش = 'salary' (< √ '-y-š عيش = 'to live') [JR/JJ/HH//JB1-A/OK//K//B]

mebes مەبەس (OK) = goal. See **mebest**.

mebest مـــەبـــەســت *f.* **(-a;-ê).** aim, goal, intention, purpose: •**Li girtîgehên Çanakkale ... yê zêdeyî 100 girtiyên siyasî bi mebesta protest[o]kirina şert û pestên îdareyê ketin greva birçîbûnê** (Wlt 2:59, 5) In the prisons of Çanakkale [et al.] more than 100 political prisoners held a hunger strike with the aim of protesting the [bad] conditions and oppression of [=at the hands of] the authorities •**Me got gel lê mebesta me ji vê peyvê ewe ku kesên tên serdana pêşangehê** (Wlt 2:71, 6) We said 'the people' but what we meant [lit. 'our intention'] by this word was 'those who come to see the exhibit'; **-merem û mebest** (AX) do. {also: mebes (IF/OK)} {syn: armanc [1]; meqsed; merem; nêt} ?< Ar mabḥaṯ مبحث = 'subject, research'; Sor mebes[t] مەبەست = 'intention, object' [AX/K(s)/IFb/TF//JB3]

mecal مەجال *f.* **(-a;-ê).** possibility, probability, chance, opportunity: •**T'i micala Memê di nava wanda ne xuyane** (Z-2) Mem had no chance among them [lit. 'no chance of Mem's appeared among them']; **-k'etin mecalê** (EP-7) to seize the opportunity. {also: mical (Z-2); [medjal] مجال (JJ); <mecal> مجال (HH)} {syn: delîve; derfet; fesal [1]; firset; kevlû [2]; k'ês} < Ar majāl مجال = 'room, space (for stg.)' [EP-7/K/A/IFb/B/JJ/HH/GF/TF]

Mecarî مەجارى (Wkt) = Hungarian. See **Macarî**.

mecbor مەجبۆر (SK/JB1-A/OK) = obliged. See **mecbûr**.

mecbûr مەجبوور *adj.* forced, obliged, obligated: •**Şivan mecbûr dibûn pêz bînine wê derê** (Ba2) The shepherds had to (were forced to) take the sheep there •**Te cebiren ez înam. Ma hek'e ez nehat'ibama da çi l min key? An da me'aşê min birî, da min j nik xo key derê, an da min kujî. Ez mecbor bom bihêm** (JB1-A #135) You brought me by force. If I hadn't come, what would you have done to me? You would either have cut off my wages, or kicked me out, or killed me. I was forced to come. {also: mecbor (SK/JB1-A/OK); [medjbouri] مجبورى (JJ)} {syn: neçar} <Ar majbūr مجبور {mecbûrî} [Ba2/K/IFb/B//SK/JB1-A/OK//JJ]

mecbûrî مەجبوورى *f.* **(;-yê).** necessity, obligation. [K/IFb/B] <mecbûr>

mecî مەجى (Wkt/G/Kmc) = she-camel. See **mencî**.

meclîs مەجليس *f.* **(-a;-ê).** (official or royal) assembly: •**Wezîr, go tê li miclisê, ...** (L) When the vizier comes to the assembly ... {also: miclis; miclîs (Z-2); mijlis (L); [medjilis] مجلس (JJ)} {syn: civat; k'omel} < Ar majlis مجلس (< √j-l-s جلس = 'to sit') [L//K/B/IF//JJ]

mecma' مەجماع (JB1-A) = tray. See **mecme'**.

mecme' مەجمەع/**me'cme** مەعجمە [Bşk] *f.* **(;-ê).** large tray, on which meals are served: •**Her êk kire d[i] sênîk'ekê ferfûrîda dane d[i] mecma'êda, bir dane ser mêzey mabeyna her duk'a** (JB1-A #78) He put each one on a porcelain plate which he put on a tray, and he put them on the table between the two of them. {also: mecma' (JB1-A)} {syn: berkeş; lengerî; mersef; sênî} Cf. P majma'ah مجمعه/majmū'ah مجموعه = '(copper) tray'; Sor mecme مەجمە/mecume مەجومە/mecum'e مەجومعە (Hej); NENA majmâhâ ܡܓܡܐܗܐ/majmâ ܡܓܡܐ (Maclean) & majuma (Garbell) & maj-ma (Oraham) = 'tray'. *Although of Arabic origin, the word majma'ah* مجمعة *does not have this meaning in Arabic per se.* [Bşk//SK//JB1-A] <lengerî; sênî; tiryan>

meçek مەچەك *f./m.(OK)* **(/-ê;).** wrist. {syn: bask; zend I} Cf. Sor meçek مەچەك [K/IFb/OK] <bazin>

meçît مەچيت (K) = mosque. See **mizgeft**.

Med مەد *m.* **().** Mede (ancient Iranian people: many Kurds believe that the Medes were their ancestors): •**Meriv dibêje qeyê agirperestekî dema medan e** (Tof) One could say he was a fire worshipper from the time of the Medes. {also: Mad (A/GF)} Sor Mad ماد [Tof/K/IFb//A/GF]

me'd•e مەعدە *m.* **(•ê;).** appetite: •**Me'dê wî qermiç'î** (Z-2) He made a face; **-me'dê/madê xwe kirin** (XF/K): a) to express one's displeasure, discontentment, etc.; b) to grieve, give o.s. over to sadness, be sad, be(come) gloomy, frown, knit one's brow, be sullen, be morose: •**Gundî me'dê xwe kir û gelekî ber xwe k'et** (XF) The villager was very sad and depressed •**Mêvanê me çiqas me'dê wî kirîye** (Z-2) How sullen our guest is; **-madê xwe tiř̄ş kirin** (XF) to frown, make a face, be dissatisfied. {also: made (XF/K); [mâdé/mîdé] معده (JJ)} <Ar mi'dah معدة --> T mide = 'stomach' [Z-2//XF/K/B/JJ] <aviř̄; bême'de; p'iř̄çû>

medek مەدەك *f.* **(-a;-ê).** female buffalo. {also: madak (IF-2); madek (K); [madek] مادك (JJ); <madak> ماداك (HH)} {syn: mange [2]; mêgamêş} [YZ/A/IF/B/ /K/JJ//HH] <gamêş>

medenîyet مەدەنيەت *f.* **(;-ê).** civilization; culture: •**Dewleta 'usmanî ḧukm li-ser hingo diket, hêşta nîşanekî medenîyetê û insanîyetê di-naw**

hingoda îcad nekirine [sic] (SK 57:662) The Ottoman government has ruled over you and has not as yet produced a sign of civilization or humanity among you. {syn: şarsanîyet; temedon (F)} < Ar madanīyah مدنية = 'civilization' [AX/K/SK]

medenos مەدەنۆس (AA) = parsley. See **bexdenûs**.

medfûnî مـەدفـوونـى (GF/ZF3) = tomato sauce. See **metfînî**.

medḧ مەدح (SK/OK) = praise. See **metḧ**.

medih مەدِه (K)/mediḧ مەدِح (OK) = praise. See **metḧ**.

medrexe مـەدرەخـە (FS) = crosspiece on shovel. See **metirke**.

meeris مەئەرِس (IFb) = pimp; atheist. See **me'ȓis**.

me'f مـەعـف/**mef** مـەف [K] *f.* **(-a;-ê).** litter, stretcher, sedan; howdah (HH): **•Me'fa min hebû, ez têda ȓazam** (EH) I had a litter [etc.], and I slept on it **•Paşê ez ḧşyar bûm, ji me'fê derk'etim** (EH) After I woke up, I got out of the litter [etc.]. {also: [mafé مـافـە/mâfé مـعـافـە] (JJ); <me'afe> مـــعـــافـــە (HH)} {syn: darbest} <Ar miḥaffah/ maḥaffah محفّة = 'litter, stretcher' [EH//K//JJ//HH]

mefer مـــەفــــەر *f.* **(-a;-ê).** opportunity, chance; possibility (A/IF): **•Meferê nadin** (XF) They don't give him a chance **•T'u mefera mêvanê te nemaye** (Z-2) Your guest has no opportunity left. {syn: delîve; derfet; firset; k'ês; mecal} <Ar mafarr مـــفـــرّ (< √f-r-r فـــرّ = 'to run away') = 'escape' [Z-2/K/A/IFb/GF/XF]

mefreq مـــەفـــرەق *m.(Zeb)/f.(OK)* **( ).** bronze. {also: [mafrak/mfrak (G)/mefrák (Lx)/müfraq (PS)] مـفـرق (JJ); <mefreq> مـەفـرەق (Hej)} {syn: birinc II; şib} Cf. P mafraγ مفرغ/مفرق <Ar mufraγ مفرغ = 'cast (in a mold)'; Sor mefreq مـەفـرەق = 'bronze' [Zeb/IFb/JJ/OK/Hej]

mefsik مەفسِك (CB/HH) = strainer. See **mifsik**.

meftiḧ مەفتِح (HR) = key; lock. See **mifte**.

meger مـەگـەر *part.* 1) apparently; It turns out that… *(commenting in retrospect on an earlier event)*: **•[Meger jina Mela Bazîd jî hatibûye guhdarîyê]** (JR-3) It turns out that Mullah Bazid's wife had also come to listen; 2) *interrogative particle expecting a negative answer*: **•Eger ew mezhebe ḧeqq neba bo çî Xudê daimî Sunnîyan dikete Şî'e? Bo çî carekê Şî'e nakete Sunnî? Meger Xudê dujminê şola çak e?** (SK 60:713) If that sect was not right, why does God always makes Sunnis into Shiahs? Why doesn't he make Shiahs into Sunnis for once? God isn't the enemy of good work, is he?; 3) {syn: ji ... pê ve; ji bilî; xêncî} *[prep.]* except for, excepting: **•Hung cedele neken digel Yehûd û Nes̱ranî, ku ehli kitab in, meger bi xeberêt baştir û nerm û xoştir** (SK 60:726) Do not argue with Jews and Christians, who are the people of the book, excepting with words which are better, softer, and kinder; 4) {syn: eger I} *[conj.]* if: **•Meger baran bê, em naçin şeher** (B) If it rains, we won't go to town. {also: [megher] مـگـر (JJ)} Cf. P magar مـگـر = 'interrogative particle expecting a negative answer' & T meğer = 'It turns out that…, apparently'; Sor meger مـەگـەر = 'but, unless, except, perhaps' [JR/K(s)/IFb/B/JJ/SK/GF/TF/OK]

megirtî مـەگِـرتـى *part.* (let's) suppose; as if. cf. Jewish NENA (of Zakho) magirti = 'as if' (Iddo Avinery. *The Aramaic Dialect of the Jews of Zakho* [Jerusalem, 1988]) Sor girîman گِريمان [Bw/Zeb]

meh مـــــــــەه *f.* **(-a;-ê).** 1) {syn: hîv [2: heyv]} month: **•meha Gulanê** = the month of May; **-vê mehê** = this month; 2) {syn: hîv} moon (K/A/B); 3) (monthly) salary: **•Meha te ezê bidime te** (Z-922) I'll give you a salary. {also: [meh] مـه (JJ); <meh> مــــــــە (HH)} [Pok. mēnōt, *gen.* mēneses, *whence* mēnes-/mēns-/mēs-/mēn- *m.* 731.] 'month': Skt mā́s/mā́sa- *m.*; O Ir *māh-/*māha- (Ras, p.133): Av må, *gen.* måŋhō; O P māha-; Mid P māh (M3); P māh ماه; Sor mang مـانـگ = 'moon, month'; Za meng *f.* = 'month' (Todd) [K/A/JB3/IFb/B/JJ/HH/GF/TF/OK/Rh]

mehandin I مـەهـانـدِن (WM) = to ferment; to freeze. See **meyandin**.

mehandin II مـەهـانـدِن (TF/ZF3/Wkt/FD) = to wear out. See **meḧandin**.

mehbûb مەهبووب (K) = beloved. See **meḧbûb**.

mehele مەهەلە (IFb) = city quarter. See **miḧel**.

mehelmî مەهەلمى (Wkt) = Mhallami. See **miḧelmî**.

mehfîr مەهفير (Czr) = carpet. See **mehfûr**.

mehfûr مـەهـفـوور *f.* **(-a;-ê).** carpet; rich, plush carpet (JJ) *{woven carpet as opposed to* ***kombar*** *= factory- made wall-to-wall carpet}*: **•Şirînê** ***meḧfîrek*** **raçand** (FS) Sh. wove *a carpet.* {also: mafûr (Wkt); mahfûr (IFb); mehfîr (Czr); meḧfîr (FS); meḧfûr (Bw); [maxfür] مـــخــــفـــور (JJ); <meḧfûr> محفور (HH)} {syn: xalîçe} Sor mafûr مـــافـــوور [BX/K//HH/GF/Bw//Czr//JJ//IFb//Wkt//FS] <beȓ IV; gelt; kombar; kulav [3]; t̲at̲î>

mehir مـەهِـر *f.* **(-a;-ê).** wedding; (civil) marriage, nuptials: -**mehr birîn** (Kmc/GF)/**mar biřîn** (K) to conclude (one's child's) marriage: •**Me'ra min bide biřîn ... gere tu me'ra min bibiřî** (HCK-5, #41, 229) Conclude my marriage ... you must conclude my marriage; -**mehr kirin** (IFb/GF)/ **mar kirin** (JJ/JR) to get married, marry: •**Mi ehd û soz dabû kû zilamê kû ev kevok birin, ez wî mehr bikim. Ava ti bûyî nesîbê min, ezê te mehr kim** (HR 3:230) I swore that I would marry the man that took those doves. Now that you are my destiny, I will marry you. {also: mar II (K/JJ/JR/Z-3); mehr (A/IFb/GF); me'r III (HCK); [mar] مار (JJ); <mehr> مهر (HH)} {syn: nikha} <Ar mahr مهر = 'bridal money'; Hau mare kerdey = 'to marry (a certain woman)' (M4). For a description of Kurdish marriage practices see: B. Nikitine. *Les Kurdes: étude sociologique et historique* (Paris : Imprimerie Nationale : Librairie C. Klincksieck, 1956), p. 108 ff. (Azerbaijan); M. Mokri. "Le mariage chez les Kurdes," in: *Recherches de kurdologie: Contribution scientifique aux études iraniennes* (Paris : Librairie Klincksieck, 1970), pp. 33-61 (Iranian Kurdistan) [SW//K/JR/JJ//A/IFb/HH/GF] <bûk I; de'wat; next = qelen; zava; zewac>

mehîn I مەهین *f.* **(-a;-ê).** mare, female horse: •**Berf li erdê hebû, mehîn likumî û lawik di bîrekê werbû** (ZZ-10, 163) There was snow on the ground, the mare stumbled and the boy rolled down into a well. {also: meȟîn II (B); miȟîn I (Z-2); mi'în (HB); [mehin مهین/mahin ماهین/ màin ماين] (JJ); <me'în> معين (HH)} {syn: hesp, f.} Mid P mādīyān (M3); P mādiyān مادیان; Sor mayîn ماین; Za mahine *f.* (Mal); Hau maînî *f.* (M4) [BX/K/A/JB3/IFb/JJ/GF/TF/ZF//B//HH//HB] <hesp; me'negî>

mehîn II مەهین *vi.* **(-meh-).** 1) to coagulate, congeal *vi.*; to ferment *vi. (of yoghurt)*: •**Mastê min nemehîye** (Zeb) My yoghurt has not fermented; 2) to freeze *vi. (fig., e.g., in politics)* (IFb). {also: meyîn (IFb-2/GF)} Cf. P māye مایه = 'ferment, leaven, yeast'; Sor meyîn مەیین = 'to set, congeal' [Zeb/IFb/M] <germixîn; meyandin>

mehîn III مەهین (TF/ZF) = to wear out (vi.), become dull. See **meȟîn I**.

mehîr مەهیر *f.* **(-a;-ê).** soup made out of buttermilk [**dew**] and cooked wheat: •**'Elbekek jî t'ije mehîr bi destê wêye** (Z-4) And she has a bucket of mehîr soup in her hand. {also: meyir (Qzl); <mehîr> مهير (HH)} {syn: girar} [Z-4/A/IFb/HH/GF/FJ/ Frq//Qzl]

mehkem مەهکەم (K) = strong, firm. See **meȟkem**.

mehlî I مەهلی *f.* **().** wooden harrow. {also: malî II (Kmc-16-2); <meȟlî> محلی (HH); <mehlî> مەهلی (Hej)} {syn: mangêřa dar} Sor małû ماڵوو [Kmc-6/ IFb//A/GF/Hej/Kmc-16//HH] <mangêř>

mehlî II مەهلی (FS) = tied bunch of branches. See **malî I**.

mehne مەهنە (TF/ZF) = meaning; reason. See **me'na**.

mehr مەهر (A/IFb/HH/GF) = wedding. See **mehir**.

mehs مەهس (GF) = slipper. See **mes I**.

mehû مەهوو (GF) = female pig. See **mahû**.

mehûj مەهووژ (K) = raisin(s). See **mewîj**.

mehvan مەهڤان (IFb) = guest. See **mêvan**.

meȟan مەحان (FS) = to wear out (vi.), become dull. See **meȟîn I**.

meȟandin مەحاندِن *vt.* **(-meȟîn-).** to wear out (vt.), erode, exhaust: •**Wekî ku ew bi zanebûn nirxên xwe yên bingehîn *dimihînin*** (rûdaw.net/Kurmanc iii.2013) As if they are consciously *eroding* their fundamental values. {also: mehandin II (TF/ZF3/ Wkt/FD); mihandin (Wkt-2); <meȟandin محاندن (dimeȟîne) (دمحینه)> (HH)} [TF/ZF3/FD/Wkt//HH] <meȟîn I>

meȟbet مەحبەت (Z-2) = love. See **muȟbet**.

meȟbûb مەحبووب *adj.* belovèd. {also: mehbûb (K); [] محبوبيك (JJ)} < Ar maḥbūb محبوب [EP-7//K//JJ]

meȟes مەحەس *f.* **(;-ê).** curry-comb, *comb made of rows of metallic teeth or serrated ridges, used to curry or dress horses*: -**meȟes kirin** (K/JJ) to curry or dress (a horse) : •[**Hespê xwe *meȟes* û gelveşîn *kir***] (PS-II, #31) He *combed* and rubbed down his horse. {also: mihes (IFb); [maḥáss] (PS-II); [mehes محس/maas معس] (JJ); <miȟes> محس (HH)} <Ar miḥassah محسّة; Sor miȟes مِحەس [PS-II/K/B/JJ//HH//IFb] <gelveşîn>

meȟfîr مەحفیر (FS) = carpet. See **mehfûr**.

meȟfûr مەحفوور (Bw) = carpet. See **mehfûr**.

meȟîn I مەحین *vi.* **(-meȟ-).** to be worn down or out, wear out (vi.), to become dull or blunt: •**Gava ku gîsin kol/kuh dibe (*dimiȟe*), dibin cem ȟedada** (Qzl) When the plowshare *gets dull*, they take it to the blacksmiths •**Serçokên şelwalê wî *meȟane*** (FS) The knees of his trousers *have worn out*. {also: mehîn III (TF/ZF); meȟan (FS); miȟîn II (Qzl); <meȟan محان (dimeȟe) (دمحه)> (HH); cf.

[maíi-bú] مايى (JJ-G) = déchiré [torn]} <Ar maḥā (u) محا = 'to erase, wipe off' & immaḥá VII امّحى = 'to be obliterated, wiped out' [Qzl//TF/ZF//FS/HH//JJ-G] <meȟandin>

meȟîn II مەحين (B) = mare. See **mehîn I**.

meȟkem مەحکەم *adj.* strong, tight, firm: **-meȟkem girtin** (Ba2) to hold tightly onto stg. {also: mehkem (K); [mouhkem] محكم (JJ)} <Ar muḥkam محكم = 'strengthened, reinforced; sturdy' {syn: ȟişk [2]; qalin [2]} [Ba2/B//K//JJ] <mukum>

meȟsûban مەحسووبان (Frq) = host. See **mazûban**.

mejan مەژان (IFb) = beam of a plow. See **mijane**.

mejî مەژى *m.* **(-yê ; mêjî** [BK]**).** 1) {syn: mex (Haz)} brain; 2) marrow, bone marrow: **-mejûyê hestû** (K) do.; 3) {syn: aqil II} sense, intelligence (K/Haz): **•*Mejîyê* te hilnade** (Haz) You can't comprehend [it] **•Mi[n] di *mejîyê* bavê te nîya/ga** (Haz) [A curse: lit. 'I fucked your father's intelligence']; 4) {syn: ser[î]} head (Haz/HH). {also: meju (Mzg); mejû (F/K/B-2/GF-2); mêjî (Ber/IFb-2/SK/TF); mijû (Haz); [mejou] مژو (JJ); <mejî> مژى (HH)} [Pok. moz-g-o- 750.] 'marrow': Skt majján- *m.* = 'marrow' & mastíṣka- *m./n.* = 'brain' & mástaka- *m./n.* = 'skull'; O Ir mazga- (Ras, p.132): Av mazga-; Mid P mazg (M3); P maɣz مغز = 'brain; marrow'; Sor mêşk مێشك = 'brain' & mêjełak مێژەڵاك = 'brain (substance)'; SoK maẍz/maqz/mazg (Fat 233); Za mezg *m.* = 'brain' (Mal); Hau mejg *m.* (M4); cf. also Rus mozg мозг = 'brain' [Haz/Srk/BK/A/JB3/IFb/B/HH/GF/OK//Mzg//F/K/JJ//Ber/SK/TF/ZF3]

mejîşûştin مەژیشووشتن *f.* **(-a;-ê).** 1) brainwashing; 2) forced assimilation. {also: mêjîşûştin (Ber/ZF3)} < mejî = 'brain' + şûştin = 'to wash' [(neol)Ber/ZF3]

meju مەژو (Mzg) = brain. See **mejî**.

mejû مەژوو (F/K/B/GF) = brain. See **mejî**.

mejxûl مەژغوول (JB1-S) = busy. See **mijûl**.

mek'an مەکان *m.* **(-ê;-î).** 1) {syn: cî; der; şûn} place: **•Min ç'e'vê xwe vekir vî *mik'anî*da** (Z-1) I opened my eyes [and found myself] in this *place*; 2) {syn: hêwirge} abode, residence; 3) {syn: niştîman} country, homeland, fatherland. {also: mikan, f. (K); mik'an II (Z-1); [mekan] مكان (JJ); <mekan> مكان (HH)} < Ar makān مكان = 'place' [Z-1//K//IF/JJ/HH/ZF3]

mekeb مەکەب = type of basket. See **mekev**.

mekesk مەکەسك (JB1-A) = scissors. See **meqes**.

mekev مەکەڤ *f.* **(;-ê).** large, wide, and shallow basket *made of slender willow branches, placed upside down over foods to air them out and protect them from insects* (MB): **•De here, ji xwe ra xiyarekî ji bin *mekevê* ... der xe û bixwe!** (MB, 11) Go get yourself out a cucumber from under *the basket* and eat it! {also: mekeb; melkeb (IFb); melkep (TF/ZF3); merkeb (Qzl/JB1-S); [mekáb] مكب (JJ)} Cf. Turoyo mkabbe, *f.* = 'basket-shaped covering, about a span long, put over food and dishes to protect them from cats' (HR2) & NENA mîkabé ܡܟܒܐ/mûkabâ ܡܘܟܒܐ = 'large basket used to cover food to protect it from mice, insects, etc.' (Maclean) & mikabbe = 'large & heavy basket placed upside down over food to keep it from cats' (Sabar:Dict); <Ar mikabbah مكبّة = 'plaited straw lid for protecting foods' < √k-b-b كبّ = 'to overturn, capsize' [MB/FS//JJ//IFb//TF/ZF3//Qzl/JB1-S] <'edil; sebet; zembîl>

Meksîkayî مەکسیکایی (ZF3) = Mexican. See **Meksîkî**.

Meksîkî مەکسیکی *adj.* Mexican. {also: Meksîkayî (ZF3-2)} Sor Meksîkî مەکسیکی [Wkt/ZF3/BF/SS]

mek't'eb مەکتەب *f.* **(-a;-ê).** school: **•Mamoste, gava ku ez dihatim *mektebê* lawikek li pey min bû, hema bela xwe di min dida, ji ber wê ez hinekî dereng mam** (LM, 16) Teacher, when I was coming *to school* a boy was behind me, he was bothering me, that's why I am a little bit late **•Roja paştir em hemî pêkve řabûyn, çûyne *mek't'ebê*, em li *mek't'ebê* řûniştîne xarê, me bo xo beȟsê hindê kir** (M-Am #715) The next day we all got up together and went *to school* and sat down in *school* and talked about it among ourselves. {also: mektew (Ad); [mekteb] مكتب (JJ)} {syn: xwendegeh} < Ar maktab مكتب (< √k-t-b كتب = 'to write')--> T mektep [K/B/JJ/M/ZF3//Ad] <dibistan; zanîngeh>

mektew مەکتەو (Ad) = school. See **mek't'eb**.

mek't'ûb مەکتووب *f.* **(-a;-ê).** letter, epistle. {also: [mektoub] مكتوب (JJ)} {syn: k'aẍez [2]; name} < Ar maktūb مكتوب (< √k-t-b كتب = 'to write')--> T mektup [L/Z-2/K/JJ/ZF3]

mela مەلا *m.* **(-yê; melê).** mullah, title of Muslim religious leader; imam, hodja; Muslim learned man (HH): **•Ji *meleyê* sibehê de erd cot dike** (HYma, 29) Since the morning *mullah* [=call to prayer, ezan], he has been plowing the earth **•Ku girêdan be, ne nivişta *melê* bi kêr tê, ne jî şêx dikare tiştekî bike** (DBgb, 15) When tying knots is involved, neither *a mullah*'s amulet with do any good, nor can a shaykh do anything •[**Lewranî qesmi xwendî û *mela* di nîv ekradan bi tima û xestî(?) meşhûrin**] (JR) Because of this, learned people and *mullahs* have a reputation among the Kurds for being greedy •**Sûq tijî qumaş e, lê *mela* bêşaş e** (BX) The marketplace is full of cloth, but *the mullah* is turbanless *[prv.]*. {also: mele (F/L/K/Ba2/IFb-2/B); melle (Dz/B-2); [mela] مـــلا (JJ); <mela> مـلا (HH)} < Ar mawlá مـولـى --> P mullā مـلا; Sor mela مـهلا {melatî; meletî} [BX/IFb/JB1A/JB2/TG2/A/JB3/JJ/HH//K/Ba2/F/L/B//Dz]

melatî مـهلاتـى *f.* **(-ya;-yê)**. profession, state or office of being a mullah, mullahship: •**Melayekî xelkê Pawe bû, ... li *melatîyê* digeřya ko wî biken e melayê gundekî, pêş-niwêjî bo wan biket û bangî bidet û millet jî fitran bidene wî w sedeqe w xêran bi wî biken** (SK 32:281) There was a mullah from Pawa who came … seeking *a post as mullah*, that they should make him mullah of a village, to lead them in prayer and give the calls to prayer, and the people give him tithes and alms; **-meletî kirin** (IFb) to serve as mullah: •**Li vî gundî salekê *melatiyê dike*** (Nbh 132:13) He *serves as mullah* (does mullahship) for a year in this village. {also: meletî (K-2/IFb/ZF)} [K/SK//IFb/ZF] <mela>

melayket مهلایكەت (M-Ak) = angel. See **melek**.

mele مهله (F/L/K/Ba2/IFb/B) = mullah. See **mela**.

melek مـهلـهك *m.* **(-ê;-î)**. angel *(religious and poetic usage)*: •[**Ewî *melekî* cewab daye**] (JR) That *angel* answered; •**Ḧakimî got, 'bismilla, ew kîye?' Gotê, 'huşşş, ez *melayketê* řuḧ-kêşanê me.'** (M-Ak #541) The governor said, 'By God, who is that?' He said, 'Hush, I am *the angel* who carries off souls.' {also: melayket (M-Ak); melyak'et (IFb-2); milêket (IFb-2); milî[y]ak'et, m./f. (B-2); milyak'et, m. (K-2); [melek] مـلـك (JJ); <melek ملك /milyaket مليـاكـت> (HH)} {syn: firîşte} < Ar mal'ak مـلأك & pl. malā'ikah مـلائـكـة [JR/F/Ba2/PS/K/IFb/JJ/B/HH/SK/OK]

melem مهلهم (IFb) = salve; comfort. See **melhem**.

meles مـهلـهس *adj.* 1) thin, elegant, refined *(of cloth)*: •**Kirasê te *meles* e** = "Your shirt is *elegant*" {song sung by Ayşe Şan}; 2) {syn: ç'arik; terḧî (Haz)} *[f.]* silken cloth *(shirt material)*; silk and cotton threaded cloth; gauze (Rh); piece of cloth (JJ) [coupon d'étoffe]. {also: melez; [melez] مـلـز (JJ)} < Ar malas ملس = 'silk fabric for women's dresses' & amlas أملس = 'smooth' --> T meles/ melez [DS/Rh//JJ]

meletî مـهـلـهتـى (K/IFb/ZF) = being a mullah. See **melatî**.

melevan مـهلـهڤان *m.&f.* **()**. 1) {syn: avjen; sobek'ar} swimmer; 2) *[adj.]* (capable of) swimming (SK): •**Ehlê Barzanê ji masîyan *melewantir in*** (SK 47:465) The people of Barzan *swim better* than fishes. {also: melewan (SK); [melevan] ملوان (JJ); <melevan> مـلـڤـان (HH)} Sor melewan مـهلـهوان {melevanî} [K(s)/IFb/HH/GF/ZF3/Wkt//JJ/SK]

melevanî مـهلـهڤانى *f.* **(-ya;-yê)**. swimming: •**Çar ji van medalîyan jibo *melevanîyê* ne** (VOA 30.vii.2012) 4 of these medals are for swimming; **-melevanî kirin** (Elk/Wn) to swim. {also: melewanî (SK); [melevani] ملوانى (JJ)} {syn: ajnê; avjenî; sobahî} [Elk/Wn/K(s)/A/GF/ZF3//JJ/SK] <melevan>

melewan مهلهوان (SK) = swimmer. See **melevan**.

melewanî مهلهوانى (SK) = swimming. See **melevanî**.

melexan مـهلـهخـان *f.* **()**. scythe, pruning hook. {syn: diryas; k'êlendî; qirim; şalok} [IFb/OK/BF]

melez مهلهز = refined; type of cloth. See **meles**.

melêf مهلێف (B) = pitchfork. See **milêb**.

melêv مهلێڤ (B/IFb) = pitchfork. See **milêb**.

melhem مـهلـهـهـم *f.* **(-a;-ê)**. 1) soothing ointment, salve, balm; balsam: •**Jin jî hene, jan jî hene, *merhema* birîna jî hene** (L) Some women are a pain, others are *a salve for* wounds *[prv.]*; 2) *[fig.]* calming, soothing; comfort: •**Derman û *melhema* minî** (FT) You are my cure and my *comfort*. {also: melem (IFb-2); melḧem (B/F); merhem (IFb/GF-2); [melhem مـــلـــهـــم/mrahm مـــرهـــم] (JJ); <melhem> مـلـهـم (HH)} <Gr malagma μάλαγμα: Ar/P marham مـرهـم; T merhem--> Bulg mehlem мехлем; Arc mālugmā מלוגמא & Syr mālagmā ܡܠܓܡܐ; Sor mełhem مـهڵـهـهـم/merhem مـهرهـهم; Za melhem *m.* (Mal) [FT/K/JJ/HH/GF//F/B//IFb/L]

melheb مهلهەب (TF) = pitchfork. See **milêb**.

melhep مهلهەپ (IFb) = pitchfork. See **milêb**.

melhêb مهلهێب (IFb) = pitchfork. See **milêb**.

melhêp مهلهێپ (A) = pitchfork. See **milêb**.

melḧem مهلحهم (B/F) = salve; comfort. See **melhem**.

melisandin مهلِساندِن *vt.* **(-melisîn-)**. to cause to crouch down, cause to lie prone on the ground *out of fear*; **-xwe melisandin** (IFb/CS) to crouch down *(vi.)*: •**Ew marê ku hawîdorê wî hatibû xazkirin, *xwe* wek miriyan *melisand*** (ZZ-7, 239-240) That snake which got spit upon, *crouched* like the dead. [ZZ/K/IFb/GF/TF/ZF/CS]

melîl مەلیل (BF) = sad. See **melûl**.

melîlî مەلیلی (BF) = sadness. See **melûlî**.

melîtk مەلیتك *m.* **(-ê;).** apron, bib: **•Sîneme *melîtkê* zařokî da ber, ku xwe pîs nekit** (FS) S. put the child's bib on, so that he wouldn't get himself dirty. {syn: berdilk [4]; berk'oş; bermalk; bervank; mêzer [4]; şalik I} [Bw/Dh/OK/FS]

melkeb مەلکەب (IFb) = basket for covering food. See **mekev**.

melk'emot/melkemot [Z-4] مەلکەمۆت *m.* **(-ê;).** 1) {syn: řuhistîn} Azrail, the angel of death; 2) *[adj.]* tough, brave, courageous: **-melk'emotê mêrê kulê** (K) fearless, not afraid of death; merciless: **•Başbazirgan bînaye *melkemotê kulêye*** (Z-4) The top merchant is *fearless* (or *merciless*). <Ar malak al-mawt ملك الموت --> T melekülmevt = 'angel of death, Azrail' [Z-4/K/IFb/ZF3]

melkep مەلکەپ (TF/ZF3) = basket for covering food. See **mekev**.

melk'es مەلکەس *f.* **(-a;-ê).** broom: **•Serokwezîr bixwe wê rahije *melkesê* û kolanên bajarê New Delhî paqij bike** (krd.sputnik.news 2014) The prime minister himself will take *a broom* and clean the streets of New Delhi. {syn: avlêk; bermalk; cerîvk (Bw); gêzî; k'inoşe; sirge (Ad); siqavêl; sivnik; sizik; şicing (Kş); şirt I} < Ar miknasah مكنسة = 'broom' (<√k-n-s كنس = 'to sweep') [Çnr/Qzl/IFb/GF/ZF3] <gêzî; maliştin>

melle مەللە (Dz/B) = mullah. See **mela**.

melûl مەلوول *adj.* 1) {syn: mon; zelûl} sad, gloomy; depressed (B): **•Tu çiřa usa *melûlî*?** (B) Why are you so *sad*?; **-melûl bûn** (B/IF) to become sad; **-simbêlê *fk-ê* melûl bûn** (Z-2) to become angry: **•Mîr Zêydîn *simbêlê wî melûl bûn*** (Z-2) M.Z. *became very angry* [lit. 'his whiskers became gloomy']; **-melûl kirin** (B/IFb) to make sad, sadden; **-melûl û mizdan** (Z-1) sad, depressed, down in the mouth: **•M. řabû ser xwe, lê gelek *melûl û mizdan* bû** (Z-1) M. got up, but he was very *sad and depressed*; 2) low (HH/GF). {also: melîl (BF); [melul] ملول (JJ); <melûl> ملول (HH)} {melîlî; melûlî} <Ar ma'lūl معلول = 'sick, ill' (√'-l-l ع ل ل = 'to fall ill') [Z-1/K/A/IFb/B/JJ/HH/GF/ZF3//BF] <p'oşman>

melûlî مەلوولی *f.* **(-ya;-yê).** sadness; depression: **•Lê sebebya *melûlya* te çîye?** (FK-kk-2) What is the reason for your *sadness*? {also: melîlî (BF)} {syn: xemgînî; zelûlî} [K/B/ZF3//BF] <melûl>

melyak'et مەلیاکەت (IFb) = angel. See **melek**.

memfiĥet مەمفیحەت (Z-2) = advantage; profit. See **menfa'et**.

memik مەمك *m./f.(B/HYma)* **(-ê/-a; /-ê).** (woman's) breast(s), bosom; breast of a young woman or girl (JJ/B); bosom of both men and women (HH): **•Destê xwe danî ser *memika* çepê** (HYma, 31) She put her hand on her left breast. {also: [memik] ممك (JJ); <memik> ممك (HH)} {syn: bistan; çiçik} Sor mem مەم/memik مەمك; Hau meme *m.* (M4) [EP-7/K/IFb/B/JJ/HH/SK/GF/TF]

memlek'et مەملەکەت *m.* **(-ê;).** 1) kingdom, realm: **•Li bajarek[î] 'azîm derk'etin. Nas nakin k'î wet'en e, k'ê dîr e, k'î *memleket* e** (JB1-S #193) They ended up in a great city. They don't know what country, what region, what *kingdom* it is **•*Memlek'etê* bavê wa jî Bex̆da ye** (HR 3:183) And their father's *kingdom* is Baghdad; 2) {syn: welat} country: **•Bajêrê Mûsilê hizar kolan hene, ew neşêt li hemîyan bigeřyêt, dê çît bo *memleketê* xo** (SK 254) The city of Mosul has a thousand streets and he cannot search them all, so he will go to his own *country*. {also: [memlekéta/memlekét (L)] مملکت (JJ)} < Ar mamlakah مملكة = 'kingdom' [HR/K/IFb/JB1-S/SK/JJ/Tsab]

me'mûr مەعموور/**memûr** مەموور [IFb/F] *m.* **().** 1) civil servant, official; 2) plenipotentiary, person authorized *(to do stg.)*, representative; 3) *[adj.]* authorized, appointed: **•[Û tu *me'mûrê* çi şolêyî?]** (JR) What work have you *been appointed to* do? {also: mamûr (JB2)} < Ar ma'mūr مأمور --> T memur [K/JR//IFb/F//JB2]

me'na مەعنا *f.* **(•a/•eya;•ê).** 1) {syn: têgih; wate} meaning, significance: **•Her do qewî 'alim o saliĥ bûn, digotin e wan 'Seydaêt Barzanî'. Seyda li-naw kurdan *bi me'na* 'ustad' *e*** (SK 46:444) Both were very wise and pious and they were called the 'Teachers of Barzan'. Sayda *means* 'teacher' among the Kurds **•*Manîya* van kursîya çi ye?** (L) What is *the significance of* these chairs?; 2) {syn: hêncet} reason, cause; motive; excuse, pretext: **•*Me'na* sergîna, çû gundê mexîna** (Dz #1123, 214) *With the excuse of* [fetching] fuel, he went to the Assyrian village *[prv.]*; **-me'na *fk-ê* geřîn** (XF)/**mane girtin** (B): a) to find fault with; to nag at, pick on; b) to find an excuse to argue with s.o., to pick a fight with: •**Ewê *me'nê* te *bigre* ... êvarê Canpolat hat, *me'nî li* Mîrze Me'mûd *girt*** (HCK-3:16, 177) He *will pick a fight with* you ... in the evening J. came and *picked a fight with* M.M.; c) to tease, mock: •**Go: "Leylê, em hatine bindarûkê, tu *me'na* me *digeřî*, teyre, teyrê minřa çi bêje, ezê teyrřa çi bêjim?"** (EP-5, #16) She said, "Leyla, we [girls] have come to play under the trees, you *must be teasing* us; it's a bird, what would the bird say to me, what would I say to him?" {also: mahne (A/IFb-2); mana (K/GF); mane (B/IFb); manî (L); mehne (TF/ZF); me'ne (B-2); me'nî (B-2); [mana معنى/mani معنى] (JJ); <me'na> معنا (HH)} < Ar ma'ná معنى (< √ '-n-y عني = 'to mean') --> T mânâ; Sor mana مانا; Za mařna *f.* (Todd) [HH/SK//B/IFb//K/JB3/JJ/GF//L//A//TF/ZF]

menat مەنات (SK) = ruble. See **manat**.

mencal مەنجال (K) = cauldron. See **mencel**.

mencel مەنجەل *f.* **(-a;-ê).** very large pot, cauldron: •**Wê av di *mencelê* da germ kir** (FS) She heated up water in the *cauldron*. {also: mencal (K); mencil (OK-2); [mendjel/manjal (Rh)] منجل (JJ)} {syn: sîtil [2]} Cf. Sor menceł مەنجەڵ = 'cooking-pot of metal, cauldron' [Msr/IF/JJ/SK/OK/ZF3/FS//K] <beroş; den I; miqilk>

mencelok مەنجەلۆك *f.* **(-a;-ê).** milk-pail: -**menceloka şîrî** (Bw) do. {also: menşolek (B)} {syn: zerik I[2]} <mencel + -ok = dim. suffix [Bw/ZF3/FS//B] <dewl I; 'elb; sîtil>

mencenik مەنجەنِك (IFb/JJ) = catapult. See **menceniq**.

menceniq مەنجەنيق *f.* **(-a;-ê).** catapult, ballista, engine for hurling stones, etc.: •**Biryar hate dan Birahîmî di nav agirê *menceniqê* da bisojin** (GShA, 229) It was decided that they would burn Ibrahim in a fire caused by *a ballista*. {also: mencenik (IFb); [mendjenik/manjanik (Rh)] منجنك (JJ)} {syn: *berayîşt; *çimçîr; hêlekan} < Ar manjanīq منجنيق < Syr mangníq ܡܢܓܢܝܩ < Gr manganikos μαγγανικός [GShA/A/SS/CS//IFb/JJ/FS/ZF3]

mencil مەنجِل (OK) = cauldron. See **mencel**.

mencî مەنجى *f.* **(-ya;).** she-camel, 2-3 year old female camel: •**Hêştira nêr lok e, hêştira mê *mencî* ye** (A. Incekan. Compact Kurdish-Kurmanji 52) A male camel is [called] lok, a female camel is [called] *mencî*. {also: mecî (Wkt/G/Kmc)} [Incekan/ZF3//Wkt/G/Kmc] <arwane; cencilok; dundil; ȟêştir; lok' II>

mend I مەند *adj.* stagnant: -**ava mend** (FS) stagnant water: •**Ji ava pêl netirse ji *ya mend* bitirse** (BF) Don't fear water with waves, fear *stagnant* [water] •**Wî di *ava mend* da mele kirin** (FS) He swam in *stagnant water*. {syn: meyav[2]; peng II} Sor meng مەنگ/mend مەند = 'still and deep (body of water)' [FS/ZF3/BF/Wkt]

mend II مەند (GF) = type of edible grass. See **mendik**.

mendehoş مەندەهۆش *adj.* surprised, amazed, astounded; bewildered, perplexed, baffled: •**Got: "Bi Xudê min hindek masî ji bin erdê da derêxistine!" Jinkê xwe xeşîm kir: "Weyla kezî kurê masî û li bin erdê da?" Mêrik got: "Keça qenc bi Xudê ez bi xwe jî *mendehoş* mame"** (Drş #427, 124) He said, "By God, I have brought up some fish from under the earth!" The wife pretended to be naïve, "You mean there are really fish under the earth?" The man said, "Dear girl, by God I was *bewildered* myself". {syn: 'ecêbmayî; ȟeyrî; ȟêbetî; met'elmayî; şaşmayî} Cf. Ar mundahiš مندهش < indahaš VII اندهش (√d-h-š دهش) + P hūš هوش? [Drş/FJ/GF/BF/FS]

mendel•e مەندەلە *f.* **(•a;).** two-story house: •***Mendela* wî li serê girî ye** (FS) His *two-story house* is on the hilltop •**Piştî şer wî wisa kiriye, her tişt daye alîkî, çûye di gundê xwe da ... bi cih bûye, ji xwe ra *mandira* saz kiriye** (Nbh 135:10) After the war he did just that, he put everything aside, and went to his village ... and settled down, built himself *a two-story house*. {also: mandira (Nbh); mendere (Kmc/CS/ZF3)} [Nbh//FJ/FS//Kmc/CS/ZF3] <xanî>

mendere مەندەرە (Kmc/CS/ZF3) = two-story house. See **mendele**.

mendê مەندێ (Bw/Hej) = type of edible grass. See **mendik**.

mendik مەندِك *f.* **(;-ê).** type of edible grass, type of watercress [T tere otu], preserved for winter use: •**Diya me jî bi me ra hat da ku pincaran şanî me bide (spink, tirşo, *mendik*, pêkesk H.D.)** (EŞ, 8) Our mother came with us too, to show us edible plants [pincar] (meadow salsify, sorrel, *mendik*, pêkesk, etc.). {also: mend II (GF-2); mendê (Bw); mendî (GF-2); <mendê> مەندێ (Hej)}

T mende/mendo [Erciş-Van] = 'nice-smelling and -tasting plant whose outer skin is removed before eating' [dış kabuğu soyularak özü yenilen, tadı ve kokusu güzel bir ot] (DS, v. 9, p. 3160, etc.) = T medik (Atılcan, p. 83)/mediyh (Gemalmaz, v.3, p. 220) [EŞ/K/B/GF/ZF3/Wkt//Hej/Bw]

mendî مەندى (GF) = type of edible grass. See **mendik**.

me‘ne مەعنە (B) = meaning; reason. See **me‘na**.

me‘negî مەعنەگى *f.* **(;-yê).** pedigreed horse, horse of noble race (IFb/A/JJ/HH); cart-horse, draught-horse [Rus bitiug битюг] (K/B): [**"Kurê min, de here tavilê, hezar û du *me‘negî* wê li tavilê da, bo xwe êkî jê bigre."**] (PS-II #34, 104, l.22-24) "My son, go to the stable, there are 1,002 *horses* in the stable, choose one for yourself." {also: manegî (A/IFb/B); manek (IFb-2); [maneki] معنقى (JJ); <me‘nek> معنك (HH)} <Ar mi‘naqī معنقي/mi‘nāq معناق = 'excellent at the pace called ‘anaq عنق (of horses)'. See Ferdinand Justi. "Les noms d'animaux en Kurde," *Revue de Linguistique*, 3 (1878), p. 7; for other references: PS, v.2a, p. 147, footnote 1. [Z-1/K/PS-II//A/IFb/B//JJ/HH] <hesp>

menfa‘et مەنفەعەت *f./m.(SK)* **(/-ê;).** 1) {syn: feyde; havil} advantage, benefit; profit, gain: **•Ew dewleta ko ho bît, ḧetta noke çu *menfe‘et* bo milletê xo nedabît, belko daimî se‘y kiribît bo meḧw û perîşanîya hingo, bes xizmet kirin bo wan fewqu-l-‘ade sefahet û ḧemaqet e** (SK 57:665) A government of this nature, which until now has done no good to its people [or, which has not benefited its people], but has rather constantly striven to destroy and disperse you--obedience to such as these is extraordinary foolishness and stupidity **•Suto ... tê-geşt ko eger Teto muroê şêx bît û daimî xulamêt şêx lalî Teto bin, ‛alê wî dê nexoş bît, *menfe‘etê* wî dê kêm bît** (SK 61:767) Suto ... realized that if Teto became a shaikh's man, and the shaikh's servants were continuously with Teto, his own [=Suto's] condition would become uncertain and his *profits* would diminish; 2) {syn: berjewendî} (vested) interest. {also: memfiḧet (Z-2); menfeet (IFb); menfe‘et (SK); menfehet; menfiet; **mifa**} <Ar manfa‘ah منفعة (<√n-f-‘ نفع = 'to be of use') [Z-2//K//IFb//SK]

menfeet مەنفەئەت (IFb)/menfe‘et مەنفەعەت (SK) = advantage; profit. See **menfa‘et**.

menfehet مەنفەهەت = advantage; profit. See **menfa‘et**.

menfîet مەنفیئەت = advantage; profit. See **menfa‘et**.

Mengolî مەنگۆلى (BF) = Mongolian. See **Mongolî**.

me‘nî مەعنى (B) = meaning; reason. See **me‘na**.

menşolek مەنشۆلەك (B) = milk-pail. See **mencelok**.

menzel مەنزەل = residence; étape, day's march. See **menzîl**.

menzil مەنزل (SK) = residence; étape, day's march. See **menzîl**.

menzîl مەنزیل *f.* **(-a;-ê).** 1) residence, apartments, lodgings, quarters: **•Ez ho munasib dibînim Ḧezretê Mehdî digel çend muroêt mezin o mu‘teber bihên e *menzila* bende** (SK 47:462) I consider it best that his Highness the Mahdi and a few leaders and honoured men should come to my *quarters*; 2) {syn: qonax [3]} stage, distance between two points or stops *(on a trip)*, a day's journey (K); distance one can travel on foot in one day (IF); day's march, distance between staging points, étape [Fr.] (JB1-A); 3) station, stop (B/HH). {also: menzel; menzil (SK); [menzel] منزل (JJ); <menzel> منزل (HH)} < Ar manzil منزل = 'house, lodgings' (<√n-z-l نزل = 'to descend, alight') [K/IFb/Ba2/B/JR//JJ/HH//SK]

meqber مەقبەر (IFb/JJ) = grave. See **meẍber**.

meqbere مەقبەره (IF/HH) = grave. See **meẍber**.

meqes مەقەس *f./m.* **(-a/-ê;-ê/).** scissors: **•Min *maqes* girt û ez ketim nav porê xwe** (LC, 6) I took a *scissors* and went after my hair [humorous]; **-meqes kirin** (B) to cut, clip: **•Ez p’erê wa *meqes dikim*** (HR 3:66) I *clip* their feathers. {also: maqes (LC); mekesk (JB1-A); meqesk (JB1-A-2/OK-2); meqest; [maqas] مقص (JJ); <meqes> مقس (HH)} {syn: cawbiř} < Ar maqaṣṣ مقصّ (<√q-ṣ-ṣ قصّ = 'to cut') --> T makas [Bg/K/A/JB3/IFb/B/HH/GF/OK//JB1-A//LC//JJ] <hevring>

meqesk مەقەسك (JB1-A/OK) = scissors. See **meqes**.

meqesok مەقەسۆك *f.* **(-a;-ê).** swallow, zool. *Hirundinidae*. {also: meqesork (F)} {syn: dûmeqesk; ḧacḧacik; *qerneqûçik} [K/B/ZF3//F]

meqesork مەقەسۆرك (F) = swallow. See **meqesok**.

meqest مەقەست = scissors. See **meqes**.

meqle مەقلە (JB1-A) = pan. See **miqilk**.

meqsed مەقسەد *f.* **(-a;).** aim, goal, purpose, intention: **•Ez nizanim em *meqseda* xo ‘erz bikeyn yan cenabê aẍa dê pisyara ḧalê mêwanan fermot** (SK 42:408) I do not know whether we should explain our *mission* [or, *purpose*] or if your honour intends to ask after his guests? **•Mîr got, "Her kesê mizgînîya ṯeyrî bo min bînît ez dê xelatekî bi keyfa wî dem ê." Xelkî jî weto texmîn kirin** [sic] **mîr beḧsê mizgînîya ṯeyrê**

biharê ye. ***Meqseda*** **mîr tê-negeştin çi ye** (SK 29:261) The Mir said, "Whoever brings me the good news of the bird I shall give him a present which will please him." People imagined that the Mir was talking of the good news of the coming of the bird of spring. They did not understand the Mir's *meaning* **•Te *mexseda* xwe bicih kir?** (HR 3:160) Have you achieved your *goal*? **•Û bê ti bi çî *meqsedê* hatîye, îşellah *meqseda* te wê icra bê** (HR 3:28) Whatever *purpose* you have come for, hopefully your *purpose* will be achieved. {also: mexsed (Z-3); [meqsed] مقصد (JJ)} {syn: armanc [1]; mebest; merem; nêt [4]} <Ar maqṣad مقصد [Z-3//K/IFb/HH/SK]

mer I مەر (F)/me'r مەعەر (B/MK/GF) = snake. See **mar I**.

meř II مەر *f.* **(-a;-ê).** iron shovel *{as opposed to **bêr** = wooden shovel}* (B); spade (A/IF); hoe (JJ): **•Çû nav baxçe û rahişt *merê* şixulî** (ZZ-7) He went into the garden and picked up *a shovel* and worked. {also: [mer] مر (JJ); <mer> مر (HH)} {syn: tevir} Cf. Sumerian mar; Akkadian marru; Ancient Egyptian (mr); Syr mara ܡܪܐ/ma'ra ܡܥܪܐ; NENA mîrâ ܡܪܐ (Maclean); Ar marr مَرّ = 'iron shovel, spade' {See: Georg Krotkoff, "Studies in Neo-Aramaic Lexicology," in: *Biblical and Related Studies Presented to Samuel Iwry* (Winona Lake, Ind.: Eisenbrauns, 1985), p. 126.} [Z-2/F/K/A/IFb/B/JJ/HH/GF/ZF] <bêr; carût; metirke>

me'r III مەعر (HCK) = wedding. See **mehir**.

meram مەرام (IFb/JJ/SK) = goal; desire. See **merem**.

meraq مەراق *f.* **(-a;).** 1) {syn: k'eder; kovan; kul I} anxiety, concern, worry: **•Di oda xo de *meraq kişand* û qiȟerî û zenzilî** (HR 4:36) In his room he *was worried* and upset and grew thin **•Min gelek *meraqa* te *xwar*** (GF) I *have been* very *worried about* you; 2) {syn: pûte} interest, caring about: **•Çawa dê mumkin bît ez wihê bibînim? Ew xebere gelek *li* min *bû meraq*. Dibît ez her bizanim** (SK 23:209) How can I see this thing? This matter has greatly *intrigued* me. I must certainly know. {also: merax (AD); mereq (B/JB1-A)} T merak = 'curiosity, interest, anxiety' < Ar √r-w-q روق = 'to excite wonder in' (Hava); Sor meraq مەراق = 'worry, anxiety; great interest, fascination' [HR/K/IFb/FJ/TF/GF/SK/CS//B/JB1-A//AD]

meraqdarî مەراقدارى (IFb) = interest. See **mereqdarî**.

meras مەراس *m./f.(ZF3)* **().** shoe(s): **•Dema ku karê erebê nedibû, *meras* (sol) boyax dikirin** (Wkt: M. Ş.Dağ: *Waris*, Bîrnebûn, 26 [2005], 41) When there wasn't any wagon work, he would polish *shoes*. {also: meres (FS); [midas] مداس (JJ)} {syn: pêlav; qondere; sol} <Ar madās مداس = 'shoe, sandal' (<√d-w-s دوس = 'to tread, step') [Krs/Plt/ZF3/Wkt//JJ//FS]

merat** مەرات *f.* **(-a;).** fishermen's net: **•Bi der nakeve *merata torane (L) *The net* doesn't go out. {syn: t'oř I} Cf. meras (FS): the way fishermen walk while fishing with nets [řêveçûna masîgiran li demê masîgirtinê bi tořê] [L/K]

merax مەراخ (AD) = anxiety; interest. See **meraq**.

merc I مەرج *f./m.(B/BF/Wkt)* **(-a/;).** 1) {syn: miçilge; şert [2]} bet, wager: **-merc girtin** (B) to place a bet; 2) condition, stipulation, terms *(of agreement)*: **•Bi *mercê ko* niştecih li malên xwe bimînin û yên derbider li cihên xwe vegerin** (yekiti-media.org 16.viii.2015) *On condition that* residents stay in their homes and those outside return to their places **•Bo parastina zimanê kurdî *merc e ku* her kes li gel zarrokên xwe bi kurdî biaxive** (Wkt) To preserve the Kurdish language *it is imperative [it is a condition]* that everyone speak to their children in Kurdish; **-merca pêşîn** (ZF3) precondition; **-mercên endamîyê** (BF) conditions of membership; 3) {syn: şert} condition, state, circumstances: **•di *mercên* dijwarda** (IF) under difficult *circumstances*. {also: [merdj] مرج (JJ)} [Z-1/K/IFb/B/JJ/GF/TF/ZF3/Wkt/BF]

merc II مەرج, f. (OK) = large hammer. See **mirc**.

mercan مەرجان (A) = coral; pearl. See **mircan**.

merd مەرد *adj.* 1) {syn: camêr} generous: **•Axa min gelek *merd* e** (AB) My soil is very *generous* [=fertile]; 2) {syn: mêrxas [2]} brave: **•lawê namerd, kalê *merd*** (SK 37) the cowardly youth and the *brave* old man; 3) {syn: emîn [2]; ewlekar; ît'bar} dependable, reliable. {also: [merd] مرد (JJ); <merd> مرد (HH)} Cf. P mard مرد = 'man'; Sor merd مەرد = 'manly, brave' {merdanî; merdayî; merdî; merdtî} [AB/K/A/IFb/B/JJ/HH/SK/GF/TF]

merdanî مەردانى (K) = generosity; bravery. See **merdayî**.

merdayî مەردايى *f.* **(-ya;-yê).** 1) generosity; 2) {syn: mêranî; mêrxasî} bravery, valor. {also: merdanî (K); merdî (B/K/IFb/GF/TF); merdtî (B)} [B/K//IFb/GF/TF] <merd>

merdî مـەردی (B/K/IFb/GF/TF) = generosity; bravery. See **merdayî**.

merdtî مـەردتـی (B) = generosity; bravery. See **merdayî**.

mereg مەرەگ (A/IFb) = hayloft; depot. See **merek**.

merek مـەرەك *f.* **(;-ê).** 1) {syn: kadîn} hayloft, haymow: **•*Merekeke* t'ek k'êleka gund hebû, me xwe li *merekê* girt, çûn, k'etine *merekê*...lê *merekêda* ardû t'u nebû, wekî me xweře agir dada, xwe pê germ bikira û kinçê xwe ziha kira** (E. Şamîlov. Berbang, 4) There was a single *hayloft* at the edge of the village, we made for *the hayloft*, we went and entered *the hayloft*...but in *the hayloft* there was no fuel, with which we could light a fire, warm ourselves and dry our clothes; 2) depot, storage room: **•[Tu vê varîlê bibe di bin oteya wîda li tabaxê jêrî dayne nîva *merekê*]** (JR) Take this barrel [directly] underneath his room, on the floor below, put it in the middle of *the storage room*. {also: mereg (A/IFb-2); [merek] مـەرەك (JR); [marak/merek] مـەرك (JJ); <merek> مـەرك (HH)} < Arm marag (W:marak) մարագ = 'hayloft' [JR/K/B/IFb/FJ/GF/HH/Tsab/ZF//A]

merem مـەرەم *m./f.(JJ/B)* **(/-a; /-ê).** 1) {syn: armanc [1]; mebest; meqsed; nêt [4]} goal, intention, aim, purpose **-merem û mebest** (AX) do.; 2) desire, ambition (K/JJ): **•Temam *merama* min ewe ye bi delîlekî waziĥ ĥeqqanîyet sabit o aşkera bibît** (SK 60:708) My whole *desire* is that the truth be proven and made clear with clear evidence. {also: meram (IFb/SK); [meram] مـەرام (JJ); <merem> مرەم (HH)} < Ar marām مرام = 'wish, desire'; Sor meram مەرام/merem مەرەم [AX/F/K/B/HH//IFb/JJ/SK]

mereq مـەرەق (B/JB1-A) = anxiety; interest. See **meraq**.

mereqdarî مـەرەقـداری *f.* **(-ya;-yê).** curiosity, great interest, concern: **•Li ser vê *mereqdariya* cîrana xwe, mêrik li wir li ser lingan bi kurtî ji cîrana xwe re kat dike** ... (Ardû, 11) In response to this *interest of* his neighbor's, the man explains it briefly to her off the top of his head **•Tew anuha dema ku li ser van tiştan difikire, *mereqdarî* lê zêdetir dibe** (Ardû, 19) Now when he thinks of those things, his *curiosity* increases. {also: meraqdarî (IFb)} {syn: *'eleqedarî; meraq} < mereq + -dar + -î [Ardû//IFb] <meraq>

meres مەرەس (FS) = shoe(s). See **meras**.

merez مـەرەز *f./m.(FS)* **(;/-ê).** angora wool, mohair, long silky hair of Angora goat [**ç'ûr I**] [T tiftik]: **•Şel û şepika ji *merezî* çê dikin** (FS) They make shal u shapiks [traditional Kurdish men's clothing] from angora wool; **-kevilekê merez** (M-Ak) goat's pelt. <Ar mir'iz مـرعـز = 'fine goat's hair'; Sor merez مـەرەز = 'mohair' [M-Ak/K(s)/IFb/OK/ZF3/FS] <ç'ûr I; hirî; kej II; kevil; kulk; liva; meles>

merga mûş مـەرگـا مـووش (GF) = arsenic, rat poison. See **mergemûş**.

Mergeh مـەرگـەه *f.* **(-a;).** a Yezidi shrine in the valley of Lalesh, near Mosul, Iraq (IFb). {also: Mergehe (IFb)} [Lalish (Mosul), Iraq/IFb] <ocax [5]; zîyaret>

Mergehe مەرگەهە (IFb) = Yezidi shrine. See **Mergeh**.

mergemûş مـەرگـەمـووش *f.(Zeb)/m.(SK)* **(-a/; /-î).** white arsenic, arsenic trioxide, ratsbane, rat poison: **•Muroêt [=mirovêt] şêxî gelek keyf-xoş bûn, 'eqlê wan yê hirçan bû, nezanîn [sic] ĥîle ye, hingûn e digel *mergemûşî* didene wan** (SK 48:509) The shaikh's men were very pleased, their intelligence was that of bears, they did not know that it was a trick, that it was honey they were being given with *ratsbane*. {also: merga mûş (GF); [merghemouch/merghamús (G)/mergamush (Rh)] مرگموش (JJ)} Cf. P marg-e-mūš مرگ موش ; Sor mergemûş مـەرگـەمـووش/mergemişk مەرگەمِشك [Dh/Zeb/JJ/SK//GF] <jehr>

me'rgîsk مەغرگیسك (B) = lizard. See **margîsk**.

merhem مـەرهـەم (IF/GF/L) = salve; comfort. See **melhem**.

merif مەرِف = man; person. See **meriv**.

merifatî مـەرِفـاتـی (IS) = manliness; humanity; humaneness; relation through marriage. See **merivtî**.

me'rifet مـەعـرِفـەت (SK) = honor; courtesy; skill; knowledge. See **me'rîfet**.

me'ȓis مەعرِس *m.* **().** *pejorative term:* pimp, cuckold; atheist, godless person; scoundrel: **•*Me'ȓis*, kurê k'erê, go, tu şivan, çolê, ew jinik t'ek, çawa te saẍ slamet berda, tu derewa dikî?** (HCK-3, #2, 28) *Pimp*, son of a donkey, shepherd, how could you let that woman go off on her own into the wilderness? You are lying **•T'u cara nave, wekî em wet'enê xwe bidine Şah Abas, wan *me'rîza*** (Tsab, 635 [Şamîlov, Dimdim, 174]) We must never give our country to Shah Abbas, to those *scoundrels*. {also: marîs (IFb); meeris (IFb-2); me'rîz (Tsab); [meariz] معـرص (JJ); <me'eȓis> مـعـرس (HH)} < Ar mu'arraṣ مـعـرّص = 'pimp, procurer;

cuckold'; Sor mařis مـــــــــارِس = 'atheist(ic); hardheaded, willful' [HCK//HH//JJ//Tsab//IFb] <forq; p'ûşt; sebav>

meriv مەرِڤ *m.* **(-ê; mêriv, vî merivî).** 1) {syn: mêr I; peya; zilam} man: **•*Merivek* řastî wî hat go ...** (Dz) *A man* chanced upon him [and] said ...; 2) {syn: benîadem; însan} person, human being: **•Boxek heye nav naxira minda, tu *merîya* naĥemlîne** (J) There is a bull in my herd [which] doesn't carry any *people* (=doesn't let *people* ride him); 3) relative, cousin, relation, kin; 4) {syn: însan [2]} one, they *(for general, impersonal statements)*: **•Çaxê mêriv jêla li ĥeç'ê ç'îyê dinihêřî, *mêriv t'irê* wê derê kela çê kirine** (Ba2:1, 203) When one looked at the mountain-top, *one would think* they had built a fortress there **•Ew usa lez dik'etin, *mêriv* qey digot ew hevřa k'etibûne lecê, çika k'îjan ji wana zû xwe digihîne germa deşta** (Ba2:1, 202) They [=the brooks] fell so quickly, that *one* might say (=it seemed as if) they were racing each other, to see which one of them will reach the warmth of the plains first [lit. 'early'] **•*Mirov* narsîstan çawa nas dike?** (www.tirsik.net: narsîzm) How does *one* recognize narcissists? **•Tu tiştekî wekî belge neketiye ber dest da *meriv* karibe firehtir li ser jiyana wî raweste** (CA, 67) Nothing like a document has been available so that *one* could go into [or, study] his life more fully. {also: merif; merî (B-2) m. (; mêrî); merof; merov (K); mirof; mirov (IFb-2/OK); muro (SK); [merif / mourouf] مـــــــرف (JJ); <mirov> مـــــــروڤ (HH)} Cf. Mid P mardō[h]m (M3) <O Ir *martiya- + *tauxma-: P mard مـــرد = 'man' & mardom مردم = 'people' ; Sor mêrd مێرد = 'husband' & mirow مِـــــروٚ = 'man; mankind'; Za merde *m.* = 'husband' & merdim *m.* = 'person, man' (Todd) {[merifaï مـرفـای]/ meriti مـرتـی] (JJ); <mirovatî> مـــروڤـــاتـــی (HH); merivatî; merivayî; merivî; merivtî; merîtî; merovî; merovtî; mirovahî; mirovatî} [Dz/IFb/B/GF/TF//JJ//HH//K//SK] <mêr I>

merivatî مـــەرِڤـــاتـــی (Z-1) = manliness; humanity; humaneness; relation through marriage. See **merivtî**.

merivayî مـــەرِڤـــایـــی (B) = manliness; humanity; humaneness; relation through marriage. See **merivtî**.

merivî مەرِڤی (K) = manliness; humanity; humaneness; relation through marriage. See **merivtî**.

merivnasî مـــەرِڤـــنـــاســـی (Wkt) = anthropology. See **mirovnasî**.

merivtî مـەرِڤـتـی *f.* **(-ya;-yê).** 1) manliness, masculinity; 2) humanity; 3) humaneness; 4) relation by or through marriage: **•*Merivatîya* wan pêşda hevřa hebû, lema jî mîr Sêvdîn sozê Zînê jî da Ç'ekan** (Z-1, 46) Since they were already *related by marriage*, mîr Sêvdîn promised Zîn to Chekan; **-pirsa merivatîyê danîn** (Z-1)/**de'wa merifatîyê li *fk-ê* kirin** (IS) to ask for a woman's hand in marriage: **•Hatine dîwana mîr Sêvdîn, *pirsa merivatîyê danîn*, seva Zîna delal bixazin Ç'ekanřa** (Z-1) They went to m.S.'s court, *to request the hand of* lovely Z. for Ch. (i.e., to marry Z. to Ch.) **•Min nav-dengê we bihîstîye, ez hatime, *de'wa merifatîyê li we dikim*** (IS-#155) I have heard of your reputation, I have come *to ask for* your sister*'s hand in marriage*. {also: merifatî (IS); merivatî (Z-1); merivayî (B); merivî (K); merîtî (B); merovî (K); merovtî (K); mirovahî (IFb/OK); mirovatî (IFb/OK); [merifaï مـــرفـــای]/ meriti مرتی] (JJ); <mirovatî> مروڤاتی (HH)} [K/B//IFb//JJ//HH] <meriv>

merivzanî مـــەرِڤـــزانـــی (Wkt) = anthropology. See **mirovnasî**.

merixîn مەرِخین *vi.* **(-merix-).** to lie down *(of horses and donkeys)* either to rest or because of illness: **•*Merixiye* naçerixe** (IFb) [The animal] *has lain down* and cannot move. {also: mexilîn (K-2/B-2); [merikhin] مـرخـیـن (JJ)} {syn: mexel bûn/hatin} [Melazgir (Mûş)/K/IFb/B/JJ] <mexel>

merî مەری m. (; mêrî) (B) = man; person. See **meriv**.

me'rîfet مەعریفەت**/merîfet** مەریفەت [K] *f.* **(-a;-ê).** 1) {syn: 'erz; giram; hurmet [3]; qedir I; řêz II} honor, respect, esteem (K/B); **-me'rîfeta *fk-ê* girtin** (XF) to show s.o. respect; 2) courtesy, politeness, civility, good manners; being cultured; 3) skill, talent; art: **•Ezê bêjim, çik hebû, *me'rîfeta* min bû** (J) I will say that whatever happened, it was [by] my *talent*; 4) knowledge, wisdom: **•Ez te'eccub dikem ji 'ilm û *me'rifeta* te, çawa ĥetta noke te ew delîl fam nekirîye** (SK 43:418) I am surprised at your learning and *wisdom*, that you have not understood that proof until now **•Mezinatî bi aqlî ye, ne bi sal e; dewletmendî bi *me'rifetê* ye, ne bi malî ye** (SK 22:207) Greatness [or, maturity] is in wisdom, not in years; wealth is in *knowledge*, not in property **•Ne milletê kurd ew hind medenîyet o *me'rifet* heye ko r̄êka ḧusola met̠loba xo bizanin**… (SK 56:646) Neither is the Kurdish nation civilized or *educated* enough to know the way to achieve their goal…. {also: malîfet (L); marîfet (IFb); me'rifet (SK); [mârifet/mãriféta] معرفت (JJ)} < Ar ma'rifah معرفة = 'knowledge, acquaintance' (<√ '-r-f عرف = 'to know, be acquainted with')--> T marifet = 'special skill, talent' [L//FK-eb-1/B/XF//K//IFb// JJ/SK] <namûs; r̄ûmet; şeref>

merîtî مەریتی (B/JJ) = manliness; humanity; humaneness; relation through marriage. See **merivtî**.

me'rîz مەعریز (Tsab) = pimp; atheist. See **me'r̄is**.

merkeb مەرکەب (Qzl/JB1-S) = basket for covering food. See **mekev**.

mermer مەرمەر *m.* **(-ê;-î).** marble *(type of stone)*: **•Wî sîngê xanîyê xwe ji *mermerî* deyna** (FS) He made the façade of his house out of *marble*. {also: [mermer] مرمر (JJ); <mermer> مرمر (HH)} [L/K/A/JB3/IFb/B/JJ/HH/GF/TF/FS/ZF3/Wkt]

me'rme'sî مەعرمەعسی (B) = eel. See **marmasî**.

merof مەرۆف = man; person. See **meriv**.

merov مەرۆڤ (K) = man; person. See **meriv**.

merovî مەرۆڤی (K) = manliness; humanity; humaneness; relation through marriage. See **merivtî**.

merovtî مەرۆڤتی (K) = manliness; humanity; humaneness; relation through marriage. See **merivtî**.

mersef مەرسەف *f.* **(-a;-ê).** tray for serving food and tea: **•Kevokê zêr̄ li ser *mersefa* zêr̄ bixun cêyê zêr̄** (HR 3:6) Golden doves on a golden *tray* eating golden barley. {also: mesef (FS); mesrefe (TF)} {syn: berkeş; lengerî; mecme'; sênî} [HR/IFb/FJ/CS//TF//FS]

merş مەرش *m./f.(FS/ZF3/Wkt/BF)* **(/-a;/-ê).** kilim, flat-weave pileless carpet; inexpensive kilim (Msr): **•Go: Ma ti çiqa dinyaê dibînê? – Go: Ez bi qasî *merşekî* dibînim** (HR 3:255) "How big does the world look to you [from up here]?" "I see it the size of *a kilim rug*". {also: merşik, f. (-a;) (Msr/A-2)} {syn: ber̄ IV; cacim; cil II; gelt; k'ilîm; p'alas; tejik} [K/A/IFb/GF/FS/BF/ZF3/Wkt//Msr]

merşik مەرشِك, f. (-a;) (Msr/A) = kilim. See **merş**.

mertak مەرتاك *f.* **(;-ê).** roof beam, wooden beam the thickness of a man's wrist used as a rafter to support roof in traditional houses (Haz); small sticks or boards placed across the main beams of the ceiling of Kurdish houses (B/HH). {also: mart'ak (B); mirdiyaq (Qzl); <martak> مارتاك (HH)} Cf. T mertek [Haz/Wkt//B/HH//Qzl] <k'êran; r̄ot>

mert'al مەرتال *f./m.(B/SK)* **(-a/;-ê/mert'êl [B]).** shield: -**[şîr metal]** (JR) sword and shield. {also: met'al (M/K[s]/JR); met̠al (SK); [mertal مرطال/ metal مطال] (JJ); <mirt̠al> مرطال (HH)} Sor me[r]tał مەرتاڵ/mertal مەرتال; Cf. NA mâţâlâ ܡܛܠܐ (Maclean); Arc meţal מטל = 'javelin for thrusting' (M. Jastrow) [EP-8/K/A/IFb/B/JJ/HH/GF//M/K(s)/JR/SK] <şûr>

merx مەرخ *f.* **(;-ê).** 1) {syn: hevris} juniper tree, bot. *Juniperus* (IF/JJ/B); 2) spruce tree, bot. *Picea* (K/B); fir tree (K/B): **-dara merxê** (K/B) do. {also: [merkh] مرخ (JJ)} [Tkm/K/IFb/B/JJ/GF/FS/ZF3] <dar I; kac>

Merxok مەرخۆك **().** a village near Tekman, province of Erzurum. [Tkm] <merx>

merzore مەرزۆره (IFb) = type of grape. See **mezrona**.

mes I مەس/**me's** مەعس [Z-2] *f.* **(;-ê).** slipper (B); slipper made of yellow leather (JJ); prayer slippers (IF): **-şim û me'sane** (Z-2) slippers and [pantoufles]. {also: mehs (GF); mest (B/IFb); mihsik (IFb-2); [mas مەس/mehs مەحس/mehsik مەحسك] (JJ); <miḧsik> مەحسك (HH)} {syn: şim[ik]} Cf. Arc mesānā מסאנא/sēnā סינא= 'shoe' (< √s-'-n סאן = 'to tread; to put shoes on') [M.Jastrow] & Syr mesānā ܡܣܐܢܐ [Costaz/Köbert]/ ܡܣܢܐ [Costaz]; NENA mâsî ܡܣܐ = 'slippers' (Maclean); also T mest = 'light, thin-soled boot (worn indoors or inside shoes)'; Sor mest مەست [Z-2//JJ//GF//B/IFb//HH] <pêlav; sol>

mes II مەس (GF) = copper. See **mîs**.

mes̠arif مەصارِف pl. (SK/JJ) = expenses. See **mesref**.

mesas مەساس (IFb) = oxgoad. See **misas**.

mesder مەسدەر *f.(K/B/ZF3)/m.(F)* **(;-ê/).** infinitive, verbal noun. {syn: jêder [2]; r̄ader} <Ar maṣdar مصدر (<√ṣ-d-r صدر = 'to emanate, originate (from)') [F/K/IFb/B/ZF3] <lêker; r̄awe>

mesef مەسەف (FS) = tray. See **mersef**.

mesel مەسەل *f.* **(•a;•ê).** 1) {syn: çîr̄ok} story; fable; parable: **•Bibêjin *mesela* xo** (M-Ak, #549) Tell your *story*; 2) {syn: gotina pêşîyan} proverb; saying; adage: **•Ḧekaêta "Cûyê şîrê xo dîtîyewe" li-naw Kurdistanê meşhûr e. Eger kesekî kirmanc, feqîr xurtî biket wê *meselê* der-**

ħeqq wî dibêjin (SK 26:241) The story of "the Jew who found his sword" is famous in Kurdistan. If a humble peasant fellow throws his weight about they quote this *adage* about him •**Lakin *mesela* mezinan e, "ji biçûkan xeta, ji mezinan 'eta"** (SK 3:25) But there is *an axiom* of the great, "Faults from the feeble, grace from the great" •**Ma tu nizanî li-naw hemî Kurdistanê ew *mesele* meşhûr e, "Hingî mêşêt hingûnî zêde dibin, şilxan diden û hingûnê çak diken ko xudanê mêşan mêşekî bikiřît û yêkî bixazît û yêkî bidizît"?** (SK 35:315) Kamo said to him, `Don't you know that all over Kurdistan this *saying* is famous that `"bees increase and swarm and make a good honey when their owner buys a bee, begs one and steals one"? •**Me'lûm li wêderê ji hemî cîyan çêtir dê qazancî kem, çonko *meselê mezinan* e, "Kê mamilet kir? muħtacî"** (SK 16:155) Obviously I shall make a better profit there than anywhere, for there is a *proverb* ``Who did business? The needy man." {also: mesele II (K/B)} <Ar maṯal مثل [M-Ak/SK]

mesela مهسهلا (IFb) = for example. See **meselen**.

mesel•e I مهسهله /**mes'ele** مهسئهله [SK] *f.* **(•a;•ê).** problem, issue, matter, question: •**Ev derdê te çi ye, *mesela* te çi ye?** (ZZ-10, 161) What is this complaint of yours, what is your *problem*? •**Welle, ez bi *mesela* Guřî ne ħesîyame** (Z-4) By God, I have not heard of this *matter* having to do with Guri (=Baldhead); **-mesele qedandin** (B) to solve a problem. <Ar mas'alah مسألة [Z-4/K/IFb/B//SK]

mesele II مهسهله (K/B) = story; proverb. See **mesel**.

mesele III مهسهله (K/B) = for example. See **meselen**.

meselen مهسهلهن *part.* for instance, for example: •**Muro bi 'emelê xo tên e ceza dan; eger çakî bît bi çakî we eger xirabî bît bi xirabî. *Meselen* eger muroekî çak li-naw qebrêt cûan difn biken hîç zerer nîye, we eger cû li-naw qebrê imam Ħuseyn difn biken hîç fayde nîye** (SK 60:724) People are rewarded according to their deeds; if [their deeds] are good, [they are rewarded] with goodness, and if bad, with bad. *For example*, if they bury a good man among the graves of the Jews there is no harm [in this], and if they bury a Jew in the tomb of Imam Hussain there is no advantage [in it]. {also: mesela (IFb); mesele III (K/B); [mesela] مثلا (JJ)} {syn: bo nimûne; wek mînak} <Ar maṯalan مثلاً --> T meselâ [SK//K/B//IFb/JJ]

meselok مهسهلۆك *f.* **(-a;-ê).** joke, humorous story, anecdote: •**Ev *meselok* (metelok, leqemok, pêkenok) piraniya wan li ser hin tiştên ku hatine serê xelkê, mîna serpêhatiyan, hatine gotin ... û timî ew di şewbêrk û civatan de têne gotin, û mirov bi wan hevdu kêfxweş dikin** (ZZ-3, 7) Most of these *anecdotes* have been told about things which actually happened to people, as true stories ... and they are always told during evening gatherings, and people entertain each other with them •**Li hin welatên dî jî ... hin *meselok* û pêkenokên sîyasî hatine afirandin** (Bkp, xxviii) In some other countries as well ... *anecdotes* and political jokes have been created. {syn: ħenek; p'êkenok; qerf} <Ar maṯal مثل = 'parable; proverb' + -ok [Bkp/ZZ/IFb/ZF3]

mesheb مهسهەب = holy book. See **mis'ef**.

mesî مهسی/me'sî مهعسی (B) = fish. See **masî**.

me'sîgir مهعسیگیر (B) = fisherman. See **masîgîr**.

mesîl مهسیل *f.* **(-a;-ê).** valley, wadi, dry riverbed: •**Ezê herim li wê *mesîla* hanê xwe dirêj kim** (AW70B2) I will go lie down in that *valley* over there. {also: [masīl] مسيل (JJ)} <Ar masīl مسيل = 'riverbed, rivulet' [K(s)/IFb/JJ/GF] <dehl>

mesîn مهسین (IFb) = brass water pitcher. See **misîn**.

mesref مهسرەف/**meṣref** مهصرەف [SK/HH] *f.* **(-a;-ê).** expense, expenditure, outlay, costs: •**Mihleta çil rojan bide min, ezê biçim ji te re bînim. *Mesrefa* min û mala min ji kîsê hemamçî** (Rnh 2:17, 308) Give me a respite of 40 days, and I'll go bring [them] for you. *The expenses for* me and my family from the pocket of the bathhouse owner. {also: meṣarif pl. (SK-2); [mesref مصرف/ mesarif *pl.* مصارف] (JJ); <meṣref> مصرف (HH)} {syn: xerac; xerc} <Ar maṣrif مصرف (*pl.* maṣārif مصارف) = 'bank; teller's window' --> P & T masraf = 'expense, outlay' [Rnh/F/K/IFb/B/JJ/ JB1-A&S/OK//HH/SK]

mesrefe مهسرەفه (TF) = tray. See **mersef**.

mest مهست (B/IFb) = slipper. See **mes I**.

mestir مهستِر (Msr/K/A/JJ-G/Z-4) = bigger. See **mezintir**.

meşandin مهشاندِن *vt.* **(-meşîn-).** 1) to cause to walk or march (BK/IF); to guide, lead (K/IFb); 2) {syn: bi rêve birin} to conduct, carry out, direct, manage, perform, run *(vt.)*: •**Li dijî têkoşerên serxwebûna Kurdistanê şerekî gemarî *dimeşîne*** (Wlt 1:36, 1)

It is *carrying out* a dirty war against those fighting for the independence of Kurdistan. < Ar mašá مشى = 'to walk' [K/IFb/GF/BK/ZF3] <meşîn>

meşihan مەشیهان (HR) = to go, walk. See **meşîn**.

meşiyan مەشیان (JB3/JJ) = to go, walk. See **meşîn**.

meşîn مەشیـن *vi.* (-meş-). 1) {syn: bi rêve çûn} to go, walk; to travel; to walk away, leave, depart: •**Xatir ji sofî xwest û *meşiha*** (HR 3:45) He took his leave of the dervish and *departed*; 2) to strut, walk proudly (JJ/B). {also: meşihan (HR); meşiyan (JB3); [mechiian] مـشیـان (JJ); <meşan مشـان (dimeşe) (دمـشـه)> < Ar mašá مشى = 'to walk' [L/K/IFb/B/ZF3//JB3/JJ//HH//HR]

meşk مـشــك *f.* (-a;-ê). 1) {syn: ‘eyar I; ‘eyarşîrk} (butter) churner made of animal skin, *as opposed to sirsûm = wooden butter churner* (Wn); animal skin in which *dew* [yoghurt and water] is made, churner (IFb); animal skin *(used as receptacle)* (A); wineskin, goatskin: •**[Nêrgisa koçer]** ... **lolep di dest de dew kîyaye bêyî ku *meşka* wê çilkan bireşîne** (Lab, 8) [Nergis the nomad girl] ... with a wooden handle bar in her hand, churned the buttermilk without her *skin sack* spilling a drop •**Piştî ku diya min dewê xwe dikila, *meşka* xwe ya reş ji darê dadixist** (Alkan, 71) After my mother churned her buttermilk, she removed her black *skin sack* from the wooden frame; -**meşka avê** (K) waterbottle [made of animal skin]; -**meşka dew** (K) butter churner [made of animal skin]; 2) bagpipe (ZF3). {also: meşke (K[s]); [mechk] مشك (JJ); <meşk> مشك (HH)} Cf. Arc mšak משך/maška משכא = 'hide, skin' (M. Jastrow) -->Mid P mašk = 'mussuck, skin bag (for liquids)' (M3); P mašk مـشــك = 'waterskin'; Sor meşke مەشكە; Za meşk *f.* = 'churn (goat skin)' (Todd) [Wn/F/K/A/IFb/B/JJ/HH/SK/GF/TF/OK/ZF3] <ḧîz; kelek; k’il III[1]; k’unk; lewleb; p’ost; sirsûm; xinûsî>

meşke مەشكە (K[s]) = butter churner; leather wineskin. See **meşk**.

meşlûl مەشـلـوول (IFb/FJ) = confection of strung nuts dipped in boiled grape juice. See **meşlûr**.

meşlûr مەشـلـوور *m./f.(ZF3)* (-ê/-a;). confection of nuts strung and dipped in boiled grape juice [W Arm rojik ռոժիկ, T cevizli sucuk]. {also: meşlûl (IFb-2/FJ)} {syn: benî II[2]} [Frq/IFb/ZF3//FJ] <gelwaz; şaran; xarûz>

met/met’ [B] مـــەت *f.* (-a;-ê). paternal aunt, father's sister. {also: metik (TF/GF-2); [met] مـــت (JJ); <met/metik مـت/متك> (HH)} [cf. Ar ‘ammah عمّة = 'paternal aunt'--> P ‘amme عمه; T hala] [Sor pûr پـــوور = (maternal or paternal) aunt]; Za ‘em *f.* (Todd); Hau metîe *f.* = 'mother's or father's sister, aunt' (M4) [Ad/F/K/A/IFb/JJ/HH/GF//TF] <ap; jinap; mam; qîzmet’; xal; xaltî>

met’al مـەتـال (M/K[s]/JR)/metal مـەطـال (SK) = shield. See **mert’al**.

met’elmayî مـــەتـەلـمـایـى *adj.* 1) {syn: ‘ecêbmayî; hicmetî; ḧeyrî; ḧêbetî; mendehoş; şaşmayî} astounded, amazed, dumbfounded, surprised; perplexed, puzzled: -**met’elmayî man** = to be amazed, dumbfounded {syn: ‘ecêbmayî man; guhişîn; hicmetî bûn; ḧeyrîn}: •**Wexta kewotka Zîna nazik dîtin, *met’elmayî man*** (Z-1) When the doves saw slender Zin, they *were dumbfounded*; 2) discouraged, disheartened. < Ar mu‘aṭṭal مـعـطـل = 'idle, inactive, inoperative, shut-down' + mayî, *past part. of* ma[yî]n = 'to remain, become'; cf. Az T məəttəl galmag = 'to be amazed' [Z-1/K/B/GF]

met’elok مـــەتـەلـۆك *f.* (-a;-ê). proverb, proverbial saying: •**Ev berevoka cara pêşine ku mesele û *met’elokên* k’urdî bi awakî fire bi xwendevanê r̄ûs dide nasîn** (Dz,40) This collection introduces the Russian reader to Kurdish sayings and *proverbs* for the first time. {also: methelok (IFb-2/TF-2/Kmc/CS-2); <metele> مـتـلـه (HH)} {syn: gotina pêşîyan} < Ar maṭal مثل = ‘proverb’; =Sor pendî pêşînan پـەنـدى پـێـشـیـنـان; cf. Sor meteł مـەتـەڵ = ‘riddle’ [Dz/K/B/IFb/GF/FJ/TF/RZ//Kmc//HH]

metfînî مـەتـفـیـنـى *f.* (-ya;). 1) tomato sauce (OK); any red sauce in which food is cooked (Zx); 2) vegetable stew cooked in earthenware pot (CB-region of Cizîra Bohtan): •**Sînemê *metfînîya* bamiya çêkir** (FS) S. made okra *stew*. {also: medfûnî (GF/ZF3)} [Zx/OK/CB/FS//GF/ZF3] <avik [2]>

meth مەتھ (IFb) = praise. See **metḧ**.

methelok مـەتـھـەلـۆك (IFb/TF/Kmc/CS) = proverb. See **met’elok**.

metḧ مـــەتـح *f.(SK/OK/IFb)/m.(K)/pl.(Bw)* (-a/-ê;). praise: -**medḧ kirin** (SK)/**meth ~** (IFb)/**metiḧ ~** (OK/JJ) to praise: •***Metḧa* meke!** (Bw) *Don't brag*!; -**metha yekî dan** (IFb)/**medihê *fk-ê* dan** (K) to praise s.o., speak of s.o. in glowing terms; -**xwe meth kirin** (IFb)/**metḧêt xo kirin** (Bw) to brag, boast. {also: medḧ (SK/OK-2); medih (K); mediḧ (OK-2); meth (IFb); metiḧ (OK); [meth/

metih] متح (JJ)} {syn: p'aye I; p'esin} <Ar madḥ مدح = 'praise'; Sor metḧ مەتح = 'praise' [Bw/JJ//SK//K//IFb//OK]

metiḧ مەتِح (OK) = praise. See **metḧ**.

metik مەتِك (TF/GF/HH) = paternal aunt. See **met**.

metirk•e مەتِركە *f.* **(•a;•ê).** 1) crosspiece on shaft of a spade or shovel on which the foot presses [Sor espere ئەسپەرە]: **•Wî pîyê xwe deyna ser *metirkê* û dewisand ku meȓ di 'erdê da biçit xwar** (FS) He put his foot on *the crosspiece* and press down, so that the shovel would go down into the earth; 2) spade (RF/IFb) *{Hakkari dialect according to IFb}*. {also: medrexe (FS-2); <metirke> مەترکە (Hej)} [Bw/IFb/OK/Hej/RF/AA/FS/BF/ZF3] <bêr; meȓ II; tevir [3]>

metirsî مەترسی *f.* **(-ya;-yê).** danger, peril; threat, menace, risk: ***•Metirsiya* ku li ser wî bû, nema** (FS) *The peril* that was on him, has disappeared **•Siberoja Kurdistana me ya ezîz di *metirsiyê* de ye!** (EN) The future of our beloved Kurdistan is in *danger*! {syn: talûke; xedarî; xeter} <Sor metirsî مەترسی = 'apprehension, dread, fear; danger, peril, menace' [EN/IFb/ZF/BF/Wkt/FS] <gef>

metreq مەترەق *m.* **().** club, stick: **•Dê kêwe çî? Ez Abû Bekr im. Dê noke te nerm kem li ber *metreqan*** (SK 11:111) Where are you going? I am Abu Bakr. Now I'll soften you up with my *club* **•Ḧeta nedît *metreq*, negot s̱eddeq** (Dh) Until he saw *the stick* [being waved at him], he would not say "ṣaddiq" [=believe it] **•Xulamêt Eḧmed Aẍayê es̱lî dest dane *metreqan*, ȓabûne mut̲irban, têr kutan, kirine der** (SK 27:251) The real Ahmad Agha's henchmen laid hold of their *clubs* and went for the Gypsy musicians, gave them a thorough beating, and drove them out. {syn: ciniḧ; çîv; ço; çogan; çomax; gopal; kevezan; şiv[dar]} Cf. Ar miṭraq مطرق = 'hammer' [Dh/SK]

meûj مەئووژ (F) = raisin(s). See **mewîj**.

mevîj مەڤیژ (FS) = raisin(s). See **mewîj**.

mevşek مەڤشەك (TF) = threshing sledge, threshing board. See **moşene**.

mevşen مەڤشەن (CCG) = threshing sledge, threshing board. See **moşene**.

mewc مەوج *f.* **().** wave *(of the sea)*. {also: mewcan (K); moc (Z-3); [mú¨g] موج (JJ); <mewc> موج (HH)} {syn: êlk'an; p'êl} < Ar mawj موج [Z-3//IFb/HH//K//JJ]

mewcan مەوجان (K) = wave. See **mewc**.

mewcûd مەوجوود *adj.* found, located, situated, present; in existence: **-mewcûd kirin** (L) to provide, have present, have waiting: **•Sibehê şibaqê, gotîye, tuê li hewşa min *mewjûd bikî*. Tuê *mewjûd ne kî*, ezê serê te jêbikim** (L-1, #1:4, l. 15-17) Tomorrow at the crack of dawn, he said, you will *have* [them] *waiting* in my courtyard. If you *don't have* them *waiting*, I'll have your head cut off. {also: mewjûd (L); [meoudjoud] موجود (JJ)} {syn: p'eyda} < Ar mawjūd موجود = 'found, located' (*passive part. of* √w-j-d وجد = 'to find') [L//K/IFb/JJ]

mewij مەوژ (Srk/IFb/GF/TF) = raisin(s). See **mewîj**.

mewîj مەویژ *m./f.(B/Tkm)* **(/-a; /-ê).** 1) {syn: k'işmîş} raisin(s); high-quality raisins (Klk); raisins with seeds, *as opposed to **k'işmîş** [seedless raisins]* (Ag); 2) {syn: tirî} grapes (JJ/Tkm): **-mewîja ȓeş** (Tkm) black grapes. {also: mawij (FS-2); mehûj (K-2); meûj (F); mevîj (FS-2); mewij (Srk/IFb-2/GF/TF); mewuj (K); mewûc (Kp); mewûj (B/Rh); mêwij (Mzg/Bw); mêwuj (Mzg); mêwîj (Zx/FS); mêwûc (Ag); mêwûj (Bw-2); mihîj (Czr); miroj (Hk); m'ûj (Klk); [meoŭj موژ/ mevij مویژ/ meviz مویز/mevij-i hechk موژی هشك] (JJ); <mewêj> مویژ (HH)} <*madwīča- (M2, p.80); P mavīz مویز = 'currants, raisins'; Sor mêwuj مێووژ = 'raisins'; =Za işkij (Todd) [A/IFb/JJ/SK/OK/Çnr/Haz/Msr/Wn/Tkm//K//B/Rh//HH//F//Hk//Klk//Czr//Kp//Ag//Mzg/Bw//Srk/GF/TF//Zx/FS] <bistaq; ç'erez; k'işmîş; mêw; miştax; ȓez; teyk; tilîk; tirî>

mewjûd مەوژوود (L) = found. See **mewcûd**.

mewuj مەووژ (K) = raisin(s). See **mewîj**.

mewûc مەووووج (Kp) = raisin(s). See **mewîj**.

mewûj مەوووژ (B/Rh) = raisin(s). See **mewîj**.

mex مەخ **().** 1) {syn: mejî} brain; 2) liquid in the brain. Cf. Ar muxx مخ = 'brain' [Haz]

mexber مەخبەر (B/JJ/ZF3) = grave. See **meẍber**.

mexdenoz مەخدەنۆز (Wkt) = parsley. See **bexdenûs**.

mexel مەخەل *f./m.(B/K/FS)* **(/-ê;/-î).** open animal pen or sty; place for animals to lie down and rest; animal shelter in the wilderness (HH): **•Çaxa bêrîyê, ez pezê xwe ber bi *mexel* tînim** (AB) At milking time, I bring my sheep toward *the pen*; **-mexel [meẍel (Qmş/K/HH/GF)] bûn** (K/A/IFb/GF)/ **hatin** (K/A/B/HH) to sit or lie down *(of cattle or beasts of burden)* {syn: merixîn}: **•Carina hinek heywan *mexel dihatin*, ên mayî jî**

li dora wan diçêriyan (Alkan, 71) Sometimes some animals would *sit down*, and the rest would graze around them; **-mexel [meẍel** (Qmş/K/HH/GF)] **kirin** (K/A/IFb/B/TF) to cause to sit or lie down *(of cattle, etc.)*: **•L[a]wik ... ji sibehê heya êvarê devehan li çolê diçêrîne, n[î]vro wan tîne ser avê û *mexel dike*** (ZZ-10, 157) The boy ... from morning until evening lets the camels graze in the wilderness, at noon he brings them to water and *has* them *sit down*. {also: mexil (FS-2); meẍel (K); [meghel] مـغـل (JJ); <meẍel> مـغـل (HH)} {syn: axil; axur; guhêr̄; kotan I; k'ox [1]; k'oz} Cf. W Arm magał մակաղ; also cf. Ar maqīl مقيل = 'halting place' < √q-yl قيل = 'to nap' [AB/A/IFb/B/TF/FS//K/JJ/HH/GF] <dolge; gom I; lêf>

mexer مـهـخـهـر *f.* **(-a;-ê).** wide and flat plain: **•Ev navçeya bedew ku ji çar aliyên wê bi çol, beyar û çiyan ve hatiye dorpêçkirin, xwedî *mexereke* têrber e. Ji vê *mexerê* re "*Mexera* sibêbiyê" tê gotin. Li vê *mexerê*, bêhtirîn bostan, rez û gelek rengên çandinî yên wekî genim, nîsk, ce, nok, kizin, [ş]oqil, ... û hwd. têne çandin** (Gundê Avadorê [blogspot]) This lovely area [Kerboran] which is surrounded by wilderness, barren land and mountains, is on [lit. 'possessed of'] a fertile *plain*. This *plain* is called "*Plain of* Sibêbî". On this *plain* are planted the best orchards, vineyards, and many types of crops such as wheat, lentils, barley, chickpeas, vetch, peas, etc. {also: meẍer (GF)} [Frq/A/IFb/FJ/HH/FS/AD//GF]

mexil مهخِل (FS) = animal pen. See **mexel**.

mexilîn مـهـخِـلـيـن (K/B) = to lie down *(animals)*. See **merixîn**.

mexîn مهخين *m.* **().** Assyrian, Nestorian, and Chaldean Neo-Aramaic speaking Christian ethnic groups who, together with the Armenians, made up the Christian population of Kurdistan: **•[Haceta sergînan diçine gundê *mexînan*]** (Noel) For need of some fuel [as an excuse], they go to visit an *Assyrian* village (i.e., to meet a girl) *[prv.]* **•[Nêzûkî kela Xoşabê dû gundêd *Mexînan* hen navê yekî Qesir û navê yekî Pagan]** (JR) Near the fortress of Hoşap there are two *Assyrian* villages, one named Qesir, and one named Pagan: **-jina mexîn** (K) Assyrian/Nestorian woman; **-zimanê mexîna[n]** (K) language of the Assyrians/ Nestorians (=Neo-Aramaic or Modern Syriac). {also: [mekhin] مـخـيـن (JJ)} Cf. Geo somexi სომეხი = 'Armenian' [JR/JJ/K/GF/ZF3] <file; kirûng (Mzg); kîlo; Suryanî>

mexînî مهخينى *adj.* Assyrian, Nestorian *(adj. & lang.)*. [K/FS] <mexîn>

mexloq مـهـخـلـوق (Tsab) = people, creatures. See **mexulqet**.

mexluqet مـهـخـلـوقـهت (B) = people, creatures. See **mexulqet**.

mexlûq مـهـخلووق (SK/Tsab) = people, creatures. See **mexulqet**.

mexlûqat مـهـخـلـووقـات (IFb/SK) = people, creatures. See **mexulqet**.

mexlûqet مـهـخـلووقـهت (K/B/Tsab) = people, creatures. See **mexulqet**.

mexmer مـهـخـمـهر *m.* **(-ê;).** velvet. {also: mexmûr (IFb/GF/OK); [mekhmer] مـخـمـر (JJ)} {syn: qedîfe} < Ar muxmal مخمل [K/B/JJ/TF/ZF3//IFb/GF/OK]

mexmûr مـهـخـمـوور (IFb/GF/OK) = velvet. See **mexmer**.

Mexolî مهخۆلى (SS) = Mongolian. See **Mongolî**.

mexrib مهخرِب (Rnh) = sunset. See **moẍrib**.

Mexribî مهخرِبى (Wkp) = Moroccan. See **Meẍrîbî**.

Mexrîbî مهخريبى (BF/Wkt) = Moroccan. See **Meẍrîbî**.

mexsed مهخسهد (Z-3) = aim. See **meqsed**.

mexulqet مـهـخـولـقـهت *m.* **(-ê; wî mexulqetî).** people, creatures, beings; masses: **•Çak e hecetekî we-bînimewe, paşî bixom. Eger bê hecet bixom dê li-nik *mexlûqê* dî mes'ol bim, paşî iḧtimal heye ji min qebûl neken** (SK 5:55) I had better find an excuse and then eat it. If I eat it without an excuse I shall have to answer for it before other *people* and they may not accept [my behavior] **•Dibo r̄oja qiyametê. *Mexlûqat* hemî cema dibon, hemî bo ḧalê xo digirîn** (SK 40:107) It was the Day of Resurrection. All *creatures* were gathered together, weeping for their present state **•Dî gemî sekinîye *mexulqet* tê dik'evêda. T'ev wî *mexulqetî* ew jî çû k'et hundur̄ê gemîê** (HCK-3, #2, 21) He saw that the ship stopped and *people* are coming and boarding it. Together with those *people* he also went and got on board. {also: mexloq (Tsab-2); mexluqet (B-2); mexlûq (SK/Tsab-2); mexlûqat (IFb/SK-2); mexlûqet (K/B-2/Tsab-2); mixulqet (B/Tsab-2); muxulqet (Tsab-2); [makhlouq] مـخـلـوق (JJ)} {syn: xelq} < Ar maxlūqāt مـخـلـوقـات = 'creatures'; Sor mexlûq مهخلووق = 'people; being' [HCK/Tsab//B//IFb//K//SK/JJ]

meẍber مـهـغـبـهر *m./f.(B)* **(-ê/-a; /-ê).** grave, tomb;

burial vault. {also: meqber (IFb); meqbere (IF); mexber (ZF3); [makhbar مخبر/ meqber مقبر] (JJ); <meqbere> مـقـبـره (HH)} {syn: gor̄ I; mezel [3]; qebr; t'irb} < Ar maqbar مقبر [Z-1/K//B/JJ/ZF3//HH//IFb] <gor̄istan>

meẍel مەغەل (K/JJ/HH) = animal pen. See **mexel**.

meẍer مەغەر (GF) = plain. See **mexer**.

meẍreb مـەغـەرەب (B) = sunset; evening; west. See **moẍrib.**

meẍrîb مـەغـریـب (K) = sunset; evening; west. See **moẍrib**.

Meẍrîbî مـەغـریـبـی *adj*. Moroccan. {also: Mexribî (Wkp); Mexrîbî (BF/Wkt); Mixurbî (Wkt-2)} Sor Meẍrîbî مەغریبی [BF/Wkt//Wkp]

mey مـەی *f.* **(-a;-ê).** wine: **•vexwarina *qurtekê* ji meyê** (B.Omerî. Rûniştina bi serxweşekî re) drinking *a gulp* of wine. {also: [meï] مـی (JJ); <mey> مـی (HH)} {syn: şerab} [Pok. médhu- 707.] = 'honey; mead; adj. sweet': Av maδu- = 'berry wine'; P mey مـی; Sor mey مەی [IFb/FJ/GF/Kmc/JJ/HH/RZ/SS/ZF3/FS]

meyandin مـەیـانـدِن *vt.* **(-meyîn-).** 1) to ferment *vt. (yoghurt)*; 2) to let stg. freeze, thicken (OK); to freeze *vt. (fig., e.g., in politics)* (IFb). {also: mehandin I (WM)} Cf. P māye مـایـه = 'ferment, leaven, yeast' [WM//K/IFb/OK/ZF3] <mehîn II>

meyav مـەیـاڤ *adj.* 1) {syn: tenik[3]; ≠k'ûr III} shallow: **•Wî li cihê *meyav* yê rûbarî sovekarî kir** (FS) He swam at a *shallow* place in the river; 2) {syn: mend I; peng II} stagnant; 3) [*f.* (;-ê).] shallow place: **•Wî di *meyavê* da melevanî kirin** (FS) He swam in *a shallow place.* [Wkt/ZF3/FS/FD]

meydan مەیدان *f.* **(-a;-ê).** 1) (town)square, plaza: **•Paşê têne meydanê** (J) Then they come to the square; 2) battlefield. {also: [midan] مـیـدان (JJ); <mîdan> میدان (HH)} Cf. Ar/P maydān میدان, T meydan [K/JB3/IFb/B//JJ/HH/SK/GF/ZF3] <qad>

meydenoz مەیدەنوز (IFb) = parsley. See **bexdenûs**.

meyik مەیك (Bw) = button. See **mêvok**.

meyil مەیِل (IFb) = inclination. See **mêl**.

meyildar مەیِلدار (IFb) = supporter; one in favor of. See **mêldar**.

meyildarî مـەیِـلـداری (JB3) = being in favor of stg. See **mêldarî**.

meyir مەیر (Qzl) = type of soup. See **mehîr**.

meyizandin مـەیِـزانـدِن (JB3) = to look at, watch. See **mêze**.

meyîn مـەیـیـن (IFb/GF) = to coagulate; to freeze. See **mehîn II**.

meykut مەیکوت (K[s]) = mallet; pestle. See **mêk'ut**.

meyl مەیل (K/A/HH/GF) = inclination. See **mêl**.

meyldar مـەیـلـدار (K/HH/GF) = supporter; one in favor of. See **mêldar**.

meyldarî مـەیـلـداری (K/GF) = being in favor of stg. See **mêldarî**.

meymûn مـەیـمـوون *f.* **(-a;-ê).** monkey, ape. {also: [maimoun/meimūn (PS)] مـیـمـون (JJ); <meymûn> میمون (HH)} < Ar maymūn میمون = 'monkey' --> T maymun; Sor meymûn مەیموون [PS/K/IFb/B/JJ/HH/GF/OK/ZF3]

meyt' مـەیـت *m.* **(-ê;).** corpse, dead body: **•Kerro *meyt'ê* K'ulik bir danî mal** (FK-kk-13:131) Kerro took Kulik's *body* and brought it home **•Silêman dîtin** [sic], **mirî ... *Meytê* Silêmanî danane** [sic] **ser darbestê, înane** [sic] **gundî** (SK 10:100) Then they saw Sulaiman, dead ... They placed Sulaiman's *corpse* on a stretcher and brought it to the village. {also: [meit] مـیـت (JJ)} {syn: berat'e [2]; cendek; cinyaz; leş; term} < Ar mayyit مـیِّـت = 'dead' (<√m-w-t مـوت = 'to die') [FK-1/K/B/JJ/SK/GF] <mirin>

meyten مەیتەن (FS) = type of robe. See **mîtan**.

meyvan مەیڤان (IFb) = guest. See **mêvan**.

meywe مەیوە (K/IFb/TF) = fruit. See **mêwe**.

meyz مەیز (A) = look, glance. See **mêze**.

meyzandin مـەیـزانـدِن (HR) = to look at, watch. See **mêze**.

mezad مـەزاد *f.* **(-a;-ê).** auction, public sale. {also: [mezad] مـزاد (JJ)} {syn: herac} < Ar mazād مـزاد = 'auction, public sale' <√z-y-d زیـد = 'to increase'; Sor mezat مەزات [Dh/Şxn/K/IFb/JJ/JB1-A/GF]

mezar مەزار, m. (GF/OK) = grave. See **mezel**[3].

mezaxtin مـەزاخـتِـن *vt.* **(-mezêx-).** to spend *(money)*: **•Ew di heyvê da du hezar dînara *dimezêxit*** (FS) He *spends* 2,000 dinars per month **•Min hinde dirave li xaniyê xo *mezaxtin*** (Zeb) I *spent* so much money on the house. {also: [mezakhtin] مضاختین (JJ); <mezaxtin> مەزاختن (Hej)} {syn: serf kirin} ?<Arc meḵes מכס (miḵsā) מכסא = 'toll, tax' & Syr maḵsā ܡܟܣܐ = 'tribute, impost, toll, tax' [Bw/Zeb/Hej/RZ/JJ/FS]

mezel مـەزەل *f.* **(-a;-ê).** 1) [<Ar manzil مـنـزل (<√n-z-l نـــزل = 'to descend, alight') = 'house, lodgings'] {syn: ode; ot'ax} {also: mezelk (JB1-A/OK-2)} room, chamber: **•Em li *mezela* binî r̄ûniştîn** (SK 54:604) We were sitting in *the room* below; 2) dwelling (HH); 3) [<Ar mazār مزار (<√z-w-r زور

= 'to visit, frequent') = 'shrine'] {also: mezar, m. (GF/OK)} {syn: gor̄ I; mex̂ber; qebr; t'irb} grave, tomb. {also: mezelk (JB1-A); [mezar مــزار/mezel مـزل] (JJ); <mezel> مـزل (HH)} [M/K/A/JB3/IFb/JJ/HH/SK/TF/OK//JB1-A//GF]

mezelk مەزەلك (JB1-A/OK) = room. See **mezel**[1].

mezin مەزن/**me<u>z</u>in** مـەظِـن [JB1-A/HH] *adj.* 1) {syn: gir I} large, big: **-mezin bûn** = to grow (up): **•Masî di avê da *mezin dibin*** (AB) Fish *grow (up)* in the water; **-t[']ilîya mezin** (F/K/B)/[telīye mazyn] (JJ-PS) thumb {syn: beranek; girdik}; 2) {syn: kal I; navsera; pîr; sere I} old, agèd; elder, older: **•Xûşka ç'ûk gote xûşka *mezin*** (Z-1) The youngest sister said to the *eldest* sister; 3) [*m.* **(-ê;)**] adult (Bw); an elder, senior member: **•Bav *mezinê* malê ye** (AB) The father is *the senior member of* the household **•Dê û bav *mezinên* me ne** (AB) [Our] parents are our *elders* **•Li pêş *mezinekî* xwe nabe ku em titûnê bikêşin** (Epl, 23) In front of *an elder* it is not all right for us to smoke tobacco; 4) {syn: pêşeng; r̄êber; r̄êvebir; r̄êzan; serek; serk'ar [1]; serok; serwer} leader, head, chief, person in charge: **•Dasinî mezhebek e, Êzedî jî dibêjinê ... *Mezinê* wan li gundê Bê'edrî dir̄ûnêt. *Mezinekî* wan zemanekî hebû, nawê wî 'Elî Beg bû** (SK 39:344) The Dasinis are a sect, also called Yezidis ... Their *leader* resides in the village of Be'adri. Once they had *a leader* whose name was Ali Beg •[Words of a policeman to thieves he has caught] **Em her̄in cem mezin** (Z-922) Let's go to the chief. {also: mazin (M-Ak/TF); [mezin] مـزيـن (JJ); <me<u>z</u>in> مـظـن (HH)} [Pok. meĝ(h)- 708.] = 'great': Skt maha- & mahā́nt- = 'great'; Av maz- & mazant- = 'big'; cf. also Lat magnus; Gr megas μέγας; Alb i madh {mezinahî; mezinatî; mezinayî; mezintî; meznayî; [mezinaï] مـزيـنـاى (JJ)} [F/K/A/JB3/IFb/B/JJ/JB1-S/SK/GF/OK//HH/JB1-A//M-Ak/TF] <girs>

mezinaî مـەزنـائـى (F/JJ) = size; greatness; leadership. See **mezinahî**.

mezinahî مەزناهى *f.* **(-ya;-yê).** 1) size: **•Qatekî din di vê *mezinahiyê* de, lê rengekî din tuneye gelo?** (KS, 34) Don't you have another suit in this *size*, but in a different color?; 2) greatness: ***•Mezinatî* bi aqlî ye, ne bi sal e; dewletmendî bi me'rifetê ye, ne bi malî ye** (SK 22:207) *Greatness* [or, *maturity*] is in wisdom, not in years; wealth is in knowledge, not in property; 3) leadership, position of authority (FK-eb-1). {also: mezinaî (F); mezinatî (K-2/SK); mezinayî (K/B/GF-2); mezinî (GF-2); mezintî (IFb-2); meznayî (A/FK-eb-1); [mezinaï] مـزيـنـاى (JJ)} [JB3/IFb/GF//K/B//F/JJ//SK//A] <mezin>

mezinatî مەزناتى (K/SK) = size; greatness; leadership. See **mezinahî**.

mezinayî مـەزنـايـى (K/B/JJ/GF) = size; greatness; leadership. See **mezinahî**.

mezinî مـەزِنـى (GF) = size; greatness; leadership. See **mezinahî**.

mezintir مەزنتِر *comp. adj.* bigger, larger; older, elder; greater: **•Geşte biraê *maztirê*, milê xo li milê wî da** (M-Ak) He reached the *eldest* brother and nudged him with his shoulder **•Hebû, qe ji xudê *mestir* t'inebû** (Z-4) There was, there wasn't anyone *greater* than God [introductory formula for folktales]. {also: maztir (M-Ak); mestir (Msr/K-2/A/Z-4); [mezintir] مزينتر (JJ); [master] مستر (JJ-G)} [Msr/A/JJ-G/Z-4//F/K/IF/JJ//M-Ak] <mezin>

mezintî مەزِنتى (IFb) = size; greatness; leadership. See **mezinahî**.

mezî مەزى = oak tree. See **mazî**.

me'zme'zîk مەعزمەعزيك (SC) = backbone, spine. See **mezmezk**.

mezmezk مەزمەزك/**me'zme'zk** مەعزمەعزك *m.(F/K)/f.(B)* **(; /-ê).** backbone, spinal column, spine. {also: bazmazk, f. (B); me'zme'zîk (SC)} = Sor pirusk پڕووسك. Cf. Av mərəzu- *n.* = 'vertebra of the neck or back'; Hau mazî *m.* = 'back' (M4) [F//K//B//SC] <derzen; kilêjî>

meznayî مـەزنـايـى (A/FK-eb-1) = size; greatness; leadership. See **mezinahî**.

mezra مەزرا (B) = hamlet, farmstead. See **mezre** [2].

mezr•e مـەزرە *f.* **(•a;•ê).** 1) field (K[s]/B): **-Mezra Bohtan** (IFb)/**Mezra Bota** (Haz) Mesopotamia; 2) {also: mezra (B-2)} hamlet, tiny settlement consisting of a few households connected to a larger village; farmstead (B/JJ). {also: [mezra] مـزرع (JJ); <mezre> مـزره (HH)} < Ar mazra'ah مـزرعـة = 'farm' (<√z-r-' زرع = 'to sow, plant') [Haz/IFb/B/HH//JJ]

mezrome مـەزرۆمـە (ZF3) = type of grape. See **mezrona**.

mezromî مـەزرۆمـى (Haz/ZF3) = type of grape. See **mezrona**.

mezrona مـەزرۆنا **().** type of grape which ripens in the autumn; variety of white grape [yapıncak] (IFb).

{also: merzore (IFb); mezrome (ZF3); mezromî (Haz/ZF3-2); mezrûn (K[s])} [Btm(Ȟatȟatkê)//Haz//K(s)//IFb//ZF3] <tirî>

mezrûn مـــــــــــــهزروون (K[s]) = type of grape. See **mezrona**.

mê مـــــــــــێ *f.* **(meya/miya;).** female: **-berxa mê** (B) female lamb; **-ȟirça mê** = female bear; **-k'era mê** = she-ass {syn: mak'er}; **-kewa mê** = female partridge {syn: mêkew}; **-k'êvroşka mê** = female rabbit. {also: [mi/meĭ] مـــى (JJ); <mê> مـــى (HH)} {≠nêr} [Pok. 3. mā- 694.] 'mother': P māde مــاده = 'female'; Sor mê مــێ; Za make/mayke *f.* (Mal) [BX/K/A/JB3/IFb/(B)/HH/GF/TF//JJ] <dêl I; mak>

mêgamêş مـێـگـامـێـش *f.* **().** female buffalo. {syn: mange [2]; medek} [OK/ZF3] <gamêş>

mêhvan مێهڤان (JB1-A&S/HH/TF/Bw/FS) = guest. See **mêvan**.

mêhvandar مـێـهـڤـانـدار (TF/FS) = host; hospitable, gracious. See **mêvandar**.

mêhvanxoş مـێـهـڤـانـخـۆش *adj.* hospitable, gracious. {syn: mêvandar; mêvanȟiz (B/F); mêvanperwer (OK); nandar} [Bw] <mêvan>

mêj I مـــێــژ **().** the past, old times—*used mostly in the following*: **-ji mêj ve** (BX/IFb)/**ji mêjva** (K) for a long time (up to and including the present moment), for years, for some time now {syn: zûda}: **•Ez *ji mêj ve* li ser vê pirtûkê dixebitim** (IF) I have been working on this book *for some time*. {also: [ji-mij ژمـيـژ/ ji-mijin ژمـيـژيـن] (JJ)} Sor mêj مێژ = 'past time' & mêjû مێژوو = 'history' [Zx/BX/K(s)/JB3/IFb/GF//JJ]

mêj II مـــێــژ = namaz, salah, Islamic prayer ritual. See **nimêj**.

mêjandin مێژاندِن *vt.* **(-mêjîn-).** to nurse *(vt.)*, suckle: **•Wê zar̄okê xwe *mêjand*** (FS) She *nursed* her child **•Wî berxê bê mak *mêjand*** (FS) He nursed the motherless lamb. {also: mijandin (IFb-2/GF/OK-2); [mijandin] ميژاندين (JJ); <mijandin مژاندن (dimijîne) (دمژينه)>} Sor mijandin مِژاندِن [K/A/IFb/B/OK//JJ//HH/GF/ZF3/FS] <dayîn III; memik; mêtin/mijîn; sawa; şîrmêj>

mêjî مێژی (Ber/IFb/SK/TF/ZF3) = brain. See **mejî**.

mêjîşûştin مێژیشووشتِن (Ber/ZF3) = brainwashing. See **mejîşûştin**.

mêker مێکەر (GF) = female donkey. See **mak'er**.

mêkew مـێـکـەو *f.* **(-a;-ê).** female partridge. {syn: marî} [BX/FS/ZF3/Wkt] <kew>

mêk'ut مـێـکـوت *m.* **().** 1) large wooden mallet used for driving stakes into the ground (K/B/JJ); 2) {syn: desteconî} pestle: **•[Û di ekserêd malan da cuhnî û *mêkut* heye bi xwe dermanî diqutin û çê dikin]** (BN 135) And in most households there is a mortar and *pestle* [which they use to] pound and make medicines. {also: meykut (K[s]); mîkut (GF-2); [miqout ميقوت/ moqout موقوت] (JJ)} Cf. Ar mīqa'ah مـيـقـعـة = 'grindstone, whetstone', but **k'utan** = 'to beat' is Kurdish; Sor mêkut مێکوت = 'mallet' [BN/K/IFb/B/GF//JJ] <ç'akûç; ger̄an I

mêkutok مێکوتۆك (GF) = chicken pox. See **mîrkut**.

mêl مـــێـــل *f.* **(-a;-ê).** inclination, tendency, propensity: **-mêl ft-îra hatin** (B) to have a propensity for stg., to desire stg., to feel like doing stg.; **-mêla *fk-ê* ser *ft-î* heye** (XF) to be a supporter of s.o., to be on s.o.'s side, to be in favor of s.o.: **•*Mêla* k'urda *ser* ûr̄isa *bû*** (XF) The Kurds *were on* the Russians' *side* **•*Mêla* axaler û begleran jî *ser* xandinê *t'une bû*** (XF) The aghas and beys *were not in favor of* learning [=education] **•*Mêla* hikûmeta we ji kê re çêtir heye, *ji* elemanan *re* an *ji* sondxwariyan *re*?** (Ronahî) Who *is* your government *in favor of*, the Germans or the Allies?; **-mêla *fk-î/ft-î* kirin/k'işandin** (B/XF) to long, yearn, or pine for, to miss. {also: meyil (IFb-2); meyl (K/A/GF); [meil] مـيـل (JJ); <meyl> مـيـل (HH)} <Ar mayl مـيـل = 'tendency; turning off, deviating (from a path)' (<√m-y-l = 'to incline, bend'); Sor meyl مەیل = 'inclination' [Rnh/IFb/B/XF//K/A/HH/GF//JJ] <ȟewas; mêldar>

mêlak مێلاك *f.* **(-a;-ê).** 1) {syn: cegera spî; k'ezeba spî; p'işa spî; sîh I} lung: **-mêlaka sor** (Bw) do.; 2) {syn: ceger[a r̄eş]/cerg; p'işa r̄eş} liver (HH/GF). {also: [melák] مـعـلاق (JJ); <mêlak> ميلاك (HH)} <Ar mi'lāq مـعـلاق = 'pluck (of an animal)' [Bw/A/IFb/HH/GF/ZF3/FS//JJ]

mêldar مێلدار *m.* **().** 1) {syn: alîgir} supporter, backer, fan, adherent, enthusiast; 2) *[adj.]* in favor of, 'pro', 'for': **•Em *mêldarên* elemanan *in*** (Rnh) We *are for* the Germans; 3) having a tendency (to), inclined (to), disposed (to). {also: meyildar (IFb); meyldar (K/GF); <meyldar> ميلدار (HH)} Cf. Sor meyldar مـــەیـــلـــدار = 'inclined, disposed (to)' {mêldarî} [Rnh//IFb//K/HH/GF] <mêl>

mêldarî مێلداری *f.* **(-ya;-yê).** support, backing (e.g., for a candidate) , being in favor of stg.: **-mêldarîya *ft-ê* kirin** (Rnh) to be in favor of stg., be on the side of stg./s.o.: **•Em *mêldariya* sondxwariyan**

dikin (Rnh) We *are in favor of* the Allies. {also: meyildarî (JB3); meyldarî (K/GF); [meildari] میلداری (JJ)} {syn: alîgirî; piştgirî} Cf. Sor meyldarî مەیلداری = 'disposition, wish' [Rnh//JB3//K/GF//JJ] <mêldar>

mêr I مێر *m.* **(-ê;).** 1) {syn: meriv; peya I; zilam} man, person; [pl.] people: **•Malxê malê wan li mal nebû. Jin û biçûk hebûn, çu *mêr* li wê-derê ḧazir nebûn** (SK 30:270) The owner of their property was not at home. There were the women and children, but no *men* present there; 2) {syn: hevser [m.]; şû} husband: **-mêr kirin** (IFb/GF) to get married *(said of a woman)* [Cf. jin anîn/ standin *(said of a man)*]: **•Ez tu carê *mêra* li dinyaê *na kim*** (L) I *shall never marry*. {also: [mir] مر (JJ); <mêr> میر (HH)} [Pok. 4. mer-/merə-, 5. mer-/merə- 735.] = 'to rub away, harm; to die' -->[Pok. mór-to- 735.] 'mortal; man, person': Skt mártya- [-i̯o- *extension of* *mór-to-] = 'man, person'; Av mašya- [-i̯o- *extension of* *mór-to-] & marəta- = 'mortal, man'; OP martiya- [-ii̯o- extension of *mór-to-] = 'man' (Kent); Mid P mard = man & mērag = 'young man, husband' (M3); P mard مرد = 'man'; Sor mêrd مێرد = 'husband'; Za merde *m.* = 'husband' (Todd); Hau mêrd *m.* = 'husband' (M4) {mêranî; mêrayî; mêrdayetî; mêretî; mêrtî} [K/A/JB3/IFb/B/HH/GF//JJ] <meriv>

mêr II مێر, See mar I.

mêranî مێرانی *f.* **(-ya;-yê).** 1) manhood; masculinity; 2) manliness, bravery: **•Eger *mêrantiya* te heba, tu yê bihata cem min** (ZZ-7, 160) If you were a man [lit. had *manliness*], you would have come to me **•Keç'ika û jina jî k'ilamêd *mêranîyê* ser wana derdixistin** (Ba2:1,p.204) Girls and women composed songs of *bravery* about them **•Zilamek got: "Ez ji kûç'kê xwe hînî *mêranîyê* bûm"** (Z-1554) A man said: "I learned *what is it to be a man* from my dog." {also: mêrantî (ZZ); mêrayî (K/B); mêrdayetî (K[s]); mêretî (A); mêrînî (SK); mêrtî (K); [mirani] مرانی (JJ)} [K/JB3/B/IFb/JJ/GF/TF/OK//A//SK//ZZ] <mêr>

mêrantî مێرانتی (ZZ)= manhood; bravery. See **mêranî**.

mêrayî مێرایی (K/B) = manhood; bravery. See **mêranî**.

mêrdayetî مێردایەتی (K[s]) = manhood; bravery. See **mêranî**.

mêrdezime مێردەزمە *m./f.(ZF3)* **().** nightmare, bad dream: **•Dîrok, Stephen got, *mêrdezimeyek* e, ya ku ez 'hewil didim jê hişyar bibim** (FB: Kawa Nemir) History, Stephen said, is *a nightmare* from which I am trying to awake. {also: mêrdezme (SS)} Sor mêrdezime مێردەزمە [FB/ZF/IFb//SS] <xewn>

mêrdezme مێردەزمە (SS) = nightmare. See **mêrdezime**.

mêretî مێرەتی (A) = manhood; bravery. See **mêranî**.

mêrg مێرگ *f.* **(-a;-ê).** meadow; prairie: **•Hesp di *mêrgê* da diçêre** (AB) The horse grazes in *the meadow* **•Min ç'ya, zozana, mêrga *biç'êrîne*** (J) *Pasture* me in the mountains, summer pastures [and] meadows; **-mêrg û çîmen** (Rnh 2:17, 307) do. {also: mêrgelan, f. (JB3); [mirk] مرك (JJ); <mêrg> میرگ (HH)} {syn: aran I[3]; ç'ayîr[1]; ç'îmen} <*margyā-: Av marəγā-; Cf. Ar marj مرج = 'meadow'; Sor mêrg مێرگ = 'meadow'. See: G. Morgenstierne. "The Name Munjān and Some Other Names of Places and Peoples in the Hindu Kush," *BSOAS*, 6 (1930), 440, reprinted in: *Irano-Dardica* (Wiesbaden : Dr. Ludwig Reichert Verlag, 1973), p.111. [K/A/JB3/IFb/B/HH/SK/GF/TF//JJ] <ç'êre>

mêrgelan مێرگەلان (JB3) = meadow. See **mêrg**.

mêrik مێرك = dim. of **mêr**.

mêristan مێرستان (AD) = anthill. See **mûristan**[1].

mêrî مێری (Bw) = ant. See **mûrî I**.

mêrînî مێرینی (SK) = manhood; bravery. See **mêranî**.

mêrkuj مێركوژ *m.* **(-ê;).** assassin, murderer, homicide. {also: [merif-kouj] مرف كوژ (JJ)} {syn: xwînî} < mêr = 'man' + kuj- = 'kill'; = Sor pyawkuj پیاوكوژ {mêrkujî} [K/A/IFb/B/GF/TF/OK/BK/ZF3//JJ]

mêrkujî مێركوژی *f.* **(-ya;-yê).** murder: **•Ew ji *mêrkujîya* bi qestî mehkûm bûye** (lemonde-kurdî #15 ii.2011) He was convicted of premeditated *murder*. [JB3/IFb/B/TF/OK/ZF3/Wkt] <mêrkuj>

mêrtî مێرتی (K) = manhood; bravery. See **mêranî**.

mêrû مێروو (SK/OK) = ant. See **mûrî I**.

mêrxas مێرخاس *m.* **(-ê;).** 1) {syn: 'efat; 'egît; fêris [1]; gernas; leheng; p'elewan} hero, brave person; 2) {syn: merd [2]} *[adj.]* brave, courageous. {also: [merxas] مرخس (JJ)} {mêrxasî; mêrxastî} [K/A/JB3/IFb/B/GF/TF//JJ] <camêr>

mêrxasî مێرخاسی *f.* **(-ya;-yê).** bravery, courage; heroism: **•Seva qedrê wan û *mêrxasîya* wan** (Z-1) Because of their honor and *courage*. {also: mêrxastî (K-2)} {syn: merdayî; mêranî} [K/JB3/IFb/B/GF/TF] <camêrî; mêrxas>

mêrxastî مێرخاستی (K) = bravery. See **mêrxasî.**

mêş مێش *f.* **(-a;-ê).** 1) fly (insect), zool. *Diptera*: •**R̄îwî çû, got, "...ĥîleyekî li qelê bikem, belkû tola xo jê wekem" ... R̄îwî çû bin dara gûzê ... xo li bin gûzê dirêj kir, xo mirand. Çavêt xo ber spî kirin, dewê xo beş kir, kêlbêt xo gir kirin, *mêş* hatine dewê wî** (SK 3:23) The fox went away, saying, "I had better go and play a trick on the crow. Perhaps I can have my revenge on her." ... The fox went beneath a walnut tree ... he stretched himself out at the foot of the walnut tree and made out to be dead. He turned up the whites of his eyes, hung his mouth open and bared his teeth. *Flies* came into his mouth; **-mêş kirine gamêş** (Zeb/Dh) to make a mountain out of a molehill, exaggerate, overreact; **-mêşa gû** (Msr) dung fly; 2) bee, zool. *Apis mellifera* (IFb) {syn: moz I[3]}: **-mêşa hingiv** (K/B) bee {also: mêş-hingiv (Ad); mêşa hingivî (A/JB3/IF); <mêşîhingifî> میشیهنگفی (HH)}. {also: [mych] مش (JJ); <mêş> میش (HH)} Av maxši- & Mid P maxš = 'fly' (M3) (different root, according to Pok); Mid P also magas (M3); P magas مگس = 'fly'; Sor mêş hengwîn مێش هەنگوین = heng هەنگ = 'bee'; Za mês *f.* = 'fly' (Todd); K mêş --> T meșe [Babik *Pötürge-Malatya] = 'bee' (DS, v.9, p.3172) [F/K/A/JB3/IFb/B/HH/SK/GF/TF/OK//JJ] <axûrk; k’ermêş; kur̄ifok; moz I; p’êşî II; şaheng; zilketk>

mêş•e مێشە *f./m.(B)* **(;•ê/wî mêşeyî).** forest, woods: •**Darbir̄ çû *mêşe* dara bibir̄e** (Dz) The woodcutter went to *the forest* to cut down trees •**Ezê usa bikim, wekî zîanê bidim *mêşê*** (Dz) I will act in such a way as to bring harm *to the forest* •**Kur̄o, darbir̄, çima ... vî *mêşeî* bedew xirav dikî?** (Dz) Lad, woodcutter, why ... are you ruining this beautiful *forest*? •**Ser Dûmanlûê t’u *mêşe* t’unebûn, vira dar jî hêşîn nedibûn** (Ba2:1, 202) On [Mount] Dumanlu there were no *forests*, trees did not even grow here. {also: [miché میشه/ michestan میشستان] (JJ)} {syn: daristan; dehl [2]; gorange; r̄êl} Skt vṛkṣa- = 'tree'; Av varəša- = 'forest'; P bīše بیشه = 'forest'; Sor bûş بووش/ bûşelan بووشەلان; T meșe [Uluşiran *Şiran-Gümüşhane] = 'forest' (DS, v. 9, p. 3172) & Az mēşe [J/F/K/B/GF/OK//JJ] <dar I>

mêşin مێشن *f.* **().** 1) {syn: mî I} sheep, *zool.* Ovis aries: •**Bav û birayên min hin ji me bijortir *pezê mêşin* diçêrandin** (EŞ, in SW1, 76) My father and brothers were even higher up [the mountain] than us, letting *the sheep* graze; 2) sheepskin (GF/JJ/IFb). {also: [mechin] مشین (JJ); <mêşin> میشن (HH)} Cf. Mid P mēš (M3); P mīš میش = 'ewe'; *see etymology under **mî I**.* [EŞ/IFb/FJ/GF/TF/HH/RZ/ZF/JJ/FS]

mêşinî مێشنی *adj.* obedient, docile, submissive *like a sheep*: •**Ew kur̄ekê *mêşinî* ye** (FS) He is a *docile* boy. [Frq/FJ/FS]

mêşkişk مێشکشك (OK) = fly swatter. See **mêşkuj.**

mêşkuj مێشکوژ *f.* **(;-ê).** 1) fly swatter, fly whisk: •**Wî mêş bi *mêşkujê* kuştin** (FS) He killed flies with a fly swatter; 2) fly (or insect) repellent: •**Wî *mêşkuj* li mêşa reşand** (FS) He sprayed *fly repellent* at the flies. {also: mêşkişk (OK-2); mêşkujk (Bw-2)} [Bw/OK/FS/FD/ZF3] <mêş>

mêşkujk مێشکوژك (Bw) = fly swatter. See **mêşkuj.**

mêşok مێشۆك *m.* **().** bag, sack. {syn: t’elîs; t’êr̄ II; xerar (IF)} Cf. Rus mešok мешок [Ba2/K/B]

mêştin مێشتن (M-Ak) = to suck. See **mêtin.**

mêşvan مێشڤان *m.&f.* **().** beekeeper: •**Li Wanê jinên *mêşvan* hingivê xwe komkir** (Anadolu Ajansı 22.ix.2017) In Van women *beekeepers* collected their honey. [AnadoluAjansı/IFb/ZF/Wkt/AD] <mêş>

mêşvanî مێشڤانی *f.* **(-ya;-yê).** beekeeping, apiculture: •**Ev jin, ji bona ku alîkariya malbata xwe bikin, *mêşvaniyê* dikin** (Anadolu Ajansı 22.ix.2017) These women are doing *beekeeping* [or, are keeping bees] in order to help their families. {also: mêşvan[î]tî (Wkt-2)} [AnadoluAjansı/IFb/ZF3/Wkt/AD] <mêş>

mêşvanîtî مێشڤانیتی (Wkt) = beekeeping. See **mêşvanî.**

mêşvantî مێشڤانتی (Wkt) = beekeeping. See **mêşvanî.**

mêtin مێتن *vt.* **(-mêj-).** to suck: •**Memik t’une bû, wekî xwer̄a *bimêje*** (EP-7) There was no breast for him *to suck*. {also: mêştin (M-Ak); mijîn (AB/K); [mitin] میتین (JJ); <mêtin میتن (dimêje) (دمیژه)> (HH)} O Ir *maik-: Av maēkant- = 'oozing out'; Mid P mēč- = 'to suck'; P makīdan مکیدن; Sor mijîn مژین = 'to suck, absorb'; Hau miştey (mij-) *vt.* (M4) [EP-8/F/A/JB3/IFb/B/HH/ GF//K/AB//JJ//M-Ak] <memik; mêjandin>

mêvan مێڤان *m.&f.* **(-ê/-a; mêvên *or* mêvîn [B], vî mêvanî/).** guest: •***Mêvanê* ‘ezîz** (B) Dear *guest*; **-çûn mêvan** (F/K)/**mêvanî çûyîn** (B) to go visiting, go on a visit (see also: **mêvanî**): •**Were em her̄ine mêvanî** (Dz) Come, let's go visiting. {also: mehvan (IFb-2); meyvan (IFb-2); mêhvan

(JB1-A&S/TF/Bw/FS); mîvan (Srk); nîvan (Mzg); [mihvan مهوان/mihman مهمان /mivan ميوان] (JJ); <mêhvan> مـيـهـڤـان (HH)} [Pok. 2. mei-, 3. mei- 710.; meigw- 713; 2. meit(h)- 715.] 'to change, go move; *with derivatives referring to the exchange of goods and services within a society as regulated by custom or law*': O Ir *maiθman-: Mid P mehmān = 'inhabitant, guest' (M3); Pashto melman; P mihmān مـهـمـان; Sor mêwan مێوان; Za meyman *m.&f.* (Todd); Hau mêman *m.* & mêmane *f.* (M4) {meyvandarî; mêvanî; mêvandarî; mêvantî} [K/(JB3)/Haz/IFb/B/GF//JJ//HH/JB1-A&S/TF/Bw/FS//Srk//Mzg] <mazûban>

mêvandar مـێـڤـاندار *m.&f.* **().** 1) {syn: mazûban} host (hostess [f.]), one who entertains guests; 2) *[adj.]* {syn: mêhvanxoş (Bw); mêvanĥiz (B/F); mêvanperwer (OK); nandar} hospitable, gracious. {also: mêhvandar (TF/FS)} [K/IFb/GF/OK//TF/FS] <mêvan>

mêvandarî مێڤاندارى (K/IFb) = hospitality; visit; being a guest. See **mêvanî**.

mêvanĥiz مـێـڤـانـحِـز *adj.* hospitable, gracious. {syn: mêhvanxoş (Bw); mêvandar; mêvanperwer (OK); nandar} [F/B] <mêvan>

mêvanî مـێـڤـانـى *f.* **(-ya;-yê).** 1) hospitality; 2) being a guest; visit: **-mêvanî çûyîn** (B)/**çûn mêvandarîyê** (IFb) to go visiting, pay a visit to, call on; **-mêvanî hatin** (B)/**hatin meyvandarî** (IF) to come on a visit, pay a visit to: **•Qîz r̄abû li ber sekinî, 'ezet, qulix, îk'ram, "Çawa seydaê min *hatîye mêvanya* min"** (HCK-1, 201) The girl stood beside him, [with] deferential treatment and respect, "As my teacher *has come to visit* me" **•Wê roja ku *hatibû mêvandariya* min, ji min re gotibû … ez ê xwe bigihînim wî** (KS, 9) The day she *came to visit* me, she told me … I should go to him. {also: mêvandarî (K-2/SK/IFb); mêvantî (K-2); mêwandarî (SK)} [B/K/IFb//SK] <mêvan>

mêvanperwer مـێـڤـانـپـەروەر *adj.* hospitable, gracious: **•Piştî ku bavê te î *mêvanperwer* bihîst ku ez mamostê gundê X'ê me, bi rewşa mîrekî mezin rûmeteke bilind da min, li ser kulavê xwe î nexşîn ciyek da min** (Lab, 11) After your *gracious* father heard that I was the teacher of X village, he treated me like a great emir, and made a place for me on his embroidered felt carpet. {syn: mêhvanxoş (Bw); mêvandar; mêvanĥiz (B/F)} [Lab/OK] <mêvan>

mêvantî مێڤانتى (K) = hospitality; visit; being a guest. See **mêvanî**.

mêvok مـێـڤـۆك *f.* **(-a;).** button. {also: meyik (Bw); mêwik (FS); [mivik] مـيـوك (JJ); <mêwik> مـيـوك (HH)} {syn: bişkoj; qumçe} according to JJ, dim. of mêwe/[meva/meivé] ميوه = 'fruit' [A/IFb/ZF3/BF//JJ//HH/FS//Bw]

mêw مێو *m./f.(FS/ZF3)* **(/-a;/-ê).** vine, grapevine, vine-stock: **•Vê *mêwê* gelek tirî daye** (FS) This vine has given many grapes; **-mêwa tirî** (FS) do. {also: [miv] مـيـو (JJ); <mêw> مـيـو (HH)} Cf. P mo مو/ mev ميو; Sor mêw مێو; Za mew/mewêrî *f.* (Todd); Hau mêwî *f.* (M4) [K(s)/A/JB3/IFb/HH/GF/TF/FS//JJ] <gûşî; lem; mewîj; r̄ez; tirî>

mêwandarî مـێـوانـدارى (K/IFb) = hospitality. See **mêvanî**.

mêwe مـێـوه *m./f.(ZF3)* **(-yê/-ya;/-yê).** fruit: **•Riweka sebrê tehl e, lê *mêweya* wê şîrîn e** (A. Gurdilî. Aforîzmayên feylesofan… 47) The plant of patience is bitter, but its *fruit* is sweet. {also: meywe (K-2/ IFb-2/TF); [meva/meivé] مـيـوه (JJ)} {syn: ber V; êmîş [1]; fikî; *xuzar} Mid P mēwag (M3); P mīve مـيـوه --> T meyve; Sor mîwe مـيـوه; Hau mêwe *m.* (M4) [K/IFb/ZF3//TF//JJ] <balete>

mêwij مێوژ (Mzg/Bw) = raisin(s). See **mewîj**.

mêwik مێوك (HH/FS) = button. See **mêvok**.

mêwîj مێويژ (Zx) = raisin(s). See **mewîj**.

mêwuj مێووژ (Mzg) = raisin(s). See **mewîj**.

mêwûc مێووو ج(Ag) = raisin(s). See **mewîj**.

mêwûj مێوووژ (Bw) = raisin(s). See **mewîj**.

mêzandin مێزاندن (HR) = to look at, watch. See **mêze**.

mêze مـێـزه *f.* **().** look, glance: **-mêze kirin** (IFb/GF) to watch, look at, contemplate, observe {also: meyizandin (JB3); meyzandin (HR); mêzandin (HR-2)} {syn: berê xwe dan [b]; fikirîn II; nêr̄în; zên dan (MK/K)}: **•Mîrê eciniya *li* her duka *meyzand*** (HR 4:9) The mir of the jinn *looked at* the two of them **•*Mêzeke*, ew k'îye tê?** (B) *Look* [and see] who that is [who is] coming. {also: meyz (A); [mizer] ميظر (JJ); <mêzekirin ميزكرن (mêzedike) (مـيـزدكـه)> (HH)} {syn: zên (MK-tape)} Cf. Ar mayyaza II ميّز = 'to distinguish' [Ad/EP-7/K/JB3/IFb/HH/GF//A//JJ] <nêr̄în>

mêzer مـێـزەر *f.* **(-a;-ê).** 1) covering, ground cloth; 2) blanket (IFb/GF/FJ); 3) {syn: cacim} kilim, type of rug (Elk/A/GF); 4) {syn: berdilk [4]; berk'oş; bermalk; bervank; melîtk; şalik I} apron (B/Kmc-#5547); 5) large bath towel (Kmc-#5548). {also:

<meyzer> میزر (HH)} Cf. Ar mi'zar مئزر = 'apron, wrapper, covering, cover' [Elk/K(s)/A/IFb/B/GF/TF/FJ/Kmc//HH]

mêzên مێزێن (JB3/IFb/OK) = pair of scales. See **mêzîn**.

mêzîn مێزین *f.* **(-a;-ê).** 1) {syn: şihîn; t'erazî} pair of scales *(for weighing)*: **•Ûsib řadive ser takî *mêzînê*, zêřa jî dikine t'aê dinê** (Ba) Joseph gets up onto one pan *of the scales*, and they put gold on the other pan; 2) Libra (astr.) (JJ). {also: mêzên (JB3/IFb/OK); [mizin/mizén] میزین (JJ)} < Ar mīzān میزان (<√w-z-n وزن = 'to weigh') [Ba/K/B/GF//JB3/IFb/GF/OK//JJ] <t'a II>

mi م = me; I; my. See **min I**.

miamel•e مِئامەلە *f.* **(•a;).** treatment, dealing (with): **-miamele kirin** [+ **bi ... ra** *or* **digel**] (Wkt) to treat (a topic or person); to deal with, have dealings with: **•Bawer bikin me dikaribû bi awayekî din jî *bi* wan *re miamele bikira*, lêbelê me nekir** (TRT Nûçe) Believe me, we *could have treated* them differently, but we didn't **•Divêt bi awayekê stratejîk *miamele digel* vê meseleyê *bêt kirin*** (www.nefel) This issue *should be treated* in a strategic manner **•Gerek mêr qet tucarî li jina xwe nede yan *bi wê miamela* tal û xirab *neke*** (JW.org) A man must never strike his wife or *treat her* severely. {also: miemele (Wkt-2); muamele (Wkt-2)} Cf. Sor mamiłe مامِڵە = 'bargain, business deal' < Ar mu'āmalah معاملة = 'treatment' (< 'āmala III عامل = 'to treat s.o.') [IFb/ZF/Wkt]

miaş مِئاش (B) = salary. See **meaş**.

micadel•e مِجادەلە *f.* **(;•ê).** debate, argument: **•Rabû k'etne *micadelê* bi hev re** (HR 4:18) They began *debating* each other/They got into *an argument*; **-micadele kirin** (IFb) to debate, argue. {also: [moudjadilé] مجادله (JJ)} {syn: gengeşe; mişt û miř; nîqaş} < Ar mujādalah مجادلة = 'debate' [HR/IFb//JJ]

mical مِجال (Z-2) = power; chance. See **mecal**.

miclis مِجلِس = assembly. See **meclîs**.

miclîs مِجلیس (Z-2) = assembly. See **meclîs**.

miç I مِچ *adj.* pricked-up *(ears, of animals)*: **•Bi du guhên *miç* li min guhdarî dike** (HYma, 11) With two *pricked-up* ears he listens to me; **-miç kirin** (GF) to prick up *(ears, of animals)*: **•Bi bihîstina deng re min bi hêz serê xwe ji ser bahlifê rakir, *guhên xwe miç kir*** [sic] **û li wî dengî guhdarî kir** (KS, 58) Upon hearing the sound, I raised my head sharply off the pillow, *pricked up my ears* and listened to that sound. {also: mûç I (IFb); <mûçkirin موچکرن (mûçdike) (موچدکە)> (HH)} {syn: bel} [HYma/Elk/KS/GF/FJ//IFb/HH]

miç II مِچ (Elk) = puckered up; shut. See **mûç II**.

miçandin مِچاندِن *vt.* **(-miçîn-).** to close, shut *(eyes, sphincter valve)*: **•Dibêjin bestekî** [sic] **beran li-tenişt gundê wan heye. Wextê diçin e seferê ji řêwe diçin e-naw besta beran, çawêt xo *dimiçînin*, pêş paş diçin** (SK 12:117) They say that there is a stony vale next to their village. When they go on a journey they go first of all to the vale of stones, *shut* their eyes, go back and forth. {also: [mitchandin] مچاندین (JJ)} {syn: damirandin} [Bw/IFb/JJ/SK/GF/ZF3] <ç'av; niqandin I>

miçilge مِچِلگە *f.* **().** 1) {syn: merc I; şert [2]} bet, wager; 2) ransom: **•Serê min û malê min t'emamê wînekê *miçilge* be** (Z-3) May my head and my property, all of it, be *a ransom*. {also: *miçilqe (A); <miçilge> مچلگە (HH)} Cf. range of meanings of Arabic root r-h-n رهن; Cf. P mučalkā مچلکا/mučalkāh مچلکاه/mučalka مچلکه = 'bond, note of hand, agreement, promise'; T müçelge [موچلکا] (15th cent.) = 'promissory note, title deed, voucher, receipt' [=Mod T senet] (TS, v. 4, p. 2822) & Chagatay mäųilrä = 'legal deed, legal document' [from: Radloff, v. 4, p. 2224]; of Mongolian origin: see: Doerfer vol. 1, #370. موچلگا = 'legal document, by which one obligates oneself to perform a particular deed by oath and by contract, with the simultaneous fixing of certain reprisals or countermeasures in case of breaking of said contract' [Z-3/IFb/HH/GF/ZF3//A]

*miçilqe مِچِلقە (A) = bet, wager. See **miçilge**.

miçiqandin مِچِقاندِن *vt.* **(-miçiqîn-).** 1) {syn: çikandin II} to cut off or stanch the flow *(of water)*; 2) {syn: çikandin II} to dry up *(vt.: a river, swamp, etc.)*, dessicate. [K/IFb/B/ZF3] <çikandin II; miçiqîn; pengandin>

miçiqîn مِچِقین *vi.* **(-miçiq-).** 1) {syn: çikîn} to stop flowing *(of water, blood, rivers, etc.)*; 2) {syn: ç'ikîn} to dry up, run dry *(of a water source)*: **•Zargotina me piř dewlemend e... Ew kaniyeke guř e. Piř milet ji wê kaniyê avê hildidin, lê kanî *namiçiqe*** (Wlt 2:59, 16) Our folklore is very rich... It is a gushing spring. Many people draw water from that spring, but it *won't run dry*. [F/K/IFb/B/GF] <çikîn; miçiqandin>

miçînk مِچينك, m. (Bw) = tweezers. See **mûçink**.

miemele مِئهمهله (Wkt) = treatment. See **miamele**.

mifa مِـفـا *m.* **(-yê;-y).** advantage, benefit: **•Me çi *mifa* ji wê gencîna di sîngê wan da *nekirîye*** (Bêhnişk, 5) We *did not take advantage of* that treasure in their breasts **•... û *mifay ji* hizrên baş *werbigrîn*** (Bêhnişk, 5) and *derive benefit from* good ideas. {also: **menfa'et**; mife't (Bw-2)} {syn: feyde; havil; menfa'et} <Ar manfa'ah منفعة [Bw/SS/FS]

mife't مِفهعەت (Bw) = advantage. See **mifa**.

mifirdî مِـفِـردى *m.* **(-yê;).** guard, watchman; bailiff, deputy, sheriff's officer (JJ); courtier, one in attendance at a royal court (L-II): **•Ezê bi hersê qesemê navê xudê kim, erke ji ser wî t'extî hiltînî, hilîne, erke hilnayînî, tê serê xo bi cindî û *mifirdîyê* Bota ji nava herdu pîlê xo bavêjî** (Z-3) I make three oaths in the name of God: if you get off of this bed, that is fine; if you don't, / You will lose your head from between your shoulders to the nobles and *guards of* Botan **•"Mamo! Ma Mîr tiştek gote te?" / *Mifirdî* dey ne kir, serî hêjand, bi lalî gote no** (L-II, 310, l.3111) "Uncle! Did the emir tell you anything?" / *the courtier* said nothing, [but] shook his head as if to say no **•*Mifirdî* tawankar weranî dadgehê** (FS) *The deputy* brought the criminal to court. {also: [mufurdi] مـفـردى (JJ); <mifirdî> مـفـردى (Hej)} {syn: pawan; qerewil} < Ar mufrad مـفـرد = 'individual, person' [L2/Z-3/IFb/ GF/TF/OK/Hej/FS//JJ]

mifriq مِـفـرق *f.* **().** north: **•Ez hatime ji welatê *mifriq*** (FK-eb-1) I have come from a *northern* land. {syn: bakur; şemal} [FK-1/K]

mifs مِفس (Bw) = colander. See **mifsik**[1]

mifsik مِـفـسِـك *f.* **(-a;-ê).** *round metal utensil with perforations, used as a strainer*: 1) {also: mifs (Bw-2)} colander, strainer; sieve; 2) skimming ladle: **•Wê birinc bi *mifsikê* kir di lalîkê da** (FS) She put the rice in the plate with *a ladle*. {also: mifs (Bw-2); mefsik (CB-2); <mefsik> مـفـسـك (HH)} <Ar miṣfāh مـصـفـاة = 'strainer, colander' (*with metathesis of* -sf- *to* -fs-) + -ik = *dim. suffix* [Bw/OK/CB/ZF3/FS//HH] <bêjing; parzinîn; parzûn>

mift مِفت = key; lock. See **mifte**.

mift•e مِفته *f.* **(;•ê).** 1) {syn: kilît[2]} key (K/JB3/IFb): **•Du girtiyên tirk her êvar *[m]ifteyên* girtîgehê didizin, derî vedikin, û bi şev diçin ji xwe re digerin** (AW74B7) Two Turkish prisoners steal the prison *keys* every night, open the door, and go out at night and wander around; **-k'ilît û mifte** (Z-1) lock and key; 2) {syn: kilît[1]} lock (IFb): **-mifte kirin** (K) to lock up: **•Li dergehê bexçe mêzand, kû deryê bexçê wê *meftiĥkirye*** (HR 3:50) He looked at the gate of the garden, [and saw] that the garden door *was locked*. {also: meftiĥ (HR); mift; mifteh (IFb); muft (B); [mufteh مـفـتـح/müftə مـفـتـا] (JJ); <mifta> مـفـتـا (HH)} < Ar miftāḥ مـفـتـاح = 'key/ (<√f-t-ḥ فـتـح = 'to open') [Z-1/ K/JB3/ZF//IFb//HR//B]

mifteh مِفتەه (IFb) = key; lock. See **mifte**.

mih مِه (JB3/HH/GF/TF) = ewe. See **mî I**.

mihafez•e مِـهـافـەزە *f.* **(•a;).** preservation; protection: **•Ji wilayeta Mûsilê jî do tabor 'esker digel do topan dê hên bo terbiya Suto û *muĥafeza* Teto** (SK 61:738) From Mosul two battalions with two guns will come to discipline Suto and *to protect* Teto; **-mihafeze kirin** (K)/**muĥafeze ~** (SK) to keep, preserve, protect: **•Ez yeqîn dizanim dîsa dê te xazin e Mûsilê, emma nebît biçî. Dê te xendiqînin. Ĥetta bişêy *xo* li cîyê xo *muĥafeze bike*** (SK 48:500) I know for certain that they will summon you to Mosul again, but you must not go. They will hang you. *Protect yourself* in your own home while you can **•Tuê van herdû mûê laşê min bixî qotîyekê û tuê *pir mihafeze bikî*** (L) You will put both hairs of my body in a box, and you'll *take very good care of* them. {also: mihafize (K); muĥafeze (SK)} < Ar muḥāfaẓah محـافظة [L//K/ /SK] <parastin>

mihafize مِـهـافِـزە (K) = preservation; protection. See **mihafeze**.

mihandin مِهاندِن (Wkt) = to wear out. See **meĥandin**.

mihbet مِهبەت = love. See **muĥbet**.

mihebet مِهەبەت (K) = love. See **muĥbet**.

mihel مِهەل (K) = city quarter. See **miĥel**.

mihelmî مِهەلمی (Wkt) = Mhallami. See **miĥelmî**.

mihes مِهەس (IFb) = curry-comb. See **meĥes**.

mihirvan مِهرڤان (GF) = kind; amiable. See **mihrivan**.

mihî مِهى (SK) = ewe. See **mî I**.

mihîj مِهيژ (Czr) = raisin(s). See **mewîj**.

mihlet مِهلەت (JB3/Rnh) = respite. See **molet**.

mihriban مِهربان (K) = kind; amiable. See **mihrivan**.

mihrivan مِـهـرڤـان *adj.* kind, benevolent; amiable; affectionate. {also: mihirvan (GF); mihriban (K); mihrîvan (TF/ZF3)} {syn: dilovan; r̄iĥsivik; xwînşîrîn} Mid P mihrbān = 'friendly, kind' (M3); P mehrabān مهربان [BX//K//TF//GF]

mihrîvan مِهریـڤـان (TF/ZF3) = kind; amiable. See **mihrivan**.
mihsik مِهسِك (IFb) = slipper. See **mes I**.
mihtac مِهتاج (IFb) = needy. See **muhtac**.
miḧal مِحال (Z-2) = city quarter. See **miḧel**.
miḧark مِحارك (HR) = bead(s). See **morî I**.
miḧel مِـحـل *f.* **(-a;-ê).** district, neighborhood, quarter *(of city)*: •**Bajarê Muxurzemînê bajarekî mezine, gelekî girane, / Ev bajarê hanê li ser sêsid û şêst û şeş kuç'ane, / Her kuç'ekê li ser sêsid û şêst û şeş *miḧelane*, / Her *miḧelakê* li ser sêsid û şêst û şeş minarane** (Z-2, 65) The city of Mukhur-zemin is a great city, very weighty, / This city contains three hundred and sixty six stone heaps, / Each heap contains three hundred and sixty six *town quarters*, / Each *quarter* contains three hundred and sixty six minarets. {also: mehele (IFb); mihel (K); miḧal (Z-2); [mahalé] محله (JJ); <meḧele> محله (HH)} {syn: t'ax} < Ar maḥall[ah] [ة]مـحـل = 'section, part, quarter (of city)' (<√ḥ-l-l حلّ = 'to stop, halt, stay') [Z-1//K//IFb/JJ/HH]
miḧellemî مِحەللەمی (Qmş) = Mhallami. See **miḧelmî**.
miḧelmî مِـحـەلـمـی *m.&f.* **().** Mhallami, members of ethnic group in Mardin and Hasakah who speak Arabic, are Muslim, and trace their origins to the Banû Bakr of Arabia (Wkp) [zimanê wan 'erebî ye, dînê wan Îslam e, 'esla wan Suryanî/Banû Hilal]: •**Çanda pêkvejiyanê li Mîdyadê ewqas bi pêş ketiye ku her kes hem Kurd, hem Siryanî, hem *Mihelmî* ye û her kes hem êzdî, hem mesihî û hem jî musilman e** (Rûdaw 25.xii.2016) The culture of co-existence is so advanced in Midyat that everyone is Kurdish, Assyrian and *Mhallami*, and everyone is Yezidi, Christian and Muslim •**Ereb û *Mihelmiyên* Mêrdînê, çûn ziyareta Parlementera Mêrdînê Gulser Yildirim ya duh serbest hat berdan** (rojname.com 5.i.2014) The Arabs and *Mhallamis* of Mardin went to visit the Mardin parlementarian Gulser Yildirim who was released yesterday. {also: mehelmî (Wkt); mihelmî (Wkt-2); miḧellemî (Qmş-2)} [Qmş//Wkt//Rûdaw/Rojname]
miḧîn I مِحین (Z-2) = mare. See **mehîn I**.
miḧîn II مِـحـیـن (Qzl) = to wear out (vi.), become dull. See **meḧîn I**.
mi'în معین (HB) = mare. See **mehîn I**.
mij مِـژ *m./f.(JB3/IFb/B/OK)* **(/-a; /-ê).** fog, mist: **-mij û dûman** (Ba2) do.: •**nava *mij û dûmanê*da** (Ba2) amid *fog and mist*; **-mij û kirove** (Zeb) do. {also: [myj مـژ/ myji مـژی] (JJ); <mij> مـژ (HH)} {syn: dûman; kirove [1]; moran; xumam, f. (JB3)} [Pok. meigh-/meik- 712.] 'to glitter, twinkle, dark (twinkling before one's eyes)': I. meigh- B. 'to become dark before one's eyes, fog, cloud': Skt mēghá- *m.* = 'cloud' & míh *f.* = 'mist'; Av maēγa- = 'cloud'; Mid P mēγ = 'cloud, mist' (M3); P meh مه; Sor mij مـژ; Za mij *m.* (Todd); cf. Arm mēg մեգ = 'fog'; Eng mist; K-->T mij [Erciş-Van] = 'fog' (DS, v. 9, p. 3198); See **mih** in I. Gershevitch. "Etymological Notes on Persian mih, naxčīr, bēgāne, and bīmār," in: *Dr. J.M. Unvala Memorial Volume* (Bombay, 1964), pp.89-91; reprinted in his *Philologia Iranica*, pp. 190-91. [F/K/A/JB3/IFb/B/JJ/HH/GF/TF/OK]
mijan مِژان (AA/Hej) = beam of a plow. See **mijane**.
mijandin مِژاندن (IFb/GF/OK/HH) = to nurse *(vt.)*. See **mêjandin**.
mijan•e مِـژانـه *f./m.(FS/BF)* **(•a/;).** part of the plow connecting the yoke to the main body of the plow: beam [Tu saban oku]; pole, shaft (AA). {also: mejan (IFb-2); mijan (AA-2); <mijane> مـژانـه (HH); <mijan مـژان/ mijane مـژانه> (Hej)} {syn: morsele; tîr I[2]} Sor mijan مـژان [Bw/AA/A/IFb/HH/GF/TF/Hej/Zeb/FS/BF/ZF3//OK] <cot [2]; halet; hincar; k'otan; nîr I; sermijank; sirnî>
mijang مِژانگ (A/IFb/GF) = eyelashes. See **bijang**.
mijank مِژانك (GF/JJ/HH) = eyelashes. See **bijang**.
mijar مِـژار *f.* **(-a;-ê).** topic, subject; matter: •**Di vê *mijarê* de hûn çi dikin?** (Wlt 1:39, 16) What are you doing about [lit. 'in'] this *matter*? •***Mijara* fîlmê Nîzametîn Arîç, li ser rewşa Kurdan e** (Wlt 2:59, 11) *The subject of* Nizamettin Arıç's film is the condition of the Kurds •**Zêrê pêwistî bi şîrovekirina *mijarê* dît** (DBgb, 14) Z. considered it necessary to explain *the matter*. {also: mijare (IFb-2)} {syn: babet I[2]; biyav; dabaş} [(neol)Wlt/IFb/GF/TF]
mijare مِژاره (IFb) = subject. See **mijar**.
Mijdar مِـژدار *f.* **(-a;-ê).** November. [(neol)Wlt/Wkt] <Ç'irî>
mijî مِژی (Srk) = eyelashes. See **bijang**.
mijîn مِژین (AB/K) = to suck. See **mêtin**.
mijlis مِژلس (L) = assembly. See **meclîs**.
mijmije مِژمِژه (OK/AA) = apricot. See **mişmiş**.
mijû مِژوو (Haz) = bone marrow. See **mejî** [2].

mijûl مِـــژووول *adj.* 1) {syn: bilî I} busy; 2) {syn: bilî} [+ **bi...ve**] concerned with, [pre]occupied with: **-mijûl bûn** (B): a) to be amused, entertained: **•Carekê tiştekî*va mijûl bin*** (Z-1) Why don't you do something to amuse yourselves [lit. '*be entertained by* stg.']; b) to be concerned with, [pre]occupied with, interested in: **•Rojhelatnasên ewropî ku *bi* "Memê Alan" *mijul bûne* çendek in** (DM) The European Orientalists who *have been interested in* "Memê Alan" are several **•Emê *bi* pirsên jêrîn *mijûl bibin* ...** (DM) We *will be concerned with* the following questions ...; **-mijûl kirin** (B) to entertain, [pre]occupy, amuse, divert; **-mijûl dan** (Haz) to speak, talk {syn: axaftin; p'eyivîn; qise kirin; şteẍilîn; xeber dan}. {also: mejẍûl (JB1-S); [mijoul] مژول (JJ); <mijûl> مژول (HH)} < Ar mašγūl مـشـغـول = 'busy' {mijûlahî; mijûlî; [mijouli] مژولى (JJ); <mijûlahî> مژولاهى (HH)} [Z-1/K/A/JB3/IFb/B/JJ/HH/SK/Haz/DM//JB1-S]

mijûlahî مِـــژووولاهـى *f.* **(-ya;-yê).** 1) amusement, diversion, entertainment, pastime; 2) conversation; 3) work, business, occupation, that with which one busies o.s. (HH). {also: mijûlî (K/B); [mijouli] مژولى (JJ); <mijûlahî> مژولاهى (HH)} [K/B/JJ//A/JB3/IFb/HH/SK] <mijûl>

mijûlank مِژوولانك, m. (OK) = eyelashes. See **bijang**.

mijûlî مِـــژووولـى (K/B/JJ) = amusement; pastime. See **mijûlahî**.

mik'an I مِكان (B) == possibility, ability; resource. See **îmk'an**.

mik'an II مِـــكـــان (Z-1)/mikan, f. (K) = place. See **mek'an**.

mikar•e مِـــكـــاره *m./f.(FS)* **(;/•ê).** chisel, auger, gimlet, tapering pod, pencil-sized metal pole with flat, sharp point, used for drilling holes in wood (before there were electric drills): **•Wî dar bi *mikarê* s̲imt** (FS) He made a hole in the wood [or tree] with *a chisel.* {also: miqar (IFb-2/RZ); miqare, f. (K); mixar (AD); nikare I (BF-2); [minqar/mnkar (GF)/makāra (Rh)] مـــنـــقـــار (JJ); <mikare> مـكـاره (HH); <miqar> مـقـار (Hej)} cf. NENA maqâr ܡܩܪ/mûqâr ܡܘܩܪ/mûghâr ܡܘܓ̰ܪ = 'chisel, graving-tool' (Maclean); Syr maqārā ܡܩܪܐ/ maqūrā ܡܩܘܪܐ = 'bird's beak; auger, gimlet' (√n-q-r) (Pyn-Sm) & Arc maqqor מקור = 'beak; tool for whetting millstones' (M. Jastrow) [Zeb/IFb/HH/OK/FS/BF//K//Hej/RZ//JJ//AD] <*alîsk; burẍî; şixab>

mikebs مِكەبس (IFb) = type of grape. See **misebq**.

mikin مِكِن (K) = to bleat. See **mikîn**.

mikîn مِـــكـــيـن *vi.* **(-mik-).** 1) {syn: k'alîn} to bleat *(of goats)*: **•Xar e, ne dar e / *Dimike*, ne kar e / Dik'şe, ne me'r e / Ew çiye?** **[Av]** (Z-1702) It's crooked, it's not a tree / It *bleats*, it's not a kid / It creeps, it's not a snake / What is it? *[rdl.; ans.: water]*; 2) [*f.* **().**] bleating (of goats). {also: mikin (K); mikmikîn (B-2)} [Z-1702/F//K/B] <bar̄în II; bor̄în I>

mikmikîn مِكمِكين (B) = to bleat. See **mikîn**.

mikur̄ مِكور: **-mikur bûn** (K)/**mikur hatin** (IFb/RF)/ **xwe mikur hatin** (K) to admit, confess: **•Ez *divê li xwe mikur werim* ku ez jî nikarim vê yekê bikim** (MUm, 17) I *have to admit to myself* that I can't do it either. {also: mukurhatin (TF)} {syn: *îtîraf; *pênasîn} Cf. Arc aker אכר < √n-k-r נכר = 'to recognize, know'; cf. also Heb mukar מוכר = 'recognized, known' [MUm/K/IFb/TF/RF]

mikur̄î مِكوڕى (K) = nostalgia. See **mukur̄î**.

mil مِل *m./f. (HR)* **(-ê/; /-ê).** 1) shoulder: **•Kalê dizvir̄e ser *milê* xwe, divê ...** (Dz) The old man looks back [lit. 'turns on [=over] his *shoulder*'] [and] says ... **•Pîrek e, çîçikê xwe avêtîye ser *milê* xwe** (L) It's an old woman, she has thrown her breasts over her *shoulders*; 2) upper arm (Ak): **•*Milê* qîza xwe girt** (J) He took [hold of] his daughter's *arm*; 3) {syn: huçik; zendik} sleeve; 4) {syn: alî} side (BX/IF): **•T'ê çê ĥewşê, mêzênê şêr li vê *milê* girêdayî ye, mehîn li vê *milê* girêdayî ye** (HR 3:141) You will go into the yard, you'll see the lion tied up on this *side*, the mare tied up on this [other] *side*; **-ji milê din** (BX) on the other hand [d'autre part]; 5) promontory, mountain plateau (JJ); mountain (HH). {also: [mil] مـــل (JJ); <mil> مـــل (HH)} Av mərəzu- *n.* = 'vertebra of the neck or back'; Sor mil مِل = 'neck'; Hau mil *m.* = '(nape of the) neck' (M4) [BX/K/A/JB3/IF/B/JJ/HH/JB1-A&S/SK/GF/TF/OK] <ç'epil; dest; navmil; pî I; pîl I; pol II>

milet/milet' مِـــلـــەت *m.* **(-ê;).** people; nation: **•Zargotina me pir̄ dewlemend e. *Miletê* me ew zargotin afirandiye, niha jî diafirîne.** (Wlt 2:59, 16) Our folklore is very rich. Our *people* has created this folklore, and is still creating it. {also: [milet] ملت (JJ); <millet> ملت (HH)} {syn: gel; net'ewe} < Ar millah ملّة --> T millet [K/JB3/IFb/B/JJ/HH]

milêb مِلێب *f.* **(-a;-ê).** pitchfork, wooden pitchfork used for winnowing grain. {also: melêf (B); melêv (B/

IFb-2); melheb (TF); melhep (IFb-2); melhêb (IFb-2); melhêp (A); milêv (IFb-2); milheb (K); milhêb (GF-2/FS); <milhêb> ملهيب (HH)} {syn: k'arêc; tebûr} cf. Syr malḥbā ܡܠܚܒܐ = 'winnowing fan' & NENA milkhâ-wâ ܡܠܚܘܐ/ܡܠܚܒܐ = 'large fork, esp. made of wood for use at the threshing floor' (Maclean) [IFb/JB3/GF//TF//A//K//HH/FS] <kunore>

milêba مِلێبا (FJ/FS) = sharecropper. See **mirêba**.

milêbayî مِلێبایی (FS) = sharecropping. See **mirêbatî**.

milêket مِلێکەت (IF) = angel. See **melek**.

milêv مِلێڤ (IFb) = pitchfork. See **milêb**.

milheb مِلهەب (K) = pitchfork. See **milêb**.

milhêb مِلهێب (GF/FS) = pitchfork. See **milêb**.

milik مِلِك *f.* **(-a;).** camel hump [T hörgüç, Ar sanām سنام]: **-milika ḧêştirê** (FS) do.; **•Hêştira *yekmilik* û hêştira *dumilik* heye** (A. Incekan. Compact Kurdish-Kurmanji 52) There is a *one-humped* camel and a *two-humped* camel. {also: milk (SS)} {syn: ḧawid} [Incekan/A/IFb/FJ/GF/ZF3/Wkt/G/FS/Kmc/CS/FS] <ḧêştir; lok' II>

milîak'et مِلیئەکەت, m.&f. (B) = angel. See **melek**.

milîs مِلیس *m.* **().** village guard [T korucu]; militia. <Fr milice = 'militia'. See: M.M. Gunter. *The Kurds in Turkey: a Political Dilemma* (Boulder, Colo.: Westview Press, 1990), pp. 81-82. [Haz/IFb/ZF3]

milîyak'et مِلییاکەت, m.&f. (B) = angel. See **melek**.

milk مِلك (SS) = camel hump. See **milik**.

milûk I مِلووك *m.* **().** 1) {syn: xwedî} owner, proprietor of land or wealth (K); 2) governor of a province (K): **•ev hersê *milûkê* ha** (Z-2) these three *governors*. Cf. Ar mulk ملك = 'property' [Z-2/K/ZF3]

milyak'et مِلیاکەت, m. (K) = angel. See **melek**.

mimkûn مِمكوون (IFb)/mimk'ûn (K) = possible. See **mumkin**.

min I مِن *prn.* me; I *(as the logical subject of past tense transitive verbs)*; my *{oblique case of ez}*: **•Ew *min* dibîne** = He sees *me* **•*Min* ew dît** = *I* saw him **•hevalê *min*** = *my* friend. {also: mi; [min] من (JJ); <min> من (HH)} Cf. P man من; Sor min مِن/emin ئەمِن = 'I'; Za min = 'me' [K/A/JB3/IFb/B/JJ/HH/JB1-A&S/SK/GF/TF/OK] <ez>

min II مِن *f.* **(-a;).** maund, mina, measure of weight approximately 3 kilograms: **•Ji Stembolê min guhark'ekê kirîye guhî ji baṯmanekê, xeleqa wê du *min* e, nala asênî** (JB1-A, #139) In Istanbul I put in his ear an earring that weighed a batman, the hoop of which is two *maunds*, shaped like a horseshoe. {also: [men] من (JJ)} <Akkadian manū = 'unit of weight': P man من; Sor min مِن/men مەن [JB1-A/OK/BF/FS//JJ] <batman I>

minal مِنال (IF) = child. See **mindal**.

minar•e مِنارە *f.* **(•eya;•ê).** minaret: **•Digel kewtina mela 'Ebbas, Muḧemmed Selîm ço, xeber da Faṯime Xanim, dayka xo. Got ê, "Seydaê me ji *minarê* kewt, mir"** (SK 15:152) When Mullah Abbas fell Muhammad Salim went and informed Madam Fatima, his mother. He told her, "Our teacher has fallen from *the minaret* and died" **•Rojekê şivanek diçe bajêr. Dinihêre ku yek derketîye ser *minarê* û diqîre** (LM, 11) One day a shepherd goes to town. He sees that someone climbs up to *the minaret* and shouts [something]. {also: [minaré] منارە (JJ); <minare> منارە (HH)} < Ar manārah منارة = 'light tower'--> T minare [Z-1/EP-7/K/A/IFb/B/JJ/HH/SK/GF] <mizgeft>

minasib مِناسِب *adj.* [+ *ezafeh*] appropriate, suitable [for s.o.] *{all-purpose positive term}*: **•çel xortê *minasib*** (L) forty *fine* young men [Quarante beaux jeunes gens] **•Ev teyr ne *minasibê* me ye** (L) This bird is not *appropriate* for us (=too good for us) **•Teyrekî pir *minasib* ê rind e** (L) It is a very *fine* and beautiful bird. {also: munasib (SK); [mounasib] مناسب (JJ)} < Ar munāsib مناسب --> T münasip [K/IFb//JJ/SK]

***mindal** مِندال *m.&f.* **().** child; children, offspring. {also: minal (IF-2)} {syn: kur̄ II; law[ik]; t'ifal, f.; zaro} Sor min[d]ał مِندال {mindaltî} [A/JB3//IF]

***mindaltî** مِندالتی *f.* **().** 1) {syn: zarotî} childhood; 2) childishness. [K(s)] <kur̄tî; mindal>

minemin مِنەمِن *f.* **(-a;).** muttering, whispering, carp(ing): **•De zû bixwîne û biqedîne, malava! Ev çi *minemina* te ye!** (Ardû, 135) Read it quickly and be done with it, old fellow! What is this *muttering of* yours! {also: minmin (TF)} {syn: mir̄emir̄; p'ilep'il} [Ardû/FJ//TF]

minesebet مِنەسەبەت (CS) = occasion. See **munasebet**.

minet مِنەت *f.* **(-a;-ê).** recognition, gratitude *(for a favor rendered)*; [feeling of] obligation to s.o. who has done you a favor: **•Qurba, min ter̄a qencî kir, ḧeyfa min te û kiḧêla te hat, yan wekî tu şer̄ dixazî em şer̄ kin, *minet* t'une** (Z-1) My dear, I did you a favor, I took pity on you and your bay horse, but if you want a battle, we will fight, there is no *obligation* **•Ra-be, ji-bedel wê çakîya kak**

Şasûar bizinek[ê] bi kar bo bibe, pêşkêş bike, 'erz bike, *me* qewî ji wî *minnet e* (SK 19:180) In return for this favor of Brother Shasuwar, get up and take a goat with a kid to him, present it to him and tell him *we are* very *grateful* to him **•Xozî tu jî řojek[ê] li min bûbay e mêwan, da min çak qedrê te girtiba, xizmeta te kiriba, da min çakîya te, *minneta* te ji-ser xo řa-kiriba** (SK 31:275) I wish that one day you would be my guest so that I could honour and serve you and rid myself of *the debt of gratitude* I owe you for your goodness; **-minet k'işandin** (K) to be obliged to s.o. (who has done a favor) ; **-mineta xwe ji *fk-ê* [ne]k'işandin** (FK-eb-1) to [not] let o.s. be indebted to s.o.: **•Memê *mineta xwe ji* kesi *nek'işand*** (FK-eb-1) Mem *would not let himself be indebted to* anyone. {also: minnet (SK); [minet] منت (JJ)} < Ar minnah منّة (<√m-n-n منّ = 'to grant (a favor)') --> T minnet [Z-1/K/IFb/B/JJ/GF//SK] <çakî>

minetdar مِنەتدار *adj.* grateful, thankful: **•Dîya min, ez bona wan qencî, mêvanhezî û dilovanîya ber bi min, *minetdarê* te me** (Elî Ebdulrahman Mamedov. Şer li çîya, 90) Mother, I am *grateful to* you for those acts of goodness, hospitality and compassion toward me. {also: minêkar (SS/TF)} {syn: spasdar} Cf. P minnatdār منتدار < Ar minnah منّة; Sor minetbar مِنەتبار [Mamedov/K/IFb//SS/TF] <minet>

minêkar مِنێکار (SS/TF) = grateful. See **minetdar**.

minmin مِنمِن (TF) = muttering. See **minemin**.

miqabil مِقابِل *adj.*1) {syn: dijber; pêşber; řaber} opposite, facing: **•alîyê *miqabil*** (B) the *opposite* direction **•Lê xan-manê Zîn xatûnê jî *miqabilî* ê Qeret'ajdînê bû** (EP-7) But Lady Zin's residence was [directly] *opposite* Qeretajdin's; 2) opposed (to), against: **-miqabilî *fk-ê/ft-î* bûn** (B) to be opposed to, to be against, to disagree with s.o. or stg.: **•Bavê te *miqabilî* çûyîna te*ye*** (B) Your father *is against* your going **•K'ê *miqabile*?** (B) Who *is opposed*? **•Řokê nişkêva bavê min gazî min kire bal xwe, got, wekî siba ew û dîa min wê heřne mala Mîloê bavê Sûsîkê, ku şîranya min û wê bixun, paşê pirsî: "Tu xwe *miqabil nînî*, lawo?"** (Ba2-#2, 207) Suddenly one day my father called me to his side, and said that the next day he and my mother would go to the house of Milo, Susik's father, to finalize the marriage between me and her [lit. 'to drink her and my sweet sherbet'], then he asked, "You'*re not opposed*, are you son?" {also: muqabil (SK); qambil (Nsb); [makabil/mokabil] مقابل (JJ); <meqabil> مقابل (HH)} < Ar muqābil مقابل [EP-7/K/IFb/B//JJ//HH//SK]

miqandin مِقاندِن *vt.* **(-miqîn-).** to grunt, snort: **•Du deve şandine, çika k'îjan deve e, k'îjan kudike ... Go, ... bera sivê du meriv lê syar bin, her yek here alîkî, go, bera sivê t'ev peyavin, wêderê deve*yê bimqîne*, kudikê têk'eve binî bimêje** (FK-K'eçelok) They have sent two camels: which is the mother, which is the baby? ... He said, let two men ride them tomorrow, each one on a different side, then let them dismount, and the [mother] camel *will grunt*, and the baby camel will come under her to nurse. {also: miqîn (FK-Keçelok-2); mirqandin (IFb/OK); <mirqandin مرقاندن/miqandin مقاندن> (Hej)} Sor mi[r]qandin مِرقاندِن = 'to grunt, snuffle' [FK-K'eçelok//IFb/ OK/Hej]

miqar مِقار (IFb/Hej/RZ) = auger, gimlet. See **mikare**.

miqare مِقارە, f. (K) = auger, gimlet. See **mikare**.

miqat مِقات *adj.* 1) careful, cautious; 2) [+ **li**] attentive (to) (JJ/TF): **-miqatî *fk-î* bûn** (B)/**li *fk-î* miqate bûn** (JB3/IFb/GF) /**miqayet li *fk-î* bûn** (WM) to look after, take care of s.o. {syn: xwedî lê kirin}: **•Gerekê hûn řind *miqatî* wî *bin*** (Ba) You must *take good care of* him **•Lê çiqa jî şivana û seêd wana *miqatî li* pêz *nekirana*, diqewimî, wekî gura mîk-dudu birîndar dikirin** (Ba2:1, 203) But no matter how much the shepherds and their dogs *took care of* the sheep, it happened that the wolves wounded a sheep or two **•*Li* van heywan-an *miqayet be*, heta ku ez herim destavê** (WM 1:2, 6) *Look after* these animals while I go to the bathroom **•*Miqatî xwebe*** (J) *Take care of yourself*; **-miqatî zara bûn** (F) to look after the children. {also: miqate (JB3/IFb/GF/TF); [mouqat] مقات (JJ)} *according to JJ,* <Ar muqayyad مقيّد = 'limited, registered'; NENA mqayid ܡܩܝܕ = 'to be careful' (Maclean); cf. also T dikkat = 'attention' < Ar diqqah دقّة = 'fineness, accuracy' in *dikkat-mikkat {miqateyî; miqatî} [K/(B)//JJ//JB3/IFb/GF/TF/OK/ /WM]

miqate مِقاتە (JB3/IFb/GF/TF/OK) = careful; attentive. See **miqat**.

miqateyî مِقاتەیی (TF) = looking after, care. See **miqatî**.

miqatî مِقاتی *f.* **(;-yê).** nursing, tending, looking (after), care (for): **-miqatî kirin** [+ lê] = to take care of: **•Dudu ji me heřin binihêřin, çika ew çi dû ye, dudu jî *miqatîyê li* kerîyê mîya *bikin*** (Ba2:2, 205) Two of us would go see what the smoke was, and two would *take care of* the flock of sheep. {also: miqateyî (TF)} {syn: sexbêrî; t'îmar} [Ba/K/B//JB3/IFb/GF//TF] <miqat>

miqayet مِقايەت (WM) = careful; attentive. See **miqat**.

miqdar مِقدار = amount. See **mixdar**.

miqilk مِــقِــلْــك *f.* **(-a;-ê).** pan, saucepan, frying pan. {also: meqle (JB1-A); miqlik (IFb-2); [meqilík] مقليك (JJ-Lx); <meqlik> مقلك (HH)} {syn: t'awe} < Ar miqlá [miqlan] مقلى & miqlāh مقلاة (<√q-l-y قلى = 'to fry') = 'frying pan' [Msr/JB3/IFb/ZF3/Wkt//JJ//HH//JB1-A] <beroş; mencel; qûşxane>

miqîn مِقين (FK-Keçelok) = to grunt. See **miqandin**.

miqlik مِقلِك (IFb) = pan. See **miqilk**.

mirad مِراد (IFb/JJ) = desire; goal. See **miraz**.

mirandin مِــرانــدِن *vt.* **(-mirîn-/-m[i]rên- [HR]).** 1) {syn: kuştin} to kill, put to death: **•Kû mere Xudê wî di îşêvda *bimrêne*, ez jê zû xilas bibim** (HR 3:290) If only God would *kill* him tonight, that I could soon be rid of him **•Noke cezaê hingo ew e, hingo di-bin daranda *bimirînim*, emma dîsa řeḧmê bi ḧalê hingo dikem, hingo nakutim** (SK 13:126) Now your punishment is this, that I should *beat you to death* with sticks, but I shall have mercy on your condition, I won't hit you; **-xwe mirandin** (SK) to act dead, pretend to be dead: **•Rîwî … xo li-bin gûzê dirêj kir, *xo mirand*** (SK 3:23) The fox … stretched himself out at the foot of the walnut tree and *pretended to be dead*; 2) {syn: t'efandin; temirandin; vekuştin; vemirandin; vêsandin} to extinguish, put out (light, fire). {also: [merāndin] مــرانــديــن (JJ-Rh); <mirandin مراندن (dimirîne) (دمرينه)> (HH)} Sor mirandin مِـرانـدِن = 'to cause the death of, deaden' [HR/K/A/IFb/JJ-Rh/HH/FJ/TF/JB1-S/SK/AD/CS]

mirar مِــرار *adj.* ritually unclean, impure *(of animals forbidden for Muslims to eat, e.g., the pig)*: **-mir[d]ar bûn** (K)/**mirar bûn** (Bw/HH/SK) to die without being ritually slaughtered *(of ritually clean animals; for ritually unclean animals, such as dogs, **sekitîn** is used, qv.)*: **•S̲ofî Şêx, zû řabe. Gaê me wê di bi řoḧê da. Eger zû nagiheyê *dê mirar bît*. Mixabin e. Wekuje, her nebît çermê wî xesar nabît** (SK 30:271) Sofi Shaikh! Our ox is at the point of death. If you do not reach it soon it will (die of itself and) *become carrion*. It is a pity. Slaughter it, at least do not let the hide be wasted **•Wextê jin çûn, şemala şemaê birine* hindav gay, dîtin* ko ga *mirar bûy*** (SK 30:273) When the women went and held a wax candle over the ox they saw that *it had died*. {also: mirdar [2] (K-2/IFb-2/GF-2); [merár] مرار (JJ-G); <mirar> مـــــرار (HH)} Mid P murdār = 'carrion' (M3); P mordār مـــــردار = 'animal carcass'--> T murdar/mundar [Bw/K/A/IFb/B/JJ-G/ HH/SK/GF/TF/OK] <sekitîn>

mirarî مِرارى (IFb/OK) = dirtiness. See **mirdarî**.

miravî مِـراڤـى *f.* **(-ya;).** wild duck; teal, short-necked river duck, zool. *Anas crecca* [T çamurcun] (IF); woodcock, zool. *Scolopax rusticola* [T çulluk] (IF). {syn: sone; werdek} Cf. P morγābī مـرغـابـى = 'wild duck, mallard'; Sor mirawî مِـراوى = 'duck' [K(s)/IFb/OK/ZF3/Wkt] <bet; mirîşk>

miraz مِــــراز *m./f.(FS)* **(-ê/-a; mirêz/).** 1) {syn: arzû; daxwaz; merem} desire, wish: **•*Miraza* wî dîtina zařokên wî bû** (FS) It was his *desire* to see his children; **-ber miraz** (Z-1) satisfied, having attained one's desire [lit. 'in front of [one's] desire']: **•Ez *ber mirazim*, ez te nakujim** (Z-1) *I've gotten what I wanted*, I won't kill you; **-mirazê xwe şabûn** (Z-1/K) = a) to rejoice in one's happiness; b) to attain one's desire, get what one wants: **•Ew herd jî nazik û bedewin, bira *mirazê xwe şa bin*** (Z-1) Both of them are fine and beautiful, let them *attain their desire*; 2) {syn: armanc [1]; mebest; meqsed; merem; nêt [4]} goal, aim. {also: mirad (IFb-2); [mirad مـــــراد/ meraz مراز] (JJ); <miraz> مراز (HH)} < Ar murād مـــراد = 'that which is desired' (<arāda IV أراد = 'to want' <√r-w-d رود); Sor mirad مِـراد/miraz مِـراز = 'desire, wish, object' [Z-1/K/A/JB3/IFb/B/HH//JJ] <ḧewas>

mirc مِــــرج *m.* **(-ê;).** large hammer, sledge hammer. {also: merc II, f. (OK)} {syn: geřan II} [Bw/ZF3//OK] <ç'akûç; mêk'ut; zomp>

mircan مِرجان *f.* **(;-ê).** 1) coral; 2) {syn: duř} pearl(s) (K/JJ/HH/GF); pearls with holes in them (IF): **•Her gulîkê--*mircanek* qîmetî pêvaye** (EP-5, #2) In every braid [of her hair]--a precious *pearl*; 3) bead(s) (K/F); 4) *name for women*. {also: mercan (A); [merjān] مرجان (JJ-Rh/PS); <mircan> مرجان (HH)} *This word has cognates throughout the Mediterranean*: Heb margalit מרגלית = 'pearl'; Arc margālītā מרגליתא/margnītā מרגניתא & Syr margānītā ܡܪܓܢܝܬܐ; P morvārīd مروارید & marjān مرجان = 'pearl'; Ar marjān/murjān مرجان = 'small pearls; coral', T mercan = 'coral'; Sp margarita = 'pearl; ox-eye daisy'; It margherita = 'pearl; ox-eye daisy'; Gr margaritēs μαργαρίτης = 'pearl'; Sor mercan مەرجان = 'coral' [EP-5/F/K/IFb/B/HH/GF//A/JJ] <duř; lal II; xişir>

mirdar مِردار *adj.* 1) {syn: bi'ok; ç'epel; dijûn II; gemarî; p'îs; qilêr; qirêj} dirty, filthy, unclean: **•Yarebî, bavê min digot, ezê teřa pênc sed xatûnê bi carî bînim, ez seva eva reşe *mirdař* hatime vira?** (EP-7) My God, my father said he'd bring me 500 women with slave girls; have I come here (=all this way) for this dark, *dirty* one?; 2) ritually unclean, impure. See **mirar**. {also: **mirar**; [mourdar] مردار (JJ)} < P mordār مردار = 'animal carcass'--> T murdar/mundar {mirarî; mirdařî; mirdarî; mirdařtî; [mourdari] مرداری (JJ)} [EP-7/K/B//JJ//Bw/A/IFb]

mirdarî مِرداری *f.* **(-ya;-yê).** dirtiness, slovenliness, untidiness, sloppiness. {also: mirarî (IFb/OK); mirdařtî (K-2); [mourdari] مرداری (JJ)} {syn: gemarî} [K/B/GF/ZF3//JJ//IFb] <mirdar>

mirdařtî مِرداریتی (K) = dirtiness. See **mirdařî**.

mirdiyaq مِردِیاق (Qzl) = wooden support beam. See **mertak**.

miřemiř مِرەمِر/**miremir** مِرەمِر [IFb/ZF]/**miře-miř** مِرە مِر [K] *f.* **(-a;-ê).** 1) purring, humming (K/B); 2) growling, snarling (K/B); 3) grunting (K); 4) {syn: minemin; p'ilep'il} muttering (K); grumbling, murmuring (ZF): **•*mirmira* baranê** (DBgb, 20) *the murmuring of* the rain; **-miremir kirin** (ZF) to grumble, mutter, murmur. {also: mirmir (DBgb)} [HR//K/B/IFb/ZF//DBgb]

mirêba مِرێبا *m.* **(-yê;).** sharecropper, laborer who receives half of crop in return for working someone else's land: **•Ew *mirêba* ye, ne xudan e** (FS) He is *a sharecropper*, not a landowner. {also: milêba (FJ-2/FS-2); mirêwa (IFb)} {mirêbatî; mirêbayî ; mirêwatî} < Ar murābi' مرابع = 'partner in agricultural enterprise (sharing quarter of earnings)' < √r-b-' ربع = 'four' [DBgb/FJ/TF/GF/CS/ZF3/FS//IFb]

mirêbatî مِرێباتی *f.* **(-ya;-yê).** sharecropping: **•Deşt bi xwe ya axê bû, Xurşo *mirêbatî* jê re dikir** (DBgb, 7) The prairie itself belonged to the agha, Khursho did *sharecropping* for him. {also: milêbayî (FS-2); mirêbayî (ZF3/FS); mirêwatî (IFb)} [DBgb//ZF3/FS//IFb] <mirêba>

mirêbayî مِرێبایی (ZF3/FS) = sharecropping. See **mirêbatî**.

mirêk مِرێك *f.* **(-a;-ê).** mirror, looking glass: **•Jêhat di hundirê mirêka şofêr de kil dibû** (SBx, 13) J. trembled inside the driver's mirror. {syn: 'eyne & 'eynik; hêlî; nênik I; qotî I} < Ar mir'āh مرآة & mirāyah مراية [SBx/IFb/FJ/ZF/RZ/CS/Kmc]

mirêwa مِرێوا (IFb) = sharecropper. See **mirêba**.

mirêwatî مِرێواتی (IFb) = sharecropping. See **mirêbatî**.

mirin مِرِن *vi.* **(-mir-).** 1) {syn: alîjiyan bûn; can dan (F); wefat bûn/kirin} to die, pass away: **•Diya Ûsib miribû** (BA) Joseph's mother was dead [lit. 'had died']: **-îsal nemirin, îsal ȟeft sale mirin** (XF) to faint, lose consciousness, fall into a swoon; to show no signs of life: **•Zîna Bek'ir jorda 'erdê k'et, *îsal nemirîye, îsal ȟeft sale mirîye*** (EP-7) Bekir's Zîn fell off onto the ground *in a dead swoon*; 2) [*f.* **(-a;-ê)**] {syn: wefat} death. {also: miran (A); [myrin] مرين (JJ); <mirin مرن (dimre) (دمره)> (HH)} [Pok. 4. mer-/merə-, 5. mer-/merə- 735.] = 'to rub away, harm; to die': Skt marati/máratē/mriyáte = 'he dies'; O Ir *mar- (Tsb 39): Av mar- (*pres.* mariya-/mirya-); OP a-mariyatā = 'he died'; Mid P murdan (mīr-) (M3); P mordan مردن (mīr-) = 'to die'; Oss māryn = 'to kill'; Sor mirdin مِردِن (-mir-); Za mirenã [merdiş] (Todd); Hau merdey (mir-) *vi.* (M4); cf. also Lat moriri; Rus umret' умереть [F/K/A/JB3/IFb/B/JJ/HH/SK/JB1-A&S/GF/TF/OK] <girêl>

mirîd مِرید *m.* **().** disciple, adherent, follower: **•Her roj piştî nimêja êvarê, şêx şîretên dînî li *mirîdên* xwe dikirin** (Rnh 2:17, 340) Every day after the evening prayer, the sheikh would advise his *disciples* on religion. < Ar murīd مريد = 'one who wants; novice (of a Sufi order), adherent, follower, disciple' {also: mirûd (Wkt-2)} {mirîdîtî} [Rnh/K/IFb/B/SK/OK/Wkt/BF] <feqî; suxte>

mirîdî مِریدی (Rnh/Wkt) = being a disciple. See **mirîdîtî**.

mirîdîtî مِریدیتی *f.* **(;-yê).** state of being a disciple, adherent, or follower: **•Ji wan şêxên ko nizanin şêxîtî û *mirîdîtî* çi ye** (Rnh 2:17, 339) One of those sheikhs who don't know what being a sheikh or *being a disciple* is. {also: mirîdî (Rnh-2/Wkt-2)} [Rnh/Wkt] <mirîd>

mirîşk مِریشك *f.* **(-a;-ê).** chicken: **•Wana *mirîşk* birin,**

yekî li tewlê şerjê kir, yekî li gomê şerjê kir (Ba3-1) They took *the chickens*, one slaughtered [his] in the stable, one slaughtered [his] in the sheepfold; -**hêka mirîşkê** (Tkm) chicken egg; -**mirîşka hindistanê** (B) turkey; -**mirîşka kurk** (B) brooding hen. {also: [mirichk مـرشـك/mirijk مرژك] (JJ); <mirîşk> مريشك (HH)} {syn: mamir} Mid P murw = 'bird' (M3); P morγ مـرغ = 'fowl'; Sor mir مـر & mirîşk مـريـشك = 'fowl (domestic)'; Za mirîçik *f.* = 'small bird' (Todd) [K/A/JB3/IFb/B/JJ/HH/SK/ GF/TF/Tkm] <cûcik/çelîk/varik = chick; dîk = rooster; hêk = egg; kurk I = brooding hen>

mirîşo مِريشۆ *m.&f.* **().** one who washes corpses *prior to burial*: •**Mela rabe ji xew îro, / Heta kengî *mirîşo* bî** (Cxn-2, 408) Mullah arise today from sleep, / How long will you be *a washer of corpses*? {also: mirîşû (FS); [myri-chou] مـريـشـو (JJ)} Sor mirdûşor مِردووشۆر [Rwn/K/IFb/FJ/GF/Wkt/BF//JJ/FS]

mirîşû مِريشوو (FS/JJ) = corpse washer. See **mirîşo**.

mirmir مِـــرمِـــر (DBgb) = humming; growling; murmuring. See **miřemiř**.

mirof مِرۆف = man; person. See **meriv**.

miroj مِرۆژ (Hk) = raisin(s). See **mewîj**.

mirov مِرۆڤ (IFb/HH/OK) = man; person. See **meriv**.

mirovahî مِـرۆڤـاهـى (IFb/OK) = manliness; humanity; humaneness; relation through marriage. See **merivtî**.

mirovatî مِـــرۆڤـــاتـــى (IFb/HH/OK) = manliness; humanity; humaneness; relation through marriage. See **merivtî**.

mirovnasî مِـرۆڤـنـاسـى *f.* **(-ya;-yê).** anthropology, the study of human beings: •**Weke jîngehnasî, divê *mirovnasî* zanîneke rastîn bibe** (Le Monde diplomatique kurdî i.2011, 20) Like ecology, *anthropology* must be a true science. {also: merivnasî (Wkt-2); merivzanî (Wkt-2); mirovzanî (Wkt-2/SS-2)} [(neol)LeMondeDipl/IFb/GF/ZF3/Wkt/SS]

mirovzanî مِـرۆڤـزانـى (Wkt/SS) = anthropology. See **mirovnasî**.

mirqandin مِـــرقـــانـــدِن (IFb/OK/Hej) = to grunt. See **miqandin**.

mirtêl مِرتێل (IFb) = mattress; bedding. See **mitêl**.

mirt'ib/mirtib [B] مِـــرتِـــب *m.&f.* **(/-a;-î/).** 1) {syn: aşiq; begzade [2]; boşe; dome (Wn); gewende; qereçî} Roma, Gypsy (Ag/Wn/Bşk); bohemian, vagabond (JJ): •**Ew *mirtiva* lêvdeqandî jî li bal e?** (ZZ-7, 224) Is that Gypsy woman with cracked lips around here?; -**jina mirt'ib** (K) Roma woman; -**zimanê mirt'iba[n]** (K) Romany, Gypsy language; 2) {syn: daholvan; defçî; deholjen; diholkut} drummer, traditional musician, minstrel (IFb/HH/SK): •**Ez û tu rahêjin tûrê parsê û herin weke aşiq û *mitirban* ji xwe re li nava eşîr û ebrê bigerrin** (ZZ-10, 136) Let's you and I pick up a beggar's sack and go as bards and *singers* and wander among the tribes and clans •***Muṯirb* geştine bederê qesra aẍa gotin** [sic]... **em jî ewe heşt neh řoj e ji laê Silêmanî û Kerkûkê li dû nawbangê Eḧmed Aẍaê Berwarî têyn da bo wî def û kemança lê deyn û lawjan bêjîn, belkû keremekî çak digel me biket** (SK 27:243) *The minstrels* arrived before the gate of the agha's mansion and said ... for 8 or 9 days now we have come from the direction of Sulaimaniya and Kerkuk following the fame of Ahmad Agha Barwari, in order to play the drum and viol for him and to sing him songs, hoping that he will reward us well. {also: mirtif (FK-kk-13); mirt'iv (Ag/Wn/ZF3); mitirb; mit'irp (Bşk); mitrib (IFb-2/GF/ZF); muṯirb (SK); [mirtib] مـرطـب (JJ); <miṯirb> مـطـرب (HH)} < Ar muṭrib مـطـرب = 'singer, musical entertainer' <aṭraba IV أطرب = 'to delight, to sing, to play music' (<√ṭ-r-b طرب = 'to be moved (with joy or grief)'); T mıtırıp [Bitlis; Mut-İçel]/mıtırıb [Silifke-İçel]/mıtrıp [Erciş-Van; Nizip-Gaziantep] = 'Roma, Gypsy' (DS, v. 9, p. 3193) {mirtibî; mirtivî} [K/IFb/JJ//B//FK-kk-13//HH//Ag/Wn/ZF3//Bsk//GF/ZF//SK] <begzade [2]>

mirt'ibî/mirtibî [B] مِرتِبى *f.* **(-ya;-yê).** 1) acting like a Roma or Gypsy ; 2) Roma or Gypsy language, Romany; 3) *[adj.]* Roma, Gypsy *(adj.)*. {also: mitirbî (Gulistan[2007]); mirtivî (B-2/ZF3)} [K/B//ZF3] <mirt'ib>

mirtif مِـرتِـف (FK-kk-13) = Roma, Gypsy; drummer. See **mirt'ib**.

mirt'iv مِرتِڤ (Ag/Wn/ZF3) = Roma, Gypsy; drummer. See **mirt'ib**.

mirtivî مِـــرتِـــڤـــى (B/ZF3) = [acting like a] Roma or Gypsy. See **mirt'ibî**.

mirt'oxe مِـرتـۆخـه (K/IFb/Hej) = omelet-like dish. See **mirtoẍe**.

mirtoẍ•e مِـرتـۆغـه *f.* **(•a;•ê).** omelet-like dish made of butter, flour, and eggs: •**Go:--Qe *mrt'oxe* teřa danîne** [sic], **ḧewle zanî? Go: --Erê! ... Anî hat t'asek t'ijî *mrt'oxe* ... řabû devê wî jev kir, ew**

mrt'oxe usa germe-germ kire devê me'rûmî (HCK-2, 87) "They've made *mirtokheh* for you, are you familiar with halvah?" "Yes!" … He brought a bowl full of *mirtokheh* … He opened the fellow's mouth, and poured the warm *mirtokheh* into his mouth. {also: mirt'oxe (K/IFb); mrt'oxe (HCK); <mirtoxe> مرتۆخه (Hej)} [Wn/ /K/IFb/Hej] <arxavk>

mirûd مِرووود (Wkt) = disciple. See **mirîd**.

mirûz مِــــــــرووز *m.* **().** 1) bad mood; melancholia, anguish, sadness, sorrow: •**[Qewî şermî dibê û bêkêf bûyî mirûzî dikitin weku êvarê paşa tête ȟaremserayê dibîne ku xanim *bi mirûz*e]** (JR) [She] was ashamed and distressed, when the pasha came into the harem in the evening, he saw that [his] wife was *in a bad mood*; **-mirûzê xwe kirin** (K/B) to be melancholy, depressed, miserable; to grieve, mourn, pine for; 2) *[adj.]* gloomy, sullen (B). {also: muȓûzî (K-2); [mourouz] مــــروز (JJ)} [JR/K/B/IFb//JJ] <bême'de>

mis مِس (IFb/GF/OK/JJ/ZF3) = copper. See **mîs**.

mis'ar مِسعار *f.* **(-a;-ê).** spinning top: •**Ew bi *mis'arê* dileyzit** (FS) S/he is playing with *the top* •***Mis'ara* wî winda bû** (FS) His *top* got lost. {also: mizar (Wkt)} {syn: vizik I; ziviȓok; zîzok} [FS//Wkt]

misas مِســـاس/**miṣaṣ** مِصـــاص [FS] *f.* **(-a;-ê).** oxgoad, goad, *a long thin stick with a needle-sharp tip used for prodding cattle*: •**Dûre tu ê bibînî ku bi qasî sê *misasan* di ser pozê çiyê re li asiman sê sitêr berwar û di rêza hev de hene** (HMp, 17) Then you will see in the sky--about three *oxgoad* lengths from the top of the mountain--there are three stars sloping and in one line. {also: mesas (IFb-2); <miṣaṣ> مــصــاص (HH)} < Ar massās مــسّــاس = 'goad' [HMp/A/IFb/GF/TF/RF/Kmc-21 (Qrj)//HH/FS] <labût>

misebiq مِسەبِق (TF/ZF3) = type of grape. See **misebq**.

misebq مِسەبق *f.* **().** type of grape (Msr/TF); summer grapes (Haz); tightly clustered grapes [sıkışık salkım üzüm] (IFb). {also: mikebs (IFb); misebiq (TF/ZF3)} ?< Ar musabbaq مــسـبّــق = 'premature [in ripening?]' [Msr/Haz//TF/ZF3//IFb] <tirî>

misexer مِسەخەر (Rnh) = slave. See **misexir**.

misexir مِــســەخِــر *m.* **().** slave, indentured servant: •**Serdara periyan emirî *misexirên* xwe kir got: "Mêrê min digel wezîr ji qesirê derêxin, qesirê digel ên din hemiwan li avê de winda bikin"** (Rnh 2:17, 308) The fairy queen commanded her *slaves*, saying: "Take my husband and the vizier out of the castle, then drown the castle in the river with everyone else inside it." {also: misexer (Rnh-2)} <Ar musaxxar مــســخّــر = 'one who has been made subservient, slave' [Rnh]

misêwa مِسێوا *adv.* continuously, constantly, incessantly, without stopping: •**Ew roja yekem *misêwa* şer dikin** (BM, 21) On that first day they fight *constantly* •**Ez *misêwa* rojnameya Welat taqîb dikim** (Wlt 1:49, 2) I *continuously* follow the newspaper Welat. [Wlt/BM/ZF3/FS/FD] <t'im>

misger مِسگەر (IFb/GF/OK/ZF3) = coppersmith. See **mîsk'ar**.

misgir مِسگِر (OK) = coppersmith. See **mîsk'ar**.

misheb مِسهەب = holy book. See **misȟef**.

mishef مِسهەف (IF/ZF3) = holy book. See **misȟef**.

misȟeb مِسحەب (EP-7) = holy book. See **misȟef**.

misȟebxan•e مِـســحــەبــخــانــە *f.* **(;•ê).** place where holy books (i.e., the Koran) are kept (EP-7). < misȟef = 'holy book' {or possibly **mezheb** = 'religion'} + xane = 'house' [EP-7] <misȟef; mizgeft>

misȟef مِــــســـــحـــەف *f.* **(-a;-ê).** copy of the Koran, holy book (K/IF/JJ). {also: mesheb; misheb; misȟeb (EP-7); mishef (IF/ZF3); [moushef] مــصــحــف (JJ); <misȟef> مـــســـحـــف (HH)} < Ar muṣḥaf/maṣḥaf مــــصـــحـــف = 'copy of the Koran'; Sor mesheb مەسهەب [EP-7//K/HH//JJ//IF/ZF3] <k'itêb>

misilman مِــســِلــمــان *m.&f.* **(-ê/;).** a Muslim, Moslem: •**Kurê min tu ji Nusêbînî yî înşalah tu ne Êzidî yî lê bila bibê. Êzidî gelek ji *Bisilmanan* çêtir in** (Ah) My son, you are from Nusaybin, I hope you are not a Yezidi, but then again, so be it. The Yezidis are much better than *the Muslims* •**Qîz dibêjê: "Ya mîr mezin/ Îro layîqê te k'efin/ *Bisurman* naye xweş li min/ Ez 'îsewî--tu sunnetî"** (FT) The girl says to him, "O great emir/ Today you deserve a shroud/ *A Muslim* is not right for me/ I am Christian--you are Sunni." {also: bisilman (Ah/FS-2); bisurman (FT); musulman (B/SK/F/GF); musurman (B-2); [mousoulman] مــســلــمــان (JJ); <misilman> مــســلــمــان (HH)} {syn: Ĥuseynî} <Ar muslim مسلم: P mosalmān مسلمان; T müslüman; Sor musułman مــوســوڵــمــان {misilmanî; misilmanîtî; misilman[t]î; musurmanî; [mousoulman] مــســلــمــان (JJ); <misilman> مــســلــمــان (HH)} [Ah//FT//K/IF/A/HH/ZF3/FS/ /B/JJ/SK/F/GF]

misilmanî مِسِلمانی *f.* **(-ya;-yê).** 1) Islam, the Muslim religion; 2) Muslim piety (B); Muslim obligations and behavior (B). {also: misilmanîtî (K); misilmantî (K-2); musulmanî (B/F); musurmanî (B-2); [mousoulmani] مسلمانی (JJ); <misilmanî> مسلمانی (HH)} [IF/HH/ZF3//K//B/F/JJ] <misilman>

misilmanîtî مِسلمانیتی (K) = Islam. See **misilmanî**.

misilmantî مِسلمانتی (K) = Islam. See **misilmanî**.

misilmênî مِسلمێنی *m.* **().** Muslim Kurds who were formerly (or whose immediate ancestors were) Christian Armenians [berê fileh bûn, piştî bûn misilman]: **•*Misilmênî*: Kesê ji dînekî derbasî dînê Îslamê bûyî. Yan jî bab û bapîrên wî misilman bûyî** (FB: A.Bingöl) *Misilmênî*: someone who has converted to Islam from another religion. Or his ancestors became Muslim. {also: misilmînî (Şnx-2)} [Şnx] <Ermenî; file>

misilmînî مِسلمینی (Şnx) = Kurds of Armenian decent. See **misilmênî**.

Misir مِسِر *f.* **(;-ê).** Egypt. {also: Misr; *Misrê (A)} < Ar Miṣr مصر --> T Mısır [Ba/Ba2/A/IF]

Misirî مِسِری (CS) = Egyptian. See **Misrî**.

misîn مِسین *m.* **(-ê;-î).** (brass) ewer, pitcher [aiguière]; metal pitcher with long, narrow neck (B); copper pitcher (HH): **•*Misînê* wî ê limêjê tije av dike** (L) He fills his prayer *pitcher* with water **•S̱ofî, here, *mesînê* min ji birka pişta gundî tejî bike, bibe edebxana mizgewtê, li wê-derê r̄a-weste ḧetta ez têm** (SK 50:524) Sofi, go and fill my *water-pot* at the pool behind the village, take it to the lavatory of the mosque and wait there till I come. {also: mesîn (IFb-2/SK/FS-2); [misin/mesin] مسین (JJ); <mesîn> مسین (HH)} <mis/mîs = 'copper' + -în = *adjectival ending for materials* [L/K/A/IFb/B/JJ/GF/FS/ZF3//HH/SK] <mîs>

miskîn مِسکین *adj.* 1) poor, wretched, miserable, pitiful; 2) nice (person), respectable (Bw). {also: [meskīn] مسكين (JJ); <miskîn> مسكين (HH)} <Ar miskīn مسكين = 'poor, wretched' [Bw/K/IFb/HH/SK/OK/Wkt//JJ] <belengaz; jar I[3]>

misoger مِسۆگەر *adj.* sure, certain, assured: **•Hatina Behremî îro *misoger* e** (FS) B.'s coming today is *assured*. {also: misoker (FS-2); mîsoger (TF)} {syn: biste [2]; piştrast} < clq Iraqi Ar mṣōgar مصوگر = 'insured; assured, guaranteed' passive participle of ṣōgar صوگر < ṣōgartā صوگرتا [written Ar sikurtāh سكرتاه] <It sicurtà = 'insurance' [IFb/OK/RZ/FS/ZF3//TF]

misoker مِسۆکەر (FS) = sure. See **misoger**.

Misr مِسر = Egypt. See **Misir**.

*Misrê مِسرێ (A) = Egypt. See **Misir**.

Misrî مِسری *adj.* Egyptian. {also: Misirî (CS)} Sor Mîsrî میسری [IFb/BF/Wkt/SS/Wkp//CS]

mist مِست/ **mis̱t** مِصت [Hk/Dh/Ak]/**misṯ** مِسط [FS] *f.* **(-a;-ê).** 1) {syn: k'ulm} fist: **•Wî *mis̱tek li* Zoroyî *da*** (FS) He *punched* Z. with his *fist*; 2) {syn: k'ulm} handful: **•*misteka* genimî, tovikan û htd.** (BF) *a handful of* wheat, seeds, etc. **•Wî *misṯeka* avê vexwar** (FS) He drank *a handful of* water; 3) palm of hand (TF). {also: mişt I (IFb-2/OK-2); moşt, m. (F); [myst] مست (JJ)} [Pok. meuk̂- 745.] = 'to scratch', cf. fist: Skt muṣṭi- *m./f.*; Av mušti- *f.*; Mid P must/mušt (M3); P mošt مشت; Sor mişt مِشت = 'fist'; Za mist (Mal); Hau mişte *f.* = 'quantity that fills the two hands cupped together' (M4) [S&E/K(s)/A/IFb/B/JJ/SK/GF/TF/OK/BF//Hk/Dh/Ak//FS//F]

mişag مِشاگ *m.* **().** farmhand, day worker. {also: [michaq] مشاق (JJ)} {syn: hodax; r̄êncber} < Arm mšak մշակ [Qzl/IFb/ZF3/Wkt/FD//JJ] <êrxat>

mişar I مِشار *f.* **(-a;).** 1) patch, bed, or strip of land on which tomatoes, cucumbers, watermelons (FS), onions, garlic, shallots (BF) are grown: **•Me *mişara* pêşîn kiriye pîvazterk. Me ya duyem kiriye bexdenûs** (K.Yildirim.Kurdî 6, 78) We made the first *patch* for green onions. We made the second one for parsley; **-mişara bacans̱orka** (FS) tomato patch; **-mişareka ‘erdî** (Zeb) a strip or patch of land; 2) furrow, trench, irrigation ditch (TF/ZF/Wkt). {also: <mişar> مشار (HH)} [Mizûrî/Syria/Zeb/IFb/FJ/GF/TF/HH/ZF/FS/BF/Wkt/CS] <p’arêz I; werz>

mişar II مِشار *f.* **(-a;-ê).** saw (tool). {also: [mychar/mishār (Rh)] مشار (JJ)} {syn: bir̄ek; *bişqî} <Ar minšār منشار [Prw/IFb/JJ/Wkt/BF/ZF3/FD]

mişe مِشە *adj.* many, plenty, abundant, a lot: **•Hingî li wê dirk’ê mişk *t mişe* bûn, çûne nav nivinkêt biçûka û meẕina** (M, #705, 322) Mice were so *abundant* there that they got into the bedding of children and adults **•Me *mişe* yêt heyn ji van** (Bw) We have *plenty* of them **•Romî xertel in, xoşîya wan ew e keleş *mişe* bin** (SK 61:740) Turks are vultures, their pleasure is in being full of carrion [lit. 'that carrion be *plenty*'] **•Xwarin *a mişe* ye** (BF) There is *plenty* of food. {also: [mish] مش (JJ-Rh)} Sor mişe مِشە = 'plentiful, common property, offered free of charge, permissible' [Bw/IFb/SK/OK/FS/BF//JJ-Rh]

mişeht مِشەهت (GF) = displaced person. See **mişext**.

mişewiş مِشەوِش *f.* **(-a;).** cooked lentils *as opposed to* ***nîsk*** = *'raw lentils'* (Msr); ground lentils [T öğütülmüş mercimek] (IFb). {also: mişewş (IFb/CB/ZF3); <mişewş> مشوش (HH)} [Msr//IFb/HH/CB/ZF3] <nîsk>

mişewş مِشەوش (IFb/HH/CB/ZF3) = cooked lentils. See **mişewiş**.

mişext مِشەخت *m.&f.* **().** displaced person; migrant; exile; fugitive; wanderer: **•Gundê wan *mişextan* xudan dikit** (FS) Their village takes care of *displaced people*; **-mişext bûn** (SK) to decamp, migrate; leave one's native land (by choice or not): **•Ew ji welatê xwe *mişext bû*** (FS) He *left his native land.* {also: mişeht (GF-2); [mouchekht] مشخت (JJ)} Cf. NENA mashkhiṭ ܡܫܚܛ = 'to sojourn' & mâshâkhaṭ ܡܫܚܛ = 'sojourner' (Maclean) [Bw/IFb/SK/GF/TF/OK/FS//JJ] <k'oçber; p'enaber>

mişextî مِشەختی *f.* **(-ya;-yê).** displacement, being displaced; migration [hijrah]: ***•Mişextîya* wî ya milyonî êk ji evan serhatîyan bû** (R 15 [4/12/96] 1) His millionth [time] *being displaced* was one of these stories. Cf. NENA mashkhatuta = 'diaspora' (Daniel Wolk) [R/Zeb/TF] <p'enaberî>

mişiriq مِشِرق (B) = east. See **mişriq**.

mişk مِشك *m./f.(LM)* **(-ê/ ; /-ê).** mouse: **•Hingî li wê dirk'ê *mişk* t mişe bûn, çûne nav nivinkêt biçûka û me͟zina** (M, #705, 322) *Mice* were so abundant there that they got into the bedding of children and adults ***•Mişkek* û çêlikên xwe li derve digerîyan. Bi carekê de çavê wê li pisîkekê ket** (LM, 28) *A mouse* and her babies were outside roaming around. Suddenly she noticed a cat; **-mişkê kor** (B) mole, zool. *Talpidae*; ***-mişkê teȓezinê (K)*** *fieldmouse:* ***•Mişkê teȓezinê*, mêrê xebera jinê, berxê ber bizinê, hersê jî ber mirinê** (K) *fieldmice*, hen-pecked husbands, and lambs [nursed] by goats, all three are headed for death *[prv.]*. {also: mişkok (B-2); [mychik] مشك (JJ); <mişk> مشك (HH)} [Pok. mūs 752.] = 'mouse': Skt mū́ṣ- *m.* = 'mouse, rat'; O Ir *mūš- (Ras, p.134): O P *mūša- &*mūšauka- *in compounds*; Mid P mušk (M3); P mūš موش; Sor mişk مِشك; Za merre *m.* (Todd); Hau miłe *m.* (M4); cf. also Rus myš´ мышь; Germ Maus [F/K/A/IFb/B/JJ/HH/SK/GF/TF/OK] <cird; sêvle>

mişkok مِشكۆك (B) = mouse. See **mişk**.

mişmiş مِشمِش *f.* **(-a;-ê).** apricot, bot. *Prunus armeniaca.* {also: mijmije (OK-2/AA); [mychmych] مشمش (JJ); <mişmiş مشمش/ mijmij مژمژ> (HH)} {syn: hêrûg[2]; qeysî; zerdelî} < Ar mišmiš مشمش = 'apricot' [K/A/IFb/JJ/HH/TF/OK/ Srk/Msr//AA]

mişriq مِشرق *f.* **(;-ê).** east; place where the sun rises. {also: mişiriq (B); [meshrik] مشرق (JJ); <mişraq> مشراق (HH)} {syn: ȓojhilat; şerq, f. (F)} <Ar mašriq مشرق = 'east, place where the sun rises' [F/K//JJ//B//HH]

mişt I مِشت (OK) = handful; fist. See **mist**.

mişt II مِشت *adj.* full, filled to the brim, filled to the top: **•Carekê diya wî sendoqek mezin *mişt* terî û guhên ker û pisîkan li qorzîkeke hewşê dîtin** (HYma, 12) Once his mother saw a big box *overflowing with* donkey and cat tails and ears in a corner of the yard; **-mişt kirin** (Bw) to fill to the brim: **•Bo min vî glasî *miştî* av *ke*** (Bw) *Fill* this glass *up to the top* for me with water **•Min ew teneke *mişt kir* ji genimî** (Bw) I *filled* that can *up to the top* with wheat. {also: [micht] مشت (JJ); <mişt> مشت (HH)} [Bw/Qrj/Elk/K(s)/A/IFb/JJ/ HH/GF/TF/FJ/BF] <t'ijî>

miştax مِشتاخ *f.* **(-a;).** spreading floor on which grapes are dried into raisins: **•Miştaxa çiya ji gotinên pêşiya** (title of proverb collection by M. M.Dêrşewî) "Mountain spreading-floor of sayings of the ancestors [i.e., proverbs]"; **-Miştax ji wan çêkir** (FS) He massacred them [lit. 'He made a spreading-floor of them']. {also: miştaxe (A/IFb-2/GF); <miştaxe> مشتاخه (HH); <mistax مستاخ/miştax مشتاخ> (Hej)} < Arc mašṭāḥā משטחא = 'grapes spread on the ground, spreading place' (M. Jastrow) & Syr mašṭāḥā ܡܫܛܚܐ = 'anything spread out to dry' (Pyn-Sm) & Jewish NENA mišṭāxa משטאכא = 'smooth floor for sorting grapes' (Sabar:Dict); cf. Ar misṭāḥ مسطاح = 'threshing floor for drying dates, figs, and grapes'; Sor miştax مِشتاخ = 'area cleared for drying raisins' [Dêrşewî/IFb/TF/OK/Hej/AA/FS//A/HH/GF] <mewîj>

miştaxe مِشتاخە (A/IFb/HH/GF) = drying place for raisins. See **miştax**.

miştin مِشتِن (-mal-) (K[s]/IF/A/JJ/HH) = to sweep. See **maliştin**.

miştomir مِشتۆمِر (BF) = argument, debate. See **mişt û miȓ**.

mişt û miȓ مِشت و مِر *f.* **(-a;-ê).** argument, debate, disagreement. {also: miştomir (BF); <mişt u miȓ>

مشت و مِر (Hej)} {syn: bêt'ifaqî; cerenîx; de'w II; doz; dubendî; gelemşe; gengeşe; k'êşe; micadele; nîqaş; xirecir} Sor mişt-u-mir̄ مِـشـت و مِـر = 'argument, passionate discussion' [Zeb/Hej//BF]

*mişwar مِـشـوار *f.(K)/m.(L)* **().** step, pace: **-mişwarekî** (L/IF) for a time, for a while: **•*Mişwarekî* meşîya** (L) He went for *a while* [lit. 'a step']. < Ar mišwār مشوار = 'errand' [L/K/JB3/IFb]

mit̠ مِـط/**mit** مِـت [Metîn] *adj.* silent, quiet: **•Ev kewe bo çî *mit̠* e? Bo çî naxwînît?** (Bw) Why is this partridge *silent*? Why isn't it singing?; **-Mit̠ bibe** (Bw) Shut up (rude) (=bêdeng bibe; ker bibe); **-xwe mit kirin** (Metîn) to keep quiet. {also: mat II (K/IFb/SK); <mit> مـت (Hej)} {syn: bêdeng} {mit̠î} [Bw/Hej//Metîn//K/IFb/SK]

mitala مِتالا (GF) = thought, pondering. See **mitale**.

mital•e مِتالـه *f.* **(;•ê).** 1) {syn: fikar; fikir; hizir; r̄aman I; xiyal} thought, thinking, reflection, pondering: **-k'etin [ber] mitala[n]** (K)/**k'etin nav mitala** (XF): a) to fall into a reverie, to lapse into deep thought or day dreams; to be pensive, thoughtful; to meditate; b) to become concerned, worried **•Memê *k'et nava mitala*** (EP-7) Mem *became pensive (*or *worried)*; 2) worry, anxiety, care (JJ); groan, moan, lament (JJ). {also: mitala (GF); [metāla] متاله (JJ); <mutale> مطاله (HH)} ?< Ar muṭāla'ah مطالعة = 'reading' [EP-7/K/IFb/JJ/B// GF//HH]

mitar•e مِتاره *m.*/**mit̠ar•e** مِطاره *f.(FS)* **(•ê/•a;•ey/).** *reciprocal* debt of labor *between village households (e.g., family A helps family B build a new house; when family A needs help in a chore, family B will help them in return for the help they received)*: **•*Mitarekê* min li def te ye** (Bw) I owe you *a debt of labor* (in payment for services you rendered me). {also: <mitare متاره> (Hej)} [Bw/Hej/FS] <p'alûte; zibare>

mitêl مِتێل *f.* **().** 1) {syn: *bincî; bin̄rex; cil III; doşek; nehlîk} mattress (IFb); 2) {syn: cil III; cî; nivîn} bedding: **•Wê *mitêlka* doşikê şûşt** (FS) She washed the mattress *bedding*; 3) strings or threads with which bed or mattress is sewn (HH). {also: mirtêl (IFb-2); mitêlk (FS); <mitêl> متيل (HH)} [K/IFb/HH/GF/ZF3]

mitirb مِترِب = Roma, Gypsy; drummer. See **mirt'ib**.

mitirbî مِـتـِربـى (Gulistan[2007]) = [acting like a] Roma or Gypsy. See **mirt'ibî**.

mit'irp مِـتـِرپ (Bşk) = Roma, Gypsy; drummer. See **mirt'ib**.

mit̠î مِطى *f.* **(-ya;-yê).** silence. {syn: bêdengî} [Bw/Zx/BF] <mit̠>

mitleq مِـتـلـەق *adv.* absolutely. {also: mitliq; muṭlaq (SK); [moutlaq] مطلق (JJ)} {syn: 'ese; helbet [2]; miqîm; t'eqez} < Ar muṭlaq مـطـلـق = 'absolute, free' [F/K//JJ/SK]

mitliq مِتلِق = absolutely. See **mitleq**.

mitrib مِـتـرب (IFb/GF/ZF) = Roma, Gypsy; drummer. See **mirt'ib**.

mix مِـــخ *m.* **(-ê;).** (iron) nail. {also: mîx (BF/Wkt); mîxe (FS)}{syn: bizmar} Cf. T mıh; Sor mêx مێخ = 'nail, peg'; Hau mêx *m.* = 'peg' (M4) [K/IFb/B/ZF3//BF/Wkt//FS]

mixabin مِخابِن *interj.* What a pity! What a shame! unfortunately: **•*muxabinê* van kiça** (Bw) *what a shame for* these girls; these poor girls **•Neçe, bo 'ilmê te gelek *mixabin e*** (SK :423) Do not go. *It is a great pity* for your learning **•Tu gelek cesûr î. *Mixabin e* te bikujim** (SK 51:552) You are very brave. *It is a pity* for me to kill you **•Xolî bi mal, mal-wêran, te bo çî mêrekî wekî 'Ebdî kuşt? *S̠ed ḧeyf û mixabin* nebû te ew qebaḧete kir?** (SK 18:172) You wretch, why have you killed a man like Abdi? Was it not *a hundred pities* that you did this shameful thing? {also: mixabûn (RZ); mix̄abin (Frq); muxabin (Bw); [moukhabin] مخابن (JJ)} {syn: cihê daxê; xebînet} NENA mûkhabn(â) ܡܘܚܒܢܐ = 'pity' (Maclean) [Bw/JJ//K/SK/GF/TF/ZF3//Frq//RZ] <ḧeyf>

mixabûn مِخابوون (RZ) = unfortunately. See **mixabin**.

mixanet مِخانەت (Wkt) = traitor. See **mixenet**.

mixar مِخار (AD) = auger, gimlet. See **mikare**.

mixare مِخاره (IF) = cave. See **mix̄are**.

mixdar مِــخـدار *m.(E/B)/f.(JB3/B)* **(-ê/; /-ê).** 1) {syn: qas; qeder I} quantity, amount; 2) while, amount of time: **•Ew *mux̄darê mehê* bal me xebitî** (B) He worked for us *for a month* **•Me *mux̄darekê*** [sic] **hevr̄a derbaz kir** (B) We passed *some time* together. {also: miqdar; muxdar; mux̄dar (K/B); [myqdar] مقدار (JJ)} < Ar miqdār مقدار = 'amount' [BX/JB3//K/B//JJ]

mixenet مِـخـەنـەت *m.* **(-ê;).** 1) {syn: destkîs; xayîn; xwefiroş} traitor: **•Mala me mala *mixeneta* nîne** (FK-eb-2) Our house is not a house *of traitors*; 2) [*adj.*] deceitful, treacherous. {also: mixanet (Wkt); mix̄enet (F)} < Ar maxānah مخانة?, verbal noun of xāna خـان (√x-w-n خـون) = 'to betray'; or <Ar muxannaṯ مـخـنّـث = 'effeminate, weak'

{mixenetî} [F//K/B/Bw/ZF3//Wkt] <cehş>

mixenetî مِـخـەنـەتـى *f.* **(-ya;-yê).** deceit, treachery: •***Mixenetîya* te li vir jî xuya dibe** (Ria Taza 5.vi.2016) Your *treachery* is evident here; **-mixenetî kirin** (K) to deceive, trick; to act in a deceptive manner {also: mix̂enetî (F)} {syn: xayîntî; xiyanet} [K/B/ZF3/FS//F] <'ewanî; geveztî; mixenet; xapandin>

mixmixk مِـخـمِـخـك *f.* **(-a;-ê).** mosquito, zool. *Culex pipiens*: •***Mixmixk* sedemê gelek nexweşiyan e** (Wkp) *The mosquito* is the cause of many diseases. {syn: p'êşî II} [Wkp/K/B/ZF3/RZ/CS] <vizik I>

mixtar مِختار (Z-4) = village chief. See **muxtar**.

mixtarî مِـخـتـارى (Z-4) = position of village chief. See **muxtarî**.

mixulqet مِـخـولـقـەت (B/Tsab) = people, creatures. See **mexulqet**.

Mixurbî مِخوربى (Wkt) = Moroccan. See **Mex̂rîbî**.

mix̂abin مِغابِن (Frq) = unfortunately. See **mixabin**.

mix̂ara مِغارا (L) = cave. See **mix̂are**.

mix̂ar•e مِـغـارە *f.* **(•eya;•ê).** cave, cavern; man-made cave, *as opposed to şkeft, a naturally formed cave* (Haz): •**di *mix̂arakê* de** (L) in *a cave* •**Qîza hakim bi tenê ma *li mix̂arê*** (L) The king's daughter remained alone (=by herself) *in the cave*. {also: mixare (IF); mix̂ara (L); [megaré] مـغـارە (JJ); <mex̂are> مغارە (HH)} {syn: şkeft; t'ûn [2]} < Ar maγārah مـغـارة --> T mağara; Hau mer̄e *f.* (M4) [L//K/Haz//IFb/JJ/HH]

mix̂enet مِغەنەت (F) = traitor. See **mixenet**.

mix̂enetî مِغەنەتى (F) = deceit. See **mixenetî**.

miz I مِـز: **-miz dan** = a) to rub, massage {syn: firikandin; p'erixandin}: •**Aşvan k'ete avê, r̄ûvî pê lepê xwe pişta wî *mizda*** (J) The miller jumped into the water, the fox *rubbed* his paw on his (=the miller's) back •**Ew pê dezmala xwe t'emiz Bor *mizdide*** (FK-eb-2) He *wipes* Bor [a horse] dry with his handkerchief; b) to stroke, caress, fondle, pet {syn: p'erixandin}; c) to grind; to pulverize: •**Careke dinê bik'eve avê, ez te *mizdim*** (J) Jump into the water again, I'*ll pulverize* you. {also: miz dayîn (B-2); mizdan I; [myz-dan] مـزدان (JJ)} [J/K/JB3/B/JJ]

miz II مـِـز *adj.* bittersweet, tart, mildly sour: •**hinara *miz*** (FS) the *tart* pomegranate. {also: [mz] مـز (JJ); <miz> مـز (HH)} <Ar muzz مـزّ = 'sourish, acidulous' [Btm(Ḧatḧatkê)/F/K/A/B/JJ-G/HH/GF/TF/ZF3/FS] <tirş>

miz III مِز (GF) = copper. See **mîs**.

mizar مِزار (Wkt) = top (toy). See **mis'ar**.

mizdan I مِزدان = to rub; to grind. See **miz I**.

mizdan II مِزدان = sad. See **melûl: -melûl û mizdan**.

miz dayîn مِز دايين (B) = to rub; to grind. See **miz I**.

mizgeft مِـزگـەفـت *f.* **(-a;-ê).** mosque: •[**Mela Bazîd ekserî we'z û şîret didaye Ekradan û li *mizgevtê* nesîḧet dikirin**] (JR-3) Most of the time Mullah Bazid gave sermons and admonitions to the Kurds and advised them in *the mosque* •**Min li *mizgefta* taxê bang da** (HYma, 44) I made the call to prayer from the neighborhood *mosque*. {also: meçît (K-2); mizgevt (B/OK-2); mizgewt (SK); [mizgheft] مزگفت (JJ); <mizkeft> مزكفت (HH)} {syn: camî} Cf. P mizkit/mazkat مـزكـت = 'small mosque' & Sp mezquita < Ar masjid مـسـجـد --> T mesçit = 'small mosque'; Sor mizgewt مِـزگـەوت; Za mescid *m.* (Mal) [Z-1/A/JB3/IFb/JJ/JB1-A/GF/TF/OK//HH//B//SK//K]

mizger مِزگەر (GF) = coppersmith. See **mîsk'ar**.

mizgevt مِزگەفت (B/OK) = mosque. See **mizgeft**.

mizgewt مِزگەوت (SK) = mosque. See **mizgeft**.

mizgîn مِـزگـيـن (A/IFb/B/JJ/JB1-A&S/GF/TF/OK) = good news; reward for bringing good news. See **mizgînî**.

mizgînî مِـزگـيـنـى *f.* **(-ya;-yê).** 1) good news, glad tidings: •***Mizgînîya xêrê* heye** (LC, 8) There is *good news* •**Mîr got, "Her kesê *mizgînîya* t̠eyrî bo min bînît ez dê xelatekî bi keyfa wî dem ê." Xelkî jî weto texmîn kirin** [sic] **mîr beḧsê *mizgînîya* t̠eyrê biharê ye** (SK 29:261) The Mir said, "Whoever brings me *the good news of* the bird I shall give him a present which will please him." People imagined that the Mir was talking of *the good news of* the coming of the bird of spring •**R̄ûvî ... *mizgînî* p'adşêr̄a bir** (J) The fox ... took *the good news* to the king; 2) reward for bringing good news: •***Mizgînîya* min wer̄a** (Z-1) You owe me a reward for bringing you good news [lit. 'my good news [reward] to you']. {also: mizgîn (A-2/IFb-2/B-2/JB1-A&S/GF-2/TF-2/OK-2); [mizghin] مـزگـيـن (JJ); <mizgînî> مـزگـيـنـى (HH)} [Pok. mizdho- 746.] = 'reward': Av mižda- *n.* = 'reward'; Pahl mizd = do.; Sgd mwjt'ak = 'messenger of glad tidings'; P možde مـژده = 'good news' --> T müjde; Sor mizgênî مِزگێنى; Za mizgîni *f.* (Mal); Hau mijde *m.*/mijdê *f.* (M4) cf. also Gr misthos μισθός = 'reward (for poet)' [J/F/K/A/IFb/B/HH/SK/GF/TF/OK//JJ/JB1-A&S]

miziçîn مِـزِجـيـن *vi.* **(-mizic-).** to smile: **•Li kurê xwe dinêrî û *dimizicî*** (SBx, 12) He kept gazing at his son and *smiling*. {also: miziçîn (GF)} {syn: beşişîn; bişkurîn; girnijîn; k'enîn} [SBx/FJ/ZF/RZ//GF]

miziçîn مِزِچين (GF) = to smile. See **mizicîn**.

mizmar مِزمار = nail *(for hammering)*. See **bizmar**.

mî I مـى *f.* **(-ya;-yê).** ewe, female sheep; *generic term for ovines*: **•Vê *mîyê* bibe çêrê** (AB) Take *this sheep* to pasture! **•*mîk*-dudu** (Ba2) *a sheep* or two: **-mî birin zozanan** (IF) to take the sheep to the summer pastures; **-mîya avê** (B) otter, zool. genus Lutra. {also: mih (JB3-2/GF-2/TF); mihî (SK); mîh (A); [meh مـه/ mih مـيـه/ mi مـى/ miia] (JJ); <mih> مه (HH)} {syn: mêşin} [Pok. moiso-s/ maiso-s 747.] 'sheep': Skt mēṣa- *m.* = 'ram' & mēṣī *f.* = 'ewe'; O Ir *maiša- = 'sheep, ram' (Ras, p.134): Av maēša- = 'ram' & maēšī- = 'ewe'; O P *maiša-, *in derivatives* *maišāna- = 'ewe'; Mid P mēš (M3); P mīš/mēš مـيش; Sor mer̄ مەڕ; Za mî *f.* (Todd); Hau meye *f.* = 'sheep, ewe' (M4) [K/JB3/IFb/ B/GF/OK/ Ag//JJ/HH/TF//A//SK] <beran, m. = ram; berx(ik), f./m. = lamb; bêçî I = 1-3 week old lamb; kavir, m. = 1-year-old sheep; berdîr, f. = 2- or 3-year-old sheep; şek = 2- or 3- year-old male sheep; bijaştîr = 3-year-old sheep; hogiç/xirt = 3-4-year-old male sheep; xamberdîr, f. = 3-year-old barren/dry sheep; pez = flock of sheep & goats; kerî II = large flock; şivan = shepherd; bêrî I = milking shed; gom I = sty, pen>

mî II مى (Czr) = hair. See **mû**.

mîçînk ميچينك (BF) = tweezers. See **mûçink**.

mîh ميه (A/JJ) = ewe. See **mî I**.

mîjank ميژانك (Çnr) = eyelashes. See **bijang**.

mîkut ميكوت (GF) = mallet; pestle. See **mêk'ut**.

mîkutok ميكوتوك (RZ) = chicken pox. See **mîrkut**.

mîmar ميمار (IFb/HH/FS) = whitlow. See **mûmar**.

mîna مـيـنـا *prep.* like, similar to: **•*mîna* min** = *like* me **•*mîna* te** = *like* you **•Qîza te ħeta niha *mîna* xûşka mine** (J) By now your daughter is *like* my sister (=like a sister to me) **•*mîna* Zîna bextr̄eş** (Ba) *like* the unfortunate Zin (from the romance of Mem û Zîn / Memê Alan)/as unfortunate as Zin **•*mîna* berê** (B) *as* before **•*mîna* gişka** (B) *like* everyone [else]: **-mîna ye** (L) it seems [cf. P mesl-e īnast مـثـل ايـنـسـت] {syn: t'irê}: **•*Mîna ye go* tu zanî çîroka bêjî!** (L) *It seems that* you know how to tell stories! {also: binanê (Z-2); mînan; mînanî (Ba2/B-2); [mina] مـيـنـا (JJ); <mîna> مـيـنـا (HH)} {syn: fena; nola; şitî II; wek} Cf. P mānand-e مانند [K/A/JB3/IFb/B/JJ/HH/GF/TF] <man[4]>

mînak مينَاك *f.* **(-a;-ê).** example: **•Bûyerên dawî, êrîşa ser Cizîrê û di cenazeyên polîsan de êrîşên ku li Diyarbekir bi ser avahiyên partiyan û welatparêzan ve birin, *mînaka* şerekî giştî û eşkere ye** (Wlt 1:39, 1) The last events, the attack on Jezira [Jizre] and, after the funerals of the policemen, the attacks which were launched in Diyarbakir against the buildings of the parties and of patriots, *are examples of* a general and open war; **-wek mînak** = for example {syn: bo nimûne; meselen}. {syn: nimûne} = Sor nimûne نِـمـوونـه [(neol)Wlt/IFb/ZF3/Wkt]

mînan مينان = like, similar to. See **mîna**.

mînanî ميناني (Ba2/B) = like, similar to. See **mîna**.

mîntan مينتان (ZF3) = robe; jacket. See **mîtan**.

mîr I مـيـر *m.&f.* **(-ê/-a;).** 1) emir, prince (m.)/princess (f.); governor, title of nobility (JB1); 2) title for tribal chieftains (JR, p. 20, note 3). {also: [mir] مـيـر (JJ); <mîr> مـيـر (HH)} < Ar amīr أمـيـر = 'prince, one who has the amr أمـــــــــر = 'power, authority, command' {mîr[î]tî} [K/A/JB3/IFb/B/JJ/HH/GF/ TF/Ba2/F/JB1/JB2] <dotmîr; jinmîr; pismîr>

***mîr II** مـــيـــر *adj.* concave (verotî) [top] side up (of knucklebones **k'ap II**): **-mîr û pik** (Wn) a winning combination of knucklebones {syn: ker û pik (Qzl)}; **-mîr û sofî** (Wn) a losing combination of knucklebones {syn: ker û çik (Qzl)}; **-du mîr** (Wn) double win {syn: du ker (Qzl)}. {syn: ker IV (Qzl)} [Wn] <k'ap II>

mîratgir مـيـراتـگـر *m.&f.* **().** heir [m.], heiress [f.], inheritor. {also: mîratgîr (GF); [mīrāt-gir] ميراتگر (JJ-Rh)} {syn: wêris} [K/JJ-Rh/OK/ZF3//GF]

mîratgîr ميراتگير (GF) = heir. See **mîratgir**.

mîrîtî ميريتى = office of emir. See **mîrtî**.

mîrkut مـيـركـوت *f.* **().** chicken pox, varicella. {also: mêkutok (GF); mîkutok (RZ-2); mîrkute (AA/OK/ RZ/FS); mîrkutok (RZ-2/ZF3); <mîrkut> ميركوت (Hej)} Cf. IFb mêkutik/nîrkutik = 'scarlatina, scarlet fever [T kızıl hastalığı]'; Sor mêkute مێکوته [Zeb/Dh/Hej//ZF3//AA/OK/RZ/FS//GF]

mîrkute ميركوته (AA/OK/RZ/FS) = chicken pox. See **mîrkut**.

mîrkutok مـيـركـوتـۆك (RZ/ZF3) = chicken pox. See **mîrkut**.

mîrnişîn مـيـرنِـشـيـن (IFb/GF) = principality. See **mîrnişînî**.

mîrnişînî میرنِشینی *f.* **(-ya;-yê).** principality: **•Ev *mîrnişînîya* he, di dema Emewîyên 'Ereb de, hatiye damezrandin** (Havîbûn 5 [1999], 73) This *principality* was established in the time of the Arab Umayyads **•Ew jî serdema *Mîrnişîna* Baban e** (AW73A3) That is the period of the Baban *Principality*. {also: mîrnişîn (IFb/GF); mîrnîşîn (OK)} [Havîbûn//IFb/GF//OK]

mîrnîşîn میرنیشین (OK) = principality. See **mîrnişînî**.

mîrtî میرتی *f.* **(-ya;-yê).** office or rank of emir, prince, or governor. {also: mîrîtî} [FK-1/K/B] <mîr>

mîs میس *m.(K/ZF3)/f.(B)* **(-ê/-a; /-ê).** copper. {also: mes II (GF-2); mis (IFb-2/GF/OK/ZF3); miz III (GF-2); [mys] میس (JJ)} {syn: sifir I} Cf. P mes مس; Sor mis مِس [K/A/B/IFb//JJ/GF/ZF3] <birinc II; misîn; mîsk'ar>

mîsger میسگەر (K)/mîsgeř میسگەڕ (B) = coppersmith. See **mîsk'ar**.

mîsk'ar میسکار *m.* **().** coppersmith. {also: misger (IFb/GF/OK-2/ZF3); misgir (OK); mizger (GF-2); mîsger (K-2); mîsgeř (B-2)} Sor misger مِسگەر/mizger مزگەر [K/A/B//IFb/GF/ZF3//OK] <sefar>

mîsoger میسۆگەر (TF) = sure. See **misoger**.

mîstin میستِن *vt./vi.(IF)* **(-mîz-).** to urinate, piss. {also: mîz kirin (A/JB3/B/HH); mîztin (IF); [miztin میزتین/ mistin میستین] (JJ); <mîz kirin> میزکرن (HH)} [Pok. meiĝh- 713.] = 'to urinate': Skt mēhati = 'he urinates'; O Ir *maiz- (Tsb 40): Av maēz- (*pres.* maēza-); Mid P mistan (mēz-) (M3); P mīxtan میختن (mīz) (میز); Sor mîzan میزان/ mîzîn میزین (-mîz-); Za mîzî kenã (Todd); cf. also Lat mingere (*pp.* mi[n]ctum) [K/IF/JJ/ZF3/FS//A/JB3/B/HH]

mîtan میتان *m.* **(-ê;-î).** 1) long, belted robe made of heavy material (called zibūn in Iraqi Arabic): **•Wî *mîtanê* xwe li xwe kir û derket** (Wane 4: www.rechid.net) He put on his *mîtan* and left; 2) woman's jacket with embroidered lapels (Qzl): **•Ka li kûne: dehrî û / Xeftan û *mîtanê* di min?** (Cigerxwîn: Di Bîr Anîn) Where are they, my gowns and / caftans and jackets? {also: meyten (FS-2); mîntan (ZF3)} [Qzl/K(s)/FJ/CS/FS]

mîvan میڤان (Srk) = guest. See **mêvan**.

mîx میخ (BF/Wkt) = (iron) nail. See **mix**.

mîxe میخە (FS) = (iron) nail. See **mix**.

mîz میز *f.* **(-a;-ê).** urine, piss: **•Gelikî *mîza wî tê*** (L) He had to go real bad [lit. 'His *piss comes very much*'] [Cf. T çişi geldi]: **-mîz kirin** (A/JB3/B/HH) to urinate, piss {syn: mîstin}. {also: [miz] میز (JJ); <mîz> میز (HH)} [Pok. meiĝh- 713.] = 'to urinate': O Ir *maiz- (Tsb 40): P mīz میز/komīz کمیز; Sor mîz میز; Za mîz(e)/mîzi *f.* (Mal) [L/F/K/A/JB3/IFb/B/JJ/HH/GF/TF/FS]

mîzdan میزدان *f.* **(-a;-ê).** (urinary) bladder. {also: mîzdang (F); mîzdank (IFb/FS); mîzildan (Ak)} P komīzdān کمیزدان; Sor mîzdan میزدان/mîzildan میزِلدان [K/B/GF//F//IFb/FS//Ak]

mîzdang میزدانگ (F) = bladder. See **mîzdan**.

mîzdank میزدانك (IFb/FS) = bladder. See **mîzdan**.

mîzildan میزلدان (Ak) = bladder. See **mîzdan**.

mîztin میزتِن (IF) = to urinate. See **mîstin**.

moc مۆج (Z-3) = wave. See **mewc**.

mohlet مۆهلەت (K/JJ) = respite. See **molet**.

mohtac مۆهتاج (K) = needy. See **muhtac**.

molet مۆلەت *f.* **(-a;-ê).** time limit, respite, extension, deadline, fixed period of time *(for carrying out an action)*: **•*Mihleta* çil rojan bide min, ezê biçim ji te re bînim** (Rnh 2:17, 308) Give me a respite of 40 days, and I'll go bring [them] for you **•*Molet* ji te re sê meh** (L) You have three months in which to do it [lit. '*Respite* for you three months']. {also: mihlet (JB3/Rnh); mohlet (K); monet (L-2); [muhul مهل/ mohlet مهلت] (JJ); <muhlet> مهلت (HH)} < Ar muhlah مهلة --> T mühlet; Sor mołet مۆڵەت [L/B/ZF3//K//JB3/Rnh//JJ//HH]

mom I مۆم *f.* **(;-ê).** flower. {also: [mōm] موم (JJ)} {syn: çîçek; gul; kulîlk} [Zx/JJ/PS]

mom II مۆم (FS) = candle. See **mûm**.

mon مۆن *adj.* 1) {syn: jar [2]; zeyf} weak, sickly; puny (K[s]): **•[Wisanî bi xef û dizî mirov dane kuştin ew karê *monane*]** (JR #27, 81) To have a man killed sneakily and secretly, this is the act *of weaklings*; 2) {syn: xirab} bad (K[s]): **•[libasêd *mon*]** (JR) *bad* (shabby) clothing; 3) {syn: melûl} sad, gloomy (K[s]); sullen, pouting, frowning (IFb/JB3/GF); morose, unfriendly, sour (OK). {also: [moun] مون (JJ)} Sor mon مۆن = 'glum' {monî} [JR/K(s)/IFb/JB3/GF/OK/ZF3/FS//JJ]

monet مۆنەت (L) = respite. See **molet**.

Mongolî مۆنگۆلی *adj.* Mongolian. {also: Mengolî (BF); Mexolî (SS); Moxolî (ZF3)} Sor Mengołî مەنگۆڵی [Wkp/Wkt//BF//SS//ZF3]

monî مۆنی *f.* **().** weakness, sickliness; puniness; gloominess. [K(s)] <mon>

mor I مۆر *adj.* purple, violet. {also: <mor> مور (HH)} {syn: binefşî; erẍewanî; şîrkî} Cf. T mor =

'purple' [Z-1/Kmc-2/K(s)/IFb/HH/GF/OK/RZ/ZF3/FS] <xemrî>

mor II مۆر *f.* **(-a;-ê).** 1) {syn: gustîl; p'îlat} signet ring; 2) seal, stamp: •**Wî *muhra* xo li namê da** (FS) He put his seal on the letter; 3) {syn: nîşan} sign, mark (K). {also: muhir (FS); muhur, m. (F-2); [moor مور/ muhur مهر] (JJ)} < Ar muhr مهر = 'signet'; Sor mor مۆر [Z-2/EP-7/F/K/A/JB3/IF/JJ/B//FS]

moran مۆران *f.* **(;-ê).** dense fog: •***Mij û moranê* çiya girt** (FS) *A thick fog* gripped the mountain •***Moraneke* hilweşand-inê, dûmaneke mirinê ji nişka ve girt ser welatên gêrîkan** (SF 23) Suddenly *a fog of* destruction, a cloud of death beset the land of the ants. {syn: dûman; kirove [1]; mij} [SF/K(s)/GF/TF/ZF3/FS/Wkt/BF]

mord مۆرد *f.* **().** myrtle, bot. *Myrtus communis* (IF). {also: mûrtik (KZ); mûtik (IFb-2/OK/RF)} Mid P mōrd = 'myrtle' (M3); P mūrd مورد; Sor mord مۆرد [Rich/IFb/ZF3/Wkt//KZ//OK/RF] <dar I>

moristan مۆرِستان (FJ/GF/SS) = anthill. See **mûristan**[1].

morî I مۆری *f.* **(-ya;-yê).** bead[s] (K/A/IF/B); glass beads (HH); necklace (K); false jewels (JJ): -**morîya xewê avîtin guhê *fk-î*** (K) to put or lull to sleep [lit. 'to throw beads of sleep on s.o.'s ears']: •**Wextê kû şêv ȟewlê sibihê da, *miȟarkê xewê kirne guhê* herduwa** (HR 4:27) When night turned into morning, they *put the beads of sleep into their ears* •***Morîya xewê li guhê wan danîne*** (Z-2) They put them to sleep. {also: miȟark (HR); mûrî II (IF-2); mûrîk (IF-2); [morik مورك/mori موری] (JJ); <morik> مورك (HH)} [Z-2/K/A/IFb/B/ZF//JJ/HH//HR] <bişkoj>

morî II مۆری (IF) = ant. See **mûrî I**.

morîstan مۆریستان (IFb/Kmc[Qrj]/ZF3/BF) = anthill. See **mûristan**[1]; (ZF3) = ant. See **mûristan**[2].

morîstang مۆریستانگ (ZF3) = ant. See **mûristan**[2].

morîstank مۆریستانك (Kmc[Qrj]) = ant. See **mûristan**[2].

morsele مۆرسەله *f.* **(;-yê).** iron pole connecting yoke to main body of plow. {also: mosele (ZF3); musele (CCG)} {syn: mijane; tîr I[2]} [CCG//ZF3//A/IFb//Flk] <bose II; cot; halet; k'otan; hevcar̄>

mosele مۆسەله (ZF3) = iron pole connecting yoke to plow. See **morsele**.

mosîqe مۆسیقه (FS) = music. See **mûzîk**.

mostran مۆستران (Wkt[Btm]) = ant. See **mûristan**[2].

mostranîk مۆسترانیك (Wkt[Btm]) = ant. See **mûristan**[2].

moşek مۆشەك (OK/ZF3) = rocket. See **mûşek**.

moşen مۆشەن (IFb) = threshing sledge, threshing board. See **moşene**.

moşen•e مۆشەنە *f.* **(•a;•ê).** (wooden) threshing sledge, threshing board *(with flint blades set in the bottom)* [T döven]: -**moşene gerandin** (ZF) to pull or drag threshing sledge *over the grain on threshing floor*: •**Li hin cihan *mevşenê* bi gayan, li hin cihan jî bi ker û hespan li ser bêderê bi kaşkirinê *digerînin*** (CCG, 71) In some places they *drag the threshing sledge* over the threshing floor with oxen, in some places with donkeys and horses. {also: mevşek (TF-2); mevşen (CCG-2); moşen (IFb); muşen (TF)} {syn: kam I} *For picture, see Kmc-16, "Alavên çandiniyê"-G [p. 4]* [CCG/Kmc/ZF/Wkt/CS/FS//IFb//TF] <cencer>

moşt مۆشت, m. (F) = handful; fist. See **mist**.

mot مۆت *m.* **(-ê;).** grape molasses, *thick syrup made from boiled grape juice* [T pekmez]. {also: motî (IF); mut (Kş); mûtî (A); <motî> موتی (HH)} {syn: aqit; dims; doşav} Cf. also [mōt] موت (JJ-Lx) = 'wine'. Cf. T mut [Babik *Pötürge -Malatya] = 'grape molasses' (DS, v. 9, p. 3225) [Srk/GF/ZF3//IF/HH//Kş//A]

motik مۆتِك *f.* **(-a;).** dummy egg in a chicken coop, to keep hens laying eggs: -**motka mirîşkê** (Qzl) do. {syn: xap (Qrj)} [Qzl/IFb/GF/FJ/ZF3/Wkt] <hêk>

motî مۆتی (IF/HH) = grape molasses. See **mot**.

movane مۆڤانه *f.* **().** old, dark honeycomb, as opposed to **şema** [3], qv. [Zeb] <şan; şema [3]>

movik مۆڤِك *f.* **(-a;-ê).** 1) {syn: hence; zend I [3]} joint *(anat.)*: -**movika piştê** (K) vertebra {syn: derzen (Z-4)}; 2) {syn: dev [3]; şilf} edge *(of a blade)*; 3) notch, node (A). {also: mûfik (A/IF); mûfirik (IF); mûfirk (IF); <movik> موڤك (HH)} [Z-2/K/A/IF/B/HH/Kmc] <geh I>

moxil مۆخِل *f.* **(-a;-ê).** flour sieve: -**moxil kirin** (K[s]) to sift. {also: mûxil (OK); [mok̄el] مخل (JJ); <moxil> موخل (HH)} <Ar munxal/munxul منخل = 'sieve; screen' [Bw/K(s)/IFb/JJ/HH/TF//OK] <bêjing; ser̄ad>

Moxolî مۆخۆلی (ZF3) = Mongolian. See **Mongolî**.

moẍrib مۆغرِب *m./f.(B)* **(; /-ê).** 1) sunset: •**Dinya bû *moẍrib*** (L) It was sunset time [lit. 'The world became *sunset*'] •**Rojekê *dema mexribê* çû ber dergehê Diyarbekirê** (Rnh 2:17, 306-7) One day *at sunset* he reached the gates of Diyarbekir; 2) evening (B); 3) {syn: řojava} west (B/JJ). {also: mexrib (Rnh); meẍreb (B); meẍrîb (K); moẍrîb; [megreb] مغرب (JJ)} < Ar maγrib مغرب = 'place or time of sunset, west' [L//B/JJ//K] <êvar; hingûr; mişriq; řojava>

moẍrîb مۆغریب = sunset; evening; west. See **moẍrib.**

moz I مـــۆز *f.* **(-a;-ê).** 1) hornet (HH); {syn: zilketk} wasp (B), zool. *Vespidae*: **-moza qirtik** (Msr)/~ **qirt** (Haz) wasp, yellowjacket {also: mozeqirtik (IF); mozqirtk (A)}; **-moza zebeş** (Msr)/**moza beş** (Haz) hornet; red stinging insect with a white forehead and larger than a bee, zool. *Vespa crabo* (IF) {also: mozebeş (IF)}; 2) gadfly, horsefly, large fly that bites or annoys livestock (K/IFb), zool. *Tabanus bovinus*; 3) {syn: mêş[a] hingiv[în]} bee, zool. *Apis mellifera*; bumble-bee: **-moza hingiv** (QtrE) do. {also: [moz مـــوز/mozi مـوزى] (JJ); <moz̲> مـوظ (HH)} Sor moz مـۆز = 'horse-fly' [DS/F/K/(A)/IFb/B/JJ/HH/GF/TF/OK] <kuřîfok; mêş; stêng>

moz II مۆز, f. (;-ê) (B) = calf. See **mozik I.**

moz III مۆز (GF/OK/AA/CB/FS) = banana. See **mûz.**

mozebeş مـــۆزەبـــەش (IF) = hornet. See **moza zebeş** under **moz I**[1].

mozeqirtik مـۆزەقِـرتِـك (IF) = wasp. See **moza qirtik** under **moz I**[1].

mozik I مـــۆزِك *m.* **().** 1) {syn: k'endik; malok (Krç)} calf, one-year-old male calf, ox, or bull (B); one-and-a-half to two-year-old ox (Wn/Bşk); two-year-old calf or ox (IF/HH); 2) stepson, son of one's wife by a previous marriage (JJ/HH). {also: moz II f. (;-ê) (B); mozîk (ZF3); [mouzik] موزيك (JJ); <moz̲îk> موظيك (HH)} < Arm mozi մոզի/mozik մոզիկ = 'year-old male calf, young bullock' <[Pok. mozĝho-s 750.] 'young bovine'; cf. also Gr moschos μόσχος = 'young steer' [Wn/Bşk/F/K/IF//JJ//HH/ZF3//B] <ga; golik; k'endik>

mozik II مۆزِك = dim. of **moz I.**

mozîk مۆزیك (ZF3) = calf (young cow). See **mozik I.**

mozqirtk مۆزقِرتك (A) = wasp. See **moza qirtik** under **moz I**[1].

mrt'oxe مـــرتـــۆخـــە (HCK) = omelet-like dish. See **mirtoẍe.**

muamele موئامەلە (Wkt) = treatment. See **miamele.**

muft موفت (B) = key; lock. See **mifte.**

muhbet موهبەت (B) = love. See **muȟbet.**

muhir موهِر (FS) = seal, stamp. See **mor II.**

muhtac مـــوهـــتـــاج *adj.* needy, lacking, in need of: **-muhtacê** ***ft-î*** **bûn** (K) to need stg.: **•Heger tu** ***muhtacê*** **çend qurûşa** ***ye***, **rabe ji ser kursîya zêr** (L) If you *are in need of* a few cents, get up from the gold chair. {also: mihtac (IFb); mohtac (K); [mouhtadj] مـحـتـاج (JJ); <miȟtac مـحـتـاج/mitȟac متحاج> (HH)} < Ar muḥtāj محتاج (< iḥtāja VIII احتاج = 'to be in need' <√ḥ-w-j حوج) [L/JJ//K//IFb/HH] <ȟewce; lazim>

muhur موهور, m. (F) = seal, signet. See **mor II.**

muȟafeze موحـافـزە (SK) = preservation; protection. See **mihafeze.**

muȟbet مـــوحـــبـــەت *f.* **(-a;-ê).** 1) love (K/B): **-eşq û muȟbet** (Z-1) do.: **•ji** ***eşq û muȟbeta*** **Zînê** (Z-1) out of *love for* Zin; **-muȟbeta kesekî hilanîn** (Z-2) for love to sustain s.o.: **•Stîya Zîn eşq û meȟbeta Memê wê hiltîne** (Z-2) Z.'s love for M. sustains her; 2) friendship; affinity, sympathy; 3) attention. {also: meȟbet (Z-2); mihbet; mihebet (K); muhbet (B-2); [mouhabet] مـــحـــبـــت (JJ); <meȟibbet> محبت (HH)} < Ar maḥabbah مَحبّة = 'love' (<√ḥ-b-b حـــبّ = 'to love')--> T muhabbet [Z-1/B//K//JJ//HH]

mukim موكِم (FS/ZF3) = strong. See **mukum.**

mukum موكوم *adj.* strong, sturdy: **•Kezan--mestir in û qelpkê wan** ***mukumtir*** **e--bêwk biçûktir in û qelpkê wan naziktir e** (Bw) Kezan [type of terebinth seed] are larger and their shell is *harder*--bêwk are smaller and their shell is softer; **-dergehê mukim** (FS) a strong, sturdy gate. {also: mukim (FS/ZF3)} [Bw//FS/ZF3] <meȟkem>

mukurhatin موكورهاتِن (TF) = to admit. See **mikuř.**

mukuřî مـوكـورى**/mukurî** مـوكـورى [B] *f.* **(-ya;-yê).** longing, yearning, nostalgia: **-mukurîya (kesekî) kirin** (F) to long for, miss, yearn for s.o.: **•Min** ***mukurya*** **gundê xwe, gundîê xwe, hevalê xweye zarotîê** ***kirye.*** **Min** ***mukurya*** **ç'ya-banîê me, kanî-ç'evkanîê me, deşt û mêrgê xwe** ***kirye*** (E. Serdar. Mukuřî, 8) I *have longed for [=long for]* my village, my villagers, my childhood friends. I *have longed for* our mountains and valleys, our wells and springs, our plains and meadows. {also: mikuřî (K)} {syn: bêrî II; hesret [2]} [Emerîkê Serdar/B/F//K]

mumkin مومكِن *adj.* possible: **•Eger** ***mumkin*** **bît dê çim e ȟeccê** (SK 31) If *possible* I shall go on the pilgrimage **•Her tişt di qudreta xudêda** ***mumkin*** **e** (SK 120) Everything is *possible* in the power of God **•Tu dizanî ku niha ne** ***mumkin*** **e mêşek jî**

sînor derbas bike (HYma 49) You know that now it's not *possible* for even a fly to cross the border. {also: mimkûn (IFb)/mimk'ûn (K); mumk'în (K-2); [moumkin] مـمـكـن (JJ)} {syn: gengaz[2]; pêkan} < Ar mumkin مـمـكن = 'possible' [HYma/SK/JJ/CS//K/IFb] <çêbûn; îmk'an>

mumk'în مومكين (K) = possible. See **mumkin**.

munasebet مـونـاسـەبـەت *f.* **(-a;-ê).** occasion: •**Ev sempozyum *bi munasebeta* bîst û yek saliya Nûbiharê tê çêkirin** (Nbh 125:3) This symposium is being held *on the occasion of* the 21st anniversary of Nûbihar. {also: minesebet (CS); [mounasibet] مـنـاسـبـت (JJ)} {syn: *helkeftin} < Ar munāsabah مـنـاسـبـة = 'occasion, opportunity' [Nbh/IFb//JJ//CS] <delîve>

munasib موناسِب (SK) = appropriate. See **minasib**.

muqabil مـوقـابِـل (SK) = opposite; opposed. See **miqabil**.

müristan مویرستان (G) = anthill. See **mûristan**[1].

muro مورۆ (SK) = man; person. See **meriv**.

murûzî مـوروزی (K) = bad mood; melancholy. See **mirûz**.

musele مـوسـەلـە (CCG) = iron pole connecting yoke to plow. See **morsele**.

musîk موسیك (AD) = music. See **mûzîk**.

musîkvan موسیكڤان (AD) = musician. See **mûzîkvan**.

musulman مـوسـولـمـان (B/SK/F/GF) = Muslim. See **misilman**.

musulmanî مـوسـولـمـانـی (B/F/JJ) = Islam. See **misilmanî**.

musurman موسورمان (B) = Muslim. See **misilman**.

musurmanî موسورمانی (B) = Islam. See **misilmanî**.

muşen مـوشـەن (TF) = threshing sledge, threshing board. See **moşene**.

mut موت (Kş) = grape molasses. See **mot**.

mutirb مـوطِـرب (SK) = Roma, Gypsy; drummer. See **mirt'ib**.

mutlaq موطلاق (SK/JJ) = absolutely. See **mitleq**.

muxabin مـوخـابِـن (Bw/JJ) = unfortunately. See **mixabin**.

muxdar موخدار = amount. See **mixdar**.

muxtar موختار *m.* **(-ê; muxtêr, vî muxtarî).** 1) village leader, village chief; headman; 2) plenipotentiary (B); 3) *[adj.]* free, independent (SK/IF). {also: mixtar (Z-4); [moukhtar] مـخـتـار (JJ); <muxtar> مـخـتـار (HH)} {syn: k'ewxwe; k'eya} < Ar muxtār مـخـتـار = 'chosen one; village chief'; Sor muxtar موختار {mixtarî; muxtarî} [K/IFb/B/JJ/HH/SK]

muxtarî مـوخـتـاری *f.* **(;-yê).** 1) office or position of village chief; execution of the office of village chief: •**Emê vêga te ji *mixtarîyê* derînin** (Z-4) Then we will remove you from *the position of village chief*; 2) authority, power, plenary powers (B). {also: mixtarî (Z-4)} [Z-4//K/B] <muxtar>

muxulqet مـوخـولـقـەت (Tsab) = people, creatures. See **mexulqet**.

muẍdar موغدار (K/B) = amount. See **mixdar**.

muz موز (TF) = banana. See **mûz**.

muze مـوزه (IFb/RZ/ZF3/Wkt) = museum. See **mûzexane**.

muzexane مـوزەخـانـە (ZF3/Wkt) = museum. See **mûzexane**.

muzîk موزیك (IFb/ZF3/Wkt/CS) = music. See **mûzîk**.

muzîker موزیکەر (ZF3) = musician. See **mûzîkvan**.

muzîkjen مـوزیـکـژەن (ZF3/Wkt) = musician. See **mûzîkvan**.

muzîkkar موزیككار (ZF3) = musician. See **mûzîkvan**.

muzîkvan مـوزیـكـڤـان (ZF3/Wkt/CS) = musician. See **mûzîkvan**.

mû مـوو *m.* **(-yê/miwê;).** a (single) hair; *many individual strands of **mû** make up one's **p'or̄*** (qv.) : •**Du *mû* ji laşê xwe hilkirin** (L) He plucked two *hairs* off his [own] body: **-mûyê xinzîr** (B) bristle. {also: mî II (Czr); [mou] مـو (JJ); <mû> مـو (HH)} Mid P mōy = 'hair' (M3); P mū مـو; Sor mû مـوو; Za mû *f.* = 'hair (single strand)' (Todd) [BX/K/A/JB3/IF/B/JJ/HH] <bisk; gilî I; kezî; pirç'; p'or̄ III; tûk I>

mûç I مووچ (IFb) = pricked up. See **miç I**.

mûç II مووچ *adj.* 1) puckered up (mouth, of humans) [T büzük ağızlı]; 2) {also: miç II (Elk)} shut *(mouth, of humans)*: **-Devê xwe miç bike** (Elk) Shut up! {also: devmûç (Elk); miç II (Elk)} [Elk/Xrz]

mûçing مـووچِـنـگ (A/IFb/TF/OK/LC) = tweezers. See **mûçink**.

mûçink مـووچِـنـك *f.(ZF3/RF)/m.(Bw/BF)* **(/-ê;-ê/).** tweezers: •**Ez jî bi *mûçingê* ketim nav porê xwe** (LC, 5) I took *a tweezers* to my hair [in search of white hairs]; **-miçînkê mîya** (Bw) tweezers (for hair); **-miçînkê neynoka** (Bw) nail clippers. {also: miçînk, m. (Bw); mîçînk (BF); mûçing (A/IFb/TF/OK); [moutchin مـوچـيـن/moutchink مـوچـيـنك] (JJ); <mûçink> مـوچـنـك (HH)} {syn: mûk'êş} P mūčīne مـوچـيـنـه = 'tweezers' [Bw//BF//RZ/RF/JJ/HH//A/IFb/TF/OK/LC]

mûfik مووفِك (A/IF) = joint *(anat.)*. See **movik**.

mûfirik مووفِرك (IF) = joint *(anat.)*. See **movik**.
mûfirk مووفِرك (IF) = joint (anat.) . See **movik**.
mûhî مويهى/مووهى (Hk) = ant. See **mûrî I**.
m'ûj معووژ (Klk) = raisin(s). See **mewîj**.
mûk'êş مووكێش *f.(OK)/m.(Bw)* **(/-ê;).** tweezers. {also: mûkêşk m. (Bw)} {also: mûçink} Sor mûkêş مووكێش = 'tweezers' [Bw//IFb/GF/OK/RZ]
mûkêşk مووكێشك, m. (Bw) = tweezers. See **mûk'êş**.
mûm مووم *f.* **(-a;-ê).** 1){syn: şema [1]} wax: **-mûm kirin** (B) to wax; 2) {syn: find; şema [2]} wax candle: **•Wî *moma* mezin hilkir** (FS) He lit the big candle. {also: mom II (FS); [moum] موم (JJ); <mûm> موم (HH)} < T mum = 'candle, wax' [S&E/K/IF/B/HH/JJ/ZF3/BF//FS] <find; şemal[k]>
mûmar موومار *f.* **(-a;).** whitlow, felon, infection on tip of finger or thumb [T dolama]. {also: mîmar (IFb-2/FS); <mîmar> ميمار (HH)>} {syn: *marok (TF/ZF3)} [Kmc/A/IFb/GF//HH/FS]
mûr موور (F) = ant. See **mûrî I**.
mûristan موورِستان *f.* **(;-ê).** 1) {syn: kurmorî[1]} anthill, formicary {also: mêristan (AD); moristan (FJ-2/GF/SS); morîstan (IFb/Kmc[Qrj]-2/ZF3-2/BF); müristan (G-2); mûrîstan (B/FD); mwîristan (G/Kmc[Qrj]-2)}: **•Ma tu li ser *mûristanê* (xuluqî) yî?** (Kmc) Do you have ants in your pants? = Why are you in such a hurry; 2) {syn: gêle; kurmorî[2]; mûrî I} ant {also: morîstan[g] (ZF3-2); morîstank (Kmc[Qrj]-2); mostran[îk] (Wkt[Btm]); mûristang (Kmc); mûrîstang (Kmc[Qrj]); mûstang (Wkt[Serhedî])}. *Cf.* ***kurmorî*** *also with both meanings.* [Haz/K/FJ/Kmc(Qrj)ZF3//B/FD] <mûrî I>
mûristang موورِستانگ (Kmc) = ant. See **mûristan**[2].
mûrî I مووری *f.(K/B/F/Bw)/m.(OK/JB3)* **(-ya/;-ê/).** ant (insect), zool. *Formicidae*: **-mêrîyêt bisurmana** (Bw) yellow ants; **-mêrîyêt êzîdîya** (Bw) red ants; **-mêrîyêt fila** (Bw) black ants. {also: mêrî (Bw); mêrû (SK/OK); morî II (IFb-2); mûhî (Hk); mûr (F); [mouri] موری (JJ); <morî> موری (HH)} {syn: gêle; kurmorî[2]; mûristan[2]} [Pok. moru̯ī- 749.] 'ant': Av maoirī-; Sgd 'm'wrč *f.*; Mid P mōr (M3); P mūrče مورچه; Sor mêrûle مێرووله; Za moncle *m.* (Todd)/mojla/morcela/morcila *f.* (Mal); cf. also Arm mrjiwn մրջիւն; Rus muraveĭ муравей; Gr myrmēx μύρμηξ, *gen.* myrmēkos μύρμηκος *m.* [K/A/JB3/IFb/B/JJ/GF//HH//F//SK/OK//Bw//Hk]
mûrî II مووری (IF) = bead(s). See **morî I**.

mûrîk موورِيك (IF) = bead(s). See **morî I**.
mûrîstan مووریستان (B/FD) = anthill. See **mûristan**[1].
mûrîstang مووریستانگ (Kmc[Qrj]) = ant. See **mûristan**[2].
mûrtik موورتِك (KZ) = myrtle. See **mord**.
mûsîkî مووسيكى = music. See **mûzîk**.
mûsîqa مووسيقا (K[s]) = music. See **mûzîk**.
mûsîqî مووسيقى (JB3/IF/GF) = music. See **mûzîk**.
mûstang مووستانگ (Wkt[Serhedî]) = ant. See **mûristan**[2].
mûşek مووشەك *f.* **(-a;).** rocket. {also: moşek (OK/ZF3)} <P mūšak موشك = 'little mouse, rocket'. *Readily understood by Bw, who actively use Arabic* ṣārūx صاروخ [(neol)VoA//OK/ZF3]
mûtik مووتِك (IFb/OK/RF) = murtle. See **mord**.
mûtî مووتى (A) = grape molasses. See **mot**.
mûxil مووخِل (OK) = sieve. See **moxil**.
mûz مووز *f.* **().** banana, bot. *Musa sapientum*. {also: moz III (GF/OK/AA/CB-2/FS); muz (TF)} Mid P mōz (M3); Ar mawz موز --> T muz; Sor moz مۆز [Kmc-2/IFb/RZ//GF/OK/AA/CB/FS//TF]
mûze موزه (K/Wkt) = museum. See **mûzexane**.
mûzexan•e موزخانه *f.* **(•eya/•a;•ê).** museum: **•Mala helbestvan û nivîskarê navdar ê kurd Hêmin Mûkiryanî ya li bajarê Mahabadê, weke "baştirîn û giringtirîn *mûzexaneya* Îranê" hate destnîşankirin** (Rûpela Nû 29.v.2017) The house of the famous Kurdish poet and writer Hêmin Mûkiryanî in the city of Mehabad has been designated as the best and most important *museum* of Iran **•Mêrdîn *mûzexaneyeke servekirî* ye û li wî bajêrî li her derê bêhna dîrokê tê, li bin her kevirekî çîrokeke veşartî heye** (Rûdaw 16.vi.2015) Mardin is *an open air museum* and li that city the smell of history is everywhere, under every rock there is a hidden story. Sor mozexane مۆزخانه {also: muze (IFb/RZ/ZF3-2/Wkt-2); muzexane (ZF3/Wkt-2); mûze (K-2/Wkt-2); mûzê (K/B)} [Rûdaw/FJ/GF/BF/Wkt/SS//IFb//ZF3//K]
mûzê موززێ (K/B) = museum. See **mûzexane**.
mûzîk موووزيك *f.* **(-a;-ê).** music: **•*Mûzîka* kurdî bandoreke mezin li ser kesatiya min kiriye** (Rûdaw 20.v.2018) Kurdish *music* greatly influenced my personality **•Yekem festîvala *mûzîka* kurdî li bajarê Seqizê ya Rojhilatê Kurdistanê hat lidarxistin** (IMPNews 23.vii.2016) The first Kurdish *music* festival was held in the city of Saqqiz in

Eastern (=Iranian) Kurdistan. {also: mosîqe (FS); musîk (AD); muzîk (IFb/ZF3/Wkt/CS); mûsîkî; mûsîqa (K[s]); mûsîqî (JB3/IF/GF); mûzîka (B); [musikí] (JJ)} Sor mozîqe مۆزیقه/mosîqa مۆسیقا; Cf. Ar mūsīqá موسيقى; T musiki/müzik <Gr mousikē (technē) μουσικη (τεχνη) = '(art) of the Muses' < mousikos μουσικος = 'of the Muses' < Mousa Μουσα = 'a Muse' [Rûdaw/K/TF/BF/RZ//B//IFb/ZF3/Wkt/CS/ /AD//GF/JJ//K(s)//FS] <kilam; mûzîkvan; stiran I>

mûzîka موزیکا (B) = music. See **mûzîk**.

mûzîkvan موزیکڤان *m.* **(-ê;).** musician: •**Bo gotina du stranan li ser Şingal û Pêşmerge, *mûzîkvanê* Kurd Dr. Dilşad Mihemed Seîd hunermendên her çar parçeyên Kurdistanê tîne cem hev** (Rûdaw 6.xi.2014) By singing two songs about Sinjar [Shingal] and the Peshmerga, the Kurdish *musician* Dr. Dilshad M. Sa'id brings artists from all 4 parts of Kurdistan together •**Helbestvan, nivîskar, *mûzîkvan* û edîbên herêma Mukriyanê gelekî binavûdeng in** (IMPNews 8.x.2016) The poets, writers, *musicians* and literati of the region of Mukriyan are very famous. {also: musîkvan (AD); muzîker (ZF3-2); muzîkjen (ZF3-2/Wkt-2); muzîkkar (ZF3-2); muzîkvan (ZF3/Wkt/CS); mûzîkjen (BF-2)} [Rûdaw/BF//ZF3/Wkt/CS//AD] <mûzîk>

mwîristan مویرستان (G/Kmc[Qrj]) = anthill. See **mûristan**[1].

N ن

na- نـــــــــــ *neg. pref.* not, do[es] not, will not. {negative particle prefixed to present indicative verbs; negativizes both the present indicative and the future, e.g., ***nabînim*** = I *don't* see/I *won't* see; the two verbs **karîn** and **zanîn** take **ni-** rather than **na-**} {also: [na] نـا (JJ); <na> نـ (HH)} Cf. P na- نـ; Sor na- نـا; Za ne (Todd) [M/BX/K/IFb/B/JJ/HH/GF/TF] <me-; ne-; ni- >

na نـا *adv.* no. {also: ne (SK); [na] نـا (JJ); <no' نـۆء/no نـۆ> (HH)} {syn: nexêr} Sor ne نـه & nexêr نـه‌خێر {≠erê} [K/IFb/B/JJ/TF//SK//HH]

nabeyn نابه‌ین (BX) = between; interval. See **navbeyn**.

nabên نابێن = between. See **navbeyn** [2].

nabos نـــابـــۆس *f.* **(-a;-ê).** cul de sac, dead end. [Frq/ZF] <kolan II; rê; zaboq; zikak>

naçar ناچار (IFb/TF/OK)/naç'ar ناچار (K[s]) = obliged, forced. See **neçar**.

naga ناگا = now. See **niha**.

nagon ناگۆن (Msr/Wkt) = heifer. See **nogin**.

naha ناها (B) = now. See **niha**.

nahiye ناهیه (IFb) = district. See **neĥî**.

nahlîk ناهلیك (RZ) = mattress. See **nehlîk**.

naĥeqq ناحه‌قق (SK) = wrong, unjust. See **neheq**.

naĥiye ناحِیه (SK) = district. See **neĥî**.

naka ناكا = now. See **niha**.

nakokî ناكۆكی *f.* **(-ya;-yê).** 1) {syn: de'w II; dubendî; k'êşe; p'evçûn} conflict, antagonism; dispute, disagreement; 2) contradiction (IFb/ZF/CS): **•Birêz Omerî xwûnerekî bidîqqet e û divê neketiba *nakokiyan*** (Nbh 125:52) Mr. O. is a careful reader and he should not have contradicted himself [lit. 'fallen into *contradictions*']. < Sor nakokî نـــاكـــۆكـــی = 'strained relations; dispute, quarrel, contention' [Nbh/K(s)/A/IFb/RZ/ZF/CS]

nal نـــــــــال *f.* **(-a;-ê).** horseshoe: **•Ji Stembolê min guhark'ekê kirîye guhî ji batmanekê, xeleqa wê du min e, *nala* asênî** (JB1-A, #139) In Istanbul I put in his ear an earring that weighed a batman, the hoop of which is two maunds, shaped like *a horseshoe* **•Mi *nalek* dît, ma hespekî û sê *nala*** (Dz-anec #21) I've found *one horseshoe*, now all I need is a horse and three more *horseshoes* [expression like 'One down and (three) to go']; **-nal kirin** (K) to shoe (a horse). {also: ne'l (B); [nal] نـعـل (JJ); <nal> نـال (HH)} < Ar na'l نـعـل = 'shoe, horseshoe'; Sor nał نـاڵ; Za nale *m.* (Todd) [K/A/IFb/JJ/HH/JB1-A/GF/TF/OK//B] <hesp; sol>

nalbend نـالبه‌ند *m.* **(-ê;-î).** blacksmith, one who shoes horses; farrier: **•Beẍdo him beyt'are, him *nalbende*** (FK-kk-13:126) Beghdo is both a veterinarian and *a blacksmith*. {also: ne'lbend (B); [nal-benda (G)/nawl-band (Rh)] نـعـلـبـنـد (JJ); <nalbend> نـالـبـنـد (HH)} {syn: solbend} Cf. P na'lband نعلبند; Sor nałbend ناڵبه‌ند = 'farrier, shoe-smith' {nalbendî; ne'lbendî} [Bw/K/A/IFb/HH/GF/TF/OK//B//JJ] <hesinger; ĥedad>

nalbendî نـــالـــبـــه‌نـــدی *f.* **(;-yê).** profession of a blacksmith, shoeing horses; profession of a farrier: **•Eve çende tu *nalbendîyê dikî*?** (BF) How long *have* you *been shoeing horses*? {also: ne'lbendî (B)} {syn: solbendî} [IFb/TF/BF//B] <nalbend>

nalç•e نـــالـــچـــه *f./m.(ZF3)* **(•a/•eyê;•ê/).** metal piece attached to sole or heel of shoe as reinforcement: ***•Nalça* sola wê şiqitîye** (Ks) *The metal piece* fell off her shoe. {also: [naljá] نـعـلـجـه (JJ)} <Ar na'l نعل = 'shoe' + P -če چه dim. suffix; --> T nalça [Ks/A/FS/ZF3//JJ]

nalenal نالەنال *f.* **(-a;-ê).** groan, moan. {also: <nalenal> نـــالـــنـــال (HH)} {syn: axîn} [K/IFb/B/HH/GF/TF/ZF3] <nalîn>

nalet ناله‌ت (CS/Wkt) = curse. See **ne'let**.

nalî نالی (SK) = moaning. See **nalîn** [2].

nalîk نالیك (BF/Wkt/JJ) = mattress. See **nehlîk**.

nalîn نـــالـــیـــن *vi.* **(-nal-).** 1) to moan, groan; to lament, bewail: **•Xecê, *tu* bi wê k'eserê ku pê *dik'alî û dinalî*, niha nêzîke, ne dûre** (IS-#271) Khej, you and your grieving! The one *you are 'pissing and moaning'* about is nearby, he is not far away; 2) [*f.* **(-a;-ê).**] {also: nalî (SK); nalînî (IS/K)} {syn: axîn; nalenal} moaning, groaning: **•Nerîn go *nalîneke* kûr ji binê bîrê tê** (L) They noticed a deep moaning coming from the bottom of the well. {also: [nalin] نـالـیـن (JJ); <nalîn نـالـیـن (dinalî) (دنالی)> (HH)} Cf. P nālīdan نالیدن; Sor nałîn ناڵین = 'to moan, whimper'; Za nalenã [nalayiş] (Srk) [L/K/A/JB3/IFb/B/JJ/HH/GF/TF/FS//SK//IS]

nalînî نالینی (IS/K) = moaning. See **nalîn** [2].

nalînk نالينك (Wkt) = mattress. See **nehlîk**.

nam نام (B/Ba2) = damp. See **nem**.

namayî نامايى (B) = dampness. See **nemayî**.

nam•e نامه *f.* **(•[ey]a;•ê).** letter *(correspondence)*, epistle: **•*Nameyek* ji birayê min gehişt destê min** (BF) *A letter* from my brother reached me. {also: neme; [namé] نامه (JJ)} {syn: k'axez [2]; mek't'ûb} Mid P nāmag = 'book, letter' (M3); P nāme نامه; Sor name نامه = 'letter, book'; Za name *f.* (Todd) [K/A/JB3/IFb/B/JJ/GF/TF/ZF3/BF/FS]

namerdî نامه‌ردى (A/IFb/TF/CS) = cowardice; baseness. See **nemerdî**.

namil نامِل (J/K/JJ/GF) = upper part of back. See **navmil**.

namil fire نامِل فِره (GF) = broad-shouldered. See **navmilfireh**.

namûs نامووس *f.* **(-a;-ê).** respectability, (sexual) honor; "*Namus*, which is a concept used by Turks and Iranians in very much the same way as **'irḍ** of the women among pastoralists in Egypt and **hurma** or **haram** among the Kabyles in Algeria, can be lost (by women's misconduct), and men are vulnerable to such loss: the *sharaf* of the men [**nif** among the Kabyles] must be asserted publicly to protect *namûs*" [adapted from: John Gulick. *The Middle East: An Anthropological Perspective* (Pacific Palisades, Calif. : Goodyear, 1976), 209-10]: **•Ewe serê zistanê ye, neşêyn bo çi cîyan biȟelêyn. Çare-y me ewe ye, ȟetta yêk ji me maye dest hel-înîn, bila *bi namûs* meȟw bibîn** (SK 48:484) Now it is the beginning of winter and we cannot flee to any other place. Our only solution is to fight to the last man. Let us be destroyed *with honor* **•Ez îslehê wan ji wan bidizim, wê *namûsa* wan bişkê, guneh e** (L) If I stole their weapons from them, it would ruin their *honor*, it would be a sin (or, a disgrace) **•Navê gund *namûsa* gund e** (AB) The village's name is the village's *honor [prv.]*. {also: namûsî (B-2); [namous] ناموس (JJ)} {syn: şeref} < Gr nomos νόμος = 'law' --> P nāmūs ناموس [K/A/IFb/JJ/B/SK/GF] <bênamûs; 'erz; r̄êz II; şeref>

namûsî نامووسى (B) = sexual honor. See **namûs**.

nan نان *m.* **(-ê; nên/nîn [B], vî nanî).** 1) bread: **-nanê ceh** (B) barley bread; **-nanê garis** (B) millet bread; **-nanê gavên/gêvên** (B) flat cake given to cattleherd as payment by cattle owner; **-nanê genim** (B) wheat bread; **-nanê hingivî** (IF) honeycomb; **-nanê k'artû/nanê kolekî** (B) stale bread; **-nanê mêşa** (IFb) honeycomb; **-nanê r̄eş** (B) black bread; **-nanê sêlê/~ tîr[î]** (Wkp) fresh bread baked on a *sêl* (convex disk); **-nanê sipî** (B) white bread;**-nanê tenûrê** (IF) freshly baked oven bread; 2) food; meal: **•Tu nexebitî, ze'vê te *nên* nade te!** (J) [If] you don't work, your son-in-law (or, brother-in-law) won't give you *bread* (or, *food*)!; **-nan xwarin** = to eat, have a meal [cf. Albanian Unë ha bukë = I have a meal, lit. 'I eat bread']: **•*Nanê* xwe danî ber xwe *nan xwar*** (Dz) He took his *bread* (or, food) out [lit. 'placed it before himself] and *ate*; **-nanê êvarê** (B) supper, evening meal; **-nanê nîvro** (B) lunch, noon meal {syn: firavîn; nawerok (A)}; **-nanê sibê** (B) breakfast. {also: [nan] نان (JJ); <nan> نان (HH)} Cf. P nān نان; Sor nan نان; Za nan *m.* = 'bread (general); food' & nan *f.* = 'loaf of bread' (Todd); Hau nan *m.* (M4) [K/A/JB3/IFb/B/JJ/HH/SK/GF/TF] <genim; girde I; loş>

nandar نان‌دار *adj.* 1) generous, hospitable {syn: mêhvanxoş; mêvandar; mêvanȟiz}: **•Mala wan maleka *nander* e** (FS) Their house is a *hospitable* house **•Slo ... *nandarî* mêvanȟiz e** (HCK-2, 195) Silo ... is *generous* and hospitable; 2) [*m.* **(-ê;).**] breadwinner, family provider (GF/SS). {also: nander (FS); [nan-dar] نان‌دار (JJ)} [HCK/K/A/B/IFb/FJ/GF/JJ/SS/ZF3/BF//FS]

nander نانده‌ر (FS) = generous; breadwinner. See **nandar**.

nankê çûçê نانكێ چووچێ (FE) = shepherd's-purse. See **nankî çûke**.

nankêçûk نانكێچووك (A) = shepherd's-purse. See **nankî çûke**.

nankî çûke نانكى چووكه *m.* **().** shepherd's-purse, bot. *Capsella bursa-pastoris* (edible plant) [T çobançantası; Ar kīs al-rā'ī كيس الراعي]: **•Ev giya pincar e. ... Çivîk jî bi tezebûn lê diçêre. *Nankî çûkê* navê xwe ji wê wergirtî** (FE) This herb is a *pinjar* [edible plant]. ... Sparrows graze on it when it is fresh. *Nankî çûkê* (lit. 'bread of the sparrow') got its name from this. {also: nankê çûçê (FE-2); nankêçûk (A)} [Efr/FE//A] <p'incar>

nanozik نانۆزك (B) = hand-to-mouth. See **nanzikî**.

nanoziko نانۆزكۆ (K/B) = hand-to-mouth. See **nanzikî**.

nanpêj نانپێژ *m.* **(-ê;-î).** baker, bread maker: **•Nan bide *nanpêja*, nanek jî zêde bide** (Z-1117) Give the bread to *the bakers*, [and] give an extra loaf *[prv.]*.

{also: [nan-pyj] نانپیژ (JJ); <nanpêj> نانپیژ (HH)} {syn: tenûrvan} Cf. P nānpaz نانپز; =Sor nanewa نانەوا {nanpêjî} [Z/K/A/IFb/B/HH/GF/TF/AD/ZF3/BF/FS//JJ]

nanpêjî نانپێژی *f.* **(-ya;-yê).** baker's profession: •**Wî deh salan *nanpêjî* kiriye** (Wkt) *He worked as a baker* for 10 years. [GF/TF/ZF3/BF/Wkt] <nanpêj>

nanuzik نانوزِك (JB1-A)/nanûzik نانووزِك (ZF3) = hand-to-mouth. See **nanzikî**.

nanzde نانزدە (M-Am & Bar) = nineteen. See **nozdeh**.

nanzik نانزِك (GF) = hand-to-mouth. See **nanzikî**.

nanzikî نانزِکی *adv.* hand-to-mouth; just barely making ends meet: -[**bi**] **nanzikî xebitîn** (IFb)/ **nanozik**[**o**] **xebitîn** (B) to earn just enough to fill one's belly, to eke out a living: •**Ji van peran mehrûm bûyî, ji bêgavîyê, zivistanê, ez li cem xelkê *nanzikî* xebitîm** (EŞ, 18) Deprived of money, with no alternative, in the winter I worked *hand-to-mouth* for people. {also: nanozik (B); nanoziko (K/B-2); nanuzik (JB1-A); nanûzik (ZF3-2); nanzik (GF)} < nan = 'bread' + zik = 'stomach, belly' [EŞ/IFb/ZF3//GF//K/B//JB1-A]

nareng نارەنگ (GF) = sour orange. See **narinc**.

narinc نارِنج *f.* **(;-ê).** bitter orange, Seville or sour orange, bot. *Citrus aurantium*: -**dara narincê** (K) bitter orange tree. {also: nareng (GF-2); naring (GF-2); narînc (B); [narindj] نارنج (JJ)} < P nāranj نارنج = 'sour orange'; Sor narinc نارِنج [AA/K/IFb/JJ/GF/TF/OK/FS/ZF3/BF//B] <lalengî; p'irteqal>

narincok نارِنجۆك *f.* **(-a;-ê).** hand grenade: •**Wan bi *narîncoka* şer kir** (FS) They fought with hand grenades; -**narincoka destan** (ZF3) do. Cf. P nāranjak نارنجك; Sor narincok نارِنجۆك [A/IFb/GF/OK/AA/ZF3/FS/Wkt]

naring نارِنگ (GF) = sour orange. See **narinc**.

naringî نارِنگی (OK/AA) = mandarin orange. See **lalengî**.

narîn نارین *adj.* 1) {syn: jar I; lawaz; lexer; nazik; qels I; qor̄ III; zeyf; zirav I} slender, thin; 2) delicate; graceful. {narînî} [K(s)/JB3/IFb/B/TF]

narînc نارینج (B) = sour orange. See **narinc**.

narînî نارینی *f.* **(-ya;-yê).** 1) slenderness, thinness; 2) grace, gracefulness, elegance: •**Narînk: Navê xwe ji *narînîya* bûkan wergirtîye** (Y.Kaplan. Strana Kurdî, 165) Narînk [type of folksong from Hekkari]: it has taken its name from *the grace of* brides. [K/B/GF/Wkt] <narîn>

nas ناس *adj.* acquainted, familiar: -**nas kirin** (B/IFb/HH/GF/TF/OK): a) to know, be acquainted with {cf. Germ kennen, Fr connaître, Sp conocer, T tanımak, P šenāxtan شناختن} {also: **nasîn** (M/JB1/K); <naskirin ناسكرن (nasdike) (ناسدكه)> (HH)}: -**xwe dan nas kirin** = to introduce o.s.: •**Tu dikarî bi kurtayî *xwe bidî naskirin*?** (Ber) Can you briefly *introduce yourself*?; b) to recognize: •**Ewê nerî go lawê wê ye, *nas kir*** (L) She saw that it was [lit. 'is'] her son, she *recognized [him]*; -**ji hev nas kirin** = to distinguish, tell apart: •**Ez wan *ji hev nas nakim*** = I *can't tell* them *apart*. {also: **nasyar** (MK); niyas (Bw); [nas] ناس (JJ); <nas> ناس (HH)} *See etymology under **nasîn**.* {nasetî; nasînî; nas[t]î} [K/A/JB3/IFb/JJ/B/HH/TF] See also **nasyar**.

nasetî ناسەتی (A) = acquaintance. See **nasî**.

nasî ناسی *f.* **(-ya;-yê).** acquaintance, familiarity; knowledge: -**nasîya xwe dayîn** (B) to meet, become acquainted with s.o. {also: nasetî (A); nasînî (JB3); nastî (K)} [K/A/B//JB3] <nas>

nasîn ناسین *vt.* **(-nas-;** *neg.* **nenas-** [M/Zeb]**).** 1) to know, be acquainted with {cf. Germ kennen, Fr connaître, Sp conocer, T tanımak, P šenāxtan شناختن}: •**Derwêş 'Alî got, "Hung Şêx R̄ezaê Kerkûkê *dinasin*?" Hemîyan gotin** [sic], **"Belê, çak *dinasîn*. Muroekî gelek 'alim û fazil e."** (SK 60:728) Darwish Ali said, "*Do* you *know* Sheikh Reza of Kerkuk?" Everyone said, "Yes, we *know* him well. He is a very wise and virtuous fellow"; -**dan nasîn** (IFb) to define; to introduce; to identify; 2) to recognize: •**Hek'o te av bo min îna tu l r̄asta singê wî r̄aweste û bi îşareta çava bêje min: Eveye, da *biniyasim*** (JB1-A) When you bring me water, stand right in front of him and tell me with a wink of the eye: This is him, *so that I recognize* him [or, know which one he is]. {also: nas kirin (B/IFb/GF/TF/OK); naysîn (Hk); niyasîn (JB1-A); nyasîn (M-2/Zx/Bw); [nasin] ناسین (JJ); <naskirin ناسكرن (nasdike) (ناسدكه)> (HH)} [Pok. 2. ĝen-/ĝenə-/ĝnē-/ĝnō- 376.] 'to know, recognize' + -sk̂o-: O Ir *xšnā- (Tsb 45): Av xšnā-, e.g., zixšnåŋhəmnå = 'those who want to learn'; OP xšnā-, e.g., xšnāsātiy = 'he shall recognize'; P āšinā آشنا = acquainted & šenāxtan شناختن (-šenās-) (شناس) = 'to know (a person)'; Sor nasîn ناسین; Za slasnenā/snasnenā (Srk); Hau ejnasay (ejnas-) *vt.* (M4); cf. also Lat gnosco, -ere; Gr gignōskō γιγώσκω; Eng know [M/JB1/K/IFb/JJ/JB1-S/SK/ GF/TF/OK/Zeb//Hk//JB1-A//Zx/Bw] See **nas**: -**nas kirin**.

nasînî ناسینی (JB3) = acquaintance. See **nasî**.

nasname ناسنامه *f.* **(-ya;-yê).** 1) identity card, paper or certificate; 2) {syn: şexsîyet [2]} identity *(e.g., ethnic or national)*: **•di çêbûna *nasnameyê* de rola ziman û dîn** (Nbh 125:6) the role of language and religion in the creation *of identity*. < nas + name: Sor nasname ناسنامه = 'identification, evidence of identity' [Nbh/FJ/GF/TF/ZF/CS]

nastî ناستی (K) = acquaintance. See **nasî**.

nasyar ناسیار *adj.* 1) familiar, acquainted; 2) [*m.&f.* **(-ê/;).**] acquaintance, person one knows: **•Ew *nasyarê* Behremî ye** (FS) He is an acquaintance of B. [MK/A/IFb/GF/FS] <nas>

naşî ناشی *adj.* 1) {syn: cahil; nestêl; nezan; xam} young, inexperienced, naïve, "greenhorn"; a novice, beginner: **•Lê ... rast e salên min ne ewqas zêde ne ku ez bibêjim ez pir jiyame û min gelek dîtiye ... tenê şeş salan ji te mezintir im. Lê ... ez ne merivekî ewqas jî *naşî* me** (Lab, 9) But it's true that my years are not so many that I can say I have lived a long time and seen a great deal ... I'm only six years older than you. But I'm not such *an inexperienced person* either; 2) [*m.* **().**] teenager, youngster (Çnr). {also: naşîn (Qzl/FJ); [nachi] ناشی (JJ)} < Ar nāši' ناشئ = 'growing, youngster, junior' < √n-š-' نشئ [Qzl/FJ//Lab/K/A/IFb/GF/OK/Çnr]

naşîn ناشین (Qzl/FJ) = young, inexperienced. See **naşî**.

nav I ناڤ *m.* **(-ê;).** 1) {syn: îsm} name: **-nav li.../ser... kirin/dan/danîn** = to name, call, give a name to {also: navkirin}; **-ser navê ...** (Ba2) by the name of ...; 2) reputation: **-nav û deng** = fame, renown; **-bi nav û deng** = famous; 3) {syn: navdêr} noun, substantive *(gram.)*: **-navê hevedudanî** (JB3/IFb) compound noun; **-navê heyînê** (K/B) substantive; **-*navê nenêr̄baran** (IFb)/**~r̄azber** (JB3/IFb) abstract noun. {also: naw (SK); [naw] ناڤ (JJ); <nav> ناڤ (HH)} [Pok. en(o)mn̥-/on(o)mn̥-/nōmn̥- 321.] 'name': Skt nāman- *n.*; O Ir *nāman-: Av & Old P nāman-; Mid P nām (M3); P nām نام; Sor naw ناو; Za name *m.* (Todd); Hau namê *f.* (M4); cf. also Gr onoma ὄνομα, -tos *n.* & Lat nomen *n.* [F/K/A/JB3/IFb/ B/JJ/HH/JB1-A&S/GF/TF//SK] <cînav; paşnav; p'ir̄enav; serenav>

nav II ناڤ *f./m.(BK)* **(-a/ ;-ê/nêv** [BK]**).** 1) milieu, middle, center, interior: **•Bûk sibe rabû, nava malê gêzîkir** (J) The bride got up in the morning [and] swept the interior of the house; **-di wê navê** (L) in this manner: **•Deh ro di wê navê çûn** (L) Ten days passed in this manner; **-ji nav birin** (GF/Dh) to eliminate, do away with; **-tilîya navê** (K)/[telīye nāve] (JJ-PS)/**tilîya navîn** (IF)/**~nêvî** (Msr) middle finger {syn: t[']ilîya ort'ê}; 2) {syn: newq} waist; 3) {also: navik (B); <navik> ناڤك (HH)} navel, belly button (B/HH). {also: [naw] ناڤ (JJ); <nav> ناڤ (HH)} [Pok 1. (enebh-) embh-/ombh-/nObh- (nēbh-?)/m̥bh- 314.] 'navel, central knob', proto IE *Hon-bh- / *Hne/obh-: Skt nábhya- *n.*/nā́bhi- *f.* = 'navel': *Iranian forms exhibit anomalous* **-f-** *in* *nāf-: Av nāfō; P nāf ناف; cf. also Lat umbilicus; Gr omphalos ὀμφαλός [BX/K/A/JB3/IFb/B/BK/JJ/HH/GF] <daxil; hindur̄; navend>

nav III ناڤ *prep.* 1) in, into, to *(motion toward)*: **•Diçine *nava* gund** (Dz) They go *to* the village **•Gavan û jina xwe daketin *nav* gund** (L) The cowherd and his wife went down *to* the village **•Min dî denek ji tatê hat, kete *nav* çem** (L) I saw a cauldron come from the rock, [it] went *into* [lit. 'fell to'] the river **•Êvarê kur̄ k'etne *nava* cîya** (Ba) In the evening the boys got *into* bed **•Şivanî çaydankê xwe kir *di nav* felemorê *r̄a* ku çaya wî germ bibit** (FS) The shepherd put his tea kettle *into* the glowing ashes so that his tea would warm up; 2) in the middle of, at the center of, inside: **•*nava* gund** (BX) *in the middle of* the village; **-nava *ft-î* da** (Z-1) in the midst of: **•*nava* ner̄eḧetîyêda** (Z-1) uncomfortable [lit. '*in the midst of* discomfort']; 3) {also: nîv [3]} between, among, amid: **•Ez diçûm *nav* gundiyên xwe** (BX) I walked *among* my [fellow] villagers. {also: nava; [naw/naf] ناڤ (JJ)} [BX/K/A/JB3/IFb/B]

nav IV ناڤ *f.* **(;-ê).** diarrhea; dysentery: **-nav çûn** (K)/**nav hatin** (B) to suffer from diarrhea or dysentery. {syn: navêş; zikçûn} [K/B/GF//HH]

nava ناڤا = into. See **nav III**.

navber ناڤبەر *f.* **(-a;-ê).** 1) middle; 2) {syn: navbeyn} interval: **-di wê navberê da** = in the meantime: **•*Di wê navberê da* mêrikê koçer çîroka xwe û direnda ji yekî dikançî ra dibêje** (JB2-O.Sebrî/Rnh 14[1943] 8-9) *In the meantime*, the nomadic man tells the story about himself and the wild animal to a shopkeeper; 3) [*prep.*] {syn: navbeyn; neqeba [*see* neqeb]} between, among: **-di navbera *ft-î* de** = between: **•*di navbera* me *de*** (JB3) between us **•*di navbera* erd û ezman *de*** (BX) *between* earth and sky **•Mem û Zîn xwe li**

textekî dirêj kirin. Memi şûrê xwe danî *navbera* xwe û Zînê, da ko beriya mehirê tu tiştê neşerî *di navbera* wan *de* neqewimit (SW) Mem and Zin lay down in bed. Mem put his sword *between* himself and Zin, so that nothing unlawful might occur *between* them before the wedding; **-ji navbera ...** = between, among; **-li navbera ...** = do. [BX/K/JB3/IFb/GF/TF]

navbeyn نـاڤـبـەيـن *f.* **(-a;).** 1) {also: nabeyn (BX/K)} {syn: navber} interval; 2) [*prep.*]{also: nabên} {syn: navber; neqeba [*see* neqeb]} between, among: ***•di navbeyna* me û we *de*** (BX) *between* us and you; **-ji nabeyna/nabêna** (BX) from among; **-li nabeyna/nabêna** (BX) among: ***•Li nabêna* me dan û standin hebû** (BX) There were relations *between* us. Cf. Ar mā bayna مـا بـيـن = 'that which is between' [BX//K(s)/JB3/IFb/GF]

navbiř I ناڤبِر *(Zeb/K/B)*/**navbir** ناڤبِر *f.* **(-a;-ê).** room divider, partition, curtain or wall *dividing a nomad's tent into discreet sections or rooms* (Ar ḥājiz حـاجز or barzax بـرزخ): **•Çadira wê ve da ... 'eynên şibet'î ya Xace 'Alî ...** ***Navbir*** **êxist'inê: eve bo kuçk'ê u eve bo ȟazirîyê u eve bo nivis-t'inê u ȟeseb tertîbeka dirûst** (JB1-A #63) He pitched her tent ... exactly like Kh. A.'s [tent] ... She put *partitions* in it: this one for the hearth and this one for receiving [guests], and this one for sleeping, according to an established arrangement. {also: navbirêk (IFb); navbirk (GF)} *See* ***navbiřî*** *for etymology.* [Zeb/K/B/JB1-A/ZF/Kmc/CS//GF//IFb]

navbiř II ناڤبِر (B) = break; interruption. See **navbiřî**.

navbirêk ناڤبِرێك (IFb) = partition. See **navbiř I**.

navbiřî نـاڤـبـِـرى *f.* **(-ya;-yê).** 1) break, recess, pause: **-navbiřîya firavînê** (K) lunch break; 2) interval, space, gap; interruption: **-bê navbiřî** (B) without interruption; **-navbiřî dan *fk-ê/ft-î*** (XF/K): a) to interrupt, cut s.o. off: **•Hevalê Babayan dike, ko ȟal û k'êfê we pirs bike, lê ez dîsa *n[a]vbiřîyê didimê*** (K2-Fêřîk) Comrade Babayan is about to ask her how she is doing, but once again I *interrupt* him; b) to divide into pieces or parts. {also: navbiř II (B)} <nav II = 'center, middle' + biř- = 'to cut' [K2-Fêřîk//K/XF//B]

navbirk ناڤبِرك (GF) = partition. See **navbiř I**.

navborî نـاڤـبـۆرى *adj./pp.* aforementioned, aforesaid: **•Li Amed a Bakurê Kurdistanê ger û seredanên şanda DBP, HDP û KCDê ya ji bo ´yekîtiya netewî´ û ´giştpirsiya pergala serokomariyê´ berdewam dike** [sic] **... Mesûd Tek jî di her dû waran de rexne li şandeya *navborî* girt** (Rûdaw, 14.ii.2017) In Diyarbakir of North Kurdistan the tours of the DBP, HDP and KCD delegation for national unity and the referendum for the presidential system continues ... M.T. criticized the *aforementioned* delegation in both fields **•Li herêmên Şehbayê ji şeva din ta vê kêliyê şer di navbera şervanên Hêzên Şoreşger û çeteyên artêşa Tirk a dagirker de didome. ... Şervanên YPJ û YPG`ê jî yekser bersiv dan êrîşên artêşa Tirk a dagirker û çeteyên wê û li ser vê yekê jî şer li herêmên *navborî* derket** (ANHA, Hawarnews .com 26.vii.2017) In the regions of Shahba the war between the fighters of the Revolutionary Forces and bands of the invading Turkish army has been continuing from last night until this moment ... And YPJ and YPG fighters immediately responded to the attachs of the Turkish army and its bands and consequently war broke out in the *aforementioned* regions. < nav + borî < borîn/bihurtin; cf. Sor nawbiraw ناوبِراو < naw + *pass. part. of* birdin بِردِن = 'to take' [Wkt/ZF3/FD]

navçav ناڤچاڤ *f.(Rnh)/m.(K/OK)* **(-a/-ê;-ê/).** forehead, brow: **•Berî ko şêr xwe bavêje ser wî, koçerê camêr darê xwe di *navçava* şêr da lêdixe** (JB2-O.Sebrî/Rnh 14[1943] 8-9) Before the lion pounces on him, the brave nomad strikes the lion in *the forehead* [lit. 'the lion's *forehead*'] with his stick. {syn: 'enî; ne'tik} [JB2/Rnh/K/IFb/GF/OK]

navç•e ناڤچە *f.* **(•[ey]a;•eyê).** district; area, region: **•Di *navçeya* me de** (IFb) In our *district* **•Yek ji wan, Qesra Ishak Paşa ye ku di nav tixûbê vê *navçeyê* de cihê xwe digire** (DE #2, 110) One of them is Ishak Pasha's Palace, which is located within the borders of this *district*. {syn: herêm; neȟî} Sor nawçe نـاوچـە = 'area, region, territory; district (administrative subdivision)' [DE/IFb/GF/TF/FJ/Kmc]

navdar نـاڤـدار *adj.* 1) {syn: berbiçav I; binav û deng} known, well known, prominent, famous: **•Helbestvan şa'irekê *navdar* bûye** (I.Badî. Remezanê Cizîrî di dwîvçûn û twêjandineka dîtir da, 12) The poet was a prominent poet; 2) of good reputation. {navdarî} [Ber/K/JB3/IFb/B/GF/TF/FS]

navdarî نـاڤـدارى *f.* **(-ya;-yê).** 1) {syn: nav û deng} fame, renown: **•Duh me qala *navdarîya* hingivê Hekarya û hûnerên wê kiribû** (lotikxane.com 29.xi.07) Yesterday; 2) granting accreditation, lending credence (to) (JJ). {also: [naw-dari] ناڤدارى (JJ)} [IFb/B/GF/ZF3/Wkt] <navdar>

navdeng ناڤدەنگ (K/FS) = fame. See **nav û deng**.

navdêr ناڤدێر *f.* **(-a;-ê).** noun, substantive: **•Di zimanê kurdî de *navdêr* birekî sereke ye ji birên axaftinê** (Welatê Me: Hozan Robar) In the Kurdish language *the noun* is a principal part of the parts of speech. {syn: nav I[3]} [IFb/ZF/Wkt]

navend ناڤەند *f.* **(-a;-ê).** center *(lit. & fig.)*; middle: **-Navenda Nûçeyan** (Wlt) News Center. Sor nawend ناوەند = 'middle' [(neol)Wlt/K/IFb/TF/ZF3/Wkt/BF] <nav II; nîv; nîvî; ort'e>

naveȓast ناڤەڕاست *f.* **(-a;-ê).** center, middle: **•2 teqînan 15 kes li *naverasta* Bexdayê kirine qurbanî** (waarmedia.com 31.xii.2016) 2 explosions left 15 victims in *the center of* Baghdad. {syn: nîv [2]; nîvî} Sor naweȓast ناوەڕاست [K(s)/IFb/FS/ZF3]

naverok ناڤەرۆك *f.* **(-a;-ê).** 1) contents: **•Roja Nû, rojnamek hefteyî ya siyasî bû. Lê gava em li *naveroka* wê dinêrin, em dibînin ciyê ku daye warê edebî û folklorî ji yê nûçe û gotarên siyasî ne kêmtir e** (RN-intro) Roja Nû was a political weekly newspaper. But when we look at its *contents*, we see that the space given to the fields of literature and folklore is not less than that [given to] news and political reporting; 2) {syn: nêta k'itêbê (F); p'êȓist; serecema k'itêbê (F)} table of contents. Sor nawerok ناوەرۆك = 'contents, ingredients' [(neol)Ber/RN/K(s)/IFb/GF/TF/RZ/ZF]

navêş ناڤێش *f.* **(;-ê).** 1) {syn: nav IV; zikçûn} diarrhea; dysentery; 2) stomachache (IFb/A). {also: navêşî (B-2)/nav êşî (FS); <navêş> ناف ايش (HH)} [A/IFb/B/HH/GF/ZF/BF//FS] <tetirxanî>

navêşî ناڤێشى (B)/nav êşî ناڤ ئێشى (FS) = diarrhea. See **navêş**.

navgîn ناڤگين *f.* **().** 1) means, vehicle, medium: **-navgînên hilberînê** (Wlt) means of production; 2) [*m.* **(-ê;).**] {syn: berevan} arbiter, middle man, go-between: **•Behrem *navgînê* Zoro û Azadî bû** (FS) B. was *the middleman between* Z. and A. [(neol)Wlt/IFb/TF/ZF3/FS/Wkt] <p'ergal II>

navik ناڤك *f.(K/B)/m.(JB3)* **(-a/ ;-ê/nêvik).** 1) {also: nav II[3]} navel, belly-button: **-nêvik biȓîn** (IF) to cut the umbilical cord: **•(Qey dibê te) *navka min biȓîye*** (XF) As if you were older than me [lit. 'as if you *cut my umbilical cord*']; 2) {also: nêv (JB1-S)} center, middle (A/JB3/JB1-S). {also: nav II; nêvik (IF-2); [naw ناڤ/nawik ناڤك] (JJ); <navik> ناڤك (HH)} [S&E/K/A/JB3/IFb/B/JJ/HH/GF/TF]

navîn ناڤين *adj.* middle, central; intermediate: **-Çiriya navîn** (JB3) November {syn: Çirîya evel (K); Çiriya paşin (IF/B); Çirîya pêşin (K); [tchiriia pachi] چريا پاشى (JJ)}; **-Rojhilata Navîn** = the Middle East; **-tilîya navîn** (IF) middle finger. {also: tilîya navê (K)/~nêvî (Msr)/[telīye nāve] (JJ-PS)} {syn: t[']ilîya ort'ê}. [K/IFb/GF/TF/ZF3] <nav II; paşîn; pêşîn>

nav•kirin ناڤكِرِن *vt.* **(nav-k-).** to name, call by name, give a name to: **•Eva gunda ser navê Mistê Kalo *hatye navkirinê* seba wê yekê, ku ...** (Ba2) This village *was called* by the name of M.K. because ... {also: nav lê kirin (GF)} [Ba2//GF] <nav I>

nav lê kirin ناڤ لێ كِرِن (GF) = to name. See **navkirin**.

nav lê (tê) dan ناڤ تێ (لێ) دان (K) = to provoke. See **nav tê dan**.

navmil ناڤمِل *f./m.(FS)* **(-a/-ê;-ê;).** upper part of back; shoulder blades, area between the shoulders (JJ): **•*Navmilê* wî têşit** (FS) His *upper back* aches **•Şivek kişand *namila* dê** (J) He fastened a stick to his mother's *back* [when hooking her up to the plow instead of an ox--*folktale*]. {also: namil (J/K/GF); [na-mil] نامل (JJ)} {syn: pî I; p'ol II} < nav = 'between' + mil = 'shoulder' [J/K/JJ/GF//IFb/B/TF] <mil>

navmilfire ناڤمِل فِره (Ba2/B) = broad-shouldered. See **navmilfireh**.

navmilfireh ناڤمِل فِرەه *adj.* broad-shouldered: **•Memo mêrekî bejnbilindî *navmilfireyî* dêmqemer bû** (Ba2:1, 204) Memo was a man tall of stature, *broad-shouldered*, dark complected. {also: namil fire (GF); navmilfire (Ba2/B)} [Ba2/B/ /GF//ZF3]

navnet'ewayî ناڤنەتەوايى (Haz) = international. See **navnet'eweyî**.

navnet'eweyî ناڤنەتەوەيى *adj.* international: **•Divê civata *navneteweyî* alîkariya Kurdan bike** (Wlt 1:37, 16) The *international* community must help the Kurds **•Zimanê hunera wan *zimanê navneteweyî* ye** (diyarname.com 4.ii.2015) The language of their art is an *international* language. {also: navnet'ewayî (Haz); navnetewî (IFb)} [Haz//Wlt/IF/ZF3/BF/Wkt//IFb] <net'ewe>

navnetewî ناڤنەتەوى (IFb) = international. See **navnet'eweyî**.

navnîşan ناڤنيشان *m.(K/FS)/f.(ZF3/BF)* **(ê/-a;/-ê).** 1) sign, token, mark(ing); 2) address: •**Wî *nav û nîşanê* xwe li ser namê nivîsî** (FS) He wrote his *address* on the letter; 3) title (of book, film, etc.): •***Navnîşana pirtûkê* eve: Rojeke sext bû** (vk.com Stena) This is the book's *title*: It was a hard day. {also: nav û nîşan (Z-1/FS)} [Ber/K/A/JB3/IF/BF//Z-1/FS]

navno ناڤنۆ *m.* **().** 1) kvetch, complainer; 2) someone with a bad reputation: -**navno bûn** (A/FS) to have a bad reputation: •**Ji ber diziya ku li ser wî aşkirabûye, ew di nav xelkî da *navnobû*** (FS) Because of the theft in which he has been implicated, he *has gotten a bad reputation* among the people; -**navno kirin** (A/GF/FJ) to give s.o. a bad reputation, to ruin s.o.'s reputation. {also: [naw-nou] ناڤنو (JJ)} [Rwn/K/A/IFb/JJ/GF/FJ/ZF3/FS]

navr̄an ناڤران *f.(Bw/K/FS)/m.(Klk)* **(-a/-ê;).** 1) {syn: dugulî; şeq[4]} perineum, inside of thighs, crotch: •***Navr̄ana* wî ziriftî ye** (FS) His crotch is irritated/ He has jock itch; 2) {syn: peyk; p'êsîr [3]} baggy part of a pair of shalvar (Klk/IFb/GF); crotch *(of a pair of pants)* (Bw). {also: navr̄ehn (FS-2); [naw-ran] ناڤران (JJ)} <nav = 'middle' + r̄an = 'thigh' [Klk/Bw/Zeb/K/IFb/JJ/GF/OK/FS/BF]

navr̄ehn ناڤرەهن (FS) = crotch. See **navr̄an**.

navser ناڤسەر (TF/JJ) = middle-aged. See **navsera**.

navsera ناڤسەرا *adj.* advanced in years, middle-aged, agèd: •**Ew merîkî *navsera*ye** (K) He is a man *advanced in years*. {also: navser (TF); navsere (K2-Fêrîk/ZF3); [naw-ser] ناڤسەر (JJ)} {syn: kal I; mezin[2]; pîr; sere I} [K2-Fêrîk/ZF3//K//JJ/TF]

navsere ناڤسەرە (K2-Fêrîk/ZF3) = middle-aged. See **navsera**.

navtang ناڤتانگ (TF) = waist; bellyband. See **navteng**.

navteng ناڤتەنگ/**navṯeng** ناڤطەنگ [FS] *f.* **(-a;-ê).** 1) {syn: bejn} waist, middle: •**Damil: pişkek e ji kirasê jinka, ji *navṯengê* û pêda ye** (FS) Hem: it is the part of a woman's dress below *the waist* [lit. 'from *the waist* and below']; 2) {syn: kejî; kolan I; qoş [1]} saddle girth, bellyband, band tied around a beast of burden's belly to hold a saddle in place: •[**Destê xwe avêt *naftenga* mahînê şidand**] (PS-II, #34) He grabbed the mare's *saddle girth* and pulled it. {also: navtang (TF); navtenk (A); **teng II**; [nāftañg] نافتنك (PS-II); [naw-tenk] ناڤتنك (JJ)} [PS-II//K/IFb/B/GF/OK//A/JJ//FS//TF] <teng II>

navtenk ناڤتەنك (A/JJ) = waist; bellyband. See **navteng**.

nav tê dan ناڤ تێ دان *vt.* **(nav di *fkî* -d-).** 1) to incite, provoke, instigate, egg on, agitate, prompt, encourage *to do evil*, put s.o. up to: •**Ez *nav tê didim* ku here ftî bike** (Qzl) I *put him up to* doing stg. •***Nav di* wan *dide*** (GF) He *encourages* them/ *eggs* them *on*; 2) [*f.* **(-a;-ê).**] incitement, agitation, provocation, instigation, prompting, encouragement *to do evil*: •**Bi *navtêdana* hin mirovên nezan û dijminê miletê kurd, Firansizan ew komele girt** (kurdstuttgart.wordpress.com: Cegerxwîn 4.vi.2013) At *the prompting of* some unknown people and enemies of the Kurdish people, the French closed down that group •**Piştî *navtêdanê* ew çû *fk* kuşt** (Qzl) After *the incitement*, he went and killed so-and-so. {also: nav lê (tê) dan (K-2); nav tê dayîn (B); [naw dihewdan] ناڤ دهڤدان (JJ) = to give the signal to attack} {syn: lê sor kirin; şarandin; têkdan} [Qzl/K/A/B/GF/TF/FD/ZF3/Wkt/CS/JJ//B]

nav tê dayîn ناڤ تێ دايين (B) = to provoke. See **nav tê dan**.

navudeng ناڤودەنگ (GF) = fame. See **nav û deng**.

nav û deng ناڤ و دەنگ/**navûdeng** ناڤوودەنگ [A] *m.* **(-ê;).** fame, renown: •***Nav û dengê* Eḧmedê Xanî di nav hemû Kurdistanê da belav e** (FS) *The fame of* Ahmedê Khani is widespread throughout Kurdistan; -**bi nav û deng** = famous. See **binav û deng**. {also: navdeng (K/FS-2); navudeng (GF)} [IFb/FS//A/BF//GF//K]

nav û nîşan ناڤ و نیشان (Z-1) = mark(ing); address. See **navnîşan**.

naw ناو (SK) = name. See **nav I**.

naxêr ناخێر (K/A/IFb/JB1-A&S/OK) = no. See **nexêr**.

naxir ناخِر *f.* **(-a;-ê).** herd of cattle: •**Boẍek heye nav *naxira* minda** (J) There is an ox in my *herd*. {also: [nakhyr] ناخير (JJ); <naxir> ناخر (HH)} {syn: gar̄an} [J/K/A/IFb/B/JJ/HH] <ga; kerî II>

naxirçî ناخِرچی (K/B) = herder, cowherd. See **naxirvan**.

naxirvan ناخِرڤان *m.* **().** herder, cowherd, goatherd, shepherd: •**Di gundê me da *naxirvanek* hebû … Wî pez û dewarên gundê me dibir** [sic] **diçêrand** [sic], **gundiyan jî jibo heqê wî ce û genim didan** (RC2. Zilma Romê û şîrîkên wê) In our village there was a *herder* … He used to take the sheep and cattle of our village to pasture, and the villagers would give him barley and wheat in payment. {also: naxirçî (K/B)} [RC2/ZF3/Wkt//K/B] <gavan; şivan>

naxoş ناخۆش (Epl) = sick; bad. See **nexweş**.

naxoşî ناخۆشی (Epl) = illness; badness. See **nexweşî**.

naxt ناخت (JB1-S/JJ-Rh) = bride-price. See **next**.

nayîn نايين *vt.* **(-nê-/-n-).** to copulate with, fuck, screw: **•E te *nim*** (Msr) [I] *screw* you *[insult]* **•Mi[n] di mejîyê bavê te *nîya*/ga** (Haz) [*A curse*: lit. 'I *screwed* your father's brain'] **•Wellah, ezê di gora bavê çwîk *nim*!** (L) By God, I'll *defile* the grave of the father of that sparrow! *[curse]*. {also: nihandin (GF); niyan (ZF3); niyandin (IFb); niyîn (IFb-2); nîhan (A); nîhandin (A); nîyan (Haz/Msr)} {syn: gan I; k'utan} Za nanã [nayiş] (Srk) [K/FD//Haz/Msr//ZF3/IFb//A//GF]

naynik نايِنك (Plt-Cambek tribe) = mirror. See **nênik I**.

naysîn نايسين (Hk) = to know. See **nasîn**.

nazanî نازانی (B) = gentle, graceful. See **nazenîn**.

nazbalgî نازبالگی (ZF3) = fancy cushion. See **nazbalîşk**.

nazbalgîv نازبالگيڤ (ZF3) = fancy cushion. See **nazbalîşk**.

nazbalîfk نازباليفك (ZF3) = fancy cushion. See **nazbalîşk**.

nazbalîşk نازباليشك *f.* **(-a;-ê).** fancy cushion or bolster. {also: nazbalgî[v] (ZF3); nazbalîfk (ZF3-2)} {syn: zemberîş} [Wn//ZF3] <balgih; balîf>

nazdar نازدار *adj.* coy, coquettish; capricious. {also: [nāz-dār] نازدار (JJ)} {nazdarî} Sor nazdar نازدار = 'sweet; pampered, coddled, spoiled' & be naz به ناز = 'coquettish' [K/B/A/IFb/FJ/TF/GF/JJ-Rh/JB1-S/FS]

nazdarî نازداری *f.* **(-ya;-yê).** coquetry, coyness: **•Marekî zêrdil dê bê pêşiya te û ew bi çelengî û *nazdarî* dê biȓeqise** (Dz #22, 389) A golden-hearted snake will come before you and will dance with agility and *coyness*. Sor nazdarî نازداری = 'sweetness; pampering, coddling' [Dz/K/B/GF/FJ/TF/SS/CS/ZF3/Wkt] <nazdar>

nazde نازده (JB1-A) = nineteen. See **nozdeh**.

nazenîn نازەنين *adj.* gentle, graceful, delicate, beautiful: **•Bengînê xulam, ez ku su'alekî ji *vê nazenînê* bikem, îzna te heye?** (MC-1) Bengin my boy, do I have your permission to ask *this gentle one* a question? {also: nazanî (B); <nazenîn> نازنين (HH)} Cf. P nāzanīn نازنين = 'delicate, tender; lovely, amiable; nice, fine' --> T nazenin = 'coy; spoiled; delicate; rascal'; Sor nazenîn نازەنين = 'graceful' [MC-1/K(s)/A/IF/HH/FS/ZF3//B]

nazik نازِك *adj.* 1) {syn: narîn} delicate, gentle, slender; 2) tender, fragile; 3) elegant, fancy. {also: [nazik] نازك (JJ); <nazik> نازك (HH)} Mid P nāzuk = 'tender, gentle, fickle' (M3); P nāzok نازك = 'thin, delicate, tender'; Sor nazik نازِك/nasik ناسِك = 'tender, gentle, delicate' {nazikayî; nazikî} [Z-1/K/A/JB3/IFb/B/JJ/HH/SK/GF/TF/FS/ZF3]

nazikatî نازِكاتی (FS) = gentleness; elegance. See **nazikî**.

nazikayî نازِكايی (B) = gentleness; elegance. See **nazikî**.

nazikî نازِكی *f.* **(-ya;-yê).** 1) {syn: ȓûnermî} gentleness; 2) tenderness, fragility: **•Ev goşt ji ber *nazikatîya* wî bibiha ye** (FS) This meat is expensive because of its *tenderness*; 3) elegance. {also: nazikatî (FS); nazikayî (B)} [A/IFb/GF/TF/ZF3//FS//B] <nazik>

naz û ne'met ناز و نەعمەت/**naz û nemet** ناز و نەمەت [K] *pl.* **().** good foods, victuals; "a feast": **•Herçê *naz û ne'metê* xarinê dinê hebû, t'emam t'op kir, t'ijî mêşokê wê kir** (EP-5, #13) She gathered up all *the finest foods*, and filled her sack with them **•Kevanîya malê hezar t'uleyî *naz û ne'met* hazirkiribû** (XF) The lady of the house had prepared a thousand types of *good foods*. [EP-5/XF//K] <xurek; xwarin>

ne- نە *neg. pref.* not, did not, may not *{negative particle prefixed to past tense, and present subjunctive verbs (and optionally to imperatives, which may also take* ***me-****, e.g.,* ***Na•bînim*** *= I don't see or I won't see;* ***[Bila] ne•bînim*** *= Lest I see, that I may not see;* ***Min ne•dît*** *= I didn't see;* ***Ne•bîne*** *or* ***Me•bîne*** *= Don't see}*. [K/JB3/IFb/B/GF/TF] <na; na-; ni->

ne نە *adv.* 1) not: **•Go *ne* ew be, kes nikare** (L) If he ca*n't* no one can [lit. 'if *not* he be']; **-ne ... ne** = neither ... nor: **•*Ne* dixum gêlaza, *ne* didim hevraza** (Dz #1208, 226) I will *neither* eat your cherries *nor* climb to the heights (=I don't want to leave your side) [*prv.*] **•*Ne* ew û *ne* keskî din** (L) *Neither* he *nor* anyone else; 2) no (SK). See **na**. {also: [nè] نه (JJ)} Za ne (Todd) [K/JB3/IFb/B/JJ/SK/GF/TF] <na; nexêr>

nebaş نەباش *adj.* bad: **•di nav vê rewşa *nebaş* da** (Ber) in this *bad* situation. {syn: nexweş [2]; xirab [1]} [Ber/K/GF/ZF3]

nebî نەبی (F) = grandchild. See **nevî**.

nebîranî نەبيرانی *f.* **(-ya;).** craving, hankering *(for particular foods, of pregnant women)*: **-nebîranîya *ft-î* kirin** (Qzl) to crave, have a hankering for *(of pregnant women)*. [Qzl/GF/ZF/FS]

nebûyî نەبوویی *pl.* false accusation, slander: •***Nebûya* nexe stûyê min** (Msr) Don't slander me [lit. 'Don't throw *things that never were* onto my neck']. {syn: neweyî (Msr)} < ne- = 'not' + bû = 'was' + -yî = abstract noun suffix : something that was not, i.e., did not happen [Msr/TF/ZF3] <derew>

necirandin نەجِراندِن *vt.* **(-necirîn-).** to carve, chisel, engrave; to hollow (stg.) out: •**Dîwarê wê tev bi kevirên *necirandî* û kilsûcesê hatiye lêkirin** (DBgb, 5) Its wall has been made with *carved* stones and limestone. {also: <necirandin> نجراندن (HH)} {syn: t'eraştin} < Ar √n-j-r نجر = 'to hew, carve, plane (wood)' [DBgb/IFb/TF/HH/CS/ZF3]

neçar/neç'ar [K/B] نەچار *adj.* obliged, compelled, coerced, forced; having no alternative; helpless: •**Çu zemanan deh sal li-dû-yêk neçûne ku li cîyekî mezinekî Kurdan ji zulm û te'eddîya 'Usmanîyan *neçar* nebûbît bi eşqîyatîyê yan ḧelatinê bo-naw dewletekî dî yan bi şer̄ kirinê ḧetta meḧw bûy** (SK 56:639) At no time have ten years on end gone by without some Kurdish leader in some place having been *obliged*, by the oppression and tyranny of the Ottomans, to take either to rebellion or flight to another state or fighting to the death •***Naçar bîn*--çi ji wana nehat, êdî--ser qesa xo man û nezivir̄înve** (M-Zx #775) *They had no alternative*--there was nothing else they could do--so they stood by their word and did not go back on it. {also: naçar (IFb-2/TF/OK); naç'ar (K[s]); [na-tchar/ne-čấr (Lx)] نچار (JJ)} {syn: mecbûr} Cf. P nāčār ناچار = 'forced by necessity, compelled, helpless'; Sor naçar ناچار [SK/A/IFb/JJ/GF//K/B//TF/OK]

neder نەدەر *f.* (;-ê). outward appearance: **-nûr û neder**, f. (EP-7) do. Cf. Ar naẓar نظر = 'seeing, sight' [EP-7/K/B] <nezer>

nederbasî نەدەرباسی (ZF3) = intransitive. See **nederbazbûyî**.

nederbazbûyî نەدەربازبوویی *adj.* intransitive: **-fêlê/-a nederbazbûyî** (B/K)/**fêla derbaznebûnê** (F) intransitive verb. {also: nederbasî (ZF3)} {syn: neger̄andî; negerguhêz} [K/B//ZF3] <derbazbûyî [2]; fêl II; lêker>

nedur نەدور (GF) = vow, pledge. See **nezir**.

nefel نەفەل *f.* **(-a;-ê).** 1) clover, trefoil, bot. *Trefolium*: •**Mêrga me tijî *nefel* e** (AB) Our meadow is full of *clover*; 2) marjoram; jasmine [Ar samsaq سمسق] (HH/GF). {also: <nefel> نفل (HH)} Cf. Ar nafal نفل = 'clover' [AB/A/IFb/HH/GF/TF/ZF3/FS] <cat'irî; ket>

nefer نەفەر *f./m.(JB1-A/F)* **(-a/;-ê/).** 1) {syn: k[']es; t'akekes} person, individual: •**Nevî-nevî t'u kes, cînarê te yanê jî *neferê* mala te min bivînin** (Ba3-3, #6) Absolutely no one, not your neighbors or *the people of* your household, may see me; 2) [*m.*] warrior, soldier (K/B/JJ); 3) *counting word for people* (K/JB1-S): •**Em çar *nefer*in** (B) There are four of us/We are four *people*. {also: [nefer] نفر (JJ)} <Ar nafar نفر [Ba3/F/K/B/JJ/JB1-S/ZF3]

nefir نەفِر (K/IFb/TF) = flute. See **nefîr**.

nefisbiçûk نەفِس بِچووک (FS) = humble. See **nefspiçûk**.

nefismezin نەفِس مەزن (Kmc/FS) = arrogant. See **nefsmezin**.

nefîr نەفیر *m./f.(ZF3)* **().** wind instrument: flute, horn or trumpet: •**Dengê *nefîr* û zurna û *burîzane** (Lwj #1, 34) It is the sound of the *flute*, the zurna and the burîzan. {also: nefir (K/IFb/TF); nefîre (GF); [nafîra] نفيره (JJ-G)} {syn: borîzan} Cf. Ar nafīr نفير = 'group, troop; trumpet'; Sor nefîr نەفیر = 'horn (musical instrument)' [Lwj/JJ/ZF3//GF//K/IFb/TF] <borîzan; zirne>

nefîre نەفیرە (GF) = flute. See **nefîr**.

nefs نەفس *f.* **(-a;-ê).** 1) {syn: can I} soul: •**Qelbêt ehlê zemanê me weto r̄eş o r̄eq bone bi zikrê Xudê nerm nabin. *Nefsa* wan bi-de'îye ye. Ḧetta de'îya *nefsê* nehêt e şkandin, zikrê Xudê hîç te'sîrê di qelbîda naket** (SK 45:436) The hearts of the people of our time have become so black and hard, that they are not softened by the mention of God. Their *soul* is full of pride. Until this pride *of soul* is broken, the mention of God will have no effect on the heart; 2) self: **-bi nefsa xwe** (K) by oneself, on one's own; **-bona nevsa xwe** (B) for one's self. {also: nevs (B); [nefs] نفس (JJ-Lx); <nefs> نفس (HH)} < Ar nafs نفس = 'soul; spirit, mind' [SK/K/IFb/GF/JJ/HH//B]

nefsbiçûk نەفس بِچووک (BZ/FJ/GF) = humble. See **nefspiçûk**.

nefsmezin نەفس مەزن *adj.* arrogant, haughty: •**Ev çîvanok di heqê kesên *nefsmezin* û kesên nefsbiçûk da tê gotin. Kesên qure yên *nefsmezin* bi şeb tên şibandin** (BZ, v. 1, 413) This anecdote is told about *haughty* and humble people. Proud and *haughty* people are likened to alum. {also: nefismezin (Kmc/FS)} {syn: difnbilind; pozbilind; qur̄e; serbilind; serfiraz} [BZ/K/GF/FJ/ZF3//Kmc/FS]

nefspiçûk نـەفـس پـچـووك *adj.* humble, modest, self effacing: **•Ev çîvanok di heqê kesên nefsmezin û kesên *nefsbiçûk* da tê gotin. ... kesên *nefsbiçûk* jî bi şekir tên şibandin** (BZ, v. 1, 413) This anecdote is told about haughty and *humble* people. ... and *humble* people are likened to sugar. {also: nefisbiçûk (FS); nefsbiçûk (BZ/FJ/GF)} {syn: dilnizm} [BZ/FJ/GF//FS//K]

neft نـەفت *f.* **(-a;-ê).** 1) oil, petroleum: **•berzbûna rolê *neftê* weku berhemekê serekî ji bo pêşketina abûrî** (Metîn 62[1997]:25) the increase of the role of *oil* as a main product for economic advancement; 2) match(es) *(for lighting fires)* (Ag/HH). See **neftik**. {also: nefte (JB1-A); nift (Ag); nivt (B-2); [nafta (G)/năft (Rh)] نـفـط (JJ); <neft̠> نـفـط (HH)} Gr naphtha νάφθα--> Ar nafṭ نفط; Sor newt نـەوت = 'mineral oil'; Za neft *m.* (Mal); Hau newte *f.* = 'oil' (M4) [F/K/IFb/B/SK/GF/TF//JB1-A//JJ//HH] <neftik>

nefte نەفتە (JB1-A) = oil. See **neft**.

neftik نـەفـتِـك *f.* **(a;-ê).** match(es) *(for lighting fires)*. {also: nift (Ag); niftek (GF); niftik (IFb); <neft̠> نـفـط (HH)} {syn: k'irpît; pitik I} [Msr/FS//Ag//GF//IFb//HH] <agir; cigare; neft; qelûn>

neger̄andî نـەگـەڕانـدى *adj.* intransitive: **-lêkera negerandî** (IFb) intransitive verb. {syn: nederbazbûyî; negerguhêz} [(neol)IFb/ZF3] <ger̄andî; lêker>

negerguhêz نـەگـەرگـوهـێـز *adj.*intransitive *(verb)*: **-lêkera negerguhêz** (TaRK/Wkt) intransitive verb. {syn: nederbazbûyî; neger̄andî; *têneper} = Sor têneper̄ تێنەپەڕ [TaRK/Wkt/ZF3] <lêker; gerguhêz>

negerî نەگەرى (HCK) = tray. See **lengerî**.

neh نەه *num.* nine, 9. {also: nehe; [nou نو/neh نه] (JJ); <neh> نـــه (HH)} [Pok e-neu̯en/neu̯n/enu̯n 318.] 'nine': Skt náva; O Ir *nawa: Av nava- (neu̯n); Mid P nō (M3); P noh نـه; Sor no نـۆ; Za new (Todd); Hau no (M4) [K/A/IFb/B/JJ/HH/SK/GF/TF] <nehêk; not; nozdeh>

neha نەها *adj.* ninth, 9th: **•r̄oja *neha*** (B) the *ninth* day. {also: nehan (K-2/IFb); **nehem**; nehê (JB1-A); ne(h)yê (JB1-S); [nehi نهی/nahnē نهنی (Rh)] (JJ)} Cf. P nahom نـهـم; Sor nohem[în] نـۆهـەمـیـن/noyem[în] نۆیەمین; Za newin (Todd) [F/K/B//IFb//JB1-A//JB1-S//JJ] <neh>

nehan نەهان (K/IFb) = ninth. See **neha**.

nehaq نەهاق (TF) = wrong, unjust. See **neheq**.

nehberk نـەهـبـەرك *f.* **(;-ê).** game played with nine (9) small stones [T dokuztaş]: **-kevirên nehberkê** (Wn) stones used in the game *nehberk*. {also: nehberkê (FS); <nehberk> نهبرك (HH)} [(A)/IFb/HH/JB1-S/GF/TF/OK/Wn//FS]

nehberkê نـەهـبـەركـێ (FS) = game with 9 stones. See **nehberk**.

nehe نەهە = nine. See **neh**.

nehek نەهەك (GF/FD) = a ninth. See **nehêk**.

nehem نـــەهـــەم *adj.* ninth, 9th. {also: **neha**; nehemîn (TF/IFb-2/GF-2/CT-2/ZF-2/Wkt-2)} Cf. P nahom نهم; Sor nohem[în] نۆهەمین/noyem[în] نۆیەمین [A/IFb/GF/CT/ZF/Wkt//TF] <neh>

nehemîn نـەهـەمـیـن (TF/IFb/GF/CT/ZF/Wkt) = ninth. See **nehem**.

neheq نـــەهـــەق *adj.* 1) wrong, in the wrong [nah̄eqq (SK)]: **•Ez ne *neheq*im, tu *neheqî*** (HCK-3, #2, 19) I am not *wrong*, you are *wrong* **•Ḧukm bo wî kesî ye yê ẍalib bît, çi ḧeqq bît çi *naḧeqq*** (SK 5:60) Power is for him who wins the upper hand, whether he be right or *wrong* **•Sultan Ḧemîd got, "'Elî, to *naḧeqq* î: ḧetta do hewyan cezaê te ew e, nêzîkî seraê nebî"** (SK 52:566) Sultan Hamid said, "Ali, you are in the *wrong*: for 2 months this is your punishment, you may not approach the palace; 2) unjust, unfair [neh̄eqq (SK)]: **•Wextê hatina kewî serê biharê ye. Êdî eger Mîr bo kewî cewabê nedet *neḧeqq* e** (SK 29:264) The time of the partridge's coming is the beginning of spring. If the Mir does not give an answer for the partridge then he is *unfair*; 3) unlawful. {also: naḧeqq (SK-2); nehaq (TF); neḧeqq (SK); niheq (K-2); [na-ahhk (G)/na-hak (Rh)] نـاحـق /[ne-haq] نـحـق (JJ)} < ne + heq < Ar ḥaqq حقّ: cf. P nāḥaqq ناحق = 'unjust, unlawful, false'; Sor naheq ناهەق = 'wrongful, unfair, wicked' [HCK/K/B/IFb//TF//SK//JJ]

nehesid نەهسِد (B) = nine hundred. See **nehsed**.

nehê نەهێ (JB1-A) = ninth. See **neha**.

nehêk نـــەهـــێـــك *f.* **(-a;).** a ninth, 1/9: **•Wî *nehêka* genimê xwe firot** (FS) He sold *a ninth of* his wheat. {also: nehek (GF/FD)} Sor no-yek نـۆیـەك (Sulaimania & Kerkuk) /no-yêk نۆیێك (Arbil) [Zeb/FS//GF/FD/Wkt]

nehêlan نەهێلان (Bw/Zeb) = to destroy. See **ne•hiştin**.

nehêngol نەهێنگۆل (Bw) = heifer. See **nogin**.

nehgon نەهگۆن (GF) = heifer. See **nogin**.

nehilmî نـــەهِـلـمـی *adj.* non-aspirated, unaspirated

(phonetics): •**Hema ev du peyv jî sabit dikin ku k'ya hilmî û k'ya *ne-hilmî* di kurmancî de fonem in, lewre maneguhêr in** (E.Öpengin. "Pirsên Rênivîsa Kurmancî", Derwaze 1, 186) These two words prove that aspirated k and *unaspirated* k are phonemes in Kurmanji, because they change the meaning of the word. •**Ji bo denganiya kurdî xera nebe û ew dengên hilmî û *nehilmî* ji holê ranebin, divê alfabeyeke fonetîk a kurdan anku alfabeya tîpguhêziyê were amadekirin...** (S.Tan. Rêzimana Kurmancî, []) In order for Kurdish phonology not to be damaged, and for these aspirated and *unaspirated* sounds not to cease to exist, a Kurdish phonetic alphabet, i.e. a transcriptive alphabet, should be created. [Öpengin/Navenda Ciwanan/Tan] <hilmî>

nehiş نـەهِـش (GF/FS/ZF3) = unconscious; crazy. See **neȟiş**.

nehişî نەهِشی (GF/ZF3) = unconsciousness; craziness. See **neȟişî**.

ne•hiştin نـەهِـشـتِـن *vt. neg.* **(na•hêl-).** 1) {syn: hilweşandin; xirab kirin} to destroy, annihilate, exterminate: •**Ez yek kevirekî tenê jî ku ji cih nehatibe livandin, *nahêlim*** (CTV260) I *will not leave* a single stone = I will destroy every single stone that has not been moved; 2) to forbid, prohibit, hinder, prevent: •**Leşkeran gava girt ser mala min *nehişt* heya nîvê şevê ez şîr bidim wî** (AW79A3) When the soldiers occupied my house, they *wouldn't let* me [=prevented me] from giving him milk until midnight. {also: nehêlan (Bw/Zeb)} [K/IFb/GF/TF/OK//Bw/Zeb] <hiştin>

nehiye نەهیە (Nbh) = district. See **neȟî**.

nehît نەهیت (TF/ZF3) = boulder. See **neȟît**.

nehk نەهك (Hk/GF) = chickpea. See **nok**.

nehlîk نـەهلیك *f.* (;-ê). small, thin mattress for sitting: •**Ew li ser *nehlîkê* rûnişt** (FS) S/he sat down on *the mattress* •**Wê palas rayêxist û *nehlîk* deyna ser** (FS) She spread out the mat and placed *the mattress* on it. {also: lalîk I (Wkt-2); lalînk (Wkt-2); nahlîk (RZ); nalîk (BF/Wkt); nalînk (Wkt-2); nohlîk (SS); nuhlîk (FJ/GF); [nalík] نالیك (JJ-G)} {syn: *bincî; binȓex; cil III; doşek; mitêl} [FS//RZ//BF/Wkt/JJ//SS//FJ/GF]

nehsed نـەهـسـەد *num.* nine hundred, 900. {also: nehesid (B); nehsid (B-2); ne-sed (SK)} Cf. P nohsad نهصد; Sor nosed نۆسەد [A//B//SK]

nehsid نەهسد (B) = nine hundred. See **nehsed**.

nehtik نەهتك (GF) = forehead, brow. See **ne'tik**.

nehwêt نەهوێت (Hk) = ninety. See **not**.

nehwirandin نـەهـوِراندِن *vt.* **(-nehwirîn-).** to mutter, whimper, mumble a plaintiff song: •**Evdal ji xwe çûbû, heş li serî mabû ... Destê Gulê, hêdî hêdî, li ser enî û rûyê Evdal digeriya û Gulê, bi hêdîka, jê re *dinehwirand*** (M.Uzun. R. Evdalê Zeynikê, 153) Evdal lost consciousness ... Gulê's hand slowly traveled over E.'s forehead and face and Gulê softly *sang plaintiffly* to him. {also: nehwirîn (TF); newirandin (K[s])} [Uzun/IFb/FJ/GF/CS//TF//K(s)]

nehwirîn نـــەهـــوِریـــن (TF) = to whimper. See **nehwirandin**.

nehyê نەهیێ (JB1-S) = ninth. See **neha**.

neȟeqq نەحەقق (SK) = wrong, unjust. See **neheq**.

neȟiş نـەحِش *adj.* 1) {syn: bêȟiş} unconscious: •**Ji dihî were ew *nehiş* e** (FS) He has been *unconscious* since yesterday; **-neȟiş k'etin** (J) to faint, lose consciousness {syn: bêȟiş k'etin; xeȓiqîn; xewirîn}; 2) {syn: dîn II; şêt} mad, crazy, insane. < ne = 'not' + ȟiş = 'sense' {also: nehiş (GF/FS//ZF3)} {neȟişî} [J/K//GF/FS/ZF3] <gêj>

neȟişî نـەحِـشـی *f.* (;-yê). 1) unconsciousness, fainting, swooning: •**Jinikê ber xweva dermana *neȟişyê* avîte nav çay** (HCK-5, #41, 230) The woman threw *fainting* potion in the tea; 2) {syn: dînayî; şêtî} craziness, insanity, madness. {also: nehişî (GF/ZF3)} [K//GF/ZF3] <gêjtî; neȟiş>

neȟî نـــەحـــی *f.* **(-ya;-yê).** district, precinct: •**Axaê *naȟiya* Zerzan Tahir Axa hebo, li gundê Masîro di-ȓû-nişt** (SK 42:404) The agha of *the district of* Zerzan was Tahir Agha, who lived in the village of Masiro •**li ser *neȟya* Aparanê ... li ser *neȟya* Talînê** (HCK-2, 195) belonging to *the district of* Aparan ... belonging to *the district of* Talin. {also: nahiye (IFb); naȟiye (SK); nehiye (Nbh); [nehi] نحی (JJ)} < Ar nāḥiyah ناحية = 'subdivision of a qaḍā', roughly corresponding to a county"; Sor naȟiye نـاحِـیـە = 'sub-district' [HCK/K/JJ//Nbh//SK//IFb] <navçe>

neȟît نـەحیت *f./m.(K/ZF3)* **(-a/ ;).** large rock, boulder: •**Adilcewazê ji bîr nekin ... da hûn wêneyên kevnar û entîk li ser *nehîtên* keviran bibînin** (SB,p.50) Don't forget Adilcewaz ... so that you may see the ancient images [etched] into the boulders [of the rocks]. {also: nehît (TF); nihêt (K); nihît (GF)} Cf. Ar naḥīt نـحـيـت = 'cut out, polished (stone)' [Omr//TF/ZF3//K//GF] <ferş; ȟelan; kevir; kuç'; lat; tat I>

nejadperest نـەژادپـەرسـت (Bkp) = racist. See **nijadp'erest**.

nekĥa نەكحا (EP-5) = marriage. See **nikha**.

nekis نەكِس (FS) = shortness of breath. See **neks**.

neks نەكس *f.* **(-a;-ê).** pain in one's side or flank *(below the ribs), from asthma, shortness of breath, or pneumonia*: •***Nekisê* ew girtiye** (FS) He's been suffering from *shortness of breath.* {also: nekis (FS); <neks> نكس (HH)} {syn: tîr lê rabûn} [QtrE/A/IFb/HH/GF/FJ/ZF3//FS]

nekse نەكسە *f.* **().** relapse, setback; defeat, blow (e.g., to one's pride): •**'Ereba *nekse* li Kurda da** (Bw) The Arabs dealt the Kurds *a blow* •**Meksîka *nekse* xar** (Bw) Mexico suffered *a setback.* <Ar naksah نكسة (<√n-k-s نكس = 'to invert, turn over, cause a relapse') [Bw/ZF3]

ne'l نەعل (B) = horseshoe. See **nal**.

ne'lbend نەعلبەند (B) = blacksmith. See **nalbend**.

ne'lbendî نـەعلـبـەندى (B) = profession of a blacksmith. See **nalbendî**.

ne'let نـەعـلـەت *f.* **(;-ê).** curse: **-ne'let lê kirin** (K) to curse: •***Ne'let* li çavê şeytên/*Lanet* li şeytan** (IFb) *A curse* on the devil['s eye]. {also: lanet (IFb/GF-2/CS); le'net (K-2); nalet (CS-2/Wkt); [lanet لعنت/nalét نعلت] (JJ); <ne'let> نعلت (HH)} {syn: ç'êr̄; dijûn I; nifir̄; qise[3]; sixêf; xeber[3]} < Clq Ar na'lah نعلة < la'nah لعنة = 'curse'; Sor le'net لەعنەت [K/B/SK/GF/HH//Wkt//IFb/CS/JJ]

nem نـەم/**ne'm** نـەعـم [B] *adj.* wet, damp: •**K'urdêd gundî avayêd bin'erde tarîye *nam*da, t'ev pêz û dêwêr dijîn** (Ba2-3, 213) The Kurdish villagers live in dark, *damp* underground dwellings, together with their sheep and cattle. {also: nam (B-2/Ba2); nim; [nem نم/nemi نمى] (JJ)} {syn: şil I; ter̄} Mid P nam = 'moisture' (M3) {nem[ay]î; ne'mayî} [Z-1/K/JJ/GF//B//Ba2]

nema نـەمـا *verbal complement* 1) no longer, no more; *often expresses the idea of stopping, ceasing*: •**Go [=ko] qehwa te bifûre, ez û tuê *ne ma* bin rizqê hevdu** (L-I, 8) If your coffee boils, you and I can *no longer* be together [lit. 'will *no longer* be each other's sustenance or reward'] •**Gur jî *nema* mîh û keran dixwin, bêhtir mirovan dixwin** (HYma, 29) And wolves *no longer* eat sheep and donkeys, they eat more people •**Ji wê rojê Hawar *nema* derket** (BX) Since that day Hawar [a journal] ceased publication [lit. 'did *not* come out *any more*'] •**Li me bû bû nîvê şevê û cihetnima jî *nema* dişixulî** (Rnh 1:11, 196) It was already past midnight and the compass stopped working [=*no longer* worked]; 2) not at all. < neg. past tense of man = 'to remain'. *See AKR (p. 59-62) for detailed discussion of* ***nema***. [BX/K/JB3/IFb/GF/FS/AKR] <êdî>

nemam نـەمـام *m.* **(-ê;).** slanderer, traitor: **-qomsî û nemam** (EP-7) troublemakers and slanderers. {also: [nemam] نـمـام (JJ)} {syn: altax; geveze; qumsî} < Ar nammām نمّام = 'slanderer' {nemamî} [EP-7/Rwn/K/JJ]

nemamî نەمامى *f.* **(-ya;-yê).** slander, betrayal, treason: •**Evî bi *nemamî* filankes kuşt** (Rwn) This one killed so-and-so as *a betrayal.* [K/Rwn/ZF3]

ne•man نـەمـان *vi. neg.* **(na•mîn-).** 1) to be destroyed, go out of existence, become extinct, perish; 2) [*f.* **(-a;-ê).**] extinction, perdition, death: •**Ew *nemana* xwe di şerî da dibînit** (FS) He meets [lit. 'finds/sees'] his *death* in the war; **-şerê man û nemanê** (Zeb) life-and-death struggle. Sor neman نـەمـان = 'extinction, coming to an end' [A/IFb/GF/TF/OK/AD/Zeb/FS/ZF3] <man>

nemayî نەمايى/**ne'mayî** نەعمايى [B] *f.* **(;-yê).** wetness, dampness. {also: namayî (B-2); nemî (K-2/Wkt)} [K//B//Wkt] <nem>

nemaze نـەمـازە *adv.* especially, particularly: •**Em hêvîdar in ku xwendawarên me *nemaze* yên ku di nav milet de dijîn ...** (DM) We hope that our readers, *particularly* those who live among the nation ... •***Nemaze* di şevên zivistanê de, li dora dengbêjan komdibin û bi saetan ... guhdariya vê stiranê dikin** (DM) *Especially* on winter nights they gather around singers and listen for hours to this song. {syn: bi taybetî; îlahî; nexasme} [DM/K(s)/JB3/IF/ZF3/FS]

neme نەمە = letter. See **name**.

nemerdî نـەمـەردى *f.* **(-ya;-yê).** cowardice; treachery, unmanliness, baseness, lowness *(of character)*: **-nemerdî kirin** (B) to act in a cowardly or dishonorable manner: •**Ĥeyran, ji boy xwedê be, *nekin nemerdî,* min navêne be'rê** (HCK-2, 182) My dear man, for God's sake, *don't act dishonorably*, don't throw me into the sea •**Şivîn *nemerdî nekir,* çû kavir̄ek anî şerjêkir** (HCK-1, 205) The shepherd *was not a coward*, he went and brought a ram and slaughtered it. {also: namerdî (A/IFb-2/TF/CS-2); [намерти] نـامـردى (JJ)} {syn: bêbextî} Cf. P nāmardī نـامـردى; Sor namerdî نـامـەردى = 'cowardliness; dastardly act unworthy of a man' [HCK/K/B/IFb/GF/Kmc/CS//A/TF/JJ] <newêrekî>

nemes نەمەس *f./m.(FS)* **(/-ê;).** dandruff; scurf: ***•Nemes* ji serê wî diwerit** (FS) *Dandruff* falls from his head. {syn: keletor; sîrik II} [Kmc/FJ/GF/ZF3/SS/FS]

nemêr نەمێر *adj.* impotent: **•Ez jî bawer dikim *nemêr* be, lewma bêdeng e ... Ma dermanê *nemêr* bûnê nîne?** (DBgb, 8) I too think that he is *impotent*, that's why he is silent ... Isn't there a cure for being *impotent*? {also: [ne-mir] نمر (JJ); <nemîr> نمیر (HH)} = Sor le pyawetî kewtû لە پیاوەتی کەوتوو [DBgb/A/IFb/FJ/TF/GF/Kmc//JJ/HH] <sist>

nemir نەمِر *adj.* immortal, eternal; *respectful way of referring to a deceased celebrity*: **•Tê xuyakirin ku, *nemir* du tîp ji alfabeya xwe avêtine, ew herdu tîp ev in: Ḧ - Ẍ** (Wlt 1:42, 10) It seems that *the dearly departed* [=Celadet Bedirxan] removed two letters from his alphabet; those two letters are Ḧ and Ẍ. Sor nemir نەمِر = 'immortal' [Wlt/A/IFb/GF/TF/OK/ZF3] <mirin>

nemî نەمی (K/Wkt) = wetness. See **nemayî**.

Nemsawî نەمساوی. See **Awistrî**.

nenas نەناس *adj.* unknown, unfamiliar, strange: **•Em hatin cîkî *nenas*** (B) We came to an *unfamiliar* place **•merîyê *nenas*** (B) *unknown* person, stranger. Cf. Sor nenasraw نەناسراو = 'unknown' & nenasyaw نەناسیاو = 'stranger' [Ba2/F/K/IFb/B/GF/TF/OK/FS] <nas[yar]>

nenûk نەنووك (A/GF/Çnr/Srk) = fingernail. See **neynûk**.

nepan نەپان (TF) = hidden, secret. See **nepenî**.

nepen نەپەن (IFb) = hidden, secret. See **nepenî**.

nependî نەپەندی (K[s]/IFb/GF) = hidden, secret. See **nepenî**.

nepenî نەپەنی/**nepe'nî** نەپەعنی [K(s)] *adj.* hidden, concealed; secret; invisible (JJ): **•Em dê gazî keyne me'donî û dê v r̄ê keyne r̄êkeka *nihanî*, biçît û nehêteve** (M-Am #739) We shall invite the guest and send him off on a *secret* road so that he goes and does not return **•Wî parên xwe deynan cihekê *nepenî*** (FS) He deposited his money in an *undisclosed* place. {also: nepan (TF); nepen (IFb-2); nependî (K[s]-2/IFb-2/GF-2); nihanî II (M-Am); [ne-peni] نپنی (JJ)} Cf. P panhān پنهان = 'hidden'; Sor nihênî نهێنی = 'secret' [IFb/JJ/GF/FS//K(s)/TF//M-Am] <r̄az; sir̄ II>

nep'ixandin نەپِخاندِن *vt.* **(-nep'ixîn-).** 1) {syn: êvitandin; p'erçifandin; werimandin} to cause to swell, blow, puff up *(vt.)*; 2) {syn: werpixandin} to exaggerate, blow out of proportion. [K/A/IFb/GF/TF/OK/ZF] <nep'ixîn>

nep'ixîn نەپِخین *vi.* **(-nep'ix-).** to swell up (vi.), be puffed up: **•Cendekê wî *nepixî* û ber bi êvarê mir** (Dz-anec #22) His body *swelled up* and toward evening he died. {also: [nepykhyn] نپخین (JJ)} {syn: êvitîn; p'erçifîn; werimîn}<Arc √n-p-ḥ נפח = 'to be blown up, swell'; cf. Ar nafaxa نفخ = 'to blow, inflate' [Dz/K/A/IFb/JJ/TF/OK/ZF3] <nep'ixandin>

neqandin I نەقاندِن *vt.* **(-neqîn-).** to select, choose (the best one), sort, pick out: **•Nûçe, nûçegihan û *neqandina* nûçeyan** (S.Tan. Azadiyawelat.com, ix.2007) News, reporting and *selecting* the news. {also: [neqandin] نقاندین (JJ)} {syn: bijartin; jêgirtin} < Ar naqqá II نقّى = 'to pick out, sift, sort' [Azadiyawelat/K(s)/A/IFb/FJ/TF/JJ/RZ/CS/ZF3]

neqandin II نەقاندِن (GF) = to blink. See **niqandin I**.

neqeb نەقەب *f.* **(-a;-ê).** passage, breach, gap; mountain pass {syn: gelî II; newal}: **•Ew di *neqebê* ra çû** (FS) He went through *the mountain pass*; **-neqeba** *[prep.]* (HR) between, among {syn: di navbera ft-î de; navbeyn}: **•Bnefşe Narîn şûr kire *neqeba* xwe û wîda** (HR 3:233) B.N. placed a sword *between* herself and him **•Rima xwe hilanî û kire *neqeba* her du polê wî da** (HR 3:74) He picked up his lance and put it *between* [the ogre's] 2 shoulders. < Ar naqb نقب = 'hole, opening, breach' [HR/A/IFb/FJ/GF/TF/Kmc/ZF/FS] <zuxir>

neqil نەقِل *f.* **(-a;-ê).** 1) account, narrative, story: **-neqil kirin**: a) to tell, recount (K/F/IFb/SK) {syn: gilî kirin; kat kirin; r̄iwayet kirin; vegotin; vegêr̄an}: **•[*Neqil dikin* ku...]** (JR) They *say* that.../The story goes that... ; b) {syn: veguhastin} to transfer, transport (IFb/JB1-A). 2) {syn: car} time, occasion [Fr fois, Germ Mal, Rus raz raz]: **•Ev *neqil* te wa kir, *neqileke* dinê ti tiştekî wa nekî** (Z-3) This *time* you've done this, next *time* don't do anything like this; **-neqlek** (GF) once, one time. {also: neql (B-2/GF/SK); neẍil (Z-3); [neqil] نقل (JJ)} < Ar naql نقل = 'carrying, transport; transmission, report' --> Az T nağıl = 'story, tale' [K/JR/Ba2/IFb/B/JJ/ZF3/FS//SK/GF] <çîr̄ok; ḧekyat>

neqiş نەقِش *m./f.* **(-ê/ ; /-ê).** 1) embroidery; embroidering: **•Eva bû çil şev û çil roj ez ji boy te serê vê p'irê rûniştime ser *nexişê* k'erge** (EP-7) I have sat on this bridge for 40 days and nights for you, [working] on an *embroidery* frame; 2) picture, image: •**Wî *neqşekê* can li çarçevê çêkir** (FS) He made a nice *picture* for the frame. {also: neqş (GF); nexiş (EP-7/B-2); nexş I (K-2/A/IF/B/TF); [neqych] نقش (JJ)} < Ar naqš نقش = 'painting, drawing, inscription' --> T nakış; Za nexş *m.* (Todd) [EP-7//K/JJ/ZF3//A/IFb/B/TF//GF]

neqişandin نـهقِـشـانـدِن *vt.* **(-neqişîn-).** 1) to draw, depict; 2) to inlay: •**Hemi *neqişandi* ye bi kevirê mermer** (L) It was all *inlaid* with marble stones. {also: neqşandin (GF); nexişandin (JB3); nexşandin (B)} < Ar naqš نـقـش = 'painting, drawing, inscription' [K/IFb/TF//GF//B//JB3]

neql نـهقـل (B/GF/SK) = story; time, occasion. See **neqil**.

neqş نهقش (GF) = embroidery. See **neqiş**.

neqşandin نـهقـشـانـدِن (GF) = to draw; to inlay. See **neqişandin**.

neřast نـهڕاست/**nerast** نـهراست [B] *adj.* 1) unreal; 2) wrong, incorrect, in error: •**Cava *nerast*** (B) The wrong *answer*; 3) untrue: •***Nerast* e ko**... (IF) It is *untrue* that...; 4) dishonest: •**Ew mirovekê *neřast* e** (FS) He is a *dishonest* person ; 5){syn: bêřêz; ≠řast [4]} irregular: -**fêlê neřast** (B) irregular verb; 6) uneven, slanted: •**'erdê *nerast*** (B) *uneven* ground. Cf. Sor nařast نـاڕاسـت = 'crooked, dishonest' {neřastî; nerastî} [F/K/IFb/B/GF/BF/FS/ZF3]

neřastî نـهڕاستـى/**nerastî** نـهراستـى [B] *f.* **(-ya;-yê).** 1) error, incorrectness, wrongness; 2) {syn: derew; viř II} lie, falsehood, untruth; dishonesty; 3) unevenness. [F/K/B/GF] <neřast>

nerdeban نـهردهبـان (JB3/IFb) = ladder rung; staircase; ladder. See **nerdewan**.

nerdevan نـهردهڤان (B) = ladder rung; staircase; ladder. See **nerdewan**.

nerdewan نـهردهوان *f.* **(-a;-ê).** 1) step, rung *(of a ladder)*; 2) {syn: derenc} staircase; 3) {syn: pêlegan; pêpelîng[3]; pêstirk; silim} ladder. {also: nerdeban (JB3/IFb); nerdevan (B-2); nerdivan (B-2); nerd(i)wan (EP-7)/nerdiwan (B-2); [nerdouvan] نـردوان (JJ)} Cf. P nardabān نـردبـان --> T merdiven = 'ladder' [EP-7//K//JB3/IFb//JJ]

nerdivan نـهردِڤـان (B) = ladder rung; staircase; ladder. See **nerdewan**.

nerdiwan نـهردِوان (B/EP-7) = ladder rung; staircase; ladder. See **nerdewan**.

nerdwan نـهردوان (EP-7) = ladder rung; staircase; ladder. See **nerdewan**.

neřehetî نهڕهههتى (K) = discomfort. See **neřeḧetî**.

neřeḧetî نهڕهحهتى/**nereḧetî** نهرهحهتى [B] *f.* **(-ya;-yê).** discomfort: •**Ew xeysetê Memê dê û bavê wî t'imê nava *neřeḧetîyê*da dihîştin** (Z-1) That trait of Mem's kept his parents in a constant state of *discomfort* •**Wezîrê tirk ji Mattis re *nerehetîya* Tirkiyê anîye ziman** (rojavanews.com 29.v.2017) The Turkish minister expressed Turkey's *discomfort* to Mattis. {also: neřehetî (K)} [Z-1//B//K/Wkt]

nerênî نهرێنى (BF) = negative. See **neyînî**.

nerîn نهرين (L) = to watch, look at. See **nêřîn**.

nerm نـهرم *adj.* soft; mild, gentle: -**goştê nerm** (Dz) desirable cuts of meat [lit. 'soft meat']. {also: [nerm] نرم (JJ); <nerm> نـرم (HH)} Mid P narm = 'meek, humble, soft' (M3); P narm نـرم; Sor nerm نـهرم {nermahî; nermayî; nermetî; nermî} [K/A/JB3/IFb/B/JJ/HH/SK/GF/TF] <teř>

nermahî نهرماهى (IFb) = softness. See **nermî**.

nermatî نهرماتى (Bw) = softness. See **nermî**.

nermayî نهرمايى (K/IFb) = softness. See **nermî**.

nermetî نهرمهتى (A) = softness. See **nermî**.

nermijîn نـهرمـژيـن *vi.* **(-nermij-).** to soften (vi.), be softened up (lit. & fig.); to become pliant: •**Bi qîrîna sloganên ku di dengê wan ê lorîkgotî de *dinermijîn*** (ŞWWM, 12) By shouting slogans which *softened* due to their lullaby-singing voices •**Wî hinar her guvaşt heta ku *nermijî*** (FS) He kept squeezing the pomegranate until it *softened.* [ŞWWM/K(s)/TF/FD/FS/ZF3] <nerm>

nermî نـهرمـى *f.* **(-ya;-yê).** softness; mildness, gentleness. {also: nermahî (IFb-2); nermatî (Bw-2); nermayî (K-2/IFb-2); nermetî (A)} Sor nermî نهرمى [K/IFb/SK/GF/TF/Bw/ZF3//B//A] <nerm>

Nerwîcî نهرويجى (BF) = Norwegian. See **Norwecî**.

nerx نـهرخ *f./m.(K/ZF3/Wkt)* **(-a/-ê;-ê/).** 1) {syn: biha [1]} price (K/A/IFb/GF); 2) value, worth: •**Hikûmeta Sûriyê *nirxê* dolar beramberî lêreya Sûriyê ji 700 lêreyî daxiste nêzî 300 lêreyan** (Kurdistan24 2.vi.2016) The Syrian government lowered *the value of* the dollar to the Syrian lira from 700 lira to nearly 300 lira. {also: nirx (GF/ZF3/BF/Wkt); [nyrkh نـرخ/nykhyr نـخـر] (JJ) < P nirx/narx نـرخ = 'price; rate'--> T narh = 'officially fixed price'; Sor nirx نِرخ = 'price, rate, value' [K/A/JB3/IFb/TF//JJ/GF/ZF3/BF/Wkt] <biha; binerx; nirxandin; qedir I; qîmet>

nerxî نهرخى (Zeb) = first-born. See **nuxurî**.

nesax نـهساخ *adj.* sick, ill. {also: nesaẍ (GF); [ne-sag]

نـصـاغ (JJ)} {syn: nexweş} Sor nasax̂ نـاساغ {nesax[t]î; nesax̂î} [Dh/K/A/IFb/TF/FS//GF//JJ]

nesaxî نـەسـاخـى *f.* **(-ya;-yê).** sickness, illness: **•Bilindbûna temenê riska vê *nesaxîyê* jî bilindtir dike** (sverigesradio.se 24.xi.2010) Advanced age increases the risk of this illness; **-nesaxîya şekirî** (FS) diabetes; **-nesaxîyên zikmakî** (FS) congenital diseases. {also: nesaxtî (A); nesax̂î (GF)} {syn: êş; jan; nexweşî; qeda [2]} Sor nasax̂î ناساغى [K/IFb/FS/ZF3//A//GF] <pejî>

nesaxtî نەساختى (A) = sickness. See **nesaxî**.

nesax̂ نەساغ (GF) = sick. See **nesax**.

nesax̂î نەساغى (GF) = sickness. See **nesaxî**.

ne-s̲ed نەصەد (SK) = nine hundred. See **nehsed**.

nesekinî نـەسـەكِـنـى *adj.* naughty, mischievous, rambunctious (of unruly children) : **•Ev zarok pir̄ *nesekinî* ye** (Msr) This child is very *naughty* (or doesn't stand still). [Msr/Wkt]

nesitêlê نەستێلێ (L) = not deserving death. See **nestêlê**.

nesîb نەسيب/**nes̲îb** نەصيب [JB1-A/JJ] *f./m.(HR)* **(/-ê;).** fortune, luck, fate; lot; destiny: **•Ava ti bûyî *nesîbê* min, ezê te mehr kim** (HR 3:230) Now that you are my *destiny*, I will marry you **•Tu *nesîbê* xwe û ew *nesîbê* xwe, bê k'î yê k'ê kujê** (HR 3:124) It *depends* on your fate and his, who will kill whom. {also: [nesib] نصيب (JJ); <nesîb> نـسـيـب (HH)} {syn: bext; *çarenivîs; enînivîs; qeder II; qismet; yazî} < Ar naṣīb نـصـيـب [HR/K/IFb/HH/JB1-S//JB1-A/JJ]

nestêle نـەسـتـێـلـە (IFb/ZF3) = not deserving death. See **nestêlê**.

nestêlê نەستێلێ *neg. adj.* not deserving *of being killed*, too young to die: **•Ya B., tu xortekî *nesitêlê* ye go ez te bikujim** (L) O B., you are a young lad who *doesn't deserve* to be killed **•Hakim hat, nerî go B. xortekî *nestêlê* ye** (L) The prince came and saw that B. was a young lad *too young to die*. {also: nesitêlê (L-2); nestêle (IFb/ZF3)} < ne + Ar ista'hala VIII استأهل (√a-h-l أهل) = 'to deserve, be worthy of' [L/GF//IFb/ZF3] <gune I>

neşerî نـەشـەرى *adj.* unlawful, running counter to the Islamic Shari'ah *(code of law)*: **•Mem û Zîn xwe li textekî dirêj kirin. Memi şûrê xwe danî navbera xwe û Zînê, da ko beriya mehirê tu tiştê *neşerî* di navbera wan de neqewimit** (SW) Mem and Zin lay down in bed. Mem put his sword between himself and Zin, so that nothing *unlawful* might occur between them before the wedding. {also: [ne-cheriié] نـشـريـعـه (JJ)} < ne = 'not' + {šar'ī شـرعـي} = 'pertaining to the Shariah (Islamic code of law)' [SW//JJ] <ĥelal; ĥeram>

neşir نـەشِـر *f./m.(F)* **(-a/;-ê/).** 1) (printing) press; 2) {syn: ç'ap II} printing, impression: **-neşir bûn** (B) to be published, printed, issued; **-neşir kirin** (B) to publish, print, issue; 3) propagation (SK). {also: neşr (SK)} <Ar našr نـشـر [F/K/B//SK] <neşirxane; weşan II>

neşiret نەشِرەت = publisher. See **neşirxane**.

neşirxan•e نـەشِـرخـانـە *f.* **(;•ê).** printing house; publisher, publishing house. {also: neşiret; neşîret (SC); neşîretxane (K)} {syn: ç'apxane} [F/B//K//SC] <neşir>

neşîret نەشيرەت (SC) = publisher. See **neşirxane**.

neşîretxane نـەشـيـرەتـخـانـە (K) = publisher. See **neşirxane**.

neşr نەشر (SK) = press; propagation. See **neşir**.

neşter نـەشـتـەر (IFb/GF/TF/FS) = spear; lancet. See **niştir**.

net'eve نەتەڤە = nation, people. See **net'ewe**.

net'ewayetî نـەتـەوايـەتـى = nationality; nationhood; nationalism. See **neteweyetî**.

netewayî نەتەوايى (Haz) = national. See **neteweyî**.

net'ew•e نـەتـەوە *f.(Wlt)/m.(Wkt/RF/FS)* **(•eya/•ê;).** 1) {syn: milet} nation: **-neteweya K'urd** (Wlt) the Kurdish nation; **-Neteweyên Yekbûyî [=NY]** (Wlt) the United Nations; 2) {syn: gel; xelq} a people. {also: net'eve} {net'eweyetî} [Ber/K(s)/A/JB3/IFb/GF/OK/RF/RZ/ZF3/BF/Wkt/FS] <navnet'eweyî; net'eweyî>

net'ewep'erest نـەتـەوەپـەرست *adj.* 1) nationalist[ic]: **•Heke tevgera kurd jî xwe bide ber vê yekê, ku hikûmeteke *neteweperest* jî desthilatdar be, wê guherînên demokratîk pêk werin** (AW75A2) If the Kurdish movement will support that idea, then even if a *nationalistic* government is in power, democratic changes will come about **•Nivîskarê rojnameya Cumhuriyetê Hikmet Çetinkaya di nivîsa xwe de sernavekî wiha bi kar anîbû: "Çepgirên *neteweperest* û rastgirên neteweperest"** (AW69A1) The writer for the newspaper Cumhuriyet, Hikmet Çetinkaya, used this title in his article: "*Nationalist* leftists and nationalist rightists"; 2) *[m.&f.]* a nationalist. {also: neteweperist (IFb/SS)} Sor neteweperist نەتەوەپەرست [AW/GF/OK//IFb/SS] <welatp'arêz>

net'ewep'erestî نـەتـەوەپـەرەسـتـی *f.* **(-ya;-yê).** nationalism: •**Rojnameya belçîkî Le Soirê dibêje, "Tirkiye *neteweperestiya* xwe nîşan dide"** (AW69A5) The Belgian newspaper Le Soire says, "Turkey is showing its *nationalism* [i.e., how nationalist it is]." {also: neteweperistî (IFb)} [AW/ZF3//IFb]

neteweperist نـەتـەوەپـەرِسـت (IFb/SS) = nationalist[ic]. See **net'ewep'erest.**

neteweperistî نـەتـەوەپـەرِسـتـی (IFb) = nationalism. See **net'ewep'erestî.**

net'eweyetî نـەتـەوەیـەتـی *f.* **(-ya;-yê).** nationality; nationhood; nationalism: •**Bêguman di nav wan de jî hindek kesên ku xwedîyê hesten *netewayetîya* kurdî bin jî hene** (pen-kurd.org: İ. Beşikçi. Kosovaya Serbixwe...) There are undoubtedly some people among them who have feelings of Kurdish *nationalism.* Sor netewayetî نـەتـەوایـەتـی = 'nationalism' {also: net'ewayetî; neteweyîtî (ZF/Wkt)} [IFb//ZF/Wkt]

net'eweyî نـەتـەوەیی *adj.* national: •**Min şexsîyeta xwe ya *netewî,* bi mana siyasî û zanistî hîn rind nedinasî** (Ber) I didn't yet know my *national* identity, in the political and scientific meaning [of the word]; **-Meclîsa neteweyî** (Wlt) National assembly. {also: netewayî (Haz); netewî (IFb)} [Ber/IFb//Wlt//Haz] <navnet'eweyî; net'ewe>

neteweyîtî نـەتـەوەیـیـتـی (ZF/Wkt) = nationality; nationhood; nationalism. See **net'eweyetî.**

netewî نەتەوی (IFb) = national. See **net'eweyî.**

net'ê نـەتـێ *adj.* invàlid, counterfeit; artificial; unreal; inadmissible: •**Dive ku min tiştekî *net'ê* got?** (Ba-1, #28) Did I say something *wrong*?; **-gilîyê net'ê kirin** (XF): a) to curse; b) to perform an evil deed; **-yeke net'ê kirin** (XF) to commit a reprehensible deed. {also: netêw (IFb); cf. also <netû> نـتـو (HH) = 'opposite of excellent'} [Ba-1/K/B/XF/ZF3//IFb//HH]

netêw نەتێو (IFb) = invalid, counterfeit. See **net'ê.**

ne'tik نـعـتِـك *f.* **(-a;-ê).** 1) {syn: 'enî; navçav} forehead, brow: •**Êşek k'etîye ne'*tka* min** (FK-eb-1) I have a pain in my *forehead* [lit. 'a pain has fallen to my forehead']; 2) front part *(of head)*; forelock (HH). {also: nehtik (GF); <ne'tik> نـعـتـك (HH)} [Z-1/Ks/K/B/HH/FS//GF]

nevis نەڤِس (FS) = stepchild. See **nevisî.**

nevisî نـەڤِـسـی *m.&f.* **().** stepchild: a) {syn: kuřhilî} stepson; b) {syn: keçhelî; qîzhilî (Frq)} stepdaughter. {also: nevis (FS); [nevisi] نـویـسـی (JJ)} Cf. P nāpesarī ناپسری = 'stepson' & navāseh نـواسـه = 'grandchild' [Bw/IFb/JJ/TF/OK/ZF//FS] <-hilî I; jinbav; ziřdayîk>

nevî نـەڤـی *m.&f.* **(-yê/-ya; /-yê).** grandchild: grandson (*m.*); granddaughter (*f.*): •**Landika *nevyê* wêderê bû** (Dz) The *granddaughter's* cradle was there. {also: nebî (F); newî (SK); [nevi (m.) نـوی/nevou (f.) نـوو] (JJ); <nevî> نڤی (HH)} [Pok nepōt-, *fem.* neptī- 764.] 'grandson, nephew': Skt nápāt (náptr̥-) = 'grandson, descendant' & naptī́- = 'granddaughter'; Av napāt-/naptar- = 'grandson' & naptī- = 'granddaughter'; OP napāt- = 'grandson'; Mid P nab (M3); P nave نوه; Sor newe نەوە = 'grandchild, descendant'; cf. also Lat nepos, nepotis. See I. Gershevitch. "Genealogical Descent in Iranian," *Bulletin of the Iranian Culture Foundation,* 1, (1973), 71 ff.; reprinted in his *Philologia Iranica,* ed. N. Sims-Williams (Wiesbaden : Dr. Ludwig Reichert Verlag, 1985), pp. 265 ff. [Dz/K/A/JB3/IFb/B/JJ/HH/GF/TF/ZF//F//SK] <bapîr; dapîr; nevîç'irk>

nevîç'iřk نـەڤـیـچِـرك *m.&f.* **(-ê/â;).** great-grandchild. {also: [nevi tchirik] نـوی چـیـریـك (JJ)} See I. Gershevitch. "Genealogical Descent in Iranian," *Bulletin of the Iranian Culture Foundation,* 1, (1973), 71 ff.; reprinted in his *Philologia Iranica,* ed. N. Sims-Williams (Wiesbaden : Dr. Ludwig Reichert Verlag, 1985), pp. 265 ff. [K/JB3/IFb/B/GF/ZF/FS//JJ] <nevî>

Nevroz نەڤرۆز (K/FS/HH) = Nawruz. See **Newroz.**

Nevrûj نەڤرووژ (B) = Nawruz. See **Newroz.**

nevs نەڤس (B) = soul; self. See **nefs.**

new نەو = new. See **nû.**

newa نـەوا *f.* **(-ya;-yê).** melody, tune, air: •**Bi barîna xwe a rîtmîk *newaya* senfonîya xewnên me pêk anîbû** (ŞWWM, 13) With its rhythmic raining it had created the symphonic *melody* of our dreams. {syn: leylan[1]; nexme} < P navā نـوا = 'air, melody, tune; song' [ŞWWM/K/FJ/GF/FD/ZF3]

newal نـەوال *f.* **(-a;-ê).** 1) {syn: dehl} ravine, gorge, canyon, narrow gully; riverbed (Haz): •**Dibêjin di *nihalekêda* řîwîyek hebû: awek nîw boş bi nîweka *nihalêda* dihate xar** (SK 2:9) They say there was a fox [living] in *a ravine*: a fairly full stream came down the middle of *the ravine* •**[Hêdî min xwe avête *nihalekê* û bi rojê di *newalêda* xwe veşartî]** (JR) Then I jumped into *a ravine*, and by day I concealed myself in *gullies*;

-**newal û nihêl** (EP-7) gorges and valleys: •**Li cîya mêşe bû, li cîya jî *newal û nihêl* bûn** (EP-7) Some places were forest, others were *gorges and valleys*; 2) {syn: aran I[2]} valley (A/JB3). {also: nihal (S/JR-2); nihêl (EP-7); [nouval] نـــوال (JJ)} Cf. Sor lêwar لـێـوار = 'edge, brink' [AB/K/A/JB3/IFb/B/JJ/GF/TF/JR/Haz//S/JR-2//EP] <aran; ç'em; dol II; gelî II; zuxir>

neweyî نەوەیی *pl.* **().** slander, false accusation: -**neweyî lê kirin** (ZF3) to slander, falsely accuse: •***Neweya li min neke*** (Msr) *Don't slander* me. {syn: nebûyî (Msr)} Cf. newihayî (A) = 'it isn't so' [Msr/ZF3] <derew>

newêr نەوێر (FJ/GF) = coward[ly]. See **newêrek**.

newêran نەوێران. See **wêrîn**.

newêrek نـەوێـرەك *m.* **().** 1) {syn: bizdonek; tirsonek} coward: •**Ez *newêrek* im ... Tirsonek im ez** (SBx, 11) I am *a coward* ... A scaredy-cat am I; 2) *[adj.]* cowardly, lacking courage. {also: newêr (FJ-2/GF-2)} {newêrek[t]î} Sor newêr نـەوێـر = 'timid, fearful, lacking courage' [SBx/K/B/IFb/FJ/GF/TF/RZ/ZF/CS/FS] <wêrîn>

newêrekî نـەوێـرەکـی *f.* **(-ya;-yê).** cowardice: •**Ji ber *newêrekîya* me zehmet e** (samandoken.com/ziyaretci-defteri- 30.iv.2013) Because of our cowardice it is difficult. {also: newêrektî (CS)} {syn: nemerdî; tirsonekî} [B/FJ/TF/GF/ZF//CS]

newêrektî نەوێرەکتی (CS) = cowardice. See **newêrekî**.

newêrîn نەوێرین. See **wêrîn**.

newhêt نەوهێت (Ag-villages) = ninety. See **not**.

newirandin نـــــەوِرانـدِن (K[s]) = to whimper. See **nehwirandin**.

newî نەوی (SK) = grandchild. See **nevî**.

newq نـەوق *f.* **(-a;-ê).** waist; lower part of chest *(below the ribs)* (B): •**Êdîka şerît bi *newqa* wî ve girêda** (L) Slowly (or, gently) he tied the rope around his *waist*. {also: noq II (Wlt-2/GF-2/ZF-2); <nûq> نـــوق (HH)} {syn: nav II[2]} [L/K/A/IFb/B/GF/TF/ ZF/Kmc-5//HH]

Newroj نەوڕۆژ (A) = Nawruz. See **Newroz**.

Newroz نەورۆز *f.* **(;-ê).** Newroz/Nawruz, the Kurdish and Iranian new year *which falls on March 21, the spring equinox*: •**Ew li *Newrozê* çûn seyranê** (FS) On *Newroz* they went on an outing/picnic •**Wextê *Newrozê* kew hat. Hemîyan gotin, "Wextê hatina kewî serê biharê ye"** (SK 29:264) At the *New Year festival* the partridge came. They all said, "The time of the partridge's coming is the beginning of spring"; -**cejna Newrozê** (CS) the Newroz festival. {also: Nevroz (K/FS-2); Nevrûj (B); Newroj (A); Nûroj (CS-2); [nourouz/naú-rúz (G)] نـوروز (JJ); <nevroz> نـڤـروز (JJ)} < P nōrūz (nawrūz) نــــوروز (naw = 'new' + rūz = 'day); Sor Newroz نەورۆز/Nwêřoj نـوێـڕۆژ [IFb/FJ/GF/TF/SK/BF/FS/ZF/SS/CS/Wkt//JJ//K/HH//B//A]

nexasim نـەخاسِم (IFb/GF/TF/OK/FS) = especially. See **nexasme**.

nexasme نـەخاسمە *adv.* especially, particularly: •**Hemî ceĥêlên li vêrê baş in, *nexasim* Behrem** (FS) All the young people here are good, particularly B. •[***Nexesme* biyanî bibînit, serî lê dihejînit**] (PS-II 38:68-69, 169) *Especially* if it [=the black horse] sees foreigners, it shakes its head. {also: nexasim (IFb/GF/TF/OK/FS); nexazim (FS-2); nexesma (RZ); [náxäsma] نـه خـصـمـه/نخصمه (JJ-PS)} {syn: îlahî; nemaze} cf. Ar xāṣṣ خـــــــاص = 'private, special' [Ak/JJ-PS//RZ//IFb/GF/TF/OK/FS]

nexaşî نــــەخــــاشــــی (HCK) = illness; badness. See **nexweşî**.

nexazim نەخازم (FS) = especially. See **nexasme**.

nexesma نەخەسما (RZ) = especially. See **nexasme**.

nexêr نەخێر *adv.* no. {also: naxêr (K/A/IFb/JB1-A&S/OK-2)} {syn: na} Cf. P naxēr نـخـيـر; Sor nexêr نەخێر [Bw/Dh/GF/TF/OK//K/A/IFb/JB1-A&S]

nexiş نەخِش (EP-7/B) = embroidery. See **neqiş**.

nexişandin نـەخِـشـانـدِن (JB3) = to draw; to inlay. See **neqişandin**.

nexm•e نەخمە *f.* **(;•ê).** melody, tune, air: •***Nexmeyine* dilhebîn û hewîndar dileyistin** (Dz #22, 389) He played amorous *melodies*. {also: neẍme (K-2)} {syn: leylan[1]; newa} < Ar naɣ[a]m نـــغـــم & naɣmah نـغـمـة = 'tone, sound, musical note' --> T nağme = 'melody, tune' [Dz/K/CS/ZF3]

nexo نـەخـۆ *conj.* 1) otherwise, or else: •**Eĥmedî gotê, 'Huşşş, *nexo* dê xudê li te ẍezeb çît'** (M-Ak, #543) Ahmed said to him, 'Hush, *otherwise* God will be angry with you' •**Kabray gotê, 'min to li nav befrê înay, *nexo* da mirî sermada'** (M-Ak, #545) The fellow said, 'I have brought you from the snow, *otherwise* you would have died of cold'; 2) after all: •**Baş e, *nexwe* tu hevalê min î, ne yê xanimê yî** (Wlt 2:73, 7) It's all right, *after all* you're my friend, not my wife's. {also: nexu (GF-2); nexwe (K/GF-2/TF/OK-2/FS/AKR); <nexo> نـــخـــو (HH)}. *See AKR (p. 63-64) for detailed discussion of* ***nexwe***. [M-Ak/HH/GF/OK//K/TF/

FS/AKR]

nexoş نـــەخـــۆش (M-Ak/JJ/SK/OK) = sick; bad. See **nexweş**.

nexoşî نـــەخـــۆشـــی (JJ/SK/OK) = illness; badness. See **nexweşî**.

nexrî نەخری (IFb/OK/Bw) = first-born. See **nuxurî**.

nexş I نەخش (A/IF/B/TF) = embroidery. See **neqiş**.

nexş II نەخش (GF/Bw) = map; plan. See **nexşe**.

nexşandin نـــەخـــشـــانـــدِن (B) = to draw; to inlay. See **neqişandin**.

nexş•e نـــەخـــشـــە *f.* **(•[ey]a;•[ey]ê).** 1) map: **-nexşeya cîhanê** (Wkt) map of the world; **-nexşeya Kurdistanê** (BF/Wkt) the map of Kurdistan; 2) plan: **•Divêt em *nexşeyek* baş bo karê xwe danin** (Wkt) We must make a good *plan* for our work. {also: nexş II (GF/Bw-2)} {syn: *xerîte} <Ar naqš نقش; Sor nexşe = 'map; plan, scheme' [Bw/K(s)/A/IFb/TF/ZF3/BF/Wkt/FD/RZ/SS/CS//GF]

next نـــەخـــت *m.* **(-ê;).** bride-price, money paid by the prospective groom to his father-in-law: **•"Mamê kund, tu keça xwe nadî kurê min?" "Ser çava" gotîyê, "lê tu dikarî hilgirî [wî] *nextê* ez dê biřim ser te? Ez temaya milka dikim"** (BG, 14) "Uncle Owl, won't you give your daughter to my son [in marriage]?" "Gladly," he replied, "but can you bear *the bride-price* I will inflict on you? I am covetous of wealth!" {also: naxt (JB1-S); [nekht/nakht(Rh)] نـخـت (JJ); <next> نـخـت (HH)} {syn: qelen} <Ar naqd نـقـد = 'cash, ready money' [Bw/A/IFb/JJ/HH/SK/GF/TF/OK//JJ-Rh/JB1-S] <bûk I; mehir; xezûr; zava; zewac>

nexu نەخو (GF) = otherwise; after all. See **nexo**.

nexundî نەخوندی (SK/JJ) = illiterate. See **nexwendî**.

nexwaş نەخواش (IFb) = sick; bad. See **nexweş**.

nexwaşî نـــەخـــواشـــی (IFb) = illness; badness. See **nexweşî**.

nexwe نـەخـوە (K/GF/TF/OK/FS) = otherwise; after all. See **nexo**.

nexwenda نەخوەندا (GF) = illiterate. See **nexwendî**.

nexwendatî نـــەخـــوەنـــداتـــی (Wkt) = illiteracy. See **nexwendîtî** .

nexwendetî نـــەخـــوەنـــدەتـــی (ZF3) = illiteracy. See **nexwendîtî** .

nexwendewar نـــەخـــوەنـــدەوار (GF) = illiterate. See **nexwendî**.

nexwendî نـــەخـــوەنـــدی *adj.* unlettered, illiterate: **•[Melayek û dû nefer mirofêd cahil *nexwendî* her sê bûyîne oldaşêd yekûdû]** (JR) A mullah and two ignorant, *unlettered* men were traveling companions. {also: nexundî (SK); nexwenda (GF); nexwendewar (GF-2); [ne-khoundi] نخوندی (JJ)} {nexwendîtî} [JR/Ba2/F/K/B/OK/ZF//GF//JJ/SK] <cahil>

nexwendîtî نـەخـوەنـدیـتـی *f.* **(-ya;-yê).** illiteracy: **•Di nav gelê me da *nexwendîtîya* olî (ya ola Êzdî) desthilatdar e** (rewanbej.net: ji-bo-65-saliya-ezize-cewo) Among our people religious *illiteracy* (of the Yezidi religion) is dominant. {also: nexwendatî (Wkt); nexwendetî (ZF3)} [K/B//ZF3//Wkt] <nexwendî>

nexweş نـەخـوەش *adj.* 1) sick, ill: **•Biraê me evřo dyar nîye, da biçîne mala wî, seḧ keynê, belke yê *nexoş* bît** (M-Ak #535) Our brother is not to be seen today. Let us go to his home and see how he is; perhaps he is *ill* **•Serma mirov *nexweş* dike** (AB) The cold makes a man *sick*; -**nexweşê şekirê** (Wkt) diabetic, person with diabetes: **•Hirmî ji ber ku toşpîya tifa dev û avzêyên (îfrazat) rûvikan zêde dike, ... jibo *nexweşên şekir* bê xisar e** (zanistuteknoloji.blogspot.com ii.2011) Pears are not harmful to *diabetics* because they increase the secretions of the oral salivary gland and intestines; 2) {syn: nebaş; xirab[1]} bad: **•Baweriya min li min xurtir dibe ku min tiştekî *naxoş* ne kiriye** (Epl, 20) My belief becomes stronger that I have not done anything *bad* **•Ez Eḧmedê Pîrikême, xudanê ṯeyrikême, eve min biraê hungo xendiqand. Eve yêt xoşin, *yêt nexoş* dê li dû hên** (M-Ak #535) I am Ahmed the son of the old woman, the owner of the bird, and now I have strangled your brother. These are the good things; the *bad ones* will come later. {also: naxoş (Epl); nexoş (M-Ak/SK/OK-2); nexwaş (IFb); [ne-khoch] نخوش (JJ)} Cf. P nāxōš ناخوش; Sor naxoş نـاخـۆش = 'unpleasant' & nexoş نـەخـۆش = 'sick, ill'; Za nêweş (Todd); Hau neweş = 'ill, unwell' (M4) {nexweş[t]î} [K/A/JB3/B/GF/TF/OK/ZF//JJ//IFb//M-Ak/SK/Epl]

nexweşî نـەخـوەشـی *f.* **(-ya;-yê).** 1) {syn: êş; jan; nesaxî; qeda [2]} illness, sickness; disease: **•Doxtira pêşîya *nexweşîyê* girt** (B) The doctors averted the *disease* [from spreading] **•Eger ḧekîmêt ḧaziq û hostayêt mahir hebin, bo zûî dişên *nexoşîya* wan derman biken** (SK 56:644) If there were skilled physicians and expert craftsmen, they could soon treat their *sickness* **•Qîzik êp'êce ji**

***nexaşîya* xwe qenc bû** (HCK-5, #41, 233) The girl has largely been cured of her *illness*; ***nexweşî-ya* giran** (JB3) serious *illness*; 2) badness, evil: **•Ew tirs û gumana *naxoşiyê* ji ser min radibe** (Epl, 20) That fear and suspicion *of evil* is lifted from me. {also: naxoşî (Epl); nexaşî (HCK); nexoşî (SK/OK-2); nexwaşî (IFb); nexweştî (A); [ne-khochi] نخوشى (JJ)} [K/JB3/B/GF/TF/OK//JJ//A//IFb//SK//HCK//Epl] <nexweş; pejî>

nexweştî نـەخـوشـتـى (A) = illness; badness. See **nexweşî**.

nexweşxan•e نەخوشخانە *f.* **(•a/•eya;•ê/•eyê)**. hospital: **-nexweşxana çêlan** (BK) children's hospital. {syn: *xeste} [K/A/IF/B/GF/BK/ZF]

neẍil نەغِل (Z-3) = story; time, occasion. See **neqil**.

neẍme نەغمە (K) = melody, tune. See **nexme**.

neyar نـەيـار *m.* **(-ê; neyêr** [B], **vî neyarî).** 1) {syn: dijmin} enemy, foe; declared enemy (HH); sworn enemy, arch enemy (B): **•Îro jî cehşê Kurd, ji bo miletê xwe, di destê *neyarê* xwe de bûye şûr** (WM 1:2, 15) Even today Kurdish jahshes [=collaborators] have become a sword in the hand *of the enemy* against their own people **•Mar *neyarê* mirov e** (AB) The snake is man's *enemy*; 2) {syn: ʻedû; hevrik} rival, competitor (IFb/TF). {also: [nä-yấr] نيار (JJ); <neyar> نيار (HH)} < ne = 'not' + yar = 'beloved, friend' {neyarî; neyartî} [AB/K/A/JB3/IFb/B/JJ/HH/GF/TF/ZF]

neyarî نـەيـارى *f.* **(-ya;-yê)**. enmity; hostility. {also: neyartî (K-2/A/B-2); [ne-iari] نـيـارى (JJ)} {syn: dijminahî} [K/JB3/IFb/B/JJ/GF/TF//A] <neyar>

neyartî نەيارتى (K/A/B) = enmity. See **neyarî**.

neyê نەيێ (JB1-S) = ninth. See **neha**.

neyînî نـەيـيـنـى *adj.* negative [Ar salbī سلبي; P manfī منفى; T olumsuz, menfi]: **•Bersîveke *neyînî*** (ZF3) A *negative* answer **•Me bi çavên xwe dît, em êdî ji nûçeyên *neyînî* bawer nakin** (krd.sputniknews.com 19.vi.2018) We saw it with our own eyes, we don't believe *negative* news anymore. {also: nerênî (BF-2)} [K/IFb/GF/TF/ZF3/Wkt/SS/FD/BF/SS/CS] <erênî>

neynesî نەينەسى *f.* **(-ya;).** cause, reason, grounds (for) (K/B): **•*Neynesîya* girîyê xwe ji minr̄a bêje!** (EP-4) Tell me *the reason for* your crying! **•Wî xwexwa dest bi serhatîya vê hurmetê, *neynesî-ya* dînbûna wê kir** (X. Çaçan. Benê min qetiya, 22) Of his own accord he began the story of this woman, *the reason for* her insanity. < T neyin nesi = 'the what of what' [EP-4/K/B] <eger II; sebeb; sedem>

neynik I نەينِك (Dyd) = fingernail. See **neynûk**.

neynik II نـەينِك (K/A/HB/IFb/B/GF/TF/Dyd/Grc/Btm/Srk/Wn) = mirror. See **nênik I**.

neynok نەينۆك (IFb/SK/ZF/Grc/Btm) = fingernail. See **neynûk**.

neynûk نـەيـنـووك *f.* **(-a;-ê).** fingernail; toenail: **•Ez naxwazim *nînoga* xortekî jî li kevirekî bikeve** (Epl, 102) [I don't want any violence] I don't want even *the fingernail of* a young man to fall on a rock. {also: nenûk (A/GF/Çnr/Srk); neynik I (Dyd); neynok (IFb-2/SK/ZF/Grc/Btm); nênik II (Tkm/Kp/Wn); nênîk (Bşk); nênûk I (Klk/Plt/Kş/Czr/Msr); nînig (IFb-2); nînog (Epl); nînok (Erg); nînûk (IFb-2); nûnîk (Hk); [neinouk] نـيـنـوك (JJ); <neynûk> نـيـنـوك (HH)} {syn: dirnaẍ} [Pok. onogh-(:ongh-/nogh-)/ongh-li 780.] 'nail, claw': Skt áṅghri- (r<l *oŋgh-li-) *f.* = 'foot'; Mid P nāxun = '(finger)nail' (M3); P nāxon نـاخـن; Sor naxun ناخون & nînok نينۆك (Arbil); Za nengwi *m.* (Todd) [K/JB3/IFb/B/JJ/HH/TF/Haz/Zx//SK//A/GF/ZF] <bêç'î; sim; tilî>

nezan نـەزان *adj.* 1) ignorant: **•Şêx û beg û aẍa zor bo ḧalê xo û menfeʻetê zatîyê xo zana û şeytan in, emma r̄eʻîyet zor bêçare û *nezan* û weḧşî ne** (SK 56:655) The shaikhs and begs and aghas are very wise and cunning in looking after their own case and their personal profit, but the peasantry are quite hapless and *ignorant* and rude; 2) {syn: cahil; naşî; nestêl; xam} naive, inexperienced, young. {also: [ne-zan] نـزان (JJ); <nezan> نـزان (HH)} Cf. P nādān نـادان; Sor nezan نـەزان {nezanî; nezantî} [K/A/JB3/IFb/B/JJ/HH/SK/GF/TF/OK] <zanîn>

nezanî نـەزانى *f.* **(-ya;-yê).** 1) ignorance: **•Gelê me ... di dema şahê gorbigor da di nav *nezanîke* mezin da dixeniqî** (Ber) Our people ... during the time of the accursed shah was drowning in a great [deal of] *ignorance* **•*Nezanî* r̄iḧetîya canê** (Msr) *Ignorance* is bliss [lit. 'ignorance, relaxation of the soul'] *[prv.]*; 2) rudeness, bad manners. {also: nezantî (B-2); nizanî (L); [nezani نـزانى/nezaniti نـزانـيـتـى] (JJ)} [Ber/K/A/JB3/IFb//B/JJ/SK/GF/TF/OK//L] <nezan; zanîn>

nezantî نەزانتى (B) = ignorance; rudeness. See **nezanî**.

nezer نـەزەر *f.* **(-a;-ê).** 1) look, glance: **•*Nezera* zar̄ê wane berê maka / Usanin, beʻrêda ç'eʻvê masî dertîne** (EP-7) *The looks of* their nursing children are such, [that] they make the eyes of fish in the sea come (=pop) out; 2) {syn: çavîn} evil eye; **•Ez nizanim *nezer* nahêle Memê Zînê bivîne** (EP-7) I don't know if *destiny* will let Mem see Zin; **-nezer ji *fk-ê* girtin** (EP-7) to put or cast the evil eye on s.o.: **•Wekî *nezer ji* te *negire*** (EP-7) *Lest the evil eye be cast on* you; 3) opinion; 4) {syn: mirin; wefat} death (B). {also: [nezer] نظر (JJ)} < Ar naẓar نظر = 'look, glance'--> T nazar = 'evil eye' [EP-7/K/IFb/B/JJ/SK] <neder>

nezir نەزر *f.* (). vow, conditional vow, pledge: **-nezr bûn** (SK) to be vowed, dedicated: **•Eger gotina wî r̄ast bît bila hemî milkê min *nezr bît* bo mizgewta Ergoş. Eger duro bît, milkê wî *nezri* mizgewtê *bît*** (SK 59:692) If what he says is true, let all my property *be vowed to* the mosque of Argosh. If it be a lie, let his property *be vowed to* the mosque; **-nezir kirin** (IFb)/**nezr** ~(Hk)/ [nader/nadúr kem] (JJ) to make a conditional vow, pledge: **•Cihû pênc mecidî *nezr kirin* ku kur̄ê wî şeveder nebît. Piştî ku kurê wî şeveder bû jî, pênc mecidî *nezr kirin* da ku venegerîte mal** (Hk) The Jew *pledged* 5 cents if his son would not stay out late at night. After his son started staying out late, he *pledged* 5 cents so that he would not return home. {also: nedur (GF); nezr (Hk/SK); [nader kem ندر/nadúr kem ندور] (JJ); <nedir ندر/nizr نزر> (HH)} < Ar nidr نذر; Sor nizir نِزر [Hk/SK//K/IFb/OK//HH//GF//JJ-G] <sond>

nezr نەزر (Hk/SK) = vow, pledge. See **nezir**.

nêçîr/nêç'îr [K/B] نێچیر *f.* **(-a;-ê).** 1) {syn: r̄av I [1]; seyd; şikar} hunting, the chase: ***•nêç'îra* k'êwrîşka** (B) rabbit *hunting*; **-çûn nêçîrê** = to go hunting: **•Evana diçine cem bavê, t'ewaqet jê dikin, ku ew îzna Ûsib bide, Ûsib wanra *her̄e nêç'îrê*** (Ba) They go to [their] father, [and] beg him to let Joseph *go hunting* with them **•Kurik *çû nêçîra* kewan** (AB) The boy *went hunting for* partridges (or, The boy went partridge-hunting); 2) {syn: r̄av I [2]; seyd} game *(caught on a hunting trip)*, wild fowl, quarry [gibier]: **•Di vê deştê de, *nêçîr* heye** (BX) On this plain, there is *[hunting] game* **•*Nêçîra* min tê, gûyê t'ejîya min tê** (Ag) Just as my *game* [i.e., deer] comes, my greyhound has to take a crap [expression denoting that an opportunity is unexpectedly lost, e.g., "I was just about to take their picture when someone walked in front of the camera"] *a more polite version*: **•Wexta *nêç'îra* min tê, xewa te'jîyê min tê** (Dz-#1565) When my *game* comes, my greyhound falls asleep **•R̄uhê k'ê heye, wekî *nêç'îra* beg u beglera jê bistîne** (FK-eb-1) Who dares to take *the game* of the bey(s) from him (them). {also: [nitchir] نچیر (JJ); <nêçîr> نیچیر (HH)} Manichaean Mid P nhčyhr = 'hunting' & Mid P naxčīr = 'game, quarry, chase' (M3); Sgd nyš'yr = 'wild game'; Shughni naxčīr = 'mountain goat'; P naxčīr نخچیر = 'wild game, prey' --> Heb naḥšir נחשיר; Sor nêçîr نێچیر = 'quarry'; Hau neçîr *m.* (M4). See: J.P. Asmussen. "Das iranische Lehnwort naḥšīr in der Kriegsrolle von Qumrān (1 QM)," *Acta Orientalia* [Copenhagen], 26 (1961), 3-20; H.W. Bailey. "Gāndhārī " *BSOAS*, 11 (1946?), 774, note 1 & "Miṣṣa Supple-tum," *BSOAS*, 21 (1958), 44-45; **2. naxčīr** in I. Gershevitch. "Etymological Notes on Persian mih, naxčīr, bēgāne, and bīmār," in: *Dr. J. M. Unvala Memorial Volume* (Bombay, 1964), p. 91-92; re-printed in his *Philologia Iranica*, p. 191-92; W. B. Henning. "Two Manichæan Magical Texts," *BSOAS*, 12, i (1947), 39-66, esp. 57, note. [Ba/K/A/JB3/IFb/B/JJ/HH/SK/GF/TF] <kevan; r̄av; tîr I>

nêçîrvan/nêç'îrvan نێچیرڤان *m.* **(-ê; nêçîrvên, vî nêçîrvanî).** hunter, huntsman: **•*Nêç'îrvanekî* te'jî berda k'êwrûşkê** (Dz) *A hunter* sent a hound after the rabbit ***•nêçîrvanê* kewan** (AB, 52) partridge *hunter*. {also: nêçîrwan (SK); [nitchir-van] نچیروان (JJ); <nêçîrvan> نیچیرڤان (HH)} {syn: seydvan; şikarçî} Cf. P naxčīrvān نخچیروان; Sor nêçîrewan نێچیرەوان [F/Dz/K/B//A/JB3/IFb/JJ/HH/GF/TF//SK] <kewgîrvan>

nêçîrwan نێچیروان (SK) = hunter. See **nêçîrvan**.

nêk نێك, f. (IFb) = hook; crocheting needle. See **nîk**.

nêm نێم *f.* **(-a;-ê).** pus, matter. {also: <nêm> نیم (HH)} {syn: 'edab; k'êm II} [A/B/IFb/HH/GF/OK/FS] <pizik>

nêngonk نێنگۆنك (Bşk) = heifer. See **nogin**.

nênik I نێنِك *f.* **(-a;-ê).** mirror; small mirror, pocket mirror (Czr/Kp/Wn): **•Keçik gava çû ber *neynikê* li xwe nerî** ... (ZZ-7, 248) When the girl went and looked at herself in *the mirror* ... **•Mîzah jî wek gelek şaxên edebî û folklorî û mûzîkî, parçeyek ji *neynika* wî milletî ye ku di wê *neynikê* de kil û kêmasîyên xwe dikarin bibînin û xwe li gor wê rast bikin** (LC, 3) Humor, like many literary, folkloric, and musical genres, is part of *the mirror of* that nation, through which they can see their shortcomings and fix them accordingly. {also: naynik (Plt-Cambek tribe); neynik II (K/A/HB/IFb/B/GF/TF/Dyd/Grc/Btm/Srk/Wn); nênuk

(Tkm); nênûk II (Hk); [neĭnik] نـيـنـك (JJ); <neynik> نـيـنـك (HH)} {syn: 'eynik; hêlî; mirêk; qotî I} Cf. P ā'īne آئـيـنـه; Sor neynok نـەيـنـۆك = awêne ئـاوێـنـه; Za lîlik *m.* (Todd) [Ad/HB/Klk/Plt/Erg/Kr/Czr/Kp//K/A/IFb/B/JJ/HH/GF/TF/Dyd/Grc/Btm/Srk/Wn//Tkm]

nênik II نێنِك (Tkm/Kp/Wn) = fingernail. See **neynûk**.

nênîk نێنیك (Bşk) = fingernail. See **neynûk**.

nênuk نێنوك (Tkm) = mirror. See **nênik I**.

nênûk I نێنووك (Klk/Plt/Kş/Czr/Msr) = fingernail. See **neynûk**.

nênûk II نێنووك (Hk) = mirror. See **nênik I**.

nêr نـێـر *adj.* male *(with connotations of bravery and authority)*; masculine; man's: **•berxê *nêr*** (B) *male* lamb **•nêrek'er/k'erê *nêr*** = *male* donkey **•ȟirçê *nêr*** = *male* bear **•kewê *nêr*/nêrekew** = *male* partridge **•k'êvroşkê *nêr*** = *male* rabbit; **•Dibêjim *nêr* e, dibêje bidoşe** (BF) I say it is a male, he says "Milk it" [*prv.*] (for people at crossed purposes); **-K'urdê nêr** (IF) brave Kurd. {also: [nir] نـيـر (JJ); <nêr> نـيـر (HH)} {≠mê; ≠dêl I} [Pok. 1. ner-(t)-/aner- (əner-?) 765.] '1) (magical) vitality; 2) man': Skt nár- (nā́) = 'man, human being'; Av nar- (nā); OP nar-; Mid P nar = 'male, manly' (M3); P nar نر; Sor nêr نێر; Za neri/nêr *m.* (Mal); cf. also Gr anēr ἀνήρ [BX/K/A/JB3/IFb/B/JJ/HH/GF/TF/BF] <camêr; mêr>

nêregur نـێـرەگـور *m.* **().** male wolf. {also: nêregurg (Wkt-2)} [IFb/GF/ZF3/Wkt] <gur>

nêregurg نێرەگورگ (Wkt) = male wolf. See **nêregur**.

nêreȟirç نـێـرەحِـرچ *m.* **().** male bear. {also: ȟirçê nêr} Sor nêrewurç نێرەوورچ [IFb] <ȟirç>

nêrek'er نـێـرەكـەر *m.* **(-ê;).** male donkey, he-ass: **•Meselekî meşhûr e li-naw me kurdan. Dibêjin ew kesê jinê dixazît maker e, ew kesê jinê didet nêreker e, belê paşî birinê şol ber-'eks e** (SK 42:411) It is a well-known proverb among us Kurds. They say that the person who asks for a woman is a she-donkey and the one who gives her is a he-ass, but after she has been taken the case is reversed. {also: k'erê nêr} {syn: guhd[i]rêj; k'er III} [BX/SK/GF/FS/ZF3] <k'er III; mak'er>

nêrekew نێرەكەو *m.* **(-ê;).** male partridge. {also: kewê nêr} [BX/K/GF/FS/ZF3] <kew>

nêřevan نـێـرەڤـان/**nêrevan** نـێـرەڤـان [FS] *m.* **(-ê;).** 1) {syn: dîdevan; zêrevan} observer, spectator, scout; 2) watchman: **•Zoro *nêrevanê* bîstanî ye** (FS) Z. is the garden's watchman; 3) reconnaissance plane (GF). {also: nêřvan (K[s]); niheřvan (K)} <nêřîn = 'to watch' {nêřevanî} [(neol)IFb/GF/ZF/BF//K]

nêřevanî نـێـرەڤـانـی *f.* **(;-yê).** observing, scouting; observation: **•Nêrevanê ko li qulûbeya *nêrevanîyê* razaye** (M.Aydogan. Berî gotin hebû 79) The watchman who fell asleep in the *observation* booth; **-nêřevanî lê kirin** (IFb) to observe stg. {syn: çavdêrî; *dîdevanî; zêrevanî} [(neol)IFb/ZF] <nêřevan>

nêrgis نێرگِس (Lab) = narcissus. See **nêrgiz**.

nêrgiz نـێـرگِـز *f.* **(-a;-ê).** narcissus, daffodil, bot. *Amaryllidaceae, Narcissus poeticus.* {also: nêrgis (Lab); [narghís/nergíz (Lx)] نـرگـس (JJ); <nêrgiz> نـيـرگـز (HH)} Cf. Mid P nargis (M3) & Ar narjis نـرجـس <Gr narkissos νάρκισσος; Sor nêrgis نێرگِس [Lab/JJ//K/A/IFb/HH/GF/TF/FS/BF/Wkt]

nêr•ik نـێـرك *f.* **(•ka;•kê).** stamen *(of a flower)*: **•Gêzegiya ... *nêrka* wî ya bilind e** (Bw) Gêzegiya [type of plant] ... its *stamen* is tall. {also: nêrî II (IFb); nêrtik (GF-2/FS-2); [niri] نيرى (JJ)} {syn: qîvar [2]} Sor nêrk نـێـرك [Bw/GF/OK/AA/ZF/BF//IFb/FS//JJ]

nêrî I نـێـری *m.* **(-yê;).** billy goat, male goat [bouc]; three-year-old male goat (JJ). {also: [niri نـيـرى/nihri نـهـرى/ pez-niri پـزنـيـرى] (JJ); <nêrî> نـيـرى (HH)} [Pok. 1. ner-(t)-/aner- (əner-?) 765.] '1) (magical) vitality; 2) man': Skt nár- (nā́) = 'man, human being' & nárya- = 'manly, masculine'; Av nar- (nā) & nairya-; Sor nêrî نـێـری = 'he-goat, billy-goat' [K/A/JB3/IFb/B/HH/GF/TF/OK/ZF//JJ] <bizin; gîsk; hevûrî; kar I; kûr I = s̲ayis̲; maz I; qert>

nêrî II نێری (IFb) = stamen. See **nêrik**.

nêřîn نـێـریـن *vt.* **(-nêř-/-ner-[L]/-n[i]hêř-).** to watch, look at, see: **•*Binere* bê gavan çi kirîye** (L) *See* what the cowherd has done **•Bav *dinihêre* îlac nabe** (Ba) The father *sees* that it's no use **•Tu k'ê *dinihêrî?*** (B) Who[m] *are* you *looking at*? {also: nerîn (L); nêrtin (A/GF-2); nhêrîn (Ag); nihêrandin; nihêrîn (B); nihêřîn; nihêrtin (JB3/IFb/GF-2); řêntin (-řên-) (Msr); [nirin نـيـريـن/nihirin نـهـريـن] (JJ); <nêrîn نـيـريـن/nêrtin نـيـرتـن (dinêre) (دنـيـره)>} {syn: berê xwe dan; dîtin; fikirîn II; mêze kirin; zên dan} Sor nuwařîn نـوواڕيـن/nořîn نـۆڕيـن/řuwanîn ڕووانـيـن; SoK runıs(t)ın/nurıs(t)ın, nurin (Fat 232) [L//K/HH/GF/TF/A//B//JB3/IFb//JJ//Ag] <bê II>

nêrtik نێرتِك (GF/FS) = stamen. See **nêrik**.

nêrtin نێرتِن (A/GF) = to watch, look at. See **nêřîn**.

nêřvan نێرڤان (K[s]) = observer. See **nêřevan**.

nêt نێت *f.* **(-a;-ê).** 1) {syn: me'na} meaning: •**Gerekê hûn *nêta* evê xewna min ji minřa bêjin** (Ba3) You must tell me *the meaning of* this dream of mine; 2) {syn: fikir; hizir} idea, thought: •**Apê Kotê *nêta* min fam kir** (Ba2:2, 205) Uncle Kotey understood my *thought* [or, hesitation]; 3) {syn: dîtin} opinion: •**bi *nêta* min** (B) in my *opinion*; 4) {syn: armanc [1]; mebest; meqsed; merem [1]} desire, goal, aim, purpose, intention: **-nêta *yekî* hebûn** [+ *subj.*] (CS) to intend (to do stg.) {syn: li ber bûn} •**Do êvarê jî min dest bi nivîsandina jiyana Qedrî Can kir. *Nêta* min *heye* ez li ser jiyan û berhemên wî kitêbekê derxim** (LC, 11) Last night I started writing Qedrî Can's biography. *I intend to* bring out a book on his life and work •**Nêta wan ne hate sêrî** (K) Their desire didn't come to pass; 5) contents *(of a book, article, etc.)*: **-nêta k'itêbê** (F) table of contents {syn: naverok; p'êřist; serecema k'itêbê (F)}. {also: niyet (IFb); nîyet (KS/SK); [niiet] نيت (JJ)} < Ar nīyah نية = 'intention'--> T niyet [Z-1/K/B/TF/CS//IFb//JJ/KS/SK]

nêv نێڤ (JB1-S) = center, middle. See **nav II** [1] & **navik** [2].

nêvik نێڤِك (IF) = center, middle; navel, belly button. See **nav II** & **navik**.

nêvî نێڤی (Msr/A/IF) = center; half. See **nîvî**.

nêz I نێز *f.* **().** hunger: **-ji nêza** = (e.g., dying) of hunger {syn: birçîna}: •**Ax ez *ji nêza* mirim!** (L) I'm dying [lit. 'I died'] *of hunger*. {also: <nêz> نيز (HH)} {syn: birçîtî; xela} [L/K/HH/GF/TF/FS]

nêz II نێز (IFb/TF) = near. See **nêzîk**.

nêzik نێزك (BX/JB1-S/OK/ZF) = near. See **nêzîk**.

nêzing نێزنگ (JB1-S/GF) = near. See **nêzîk**.

nêzîk نێزیك *adj.* [+ **ji** or **-î**] near, close to: **-nêzîk bûn** (K/B/IFb/GF) to approach, near [**nêzîkî *fk-î/ft-î* bûn**]: •**Sultan Ḧemîd got, "'Elî, to naḧeqq î: ḧetta do hewyan cezayê te ew e, *nêzîkî* serayê *nebî*"** (SK 52:566) Sultan Hamid said, "Ali, you are in the wrong: for 2 months this is your punishment, you *may not approach* the palace" •**Şivan *nêzîkî* wî *bû*, girt avîte 'erdê, dest-p'ê wî ḧişk girêda** (Dz) The shepherd *approached* him, grabbed him and threw him to the ground, and bound his hands and feet tightly; **-nêzîk kirin** (K/B/IFb/FJ/CS/GF) to bring stg. close to stg. else [***ft-î* nêzîkî *bk-î* kirin**]: •**Lê her ku kevçiyê şerbetê yan jî liba derman *nêzîkî* devê xwe *dikir*, dikir ku vereşe** (HYma, 34) But every time he *brought* the sherbet spoon or the pill *close* to his mouth, he was about to throw up •**Mêvan t'ebax *nêzîkî* xwe *kir* û dest bi xwarinê kir** (B) He *brought* the plate *close* to him and began to eat. {also: nêz II (IFb-2/TF); nêzik (BX/JB1-S/OK-2/ZF); nêzing (JB1-S-2/GF-2); nêzîng; nêzûk; nizîk; nîzing (H2); [nizouk نزوك/ nezīk نزيك] (JJ); <nîzîk> نيزيك (HH)} {≠dûr} Skt nēdīyas- = 'nearer' & nēdiṣtha- = 'nearest': O Ir *nazda- = 'near' & *nazdi̯ah- = 'nearer' (Ras, p.132): Av nazdyō = 'nearer' & nazdišta- = 'nearest'; Mid P nazd/nazdīk (<*nazdi̯a-ka-); P nazdīk نزديك; Sor nizîk نزيك; Za nezdi/nezdî (Todd); Hau nizîk (M4) {nêzîkahî; nêzîkayî; nêzîkî; nêzkayî} [BX/JB1-S/ZF//K/A/IFb/B/JB1-A/SK/GF/OK//JJ//HH//TF//H2]

nêzîkahî نێزیکاهی (IFb) = nearness. See **nêzîkayî**.

nêzîkaî نێزیکائی (L) = nearness. See **nêzîkayî**.

nêzîka•yî نێزیکایی *f.* **(;•yê).** 1) nearness, proximity, closeness: **-lê nêzîkayî kirin** = to approach, draw near to: •**Dîya wî *nêzîkaî lê kir* û hat** (L) His mother *approached him* •**Gava go hatin *nêzîkaî li* qesra qîza hakim *kirin*** [sic] (L) When they *drew near to* the princess' palace •**Hat, *nêzîkaî li* mixara Canpola *kir*** (L) He *approached* Janpola's cave; 2) nearing, approaching (JJ) [approchement]. {also: nêzîkahî (IFb); nêzîkaî (L); nêzîkî I (K/A/IFb); nêzkayî (K); [nizoukahi نزوکاهی/ nizouki] نزوکی (JJ)} [L//K/A/IFb//JJ] <nêzîk>

nêzîkî I نێزیکی (K/A/IFb) = nearness. See **nêzîkayî**.

nêzîkî II نێزیکی (K) = near (to). See **nêzîk**.

nêzîng نێزینگ = near (to). See **nêzîk**.

nêzkayî نێزکایی (K) = nearness. See **nêzîkayî**.

nêzûk نێزووك = near (to). See **nêzîk**.

nhêrîn نهێرین (Ag) = to watch, look at. See **nêřîn**.

nhú نهو (Ad) = new. See **nû**.

ni- نِ *neg. part.* not, do[es] not, will not {*negative particle prefixed to present indicative of the two verbs* ***karîn*** *and* ***zanîn****; negativizes both the present indicative and the future, e.g.,* ***nizanim*** *= I don't know or I won't know; all other verbs take* ***na-*** *rather than* ***ni-****}* Cf. P na- نـ [IFb/B/SK/GF] <me-; na-; ne->

niç' نِچ *interj.* plaintive sound, sigh, tsk tsk *(sound of pity, regret or disapproval)*: •***Niç, niç, niç!* ... Heyf û xebînet e! Va roviyek li vir miriye!** (ZZ-4, 203) *Tsk, tsk, tsk*! What a crying shame! There's a fox here who has died! [ZZ/FJ/GF/ZF] <niç'eniç'>

niç’andin نـچـانـدِن *vt.* **(-niç’în-).** 1) {syn: niç’ikandin} to stick, drive in, thrust, forcibly insert *(e.g., a stake into the ground)*: •**Şêr ze‘f brîndar bû. Ewî serê qamîş *niç’ande* brîna wê** (HCK-3, #16, 182) The lioness was badly wounded. He [=Mirza Me’mud] *thrust* the head of the reed into her wound; 2) to reproach, scold: •**Ewî niç’ande wî – ew neçû, ewî gote wî – neçû** (HCK-2, 84) He *scolded* him, but he didn’t go, he told him, but he wouldn’t go. [HCK/B]

niç’eniç’ نـچـهـنـچ *f.* **().** tsk tsk, *sound of pity, regret or disapproval*: •**Tenê yekî rîsipî, wî tenê bi *niçeniç* serê xwe li ba dikir** (Ardû, 134) Only one old man, he was the only one to shake his head in disapproval [lit. ‘with *tsk tsk*’]. {also: niç-niç (AD)} [Ardû/IFb/ZF//AD] <niç’>

niç’ikandin نِچِكاندِن *vt.* **(-niç’ikîn-).** 1) {also: niç’andin} to stick, drive in, thrust, forcibly insert *(e.g., a stake into the ground)*; 2) {syn: daç’ikan-din} to hoist, erect *(a banner)*; 3) to plant *(a tree)*: •**Dora t’irba darê sipindara *diniç’ikîne*** (Z-4) Around the graves he *plants* poplar trees. [Z-4/K/FS] <daç’ikandin>

niç-niç نِچ نِچ (AD) = tsk tsk. See **niç’eniç’**.

nifiȓ نـفـر/**nifir** نـفـر [A/IFb/HH/GF/TF/OK] *f.* **(;-ê).** curse, malediction, anathema [T beddua, Ar la‘nah لـعـنـة]: **-nifiȓ lê kirin** (B)/**nifiȓ[î] kirin** (K)/**dayîn nifiȓa** (K-2) to curse, call down curses upon: •**Ew mexseda we, ko dîya te û bavê te *nifiȓ kirine*** [sic] (Z-3) This purpose of yours which your parents *have cursed* •**Jina k’esîv *nifiȓya* Aqûb *dike*** (Ba3-3, #16) The poor man’s wife *curses* Jacob. Examples of curses: **Xudê pişta dujminan bi şikêne** (FS) May God break the enemies' back; **Xudê wî nehêlit!** (FS) May God not keep him alive! {also: nifiȓî (B-2); nifîn (Hk); nifrîn (FS/BF); [nifran] نـفـران (JJ); <nifir> نـفـر (HH)} {syn: ç’êȓ; dijûn I; ne‘let; qise[3]; sixêf; xeber[3]} Mid P nifrīn = 'curse' (M3); cf. also Ar nafara نـفـر = 'to have a distaste or aversion for' [Z-3/K/A/IFb/B/HH/GF/TF/OK//JJ//FS/BF//Hk] <ç’êȓ; dijûn I>

nifiȓî نِفِرى (B) = curse. See **nifiȓ**.

nifîn نِفين (Hk) = curse. See **nifiȓ**.

nifrîn نِفرين (FS/BF) = curse. See **nifiȓ**.

nifs نِفس (Şnx) = low. See **nizm**.

nifş نـفـش *m.(Hk/FS)/f.(Wlt/ZF)* **(-ê/-a;-î/).** 1) {syn: cîl} generation: •**Divê *nifşa* (cîla) nû xwe pêve mijûl bike!** (Wlt) The new *generation* must concern itself with this!; 2) lineage, line (of descent): •**ji *nifşê* Şêx Seid** (IFb) from Shaikh Sa‘id’s *line*. {also: nivş (FS)} [Wlt/IFb/GF/TF/ZF//FS]

nift نِفت (Ag) = oil; match(es). See **neft** & **neftik**.

niftek نِفتەك (GF) = match(es). See **neftik**.

niftik نِفتِك (IFb) = match(es). See **neftik**.

nig نگ (Ad/Bg/IF) = foot. See **ling**.

niha نـهـا *adv.* now: **-ji niha û wêvatir** = from now on, henceforth. {also: ana (MK2); anaka (A-2); anêka; aniha (A-2/JB3); anika (HB); naga; naha (B); naka; niho (GF); nika; noke (Bw/SK); [neha نـهـا/ nouka نكا/ânekа انكا/ ânuha انـها/ nōhá نـوهـه] (JJ); <neha> نـها (HH)} {syn: taze [4]} = Sor êsta ئێستا [K/A/JB3/IFb//B//JJ/HH//GF//Bw/SK//HB//MK2]

nihal نـهـال (S/JR) = ravine, gully; riverbed; valley. See **newal**.

nihan نِهان, m. (Dh) = shelter. See **nivan**.

nihandin نِهاندِن (GF) = to copulate. See **nayîn**.

nihanî I نِهانى (Zeb/Hej/BF) = shelter. See **nivan**.

nihanî II نِهانى (M-Am) = hidden, secret. See **nepenî**.

niheq نِهەق (K) = wrong, unjust. See **neheq**.

nihêl نـهێل (EP-7) = ravine, gully; riverbed; valley. See **newal**.

nihêrandin نِهێراندِن = to watch, look at. See **nêȓîn**.

nihêrîn نـهێرين (B)/nihêȓîn نـهێرين = to watch, look at. See **nêȓîn**.

nihêrtin نـهێرتن (JB3/IFb/GF) = to watch, look at. See **nêȓîn**.

nihêȓvan نِهێرڤان (K) = observer. See **nêȓevan**.

nihêt نِهێت (K) = boulder. See **nehît**.

nihît نِهيت (GF) = boulder. See **nehît**.

nihk نِهك (FS) = hook; crocheting needle. See **nîk**.

niho نِهۆ (GF) = now. See **niha**.

nijad نـژاد *m./f.(ZF)* **(-ê/-a;).** (biological) race: •***Nijadê* mirovî ji Ademî ye û Adem ji axê ye** (FS) The race of mankind is from Adam, and Adam is from the earth/soil. {also: nîjad (ZF)} {syn: dol I} Cf. P nežād نژاد ; Sor nîjad نـيـژاد = 'race, stock' [K/JB3/IFb/GF/TF/AD/FS//ZF] <gel; net’ewe>

nijadparest نژادپارەست (TF) = racist.

nijadp’erest نـژادپـەرەسـت *adj.* 1) racist: •**Her wiha helwesta Tirkiyeyê ya *nijadperest* derkete ber çavê gelê cîhanê** (AW69C1) Likewise, Turkey's *racist* attitude has been noticed by the peoples of the world; 2) [*m.&f.* ().] a racist: •***Nejadperestên* Tirk û Ereb û Farisan, jibo ku gelê Kurd biçûk bixin, hin peyvên heqaretê çêkirine û belav kirine** (Bkp, 4) Turkish, Arab and Persian *racists*, in order to denigrate the Kurdish people, concocted some slanderous phrases and spread them around. {also: nejadperest (Bkp); nijadparest (TF); nijadperist (IFb); nîjadperest (ZF)} [AW/K//IFb//TF//Bkp//ZF]

nijadp'erestî نـژادپـــەرســتــى *f.* **(-ya;-yê).** racism: **•Dewleta tirk bi *nijadperestiyê*, bi binpêkirina mafên mirovan û bi durûtiya xwe êdî li cîhanê deng daye** (AW69C2) The Turkish state has made a name for itself in the world for its *racism*, its suppression of human rights and its hypocrisy. {also: nijadperistî (IFb)} [AW/K//IFb]

nijadperist نژادپەرِست (IFb) = racist. See **nijadp'erest**.

nijadperistî نـژادپـــەرِســتـــى (IFb) = racism. See **nijadp'erestî**.

nijandin نـژانـدِن *vt.* **(-nijîn-).** 1) to build (a stone wall) *by piling stones one on top of the other*: **•Li hindav û nêzî Wanê û Gola Wanê kelehên mezin û dîrokî hene, du keleh ji van kelehan li raserî lêva golê ne, herdu jî li ser tatên pan û mezin *hatine nijandin*** (SB, 50) Above and beside Van and Lake Van there are large and historic fortresses, [and] two of those fortresses overlook the shore of the lake, both of them *have been built* on flat and large cliffs; **-nijinîn û heraftin** (SK)/ **nijandin û herifandin** (Bw) to mull over, ponder, contemplate, turn over in one's mind [lit. 'to build and tear down']: **•Her *dinijand û herifand*** (Bw) He *was deep in thought* **•Mûsilî di dilê xo da *nijinî û heraft*, gele hizr kir** (SK 31:276) The Mosuli *turned the matter over in his mind* and thought a great deal; 2) to pile up, stockpile (IFb/OK) [nijinandin]. {also: nijinandin (-nijinîn-) (IFb/GF-2/OK); nijinîn (SK/K[s]/Bw); nijintin (Bw-2); [nijinin/nizhinīn (Rh)] نـــژيـــنـيـن (JJ); <nijandin> نژاندن (Hej)} [Hk/Zeb/GF/Hej//IFb/OK//K(s)/JJ/SK/Bw]

nijdar نژدار (FS) = doctor; medicine man. See **nojdar**.

nijd•e نـــژده *f.* **(•a;•ê).** raiding-party, band or gang of robbers: **•Heware, *nijde* hat ser me** (M-Zx #768, 354) Help, *a raiding party* is upon us! **•Karwanekî Şêxê Barzanê diçû Akrê. *Nijda* Sûrçîyan hat, karwan şeland û deh muro kuştin. Sebeb wihê Zêbarî hizar mêr řabûn, çûne ser gundê Bicîlê** (SK 50:533) A caravan of the Shaikh of Barzan was going to Akre. A Surchi *raiding party* came, plundered the caravan and killed ten men. On account of this a thousand Zebaris rose and went against the village of Bijil. {also: [nijdé] نژده (JJ)} {syn: cerd I} Sor nijde نـــژده (K3) [M-Zx/K(s)/A/IFb/JJ/SK/GF/OK] <t'alan>

nijdekar نِژدەكار (Dh) = bandit. See **nijdevan**.

nijdekarî نِژدەكارى (Dh) = banditry. See **nijdevanî**.

nijdevan نـــژدەڤــان *m.* **(-ê;).** bandit, robber, brigand: **•Se'doyê Meysê serekdarê *nijdevana*** (FS: song of Filîtê Quto) Sadoyê M., leader of the bandits. {also: nijdekar (Dh); nijdivan (TF)} {syn: ħerebaşî; k'eleş II; řêbiř} {nijdevanî; nijdekarî; nijdivanî} [Dh//K/A/IFb/GF/OK/FS/BF//TF]

nijdevanî نـــژدەڤــانــى *f.* **(-ya;-yê).** banditry, brigandage, highway robbery. {also: nijdekarî (Dh); nijdivanî (TF)} {syn: k'eleşî; řêbiřî} [Dh//IFb//TF] <nijdevan>

nijdivan نژدِڤان (TF) = bandit. See **nijdevan**.

nijdivanî نژدِڤانى (TF) = banditry. See **nijdevanî**.

nijinandin نـژنـانـدِن (-nijinîn-) (IFb/GF/OK) = to build (stone wall); to pile up. See **nijandin**.

nijinîn نـژنـيـن (SK/K[s]/JJ) = to build (stone wall); to pile up. See **nijandin**.

nik I نــك *prep.* at, at the house of, over [chez]: **-li nik** (IF) do.; **-nik dilê min** (BX) in my opinion [lit. 'at my heart']. {also: [nik نيك/ li-nik لنيك/bi-nik بنيك] (JJ); <nik> نـــك (HH)} {syn: bal I; cem; hinda I; ħafa [*see* ħaf]; lalê; li def (Bw); řex I} Sor kin كِـن [BX/K/A/JB3/IFb/JJ/HH/SK/GF/ZF]

nik II نِك (Bg) = chickpeas. See **nok**.

nika نكا = now. See **niha**.

nikare I نِكاره (BF) = auger, gimlet. See **mikare**.

nikare II نِكاره = S/he cannot. See under **karîn**.

nikeh نِكەه (K) = marriage. See **nikha**.

nikha نـكـهـا *f.* **(; nikhê/nikhaê).** wedding, nuptials; marriage: **-nikha kirin** (B)/**nikeh kirin/biřîn** (K) to marry off: **•Bavê 'Eynêye --/ ... / 'Eynê ser Meħmed Emîn *nekħa kirîye*** (EP-5, #5) Ayneh's father --/ .../ *married* Ayneh to Mehmed Emin. {also: nekħa (EP-5); nikah (IF); nikeh (K); [никïахь/nekah (Lx)] نكاح (JJ)} {syn: mehir} <Ar nikāḥ نـكـاح = 'marriage; marriage contract'--> T nikâh [EP-5//B//IFb//JJ//K] <bûk I; de'wat; zava>

nikil نـكِـل *m.* **(-ê;).** 1) {syn: dim} beak, bill *(of bird)*: **•Kew û ferûçkê bi *nikulên* xwe kevir werger-andin, derketin û revîyan** (SW1, 24-25) The partridge and chicken overturned the rock with their *beaks*, exited, and fled; **-nikilê** (A) long-nosed, ugly woman; **-nikilo** (A) long nosed, ugly man; 2) point, sharp tip (B): **•nikulê derzîyê** (B) point of a needle. {also: nikul (K/Ks/B/GF-2);

nîkil (IFb-2/OK/Bw); nukul (Z-3/IFb-2); [noukoul] نكول (JJ); <nikil> نكل (HH)} [Ks/K/B//A/JB3/IFb/HH/SK/GF/TF//JJ//Bw/OK] <xişt III>

nikul نِكول (K/Ks/B/GF) = beak, bill; point, tip. See **nikil**.

nim نِم = wet. See **nem**.

nimandin نِماندِن *vt.* **(-nimîn-).** to show, indicate, represent: •**Dengê [e] dengdêr e û bi V (îng. Vowel) *tê nimandin*** (N.Hirorî. Nihêniyên Befrê/Berfê, Kulturname 18.i.2013) The sound [e] is a vowel and *is represented* by V •**Digere lê, ew yekê ku bavê wî yê rihmetî jê re *nimandi bû*, nabîne** (Ardû, 27) He is searching, but he doesn't find that which his late father *had indicated* •**Me berê jî qala strana "Sînem"ê kiribû û mînak jê *numandibû*** (BZ, 409) Earlier we also spoke of the song "Sinem" and *showed* an example from it. {also: numandin (BZ)} Cf. P numāndan نماندن/numūdan نمودن = 'to show, appear'; Sor nûwandin نووواندِن = 'to show, appear, seem' [Ardû/K(s)/IFb/FJ/GF/CS/Kmc//BZ]

nimê نِمی (Ad/GF) = namaz, salah, Islamic prayer ritual. See **nimêj**.

nimêj نِمێژ *f.* **(-a;-ê).** namāz, ṣalāh, Islamic prayer ritual: •**Her roj piştî *nimêja* êvarê, şêx şîretên dînî li mirîdên xwe dikirin** (Rnh 2:17, 340) Every day after the evening *prayer*, the sheikh would give religious advice to his disciples [or, would advise his disciples on religion]. {also: **limêj**; mêj II; nim•ê (•îyê;) (Ad/GF); nivêj (M-Zx/JB1-A/GF-2); niwêj (SK); nmêj; [nymij نميژ/nymi نمی/lämüž لموژ] (JJ); <limêj> لميژ (HH)} Cf. P namāz نماز --> T namaz; Sor niwêj نوێژ; Za nimaz (Todd/Mal)/nimac/nimaj *m.* (Mal); Hau nima *f.* (M4) {See: Mohammad Mokri's Introduction to HH, p. 27 (in French) & p. 52 (in English)} [K/IFb/B/OK//Ad/GF//JJ//HH//M-Zx/JB1-A//SK] <destnimêj; mizgeft> See also **limêj**.

nimone نِمونە (AD) = example, sample. See **nimûne**.

nimûne نِموونە *f.(ZF/CS)/m.(K)* **(-ya/-yê;-yê/).** 1) {syn: mînak} example: **-bo nimûne** (Bw) for example, for instance {syn: meselen; wek mînak}; 2) sample, specimen, model. {also: nimone (AD); [nemouné] نمونه (JJ)} Cf. P numūne نمونه --> T nümûne; Sor nimûne نِموونە [K/IFb/GF/ZF/RZ/SS/CS//JJ//AD]

nimz نِمز (F/Ba/B) = low. See **nizm**.

nimzayî نِمزایی (B) = lowness. See **nizmî**.

ning نِنگ = foot. See **ling**.

niqandin I نِقاندِن *vt.* **(-niqîn-).** to blink, twitch *(of eyes)*. {also: neqandin II (GF)} ?<leqandin = 'to cause to move'; cf. Sor nûqandin نووقاندِن = 'to close (only of eyes)' [Bw//GF] <çav; miçandin>

niqitîn نِقِتین (K/B) = to drip. See **nuqutîn**.

niqitk نِقِتك *f.* **(-a;-ê).** 1) {syn: çilk; çipik; dilop; p'eşk I} {also: niqut (A/IFb/TF)} drop *(of a liquid)*: •***Niqitkeke* xûna wî dîsa pekîya ort'a M. û Z.** (Z-1) *A drop of* his bood (again) fell between M. and Z.; 2) {syn: xal II[2]} {also: niqte (IFb/JB3/GF)} dot, point; point *(grammatical term)* (JJ) [nouqet]; point (in writing) (JJ) [nukát]. {also: [1] niqte (IFb/JB3/GF); [2] niqut (A/IFb/TF); niqutik (A-2); [nouqet/nukát] نقط (JJ); <nuquṯ> نقط (HH)} Cf. Ar nuqṭah نقطة = 'point, dot' [Z-1/F/K/B/XF//IFb/JB3//A//JJ//HH]

niqo bûn نِقۆ بوون (K/FS) = to dive, plunge (vi.). See **noq bûn** under **noq I**.

niqo kirin نِقۆ کِرِن (K/FS) = to sink, submerge (vt.). See **noq kirin** under **noq I**.

niqte نِقتە (IFb/JB3/GF) = dot, point. See **niqitk**.

niqut نِقوت (A/IFb/TF) = drop. See **niqitk**.

niqutik نِقوتِك (A) = drop; dot, point. See **niqitk**.

niqutîn نِقوتین (A/IFb/TF) = to drip. See **nuqutîn**.

nirx نِرخ (GF/JJ/ZF3/BF/Wkt) = price, value. See **nerx**.

nirxandin نِرخاندِن *vt.* **(-nirxîn-).** to evaluate, appraise; to appreciate: •**Her berhem *divê* li gor dem û rewşa ku tê de hatiye afirandin, *were nirxandin*** (Wlt 1:39, 11) Every work of art *should be evaluated* according to the time and conditions in which it was created. [(neol)Wlt/GF] <nerx>

nisar نِسار (IFb) = crag. See **zinar I**.

nişêw نِشێو (IFb) = downhill slope. See **nişîv**.

nişîv نِشیڤ *m.* **(-ê;).** 1) {syn: jordanî} downhill slope, incline, declivity: •**Evraz bê *nişûv* nînin** (IFb) Every uphill slope has a downhill slope [lit. 'there are no uphill slopes without *downhill slopes*'] *[prv.]*; 2) steep slope, precipice; cliff; 3) {syn: başûr; cenûb; jêr [3]} south (Bw); 4) *[adv.]* {also: nişîwî (SK)} down[ward(s)], downhill. {also: nişêw (IFb-2); nişûv (IFb-2/GF-2); [nichouw نشوف/nichiw نشيف] (JJ); <nişov> نشوف (HH)} Mid P nišēb = 'declivity, dejection' (M3); P nešīb نشيب = 'declivity, descent'; Sor nişêw نشێو = 'downward slope, declivity' [Bw/K(s)/IFb/JJ/GF/OK//HH//SK]

nişîwî نِشیوی (SK) = downhill. See **nişîv**[4].

nişka ve نِشکاڤە (JB3/GF) = suddenly. See **nişkêva**.

nişkêva نِـشـكـێـڤـا *adj.* suddenly, all of a sudden: **•Ditirsyam, ku pey çûyîna min r̄a *nişkêva* gur xwe bavêjne ser kerîyê pêz** (Ba2:2, 205) I was afraid that after I left [lit. 'my going'] the wolves would *suddenly* pounce on the flock of sheep **•Lê îro *ji nişka ve* wekî piştevanên demokratîkbûnê derdikevin holê** (AW70D2) But today they *suddenly* appear on the scene as supporters of democratization **•*Nişkêva* bîna k'ivava k'ete pozê wan** (Dz) *Suddenly* they smelled kebabs. {also: nişkêve (A); (ji) nişka ve (JB3/GF/OK); ji nişke ve (IFb); [ji-nichkiwé] ژنشكڤه (JJ); <nişkêve> نشكيڤه (HH)} < ji + nû = 'new' + -şk + ve/va [F/Dz/K/B//A/HH//JB3/GF/OK//IFb]

nişkêve نِشكێڤه (A/HH) = suddenly. See **nişkêva**.

nişov نِشۆڤ (HH) = downhill slope. See **nişîv**.

niştecih نِـشـتـەجِه *m.&f.* **(-ê/-a;).** inhabitant, resident: **•*niştecihên* gund** (ZF) *the residents of* the village **•*niştecihên* vî welatî** (Mîr Qasimlo. Dilya û Zalar, 182) *the inhabitants of* this country. {also: niştecî (FJ); nîştecih (BF/Wkt)} {syn: akincî; *rûniştvan} Sor nîştecê نیشتەجێ [M.Qasimlo/ZF//FJ//BF/Wkt] <binecî; binelî>

niştecî نِـشـتـەجـى (FJ) = resident, inhabitant. See **niştecih**.

niştel نِشتەل (FS) = lancet. See **niştir**.

nişter نِشتەر (OK/JJ/BF/FS) = lancet. See **niştir**.

niştêr نِشتێر (IFb) = spear; lancet. See **niştir**.

niştiman نِشتِمان (JB3/TF) = homeland. See **niştîman**.

niştir نِـشـتِـر *m./f.(K/B/FS)* **(; /-ê).** 1) {syn: nize, f. (F); r̄im} spear, pike, lance (K): **-kax̄ezê niştir** (F) spades *(suit in card games)*; 2) lancet, scalpel: **•Noşdarî kulka binkefşê wî bi *niştere* kelaşt û derkir** (FS) The doctor lanced the boil in his armpit with *a lancet* and removed it; 3) harpoon (A). {also: neşter (IFb/GF/TF/FS-2); niştel (FS-2); nişter (OK/BF/FS); niştêr (IFb-2); [nichter] نشتر (JJ); <neştel> نشتل (HH)} Cf. Skt √nikṣ-: nikṣati = 'to pierce' & nékṣaṇa- = 'sharp stick, spear'; Pashto nēš̌ = 'the sting of any venomous animal, puncture, lancet'; P nīštar نیشتر (Horn #1067) --> T neşter; Sor neşter نـەشـتـەر = 'surgeon's knife, lancet' [F/K/A/B//IFb/GF/TF//JJ/OK/BF/FS//HH] <tîr; zerg>

niştîman نِـشـتـيـمـان *f./m.(BF/ZF3/Wkt)* **(-a/-ê;).** homeland, one's native country: **•*Nîştimanê* me Kurdistane** (BF) Our homeland is Kurdistan. {also: niştiman (JB3/TF); nîştiman (A/ZF3/BF); nîştman (K)} {syn: welat} [K//A/ZF3/BF//JB3/TF//IFb/Haz] <r̄ûniştin>

niştman نِشتمان (JB3) = homeland. See **niştîman**.

nişûk نِـشـووك *f.* **(-a;-ê).** snuff: **•Dev ji çixarê yan jî *nişûkê* ... berde** (alkoholhjalpen.se) Leave off cigarettes or *snuff*. {syn: birmût} [Qzl/A/IFb/FJ/ZF/RZ/Wkt]

nişûv نِشووڤ (IFb/GF) = downhill slope. See **nişîv**.

nitirandin I نِـتِـرانـدِن *vt.* **(-nitirîn-).** 1) {syn: ç'êla ft-î kirin [see ç'êl III]; kat kirin [see kat I]} to describe, depict, portray, represent: **•Li vî şovîda qewimandin û reng û rûyê qeremanêd dastanê bi yeko-yeko, qeşeng û rind *hatine nitirandin*** (K-dş) In this version, the happenings and qualities of the characters of the story *were depicted* beautifully one by one; 2) {syn: xemilandin} to adorn, decorate, embellish; to cover with drawings or paintings. [K-dş/K/GF/ZF3/FS]

nitirandin II نِـتِـرانـدِن *vt.* **(-nitirîn-).** to cause to guard, watch over; **-xwe lê nitirandin** (ZF3/FS) to ambush, lie in wait for {syn: bose danan/vedan}: **•Nêçîrvan di kozikan de *xwe li* nêçîran *dinitirînin*** (ZF3) The hunters *lie in wait for* their quarry in the trenches **•Rojek ji rojan, pisîkê *xwe li* şîrê pîrê *nitirand*** (FS: Mîr Zoro. Boz) One day, the cat *lay in wait for* the old lady's milk **•Rovîyê *xwe li* mirîşkê *nitirand*** (glosbe.com) The fox *ambushed* the chicken. < Ar √n-ṭ-r نـطـر = 'to watch, guard' [glosbe/FS/ZF3]

nivan نِڤان *f.* **().** shelter, refuge: **•Ewrê sorê spêdeyan, gazî dikite karwanîyan, xwe bidene *nihanîyan*** (BF) A red cloud in the morning calls on caravans to head for *shelter* [*weather superstition*] **•Mirov pezê xwe dibe ber *nivanekê*** (Wkt) The man leads his sheep to *a shelter*. {also: nihan, m. (Dh); nihanî I (Zeb/BF); <nihanî نـهـانـى/nivanî نـڤـانـى> (Hej)} {syn: sit'ar} [Dh//Zeb/Hej/BF//IFb/GF/OK/Wkt]

nivandin نِـڤـانـدِن *vt.* **(-nivîn-).** 1) {syn: r̄azandin} to cause to sleep, put to bed; to anesthetize, put to sleep *(by means of narcotics)* (K/OK); to cause to lie down; 2) to put into the hospital (Bw). {also: [nevandin] نـڤـانـدين (JJ)} Mid P nibāstan (*nibāy-) = 'to lay down' (M3); Sor nuwandin نـــووانـدِن (-nuwên-) = 'to put to sleep' [Bw/K/IFb/JB1-A&S/GF/TF/OK//JJ] <nivistin; xew>

nivêj نِـڤـێـژ (M-Zx/JB1-A/GF) = namaz, salah, Islamic prayer ritual. See **nimêj**.

nivêsîn نِـڤـێـسـيـن (-nivês-) (Bw/Dh) = to write. See **nivîsîn**.

nivink نِڤِنك (JB1-A) = bed[ding]. See **nivîn**.

nivisandin نِـڤِـسـانـدِن (BK) = to write; to dictate. See **nivîsandin**.

nivistin نِـڤِـسـتِـن *vi.* (**-niv**-[M/Bw/JB1-A&S]/**-nivis**-[HH]). to sleep; to go to bed (IFb/JJ); to lie down (JJ): **•Te bo çî xew li xelkî ḧeram kirîye? Nîwşewê dest bi qîjeqîjê dikey, nahêlî xelk *biniwît*** (SK 4:50) Why have you made sleep impossible for people? You start crowing in the middle of the night and do not let people *sleep*. {also: niwistin (-niw-) (SK); [nywistin] نـڤـسـتـيـن (JJ); <nivistin نـڤـسـتـن (dinivise) (دنـڤـسـه)> (HH)} {syn: r̄ak'etin; r̄azan} O Ir *ni- (Tsb 72) + pad- (Tsb 38): Sor nwîstin نـویـسـتِـن (-no-: *3rd p. sing.* -nwa-)/nustin نوستِن (-nu-) (W&E)/nûstin نووستِن (-nû-) (M-Sor/Muk); **pad**-: [Pok. 2. pĕd-/pŏd- *m.* 790.] 'foot' --> [pédi̯o- 2.verbal]: Skt pádyate = 'goes, falls'; Av pai∂yeiti = 'moves downward, lies down'; Mid P nibastan (nibay-) = 'lie down, sleep' (M3); cf. also Rus past' пасть (padu) (паду) = 'to fall' [K/JB3/IFb/JJ/HH/JB1-A&S/M/Bw//SK] <nivandin; nivîn; xew; xilmaş>

nivişk نِڤِشك (GF) = butter. See **nivîşk**.

nivişt نِـڤِـشـت *f.* (**-a;-ê**). amulet, charm, talisman: "The most ordinary type of healing power is believed to be contained in the muskas (amulets) written by a mela (religious priest, imam in Turkish). ... The muska (nivişt in Kurdish) is written for simple complaints from headaches to more serious illnesses like psychological disorders, but in this latter case muska could be written or prepared only by powerful, respected shaikhs and other religious personnel." [from: Lale Yalçın-Heckmann. *Tribe and Kinship among the Kurds* (Frankfurt a.M. et al. : Peter Lang, 1991), p. 86]: **•Ku girêdan be, ne *nivişta* melê bi kêr tê, ne jî şêx dikare tiştekî bike** (DBgb, 15) When tying knots is involved, neither a mullah's *amulet* with do any good, nor can a shaykh do anything. {also: nivişti (Bw); niwîştî (SK); <nivişt> نـڤـشـت (HH)} {syn: t'ilism; t'iberk} Cf. P neveštan نـوشـتـن = 'to write'. See H. H. Hansen. *The Kurdish Woman's Life* (Copenhagen : Ethnografiske Kaekke, 1961) for pictures of Kurdish nivişts. Also, see 2 short stories by M. E. Bozarslan in **Meyro** (MB): "Ji me çêtira," pp. 21-24; and "Tabirr" pp. 42-48. See also B. Nikitine. *Les Kurdes, Étude sociologique et historique* (Paris : Imprimerie Nationale, 1956), pp. 244-47 and M. Beyazidî. *Adat û risûlnameyê Ekradiye*, ed. & tr. M. B. Rudenko (Moscow, 1963), pp. 27-28, who mention visits to shaikhs or ziyarets for treatment of illnesses; the latter also describes the occasions for writing nivişt. [Haz/K/A/IFb/B/HH/GF/TF//Bw//SK] <berbejn; t'iberk>

nivişti نِڤِشتی (Bw) = amulet. See **nivişt**.

nivîn نِـڤـيـن *f.(K/B/JJ)/m.(Z-1/B/Wn/KS)/pl.(B)* (**-a/ -ê;-ê/**). bed (B [m./pl.]); bedding (B [f.]): **•Dostê wî jî gelek qedrê wî digirt: her tuxme te'amê xoş ba, bi-lezet ba, ew bo wî dirust dikir ... bo niwistinê jî *niwînêt* çak bo wî dir̄aêxistin: liḧêf, doşek, balge, herçî çak ban ew bo wî dîinan** (SK 31:274) His friend would treat him with great respect. He would prepare for him every kind of good and tasty food ... He would spread fine *bedding* for him also, to sleep on: quilts, mattresses, cushions, whatever fine things there were he would bring for him **•Zînê k'ete nav *nivînê* xwe** (Z-1) Zin lay down on her *bed*. {also: livîn II (Msr); nivink (JB1-A); niwîn (SK); [niwin] نڤين (JJ); <nivîn> نڤين (HH)} {syn: cî [2]; text} *for etymology see* ***nivistin***. [Z-1/K/A/JB3/IFb/B/JJ/HH/GF/Wn//JB1-A//SK//Msr] <nivistin; xew>

nivîs نِـڤـيـس *f.* (**-a;-ê**). piece of writing, article: **•Di vê *nivîsê* de emê qala îdiayên li ser eslê Ebû Suûd Efendî bikin** (Nbh 125:17) In this *article* we will discuss assertions about the origins of Abu Su'ûd Efendi. {syn: bend I[2]; gotar [2]; nivîsar} = Sor nûsraw نـووسـراو = 'article, written composition, report' [Nbh/A/IFb/FJ/GF/Kmc/RZ/ZF/CS] <nivîsar>

nivîsandin نِڤيساندِن *vt.* (**-nivîsîn-**). 1) {syn: nivîsîn} to write: **-mekîna nivîsandinê** (IFb) typewriter; 2) to cause to write, to dictate (BK). {also: nivisandin (BK); [nevisandin] نـويـسـانـديـن (JJ); <nivîsandin نڤيساندن (dinivîse) (دنڤيسه)> (HH)} Cf. P neveštan نـوشـتـن (-nevīs-) (نـويـس); Sor nûsîn نـووسـيـن; Za nûsenã (Dersim)/nûşenã (Srk) [nûştiş] (Todd/Srk) [K/A/JB3/IFb/B/HH/GF//BK//JJ] See also **nivîsîn**.

nivîsar نِـڤـيـسـار *f.* (**-a;-ê**). 1) {syn: nivîs} writing, something written; article, piece of writing; 2) {syn: afirandin; berhem} (literary) work, opus: **•Bi kêfxweşî û xweşḧalî bi *nivîsara* Eḧmedê Xanî dixûnin** (K-dş) They happily read from *the work of* Ahmed-i Khani. {also: [nyvisar] نـويـسـار (JJ)} Cf. Sor nûsyar نـووسـيـار = 'writing, thing(s) written' [K-dş/K/IFb/B/JJ/GF] <nivîsîn; nivîsk; nivîsk'ar>

nivîsarçî نِڤيسارچی (B) = writer. See **nivîsk'ar**.

nivîsark'ar نِڤیسارکار (B) = writer. See **nivîsk'ar**.

nivîsarxane نِڤیسارخانه (K) = office. See **nivîsxane**.

nivîser نِڤیسەر (A) = writer. See **nivîsk'ar**.

nivîsevan نِڤیسەڤان (K/GF) = writer. See **nivîsk'ar**.

nivîsgeh نِڤیسگەه (GF/IFb) = office. See **nivîsxane**.

nivîsîn نـڤـیـسـیـن *vt.* **(-nivîs-)**. to write. {also: nivêsîn (-nivês-) (Bw/Dh); niwîsîn (SK); [nyvisin] نویسین (JJ); <nivîsandin نـڤـیـسـانـدن (dinivîse) (دنـڤـیـسـه)> (HH)} O Ir *ni- (Tsb 72) + *pais- (Tsb 40): OP ni-pištam = 'written down'; Mid P nibištan (nibēs-) (M3); P neveštan نـوشـتـن (-nevīs-) (نـویـس); Sor nûsîn نـووسـیـن; Za nûsenã (Dersim)/nûşenã (Srk) [nûştiş] (Todd/Srk); Hau niwîstey (niwîs-) *vt.* (M4);***pais-**: [Pok. 1. peig-/peik- 794.] 'to cut, mark (by incision)': Skt piśáti = 'cuts, adorns'; OP paiθ- = 'to cut, engrave, adorn'; Av paēs- = 'to dye, adorn'; cf. also Lat pingo, -ere, pinxi, pictum = 'to paint, draw, color, decorate'; Rus pisat' писать (pišu) (пишу) = 'to write' [K/IFb/JJ//HH//Bw/Dh//SK] See also **nivîsandin**.

nivîsk نـڤـیـسـک *f.* **(-a;-ê).** 1) inscription: •**Aliyek yê *nivîskê* bi zimanê ûrartû û aliyê din jî bi zimanê asûrî bû** (nefel.com 8.ix.2010) One side of *the inscription* was in the Urartian language and the other side was in Assyrian; 2) book; pamphlet, brochure. {syn: k'itêb; p'irtûk} [JB3/IFb/ZF3/Wkt]

nivîsk'ar نـڤـیـسـکـار *m.* **(-ê; nivîskêr)**. writer, author: •**Hinek *nivîskar* diyar dikin ku MHP xwe ji nû ve saz dike û ber bi demokratîkbûnê ve diçe** (AW69A1) Some *writers* declare that the MHP [Nationalist People's Party] is re-making itself and becoming more democratic. {also: nivîsarçî (B-2); nivîsark'ar (B-2); nivîser (A-2); nivîsevan (K/GF-2)} Cf. P nevīsande نویسنده; Sor nûser نووسەر [Ber/BX/JB3/B/IFb/GF//K//A] <çîroknivîs; nivîsandin; nivîsîn; romannivîs>

nivîskî نـڤـیـسـکـی *adj.* written, in writing: •**ezmûna *nivîskî*** (ZF) *written* exam •**Rexnê an jî pesinandina vê berhemê, divê wekî berhemeke edebiyata *nivîskî* were kirin** (Ş. Cizîrî. Edebiyata Devkî û Sosyalîzasyon, 166) Criticism or praise of this work must be done as a work of *written* literature; **-bi nivîskî** (ZF) in writing. < nivîsîn [Ş.Cizîrî/IFb/FJ/GF/RZ/Kmc/ZF/SS/CS] <devkî>

nivîsxan نِڤیسخان (K) = office. See **nivîsxane**.

nivîsxan•e نِڤیسـخـانـه *f.* **(•a;•ê).** office, bureau: •**Rojekê gazî min kir, bire *nivîsxana* xwe** (K2-Fêrîk) One day he called me, and took me to his *office*. {also: nivîsarxane (K); nivîsgeh (GF/IFb-2); nivîsxan (K-2)} <nivîs- = 'to write' + P xane = 'house' [K2-Fêrîk/F/IFb/B//K//GF]

nivîşk نـڤـیـشـک *m.* **(-ê;).** 1) {syn: r̄ûn I} butter: **-r̄ûnê nivîşk[î]** (K/B/F) fresh butter; 2) cream (Msr). {also: nivişk (GF); nîvişk (A/Msr); [niwik نـڤـک/ niwichk نڤشك] (JJ); <nîvişk> نیڤشك (HH)} [K/IFb/B//GF//A/HH/Msr]

nivîşkan I نِـڤـیـشـکـان *adj.* disabled, handicapped, crippled. [Slm/Rwn/Urm/QtrE/ZF3] <goc; nîvişkan; qop; şeht>

nivîşkan II نِـڤـیـشـکـان (FS/ZF3) = incomplete. See **nîvişkan**.

nivş نِڤش (FS) = generation; lineage. See **nifş**.

nivt نِڤت (B) = oil. See **neft**.

nivz نِڤز (GF) low. See **nizm**.

nivzînî نِڤزینی (EP-4) = saddle-trained. See **nîvzînî**.

niwazde نِوازده (JB1-S) = nineteen. See **nozdeh**.

niwêj نِوێژ (SK) = namaz, salah, Islamic prayer ritual.

niwistin نِوستِن (-niw-) (SK) = to sleep. See **nivistin**.

niwîn نِوین (SK) = bed[ding]. See **nivîn**.

niwîsîn نِویسین (SK) = to write. See **nivîsîn**.

niwîştî نِویشتی (SK) = amulet. See **niviştֹ**.

nixaftin نِخافتِن (Zeb/JJ/GF) = to cover. See **nixamtin**.

nixamtin نِـخـامـتِـن *vt.* **(-nixêm-)**. to cover: •**Wexta mij û dûmanê 'erd *dinixamt*** (Ba2:1, 203) When fog and mist *covered* the earth. {also: nixaftin (Zeb/GF-2); nixumandin (IFb-2); nuxumandin (-nuxumîn-) (A/JB3/IFb/TF/OK-2); [nykhaftin] نخافتین (JJ); <nuxumandin نخماندن (dinuxumîne) (دنخمینه)> (HH)} {syn: pêçavtin; werkirin} Mid P nihuftan (nihumb-) = 'to cover hide, conceal, clothe' (M3); Za nimitiş (nimnenã) = 'to hide, cover' [JB2/K/B/GF/OK//A/JB3/IFb/ HH/TF//JJ/Zeb]

nixan نِـخـان *vi.* **(-nix-).** to kneel (of camels): •**Ḧêştir *nixa*** (FS) The camel knelt. {also: nîxan (TF)} {syn: xiya bûn} Cf. Ar nayyax II نيّخ [FS//TF]

nixandin نِـخـانـدِن *vt.* **(-nixîn-).** to cause (a camel) to kneel: •**Wî ḧêştir *nixand*** (FS) He made the camel kneel. {also: nîxandin (TF)} {syn: tixandin; xiya kirin} Cf. Ar nayyax II نيّخ [FS/BF//TF]

nixrî نِخری (GF/IFb/HH) = first-born. See **nuxurî**.

nixumandin نِخوماندِن (IFb) = to cover. See **nixamtin**.

nixurî نِخوری (IFb) = first-born. See **nuxurî**.

niyan نِیان (ZF3) = to copulate. See **nayîn**.

niyandin نِیاندِن (IFb) = to copulate. See **nayîn**.

niyas نِیاس (Bw) = acquainted, familiar. See **nas**.

niyasîn نِیاسین (JB1-A) = to know. See **nasîn**.

niyet نیەت (IFb) = aim, purpose. See **nêt**.

niyetxerab نـیـەت خـەراب (ZF) = ill-intentioned. See **niyetxirab**.

niyetxirab نِـیـەت خِـراب *adj.* ill-intentioned, evil, wicked: **•Çi nezanên vê meseleyê, çi jî ewên *niyetxirab* eger li 150 salên Kurdan yên dawîn binêrin, wê bibînin ku ev nêrîna çiqas şaş e** (Nbh 134:3) If those ignorant of this issue, or those *with evil intentions*, look at the last 150 years of the Kurds, they will see how wrong this view is. {also: niyetxerab (ZF)} [Nbh/Wkt//ZF] <nêt>

niyîn نیین (IFb) = to copulate. See **nayîn**.

nizanî نِزانی (L) = ignorance; rudeness. See **nezanî**.

nizar I نِـزار *m.* **(-ê ; nizêr, vî nizarî).** shady side *(of mountain or valley)*; mountain that never sees sunlight: **•Dibêjin di nihalekêda řîwîyek hebû…car diçû beřojî, car diçû *nizarî*** (SK 2:9) They say there was a fox [living] in a ravine…sometimes he would go on the sunny side, sometimes on *the shady side* **•Ew çûn nav *nizêr* û li rex newalekê rûniştin** (docshare.tips: Serhatiya jiyana Doktor Seîd) They went to *the shady side* and sat down beside a ravine. {also: zinar II (A-2/IFb/TF); <nizar> نـزار (HH)} {syn: dubur; zimank} {≠beřoj} Sor nisar نِـسار/ nisê نِـسێ = 'shady side of mountain, ubac'; Hau nisar *m.* = 'the shady side of a hill' (M4) [Zeb/Bw/A/HH/SK/Kmc-#7622//IFb/TF] <berberoşk; beřoj; qunt'ar>

nizar II نِزار (K[s]/JJ) = crag. See **zinar I**.

nize نِـزە *f.* (). 1) {syn: niştir; řim} spear, lance; 2) bayonet (IFb). {also: nîze (IFb/GF/Wkt)} Mid P nēzag = 'lance' (M3) [F/K/ZF3//IFb/GF/Wkt]

nizim نِزم (A) = low. See **nizm**.

nizîk نِزیك = near (to). See **nêzîk**.

nizm نِـزم *adj.* low: **-nizm bûn** = to sink, drop *(vi.)*, be lowered, come down: **•Îro banê odê *nimz bûye*** (Ba) Today the ceiling/roof of the room *has fallen*. {also: nifs (Şnx); nimz (F/Ba/B); nivz (GF-2); nizim (A); [nizm] نـزم (JJ); <nizm> نـزم (HH)} {≠bilind; ≠quloz} <*ni-zma- = 'on the ground', cf. Av upa-sma- = 'in the ground', *further* upairi-zəma = 'upon/above the earth', aδairi-zəma- < zam- = 'earth'; Sor nizm نِـزم {nimzayî; nizmahî; nizmayî; nizmetî; nizmî} [F/B/Ba//K/JB3/IFb/JJ/HH/GF//A//Şnx]

nizmahî نِزماهی (IFb/FS) = lowness. See **nizmî**.

nizmatî نِزماتی (GF/FS) = lowness. See **nizmî**.

nizmayî نِزمایی (K) = lowness. See **nizmî**.

nizmetî نِزمەتی (A) = lowness. See **nizmî**.

nizmî نِزمی *f.* **(-ya;-yê).** lowness, baseness: **•*nizmatîya* dîwarî** (FS) *the lowness of* the wall. {also: nimzayî (B); nizmahî (IFb/FS-2); nizmatî (GF-2/FS); nizmayî (K/IFb-2); nizmetî (A); [nizmi] نزمی (JJ)} Sor nizmayî نِزمایی = 'depression, low ground' [K/IFb/JJ/GF//FS//B//A] <nizm>

nî نی (BF) = new. See **nû**.

nîhan نیهان (A) = to copulate. See **nayîn**.

nîhandin نیهاندِن (A) = to copulate. See **nayîn**.

nîjad نیژاد (ZF) = race. See **nijad**.

nîjadperest نـیـژادپـەرسـت (ZF) = racist. See **nijadp'erest**.

nîk نـیـك *m.(K)/f.(AB/JJ)* **(-ê/-a;).** 1) hook; point; hooked needle, crocheting needle (IFb): **•*Nîka* teşîya min jê derket** (AB) *The point* [or *hook*] of my distaff came out; 2) wooden stick used in raising and lowering millstone. {also: nêk, f. (IF-2); nihk (FS-2); [nik] نـك (JJ); <nêk [1]; nîk [2]> نیك (HH)} Sor nûk نووك = 'tip, point' [AB/K/A/IFb/HH/GF/ZF/FS//JJ] <çengel I; ç'iqil [2]; şewk>

nîkah نیکاه (IFb) = marriage. See **nikha**.

nîkil نـیـکِـل (IFb/OK/Bw) = beak, bill; point, tip. See **nikil**.

nînig نینِگ (IFb) = fingernail. See **neynûk**.

nînog نینۆگ (Epl) = fingernail. See **neynûk**.

nînok نینۆك (Erg) = fingernail. See **neynûk**.

nînûk نینووك (IFb) = fingernail. See **neynûk**.

nîqaş نـیـقـاش *f.* **(-a;-ê).** debate, argument: **•Em dixwazin gavên *nîqaşeke* destpêkê li ser edebiyata Kurmanciyê bavêjin** (Dqg, 154) We want to take the initial steps towards *a debate on* Kurmanji literature; **-nîqaş kirin** (ZF) to debate, argue (a topic). {syn: gengeşe; micadele; mişt û miř} < Ar niqāš نـقـاش < nāqaša III نـاقـش = 'to debate' [Dqg/ZF/Wkt]

nîr I نیر *m.* **(-ê;).** 1) {also: nîre II (OK)} yoke *(of oxen pulling plough)*: **•Kuř řabû cotê xwe û *nîrê* xwe derxist** (J) The boy got up and took out his plough and his *yoke*; **-gayê nîr** (IFb) plow-pulling ox; **-nîr û halet** (Haz) yoke and plow/plough; 2) {syn: hoker (neol.); řengpîşe (neol.); zerf (F)} *adverb (IFb/OK). {also: nîre II (OK); [nir] نـيـر (JJ); <nîr> نـیـر (HH)} Cf. Ar nīr نـیـر = 'yoke'; Syr nīrā ܢܝܪܐ = 'yoke; beam of a loom' [J/F/K/A/IFb/B/JJ/HH/GF/TF/Haz//OK] <halet; mijane; sermijank; xenîke>

nîr II نـیـر *m.* **(-ê;).** time, period, season: **•Mi her çar *nîrê* salê dî** (Z-885) I have seen all four *seasons* of the year. [Z-885/IFb/Hej/ZF3] <demsal; serdem; werz[2]>

nîr•e I نـيـره *m.* **(•ê;).** thin wooden beam[s] *(in ceiling of traditional Kurdish house, as opposed to **garîte**, thick wooden beams (Bw))*; rafter[s] [Germ. Dachsparren] (OK): **•Ev *nîre* yê kurt e** (Bw) This *beam* is short **•Wî xaniyê xwe *nîre kir*** (FS) He *fitted* his house *with thin wooden beams*. Cf. Syr nīrā ܢܝܪܐ = 'yoke; beam of a weaver's loom, weft'; Sor nîrge نـيـرگـه = 'roof-tree, main beam of roof' [Bw/OK/FS] <garîte; k'êran>

nîre II نيره (OK) = yoke. See **nîr I**[1]

nîrî نـيرى (Bw/Dh) = third of a dozen, unit of four. See **nûrî**.

nîro نيرۆ (JB3) = noon; south. See **nîvro**.

Nîsan نـيـسان *f.* **(-a;-ê).** April: **•[Tavîya *Nîsanê*, hêjaya malê Xuristanê]** (BG) An *April* cloudburst is worth all the riches of the universe *[proverbial saying]*. {also: [nisan] نـيـسـان (JJ); <nîsan> نـيـسـان (HH); [niçâne] (BG)} Syr nīsan ܢܝܣܢ [Heb nisan ניסן] --> Ar nīsān نيسان; *corresponds to last part of* Newroz[mang] [نەورۆز[مانگ]/Xakelêwe خاکەلێوە (P farvardīn فروردين) [Aries] *& 1st part of* Gułan گولان/Banemeř بانەمەڕ (P ordī behešt اردى بهشت) [Taurus] [K/A/JB3/IFb/B/JJ/HH/GF/ OK//BG]

nîsk نـيـسـك *f.* **(-a;-ê).** lentil(s), bot. *Lens culinaris*: **•baqê *nîskane*** (Dz) a handful *of lentils* **•Jinekê legeneka *nîskê* digel sê çar naneka birin, li ber danan** (M-Ak 278, #613) The woman took a basin *of lentils* with 3 or 4 pieces of bread and placed them before him; **-nîska kesk** (CB) green lentils; **-nîska sor** (CB) yellow lentils. {also: nîzk (JB3/OK-2); [nisk] نسك (JJ); <nîsk> نيسك (HH)} Cf. P nask نسك /nazag نزگ/narask نرسك; Sor nîsk نـيـسـك [Dz/K/A/IFb/B/HH/SK/GF/TF/OK/AA/CB//JB3//JJ] <mişewiş>

nîsyan نيسيان (AZ) = to stick to *(vi.)*. See **nûsyan**.

nîşa نـيـشـا: -nîşa dan (Bw) = to show; to teach. See **nîşan dan** under: **nîşan**.

nîşan نـيـشـان *f.* **(-a;-ê).** 1) sign, symbol; mark: **-nîşan dan/nîşa dan** (Bw/Dh)/**nîşê dan** (Bar)/**şanî dan** (L/EŞ)/**nîşan kirin**: a) to show {syn: rayî yekî dan}: **•Eva jî kirasê wîye, me anîye *nîşanî tedin*** (Ba) And this is his shirt, we brought it *to show you* **•Ez *dê nîşa te dem*** (Bw) I *will show it to you*; b) to teach, instruct: **•Diya me jî bi me ra hat da ku pincaran *şanî me bide* (Spink, tirşo, mendik, pêkesk H.D.)** (EŞ, 8) Our mother came with us too, *to teach us about* edible plants [pincar] (meadow salsify, sorrel, mendik, pêkesk, etc.) **•Hûn zimanê Kurdî *nîşa* zarokêt xwe *diden*?** (Dh) *Do* you *teach* your children Kurdish?; **-nîşan kirin** (ZF3) to signal: **•Dûrva *nîşan kire*** (J) He *signalled* from afar; **-t'ilîya nîşanê** (F/B)/~**nîşandekê** (IF)/~**nîşankirinê** (K) index finger, pointer {syn: tilîya şadê (Msr)}; 2) medallion; 3) {also: nîşanî} engagement ceremony (JJ): **-nîşana *fk-ê* danîn** (Z-2) to betroth, engage: **•A vêga *nîşana* wê *dayne*** (Z-2) Then *betroth* her; 4) aim *(in shooting)* (Bw): **-nîşan girtin** (K/IFb/FJ/GF) to take aim (at): **•Li ber singa xwe tijî kevir kiribû, yek yek *nîşan girt* avêtin qula ber** (DBgb, 16) He had filled his lap with stones, he *took aim* and threw the stones into the hole of the rock; 5) birthmark (Bw). {also: nîşa (Bw/Dh); nîşê (Bar); şanî (L/EŞ); [nichan نـشـان/nichi نـشى] (JJ); <nîşan> نـيـشـان (HH)} Mid P nīšān = 'sign, mark, banner' (M3); P nīšān نيشان --> T nişan; Sor nîşan نـيشان = 'sign, target, medal worn as honour' & pîşan [=pê nîşan] dan پيشان دان = 'to show' See **nišān** in: I. Gershevitch. "Iranian Words Containing -ān-," C. E. Bosworth (ed.). *Iran and Islam: In Memory of the Late Vladimir Minorsky* (Edinburgh, 1971), pp.272-79; reprinted in his *Philologia Iranica*, ed. N. Sims-Williams (Wiesbaden : Dr. Ludwig Reichert Verlag, 1985), pp. 242-49. [F/K/A/JB3/IFb/B/JJ/HH/SK/JB1-A&S/GF/TF/OK/ /Bw//Bar//L/EŞ] <deq; xal II>

nîşanî نيشانى = engagement ceremony. See **nîşan** [3].

nîşev نيشەڤ (EP-7) = midnight. See **nîv** [1]: nîvê şevê.

nîşê dan نـيـشـێ دان (Bar) = to show; to teach. See **nîşan dan** under: **nîşan**.

nîştecih نـيشتەجە (BF/Wkt) = resident, inhabitant. See **niştecih**.

nîştiman نـيـشـتِـمـان (A/ZF3/BF) = homeland. See **niştîman**.

nîştman نيشتمان (K) = homeland. See **niştîman**.

nîv نـيـڤ *m.* **(-ê;).** 1) half: **•Heyanî *nîv saetê* îşê wan heye** (L) They have up to (=no more than) *a half hour*'s work; **-nîvê şevê/nîveka şevê** (Bşk) = midnight {also: nîşev (EP-7)}; 2) {syn: naveřast; nîvî} center, middle: **•Ûsufşa k'ete *nîvê* avê da** (HR 3:191) U. fell into *the middle of* the river; 3) *[prep.]* among, amid[st]: **-di nîv[a] ... da** = do. {also: nav II & III}: **•[di nîv[a] Ekradan]** (JR) among the Kurds. {also: nîw (SK); [niw] نيڤ (JJ);

<nîv> نـيـڤ (HH)} Cf. Skt nēma- = 'half'; Av naēma- = 'half' (*in* naēmē asni); Mid P nēm = 'half' & nēmag = 'half, side, direction' (M3); P nīm نيم (Horn #1069 & Hübsch); Sor nîw نیو; Za nîm (Mal); Hau nîm *m.* (M4) [F/K/A/JB3/IFb/B/JJ/HH/JB1-A&S/GF/ZF//SK] <nav II; navend; navîn> See also **nîvî**.

nîvan نيڤان (Mzg) = guest. See **mêvan**.

nîvco نیڤجۆ *adj.* incomplete, unfinished: •**De bila vê carê jî wekî her carî nivîsa min *nîvco* bimîne** (LC, 13) Let my writing remain *unfinished* this time too, like every other time •**Do êvarê jî min dest bi nivîsandina jiyana Qedrî Can kir. Nêta min heye ez li ser jiyan û berhemên wî kitêbekê derxim. Lê min ew jî *nîvco* hîşt** (LC, 11) Last night I started writing Qedrî Can's biography. I intend to bring out a book on his life and work. But I left that *unfinished* too •**Lê heta ku rêza pêşîn dinivîsim, malmîrata şerîta fîlmê ya di nav mêjîyê min de zû diçe. Îcar ez pê re nagihîjim, loma weha *nîvco-qurço* derdikeve** (LC, 14) But by the time I write down the first line, the darn movie in my mind goes by [too] quickly. I don't make it in time, and that's why it comes out *all incomplete*. {also: nîvçe (IFb/B)} {syn: *nîvero; nîvişkan} [LC/GF/FJ/FS//IFb/B]

nîvderzin نیڤدەرزن *f.* **().** half-dozen, six. [Bw] <derzin; şeş>

nîvgirav نیڤگراڤ *f.* **(-a;-ê).** peninsula [Ar شبه جزيرة šibh jazīrah; T yarımada]: •**Li *nîvgirava* Sînayê 16 mîlîtan hatin kuştinê** (rojname.com 11.ii.2018) In the Sinai *Peninsula* 16 militants were killed •***Nîvgirava* Erebistanê ... mezintirîn *nîvgirava* cîhanê ye. Li rojhelata *nîvgiravê* Kendava Farisî û Kendava Omanê heye** (Wikiwand) The Arabian *Peninsula* ... is *the* largest *peninsula* in the world. To the east of *the peninsula* there are the Persian Gulf and the Gulf of Oman. {*other proposed terms*: nîvada (K)/nîvade (B); nîvdûrge[h]} = Sor nîmçedorge نیمچەدورگە & kerke کەرکە [K(s)/TF/ZF3/Wkt/Wkp/SS/CS]

nîvişk نیڤِشك (A/HH/Msr) = butter. See **nivîşk**.

nîvişkan نیڤِشکان *adj.* incomplete, unfinished: •**Bê navê te pertûk û nivîsîn *nivîşkan* in** (FS) Without your name the book and writing are *incomplete* •**Wî name *nivîşkan* hêla** (FS) He left the letter *unfinished*. {also: nivîşkan II (FS/ZF3); [niwichkan] نيفشكان (JJ)} {syn: nîvco} [Hk/JJ//FS/ZF3] <nivîşkan>

nîvî نیڤی *f.(K)/m.(B)* **().** 1) {syn: naveřast; nîv[2]} center, middle: **-tilîya nêvî** (Msr) middle finger {also: tilîya navê (K)/~navîn (IF)} {syn: t'ilîya ort'ê (F/K/B)}; 2) half *(of a whole)*. {also: nêvî (Msr/A/IF-2); [niwi] نیڤی (JJ); <nî[v]î> نیڤی (HH)} [K/IF/B/JJ/HH//Msr/A] <nav II; navik; navend; navîn> See also **nîv**.

nîv'în نیڤعین *f.* **().** unripe, green almond [T çağla]. {also: bin'în (Twn)} {syn: behîvteř; çil'în (Haz); gêrih (Frq)} [Mtk//Twn] <behîv>

nîvmalik نیڤمالك *f.* **(-a;-ê).** hemistich, half a poetic line [malik]: •**Ji misrayê re bi Kurdî peyvên wek "*nîvmalik*", yan jî "riste" ... tên bikaranîn** (Adak, 366) In Kurdish for hemistich [Ar miṣrā' مصراع] words such as "*nîvmalik*" or "riste" ... are used •**Li toreya Kurdî da ji beytê ra malik tê gotinê û ji misra'ê ra *nîvmalik* hatiye gotinê** (Chn, 55) In Kurdish literature a verse [Ar bayt بيت] is called a malik and a hemistich [Ar miṣrā'] has been called *a nîvmalik*. [Adak/Chn] <malik; řêzik>

nîvro نیڤرۆ *m./f.(B/FS)* **(/-ya; /-[y]ê).** 1) {syn: de'n [1]} noon: •**Heyanî *hukmê nîvro* rûniştin** = They sat until noon •**Řo hatibû *nîvroj*** (FK-eb-1) The noon hour came [lit. 'the day came to *noon*']; **-piştî nîvro** (BX) (in the) afternoon; 2) {syn: başûr} south [cf. It pomeriggio]. {also: nîro (JB3); nîvřoj (FK-eb-1/JB1-S/TF/OK-2); nîwřo (SK); [niw-rouj] نيف روژ (JJ); <nîvro> نیڤرو (HH)} Mid P nēm-rōz = 'midday, south' (M3); Sor nîweřo نیوەڕۆ; Hau nîmeřo *m.* (M4) [L/K/A/IFb/B/HH/GF/FS//JB3//JJ/JB1-S/TF/FK-eb-1//SK] <řoj>

nîvřoj نیڤڕۆژ (FK-eb-1/JB1-S/TF/OK) = noon. See **nîvro**.

nîvsaet نیڤساعەت *f.* **(-a;ê).** half hour, thirty minutes: •**Piştî *nîvsaeta* din divê ez herim** (KS, 52) In another *half hour* I must go. {also: nîvsehet (K); nîw sa'et (SK)} [KS//K//SK]

nîvsehet نیڤسەهەت (K) = half hour. See **nîvsaet**.

nîvzînî نیڤزینی *adj.* being trained to wear a saddle, being 'broken in' *(of horses)*: •**Hespa *nîvzînî*** (K) Horse *being trained to wear a saddle* •**Sîabendê Silîvî ce'nûke *nivzînî* sîyare** (EP-4, #30) Siyabend the Silivi is out riding a *newly saddled* colt. {also: nivzînî (EP-4)} [EP-4//K/Wkt] <zîn I>

nîwřo نیوڕۆ (SK) = noon. See **nîvro**.

nîw sa'et نیو ساعەت (SK) = half hour. See **nîvsaet**.

nîxan نيخان (TF) = to kneel (of camels). See **nixan**.

nîxandin نیخاندِن (TF) = to cause to kneel (of camels). See **nixandin**.

nîyan نییان (Haz/Msr) = to copulate. See **nayîn**.

nîyet نییەت (KS/SK) = aim, purpose. See **nêt**.

nîze نـیـزە (IFb/GF/Wkt) = spear, lance; bayonet. See **nize**.

nîzing نیزِنگ (H2) = near. See **nêzîk**.

nîzk نیزك (JB3/OK) = lentil. See **nîsk**.

nmêj نـمـێـژ = namaz, salah, Islamic prayer ritual. See **nimêj**.

no نـــۆ *adj.* 1) sharp, hot (peppers): **-filfila *no*** (FS)/ **îsota *no*** (ZF3) *hot* pepper; 2) severe: **•Îsal wê zivistan *no* derbas be** (Wkt: S.Bulut: Bihuşta lal, 46) This year the winter will be [lit. 'pass'] *severe*. {also: [no] نـو (JJ)} {syn: tûj} [Rwn/Qmş/A/IFb/JJ/GF/FJ/ZF3/FS/Wkt]

noba نۆبا = a turn; patrol. See **nobet**.

nobe نۆبە (GF/SK) = a turn; patrol. See **nobet**.

nobedar نـــۆبـــەدار (B/JJ/GF/ZF3) = person on duty; guard. See **nobetdar**.

nobedçî نـۆبـەدچـی (Z-3) = person on duty; guard. See **nobetdar**.

nobet نـــۆبـــەت *f.* **(-a;-ê).** 1) {syn: dor; ger̄ II[3]; sirê}(one's) turn *(in line)*; 2) patrol, watch, guard duty: **•*Nobeta* we kişand** (L) He took your (pl.) *turn* [at standing guard]: **-nobe girtin** (SK) to keep watch. {also: noba; nobe (GF-2/SK-2); [nouba/noube] نـوبـە (JJ); <newbet> نـوبـت (HH)} < Ar nawbah نوبة --> T nöbet [L/K/IFb/B/SK/GF//JJ/HH]

nobetçî نـــۆبـــەتـــچـــی = person on duty; guard. See **nobetdar**.

nobetdar نۆبەتدار *m.* **(-ê;).** 1) person on duty; orderly; 2) guard, sentinel, sentry, watchman: **•Ew *nobedarê* bîstanî ye** (FS) He is the garden *watchman*. {also: nobedar (B/GF/ZF3); nobedçî (Z-3); nobetçî; [nōbeči نـــوبـــەچـــی/nobe-dar/nobadar نوبەدار] (JJ)} [Z-3/IFb//K//B/JJ/GF/ZF3] <nobet>

nod نۆد (K/B/IFb/HH) = ninety. See **not**.

nodemîn نۆدەمین (IFb) = ninetieth. See **notem**.

nogen نۆگەن (GF) = heifer. See **nogin**.

nogin نـــۆگِـــن *f.* **(-a;-ê).** 1) heifer; two-year-old cow (Bşk/Wn); three-year-old cow (IFb/HH/OK); young cow which has not yet calved (Bw): **•Li navçeya Sariqamişê kesên ku *nogina* şeşpê dibînin ecêbmayî dimînin** (tigrishaber.com 12.viii.2014) In the Sarıkamış district, people who see a six-footed *heifer* are amazed; 2) girl (slang) (Kş). {also: nagon (Msr/Wkt); nehêngol (Bw); nehgon (GF-2); nêngonk (Bşk); nogen (GF); nogon (A); nogun (Wn); nugul (Kş); nugun (Mzg); nuhgon (GF-2); nûgin (FS); nûgon (FS-2); <n[o]gin> نـــوگـــن (HH)} Sor nwêngîn [nöngîn] نوێنگین = 'yearling heifer' [K/IFb/B/HH/OK//FS//GF//Bşk/ /A//Msr/Wkt//Wn//Bw] <ç'êlek; ga; golik; parone>

*nogon نۆگۆن (A) = heifer. See **nogin**.

nogun نۆگون (Wn) = heifer. See **nogin**.

nohlîk نۆهلیك (SS) = mattress. See **nehlîk**.

nojdar نـــۆژدار *m.&f.* **(;/-î).** 1) {syn: bijîşk; duxtor; ḧek'îm} doctor, physician: **•*Noşdarî* kulka binkefşê wî bi niştere kelaşt û derkir** (FS) *The doctor* lanced the boil in his armpit with a lancet and removed it; 2) traditional medicine man or woman: **•Heta hingê Zêrê nepeyivî bû. *Nojdarek* Kurdî bû. Ne xwenda bû, lê belê nexweşên herêmê tev dihatin cem. Dermanên wê tev giyayên çolê bûn** (DBgb, 13) Until then Z. hadn't spoken. She was a Kurdish *nozhdar*. She was illiterate, but all the sick people of the district came to her. All of her cures were wild herbs. {also: nijdar (FS-2); noşdar (FS)} [Zeb/Zx/DBgb//FS] <cebar II>

nok نـــۆك *m./f.(B/FS/ZF3)* **(-ê/; /-ê).** 1) chickpea(s), garbanzo bean(s): **•Cêva xwe t'ijî çerez dikir, k'şmîş, *noqit*** (HCK-2,181) He filled his pockets with snacks, raisins, *chickpeas* **•*Nok* çû bajêr, bû leblebû** (AB) The *chickpea* went to town, and became a sunflower seed; 2) peapod (B). {also: nehk (Hk/GF-2); nik II (Bg); noqit (HCK); [nouk] نـوك (JJ); <nok> نـوك (HH)} Mid P naxōd (M3); P noxod نـخـد -->T nohut; Sor nok نـۆك [AB/K/A/JB3/IFb/B/HH/SK/GF//JJ//Bg//Hk//HCK] <alînok; ç'erez>

noke نۆكە (Bw/SK) = now. See **niha**.

nola نـــۆلا *prep.* like, similar to; as: **•Bor *nola* teyra difir̄îya** (Z-1) The horse flew *like* a bird [lit. '*like* birds']. {also: nolanî (B-2/GF); nolî (JB3/IFb-2/ZF); nona (HCK); notla (K); notlanî (K-2)} {syn: fena; mîna; şitî II; wek} ?< metathesis of clq. Ar lōn [lawn] لـــون = 'color' [Z-1/BX//K/IFb/B//JB3/ZF//GF/ /HCK]

nolanî نۆلانی (B/GF) = like, as. See **nola**.

nolî نۆلی (JB3/IFb/ZF) = like, as. See **nola**.

nona نۆنا (HCK) = like, as. See **nola**.

noq I نـــۆق *adj.* submerged, sunk, under water: **-noq bûn** (K/GF/FJ/ZF3) to plunge, dive into water (vi.); to sink, drown (vi.) {also: niqo bûn (K-2/FS-2); noqi bûn (IFb); noqî bûn (FS); [nouq bouin] نوق بوین (JJ); <noqîbûn> نوقیبون (HH)}; **-noq kirin** (K/GF) to plunge, dip, submerge (vt.); to sink, drown (vt.). {also: niqo kirin (K-2); noqî kirin (FS); [nouq kirin] نوق کرین (JJ)} {syn: bin av; nuqim} [K/JB3/FJ/GF/JJ/ZF3//HH//IFb//FS]

noq II نۆق (Wlt/GF/ZF) = waist. See **newq**.

noqav نـــۆقـــاڤ *f.* **(-a;-ê).** submarine: •***Noqavên* me hinde zehf gemiyên Japonî ên bar û banzînkêş bin av kirine ko...** (Rn) Our *submarines* have sunk so many Japanese freight ships and tankers that... [(neol)Rn/K/JB3/IFb/GF/ZF3] <noq I>

noqit نۆقِت (HCK) = chickpeas. See **nok**.

noqî bûn نۆقی بوون (FS) & noqî kirin نۆقی کِرِن (FS). See **noq I**.

Norwecî نـــۆروەجـــی *adj.* Norwegian. {also: Nerwîcî (BF)} Sor Nerwîcî نەرویجی [Wkt/ZF3//BF]

noşdar نـــۆشـــدار (FS) = doctor; medicine man. See **nojdar**.

not نـــۆت *num.* ninety, 90. {also: nehwêt (Hk); newhêt (Ag-villages); nod (K/B/IFb); [noud نـــود/ nehvid نـــهـــود] (JJ); <nod> نـــود (HH)} Skt navatáy-; Av navaitīm *[acc.]*; Mid P nawad (M3); P navad نـــود; Sor newed نـــەوەد; Za neway (Todd); Hau newed (M4) [K/B/IFb/HH//A/JB3/GF//JJ/Hk] <neh; notem>

notem نۆتەم *adj.* ninetieth, 90th. {also: nodemîn (IFb); notemîn (GF-2/Wkt-2)} Cf. P navadom نـــودم; Sor newed[h]emîn نەوەدهەمین [GF/Wkt//IFb] <not>

notemîn نۆتەمین (GF/Wkt) = ninetieth. See **notem**.

notla نۆتلا (K) = like, as. See **nola**.

notlanî نۆتلانی (K) = like, as. See **nola**.

nozde نـــۆزدە (A/B/HH/M-Sur & Shn [nōzda]; M-Ak [nôzda])/nozde نـــۆظـــدە (M-Zx & Gul) = nineteen. See **nozdeh**.

nozdeh نـــۆزدەه *num.* nineteen, 19. {also: nanzde (M-Am & Bar); nazde (JB1-A); niwazde (JB1-S); nozde (A/B-2/M-Sur & Shn [nōzda]; M-Ak [nôzda]); nozde (M-Zx & Gul); [nouz-deh نـــوزده/ dehounou دهـــونـــو] (JJ); <nozde[h]> نـــوزده (HH)} Skt návadaśa; Av navadasa = nineteenth; Mid P nōzdah (M3); nūzdah نـــوزده; Sor nozde نـــۆزده; Za newês/desunew (Todd); Hau noze (M4) [F/K/IFb/B/HH/GF/SC//A//JJ] <neh; not>

nozdehem نـــۆزدەهـــەم *adj.* nineteenth, 19th. {also: nozdehemîn (IFb/ZF-2/Wkt-2); nozdemîn (IFb-2); nozdeyem (Wkt-2); nozdeyemîn (Wkt-2)} Cf. P nūzdahom نـــوزدهـــم; Sor nozdehem نـــۆزدەهـــەم/ nozdemîn نۆزدەمین [CT/GF/ZF/Wkt//IFb] <nozdeh>

nozdehemîn نـــۆزدەهـــەمـــیـــن (IFb/ZF/Wkt) = nineteenth. See **nozdehem**.

nozdemîn نۆزدەمین (IFb) = nineteenth. See **nozdehem**.

nozdeyem نـــــۆزدەیـــــەم (Wkt) = nineteenth. See **nozdehem**.

nozdeyemîn نـــۆزدەیـــەمـــیـــن (Wkt) = nineteenth. See **nozdehem**.

nozîn نۆزین (Trg) = four-year-old colt. See **nûzîn**.

nu نو (IF) = new. See **nû**.

nugul نوگول (Kş) = heifer. See **nogin**.

nugun نوگون (Mzg) = heifer. See **nogin**.

nuh نوه (A/B) = new. See **nû**.

nuhgon نوهگۆن (GF) = heifer. See **nogin**.

nuhî نوهی (IFb) = newness. See **nûtî**.

nuhlîk نوهلیك (FJ/GF) = mattress. See **nehlîk**.

nuhtî نوهتی (IF) = newness. See **nûtî**.

nuhú نوهو (Ad) = new. See **nû**.

nukrosk نوکرۆسك (Zeb) = nodding off. See **nuqrosk**.

nukrusk نوکروسك (Zeb) = nodding off. See **nuqrosk**.

nukul نـــوکـــول (Z-3/IFb/JJ) = beak, bill; point, tip. See **nikil**.

numandin نـــومـــانـــدِن (BZ) = to show, indicate. See **nimandin**.

nuq•im نوقِم *adj.* submerged, sunk: **-nuqim bûn** (FS): a) {syn: noq bûn} to sink, drown (vi.): •**Ew di avê da *nuqim bû*** (FS) S/he *drowned* in the water; b) [**nuqmî *ft-î* bûn**] to be lost, engrossed, distracted (in thought, etc.): •**Ez *nuqmî* temaşekirina jinên ku li meydanê li hev dicivîyan *bûbûm*** (ŞWWM, 12) I *had gotten engrossed in* watching the women who were gathering in the square. Sor nuqum نوقوم = 'submerged, sunk' [ŞWWM/ZF3/FS] <noq I>

nuqrosk نـــوقـــرۆسـك *pl.(JB1-A)/f.(OK)* **().** nodding off, nodding of the head as one dozes off: •**Her neqlekê yê *nuquluska didet* li pişt kûrhê û hostayê wî yê bistekê ho li 'ûrê wî didet** (JB1-A, #103) Every time he *nods off to sleep* behind the hearth, his boss poked his belly like so with an iron skewer. {also: nukrosk (Zeb-2); nukrusk (Zeb-2); nuqrusk (Zeb-2); nuqulusk (JB1-A/OK); <nuqirsk نوقرسك/nuqursk نوقورسك> (Hej)} [Zeb/ /JB1-A/OK//Hej] <xew; xilmaş>

nuqrusk نوقروسك (Zeb) = nodding off. See **nuqrosk**.

nuquç نـــوقـــوچ *f.* **().** pinch, tweak: •**Bavê wî *nuquçek lêxist*** (L) His father *pinched* [or, *nudged*] him •**Lawo, ca were *nuquç'kekê serê minxe*** (J) Son, come *pinch me.* {also: nuqurç (K[s]/IFb)} {syn: quncirik} [J//K(s)/IFb]

nuqulusk نـــوقـــولـــوسـك (JB1-A/OK) = nodding off. See

nuqrosk.

nuqurç نوقورچ (K[s]/IFb) = pinch. See **nuquç**.

nuqutîn نـوقـوتـيـن *vi.* **(-nuqut-).** to drip: **•Xilolîkên hêsirên çavên mêrik di ser riwê wî yê nekurkirî de gêrdibûn ser çena wî û paşê *dinuqutîn* 'erdê** (KS, 10) The tiny hailstones of the man's tears rolled down his unshaven face onto his chin and then *dripped onto* the ground. {also: niqitîn (K/B); niqutîn (A/IFb/TF); <niqetîn نـقـتـيـن (dineqitî) (دنقتى)> (HH)} {syn: çikîn[3]} Cf. niqitk = 'drop (of a liquid)' < Ar nuqṭah نقطة = 'point, dot' [KS//A/IFb/TF//K/B//HH]

nuxumandin نـوخـومـانـدِن (-nuxumîn-) (A/JB3/IFb/HH/TF/OK) = to cover. See **nixamtin**.

nuxurî نـوخـورى *m.&f.* **(-yê/-ya;).** first-born child, oldest son/daughtere (or brother/sister): **•Birê mezin--*nuxurîyê* damarîya Ûsib simêlê xwe ba dan** (Ba-1, #31) The oldest brother--*the first born of* Joseph's stepmother--twirled his moustache **•Ez *nûxuriyê* diya xwe me** (Lab, 56) I am my mother's *first-born child*. {also: nerxî (Zeb); nexrî (IFb-2/OK/ Bw); nixrî (GF-2/IFb-2); nixurî (IFb-2); nûxurî (Lab); nûxwirî (K); [noukhri] نـخـرى (JJ); <nixrî> نـخـرى (HH)} M. Schwartz: < O Ir *nahwa- = 'first, up front', cf. [Pok. nas- 755.] 'nose' + cf. Mid P rēdag = 'child'; Cf. P naxirī نـخـرى = 'a first-born child' (Steingass) & noxost نـخـسـت = 'first'; = Sor nobere نۆبەرە [Ba-1/Rwn/A/IFb/B/GF//K//Lab//JJ//HH//OK/Bw//Zeb]

nû نـوو *adj.* new, fresh: **•Cilên *nû* zarûkan kêfxweş dikin** (AB) *New* clothes make the children happy. {also: new; nî (BF); nu (IFb-2); nuh (A-2/IFb-2/B-2); n(u)hú (Ad); [nou/neoŭ] نـو (JJ); <nû> نـو (HH)} {syn: t'aze} [Pok. neu̯os/-i̯os 769.] 'new': Skt náva-; Av nava-; Mid P nōg (M3); P nō/naw نو; Sor no نۆ/nwê [nö] نوێ; Za newe (Mal/Todd); Hau no (M4); cf. also Lat novus; Gr neos νέος; Arm nor նոր (*nou̯ero-) {nuh[t]î; nû[yî]tî} [Ad//AB/K/A/JB3/IFb/B/HH/SK/GF//JJ//BF] <ji nû ve>

nûbar نـووبـار *f.* **(-a;-ê).** first fruits, early fruits or vegetables: **•Ezê vê *nûbarê* bivim qîza p'adşê ç'ûkr̄a. Ewî r̄abû dîsa nûbara xwe hilda bir çû** (HCK-3, #16, 180) I will take these *first fruits* to the king's youngest daughter. He got up, picked up the first fruits, took them and went. {also: nûber (IFb/FJ-2/TF/Kmc-2/GF-2); [nou-bar] نوبر (JJ)} Cf. P nōber نوبر = 'first fruits'; Sor nobere نۆبەرە = 'first-born; first fruits' [HCK/B/FJ/GF/Kmc/JJ//IFb/TF]

nûber نـووبـەر (IFb/FJ/TF/Kmc/GF) = first fruits. See **nûbar**.

nûçe نـووچـە *f.* **(-ya;-yê).** 1) (piece of) news, information, news report: **•Ji bo vê nûçeyê pêdivî bi *şîrovê* tune ye** (orient-news.net 22.iv.2016) There is no need for *an explanation* of this report **•*Nûçeya* me ya ku di hejmara 42 an de, li ser HEP'ê ... derket** (Wlt 1:43, 8) Our *report* in issue 42, about HEP ... went out; 2) {syn: cab[2]; xeber[1]} [in *pl.*] news: **•*Nûçeyên* şehîdbûna wan hêstirên me diherikînin** (Wlt 1:32, 2) *News of* their martyrdom causes our tears to flow **•Roja Nû, rojnamek hefteyî ya siyasî bû. Lê gava em li naveroka wê dinêrin, em dibînin ciyê ku daye warê edebî û folklorî ji yê *nûçe* û gotarên siyasî ne kêmtir e** (RN-intro) Roja Nû was a political weekly newspaper. But when we look at its contents, we see that the space given to the fields of literature and folklore are not less than that [given to] *news* and political reporting. [(neol)RN/K/JB3/IFb/GF/TF/OK]

nûgin نووگِن (FS) = heifer. See **nogin**.

nûgon نووگون (FS) = heifer. See **nogin**.

nûjen نـووژەن *adj.* modern, contemporary; brand new. {syn: hemdem; hevçerx} [K/A/IFb/GF/TF/ZF]

nûner نـوونـەر *m.&f.* **(-ê/-a;).** representative: **•Par havîne jî ez *nûnêra* Norwecê yê NY'ê bûm** (Wlt 1:37, 16) Last summer I was the Norwegian *representative* to the UN. {also: nûnêr (Wlt-2)} <Sor n[i]wêner نوێنەر <niwandin نِواندِن (-niwên-) = 'to show, display, represent'; 'to be appealing, to look like, appear (EM)' {nûnertî} [(neol)Wlt/ZF3/Wkt] <şandiyar>

nûnerî نوونەرى (ZF3) = representation. See **nûnertî**.

nûnertî نوونەرتى *f.* **(-ya;-yê).** representation: **•Mesûd Barzanî û Celal Telabanî tenê *nûnertiya* xwe û ya malbata xwe *dikin*** (Wlt 1:37, 2) Massoud Barzani and Jelal Talabani *represent* only themselves and their own families. {also: nûnerî (ZF3)} [(neol)Wlt//ZF3] <nûner>

nûnêr نوونێر (Wlt) = representative. See **nûner**.

nûnîk نوونيك (Hk) = fingernail. See **neynûk**.

nûr نـوور *f.* **(-a;-ê).** (source of) light: **-nûra sibê** (B) morning light. {also: <nûr> نـور (HH)} {syn: r̄ohnî; r̄onahî} < Ar nūr نور [EP-7/K/IFb/B/HH]

nûrî نـويرى/نوورى **().** unit of four items, or one-third of a dozen (unit for counting): **•Çar nan *nûrî* ne** (Bw) Four loaves of bread are a *nûrî* (1/3 of a dozen). {also: nîrî (Bw-2/Dh-2)} Cf. Sor nordû نـۆردوو/nirdû نِـردوو = 'flaps of bread folded for journey' [Bw/Dh/MJ] <derzin>

Nûroj نووروٚژ (CS) = Nawruz. See **Newroz**.

nûsandin نـووسـانـدِن *vt.* **(-nûsîn-).** to (cause to) stick, adhere, cling to, glue: **-xwe bi *ft-î* ve nûsandin** (SK) to cling to: •**Herçend kore xo newî kir û *xo bi* 'erdîwe *nûsand* emma fayde nekir** (SK 13:132) However much the blind man crouched and *clung to* the earth it was pointless. {also: <nwîsandin> نـويـسـانـدن (AId)} {syn: pêvekirin; zeliqandin} [SK/OK/ZF//AId]

nûsiyan نووسِيان (JB1-A&S/OK) = to stick to *(vi.)*. See **nûsyan**.

nûsîn نـووسـيـن (IFb/Kmc-5263/ZF) = to stick to *(vi.)*. See **nûsyan**.

nûsyan نـووسـيـان *vi.* **(-nûsyê-).** to stick, adhere, cling to *(vi.)*: •**Tiştekê mino tişt e/bi hemî tişta ve *dinîsît* [nav e]** (AZ, #50, 29) Something that's mine-and-something/it *sticks* to everything *[rdl.; ans.: It's a name]*; **-pêve nûsiyan** (JB1-S)/**pêkwe nûsyan** (SK) to stick together, be united: •**Mû wextê yekta bît ji qoweta pîrejinek[ê] dibizdyêt, emma wextê *pêkwe* [*nûsyan* ji qoweta Rostem nabizdyêt**] (SK41 :394) When a hair is single it can be severed by the strength of an old woman, but when *they are united* they cannot be severed by the strength of Rostam. {also: nîsyan (AZ); nûsiyan (JB1-A&S/OK); nûsîn (IFb/Kmc-5263/ZF); <nwîsyan> نـويـسـيـان (AId)} {syn: *zeliqîn} Sor nûsan نـووسـان = 'to adhere, be stuck' [SK/M//AId//AZ//JB1-A&S/OK//IFb/Kmc-5263/ZF]

nûtik نـووتِك *f.* **(-a;-ê).** young louse: •**Sipî rişka dikin, rişk dibin *nûtik*, *nûtik* dibin sipî** (Qrj) Lice lay nits, nits become *nûtik* [=young lice], *nûtik* become lice. [Qrj/IFb/GF/FJ] <rişk; spî II>

nûtî نـووتـى *f.* **(-ya;-yê).** newness. {also: nuhî (IFb); nuhtî (IF); nûyîtî (Wkt/ZF3-2)} [IFb//ZF3//Wkt] <nû>

nûxurî نووخورى (Lab) = first-born. See **nuxurî**.

nûxwirî نووخورِى (K) = first-born. See **nuxurî**.

nûyîtî نوويیتى (Wkt/ZF3) = newness. See **nûtî**.

nûzîn نـووزيـن *m.* **().** 1) a colt or foal old enough to be saddled, i.e., a three or four-year-old colt; 2) newly-saddled (of colt): •**Wî canîkeka *nûzîn* kirî** (FS) He bought a *newly-saddled* colt. {also: nozîn (Trg); [nou-zin] نوزين (JJ); <nûzîn> نوزين (HH)} [Trg//IFb/JJ/HH/GF/FJ/FS/ZF3] <berzîn I; canî>

nyasîn نياسين (M/Zx/Bw) = to know. See **nasîn**.

O ئۆ

ob•e ئـــــۆبــــه *f.* (;•ê). oba, Kurdish nomadic group consisting of 10 to 20 tents: •**Obeke t'eze [hatîye] li wêye** (EP-5, #2, #3) *A new oba has come here.* {also: [obé] اوبه (JJ); <obe> اوبه (HH)} < T oba = 'group of nomads (under authority of a chief)' [EP-5/K/A/IFb/B/JJ/HH/GF] <'eşîret; qebîle; t'ayfe>

ocax ئـۆجـاخ *f.(JJ/SK)/m.(B/ZZ)* (-a/-ê; /ocêx). 1) oven, furnace; 2) {syn: pixêrîk} hearth, fireplace (A/IFb/JJ); 3) {syn: berek; binemal; îcax} family (IFb), clan; offspring, descendants: •**Du muro hebûn ji 'eşîreta Mizûrî Jorî, ji gundê Argoş, navê yekî 'Abdî bû, navê yê dî 'Azîz. Her du ji ocaẍekê bûn, ocaẍa wan dibêjinê Mam Şaran** (SK 18:166) *There were two men of the Upper Mizuri tribe, from the village of Argosh, one of whom was called Abdi and the other Aziz. They were both of one clan, called Mam Sharan.* Sometimes used as collective noun, e.g.: •**Noke jî li nav Zêbarîyan, li gundê Perîse, ocaẍa wan mayne, dîsa dewletmend in** (SK 38:342) *Even now his descendants are still to be found in the village of Parisa, among the Zebaris, and they are still rich;* -**ocax kor bûn** (K) to be wiped out, become extinct *(of a family line)*; -**ocax kor kirin** (K) to wipe out, render extinct *(a family/lineage)*: •**Te ûcaxê bavê min kwîr kiro** (ZZ-10, 134) *You who have wiped out my father's line;* 4) saint's tomb, shrine, place of pilgrimage (JJ): •**[Îcarî jinê gotîye ku "ji boy çi em biçîne mala şêxî?" Isma'îl dibêje: "Ew ocaẍ e. Hûn biçîne wê derê"]** (JR 6) *Then the wife said, "Why should we go to the sheikh's house?" Ismail says: "It is a shrine [or, holy place]. You go there."* {also: ocaẍ (B-2/SK); ûcax (ZZ-10); [odjag] اوجـاغ (JJ)} < T ocak = 'oven' [K/A/JB3/IFb/B/GF/OK//JJ/JR/SK//ZZ] <hoz; îcax; qebîle; war>

ocaẍ ئۆجـاغ (B/JJ/SK) = oven; furnace; hearth; family; shrine. See **ocax**.

oda ئۆدا = room. See **ode**.

od•e ئـــــۆده *f.* (•a/•eya;•ê). 1) {syn: mezel[1]; ot'ax} room, chamber; 2) diwan, hall in which a dignitary receives guests (HH): •**Zivistana … carcara êvara oda meda mêrêd gund berev dibûn** (Ba2:1, 204) *In winters … sometimes the* men of the village would congregate in our *diwan* in the evenings. {also: oda; [oda اودا/odé اوده] (JJ); <ode> اوده (HH)} < T oda < P otāq اطـاق -- > clq. Ar ōḍa أوضه [L/K/A/JB3/IFb/B/HH/SK/GF/OK/RZ//JJ]

ogeç ئۆگەچ (K) = young ram. See **hogiç**.

ol ئـۆل *f./m.(HYma)* (-a/-ê;-ê/). religion, faith: •**Divê em vî neyarê ola xwe ji gundê xwe biqewitînin** (Ardû, 57) *We must expel this enemy of our religion from our village* •**Ez nizanim bê çawa zanibû ku baweriya min bi olê min ewqasî xurt e** (HYma, 44) *I don't know how he knew that my belief in my religion was so strong.* {syn: dîn III} Cf. T yol = 'way, road' [Msr/K/A/IFb/GF/TF/OK/RZ/AId/ZF3] <dîndar III>

olam ئـۆلام *f.* (-a;-ê). 1) {syn: bac; bêş; xer[a]c; xûk} tax: •**[P'êsîra me ji olama Romî xelas dibe]** (JJ) *We will free ourselves of Turkish domination* [lit. 'Our collar will be rid of Turkish *taxes*']; 2) {also: olam[t]î (B); [olami اولامـى/houlam هـولام] (JJ)} {syn: suxre} corvée, forced labor: •**Eger dîwan, merîyêd wê pê biḥesin ku k'urd dixwazin heṙne Ermenîstanê, wê pez û dewarê wana jê bistînin, mêra bigirin bavêjne kelê yanê jî bibine olamê** (Ba2-3, 214) *If the porte [Ottomans] or its people find out that the Kurds want to go to Armenia, they will take their sheep and cattle from them, arrest the men and throw them into the citadel or carry them off into corvée;* 3) indentured servant, person forced into corvée (B). [Z-922/K/B//JJ]

olamî ئـۆلامـى (B/JJ) = corvée, forced labor. See **olam** [2].

olamtî ئـۆلامـتـى (B) = corvée, forced labor. See **olam** [2].

olan ئـــــۆلان *f.* (;-ê). echo, reverberation: -**olan dan** (Epl/FS) to echo {syn: deng vedan}: •**Dengê vê hewara wî li zinarên çiyayên hember olan dide û bi du sê dengan dîsa li me vedigere** (Epl, 34) *The sound of his cry for help echoes off the cliffs of the mountains opposite, and comes back to us in two or three voices.* {also: alan (IFb/RF-2)} {syn: dengvedan} [Epl/RF/ZF3/FS//IFb]

olçek ئـۆلچـهك *f.* (-a;). unit of weight for measuring grain, appr. 25 kg. in Nusaybin (A), 35 kg. in other places (IFb); 40 kg. in some places, 50 kg. in others (CCG); 5 *olçeks* equal a full sack or 10 *şafîḥas* (GF). {also: welçek (CCG)} <T ölçek = 'unit of dry measure, 1/4 of *kile*' < ölçmek = 'to measure' [Qzl/A/IFb/GF/TF/FJ/ZF//CCG] <kêl III; kod[2]; somer; t'as[2]; tilm>

oldaş ئـۆلـداش *m.* **(-ê;).** friend, companion, comrade: •[**Melayek û dû nefer mirofêd cahil nexwendî her sê bûyîne *oldaşêd* yekûdû**] (JR) A mullah and two ignorant, unlettered men were traveling *companions*. {also: [oldach] اولـــداش (JJ)} {syn: dost; heval; hogir} < T yoldaş = 'traveling companion' [JR/TG2/JB1-S/PS/JJ/Mosul (Lalish)/FS]

olg ئۆلگ (FS/ZF3) = chain. See **olk I**[2].

olk I ئـۆلـك *f.* **(-a;-ê).** 1) {syn: xelek} hoop, circle, ring *(final link in a chain, used to connect the chain to such things as a wooden post or a pocket watch)*; 2) chain (FS/ZF3): •***olga* dirêj** (FS) long *chain*. {also: olg (FS/ZF3)} cf. Sor ełqe ئـەڵـقـە = 'ring, circle' [AB/Xp//FS/ZF3] <heçî I>

olk' II ئۆلك (K-2/EH) = empire. See **ork'e**.

olke ئۆلكە (GF) = region; empire. See **ork'e**.

olp'erest ئۆلپەرست *m.&f.* **().** 1) religious fanatic; 2) *adj.* religious, pious. {also: olperist (IFb/BF)} [RC2/FJ/GF/TF/RZ/ZF/CS//IFb/BF]

olperist ئـۆلـپـەرِسـت (IFb/BF) = religious fanatic. See **olp'erest**.

Omanî ئۆمانى (Wkp) = Omani. See **'Umanî**.

omet ئـۆمـەت *f.* **(-a;-ê).** community, people *(of Islam)*: •**K'î ne ji xîretêye, ne ji *ometêye*** (Dz, #17:384) He who doesn't show zeal (or concern) is not part of *the community [prv.]* •**Ma em jî ne ji *ometa* Mihemed in?** (Lab 60) But aren't we also part of Mohammed's *people*? {also: ummet (SK); <ummet> امت (HH)} < Ar ummah أمّة = 'people, nation, community'; Sor omet ئـۆمـەت [Dz/Lab/K/IFb/OK//HH/SK] <civak>

omid ئۆمِد = hope. See **omîd**.

omîd ئـۆمـیـد *m.(F)/f.(K)* **().** hope. {also: omid; omûd; ûmûd f. (K); [oumoud امـود/oumid اومـیـد] (JJ)} {syn: hêvî} < P omīd امید [F//JJ//K]

omûd ئۆموود = hope. See **omîd**.

ordek ئۆردەك (A) = duck. See **werdek**.

ordî ئـۆردى *f.* **(-ya;-yê).** army: •**Qeret'ajdîn bi *ordîya* xweba** (FK-eb-1) Q. and his *army* •[**Weku şeřê Rom û Îranê li deşta Aleşkerê bûyî *ordûya* Romê revî û belav bûyî**] (JR #39,120) When the Turco-Iranian war took place on the plain of Eleşkirt, the Turkish *army* was routed and dispersed. {also: [ordou اوردو/ordouï اوردوى] (JJ)} {syn: artêş; esker [2]; leşker} < T ordu = 'army' [FK-1/K/B//JJ]

orîn ئـۆریـن *vi.* **(-or-).** 1) to moo, low; to bellow; 2) [*f.* **(-a;)**] mooing, lowing; bellowing: •**Bû *orîna* çêlekan û golikan** (AB) *The mooing* of cows and calves [suddenly] was heard. [AB/K/B/ZF3] <k'alîn>

ork'•e ئـۆركـە *f.* **(•a;).** 1) empire, monarchy, kingdom: •[ör kī 'ağämüstāne] (LC-1) The kingdom of Persia •**Çiqas *olk'a* wîda t'elal hene** (EH) How many heralds there are in his *kingdom*; 2) region. {also: olk' II (K-2/EH); olke (GF); ork'et (K-2); [orka اركە/orkét/orkéta] (JJ)} cf. Geo olki ოლქი = 'region'; P olkā الکا = 'region; kingdom'; T ülke = 'country'; Sor wułge ووڵگە = 'province, region'; NENA olka *f.* = 'city, country' (Garbell) [EH//K//JJ//GF]

ork'et ئۆركەت (K) = empire. See **ork'e**.

ort ئۆرت (BX)/ort' (B) = center; among. See **ort'e**.

ort'a ئۆرتا (Z-1) = among, between. See **ort'e** [2].

ort'•e ئـــۆرتـــە *f.* **(•a;•ê).** 1) {syn: nîv; nîvî} center, middle: **-ji ort'ê řakirin** = to do away with, remove {syn: ji holê řakirin}{cf. T ortadan kaldırmak; P az miyān bordan از ميان بردن}: •**Ev zordestî ... *ji ortê hate rakirin*** (Ber) This force ... *was done away with*; **-k'etin ort'ê** = a) to pass (time) {syn: derbaz bûn}: •**Çend deqe *nek'etine ort'ê*** (Z-1) A few minutes *had barely passed* •**Çend sal *k'etin ortê*** (K) A few years *passed/intervened* [lit. 'fell in the middle']; b) to interfere, meddle; **-t'ilîya ort'ê** (F/K/B) middle finger {syn: tilîya navê (K)/~navîn (IF)/~nêvî (Msr)}; 2) {also: ort'a ... (Z-1)} *[prep.]* among, between, *according to BX, used mainly in Western dialects*: •**Niqitkeke xûna wî dîsa pekîya *ort'a* M. û Z.** (Z-1) A drop of his bood (again) fell *between* M. and Z. {also: ort' (B)} < T orta = 'center' [BX/Ad/Z-1/K//B] <hol II; nav II; navend; nîv>

orxan ئـۆرخـان *f.* **(;-ê).** quilt: **-orẍan-doşek** (IS) quilts and mattresses, bedroom appurtenances. {also: orẍan (K/GF/IS); [ourgan] اورغـــــــــان (JJ)} <T yorgan [Ag/F/B//IS/K/GF/FS/ZF3//JJ] <liĥêf>

orẍan ئۆرغان (K/GF/IS) = quilt. See **orxan**.

ost•a ئـۆسـتـا *m.* **(•ayê;•ê/•ay).** master *(of a trade or profession)*, master artisan; one in charge: •***Hustay* dest bi ava kirina p'irê kir û p'ira xo ava kir** (M-Zx #775) *The master-builder* began to build the bridge and he built his bridge. {also: hosta (B-2); husta (M-Zx); [ousta] اوستا (JJ)} Cf. P ostād استاد --> Ar ustāḏ أستاذ --> Clq Ar usṭā أسطى; Ar--> Sp Usted = 'you *(polite form)*' {hostatî; ostatî; [oustaï] اوستای (JJ)} [L/Z-1/K/B/ZF3//JJ//M-Zx] <mamosta>

ostatî ئــۆســتــاتــى *f.* (-ya;). master artisanship, skilled craftsmanship; masterliness, expertise. {also: hostatî (K-2); hostayî (BF); [oustaï] اوستای (JJ)} [K/B/ZF3//JJ//BF] <osta>

Ostralî ئــۆســتــرالــى (Wkp) = Australian. See **Awistralyayî.**

ot'ax ئــۆتــاخ *f.* (-a;-ê). room, chamber: •**Ew** *ot'axe* **çarnikal eynekirî bûye** (Ba-1, #17) That *room* was covered with mirrors on all four sides. {also: ot'aẍ (B-2); [otag] اوتــاغ (JJ)} {syn: mezel [1]; ode} < P otāq اطاق [Ba/F/K/B//JJ]

ot'aẍ ئــۆتــاغ (B) = room. See **ot'ax.**

otel ئــۆتــل (ZF3) = hotel. See **ûtêl.**

otêl ئــۆتــێل (K/JB3/Wkt) = hotel. See **ûtêl.**

otî ئــۆتــى (IFb/OK) = [flat]iron. See **ût'î.**

otobês ئــۆتــۆبــێس (SS) = bus. See **otobûs.**

otoboz ئــۆتــۆبــۆز (CS) = bus. See **otobûs.**

otobus ئــۆتــۆبــوس (IFb/ZF3/RZ) = bus. See **otobûs.**

otobûs ئــۆتــۆبــووس *f.* (-a;-ê). bus, autobus: •**Gava** *otobês* **gihîştibû Edenê tarî bûbû** (N.Mîro.Gava mirî biaxife, 34) When *the bus* reached Adana it was already dark •*Otobûsa* **haciyên Kerkûkê qulipî** (Rûdaw 7.viii.2017) *The bus of* pilgrims from Kerkuk turned over. {also: otobês (SS); otoboz (CS); otobus (IFb/ZF3/RZ); otopêz (G)} < Eng autobus < Gr auto- + bus (from Lat omnibus, ablative & dative pl. of omnis = 'all') [Rûdaw/Wkt/IFb/ZF3/RZ//CS//SS//G]

otopêz ئــۆتــۆپــێز (G) = bus. See **otobûs.**

Otrîşî ئــۆتــریــشــى. See **Awistrî.**

oxçir ئــۆخــچــر *f.* (). drawstring. {syn: doxîn} <T uçkur [Dy] <şalvar>

oxir ئــۆخــر (Z-1/IF/B) = (good) luck. See **oẍir.**

oẍir ئــۆغِــر *f.* (-a;-ê). luck, good luck, fortune: •**Berê xwe dane** *oẍirê* **û pişta xwe dane felekê** (HR 3:9) They turned their faces towards *good luck* and

turned their backs on the heavens *{folktale formula}*; -**Oẍira te a xêrê be** (L)/**Oẍra te b xêr** (JB1-S)/**Weẍera te bi xêr** (M-Ak, #545) Bon voyage! Farewell!; -**Oẍir be** = Good bye *{said by the host remaining behind after a guest signals his intention to leave by saying* **Xatirê te,** *qv. [cf. T* **güle güle,** *in answer to* **Alla[h'a ı]smarladık]}*; -**ser oxrê** (EP-7)/**serîke we oxire!** (XF) without fail, absolutely, certainly. {also: oxir (Z-1/IF/B); oẍra (JB1-S); oẍur (GF-2); weẍer (M-Ak); [ogour] اوغــور (JJ)} < T uğur = 'good luck, good omen'; Sor oẍir ئــۆغِــر = 'fortunate going (polite term for movements of another person)' [L/K/GF//IFb/B//JJ//JB1-S//M-Ak]

oẍra ئــۆغــرا (JB1-S) = (good) luck. See **oẍir.**

oẍur ئــۆغــور (GF) = (good) luck. See **oẍir.**

oyîn ئــۆیــیــن *f.* (-a;-ê). calamity, disaster, misfortune; mishap; trouble, unpleasantness: •**Gelekî duşurmîş bû: "Ḧeyran, go, hela were vê** *oyînê* **binhêre, … ezê ça t'ev vê meymûnê ṟazêm?"** (Z-920, 288) He was very distraught, thinking "oh boy, look at this *mess* [I'm in] … how can I sleep with this monkey?" •*Oyîn* **hate serê wî** (K/XF) *Misfortune* befell him; -oyîn anîn serê *fk-î* (K/XF)/oyîn kirin serê *fk-î* (Z-821) to bring disaster upon s.o.: •**Go, k'afirê te xe, te bikuje,** *oyîneke* **serê te bike, vegere heṟe** (Z-821, 131) He said, "The infidel will strike you, kill you, *bring a calamity upon you,* [and] then go back [where he came from]" •**Xudê zane, naka çi** *oyîn* **serê wî anîne** (Z-821, 133) God knows what *disaster they have brought* down on him now. {also: oyn (B)} {syn: bela I; bêt'ar; boblat; qeda; t'ifaq} <T oyun = 'game; dance'; cf. Sor ayn-û-oyîn ئــایــن و ئــۆیــیــن = 'prevarication, equivocation' [Z-821/Z-920/K//B]

oyn ئــۆیــن (B) = disaster, trouble. See **oyîn.**

Ozbekistanî ئــۆزبــهکِــســتــانــى (BF) = Uzbek. See **Ûzbekî.**

Ozbekî ئــۆزبــهکــى (Wkt/BF/SS) = Uzbek. See **Ûzbekî.**

P/P' پ

p'a پا (Ba2) = part, portion. See **p'ay**.
pac پاج (A) = skylight. See **p'ace**.
paca پاجا (TG2) = skylight. See **p'ace**.
p'ac•e پـاجـه *f.* **(•a;•ê).** skylight (IFb/TG2); dormer window [lucarne] (JJ); window (IFb/A/Msr): **•Stîya Zîn derk'etîye *p'acê* li wan di'îşîne** (Z-2) Lady Zîn went out to look at them through *the skylight.* {also: pac (A); paca (TG2-2); paça (TG2-2); peçe I (TG2-2); [badjé بـاجـه/pajā پـاچـه/ پـاچـا] (JJ)} {syn: k'ulek II; r̄ojin} Cf. P bājeng بـاجـنـگ = 'small window' [Z-2/IFb/TG2/Msr//JJ//A] <p'encere; pixêrîk>
paç' I پـاچ *f.* **(;-ê).** kiss: **-paç' kirin** (K/B/IFb) to kiss s.o. (vt.) {syn: hatin r̄ûyê fk-ê; maç' kirin; r̄amûsan}: **•Zînê sûrtê xwe dirêjî dewrêş kir, dewrêş *têr paç' kir*** (FK-eb-1) Zîn held up her cheeks for the dervish, and he *showered* them *with kisses*; **-hev paç' kirin** (K/B) to kiss [one another] *(vi.)*. {syn: maç'; r̄amûsan} [K/B/IFb/ZF3]
p'aç' II پـاچ *m.* **(-ê;).** 1) {syn: kerkon; kevnik [2]; p'aç[']ik; p'ate II; p'er̄ok; pîne; p'ot; qerpal} rag, coarse cloth (A/IFb/HH): **-p'aç'ê hevîr** (A/IF) cheesecloth; 2) *pach*, a type of man's overcoat (K); long oriental robe (JJ). {also: paçe (GF-2); [patch] پـاچ (JJ); <paç> پـاچ (HH)} [K/A/IFb/B/JJ/HH/GF/TF/ZF3/FS] <p'aç[']ik; p'ate II>
paça پاچا (TG2) = skylight. See **p'ace**.
paçe پاچه (GF) = patch; rag. See **p'aç' II** & **p'ate II**.
p'aç[']ik پـاچـك *m.(K)/f.(B)* **(; /-ê).** 1) {syn: kerkon; kevnik [2]; p'aç' II; p'ate II; p'er̄ok; pîne; p'ot; qerpal} rag (K/IFb); 2) {syn: pêçek; pêçolk} diaper, nappy (K/B). [K/B/IFb/ZF3] <p'aç' II; pêçek>
paçvan پـاچـڤـان (FJ/GF/FS/ZF3/SS/CS) = interpreter. See **p'açveker**.
p'açv•e پاچـڤـه *f.* **(•eya/•a;•ê).** translation; interpreting, interpretation *(between languages)*: **•*Paçva* pertûkê bir̄êk û pêk bû** (FS) *The translation of* the book was splendid; **-p'açve kirin** (IFb/FJ/GF/ZF3/FS) to translate; to interpret {syn: t'ercime kirin; werger̄andin}: **•Wî çend pertûkek *paçvekirine* bo ser zimanê Kurdî** (FS) He *translated* some books into Kurdish. {also: peçve (IFb-2)} [(neol)IFb/FJ/GF/ZF3/Wkt/FS/CS]
p'açveker پـاچـڤـەکـەر *m.&f.* **().** interpreter; translator: **•Ev filim çîroka wan rûdanên tirajîdî-komêdî ye ko Zelala *paçveker* di dema paçvandinê ya di navbera jineka mişext li Firensayê ko nikarit bi Firensayî biaxivit û pijîşkekê jinan da bi çavên xwe dîtine** (duhokiff.com) This film is the story of those tragicomedic events which *the interpreter* Zelal witnessed while interpreting between an immigrant woman in France who can't speak French and a gynecologist **•Wî wek *paçveker* ji bo desteya Neteweyên Hevgirtî li Îraqê ... kar kiriye** (X̆.M.Mistefayî. Leyla bûka Kurd, 108) He worked as *an interpreter* for the United Nations in Iraq.... {also: paçvan (FJ/GF/FS/ZF3-2/SS/CS); paçvevan (ZF3); paçvezan (GF-2/FS-2/ZF3-2); paçzan (SS-2); peçvan (IFb)} {syn: t'ercimeçî; wergêr̄} [X̆.M.Mistefayî/Wkt//ZF3//FJ/GF/FS/SS/CS//IFb]
paçvevan پاچڤەڤان (ZF3) = interpreter. See **p'açveker**.
paçvezan پـاچـڤـەزان (GF/FS/ZF3) = interpreter. See **p'açveker**.
paçzan پاچزان (SS) = interpreter. See **p'açveker**.
p'adişa پادِشا (B) = king, ruler. See **p'adşa**.
padişah پـادِشـاه (-ê;) (B/JB3/GF) = king, ruler. See **p'adşa**.
padişahî پادِشاهی (GF) = kingship. See **p'adşatî**.
p'adişahtî پادِشاهتی (B) = kingship. See **p'adşatî**.
p'adişatî پادِشاتی (B/GF) = kingship. See **p'adşatî**.
p'adişayî پادِشایی (B) = kingship. See **p'adşatî**.
padîşah پادیشاه (IFb/ZF3) = king, ruler. See **p'adşa**.
padîşahî پادیشاهی (ZF3) = kingship. See **p'adşatî**.
padîşe پادیشه (A) = king, ruler. See **p'adşa**.
p'adş•a پـادشـا *m.* **(;•ê).** king, padishah, ruler: **•*P'adşê* go** (J) *The king* said. {also: p'adişa[h] (B); padişah (-ê;) (B/JB3/GF); padîşah (IFb/ZF3); padîşe (A); p'adşah (K); p'atşah (-ê;) (FK-eb-1); [patsca پـادشـا/padišāh پـادشـاه] (JJ); <padişa> پـادشـا (HH)} {syn: ĥakim; qiral} Cf. Mid P pādixšā(y) = 'ruler' (M3); P padišāh پـادشـاه {p'adişayî; p'adişa[h]tî; p'adşahîtî; p'adşatî; [pādišāhītī پادشاهیتی/ pādišāhī پـادشـاهـی] (JJ)} [J//K//A//JB3/JJ/B/GF//IFb/ZF3//HH] <p'aşa; silt'an>
p'adşah پادشاه (K) = king, ruler. See **p'adşa**.
p'adşahîtî پادشاهیتی (K) = kingship. See **p'adşatî**.
p'adşatî پـادشـاتـی *f.* **(-ya;-yê).** kingship, rule, office of the king: **•Hûn gerekê Ûsib bikujin, wekî dewlet**

û *p'atşatî* weȓa bimîne (Ba3-1) You must kill Joseph, so that the government and *kingship* go [lit. 'remain'] to you. {also: padişahî (GF-2); p'adişahtî (B-2); p'adişatî (B/GF-2); p'adişayî (B-2/GF-2); padîşahî (ZF3); p'adşahîtî (K-2); p'atşatî (Ba3-1); [pādišāhītī پادشاهيتى/ pādišāhī پادشاهى] (JJ)} [K//GF//B//JJ//ZF3] <p'adşa>

padval [K/B/HCK-2]/**p'adval** پادڤال *f.* **(-a;-ê).** cellar, basement: **•Mîrê min, 'emir bike, bira *padvala* û zêȓzemîna t'emam valakin û bidne t'emizkirinê** (Ba3-3, #34) My emir, give the order that all *the cellars* and dungeons should be emptied out and [then] have them cleaned. {syn: zêȓzemîn} <Rus podval подвал [Ba3/K/B] <zîndan>

page پاگه (HH/GF) = horse stable. See **pange** [1].

pageh پاگهه (A/IFb) = horse stable. See **pange** [1].

pahn پاهن (A/IFb) = wide; flat. See **pehn**.

pahnayî پاهنايى (A) = width. See **pehnî II**.

pahtin پاهتِن (Bw) = to bake. See **patin**.

paî پائى, m. (F) = pride; praise. See **paye I**.

paîz پائيز (F) = autumn, fall. See **payîz**.

p'ak پاك *adj.* 1) {syn: p'aqij; t'emiz} pure, clean; 2) {syn: saxlem; saẍ} healthy, well (K/A/Ag): **•Memê *wê* bi îzina xwedê *p'ak be*** (Z-1) Mem *will get well*, with God's help [lit. 'permission']; 3) {syn: baş; qenc; ȓind; xweş} good, excellent (B/HH): **•Ew ser 'erdê sar, ser xisîla yanê jî, ḧalê k'ê hinekî *p'ak bû*, ser kulava ȓadizan** (Ba2-3, 213) They would sleep on the cold floor, on mats, or if they were a little better off [lit. 'he whose condition *became* a little *good*'], on rugs. {also: [pak] پاك (JJ); <pak> پاك (HH)} Cf. Mid P pāk = 'clean, pure, holy' (M3); P pāk پاك {p'akî; pakîtî; p'aktî; [paki] پاكى (JJ)} [Z-1/K/A/JB3/IFb/B/ JJ/HH/SK/JB1-S/GF/TF/OK]

pakij پاكِژ (OK) = clean. See **p'aqij**.

pakijî پاكِژى (OK) = cleanliness. See **p'aqijî**.

P'akistanî پاكِستانى *adj.* Pakistani. [IFb/Wkt/BF/Wkp/CS]

p'akî پاكى *f.* **(;-yê).** 1) {syn: p'aqijî} purity, cleanliness; goodness; 2) *[adv.]* {also: bi p'akî} well, properly: **•Em nikarin *bi p'akî* kêrî we bên** (Ba2:2, 206) We can't *really* be of help to you **•K'ê ku *p'akî* haj ji şivantîyê t'unebû, hew zanibû, ku ew tiştekî çetin nîne** (Ba2:1, 203) Those who were not *well* acquainted with shepherding thought that it was something not very difficult. {also: pakîtî (GF-2); p'aktî (K-2); [paki] پاكى (JJ)} [K/B/IFb/JJ/GF/TF/OK] <p'ak>

pakîtî پاكيتى (GF) = purity. See **p'akî**.

p'aktî پاكتى (K) = purity. See **p'akî**.

p'al پال *f./m.(SK)* **(-a/-ê;-ê/).** 1) side, flank: **-p'al** [**ve**] **dan** (K) = a) to lie on its side; b) to lean (against). See under **p'aldan**; 2) {syn: berwar; hevraz; jihelî; pesar; p'êş II[2]; qunt'ar; sîng; teȓazin} slope, side of mountain (K/B/JJ); hill (HH): **•Li *pala* hember colek mîhên mor di mexeliyê de bû** (Lab, 11) On *the slope* opposite, a flock of purple sheep was in the open-air pen **•ser *p'ala* çîyê** (EP-8) on *the side of* the mountain; 3) thigh, thigh bone (IFb). {also: [pal پال/palé پاله] (JJ); <pal> پال (HH)} [Z-1/K/A/JB3/IFb/B/JJ/HH/SK/GF/TF/OK]

palandin پالاندِن *vt.* **(-palîn-).** 1) {syn: dakirin; parzinandin} to strain, filter; to drain (JJ); 2) to settle, precipitate *(of liquids)* (B). {also: [palandin] پالاندين (JJ)} Cf. P pālūdan پالودن; Sor paławtin پالاوتِن (-pałêw-) = 'to filter, strain' [S&E/K/JB3/IFb/B/JJ/GF]

palan dûv پالان دووڤ (GF) = girth strap. See **p'aldûm**.

p'alas پالاس *f./m.(B/Kmc)* **(; /p'alês).** thin rug or mat made of coarse cloth: **•Li pey genim û ka ji hev hatin qetandin, genim wek qûrçek li ser *palasan* tê civandin, ji vê komrişka genim re "têx" tê gotin** (CCG, 72) After the wheat and straw have been separated from each other, the wheat is gathered in [lit. 'like'] a pile on *mats* [or *rugs*], this stack of wheat is called a *têx* **•Wê *palas* raêxist û nehlîk deyna ser** (FS) She spread out a *rug/mat* and placed a sitting mattress on it; **-pelasekî kerkît** (Kmc) flat weave rug or kilim woven on hand loom. {also: pelas (Kmc)} Cf. T palas = 'coarse textile rug'; P palās پلاس = 'sackcloth; coarse woollen cloth'; Sor pełas پەلاس = 'thin rug used to sit on' [CCG/K/B/IFb/FJ/ZF/FS//Kmc] <doşek; nehlîk; qisîl>

palavtin پالاڤتِن (dipalêve) (IFb/AD) = to drip, be filtered. See **palîn II**.

p'al•dan پالدان *vt.* **(p'al-d-).** 1) {syn: ȓak'etin; ȓazan} to lie down, go to sleep; to sleep: **•Ewî *p'aldabû* li ser piştêye** (FT, 150) He *had lain down* on his back; 2) to lean against, rest against, be supported (IFb/JJ/GF/TF/OK); to put one's back up against (JJ): **•Wan kevira usa *ser hevda p'al dabûn*, hev meḧkem girtibûn û 'erdê da çûbûn, ku t'u qeweta nikaribû wana ji cî bileqîne** (Ba2:1, 203) Those rocks *were leaning against one another* in such a way, held each other so tightly and had lodged themselves [lit. 'gone'] [so deeply] into the earth that no force could budge them; 3) to push, stimulate (JJ); to encourage. {also: p'al da[yî]n (B); [pal-dan] پالدان (JJ); <paldan پالدان (paldide) (پالددە)> (HH)} Hau pałò day *vt.* = 'to lean back' [Ag/EP-7/F/K/A/IFb/JJ/HH/GF/TF/OK//B] <r̄amedîn>

p'al dayîn پال دایین (B) = to lie down. See **p'aldan**.

p'aldûm پـالـدووم *m.(K)/f.(Ardû)* **(/-a; /-ê).** crupper strap, girth strap, leather strap fastening the saddle to the pack animal's back: **•Ker bi kurtaneke jihevketî ye, *paldûma* wê qetyaye, navtenga wê sist e** (Ardû, 66) The donkey is with a broken down pack saddle, its *girth strap* is cut, its belly strap is weak. {also: palan dûv (GF); [paldoum پـالـدوم/palouw پـالـوف] (JJ)} {syn: palî II} Cf. P pāldom پالدم --> T paldım = 'crupper strap' [Ardû/K/IFb/JJ//GF] <heçî I = werqîl; navteng; qoş>

p'al•e پـالـه *m.* **(•ê/•eyê [BK];).** 1) {syn: k'arker; r̄êncber; xebatk'ar} worker, workman; day-laborer: **•*Pale* hatin taştê** (AB) *The workers* came to breakfast: **•*Van p'ala* dest pê kirin** [sic] **kela çêkirin** [sic] (EP-8) *These workers* began to build the fortress; **-paleyê peyya** (BK) male worker; **-paleya pîrek** (BK) female worker; **-sinifa p'ala** (B) working class; 2) {also: p'alevan II (K-2/A-2)} {syn: êrxat; mişag} harvester, agricultural worker, farmhand (A/JB3/Haz/Srk). {also: [palé] پـالـه (JJ); <pale> پـالـه (HH)} <Arc plaḥ פלח = 'to till, work; to serve, worship' & pālḥā פלחא = 'worker, servant; worshipper': NENA √p-l-x: pla:xa = 'to work' & pala:xa m. = 'worker' (Krotkoff); cf. Ar falaḥa فـلـح = 'to plow, till, cultivate' & fallāḥ فـلاّح = 'peasant, farmer, tiller of the land'; Sor fe'le فعله/fa'le فاعله/fele فهله = 'worker' & feḷe فـه‌ڵـه/pałe پـاڵـه = 'agricultural worker'; also Az T fəhlə = 'worker' {p'aletî; paleyî} [EP-8/AB/K/A/JB3/IFb/BK/B/JJ/HH/GF] <cot'k'ar; hodax>

p'aletî پـالـەتـى (B) = worker's profession; agricultural work. See **p'aleyî**.

p'alevan I پـالـەڤـان (K/JB3/IF) = hero; knight; athlete. See **p'elewan**.

p'alevan II پـالـەڤـان (K/A) = agricultural worker. See **p'ale** [2].

palevanî پالەڤانى (IF) = heroic deed. See **p'elewanî**.

p'aleyî پالەیى *f.* **(-ya;-yê).** 1) being a worker, worker's profession; 2) agricultural work, work in the fields harvesting or reaping with a scythe and sickle (Haz): **•Îcar wek *palîya* genimê sor ku çawa meriv dide ber dasan, wele ez jî bi mûçingê ketim nav porê xwe** (LC, 5) Like *harvesting* red wheat, the way one strikes it with a sickle, that's how I went after my hair with a tweezers **•Ma zatî *palî* jî nemaye. Traktor derketiye** (LC, 22) In any case, *harvesting* no longer exists--the tractor came along [and replaced it]; **-p'aleyî kirin** (IFb/JB3) to do agricultural work, to do work harvesting in the fields, to harvest. {also: p'aletî (B); palî I (LC/GF-2)} [K/A/JB3/AB/IFb/GF/TF/Haz//B] <hodaxtî; p'ale>

palihan پالِهان (HR) = to drip, be filtered. See **palîn II**.

p'alik [K(s)]/**palik** [IFb/GF] پـالِـك *m.* **(-ê;).** wooden pack saddle. {also: [palik/palek] پـالـك (JJ)} {syn: kurtan} [Qrj/K(s)/IFb/GF]

palî I پالى (LC/GF) = harvesting. See **p'aleyî**.

palî II پـالـى *f.* **(-ya;).** crupper, breeching, *one of the straps which keep packsaddle [**kurtan**] on animal's back--fastened around horse's tail* (string extends from corners of back end of packsaddle). {also: <pałî> پاڵى (Hej)} {syn: p'aldûm} Sor pałû پـاڵـوو = 'breeching, strap passing round hindquarters of pack-animal' [Bw/Zeb//Hej] <berok I; kurtan; palîkurtk; t̲eng II>

palîkurtk پاليكورتك *f.* **().** crupper, breeching, *one of the straps which keep packsaddle [**kurtan**] on animal's back--fastened around horse's tail* (string extends from middle of back end of packsaddle). [Bw] <berok I; kurtan; palî II; t̲eng II>

palîn I پـالـين *f.* **(-a;-ê).** grazing of sheep before dawn: **•Şivanî pez rakir *palînê*** (GS) The shepherd took the sheep out for their *morning grazing*; **-palîna pezî** (Bw) do. {syn: şevîn} [Bw/FS] <ç'êrîn; hevêz = hevşî>

palîn II پالين *vi.* **(-pal-).** to drip; to precipitate, settle; to be filtered: **•Av wa ji qaşlê şebeşa bi der qûna wî da *dipalihê*** (HR 3:164) Water *is dripping* down from the watermelon rind onto his backside. {also: palavtin (dipalêve) (IFb/AD); palihan (HR); [palin] پـالـيـن (JJ)} {syn: ç'ikîn; nuqutîn} Cf. P pālūdan پـالـودن; Sor paławtin پـاڵاوتـن (-pałêw-) = 'to filter, strain' [HR//K/B/GF/JJ/ZF3//IFb/AD] <palandin>

palkon [B]/**p'alkon** پـالـكـۆن *f.* **(;-ê).** balcony. {also: balkon (B-2/IFb)} {syn: behwe; r̄ewaq [4]; telar; yazlix̌} [EP-7/B//IFb]

p'alûd پالود *f.* **(;-ê).** acorn. {also: belot (ZF3); palût

(ZF3-2); [palout] پـلـوط (JJ)} {syn: berû} Cf. Ar ballūṭ بلّوط; T palamut [MC-1/K/B/JJ//ZF3]

palûke پالووكه (IFb) = factory. See **pavlike**.

palût پالووت (ZF3) = acorn. See **p'alûd**.

p'alût•e پـالـووتـه *f.* **(•[ey]a;).** social institution whereby a group of villagers pools their efforts to complete a task for one member of the group, e.g., building a house or harvesting the crop of each member of the group in turn, similar to American [quilting] bees [T imece]: **•Gundî tev *palûta* hev dikin** (FS) Villagers all help each other to complete their tasks. {also: palûze (FS-2)} {syn: zibare} = Sor herewez هـەرەوەز [Qzl/A/IFb/GF/TF/OK/ZF3/FS]

palûze پـالـووزه (FS) = communal work situation. See **p'alûte**.

p'an I پـان *vt.* **(-p'ê- / -p'ihê- / p'eyî- [IF-2]).** 1) {syn: ç'avnihêrî li r̄îya... kirin; hêvîyê bûn/sekinîn/man; li benda...man; sekinîn} to await, wait for, lie in wait for: **•Ew bersiva ku wî bi dilpekîn *dipa*, îro nû gîhîştiye destê wî** (Lab, 5) The answer he *has been awaiting* with beating heart has just reached him today **•[Meger heşt suwarêd êzîdîyan r̄êbir̄ ji boy xirabîyê di nîva ker̄eyêda(?) *dipan*]** (JR) Eight Yezidi bandits on horseback *were waiting* in the canyon to do evil [lit. 'for evil']; 2) to watch out for. {also: payin (BK); payîn (K[s]/IFb-2); pihan (K-2); [pàin] پـايـن (JJ)} Mid P pādan (pāy-) = 'to stand, wait' (M3); Za pawenã [pawtiş] = 'to await, wait for' (Todd) [JR/BX/JB3/IFb//K(s)/GF//BK/JJ]

pan II پان (A/IFb/SK/GF) = wide; flat. See **pehn**.

panayî پانايى (A) = width. See **pehnî II**.

pang•e پـانـگـه *f.* **(•a;).** 1) {also: page (GF); pageh (A/IFb); [pag] پـاگ (JJ); [pawga] پـاوگـا (JJ-Rh); <page> پاگه (HH)} {syn: stewl; t'ewle} stable for horses; 2) {also: pangeh (JB3/IFb/FS/ZFe)} {syn: 'embar} barn, granary: ***•panga* genimî** (FS) wheat granary. [Msr//IFb/JB3/FS/ZF3//A//HH/GF//JJ] <extexane>

pangeh پانگەھ (JB3/IF/FS/ZF3) = barn. See **pange** [2].

p'anglot پانگلۆت (Ad) = lira. See **baqnot**.

panî I پـانـى *f.* **(-ya;-yê).** heel *(of foot or shoe)*: **•Wextê diçin e seferê ji r̄êwe diçin e-naw besta beran, çawêt xo dimiçînin, pêş paş diçin, *panîya* pîyê wan geheşt e kîşk berî dê înin, bi terazîyê kêşin** (SK 12:117) When they go on a journey they go first of all to the vale of stones, shut their eyes, go back and forth and, whichever stone *the heel of* their foot touches, they will bring it and weigh it in a balance ***•Pe'nî da* hespê û hesp fir̄îya bû** (Z-2) He *dug his heels into* [lit. 'gave heel to'] the horse, and the horse flew; **-pehniya solê** (JB3) heel of shoe. {also: pehnî I (K-2/[JB3]/GF-2/TF/OK-2); penî (F); pe'nî (EP-7/K/B/Wn/Rh); [pani] پانى (JJ); <peȟnî> پحنى (HH)} {syn: çim II} [Pok. persnā/-snī̆-/-sno- 823.] 'heel': Skt pā́rṣṇi- *f.*; Av pāršni- (Morg3, p. 340); Mid P pāšnag (M3); P pāšne پاشنه; Sor panê پانێ/pajne پاژنه; Za paşna *f.* (Todd); cf. also Lat perna (<*pērsnā) = 'haunch'; Rus piátka пятка = 'heel' [EP-7/K/B/Wn/ Rh//F//A/IFb/JJ/SK/GF/OK//HH//JB3/TF]

panî II پانى (K) = width. See **pehnî II**.

pank I پانك *f.* **(-a;).** palm *(of the hand)*: **-panka destî** (Dh)/[pana dest] (JJ-G) do.; **-panka devî** (Zeb) palate (of the mouth); **-panka pê** (OK) sole of the foot. {syn: çeng I; ç'epil; k'ef II} <pehn I = 'wide, broad, flat' [Dh/Zeb/OK//JJ-G]

p'ank II پـانـك *f.* **(-a;-ê).** electric fan: **•Vî zarok[î] werîs yan heble xistiye *pankê*** (Wkt:N.Sindî *Xwekuştina zarokan*, Evropress.com x.2011) This child threw a string or rope into *the electric fan*. {also: p'anke (FS)} {syn: p'erwane} <Hindi pankhā = 'fan'; Sor panke پانكه [Wkt//FS] <baweşînk>

p'anke پانكه (FS) = electric fan. See **p'ank II**.

p'anot پانۆت (Epl) = paper money. See **baqnot**.

p'anqanot پـانـقـانـۆت (Qtr-E) = paper money. See **baqnot**.

p'antalon پانتالۆن (K) = pants, trousers. See **p'antol**.

p'antol پـانـتـۆل *m.* **(-ê;).** European style pants, trousers: **•Xelîl Beg ... kujên kurtikê xwe xiste** [sic] **bin kembera *pantorê* xwe** (SBx, 8-9) X.B. ... pushed the corners of his shirt under the waistband of his pants. {also: pantalon (K); p'antolon (RZ/ZF); p'antor (SBx/GF-2/ZF-2); p'entol (IFb-2)} {syn: şal I} < Fr pantalon; Sor pantoł پانتۆڵ [SBx//IFb/FJ/GF/ZF3]

p'antolon پـانـتـۆلـۆن (RZ/ZF) = pants, trousers. See **p'antol**.

p'antor پـانـتـۆر (SBx/GF/ZF) = pants, trousers. See **p'antol**.

panzde پـانـزده (K/B/JB1-A&S/GF/M-Ak & Am & Bar & Shn) = fifteen. See **panzdeh**.

panzdeh پـانـزدەھ num. fifteen, 15. {also: panzde (K/B-2/JB1-A&S/GF/M-Ak & Am & Bar & Shn); panzdê (JB1-S); pazde (M-Sur); paz̲de (M-Zx & Gul); [panzdeh پـانـزده/dehoupyndj/deh-pyndj

دهوپنج] (JJ)} Skt páñcadaśa; Av pancadasa; Mid P pānzdah (M3); P pānzdah پانزده; Sor pazde پازده/ panze پانزه; Za pancês/desupanj (Todd); Hau panze (M4) [F/IFb/B/JJ/SC//K/JB1-A&S/GF/M-Ak & Am & Bar & Shn/M-Sur/M-Zx & Gul] <pênc; pêncî>

panzdehem پانزدههم *adj.* fifteenth, 15th. {also: panzdehemîn (CT-2/GF-2/ZF-2); panzdemîn (IFb); panzdeyem (Wkt-2); panzdeyemîn (Wkt-2); pazdehem (A/Wkt); pazdehemîn (Wkt-2); pazdeyem (Wkt-2); pazdeyemîn (Wkt-2)} Cf. P pānzdahom پانزدهم; Sor panzehem[în] پانزەهەم[ین]/panzemîn پانزەمین [CT/GF/ZF//IFb//A/Wkt] <panzdeh>

panzdehemîn پانزدههمین (CT/GF/ZF) = fifteenth. See **panzdehem**.

panzdemîn پانزدهمین (IFb) = fifteenth. See **panzdehem**.

panzdeyem پانزدهیهم (Wkt) = fifteenth. See **panzdehem**.

panzdeyemîn پانزدهیهمین (Wkt) = fifteenth. See **panzdehem**.

panzdê پانزدێ (JB1-S) = fifteen. See **panzdeh**.

papûç پاپووچ (A/IFb/GF) = infant's shoe. See **p'apûç'k**.

papûçik پاپووچك (ZF3) = infant's shoe. See **p'apûç'k**.

p'apûç'k پاپووچك *f.* **(-a;-ê).** infant's shoe, baby shoe (HH/IF); slipper (A). {also: papûç (A/IFb/GF); papûçik (ZF3); <papûçik> پاپوچك (HH)} Cf. T pabuç & Ar bābūj بابوج = 'slipper' [Z-3/HH/ZF3//A/IFb/GF] <p'êlav; sol>

paq پاق *f./m.(K/ZF3)* **(-a/ ;).** calf of leg, part of the leg below the knee. {also: baq III (FS); [paq] پاق (JJ)} {syn: belek II; boqil; ç'îm I} [Qzl/K/A/IFb/JJ/TF/GF/FJ//FS] <ling>

p'aqij پاقِژ *adj.* clean, neat, tidy: **-p'aqij kirin** (JB1-S/GF/TF/OK) = a) to clean, wipe up: **•Êsirê xwe *paqij dike*** (L) He *wipes away* his tears; b) to sweep up (B): **•Ew ot'axê pê gêzîyê *paqiş dike*** (B) He *sweeps* [lit. '*cleans*'] the room with a broom. {also: pakij (OK-2); paqiş (B); [pakij] پاكيژ (JJ); <paqij> پاقژ (HH)} {syn: p'ak; t'emiz} {p'aqijî; [pakiji] پاكيژى (JJ)} Cf. Mid P pākīzag = 'pure' (M3) [L/K/A/JB3/IFb/HH/JB1-S/GF/OK/FS//JJ//B]

p'aqijî پاقِژى *f.* **(-ya;-yê).** cleanliness; cleaning. {also: pakijî (OK-2); [pakiji] پاكيژى (JJ)} {syn: p'akî} [K/A/IFb/GF/TF/OK/ZF3/FS//JJ] <p'aqij>

paqiş پاقِش (B) = clean. See **p'aqij**.

par I پار *adv.* last year: **•Wî *par* jin îna** (FS) He got married *last year*. {also: [par] پار (JJ); <par> پار (HH)} {syn: sala borî (JB3); sala çûyî (A)} <O Ir *para- (A&L p. 82 [I, 1]): P pārsāl پارسال; Sor par پار/salî par ساڵى پار; Za par (Todd). See I. Gershevitch. "Iranian Chronological Adverbs," *Indo-Iranica: Mélanges présentés à Georg Morgenstierne* (Wiesbaden, 1964), pp.78-88; reprinted in his *Philologia Iranica*, ed. N. Sims-Williams (Wiesbaden : Dr. Ludwig Reichert Verlag, 1985), pp. 179-89. [K/A/JB3/IFb/B/JJ/HH/SK/GF/BK/ZF3/Wkt] <betrapêrar; pêrar; sal>

p'ar II پار *f.* **(-a;-ê).** portion, part, share: **•'Ûr û pizûr, *para* xezûr, ser û pepik, *para* metik** (Msr) Intestines and undesirable parts [are] the father-in-law's *portion*, the head and trotters are the maternal aunt's *portion* (this is part of a folk poem which indicates how the parts of a slaughtered goat or sheep are divided among family members); **-p'ar kirin** = to divide up, deal out: **•Bira tu goştê me *p'ar bike*** (Dz) Brother, you *divide up* our meat **•Şêr ji vê *p'arkirinê* p'ir̄ xeyîdî** (Dz) The lion was furious at this *division* [of the spoils]. {also: p'arçe; p'erçe; [par پار/paré پاره] (JJ); <parçe> پارچه (HH)} {syn: behr I; beş I[2]; p'ay; pişk} [K/A/JB3/IFb/B/JJ/JB1-A/GF//HH] <parî; p'ay; p'erçe; qet II>

par̄a پارا *adv.* (from) behind; after: **•Ûsib dide pey wê, dest davêje *par̄a* dêrê wê** (Ba3) Joseph follows her, grabs hold of her dress *from behind*; **-par̄a man** = to stay, be, or fall behind. {also: (ji) par re (JB3/IF)} [Z-1/K/A/B//JB3/IFb]

parang پارانگ (TF) = ember. See **p'ereng**.

p'arastin پاراستِن *vt.* **(-p'arêz-).** 1) {syn: p'awandin} to protect, defend: **-xwe p'arastin** (JB3) to protect o.s., defend o.s.: **•B. kete nav bajêr û ... *xwe* ji haris *parast*, ji bona go wî nebînin** (L) B. entered the city and *protected himself* (=hid) from the guards, so they wouldn't see him; 2) {syn: r̄agirtin} to keep, preserve, store, save (M); 3) to take care of o.s., preserve o.s. (JJ). {also: p'araztin (GF-2); [paristin] پارستين (JJ)} Mid P pahrēxtan (pahrēz-) = 'to care for, tend, protect' (M3); Sor parastin پاراستِن = 'to protect, save' [L/K/A/JB3/IFb/GF/TF/M//JJ]

paraztin پارازتِن (GF) = to protect. See **p'arastin**.

p'arçe پارچه (B/IFb/JJ/SK/GF) = piece. See **p'ar II** & **p'erçe**.

parçêmk پارچێمك (GF) = bat (flying mouse). See

barç'imok & **pîrçemek**.

pare پاره (IFb/JJ/SK) = money. See **p'ere I**.

p'areve kirin پارەڤە کِرِن (K/B)/pare vekirin پاره ڤەکِرِن (RZ) = to divide; to share. See **p'arve kirin** under **p'arve**.

parêv پـاريـَـڤ (K/IFb/GF/Kmc/ZF3/FS) = lamb dish. See **parîv**.

p'arêz I پـاريَـز *f./m.(ZF3/FS)* **(-a/; /-î).** [water]melon patch; field, garden or bed of watermelons and melons. {also: p'arîz (K/GF); [pārēs] پـاريس (JJ); <parêz> پــاريــز (HH)} {syn: werz [1]} Cf. Av pairi-daēza ='walled-in park, circumvallation' <pairi = 'around' + daēza = 'wall': P pālīz پـاليـز = 'kitchen garden; melon bed'; W Arm bardēz պարտէզ = 'garden'; Heb pardes פרדס = 'orchard, earlier: enclosure, park, garden'; Ar firdaws فـردوس = 'paradise'; Eng paradise [Msr/A/IFb/HH//K/GF//JJ] <lem; le'tik; mişar I>

p'arêz II پاريَز *f.* **(-a;-ê).** diet, regimen: **-parêz girtin**/ ~ **kirin** (ZF3) to diet, be on a diet: **•Camêr nexweş e, *parêz dike*** (ZF3) The man is ill, he*'s on a diet* **•Ez dixwazim *parêzê bigirim* lê dîsan jî dilê min diçe tiştên şirîn û dondar** (Wkt) I want *to diet*, but I also am attracted to sweet and fatty things. Cf. P parhīz پرهيز = 'abstinence; diet'; Sor p'arêz پارێز [ZF3/FS/Wkt]

parî پــاری *m.* **(-yê;).** 1) {syn: beş I; kerî; p'ar II; qet II} piece, morcel; mouthful (JJ/SK); 2) slice *(of bread)*: ***•parîyekî* nan** (MC-1) *a slice of* bread; 3) piece of bread folded over (for use in scooping up food while eating) (Bw); 4) piece of food situated in the mouth (B); 5) a little bit *(of food)* (B). {also: pe'rî I (B); [pari] پــاری (JJ); <parî> پــاری (HH)} Cf. Sor par پــــار = 'piece, part, chapter' & parû پــاروو = 'morsel' [MC-1/Bw/K/A/IFb/JJ/HH/SK/GF/FS//B] See also **p'ar II**.

parîv پـاريـڤ *f.* **(-a;-ê).** dish of roasted lamb (T tandır kebap): **•Wî *parêva* goştê pezî çêkiribû** (FS) He had made roasted lamb *parêv*. {also: parêv (K/IFb/GF/Kmc/ZF3/FS); [pariw] پــــاريــــڤ (JJ); <parêf> پـاريـف (HH)} {syn: biryan I} [Kurd1/JJ//K/IFb/GF/Kmc/ZF3/FS//HH]

p'arîz پاريز (K/GF) = melon patch. See **p'arêz I**.

p'ar kirin پــــار کِــــرِن (K) = to divide; to share. See **p'arve kirin** under **p'arve**.

parne پــــارنــــه (FS) = one or two-year-old calf. See **parone**.

paron•e پـارۆنـه *f.* **(•a;).** one-year-old calf (IFb/Kmc); two-year-old calf (A/FJ/GF): **•Du salan jî wan xwedî bikim-- golik, *parone*, nogin** (Ardû, 153) I'll care for them for 2 years—one, *two* and three-*year old calves* **•Wê *parona* xwe firot** (FS) She sold her *two-year old calf*. {also: parne (FS-2); paronek (A/IFb/GF-2)} [Ardû/FJ/GF/Kmc/FS//A/IFb] <conega; golik; nogin>

paronek پــــارۆنــــهك (A/IFb/GF) = one or two-year-old calf. See **parone**.

p'ars پــارس *f.* **(-a;-ê).** begging; alms collecting: **•Ez û tu rahêjin *tûrê parsê* û herin weke aşiq û mitirban ji xwe re li nava eşîr û ebrê bigerrin** (ZZ-10, 136) Let's you and I pick up a *beggar's sack* and go as bards and singers and wander among the tribes and clans **•K'ete *p'arsa* nane** (EP-5, #7) She took to *begging for* bread; **-p'ars kirin** (B/HH) to beg, be a beggar. {also: [pars kirin] کـريـن پـارس (JJ); <pars> پـارس (HH)} {syn: deroze; geşt} [J/F/K/A/IFb/B/JJ/HH/ZF]

p'arsçî پارسچی = beggar. See **p'arsek**.

p'arseçî پارسەچی = beggar. See **p'arsek**.

p'arsek پـارسـەك *m.* **(;-î).** beggar, mendicant: ***•Parsekî* destê xwe li ber wî vegirt ku para biditê** (FS) *The beggar* opened his hand wide before him to give him (=the beggar) money. {also: p'arsçî; p'arseçî; p'arsekçî (F/B/FS-2); [parsek پــــارســــك/ parsedji پارسجی] (JJ)} {syn: gede; xwazok} Cf. P pārse پــــارســــه = 'poverty; beggar' {p'arsekçîtî; p'arsek[t]î} [F//K/A/JB3/IFb/B/JJ/GF/FS]

p'arsekçî پارسەكچی (F/B/FS) = beggar. See **p'arsek**.

p'arsekçîtî پارسەكچيتی (B) = begging. See **p'arsekî**.

p'arsekî پارسەكی *f.* **(-ya;-yê).** begging; beggary: **•Te em xizan kirin û te em anîn *parsekîyê*** [for: *bariskiyê] (Lwj #41, 39) You made us poor and led us *into beggary*. {also: p'arsekçîtî (B-2); p'arsektî (K-2)} [K/B/IFb/GF/TF/ZF/Wkt] <p'arsek>

p'arsektî پارسەكتی (K) = begging. See **p'arsekî**.

parsû/p'arsû [K/B] پـارسـوو *f./m.(ZF)* **(-ya/;-yê/).** rib: **•Dizanin ko êdî çî dî neşên leqan li t̲eniştêt feqîran biden û goştê *perasîyêt* wan biken e kebab** (SK 56:656) They know that they will no longer be able to kick the poor in the sides and make kebabs with the flesh of their *ribs*. {also: **parxan**; pasû; perasî (SK/FS); perasû (Elk); pirasî (Bw); [parsou] پـارسـو (JJ)} [Pok. I. perḱ- 820.] 'rib; area of the rib, breast': Skt párśu- *f.* = 'rib'; O Ir *parsu- (Hübsch #342): Av parəsu- *f.* = 'rib'; Oss fars = 'side, spot, area'; Mid P pahlūg = 'side, rib'

(M3); P pahlū پهلو = 'side' (Hübsch #342) [Z-1/K/B//(A)/IFb/JJ/GF/TF/RZ/OK//Elk//SK/FS//Bw] <memik; pişik; sîng> See also **parxan**.

p'arsû-qalim پارسوو قالِم *adj.* thick-skinned, harsh, callous, rough, coarse, unrefined (EP-4): **•Mîr hene *p'arsû-qalim*in** (EP-4) There are princes who are *harsh* {cf. **•P'arxana wî qalime** (K/XF) He is insensitive, unfeeling/He is dull [lit. 'His rib is thick']}. [EP-4/(K)/(XF)]

p'arsû sitûr پارسوو سِتوور (EP-7) = insolent; arrogant. See **p'arsûstûr**.

p'arsûstûr پارسووستوور *adj.* impertinent, impudent; insolent *(of a subordinate)* (EP-7); conceited, arrogant (IFb) [lit.: 'thick-ribbed']: •[Who has ever seen the daughter of aristocrats passing around cups, /Bringing a cup to her father's servants?/] **Xulam *p'arsû sitûr* be** (EP-7) The servant will become *insolent*. {also: p'arsû sitûr (EP-7)} [EP-7/IFb] <ĥur; zimandirêj>

p'arsûxar پارسووخار (B/IFb/Z-1) = unhappy; insincere; stubborn. See **p'arsûxwar**.

p'arsûxwar پارسووخوار *adj.* 1) meek, powerless, easily dominated; 2) insecure, unsure of oneself; 3) insincere, false, fickle; evil (B): **•Herê Zînê, lema divên: qismî jin heye *p'arsû xare*** (Z-1) Yes Zin, for they say that some women are *fickle*. {also: p'arsûxar (B-2/IFb/Z-1); p'arxan xar (K)} [Z-1/K/A/B//IFb]

P'art پارت (Bw) = the KDP. See **p'artî**[2].

p'artî پارتی *f.* **(-ya;-yê).** 1) political party: **-Partiya Demokrat a Kurdistana Îranê** (Wkp) Democratic Party of Iranian Kurdistan KDPI;**-Partiya Demokrat a Kurdistanê** (Wkp) Democratic Party of Kurdistan [of Iraq/Başûr], KDP;

-Partiya Karkerên Kurdistanê (=PKK) = Kurdistan Workers' party; **-Partiya Keda Gel** (=HEP) = People's Labor party; 2) {also: P'art (Bw)} [Partî] The Party, i.e., the KDP [=Kurdistan Democratic Party (of Iraqi Kurdistan)]. {also: partîya f. (;-ê) (B)} <Fr parti m. & Eng party [Wlt/K/IFb/TF//B]

partîya پارتییا, f. (;-ê) (B) = political party. See **partî**.

p'arve پارڤه: **-p'arve kirin** [GF/RZ]/**p'ar ve kirin** [IFb]/**parvekirin** [FJ]. 1) to divide *(also math.)*{syn: p'arçe p'arçe kirin; p'irt kirin}: **•Çil û pêncan li nehan *parve bike*** (Kmc) *Divide* 45 by 9 **•Sedî li bîstî *par veke*** = *Divide* 100 by 20; 2) to share. {also: p'ar kirin (K-2); p'areve kirin (K/B)/pare vekirin (RZ-2); [paré we-kirin] پاره ڤەكرین (JJ)} [IFb/GF/FJ/RZ//K/B/JJ] <p'ar II>

p'arvekirin پارڤەكِرِن *f.* **(-a;-ê).** division *(math.)* [Ar taqsīm تقسیم, T bölme, P taqsīm تقسیم]. = Sor dabeş kirdin دابەش كِردِن [Kmc/IFb/GF/ZF3]

parxan/p'arxan [K/B] پارخان *f./m.(ZF)* **(-a/;-ê/).** rib; huge ribs (IFb): ***-P'arxana* wî qalime** (K/XF) He is insensitive, unfeeling/He is dull [lit. 'His *rib* is thick']. {also: parxwan (A)/p'arxwan (B-2); **parsû**} [Z-1/K/B/F/IFb/XF/ZF/Wkt/FD/FS//A] <memik; p'iş I; sîng> See also **parsû**.

p'arxan xar پارخان خار (K) = meek; insincere. See **p'arsûxwar**.

parxêl پارخێل *f.* **(;-ê).** timber sled[ge], dray; oxcart: **•Qol û *parxêl* cida ne li nik me. *Parxêlê* havînan girê didin, didin dû gayan daku ga ji cihên dûr giya bînin nav gundî. Lê qol li ser berfê ye...** (M. Gür, ji Hekaryan, "Zimanê Kurdî", Rûname 5/2012) Qol and *parkhel* are different for us. They tie up a *parkhel* [timber sledge] in the summer, and put it behind oxen so they they will transport the grass from distant places to the village. But the qol [sleigh] is on the snow..... {also: paxêl (A/GF-2/Kmc-16-2); perxîl (GF); [pakhil] پاخیل (JJ); <paxêl> پاخیل (HH)} cf. W Arm palkhir բալխիր [Kmc-2/Kmc-6/Kmc-16/IFb/ZF3//A/GF/JJ/HH]

parxwan (A)/p'arxwan (B) پارخوان = rib. See **parsû** & **parxan**.

parzandin پارزاندِن (K/B) = to filter. See **parzinandin**.

parzin پارزِن (B) = filter, strainer. See **parzûn**.

parzinandin پارزِناندِن *vt.* **(-parzinîn-).** to filter, strain. {also: parzandin (K-2/B); parzinandin (A); parzûnandin (IFb-2); [parzinin پارزنین/palandin پالاندن] (JJ)} {syn: dakirin; palandin} Cf. P pālūdan پالودن; Sor paławtin پاڵاوتِن (-pałêw-) [K/JJ//A/GF//IFb//B] <mifsik; parzûn>

parzinîn پارزِنین (IFb/JJ) = to filter. See **parzinandin**.

parzink پارزِنك (FS) = filter, strainer. See **parzûn**.

parzîn پارزین (Wkt) = filter, strainer. See **parzûn**.

parzû پارزوو (OK) = filter. See **parzûn**.

parzûn پارزوون *m.(BF/Wkt)/f.(ZF3)* **(-ê/ ;).** 1) filter, strainer; thin cloth for straining milk; 2) {also: parzûnk', f. (JB1-A/OK)} woman's pack (carried on back) (Bw/JB1-A/OK). {also: parzin (B-2); parzink (FS); parzîn (Wkt-2); parzû (OK); parzûng (GF-2); [parzoun] پارزون (JJ); <parzûn> پارزون (HH)} [F/K/A/IFb/B/JJ/HH/GF/TF/Bw/ZF3/BF/Wkt//JB1-A//OK//FS] <cente; mifsik; palandin; parzinîn>

parzûnandin پـــارزوونـــانـــدِن (IFb) = to filter. See **parzinandin**.

parzûng پارزوونگ (GF) = filter. See **parzûn**.

parzûnk' پـــارزوونـــك, f. (JB1-A/OK) = woman's pack. See **parzûn**.

p'asaport پاساپۆرت *f.* **(-a;-ê).** passport: **•Ez ê biharê bi *pasaportê* herim** (Nofa, 93) In the spring I will go with *a passport* [i.e., legally] **•Gotibû ez ê *pasaporta* xwe derxim** (Nofa, 90) She had said that she would get *a passport.* {also: paseport (AD); pasport (K/B); paşeport (G)} Cf. T pasaport < Eng passport [Nofa/A/IFb/FJ/TF/ZF3/Wkt/CS//K/B//AD//G]

pasar I پــــــاســــار *f.* **().** wilderness, unpopulated area, deserted area, desert *{word used in area of Sason, Siirt [Sêrt] province by mbrs. of the Xîyan tribe (Haz)}* {syn: ç'ol} [Haz/ZF3]

pasar II پاسار (IFb/TF) = slope. See **pesar**.

paseport پاسەپۆرت (AD) = passport. See **p'asaport**.

pasimam پاسِمام (EP-8) = cousin. See **pismam**.

pasport پاسپۆرت (K/B) = passport. See **p'asaport**.

pasû پاسوو = rib. See **parsû** & **p'arxwan**.

paş پـــــــاش *adv.* 1) {syn: pişt II} behind *[in place (for both location and motion)]*: a) *[location (place where)]*: **•Herdu ga *li paş* in, gamêş jî li pêş in** (AB) Both of the oxen are *in the back*, while the buffaloes are up front **•Tirsonek tim *li paş* in** (AB) The cowards are always *at the rear*; **-paş û pêş** (ZF) back and forth. See under **paş û pêş**; **-paş ve** (BX) in back, in the rear; b) *[motion (place to which)]*: **•Ez çûm *paş* xênî** (BX) I went *behind* the house; **-xwe dane paş** (K/XF) to retreat; to remain aloof, stay away; to avoid, keep away from; to avoid the limelight, to keep a low profile; to be reluctant [see also: **xwe-dane-paş**] {syn: xwe dûr xistin ji *f-tî*}: **•Ez *xo dideme paş* ji van tiştan** (Bw) I *avoid* [or, *keep away from*] these things **•Wextê r̄ûs kir, zabitî dît bazîbendek ya bi milê r̄astêve. Ḧalen hema *xo da paş*, destê xo li ser êk da na** (M-Ak #677, 306) When he was stripped, the officer saw an armlet on his right shoulder. Immediately *they all retreated*, placing their hands one upon the other (in homage); 2) after, afterward *[in time]*: **-paşê** = afterward, then, later {syn: dûr̄a; hingê, etc.; (di) pişt re; şûnda}: ***•Paşê* têne meydanê** (J) *Then* they come to the square (or battlefield); 3) used in conjunction with postpositions:

-di paş ... de = behind *(location, no motion)* {also: li paş}: ***•Di paş* xaniyê me *de* kaniyek heye** (BX) *Behind* our house there is a spring;

-di paş ... re = behind *(in motion)*: **•Gur *di paş* şivên *re* derbas bû** (BX) The wolf passed *behind* the shepherd;

-ji paş = from behind: **•Dijmin *ji paş* çiyê derket** (BX) The enemy came out *from behind* the mountain. {also: paşî I (F/JB1-A); [pachi] پاشی (JJ); <paş> پـــاش (HH)} Av pasča = 'after'; O P pasā = 'behind'; Mid P pas = 'then, afterward, behind' (M3); P pas پس (Horn); Sor paş پاش = 'behind, after'; [Za peydi = 'back, backward, behind' (Todd)]. See I. Gershevitch. "Iranian Chronological Adverbs," *Indo-Iranica: Mélanges présentés à Georg Morgenstierne* (Wiesbaden, 1964), pp.78-88; reprinted in his *Philologia Iranica*, ed. N. Sims-Williams (Wiesbaden : Dr. Ludwig Reichert Verlag, 1985), pp. 179-89. [BX/K/(A)/JB3/IFb/B/JJ/HH/SK/GF//F/JB1-A]

p'aşa پـــاشـــا *m.* **(-yê; p'aşê).** 1) pasha, Turkish high ranking official; 2) *man's name.* {also: paşe (A); [pacha] پاشا (JJ)} Cf. T paşa < P padišāh پـادشـاه {p'aşatî; [pachati] پاشاتی (JJ)} [Z-1/K/IFb/B/JJ/SK/GF//A] <p'adşa>

p'aşatî پـاشـاتـی *f.* **(-ya;-yê).** rank of pasha, pashadom: **•Ez te'eccubê dikem, paşa, te çawa ḧetta noke *paşatî kiriye*, te r̄idîna xo spî kiriye û 'emrê xo r̄a-bariye di *paşatiyê*da, hêşta nizanî dê çawa hijîrê xoy?!** (SK 20:184) I wonder, Pasha, how can you *have ruled as Pasha* until now and let your beard grow white and passed all your life as Pasha [lit. 'in *pashadom*'] and still not know how to eat a fig? **•Kincên *paşatiyê* lê kirin, taca dewletê dane** [sic] **serê wî û li ser text dane** [sic] **rûniştandin** (ZZ-7, 256) They put the clothes *of pashadom* on him, placed the crown of the kingdom on his head and seated him on the throne. {also: [pachati] پاشاتی (JJ)} [K/JJ/SK/GF/ZF3] <p'aşa>

paşbend پاشبەند *f.* **(-a;-ê).** rhyme: **•Li Kurdî da jî ji qafiyeyê ra *paşbend* û paşhel gotine** (Chn, 55) In Kurdish, for qafiye (rhyme), they have also said *paşbend* and paşhel. {syn: beşavend; qafiye; serwa} [Chn/FJ/GF/SS]

paşda پـــاشـــدا *adv.* back (e.g., 'to give back'), in return: **•Dibe ku te t'emî dane Ûsib, wekî ... *paşda* bîne**

(Ba) Perhaps you instructed Joseph to ... bring [it] *back*; **-paşda man** (K)/**paşde man** (ZF3/FD) to stay behind {syn: pař̄a man; veman}. {also: paşde (IFb/GF)} [K/B//IFb/GF]

paşdamayî پاشدامایی *pp./adj.* backward, left behind, underdeveloped: **•Zivingê gundê herî *paşdemayî* yê Stilîlê ye** (Nbh 132:12) Z. is the most *backward* village of Stilîlê. {also: paşdemayî (Nbh/GF/K-2); paşvemayî (ZF)} [Nbh/GF//K/B/FJ//ZF] <paşverû>

paşde پاشده (IFb/GF) = back, in return. See **paşda**.

paşdemayî پاشدەمایی (Nbh/GF/K) = backward, underdeveloped. See **paşdamayî**.

paşe پاشە (A) = pasha. See **p'aşa**.

paşeport پاشەپۆرت (G) = passport. See **p'asaport**.

paşeřoj پاشەڕۆژ *f.* **(-a;-ê).** future: **•Bêguman niha piraniya xelkê Kurd li Turkiya wê yekê meraq diken ka dê *paşeroja* Kurdan li Turkiya çawa bît** (Evro 24.ii.2013, 3) No doubt, the majority of Kurds in Turkey are now wondering what [lit. 'how'] t*he future of* the Kurds in Turkey will be **•Kurd bûyne faktereké serekî di diyarkirina *paşeroja* Rojhelata Navîn da** (Evro 24.ii.2013, 3) The Kurds have become a major factor in determining *the future of* the Middle East **•Kurd qewmekî nexundî ye, tedbîra *paşeřoja* xo nizanin, bêtifaq in** (SK 56:643) The Kurds are an illiterate people, improvident of their *future* and disunited. {also: paşroj (GF); pêşeroj (Ber/RZ)} {syn: siberoj} Cf. Sor paşeřoj پاشەڕۆژ & dwařoj دواڕۆژ= 'future'. See Sidqî Hirorî, "Pêşeroj yan Paşeroj?" *RN2* 44-45 (1996) & Keça Kurd. "Pêşeroj û Paşeroj," *Rastî* 3 (1998), 45. [Ber/RZ//K/IFb/JB3/SK/OK/BF/ZF//GF]

paşgotinî پاشگۆتنی *f.* **(-ya;-yê).** gossip, backbiting: **-paşgotinîya *fk-î* kirin** (LC/IFb/RZ) to gossip about s.o., talk about s.o. behind his back, "to dish" s.o.: **•Me dîsa bi hev re *paşgotiniya* nivîskarekî din *kir*** (LC, 21) Once again we *gossiped about* another writer. {syn: *dedîqodî; galegûrt; galigal; gotgotk; kurt û p'ist; xeyb} [LC/IFb/GF/OK/RF/RZ/ZF]

p'aş•il پاشِل *f.* **(•[i]la;•ilê).** 1) {syn: p'êsîr [1]; pizî III; sîng} bosom, breast; chest: **•Zîna delal ȟişîyar bû, lênihêřî, xortekî nazik *paşla* wêdane** (Z-1) Zin woke up, looked around [and saw] a fine youth was at her *bosom* **•Her çar birê wî jinê xwe xistin *paşila* xwe û razan** (Z-1) All four of his brothers took their wives to their *bosom(s)* and went to sleep; 2) {syn: ȟemêz [2]} embrace. {also: p'axil, f. (;-ê) (SK); [pachil پاشل/pakhil پاخل] (JJ); <paşil پاشل/paxil پاخل> (HH)} [Z-1/K/IFb/B/JJ/HH/GF//SK]

paşin پاشِن (B/IFb) = last, final. See **paşîn**.

paşî I پاشی (F/JB1-A) = behind; after. See **paş**.

paşî II پاشی (SK/A) = last, final. See **paşîn**.

paşîn پاشین *adj.* 1) {syn: dawîn} last, final: **-cara paşin** (B) the last time; 2) next, following. {also: paşin (B/IFb-2); paşî II (SK/A); [pachin] پاشین (JJ); <paşî> پاشی (HH)} Mid P pasēn = 'final, last' (M3); P pasīn پسین = 'last, latest'; Sor paşîn پاشین = 'subsequent, future; last' [F/K/JB3/IFb/JJ/GF//B//A/HH/SK] <pêşîn>

Paşînî پاشینی **(;-yê).** Saturday. {syn: Sebt; Şemî} < paş = 'after' + în[î] = 'Friday'; Za paşêne *m.* (Mal) [cf. T cumartesi < cuma = 'Friday' + ertesi = 'the day after'] [Rh/Kr/Mzg/ZF3]

paşîv پاشیڤ *f.* **(-a;-ê).** 1) meal eaten just before dawn during the fast of Ramadan {Ar saḥūr سحور, T sahur}: **•Şivan fitara xwe jî *paşîva* xwe jî li çol û mexelan dixwin** (aa.com.tr 3.vi.2018) The shepherds both break their fast and eat their *early morning meal* in the wilderness and by the sheepfolds; 2) dessert (A/IFb/HH). {also: [pachiw] پاشیڤ (JJ); <paşîv> پاشیڤ (HH)} < paş = 'after' + şîv = 'dinner' [Msr/K/A/IFb/B/JJ/HH]

paşlandik پاشلاندِك *m.&f.* **().** youngest child, last-born child, baby of the family. {syn: binhemban} [Qzl/Kmc-#5356/ZF3]

paşnav پاشناڤ *m.* **(-ê;).** last name, surname: **•Lewre jî dibêjin, divê polîtîkaya nû li gor *paşnavê* Demîrel sert û dijwar (weke hesin) be** (Wlt 2:71, 13) Hence they say that the new policy must be hard and firm (like iron), in accordance with Demirel's last name [*note: in Turkish demir = 'iron' & el = 'hand']. [(neol)Wlt/ZF3] <nav I>

paşop'ê پاشۆپێ (K/B) = back and forth. See **paş û pêş**.

paşopêş پاشۆپێش (K) = back and forth. See **paş û pêş**.

paşpêşî پاشپێشی (IFb) = back and forth. See **paş û pêş**.

paşpirt پاشپرت (BF/SS) = suffix. See **paşp'irtik**.

paşp'irtik پاشپرتك *f.* **(-a;-ê).** suffix. {also: paşpirt (BF/SS); paşp'irtî (B-2)} [K/B/ZF/Wkt//BF/SS] <pêşp'irtik; qertaf>

paşp'irtî پاشپرتی (B) = suffix. See **paşp'irtik**.

paşroj پاشرۆژ (GF) = future. See **paşeřoj**.

paşstû پاشستوو *m.* **(-yê;).** nape of neck: **•Kilso *paşstûyê* xwe dixurîne** (mamostemaruf.blogspot.com

17.xi.2013) K. scratches *the back of his neck.* {also: paşustû (K-2)} {syn: p'ate I; stukur} [K/GF/AD/ZF3]

P'aştûyî پاشتوویی *adj.* Pashto/Pushtu. {also: Peştûyî (Wkt-2)} [Wkt/SS]

paşustû پاشوستوو (K) = nape of neck. See **paşstû**.

paş û pêş پاش و پێش *adv.* back and forth: **•Wextê diçin e seferê ji r̄êwe diçin e-naw besta beran, çawêt xo dimiçînin, *pêş paş diçin*, panîya pîyê wan geheşt e kîşk berî dê înin, bi ṯerazîyê kêşin** (SK 12:117) When they go on a journey they go first of all to the vale of stones, shut their eyes, *go back and forth* and, whichever stone the heel of their foot touches, they will bring it and weigh it in a balance; **-paşop'ê çûyîn** (B): a) to move backwards; b) to be unsuccessful, fail: **•Şixulê wî *paşop'ê diçe*** (B) His affairs *are failing*; **-paş û pêş xistin** (X.Duhokî) to invert, change the order of, transpose; to confuse, mix up: **•Lê piraniya çîrokên wî, bi teknîka modêrn, monolog û dalog** [sic], ***paş û pêşxistina* demî û zincîra rûdanan, ḧeta dawiyê bi hev re girêdayîye** (X. Duhokî. Qefteka gulan, 129) But most of his stories are connected to each other in a modern technique, monologue & dialogue, *transposing* the time and order of events. {also: paşop'ê (K/B); paşopêş (K-2); paşpêşî (IFb); pêş paş (SK); pêş û paş (A)} [X.Duhokî/ZF//IFb//K/B//A//SK]

paşvemayî پاشڤەمایی (ZF) = backward, underdeveloped. See **paşdamayî**.

paşveroh پاشڤەرۆه (OK) = reactionary. See **paşver̄û**.

paşver̄û پاشڤەڕوو *adj.* backward, reactionary. {also: paşveroh (OK)} {≠pêşver̄û} [TF/OK/ZF] <paşdamayî>

paşxan پاشخان (RZ/Wkt) = background. See **paşxane**.

paşxane پاشخانە *f.* **(-ya;-yê).** background *(lit. & fig.)* [*T arkaplan, Ar xalfîyah* خلفية]: **•Heta ku *paşxaneya* wê neyê ronkirin ev birin** [=birîn] **dê her hebe** (Partîya Demokratîk a Gelan, 1.vii.2017) Until its *background* is made clear, this wound will always remain **•... lêkolîner-nivîskar M. Malmîsanij û ji başûrê Kurdistanê Abdulla M. Zangana wê li ser *paşxane* û peywendiyên ku Rojî Kurd anîne holê nîqaş bikin** (Rûdaw 12-3-2013) ... the researcher and writer M. M. and A.M.Z. from southern Kurdistan [i.e., Iraqi K-n] will debate about *the background* and connections which [the newspaper] Rojî Kurd brought to the fore **•Nûçegihînê/a ku wê bûyerê bike nûçe divê bi wî warî re têkildar be, li ser *paşxana* bûyerê hinekî agahdar be** (S. Tan. *Nûçe, nûçegihan û neqandina nûçeyan*, Azadiyawelat.com, ix.2007) The reporter who makes that event into news must be familiar with the field, [must] be informed about *the background of* the event. {also: paşxan (RZ/Wkt-2)} [(neol.)ZF3//RZ/Wkt]

pat پات (GF/AD/FS) = tie or draw (in games). See **pate III**.

pata پاتا (IFb/FD/ZF3) = tie or draw (in games). See **pate III**.

p'ate I پاتە *f.* **().** 1) {syn: paşstû; stukur} {also: patik, f. (-a;-ê) (B/SK/Hk); p'atik (JB1-A); paṯik (FS); patûk (Hk-2)} back of the neck, nape: **-p'ate vedan** (XF) to incline one's head, take a bow [Rus prikloniat'sia приклоняться]; 2) military salute (IFb/GF): **-pate lê xistin** (IF) to salute [T selâm çakmak]; **-p'ate avêtin** (GF) to salute, greet: **•Mek't'ûbê dide destê wî û *p'ate davêje*, li cîyê edebê disekine** (Z-3) He hands him the letter and *salutes*, standing in a position of respect. [Z-3/IFb/GF/XF//JB1-A//B/SK/Hk]

p'at•e II پاتە/**paṯ•e II** پاطە [Bw/Dh] *m.* **(•ê;•ey).** 1) {syn: pîne} patch (Bw/IFb/GF): **•Kun ji *patey* maṯir lê hat** (Bw) There are more *patches* than holes *[expression]* ***•patek* û ṣed kun** (Bw) *one patch* and 100 holes *[expression for trying to solve a problem with inadequate means]*; 2) {syn: kerkon; kevnik [1]; p'aç' II[1]; p'er̄ok; pîne; p'ot; qerpal} rag, tatter (OK/GF); small piece of cloth (Bw). {also: paçe (GF-2)} [Bw/Dh//IFb/GF/OK] <p'aç' II & p'aç[']ik; pîne>

pate III پاتە *f.* **().** a tie, a draw, a stalemate, a deadlock (in card games): **•Lîstik *pate* ket** (Qmş) The game was a *draw/tie*; **-pate bûn** (Qmş) to be tied, be deadlocked: **•Ev lîstik *pate ye*** (Qmş) This game *is a stalemate.* {also: pat (GF/AD/FS); pata (IFb/FD/ZF3-2)} T pata = 'stalemate, deadlock (in card games)' [Qmş/FJ/ZF3//IFb/FD//GF/AD]

patik پاتِك, f. (-a;-ê) (B/SK/Hk)/p'atik (JB1-A)/paṯik پاطِك (FS) = nape of the neck. See **p'ate I**.

patin پاتِن *vt.* **(-pêj-).** 1) {syn: pijandin} to bake, cook: **•Dibêje lê *napêje*** (Z-) He says but he *doesn't bake* [=he's all talk and no action] **•Nanê min *bipêje*** (Dz) *Bake* my bread (=Bake me some bread); 2) to burn, bake, beat down *(of the sun)* (B): **•Te'v *dipêje*** (B) The sun *is beating down.* {also: pahtin (Bw); pehtin (JB3-2/DZK); peḧtin (M-Am/M-Zx);

petin (F); pe'tin (B/Dz); pêjîn (IF-2); pijan (A); pijîn (K-2/JB3-2/IFb-2); [patin پاتين /pejiian پژيان] (JJ); <peȟtin پحتن (dipêje) (دپیژه)> (HH)} [Pok. pekṷ- 798.] 'to cook, ripen': O Ir *pak- (Tsb 42) & *paxta- (A&L p. 88 [X, 6]): Av pak- (*pres.* pača-); Mid P poxtan (paz-) (M3); P poxtan پختن (-paz-) (پز); Sor pîşan پیشان (-pîşê-) = 'to be cooked' (see under **pijîn**); Za pewjenã [pewtiş] = 'to cook (vt.)' & peyşenã [peyşayiş] = 'to roast, cook (vi.)' (Todd/Srk); cf. also Lat coquere (<*poquere); Gr peptein πεπτειν = 'to cook, ripen, digest'; Rus peč' печь (pekú, pečëš') (пеку, печёшь) [F//K/JB3/IFb/JJ/SK/GF/M//Bw// B/Dz/DZK//HH/M-Am/M-Zx] See also **pijîn** & **pijandin**. <aşpêj; biraştin; lênan; qijilandin>

patos پاتۆس (IFb/Kmc-6) = threshing machine. See **patoz**.

patoz پاتۆز *f.* **().** thresher, threshing machine, threshing sled. {also: batoz (Frq); patos (IFb-2/Kmc-6); <patoz> پاتۆز (Hej)} {syn: cencer} Cf. T batos [Edirne] = 'threshing machine' [harman makinası] (DS, v. 2, p.572) [Frq-->Bw/Hej//IFb/Kmc-6] <bênder>

patrom•e پاترۆمه *f.* **(•a;).** graft[ing], scion: **•*Peṯroma* hirmîkê şîn bû** (FS) The pear *graft* turned green; **-patrome kirin** (Kmc-6) to graft {syn: tamandin}. {also: patrûme (K); petirme (GF-2/FS-2); peṯrome (FS); petrume (GF); peturme (M. 'Ebdulreȟman. Peturmekirina gunehan); [patruma] پترومه (JJ); <petirme> پەترمە (Hej)} {syn: *lûl (IFb/Kmc-6)} =Sor mutirbe موتربە/miturbe متوربە [Kmc-6/IFb//K//JJ//GF/Hej//FS]

patrûme پاتروومه (K) = grafting. See **patrome**.

p'atşah پاتشاه (-ê;) (FK-eb-1) = king, ruler. See **p'adşa**.

p'atşatî پاتشاتی (Ba3-1) = kingship. See **p'adşatî**.

patûk پاتووك (Hk) = nape of the neck. See **p'ate I**.

pavlik•e پاڤلکه *f.* **(;•ê).** factory, plant: **•Bavê te çi k'arî dike? -K'arker e, di *pavlikê* da dixebite** (DZK) What does your father do for a living? -He is a worker, he works in *the factory*. {also: palûke (IF)} [(neol)DZK//IFb]

p'awan I/pawan [K] پاوان *m.* **(-ê;).** guard, watchman: **•[Lakin *pawan* jî pê naȟesin]** (JR #27, 80) But even *the watchmen* are not aware of him. {also: [pavan] پاوان (JJ/JR)} {syn: qerewil} <O Ir *pā̊- = 'to guard' + *suffix* -wān² (<*pāna-) (A&L p. 82 [I, 1]); Arm pahpan (W Arm: bahban) պահպան [JR/K/JJ/ZF3]

p'awan II پاوان *m.* **(-ê;).** grassy piece of land which is off limits for grazing in spring and summer, used as pastureland in the wintertime (Zeb). {also: <pawan> پاوان (Hej)} {syn: qorix} Sor pawan پاوان [Zeb/IFb/OK/Hej/AA]

p'awandin/pawandin [K] پاواندن *vt.* **(-pawîn-).** to guard, protect, defend: **•Ev mêrga hanê, mi *pawandîye* ji boy Sîyabend û Qedêye** (Z-4) This meadow, I *have guarded it* for S. and Q. [Z-4/K/ZF3] <p'arastin>

pawîz پاویز (Bw) = autumn, fall. See **payîz**.

paxêl پاخێل (A/HH/GF/Kmc-16) = timber sled. See **parxêl**.

p'axil پاخل, f. (;-ê) (SK) = bosom, breast; chest. See **p'aşil**.

p'ay پای *f.(K)/m.(B/Ba2)* **(/-ê; /p'êy).** 1) {syn: behr I; beş I; p'ar II; pişk} part, portion: **•*p'aê* salêyî p'iȓ** (Ba2) a large *part* of the year; 2) pride; praise. See **p'aye I**. {also: p'a (Ba2); [paï] پای (JJ); <pay> پای (HH)} Cf. T pay = 'portion' [Ba2/K/A/IFb/B/JJ/HH/GF]

p'aye I پایه *f.* **().** 1) pride; showing off, swaggering: **-xwe paye kirin [bi]** (Wlt) to be proud of, boast of: **•Û hêja ye ku gelê Kurd, *xwe paye bike* bi vî lehengê bi nav û nîşan** (Wlt 1:42, 10) And it is fitting that the Kurdish people *be proud of* this famous hero; 2) {syn: meȟ; p'esin[1]} praise, eulogy (B): **-p'a[y]ê *fk-ê/ft-î* dayîn** (B) to praise: **•Ewe gelekî ji mîr ȓazî bûn û ȓêva *p'ayê wî didan*** (Ba-1, #33) They were very pleased with the emir, and *were praising him* [while] en route. {also: paî, m. (F); **p'ay**[2] (B); p'ayî (K); peya II (IFb); [paia] پایه (JJ)} [Wlt/A/JJ/OK//F//K//B//IFb]

paye II پایه: -paye bûn (Haz) = to disembark. See **peya**[2].

p'ayebilind پایەبلند *adj.* respected, worthy of esteem; first rate; high ranking: **•Aramê Dîkran nûnerekî *payebilind* yê şaristaniya Rojhilatê bû** (mediakurd.com 8.viii.2010) A. Dikran was a *first rate* representative of the civilization of the East. < p'aye I + bilind [mediakurd/IFb/ZF3/Wkt/BF/FD] See also **bilindpaye.**

payin پاین (BK/JJ) = to wait for. See **p'an I**.

payitext پایتەخت (IFb) = capital city. See **p'ayt'ext**.

payiz پایز (B/JJ/GF/TF/OK) = autumn, fall. See **payîz**.

p'ayî پایی (K) = pride; praise. See **p'aye I**.

payîn پایین (K[s]/IFb/GF) = to wait for. See **p'an I**.

payîz پاییز *f.* **(-a;-ê).** autumn, fall: **-payîzan** (AB)/ **payizê** (B) = in the autumn, in the fall: **•*Payizan* pel ji daran diweşin** (AB) *In the fall,* the leaves fall from the trees. {also: paîz (F); pawîz (Bw); payiz (B/GF/TF/OK-2); pehîz (GF-2/ OK-2); [pàiz] پـــايـــز (JJ)} Av *paitidaeza- & O P *patidaiza- (Fr. Müller. WZKM 5, 261); Mid P pādēz (M3); P pā'īz پائيز; Sor payîz پاییز; Za payiz (Todd)/payîz (Mal) *m.*; Hau paîz *m.* (M4) [K/A/JB3/ IFb/OK//B/JJ/GF/TF//F//Bw]

p'ayt'ext [K/B]/**paytext** پایتەخت *m.(K/B/Wkt)/f.(ZF)* **(-ê/-a; /-ê).** capital city: **•Li Kiyêv *paytexta* Ukraynayê, îro rojnamevanekî navdar di encama teqîna bombeyeke, ku di tirimbêla wî de hatibû biciĥkirin..., jiyana xwe ji dest da** (Orient.net) In Kiev *the capital of* Ukraine, today a well known journalist lost his life as the result of the explosion of a bomb which had been placed in his car. {also: payitext (IFb)} Sor paytext پایتەخت < P pāytaxt پایتخت (<pā = 'foot' + taxt = 'throne') [Orient.net/K/B/FJ/GF/SS/RZ/ZF/Wkt//IFb]

p'aytûn پایتوون, m. (SK) = carriage. See **fayton**.

paz پاز (TF) = sheep and goats. See **pez**.

pazde پازده (M-Sur)/pazde پاظده (M-Zx & Gul) = fifteen. See **panzdeh**.

pazdehem پازدەهەم (A/Wkt) = fifteenth. See **panzdehem**.

pazdehemîn پازدەهەمین (Wkt) = fifteenth. See **panzdehem**.

pazdeyem پازدەیەم (Wkt) = fifteenth. See **panzdehem**.

pazdeyemîn پازدەیەمین (Wkt) = fifteenth. See **panzdehem**.

peçavtin پەچاڤتِن (Hk/JJ) = to cover. See **pêçavtin**.

peçe I پەچە (TG2) = skylight. See **p'ace**.

peçe II پەچە (OK) = veil. See **pêçe**.

*peçiqandin پەچِقاندِن (RN) = to crush. See **p'erçiqandin**.

peçvan پەچڤان (IFb) = interpreter. See **p'açveker**.

peçve پەچڤە (IFb) = translation. See **p'açve**.

pehen پەهەن (IFb) = dung, manure. See **peyîn.**

p'ehîn پەهین (K/A/IF/GF) = kick. See **p'eĥîn**.

pehîz پەهیز (GF/OK) = autumn, fall. See **payîz**.

pehlewan پەهلەوان (ZF3) = hero; knight; athlete. See **p'elewan**.

pehlewanî پەهلەوانی (ZF3) = heroic deed. See **p'elewanî**.

pehliwan پەهلِوان = hero; knight; athlete. See **p'elewan**.

pehn I پەهن *adj.* 1) {syn: [ber]fireh; berîn} wide, broad: •...**Lixawekî asin dû gez dirêj, gezek *pan*, bi qeder zenda destî stûr bide çêkirin** (SK 33:297) Go and get an iron bridle made, two yards long, a yard *wide* and as thick as a man's wrist; 2) {syn: dûz} flat; 3) smooth. {also: pahn (A-2/ IFb-2); pan II (A/IFb-2/SK/GF-2); pen (F); pe'n (B/Msr); [pan] پان (JJ); <peĥn> پحن (HH)} [Pok. pet-/p$_e$t-/petə- 824.] 'to stretch out, esp. the arms': Av paθana- = 'wide, broad'; Mid P pahn (M3); P pahn پهن; Sor pan پان {pa[h]nayî; panî; pehnayî; pehnî II; pe'nayî; [pehnaï] پهنای (JJ)} [S&E/K/JB3/IFb/ /F//B/Msr//A/JJ/SK//HH]

pehn II پەهن (Bw) = kick. See **p'eĥîn**.

pehnahî پەهناهی (GF) = width. See **pehnî II**.

pehnatî پەهناتی (GF) = width. See **pehnî II**.

pehnayî پەهنایی (K/JJ) = width. See **pehnî II**.

pehnî I پەهنی (K/[JB3]/GF/TF/OK) = heel. See **panî I**.

pehnî II پەهنی *f.* **(-ya;-yê).** 1) width, breadth; 2) plain, flat land; 3) visibility at a distance. {also: pa[h]nayî (A); panî II (K-2); pehnahî (GF); pehnatî (GF-2); pehnayî (K-2); peĥnî (FS); pe'nayî (B); [pehnaï] پهنای (JJ)} Cf. P pahnā پهنا/ pahnī پهنی [K/JB3/IFb//A//B//JJ//GF//FS] <pehn I>

pehtin پەهتِن (JB3/DZK) = to cook. See **patin**.

p'eĥeyn پەحەین (Z-821) = kick. See **p'eĥîn**.

p'eĥîn پەحین *f.* **(;-ê).** kick, blow with the foot: **-p'ehîn lê dan/xistin** (K) to kick: **•K'êleka şeher baẍek hebû, go: "Ezê heřim wî baẍî...." *P'eĥînek* derê bêẍ *da*, derê bêẍ vebû, çû hunduřê bêẍ** (Z-821, 134) At the edge of the city there was a garden, he said, "I will go into that garden..." He *kicked* the door of the garden, it opened, and he went into the garden **•Kuřik'î *pêhnek* marî *da*, kuşt'** (M-Zx, #762, 352) The boy *kicked* the snake and killed it. {also: p'ehîn (K/A/IF/GF); pehn II (Bw); p'eĥeyn (Z-821-2); pêhn (M-Zx); pihîn (GF-2); pîn II (IFb-2); [peïnek/painek] پینك (JJ); <peĥîn> پحين (HH)} {syn: çivt; lotik; řefes; tîzik} [Z-821/B/HH//K/ A/IFb/GF//JJ//Bw//M-Zx] <lotik>

peĥnî پەحنی (FS) = width. See **pehnî II**.

peĥtin پەحتِن (M-Am/M-Zx/HH) = to cook. See **patin**.

peîn پەئین (F) = dung, manure. See **peyîn**.

pej پەژ *m.* **(-ê;).** 1) twigs and branches cut off during pruning, clippings; 2) {syn: ĥejik} twigs used as firewood: **-hejik û pejik** (GF-Cigerxwîn) small branches, twigs. {also: pejalok (FJ-2/GF-2); pejik (TF/ZF-2/CS/FS/Kmc); [pej] پژ (JJ); <pejik> پژك (HH)} [CCG/GF/JJ/ZF/Wkt//TF/HH/CS/FS/Kmc] <pejikandin>

pejalok پەژالۆك (FJ/GF) = twig(s). See **pej**.

pejik پەژک (TF/ZF-2/CS/FS/Kmc/HH) = twig(s). See **pej**.

pejikandin پەژکاندِن *vt.* **(-pejikîn-).** to prune, trim, clip, cut off, lop off *(branches)*: **•Gelê me di meha adarê de dest bi *pejikandina* daran dikin. Yanê hin gulî û pejên daran tên jêkirin** (CCG, 287) Our people start *pruning* trees in the month of March. In other words, some branches and twigs are removed. {also: pejilandin (GF/BF/SS); pejinîn (FS); pejiqandin (Wkt-2); pejlandin (FJ); pejnandin (Kmc); pijikandin (Wkt-2); pijiqandin II (Wkt-2)} {syn: çipilandin; k'ezaxtin; t'eřişandin} [CCG/ZF/Wkt//GF/BF/SS//FJ//Kmc//FS] <pej>

pejilandin پەژلاندِن (GF/BF/SS) = to prune, clip. See **çipilandin** & **pejikandin**.

pejin پەژِن (IFb/TF/OK) = sound whose origin is unclear. See **pêjin**.

pejinîn پەژنین (FS) = to prune, clip. See **pejikandin**.

pejiqandin پەژِقاندِن (Wkt) = to prune, clip. See **pejikandin**.

p'ejirandin پەژِراندِن *vt.* **(-p'ejirîn-).** to accept, approve of: **•Gelê me xebata me *dipejirîne*** (Wlt 1:37, 16) Our people *accepts* [or, *approves of*] our effort. {also: pejîrandin (GF-2)} {syn: qebûl kirin [b]} Cf. P paẕīroftan پذيرفتن = 'to accept' [Wlt/K/IFb/GF/TF]

pejî پەژی *m.(Zeb)/f.(OK)* **(-yê/ ;).** 1) {syn: êş; jan; qotik II; şewb; weba} epidemic, plague; contagious or infectious illness; 2) *[adj.]* infectious, contagious (disease). {also: pejîk (OK-2); <pejîk پەژیك> (Hej)} [Zeb/OK/FS//Hej]

pejîk پەژیك (OK/Hej) = epidemic. See **pejî**.

pejîrandin پەژیراندِن (GF) = to accept. See **p'ejirandin**.

pejlandin پەژلاندِن (FJ) = to prune, clip. See **çipilandin** & **pejikandin**.

pejn پەژن (IFb/OK) = sound whose origin is unclear. See **pêjin**.

pejnandin پەژناندِن (Kmc) = to prune, clip. See **pejikandin**.

p'ekandin پەکاندِن *vt.* **(-p'ekîn-).** 1) to burst, split, crack *(vt.)*; 2) {syn: dan ber lingan; dewisandin; 'eciqandin; heřişandin; p'elaxtin; p'erçiqandin; pêpes kirin; t'episandin} to crush, squash; 3) to cut off, chop off, sever, break off. {also: peqandin (-peqîn-) (JB1-A); paqānd- (JJ-PS)/pakánd- (JJ-G)} < Arc √p-q-' פקע/Syr √p-q-' ܦܩܥ [F/K/JB1-S/GF//JB1-A//JJ] <p'ekîn>

p'ekîn پەکین/pekîn [B] *vi.* **(-p[']ek-).** 1) to come off, break off *(vi.)*, come undone: **•Gustîlek di destê hakim de bû ... ji destê wî *pekîya*** (L) There was a ring on the king's hand ... it *came off* his hand; 2) {syn: k'etin; weşîn} to drop *(vi.)*, fall (into); 3) to splash, splatter *(of liquids) (vi.)*: **•Niqitkeke xûna wî dîsa *pekîya* ort'a M. û Z.** (Z-1) A drop of his blood (again) *splattered* between M. and Z.; 4) to explode, flash *(of sparks, etc.)*: **•Ew milê Ûsiv digire sîleke usa lê dixe, wekî ji ç'avê wî pirîsk *dipekin*** (Ba3-3, #25, 196) He grabs Joseph's arm and slaps him so hard that sparks *fly out* his eyes. {also: **p'eqîn**; [pŭkīn] پقين (JJ)}< Arc √p-q-' פקע/ Syr √p-q-' ܦܩܥ = 'to burst, break; to escape': NENA pâqé/păqî ܦܩܥ (Maclean). For the medial -q- of the original Arc, there are forms in both -k- and -q-. The disappearance of the final 'ayn (ع) is not uncommon, for other examples see **civîn** & **qetîn**. [L/K/JB1-S/GF//IFb/B//JJ] See also **p'eqîn**. <p'ekandin>

p'el I پەل *m./f.(Qzl)* **(-ê/-a;).** 1) {syn: belç'im; belg} leaf (pl. leaves): **•Payizan *pel* ji daran diweşin** (AB) In the fall, *the leaves* fall from the trees; **-p'elê dara** (IFb) tree leaf; **-p'elê kelema** (IFb) cabbage leaf; **-p'elê reza** (IFb) grape leaf {syn: belgêt mêwa (Bw)}; 2) {syn: t'ebax II} cigarette paper (Msr): **-p'elê cixarê** (IF)/**pela cix̄arê** (Qzl) do. {also: p'eř (IFb-2); [päl] پل (JJ)} --See etymology under **p'eř**. [AB/K/A/JB3/IFb/GF/Msr//JJ] See also **p'eř**.

p'el II پەل *m./f.(Zeb)* **(-ê/-a;-î/-ê).** firebrand, charred wood, smouldering piece of wood, live coal; ember: **•Min *pelek* bi ezmanê xo vena** (Dh) I spilled the beans/I let the cat out of the bag (i.e., I revealed a secret); **-p'elek agir** (K/JJ) do. {also: [pel پيل/pol پول/pelek aghir پلك آگر/polek aghir پولك آگر] (JJ); <pel> پەل (Hej)} {syn: bizot; p'ereng} =Sor sikił سِکِڵ/polû پۆلوو/bengir بەنگِر = 'ember' [Bw/Dh/K/GF/Hej//JJ] <agir; řejî; tenî>

p'elandin پەلاندِن *vt.* **(-p'elîn-).** to search s.o.'s person, frisk, grope; to inspect with one's hands [T el yordamiyle]: **-destê xwe p'elandin** (Qzl/B): a) to grope, feel s.o. up: **•Cilên min ji min kirin. Destên xwe *pelandin* her deverê hetanî ku yekî ji wan "mêrikê" min jî pîva bû** (HYma, 49) They stripped off my clothes. They *groped* every place until one of them even measured my "manhood"; b) to grope in the dark: **•Kuřik li vî**

axûrê qesrê digeřehe. Wê şevê destêd xo *dip'elîne* (JB1-S, #207, 162) The boy wanders around this stable of the castle. That night he *gropes around* with his hands. {also: pellandin (GF)} [Qzl/HYma/K/B/IFb/FJ/TF/JB1-S/Kmc/BF/AD/CS//GF]

pelangirk پەلانگرك (FS) = fire tongs. See **p'elegirk**.

pelapîtik پــەلاپــيــتِــك (RZ) = butterfly, moth. See **p'iřp'iřok**.

pelas پەلاس (Kmc) = thin rug or mat. See **p'alas**.

pelatînk پــەلاتــيــنــك (BF) = butterfly. See **belantîk** & **p'erîdank**.

pelav پەلاڤ (SS) = cooked rice. See **p'elaw**.

p'elaw پــەلاو *f.* (;-ê). cooked rice, pilaf: •**"Bo melan goştî da-nên e-ser birincî, emma bo koçekan birincî da-nên e-ser goştî." Wextê mecme'êt *pilawê* înan koçekan dîtin bo melan goşt înane, bo koçekan birinc bi-tinê, çi goşt dîhar nîye. Hemî koçekan sil bon, destêt xo kêşan e paş** (SK 39:350) "For the mullahs put the meat on top of the rice, but for the kochaks put the rice on top of the meat." When they brought the trays *of pilaf* the kochaks saw that they had brought meat for the mullahs but for the kochaks only rice with no meat visible. All the kochaks were offended. They withdrew their hands •**Ez dê *p'ilavekê* lênim** (JB1-A #142, 142) I will make a *pilaf* •**Her tuxme te'amê xoş ba, bi-lezet ba, ew bo wî dirust dikir. Xarina bajerîya, ko şirînî, *pilaw*, goşt, êprax, şorbawa bi dermanêt bên-xoş o tiştêt wekî wan e, bo wî di-da-nan e-ser sifrê** (SK 31:274) He would prepare for him every kind of good and tasty food. He would set on the table-cloth townsmen's food, which is sweetmeats, *pilaf*, meat, stuffed vine-leaves, soup with fragrant spices and other such things •**Xezêyn** [=**Xwedî**] **çû dîsa *p'elaw* çêkir ji xwe, wî řa, anî nan danîn** (HCK-2, 179) The master went and made *rice* again, he brought it for himself and for him, put out bread. {also: pelav (SS); pilav (GF); pilaw (SK); pîlav (IFb/AD); [pelaw] پــــەلاڤ (JJ)} {syn: birinc I} Cf. T pilav; P pelāv پلاو /pelow پلو; Sor piław پــــڵاو = 'boiled drained rice with burnt oil/butter poured over it' [HCK//SS/JJ//SK//GF//IFb/AD]

p'elaxtin پــەلاخــتِــن *vt.* **(-p'elêx-).** 1) {syn: dan ber lingan; dewisandin; 'eciqandin; heřişandin; p'ekandin; p'erçiqandin; pêpes kirin; t'episandin} to crush, crumple, mash, trample; 2) [*vi.*] {also: pelexîn (M); p'elixîn (B/IFb-2)} to be crushed, crumpled, mashed, trampled (IFb); to be shattered (M); to be crumpled *(of tin-ware)* (B). [BK/K/JB3/IFb//M//B] <p'erçiqandin>

pelçimok پەلچِمۆك (Qzl) = bat *(zool.)*. See **barç'imok**.

p'elç'iqandin پــەلــچِــقــانــدِن (K/B) = to crush. See **p'erçiqandin**.

p'elç'iqîn پــەلــچِــقــيــن (K/B) = to be crushed. See **p'erçiqîn**.

p'elegirk پەلەگِرك *f.* **(-a;-ê).** fire tongs for picking up firebrands [p'el I]. {also: pelangirk (FS); pelgir, m. (GF/OK)} {syn: maşik II} [Zeb//GF/OK//FS] <p'el II>

peleng پەلەنگ (F) = tiger; leopard. See **piling**.

p'elewan پــەلــەوان *m.* **(-ê; p'elewên, vî p'elewanî).** 1) {syn: 'efat; 'egît; fêris [1]; gernas; leheng; mêrxas} hero, brave man; champion; 2) knight: •**Ħevt dergê bavê min hene ji polane / T'emamî bi qerebaşî, *p'elewane*** (Z-1) My father has 7 gates of steel, / replete with servants and *knights*; 3) athlete ; 4) acrobat, tightrope walker (B/JJ). {also: p'alevan I (K-2/JB3/IFb); p'ehlewan (ZF3); pehliwan; [palvan پالوان/pehlivan پهلوان] (JJ)} Cf. P pahlavān پــهــلــوان --> T pehlivan {palevanî; p'elewanî} [Z-1/K//JB3/IF//JJ]

p'elewanî پــەلــەوانــی *f.* **(-ya;-yê).** 1) heroic deed or feat; 2) profession of tightrope walking (B) {also: palevanî (IF); pehlewanî (ZF3)} [B//IF//ZF3] <p'elewan>

pelexîn پــەلــەخــيــن (M) = to be crushed, trampled. See **p'elaxtin**[2].

p'elê 'ewr پەلێ عەور (B) = storm cloud. See **p'elte**.

pelgir پەلگِر, m. (GF/OK) = fire tongs. See **p'elegirk**.

p'elixîn پەلِخين (B/IFb) = to be crushed, trampled. See **p'elaxtin**[2].

pelîtan پەليتانك (ZF3/SS) = butterfly. See **p'erîdank**.

pelîtank پەليتانك (BF/FS) = butterfly. See **p'erîdank**.

pelk پەلك *f.* (). Euphrates poplar, tree which grows on riverbanks [T Fırat kavağı, Ar γarab غــرب]. {also: pelt (Dh/OK/AA-2); <pelk> پــــلــك (HH); <pełk> پەڵك (Hej)} Sor pełk پەڵك [Zeb/A/IFb/HH/GF/AA//Dh/OK] <evran; qewax; sipindar>

pellandin پــەلــلانــدِن (GF) = to search, frisk. See **p'elandin**.

pelok پەلۆك (Kmc) = type of sweet soup. See **pelor**.

pelor پــەلــۆر *f.* **(-a;-ê).** thick soup made of flour, butter and sugar or grape molasses, *given to new mothers after childbirth to give them strength, or to people who have lost their teeth*: •**Hebe tunebe,**

[x]warina bêesil *pelor* e. Wezîr çû ser poxanê qutîkek dît, piştre *peloreke* ji arvanê garis çêkir û xistê** (ZZ-&, 264) I bet the baseless food is *pelor*. The vizier went to the junk heap and found a little box, then he made *a pelor* of corn [or millet] flour and put that in it. {also: pelok (Kmc-2); pelûl (A-2/GF/Kmc-2); pilor I (A/IFb/ZF/Kmc)} {syn: ḧewdel} [ZZ//A/IFb/ZF/Kmc//GF]

pelpelîtank پەلپەلیتانك (RZ) = butterfly, moth. See **p'iȓp'iȓok**.

pelpelîtk پەلپەلیتك (SS) = butterfly, moth. See **p'iȓp'iȓok**.

pelpelûsk پەلپەلوسك (Zimanê Kurdî) = butterfly, moth. See **p'iȓp'iȓok**.

pelpîne پەلپینە (IFb/GF/OK) = purslane. See **pêrpîne**.

pelpîtanîk پەلپیتانیك (FJ) = butterfly, moth. See **p'iȓp'iȓok**.

pelt پەلت (Dh/OK/AA) = Euphrates poplar. See **pelk**.

p'elte پەلتە *f.* **().** (storm) cloud: **•*P'elte* 'ewrê ȓeş derk'et û baranê usa destpê kir** (Z-1) Black *storm clouds* came out and it began to rain. {also: p'elê 'ewr (B)} {syn: 'ewr; hecac} [Z-1/K//B]

pelûl پەلوول (A/GF/Kmc) = type of sweet soup. See **pelor**.

pembî پەمبی (SK) = cotton. See **pembû**.

pembo پەمبۆ (A/JB1-S) = cotton. See **pembû**.

pembu پەمبو (B/IFb) = cotton. See **pembû**.

pembû پەمبوو *m.* **(-yê;).** cotton (processed, *as opposed to* **loke** *= cotton on plant)*; cotton material: **•Bes hung jî wekî hemî milletan çawêt xo weken, *pembîyê* ẍefletê ji guhê xo derînin, da ew nawê kirêt ji ser hingo rabît** (SK 56:661) You too must open your eyes, like all the nations, and take *the cotton of* negligence out of your ears so that you may lose that ugly name. {also: pembî (SK); pembo (A/JB1-S); pembu (B-2/IFb-2); penbu (IFb-2); [penbou] پنبو (JJ); <penbû> پنبو (HH)} < Mid P pambag (M3); P panba پنبه; T [& Hungarian] pamuk, clq. pambuk; Sor pemû پەموو = 'cotton on the plant (cf. loke)'; Za peme *m.*; Cf. W Arm pambag բամպակ [K/JB3/IFb/B/GF/OK//SK//A/JB1-S//JJ/HH] <loke>

pen پەن (F)/pe'n پەعن (B/Msr) = wide; flat. See **pehn**.

p'ena پەنا *f.* **(-ya;-yê).** refuge, asylum, shelter, sanctuary: **•Selaḧ o munasib ew e ko pêş wext em bo xo *penahek[ê]* peyda bikeyn** (SK 48:497) It is advisable and proper that we find *a place of refuge* for ourselves ahead of time; **-p'ena birin bo/ber** (GF) to defect to, take refuge in: **•Hindek harîkarêt leşkirî yêt mezin yêt serokê 'Îraqê *pena bire ber* Ûrdunê** (VoA) Some high ranking Iraqi military attaches *defected to* Jordan **•Li sala 1992 zanyarekî atomî yê 'Îraqê ku *pena bir bo* Urdunê li ser cadeka 'Amman hate kuştin** (VoA) In 1992 an Iraqi atomic scientist who *had defected to* Jordan was killed on a street in Amman. {also: p'enah (K/GF-2/TF/FD/SK/CS-2); [penah] پناه (JJ)} Cf. P panāh پناه; Sor pena پەنا = 'hidden corner; refuge, asylum, shelter' [Zeb/IFb/GF/ZF3/BF/RZ/SS//K/JJ/TF/FD/SK] <p'enaber>

p'enaber پەنابەر *m.&f.* **().** refugee: **•Ji aliyê *penaberên* Kurd ve agahdarî mesela Kurdan bûm** (Wlt 1:37, 16) I became aware of the Kurdish issue through Kurdish *refugees* **•*Penaberên* ku di ser behra Egeyê re bi belemê derbasî giravên Yewnenîstanê dibûn ketin nav behrê** (basnews 7.iii.2016) *Refugees* who were crossing the islands of Greece on the Aegean Sea by boat fell into the sea. <Sor penaber پەنابەر = 'refugee'; cf. P panāhande پناهنده [(neol)Wlt/IFb/ZF3] <k'oçber; mişext>

p'enaberî *f.* **(-ya;-yê).** being a refugee, requesting or seeking asylum: **•Belge fîlm li ser mijara *penaberîyê* disekine** (Rûpela Nû 23.xi.2017) The documentary deals with the issue of *being a refugee*. [RûpelaNû/ZF3/Wkt/FD] <k'oçberî; mişextî>

p'enah پەناه (K/GF/JJ/TF/FD/SK/CS) = refuge, asylum, shelter. See **p'ena**.

pe'nayî پەعنایی (B) = width. See **pehnî II**.

penbu پەنبو (IFb/JJ) = cotton. See **pembû**.

p'encer•e پەنجەرە *f.* **(•a/•eya;•ê).** window: **•Mûsilî serê xo ji *pencerê* îna der, got, "Ew kiye?"** (SK 31:279) The Mosuli put his head out of *the window* and said, "Who is it?" **•Roja eynî Mela 'Ebbas bi hemî keyf û hewesa xo çû ser munarê, muqabilî *pencera* F<u>a</u>time xanimê wekî kewê ȓibad kebar dikir, diqîȓand** (SK 15:149) On Friday Mullah Abbas went up the minaret full of his pleasure and began to bawl the takbir opposite Madam Fatima's *window*, like a decoy partridge. {also: pençire (DZK); [pendjeré] پنجره (JJ); <pencere> پنجره (HH)} {syn: akoşke; şibak} Cf. P panjare پنجره -->T pencere; Sor pencere پەنجەرە; Za pencera *f.* (Todd) [Z-1/F/K/JB3/IFb/B/JJ/HH/SK/JB1-S/GF//DZK] <p'ace>

p'enceşêr پەنجەشێر *f.* **(-a;-ê).** 1) cancer (Bw/ZF/SS);

2) leprosy [Ar juddām جـذّام] (IFb/FJ/GF/HH); 3) anthrax carbuncle (IFb/ZF); 4) lady's mantle, bot. Alchemilla (IFb). {also: pençeşêr (ZF); şêrpence (SS-2); <penceşêr> پـنـجـشـيـر (HH)} Sor şêrpence شێرپەنجە = 'anthrax, malignant ulcer; cancer' [Bw/IFb/FJ/GF/HH/SS//ZF] <řîş>

pencî پەنجی (GF) = fifty. See **pêncî I**.

pençeşêr پـەنـچـەشـێـر (ZF) = cancer; leprosy. See **p'enceşêr**.

pençire پەنچرە (DZK) = window. See **p'encere**.

p'enese پـەنـەسـە *adj.* 1) transient, ephemeral; 2) vanished, disappeared (S&E): **-p'enese bûn** (B) to disappear, vanish from view. {syn: beta vebûn; řoda çûn; (ji ber) winda bûn} [S&E/K/B]

penêr پەنێر (K/B) = cheese. See **penîr**.

peng I پـەنـگ *f.(Bw)/m.(OK)* **(-a/;).** skein, hank *(of yarn)*: **-penga řês** (Bw) do. {also: <penk> پـنـك (HH)} {syn: girov; gulok} [Bw/A/IFb/GF/TF/OK//HH]

peng II پـەنـگ *m.* **(-ê;).** 1) small dammed up pool of water (Bw); reservoir (Bw); 2) [*adj.*] stagnant, sluggish *(of water)*{syn: mend I; meyav[2]}: **-ava peng** (IFb/GF) stagnant water. Sor peng پـەنـگ = 'banking up, piling up (water)' [Bw/IFb/GF] <ḧewz>

pengandin پەنگاندِن *vt.* **(-pengîn-).** to dam up, stop up, plug up, block up *(a water course)*. {also: pengihandin (IFb/GF)} {syn: xitimandin} [Bw//IFb/GF] <ç'ikandin II; miç'iqandin>

pengihandin پـەنـگِـهـانـدِن (IFb/GF) = to dam up. See **pengandin**.

pengizandin پـەنـگِـزانـدِن *vt.* **(-pengizîn-).** to cause to leap, jump, or spring up: **•Geh wî li min dixist ez bi çend gavan bi paş de *dipengizandim*, geh min lê dixist ew bi çend gavan bi şûn de dişand** (KS, 59) Sometimes he [=a snake] struck at me and *sent me jumping* back several steps, sometimes I struck at him sending him backward several steps. [KS/A/IFb/GF/TF/OK] <pengizîn>

pengizîn پـەنـگِـزيـن *vi.* **(-pengiz-).** to leap up, jump up, spring up: **•Gava mêrik ev yeka han ferq kir, hema ji cihê xwe *pengizî* û pencere vekir** (KS, 8) When the man realized [or, noticed] this, he *leapt up* from his place and opened the window. {syn: ba[n]z dan; çeng bûn [*see* çeng III]; firqas kirin; hilpekirin; lotik dan xwe; qevz dan [*see* qevz II]; xwe qevaztin} [KS/A/IFb/GF/TF/OK] <pengizandin>

penî پەنی (F)/pe'nî پـەعـنی (EP-7/K/B/Wn/Rh) = heel. See **panî I**.

penîr پەنیر *m.* **(-ê; pênîr/pênêr).** cheese: **•Qijik *penîr* didize** (AB) The rook (bird) steals *cheese*; **-penîr avîtin** (B) to make cheese; **-penîrê kesidandî** (IFb) cheese in brine [T salamura peynir]; **-penîrê kelandî** (IFb) Kashar cheese, yellow sheep's milk cheese; **-penîrê meşkê** (IFb) cheese encased in a skin; **-penêrê řiçal** (K) string cheese; **-penîrê sîrik** (IFb) herb cheese. {also: penêr (K/B-2); [penir] پـنـير (JJ); <penîr> پـنـير (HH)} Cf. Mid P panīr (M3); P panīr پـنـير --> T peynir; Sor penîr پەنیر; Za penîr *m.* (Mal) [K//A/JB3/IFb/JJ/B/HH/SK/GF]

penpulî پەنپولی (RZ) = butterfly, moth. See **p'iřp'iřok**.

p'entol پەنتۆل (IFb) = pants, trousers. See **p'antol**.

p'ep پەپ (B) = foot of small child. See **pepik** [2].

pepik پـەپـك *m.* **(-ê;).** 1) trotter *(foot of sheep or goat)*: **•'Ûr û pizûr, para xezûr, ser û *pepik*, para metik** (Msr) Intestines and undesirable parts [are] the father-in-law's portion, the head and *trotters* are the maternal aunt's portion *(this is part of a folk poem which indicates how the parts of a slaughtered goat or sheep are divided among family members)*; 2) {also: p'ep (B)} foot of small child (Msr/B); hand of small child (IFb). {also: <pepik> پپك (HH)} [Msr/K/A/JB3/IFb/HH/GF//B] <p'ê II>

pepûg پەپووگ (IFb) = cuckoo; hoopoe. See **p'epûk II**.

p'epûk I/p'ep'ûk [Z-1] پـەپـووك *adj.* 1) weak, feeble, sickly: **•Al-p'aşa û dîya Memêva ber serê Memê bûbûne *p'ep'ûk*** (Z-1) A.p. and Mem's mother were *sick* over Mem; 2) {syn: kezîkurê} upset, messed up (A/IFb); miserable, wretched: **•[Vê] *pepûka jinê* bi şev û roj kar dikir û zarok mîna çîçikên birçî bidû de baz didin** (HYma 30) This *poor woman* worked day and night and [her] children run after her like hungry chicks; 3) [*m.*] {syn: p'arsek} beggar, pauper. {pepûktî} [Z-1/K/A/IFb/GF/TF] <kezîkurê>

p'epûk II پـەپـووك *f.* **().** *name for several birds:* 1) {also: pûpû (B)} cuckoo, zool. *Cuculus canorus* (JB3/IFb/ JJ/GF); 2) {also: [pipo] پـيـپـو (JJ)} hoopoe, zool. *Upupa epops: this bird nests in the nests of other birds* (IFb/JJ/GF/TF/KZ); 3) {syn: bûm; kund} owl, zool. order *Strigiformes* (A/HH). {also: pepûg (IFb-2); [pepouk] پپوك (JJ); <pepûk> پپوك (HH)} Cf. P pūpū پوپو ; Sor pepû پەپوو = 'owl, cuckoo (of clock)' [A/JB3/IFb/JJ/HH/GF/TF]

p'eq پەق *f.* **().** blister. {also: peqik II (IFb/TF)} [Bar/FS//IFb/TF] p'eqan پەقان (Bw) = to burst (vi.). See **p'eqîn**.

peqandin پــەقــانــدِن (-peqîn-) (JB1-A) = to burst, break off *(vt.)*. See **p'ekandin**.

peqijok پەقِژۆك (GF) = bubble. See **beqbeqok**.

peqik I پەقِك (IFb) = bubble. See **beqbeqok**.

peqik II پەقِك (IFb/TF) = blister. See **p'eq**.

peqîk پەقیك (TF) = bubble. See **beqbeqok**.

p'eqîn پــەقــیــن *vi.* **(-p'eq-).** 1) {syn: teqîn} to break, burst (open), split, crack *(vi.)* (K/Mc/JB1-S); to explode (JB1-S/JB3/IFb); to break off, come undone (K); 2) to rebound, bounce back (K); 3) {syn: mirin} to die (M-Ak): **•Îna şerm kir, ħalen *peqî*** (M-Ak) He was ashamed and *died* immediately. {also: **p'ekîn** (K/JB1-S); p'eqan (Bw); [pŭkīn] پــــقــــیــــن (JJ)} [IFb/JB3/GF/M-Ak//Bw//K/JB1-S//JJ] <p'eqandin> See also **p'ekîn**.

peqîşk پەقیشك (Bw/Zx) = bubble. See **beqbeqok**.

peqpeqok پەقپەقۆك (GF/Bw) = bubble. See **beqbeqok**.

peqpeqoşk پەقپەقۆشك (Bw) = bubble. See **beqbeqok**.

p'eř پــەڕ *m./f.(L)* **(-ê/ ; p'êř/).** 1) {syn: bask} feather: ***•Her pereke* wî ji hawakê ye** (L) *Every one of his feathers* is of a [different] color; 2) {syn: qanat} wing; 3) {syn: belg [2]; t'ebax II} sheet *(of paper)*: **•Em êvarê *p'eře* k'axaza cigarê bikne bin doşeka Ûsib** (Ba) This evening we will place *a sheet of* cigarette paper under Joseph's mattress; 4) {syn: kevî I; k'êlek} edge, outskirts (of town, road, dress): **•Ewana gihîştine *p'eřê* şeherê Cizîrê** (Z-1) They reached *the edge of* the city Jezirah **•p'eřê gund** (B) the edge of the village; **-ber p'eřê 'ezmana fiřîn/k'etin** = to do stg. extravagant [lit. 'to fly to the edge (or wings) of the sky']: ***•Bifiře ber p'eřê 'ezmana* jî** (XF) No matter what he does (there is no saving him); 5) leaf (Msr). See **p'el I**. {also: p'el; pere II (A); [per] پــر (JJ); <per> پــر (HH)} [Pok. 2. (s)p(h)er- 993.] 'to jerk, start; to strew': Skt parṇá- *n.* = 'feather, wing'; Av parəna- = do.; Mid P parr = 'feather, wing' & parrag = 'wing' (M3); Sor peř پەڕ = 'feather'; Za perr *m.* = 'leaf, sheet (of paper)' (Todd); Hau pel *m.* = 'feather' & peř *m.* = 'side, edge' (M4); cf. also P parrīdan پــریــدن = 'to fly'; Gr pteron πτερόν = 'feather'; Rus pero перо = 'feather' [L/Z-1/Ba/K/IFb/JJ/B/HH/SK/GF//A] See also **p'el I**. <fiřîn; [3] k'axez; řûp'el>

p'eřanî پــــەڕانــــی *f.* **(-ya;-yê).** pack of wolves: **•Wextekê *peranîya* guran rastî wan hat** (J2, 13). Once *a pack of* wolves encountered them [i.e., they encountered a pack of wolves]. {syn: gel} [J2/K/B] <gur I>

perasî پەراسی (SK/FS) = rib(s). See **parsû**.

perasû پەراسوو (Elk) = rib(s). See **parsû**.

p'eřav پــــەڕاڤ [K] *f.* **(;-ê).** 1) {syn: bar II; kevî I[2]} bank *(of river)*: **•Ev deşt ji *peravên* Nîlê jî ji Çûkûrovayê jî hîn bi berekettir in** (SF 18) These plains are even more fertile than *the banks of* the Nile, than the [plain of the] Çukurova; 2) {syn: *dev-av} coast, shore: **•Balafirên ingilîzî di *peravên* Tirkiyê de vaporeke frensizî ... bin av kirin** [sic] (H2 9:31, 776) English planes sank a French steamship on the Turkish *coast*. Cf. Sor peř پەڕ = 'side, end, coast, shore' [SF/IFb/GF/TF/FS//K]

p'eřawî پــــەڕاوی *f.* **().** notebook. {syn: deft'er} [K(s)/A/IFb/ZF3]

p'ercan/perçan [JB1-A] پــــەرجــــان *m./f.(K)* **(-ê/-a;).** wooden fence, enclosure; hedge: **•Piştî çarîkekî herdu cîran ji paş *perçîna* rezan derdikevin** (Ardû, 12) After a quarter of an hour, the 2 neighbors come out from behind the vineyard *fence*; **-pêjanê rezî** (Bw) vineyard fence. {also: percar (OK-2); perciyan (GF); perçiyan (FJ); perçîn (RZ-2/Ardû); perijîn (SS); perjîn (RZ-2); pêjan (Bw); [pergiana] پــرجــان (JJ-G)} {syn: çeper [1]; k'ozik; t̲an} Mid P parzīn = 'fence, hedge' (M3); P parčīn پرچین; Sor perjîn پەرژین = 'hedge, fence' [Bw//K/IFb/JJ/JB1-A/OK/RZ//SS] <k'ozik I; sênc; sîme>

percar پەرجار (OK) = fence. See **p'ercan**.

perciyan پەرجیان (GF) = fence. See **p'ercan**.

p'erç•e پــــەرچــــە *m./f.(JB3)* **(•ê;).** 1) {syn: beş; kerî I; p'ar II; parî; qet II} piece, morsel: **-p'arçe 'erd** (B) plot of land: **•Şwîr bû du *perçe*** (L) The sword broke in two [lit. 'became two *pieces*']; 2) splinter, fragment; clod; 3) {syn: ç'arşev[2]} fabric, cloth (F). {also: p'arçe (B/IFb-2/SK/GF); [partché] پــارچــه (JJ); <parçe> پــارچــه (HH)} Cf. P pārče پــارچــه--> T parça [L/K/JB3/IFb//B/JJ/HH/SK/GF] See also **p'ar II** & **parî**.

p'erçemûk پــــەرچــــەمــــووك (Dz) = bat *(zool.)*. See **pîrçemek**.

p'erç'evandin پەرچەڤاندِن (K) = to inflate, swell; blow up. See **p'erçifandin**.

p'erç'evîn پەرچەڤین (-p'erç'iv-) (K) = to swell *(vi.)*. See **p'erçifîn**.

p'erçifandin پــــەرچِــفــانــدِن *vt.* **(-p'erçifîn-).** 1) {syn: êvitandin; nep'ixandin; werimandin} to inflate, puff up, blow up (with air), swell *(vt.)*: •**Beqê nêr bîhn girt, *xwe* piçek din *perçifand* ... û *xwe* piçek din *perçifand* û bû wek balonekî** (K.Burkay. Aso, 66) The bullfrog took a breath, *puffed himself up* a little bit more ... and *puffed himself up* a little bit more and became like a balloon; 2) to blow stg. up, explode stg. {also: p'erç'evandin (K); perçivandin (IFb-2/GF/CS/ZF)} [K.Burkay/IFb/AD/OK//GF/CS/ZF//K] <perçifîn>

p'erçifîn پـەرچـفـيـن *vi.* **(-p'erçif-).** 1) {syn: êvitîn; nep'ixîn; *pendifyan (M); werimîn} to be swollen, swell *(vi.)*; to swell until it bursts [T yarılmak]: •**Ser û çavê wan *perçifî* bû** (DZK, 135) Their faces were *swollen*; 2) to sleep *(contemptuous)* (Dh). {also: p'erç'evîn (-p'erç'iv-) (K); perçiftin (Mzg/ZF-2); perçivîn (IFb/ZF); perçiwtin (SK); [pertchewin] پـرچـڤـيـن (JJ)} [DZK/OK/Qzl/Xrz//IFb//K/JJ//Mzg/ZF//SK] <p'erçifandin>

perçiftin پـەرچـفـتِـن (Mzg/ZF) = to swell *(vi.)*. See **p'erçifîn**.

perçikandin پـەرچـكـانـدِن (GF) = to crush. See **p'erçiqandin**.

p'erçiqandin پەرچقاندِن *vt.* **(-p'erçiq-).** 1) to crush, press, smash, squash *(insects, soft fruit)*: •**[K'eftar̄] fêm dike ku şêr bi hîleyên wî hesiyaye ... Şêr bang dike, dibêje: "... Qeşmerê teres, divê ku ez careke din te li hizûra xwe nebînim. Bicehime here, hêj ku min tu *neperçiqandiye*"** (Wlt 2:100, 13) [The hyena] understands that the lion has caught onto his ruses ... The lion shouts, "... Worthless bum, I don't want to see you in my presence ever again! Now get the hell out of here, before I *smash you* to a pulp" •...**koşk ewê ji nişkave hilşe, her çî kesê der û hundurê xwe *bipeçiqîne*** [sic] (RN) ...The palace could suddenly collapse, and everyone inside and out would be *crushed*; 2) to oppress, repress, suppress: •**Bizava wê ya piçuktrîn a ji bo pêşeroja wê ya sîyasî, bi cezayên girantirîn *têt pelçiqandin*** (Ber #7, 10) Its slightest movement for its political future *is repressed* with the heaviest of punishments. {also: *peçiqandin (RN); p'elç'iqandin (K/B); perçikandin (GF-2)} {syn: dan ber lingan; dewisandin; 'eciqandin; her̄işandin; p'ekandin; p'elaxtin; pêpes kirin; t'episandin} [RN//K/B//JB3/IFb/JB1-A/GF/TF] <p'elaxtin; p'erçiqîn; tepeser kirin>

p'erçiqîn پـەرچـقـيـن *vi.* **(-p'erçiq-).** to be crushed, pressed, smashed, squashed (insects, soft fruit). {also: p'elç'iqîn (K/B); pirçiqîn (M)} [K/B//IFb/TF//M] <p'erçiqandin>

perçivandin پـەرچـڤـانـدِن (IFb/GF/CS/ZF) = to inflate, swell; blow up. See **p'erçifandin**.

perçivîn پـەرچـڤـيـن (IFb/ZF) = to swell *(vi.)*. See **p'erçifîn**.

perçiwtin پەرچوتِن (SK) = to swell *(vi.)*. See **p'erçifîn**.

perçiyan پەرچيان (FJ) = fence. See **p'ercan**.

perçîn پەرچين (RZ/Ardû) = fence. See **p'ercan**.

p'erdax پـەرداخ *m.* **(-ê;).** drinking glass, tumbler. {syn: avxork; gilas; p'eyale[2]} <T bardak; Sor perdax پەرداخ (K3) [Bw/K(s)/GF] <p'eyale>

p'erd•e پـەردە**/p'er̄de** پـەردە [XF] *f.* **(•a;•ê).** 1) curtain; 2) screen, partition; curtain separating the compartments of a tent (PS); 3) film, membrane: **-p'erda ç'e'va** (B) cataract (in the eye); **-p'erda dil** (B) pericardium; **-p'erda guh** (B) eardrum; **-p'erda r̄û** (B) shame, honor; 4) {syn: ç'adir[1]; ç'arik[2]; ç'arşev[1]; p'êçe} veil (JB1-S). {also: [perdé] پـردە (JJ); <perde> پـردە (HH)} Mid P pardag = 'veil, curtain' (M3); P parde پـرده --> T perde; --> Eng purdah; Sor perde پـەردە = 'curtain, screen, scene (theater)'. *This word is associated with the harem and the seclusion of womenfolk behind a curtain or veil.* [FK-1/IS/F/K/A/IFb/B/JJ/HH/JB1-S/GF//XF] <r̄ûpoş>

p'er•e I پـەرە *pl./m.(B/JB3)* **(•ê;).** money: •**Hakim qîza xwe na de bi *pera*** (L) The king doesn't give his daughter [in exchange] for *money* •***Perên* ku didane me ne pir bin jî, dîsa jî ji meaşên hemû karmend û karkerên wan zêdetir bûn** (AW72B3) Even if *the money* they gave us was not a lot, it was still more than the wages of all their workers •**Tuê here ji mi re li van *pera* tişta bikire!** (L) Go buy me some things with this *money*!; **-pere anîn** (IF) to earn money; **-p'ere dan** (K)/**pare dan** (IFb) to pay; **-p'erê hûr** (B) small change. {also: pare (IFb-2/SK); [paré] پـاره (JJ)} Cf. T para, *originally a small coin, 1/40 of a kuruş, now = 'money'* [L/K/JB3/IFb/B/GF//JJ/SK] <baqnot; çerxî; kapêk; manat; şeyî>

pere II پەرە (A) = feather; wing; paper; edge. See **p'er̄**.

p'ereng پـەرەنـگ *f.(K/ZF3)/m.(BF/FS)* **(/-ê;-ê/).** firebrand, live ember: •**Bi kişandina wê çixarê re û vexwarina qurtekê ji meyê, çav wek *perengê* li serî sor bûn** (B. Omer̄î. Rûniştina bi serxweşekî re) While smoking that cigarette and drinking a gulp of wine, his eyes reddened like the head of a *firebrand*; **-perengê agirî** (FS) firebrand. {also: [pāráng] پـارـنـگ (JJ-S); parang (TF)} {syn: bizot; p'el II} [B.Omerî/K/IFb/FD/BF/FS/ZF3/Wkt//JJ-S//TF] <helemor>

perestge پەرستگە (OK) = temple. See **p'erestgeh**.

p'erestgeh پـەرەسـتـگـەه *f.* **(-a;-ê).** temple, place of worship: **•Min *perestgeheke* mezin ava kir, agir li hundurê wê gurmujand û hevîya xwe pê ve girêda û dua kir** (K-ça) I built a great *temple*, and lit a fire inside it, tied my hopes to it and prayed. {also: perestge (OK); peřêzgeh (FS); peristge (OK-2); peristgeh (Dh/GF)} P parastešgāh پرستشگاه; Sor peristiştga پەرِستِشتگا = 'place of worship' [Dh/GF//K-ça/IFb/RZ//OK//FS]

p'erestin پەرەستِن vt. **(-perês-[IFb]).** to worship: **•Em Xudê *dipeřîzîn*** (FS) We *worship* God. {also: peristin (GF)/peřistin (-peřîz-) (FS); [peristin] پـرسـتـيـن (JJ)} Cf. Mid P paristīdan = 'to serve, worship' (M3); Sor peristin پەرِستِن [K/A/IFb/OK//JJ/GF//FS]

perêz پەرێز (AA/OK/Hej) = field stubble. See **p'irêz**.

peřêzgeh پـەڕێـزگـەه (FS) = temple (place of worship). See **p'erestgeh**.

p'ergal I پـەرگـال *f.* **(-a;-ê).** 1) order, arrangement; the system, the social order (Haz); 2) {syn: hiner; îlac} *(fig.)* way out of, remedy to a difficult situation (K): **•Sitîyê got: "Mala me şewitî, *pergala* me ma bi neyarane"** (LT-Mîşo) Siti said, "May our house be burnt down, we are at the mercy of our enemies [lit. 'our *way out* has remained with the enemies']." {also: p'ergel} [Ber/K/IFb/B/GF/Haz]

p'ergal II پەرگال *f.* **(;-ê).** 1) {also: pergar (IFb)} (pair of) compasses, dividers (K/IFb); 2) {syn: alav II; amîr} tool, instrument (K/IFb): **•Herçiqas av ji bo hemû jîndaran çavkaniyeke bingehîn be jî, îro di destê mirovên "hemdem" de wek *pergaleke* ji holê rakirina berhemên dîrokê tê bi kar anîn** (Wlt 1:21, 16) Although water is a basic resource for all living things, today it is being used by "modern" man as *an instrument for* destroying historical artifacts **•*pergalên* berkêş-anê** (IFb) *instruments of* production. {also: pergal = 'instrument' & pergar = 'pair of compasses' (IFb); [pergar] پرگار (JJ)} < P pergār پرگار/pergāl پرگال--> T pergel = 'pair of compasses' & Ar firjār فرجار [K/GF//IFb/JJ/GF]

pergar پەرگار (IFb) = compass. See **p'ergal II**.

p'ergel پەرگەل = social order; remedy. See **p'ergal I**.

perijîn پەرژین (SS) = fence. See **p'ercan**.

p'eř•ik پەڕِك *f.(BF)/m.* **(•ka/•kê;).** playing cards. [Bw/BF]

peristge پەرِستگە (OK) = temple. See **p'erestgeh**.

peristgeh پـەرِسـتـگـەه (Dh/GF) = temple. See **p'erestgeh**.

peristin پـەرِسـتِـن (GF)/peřistin پـەڕِسـتِـن (FS) = to worship. See **p'erestin**.

p'eřitandin پـەڕِتـانـدِن/**peritandin** پـەرِتـانـدِن *vt.* **(-p'eřitîn-).** 1) to sever, break: **•Hema zaro şûrê xwe avêt ser dûvê marî, dûvê marî *peritand*** (KH, 34) The child immediately swung his sword at the snake's tail, and *severed* the snake's tail; 2) {syn: ç'iřandin} to tear, rend *(dress, shoes, etc.)* (K/B); 3) {syn: p'ûrtikandin; řûç'ikandin} to pluck *(feathers)* (A/IFb/K). [KH/K/A/IFb/B/JB1-S/GF/OK] <p'eřitîn>

p'eřitîn پـەڕِتـيـن *vi.* **(-p'eřit-).** 1) to be torn, frayed, worn out; to be exhausted; 2) to be boiled up; to come apart, fall to pieces *(of meat that is well cooked)*; 3) to be wretched, miserable; to suffer; 4) to freeze *(vi.)*, be freezing; 5) to burn *(in pain or with love, passion, etc.)*: **•Çiqas Memê zîndanêda diĥelîya usa jî Zîna delal diha ze'f bona Memê xwe diĥelîya û *dip'eřitî*** (Z-1) The more Mem 'melted' in prison, the more darling Zin pined [lit. 'melted and *burned*'] for him **•Go t'êr xwê mi kirîye tilya xwede, kû xwê dik'evê dereka kulda dişewitê *dipeřitêê*** (HR 3:281) He said, I put a fair amount of salt on my finger, when salt enters a sore place it burns and *smarts*. {also: <peritîn پـرتـين (diperite) (دپرته)> (HH)} [Z-1/K/B/HH/JB1-S/OK/ZF]

p'erixandin پـەرِخـانـدِن *vt.* **(-p'erixîn-).** 1) {syn: firikandin; miz I: miz dan} to rub, massage; 2) {syn: miz I: miz dan} to pet, stroke. {also: p'erxandin (K)} < Syr √p-r-k ܦܪܟ = 'to rub, bruise' & NENA pârikh ܦܪܟ = 'to rub, chafe', *cognate with* Ar √f-r-k فرك = 'to rub' (>firikandin) [Elk/IFb//K]

pe'rî I پەعری (B) = piece; slice. See **parî**.

p'erî II پـەری *f.* **().**1) fairy; 2) {syn: husulcemal} beauty, beautiful woman. {also: [peri] پـری (JJ)} Mid P parīg = 'witch' (M3) [EP-7/K/JB3/IFb/JJ/GF]

p'erîdank پـەریـدانـك *f.* **(-a;).** butterfly, zool. *Lepidoptera*. {also: **belantîk**; belîtank (RZ);

pelatînk (BF-2); pelîtan (ZF3/SS); pelîtank (BF/FS-2); perîtang (FS)} {syn: belantîk; fir̄fir̄ok; p'ir̄p'ir̄ok; pîrik[4]} = Sor pepûle پەپوولە [Wkp/Wkt//FS//BF//ZF3/SS//RZ] <bizûz> See also **belantîk**.

perîn پەرین *vi.* **(-per-).** 1) to mate, mount, couple with *(of equines)*: **•xesandin: karekê nojdarîyê ye endamê guhnelîyê yê lawira ji kar diêxin, ku nikarit** [sic] ***biperit*** (BF) to geld: it is a surgical prodecure [by which] they disable the sexual organs of animals, so that it [sic] cannot *mate*; 2) [*f.* **(-a;-ê).**] mating, coupling, sexual union *(of animals)*: **•Dema *perîna* kewalane** (BF) It is the *mating* season of animals; **-gera perînê** (SS) mating season. {also: [perin] پرین (JJ)} Sor per̄în پەڕین = 'to mate, mount (esp. of single-hoofed male animal)' [BF/SS/ZF/JJ] <guhnêr>

p'erîşan پەریشان *adj.* 1) upsèt, chaotic, messed up, in bad shape, distressed, disturbed; 2) {syn: belengaz; r̄eben} wretched, miserable, poor: **•B. giha bajarê Mîrê Sêrê. Gelikî *perîşan* bûye** (L) B. reached the city of the prince of Magic. He (=B.) was *in a sorry state* {en piteux [sic] appareil}. {also: [perichan] پریشان (JJ); <perîşan> پریشان (HH)} Cf. P parīšān پریشان--> T perişan; Sor perêşan پەرێشان = 'scattered, distracted, anxious, worried' {p'erîşanî; perîşantî} [K/A/JB3/IFb/B/JJ/HH/SK/GF]

p'erîşanî پەریشانی *f.* **(-ya;-yê).** 1) ùpset, distress (n.) ; 2) misery; 3) poverty, indigence. {also: perîşantî (A); [perichani] پریشانی (JJ)} [K/JB3/IFb/JJ/SK/GF//A] <p'erîşan>

perîşantî پەریشانتی (A) = misery; poverty. See **p'erîşanî**.

perîtang پەریتانگ (FS) = butterfly. See **p'erîdank**.

perîzad•e پەریزادە *f.* **(•a;).** goiter *(growth on the thyroid gland)*. ?< perde zêde [Bw/SS/ZF3]

perjîn پەرژین (RZ) = fence. See **p'ercan**.

p'er̄lemîş پەڕلەمیش: **-p'er̄lemîş bûn** = to shine: **•Weke rojê *p'er̄lemîş dibû*** (EP-7) She *shone* like the sun. {syn: biriqîn; birûskîn; ç'irûsîn} < T parlamış = 'having shined' [EP-7]

p'er̄o پەڕۆ (Zeb) = rag. See **p'er̄ok**.

p'er̄ok پەڕۆك *m.* **(-ê;-î).** rag, piece of cloth: **•Wextê çû jor dît jinek meşkê dihijînît, ya r̄ûs bû, tiştek di berda nebû. T̲ayekî bendikî li pişta xo girê dabû *per̄okekî* kewn[î] qirêjî li laê berwe, yêk li laê piştwe di bendikî alandibûn. Çi wextê kurk li meşkê da her du *per̄ok* bilind dibûn, pêş û paşêt wê der-dikewtin** (SK 16:156) When he went inside he saw a woman shaking a goatskin churn, naked, without a thing on. She had tied a woollen thread round her waist and hung a filthy old *rag* on the thread in front and another one behind. Whenever she gave the skin-bag a jerk both *rags* flew up revealing her fore and aft. {also: p'er̄o (Zeb-2); p'er̄ûk (Bw)} {syn: kerkon; kevnik [2]; p'aç' II & p'aç[']ik; p'ate II; pîne; p'ot; qerpal} Sor per̄o پەڕۆ = 'rag, cloth' [Zeb/SK/OK/FS//Bw]

perpelisk پەرپەلِسك (RZ) = butterfly, moth. See **p'ir̄p'ir̄ok**.

perperik پەرپەرِك (RZ) = butterfly, moth. See **p'ir̄p'ir̄ok**.

perperok پەرپەرۆك (IFb/HH/RZ/SS) = butterfly, moth. See **p'ir̄p'ir̄ok**.

perpitîn پەرپتین (IFb/JJ/HH) = to thrash about. See **p'irpitîn**.

perpîne پەرپینە (GF/OK/JJ) = purslane. See **pêrpîne**.

p'erpînek پەرپینەك (K) = purslane. See **pêrpîne**.

perpûşik پەرپووشِك (RZ) = butterfly, moth. See **p'ir̄p'ir̄ok**.

p'ersim پەرسِم, f. (K) = common cold. See **p'ersîv**.

p'ersiv پەرسِڤ = common cold. See **p'ersîv**.

p'ersîv پەرسیڤ *m.(Bw)/f.(FS)* **(-ê/-a; /-ê).** common cold, catarrh; flu, influenza: ***•P'ersîv* yê li min** (Bw) I have *a cold* ***•Persîva* wî hat min** (FS) I caught his cold [lit.'His *cold* came to me'] ***•Persîvê* ew girtiye** (FS) He caught a *cold* [lit. '*The cold* has seized him']. {also: p'ersim, f. (K); p'ersiv; [persiw] پرسیڤ (JJ)} Sor pasîw پاسیو [Bw/JJ/GF/OK/FS//K] <sat'ircem; serma; sitam>

pertal پەرتال *pl.* **().** 1) {also: p'irt-p'al} goods, merchandise, wares; property: **•Wî *pertalên* xwe birin gumrikê** (FS) He took his *merchandise* to customs; 2) [*m.* **(-ê;).**] cloth, fabric, textile (Zeb): **-pirtî û pertal** (IFb) textiles and clothes [kumaş ve giyim eşyası]; wares and merchandise [mal ve eşya]; 3) {syn: kerkon; p'ot; qerpal} old clothes, rags. {also: pirtal (IF-2/Zeb); [pertal] پرتال (JJ); <pirtal> پرتال (HH)} [K/A/JB3/IFb/JJ/GF//HH]

p'ertok پەرتوك = book. See **p'irtûk**.

pertukxane پەرتوكخانە (TF) = library; bookstore. See **pirtûkxane**.

p'ertûk پەرتووك (K[s]/GF) = book. See **p'irtûk**.

p'ertûkxane پەرتووكخانە (K[s])/pertûkxane (GF) = library; bookstore. See **pirtûkxane**.

perû پەرروو/**peřû** پەڕوو [A/HH] *f.* **(-ya;).** 1) {syn: pêşk'êş; xelat [1]} reward: **•De zû rabe here cem mîr û *perûya xwe* bistîne** (JB2-Osman Sebrî/Rnh 14 [1943], 8-9) Hurry! Go to the emir and claim *your reward*!; 2) {syn: dayîn II; pêşk'êş; xelat [2]} gift, present. {also: <peřû> پرّو (HH)} [Rnh/JB-2/A/IFb/HH/GF/OK]

p'eřûk پەڕووك (Bw) = rag. See **p'eřok**.

p'erwan•e پەروانە *f.* **(;•ê).** 1) {syn: p'ank II} fan, ventilator (Bw): **•Tu dibînî çawa li dora xwe zîz dibe, eynî wekî *perwanê* ye** (LM, 6) Do you see the way he's spinning around, just like *a fan*; 2) {syn: belantîk; fiřfiřok; p'iřp'iřok} moth (K/JJ/HH). {also: [pervané] پروانه (JJ); <perwane> پروانه (HH)} [Bw/LM/K/IFb/HH/GF//JJ] <baweşînk; bizûz>

p'erwaz پەرواز *f./m.(FS)* **(/-ê;).** frame; border *(of a picture)*: ***•perwazê* wêneyî** (FS) picture *frame*. {syn: ç'arçove} Cf. Sor perawêz پەراوێز = 'hem' [Qmş/K(s)/IFb/GF/OK]

p'erwerd•e پەروەردە *adj.* 1) educated, bred, trained; 2) [*f.* **(•a/•eya;).**] education, training: **•Bingeha dewletê, *perwerdeya* zarokan e** (Hk) The foundation of [every] state is *the education of* its youth; **-p'erwerde kirin** (IFb) to educate, train: **•Em li gor îdeolojîya netewî û ferma (resmî) *dihatin perwerde* (talîm) *kirdin*** [sic] (Ber #7, 9) We *were educated* according to the nationalist and official ideology. <Mid P parwardan (parwar-) = 'to foster, nourish, cherish, educate' (M3); P parvarde پرورده = 'nourished, nursed; educated, bred, trained'; Sor perwerde پەروەردە = 'nourished' & perwerde kirdin پەروەردە کِردِن = 'to nurture' [(neol)Ber/IFb/GF] <hîn I>

p'erxandin پەرخاندِن (K) = to rub; to pet. See **perixandin**.

perxîl پەرخيل (GF) = timber sled. See **parxêl**.

pesar پەسار *m.* **().** slope, hillside: **•Li her du *pesarên* dolê – hem nizar, hem beroj – hatibûn kolan** (DBgb, 6) On both *slopes of* the valley – both the shady side and the sunny side – they had been dug. {also: pasar II (IFb-2/TF)} {syn: berwar; hevraz; jihelî; p'al; p'êş II[2]; qunt'ar; sîng; teřazin} [DBgb/IFb/FJ/Kmc/SS//TF]

pesardin پەساردِن (IFb) = to lean, support. See **p'esartin**.

pesarî پەسارى *pl./f.(B)* **(; /-yê).** dried cow dung: **•Li Kurdistanê, qelaxan ji kerme, sergîn û *pesariyan* çêdikin û bi rêxê sewax dikin ku bi wê rêxê ji berf û baranê bête parastin** (Wlt 1:37, 13) In Kurdistan, they make piles of pressed dung patties from [various types of *dried manure*], then coat them with moist dung so that they will be protected from rain and snow. [Wlt/K/B] <bişkul/pişkul; ç'êrt; dirg; guhûr; k'erme; keşkûr; peyîn; qelax; řîx; sergîn; sergo; sêklot; tepik; t'ers; t'ert[ik]; zibil; zirîç>

p'esartin پەسارتِن *vt.* **(-p'esêr-).** to prop, lean, support *(vt.) (stg. against a wall, etc.)* (BK): **•Wî tevrê** [sic] **xwe yê hêj heriya wê bi devê wê ve hişknebûyî *pesart* dîwarê** (MG. Jiyaneka pêguhork) He *leaned* his hoe, on whose blade the mud was not yet dry, against the wall; **-xwe spartin dîwêr** (K) to lean *(vi.)* against the wall. {also: pesardin (IFb); s[i]partin II (B/CS); [sipartin سپارتين/ispartin اسپارتين] (JJ)} {syn: hilp'esartin} Sor heł•pesardin هەڵپەساردِن [MG/AD//IFb//B/JJ/CS]

p'esin/pesin [K/B] پەسِن *m./f.(B/IF)* **(-ê/ ;/-ê).** praise: **-pesin[ê kesekî] dan** (K/JB3)/**kirin** (B)/**vedan** (B) to praise; **-pesinê xwe dan** (K/JB3) to boast, brag. {also: pesn (F/JB3/B-2/GF); [pesin] پسن (JJ); <pesn> پصن (HH)} {syn: meth; p'aye I} Cf. P pasand پسند = 'approbation'; Sor pesend پەسەند/pesind پەسِند/pesin پەسِن [AX/IFb/A/JJ//K/B//JB3/F/HH/GF]

pesn پەسن (F/JB3/B/GF) = praise. See **p'esin**.

p'est پەست *f.* **(-a;).** pressure; oppression: **•Çima ku ez Kurd im min pirr çews (*pest*) û îşkence ji destê Dewleta Tirk kişandiye** (Wlt 1:36, 16) Because I am a Kurd, I have suffered much *oppression* and torture at the hands of the Turkish state **•Ev serokatî ne bi tenê Serokatiya Neteweyî ye; her wiha serokatiya her kesê ku azadiyê dixwaze, *pêst* û kotekiyê dibîne, ye** (AW78A3) This leadership is not only national leadership; it is likewise the the leadership of every person who desires freedom, who has experienced *oppression* and beatings. {also: pêst I (AW)} {syn: ç'ews; fişar; pêk'utî; zext I} [(neol)Wlt/IFb//AW]

peşêman پەشێمان (Bw) = sorry. See **p'oşman**.

peşik پەشِك (K) = drop *(of liquid)*. See **p'eşk I**.

peşîman پەشيمان (SK) = sorry. See **p'oşman**.

peşîmanî پەشيمانى (SK) = regret. See **p'oşmanî**.

p'eşk I پەشك *f.* **().** drop; raindrop; drops of water, *such as those released when one shakes one's wet hands* (Zeb): **•Ez ḧeta *p'eşkek* av biřêjim** (Z-2) Until I take a piss [lit. 'spill *a drop of* water'] **•Her kesê *peşkekê* ji awa tizbîyêt min wexotewe,**

cendekê wî agirê cehennemê nabînît (SK 12:119) Whoever drinks *a drop of* the water from my rosary, his body will not see the fire of Hell. {also: peşik (K); <peşk> پـشـك (HH)} {syn: çilk; çipik; dilop; niqitk} [Z-2/Zeb/A/IFb/HH/SK/GF/OK//K]

peşk II پەشك *f.* **(;-ê).** 1) lot(s) *(lit.)*: **-peşk avêtin** (F)/ **avîtin/danîn** (K)/**derxistin** (B) to cast lots; **-peşk k'işandin** (F) to draw lots; 2) lot *(fig.)*, fate, fortune, destiny, portion; 3) lottery, raffle (JJ); 4) ballot, vote (JJ). {also: [pychk] پـشـك (JJ)} P pešk پشك = 'casting lots'; Sor pişk پشك [F/K/A/IFb/B//JJ] See **pişk**.

peşk III پەشك *f.* **(-a;).** {syn: p'êt I[2]; p'irîsk} spark. [K/JB3/IFb/OK/FS/SS] <agir; birûsk; bizot>

peşkerî پەشكەری (K) = indicative (mood). See **pêşker**.

p'eşkilîn پـەشـكِـلـيـن *vi.* **(-p'eşkil-).** to disperse, recess, break, pause *(of a meeting)*: **•Ȟeyanî êvarkî civata wana *dip'eşkile*, diçine malê** (Z-3) Their assembly *disperses* by evening, they go home. {also: [pishikin] پشيكين (JJ/PS)} [Z-3/IFb//JJ/PS]

peşme w bergûz پەشمە و بەرگووز (M-Ak) = Kurdish man's suit of clothes. See **bergûz**.

Peştûyî پەشتوویی (Wkt) = Pashto. See **P'aştûyî**.

petêx پـەتـێـخ *m.* **(-ê;).** melon; yellow melon. {also: petîx (Btm/TF); [betikh بطيخ /peţig پطيغ] (JJ); <petîx> پـتـيـخ (HH)} {syn: gindor; qawin; şimamok} < Ar baṭṭīx بطّيخ = 'watermelon' [IFb//JJ//HH/TF/Btm] <zebeş>

petin پـەتِـن (F)/pe'tin پـەعـتِـن (B/Dz) = to cook. See **patin**.

petirme پەتِرمە (GF) = grafting. See **patrome**.

p'etî پـەتـی *adj.* pure, unadulterated *(of language)*. {syn: xwer̄û [1]} [Bw/IFb/OK/ZF3] <zelal>

petîx پەتيخ (Btm/HH/TF) = melon. See **petêx**.

petot پەتۆت *adj.* rotten, decayed. {also: [petout] پتوت (JJ); <peṯot> پـطـوط (HH)} {syn: p'ûç' [3]; r̄izî} <W Arm p'dut'iwn փտութիւն = 'putrefaction' [HB/IFb/FS/ZF3//HH//JJ]

peṯrome پەطرۆمە (FS) = grafting. See **patrome**.

petrume پەترومە (GF) = grafting. See **patrome**.

peturme پـەتـورمـە (M.'Ebdulreȟman. Peturmekirina gunehan) = grafting. See **patrome**.

p'ev پـەڤ *adv.* together. {also: [pew پڤ/be-pew بپڤ] (JJ)} {syn: pêk; vêk} < bi + hev [BX/(K)/JB3/IFb/B/JJ/GF]

p'ev•çûn پەڤ چوون *vi.* **(p'ev-ç-).** 1) to argue, quarrel, fight; 2) {syn: ceng [2]; de'w II; doz; gelemşe; gelş; nakokî} [*f.* **(;-ê).**] argument, quarrel, fight, dispute (GF/TF/OK): **•Bi gotinên sivik *pevçûnê* destpêkir lê sofî Gundoro bi xeberan pevçûn germ kir** (HYma, 25) The *quarrel* began with light words but sofi Gundoro fanned the flames of the quarrel with curses **•[Ew dibêje ji mira ye, û ê dî dibêje ji mira ye, *pevçûn dikin*]** (PS-I, #3, 11, l. 4-5) He says "It's for me," and the other one says "It's for me," and they *start fighting*. {also: bihevçûn (A); [pew tchouin] پڤ چوين (JJ)} [PS-I/K/IFb/GF/TF/OK//JJ//A]

p'evgirêdan پـەڤ گـرێـدان *f.* **(-a;-ê).** 1) connection, contact, relationship; link, tie, bond: **•Bi alîk'arîa hevala Sûsîkê *p'evgirêdana* me bere-bere meȟkem bû û em îda r̄ind haj hev hebûn** (Ba2-#2, 209) With the help of Susik's friend, our *connection* became gradually stronger, and we were well aware of one another **•Weke salekê min derheqa Sûsîkêda t'u tişt nizanbû, ne *p'evgirêdana* me hevr̄a hebû, ne jî me hev didît** (Ba-2, #2, 209) for about a year I knew nothing about Susik, we neither had any *contact* with each other, nor did we see one another; 2) {syn: gihanek} conjunction *(gram.)* (B). {also: pevgirêdanî (IFb)} [Ba2/F/K/B/GF//IFb]

pevgirêdanî پەڤ گرێدانی (IFb) = connection, link. See **p'evgirêdan**.

p'ev k'etin پـەڤ کـەتِـن *vi.* **(p'ev -k'ev-).** 1) to be reconciled, make up; 2) to reach an accord, come to an agreement: **•Min t'irê ew bona qelen *nikarin p'evk'evin* yanê jî apê Mîlo naxwaze qîza xwe bide min** (Ba2-#2, 207) I imagine that they *cannot agree* on the bride-price or that Uncle Milo does not want to give his daughter to me; 3) to clash, fight, argue, disagree: **•Ew *pevketin*** (FS) They *clashed* **•Li cem her kesekî bi awayekî, reng û şêweyekî cihê şingilîme, *pev ketime*** (C. Kulek. Nameyek ji Xwedê re, 131) I have been left hanging, *I have clashed* with everyone in different ways, shapes and forms; 4) to collide, crash into each other: **•Du ṯirimbêl *pev ketin*** (FS) The two cars *collided.* [F/K/B/JJ/FS/ZF3]

p'evr̄a پەڤرا (K) = together. See **bihevr̄a**.

pev re پەڤ رە (IFb) = together. See **bihevr̄a**.

p'exşan پەخشان *f.* **(-a;-ê).** prose, *as opposed to verse (helbest or şêr II)*: **•Dîroka *pexşana* Kurdî ji layê kevnatiya xo ve gelek ya cuda nîne ji dîroka şi'ra Kurdî** (Doskî. Ji pêşengên pexşana Kurdî, 5) When it comes to age, the history of Kurdish *prose* is not very different from Kurdish poetry. <Sor pexşan پەخشان = 'prose' < pexş پەخش = 'scattered,' cf. Ar natr نثر [(neol)Doskî/IFb/FJ/ZF/CS]

p'exşannivîs پەخشان نڤیس *m.&f.* **(-ê/ ;).** prose writer: **•Mela 'Eliyê Teremaxî ewê li sedsala şazdê zayînî jiyay ... diête hijmartin êkemîn *pexşannivîsê* Kurd** (Doskî. Ji pêşengên pexşana Kurdî, 5-6) Mulla Ali Taramakhi, who lived in the 16th century AD ... is considered the first Kurdish *prose writer*. Sor pexşannûs پەخشان نووس [(neol)Doskî/ZF]

pey I پەی *prep.* after *(with motion)*, behind: **•Xwe jî çûne *pey* nêç'îrê** (Ba) As for themselves, they went hunting [lit. 'they went [out] *after* the hunt'] **•Halet û gîsinan li *pey* xwe xweş dikêşin** (AB) They pull the plow and plowshares *behind* themselves well (=They do a good job of pulling the plow...) **•Lê berêda mêr *pey* jina diçin, jin *pey* mêra naçin** (EP-7) But from the earliest times, men go *after* (=pursue) women, women don't go *after* men; **-dan pey** = to pursue, follow: **•Min *da pey* wî** (BX) I *pursued* him **•Ûsib *dide pey* wê** (Ba3) Joseph *follows* her; **-hatin pey** = do.: **•pey wî hatin** (BX) They followed him **•Qîza qenc, em *hatine pey* te** (EP-7) Good girl, we have *come for/after* you ; **-pey .. re/ȓa** = after (in time) , as a result or consequence of {syn: paşê}: **•Ditirsyam, ku *pey* çûyîna min *ȓa* nişkêva gur xwe bavêjne ser kerîyê pêz** (Ba2:2, 205) I was afraid that *after* I left [lit. 'my going'] the wolves would suddenly pounce on the flock of sheep **•*Pey* mirina birê me Ûsib*ȓa* ew kor bîye** (Ba3) *After* (or, as a result of) the death of our brother Joseph, he [=our father] became blind **•*Pey* vê xeberdanê*ȓa* Ûsib gazî xulama kir** (Ba3) *After* this conversation Joseph called [his] servants **•*pey* vê yekê*ȓa*** (Ba/Ba3) *after* that, afterward. {also: [peï] پی (JJ); <pey> پی (HH)} {syn: dû III} [BX/K/(JB3)/IFb/JJ/B/HH/GF/OK]

pey II پەی = foot. See **pê II**.

pey•a I پەیا *m.* **(•ê/•ayê; •ê).** 1) {syn: meriv; mêr I; zilam} man; person: **•*Peyakî* mizgîn ji me ra anî** (AB) A *man* (or, [3] *footsoldier*) brought me the news; 2) pedestrian: **-peya bûn** = to get (down) off, alight, descend, disembark, dismount; to get out of *(a car, bus, train, etc.)* {also: paye [II] bûn (Haz)} {syn: dahatin; hatin xwarê}: **•Memê ji banê k'oçkê *peya bû*** (Z-1) Mem *came down* from the roof of the palace; 3) infantry footsoldier. {also: peyya (BK); [peia] پیا (JJ); <peya> پیا (HH)} Sor pyaw پیاو/pyag پیاگ [Sinneh] = 'man'; Hau pîa *m.* = 'man' (M4) {peyatî} [K/A/JB3/IFb/JJ/B/HH/GF//BK]

peya II پەیا (IFb) = pride; praise. See **paye I**.

peyak پەیاك *f.* **(;-ê).** pawn *(in chess)*: **•Ç'e'vêd min bûne tarî, fîla davêm / dewsa *peyaka*** (FK-eb-1, 286) My eyes have gotten dark, I am playing [lit. 'throwing'] bishops / instead of *pawns*. [B/IFb] <k'işik>

peyal پەیال (K) = tea glass. See **p'eyale**.

p'eyal•e پەیالە *f.* **(•a;•ê).** 1) {syn: îstekan; şûşe[3]} small glass for tea (Bw/Zx/K/Lab); "The tea was served in tiny, pear-shaped glasses--*piyala* in Kurdish--which sat delicately on painted saucers" [from: Teresa Thornhill. *Sweet Tea with Cardamom* (Hammersmith, London : Pandora, 1997), p. 8] : **•Her yekî *piyalek* çay datîne ber wan** (Lab, 41) He sets down a *glass* of tea before each one of them; 2) {syn: avxork; p'erdax} tumbler, water glass (IFb). {also: peyal (K-2); piyal (GF); piyale (Lab/IFb-2); piyan (IFb-2/ GF-2); pîyale (A); pîyan (TF); [pián] پیان (JJ-G) [Jezira] & [payāl] (JJ-PS) [Bohtan = Zx]} Mid P *paygāl = 'cup, goblet' (M3); P piyāle پیاله --> T piyale [Bw/Zx/K/IFb//Lab//A//JJ-PS//GF//JJ-G//TF]

p'eyam پەیام *f./m.(K)* **().** message; news; information. Cf. P peyām پیام/peyγām پیغام; Sor peyam پەیام [K/ IFb/GF/TF/RF/RZ]

p'eyamhinêr پەیام هنێر *m.&f.* **().** reporter, news writer. {syn: *nûçegiha} Sor peyamnêr پەیام نێر [VoA/GF/ ZF3]

peyatî پەیاتی *f.* **().** being a pedestrian. {also: [peiati] پیاتی (JJ)} [K/A/JJ] <peya[2]>

p'eyda پەیدا *adj.* visible, apparent: **-p'eyda bûn** = a) {syn: bît'er bûn} to appear: **•Paşî me dît ȓonaîyek ji 'esmanî *peyda bû*** (SK 11:107) Then we saw a light *appear* from heaven; b) {syn: bît'er bûn; çêbûn} to come into existence, be born, be created: **•... Memê Alan, Xec û Siyamend, Koroxlî, Topa Sultanê Îslamê û hwd; ko heryekê ji bûyerekê an ji xeyala kesekî *peyda bûye*** (SB, 50) [Stories like] Memê Alan, Khej and Siyamend, Köroğlu, Topa Sultanê Islamê, etc., each of which *was created* from an event [i.e., is a true story] or from someone's imagination; **-p'eyda kirin** = a) {syn: dîtin; vedîtin} to find; b) to get, obtain, acquire, procure: **•Divê em çil çekî**

peyde bikin (Ber) We must *find/get* 40 [coats of] armor. {also: peyde (Ber/TF); pêda II; pêde; [peida] پیدا (JJ); <peydabûn پیدا بون & peydakirin پیدا کرن> (HH)} {syn: mewcûd} Mid P paydāg = 'visible, obvious, revealed' (M3); P peydā پیدا--> T peyda [Ber/TF//K/A/JB3/IFb/B/JJ/JB1-A/SK/GF/OK]

peyde پەیدە (Ber/TF) = visible. See **p'eyda**.

peyiftin پەیفتن (IFb) = to speak. See **p'eyivîn**.

peyik پەیك (IFb) = baggy part of shalvar. See **peyk**.

p'eyiv پەیڤ *f.* **(-a;-ê).** word; spoken word(s), *as opposed to the written words* [Cf. Fr parole vs. mot]: **•Lê bi rastî *peyva* ku hêrseke xurt xistibû nava min ev bû: -Vî kerê te ev zuwabûn bi ser me de anî** (HYma, 12) But to tell the truth *the words* that really got me mad were these: "This donkey of yours brought this drought upon us" **•Me got gel lê mebesta me ji vê *peyvê* ewe ku kesên tên serdana pêşangehê** (Wlt 2:71, 6) We said 'the people' but what we meant [lit. 'our intention'] by this *word* was 'those who come to see the exhibit'. {also: peyîv (K[s]/OK-2); peyv (Wlt/GF/IFb-2/OK-2)} {syn: bêje; gilî[1]; gotin; pirs[2]; xeber; zar I} Cf. Mid P paygām = 'message' (M3); P peyām پیام/peyγām پیغام = 'message' [JB3/IFb/TF/OK//K(s)//Wlt/GF] <bêje; lavz; peyiftin>

p'eyivdar پەیڤدار *m.&f.* **().** speaker, spokesman. {syn: berdevk I; qiseker} = Sor qiseker قسەکەر [(neol)IFb/TF/OK]

p'eyivîn پەیڤین *vi.* **(-p'eyiv-).** to speak, talk: **•Lê ew bi xwe di konferanseke wiha girîng da bi kurdî *napeyive*, bi tirkî *dipeyive*** (Z.Xamo: Hindik Rindik) But in such an important conference he *doesn't speak* in Kurdish, he *speaks* in Turkish. {also: peyiftin (IFb-2); peyivtin (OK-2); peyîftin (-peyîf-) (K/JB1-S); peyîvtin (-peyîv-) (IFb-2); peyvîn (RZ)} {syn: axaftin; k'êlimîn; mijûl dan; qezî kirin (Bg); qise kirin (Ks); şor kirin; ştexilîn; xeber dan} [BX/JB3/IFb/TF/OK//K/JB1-S//RZ]

p'eyivsazî پەیڤسازی *f.* **(-ya;-yê).** morphology: **•Di rêzimana klasîk de bingeha rêzimanê *peyvsazî* anku morfolojî ye** (AzadiyaWelat) In classic grammar the basis of grammar is *morphology* **•Zimanê standard bi wî zimanî têt gotin yê ku çi di warê rêziman û çi di warê dengnasî û çi di warê hevoksazî û çi di warê *peyivsazî* û çi di warê rênivîsê de şêweyekê qalibdariştî wergirtibe** (Kurdish Academy of Language) 'Standard language' is applied to that language which has been unified in the fields of grammar, phonology, syntax, *morphology* and orthography. {also: peyvesazî (Welatê Me); peyvsazî (Wkt)} [SS//Wkt///WelatêMe] <hevoksazî>

peyivtin پەیڤتن (OK) = to speak. See **p'eyivîn**.

peyîftin پەیفتن (-peyîf-) (K/JB1-S) = to speak. See **p'eyivîn**.

peyîn پەیین *m.* **(-ê; p'êyn** [B]**).** dung, manure: sheep dung *used as fuel and fertilizer* (K/A/B); horse manure (JJ): **•Wekî *peynî* zêde ne** [or **gelek in**] (Hk) They are a dime a dozen [lit. 'as abundant as *manure*']. {also: pehen (IFb-2); peîn (F); p'eyn, m. (; p'êyn) (B)/peyn (IFb/FS); [pèin] پین (JJ)} cf. Az T peyin; T peyin [Doğubayazıt-Ağrı] = 'manure, dung' [gübre, dışkı] (DS, v. 9, p. 3438); Sor peyîn پەیین = 'manure, dung of horse' [F//K/A/SK//B/IFb/JJ/FS] <bişkul/pişkul; ç'êrt; dirg; guhûr; k'erme; keşkûr; pesarî; qelax; r̄îx; sergîn; sergo; sêklot; tepik; t'ers; t'ert[ik]; zibil; zirîç>

peyîv پەییڤ (K[s]/OK) = spoken words; talk. See **p'eyiv**.

peyîvtin پەییڤتن (-peyîv-) (IFb) = to speak. See **p'eyivîn**.

peyk پەیك *f.* **().** baggy part or crotch of a pair of shalvar [=baggy pants]. {also: peyik (IFb)} {syn: navr̄an [2]; p'êsîr [3]} [Rh//IFb]

p'eyker پەیکەر *m.* **().** 1) {syn: heyk'el} statue; piece of sculpture: **•Di vê pêşangehê de 21 wêne û 11 *peyker* (heykel) cih digirin** (Wlt 2:71, 6) In this exhibit, 21 pictures and 11 *sculptures* are on display; 2) form, image (JJ/OK). {also: [peiker] پیکر (JJ)} <P paykar پیکر =' portrait, figure, model, idol' [<Mid P pahikar [ptkl] = 'picture, image' (M3) < O P patikara- = 'picture, (sculptured) likeness']; Mid P pahikar = 'picture, image' (M3); Sor peyker پەیکەر = 'statue' [Wlt/IFb/JJ/TF/OK] <hiner>

p'eyman پەیمان *f.* **(-a;-ê).** pact, contract, treaty, (formal) agreement: **•Dewleta Tirk li gorî *peymana* Cenewre nameşe** (Wlt 1:39, 16) The Turkish state does not abide by [or, go along with] the Geneva *Convention*. <Mid P paymān = 'measure, period, moderation, treaty' (M3); P peymān پیمان; Sor peyman پەیمان = 'promise, agreement, treaty' [(neol)Wlt/K/A/IFb/TF]

p'eyn پەین, m. (; p'êyn) (B)/peyn (IFb/FS) = dung, manure. See **peyîn**.

peyt پەیت (BF) = healthy, strong. See **p'ît I**.

peyv پەیڤ (Wlt/GF/IFb/OK) = spoken words; talk. See **p'eyiv**.

peyvesazî پەیڤەسازى (Welatê Me) = morphology. See **p'eyivsazî**.

peyvîn پەیڤین (RZ) = to speak. See **p'eyivîn**.

peyvsazî پەیڤسازى (Wkt) = morphology. See **p'eyivsazî**.

p'eywendî پەیوەندى *f.* **(-ya;).** relationship, relation(s), connection: **•Di navbera folklor û edebiyatê de *pêwendiyeke* xurt heye** (YPA, 11) There is a tight *connection* between folklore and literature **•*Pêwendiya* min ligel wan nîne** (IFb) I have no *connection* with them whatsoever **•*Peywendiyên* (têkilî) we bi têkoşînê, ku Kurd ji bo rizgariya xwe didomînin, wek partiya Karkerên Kurdistan (PKK) û partiya Keda Gel (HEP), çawa ne?** (Wlt 1:37, 16) How are your *relations* with [those representing] the struggle which the Kurds are carrying on for their freedom, such as the Kurdistan Workers' Party (PKK) and the People's Labor party (HEP)? {also: pêwendî (IFb-2)} {syn: t'êkilî II[3]} <Sor peywendî پەیوەندى = 'connexion, relationship'; cf. P payvand پيوند 'link, connection, relationship' [(neol)Wlt/A/IFb/TF] <hatin û çûn>

peywir پەیوەر *f.* **(-a;).** 1) {syn: vatinî; wezîfe} duty, responsibility: **•Di encamê de ji bo hilgirtina van *peywiran* (wezîfeyan) ev endam hatin hilbijartin** (Wlt 1:36, 5) In the end, these members were elected to carry out these *duties*; 2) job, employment: **•Endamên malbata min ji min hêvî dikirin ku ez zanîngehê biqedînim, bibim xwedî *peywir* û alîkarîya aborî bi wan re bikim** (Wlt 1:35, 16) Members of my family expected me to finish college, get a *job*, and help them out financially. [(neol)Wlt/ZF3]

peyxember پەیخەمبەر (BX) = prophet. See **p'êxember**.

peyya پەییا (BK) = person; pedestrian. See **peya**.

pez پەز/**pez̲** پەظ [SK-2] *m.* **(-ê; pêz, vî pezî).** (flock of) sheep: **•Xwe bû şivan û jina xwe kire *pez*** (L) He himself became a shepherd, and he made his wife (=turned her into) *a sheep*; **-goştê pêz** (B) mutton; **-k'etina serê pêz** (B) lambing time, period when ewes bring forth lambs; **-pezê doşanî** (B) Milk-bearing sheep; **-pezê k'ûvî** (B/JJ) wild ram. See **pezk'ûvî**; **-pezê nêr** (BX) ram, male sheep {syn: beran}: **•*Pezê nêr* ji bo kêrê ye** (BX) *The ram* is [destined] for the knife *[prv.]*; **-pezê r̄eş** (JB3) goat(s) {syn: bizin}; **-pezê spî** (JB3) sheep {syn: mî I}; **-pezê stewr** (B) sterile sheep {also: paz (TF); pêz, f. (F/AB-2); [pez] پز (JJ)} [Pok. 2. peḱ-797.] 'wealth, movable property': Skt paśu- *m.* = 'cattle'; O Ir *pasu-/zero grade *fšu-: Av pasu- = 'small livestock, domestic quadruped'; Mid P pah = 'sheep' (M3); S Baluchi pas = 'small livestock'; W Oss (Digor) fus = 'sheep'; Sor pez پەز = 'sheep and goats'; Za pes *m.* = 'livestock' (Mal); cf. also Lat pecus, pecoris n. = 'flock (of cattle or sheep)'; Germ Vieh *n.* = 'cattle' [K/A/JB3/IFb/B/JJ/JB1-S/SK/GF//AB/F//TF] <bizin; celeb II; col; çêrîn; kewal; mî I; sewal I; sûrî I; şivan>

pezkovî پەزكوڤى (IFb) = ibex. See **pezk'ûvî** [2].

pezk'ûvî پەزكووڤى *m.* **().** ibex, mountain goat: **•Carna bi strandin an bi fîkandin, bê tirs û telaş, wek *pez kuviya*, ji tehteke me xwe davête tehteke din** (SW:Erebê Şemo. Şivanê Kurd, 43-44) Sometimes with singing or whistling, without fear or worry, they would leap from one rock to another like mountain goats. {also: pezê k'ûvî (B); pezkovî (IFb); [pez kouwi پزكوڤى/paz kuí (JJ-G)/paz-a kōvi *or* pes-kōvi (JJ-Lx)] (JJ)} Cf. Sor pezekêwî پەزەكێوى = 'mouflon & ibex' [DZK/K/JJ/GF//B//IFb] <*deer*: ask; gak'ûvî; *goat*: bizin; *sheep*: beran; pez>

pê I پێ 1) [<bi + wî/wê] with him/her/it; 2) *[prep.]* with, by, by means of (=**bi**) (K2): **•Ax çawa gustîlka Memê ji Zîna qîza mîr nedizî, minê îro *pê* wê gustîlkê Memê bistenda** (FK-eb-1, 271) Oh! Had I only stolen Mem's ring from Zîn, the mîr's daughter, I could have gotten Mem today *with* it **•Birînê min girêde *pê* dezmalê destane** (Z-1, 51) Bind my wounds *with* a handkerchief **•Merî xûnê pê xûnê naşo, merî xûnê *pê* avê dişo** (Z-1257) One doesn't wash blood with blood, one washes blood *with* water *[prv.]* **•Pîrê, lê *pê* t'ertê sergîn be'r tê şewitandin?** (Dz-anec. #4) Granny, can the sea be set on fire *with* a dung patty? **•T'asêd xwe digirtne destêd xwe, *pê* şiva li wan dixistin, wekî bi wî dengî gura bitirsînin** (Ba2:1, 203) They would take their bowls and bang on them *with* their staffs, so as to scare away the wolves with this noise. < bi + wê/wî [K2/FK/EP/Z/EH/Dz/Ba2/K/IFb/B/JB1-A&S/OK] <bi; p'ev; pêk>

pê II/p'ê [K/B/JB1-A] پێ *m.* **(pîyê;).** foot, leg:

•Hingo 'adet kiriye, kesê destê merĥemetê bi serê hingoda bînît dê leqekî li wî destî den, û kesê *pîyê* bi-gû di serê hingo bihusût mirç-mirç dê wî pê[yî] maç ken (SK 57:661) If anyone lays a compassionate hand upon your head you have been accustomed to bite that hand, and if anyone wipes a dung-covered *foot* on your face then you kiss that foot noisily; **-p'ê li zimanê hev kirin** (XF/EP-7) to be so crowded, that there's no room for a pin to fall, to be up to one's nose in ... [lit. 'to put [their] feet on one another's tongues'] **•Şikyatçî *p'ê zimanê hev dikin*** (Z-1) We're up to our necks in plaintiffs [lit. 'plaintiffs *are stepping on each other's tongues*'] [people coming to the court to air their complaints]. {also: pey II; [peï] پى (JJ); <pî> پى (HH)} [Pok 2. pēd-/pōd- (*nom. s.* pōts [Kent: *pōd-s], *gen.* ped-és/-ós) 790.] 'foot': Skt pad-/pā́da-; Av pad- ='foot' & pāδa- = 'step, pace' (Kent); OP pad-/pāda- (Kent); Mid P pay [pdy] = 'foot; footstep, track' (M3); P pā پا; Sor pa پا ='foot' & pê پێ = 'foot, footing, degree, note (music)'; Za pa *m.* = 'foot, kick' (Mal); Hau pa *m.* (M4); cf. also Lat pes, pedis; Gr pous πούς (*gen.* podos ποδός); Arm odk' ոտք [vodk']; Germ Fuss [K/A/JB3/IFb/B/SK/GF//JJ//HH] <ling>

pêçan/pêç'an [B] پێچان *vt.* **(-pêç-).** 1) to wrap, pack; 2) to swaddle; 3) to fold; 4) to roll *(cigarettes)*: **•Te cixarên xwe temam bi jahrê *pêçane*** (ZZ-10, 138) You *have rolled* your cigarettes with poison. {also: pêç'andin (B-2); p'êç'andin (K); pêçîn; [petchan پچان /pitchan پيچان/pitchiian پيچيان] (JJ); <pîçan پيچان (dipîçe) (دپيچه)/pêçandin پيچاندن (dipîçîne) (دپيچينه)> (HH)} Mid P pēčīdan (pēč-) = 'to twist, entwine' (M3); P pīčīdan پيچيدن; Sor pêçan پێچان = 'to wrap, cover by winding' & pêçanewe پێچانەوە = 'to fold up, roll up; conceal'; SoK pèč[ân]-/pič[ân]- (Fat 355); Za pêşenã [piştiş] (Srk); Hau pêçay/pêtay (pêç-) *vt.* (M4) [Z-1/EP-8/IFb/B/JJ/SK/GF//A/JB3//K//HH] <pêçavtin>

pêç'andin (B)/p'êç'andin (K) پێچاندِن = to wrap; to fold. See **pêçan**.

pêçavtin پێچاڤتِن *vt.* **(-pêç'iv-).** 1) {syn: nixamtin; werkirin} to cover, envelop, wrap (up): **•[Xûnê ser û çavêd Behramî *pêç'avt*]** (JR) Blood *covered* Behram's face [lit. 'head and eyes']; 2) to wind *(around)*. {also: peçavtin (Hk); [petchawtin] پچاقتن (JJ)} [JR/K(s)//JJ/Hk] <pêçan>

pêç•e پێچە *f.* **(•a;).** veil: **-pêça bûkê** (Bw) bridal veil. {also: peçe (OK-2)} {syn: ç'adir[1]; çarik[2]; ç'arşev[1]; p'erde[4]} [Bw/Dh/GF/OK/(JB1-A)] <hêzar; r̄ûpoş; xêlî I>

pêçek/pêç'ek [B] پێچەك *f.* **(-a;-ê).** 1) package, parcel, bundle; roll *(of paper)*; 2) {syn: p'aç'ik; pêçolk} diaper, nappy; swaddling clothes, swaddling band: **•Dijmin...zarokên li ser *pêçekê* kuştin** (Wlt 2:59, 7) The enemy...killed infants in *swaddling clothes* **•Mi anî mi bi şîrê ẍizala xwey kir, wilo bç'ûk di *pêçekê* da** (HR 3:275) I brought him and nursed him with gazelle milk, such a small one in *swaddling clothes* **•...Pê devê xwe *p'êç'eka* t'falê girt bû** (EH) [the goat] picked up in its mouth the child's *swaddling band.* {also: [pétchek] پيچك (JJ)} Sor pêçek پێچەك = 'bandage; package; envelope' [EH/K/A/IFb/B/JJ/GF] <p'aç'ik>

pê ç'êbûn پێ چێ بوون *vi.* **(pê çê-b-).** 1) {syn: karîn; şiyan} can, to be able [*rev. con.*]: **•Min *pê çê nabît*** (Zeb) I *cannot*; 2) [*f.* **(-a;).**] {syn: şiyan} ability: **•li dûv *şiyan û pêçêbûna* xo** (R 15 [4/12/96] 2) to the best of one's *ability*. [Zeb/R/FS]

pêç'î پێچی (K) = finger. See **bêç'î II**.

pêçîn پێچین = to wrap; to fold. See **pêçan**.

pêçol پێچۆل (AD) = diaper. See **pêçolk**.

pêçolk پێچۆلك *f.* **(-a;).** 1) {syn: p'aç'ik; pêçek[2]} diaper, nappy: **•Wê *pêçolk* li zar̄okê xwe pêça** (FS) She wrapped her baby in *a diaper* [lit. 'She wrapped a diaper on her child']; 2) baby in diapers (FS): **•Wî *pêçolka* xwe da milê xwe** (FS) He picked up his *diapered baby* in his arms. {also: pêçol (AD)} [Y.Saliĥ/FS//AD] <sawa>

pêda I پێدا *adv.* below: **-ji *ft-î* pêda** (Bw/SK) below, downward of, lower than: **•Damil: pişkek e ji kirasê jinka, *ji* navṯengê *û pêda* ye** (FS) Hem: it is the part of a woman's dress below the waist [lit. '*from* the waist *and down*'] **•Dibêjin carekî gurg çû serkanîyekî av dixareve. Di wî wextîda berxek hate ser avê, qiyasê do werîsan *ji* gurgî *pêda* dest bi av-xarinewê kir** (SK 5:55) They say that a wolf once went to a spring and was drinking some water. At the same time a lamb came to the water and began to drink about two rope-lengths *below* the wolf. {≠pêhel} [Bw/SK] <binat'ar>

pêda II پێدا. See **p'eyda**.

pêde پەدە. See **p'eyda**.

pêdivî پێدِڤی *f.* **(-ya;-yê).** 1) {syn: ĥewce} a need, necessity: **•Ayeta jorîn jî vê *pêdivîyê* derdixe pêşiya me** (fetwayenkurdi.com 10.ii.2014) The above

[Quranic] verse presents this *necessity* to us; -**pêdivî pê hebûn** (ZF3) to need: •***Pêdiviya me bi* wan *heye*** (Wkt) We *need* them/have need of them; 2) [*adj.*] {syn: gerek; lazim; p'êwîst} necessary, essential [often + *subj.*]: •**Ma *pêdivî* ye ez jî bêm?** (Wkt) Is it *necessary* that I come as well? •**Oksijen ji bo jinê *pêdivî* ye** (ZF3) Oxygen is *necessary/essential* for life •***Pêtivîye* ku harîkariya hejaran bêt kirin** (FS) *It is necessary* that the poor be given aid; 3) in need of, needing: •**Behrem *pêtivî* harîkariyê ye** (FS) B. is *in need of* help. {also: pêdvî (BF); pêtivî (FS)} Sor pêwîst پێویست = 'necessary' [Zeb/ZF3/Wkt//BF//FS] <p'êwîst>

pêdvî پێدڤی (BF) = need; necessary. See **pêdivî**.

p'êge پێگه (B) = path, trail. See **pêgeh**.

pêgeh/p'êgeh [K] پـێـگـه‌ه *f.* **(-a;-ê).** path, trail: •**Ez nahêlim *pêgeha* te li mala min k'eve** (K) I won't allow you to set foot in my house [lit. 'your *path* to enter my house'] •**Mala 'Elî – bavê K'oroxlî – li Mek'ûê bûye, li ser *p'êga* zozanê kurmancîyê bûye** (K'yoroghli ēposi K'rdakan patumnerē, 1953, 157) The house of Ali – Koroghlu's father – was in Maku, on *the path to* the Kurds' summer pasture. {also: p'êge (B)} {syn: dirb I; r̄êç' II; şiver̄ê} Cf. Sor page پاگه = 'threshold' [K'yoroghli ēposi/K//FJ/GF/AD//B]

pêgirî پـێـگـرى *f.* **(-ya;-yê).** adherence (e.g., to a rule), compliance (with), following, obeying; allegiance, faithfulness, fidelity, loyalty: •***Pêgirîya* xwe hember biryarê da zanîn** (BF) He announced his *compliance* with the decision; **-pêgirîya ft-î kirin** (RR)/**pêgirîyê li ft-î kirin** (Nefel) to adhere to, comply with, follow, obey (a rule): •**Malikîyê serokwezîrê Iraqa niha, ne tenê *pêgiriyê* li destûrê *nake* û mafê Kurdan asteng dike, ...** (nefel.com:M.Evdila. Rola Hewlêrê di perspektîfa global de. iv.2012) Not only does Maliki, the current prime minister of Iraq, *not adhere to* the constitution and [thereby] limit the Kurds' rights, ... [RR/nefel.com/ZF/Wkt/BF]

pêhel پـێـهـل *adv.* above: **-ji *ft-î* [û] pêhel** (Bw/SK) above, upward of, higher than: •**Hevalêt min hemî ji hejdê ne û *pêhel[tir]*** (Bw) My friends are all eighteen (years old) and *above*. {≠pêda I} [Bw/SK/FS] <wêvatir>

pêhn پێهن (M-Zx) = kick. See **p'eḧîn**.

pê ḧesîn پـى حـەسـيـن = to find out about, learn of, be aware of. See **ḧesîn**.

pêjan پێژان (Bw) = fence. See **p'ercan**.

pêjgeh پـێـژگـه‌ه *f.* **(-a;-ê).** 1) {syn: aşxane; pixêrîk} kitchen; cookhouse; 2) cuisine: •**Şilikî navê şîraniyeke kurdan e û ji *pêjgeha* Rihayê ye** (Wkp) Shiliki is the name of a Kurdish dessert and is from *the cuisine of* Urfa •**Tirî, dendikên tiriyê, ... di *pêjgeha* soranan de gelek cih digirin** (Wkp:Şifte birașk) Grapes, grape seeds ... are very prominent in the cuisine of the Soran [i.e., Sorani speakers]. [(neol)Wkp/ZF3/AD]

p'êjgîr پـێـژگـیـر *f.* **(-a;-ê).** towel. {also: pêşkir (IFb); pêşkîr (A); [pychkir] پیشگر (JJ)} {syn: xawlî} <P pīšgīr پـیـشـگـیـر = 'napkin; apron'--> T peşkir = 'towel'--> Ar baškīr بشكير [EP-7/K/B//A//IFb//JJ]

pêjin پـێـژن *f.* **(-a;-ê).** 1) slight sound, sound heard while dozing off [sound one is not sure one has heard or not, or sound whose origin is unclear]; sound of stg. moving: •**[Lakin weku *pêjna* kitin û deng têtin meger xweha Meḧmed begî bi *pêjnê* hişyar dibê]** (JR) But when he made *noise* [by climbing in the window] and the sound carried, Mehmed beg's sister woke up at *the sound*; 2) rumble; echo; rumor; event (K). {also: pejin (IFb/TF-2/OK-2); pejn (IFb-2/OK-2); [pejin پیژین/pejnek پیژنك] (JJ); <pêjn> پیژن (HH)} [JR/JJ/IFb/GF/TF/OK//K//HH] <sînahî>

pêjîn پێژین (IFb) = to cook. See **patin** & **pijîn**.

pêk/p'êk [K] پـێـك *adv.* together. {syn: p'ev} < bi + [y]êk [Ber/K/A/JB3/IFb]

pêkan پێکان *adj.* possible: •**Ma gelo *pêkan* e ku gel bi hev re rûniştibin û berhemek afirandibin** [sic]? (YPA, 12) Isn't it *possible* for a people to live together and [jointly] to create an object? (syn: gengaz[2]; mumkin} <pê + kanîn/karîn = 'to be able to, can' [(neol)ZF/Wkt]

pêk•anîn پـێـك ئـانـیـن/پـێـكـئـانـیـن *vt.* **(pêk[t]în-).** 1) to prepare: •**[Çend belgîr ku lazim *pêk bînin*]** (JJ) *Prepare* as many horses as are necessary; **-xwe pêkanîn** = to prepare o.s., get ready: •**Kurd *xwe pêk tînin*, da bi keriyên xwe ve herin lêfa** (SW-#18 [Ereb Şemo]) The Kurds *get ready* to go to the lambing pen with their flocks; 2) to accomplish, achieve, carry out, bring to pass: •**Xwedê dilxwaza te *pêk bîne*** (GF) May God *grant* your wish [i.e., bring it to pass]; 3) {syn: li dar xistin} to organize, put together, hold (a conference); 4) to unite (JB1-A); to bring together, reconcile (SK); 5) to constitute, make up, comprise: •**Ez dikarim armanca me di çend xalan de şîrove**

bikim ku ew bingehê xebata me jî *pêktînin* (Wlt 1:37, 16) I can explain our goals in a couple of points that *comprise* also the bases of our work. {also: pêk înan (SK); [peik anin] پـيـك آنـيـن (JJ); <pêk anîn پێکئانین (pêktîne) (پێکتینه) (HH)} [Wlt/K/A/JB3/IFb/JJ/HH/JB1-S/GF/TF//SK] <pêkanîn>

pêkenik پـێـکـەنِـك (GF) = laughing stock; joke. See **pêk'enok**.

pêkenînk پێکەنینك, f. (GF) = laughing stock; joke. See **pêk'enok**.

pêk'enok پێکەنۆك *f./m.(K)* **(-a/;).** 1) laughing stock, person who everyone laughs at; 2) {syn: ĥenek; meselok; qerf} thing laughed at, humorous anecdote, joke: **•Kesên ku di nav civatên me Kurdan de henekan dikin an jî *pêkenokan* dibêjin, ew "henekvan" in. Kesên ku bêhtir di dîwanxaneyên mîran de *pêkenok* digotin û carna weke şanogerekî bi rola xwe ve radibûn, ew "qeşmer" bûn** (CP, 6) People who crack jokes or tell *humorous anecdotes* at the gatherings of us Kurds are "comedians." People who told *jokes* and sometimes acted out their stories in the courts of emirs, were "jesters" **•Li hin welatên dî jî ... hin meselok û *pêkenokên* sîyasî hatine afirandin** (Bkp, xxviii) In some other countries as well ... political jokes and *anecdotes* have been created. {also: pêkenik (GF); pêkenînk, f. (GF-2)} [CP/K/A/IFb//GF] <ĥenek>

pêk'esk پـێـکـەسـك *f.* **().** edible mountain plant: **•Diya me jî bi me ra hat da ku pincaran şanî me bide (Spink, tirşo, mendik, *pêkesk* H.D.)** (EŞ, 8) Our mother came with us too, to show us edible plants [pincar] (meadow salsify, sorrel, mendik, *pêkesk*, etc.). [EŞ/GF/FS]

pê•k'etin پـێ کـەتِـن *vi.* **(bi ... -k'ev-).** 1) to get sick (from), for food to disagree with one: **•Bizin *bi* cehî *ket*** (FS) The goat *got sick from* the barley **•Ez *bi* vê xwarinê *ketim*** (ZF3) I *got sick from* this food/This food did not agree with me **•Ez her rojê ... ji te re dibêjim golikan li ber onca Apê Sêvdîn re nebe, îro giş *bi* oncê *ketin*** (Wkt) Every single day I tell you not to take the calves to Uncle S.'s clover, today they all *got sick from* the clover; 2) to feel nauseous, to be airsick (of airplanes), be carsick (of automobiles): **•Ew *bi erebeyê dikeve*** (ZF3) He *is car sick*; 3) to die from, succumb to, perish: **•Li Helebçe nêzîkî pazde hezar Kurda *bi* kîmyayî *k'etin*** (Bw) In Halabcha nearly 15,000 Kurds *perished from* chemicals **•Li Mêrdînê, dijminî jehr kir nav avê, bi sedan Kurd *pê k'etin*** (Bw) In Mardin, the enemy poisoned the water, and hundreds of Kurds *perished*. [Bw//ZF3/FS/Wkt] <nesax; nexweş>

pêkewk پێکەوك *f.* **().** ragged robin, cuckooflower, bot. *Lychnis flos-cuculi*. {also: <pêkewk> پـێ کـەوك (Hej)} {syn: *pêqijik (IFb)} [Bw/IFb/OK/Hej/AA]

pêk•hatin پێك هاتِن/پێکهاتِن *vi.* **(pêk[t]ê-).** 1) to take place, come about, occur: **•Belê, ev rast e ku bûyerên wiha *pêk tên*** (Wlt 1:37, 16) Yes, it is true that such events *take place* **•Êrîş roja 12.11.1992 an, êvarê saet di 22.30 an de *pêk hat*** (Wlt 1:39, 9) The attack *took place* on November 12, 1992, at 10:30 in the evening **•Ji Newrozê û hetanî roja îro pêl bi pêl ji alî "hêzên tarî" ve gelek cînayet *pêk hatin*** (Wlt 1:39, 16) Ever since Newroz, murders *have been occurring* in waves at the hands of "dark forces"; 2) to be organized, founded, established, arranged; 3) to be prepared, made ready (JJ/HH): **•[Hêj zad *pêk nehatiye*]** (JJ) The food *is not* yet *ready*; 4) to be reconciled, to make up (SK); 5) [+ **ji**] to consist (of): **•Weşanxaneya Zelalê ... pirtûkek ku ji du cîldan *pêk tê* derxist** (AW75B6) Zelal Publishers have published a book ... which *consists of* two volumes. {also: [peik hatin] پـيـك هـاتـيـن (JJ); <pêkhatin پـيـکـهـاتـن (pêktê) (پێکتێ) (HH)} Cf. Sor pêk hatin پێك هاتِن = 'to come together, agree, turn out well, be formed, be completed, be accomplished' [Wlt/K/A/IFb/JJ/HH/SK/GF] <pêkanîn>

pêkijîn پـێـکِـژیـن *vi.* **(-pêkij-).** to sneeze. {also: pişikîn (Qmş/Wn); pişkîn (IFb/GF/Slm); p'işkyan (Qzl)} {syn: bêhnijîn; hênijîn [3]} =Sor pijmîn پـژمـیـن/ pişmîn پـشـمـیـن [M-Ak//Qmş/Wn//Slm/IFb/GF//Qzl] <sebr [3]>

pêk înan پێك ئینان (SK) = to prepare; to accomplish; to reconcile. See **pêkanîn**.

pêk'ol پـێـکـۆل *f.* **(;-ê).** 1) pawing the ground *(of animals)*: **-pêk'ol kirin I** (B/GF) to paw the ground; 2) {syn: bizav} effort: **•Berdewam li pêşahîya her *pêkoleka* aştîxwazîyê bûye bo ragirtina şerê navxo** (R 15 [4/12/96], 2) It has consistently been at the forefront of every peacemaking *effort* to stop the civil war; **-pêk'ol kirin II** (Zeb) to strive, make an effort: **•Berdewam jî dê *pêkol* hête kirin bo rohnkirin û têgihandineka dirust bo vê projê** (R 15 [4/12/96], 2)

Efforts will continually be made to clarify and correctly expalin this project **•Me *pêkolkiriye*, ku li dwîv şiyanan di şilovekirina hozanên wanda babetî bîn** (B.Y.'Ebdulla, Hozana afretan di edebê Kurdîda, 6) We *have strived*, as much as possible to be objective in interpreting their poems. < p'ê = 'foot' + k'ol- = 'to dig' [Zeb/R/K/B/GF]

pêk'utî پێکوتی *f.***(-ya;-yê).** pressure; oppression: **•*Pêkutî* û îşkenceyên ku li wan dibin hemû ji me re tînin** (Wlt 1:49, 16) Whatever *oppression* and torture befalls them, they bring all these things to us. {syn: ç'ews; fişar; p'est; zext I} [(neol)Wlt/ZF3]

pêkve پێکڤه *adv.* together: **•'Çare-y me ji ẍeyri ḧelatinê çî dî nîye.' Xulase şûtikêt xo *pêkwe* bestin, li pencerê girê dan** (SK 47:465) 'There is no other way out for us but to escape.' In short, they tied their cummerbunds *together* and lashed them to the window **•Koçer û binecî yêk in. Lazim e em *pêkwe* wê tolê we-keynewe** (SK 40:376) The nomads and the settled are one. We must avenge this *together*. {also: pêkwe (SK); [peikwé] پیکڤه (JJ)} {syn: bihevra; t'evde} Sor pêkewe پێکەوە [Bw/Dh/Zeb/GF//JJ//SK]

pêkwe پێکوه (SK) = together. See **pêkve**.

p'êl پێل *f.* **(-a;-ê).** 1) {syn: êlk'an; mewc} wave *(at sea)*: **-pêl bi pêl** (IFb) in waves: **•Ji Newrozê û hetanî roja îro *pêl bi pêl* ji alî "hêzên tarî" ve gelek cînayet pêk hatin** (Wlt 1:39, 16) Ever since Newroz, murders have been occurring *in waves* at the hands of "dark forces"; **-p'êl dan** = to wave, flap *(vi.)*, be agitated: **•Ala min *pêl dide*** (AB) My flag *is waving* [in the wind] **•Rêşiyên li dora şahra serê wî *di ser hev de pêl didin*** (Tof, 7) The tassels around his head band *hit against one another*; **-p'êla be'rê** (B) wave of the sea, sea-wave; 2) {syn: gav; wext} time: **-vê p'êlê** (K) the other day: **•Erê, biřa *vê p'êlê* hevalekî cabdar nemek ji Moskvaê, ji komûnîstekî kevn stendibû** (K2-Fêrîk) Just *the other day* a comrade in a position of responsibility received a letter from Moscow, from an old communist; 3) series *(of attacks, etc.)* (Zeb). {also: [pél] پیل (JJ); <pêl> پیل (HH)} [K/A/JB3/IFb/JJ/B/HH/GF/Zeb] <beḧr; k'ef>

pêlav/p'êlav [K/B] پێلاڤ *f.* **(-a;-ê).** shoe, footwear; slipper [babouche], boot [bottine], sandal [sandale], pointed shoe which rises above the heel [soulier pointu qui s'élève par dessus le talon] (JJ); type of shoe, high and pointed in back (PS); type of canvas shoe [Fr espadrille] made of woven cords and with a sole of leather or rubber (the latter made of automobile tires) (JB1-A): **-p'êlav p'ê kirin/ p'êlav xistin p'ê** (K) to put on shoes. {also: pêlaw (SK); [pélaw/pēlāw/pēlāv] پیلاف (JJ); <pêlav> پیلاف (HH)} {syn: meras (Kş/Plt); qondere; sol} See JB1, note #155, p. 201. Cf. Sor pêław پێڵاو = 'footgear'; Hau pała *m.* = 'leather shoes' (M4) [Msr/Bw/A/IFb/JJ/HH/JB1-A/GF//K/B//SK] <gore; k'alik II; sol; şîrox>

pêlaw پێلاو (SK) = shoe. See **p'êlav**.

pêlegan پێلەگان *f.* **(;-ê).** 1) {syn: nerdewan; pêpelîng; pêstirk; silim} ladder; 2) {syn: nerdewan; pêpelîng} staircase; 3) {syn: pêpileke (A); pêstirk} step in a staircase. {also: p'êlekan (K/B)/ pêlekan (A/IFb); pêlûk (IFb)} Mid P pillagān = 'steps, ladder' (M3) [Hk/Wn//K/A/IFb/B//F//Ad] <hewq>

p'êlekan (K/B)/pêlekan (A/IFb) پێلەکان = ladder; staircase. See **pêlegan**.

pêlpêlik پێلپێلك (Şnx) = ladder; staircase. See **pêlegan**.

pêlûk پێلوك (IFb) = ladder; staircase. See **pêlegan** & **pêpelîng**.

pêmirîşk پێمریشك *f.* **().** buttercup, crowfoot, bot. *Ranunculus*: **•*Pêmirîşk*: ...Hin cureyên wan di nava avê de aj didin, heşîn dibin. Ji 600'î zêdetir cureyên wê hene. ... ji xeynî cihên pirr sar û pirr germ, li her derê aj dide** (Wkp:Çûng) *Buttercups*: Some types put forth shoots in the water [and] grow. There are more than 600 types of it. ... except for very cold and very hot places, it sends forth shoots everywhere. {syn: *çûng; *genimok} [Bw/AA/BF/Kmc]

pênase پێناسه *f.* **(-ya;).** definition (of a word): **•*Pênaseya* "Destan"ê** (Nbh, 136:26) *The definition of* "story"; **-pênase kirin** (Wkt) to define. {syn: salix[2]} Sor **pênase** پێناسه = 'definition; characteristic (n.), distinguishing trait or quality' [Nbh/ZF/Wkt]

pênc پێنج *num.* five, 5. {also: pênç (A); pyenc (S&E); pyênc (S&E); [pendj] پنج (JJ); <pênc> پینج (HH)} [Pok. penk^{u}e 808.; pṇksti- 839.] 'five': Skt páñca-; O Ir *paṇča; Av panča; Mid P panǰ (M3); P panj پنج; Sor pênc پێنج; Za panj (Todd); Hau penc (M4) [K/JB3/IF/B/HH//A//JJ] <panzdeh; pêncêkî; pêncî I>

pênca پێنجا *adj.* fifth, 5th. {also: pêncan (K-2/IF/BX); pêncanî (K-2); **pêncem**; pêncê (JB1-A/SK/M-

Ak); pêncî II (IF-2); pêncyê (JB1-S); [pēňjāň پـنـجـان (Lx)/pēnjē (Rh)] (JJ)} Cf. P panjom پـنـجـم; Sor pêncem[în] پێنجەمین; Za pancin (Todd) [F/K/B/BK//IF/BX/JJ//JB1-A/SK/M-Ak//JB1-S] <pênc>

pêncan پێنجان (K/IF/BX) = fifth. See **pênca**.

pêncanî پێنجانی (K) = fifth. See **pênca**.

pênce پێنجە (IFb/SK) = fifty. See **pêncî I**.

pêncehem پێنجەهەم (Wkt) = fiftieth. See **pênciyem**.

pêncehemîn پـێـنـجـەهـەمـیـن (IFb/Wkt) = fiftieth. See **pênciyem**.

pêncek پێنجەك (GF) = a fifth. See **pêncêkî**.

pêncem پێنجەم *adj.* fifth, 5th. {also: **pênca**; pêncemîn I (TF/RZ/IFb-2/GF-2/CT-2/ZF-2/Wkt-2)} Cf. P panjom پـنـجـم; Sor pêncem[în] پێنجەمین [A/IFb/GF/CT/ZF/Wkt//TF/RZ] <pênc>

pêncemîn I پـێـنـجـەمـیـن (TF/RZ/IFb/GF/CT/ZF/Wkt) = fifth. See **pêncem**.

pêncemîn II پێنجەمین (IFb) = fiftieth. See **pênciyem**.

pêncê پێنجێ (JB1-A/SK/M-Ak) = fifth. See **pênca**.

pêncêk پێنجێك (AR) = a fifth. See **pêncêkî**.

pêncêkî پـێـنـجـێـکـی *f.* **(-ya;).** a fifth, 1/5: **•*Pênc-yeka* (*pêncêka*) samanê wî behra min bû** (AR, 288) *A fifth of* his wealth was my share. {also: pêncek (GF); pêncêk (AR); pênc-yek (AR-2)} Sor pênc-yek پـێـنـجـیـەك (Sulaimania & Kerkuk)/pêncêk پێنجێك/pênc-yêk پێنجییێك (Arbil) [Zeb//AR//GF]

pêncih پێنجِه (HH/TF) = fifty. See **pêncî I**.

pêncihem پێنجِهەم (Wkt) = fiftieth. See **pênciyem**.

pêncihemîn پـێـنـجِـهـەمـیـن (TF/Wkt) = fiftieth. See **pênciyem**.

pênciyem پێنجِیەم *adj.* fiftieth, 50th. {also: pêncehem (Wkt-2); pêncehemîn (IFb/Wkt-2); pêncemîn II (IFb-2); pêncihem (Wkt-2); pêncihemîn (TF/Wkt-2); pênciyemîn (IFb-2/Wkt-2); pêncîhem (Wkt-2); pêncîhemîn (Wkt-2)} Cf. panjāhom پنجاهم; Sor pencahem[în] پەنجاهەم[ین] [Wkt//IFb//TF] <pêncî I>

pênciyemîn پـێـنـجِـیـەمـیـن (IFb/Wkt) = fiftieth. See **pênciyem**.

pêncî I پـێـنـجـی *num.* fifty, 50: **•Ji *pêncî* carî bêhtir gotina "mist" di şûna gotina "mizdanê" de, bi çewtî hatiye bikaranîn** (AW73C2) More than *50* times the word 'mist' was incorrectly used instead of the word 'mizdan'. {also: pencî (GF); pênce (IFb/SK); pêncih (TF); [pyndji پـنـجـی/pyndjehi پنجهی] (JJ); <pêncih> پینجه (HH)} Skt pañcāśát; Av pančāsatəm *[acc.]*; Mid P panjāh (M3); P panjāh پنجاه; Sor penca پەنجا; Za pancas (Todd); Hau penca (M4) [(K)/A/JB3/B//IFb/SK//JJ//HH/TF//GF] <pênc>

pêncî II پێنجی (IF) = fifth. See **pênca**.

pêncîhem پێنجیهەم (Wkt) = fiftieth. See **pênciyem**.

pêncîhemîn پێنجیهەمین (Wkt) = fiftieth. See **pênciyem**.

pêncsed پـێـنـجـسـەد/**pêncṣed** پـێـنـجـصـەد [SK] *num.* five hundred, 500. {also: pênc sed (BK); pênc sid (BK-2); pênsed (IFb); pênsid (B)} Av panča sata; P pānṣad پانصد; Sor pênsed پێنسەد; Za panj sey [K/A/BK//SK//IFb//B]

pênc sid پێنج سِد (BK) = five hundred. See **pêncsed**.

Pêncşem پـێـنـجـشـەم *f.* **(-a;-ê).** Thursday. {also: Pêncşemb (IFb); Pênşem (B-2/Rh); Pênşemb; Pêşem II; [pechem پشم/pechemb پشنب] (JJ)} Cf. P panjšanbe پـنـجـشـنـبـه --> T perşembe; Sor pêncşem[m]e پێنجشەممە/pêncşemû پێنجشەموو; Za panjşeme [F/K/JB3/B//JJ//IFb//Rh]

Pêncşemb پەنجشەمب (IFb) = Thursday. See **Pêncşem**.

pênc-yek پهێنجیەك (AR) = a fifth. See **pêncêkî**.

pêncyê پێنجیێ (JB1-S) = fifth. See **pênca**.

pênç پێنچ (A) = five. See **pênc**.

pêngav پـێـنـگـاڤ *f.* **(-a;-ê).** step, pace; measure: **•Řîwî sê çar *pêngawan* diçû, řadiwesta, diçû sicdê, du'a dikir, da dilê hewalan zêdetir qahîm bibît derĥeqq wî** (SK 4:48) The fox would walk three or four *paces*, stop, prostrate himself and pray, so that his companions' hearts would become more firmly attached to him; **-pengav avêtin** (Zeb) to take steps or measures. {also: pêngaw (SK)} {syn: gav [2]} = Sor hengaw هـەنـگـاو [Zeb/Dh/Hk/IFb/TF/OK//SK]

pêngaw پێنگاو (SK) = step. See **pêngav**.

pênivîs پێنڤیس (ZF3) = ink pen. See **pênûs**.

pênsed پەنسەد (IFb) = five hundred. See **pêncsed**.

pênsid پێنسِد (B) = five hundred. See **pêncsed**.

Pênşem پێنشەم (B/Rh) = Thursday. See **Pêncşem**.

Pênşemb پێنشەمب = Thursday. See **Pêncşem**.

pênûs پـێـنـووس *f.* **(-a;-ê).** pen. {also: pênivîs (ZF3-2)} {syn: qelem} Sor pênûs پـێـنـووس < pê = 'with it' + nûs- = 'write' [A/JB3/IFb/ZF3]

pêpelank پێپەلانك (Zeb) = staircase. See **pêpelîng**[2]

pêpeling پـێـپـەلِـنـگ (BF) = step; staircase; ladder. See **pêpelîng**.

pêpelîng/p'êpelîng [K/B] پێپەلینگ *f./m.(Mş)* **(-a/-ê;-ê/).** 1) {also: pêpilok (Haz)} {syn: derenc; hewq; nerdewan (EP-7)} step, rung *(of ladder)*; 2) {also: pêpelank (Zeb)} {syn: derenc; nerdewan; pêlegan; pêstirk} staircase, steps: **•Gava seyda *p'êp'elînga***

peya bû, qîzikê qirmîk li serê wî da (HCK-1, 201) When the teacher descended the *staircase*, the girl struck his head with a teapot; 3) {syn: nerdewan; pêlegan; pêstirk; silim} ladder (Ad). {also: pêlûk (IFb-2); pêlpêlik (Şnx); pêpeling (BF-2); pêpelîsk (BF); p'êp'elûk (Z-1/IFb/F/Mş); pêpileke (A); pêpilik (A); pêpilok (Haz)} [Ad/K/B//A//Haz//Z-1/IFb/F/Mş//BF//Zeb//Şnx]

pêpelîsk پێپەلیسك (BF) = step; staircase; ladder. See **pêpelîng**.

p'êp'elûk پێپەلووك (Z-1/IFb/F/Mş) = step; staircase; ladder. See **pêpelîng**.

pêpes/p'êpes [F/K/B] پێپەس: **-p'êpes bûn** (K) to be trampled under foot; **-p'êpes kirin** (F/K/B) to crush, crumple, mash, trample under foot {syn: dan ber lingan; dewisandin; 'eciqandin; her̄işandin; p'ekandin; p'elaxtin; p'erçiqandin; t'episandin}. {also: [pei-pez kirin] پی پز کرین (JJ)} [F/K/B//ZF3/Wkt//JJ]

pêpileke پێپلەکە (A) = staircase step; ladder rung. See **pêpelîng**.

pêpilik پێپلك (A) = step; staircase; ladder. See **pêpelîng**.

pêpilok پێپلۆك (Haz) = step, rung of ladder. See **pêpelîng**.

pêr پێر *adv.* the day before yesterday, two days ago: **-duh[u] na pêr** (B) do. {also: [pēr] پیر (JJ); <pêr> پیر (HH)} Av *parō.ayare; Pahl parēr; P parīrūz پریروز (Horn #311); Sor pêrê پێرێ; Za perey (Todd). See I. Gershevitch. "Iranian Chronological Adverbs," *Indo-Iranica: Mélanges présentés à Georg Morgenstierne* (Wiesbaden, 1964), pp.78-88; reprinted in his *Philologia Iranica*, ed. N. Sims-Williams (Wiesbaden : Dr. Ludwig Reichert Verlag, 1985), pp. 179-89. [S&E/BK/K/JB3/IFb/B/JJ/HH/GF] <betrapêr; dihî>

pêr̄a پێڕا *adv.* 1) together, jointly; 2) instantly, at once, immediately: **-pêr̄a-pêr̄a** (B/Ba3/HR-1) do.: **•Lê Ûsiv *pêr̄a-pêr̄a* dest bi xwarinê nekir** (Ba3) But Joseph did not begin *immediately* to eat.{also: pê re (IFb-2)} [Ba3/K/A/IFb/B]

pêrar پێرار adv. two years ago, year before last: **-par na pêrar** (B) do. {also: [pirar] پیرار (JJ); <pêrar> پیرار (HH)} <O Ir *para-yār- (A&L p. 82 [I, 1]): P pīrār پیرار; Sor pêrar پێرار. See I. Gershevitch. "Iranian Chronological Adverbs," *Indo-Iranica: Mélanges présentés à Georg Morgenstierne* (Wiesbaden, 1964), pp.78-88; reprinted in his *Philologia Iranica*, ed. N. Sims-Williams (Wiesbaden : Dr. Ludwig Reichert Verlag, 1985), pp. 179-89. [K/A/JB3/IFb/B/HH/SK/GF//JJ] <betrapêrar; par>

pê re پێ رە (IFb) = together; instantly. See **pêr̄a**.

pêrêst پێرێست (A) = table of contents; index. See **p'êr̄ist**.

p'êrgî پێرگی (A/L/GF) = encounter; welcoming. See **p'êrgîn**.

p'êrgîn پێرگین *f.* (;-ê). 1) {syn: berahik} encounter, meeting: **-p'êrgî bûn** = to encounter, meet: **•Bi rê de, wezîrê hakim *pêrgî* keçelok *bû*** (L) On the way, the king's vizier *encountered* Kechelok; 2) {syn: berahik; pêşwaz} welcoming, going out to meet s.o. arriving: **-çûn pêrgînê** (IFb) to go out to greet s.o.: **•Rabûn *pêrgî* B. *ve çûn*** (L) They got up and *went out to meet* B. {also: p'êrgî (A/L/GF-2)} [L/A//K/BX/IFb/GF] <berbir̄î>

p'êr̄ist پێڕست *f.* (). 1) {syn: naverok; nêta k'itêbê (F); serecema k'itêbê (F)} (table of) contents; 2) {syn: naverok} index. {also: pêrêst (A)} [K(s)/IFb/GF/ZF3//A]

pêrpîn•e پێرپینە *f.* (•a;). purslane, bot. *Portulaca oleracea*: **•Bila *pêrpîne* li ser dilê wî hişîn bibe** (BF) Let *purslane* grow on his heart, i.e., He should not back down or give up [*idiom*]; **-r̄ihka pêrpîne** (Bw) a loner [lit. 'root of purslane'] *[expression] because pêrpîne grows in individual, isolated clumps.* {also: pelpîne (IFb/GF-2/OK-2); perpîne (GF/OK); p'erpînek (K); pêrpûn (Wkt-2); pirpar (Wkt); pirpir (Ad); [perpiná] پرپنا (JJ)} Cf. P parpahn پرپهن; Sor pełpîne پەڵپینە [Bw/FS/BF//GF/OK/JJ//K//IFb//Wkt//Ad]

pêrpûn پێرپوون (Wkt) = purslane. See **pêrpîne**.

pêrtevînk پێرتەڤینك *f.* (). spider. {also: p'êtavent (K); **t'evnpîrk**; [petavent] پیتاونت (JJ)} {syn: dapîroşk; p'indepîr; pîr [4]; pîrhevok; pîrik [3]; t'evnpîrk [1]} [Slv//K/JJ]

pêser پێسەر (A) = breast; collar. See **p'êsîr**.

pêsikandin پێسکاندن *vt.* (**-pêsikîn-**). to adopt *(a child)*: **•Min xwarziyê xwe Nadan wek kurê xwe *pêsikand*** (Qzl) I *adopted* my nephew Nadan as my son. {syn: di ber pêsîra xwe re derbaz kirin (Qzl)} [Qzl/RZ/Ag]

p'êsîr پێسیر *f.* (**-a;-ê**). 1) {syn: p'aşil; sîng} breast, chest; chest cavity; 2) {syn: berstû; bestik; girîvan; pisto; yax} collar; lapel; edge, border of a garment (JJ): **-di ber pêsîra *fk-î* re derbaz kirin**

(Qzl) to adopt *(a child), when a child is passed between a woman's body and her collar (i.e., dress), the child is considered to be her own (see example under **girîvan**)*; -**p'êsîr girtin** (JJ) to collar, seize, catch hold of; -**p'êsîra *fk-ê* ji *fk-ê/ft-î* xilaz kirin** (B) to save, rescue s.o. from s.o./stg.: •[***P'êsîra* me *ji* olama Romî *xelas dibe***] (JJ) We *will free ourselves of* Turkish domination [lit. 'Our collar will be rid of Turkish taxes']; 3) {syn: navřan [2]; peyk} crotch (of trousers) (Bw/Zeb). {also: pêser (A); [pesir] پسير (JJ); <pêsîr> پيسير (HH)} [JR/K/JB3/IFb/B/JJ/HH/GF/TF/OK/Bw//A] <pizî III; yax>

pêst I پێست (AW) = oppression. See **p'est**.

p'êst II پێست (K[s]) = skin, hide. See **pîst**.

p'êstir پێستر (K/JJ-Rh) = ladder; stairs. See **pêstirk**.

pêstirk پێستِرك *f.* **(-a;-ê).** 1) {syn: pêlegan; pêpelîng; silim} ladder: •**Ew di *pêstirkê* ra çû serbanê xwe** (FS) He went up *the ladder* to his roof; 2) {syn: derenc; pêlegan; pêpelîng} steps, stairs. {also: p'êstir (K); spêtirk (Snd); [pe-stir] پيستر (JJ-Rh)} [Snd//Bw/OK/FS//K/JJ-Rh]

pêş I پێش *prep./adv.* 1) {syn: ber} in front of, before *(place)*: •**Herdu ga li paş in, gamêş jî *li pêş* in** (AB) Both of the oxen are in the back, while the buffaloes are *up front*; **-pêş *fk-ê* kirin** = to show [lit. 'to put in front of s.o.']: •**Bêbextiya xwe *pêş* çavên min *kir*** (BX) He *revealed* to me (=*put before* my eyes) his treachery •**Lazim e lawê te bi min re bê, wê tatê *pêş* min *bike*** (L) Your son must come with me [and] *show* me that rock;

2) *used in conjunction with postpositions*:

-**pêş ... de** = in front of, before *(place)*: •***pêş* min *de* /*di pêşiya* min *de*** = *in front of* me;

-**pêş ... ve** (BX) in exchange for;

-**ji pêş ... ve** (Bw/Dh) on behalf of: •***ji pêş* min *ve*** (Dh) on my behalf;

-**li ... pêşve** (EP-7) in front of, before *(place)*: •**Zînê wê *li* rewaqa *pêşva* sekinye** (EP-7) Zin stood *before* the balcony. {also: [pech پش/pych پيش] (JJ)} Cf. P pīš پيش; Sor pêş پێش. See I. Gershevitch. "Iranian Chronological Adverbs," *Indo-Iranica: Mélanges présentés à Georg Morgenstierne* (Wiesbaden, 1964), pp.78-88; reprinted in his *Philologia Iranica*, ed. N. Sims-Williams (Wiesbaden : Dr. Ludwig Reichert Verlag, 1985), pp. 179-89. [BX/K/A/JB3/IFb/B/SK/GF//JJ] <pêşî I>

p'êş II پێش *f.* **(-a;-ê).** 1) {syn: damen; daw I} skirt, flap, lap *(of a garment)*; 2) {syn: berwar; hevraz; jihelî; p'al; pesar; p'êş II[2]; qunt'ar; sîng; teřazin} slope *(of mountain)*: •**ser *p'êşa* Dûmanlûê** (Ba2) on *the slope of* [Mount] Dumanlu *(located between Erzurum and Erzincan in northeastern Turkey)*. {also: [pech] پيش (JJ); <pêşik> پێشك (HH)} [Ba2/K/IFb/B/JJ//HH]

pêşangeh پێشانگەه *f.* **(-a;-ê).** exhibit, exhibition; display: •**Di vê *pêşangehê* de 21 wêne û 11 peyker (heykel) cih digirin** (Wlt 2:71, 6) In this *exhibit*, 21 pictures and 11 sculptures are on display. <Sor pîşange پیشانگه [(neol)Wlt/IFb//(A)]

pêşbazî پێشبازى *f.* **(-ya;-yê).** competition, contest, race; rivalry: **-pêşbazî kirin** (Wkt) to compete. {also: pêşbezî (Wkt-2/SS-2); pêşbezîn (GF/FJ-2/SS); pêşwazî II (Siya Mem û Zîn-2)} {syn: berêkanê; lec; řik'êb} = Sor pêşbiřkê پێشبِڕکێ [Siya Mem û Zîn/IFb/FJ/ZF/Wkt/CS//GF/SS] <hevrikî>

pêşber پێشبەر *prep.* [+ **li** / **-î**] opposite, facing: **-pêşberî hev** (BX/JB3) facing each other, face to face. {also: pêşberî (B)} {syn: dijber; miqabil; řaber} [BX/K/JB3/IFb/GF//B]

pêşberî پێشبەرى (B) = opposite. See **pêşber**.

pêşbezî پێشبەزى (Wkt/SS) = competition, contest. See **pêşbazî**.

pêşbezîn پێشبەزين (GF/FJ/SS) = competition, contest. See **pêşbazî**.

pêşbînayî پێشبينايى (K) = prediction. See **pêşbînî**.

pêşbînî پێشبينى *f.* **(-ya;-yê).** forecast, prediction: •**Her dem encamên ne li gorî *pêşbîniyên* (texmîn) çapemeniyê hatin wergirtin** (AW71A2) Every time the results [lit. 'results were received'] were not according to the *predictions* of the press; **-pêşbînî kirin** (OK) to predict. {also: pêşbînayî (K)} Sor pêşbînî پێشبينى = 'foresight, precautions' [IFb/GF/OK/ZF3//K]

pêşda پێشدا *adv.* 1) {syn: berî} before *(time & place)*: **-pêşda çûyîn** (B) to advance, move forward; 2) {syn: li ber vê (Ad); ≠şûnda} ago *(referring to the past)*. {also: pêşde (A/JB3/IFb); pêşta (Ber)} [Z-1/K/B//A/JB3/IFb//Ber]

pêşdaçûn پێشداچوون *f.* **(-a;-ê).** advancement, progress. {also: pêşdaçûyîn (B); pêşdeçûn (A/JB3/IFb/GF); pêştaçûyîn (Ber)} {syn: pêşk'etin; pêşveçûn} [Ber/K//B//A/JB3/IFb/GF//Ber]

pêşdaçûyîn پێشداچوويين (B) = progress. See **pêşdaçûn**.

pêşde پێشده (A/JB3/IFb) = before; ago. See **pêşda**.

pêşdeçûn پێشدەچوون (A/JB3/IFb/GF) = progress. See **pêşdaçûn**.

pêşdeçûyî پێشدەچوویی (FJ) = advanced, progressive. See **pêşveçûyî**.

p'êşe پێشە (K/FS) = profession, calling. See **p'îşe**.

p'êşek'ar پێشەکار = artist; artisan; servant. See **p'îşek'ar**.

Pêşem II پێشەم (JJ) = Thursday. See **Pêncşem**.

pêşeng پێشەنگ *m.&f.* **().** 1) leading animal in a caravan; bell wether; 2) pioneer, scout, vanguard: **•Û ji *pêşengên* pexşana Kurdî di ... dwîmahiya sedsala nozdê û despêka sedsala bîstê [da] navekê jêhatî heye** (Doskî. Ji pêşengên pexşana Kurdî, 5-6) And among *the pioneers of* Kurdish prose at ... the end of the 19th and start of the 20th century, there is an outstanding name; 3) {syn: mezin [4]; r̄êber; r̄êvebir; r̄êzan; serek; serk'ar [1]; serok; serwer} leader: **•Kurdan li pey mirina lehengên netewî û *pêşengên* gel jî wekî Şêx Seîd, Seyîd Riza, Mele Mustefa Barzanî û hwd şînên mezin girêdane** (Nbh 125:26) On the death of national heroes and *leaders of* the people such as Shaikh Sa'id, Seyit Riza, Mulla Mustafa Barzani, etc., the Kurds have gone into mourning. {also: pêşenk (A); <pêşenk> پیشنك (HH)} < pêş I; Sor pêşeng پێشەنگ = 'leading animal in caravan; leader; precedent, antecedents' [Doskî/K(s)/IFb/FJ/TF/GF/ZF/SS/CS/ /A/HH]

pêşenk پێشەنك (A/HH) = pioneer, scout; leader. See **pêşeng**.

pêşeroj پێشەرۆژ (Ber/RZ) = future. See **paşer̄oj**.

pêşgotin پێشگۆتن *f.* **(-a;-ê).** introduction, preface, foreword *(e.g., of a book)*: **•Piştî ku min *pêşgotina* pirtûkê xwend** ... (Epl 11) After I read the book's *introduction* .... Sor pêşekî پێشەکی [Epl/ AZ/K/IFb/GF/OK/ZF3]

pêşin پێشن (B) = first. See **pêşîn**.

pêşî I پێشی *f.* **(-ya;-yê).** face, front part: **-çûn pêşîya *fk-ê*** (K)/**pêşîyêda çûyîn** (B) to welcome, greet, go out to meet s.o. {syn: çûn pêrgînê; çûn pêşwazîyê}: **•Seyda *çû pêşîya* ḧecîya** (HCK-1, 207) The teacher *went to welcome* the returning pilgrims; **-di pêşîya *fk-ê/ft-î* de** = in front of, before: **•*di pêşîya* min *de*** = *in front of* me; **-[li] pêşîya *fk-ê* k'etin** (B) to precede, lead, go before: **•Lawê ê kor *li pêşîya* qîza hakim *ket*** (L) The son of the blind man *preceded* [=led] the princess **•R̄okê *k'ete pêşya* bizinê xwe, bir ser kanyê avde** (Dz) One day he *lead* his goats to a spring to water them [lit. 'he preceded them, brought them'] **•... Zînê ... *pêşya* bazrgên *k'etye*, tê ser kanîê** (EP-7) Zin ... *preceded* the caravan, headed for the spring; **-pêşî [lê] bir̄în/~ya *fk-ê/ft-î* girtin/~ lê/jê stendin** (K/B/XF): a) to bar or block s.o.'s path: **•Me *pêşîya* pêz *girt*, wekî ew nêzîkî xilxile nebe** (Ba2:2, 205) We *barred* the sheeps' *path*, so that they could not approach the rock pile; b) to dam, block up: **•Me *pêşîya* ç'êm *bir̄î*** (B) We *dammed up* the river; c) to prevent, avert, stave off: **•Doxtira *pêşîya* nexweşîyê *girt*** (B) The doctors *averted* the disease [prevented from spreading]. {also: [pichi] پیشی (JJ); <pêşî> پیشی (HH)} {syn: ber I} [EP-7/BX/K/A/JB3/IFb/B/HH/SK/GF/OK//JJ] <pêş I>

p'êşî II پێشی *m.* **(-yê;).** gnat, mosquito: **•Tev mêş û kelmêş *pêşî* û dûpişk**/ (Cegerxwîn. Halê gundiya) Amid flies and midges, *gnats* and scorpions. {also: p'êşû (IFb-2/Erh); [picho/pēshu (Rh)/pesci (G)] پشو (JJ); <pêşû> پیشو (HH)} {syn: k'ermêş [1]; mixmixk} Mid P paxšag = 'mosquito, gnat' (M3); P paše پشه = 'gnat, mosquito'; Sor pêşûle پێشوولە = 'gnat'; SoK pašxa/paxša/paqša = 'fly; mosquito' (Fat 232) [Cxn/A/IFb/GF//HH/Erh//JJ] <axûrk; mêş; moz; vizik I>

pêşî III پێشی (GF) = first. See **pêşîn**.

pêşî ketin پێشی کەتن (A) = to advance; advancement. See **pêşk'etin**.

pêşîn پێشین *adj.* first; foremost. {also: pêşin (B); pêşî III (GF); [pichin/pešīn (Lx)] پیشین (JJ)} {syn: 'ewil; sift (Ad); yekem} [K/A/JB3/IFb//JJ//B] <paşîn; yek>

pêşkese پێشکەسە *m.* **().** person sent to house of father of prospective bride to announce that the wedding procession will come on the following day, wedding herald. {syn: r̄ovî I [2]} *jocular folk etymology*: <pêçke•se = 'little-foot•of a dog'; actually <pêş = 'before' + kes = 'person', i.e., the person who precedes the wedding procession [Zeb] <dolebaşî>

pêşkeş پێشکەش (GF) = present. See **pêşk'êş**.

pêş•k'etin پێشکەتن *vi.* **(pêş-k'ev-).** 1) to go forward; to advance *(vi.)*, get ahead, make progress; to be developed, develop *(vi.)*; 2) [*f.* **(-a;-ê).**] progress, advancement; development: **•Ji bo *pêşketinê*, li herêma ku kurd lê dijîn, divê reformên aborî, siyasî û civakî pêk bên** (AW71A1) For *development*, in the region which the Kurds inhabit, economic, political, and social reforms must take place **•Orkestraya Neteweyî ya Kurd li derveyî welêt her tim di halê *pêşketinê* de ye** (AW69B3) The Kurdish National Orchestra abroad is making progress [lit. 'is in the state of *advancement*']. {also: k'etin pêş (IFb); pêşî ketin (A); pêşk'ewtin (SK)} {syn: pêşdaçûn; pêşveçûn} Sor pêş•kewtin پـێـشـکـەوتـن = 'to go forward, make progress' [K/B/GF/AD/ZF3//IFb//A//SK]

pêşk'etî پـێـشـکـەتـی *adj./pp.* advanced, progressive: **•Bêguman îro çapemeniya kurdan, li gorî neteweyeke wekî kurdan bêdewlet, bêmaf gelek *pêşketî* ye** (AW70A2) No doubt, for a stateless, rightless nation like the Kurds, the Kurdish press today is very *advanced* **•Hêvîdar im ku rola afreta kurd, dê di warê şanogeriyê de *pêşketîtir* be** (AW73A3) I hope that the role of the Kurdish woman will be *more progressive* in the field of theater. {syn: pêşveçûyî} Sor pêş•kewtû پـێـشـکـەوتـوو = 'advanced, antecedent' [K/AD/ZF3] <pêşveřû>

pêşk'ewtin پێشکەوتن (SK) = to advance; advancement. See **pêşk'etin**.

pêşk'êş پـێـشـکـێـش *f.* **(-a;-ê).** gift, present, offering: **-pêşk'êş kirin**: a) to give as a gift, to make a present of {syn: bexşandin [2]}: **•Ji bedel wê çakîya Kak Şasuwar bizînekî bi kar bo bibe, *pêşkêş bike*, 'erz bike, me qewî ji wî minnet e** (SK 19:180) In return for this kind favor of Kak Shasuwar's, take a goat with a kid to him, *present it to him* and tell him we are very grateful to him **•To hind lê hatî ez carîya xo *pêşkêşî* te *bikem*, eto pê řazî nebî?** (M #670) Has so much happened to you that when I *give* you my own maidservant you're not satisfied with her?; b) to present, offer {syn: berpêş kirin}: **•Silavên germ *pêşkêş dikim*** (IFb) I *offer* warm greetings. {also: pêşkeş (GF-2); [pichkech] پـیـشـکـش (JJ)} {syn: dayîn II; diyarî; xelat} Cf. P pīškeš پـیـشـکـش = 'present, gift, offering (from inferior to superior)' & pīškeš kardan پیشکش کردن = 'to offer, present'; Sor pêşkeş پێشکەش [K/A/IFb/SK/GF/B//JJ]

pêşkir پێشکر (IFb) = towel. See **p'êjgîr**.

pêşkîr پێشکیر (A) = towel. See **p'êjgîr**.

pêşmerge پێشمەرگە *m.&f.* **().** soldier; freedom fighter, guerrilla, partisan; "Qazî, the president of the short-lived Mehabad Republic, ... formed a committee of hand-picked littérateurs and writers, to come up with Kurdish terms for his military officers to use ... the first word they encountered for which they wanted to find a Kurdish equivalent was 'serbaz,' the Persian word for **soldier** ... A great deal of deliberating ensued, but it proved to be a fruitless undertaking. Exhausted and frustrated, they ordered tea. An elderly fellow--the sort with a fair amount of experience to show for his years on this earth--brought them their tea, and, reading the frustration in their faces, said with a smile, "I may have no formal education, but I'm anything but an ignoramus. What is the problem which you professor-types are wrangling with?" They replied, "Actually, you may even be able to help us! Instead of 'serbaz,' what would you call a **soldier** in Kurdish?" The elderly fellow smiled again, and said simply, "The Kurds call a man who is willing to sacrifice his life for a cause a 'peshmerga'." *from:* KDPI, *Kurdistan*, 1 (January 1971). <Sor pêşmerge پێشمەرگە: pêş = 'before' + merge <P marg مرگ = 'death' [K(s)/A/IFb/GF/TF/OK]

pêşniyar پێشنیار *f.* **(-a;-ê).** proposal, suggestion: **•Sala par (çûyî) min *pêşniyarek* anî meclîsê** (Wlt 1:37, 16) Last year I brought *a proposal* to the assembly; **-pêşniyar kirin** (ZF3) to propose, suggest. {also: pêşniyaz (VoA/ZF3/FS-2)} <Sor pêşniyar پێشنیار; cf. P pīšnehād پیشنهاد [(neol)Wlt/IFb/TF/FS//VoA/ZF3]

pêşniyaz پـێـشـنـیـاز (VoA/ZF3/FS) = proposal. See **pêşniyar**.

pêş paş پێش پاش (SK) = back and forth. See **paş û pêş**.

pêşp'irtik پـێـشـپـرتـك *f.* **(-a;-ê).** prefix. {also: pêşp'irtî (B-2)} [K/B/GF/Wkt/ZF3] <paşp'irtik; qertaf>

pêşp'irtî پێشپرتی (B) = prefix. See **pêşp'irtik**.

pêşta پەشتا (Ber) = before; ago. See **pêşda**.

pêştaçûyîn پێشتاچوویین (Ber) = progreş. See **pêşdaçûn**.

pêştir پێشتر *adj.* 1) prior, earlier: **•Eger sa'etekî *pêştir* hung nexoşîya xo bi ḧekîmêt ḧaziq o xêrxaz derman neken ... pîçek maye hingo bikujît** (SK 57:660) If you didn't have your illness treated by skillful and well-meaning doctors an hour *earlier* ... it would just about kill you; 2) pre-eminent, more honored: **•Li-nik Smail Paşa kes ji 'Îsa *pêştir* o mu'tebertir nebo** (SK 21:188) There was nobody *more honored* or trusted by Ismail Pasha than Isa; 3) *[prep.]* [+ **ji** or **–î**] except for, besides {syn: bê I[2]; ji ... pê ve; ji bilî; meger

[3]; xêncî}: **•Hespê wî meriv nedihemilandin *pêştirî* p'adşê** (HCK-1, 75) His horse didn't let anyone *except* the king ride him. Cf. P pīštar پيشتر = 'formerly' [HCK/B/SK]

p'êşû پێشو (IFb/HH/Erh) = gnat. See **p'êşî II**.

pêş û paş پـێـش و پـاش (A) = back and forth. See **paş û pêş**.

pêşvaçûn پـێـشـڤـاچـوون (Ber/K/JB3) = progress; improvement. See **pêşveçûn**.

pêşveçûn پـێـشـڤـهچـوون *f.* **(-a;-ê).** 1) {syn: pêşdaçûn; pêşk'etin} advance(ment), progress: **•Ziman neynika çand, pîşe, dîlan, wêje, afirandin û *pêşveçûnê* ye** (F.H. Sagniç: gotinenpesiyan.com) Language is the mirror of culture, skill, songs, literature, creativity and *advancement*; 2) improvement. {also: pêşvaçûn (Ber/K/JB3); [pychwé tchouin] پيشڤه چوين (JJ)} [Ber/K/JB3//IFb/GF//JJ] <werar>

pêşveçûyî پێشڤهچوويى *pp./adj.* advanced, progressive: **•Roşinbîrên wan ên bijare ku xwediyê fikrên gelek *pêşveçûyî* ne** (Nbh 132:11) Their fine intellectuals, who have very *advanced* ideas. {also: pêşdeçûyî (FJ)} {syn: pêşk'etî; pêşverû} [Nbh/IFb/GF/ZF//FJ]

pêşverû پێشڤهروو *adj.* progressive *(politically)*: **•Ji we re jiyaneke serfiraz û *pêşverû* daxwaza me ye** (Wlt 1:37=38, 2) Our wish for you is a proud and progressive life. {syn: pêşk'etî; pêşveçûyî; ≠paşverû} [(neol)Wlt/IFb/TF/ZF3]

pêşwaz پـێـشـواز **().** welcoming, greeting, receiving guests, going out to meet s.o. arriving. {also: pêşwazî I (SK); [pich-vaz] پـيـشـواز (JJ)} {syn: berahik; p'êrgîn} Cf. P pīšvāz پيشواز; Sor pêşwaz پێشواز [IFb/GF/Wkt//SK//JJ]

pêşwazî I پێشوازى (SK) = welcoming. See **pêşwaz**.

pêşwazî II پـێـشـوازى (Siya Mem û Zîn) = competition, contest. See **pêşbazî**.

pêşxistin پێشخِستِن/**pêş xistin** پێش خِستِن [K/B] *vt.* **(pêş-xîn-/-x-).** 1) to present, introduce (IFb/GF); 2) to promote, advance (vt.). Sor pêşxistin پێشخِستِن = 'to put forward, put in front, give priority to, prefer' [Wlt/K/IFb/B/GF]

pêşxizmet پێشخِزمهت *m.* **().** attendant, valet; servant: **•Wextê ko Smail Paşa zanî dîharîya maqûlêt Mizûrîyan kûr in, pîçek di dilê xo da sil bû. Gote *pêşxizmetêt* xo, "Têşta wan sewar bît"** (SK 24:222) When Ismail Pasha learnt that the present of the Mizuri elders was kids [=goats], he became a little annoyed in his heart. He said to his *attendants*, "Let their morning meal be of crushed wheat." {also: [pych-khizmet] پـيـشـخـذمـت (JJ)} {syn: xizmetk'ar; xulam} Cf. P pīšxedmat پيشخدمت [SK/K/JJ]

p'êt I پـێـت *f.* **(-a;).** 1) {syn: agir; alav I; ar I} flame, fire; 2) {syn: peşk III[1]; p'irîsk} spark (A): **•Ker çend caran baz da, di wê mêrga fireh de, û *pêt* ji bin lingên wi derdiket** (SW) The donkey leaped a few times in that spacious meadow, and *sparks* flew out from under his feet; 3) sorrow, grief, woe: **-p'êt û agir** (Msr) deep sorrow [lit. 'fire and flame']. {also: [peit] پيت (JJ); <pêt> پيت (HH)} [Msr/SW/K/A/JB3/IFb/JJ/HH/GF]

pêt II پێت (IFb/BF/FS/ZF) = healthy, strong. See **p'ît I**.

p'êtavent پێتاڤهنت (K/JJ) = spider. See **pêrtevînk.**

pêtik پێتِك (IFb/RZ/CS) = match(es). See **pitik I**.

pêtivî پێتِڤى (FS) = need; necessary. See **pêdivî**.

pêva پـێـڤـا *adv.* completely, totally, entirely: **•Boẍ da lodka, gur *pêva* darda bû** (J) The ox gave a leap, [and] the wolf was *completely* [left] hanging. {syn: lap} [J/K]

pêvajo پـێـڤـاژۆ *f.* **(-ya;).** process, progression, course: **•*Pêvajoya* avakirina dewletê dirêj e** (Wkt) *The process of* building the state is long; **-di pêvajoya *ft-î* de** (Wlt) during, in the course of: **•*Di pêvajoya* têkoşînê *de* bi rastiyan re çewtî jî xwe diyar dikin** (Wlt 1:20, 3) *In the course of* the struggle, together with the truths mistakes also present themselves. <pêv + ajo- [Wlt/IFb/ZF3/Wkt]

pêve•kirin پێڤهكِرِن *vt.* **(pêve-k-/-ke- [Bw]).** to attach, stick *(vt.)*, adhere, affix, paste. {syn: nûsandin; pêvenan; zeliqandin} [Bw/A/IFb/TF/OK]

pêve•nan پـێـڤـهنـان *vt.* **(pêve-n-).** to attach, stick *(vt.)*, adhere, affix, paste: **•Wî wêne *bi* dîwarî *ve na*; wî wêne *pêvena*** (FS) He *attached* the picture *to* the wall; he *attached* [or, hung] the picture. {syn: pêvekirin; zeliqandin} [Bw/FS/BF/Wkt]

pêvir پێڤِر *f.* **(-a;-ê).** Pleiades *(constellation)*: **-pêvir û mêzîn** (B) Libra, the Scales *(constellation)*. {also: pêwir (A/IFb/FS); pêwr (IFb-2); [peívir پـيـور/ peirou پـيـرو] (JJ); <pêwir> پـيـور (HH)} <O Ir *parwi- (A&L p.82 [I, 1]): Sgd pr-prw('k) = 'behind the Pleiades'; Baluchi panvar; P parvīz پرويز; Sor pêrû پێروو = 'pleiades' & pêwir پێور = 'comet' See I. Gershevitch. "Iranian Chronological Adverbs," *Indo-Iranica: Mélanges présentés à Georg Morgenstierne* (Wiesbaden,

1964), pp.83-84; reprinted in his *Philologia Iranica*, ed. N. Sims-Williams (Wiesbaden: Dr. Ludwig Reichert Verlag, 1985), pp. 184-85. [K/B/JJ//A/IFb/HH/FS]

pêwendî پێوەندی (IFb) = relation(ship). See **peywendî**.

pêwir پێوِر (A/IF/HH/FS) = Pleiades. See **pêvir**.

pêwist پێویست (Ber/GF) = forced; necessary. See **p'êwîst**.

p'êwîst پێویست *adj.* 1) forced, coerced, oblig[at]ed; having to, must: **•Îro zarokên kurd li Kurdistanê *pêwistin* zimanên biyanî wek zimanê tirkî, farisî û zimanê erebî** (Ber) Today Kurdish children in Kurdistan are *forced* [to learn] foreign languages like Turkish, Persian, and Arabic **•Di nav vê rewşa nebaş da zarokên kurd *pêwistin* zimanê tirkî hînbin** (Ber) Under these bad conditions, Kurdish children *are forced to* learn Turkish; 2) {syn: divêt [*see at* **viyan**]; gerek; ḧewce; lazim} necessary, obligatory, compulsory (IFb): **•Lê *ne pêwîst e* ku meriv bixwîne** (Epl 17) But *it is not necessary* for one to read/study. {also: pêwist (Ber/GF)} <Sor pêwîst پێویست = 'necessary' [Ber/GF//IFb/ZF3/BF/Wkt] <pêdivî>

pêwr پێور (IF) = Pleiades. See **pêvir**.

pêxametî پێخامەتی (Zeb) = because of; for the sake of. See **pêxemet**.

pêxamî پێخامی (FS) = because of; for the sake of. See **pêxemet**.

pêxamînî[ya] پێخامینیا (Zeb) = because of; for the sake of. See **pêxemet**.

p'êxas (K)/pêxas (IFb/HH/SK) پێخاس = barefoot; beggar. See **pêxwas**.

pêxem پێخەم (ZF3) = because of; for the sake of. See **pêxemet**.

p'êxember پێخەمبەر *m.* **(-ê;).** prophet; the prophet Muhammad. {also: peyxember (BX); p'êẍember (K/SK); [peigamber] پیغمبر/پیغامبر (JJ); <pêẍember> پیغمبر (HH)} < P peyɣambar پیغامبر = 'message bearer' --> T peygamber {pêxemberîtî; p'êxember[t]î; p'êẍembertî} [Ba/A/IFb/B/GF//K/HH/JJ/SK]

p'êxemberî پەخەمبەری (B/ZF3) = prophethood. See **p'êxembertî**.

pêxemberîtî پێخەمبەریتی (GF) = prophethood. See **p'êxembertî**.

p'êxembertî پێخەمبەرتی *f.* **(-ya;-yê).** prophethood. {also: p'êxemberî (B-2/ZF3-2); pêxemberîtî (GF); pêẍemberî (SK); p'êẍembertî (K); [pēkhamberī] پیغمبری (JJ)} [B/ZF3//GF//K//JJ/SK] <p'êxember>

pêxemet پێخەمەت *prep.* because of, due to, thanks to; for the sake of: **•Em vê xebatê *pêxemet* rizgarbûna Kurdistanê dikin** (Wkt) We do this work *for the sake of* the liberation of Kurdistan **•Me, *pêxemet* diyarkirina egerên hatina xwarê ya vê rêjeyê xwast dîtina bisporekî werbigirin** (Wkt: Kulturname.com, viii.2009) We wanted to get the opinion of an expert *for the sake of* revealing the reasons for the decline in this rate ***•Pêxamînîya* te eve bi serê min hat** (Zeb) *Because of* you this happened to me; **-di pîxameta ... da** (Elk) do.: **•Ew *di pêxemeta* filan kesî *da* ket di zîndanê da** (FS) He landed up in prison *thanks to* so and so; **-ji pêxemet** (BF)/**ji pêxema ... de** (ZF3) because of; for the sake of: **•Em xebatê dikeyn *ji pêxemet* azadîya gelê xwe** (BF) We are struggling *for [the sake of]* the liberation of our people **•Ev pertoke hewldaneke jibo xirvekirin û parastina wan vekolîn û rexne û rêbazên edebî ewên di govarên deverê da hatîne belavkirin, *ji pêxemet wê yekê* xwandevan mifay jê wergirît û karê vekolerên edebî jî bi sanahîtir lê biket** (E.'Ebdulqadir. Têkist di navbera gotara rexneyî û rêbazên edebî da, 1980, 7) This book is an attempt to collect and preserve those literary studies, critiques and policies which have been published in local journals, *so that because of this* the reader may benefit and the work of researchers may be made easier ***•Ji pêxema* te *de* ez li vir mam** (ZF3) *Because of* you I stayed here **•Xebat *ji pêxemet* azadîya welat** (BF) Struggle *for* the liberation of the homeland. {also: pêxametî (Zeb); pêxamî (FS-2); pêxamînî [ya] (Zeb-2); pêxem (ZF3); pêxemînî[ya] (Zeb-->Mizûrî); pîxamet (Elk); pîxemet (FS)} {syn: bi xêra; dewlet serê; sexmerat} [Zeb//Elk//FS//BF/Wkt//ZF3] <sexmaret>

pêxemînî[ya] پێخەمینیا (Zeb-->Mizûrî) = because of; for the sake of. See **pêxemet**.

pê•xistin پێخستِن *vt.* **(pê-x- / pê-xîn-).** 1) {syn: dadan; hilkirin [2]} to kindle, light up, ignite: **•Bavê min ... çixara xwe *pêxist*, hilmek-dudu kişandin** (Alkan, 72) My father ... *lit* his cigarette, and took a puff or two **•Cara mayn ç'e'vê dê û bavê *pêxîne*** (EP-7) Until he again stands before the eyes of his parents [lit. 'once again he *kindles* the eyes of his mother and father']; 2) to rub two things together *(e.g., two sticks, to light a fire).* {also: vêxistin}

[EP-7/A/JB3/IFb/TF] See also **vêxistin**. <sûtin; vêxistin>

pêxrîk پێخریك (Wn) = fireplace; chimney. See **pixêrîk**.

p'êxûn پـێـخـوون (Dz) = dish made of roasted wheat ground into flour. See **p'oxîn**.

pêxwas/p'êxwas [B] پـێـخـواس *adj.* 1) barefoot: •**Ditirsim solêt min bidizin, paşî dê *pêxas* mînim** (SK 60:717) I'm afraid they'll steal my shoes, [and] then I'll be *barefoot*; **-p'êxwas bûn/xwe p'êxwas kirin** (B) to take one's (own) shoe's off; **-p'êxwas kirin** (B) to take s.o.'s shoes off; 2) *[m.]* pickpocket; beggar; 3) strong, tough person [T kabadayı]. {also: p'êxas (K)/pêxas (IFb/SK); [pei-khas /pēkhwas] پی خواس (JJ); <pêxwas پیخواس /pêxas پیخاس> (HH)} <p'ê = 'foot' + xwas: **xwas**: <O Ir *xwā-auθra- (A&L p. 86 [VI, 4b]): Sor pêxawis پێخاوِس/pêxawus پێخاووس; Hau pawirûa (M4); See **Outside** in: I. Gershevitch. "Outdoor Terms in Iranian," A *Locust's Leg: Studies in Honour of S.H. Taqizadeh* (London, 1962), pp.82-84; reprinted in his *Philologia Iranica*, ed. N. Sims-Williams (Wiesbaden : Dr. Ludwig Reichert Verlag, 1985), pp. 176-78. [F/B//A/JB3/JJ/HH/GF//K//IFb/SK]

p'êxember پـێـغـەمـبـەر (K/JJ/HH/SK) = prophet. See **p'êxember**.

pêxemberî پـێـغـەمـبـەری (SK) = prophethood. See **p'êxembertî**.

p'êxembertî پـێـغـەمـبـەرتـی (K) = prophethood. See **p'êxembertî**.

pêz پێز, f. (F/AB) = sheep and goats. See **pez**.

piçan پـچـان *vi.* **(-piçê-).** to break, burst, split, snap *(of thread, string, rope, etc.)*: •**Doxîna şalwarê min *piça*** (Bw) The drawstring of my shalvar [=Kurdish trousers] broke. {also: piçihan (FS-2); pirçyan (-pirçyê-) (OK/M/FS-2)} Sor pisan[ewe] پـسـان[ەوە] = 'to burst asunder, break (rope), suffer severe or fatal strain' [Bw/FS//OK/M] <bizdîn; piçandin; pizirîn; qetîn>

piçandin پـچـانـدِن *vt.* **(-piçîn-).** 1) to cut in two, cut in half, sever, snap (vt.): •**Ka meqesê, ez *dê* vî benî *bipiçînim*** (Wkt) Where is the scissors, I *will cut* this string *in two* •**Wê bi didanan dezî *piçand*** (BF) She *severed* the thread with her teeth •**Wî dezî/werîs *piçand*** (FS) He *cut* the thread/rope *in two*; 2) to terrify, scare to death: •**Dengê kifêna marî *dilê min piçand*** (BF) The sound of the snake's hissing *terrified me* •**Dengê topê em *piçandin*** (Wkt) The sound of the cannon *scared us to death* •**Te deziyê *dilê wî piçand*** (FS) You *scared him to death* [lit. 'you severed the thread of his heart']. Sor pisandin پـسـانـدِن = 'to snap, break (vt.)' [Wkt/FS/BF] <çipilandin; piçan>

piçek پـچـەك *adv.* a little, a little bit: •**Payîz da-hat, dunya *pîçek* sar bû** (SK 2:12) Autumn came and the weather became *a little* cold •**Xizmeta te *pîçek* pitir e ji xizmeta kolare** (SK 1:4) Your service is *a little* greater than that of the kite. {also: bîçek (BK); piçik (JB3); piçikî (A-2); pîçek (JB1-A/Bw); <piçek> پـچـك (HH)} {syn: çîçik II; hindik; hinek; ≠gelek; ≠p'iř II; ≠ze'f} [IFb/A/HH/GF//BK//JB3//JB1-A/SK/Bw] <piçûk>

piçihan پچِهان (FS) = to snap, break. See **piçan**.

piçik پچِك (JB3) = a little. See **piçek**.

piçikî پچِكی (A) = a little. See **piçek**.

piçûk پـچـووك *adj.* 1) small, little: -[telīye pečūk] (JJ-PS) pinkie, little finger {syn: qilîç'k/tilîya qilîç'kê; *tilîya başikan (IF); t'ilîya çûk (B)}; 2) *[m.]* child [*pl.* children]. {also: biçîk (Zx); biçûk (K/SK); [pučúk/piciúk] پچوك (JJ); <piçûk> پچوك (HH)} {syn: çûçik; qicik (Kg)} Sor biçûk بِـچـووك; Hau wuçkle (M4) {biçûkayî; biçûk[t]î; piçûkayî; piçûk[t]î; [püčúki] پچوكی (JJ)} [BX/A/JB3/IFb/B/HH/GF//K/SK//JJ]

piçûkanî پـچـووكـانـی (GF) = childhood. See **piçûkayî** [2].

piçûkayî پـچـووكـايـی *f.* **(-ya;-yê).** 1) smallness, littleness; 2) {syn: çûçiktî; zařotî} {also: biçûkînî (SK); piçûkanî (GF)} childhood: •**Du keçên wan di *piçûkayîya* xwe de mirine** (kurdi.yekiti-media.org 6.i.2017) Two of their daughters died in childhood. {also: biçûkayî (K-2); biçûkî (K-2); biç'ûktî (K-2); piçûkî (K-2/B-2/IFb/GF); piç'ûktî (B-2); [püčúki] پچوكی (JJ)} [K/B//IFb/GF//JJ//SK] <piçûk>

piçûkî پـچـووكـی (K/B/IFb/GF) = smallness. See **piçûkayî**.

piç'ûktî پچووكتی (B) = smallness. See **piçûkayî**.

p'idî/pidî [K] پـدی *f.* **(-ya;-yê).** 1) {syn: alûme[1]} {=Sor pûk} gums (flesh around the teeth); 2) {syn: alûme[2]; *polke (IF); = Sor mełaşû مەڵاشوو} palate *(roof of the mouth)* (IFb/F/K) [(K) p'idû/pizî]. {also: bidû (Kş); pidû (IFb-2/K-2/GF/Mzg); pirî (F); pizî II (K-2); p'udu (B/SC); [poudi] پودی (JJ); <pudû> پـدو (HH)} Sor pûk[-î dan] پـووك[ی دان] = 'gums'. See: Eduard Schwyzer. "Die Bezeichnungen des Zahnfleisches in den indogermanischen Sprachen," *Zeitschrift für vergleichende Sprachforschung auf dem Gebiete der Indogermanischen Sprachen*, 57 (1930), 256-75; reprinted in his *Kleine Schriften*, hrsg. von Rüdiger Schmitt, Innsbrucker Beiträge zur Sprachwissenschaft, Bd. 45 (Innsbruck, 1983), pp. [216]-235. [BK/K/IFb/Bw//Kş//B/SC//F/GF/Mzg//JJ//HH]

p'idû پدوو (K/IFb/GF/Mzg) = gums; palate. See **p'idî**.

p'if پف *f.* **(-a;-ê).** puff (of air), (exhaled) breath: **-p'if dan/kirin** (B/SK) to blow, puff *(on, into, etc.)*: **•Boçî tû hosa heywaneke piçûk** ***pif dikeye*** **agirî? Ma dê** ***pifa*** **te çî ket?** (GShA, 230) Why are you *blowing on* the fire? What will your *blowing* do? **•Çaxa şevînê jî** ***pif dikim*** **bilûrê** (AB) At the night feeding [of the animals] I *blow on* my flute. {also: piv II (FS); [pouw] پف (JJ); <pif> پف (HH)} Sor pif پف = 'puff, blow' [AB/K/A/IFb/B/HH/SK/GF//FS//JJ]

pifdanik پفدانِك (IFb) = balloon. See **p'ifdank**.

p'ifdank پفدانك *f.* **(-a;).** balloon: **•Zar̄okî** ***pivdank pivda*** (FS) The child blew up [or, inflated] *the balloon*. {also: pifdanik (IFb); pivdank (FS)} [Bw/BF//IFb//FS] <p'if>

pihan پهان (K) = to wait for. See **p'an I**.

pihîn پهین (GF) = kick. See **p'eĥîn**.

pijan پژان (A) = to cook. See **patin** & **pijîn**.

pijandin پژاندن *vt.* **(-pijîn-).** to cook *(vt.)*. {also: <pijandin پژاندن (dipijîne) (دپژینه)> (HH)} Sor pijandin پژاندِن (-pijên-) & pîşandin پیشاندِن = 'to roast in hot ash without receptacle' [K/A/JB3/IFb/HH/GF] <biraştin; patin>

pijikandin پژکاندِن (Wkt) = to prune, clip. See **pejikandin**.

pijiqandin I پژِقاندِن *vt.* **(-pijiqîn-).** to squirt, spurt, splash *(vt.)*: **•Kurka [heştpê] tijî aveke mîna hibrê ye. Li dijî êrîşekê, ji bo ku xwe veşêre, vê hibrê** ***dipijiqîne*** (Wkp: Heştpê) [The octopus'] tail is full of a liquid like ink. Against an attack, to hide, it *squirts* this ink **•Te ters kirin maseyên wan.. / Ew badeya ji xwîna me...ew meya ji xwêdana me..*pijiqand*** **ser çavên wan...** (B.Bênij. Kemenda nemerda) You overturned their tables / That goblet of our blood...that wine of our sweat..you *squirted* into their eyes. {syn: beliqandin I} Cf. Sor pirjandin پرژاندِن = 'to sprinkle, spray' [Wkp/MG/IFb/TF/ZF3/Kmc/FD/G/CS] <ç'eliqandin; pijiqîn; vizik II>

pijiqandin II پژِقاندِن (Wkt) = to prune, clip. See **pejikandin**.

pijiqîn پژِقین *vi.* **(-pijiq-).** to gush, spurt out, squirt *(vi.)*, shoot forth *(vi.)*; to erupt: **•Ji bin erdê, ji dêlva avê ve, petrol** ***dipijiqe*** (nefel.com: M. Ali Kut. 7.viii.2011) From beneath the earth, instead of water, oil *shoots forth* **•Li Kamçatkayê Volkanê bi navê Şîvilûç** ***dipijiqe*** (Radyo Dengê Rûsya 26.vi.2011) In Kamchatka the Shiviluch volcano *is erupting*. {syn: ver̄estin[3]} [Nefel/IFb/ZF3/CS] <pijiqandin I; vizik II>

pijîn پژین *vi.* **(-pij-).** 1) to cook *(vi.)*, be cooked; 2) to mature. {also: pêjîn (IFb-2); pijan (A); [pejiian] پژیان (JJ)} Sor pîşan پیشان (-pîşê-) = 'to be baked, to be roasted in hot ash without receptacle'; Za pewjenã [pewtiş] = 'to cook' & peyşenã [peyşayiş] = 'to roast' (todd) [K/JB3/IFb/GF//A//JJ] <pijandin> See also **patin**.

pik پك **().** side of knucklebone (k'ap II) that sticks out (hildayî) [T yüz üstü - âşık kemiğinin çukur tarafının yere gelmesi hali]. {syn: sofî (Wn)} {≠çik II} [Qzl/A/GF/TF] <k'ap II>

pilav پلاڤ (GF) = cooked rice. See **p'elaw**.

pilaw پلاو (SK) = cooked rice. See **p'elaw**.

p'ilep'il پلەپل *f.* **().** muttering: **•Lê jina wî** ***her dike pilepil*** (Ardû, 14) But his wife *keeps on muttering*. {also: pilpil (FJ/GF); [pelpel] پلپل (JJ)} {syn: minemin; mir̄emir̄} [Ardû/K//FJ/GF/JJ]

piling پلِنگ *m.* **(-ê;).** *name for large cats:* 1) tiger; 2) type of leopard (EI2): **•Wextê çû hindawê latê dît hirçek liser dara keskanêye û** ***pilingek*** **jî li bin darê ye. Hirçê nir-nir dikir,** ***pilingî*** **jî zir-zir dikir** (SK 10:95) When he went above the stretch of meadow he saw that there was a bear in the top of a terebinth tree and also *a leopard* at the foot of the tree. The bear was whimpering and *the leopard* [was] snarling; 3) heroic warrior: **•Ew dewleta ku 'eskerê wê cendirmêt wekî hingo di ling-dir̄yay û ji-birsa-mirî bin çawa dişên** ***pilingêt*** **wekî 'Alî bê şer̄ û zeĥmet bigirin û xirab biken?** (SK 14:139) How can a government, whose army consists of ragged-trousered, starving zaptiehs like you, catch and destroy *leopards* like Ali without fighting and trouble? {also: peleng (F-2); [pilink] پلنك (JJ)} Skt pṛdāku- *m.* = 'tiger, panther; adder'; Sgd pwrd'nk/pwrdnkh; Pashto pṛōng; P palang پلنگ = 'panther'; Sor piłing پڵنگ; cf. also Lat pardus; Gr pardos παρδος [S&E/F/K/A/JB3/IFb/B/SK/GF/TF/OK//JJ] <p'isîk; şêr I; weşeq>

pilîsk پلیسك (GF) = spark. See **p’irîsk**.

pilor I پــلـــۆر (A/IFb/ZF/Kmc) = type of sweet soup. See **pelor**.

pilor II پلۆر (SS) = squirrel. See **pilûr**.

pilpil پلپل (FJ/GF) = muttering. See **p’ilep’il**.

pilpilînk پلپلینك (RZ) = butterfly, moth. See **p’ir̄p’ir̄ok**.

pilpilok پلپلۆك (RZ) = butterfly, moth. See **p’ir̄p’ir̄ok**.

pilqe pilq پــلــقــه پــلــق (SBx) = bubbling sound. See **bilqebilq**.

pilte پلته (F/JJ/Z-1796) = wick. See **fitîl**.

pilûr پــلـــــووور *f./m.(FS)* **().** squirrel, zool. *Sciurus vulgaris*. {also: pilor II (SS)} {syn: siwûrî} [Wkp/IFb/ZF3/FS/FD/Wkt//SS]

pin II پن (IFb) = chicken coop. See **pîn I**.

p’in II پن *m.* **(-ê;).** plant, particularly melon-like fruits that grow (and creep) on the ground: **•Ez çûme serê dîyarekî, min dî heft beran li pey beranek[î] [*pinê* zebeş]** (L) I went to the top of the hill, I saw seven rams after one another *[rdl.; ans.:* watermelon *plant]*. [L/K(s)/GF/TF]

p’incar پنجار/**p’incar̄** پینجار [B] *m./f.(K/B)* **(; /-ê).** 1) wild edible greens or plants (IFb); edible plants, whether raw or cooked (EŞ - Turkish ed., p. 12): **•Diya me jî bi me ra hat da ku *pincaran* şanî me bide (Spink, tirşo, mendik, pêkesk H.D.)** (EŞ, 8) Our mother came with us too, to show us *wild edible plants* [pincar] (meadow salsify, sorrel, mendik, pêkesk, etc.); 2) beet, bot. Beta vulgaris (IFb/JJ). {also: [pindjar] پــنــجــار (JJ); <pincar> پــنــجـار (HH)} Cf. T pancar = 'beet'; W Arm panǰarełēn բանջարեղէն = 'vegetables' [F/K/A/IFb/JJ/HH/GF//B] <ç’aqir; deramet I; dikak; êmîş [2]; heşînatî>

pind پــنــد *f.* **(-a;).** anus *(of human being or animal)*. {also: <pind> پــنـد (HH)} {syn: zotik} [Msr/A/IFb/HH/GF/OK/ZF3/FS] <qûn>

p’indepîr پــنــدەپــیــر *f.* **(-a;-ê).** spider: **•Bala wê çû ser *pindepîrê*** (Mişkê pisîkxwir: denge-mamoste.com) She turned her attention to *the spider*. {syn: dapîroşk; pêrtevînk; pîr [4]; pîrhevok; pîrik [3]; t’evnpîrk [1]} [K/JB3/IFb/GF/OK/ZF3/FS/BF/Wkt]

pindk پندك = type of children's game. See **tilî pindk**.

pinî پنی (FS) = rag; patch. See **pîne**.

pinpinî پنپنی (HD/RZ) = butterfly. See **p’ir̄p’ir̄ok**.

pinpinîk پــنــپــیــنــك (GF/RZ/RF) = butterfly. See **p’ir̄p’ir̄ok**.

p’ir I پــــــر *f.* **(-a;-ê).** bridge: **•*P’ira* Mezin *p’irek* e ji zemanê kevn were wê** [sic] **hatî ava kirin** (M-Zx #77) The Big *Bridge* is *a bridge* which has been built in the olden days; **-Pira Batmanê** (BK) the bridge at Batman (in Batman province [formerly in Siirt province], Kurdistan of Turkey); **-P’ira R̄eş** = Diyarbakir’s Black Bridge. {also: p’ira (K/B); p’ire (Ag); [pyr] پــیــر (JJ); <pir> پــــر (HH)} [Pok. per-tu-/por-tu-, *gen.* pr̥-teus 817.] 'crossing, ford' <[Pok. B. per-/perə- 816.] 'to transport, convey across' <[Pok. 2. per 810.] 'carrying across, transporting': Av pərətu- *m./f.* (<O Ir *pr̥θu-) & *compound* pəšu- *m.* (<O Ir *prtu-) = 'crossing, ford, bridge'; Mid P puhl (M3); P pol پـــل; Sor pird پــرد; Za pird *m.* (Mal); Hau pirdî *f.* (M4). *According to A&L, the final -d of Sor **pird** appears by analogy with **mêrd**, etc.* [K/B//A/JB3/IFb/JJ/HH/GF/TF/OK//Ag]

p’ir̄ II پر *adv.* very, very much: **•Şêr ji vê p’arkirinê *p’ir̄* xeyîdî** (Dz) The lion got *very* angry at this division [of the spoils] ***•p’ir̄* diçin, hindik diçin** (Dz) They keep on going and going [lit. 'They go *much*, they go little'] [cf. T az gitmiş, uz gitmiş, dere tepe düz gitmiş]; **-pir û zêde** (IF) more than enough; **-p’ir̄tir** = more {syn: bêtir; ze‘ftir; zêdetir}. {also: [pur/pir] پـر (JJ); <pir> پـر (HH)} {syn: gelek; qewî; ze‘f; zor II (Bw); ≠hindek; ≠piçek} [Pok. 1. pel- 1798.] 'to fill' --> *pl̥E(-)no-: Skt pūrṇá- = 'full'; OIr *pr̥na- *for expected* *parna-: Av pərəna-; Sgd pwrn [purn]/pwn; Mid P purr = 'full' (M3); P porr پر = 'full'; Sor pir̄ پڕ = 'full'; Za pirr = 'full' (Mal/Todd); Hau per̄ = 'full' (M4); cf. also Lat plenus = 'full'; Gr polys πολύς = 'much' & pleōs πλέως = 'full'; Lith pilna-; Rus polnyĭ полный = 'full'; Germ voll = 'full' & viel = 'much'; Eng full. [K/A/JB3/IFb/B/HH/JB1-A/SK/GF/TF/OK//JJ]

p’ira پرا (K/B) = bridge. See **p’ir I**.

p’ir̄alî پــڕالــی *adj.* multilateral: **•Lê tu car Komara Tirk pêwist nedîtiye ku bi hêzeke wisa xurt û *pirralî* here ser wan serhildanan** (Wlt 1:37, 8) But the Turkish Republic never before found it neces-sary to act against those uprisings with such a strong and *multilateral* force **•Wek ji navê wî jî tê fêm kirin ew şer *pirralî* ye** (Wlt 1:37, 8) As its name implies [lit. 'as is understood from its name'], this war is *multilateral*. {also: pirralî (Wlt/Wkt)} [(neol)Wlt/ZF3/Wkt]

p’ir̄anî پــڕانــی *f.* **(-ya;-yê).** majority, most: **•Ji ber ku *piraniya* gelê Keşmîrê misilman e, dewleta Pakistanê piştevaniya şervanên Keşmîrê dike**

(AW77A5) Because *the majority of* the Kashmiri people are Muslims, the Pakistani government supports the Kashmiri fighters ***•Pirraniya* nûnêran ew terorê, ku li dijî gelê Kurd ji aliyê dewletên wek Tirkiyê û Iraqê ve tê ajotin, dieyibînin (protesto dikin)** (Wlt 1:37, 16) *Most of* the representatives protest this terror which is being carried out against the Kurdish people by such states as Turkey and Iraq. {also: pirayî (A); p'iřayî (K-2/B); pirranî (Wlt)} {syn: gelemperî; zorbe} [Wlt//F/K/IFb/GF/TF//A/B] <bêt'ir; kêmanî; p'iř II>

pirasî پراسی (Bw) = rib(s). See **parsû**.

pirayî پـرایـی (A)/p'iřayî پـڕایـی (K/B) = majority. See **p'iřanî**.

pirç' پـــــــرچ/**p'irç** [B]/**p'irç'** [B] *f./m.(Bw-2)* **(-a/-ê; -ê/).** 1) {syn: t'ûk I} hair, fur *(of animals)*; body hair *{neg. connotation: may denote pubic hair (Krç)}*; hair of the body from the neck down, *as opposed to **p'oř** = hair on the head (Haz)*: ***•pirç'a* pîlê min** (Krç) my armpit *hair*; **-p'irç[']a xinzîr** (B) bristle; 2) {syn: p'oř I} hair on the head, as opposed to **tûk** (Bşk)/**mû** (Bw) = hair on the head (HH/Bşk/Bw): ***•Pirça* min diwerit** (Bşk) *My hair* [=on my head] is falling out. {also: [pyrtch] پـرچ (JJ); <pirç> پـرچ (HH)} [Krç/Haz/Bşk/K/A/JB3/IFb/JJ/HH/GF//B] <mû; p'oř III; tûk I>

pirçemek پرچەمەك (SW) = bat *(zool.)*. See **pîrçemek**.

pirçiqîn پرچقین (M) = to be crushed. See **p'erçiqîn**.

pirçu پرچو (EH) = frown. See **p'iřçû**.

p'iřçû پڕچوو/**pirç'û** پرچوو [F/K/B] *m.* **(-yê;).** gloomy or sullen look; frown, scowl: **-p'iřçûyê xwe kirin** (XF) to make a sour face, to grimace, frown, scowl. {also: pirçu (EH-2); purç'u (EH-2)} {syn: aviř} [EH/XF//F/K/B] <me'de>

pirçyan پرچیان (-pirçyê-) (OK/M/FS) = to snap, break. See **piçan**.

p'ire پرە (Ag) = bridge. See **p'ir I**.

pirejimar پرەژمار (BF/CS) = plural. See **p'iřhejmar**.

pirejmar پرەژمار (IFb)/p'iřejmar پڕەژمار (K) = plural. See **p'iřhejmar**.

p'irêz پـــــــریـــــز *f.* **(-a;-ê).** stubble in a field after harvesting: ***•Pirêzên* te ne paqij in** (Qzl) You have a dark past [lit. 'your *stubbles* are not clean'] [*expression*]. {also: **firêze** (IFb); perêz (AA/OK); p'irêze (Qzl); <firêz فـریـز/firêze فـریـزە/perêz پەریز> (Hej)} Sor perêz پەریز [Zeb//OK/AA//Qzl//IFb]

p'irêze پریزە (Qzl) = field stubble. See **p'irêz**.

p'iřhejmar پـڕهـەژمـار *adj.* plural *(in grammar)* [Ar jam' جـمـع, T çoğul]: **•navên *pirrhejmar*** (CT) *plural* nouns. {also: pirejimar (BF/CS); pirejmar (IFb)/p'iřejmar (K); pirhêjmar (AD); pirjimar (FD/ZF3-2); pirrhejmar (CT); pirrjimar (Wkt-2)} {syn: *gelejimar} = Sor ko کۆ [TF/ZF3/RZ/Wkt//AD//CT//K/IFb//BF/CS//FD]

pirhêjmar پرهێژمار (AD) = plural. See **p'iřhejmar**.

p'irik پـرك *f./m.(FS)* **(-a/ ;).** 1) small bridge; 2) {also: birk II (A-2/GF-2); pirk (GF/FJ/FS)} bridge-like part of plow, connecting the handle or haft with the plow share; **-pirika hevcar** (CCG) do. [CCG/A/IFb/TF//GF/FJ/FS]

pirî پری (F) = gums; palate. See **p'idî**.

pirîs پریس (GF) = spark. See **p'irîsk**.

p'irîsk/pirîsk [K/B] پـریـسـك *f.* **(-a;-ê).** spark(s): **•Ew milê Ûsiv digire sîleke usa lê dixe, wekî ji ç'avê wî *pirîsk* dipekin** (Ba3-3, #25, 196) He grabs Joseph's arm and slaps him so hard that *sparks* fly out his eyes. {also: pilîsk (GF-2); pirîs (GF-2); [pyrizk] پـریـزك (JJ)} {syn: ç'irûsk & çirs; peşk III[1]; p'êt} [Ba3/F/K/B//A/IFb/GF//JJ] <birûsk>

pirjimar پرژمار (FD/ZF3) = plural. See **p'iřhejmar**.

pirk پــــرك (GF/FJ/FS) = bridge-like part of plow. See **p'irik**.

pirkîn پركین (TF) = giggling, chuckling. See **p'îrqîn**.

pirkîte پركیتە (IFb) = polysyllabic. See **p'iřk'îteyî**.

p'iřk'îteyî پـڕكـیـتـەیـی *adj.* polysyllabic: **•Di peyvên *pirkîteyî* de kirpandin bi gelemperî li ser kîteya paşîn e** (Samî Tan.Rêzimana Kurmancî) In *polysyllabic* words, the accent is for the most part on the final syllable. {also: pirkîte (IFb)} [Wkt/SS//IFb] <k'îte>

pirot پروت (IFb/FS) = potter. See **p'irûd**.

pirpar پرپار (Wkt) = purslane. See **pêrpîne**.

pirpir پرپر (Ad) = purslane. See **pêrpîne**.

p'iřp'iřk پڕپڕك (K) = butterfly, moth. See **p'iřp'iřok**.

p'iřp'iřk پـــــــڕپـــــــڕك (B/F) = butterfly, moth. See **p'iřp'iřok**.

p'iřp'iřok پـڕپـڕۆك *f.* **(-a;-ê).** butterfly, moth. {also: pelapîtik (RZ-2); pelpelîtank (RZ-2; pelpelîtk (SS); pelpelûsk (Zimanê Kurdî); pelpîtanîk (FJ); penpulî (RZ-2); pepûle (A/IFb); perpelisk (RZ-2); perperik (RZ-2); perperok (IFb/RZ-2/SS-2); perpûşik (RZ-2); pilpilînk (RZ-2); pilpilok (RZ-2); pinpinî (HD/RZ); pinpinîk (GF/RZ-2/RF); p'iřp'iřk (K); p'iř'p'iřk (B/F); [pilpiluk پـلـپـلـك/perpúšik پـرپـوشـك] (JJ-Lx); <perperok> پـرپـروك (HH)} {syn: belantîk; fiřfiřok; p'erîdank; pîrik

[4]} Cf. Sor pepûle پەپوولە = 'butterfly' & perwane پەروانە = 'moth; revolving fan; propeller'; Za filfilik *f.* (Mal); also Heb parpar פרפר [Msr//IFb/HH/SS//K//B/F//JJ//HD/RZ//GF/RF] <bizûz>

p'irpitîn پرپتین *vi.* **(-pirpit-).** to flap about, thrash about, flutter about, struggle as in the throes of death [T debelenmek, çırpınmak]: •**Piştî ko bi qasekî di vê germî û vê nermiya xwe de li erdê *pirpitîye*…** (Tof, 12) After he *thrashed about* for a while on the ground in this warmth and comfort. {also: perpitîn (IFb); [perpytin] پرپتین (JJ); <perpitîn پرپتين (diperpite) (دپرپته)> (HH)} [Tof/K//IFb/JJ/HH] <gevizîn; sekerat>

pirqênî پرقێنی (DBgb) = giggling, chuckling. See **p'îrqîn**.

pirqîn پرقین (FJ/GF) = giggling, chuckling. See **p'îrqîn**.

pirralî پڕالی (Wlt/Wkt) = multilateral. See **p'iřalî**.

pirranî پڕانی (Wlt) = majority. See **p'iřanî**.

pirrhejmar پڕهەژمار (CT) = plural. See **p'iřhejmar**.

pirrjimar پڕژمار (Wkt) = plural. See **p'iřhejmar**.

pirs پرس *f.* **(-a;-ê).** 1) {syn: sual; ≠bersiv I; ≠cab} question: •**Xwedê ez şandime bal te, ku ez caba *pirsêd* te bidim** (Dz) God has sent me to you to answer your *questions*; -**pirs danîn/dayîn** (B) to put forth a question *(for discussion)*: •**Hatine dîwana mîr Sevdîn, *pirsa* merivatîyê *danîn*, seva Zîna delal bixazin Ç'ekanřa** (Z-1) They came to prince Sevdin's court, *put forth a question of* manliness, to request darling Zin for Chekan [in marriage]; -**pirs kirin** (K/A/JB3/B/Msr/SK/TF) to ask {also: pirsîn}; 2) {syn: bêje; gilî [1]; lavz; p'eyiv; xeber; zar I} word; 3) {syn: mesele} issue, matter, question, affair, problem (VoA); 4) {syn: şerd (L)} task (B). {also: [pyrs] پرس (JJ); <pirs> پرس (HH)} Cf. P porseš پرسش; Sor pirs پرس = 'question'; Za pers kenã = 'to ask' (Todd) [F/K/A/JB3/IFb/B/JJ/HH/SK/GF/TF] <pirsîn; pirsyar>

pirsgirêk پرسگرێك *f.* **(-a;-ê).** problem, issue: •**Hêviya me ya herî mezin ew e ku em bikaribin *pirsgirêka* Kurdan bînin nav dezgah û sazgehên navneteweyî** (Wlt 1:37, 16) Our greatest hope is that we will be able to bring the Kurdish *problem* to international organizations and associations •**Ya dîtir av germ dikir û baz dida mala Şêx Qineb, ji bo ku wî bîne da vê *pirsgirêkê* çareser bike** (HYma 34) The other woman was heating water and hopping over to Shaykh Qineb's house, to bring him so that he might solve this *problem*. {syn: alozî; arêşe; t'eşqele} [(neol)Wlt/IFb/TF/ZF3]

pirsiyar پرسِیار (A/IF/GF/OK) = interrogation; question. See **pirsyar**.

pirsiyarî پرسِیاری (JB3) = interrogation; question. See **pirsyar**.

pirsîn/p'irsîn پرسین *vt.* **(-pirs-).** [+ **ji**] to ask (s.o.): •**Kalê *jê dipirse*, divê ...** (Dz) The old man *asks him*, saying ... [lit. 'he says ...'] •**Min *ji* Tacîn li te *pirsî*** (BX) I *asked* Tajin about you. {also: pirs kirin (K/A/JB3/B-2/Msr/TF); pi[r]syar kirin (Zx); [pyrsin] پرسین (JJ); <pirsîn پرسین (dipirsî) (دپرسی)> (HH)} [Pok. perḱ-/preḱ-/pr̥ḱ- 821.] 'to ask, entreat': Skt praś- *& with inchoative pres.* [pr̥ḱ-sḱe-] prach- pr̥ccháti = 'he asks'; Av fras- *& with inchoative pres.* [pr̥ḱ-sḱe-] pərəsaiti; O P fraθ- *& with inchoative pres.* [pr̥ḱ-sḱe-] parsa-; Mid P pursīdan (purs-) (M3); P porsīdan پرسیدن; Sor pirsîn پرسین; Za pers kenã = 'to ask' (Todd); Hau persay (pers-) *vt.* (M4); cf. also Arm harc'nel հարցնել; Lat precor, -ari *& with inchoative pres.* posco, -ere; Germ fragen; Rus prosit' просить [K/JB3/IFb/B/JJ/HH/SK/GF/OK]

pirsyar پرسیار *f.* **(-a;-ê).** question: -**pirsyar kirin** = a) to interrogate, question (B); b) to ask, enquire (Zx). {also: pirsiyar (A/IF/GF/OK); pirsiyarî (JB3); pisyar (Bw/SK); [pyrsiar] پرسیار (JJ)} {syn: pirs} Cf. Sor pirsyar پرسیار [F/K/B/JJ/FS//A/IFb/GF/OK//JB3//Bw/SK]

pirtal پرتال (IF/HH/Zeb) = goods, merchandise. See **pertal**.

p'irtep'irt I [B/OK]/**p'irte-p'irt** [K] پرتەپرت *f.* **(-a; -ê).** fast beating of the heart *(out of excitement, fear, etc.)*: •**Bû *p'irtep'irta* dilê min** (Ba2:2, 207) My heart started *beating fast* •**Dilê min *dike p'irtep'irt*** (B) My heart *is beating*. {syn: gurpegurp} [Ba2/K/B/GF/OK] <dil>

pirte pirt II پرتە پرت (SBx) = chatter. See **pitepit**.

p'irteqal پرتەقال *f.* **(-a;-ê).** 1) orange (fruit), sweet orange, bot. *Citrus sinensis*: -**p'irteqala navik sor** (AA) blood orange; 2) orange color. {also: pirteqan (HR); porteqal (IFb-2/Kmc-2/RZ/CB); p'ortoxal (K); [portoghal] پرتغال (JJ)} <Portugal, *source of oranges in the Mediterranean region*: cf. Ar burtuqāl برتقال/burtuqān برتقان; P porteqāl پرتقال = '(sweet) orange'; T portakal; Gr portokali πορτοκάλι; Sor pirteqał پڕتەقاڵ; Za pırtıqalı *f.* (Mal) [AA/K(s)/A/IFb/OK//Kmc-2/RZ/CB//K/JJ//HR] <lalengî;

narinc>

pirteqan پرتەقان (HR) = orange. See **p'irteqal**.

p'irtik پـرتِـك *f.(K/B)/m.(EP-7)* **(-a/-ê;-ê/).** particle, little piece: **•Emê *p'iṙtkê* teyî mezin guhê te bêhêlin** [sic] (EP-7) We will cut you into pieces [lit. 'We will leave your ear the biggest *piece of* you']. {also: [pyrti pyrtik] پـرتـی پـرتـك (JJ)} Cf. Arm p'ert' փերթ = 'morsel' [EP-7/K/B/ZF3//JJ] <paşp'irtik; pêşp'irtik; piçek>

pirtikandin پـرتِـكـانـدِن (IFb/TF/ZF) = to pluck. See **p'ûrtikandin**.

p'iṙtir پرتر = more. See under **p'iṙ II**.

p'irtok پرتۆك = book. See **p'irtûk**.

p'irt-p'al پـرت پـال = clothes; wares. See **pertal: pirt û pertal.**

p'irtûk پـرتـووك *f.* **(-a;-ê).** book, publication: **•Altiok niha jî li ser Çewligê *pirtûkekê* amade dike** (AW78A4) Altiok is now writing *a book* on Bingöl [Çewlig] **•We heta niha gelek *pirtûk* nivîsîne an jî wergerandine** (AW69A3) Up till now you have written or translated many *books*. {also: p'ertok; p'ertûk (K[s]/GF); p'irtok} {syn: k'itêb; nivîsk} Sor pertûk پەرتووك; Za pîrtok *m.* (Todd) [K(s)/GF/ /A/IFb]

p'irtûkxan•e پـرتـووكـخـانـه *f.* **(•[ey]a;•ê). 1)** {syn: k'itêbxane} library *(lit. & fig.)*: **•refikên pirtûkxanê** (Epl 8) library shelves **•Te pirtûkxaneyeke dewlemend heye** (Epl 16) You have a rich library; 2) bookstore, bookshop. {also: pertukxane (TF); p'ertûkxane (K[s])/ pertûkxane (GF)} Sor pertûkxane پەرتـووكـخـانـە [Epl/A/IFb/CS/AD/ZF3//TF//K(s)/GF]

p'irûd پـــــــــروود *m.&f.* **(/-a;-î).** potter: **•Dîya qîza - *p'irûda* dîza, dîz çê kirin, xelqê birin** (Z-1004) The mother of girls [is] *a fashioner of* clay pots, [after] she made the pots, others took them away *[prv.]*. {also: pirot (IFb); pîrot (IFb-2/AD/ZF3); prot (GF); <pirot> پـــــــروت (HH)} {syn: qewaq} < W Arm prut/E Arm brud բրուդ [Rwn/Z//IFb/HH/ FS//GF//AD/ZF3]

pirxepirx پرخەپرخ (SK) = snoring. See **p'ixep'ix**.

pirzik پـرزِك (IF/A/HH)/p'irzik (K) = pimple; boil. See **pizik**.

pisdan پسدان (GF) = placenta. See **p'izdan**.

p'isep'is پسەپس *f.* **(;-ê).** whisper: **-p'isep'is kirin** (B) to whisper {also: pispis kirin (IF); pispisan kirin (A); p'isp'isandin}: **•Bek'o ... guhê mîrda *kire p'iste-p'ist*** (FK-eb-1) Beko *whispered* in the mîr's ear. {also: pispis (IFb); p'iste-p'ist (K); [pysapys] پـسـاپـس (JJ); <pispis> پـسـپـس (HH)} {syn: kurt û p'ist} [B/JJ//IF/HH//K]

p'isik پسِك (Ad/Rh) = cat. See **p'isîk**.

pising پسِنگ (JB3) = cat. See **p'isîk**.

p'isîk پسيك *f.* **(-a;-ê).** cat; kitty-cat *{in the north this is the normal word for cat; in the south it is baby talk: adults use **k'itik II**}* (Bw) [p'işîk]: **•Mişkek û çêlikên xwe li derve digerîyan. Bi carekê de çavê wê li *pisîkekê* ket** (LM, 28) A mouse and her babies were outside roaming around. Suddenly she noticed *a cat*. {also: p'isik (Ad/Rh); pising (JB3); pisîng (Krç/IFb-2); pişik (GF); p'işîk (K/F/ Bw); pşîk (Ag); [pisik پـسـيـك/pichik پـشـيـك] (JJ); <pissîk پسّيك/pişîk پشيك> (HH)} {syn: k'itik II} P pušek/pōšek (dialect of Transoxania: Horn #322); Sor pişîle پـشـیـلـه; Za psîng *m.* & psîngi *f.* (Todd); Hau pişîlê *f.* (M4); cf. Ar biss بـــــــسّ; T pisi; Az T pişik; Eng puss; Romanian pisică [Ad/Rh//GF//JB3// AB/A/IFb/Haz/JJ//Krç//K/F/B/HH//Ag] <piling; şêr I; weşeq>

pisîng پسینگ (Krç/IFb) = cat. See **p'isîk**.

pismam پـسـمـام *m.* **(-ê; pizmêm** [B]**).** cousin, male first cousin, relative [cf. Ar ibn al-'amm ابن العمّ]: **•Ma em Şî'e ḧeqq nîne tebeṙiyê ji wane bikeyn? Çonko wan bê-bextî digel *pismamê* pêẍember kirin** [sic] (SK 60:706) Don't we Shias have a right to oppose them? Because they acted dishonorably with *the first cousin of* the Prophet [=with Ali] **•Yêkê dî ji *pismamêt* wan heye, Yosuf Beg kuṙê Mu**<u>**s**</u>**tefa Beg, li Badilyan, ew jî cesor e** (SK 51:558) There is another one of their *cousins*, Yusuf Beg son of Mustafa Beg, in Badilyan. He too is brave. {also: pasimam (EP-8); pizmam (F/B/FS); [pesmam] پـــــســـــمـــــام (JJ); <pismam> پـــســـمـــام (HH)} {syn: kuṙap; kuṙmam; lawê ap} < pis- = 'boy, son' + mam = 'father's brother': **pis**-: [Pok. pōu- 842.] 'few, little' --> proto IE *putlo- (Oscan-Umbrian & Iranian) --> proto IndIr *putra-: Skt putra- *m.* = 'son'; Av puθra- = 'son'; O P puça- = 'son'; Mid P pus = 'son' (M3); Parthian puhr = 'son'; P pesar پـــســـر = 'son' (with - ar by analogy with doxt**ar**, mād**ar**, ped**ar**); = Sor amoza ئـــــامـــــۆزا ='cousin' {pismametî; pismam[t]î; pizmam[t]î} [K/A/JB3/IFb/SK/GF// F/B/ FS//JJ//EP-8] <binam; dotmam; mam>

pismametî پـــســـمـــامـــەتـی (A/IFb) = cousinhood *(on paternal side)*. See **pismamtî**.

pismamî پسمامی (K) = cousinhood *(on paternal side)*. See **pismamtî**.

pismamtî پسمامتی *f.* **(-ya;-yê).** cousinhood, being related on one's father's side. {also: pismametî (A/IFb); pismamî (K-2); pizmam[t]î (B)} [K//A/IF//B] <pismam>

pismîr پسمیر *m.* **(-ê;).** son of an emir; prince: **•Her du zarokan *pismîr* û xulamkole ji yek guhanî şîr dimêtin** (Rnh 3:23, 5) Both infants, *the emir's son* and the servant's child, sucked milk from the same breast [lit. 'nipple']. [Rnh/OK/ZF3/Wkt] <dotmîr; jinmîr; mîr I>

pispis پسپس (IFb/HH) = whisper. See **p'isep'is**.

p'isp'isandin پسپساندن *vt.* **(-p'isp'isîn-).** to whisper; to gossip. {also: <pispisandin> پسپساندن (HH)} {syn: p'isep'is kirin; p'istîn} [JB3/IFb/HH] <p'isep'is>

pispisan kirin پسپسان کِرن (A) = to whisper. See **p'isep'is: -p'isep'is kirin**.

pispisok I پسپسۆک *f.* **().** firefly, lightning bug. {also: <bisbisok> بسبسوک (HH)} [HB/Xrz/ZF3//HH]

p'isp'isok II پسپسۆک *m.* **().** whisperer, one who whispers. [A/IFb/Wn] <p'isep'is>

p'ispor/pispor [K/B] پسپۆر *m.* **(-ê;).** 1) young man who knows a lot about animal husbandry and herding (K/B/JJ); child old enough to help about the house or with the flocks (M): **•Apê minî Memo jî şivan bû. Ew nava şivanêd êla Ĥesinîya da dihate ĥesabkirinê çewa *şivanekî başî p'ispor*** [sic] (Ba2:1, 204) My uncle Memo was also a shepherd. Among the shepherds of the Hesini tribe he was considered an *experienced shepherd*; 2) expert, specialist: **•Ew ... pisporê zimanên Rojhilata Navîn e** (Wlt 1:35, 7) He ... is a specialist on Middle Eastern languages. {also: bispor (M); [pyspor] پسپور (JJ)} <O Ir *wisa(h)-puθra- = 'house boy' [Fr fils de maison] (A&L p. 86 [VI, 4a] + 91 [XIII, 5] + 94-95 [XVIII, 1] + note 28 [p. 102]): Sor pispor̄ پسپۆڕ = 'expert'. See: W. B. Henning. "The Survival of an Ancient Term," in: *Indo-Iranica: Mélanges présentés à G. Morgenstierne* (Wiesbaden, 1964), pp. 95-97; D. N. MacKenzie. *KDS*-II [=M, vol. 2], pp. 376-77, note 759. [Wlt/K/IFb/B/JJ/GF/TF/OK/FS//M]

pissik پسِک (GF) = cat. See **p'isîk**.

p'iste پسته *f.* **().** pistachio, bot. *Pistacia vera.* {also: p'istik (K); pişte (A/IFb); pîste (CB)} {syn: fistiq} Mid P pistag (M3); P peste پسته; Sor biste بِسته [Kmc-2/K(s)/GF/Wkt//CB/K//A/IFb]

p'iste-p'ist پستهپست (K) = whisper. See **p'isep'is**.

pisteq پستهق (HH/CB) = low-quality raisins. See **bistaq**.

p'istik پستِک (K) = pistachio. See **p'iste**.

pistiyan پستیان (FS) = to whisper. See **p'istîn**.

pisṯî پصطی (Dh) = collar. See **pisṯo**.

p'istîn پستین *vi.* **(-p'ist'-).** 1) {syn: p'isep'is kirin; p'isp'isandin} to whisper (B); 2) {syn: p'isep'is} [*f.* **(;-ê)**] whisper (B). {also: pistiyan (FS)} [K/B/ZF3//FS] <p'isep'is>

pisṯo پسطۆ [Bw]/**pisto** پستۆ [Zeb] *f.* **(-ya;).** collar. {also: pisṯî (Dh); pistok (Wkt); piştstû (GF)} {syn: berstû; bestik; girîvan; p'êsîr [2]; yax} <pişt + stû [Bw/FS//Zeb/ZF3//Dh//Wkt//GF]

pistok پستۆک (Wkt) = collar. See **pisṯo**.

pisyar پسیار (Bw/SK) = question. See **pirsyar**.

p'iş I پش *f.* **(-a;).** *term for various internal organs*: 1) {syn: cegera spî; k'ezeba sipî; mêlak[a sor]; sîh I} lung {Cf. T akciğer}: **-pişa spî** (IFb/GF) do.; 2) {syn: ceger[a reş]/cerg; k'ezeb[a r̄eş]; mêlak} liver [Cf. T karaciğer]: **-pişa reş** (JB3) do. {also: pişe (GF/FJ-2); p'işik (K/FJ-2); pûş II (JB3)}; 3) spleen (Hk). [IFb/GF/AA//K/HH/FJ] <hinav; p'işik>

piş II پش (B) = behind. See **pişt II**.

p'işaftin پشافتِن *vt.* **(-p'işêf-/-p'işêv-).** 1) {syn: bihoştin; ĥelandin} to melt (together); to dilute, dissolve, thin; 2) to mix something dry and hard with water (e.g., **keşk**), and turn it into dough or liquid (Zeb); 3) to assimilate: **-di nîva xwe de pişavtin** (IFb) to assimilate, melt together; 4) {syn: asîmîlasyon} [*f.* **(;-ê).**] assimilation: **•Dewleta Tirk, tevî hemû têkçûnên polîtîkayên xwe yên *pişaftinê* (asîmî-lasyonê) dev ji van kirinên xwe bernade** (Wlt 1:35, 5) The Turkish state, in spite of all its political failures at *assimilation*, will not give up those activities. {also: bişaftin (Zeb); bişavtin (K/IFb-2/TF/OK-2); pişavtin (IFb-2); [bechawtin] بشافتین (JJ)} [(neol)Wlt/IFb/OK//K/JJ/TF//Zeb]

pişavtin پساڤتِن (IFb) = to melt, dissolve; to assimilate. See **p'işaftin**.

pişdawî پشداوی (Rnh/OK) = the hereafter. See **piştdawî**.

pişe پشه (GF/FJ) = lung. See **p'iş I**.

p'işik پشِک (K/HH/FJ/Hk) = lung; spleen. See **p'iş I**.

pişikdar پشِکدار (Dh/Hk/Zeb) = participant. See **pişkdar**.

pişikîn پشِكين (Qmş/Wn) = to sneeze. See **pêkijîn**.

p'işirûk پشِرووك (K) = cooked groats. See **pişrûng**.

p'işîk پشيك (K/F/Bw) = cat. See **p'isîk**.

pişk پشك *f.* **(-a;-ê).** 1) {syn: behr I; beş I[2]; p'ar II; p'ay} share, lot, portion: **•Çûnkû cenabê mîr zatekî mezin e, ez û ȓîwî xulam în, dibît *pişka* zatê wî zêdetir bît** (SK 7:71) ... **We ye, emma dîsa lazim e, çi kêm çi zor, *pişkek* ji bo xulamî bête danan** (SK 7:73) Since his excellency the chief is a great person, while the fox and I are servants, his personal *portion* must be greater ...That is so, but it is still necessary that some *portion*, whether small or great, be put aside for the servant **•Şêx Silêman digel sê çar derwêşan miqdarekî kullî ji cewahir û ji zêȓ bo xo helgirtin, gotine derwêş[ê]t dî, "Hung jî *pişka* xo helgirin, herçî ku em neşêyn helgirîn, bibeyn, li cîyekî dûr çal keyn"** (SK 38:341) Shaikh Sulaiman and three or four dervishes took a goodly amount of the jewels and gold for themselves and said to the other dervishes, "You too take your *share* and whatever we cannot take away, let us take it and bury it in some distant place"; 2) {syn: beş I} part; section: **-pişka bitir/ pitir** (SK) greater part, majority: **•Ḧetta em bi karwanê keran diçîne Ormîyê yan Mûsilê û têynewe, *pişka pitir* ji kerêt me di bin barî da seket dibin** (SK 11:176) By the time we go to Urmiya and Mosul with a donkey caravan and return, *the greater part of* our donkeys die under the loads **•Kesê şêstsalî, ȓidîna wî kêm-kême ȓeş dibît, *pişka bitir* spî dibît. Ewe bo çî ȓidîna te nîwe-nîwe ye?** (SK 23:214) A person sixty years old usually has a *mainly* white beard with only a little black. Why then is your beard half-and-half?; 3) piece: **•Têşta wan s̱ewar bît, sênîyan tejî biken, serê wan qubbeyî biken, *pişkêt* qelîya goştê kûran bi ȓexêt s̱ewarê wenên** (SK 24:222) Let their morning meal be of crushed wheat. Fill the trays, pile them up like a dome and put *the pieces of* fried kid-meat round the boiled wheat. {also: [pychk] پشك (JJ)} Cf. P pešk پشك = 'casting lots' [A/IFb/SK/GF/TF] See **peşk II.**

pişkdar پشكدار *m.* **(-ê;).** 1) {syn: beşdar} shareholder; 2) {syn: beşdar} participant; 3) [*adj.*] {syn: beşdar} participating, taking part. {also: pişikdar (Dh/Hk/Zeb)} [Dh/Hk/Zeb//GF/TF/FS]

pişkil پشكِل (FS) = sheep or goat manure. See **bişkul** & **pişkul**.

pişkîn پشكين (IFb/GF/Slm) = to sneeze. See **pêkijîn**.

pişkoj پشكۆژ (K) = button. See **bişkoj**.

pişkok پشكۆك (Msr) = button. See **bişkoj**.

pişkul پشكول *f.* **(-a;-ê).** goat manure *(in the shape of little balls)* (Msr/Mzg); sheep or camel dung (K/ A/JJ); sheep, goat, camel, or rabbit dung (B): **-bişkul kirin** (B) to defecate *(of sheep, goats, camels, or rabbits)*. {also: **bişkul**; k'uşpil (FS-2); pişkil (FS); pişqil (IFb-2); pişqul (IF-2/Mzg); [pychkoul] پشكول (JJ); <pişkul> پشكل (HH)} Cf. P piškil پشكل = 'orbicular dung of sheep'; Sor pişkil پشكِل/pişqil پشقِل; Za pişkul *f.* = 'goat droppings' (Todd); Hau pişqeɫî *f.* = 'sheep dung' (M4) [A/IFb/JJ/GF//FS//K/B/F/Msr//Mzg] <k'erme; peyîn; qelax; sergîn; tepik> See also **bişkul**.

p'işkyan پشكيان (Qzl) = to sneeze. See **pêkijîn**.

pişpişî پشپشى *adj.* puffy, tired (eyes); swollen, puffed up: **•Ç'avê min *pişpişî* ne** (Msr) My eyes are *puffy/tired.* [Msr/ZF3/Wkt]

pişqil پشقِل (IF) = sheep or goat manure. See **bişkul** & **pişkul**.

pişqul پشقول (IF) = sheep or goat manure. See **bişkul** & **pişkul**.

pişrûk پشرووك (A/IFb/JJ)/p'işrûk (B) = cooked groats. See **pişrûng**.

pişrûng پشروونگ *f.* **(-a;-ê).** dish of cooked grain or groats. {also: p'işirûk (K); pişrûk (A/IFb)/p'işrûk (B); pişûrig (IFb-2); [pychrouk] پشروك (JJ); <pişrûn> پشرون (HH)} Cf. Arm p'šrel փշրել = 'to chop finely, mince' & p'šowr փշուր = 'crumb' [Qrj//HH//A/IFb/B/JJ//K] <girar>

pişt I پشت *f.(K/JB3)/m.(BX)* **(-a/ ;-ê/).** 1) back *(anat.)*: **•Bavê xwe li *pişta* xwe kir** (L) He put his father on his *back* [to carry him across a stream] **•Keçelok *pişta* stuê xwe xorand û hat** (L) Kechelok scratched *the back of* his head [lit. 'neck'] [in bewilderment] and came **•*Pişta xwe da* wan û çû** (FK-eb-1) He *turned his back on* them [lit. 'he gave them his back'] and went; 2) top, roof *(of building)*: **•ser *pişta* qesrê** (L) on *the roof of* [=on top of] the castle; 3) support, backing: **•*Pişta* min pê germ bû, lê wî soza xwe xwar** (Qzl) I trusted him, but he disappointed me **•*Pişta* wî heye** (Qzl) He has *support[ers]*; 4) sperm; descendants: **•*Pişta* wî hat** (Qzl) He ejaculated/He 'came'. {also: [pycht] پشت (JJ); <pişt> پشت(HH)} cf. Skt pṛ-ṣṭi- *f.* = 'rib' --> **-ṣṭi-**: [Pok. D. -st-o-

1005-6.] <[Pok. stā-:stə- 1004.ff.] 'to stand, to put': Skt pṛ-ṣṭhá- *n.* = 'back'; OIr *pṛšti- (A&L p. 82 [I, 1]/Ras, p.134): Av paršti-; Mid P pušt = 'back, support, protection' (M3); P pošt پشت; Sor pişt پشت; Za paşt[î] *f.* = back (Mal); Hau peşt = 'back' *in* peşt be = 'away from' (M4) [K/A/JB3/IFb/B/JJ/HH/JB1-A&S/SK/GF/TF/OK]

pişt II پشت *prep.* behind, after *(place & time)*:

1) used in conjunction with postpositions:

-di pişt ... de = behind *(without motion)*: •**Gundê me *di pişt* çiyê *de* ye** (BX) Our village is *behind* the mountain;

-di pişt ... re = behind, after *(time or motion)*: •**Ez *di pişt* te *re* derbas bûm** (BX) I passed *behind* you •**di pişt re** = afterward {syn: hingê; paşê; şûnda, etc.};

-di pişt ... ve = afterward {syn: hingê; paşê; şûnda, etc.}: •**Ezê, *di pişt* xwe *ve*, jin û zarok bihêlim** (BX) I'll leave *behind* a wife and children;

2) *used in conjunction with prepositions*:

-ji pişt = from behind;

-li pişt = behind (with motion). {also: piş II (B); [pycht /pisct] پشت (JJ)} [BX/K/A/JB3/JJ/GF] See also **piştî II**.

piştdawî پشتداوی *f.* (;-yê). the hereafter, the next world: •**Her roj piştî nimêja êvarê, şêx şîretên dînî li mirîdên xwe dikirin û dijwariya roja *pişdawiyê* û agirê dûjehê jî diêxist bîra wan** (Rnh 2:17, 340) Every day after the evening prayer, the sheikh would advise his disciples on religion and admonished them about the difficulties of the hereafter and the fire of hell. {also: pişdawî (Rnh/OK)} {syn: axret} [Rnh/OK//GF/TF]

pişte پشته (A/IFb) = pistachio. See **p'iste**.

piştevan پشتەڤان (AW) = defender; supporter. See **piştîvan**.

piştevanî پشتەڤانی (AW) = protection; support. See **piştîvanî**.

piştgir پشتگِر *m.&f.* (-ê/;). supporter, backer: •**Ji wê demê pê ve C. Ç. bûye hevalbend û *piştgirê* K.P.** (Bkp, 29) Ever since that time, J.Ch. became an ally and *supporter of* K.P. {also: piştgîr (SS)} {syn: alîgir; mêldar; piştîvan [3]} Sor piştgîr پشتگیر {piştgirî} [Bkp/K/ZF/CS//SS]

piştgirî پشتگِری *f.* (-ya;-yê). support[ing], backing: •**Çareya wê jî biratî ye, yekbûn e, welatparêzî ye, xebat e, *piştgirîya* şoreşê ye, mirin û mayîn e** (Wlt 1:35, 4) The solution for it is brotherhood, unity, patriotism, struggling, *supporting* the revolution, dying and remaining alive; **-piştgirîya *fk-î* kirin** (RN2) to support: •**A. Soljênîtsîn *piştgirîya* gelê Kurd *dike*** (RN2, 51[1998], 28) A. Solzhenitsyn *supports* the Kurdish people. {syn: alîgirî; mêldarî} [(neol)Wlt/IFb]

piştgîr پشتگیر (SS) = supporter. See **piştgir**.

piştî I پشتی *m.(Qzl)/f.(B)* (/-ya; /-yê). load, burden; package, bundle; package carried (by a porter) on the back (HH/JJ): •**R̄ojê *pişto* dar tînim difroşim** (Z-922) In the daytime I take *a load of* wood [and] sell [it]. {also: pişto (Z-922/GF-2); [pychti] پشتی (JJ); <piştî> پشتی (HH)} Mid P puštag = 'load (carried on the back)' (M3) [Z-922//K/A/IFb/B/JJ/HH/SK/GF/TF/OK/Qzl] <bar I; pişt I>

piştî II پشتی *prep.* 1) {syn: paş I} behind, after *(place & time)*: **-piştî nîvro** (BX) (in the) afternoon; **-piştî ko** + *subj.* = after + -ing; 2) instead of, rather than (Z-2): •**Te *piştî* stîya Zîn çû xast qîza Bek'oê** (Z-2) You have requested the daughter of Beko *rather than* Lady Zîn. [IFb/B/ZF3] See also **pişt II**.

piştîvan پشتیڤان *m.* (-ê;). 1) defender, protector: •**...ew *piştîwanêd* ĥukumet û dewleta mîrê Cizîra Botan bûn** (K-dş) They were *the protectors of* the government of the prince of Jezira Bohtan; 2) patron; 3) {syn: alîgir; mêldar; piştgir} supporter (IF/SK): •**Lê îro ji nişka ve wekî *piştevanên* demokratîk-bûnê derdikevin holê** (AW70D2) But today they suddenly appear on the scene as *supporters of* democratization. {also: piştevan (AW); piştîwan (K-dş/SK); piştovan (F); piştvan (IF); [pychtouvan] پشتوان (JJ)} Mid P puštībān = 'supporter, bodyguard' (M3); P poštbān پشتبان/ poštvān پشتوان = 'prop, buttress, support; bar of a door; helper, supporter'; Sor piştîwan پشتیوان = 'supporter; reserve (military)' {piştîvanî; piştvanî} [K-dş/SK//K//F//JJ//IFb//AW]

piştîvanî پشتیڤانی *f.* (-ya;-yê). 1) protection; 2) patronage; 3) support: •**Her wiha ew balê dikişînin ser *piştevaniya* dewletên Ewrûpayê jî** (AW71A3) Likewise they draw attention to *the support of* the European states as well •**Ji ber ku piraniya gelê Keşmîrê misilman e, dewleta Pakistanê *piştevaniya* şervanên Keşmîrê *dike*** (AW77A5) Because the majority of the Kashmiri people are Muslims, the Pakistani government *supports* the Kashmiri fighters. {also: piştevanî (AW); piştvanî (IF)} [K//IFb//AW] <piştîvan>

piştîwan پشتیوان (K-dş/SK) = protector; supporter. See **piştîvan**.

piştkul پـشـتـكـول *adj.* hunched-over, suffering from a bad back: •**Hespekî jar, t'opal, *piştkul* hat** (J) A thin, lame, *hunched-over* horse came. < pişt = 'back' + kul- = 'pain' / kulîn = 'to limp' [J/ZF3/FS]

piştkûz پشتكووز (F) = hunchbacked. See **kûz I**.

piştmêr پـشـتـمـێـر *m.* **(-ê;).** 1) protector, defender; henchman; bodyguard (A/IF/BK); 2) retinue, suite. {also: <piştmêr> پـشـتـمـیـر (HH)} < pişt = 'back' + mêr = 'man'; cf. T arka 'back, backer, supporter' [BX/BK/K/A/IFb/HH/GF/FS]

pişto پشتو (Z-922/GF) = load, burden. See **piştî I**.

piştovan پـشـتـوڤـان (F) = protector; supporter. See **piştîvan**.

piştpez پشتپەز *adj. pattern of* **bergûz** *material*: brown monochrome (êkreng). [Bw/Wkt] <bergûz>

piştr̄ast پـشـتـراسـت *adj.* sure, assured: **-piştrast bûn** (AId) to be sure, be assured; **-piştrast kirin** (VoA) to verify, ensure: •**Karbidestêt Elmanî dibêjin, ew neşîyan peyamêt ku dibêjin du hevwelatêt Elmanî hatibûne revandin li başûra rojhelata Turkiye *piştrast ken*** (VoA) German officials say they have not been able *to verify* reports that two German citizens were abducted in southeastern Turkey •**Neteweyêt Êkgirtî dê zêrevanîya firotina nefta 'Îraqê li derve û berhemêt van firotina ket, *da piştrast bête kirin* ku ew bo kel û pelêt mirovanî ... bête xerc kirin** (VoA) The United Nations will oversee the sale of Iraqi oil abroad and the results of these sales, *in order to ensure* that they be spent on humanitarian supplies. {syn: biste [2]; misoger I} [Bw/VOA/A/GF/OK/RZ/AId/FS] <emîn; ewlekar; fireqet>

piştstû پشتستوو (GF) = collar. See **pisto**.

piştvan پـشـتـڤـان (IFb) = protector; supporter. See **piştîvan**.

piştvanî پـشـتـڤـانـی (IFb) = protection; support. See **piştîvanî**.

pişûrig پشوورگ (IFb) = cooked groats. See **pişrûng**.

pitepit [Ardu/Frq/B]/**pite-pit** [LC/K/IFb] پـتـەپـت *f.* **(-a;-ê).** blabber, chatter, prattle, idle talk: •**Bêhna kurik ji vê *pitepita* diya wî teng dibe û derdikeve der** (Ardu, 117) The boy, non-plussed by his mother's *outburst*, walks out •**Bû *pirte pirta* çûkên di nav de lûsiyayî** (SBx, 18) Fledgelings perched in it [=the tree] began to *chatter*. {also: pirte pirt II (SBx); pitpit (GF/TF/AD); <pitapit> پطاپط (HH)} {syn: galegûrt; galigal} [LC/K/IFb/Ardu/Frq/B//GF/TF/AD//HH//SBx]

pitê پـتـێ *f.(voc.).* woman, girl: *affectionate term for one's wife; term by which Kurdish men call their wives instead of using their names* (HH) {also: [pīte] پیته (JJ); <pitê> پتێ (HH)} [Kg/K/A/IFb/HH/GF//JJ] <keç>

pitik I پـتِـك *f.* **(;-ê).** match(es): •**[Îşeve çewalekî û ben û berheste û şemal û *bitik* {بـطـك} evene ĥazir bike]** (JR #37, 110) This evening prepare a sack and a rope and a flint and a candle and *matches*. {also: pêtik (IFb/RZ-2/CS); [bitik] بـطـك (JR)} {syn: k'irpît; neftik} [JR//K/B/RZ/ZF3/FS//IFb/CS]

pitik II پـتِـك *m.&f.* **(-ê/-a;).** baby, infant; babe in arms: •**Hîn ez *pitik* bûm, di pêçekê de bûm, bavê min ji ber karê xwe malê ji gund bar dike tîne Diyarbekirê** (M.Gazî Baweriyên batil ên Kurdan) I was still *an infant*, in diapers, due to his work my father moves the household from the village and brings [us] to Diyarbakir; **-pitika min** (ZF3) my baby/my child. {syn: dergûş; sava; şîrmêj} [Ag/M.Gazî/K/B/IFb/GF/RZ/ZF3/G/FD/Wkt/CS]

pitikî پـتِـكـی *f.* **(-ya;).** infancy, early childhood: •**Ez ji *pitikiya* xwe û vir de ye li Diyarbekirê dijîm** (M.Gazî Baweriyên batil ên Kurdan) Ever since my *infancy* I have been living in Diyarbakir. {also: pitikîtî (Wkt-2); pitiktî (ZF3/Wkt-2)} [M.Gazî/Wkt//ZF3] <pitik II>

pitikîtî پتِكیتی (Wkt) = infancy. See **pitikî**.

pitiktî پتِكتی (ZF3/Wkt) = infancy. See **pitikî**.

p'itir [K]/**pit'ir** [JB1-A] پـتِـر *adj.* more, greater in number: •**Ewane ji me *pitir* in** (SK 40:374) They are *more* than us; **-ji hemî caran pitir** (SK) more than ever. {also: [pytir] پتر (JJ)} {syn: bêtir} <p'ir̄ + -tir: Sor pitir پتر [Bw/Zeb/Dh/IFb/JJ/SK/GF/OK/FS//K//JB1-A]

pitpit پتپت (GF/TF/AD) = prattle, chatter. See **pitepit**.

piv I پڤ *f.* **(-a;).** audible flatulence, fart: •***Piva* wî hat** (FS) He broke wind; **-piv kirin** (FD/Wkt) to pass gas, break wind, cut a fart: •**Wî *piv kir*** (FS) He passed gas/He cut a fart. {syn: tir̄} [Wkt/FS/BF/FD]

piv II پڤ (FS) = puff (of air). See **p'if**.

pivdank پڤدانك (FS) = balloon. See **p'ifdank**.

pivikî پڤِكی *adj.* arrogant, haughty; conceited, stuck up, self important: •**Mirov narsîstan çawa nas dike? Narsîst pir pozbilind û bi paye ne. Ji xwe razî, qurre û *pivikî* ne** (www.tirsik.net: narsîzm) How does one recognize narcissists? The narcissist is very arrogant and haughty. He is self important, proud and *stuck up*. {syn: difnbilind; pozbilind; qur̄e} [Çira/tirsik/ZF3]

p'ixep'ix پخهپخ *f.* **(-a;).** snoring: **•K'eçelonek jî xwe li odê avêtye 'erdê, *pixpixa wî ye* razae** (HR 3:221) And Bald boy threw himself onto the floor, *snoring* as he fell asleep **•Mam Tal dibihîst, emma xo nebizawt, *pirxepirx* ji xo diîna ko, "Ez di xewêda me, min agah ji hingo nîye"** (SK 28:256) Mam Tal could hear but he did not move, he pretended *to snore* (as if to say), "I'm asleep, I cannot hear you" **•Piştî du deqan tenê, *bû pixte pixta wê*** (HYma 19) After only 2 minutes, *she was snoring*; **-p'ixep'ix kirin** (IFb) to snore. {also: pirxepirx (SK); pixpix (GF); pixte pixt (HYma)} [HR/GF//FJ/IFb//HYma//SK] <nivistin; r̄azan; xew>

pixêrî پخێرى (IFb) = fireplace; chimney. See **pixêrîk**.

pixêrîg پـخـێـريـگ (IFb) = fireplace; chimney. See **pixêrîk**.

pixêrîk پـخـێـريـك *f.* **(-a;-ê).** 1) fireplace, hearth: **•Ew r̄adive *beẍîra* oda xwe dadide** (HCK-3, 176) He lights *the fireplace* in his room; 2) chimney (K/A/JB3) [pixêrîg]; flue, channel in a chimney for conveying smoke outside (K); 3) {also: aşxane; pêjgeh} kitchen [pixêrî]. {also: bexêrî; bexîr•e (;•ê) (K/F); beẍîre (B); bixêrî (A/JB3/FS); pêxrîk (Wn); pixêrî (IFb); pixêrîg (IFb); [boukhari] بخارى (JJ); <bixêrî> بخيرى (HH)} {syn: k'ulek II; r̄ojin} < Ar buxār بـــخـــار = 'steam'; Cf. W Arm puxerig բուխերիկ/puxarig բուխարիկ = 'smokehole in roof' [Bt//K/F/ZF3//B//A/JB3/HH/FS//Wn//IFb//JJ] <k'ulek II; p'ace>

pixpix پخپخ (GF) = snoring. See **p'ixep'ix**.

pixte pixt پخته پخت (HYma) = snoring. See **p'ixep'ix**.

piyal پيال (GF) = tea glass. See **p'eyale**.

piyale پياله (Lab/IFb) = tea glass. See **p'eyale**.

piyan پيان (IFb/GF) = tea glass. See **p'eyale**.

p'izan پزان, m. (Qzl/GF) = placenta. See **p'izdan**.

p'izdan پـــــــــزدان *f.* **(-a;-ê).** placenta, afterbirth, secundines; placenta of cattle (B); womb, uterus *of animals*. {also: pisdan (GF-2); p'izan, m. (Qzl/GF-2); p'izdang (B-2); <pizdan پـــــزدان/pizan پـــزان> (HH)} {syn: hevalçûk} <*pus-dān <O Ir *puθra-dāna-(ka-) (A&L p. 82 [I, 1]): Mid P pusyān; Sor pisdan پسدان/pizdan پزدان = 'placenta, womb' [K/IFb/B/HH/GF//Qzl] <fir̄o; malzarok; welidîn; zayîn>

p'izdang پزدانگ (B) = placenta. See **p'izdan**.

pizik پزِك *f.* **(-a;-ê).** 1) pimple; pustule: **•*Pirzika* destê wî sax bû** (FS) *The pimple on* his hand has healed; 2) boil, sore, ulcer. {also: bizrik (IF-2); pirzik (IF-2/A); p'irzik (K); pizrik (IF-2); **zipik**; [pizik] پزك (JJ); <pirzik> پـرزك (HH)} [F/K/A/IFb/B/JJ/GF/TF//HH] See also **zipik**. <k'êm II; nêm>

p'izinîn پزِنين (K/B) = to wear out (cloth). See **pizirîn**.

pizirîn پـزريـن *vi.* **(-pizir-).** to wear thin, wear out *(of cloth) (vi.)*. {also: p'izinîn (K/B)} [Qrj//K/B] <piçan>

pizî I پـــــــــزى *f.* **(-ya;-yê).** tunnel or seam for the drawstring at the waistline of a pair of shalvar. {syn: maldoxîn} [Qzl/Kmc-#5647/IFb/GF/ZF3]

pizî II پزى (K) = gums; palate. See **p'idî**.

pizî III پـــزى *f.* **(-ya;).** breast pocket; breast, bosom, embrace *(between outstretched arms)*: **•Eve hêj berê wî li *pizya* – paxila – min da ye** (Drş #427, 125) Here is his stone still in my *breast pocket* **•Wî *pizîya* xwe tejî sêv kirin** (FS) He filled his *pocket* with apples. {syn: berîk; p'aşil} [Drş/GF/Bw/FS]

pizmam پزمام (F/B/FS) = cousin. See **pismam**.

pizmamî پـزمـامـى (B) = cousinhood *(on paternal side)*. See **pismamtî**.

pizmamtî پزمامتى (B) = cousinhood *(on paternal side)*. See **pismamtî**.

pizor پزۆر (IF/HH) = bowels. See **pizûr**.

pizrik پزرك (IF) = pimple; boil. See **pizik**.

pizûr/p'izûr [K/B] پـزوور *pl.(K)/f.(B)* **(; /-ê).** bowels, entrails, 'innards', intestines; pluck *(animal viscera)*; general name for the internal organs of animals; small intestine (B): **-'ûr û pizûr** (Msr)/ **ḧûr û p'izûr** (B) entrails, tripe, organs situated in the abdominal cavity: **•'Ûr û *pizûr*, para xezûr, ser û pepik, para metik** (Msr) Intestines and *undesirable parts* [are] the father-in-law's portion, the head and trotters are the maternal aunt's portion *(this is part of a folk poem which indicates how the parts of a slaughtered goat or sheep are divided among family members)*. {also: pizor (IF); <pizor> پـزور (HH)} {syn: r̄odî; r̄ovî II; ûr} [Msr/K/B//IF/HH] <r̄ovî II; ûr>

pî I پـــى *m.* **(-yê;).** shoulder blade. {syn: navmil; p'ol II} [Kmc-5/A/IFb/GF/OK/ZF3] <mil; pîl I>

p'î II پـــــى *adj.* well-off, well-to-do, prosperous, rich. [S&E/K]

pîcî پیجی (K) = finger. See **bêç'î II**.

p'îç پـیـچ *m.* **(-ê;).** 1) illegitimate child, bastard: •**K'î zane *bîcê* k'êye?** (EP-5, #6) Who knows who his father is? [lit. 'whoșe *bastard* he is']; 2) mongrel, hybrid, e.g., *a mule as the product of a horse and a donkey*; 3) (fig.) clever, sly person; swindler (B); 4) *[adj.]* worthless, ruined. See **p'ûç'**. {also: bîc (K-2/B/EP-5); bîjî (IF-2/GF-2); pînc I (IFb-2); [pitch] پـیـچ (JJ); <pîç> پـیـچ (HH)} <T piç = 'bastard'; Sor bîc بیج/bîç بیچ/bîjû بیژوو {pîçî (A/IF)} [EP-5/B//K/A/IFb/JJ/HH/GF]

pîçek پیچەك (JB1-A/Bw) = a little. See **piçek**.

p'îçî پیچی *f.* **().** illegitimacy, bastardy. [A/IF] <p'îç>

pîj I پـیـژ *m.* **(-ê;).** 1) {syn: qirş} splinter, sliver; 2) {syn: caẍ} knitting needle; other long, sharp objects, such as tent stakes; 3) hangnail; 4) awl (JJ); chisel; 5) *[adj.]* sharp *(of knives)* (K/IFb). {also: pîjik II (Qzl/IFb-2); pînc II (Wn); [pij] پـژ (JJ)} [Ag/K/A/IFb/B/GF/TF/FS//Qzl//Wn]

pîj II پیژ (K/B) = fork used in weaving. See **pîjik**.

pîj III پـیـژ *adj.* stretched out at full length *(e.g., of a corpse)*: **-pîj kirin** (ZF) to stretch out: •**Piştre rovî rabû çû û li ser devê riya Melê *xwe* avêt erdê *pîj kir*, mîna ku ew heftiyek be miriye, xwe bê rih hişt** (ZZ-4, 203) Then the fox went and threw himself on the side of the road for the Mullah [lit. 'the Mullah's road'] and *stretched himself out*, as if he had been dead for a week, he played dead. [ZZ/ZF]

pîjan پیژان (MG/IFb) = mint. See **pûjan**.

pîj•ik I پـیـژك *m.* **(•kê; •kî).** three-pronged fork used in tamping down threads while weaving on a loom [T kirkit/kerkit]. {also: pîj II (K/B); [pijik] پـژك (JJ)} [Bw/Zx/A/IFb/JJ/FS//K/B] <befş; hepik; t'evn>

pîjik II پـیـژك (Qzl/IFb) = splinter; knitting needle; hangnail; awl. See **pîj I**.

pîkap پیکاپ (IFb) = pickup truck. See **p'îqab**.

pîkem پیکەم (Slv) = pickup truck. See **p'îqab**.

pîl I پـیـل *m.* **(-ê;).** arm *(from shoulder to wrist)*; shoulder; shoulder-blade (B). {also: [pil] پـیـل (JJ)} [Kg/Krç/K/IFb/B/JJ/SK] <ç'epil; dest; mil; pî I; p'ol II>

pîl II پـیـل *f.* **(-a;).** 1) battery, electric cell: •**Ev radyo bi *pîlan* dixebite** (Wkt) This radio works on *batteries* •***Pîla* çiradestê sot** (FS) The flashlight *battery* burned out; 2) flashlight (GF). <Fr pile = 'battery' [IFb/GF/Wkt/RZ/BF/FS/CS]

p'îlat پـیـلات *f.* **(-a;).** 1) seal, stamp; 2) {syn: gustîl; mor II[1]} signet ring: •**K'anê *pîlata* min** (FK-eb-2) Where is my *signet ring*? •**Were emê *mor-p'îlatê* xwe bi hev biguhêȓin** (FK-eb-2) Come, let's exchange *signet rings*. [FK-2/K]

pîlav پیلاڤ (IFb/AD) = cooked rice. See **p'elaw**.

pîldar پیلدار *m.* **().** fortune teller *(originally, person in possession of shoulder-blade bones)*: •**[Lewranî min bi xwe bi çavêd xwe paşayek ji ehlê Ûrmayî dît ku navê Seyfeddîn Paşa bû, ew jî *pîldar* bû û pîl digel hebû]** (BN, 77) For I saw with my own eyes a pasha from the Turks, named Seyfeddin Pasha, and he was *a fortune teller*, and had [shoulder-blade] bones with him. {also: [pildar] پیلدار (JJ)} {syn: falçî; ȓemildar} [BN/JJ/ZF3] <pîl I>

pîn I پـیـن *f.* **(-a;).** chicken coop: •**Mala me piçûk e, mîna *pîna* mirîşkan e** (DZK, les. 8) Our house is small, like a chicken coop. {also: pin I (IF)} [DZK/K/GF/FS//IFb]

pîn II پین (IFb) = kick. See **p'eḧîn**.

pînc I پینج (IFb) = bastard. See **p'îç**.

pînc II پـیـنـج (Wn) = splinter; knitting needle; hangnail; awl. See **pîj I**.

pîn•e/p'îne [F/K/B] پـیـنـە *m.* **(•ê;).** 1) {syn: kerkon; kevnik [2]; p'aç' II; p'ate II; p'eȓok; p'ot} rag(s), tatters (F/K/B): •**Wekî meriv t'êlek ji k'incê wê bik'şanda, ḧezar *p'îne* wê jê bik'etana** (EH) If one were to pull a thread from her clothes, a thousand *rags [or, patches]* would fall from her; 2) {syn: p'ate II} patch: **-p'îne kirin** (Mzg) to patch, sew patches on. {also: pinî (FS); [piné] پینه (JJ); <pîne> پینه (HH)} Cf. P pīne پینه = 'patch'; Sor pîne پینە = 'patch' [EH/F/K/B//A/IF/JJ/HH/Mzg//FS]

pîneçî/p'îneçî [K/B] پـیـنـەچـی *m.* **().** 1) old clothes salesman, ragseller (JJ/K); 2) cobbler (JJ/K); cobbler who works on the street (B): •***Pîneçî* pêlava wî pîne kir** (FS) *The cobbler* repaired his shoes; 3) *[fig.]* someone who mangles or botches up his job, a quack in his profession (B). {also: [pinedji/pīnăčī (PS)] پینەچی (JJ); <pîneçî> پینچی (HH)} [K/B/HH/FS//JJ] <pîne>

pîpik پیپك (IF) = pupil. See **bibiq**.

pîpok پـیـپـۆك *f.* **(-a;-ê).** opening, window: •**Banê holê kulêr û *pîpokên* kulekên wê şikestibûn** (H v. 1, 83-84 [1932 1:4]) The roof of the hut, the *small windows* in the smoke holes of its skylight were broken. {syn: ȓojin} [H/K/GF/ZF]

p'îqab پـیـقـاب *f.* **(-a;-ê).** pickup truck: •***Pîqab* zû**

derketibû ser rê û bi sureteke xurt ji wir bi dûr ketibû. Apê keçikê pîlaka *pîqabê* nivîsandibû û ji mêrikê kal yê li ber benzînxanê pirsa wê *pîqabê* kiribû (KS, 12) *The pickup truck* quickly hit the road and at a high speed distanced itself from there. The girl's uncle wrote down the *truck's* license plate number and inquired about *the truck* from the old man at the gas station. {also: pîkap (IFb); pîkem (Slv); pîqap (TF)} < Eng pickup [KS//TF//IFb//Slv] <cemse; t'aksî; trimbêl>

pîqap پیقاپ (TF) = pickup truck. See **p'îqab**.

pîr پـیـر *adj.* 1) {syn: kal I; mezin[2]; navsera; sere I} old *(of people & animals)*: **-pîr bûn** = to grow old, age: **•Ez *pîr bûme*** = I'*ve grown old*/I'*ve aged* **•Ezê darê cahil jî bibiȓim, *yê pîr* jî** (Dz) I will cut down both young trees and *old ones*; 2) {syn: îxtiyar; kalik} [*m.*] old man; [*f.* (;-ê).] old woman: **•mirîşka pîrê** = the old woman's chicken; **-Lawê pîrê** = Son of the old woman *{a character in Kurdish folklore; see also **Keçelok**}*; 3) {syn: jin} [*f.*] wife; 4) [*f.*] {syn: dapîroşk; pêrtevînk; p'indepîr; pîrhevok; pîrik [3]; t'evnpîrk [1]} spider (B). {also: [pir] پـیـر (JJ); <pîr> پـیـر (HH)} <proto IE *pr̥u̯os (Kent), cf. [Pok. perə-u̯o- 815.] -> [Pok. 2. per 810.] 'to lead, paş over': Skt pū́rva- = 'being before or in front'; O Ir *parvya- (M. Schwartz: this updates *pr̥vya- Hübsch #286): Av paurva-; O P p(a)ruva- = 'being before in time or place' (Kent); Mid P pīr = 'old, aged, ancient' (M3); P pīr پیر; Sor pîr پیر; Za pîr (Todd); Hau pîr (M4). See I. Gershevitch. "Iranian Chronological Adverbs," *Indo-Iranica: Mélanges présentés à Georg Morgenstierne* (Wiesbaden, 1964), pp.81-82; reprinted in his *Philologia Iranica*, ed. N. Sims-Williams (Wiesbaden : Dr. Ludwig Reichert Verlag, 1985), pp. 182-83. {pîranî; pîrayî; pîretî; pîrî[tî]; [piráia] پیرای (JJ)} [F/K/A/JB3/IFb/B/JJ/HH/SK/JB1-A&S/GF] <bapîr; dapîr; kevn>

pîrabok پیرابۆك (A/TF) = witch. See **pîrhevok**.

pîranî پیرانی (K) = old age. See **pîrayî**.

pîratî پیراتی (ZF3) = old age. See **pîrayî**.

pîravok پیراڤوك (TF) = spider. See **pîrhevok**.

pîrayî پـیـرایـی *f.* **(-ya;-yê).** old age, elderliness. {also: pîranî (K-2); pîratî (ZF3); pîretî (A); pîrî (JB3); pîrîtî (JB3-2); [piráia] پـیـرای (JJ)} [K/JJ//A//JB3//ZF3] <pîr>

pîrçemek پیرچەمەك *f.* **(;-ê).** bat, zool. *Chiroptera*: **•Lê *pirçemekê* xwe ruçikand dibû [=ruçikandi bû]: ji wê rojê de şerm dike ko bi ro derkeve, nav heval û hogiran, ji lew re bi şev der tê** (SW) But *the bat* had already plucked out its feathers: from that day on it was ashamed to come out during the day, [to be seen] among its friends, for this reason it comes out at night **•Wek *p'erçemûk* xwe pêşda ȓuquç'and** (Dz) He took off [his feathers] first like *the bat* [*prv.*]. {also: **barç'imok** (Wn); parçêmk (GF); p'erçemûk (Dz); pirçemek (SW); [bārçémik] بـارچـمـك (JJ)} {syn: çekçekîle; çil II; dûvmesas (IF); şevrevînk; şevşevok} [IFb//SW//Dz//GF] See also **barç'imok**.

pîrebok پیرەبۆك (Lab/IFb) = witch. See **pîrhevok**.

pîr'ebotk پیرعەبۆتك (Qrj) = witch. See **pîrhevok**.

pîreda پیرەدا (K/A) = old woman. See **pîredê**.

pîredak پیرەداك (JB1-S) = old woman. See **pîredê**.

pîred•ê پـیـرەدێ *f.* **(•îya;).** old woman, old mother; grandmother: **•Roêda gede diçû cem hevalê xwe, *pîredya* wî jî diçû nava cînara, nav gund** (HCK-3, #2, 18) During the day the fellow would go to his friends, and his *old mother* would go to the neighbors, around the village. {also: pîreda (K-2/A); pîredak (JB1-S)} {syn: pîrik} [HCK/K/B/FJ/GF//A//JB1-S] <dapîr>

pîrejin پـیـرەژن *f.* **(-a;-ê).** old woman: **•Em Al-p'aşa, *pîrejina* wî û M. delalva bihêlin şeherê Muxurzemînêda** (Z-1) Let's leave A.p., his *wife* [lit. '*old lady*'] and dandy M. in the city of M. [Z-1/K/A/IF/B] <jin>

pîrek پـیـرەك *f.* **(-a;).** wife; married woman: **•*Pîrek* diçin bêrîyê** (AB) *The women* go to the sheepfold **•*Pîreka* wî kete ber pîrka** (L) *His wife* gave birth [lit. 'fell before the midwives']. {also: <pîrek> پـیـرك (HH)} {syn: jin; kevanî; k'ulfet; zêç}[L/Erh/IFb/TF/HH/ZF] <afret>

pîrekî پـیـرەکـی *f.* **(-ya;-yê).** womanhood, being a woman; being a wife: **•Kes şihba *pîrekiyê* ji min nake** (ZZ-10, 152) No one suspects that I am a woman [lit. 'No one suspects me of *womanhood*']. {also: pîrektî (A/IFb-2)} {syn: jintî I} [ZZ/IFb/TF/ZF3//A] <pîrek>

pîrektî پیرەکتی (A/IFb) = womanhood. See **pîrekî**.

pîretî پیرەتی (A) = old age. See **pîrayî**.

pîrevok پیرەڤۆك (Msr) = spider. See **pîrhevok**.

pîr'evûk پیرعەڤووك (Ad) = spider. See **pîrhevok**.

pîrhebok پیرهەبۆك (K) = spider. See **pîrhevok**.

pîrhevo پیرهەڤۆ (K/JJ) = spider. See **pîrhevok**.

pîrhevok پیرهەڤۆك *f.* **(-a;-ê).** 1) {syn: dapîroşk; pêrtevînk; p'indepîr; pîr [4]; pîrik [3]; t'evnpîrk [1]} {also: pîravok (TF); pîrevok (Msr); pîr'evûk (Ad); pîrhebok (K); pîrhevo (K-2); pîrḧebok (B); [pir-hewou] پیرهڤو (JJ); <pîrhevûk> پیرهڤوك (HH)} spider; 2) {also: pîrabok (A/TF); pîrebok (Lab/IFb-2); pîr'ebotk (Qrj); pîrḧebok (B)} witch: •**Weke cin û *pîrebokan* li vê rewşa te dinêrin** (Lab, 51) They will look at you [lit. 'at your situation'] as if you were a jinn or *witch.* =Sor całcałoke جاڵجاڵۆكە & dapîroçke داپیرۆچكە/ dapîroke داپیرۆكە = 'spider'; Za pīriké = 'spider' (JJ) [Ad//J//K/IFb//B//HH//JJ//Msr//A/TF//Lab//Qrj] See also **pîrik** [3].

pîrḧebok پیرحەبۆك (B) = spider; witch. See **pîrhevok**.

pîrik پیرك *f.* **(-a;-ê).** 1) {syn: dapîr; pîredê} grandmother; old woman; 2) midwife: **-ber pîr[i]ka k'etin** (L) to be in childbed, to give birth (originally 'to be under the care of old women / midwives'): •**Pîreka wî *kete ber pîrka*** (L) His wife gave birth [lit. '*fell before the midwives*']; 3) {syn: dapîroşk; pêrtevînk; p'indepîr; pîr [4]; pîrhevok; t'evnpîrk[1]} spider; 4) {syn: belantîk; fir̄fir̄ok; p'erîdank; p'ir̄p'ir̄ok} butterfly. {also: pîrek (Erh); [pirik /pīrik] پیرك (JJ); <pîrik> پیرك (HH)} Cf. Za pīriké = 'spider' (JJ), pīrik = 'grandfather' (JJ) [L/K/A/JB3/IFb/JJ/HH/Tkm/Wn/Msr/Bt/Rh] <bapîr; kalik>

pîrî پیری (JB3) = old age. See **pîrayî**.

pîrîtî پیریتی (JB3) = old age. See **pîrayî**.

pîrot پیرۆت (IFb/AD/ZF3) = potter. See **p'irûd**.

pîroz پیرۆز *adj.* blessed: **-pîroz kirin** (Ber/K) to bless; to congratulate, wish well *(on a festive occasion)*: •**Bûk li zavê *pîroz* be** (AB) May the bride be *blessed* to the groom •**Cejna we *pîroz* be** (AB) Congratulations on your wedding [lit. 'May your celebration be *blessed*'] •**'Eyda te *pîroz* be!** (B) Happy holiday! •**Sersala we *pîroz* be** (AB) Happy anniversary or birthday [lit. 'May your anniversary be *blessed*']. {also: [pirouz] پیروز (JJ); <pîroz> پیروز (HH)} {syn: bimbarek} Mid P pērōz = 'victorious' (M3)' < *pari-aujah- (aujah- 'strength'); P pīrōz پیروز = 'victorious, prosperous'; Sor pîroz پیرۆز = 'blessed, fortunate, victorious' {pîrozî} [AB/K/A/(JB3)/IFb/B/HH/SK/GF//JJ]

pîroze پیرۆزە *f.* **( ).** turquoise: •**Şîrekî gelek kewn hebû, kalwanê wî zîw bû, destikê wî zêr bû, qaşêt elmas û *pîroze* hatibûne têgirtin** (SK 26:234) There was a very ancient sword with a silver scabbard, its hilt of gold inlaid with gems of diamond and *turquoise*. {also: [pirouzé] پیروزه (JJ)} {syn: tebesî} Cf. P pīrūze پیروزه/fīrūze فیروزه; Ar fayrūz فیروز/fīrūzaj فیروزج (<Mid P *pērōzag); Sor pîroze پیرۆزە [SK/IFb/JJ]

pîrozî پیرۆزی *f.* **().** congratulations, felicitations. {also: [pirouzi] پیروزی (JJ)} [K/A/JB3/JJ] <ç'avr̄onayî; pîroz>

p'îrqîn پیرقین *f.* **(-a;-ê).** giggle, chuckle; giggling, chuckling: •**Mîna carê dinê *dibe p'îrqîna wê*** (K2-Fêrîk) As other times [in the past], she *giggles* •**Stîya qîza Bek'o diçe ba stîya Zîne, / Dik'ene û *bi p'îrqîne*** (Z-2) The daughter of Beko went to Lady Zîn, / laughing and *in giggles*. {also: pirkîn (TF); pirqênî (DBgb); pirqîn (FJ/GF); p'îrqînî (B-2)} [Z-2/K/B//FJ/GF//DBgb//TF] <k'en>

p'îrqînî پیرقینی (B) = giggling, chuckling. See **p'îrqîn**.

p'îs پیس *adj.* 1) {syn: bi'ok; ç'epel; dijûn II; gemarî; mirdar̄; qirêj} dirty, impure, foul: •**Zani bû go hûn *pîs* in û hûn emalê serê wî ne** (L) He knew that you were [lit. 'are'] *foul* and that you brought [lit. 'bring'] him nothing but trouble; **-p'îs û pelos** (Zeb) filthy; 2) dishonorable. {also: [pis] پیس (JJ); <pîs> پیس (HH)} Cf. T pis; Sor pîs پیس = 'dirty, mean' {p'îsî[tî]; p'îsîyî} [L/K/A/JB3/IFb/JJ/B/HH/SK/GF]

p'îsî پیسی *f.* **(-ya;-yê).** 1) dirt; 2) excrement: •**Meriv ji *pîsîya* heywanan çawa feyde digre?** (Çandname 3.vi.2016) How does one derive benefit from animal *excrement*?; 3) uncleanliness (HH); 4) ugliness (JJ). {also: p'îsîtî (JB3/IFb/GF-2); p'îsîyî (A); [pisi] پیسی (JJ); <pîsî> پیسی (HH)} [B/IFb/JJ/HH//JB3/GF//A] <p'îs>

p'îsîtî پیسیتی (JB3/IFb/GF) = dirt[iness]. See **p'îsî**.

p'îsîyî پیسیی (A) = dirt[iness]. See **p'îsî**.

pîst پیست *m.* **(-ê;).** 1) {syn: ç'erm} skin, hide, pelt (K/IFb/TG2): •**Gurg e çûye di *pîstê* mihîyê da** (SK 50:521) He is a wolf in sheep's *clothing* •**Werşeq-weşeq kûviyeke ku *postê* wê pirr rind e** (Wlt 2:100, 13) The lynx is a wild animal with a very nice *pelt*; 2) skin *(of fruit)*, peel, shell (K); 3) sheepskin coat (K); 4) goatskin, leather bottle, wineskin, water bottle (K/IF/JR/TG2): •**[Melayî dît ku çar *pîstêd* biçûk rûnê bi ser avê ketîye têtin]** (JR) The mullah espied four *goatskins* [full] of butter floating on the water, headed in their direction. {also: p'êst II (K[s]/JR); post (IFb-2/GF-2/OK-2/Ba2/TG2)/p'ost (F/K); [pyst /پیست

پێست/post پوست (JJ)} Skt (Vedic) pavásta-; OP pavastā- = '(clay) envelope of tablet' (Kent/ Benveniste); Wakhi pīst = 'skin, shell'; Ormuri, Shughni pōst = 'tree bark'; Yidgha pisto/pusto = 'tree bark' & pisto = 'nutshell'; Mid P pōst = 'skin, hide, bark, shell' (M3); P pūst پوست = 'skin, shell'; Sor pêst پێست/post پۆست = 'skin'; Za poste *m.* = 'skin, hide' (Mal); Hau pos *m.* (M4). See: E. Benveniste. "Études sur le Vieux-Perse," *Bulletin de la Société de Linguistique de Paris* 47 (1951), 40-49. [JR/IFb/SK/GF/OK/Hk//F/K/Ba2/TG2//K(s)]

pîste پیسته (CB) = pistachio. See **p'iste**.

p'îşe پیشه *f.* **(-ya;-yê).** profession, occupation, trade, calling, vocation: **•Dema tu mezin bibî, tu dixwazî *pîşeya* te çi be?** (Wkt) When you grow up, what do you want your profession to be? **•Lê di destê yekê ji we da jî karek, *pîşeyek* tune** (FS:Boz. Kuřê mîrê masiyan) But not a single one you has a job or *a trade*. {also: p'êşe (K/FS-2)} Cf. Mid P pēšag = 'trade, craft; guild, caste' (M3); P pīše پیشه; Sor pîşe پیشه [IFb/Wkt/ZF3/BF/FS/FD//K]

pîşeger پیشەگەر (IFb) = artisan. See **p'îşek'ar**.

p'îşek'ar پیشەکار *m.&f.* **(-ê/;).** 1) {syn: sen'etkar} artisan, craftsman; 2) {syn: hunermend} artist; 3) servant, valet. {also: p'êşek'ar; pîşeger (IFb-2); [pīshkar] پیشکار (JJ)} Sor pîşeger پیشەگەر = 'craftsman' [Ber/K/JB3/IFb/GF/ZF3/FS//JJ]

p'îşesazî پیشەسازی *f.* **(-ya;-yê).** industry, manufacturing [Ar ṣinā'ah صناعة, T sanayi/endüstri, P ṣan'at صنعت]: **•Pêwîste êdî em fêhm bikin, cîvaka kû *şoreşa pîşesazîyê* ava kiribu di paş de maye** (civakademokratik.com 1.iii.2018) We must understand by now that the society which had created *the industrial revolution* has fallen behind **•*pîşesazîya* biçûk ji bo Kurdîstanê** (FB) *light industry* for Kurdistan. {syn: sen'et} Sor **pîşesazî** پیشەسازی [civakademokratik/IFb/GF/ZF3/Wkt/SS/CS]

pîşk پیشك (Hej) = rice husk. See **p'ûşk**.

p'ît I پیت *adj.* healthy, strong, robust, fit, hale and hearty [T dinç]: **•Şeş zarû anîbûn. Lê hê jî mîna bûkekî, rind û bedew û *pît* bû** (MB-Meyro) She had borne six children, but she was still beautiful, winsome, and *robust*, like a bride. {also: peyt (BF); pêt II (IFb-2/BF-2/FS/ZF)} [MB/IFb/FS//ZF//BF] <saẍ>

pît II پیت (A) = letter *(of alphabet)*. See **tîp**.

pîte پیته (M-Ak) = attention. See **p'ûte**.

pîvan پیڤان *vt.* **(-pîv-).** to measure: **•Ezê zêřêd xwe *bipîvim*, çika zêřê min çiqasin** (J) I *will measure* my gold [pieces], to see how much my gold is (=how much gold I have). {also: pîvandin (F/B-2/ IFb); pîwan (SK); [piwan] پیڤان (JJ)} OIr *pati- +*mā- (Tsb 42): Mid P paymūdan (paymāy-) (M3) & pad-māy-; P peymūdan پیمودن (-peymā-) (پیما); Sor pêwan پێوان/pîwan پیوان (Arb); Za peymenã [peymitiş] (Todd); Hau pîmay (pîm-) *vt.* (M4); ***mā-**: [Pok. mē-/m-e-t- 703.] 'to measure': Skt mā-; Av mā-; O P mā- [M/J/K/A/JB3/JJ/GF//F/IFb/B/ /SK] <fesilandin>

pîvandin پیڤاندِن (F/B/IFb) = to measure. See **pîvan**.

pîvaz پیڤاز *f.* **(-a;-ê).** onion: -**zîla pîvazê** (Wkt) onion sprout. {also: pîwaz (SK); pîzav (Kg/Mzg); [pivaz] پیواز (JJ); <pîvaz> پیڤاز (HH)} M. Schwartz: <O Ir *piyāv[a]- (Bailey: *Dictionary of Khotan Saka*. Cambridge, 1979) (+ *possible metathesis to* *pivāy-) + *suffix* -č: Khotanese pāu-; Sgd py'kh [pyākh]; Pamir dialects: Yazgulami piyeg; Wakhi piūk; P piyāz پیاز; Sor piyaz پیاز/ pêwaz پێواز; Za pyaz (Todd)/piyanz (Mal) *m.* [F/K/ A/JB3/IFb/B/HH/GF/Wkt//JJ//Kg/Mzg//SK] <k'ixs; sîr>

pîvazî پیڤازی *adj.* pink, rose-colored. <pîvaz = 'onion', cf. NENA sōγānī = 'pink' (<T soğan = 'onion') [Bw/ JB1-A/GF/OK/ZF3/FS]

pîvaztark پیڤازتارك (TF) = green onion. See **pîvazteřk**.

pîvazteřk پیڤازتەرك *f.* **(-a;-ê).** green onion, spring onion, bot. *Allium cepa:* **•Me mişara pêşîn kiriye *pîvazterk*. Me ya duyem kiriye bexdenûs** (K.Yildirim.Kurdî 6, 78) We made the first patch for *green onions*. We made the second one for parsley. {also: pîvaztark (TF)} <pîvaz + teř = 'wet, fresh'; Sor teřepiyaz تەرەپیاز [K.Yildirim/IFB/GF/Wkt/ZF3/BF/FS/ AA/CS//TF]

pîvik پیڤِك (Xrs) = tulip. See **pîvok**.

pîvok پیڤۆك *f.* **(;-ê).** *a term for several types of flower:* 1) {syn: canemerg [2]} crocus (A/IFb/ Haz); 2) tulip (Xrs) [pîvik]; edible tuberous plant the size of the hazelnut (IFb); 3) snowdrop, zool. *Galanthus nivalis* (B) [pîvonge: Rus podsnezhnik подснежник; 4) white plant with roots like those of the hazelnut (HH). {also: pîvik (Xrs); pîvong (GF-2/FS-2); pîvonge (B); [pivok] پیوك (JJ); <pîvok> پیڤوك (HH)} [Xrs//K/A/IFb/HH/GF/Haz/FS//JJ//B]

pîvong پیڤۆنگ (GF/FS) = snowdrop, zool. *Galanthus nivalis* (type of flower). See **pîvok**.

pîvonge پیڤۆنگە (B) = snowdrop, zool. *Galanthus nivalis* (type of flower). See **pîvok**.

pîwan پیوان (SK) = to measure. See **pîvan**.

pîwaz پیواز (SK) = onion. See **pîvaz**.

pîxamet پـیـخـامـەت (Elk) = because of; for the sake of. See **pêxemet**.

pîxemet پـیـخـەمـەت (FS) = because of; for the sake of. See **pêxemet**.

pîyale پییاله (A) = tea glass. See **p'eyale**.

pîyan پییان (TF) = tea glass. See **p'eyale**.

pîz پیز *m.* **(-ê;).** watercress, bot. *Nasturtium officinale*. {also: pûz (IFb/FS)} {syn: kîzmas; t'ûzik} [Bw//IFb/FS] <dêjnik; r̄eşad>

pîzav پیزاڤ (Kg/Mzg) = onion. See **pîvaz**.

poç'ik پۆچك (Dz-#897) = tail. See **boç'ik**.

p'ojman پۆژمان (K) = sorry. See **p'oşman**.

p'ojmanî پۆژمانی (K) = regret. See **p'oşmanî**.

p'ol I پـــۆل *m.* **().** coin. {also: pûl (IFb-2/SK); [poul] پول (JJ); <pol> پول (HH)} Sor pûl پوول = 'coin, money; postage stamp' [A/IFb/HH/GF/ZF3//JJ/SK] See also **p'olik I**.

p'ol II پـۆل *m.* **(-ê;).** shoulder, shoulder blade: •**Rima xwe hilanî û kire neqeba herdu *polê* wî de** (HR 3:74) He picked up his spear and thrust it between his [another's] *shoulder blades*. {also: [pōl پول/pil پـیـل] (JJ); <pol> پـول (HH)} {syn: navmil; pî I} Sor pûl پوول = 'scapula, shoulder blade' [HR/K/A/IFb/GF/TF/JJ/HH/CS/ZF3] <mil; pîl I>

p'ol III پـــــــــۆل *f.* **(-a;-ê).** class *(in school)*: -**pola yekemîn** (ZF)/~ **yekem** (RC2) first grade *(of elementary or primary school)*: •**Şagirtên Kurd ji van mamostan tiştek negirtine** [sic] **her di pola yekem da mane** (RC2. Ku heye Xwedê hiş bide gelê Kurd) Kurdish pupils have gotten nothing from these teachers, they have remained in the first grade. {syn: dersxane; sinif} < Sor pol پـــۆل = 'class, body of students studying same subject; flock (of birds); regiment (mil.)' [(neol)RC2/A/IFb/FJ/TF/RZ/ZF/SS] <dersxane; xwendegeh; xwendinxane>

p'ola/pola [K/B] پـــۆلا *m.(B)/f.(JB3)* **().** steel: -**ji pola** (B) made of steel: •**Ḧevt dergê bavê min hene ji polane** (Z-1) My father has 7 gates of steel. {also: p'olad; polat (IFb-2/B-2); pûla (SK); [pola پـــولا/poulad پولاد/pila پیلا] (JJ); <pola> پولا (HH)} Mid P pōlāwad (M3); P pūlād پـــــــولاد--> T polat, Ar fūlād فـــولاذ, Heb peladah פלדה, W Arm bołbad պողպատ; Sor poła پۆڵا; Za pola[t] *m.* (Mal); Hau poła *m.* (M4) [K/B//A/JB3/IFb/JJ/HH/GF//SK] <deban; hesin>

p'olad پۆلاد = steel. See **p'ola**.

polat پۆلات (IFb/B) = steel. See **p'ola**.

Polendayî پـۆلـەنـدایـی (BF/Wkt) = Polish, from Poland. See **P'olonî**.

Polendî پـــۆلـــەنـــدی (Wkt) = Polish, from Poland. See **P'olonî**.

p'olik I پـــۆلِـك *f.* **(;-ê).** copper coin or pendant, as an adornment to a woman's headdress *{k'ofî, qv.}*; small coin, farthing: •**Bira zêr̄ hildidin, paşda vedigerin. R̄êva ew dinihêr̄in, wekî ew zêr̄ t'emam *polkê* qelpin** (Ba3-3, #23) The brothers take the gold [coins] and head back. On the way they see that all *the gold coins* are counterfeit [lit. 'that the golds are counterfeit coins']. {also: polk (Ba3-3); [poulik] پـــولـــك (JJ)} [Ba3//K/B//JJ] See also **p'ol**.

polik II پـــۆلِـــك *f.* **(-a;).** pea(s), bot. *Pisum sativum*. {also: lobik (CB-2); lopik (GF/OK/AA); [polik پـلـك/lupék لـوپـك] (JJ); <lopik> لۆپك (Hej)} {syn: gilol II; kelî I} Sor połke پۆڵکە [Kmc-6/K/IFb/JJ/CB//GF/OK/Hej/AA] <kizin; lowûk; maş; şolik>

polk پۆلك (Ba3-3) = coin. See **p'olik I**.

P'olonî پـــۆلـــۆنـــی *adj.* Polish, from Poland. {also: Polendayî (BF/Wkt-2); Polendî (Wkt-2); Polonyayî (Wkt-2/ZF3-2)} Sor Połendî پـۆڵـەنـدی [Wkt/ZF3/BF/SS/CS//BF]

Polonyayî پۆلۆنیایی (Wkt/ZF3) = Polish, from Poland. See **P'olonî**.

pol poşman پـۆل پـۆشـمـان (GF) = disappointed; sorry. See **p'or̄ II: p'or̄ û p'oşman**.

poncîn پۆنجین (OK) = to think. See **p'onijîn** [2].

p'onijîn پۆنژین *vi.* **(-p'onij-).** 1) {syn: hênijîn [1]} to doze, nap: •**Ewî serê xwe berjêr kir û *p'onijî*** (FK-eb-1) He put down his head and *dozed off*; 2) {also: poncîn (OK)} {syn: duşirmîş bûn; fikirîn I [1]; hizir kirin; r̄aman I} to think, ponder (A/IFb): •**Gelek *ponijiye* (fikiriye), ku gelo çima rengê hêkên wê reş in** (Wlt 1:37, 13) She *thought* for a long time [about] why her eggs [lit. 'the color of her eggs'] were black •**Lê eger mirov li gor mentiq *biponije* bersîva vê pirsê dikare bi kurtî wisa bête dayîn** (ŞBS, 61) But if one *thinks* logically, that question can briefly be answered like this. {also: p'oniştin (K[s]-2); <ponjîn پونژین (diponjî) (دپونژی)> (HH)} [K(s)/A/IFb/(GF)/TF/OK//HH] <xilmaş>

p'oniştin پۆنشتِن (K[s]) = to doze. See **p'onijîn**.

p'or̄ I پـــــــۆڕ *f.* **(;-ê).** francolin, type of quail, zool. *Francolinus*; blackcock, wood grouse [Germ

Haselhuhn] (OK). Sor por̄ پۆڕ = 'francolin, black-partridge' [Bw/IFb/GF/OK/FS] <‘ebdal; kew I; k’êr̄asû>

p’or̄ II پۆڕ: **-p’or̄ û p’oşman** پۆڕ و پۆشمان *adj.* 1) disappointed, despairing; 2) regretful, sorry. {also: pol poşman (GF); p’or û p’ojman (K); p’or-p’oşman} [B//GF//K]

p’or̄ III پــــۆڕ *m.* **().** hair (coll.), head of hair; hair on the head *as opposed to* ***pirç’*** *= hair of the body from the neck down (Haz);* ***p’or̄*** *is made up of many individual strands of* ***mû*** *(qv.)*; hair of the head when it is long (HH): •***Por*** **xemla keçan e** (AB) *Hair* is the ornament of girls; **-p’or̄ şe kirin** (B) to comb s.o.'s hair; **-p’or̄ê kurîşkî** (B) curly hair; **-p’or̄ê r̄êş** (B) black hair; **-p’or̄ê xwe kur̄ kire**! (XF) May she lose her closest [male] relatives [curse:*{indicates a wish that she lose her male relatives, and cut her hair while mourning them}* Cf. p’or̄kur̄]: •**Ez nizanim saxe yan mirîye ... Weyla min** ***p’or̄ê xwe kur̄kire***! (XF) I don't know if he's alive or dead *...woe is me.* ; **-p’or̄ê zer** (B) light hair. {also: [por] پور (JJ); <pûr> پور (HH)} {syn: t’ûk I} [AB/K/A/JB3/IFb/B/JJ/GF/ZF3//HH] <bisk; gijik; gulî I; kezî; mû; pirç’; şeh; t’ûk I; t’ûncik>

p’or̄kur̄ پۆڕکوڕ *adj.* 1) shaved, with short hair *(said of a woman)* (K); 2) [*f.*] a woman or girl bereft of male relatives (K); curse said to a woman *{indicates a wish that she lose her male relatives, and cut her hair while mourning them}* (IF); 3) unlucky, miserable woman (K) •**Zînê tûyî, hêsîr,** ***p’or̄kur̄*** **Memo ezim** (Z-3) You are Zîn, miserable, *short-haired*, I am Mem.{also: porkurê (IF)} [Z-3/K//IF]

porkurê پــۆڕکــوری (IF) = woman with short hair. See **p’or̄kur̄.**

p’or-p’oşman پۆڕپۆشمان = disappointed; sorry. See **p’or̄ II: p’or̄ û p’oşman**.

Portegîzî پــۆرتــهگــیــزی (Wkt) = Portuguese. See **P’ortugalî**.

Portekîzî پــۆرتــهکــیــزی (ZF3) = Portuguese. See **P’ortugalî**.

porteqal پۆرتەقال (IFb/Kmc-2/RZ/CB) = orange. See **p’irteqal**.

p’ortoẍal پۆرتۆغال (K/JJ) = orange. See **p’irteqal**.

P’ortugalî پۆرتوگالی *adj.* Portuguese. {also: Portegîzî (Wkt-2); Portekîzî (ZF3); Portuxalî (Wkt-2); Portûgalî (Wkp)} Sor Purtugalî پورتوگالی [Wkt/BF/SS//Wkp//ZF3]

Portuxalî پــۆرتــوخــالــی (Wkt) = Portuguese. See **P’ortugalî**.

Portûgalî پــۆرتــووگــالــی (Wkp) = Portuguese. See **P’ortugalî**.

p’or û p’ojman پــۆر و پــۆژمــان (K) = disappointed; sorry. See **p’or̄ II: p’or̄ û p’oşman**.

p’osîde پــۆســیــده *adj.* troubled, upset, sad, sorry: •***Pûsîde*:** **her dem bi xeman mijûl e** (A.Kızılkaya.BûkaBaranê, 111) *Pûsîde*: always busy worrying. {also: p’ûsîde (Hk/A.Kızılkaya)} Cf. P pūsīda پوسیده = ‘rotten, worn out’ [Hk/Kızılkaya//ZF/Wkt/BF/FD] <p’oşman>

p’osîdeyî پــۆســیــدهیــی *f.* **().** being troubled or upset, sorrow: •**Kenîn ji bo çakkirina rewşê mirovî hatiye himberî girî û** ***posîdeyî*** **û dilgiraniyê** (E.Zero. Tir̄ane û pêkenîn li cem milletan, 2) Laughter has come to improve a person’s condiiton, as opposed to crying and *being troubled* and heaviness of heart. [E.Zero] <p’oşmanî>

post (IFb/GF/OK/Ba2/TG2)/p’ost (F/K) پۆست = skin, hide. See **pîst**.

p’ostaxane پــۆســتــاخــانــه (TF/ZF3) = post office. See **p’ostexane**.

p’ostexane پــۆســتــهخــانــه *f.* **(-ya;-yê).** post office: •***Postexaneya*** **herî nêzîk li kû ye?** (Sözlüklü Kürtçe konuşma kılavuzu, 40) Where is the nearest post office? {also: p’ostaxane (TF/ZF3); p’ostxane (K/BF)} [IFb/GF/RZ/FD/SS/CS//TF/ZF3//K/BF]

p’ostxane پــۆســتــخــانــه (K/BF) = post office. See **p’ostexane**.

p’oşî پــۆشــی *m./f.(ZF3/FS)* **(/-ya; /-yê).** 1) Kurdish man's headdress or turban, often made of silk; 2) black head kerchief worn by Kurdish women (HH/GF/FS). {also: pûşî (A/GF-2); [posh پــوش/ pushī پــوشــی] (JJ); <poşî> پــوشــی (HH)} {syn: cemedanî; dersok; kevîng; şemil} [K/IFb/GF/HH/FS/ZF3//A/JJ] <hêratî; k’ofî; k’um; laç’ik; xavik>

poşîman پۆشیمان (IFb) = sorry. See **p’oşman**.

p’oşman پــۆشــمــان *adj.* sorry, regretful, penitent: **-p’oşman bûn** (B) to regret, be sorry (for doing stg.) [+ **ji**]: •**‘Emer Aẍa qrarê xwe** ***p’oşman bûye*** (FK-kk-13:131) Omar Agha *regretted* his decision •**S̱ofî ‘Ebdullah Şikak û muroêt wî gelek li Wanê [r̄ûniştin] ... pîwazek bo wan ḧasil nebû. Gelek** ***peşîman bûn*****, gotin** [sic], **"Ewe çi gû bû me xarî!"** (SK 48:511) Sofi Abdullah Shikak and his men sat in Van for a long time … but not an onion did they get. They *were* most *regretful*, saying, "What dung we have eaten!"; **-p'oř û p'oşman** = disappointed, despairing: **•K'esîv řadive *p'oř-p'oşman* tê mala xwe** (Z-922) The poor man gets up and comes home, *all disappointed.* {also: peşêman (Bw); peşîman (SK); p'ojman (K); poşîman (IFb2); [pochiman] پشيمان (JJ)} <O Ir *pasča = 'after' + √man- = 'to think' ('after-pondering': Hübsch #312): Mid P pašēmān = 'penitent, repentant' (M3); P pāšīmān پاشيمان/pežmān پژمان --> T pişman; Sor peşîman پەشیمان = 'contrite, repentant, regretful' {p'ojmanî; poşmanî; [pochimani] پشيمانى (JJ)} [Z-922/A/JB3/B/IFb/GF/TF//K//JJ//SK//Bw] <melûl; p'osîde; zelûl>

p'oşmanî پۆشمانی *f.* **(-ya;-yê).** sorrow, regret; repentance. {also: peşîmanî (SK); p'ojmanî (K); [pochimani] پشيمانى (JJ)} Mid P pašēmānīh = 'penitence, repentance' (M3) [A/JB3/IFb/B/TF/ZF//K//JJ//SK] <melûlî; p'osîdeyî; p'oşman; zelûlî>

p'ot پۆت *m.* **(-ê;).** 1) {syn: kerkon; kevnik; p'aç' II; p'ate II; pertal; pîne; qerpal} rag; 2) shabby, threadbare overcoat: **•Birayo, go, ev k'incê min ji teřa, şe'lekî kevin, *p'otekî* kevin bide min ez xwekim. Şivîn *p'otê* xwe êxist, şe'lê xwe êxist** (HCK-1, 205) Brother, she said, here are my clothes for you; give me an old pair of trousers, an old *overcoat*, that I can put on. The shepherd took off his *overcoat*, took off his pants. [HCK/K/B/GF/FJ]

p'otîn پۆتین *f.(ZF3)/m.(AD)* **(-a/;).** work boots, army boots. {syn: sapok} [Krç/K(s)/IFb/GF/AD/ZF3]

poxan پۆخان *f.* **(;-ê).** garbage dump, dung heap: **•Keçelok ... rabû çû li ser *poxanên* gundiyan geriya, çi kaxezên dîtin hemû berev kirin û hanîn malê** (ZZ-4, 245) The bald boy ... went around to *the garbage heaps of* the villagers, and gathered all the paper he found and brought it home **•Wezîr çû ser *poxanê* qutîkek dît** (ZZ-&, 264) The vizier went to *the junk heap* and found a little box. {syn: axpîn; sergo; ting} [ZZ/CS/ZF]

p'oxîn پۆخین *f.* **(;-ê).** *pekhun/pokhin*, a dish made of roasted wheat ground into flour; a sweet made with flour, butter, and sugar (IF) [T un helvası]; a sweet pastry (JJ) [pâte douce]: **•Hine rûnê min hebû min anî teřa kire *p'êxûn*** (Dz) [If] I had some butter I would bring [it and] make you *pekhun.* {also: p'êxûn (Dz); p'oxîn (K-2); [pokhin] پوخين (JJ); <poxîn> پوخين (HH)} Cf. W Arm p'oxint փոխինդ [Dz//K/A/IFb/B/JJ/HH/GF]

p'oxîn پۆغین (K) = dish made of roasted wheat ground into flour. See **p'oxîn**.

poz I پۆز *m.* **(-ê;).** nose: **-anîn serê pozê *fk-î*** (Kmc) to be fed up, sick and tired, angry: **•Vê tisqîtî û neheqîya Xudo sebra Eto êdî *anî serê pozê wî*** (W.Eşo. Sîber, 47) Kh.'s nastiness and injustice *was the last straw for* E.; **-bîn pozê *fk-ê* k'etin** (Dz) to catch a smell/scent of, to smell stg.: **•Nişkêva *bîna* k'ivava *k'ete pozê* wan** (Dz) Suddenly they *smelled* kebabs [lit. 'The smell of kebabs fell on their noses']; **-pozê xwe paqiş/t'emiz kirin** (B) to blow one's nose. {also: [boz بوز/poz پوز] (JJ); <poz> پوظ (HH)} {syn: bêvil[2]; difn; kepî[1]; =Sor lût لووت} Cf. Mid P pōz(ag) (M3) = 'snout, muzzle'; P pūz(e) پوز(ه) = 'snout'; Sor poz پۆز = 'muzzle (nose and mouth)' [F/K/JB3/IFb/B/JJ/GF//HH]

poz II پۆز *f.* **(-a;).** anus; backside, rump. {syn: qûn} [Bw/Zeb/FS]

pozbilind پۆزبلند *adj.* arrogant, haughty, stuck up, conceited. {syn: difnbilind; nefsmezin; quře} {pozbilindî} [K/IFb/B/GF/TF/ZF]

pozbilindî پۆزبلندی *f.* **(-ya;-yê).** arrogance, haughtiness, pride. [K/IFb/B/GF] <pozbilind>

p'ronav پرۆناڤ *f.(K)/m.(IFb)* **(-a/-ê;).** pronoun: **-pronava girêkî** (K) relative pronoun (i.e., ko); **-pronavê hevdutîyê** (IF) reciprocal pronoun (i.e., hev); **-pronava işarkî** (K) demonstrative pronoun (i.e., ev & ew); **-pronava k'esîn** (K) personal pronoun; **-pronava pirsyarkî** (K) interrogative pronoun (i.e., kî & ç'i). {syn: bedelnav; cînav} <Lat pro = 'for' + nav = 'name, noun' [(neol)K/A/JB3/IFb/GF]

prot پرۆت (GF) = potter. See **p'irûd**.

pşîk پشيك = cat. See **p'isîk**.

p'udu پودو (B/SC) = gums; palate. See **p'idî**.

purç'u پورچو (EH) = frown. See **p'irçû**.

p'ûç'/p'ûç پووچ *adj.* 1) empty, hollow (K/B/JB1-S); without seed or kernel *(of nuts, grain, etc.)* (B/HH/A); with a rotten seed or kernel (HH); 2) {syn: bêkêr; qels I[3]} worthless, useless *(of people)* (K/B/SK); clumsy (IF); silly, vain, devoid of content (K/JB1-S); 3) {syn: petot; řizî} rotten (Msr/JJ/JB1-S); ruined, spoiled: **-pûç [pîç] kirin** (Bw) to ruin, spoil, mess up {syn: xirab kirin}. {also: p'îç[4] (Bw); [poutch] پوچ (JJ); <pûç> پوچ (HH)} Sor pûç پووچ = 'empty, silly' [Msr/RN/K/A/JB3/IFb/ B/JJ/HH/JB1-S/SK/GF/Bw] <cilq>

pûjan پووژان *f.* **(-a;-ê).** mint, bot. *Mentha arvensis.*

{also: pîjan (MG/IFb); [poujan] پـوژان (JJ)} {syn: pûng; tihtavik} [MG//IFb/Kmc/JJ/CS/ZF]

pûl پوول (IFb/SK) = coin. See **p'ol I**.

pûla پوولا (SK) = steel. See **p'ola**.

pûn پـوون *vt.* **(-pû-).** to tan *(hides)*, dress *(pelts)*: •**Wî eyarê gîskî *pûyî*** (FS) He *tanned* the goat hide. {also: pûyîn (BX-2/Kmc-2/CS-2/FS)} {syn: *debax kirin} [BX/FJ/GF/Kmc/ZF/CS//FS]

pûng پـوونـگ *f.* **(-a;-ê).** 1) {syn: pûjan; tihtavik} mint *(plant)*, bot. *Mentha*; 2) basil (HH). {also: [pounk] پونك (JJ); <pûnk> پونك (HH)} Cf. P pūne پونه; Sor punge پونگه [S&E/K/A/IFb/B/GF//HH/JJ]

pûpû پـووپـوو *f.* **(;-yê).** *type of bird:* 1) {also: **pepûk II**[1]} cuckoo, zool. *Cuculus canorus* (B); 2) owl (ZF3). Cf. P pūpū پوپو [B/ZF3]

p'ûrt پـــــــوورت *f.* **(-a;-ê).** 1) feathers, plumage; 2) eiderdown, soft and fluffy feathers: •**Belkîs jê xwest ko ji *pûrta* teyran jê re nivîneke çêke** (SW) Belkis asked him to make a bed for her out of down [lit. '*the down of* birds']; 3) fur, hair *(of animals)*; 4) short wool (IF). {also: [pourt] پـورت (JJ); <pûrt> پـــــورت (HH)} <W Arm purt բուրդ [SW/K/JB3/IF/B/JJ/HH]

p'ûrtikandin پوورتِکاندِن *vt.* **(-p'ûrtikîn-).** to pull out, pluck *(feathers, from a bird)*: •**Kêfa min ji *pirtikandina* kewan re pir tê** (ZZ-7, 262) I very much like *to pluck* partridges. {also: pirtikandin (IFb-2/TF/ZF); [pourtkandin] (JJ)} {syn: p'eȓitandin [3]; ȓûç'ikandin} [ZZ/TF/ZF//K/IFb/JJ] <p'ûrt>

p'ûsîde پـووسـيـده (Hk/A.Kızılkaya) = troubled, sorry. See **p'osîde**.

p'ûş I/pûş [K] پـــــووش *m.* **(-ê;).** hay, dry grass; dry leaves; unmowed grass that grows in a meadow (JJ): •**Kê ḧedd hebû ji qirşekî ḧetta *pûşekî* tiştekî bêjite wî?** (SK 36:323) Who would have dared to say anything [lit. 'from shavings to *dry grass*'] to him? •**Rabû *p'ûşê* hêlîna ç'ivîkê ji ç'e'vê wî derxist** (EP-5, #18) She removed *the dry grass of* the bird nest from his eyes; **-pûş û pelax** = dry grass and tree leaves (IFb); straw. {also: [pouche] پـــــوش (JJ)} Sor pûş پـــــووش = 'withered grass, hay' [L/IFb/JJ/SK/GF/OK/ZF3//K] <ka I>

pûş II پووش (JB3) = liver. See **p'iş I**[3].

pûşî پووشی (A/GF) = Kurdish headdress. See **p'oşî**.

p'ûşk پويشك/پـووشـك *m.* **().** rice husk after it has been removed from the rice. {also: <pîşk> پيشك (Hej)} [Zeb/OK//Hej] <birinc I; ç'eltûk; tûşk>

P'ûşpeȓ پووشپـهڕ. A Sorani name for Persian month of *Tīr* تـيـر [Cancer] (June 21-July 22). See chart of Kurdish months in this volume. <Ḧezîran; Tîrmeh>

p'ûşt پووشت *m.&f.* **(; /-ê).** *pejorative term*: catamite, slanderer, dolt *(of males)*; slut *(of females)*: •**Qe k'êfê qîza min çine? Go:--Be'sa wê *p'ûştê* nekî nave?** (HCK-1, 201) "How is my daughter doing? [lit. 'what are my daughter's conditions/ pleasures?']" "Would you mind not talking about that *slut*?". Sor puşt پوشت = 'catamite' [HCK-1/IFb/FJ/GF] <forq; me'ȓis; qab II; sebav>

p'ût I پـــــــــــــــووت *m.* **(-ê;).** dried winter fodder for domestic animals : •**Îsal *pûtê* terşê me bese** (Haz) This year we have enough *winter fodder* for our cattle [lit. 'this year the fodder of our cattle is enough']. {also: [pouti پوتی/pout پوت] (JJ); <pût> پوت (HH)} Sor pût پووت = 'hay stacked for winter fodder' [Haz/A/IFb/JJ/HH/GF] <alif; alîk I; çilo II; êm>

p'ût II پـــووت *f.* **(;-ê).** pood, unit of weight, 16.38 kg or ± 36 lb.: •**Heȓe fȓinê weke sê *p'ût* loş bîne … Du-sê *p'ût* nanê loş anî** (HCK-3, #2, 22) Go to the oven and bring 3 *poods* of lavash … He brought 2-3 *poods* of lavash bread. < Rus pud пуд [HCK/K/B/GF]

p'ûte پويته/پووته *f.* **().** concern, care, attention, regard, interest: **-pûte pê kirin** (Bw/Dh/IFb/GF/OK) to pay attention to, care for, take an interest in: •**Pismam, ez a tbînim eto *pîte p* min *nakey*, eto yê çûye bajera, bîladêt mazin, ete jinêt cwan yêt dîtîn, noke te ez nevêm** (M-Ak #633, 286) Cousin, I see that you *are not interested in* me, you have been to towns and great countries and seen beautiful women, now you do not want me. {also: pîte (M-Ak); cf [pouti dàin] پـوتـی دايـن (JJ) = 'to board an animal during the winter' (i.e., to care for it, give it special attention?)} {syn: 'elaqe; ḧewas; meraq} [Bw/Dh/IFb/GF/OK//M-Ak]

pûyîn پـوويـيـن (BX/Kmc/CS/FS) = to tan *(hides)*. See **pûn**.

pûz پووز (IFb/FS) = watercress. See **pîz**.

pyenc پيهنج (S&E) = five. See **pênc**.

pyênc پيێنج (S&E) = five. See **pênc**.

Q ق

qab I قـــاب *f.* **(-a;-ê).** 1) {syn: kalan} sheath, scabbard *(of sword)*: **•Şûrê xwe bikine *qavêd* wan û guh bidine ser min** (Z-1) Put your swords in their *sheaths* and listen to me; 2) {syn: qut'î; sindoq} case, container, box. {also: qav I (B/Z-1); [qab] قاب (JJ)} [Z-1/B//K/JJ/GF] <qebd; şûr>

qab II قـــاب *m.* **().** 1) {syn: forq} profligate, libertine: **•Çavê te çavê *qeĥbaye*** (Msr) You have the eyes of a *profligate (said in admiration to a womanizer)*; 2) [*f.* **(-a;-ê).**] {syn: qalt'ax [3]; qûnek [2]} prostitute, whore. {also: qav II (B); qaxpe (B-2); qehbe (K[s]); qehpe (GF); qeĥb (Msr); qexpe (IFb); [qahb قحب/qahbé قحبه] (JJ); <qeĥb> قحب (HH)} < Ar qaḥbah قـحـبـة = 'whore, harlot' --> T kahpe; Sor qeĥbe قەحبە = 'harlot' {qab[t]î; qav[t]î; qehbetî} [FK-1/K//B//(K[s])//GF//IFb//JJ/HH] <p'ûşt; qebrax>

qabî قابى (FK-eb-1) = adultery; prostitution. See **qabtî**.

qabtî قابتى *f.* **(;-yê).** 1) adultery: **-qabtî kirin** (K) = a) to commit adultery; b) to be a prostitute; 2) prostitution. {also: qabî (FK-eb-1); qabtî (K); qavî (B-2); qavtî (B); qehbetî (K[s])} [FK-1//K//B//K(s)]

qac قاج (IFb) = pine tree. See **kac**.

qaçaq قاچاق (SK) = fugitive; robber. See **qaç'ax**.

qaç'ax قـــاچـــاخ *m.&f.* **(/-a;-î/).** 1) {syn: firar; r̄evî; *r̄evok(e) (IF)} fugitive, runaway: **•Emê pey *qaçaxa* jina min k'evin** (HCK-1, 206) We will go after my *runaway* wife; 2) robber, brigand (B): **•Nevêjin K'ulik bir, bêjin *qaçaxa* bir** (FK-kk-13:129) Don't say that Kulik took her, say that *robbers* took her. {also: qaçaq (SK); qaçax̂ (B)} < Az T qaçaq = 'fugitive; contraband' [HB/K/IFb/GF//B//SK]

qaç'axçî قـاچـاخـچـى *m.* **(-yê;).** smuggler, bootlegger: **•Neco û *qaçaxçiyên* din dema ji ser xetê vedigeriyan barên wan giran bûn, hinek pere didan serbazê leşkerên nobedar, wan jî du-sê deqeyan çavên xwe digirtin heta *qaçaxçî* derbas dibûn** (Nofa, 90) When N. and the other *smugglers* would return over the border their loads were heavy, they gave some money to the border guards on duty, they would close their eyes for 2-3 minutes until the *smugglers* passed **•*Qaçaxçiyan* bi qaçaxî zelamek li tixûbî derbas kir** (FS) The *smugglers* sneaked a man across the border. {also: qaçax̂çî (FS-2)} <T kaçak + -çı [Nofa/GF/Wkt/FS/CS]

qaçax̂ قاچاغ (B) = fugitive; robber. See **qaç'ax**.

qaçax̂çî قاچاغچى (FS) = smuggler. See **qaç'axçî**.

qaçor قاچۆر (GF) = animal tax. See **qamçûr̄**.

qad قاد *f.* **(-a;-ê).** field, open space: **-qada şer̄** (K/GF)/ ~ **şerî** (IFb) battlefield, battleground: **•Refên me bi ser *qada şerî* re firiyane** (RN) Our squadrons flew over *the battlefield.* [RN/K/JB3/IFb/GF/TF] <meydan>

qadî قادى (GF) = judge. See **qazî**.

qaf قاف (A/IFb/B/GF/HH) = skull; top, peak. See **qehf**.

qafiye قـافـيـه *f.* **(-ya;-yê).** rhyme: **•Li Kurdî da jî ji *qafiyeyê* ra paşbend û paşhel gotine** (Chn, 55) In Kurdish, for *qafiye* (rhyme), they have also said paşbend and paşhel **•Serwa di şûna peyva *qafiyeyê* de tê bikaranîn û ji aliyê etîmolojiyê ve têkiliya wan bi hev re heye** (Adak, 358) Serwa is used instead of the word *qafiye* [=rhyme], and from the point of view of etymology, they are related to each other. {also: qafî (IFb-2/FJ)} {syn: beşavend; paşbend; serwa} < Ar qāfiyah قـافـيـة = 'rhyme'; Sor qafiye قافیه [Adak/Chn/IFb/ZF//FJ]

qafî قافى (IFb/FJ) = rhyme. See **qafiye**.

qail قائِل (JB3) = willing; satisfied. See **qayîl**.

qailî قائِلى (JB3) = willingness. See **qayîlî**.

qaîl قائيل (F/A) = willing; satisfied. See **qayîl**.

qaîltî قائيلتى (A) = willingness. See **qayîlî**.

qaîş قائيش (A) = leather belt. See **qayîş**.

qaj قاژ (IFb) = pine tree. See **kac**.

qajeqaj قـاژەقاژ *f.* **(-a;-ê).** noise, din, commotion: **•Bû *qajeqaja* zarokan... Hawara wan gihîşt ezmanan** (trtnûçe.com 14.xi.2015) *The loud noise of* children could be heard...Their cries reached the heavens. {syn: galegûrt; galigal[4]; hêwirze; hose; k'im-k'imî; qalmeqal; qareqar; qerebalix; qîr̄eqîr̄; şerqîn; t'eqer̄eq} [F/IFb/GF/BF/ZF3]

qal I قـــــال *f.* **(-a;-ê).** topic, subject: **-qala *fk-ê/ft-î* kirin** = to talk or speak about or of, to discuss {syn: beĥs kirin}: **•Belê, ez dixwazim pêşî ji we re piçekî *qala* planên xwe yên nivîsandinê *bikim*** (LC, 11) Yes, I want first *to tell* you a little bit about my writing plans **•Ferzo û Biro *qala* hev *dikir* = Ferzo and Biro *were speaking about* each other •**Rojekê wezîrên wî jê re *qala* ziwacê *kirin*** [sic] (SW) One day his viziers *broached the subject of* marriage (or, spoke to him of marriage). {also: [qal] قـال (JJ)} < Ar qāla قـال = 'he said, to say' [K/A/JB3/IFb/B/JJ/ZF3]

qal II قـال *adj.* pure, refined *(gold or silver)*: •**Wextê kevokê zêr xwend, derĥal ç'e'vê bavê wî bûne weke zêrê *qal*, r̄iĥet bûn** (HR 3:204) When the golden dove sang, the father's eyes immediately became like *pure* gold, they were eased; **-qal bûn** (HH/FJ/GF) to be purified or refined *(gold or silver)*; **-qal kirin** (A/JJ/HH/GF) to purify or refine *(gold or silver)*. {also: [qal] قـال (JJ); <qal> قـال (HH)} Cf. P qāl قـال = 'refining, purification or assaying of metals'; Sor qał قـاڵ = 'pure, refined' [HR/K/A/IFb/JJ/HH/GF/FJ/FS]

qalax قالاخ (A/IFb/GF) = pressed dung. See **qelax**.

qalç'ik قـالـچك, m. (; qêlç'ik) (K/B) = shell, rind, peel; scab. See **qalik**.

qalç'ix قالچخ = shell, rind, peel; scab. See **qalik**.

qalen قالەن (A) = bride-price. See **qelen**.

qalib قـالِـب *m.* **(-ê; qêlib, vî qalibî).** 1) {syn: qurs} form, mold; bar *(of soap, etc.)*: •**Ĥiş û aqilê min çû, *qalib* ma cîda** (Z-1) My sense and mind went, *an empty body or shell* [lit. 'mold'] remained in [its] place; **-qalibê sabûn** (IF) bar of soap; 2) boot-tree, last (B). {also: [qalib] قـالـب (JJ)} < Ar qālib قالب [Z-1/K/B/IFb/JJ/ZF]

qal•ik قـالِـك *f.(K)/m.(B/JB3)* **(/•kê; /qêlik, vî qalikî).** 1) {syn: qaşil [2]; qelp II; tîvil} shell, rind, peel, skin *(of fruit, nut, egg)*: **-qalik kirin** (B) to peel, shell; **-qalkê hêkê** (Haz) eggshell; 2) scab (B). {also: qalç'ik, m. (; qêlç'ik) (K-2/B-2); qalç'ix; [qalik] قالك (JJ); <qalik> قالك (HH)} [HB/A/JB3/IFb/B/JJ/HH/GF/Haz//K]

qalim قالِم (EH) = thick; tight. See **qalin**.

qalimayî قالِمايى (K) = thickness. See **qalinî**.

qalimî قالِمى (K) = thickness. See **qalinî**.

qalin قالِن *adj.* 1) thick, coarse, rough; fat: •**Dengê dya me zirave, lê ê evê *qaline*** (J) Our mother's voice is soft, but this one's is *rough*; **-qalin bûn** (B) to grow thick or fat; **-qalin kirin** (B) to thicken; **-t'êlê qalin** (B) heavy thread; 2) {syn: ĥişk [2]; meĥkem} tight, firm *(grip)*: •**Ewî dîsa *qalim* bi lingê teyr girt** (EH) Once again he held on *tightly* to the bird's leg. {also: qalim (EH); qalind I (IFb/GF/ZF3/Wkt); [qalyn] قالن (JJ); <qalin قالن/qalind قالند> (HH)} < T kalın = 'thick' {qalimayî; qalimî; qalinayî; qalin[t]î} [J/K/JJ/B/HH//IFb/GF/ZF3/Wkt//EH]

qalinayî قالِنايى (K/B) = thickness. See **qalinî**.

qalind I قـالِـنـد (IFb/HH/GF/ZF3/Wkt) = thick. See **qalin**.

qalind II قالِند (HB) = bride-price. See **qelen**.

qalindî قالِندى (ZF3/Wkt) = thickness. See **qalinî**.

qalinî قـالِـنـى *f.* **(-ya;-yê).** thickness, coarseness, roughness: •***Qalindîya* berfê jî nêzîkî 2 metreyan bû** (www.ku.ilkha.com 5.iii.2018) *The thickness of* the snow was nearly 2 meters. {also: qalimayî (K-2); qalimî (K); qalinayî (K-2/B); qalindî (ZF3/Wkt); qalintî (B-2)} [K//B//ZF3/Wkt] <qalin>

qalintî قالِنتى (B) = thickness. See **qalinî**.

qalmeqal قـالـمـەقـال *f.* **(-a;-ê).** noise. {also: qalmeqalm (B-2)} {syn: galegûrt; galigal[4]; hêwirze; hose; k'im-k'imî; qajeqaj; qareqar; qerebalix; qîr̄eqîr̄; şerqîn; t'eqer̄eq} [F/B/GF/ZF3/FS]

qalmeqalm قالمەقالم (B) = noise. See **qalmeqal**.

qaloçk قالۆچك (FS) = small sickle. See **qalûnç**.

qalt'ax قـالـتـاخ *m.* **(-ê;).** 1) pommel *(of saddle)* (K); 2) bow-shaped tool used by saddlers [Fr arçon] (JJ); 3) [*f.* **(-a;-ê).**] {syn: qab II; qûnek [2]} whore, harlot, slut: •***Qalt'ax* ji te *qalt'axtir* jî p'eyda nabî** (Z-3) There is nowhere to be found *a slut sluttier* than you. {also: [qaltaq] قـلـتـق (JJ)} <T kaltak = 'whore; saddletree' [Z-3/K/IFb/ZF3//JJ]

qalûc قـالـووج, f. (-a;) (Mlt-Akçadağ/Mrş-Pazarcık) = small sickle. See **qalûnç**.

qalûç قالووچ (A/IFb/ZF3) = small sickle. See **qalûnç**.

qalûnç قـالـوونچ *m./f.(ZF3)* **(-ê/-a; /-ê).** 1) small sickle [T orak]: •**Wî giya bi *qaloçkê* dirû** (FS) He mowed the grass with *a small sickle*; 2) small hammer (Mzg). {also: qaloçk (FS); qalûc, f. (-a;) (Mlt-Akçadağ/Mrş-Pazarcık); qalûç (A/IFb/ZF3)} [Krş/Mzg//A/IFb/ZF3//FS//Mlt/Mrş] <das; diryas; şalok>

qam قـام *f.* **(-a;-ê).** 1) {syn: bejn; qedqamet} height, stature: •**Remilê bikol, li gora *qama* xwe** (L) Dig [a hole in] the sand as deep as your *height* [lit. 'according to your height']; **-ji qamê derê** (Slv) excessive(ly), too much; 2) water that goes no higher than one's neck (when one stands in a pool of water) (Haz). {also: qamet (K/SK); [qam قـام/ qamet قـامـت] (JJ); <qamet> قـامـت (HH)} <Ar qāmah قامة [L/IFb/JJ/JB1-S/FS//K/HH/SK/Haz]

qambil قامبِل (Nsb) = opposite; opposed. See **miqabil**.

qamçî قامچى *m.* **(-yê ; qêmçî).** 1) whip: **-qamçî kirin** (B) to lash, whip; 2) whipping, lash(es) with a whip: •...**û *çend qamçîya* davêje wê** (Ba-1, #26) ...and he gives her *several whippings* •**Paşî van qamçîya** (Ba-1, #27) After those whippings. {also: [qamtchi] قـامـچـى (JJ); <qamçî> قـامـچـى (HH)} < T kamçı [Z-922/K/A/IFb/B/JJ/HH/GF//ZF]

qamçur قامچور (TF) = animal tax. See **qamçûr̄**.

qamçûr̄ قامچوور *f.* **(-a;-ê).** tax, animal tax; "The agha [or tribal chief] collects certain taxes on the tribe's internal affairs, notably on the sale of livestock: These taxes are called **qemçor** ..." (LY, p. 164, body of text & note 2 [*my translation*]): •**Ezê van p'erê hûr bibim *qamçûr̄a* paz** (Z-2) I will take this small change [to pay] *the tax on* our sheep •**Li gor vê hijmarê, *qamçûr* li çar serî pezê te dikeve ... dema tu êvarê vedigerî, wek mafê qamçûrê, wê çaxê tu ê çar bizinan ji me re veqetînî** (Ardû, 114-5) According to this number [of sheep], your *animal tax* amounts to 4 animals from your flock ... when you return in the evening, as the duty of tax [?], you can pick out 4 goats for us then. {also: qaçor (GF); qamçur (TF); qemçor (LY); xemçûr (IF-2)} Cf. Arm xamč'ur խամչուր/xap'č'ur խափչուր = 'sheep tax' (Avak), cf. Tatar qubġur = 'animal tax', Uigur qubčïr = 'general tax on behalf of the government' (Nadeliaev p. 462) & 14th-15th cent. T kapçur [قپچور] = 'tax according to the number of animals one owned' [sayım vergisi] (TS, v. 4, p. 2246-47); T gamçûr [Erzincan; Bitlis; Ağın, Keban-Elâzığ] & kamçor [Erciş-Van] = 'animal tax' [hayvan vergisi] (DS, v. 6, p. 1907; v. 8, p. 2615) & gamçor [Kars: Kacar Uruğu] & gançur/gaŋḫçur [Kars: Terekeme Uruğu] (AC-1, p. 248) = 'tax on cattle and sheep' [davar ve koyun vergisi]; P qubjūr قـبـجـور/qūbjūr قـوبـجـور/ q[u]fjūr قـفـجـور = 'a tribute consisting in one head of cattle per hundred; such tribute converted into money' (Steingass) < Mongol govčuur говчуур/ guvčuur гувчуур = 'impost, tax' [from: Hangin, p. 121]; of Mongolian origin: see: Doerfer vol. 1, #266. قـبـچـور = 'type of tax, originally most commonly collected in kind (primarily in cattle), it later came to denote set taxes levied on nomads and farmers' [Z-2/IFb//TF//GF//LY] <bac; bêş; kode; olam; xerc>

qame قامه (IFb) = dagger. See **qeme**.

qamet قامەت (K/SK/HH/JJ) = height. See **qam**.

qamir̄ قـامِر [Qzl/Qrj/Slm]/**qamir** قـامِر [K/IFb/GF/FJ] *m.* **(-ê;).** type of reed, bulrush, bot. *Scirpus (used in making mats)*: •...**Kanîk e, di hewşa wê odê de heye, weke *qamir* li wê derê heye. Xwe di nav de veşart** (L-I, #4, 112, l. 31-33) There is a spring in the yard of that room [sic], and there a *stand of bulrushes* there. He hid in it. {also: qeram (GF/IFb/Kmc)} {syn: leven; qamîş; zil} Cf. Sor qer̄em قەڕەم = 'reed pen' [Qzl/Qrj/Slm/FS//K/IFb/GF/FJ//GF/IFb/Kmc] <gorange [2]; qisîl>

qamîş قـامـيـش *m.* **(-ê; qêmîş).** 1) {syn: leven; qamir̄; zil} cane, reed, bot. *Phragmites & Arundo*: •***Qamîşê* zurnê teherekî hişk bibû** (www.dengekurdistan.nu: T.Reşîd. Mirazê dilê min) *The reed of* the zurna [oboe-like musical instrument] had gotten somewhat dry; 2) {syn: kîr} penis (JJ). {also: qamûş (F); [qamouch] قامش (JJ); <qamîş> قاميش (HH)} <T kamış = 'reed'; Sor qamîş قـامـيـش [EH/K/IFb/B/HH/SK/GF/ZF//F/JJ]

qam-qanat قـــام قــــانـــــات (K) = stature; build. See **qedqamet**.

qamûş قامووش (F/JJ) = reed. See **qamîş**.

qanad قاناد (JJ/ZF3) = wing. See **qanat**.

qanat قــــانـــــات *m.* **(-ê;).** wing. {also: qanad (ZF3); [qanad] قناد (JJ)} {syn: p'er̄ [2]} < T kanat [Z-1/K/B//JJ/ZF3] <bask>

qane قانه (K)/qane' قـانـع (JB1-A) = satisfied; willing; convinced. See **qani'**.

qaneh قانهه = willing; satisfied; convinced. See **qani'**.

qani' قـانِـع *adj.* 1) contented, satisfied; 2) {syn: qayîl; r̄azî} willing; 3) convinced, persuaded: •**Ez te'eccub dikem, hêşta tu *qani' nebûy* ko xeberê min dirust der-kewt?** (SK 59:696) I am amazed that you still *haven't been convinced* that what I said has turned out correct; **-qani' kirin**: a) to convince (SK) {syn: êqîn kirin; îqna' kirin}: •**Cenabê muctehid hêşta delîlekî weto neînaye ko biçûkê landikê jî *qani' biket*** (SK 60:708) Your honor has not yet brought forth a proof that *would convince* even a baby in its cradle; b) to appease, placate: •**Bavê xwe *qane kir*** (L) He *placated* his father (=calmed him down, rid him of his anger). {also: qane (K); qane' (JB1-A); qaneh; qanî (IFb); [qāneḥ kir] قانح (JJ)} < Ar √q-n-' قـنـع = 'to be satisfied; be convinced' [SK//L/K//JB1-A//IFb//JJ]

qanî قــانــى (IFb) = willing; satisfied; convinced. See **qani'**.

qant'ir قانتِر/**qant'ir̄** قانتِر [B/Wkt] *m./f.(B/JB3)* **(-ê/-a; /-ê).** mule. {also: qatir (IF-2); [qatir قـاطـر/qantir قانطر] (JJ); <qantir> قانتر (HH)} {syn: exte; hêstir

II} Cf. P qāṭir قــاطــر = 'mule' < *xar-tar: xar = 'donkey' + -tar = -er *(suffix for comparative degree)*: 'more like a donkey';--> T katır [L/K/A/JB3/IFb/JJ/HH//B/Wkt] <k'er III>

qanûn قــانـــوون *f.* **(-a;-ê).** law; rule, regulation: **•Belê, muro lazim e daimî hişyar bît, tiştê muxalifî *qanûna* xudê bît qebûl neket** (SK 9:93) Yes, a man must always have his wits about him and not accept anything which goes against *the law of* God **•Emma dibêjin *qanûna* Eḧmed Midḧet Paşa ji Qur'anê çêtir e û ew pîçek ji Xudê bi 'aqltir e** (SK 48:514) But they say that *the laws of* Ahmad Midhat Pasha are better than the Koran and he is a little more intelligent than God **•Ew deł̄îlêt şer' û *qanûnan* hemî pir̄-û-pûç in, bê fayde ne** (SK 43:418) Those proofs of the religious and civil *law* are all rubbish and quite useless. {also: [qanoun] قانون (JJ); <qanûn> قانون (HH)} {syn: zagon} < Ar qānūn قــانـــون = 'law' < Gr kanōn κανών = 'straight rod or bar, ruler; rule, standard (=Lat. regula, norma)' [K/IFb/B/JJ/HH/JB1-S/SK/GF]

qaput قاپوت (A) = overcoat. See **qap'ût**.

qap'ûd قاپوود (B) = overcoat. See **qap'ût**.

qap'ût قـاپــووت *f.(K)/m.(B/BF/FS)* **(-a/-ê;).** overcoat: **•Zînê k'etibû bin *qap'ûtê* Memê, telîya bû** (Z-1, 57) Zin jumped under Mem's *coat* and hid. {also: qaput (A); qap'ûd (B-2); [qapout] قــاپـــوت (JJ)} {syn: hewran I} [Z-1/K/A/IFb/B/JJ/GF/FS/BF]

qaqareş قــاقــارەش *f.* **(;-ê).** type of melon or squash [T kara kırman]: **•Me jê dabû *qaqareş*** (B.Bereh. Xewna dawî: "Kerek me hebû", 116) We gave him *melon* [to eat]. {also: qaqereş (A/FJ/ZF3); qaqreş (IFb/GF); <qaqereş> (HH)} [B.Bereh/TF//A/FJ/HH/ZF3//IFb/GF] <gindor I; k'al III; petêx; qawin>

qaqereş قــاقــەرەش (A/FJ/HH/ZF3) = type of melon. See **qaqareş**.

qaqreş قاقرەش (IFb/GF) = type of melon. See **qaqareş**.

qar I قار = deaf; silent. See **ker̄ II**.

qar II قار (IFb) = anger; disgust. See **qehr**.

qarç قارچ (A) = tailbone. See **qarç'ik**.

qarç'ik قــارچــك *f./m.(FS)* **(-a/;-ê/).** tailbone, coccyx: **•Hêt, qorik û *qarçika* min welê jan dikir ko qûna min li ser doşega nermik a sedirê jî nedihewiya** (M.Uzun. Hawara Dicleyê 166) My thigh, hip and *tailbone* ached so much that my rear end did not even feel relief on the soft cushion of the divan. {also: qarç (A); <qarçik> قــارچــك (HH)} {syn: kilêjî} [Msr/K/B/HH/ZF3/FS//A]

qareqar قــارەقــار *f.* **(-a;-ê).** noise; din, screaming and shouting, hullaballoo: **•Ji êvarê ve bela va zarowê te frotye mi, *qarqar̄a* wa bar̄bara wa bi serê mi da** (HR 3:289) Since the evening these kids of yours have been driving me crazy, their *noise* and shrieks make my head split. {also: qarqar (HR)} {syn: bar̄ebar̄; bir̄bir̄; hengame; hêwirze; hoqeboq; k'im-k'imî; qajeqaj; qalmeqal; qerebalix; qîr̄eqîr̄; şerqîn; t'eqer̄eq} [F/IFb/ZF//HR]

qar̄im قارِم (Haz) = scythe. See **qirim**.

qarin قارِن (M-Sh) = to be able. See **karîn**.

qariş قــارش: **-qarişî *ft-î* bûn** (Z-3) to interfere, meddle in: **•K'ese *qarişî* Memo *nebe*** (Z-3) *Don't let* anyone *interfere with* Mem. {also: [qarišmíš de-bé] قارشمش (JJ)} < T karışmak [Z-3//JJ]

qarix قارخ *m.* **(-ê;).** flower bed. [Krş/Mzg/IFb/FD]

qarqar قارقار (HR) = noise. See **qareqar**.

qarûme قــــــــاروومــــــــە **().** edible wild plant. {also: <qarûme> قارومە (HH)} [HB/A/IFb/HH]

qas قــاس *m./f.* **().** amount, quantity: -[**bi**] **qasî** (IFb/JJ) = a) as ... as {syn: temet}: **•Ew *qasî* min e** (IFb) He is *as* [big] *as* I am •[***Bi qasî* we xûndî nînim**] (JJ) I am not *as* educated *as* you are; b) according to: •[***bi qasî* qudreta xwe**] (JJ) *according to* his strength, with all his might; **-çiqas**[**î**] = how much; **-ewqas** = so much; **-haqas** = do.: **•Çima ez nagihim te, ez *haqas* dibezim?** (Dz) Why don't (=can't) I catch up with you; I run *so much* (=so fast)?; **-qasekê/ qasekî** (B) (for) a while, a short time: **•Tu jî *qasekî* şûn de here** (IF) And you go *a while* later. {also: [qas] قـــــاس (JJ)} {syn: mixdar; qeder I} [K/A/IFb/B/JJ/GF] <temet>

qasid قــاسِد *m.* **(-ê ; qêsid).** messenger, courier, errand boy: **•Wextê cewaba ax̄a ji r̄êwe dixast ho digot e *qasidê* ax̄a, 'Here, bêje ax̄aê xo ez xercê nadem.' *Qasidî* digot, 'Belê, wezîfa min xeber dan e. Dê çim, we bêjim e ax̄ay. Paşî to w ax̄a dizanin.'** (SK 14:136) When first an answer was requested for the agha he used to say to the agha's *messenger*, `Go and tell your agha I'm not paying any taxes.' *The messenger* would say, `Right, my duty is to bear news. I shall go and tell this to the agha. Afterwards you and he know best'; -[**qasidê xwedê**] (JJ) apostle, messenger of God. {also: [qasid] قاصد (JJ)} {syn: qewaz} < Ar qāṣid قاصد [EP-8/K/JB3/IFb/B/JJ/SK]

qaş قــاش *f.* **(-a;-ê).** 1) precious stone *(on ring)*: ***•Qaşa***

gustîla min ya şîne (BF) *The stone on* my ring is green .•**Şîrekî gelek kewn hebû, kalwanê wî zîw bû, destikê wî zêȓ bû, *qaşêt* elmas û pîroze hatibûne têgirtin, tîyê wî kerman bû** (SK 26: 234) There was a very ancient sword with a silver scabbard, its hilt of gold inlaid with *gems of* diamond and turquoise, and its blade of Kermani steel; 2) gold or silver mounting, setting (B); 3) {syn: gustîl} ring *(on finger)* (Hk[Gewer]). {also: qaşe (SK); [kāš] كاش (JJ); <qaş> قاش (HH)} [HB/K/A/IFb/B/HH/GF/Hk/BF//JJ//SK]

qaşe قاشه (SK) = precious stone. See **qaş**.

qaşik قـاشِـك (IFb/GF) = melon rinds; tree bark. See **qaşil**.

qaşil قـاشِـل *m./f.(B)* **(-ê/; /-ê).** 1) shavings, filings, chips; 2) {syn: qalik; qelp II; tîvil} shell, rind, peel; rinds of melons and the like; bark of a tree (GF/FS): •**Av wa ji *qaşlê* şebeşa bi der qûna wî de dipalihê** (HR 3:164) Water from the watermelon *rinds* is dripping out the back [of the bag]. {also: kaşûl (IFb-2); qaşik (IFb-2/GF-2); qaşul (TF); qaşûl (GF-2 [Bot]/RZ-2); <qaşil> قاشل (HH)} [HB/K/IFb/B/HH/GF/RZ//TF] <petêx; qawin; şimamok; zebeş>

qaşo قـاشـۆ *interj.* supposedly, allegedly, ostensibly: •**De ka ez binêrim bê te çend co xwarine, tu mêrekî çawa ye** [sic]**! *Qaşo* tu jî kurê wî ye** [sic]**!** (Ardû, 117) Let me see how many times you've been hit with their stick, let me see what kind of a man you are! You're *supposed to be* his son! •***Qaşo* min tîra xwe berdida vî** (ZZ-7, 242) I was *supposed to be* shooting my arrow at *him.* {syn: xwedêgiravî} [Ardû/A/GF/ZF]

qaşul قاشول (TF) = melon rinds. See **qaşil**.

qaşûl قاشوول (GF/RZ) = tree bark. See **qaşil**.

qat قـات *m.(B)/f.(JB3)* **(-ê/-a; qêt, vî qatî/).** 1) fold; times *(multiplication, X)*: •**sê *qat*** = three*fold*: **-qat kirin** (IFb) to fold: •**Li vî welatê gawiran cil-şuştin jî bi serê xwe derdekî giran e ... paşê bavêjin makîna zuhakirinê, paşê derxin *qat kin*, dûz kin û bînin mal** (LC, 12) In this country of infidels, doing laundry is a big headache ... then throw it in the dryer, then take it out, *fold* it, flatten it, and bring it home; 2) floor, story *(of a building)*: **-qata jêrîn** (IFb) lower level, downstairs; **-qata jorîn** (IFb)/**qatê jorin/ jorîn/ jorê** (B) upper level, upstairs; 3) {syn: dest [2]} *counting word for suits of clothing* (KS): •**Lê diviyabû Doktor Sertaç ji xwe re *qatek* kinc bikiriya** (KS, 36) But Dr. Sertaç had to buy himself *a suit of* clothes. < T kat = 'fold, story (of bldg.)' [Z-1/K/JB3/IFb/B/GF/KS]

qatir قاتِر (IF/JJ) = mule. See **qant'ir**.

qat'ix قـاتِـخ/**qatix** [B] *m.* **(-ê; qêt'ix** [EP-7], **vî qat'ixî).** 1) {syn: mast} yoghurt (Wn/Ag/K); curdled milk, light meal (JJ); 2) milk products (A/IFb). {also: [qàtik] قــاتــق (JJ)} < T katık = 'condiment (with bread); yoghurt' (in Kars & vicinity) & Az T qatıq = 'yoghurt' [Wn/Ag/K/A/IFb//JJ//B] <dew; nast; şîr; tawaş; to I>

qav I قاڤ (B/Z-1) = sheath; box. See **qab I**.

qav II قاڤ (B) = profligate; prostitute. See **qab II**.

qavî قاڤی (B) = adultery; prostitution. See **qabtî**.

qavtî قاڤتی (B) = adultery; prostitution. See **qabtî**.

qaw•e قـاوه *f.* **(•a;•ê).** coffee: •**Te cixarên xwe temam bi jahrê pêçane, te *qehwa* xwe giş bi jahrê çêkir** (ZZ-10, 138) You have rolled your cigarettes with poison, you made your *coffee* completely with poison •**Xidmetçî çon, zadêt laîq înan. Têşt xarin, destêt xo şuştin. *Qehwe* w çay înan, xarinewe** (SK 60:719) The servants went [and] brought fitting foods. They ate breakfast [and] washed their hands. They brought *coffee* and tea [and] they drank; **-cimcimê qehwê** = coffee pot. {also: qehwa; qehwe (IFb-2/GF/SK/ZF); [qavé] قــاوه (JJ)} {syn: avê reş (Hirço)} Cf. Ar qahwah قـهـوة, P qahve قـهـوه, T kahve; Sor qawe قـاوه [Z-1/EP-7/K/IFb/B/JJ//GF/SK/ZF]

qaweçî قــاوهچــی *m.* **(-yê;).** 1) person who serves coffee, one who works in a coffee house; 2) owner of a coffee house. {also: qehweçî (GF/FS); qehwevan (IFb/BF); [qavedji] قــاوهجــی (JJ)} < T kahveci [Z-2/K//JJ//GF/FS//IFb/BF]

qawexan•e قـاوەخـانـه *f.* **(•[ey]a;•ê).** coffeehouse, café, coffee shop: •**Memê ku nasî *cîyê qawexanê* bû, Zînê jî dihat wêderê, bona Memê bibîne** (FK, 277) Mem was familiar with *coffeehouses*, and Zin would come there in order to see Mem •**Muroêt *qehwe-xanê* qewî şeytan o ĥîlebaz bon** (SK 28:253) The men of *the coffee-house* were great tricksters. {also: qehwexane (IFb/FJ/GF/SK/RZ/ZF/SS/BS)} Cf. P qahvah´xāne قـهـوهخـانـه; Sor qawexane قاوەخانه [FK/K/B/CS//IFb/FJ/GF/SK/RZ/ZF/SS/BS] <ç'ayxane>

qawin قـــاوِن *m./f.(ZF3)* **(-ê/-a;).** melon: •***Qawinên* Diyarbekrê binavûdeng in** (FS) *The melons of*

Diyarbakir are famous. {also: qawûn (IFb-2); [qaoun] قـــاون (JJ); <qawin> قـــاون (HH)} {syn: gindor; petêx; şimamok} < T kavun [HB/K/IFb/B/HH/ZF3/FS//JJ] <qaşil [2]; zebeş>

qawit قاوِت (ZF3/Wkt) = cake-like pastry. See **qawît**.

qawît قـاويـت *f./m.(K/B)* **(; /-ê).** cake-like pastry made of fried wheat which is ground, and then mixed with grape syrup [**dims**] [T kavut]. {also: qawit (ZF3/Wkt); qawût, m. (K/B); qewît (TF); [qavout] قـاوت (JJ); <qawît> قـاويـت (HH)} Cf. Sor qawut قـــــــاووت = 'crumbled dry bread as provision for journey'; Za qawite *f.* (Mal) [Krb/A/IFb/HH/GF//TF//ZF3/Wkt//K/B/JJ]

qawûn قاووون (IFb) = melon. See **qawin**.

qawût قاووت, m. (K/B) = cake-like pastry. See **qawît**.

qax قـــــــــــــاخ *f./m.[B]* **(;-ê/qêx).** natural hole in a boulder in which rain water collects: **-ava qaxê** (Rwn) rain water collecting in such a hole. [Rwn/K/B]

qaxpe قاخپه (B) = profligate; prostitute. See **qab II**.

qayik قايك (FS) = boat. See **qeyk**.

qayil قايل (GF/HH) = willing; satisfied. See **qayîl**.

qayilî قايلى (GF) = willingness. See **qayîlî**.

qayilîtî قايليتى (GF) = willingness. See **qayîlî**.

qayiş قايش (GF) = strap, belt. See **qayîş**.

qayîl قـــايـــيـــل *adj.* 1) {syn: qane; r̄azî} consenting, willing, in agreement: **-qayîl bûn** [+ **bi**] (B/HH) to agree [to], assent [to], consent [to]: **•Aqû p'êxember *qayîl nabe*** (Ba) Jacob the prophet *does not assent* **•Aqûb *bi* gilîê Meyanê *qayîl bû*** (Ba3-3, #7) Jacob *agreed to* Meyaneh's conditions [lit. 'words'] **•Bavê min *qayîl bûye*, emê îro her̄in** (B) My father *has agreed*, we will go today **•Ez *qayîlim*, tu dikarî her̄î** (B) I *consent*, you can go **•Xûşka mezin herd xûşkê xwer̄a *qayîl bû*** (Z-1) The older sister *agreed with* her two sisters; **-qayîl kirin** (B/HH) to make agree, force to agree; 2) {syn: ber miraz; qane} satisfied (JJ). {also: qail (JB3); qaîl (F/A); qayil (GF); [ká'il] قـــايـــل (JJ); <qayil> قـــايـــل (HH)} < Ar qā'il قـــائـــل = 'saying' (√q-w-l قــول = 'to say')--> T kail = 'ready, willing' {qailî; qaîltî; qayîlî} [F/A//K/IFb/B//JB3//HH/GF//JJ]

qayîlî قـــايـــيـــلـــى *f.* **(-ya;-yê).** agreement, willingness, consent. {also: qailî (JB3); qaîltî (A); qayilî (GF); qayilîtî (GF-2)} [K/IFb/B//JB3//A//GF] <qayîl>

qayîş قـايـيـش *f.* **(-a;-ê).** 1) leather strap, man's belt; belt made of red and white hide, covered with spun silver (JJ) [kaīsh]; long thin piece of leather hung from the waist, in which daggers and the like are carried (HH): **•Paşê ew berê *qayşa* xwe dike ser brîna Qeret'ajdîn** (FK-eb-2) Then he wraps the top of his *leather belt* around Qeretajdîn's wound; 2) piece of leather (JJ) [qàich]; 3) [*adj.*] leather, made of leather (B): **-p'otê qayîş** (B) a leather coat or jacket. {also: qaîş (A-2); qayiş (GF); [qàich/kaīsh] قـايش (JJ); <qayîş> قـايـيـش (HH)} <T kayış = 'strap' [FK-2/K/IFb/B/HH//GF//A//JJ]

qaz قـــــــاز *f.* **(-a;-ê).** goose (pl. geese), zool. *Anser & Branta*: **•*Qaz* li ser avê digerin** (AB) *The geese* move about on the water. {also: [qaz] قـــــــاز (JJ); <qaẕ> قـاظ (HH)} [Pok ĝhan-s- 412.] 'goose': Skt haṁsá- *m.*/haṁsī *f.* = 'goose, swan'; Sgd z'γ = 'type of bird'; P γāz غاز -->T kaz; Sor qaz قاز; Za qanz (Lx)/qaz/qanzi *f.* (Mal); Hau qaz (M4) [AB/K/JB3/IFb/B/JJ/GF/TF//HH] <bet; qazvan; werdek>

qazanc قـازانـج *f.(K/B)/m.(SK)* **(-a/-ê;-ê/).** profit, gain: **-qazanc kirin** (K/B/SK)/**qezenc kirin** (IFb) to earn, gain, make a profit: **•Bes muro jî çak e bo xo ji xelkî 'ibret-girtî bibît da meqbûl bibît û daimî wucoda xo kêmas bizanît da wekî r̄iwî *sê-çendan qazanç biket*, ne wekî gurgî xo mezin ħisab biket, paşî serê wî bihêt e şkandin û mêjîyê wî bihêt e înan-e-der** (SK 7:77) But it is good for a man too to take a warning from people, so that he may be acceptable, and always to consider himself wanting so that, like the fox, he may *make treble* the profit, and not consider himself great, like the wolf, so that in the end his head is broken and his brains knocked out **•"Çak ew e ew sale r̄a-bim, biçim e kûstanê, kerê xo bar kem ji cang-û-colî û ji şure-pêlaw-û-mêlaw, bibem e-naw 'eşîreta Girdî Jorîyan, belko *qazancekî bikem*, bo biçûkêt xo r̄izqekî peyda bikem"** (SK 16:154) "This year it would be good to go into the mountains, to load up my donkey with cloth and haberdashery and footwear and take it among the Upper Girdi tribe. Maybe I *shall make a profit* and gain sustenance for my child-ren" **•Ewe sê sal e hung şer̄î diken har̄î 'Usmanî, hingî [=hingo?] ji x̄eyri zerer û perîşanî çî dî *qazanc nekir*, û ji noke paşwe dê xirabtir bît** (SK 57:674) For three years now you have fought for the Turks and apart from injury and regret you *have gained nothing*, and from now on it will be worse **•Gundek heye li-naw 'eşîreta Berwarîyan, daxili qeza Amedîyê,**

Spîndar dibêjin ê. Muroek hebû ji wî gundî, nawê wî Mam Tal bû. Gelek caran diçû Mûsilê, şure-mure dikiřî, diîna gundê xo, difirot, *qazanc dikir* (SK 28:252) There is a village among the Barwari tribe, in the district of Amadiya, called Spindar. There was once a man from that village whose name was Mam Tal. He used to go often to Mosul and buy goods, bring them back to his village, sell them and *make a profit* •**Wê keredê *qazancek min kiriye* kes nekirî** (SK 28:257) This time *I've made* such *a profit* as no man has ever made; -**xwera nav qazanc kirin** (K) to make a name for oneself. {also: qezanc (GF); qezenc (IFb); [qazandj] قزانج (JJ)} < T kazanç [K/B/SK//GF/JJ//IFb]

Qazaxistanî قازاخِستانى (Wkp/Wkt) = Kazakh. See **Qazaxî**.

Qazaxî قازاخى *adj.* Kazakh. {also: Kazaxî (BF/Wkt-2); Qazaxistanî (Wkp-2/Wkt-2); Qezaxî (ZF3); Qezexî (Wkt-2)} [Wkt/Wkp//ZF3//BF]

qazik قازِك *f.* **(-a;-ê).** pot with handle: •**Wê girar di *qazikê* da lêna** (FS) She cooked the porridge in *the pot*. {also: <qazik> قازك (HH)} {syn: qûşxane} [Frq/Efr/K/HH/GF/ZF3/FS]

qazix قازخ (B) = stake, stick. See **qazux**.

qazî قازى *m.* **(-ê;).** judge, Islamic judge, cadi: •**Dibêjin cenabê *qazî* muroekî qabil o zîrek e w şola feqîran çak dirust diket** (SK 54:584) They say that your honor *the judge* is a capable and wise person who carries out the work of the poor •**Ez *qazî* me, çend kitêbêt şer' o qanûn min xundine w mutale'e kirine, ji ẍeyri wane min çu delîl, ne ze'îf, ne muȟkem, nedîtine** (SK 40:417) I am *a cadi*, I have read and studied some books of divine law, other than them I have seen no proof, neither weak nor solid •**Ser řûê *qazî* t'emiz kuvkir** (HCK-5, #41, 230) She shaved *the judge*'s face clean. {also: qadî (GF-2); [qazi/qadi] قاضى (JJ); <qaẓî> قاظى (HH)} {syn: dadger; dadpirs; ȟakim} < Ar qāḍin قاض (qāḍī قاضى); Sor qazî قازى = 'judge, magistrate (also of religious courts)' [HCK/K/B/IFb/GF/TF/SK/JJ/HH]

qazox قازوخ (A/HH) = stake, stick. See **qazux**.

qazoxe قازوخه (FS) = stake, stick. See **qazux**.

qazquling قازقولنگ **().** swan; wild goose (FS): •**Koça *qazqulinga* ji Afrikaya Bakur dest pe dike ü ber bi Iranê va diçin** (Haberler.com) The migration *of swans* begins in North Africa and they go toward Iran. {syn: qubeqaz; qû} < qaz = 'goose' + quling = 'crane' [RZ/Wkt/FS]

qazux قازوخ *m./f.(B)* **(; /-ê).** 1) stake, pale, stick, rod, post, pole: •**Wan filan kes *qazoxe da/li qazoxê da*** (FS) They *had* so-and-so *impaled on a stake*; -**qazox kirin** (A) to impale *(a form of capital punishment)*; 2) spoke *(of wheel)* (K); 3) rod attached to the shaft of the front axle of a horse-drawn cart (B). {also: qazix (B); qazox (A); qazoxe (FS-2); xazoqe (FS); [qazouk] قازق (JJ); [ḥazōq] حزوق (JJ/PS); <qazox> قازوخ (HH)} Cf. Ar/P xāzūq خازوق = 'stake', T kazık [HB/K//A/HH//B//JJ//PS//FS]

qazvan قازڤان *m.* **(-ê;).** gooseherd, one who tends geese: •**De heře holka qaza bidê, qazê min bidê, bra bive *qazvan*, heře ber qazê min** (HCK-3, #16, 181) Go give him the geese shack, give him my geese, let him become *a gooseherd*, and tend my geese [lit. 'go before my geese']. Sor qazewan قازهوان = 'one who tends a flock of geese' [HCK/K/GF] <qaz>

qe قه = ever; (not) at all. See **qet I**.

qebd قهبد *f./m.(JB3)* **(-a/;).** handle, haft, hilt *(of sword, dagger, etc.)*: •[***Qebda* xencera wî şkest**] (HM) *The handle of* his dagger broke •**Ç., 'E. destê wan ser *qevza* şûrin** (Z-1) Ch. and E.'s hands are on *the hilt[s] of* [their] sword[s] (=they are about to draw their swords). {also: qeft [2]; qevd, m. (JB3/IFb-2/GF); qevz I (Z-1/K/GF-2); [qabze] قبضه (JJ); <qevd> قڤد (HH)} {syn: balçîq} < Ar qabḍah قبضة --> T kabza [HM/A/IFb//K//JB3/HH/GF//JJ] <kalan; qab I; şûr>

qebel قهبهل. See **qebûl**.

qebeqaz قهبهقاز (Wkt) = swan. See **qubeqaz**.

qebe-qeb قهبهقهب (Alkan) = cooing. See **qebqeb**.

qebir قهبِر, f. (-a;-ê) (K/B/IFb) = grave. See **qebr**.

qebiristan قهبِرستان (K/IFb/CS) = cemetery. See **qebristan**.

qebîl قهبيل (Ba2/B) = tribe. See **qebîle**.

qebîle قهبيله *f.* **(-a;-ê).** tribe; medium-sized tribe (JR). {also: qebîl (Ba2/B); [qabilé] قبيله (JJ)} < Ar qabīlah قبيلة [Ba2/B//F/IFb/JJ] <berek; binemal; 'eşîret; hoz; îcax; ocax[4]; tayfe>

qebîn قهبين *vi.* **(-qeb-).** to coo, call *(of partridges [kew])*. {also: qeqibîn (IFb-2); qibîn (IFb)} [Bw//IFb] <kew I>

qebqeb قهبقهب *f.* **(-a;-ê).** billing and cooing *(of doves, etc.)*: •**dengê *qebe-qeba* kewan** (Alkan, 71) the sound of *the cooing of* partridges **•Dîsa Derwêş 'Elî wekî kewê r̄ibad *qebqeb kir*** (SK 60:726) Once again Dervish Ali *cooed* like a decoy partridge. {also: qebe-qeb (Alkan); qepqep (IFb)} [Alkan//K(s)/SK//IFb]

qebr قەبر *m.* **(-ê;).** grave, tomb: **•Dasinî mezhebek e, Êzedî jî dibêjin ê. Eslê wan mirîd o tabi'êt Şêx Hadî bon. *Qebrê* wî nêzîkî Dehokê ye li-naw 'eşîreta Berwarîyan** (SK 39:344) The Dasinis are a sect, also called Yezidis. By origin they were disciples and followers of Shaikh Adi. His *tomb* is near Duhok among the Barwari tribe **•Rabî, her do biraêt wî *qebr* bo kolan, veşart'in** (M-Zx, #755, 350) He rose and dug *graves* for both of his brothers and buried them. {also: qebir, f. (-a;-ê) (K/B/IFb); [qebr/qăbir/k'abr (G)] قبر (JJ); <qebr> قبر (HH)} {syn: gor̄ I; mex̂ber; mezel; t'irb} < Ar qabr قبر [M-Zx/SK/JJ/HH/RZ//K/B/IFb]

qebrax قەبراخ *m.* **(-ê;).** 1) {syn: qurumsax} pimp; 2) bastard. {also: qebro (Msr-2)} cf. <qibrax kirin> قبراخ کرن (HH) = 'to tie one's clothes on one's back in preparation for departing on a journey' [Msr/IFb] <qab II>

qebrestan قەبرەستان (GShA) = cemetery. See **qebristan**.

qebristan قەبرستان *f.* **(-a;-ê).** cemetery, graveyard: **•Ez diqarim, we nakem / Miriyekî ji *qebrestanê* rakem** (GShA, 229) I can do things I won't do / I can raise a dead man from *the graveyard.* {also: qebiristan (K/IFb-2/CS); qebrestan (GShA); [qaberistan/kabirstān (Lx)] قبرستان (JJ); <qebristan> قبرستان (HH)} {syn: gor̄istan} < Ar qabr قبر = 'grave' + P –[i]stān ستان = 'place' [GShA//IFb/HH//K/CS//JJ]

qebro قەبرۆ (Msr) = pimp; bastard. See **qebrax**.

qebûl قەبوول *f.* **().** acceptance, consent: **-qebûl bûn** (B/IFb) to be accepted or acceptable: •[***qebûl dibe***] (JJ) *acceptable*; **-qebûl kirin** (IFb): a) to accept, agree, approve, assent {syn: qayîl bûn}: **•Dîya min *qebûl nake*** (L) My mother *doesn't accept* (=says no); b) to approve of (B) {syn: p'ejirandin}: **•Tu xebata min *qebûl dikî*?** (B) Do you *approve of* my work?; c) to receive, welcome (B) {syn: çûn p'êrgînê}: **•Ewana mêvan r̄ind *qebûl kirin*** (B) They *received* the guests well. {also: qebel; [qaboul] قبول (JJ); <qebûl > قبول (HH)} < Ar qubūl قبول = 'acceptance, reception' --> T kabul [K/JB3/IFb/B/JJ/HH/SK]

qeda قەدا *f.(K/B)/m.(JB1-A)* **(; qedaê** or **qedê** [B]/**).** 1) {syn: bela I; bêt'ar; boblat; gosirmet; oyîn; siqûmat; t'ifaq} misfortune, disaster; accident: **•*Qeda* te k'eve!** (B)/***Qede* li te bik'eve** (Msr) May *a disaster* befall you! *[curse]* **•Ne sîr û ne pîvaz, *qede* li dermanê germ bik'eve** (Msr) May *disaster* befall neither garlic nor onions, but rather [red] peppers (=All three are equally bad) *[prv.]*; 2) {syn: nesaxî; nexweşî} disease, illness, sickness (B). {also: qede (Msr); qedeh I (K); **qezîya**; [qeda قدا/qaza قضا] (JJ); <qeda> قدا (HH)} < Ar qaḍā' قضاء 'destiny; decree' --> T kaza = 'accident'; Sor qeza قەزا = 'accident' [Msr//IFb/B/JJ/HH/JB1-A/GF//K] See also **qezîya.**

qedandin قەداندِن *vt.* **(-qedîn-).** 1) to carry out, execute, complete: **•Îşê xwe *biqedîne*** (L) Attend to (or, *carry out*) your affairs **•Destxweda gilîyê kalê dinîyadîtî *hate qedandin*** (Z-1) Immediately the words (=advice) of the experienced old man *were carried out*; 2) to end, conclude, finish: **•Jan Dost roman Kobanî *qedand*** (avestakurd.net 19.viii.2016) J.D. *finished* [writing] the novel "Kobanî"; 3) to solve (a problem) (B): **-mesele qedandin** (B) to solve a problem. {also: <qedandin قداندن (diqedîne) (دقدينه)> (HH)} < Ar qaḍá قضى = 'to finish, terminate' [L/K/A/JB3/IFb/B/HH/GF]

qeddimîn قەددِمين (K) = to move, advance. See **qedimîn**.

qede قەدە (Msr) = misfortune. See **qeda**.

qedege قەدەگە (A) = forbidden. See **qedexe**.

qedeh I قەدەه (K) = misfortune. See **qeda**.

qedemg•e قەدەمگە *f.* **(•a;•ê).** toilet, water closet, lavatory: **•Dotirê rojê, bêhna tirş ji *qedemgê* dihat** (dinadintir.blogspot.com 17.vi.2015) The following day, a sour smell was emanating from *the lavatory*. {also: qedemgeh (TF); [qadem-gah] قدمگاه (JJ); <qedemgah> قدمگاه (HH)} {syn: avdestxane; avr̄êj I; ç'olik III (Msr); daşir (Dy); destavxane; edebxane [1]} Cf. P qadamgāh قدمگاه = 'footing; place of arrival' [Msr//JJ/HH//TF]

qedemgeh قەدەمگەه (TF) = toilet. See **qedemge**.

qeder I قەدەر *m.(E)/f.(W/JB1-A)* **(-ê/;).** 1) {syn: mixdar; qas} quantity, amount: **-qederê** (B) about, approximately {syn: qiyasê}: **•*qederê* mehekê** (B) *about* a month; **•Emê *qederê* 10 r̄oja vira bijîn** (B) We will live here *about* 10 days **•*Qederê* nîv saetê ma** (L) It stayed for *about* half an hour [lit. 'the amount of a half hour']; 2) moment, small amount of time (B): •***Qederek* k'ete ort'ê** (B) *Some time* passed (after stg. happened). {also: qedir II, m. (JB3); qender (K2-Fêrîk); [qadr] قدر (JJ); <qeder> قدر (HH)} < Ar qadr قدر --> T kadar [BX/K/JB3/IFb/B/HH/JB1-A/SK/OK//JJ]

qeder II قەدەر *f.* **(-a;-ê).** destiny, fate: •**Em ji *qedera* xwe xeyidîne** (IF) We cursed our *fate* •**Wisa xuya dibe *qedera* wan wisa hatiye nivîsîn** (Nbh 132:16) It seems that their *fate* was written that way. {also: <qeder> قدر (HH)} {syn: bext; enînivîs; nesîb; qismet; yazî} < Ar qadar قدر --> T kader [K/JB3/IFb/HH/GF/OK/ZF]

qedexe قەدەخە *adj.* forbidden, prohibited, banned [Cf. T yasak]: **-qedexe kirin** (IFb/GF) to ban, prohibit, forbid {syn: berbend kirin}. {also: qedege (A); qedexe (FS); <qedexe> قدغە (HH)} {syn: ĥeram} Cf. P qadaγan قدغن [Ber/IFb/GF/OK//A//HH/FS]

qedexe قەدەغە (HH/FS) = forbidden. See **qedexe**.

qedimîn قەدمین *vi.* **(-qedim-).** to step, go, move, advance. {also: qeddimîn (K)} < Ar qadama قدم [L//K] <pêşdaçûn>

qedir I قەدر *m.* **(-ê;).** 1) {syn: giram; hurmet; r̄êz II; r̄ûmet} respect, gravity: •**bona *qedirê* te** (B) out of *respect to* you •**Wê jê re *qedir* û malîfetê bike** (L) [She] will show [lit. 'do'] *respect* and honor to him; **-qedir girtin** (B/FS) to respect, honor: •**Dostê wî jî gelek *qedrê* wî *digirt*: her tuxme te'amê xoş ba, bi-lezet ba, ew bo wî dirust dikir … bo niwistinê jî niwînêt çak bo wî dir̄aêxistin…** (SK 31:274) His friend *would treat* him *with* great *respect*. He would prepare for him every kind of good and tasty food … He would spread fine bedding for him also, to sleep on •**Ew *qedirê* hev *digirin*** (B) They *respect* each other; 2) {syn: qîmet} worth; dignity: **-qedir êxistin** (B) to lower in prestige. {also: qedr (JB3/IFb/SK/GF)} < Ar qadr قدر [K/B//JB3/IFb/SK/GF/FS] <'erz; qeder I>

qedir II قەدر, m. (JB3) = amount. See **qeder I**.

qedirgiran قەدرگران *adj.* respected, honored, valued; respectable, honorable: •**Lo yeman, lo hoste û *qedirgiran*** (M.Uzun. Roja Evd. Zeyn., 73) O masters and *honored* ones. {also: qedrgran (GF)} {syn: bir̄êz; r̄êzdar II} [Uzun/K/CS//GF]

qediyan قەدیان (JB3/IFb) = to be finished; to pass (of time) . See **qedîn**.

qedîfe قەدیفە *m.* **().** velvet. {also: [qadifé] قدیفە (JJ)} {syn: mexmer} < Ar qaṭīfah قطيفة --> T kadife [K/IFb/B/JJ/(GF)/OK]

qedîn قەدین *vi.* **(-qed-).** 1) to be completed, finished, exhausted, come to an end: •**Dema me serxwebûn bidest xist wê gavê erka min *diqede*** (bianet.org 6.ix.2017) When we have achieved independence, that is when my work *comes to an end* •**Ne mumkune ku beriya Remezanê operasyon *biqede*** (trtnûçe.com 21.v.2017) It is not possible for the operation *to be completed* before Ramadan; 2) to pass, elapse *(vi.) (of time)*: •**Ev e nîv saeta min *qedîya*, ez ji xwe re li te temaşe bikim** (L) I've been watching you for half an hour [lit.' A half hour of mine *passed*, that I watch you for myself']. {also: qediyan (JB3/IFb); qedyan (SK)} < Ar qaḍá قضى = 'to finish, terminate' [L/K//JB3/IFb]

qedqamet قەدقامەت *f.* **(-a;).** 1) {syn: bejn; qam} height, stature: •**Talîma beden … *qed û qameta* meriv rasttir û xweşiktir dike** (dilawerkurdi.files.wordpress.com: Qedrî Can 217) Training the body … makes one's stature straighter and more attractive.; 2) figure, build, frame *(of a person)*; 3) carriage, bearing. {also: qam-qanat (K-2); qed û qamet (K/ZF3/FD); qem-qanat (EP-4)} < Ar qadd wa-qāmah قدّ و قامة [JR//K/ZF3/FD] <bejnbal>

qedr قەدر (JB3/IFb/SK/GF) = respect. See **qedir I**.

qedrgran قەدرگران (GF) = respected, honorable. See **qedirgiran**.

qedûm قەدووم *m.* **(-ê;).** 1) {syn: ling; p'ê II} feet, legs; 2) {syn: birî I; ĥêl; hêz; qewat; t'aqet; zexm I [2]; zor I} strength *(fig.)*: •***Qudûm* hat ber çokêd min** (K) I felt strong [lit. '*strength* came to my knees'] •***Qudum* çokê wanda nema** (Z-1) They felt weak [lit. 'there was no *strength* left in their knees'] •**Wexta me eva yeka dît, *qudûmê* çokêd me sist bûn** (Ba2:2, 206) When we saw that, we felt weak in the knees; **-[ji] qudûm êxistin** (B) to drain of energy; **-qudûm şkestin** (B) to become weak: •***Qudûmê* min *şkestin*** (K) I am weak/I've lost all my strength [lit. 'my *legs are broken*'] •***Qedûmê* birê wî *şikestin*** (L) His brothers *were unable to walk*; 3) sadness, grief (B); 4) form, shape, aspect (HH/IFb) [hay'ah]. {also: qidûm (IFb); qudum (Z-1); qudûm (K/B); <qidûm> قدوم (HH)} Cf. Ar qadam قدم = 'foot' *(anat. & unit of measure)* [L//K/B//IFb/HH]

qed û qamet قەد و قامەت (K/ZF3/FD) = height, stature. See **qedqamet**.

qedyan قەدیان (GF) = to be finished; to pass *(of time)*. See **qedîn**.

qefaltin قەفالتِن *vt.* **(-qefêl-).** to catch, capture, apprehend, seize: •**Carekê digihê çend hevalên xwe û bi hev re direvin bi aliyê Sêwregê ve diçin. Apê wî Xalit dikeve dû, wî *diqefêle* tîne** (Nbh 132:12) Once he joins some friends of his and together they run away in the direction of Siverek. His uncle Khalit goes after him, *catches him* and brings him back. {syn: girtin[2]} [Nbh/GF/ZF]

qefes قەفەس *f.* **(-a;-ê).** 1) cage: •**Ji teyrê te re lazim e *qesefek* ji hestîyê fîla** (L) Your bird needs an ivory *cage*; 2) rib cage. {also: qesef (L); [qafes] قفص (JJ); <qefes> قفس (HH)} < Ar qafaṣ قفص --> T kafes [L//K/IFb/B/JJ/HH] <r̄eke>

qefil قەفِل *m./f.(ZF3)* **(/-a;).** several *destî's* (armfuls) of wheat (barley, etc.) as a unit [unit of measure--larger than *destî*, smaller than *gidîş*]. {also: qefle II (ZF3-2); cf. [qaflé] قفله (JJ) = 'fardeau' [=burden, load]} Cf. Turoyo quflo = 'armful' (HR2) [Qzl/Kmc-5769/ZF3/FS] <destî; gidîş>

qefilin قەفِلِن (A) = to freeze. See **qefilîn**.

qefilî قەفِلی *adj.* 1) tired, weary (Kg); 2) frozen (K/A). {also: qefîlî (Kg)} [Kg//K/A/ZF3] <westîyan>

qefilîn قەفِلین *vi.* **(-qefil-).** 1) {syn: cemidîn; qerimîn; qeşa girtin; simirîn} to freeze *(vi.)* (Bzd/Kş/Srk/IFb); 2) {syn: betilîn; r̄e't bûn; westîn} to be or become tired (Kg/Mzg/IFb): •***Qefilyame*** (Kg) *I am tired*. {also: qefilin (A); qefilyan (Kg); <qufilîn قفلين (diqufilî) (دقفلی)> (HH)} Za qeflyenã [qeflyayiş] (Srk) = 'to be cold' [Kg//Mzg/Bzd/Kş/Srk/K/IFb/B/ZF3//HH//A] <t̠ezî II>

qefilvan قەفِلڤان (Kmc-5770/ZF3) = carrier of sheaves. See **qeflevan**.

qefilyan قەفِلیان (Kg) = to be tired. See **qefilîn** [2].

qefiş قەفِش (FS) = handful, bunch. See **qefş**.

qefîlî قەفیلی (Kg) = tired. See **qefilî**.

qefle I قەفلە *f.* **().** herd *(of cows, buffalo, or horses)*: **-qeflekî dawar** (Haz) a herd of cattle; **-qeflekî gamêş** (Haz) a herd of buffalo(es); **-qeflekî hesp** (Haz) a herd of horses. {also: qifle (Btm/Czr)} {syn: îrxî; r̄evo} <Ar qāfilah قافلة = 'caravan' [Haz/Rwn/ZF3//Btm/Czr] <ga; gamêş; kerî II; r̄af>

qefle II قەفلە (ZF3) = armful as unit of measure for grain. See **qefil**.

qeflevan قەفلەڤان *m.* **().** agricultural worker who piles ***qefils*** together in a field [ew kesê ku qeflan dide hev di zevîyê da], carrier or collector of sheaves in the field. {also: qefilvan (Kmc-5770/ZF3)} [Qzl//Kmc-5770] <qefil>

qefş قەفش *f.* **(-a;-ê).** handful; bunch, bundle: •**Bizinê *qefşeka* giyayî xwar** (FS) The goat ate *a bunch of* grass. {also: qefiş (FS); qevş (B)} {syn: baq; qeft[1]} [IFb/ZF3//FS//B]

qeft قەفت *f./m.(FS)* **(/-ê;).** 1) {syn: qefş} (small) handful; bouquet, bunch: •***qeftek* sosinan** (Zx-song) *a handful of* lilies •***Qeftek* gulan da yara xwe** (Wkt) He gave his beloved *a bouquet of* roses; 2) handle, haft. See **qebd**. {also: [qawdi] قفضی (JJ); <qevd> قفد (HH)} [Zx/A/IFb/FS/ZF3/Wkt//JJ//HH]

qefz قەفز (IFb/HH) = jump; step. See **qevz II**.

qehbe قەهبە (K[s]) = profligate; prostitute. See **qab II**.

qehbetî قەهبەتی (K[s]) = adultery; prostitution. See **qabtî**.

qehf قەهف *m.* **(-ê; qêf** [B]**).** 1) {syn: k'elle II; k'ilox} skull, cranium: •**Bê şerm, wek dehbekî ecêb, ji serê *qehfê* min, heya neynûkên lingên min, li min dinêrin** (EŞ, 19) Shamelessly, like some strange beast, they look me over, from the top of my *skull* to the tips of my toes [lit. 'the nails of my feet']; 2) top, crest, peak: •**Mi mêzand kû wê di *qeḧfê* latê de dixwênin** (HR 3:197) I saw that [the doves] were singing at *the top of* the cliff. {also: qaf (A/IFb/B/GF-2); qeḧf (HR); <qaf> قاف (HH)} <Ar qiḥf قحف = 'skull' [EŞ/K/GF/TF/ZF3//A/IFb/B/HH//HR] <qerqode>

qehir قەهِر (K/OK/CS) = anger; disgust. See **qehr**.

qehirandin قەهِراندِن *vt.* **(-qehirîn-).** 1) to sadden, depress, anger, annoy; to rouse indignation; to disappoint, frustrate: •**Te *em qehirandin*** (L) You *have frustrated us*; 2) to torment. {also: <qeḧirandin> قحراندن (HH)} < Ar qahara قهر = 'to conquer; (clq.) to disappoint, upset' [K/JB3/IFb/ZF3//HH] <qehirandin>

qehirîn قەهِرین *vi.* **(-qehir-).** 1) to be depressed, sad, angry, upset: •**Tu gelikî *diqehirî*, her êvar tu kêfa me jî dişkenînî** (L) You *are* very *depressed*, every evening you upset us also •**Wextê ku bavê wî wilo got, gelekî M. 'aciz bû û *qiḧerî*** (HR 4:35) When his father said that, M. *got* very upset and *angry*; 2) to be disgusted, disappointed, frustrated. {also: qiḧerîn (HR); [qaherīn] قهرين (JJ); <qeḧirîn> قحرين (HH)} < Ar qahara قهر = 'to conquer; (clq.) to disappoint, upset'; Za qaḧrîyenã

= 'to become angry' (Todd) [L/K/JB3/IFb/JJ/M//HH//HR] <aciz; qehirandin; tengav>

qehpe قەهپە (GF) = profligate; prostitute. See **qab II**.

qehr قــەهــر *f.* **(-a;-ê).** anger, rage, wrath; disgust, frustration: **•Eger min çente-y maşan nebiriba harî xudê w min bi hîwîya xudê bi-tinê hêlaba, Mela 'Ebbas da qûna te diřînît. Belê min çente-y maşan bir e harî Xudê, lewanê xudê zû *qehra* xo li wî kir, em ji şeřê wî xilas kirîn** (SK 15:152) If I hadn't taken a bag of green gram to the assistance of God and if I had left it in hope of God alone, Mullah Abbas would have split you apart. But I did take a bag of gram to the help of God and that is why God soon visited him with His *wrath* and freed us from the evil of him **•Xewnê şêvane, bila şteře [=ji te re] *nebê qeḧr*!** (HR 4:33) *Don't let* nighttime dreams *get* you *upset*. {also: qar II (IFb); qehir (K/OK/CS); qeḧr (HR)} < Ar qahara قــهــر = 'to conquer; (clq.) to disappoint, upset' (Todd); Sor qar قار = 'vexation, distress' [HR//FJ/TF/SK/GF//K/OK/CS//IFb] <qehirîn>

qehwa قەهوا = coffee. See **qawe**.

qehwayî قەهوایی (GF/OK) = brown. See **qehweyî**.

qehwe قەهوە (IFb/GF/SK/ZF) = coffee. See **qawe**.

qehweçî قــەهــوەچــی (GF/FS) = coffee server; coffee house owner. See **qaweçî**.

qehwevan قــەهــوەڤــان (IFb/BF) = coffee server; coffee house owner. See **qaweçî**.

qehwexane قەهوەخانە (IFb/FJ/GF/SK/RZ/ZF/SS/BF) = coffeehouse. See **qawexane**.

qehweyî قــەهــوەیــی *adj.* 1) brown, coffee-colored; 2) type of brown-colored material used in making traditional *bergûz* [qv.]. {also: qehwayî (GF/OK-2)} Sor qaweyî قاوەیی [Kmc-2/IFb/TF/OK//GF]

qeḧb قــەحــب (Msr/JJ/HH) = profligate; prostitute. See **qab II**.

qeḧf قەحف (HR) = skull; top, peak. See **qehf**.

qeḧr قەحر (HR) = anger; disgust. See **qehr**.

qeîq قەئیق (F) = boat. See **qeyk**.

qel قــەل *f.* **(-a;-ê).** crow, raven: **•Nêzîkî spêdê gazî *qelê* kir. Got ê, "To bo çî zira'eta xelkî dixoy o xirab dikey? Ma xelkî ew çandine bo te kiriye? Ma to ji xudê natirsî?" *Qelê* got, "Waqi'en gunahêt min zor in…"** (SK 4:52) Near dawn he summon-ed *the crow*. He said to it, "Why do you eat what people sow and spoil it? Have people done this planting for you, then? Have you no fear of God?" *The crow* said, "My sins are indeed many…" {also: qela II (IFb); qele II (GF)} {syn: qijik; qiřik II} Sor qel قــەل = 'crow, raven' [SK/RZ/SS//GF/FS/ZF3/Wkt//IFb]

qela I قەلا (HB//GF/OK) = fortress. See **kela**.

qela II قەلا (IFb) = crow *(bird)*. See **qel**.

qelafet قەلافەت *m.* **(-ê;).** outward appearance, figure, shape, form, looks, build *(of one's body)* [şiklê laş]: **•Ew bi *qelafetê* xwe yê girs ji cihê xwe pengizî bû û mîna zarokekî kêfxweş dibû** (SF 7 [intro]) He, with his large *build*, jumped up from his place and rejoiced like a child. {also: qilafet (K); [qalafat قلافت/qiiafé قیافه] (JJ)} {syn: bejnbal; dilqe; qilix I} Cf. T kıyafet < Ar qiyāfah قــیــافــة = 'costume, guise'; Sor qeĺafet قەڵافەت = 'strapping figure, imposing stature' [SF/IFb/GF/TF//JJ//K]

qelak قەلاك (L) = pressed dung. See **qelax**.

qelandin قەلانـدِن *vt.* **(-qelîn-).** 1) [< Ar qalá قــلــى = 'to roast'] {syn: biraştin} to roast; {syn: qewrandin II} to fry (JB3): **-goşt qelandin** (IF) to roast meat; 2) [< Ar qala'a قــلــع = 'to uproot'] {syn: qiř kirin} to destroy, uproot, extirpate: **-k'ok qelandin** (K/B) to annihilate, destroy [lit. 'to pull up by the roots']: **•Wekî Q. Memo wî ḧalîda dît, wê şeher xirab ke û *k'ok'a* me *biqelîne*** (Z-1) If Q. sees Mem in this condition, he'll sack the city and *annihilate* us. {also: [qalandin] قــلانــدیــن (JJ); <qelandin قــلانــدن (diqelîne) (دقــلــیــنــه)> (HH)} [Z-1/K/A/JB3/IF/B/HH] <patin; pijandin>

qelaşînk قــەلاشــیــنــك *m.* **(-ê;).** *type of bird:* European roller, zool. *Coracias garrulous*: **-qelaşînkê Ewropayê** (Wkp) do. {also: qeleşîn (GF); qeleşînk (ZF3)} Cf. qel قــەل = 'crow, raven' [Wkp/IFb//ZF3//GF]

qelaştin قــەلاشــتِــن *vt.* **(-qelêş-).** 1) to tear, rip, split, crack: **•Zikê wî *diqelêşe*** (J) She *rips open* his stomach. {also: qelişandin; [qalachtin] قــلاشــتــیــن (JJ); <qelaştin قلاشتن (diqelîşe) (دقلیشه)> (HH)} [J/F/K/A/JB3/IFb/B/HH/GF//JJ]

qelat قەلات (A/SK) = fortress. See **kela**.

qelax قــەلاخ *f.* **(;-ê).** large pile of pressed dung (K); dung piled up in the form of a pyramid (K); large dung heap (Ag): **•Bavo, ev çel keleş hebûn, bajarê Dîyarbekrê xisti bûn *qelakê*** (L) Father, there were 40 brigands, who made a shambles out of Diyarbakir (=turned the city into *a dung heap*) [Amis, il y avait 40 brigands qui avaient mené la ville de Diyarbekr à deux doigts de sa perte]. {also: qalax (A/IFb/GF); qelak (L); <qalax> قــالاخ

(HH)} {syn: lodê keşkûran (IF); sergo} [Ag/K/B/ZF3// A/IFb/HH/GF] <deve II; dirg; k'erme; peyîn; sergîn; t'epik II>

qelb I قهلب (IFb/HH) = false; dishonest. See **qelp I**.

qele I قهله (IFb) = fortress. See **kela**.

qele II قهله (GF) = crow (bird). See **qel**.

qelebalix̄ قهلهبالغ (SK) = noise; crowd. See **qerebalix**.

qelefiskî قـهـلـهـفِـسـكـى: **-qelefiskî** (K//JJ)/**qelefîstikî** (Btm)/**qulofîskî r̄ûniştin** (Ag) to squat, kneel; **-li ser qelevîska** (Qmş)/**qilafîska r̄ûniştin** (Qzl) do. {also: qelefîstikî (Btm); qelevîsk (Qmş); qerefîskî (B); qilafîsk (Qzl); qulofîskî (Ag); [kalafisk rou-nichtin] كالفسك رونشتين (JJ)} {syn: *tutik (Qrj)} cf. Ar qurfuṣā' قرفصاء = 'squatting position' [K//JJ//B] <ç'armêrgî; çok>

qelefîstikî قهلهفيستكى (Btm) = squatting, kneeling. See **qelefiskî**.

qelem قهلهم *f./m.(Bw)* **(-a/-ê;-ê/).** (ink) pen; pencil (B). {also: [qalem] قلم (JJ); <qelem> قلم (HH)} {syn: pênûs} < Ar qalam قـــلـــم <Lat calamus & Gr kalamos καλαμος [K/JB3/IFb/B/HH/GF/Bw//JJ]

qelemaç قـهـلـهمـاج (HYma) = spades (in card games). See **qeremaç**.

qelemzirêç قـهلـهمـزريـچ *f./m.(BF)* **(-a/;-ê/).** pencil: **•Ji ber ku ew bi *qelemzirîçê* hatine nivîsîn baş nayên xwendin** (R.Pertev. Mîrsadu'l-etfal 88) Because they were written in *pencil* they cannot be read well [=they are hard to read]. {also: qelemzirîç (ZF3); qelemzrêç (JB3/IFb)} < qelem = 'pen' + zirêç = 'lead' (mineral) [BX/K/GF/BF/FD//JB3/IFb//ZF3] <qelem>

qelemzirîç قهلهمزريچ (ZF3) = pencil. See **qelemzirêç**.

qelemzrêç قــهــلــهمــزرێــچ (JB3/IFb) = pencil. See **qelemzirêç**.

qelen قــهــلــهن *m.* **(-ê;).** money paid by bridegroom to bride's family; trousseau given to the fiancée, which the parents keep for [the newly wed couple?] (JJ); price of purchasing a wife (JJ); bride-price, bridewealth (B) [Cf. T başlık]: **•Hema *qelenê* qîzê min--ħeft qent'er deve, barê wana lal û dir̄, cewahir** (IS-#179) But *the price of* my daughters is: seven trains of camels loaded up with rubies and pearls **•Keça mîran bi *qelenê* gavana nayê** (L[1937]/Dz) For the daughter of an emir, a cowherd's *trousseau* won't do *[prv.]* **•Min t'irê ew bona *qelen* nikarin p'evk'evin yanê jî apê Mîlo naxwaze qîza xwe bide min** (Ba2-#2, 207) I imagine that they cannot agree on *the bride-price* or that Uncle Milo does not want to give his daughter to me. {also: qalen (A); qalind II (HB); qelend; qeleng (OK); qelin (FK-kk-1); qelind (IFb); [qalin/qalän] قلن (JJ); <qalan> قالان (HH)} {syn: next} Sor qelen قــهــلــهن; Cf. T galın [Emirdağı-Afyon; Sungurlu-Çorum; Malatya; Gaziantep; Telin, Gürün-Sıvas; Pınarbaşı-Kayseri; Niğde] = 'the money which the groom gives to the bride's family' (DS, v. 6, p. 1901); Rus kalym калым. for a description of this practice see: B. Nikitine. *Les Kurdes: étude sociologique et historique* (Paris : C. Klincksieck, 1956), pp. 108-9 [HB//K/B/ JB1-S/GF/TF//A//IFb//FK-kk-1//HH//JJ//DS//OK] <cihaz; dermalî>

qelend قهلهند = bride-price. See **qelen**.

qeleng قهلهنگ (OK) = bride-price. See **qelen**.

qeleşîn قـهـلـهشـيـن (GF) = European roller (bird). See **qelaşînk**.

qeleşînk قهلهشينك (ZF3) = European roller (bird). See **qelaşînk**.

qelet قهلهت (F/K) = mistake; wrong. See **xelet**.

qelevîsk قـهـلـهڤـيـسـك (Qmş) = squatting, kneeling. See **qelefiskî**.

qelew قـهـلـهو *adj.* plump, fat, stout, obese *(of people & animals)*: **•S̲ubey zû S̲adiq Beg deh peẕêt *qelew* înan, do xulam bê çek digel xo birin, çû ber derê kinîştê, r̄awesta** (SK 26:238) Early next morning Sadiq Beg brought ten *fat* sheep, took two unarmed followers with him and went to the door of the synagogue and stopped. {also: <qelew> قلو (HH)} {syn: k'ok I[1]; xurt [3]; ≠jar; ≠zirav} Sor qełew قــهــڵــهو; Za qelaw (Todd) {qelew[t]î} [K/A/JB3/IFb/B/HH/SK/GF/TF/OK]

qelewî قــهــلــهوى *f.* **(-ya;-yê).** fatness, plumpness, obesity, stoutness: **•Çend zanayên zankoya Harfard ya Amerîka, rêya kontrolkirina *qelewîyê* aşkere kir** (diarbaker.net 9.v.2015) Some scientists at Harvard University in America have revealed a way to control *obesity*. {also: qelewtî (B-2)} [K/IFb/B/GF/TF/ZF3] <qelew>

qelewtî قهلهوتى (B) = fatness. See **qelewî**.

qelibandin قـهـلِـبـانـدِن *vt.* **(-qelibîn-).** to force s.o. to meet s.o. else; to cause to collide, knock together: **•Çwîkê beytik çû *xwe li* çêlîkê teyrê Sêmir *qeliband* û car di vegerîya û car di *xwe lê qeliband*** (L) The sparrow went and *threw herself at* the Simurgh's chick, and came back, and *darted at it* again **•Hûnê me li belakê *biqelibînin*** (L)

You *will drag* us into a disaster. [L/K/IFb/ZF3] <qulibîn>

qelin قەلِن (FK-kk-1) = bride-price. See **qelen**.

qelind قەلِند (IFb) = bride-price. See **qelen**.

qelişandin قەلِشاندِن *vt.* **(-qelişîn-).** 1) to tear, rip *(vt.)*; 2) to crack, split *(vt.)*. {also: kelişandin (Bw/Zx); **qelaştin**; <qelişandin قلشاندن (diqelişîne) (دقلشینه)> (HH)} [Ba3/K/IFb/HH/GF//Bw/Zx] <qelişîn> See also **qelaştin**.

qelişîn قەلِشین *vi.* **(-qeliş-).** 1) {syn: ç'irîn; dirîn} to tear, rip *(vi.)*; 2) to crack, split *(vi.)*; to break, snap *(vi.)*; 3) to come apart. {also: kelişîn (Bw/Zx); <kelişîn> کلشین (JR); [qelechin] قلشین (JJ); <qelişîn قلشين (diqelişî) (دقلشى)>} [JR/Bw/Zx//K/IFb/HH/GF//JJ] <qelişandin>

qelişţek قەلِشتەك (K) = hole; crack. See **qelîştek**.

qelişţok قەلِشتۆك (B) = hole; crack. See **qelîştek**.

qelî قەلی *f.* **(-ya;).** meat which is roasted in fat [**dohn**] and then kept in a cold place (or frozen) for as long as a year, to be saved for consumption during the winter [cf. drippings]; fried meat: **•Wextê ko Smail Paşa zanî dîharîya maqûlêt Mizûrîyan kûr in pîçek di dilê xoda sil bo. Got e pêş-xizmetêt xo, 'Têşta wan sewar bît. Sênîyan tejî biken, serê wan qubbeyî biken, pişkêt qelîya goştê kûran bi řexêt sewarê we-nên'** (SK 24: 222) When Ismail Pasha learnt that the present of the Mizuri elders was kids [=goats] he became a little annoyed in his heart. He said to his attendants, `Let their morning meal be of crushed wheat. Fill the trays, pile them up like a dome and put the pieces of fried *kid-meat* round the boiled wheat'. {also: [qeli] قلى (JJ); <qelî> قلى (HH)} [Bw/K/A/IFb/B/JJ/HH/SK/TF/OK] <goşt; qelandin[1]>

qelîbotk قەلیبۆتك *f.* **(-a;-ê).** humorous anecdote, joke: **•Hecî, lawo, hema bi van çîroka, *qelîbotka* tu ebûra xwe dikî?** (mirbotan.com 24.i.2009) Haji [Jndiye], my boy, do you make your living from these tales, these *jokes*? {syn: qirwelk} [Rwn/Z-#839-#925/ZF3] <çîvanok>

qelîştek قەلیشتەك *f.* **(-a;-ê).** aperture, opening, orifice; hole; crack, slit, fissure, crevice *(in a wall)*: **•Li ort'a kevir *qelîştekek* hebû** (EP-8) in the middle of the rock there was *an opening*. {also: kelişţek (JB3); qelişţek (K); qelişţok (B); qelîştok (B-2)} {syn: derz; kelş; terk} [EP-8//K//JB3]

qelîştok قەلیشتۆك (B) = hole; crack. See **qelîştek**.

qelp I قەلپ *adj.* 1) false, falsified, counterfeit, forged, spurious, fake(d); 2) dishonest, insincere, dissimulating, hypocritical: **•Birê *qelpe* bêřahm divên: "Mîrê me, birakî wî jî hebû, navê wî Ûsiv bû, ew jî mîna vî xirav bû, lê me řokê ew batmîş kir bê ser-berate"** (Ba3-3, #38) The *dishonest*, merciless brothers say: "Our emir, he had a brother named Joseph who was as bad as him, but one day we did away with him without leaving a trace." {also: qelb I (IF-2); [qalb] قلب (JJ); <qelb> قلب (HH)} <Ar qalb قلب, verbal noun of qalaba قلب = 'to turn, overturn; to change' --> P qalb قلب = 'counterfeit, base'; T kalp = 'counterfeit; (person) who is not what he appears to be'; Sor qełb قەڵب = 'false, faked, counterfeit' {qelp[t]î} [MC-1/F/K/IFb/B/GF//JJ/HH]

qelp II قەلپ *m.* **(-ê;).** shell, rind, peel; bark: **•Kezan--mestir in û *qelpkê* wan mukumtir e--bêwk biçûktir in û *qelpkê* wan naziktir e** (Bw) Kezan [type of terebinth seed] are larger and their *shell* is harder--bêwk are smaller and their *shell* is softer; **-ji qelp [şqelp] kirin** (Bw) to peel *(e.g., a banana)* {syn: spî kirin}. {also: qelpik (Bw-2/IFb); qelpîşk (Bw-2)} {syn: qalik; qaşil; tîvil} <NENA qŭlpâ ܩܠܦܐ = 'skin, rind, bark' (Maclean) < Syr qālpā ܩܠܦܐ = 'bark, rind, husk, peel' & Arc qlaf קלף = 'to peel, pare' [Bw//IFb]

qelpik قەلپك (Bw/IFb) = shell, peel. See **qelp II**.

qelpî قەلپی *f.* **(-ya;-yê).** 1) falsity, trickery, deception, cheating; 2) insincerity, dishonesty, hypocrisy, dissimulation: **•Îsa *qelpîya* wan zanibû** (NewTestament: Metta 22:18) Jesus knew of their dishonesty. {also: qelpîtî (ZF3-2); qelptî (K-2/B-2)} [F/K/B/ZF3] <qelp I>

qelpîşk قەلپیشك (Bw) = shell, peel. See **qelp II**.

qelpîtî قەلپیتی (ZF3) = falsity, trickery; dishonesty. See **qelpî**.

qelptî قەلپتی (K/B) = falsity, trickery; dishonesty. See **qelpî**.

qelq قەلق *f.* **().** 1) agitation, upset ; 2) motion, movement: **•Nexweşiya hewayî li reşayiyê *qelqên* eskerî ên mezin aciz dike** (RN) Airsickness on land frustrates large military *movements*. < Ar qalaq قلق = 'upset, concern, worry' [RN/K(s)/JB3/GF]

qelqilîn قەلقلین (FS) = to worry; to be nauseous. See **qilqilîn**.

qels I قەلس *adj.* 1) {syn: lawaz [2]; sist [1]; zeyf [2]; ≠xurt} weak, feeble, decrepit: **•Şewata ku di 1'ê**

Gulanê de destpê kir, *qels dibe* (anfkurdi.com 9.v. 2016) The fire which began on May 1st is *weakening*; 2) {syn: jar I; lawaz; leẍer; narîn; qoř III; zeyf; zirav I} lean, puny (JB3/HH); 3) {syn: bêkêr; p'ûç['] [2]} useless, worthless (K/IF): •...**Her çiqas qenc hatibe dîtin jî, niha ew bingeh û awayê îdareyan *qels* b[û]ye, bêkêr ma ye** (RN) No matter how good it may have seemed, now the foundation and structure of leadership is *of no use*, has become worthless. {also: <qels> قلس (HH)} {qelsî} [Msr/RN/K/A/JB3/IFb/HH/GF/TF/OK]

qels II قەلس *f.* **(-a;).** dense crowding together of fish (in a river) during the coldest [40 days] of the winter (komcivîna masiya li çillê zivistanê). [Zx] <guhnêr; masî>

qelsî قەلسى *f.* **(-ya;-yê).** 1) {syn: sistî [1]; zeîfî [2]} weakness; 2) leanness (JB3); 3) uselessness, worthlessness (IF). [A/JB3/IF/GF/ZF3] <qels I>

qelş قەلش (K/A/IFb/GF/TF) = crack. See **kelş**.

qelûn قەلوون *f.* **(-a;-ê).** 1) smoking-pipe: •***Qelûna* bavê min tijî titûn e** (AB) My father's *pipe* is full of tobacco; 2) {syn: lûle} pipe, tube. {also: qelin (K/B); [qaloun] قلون (JJ); <qelûn> قلون (HH)} Cf. Ar ɣalyūn غليون; Za qeylani *f.* (Todd) [AB/JB3/IFb/HH/JJ/GF//K/B] <baçek; cigare; lûle; serik [2]>

qemandin قەماندِن *vt.* **(-qemîn-).** 1) {syn: kuzirandin} to toast *(bread)*; to char, singe, sear; 2) to treat a swollen limb with: a) warm water (GF); b) heat (DBgb/FS): •**Xwe dirêj bike *ezê* birînan *biqemînim*. Paçek stûr anî da ber agir heta baş germ bû, pişt re danî ser birînê. Paç pir germ bûbû, laşê wî ji ber dişewitiya, lê dîsa *qemandin* lê xweş dihat** (DBgb, 46) Lie down, *I'll treat* your wounds. She took a thick cloth and held it before the fire until it heated up, then she put it on the wound. The cloth had gotten hot, his body was baking under it, but still *the burning* felt good. {also: qemihandin (GF-2); qemirandin I (A/TF/ZF/CS/BF-2)} Cf. Ar qammar II قمّر = 'to toast' [DBgb/FJ/GF/BF/FS//A/TF/ZF/CS]

qemç قەمچ *f.* **(-a;-ê).** tail *(of animal: horse, donkey, goat)*: •**Hat tespîtkirin ku dirêjiya dînazorê ji *qemçê* heta serî 35 mêtre ye** (www.aa.com.tr 9.viii.2017) It has been proven that the dinosaur's length from *tail* to head is 35 meters; **-qemça hespê** (Frq/Srk) horse's tail; **-qemça kerê** (Frq/Srk) donkey's tail. {also: qemç[i]k (Srk-2); [qamtchik] قمچك (JJ); <qemçik> قمچك (HH)} {syn: boç'[ik]; dêl II; k'ilk; kurî I (Bw); teřî I} [Frq/Srk/IFb/ZF3//JJ/HH] <dûv; qemçik>

qemçik قەمچِك *f.* **(-a;).** 1) {also: qemç} tail *(of goats)* (IFb/JJ/HH): **-qemçka bizinê** (Srk) goat's tail {syn: dûvê bizinê (Frq)}; 2) ponytail (Frq/Srk/A/IFb). {also: qemçk (Srk-2); [qamtchik] قمچك (JJ); <qemçik> قمچك (HH)} [Frq/Srk/A/IFb/JJ/HH] <qemç>

qemçk قەمچك (Srk) = tail. See **qemç[ik]**.

qemçor قەمچۆر (LY) = animal tax. See **qamçûř**.

qem•e قەمە *f.* **(•eya;•[ey]ê).** dagger: •***Qemeya* Kurdî ya 200 salî!** (antikakurd.blogcu.com) 200 year-old Kurdish dagger. {also: qame (IF); qime (B); <qame> قامە (HH)} {syn: kahûr (IF); xencer} [K/F/Ba2/JR//IFb/HH/ZF3//B] <k'êr; sîleḧ; şûr>

qemer قەمەر *adj.* 1) {syn: dêmqemer} swarthy, dark-complected, dark-complexioned; 2) black *(of horses)* (K/JJ/HH/GF). {also: qimer (B); [qamer/qamär (PS)] قمر (JJ); <qemer> قمر (HH)} Cf. NA kûmâ ܟܘܡܐ = 'black' < Arc 'ūkāmā אוכמא; cf. also T kumral = 'brown (haired)' < kum = 'sand' [Kmc-2/K/A/IFb/JJ/HH/GF/TF/OK//B] <řeş>

qemihandin قەمهاندِن (GF) = to toast. See **qemandin**.

qemirandin I قەمِراندِن (A/TF/ZF/CS/BF) = to toast. See **qemandin**.

qemirîn قەمِرين (IFb) = to freeze; to be numb. See **qerimîn**.

qemî قەمى *adv./conj.* [+*subj.*] perhaps, maybe; in hopes of: •**Çak ewe em her do xo tecribe bikeyn, *qemî* çareyekî bikeyn, bişkînîn** (SK 6:66) It would be best for us both to try, *perhaps* we can find a solution, by rending it •**Ew çû mala Azadî *qemî* bibînit** (FS) He went to A.'s house in hopes of seeing him. {also: <qemî قەمى> (Hej)} {syn: belkî; çêdibît [see çê]} [Hk/Zeb/SK/OK/Hej/FS]

qemîs قەميس *m.* **(-ê;).** shirt: •**Carna şêx bi xwe *qemîsê* xwe dike dîyarî** (kurdinfo.com: Êzîdî û ola Êzîdîtî) Sometimes the sheikh himself makes a gift of his own *shirt*. {syn: îşlik; kiras[1]; qutik I} <Ar qamīṣ قميص < Sp camisa [Bw/Zeb/RZ/ZF3]

qem-qanat قەم قانات (EP-4) = stature; build. See **qedqamet**.

qenaet قەنائەت/**qena'et** قەناعەت [SK/OK] *m./f.(SK/GF)* **(-ê/-a; /-ê).** 1) satisfaction, contentment: **-bi ft-î qenaet kirin** (JR)/**qenaetê xwe kirin** (K) to be satisfied or contented with, to make do with: •**Emma keşkele, egerçî pîs e, belê hemî wext digel me ye, li řaḧetîyê w zeḧmetê digel me řefîq e, xudan-wefa ye. Ew *qena'etê diket bi* pîsî**

ser kulîngêt me (SK 29:269) But the magpie, although it is dirty, is always with us. It is our faithful companion in easy times and hard. It *is satisfied with* the dirt on our middens •[**Melayî sê pîst girtine, dîsanî** ***bi*** **wan** ***qenaet nake***] (JR-1) The mullah grabbed three goatskins, but he still *wasn't satisfied with* them; 2) conviction, being convinced (OK). {also: qinyat (IFb-2/GF/TF); [qanaet] قناعت (JJ); <qina'et> قناعت (HH)} < Ar qanā'ah قناعة = 'satisfaction, contentment; being convinced' --> P qanā'at قناعت & T kanaat [K/IFb/JR/TG2//SK/OK//JJ//HH//GF/TF] <qane>

qenc قهنج *adj.* 1) {syn: baş; ç'ak; ç'ê; r̄ind; xweş; =Sor çak; xas} good: •**Heya go** ***qenc*** **Teyrê Sêmir** ***jê bihecî*** (L) Until the Simurgh *got good and mad at her*; 2) well, healthy; whole, unharmed: **-qenc bûn** (B) to get well, to (be) heal(ed) {syn: k'ewîn; sax bûn}: •**Û ç'evê wî jî** ***qenc bûye*** (Ba) And his eye also *was healed.* {also: [qendj] قنج (JJ); <qenc> قهنج (HH)} {qencî} [BX/K/A/JB3/IFb/B/JJ/HH/JB1-S/GF/TF/OK]

qencî قهنجى *f.* **(-ya;-yê).** 1) {syn: ç'akî; xêr I} goodness: •**Em wer̄a** ***qencîyê*** **dixwazin** (Ba2:2, 206) We mean you no harm [lit. 'we want *goodness* for you']; 2) {syn: ç'akî} a favor; a good turn: •**Vê** ***qencîyê*** **bi min bikî, ez jî ezê** ***qencîke*** **mezin li te bikim** (L) [If] you do me this *favor*, I will do you a big *favor*; **-bin qencîya** ***fk-ê*** **der-k'etin** (XF) to absolve oneself of one's indebtedness to s.o., to repay one's debt [lit. 'to come out from under s.o.'s favor or goodness']: •**Tiştek mi ne lazime, lao, lê wekî tu min r̄astî mîrê misrê bînî, ḧesabke ku tu** ***bin qencîya*** **min** ***derk'etî*** (Ba-1, #24) I don't need anything, boy, but if you arrange for me to meet the emir of Egypt, consider yourself *to have repaid your debt*. {also: [qendji] قنجى (JJ)} [K/A/JB3/IFb/B/JJ/GF/TF/OK] <qenc>

qendarî قهندارى *m.* **().** *type of wheat*: dark brown [reddish] in color, its spikes are widely spaced apart; ripens early and is full of starch (A). {also: qendeharî (A/IFb/GF); <qendeharî> قندهارى (HH); <qendeharî> قهندههارى (Hej)} <P Qandahār قندهار = city in Afghanistan [Qzl//A/IFb/HH/GF/Hej] <genim>

qendeharî قهندههارى (A/IFb/GF/HH/Hej) = type of wheat. See **qendarî**.

qender قهندهر (K2-Fêrîk) = amount. See **qeder I**.

qent'er قهنتهر *f.* **(-a;-ê).** train of camels: •**Hema qelenê qîzê min--ḧeft** ***qent'er*** **deve, barê wana lal û dir̄, cewahir** (IS-#179) But the price of my daughters is: seven *trains of* camels loaded up with rubies and pearls; **-qent'era deva** (B) do. {syn: boş III} <Ar qiṭār قطار --> T katar = 'string, file, or train of animals' [IS/F/K/B] <deve I; ḧêştir; lok' II>

qentirme قهنترمه (Wlt) = rein. See **qet'irme II**.

qeper قهپهر *f.* **(-a;-ê).** throat, neck: •**Ji hêrsan Şêrîfo dilerizî. Bi** ***qepera*** **Sofî girtibû û bi hêz ew hejand** (HYma 43) Sherifo was trembling with rage. He grabbed Sofi by *the throat* and shook him vigorously. {also: gepir (ZF3/Wkt/FS)} {syn: gewrî; ḧefik} [HYma/FJ//ZF3/Wkt/FS]

qepqep قهپقهپ (IFb) = cooing. See **qebqeb**.

qeqibîn قهقِبين (IFb) = to coo (of partridges). See **qebîn**.

qer I قهر *m.* **(-ê;).** debt; loan: •**Me ew pare hemî ji ser̄afan** ***qer kirîye***, **noke** ***qerî*** **dixazin. Me jî çu pare nîye. Ew** ***qere*** **jî me bi hîwîya cenabê begî kirîye** (SK 54:599) We *borrowed* all this money from the bankers and now they want their *loan* back. We have no money. We incurred this *debt* in anticipation of your honor's (honoring it); **-qerê xwe razî kirin** (Hk) to pay off one's debt. {also: qerd II (IFb-2/GF-2/OK-2); qerz (K[s]/IFb-2/GF-2); [qar قر/qarz قرض] (JJ)} {syn: deyn II} < Ar qarḍ قرض [Hk/IFb/JJ/SK/GF/OK//K(s)]

qer II قهر *adj.* shiny black *(of animal's coat)*: •**hespekî** ***qer***, **hespekî, boz, hespekî k'umeyt** (HCK-3, #16, 177) a *black* horse, a gray horse, a bay horse •**mîya** ***qer*** (B/GF) *black* sheep. {syn: ḧemis; r̄eş} [HCK/K/B/IFb/FJ/GF/TF/Kmc] <bel; kever; k'ol IV; taq; xez>

qeraçî قهراچى (K/B) = Gypsy. See **qereçî**.

qeralt'uk قهرالتوك, f. (B) = indistinct figure in the distance; ghost. See **qeret'û**.

qeram قهرام (GF/IFb/Kmc) = reed, bulrush. See **qamir̄** قامِر.

qeran قهران *vt./vi.* **(-qer-).** [+ **jê**] to stop, cease, leave off or quit doing stg.; to leave, abandon: •[**Ezê** ***jê qerim***] (JJ) I *will leave off it* •...**Her şeş serî jêkirin, ew jî bi yek serî hişt û** ***jê qariha***, **r̄ast çû qesrê** (HR 3:132) He chopped off all 6 heads, he left him with one head and *left him* that way, and went straight to the palace •**Hecî Ezîz** ***dev ji gund qeriya*** **ji ber ku şeş-heft dikan avakirin** (HYma 18) Haji Aziz *left* the village because they built

6-7 shops •**Min *jê qereha* = Ez *jê qeram*** (Mdt) I *quit doing it*. {also: jê qarihan (HR); qerehan (Mdt-2); jê qeriyan (HYma); qeřandin (K); [qarin] قـريـن (JJ)} {syn: dest jê k'işandin; dev jê berdan; hiştin; ji ... řabûn; t'erkandin} [Mdt/TF/FJ//HR//JJ//K]

qeřandin قـەڕانـدِن (K) = to stop, quit, abandon, leave off. See **qeran**.

qerar قـەرار (JB3/HH/SK/GF/LY) = decision; command; reign; agreement; promise; custom. See **qirar**.

qerargeh قەرارگەه *f.* **(-a;-ê).** (military) headquarters: •***qerargeha* Hevalbendan a mezin** (RN) main Allied *headquarters*. {also: qirarge (K)} {syn: fermangeh} Cf. P qarārgāh قـرارگـاه = 'residence, abode'; T karargâh = 'headquarters' [RN/IFb/GF/ZF3/Wkt//K]

qerase I قـەراسە *adj.* huge, enormous, gigantic: •**Em çawa dikarin êrîşî fîlên weha *qerase* ku bi qasî Xwedê mezin in, bikin Siltanê min?** (SF 29) My Sultan, how could we attack elephants, that are as *huge* as God? {also: qirase I (IFb-2)} {syn: girs; gumreh; teřikî II} [SF/IFb/TF/ZF3]

qeřase II قـەڕاسـە *m./f.(Wkp)* **(/-ya;-yî/-yê).** crank, lever: •**Bi alîkariya *qeraseyê* mirov dikare gelek tiştên giran ji cî bilivîne û rake** (Wkp) With the help of a lever one can move heavy things and lift them. {also: qirase II (IFb-2/BF)} [CCG/IFb/GF/TF/FS//BF]

qeraş قـەراش (K[s]/A/JB3/IFb/GF/TF/FS) = miller. See **keraş**.

qeřate قـەڕاتـە (FS) = indistinct figure in the distance; ghost. See **qeret'û**.

qeratî قـەراتـی = indistinct figure in the distance; ghost. See **qeret'û**.

qerat'û قـەراتـوو (K) = indistinct figure in the distance; ghost. See **qeret'û**.

qeratûk قـەراتـووك (EP-7) = indistinct figure in the distance; ghost. See **qeret'û**.

qerat'ûlk قـەراتـوولـك = indistinct figure in the distance; ghost. See **qeret'û**.

qerawil قەراوِل (B) = guard, sentry. See **qerewil**.

qerawilî قەراوِلی (B) = guard duty. See **qerewiltî**.

qerawiltî قەراوِلتی (B) = guard duty. See **qerewiltî**.

qerawîl قەراویل (GF) = guard, sentry. See **qerewil**.

qerawîlî قەراویلی (GF) = guard duty. See **qerewiltî**.

qerax قەراخ, m. (K/IFb/GF) = edge. See **qirax**.

qerbaş قەرباش (L-Mîşo) = servant. See **qerwaş**.

qerç'im قەرچِم (B) = wrinkle. See **qermîçok**.

qerç'imandin قـەرچِـمـانـدِن (B/K) = to wrinkle; to fade. See **qermiç'andin**.

qerç'imîn قـەرچِـمـيـن (K/B) = to be wrinkled; to fade (vi.) . See **qermiç'în**.

qerç'imok قەرچِمۆك (B) = wrinkle. See **qermîçok**.

qerçîmek قەرچیمەك (GF) = wrinkle. See **qermîçok**.

qerd I قـەرد *adj.* mature, adult; large (B): -**qerd bûn** = to mature, grow up: •**Qîza te jî *qird bûye*, ce'nûa te jî mezin bûye** (Z-921) Both your daughter has *matured*, and your colt has grown; -**ĥeywanê qird** (B) cattle (=cows, oxen, water buffalo) *as opposed to pez = sheep and goats*. {also: qird (B/Z-921)} {≠cahil; ≠nestêl; ≠xam} [Z-921/B//K]

qerd II قەرد (IFb/GF/OK) = debt. See **qer**.

qerdar قـەردار *adj.* in debt, indebted, owing: •**Hûn *qerdarî* me ne** (SK 54:599) You owe us some money/You are *indebted to* us. {also: qerddar (IFb); qerzdar (K[s]/GF/TF); [qarz-dar قـرضـدار/ qardar قـردار] (JJ)} {syn: deyndar I} Cf. P qarzdār قرضدار [SK/JJ/OK//IFb//K(s)/GF/TF]

qerddar قەرددار (IFb) = in debt. See **qerdar**.

qerebalix قـەرەبـالِـخ *f.* **(-a;-ê).** 1) {syn: bařebař; biřbiř; gelemşe; hengame; hêwirze; hoqeboq; k'im-k'imî; qajeqaj; qalmeqal; qareqar; qîřeqîř; şerqîn; t'eqeřeq} din, noise, uproar, commotion: •**Wan gelek *qerebaliẍ* kir** (FS) They made a lot of noise; 2) {syn: ferc; sixlet; t'op I} crowd, mob: •**Di *qerebalixa* zêde û kombûnên teng de ew dest tavêjin berîkên xelkê** (sverigesradio.se 14.vii.2014) In dense crowds and tight gatherings they direct their hands to people's pockets; 3) [*adj.*] crowded: •**Ez o çend derwêşêt feqîr li wê-derê řû-nêyn, 'ibadetê xudê bikeyn, çonko naw bajêrî *qelebaliẍ* e, qelbê muro mişewweş dibît, muro neşêt bi dirustî zikrê xudê biket** (SK 38:339) Some poor dervishes and I shall settle there and worship God, for in the city it is crowded and commotion and a man's heart is disturbed and he cannot properly worship God. {also: kerebaliẍ (L); qelebaliẍ (SK); qerebaliẍ (FS); [qarabaliq] قـرەبـالـق (JJ)} < T kalabalık = 'crowd(ed)' <Ar ɣalabah غـلـبـة (= large amount, majority) verbal noun of √ɣ-l-b غـلـب = 'to vanquish; to prevail, predominate' + T -lık abstract noun ending; cf also Turoyo ɣalabe = 'much, very' [L//K/B/GF//JJ//FS//SK]

qerebaliẍ قەرەبالِغ (FS) = noise; crowd. See **qerebalix**.

qerebaşî قـەرەباشـی *m.* **().** servant; slave: •**Ĥevt dergê**

bavê min hene ji polane / T'emamî bi *qerebaşî*, p'elewane (Z-1) My father has 7 gates of steel, / replete with *servants* and knights. [Z-1/L] See also **qerwaş**.

qereç قەرەچ (SK/BF/FS) = Roma, Gypsy. See **qereçî**.

qereçî قـەرەچـى *m.* **(-yê;).** 1) {syn: aşiq; begzade [2]; boşe; dome; gewende; mirt'ib} Roma, Gypsy; 2) {syn: aşiq[2]; begzade[2]} musician: **•Ez hîwî dikem, çî dî beḧsê qerî digel musîbet neke, bila bo wî bît. We diyar e wî di 'umrê xoda eslen pare nedîtiye, ḧetta noke delû we *qereç* boye** (SK 54:626) I ask you, don't talk about debts and misfortunes anymore, let him have it. It is clear that he has never seen money in his life, up til now he has been a minstrel, a *musician*. {also: qeraçî (K/B); qereç (SK/BF/FS); [karach] قـــراچ (JJ); <qereçî> قرچى (HH)} Cf. Iraqi Ar qaraj قرج = 'Roma, Gypsy'; Sor qerec قـــەرەج [IFb/A/HH/GF//K/B/FD//SK/BF/FS//JJ]

qerefil قەرەفِل, m. (B) = carnation; clove; nosering. See **qerefîl**.

qerefîl قـــەرەفـيـل *f.* **(-a;-ê).** 1) {also: qerenfil (K/F); qerenfîl (IFb/GF); [qarafil/karafil (Lx) قـــرافـل/ karúnfol (G)/karanfīl (Rh) قـرنـفـل] (JJ); <qerafil> قـرافـل (HH)} carnation, bot. *Dianthus plumarius*: **•Me *qerenfîla* sor jî wek nîşaneya rengê ala xwe danî ser mezel** (www.aa.com.tr 28.xi.2013) We placed a red *carnation* on the grave as a symbol of the color of our flag; 2) clove (spice); 3) {also: qerefil, m. (B); qerenfîl (IF); [karafil (Lx) قـرافـل/ karúnfol (G)/karanfīl (Rh) قـرنـفـل] (JJ); <qerafil> قـرافـل (HH)} {syn: xizêm} nosering; golden nose ornaments in the shape of chamomile flowers [Rus romaški ромашки], for women (Ba): **•Xizêma poz, qaş, *qerefîl*, guharê zêr̄ xala sûretr̄a şer̄bûn** (Ba-1, #17) The nosering, precious stone, *nose ornament*, [and] golden earrings were fighting with the birthmark on [her] cheek. <Gr karyophyllon καρυόφυλλον + Mod Gr kariofîli καρυοφύλλι <karyo- = '(wal)nut' + phyllon = 'leaf': Ar/P qaranful قـرنـفـل = 'carnation; clove'; T/S-Cr karanfil; Bulg karamfil карамфил [Ba/K/B/GF/FS//F//IFb//JJ/HH]

qerefiskî قـەرەفـيـسـكـى (B) = squatting, kneeling. See **qelefiskî**.

qerehan قەرەهان (Mdt) = to stop doing stg. See **qeran**.

qeremac قـەرەمـاج (GF) = spades (in card games). See **qeremaç**.

qeremaç قـــــەرەمـــاچ *m.* **().** spades *(suit in deck of cards)*: **•Bi *qelemaçan* dilîstin heta banga dîkan** (HYma, 31) They played *spades* [card game] until the crow of the roosters. {also: qelemaç (HYma); qeremac (GF); <qeremaç> قـەرەمـاچ (Hej)} {syn: maçe} < T kara = 'black' + T maça = 'spades (in cards)' [Elk/Hej//GF//HYma]

qeremtin قـەرەمـتِـن (M-Am) = to freeze; to be numb. See **qerimîn**.

qerenfil قـەرەنـفِـل (K/F) = carnation; clove; nosering. See **qerefîl**.

qerenfîl قـــەرەنـــفـــيـــل (IFb/GF) = carnation; clove; nosering. See **qerefîl**.

qereqûş قـــەرەقـــووش *m.* **().** bird of prey; hawk, kite, zool. family *Accipitridae* (K): **-teyrekî qereqûş** (EP-7) do. < T karakuş = 'black eagle' [EP-7/K/FS]

qeresî قـەرەسـى *f.* **(-ya;-yê).** cherry; sour cherry (IFb). {syn: gêlaz} Cf. Ar karaz كرز, T kiraz [K/(A)/JB3/IFb/GF/TF/OK/RZ/ZF3/FD]

qeret'û قـــەرەتـــوو *m./f.(B/ZF3)* **(-ê/ ; /-ê).** 1) {syn: r̄eş[2]; r̄eşayî} indistinct figure *(obscured by darkness, distance, or mist)*; silhouette: **•Dûrva *qeret'ûk* xuya dike** (Z-1) in the distance *a silhouette* (=figure) is visible **•*Qeratûkê* wê k'ifş dike** (EP-7) His *indistinct figure* appears; 2) {syn: r̄eşe; sawîr} apparition, ghost (K/B). {also: qeralt'uk, f. (B); qer̄ate (FS); qeratî; qerat'û (K); qeratûk (EP-7); qerat'ûlk; [qaraltou ditin] قـرالـتـو ديـتـن (JJ) = [voir peu à cause de l'éloignement = to see little because of the distance]} < T karaltı = 'indistinct figure' [Z-1/EP-7/ZF3//FS//K//B//JJ] <r̄eş[2]; sînahî>

qeretûn قـــەرەتـــوون *f.* **(-a;-ê).** 1) {syn: berfiravînk (Bw)} mid-morning coffee break (Msr); 2) first breakfast, meal before breakfast (IFb/JB3/FJ/GF). Cf. Sor qawełtî قـاوەڵـتـى = 'lunch; mid-afternoon snack' & qawełtûn قـاوەڵـتـوون/qawełtî قـاوەڵـتـى = 'mid-morning coffee break' (Mukrî) < T kahvaltı = 'breakfast' (<kahve = 'coffee' + altı = '6') [Msr/K(s)/JB3/IFb/TF/FJ/GF] <taştê>

qerewêl قەرەوێل (ZF3) = guard, sentry. See **qerewil**.

qerewêlî قەرەوێلى (ZF3) = guard duty. See **qerewiltî**.

qerewil قـــەرەوِل *m.* **(-ê;).** guard, sentinel, sentry, watchman: **•Delalê, ḧevt dergê bavê min jî hene bi ḧesinî, / T'emam *qerewil*, qerebaşe ber sekinî** (Z-1) My darling, my father has seven gates of iron, / *Watchmen* and guards stand before them.

{also: qerawil (B); qerawîl (GF); qerewêl (ZF3); [qaraoul] قـــــــراول (JJ)} {syn: p'awan I} < T karavul = 'guard, outpost' --> Rus karaúl караул = 'guard' {qerawil[t]î; qerawîlî; qerewil[t]î} [Z-1/K//B//JJ//GF//ZF3]

qerewilî قەرەولى (K) = guard duty. See **qerewiltî**.

qerewiltî قـەرەولـتـى *f.* **(;-yê).** guard duty: **•Her merîk du seʿheta *qerewiltîyê dikşînin*** (FK-kk-13:128) Each man *stands guard* for 2 hours. {also: qerawil[t]î (B); qerawîlî (GF); qerewêlî (ZF3); qerewilî (K)} {syn: nobet} [K//B//GF//ZF3] <qerewil>

qerex قەرەخ = edge. See **qirax**.

qerf قـــــــەرف *f.* **(;-ê).** joke, pleasantry: **•Her wiha peyvên mecazî ku ji bo nifir, çêr û *qerfan* têne bikaranîn jî bi berfirehî di nava vê beşê de cih digirin** (AW70C2) Also, metaphorical words which are used for curses, abuses and *jokes* are abundantly represented in this section **•Vî alî û wî alî avêtin** [sic] **henek û *qerfikan*, bi hev re lîstin** (AW69B4) They cracked all kinds of *jokes* [lit.'to this side and that side they threw jokes'], and frolicked together; **-qerf lê/pê kirin** (K) to tease s.o., make fun of, play a joke on s.o.: **•Divê mirov *qerfan* bi kesî *neke*** (ZF3) One must *not make fun of* anyone. {syn: ħenek; meselok; pêk'enok; tewz; tinaz; t'iȓane; yarî II} [K/A/IFb/B/GF/ZF3]

qerik قەرك (L) = throat. See **qiȓik I**.

qerimçik قەرمچِك (GF) = wrinkle. See **qermîçok**.

qerimîn قـەرمـيـن/**qeȓimîn** قـەرِمـيـن [K] *vi.* **(-qerim-/-qeȓim-).** 1) {syn: cemidîn; qefilîn [1]; qerisîn; qeşa girtin} to freeze up *(vi.)*, be frozen; to turn to ice: **•Îna piştî hingî em hemî hatîne mal, em *qeremtîn* sermada, me bo xo sope helkirin, me xo li ber dirêj kir** (M-Am #716) Then, after that, we all came home and we *were frozen* with cold, and we stoked up the stove for ourselves and stretched out in front of it; 2) {syn: qefilîn [2]; westîyan} to tire *(vi.)*, become tired: **•Çavê min li rîya te *qerimîn*** (Frq) I'm sick and tired [lit. 'My eyes *have tired*'] of waiting for you; 3) to be sluggish *(of rivers, feet, etc., under strong pressure)* (B); to be numb, go to sleep *(of feet, etc.)* (A/IFb/GF); 4) to thicken, harden (B). {also: qemirîn (IFb-2); qeremtin (M-Am); [qaremin] قرمين (JJ); <qerimîn قرمين (diqerimî) (دقرمى)> (HH)} [K//A/B/IFb/HH/GF/Frq//JJ//M-Am] <qefilîn; simirîn>

qerisîn قـەرسـيـن/**qeȓisîn** قـەرِسـيـن [K] *vi.* **(-qeris-/-qeȓis- [K]).** 1) to be cold (Kg/IFb); 2) {syn: cemidîn; qefilîn [1]; qerimîn; qeşa girtin} to freeze *(vi.)*, be frozen (K/HH). {also: <qerisîn قـرسـيـن (diqerisî) (دقـرسـى)> (HH)} [Kg/IFb/HH//K] <qeşa; sar; suȓ I>

qerisokî قـەرسـۆكـى *adj.* cold, frigid, freezing: **•Di ser bayên germ û yên *sar û qerisokî* re firîn** (EN) In spite of the warm and *freezing cold* winds, they flew. [EN/ZF] <qerisîn>

qermiç'andin قـەرمـچـانـدِن *vt.* **(-qermiç'în-).** 1) to wrinkle, rumple *(clothes or skin) (vt.)*: **-ȓû qermiç'andin** (JJ) to scowl, make a face; 2) to fade, wither (vt.) (K). {also: qerç'imandin (B/K); qurçimandin (F); qurmiçandin (IF-2); [qyrmitchandin] قـرمـچـانـديـن (JJ); <qurmiçandin قرمچاندن (diqurmiçîne) (دقرمچينه)> (HH)} [A/IFb//HH//JJ//B/K//F]

qermiç'în قـەرمِـچـيـن *vi.* **(-qermiç'-).** 1) to be wrinkled, puckered *(clothes or skin)*: **•Me'dê wî *qermiç'î*** (Z-2) He made a face [lit. 'His appetite *wrinkled* (or faded)']; 2) {syn: ç'ilmisîn} to fade, wither (K). {also: qerç'imîn (K-2/B); qermijîn (K[s]); qurçimîn (F); qurmiçîn (IFb-2); [qyrmitchin] قـرمـچـيـن (JJ); <qermiçîn قـرمـچـيـن (diqermiçî) (دقــــرمــــچــــى)> (HH)} [Z-2/K/IFbHH//JJ//B//K(s)//F] <qermiç'andin>

qermiçok قەرمچۆك (A/IFb) = wrinkle. See **qermîçok**.

qermijîn قەرمژين (K[s]) = to be wrinkled; to fade *(vi.)*. See **qermiç'în**.

qermîçok قـەرمـيـچـۆك *f.* **(;-ê).** wrinkle, fold, crease; furrow *(in brow)*: **•Birû li mirov dibin cot, mirûz tirş û talo, *qermûçek* li eniya mirov çêdibin** (Wlt 2:59, 12) One's brow becomes pair[ed], morose, sour and bitter, *wrinkles* form on one's brow **•Enî *bû qermîçok* / Herdû birû gihan hev** (Cxn-KE: rencberê birûmet) The forehead *became wrinkle[d]* / The eyebrows came together [lit. 'reached one another']. {also: qerç'im[ok] (B); qerçîmek (GF); qerimçik (GF-2); qermiçok (A/IFb); qermûçek (Wlt 2:59, p.12); qurmîçong (TF); [qarmoutchek قرمچك/ qyrmach قرماش] (JJ)} Cf. Ar karmašah كـرمـشـة = 'fold, crease, wrinkle' [Cxn-KE//B//GF//A/IFb//Wlt/JJ//TF]

qermûçek قـەرمـووچـەك (Wlt 2:59, p.12/JJ) = wrinkle. See **qermîçok**.

qernî قەرنى (GF) = tick. See **qirnî**.

qerpal قـەرپـال *m.* **(-ê;).** 1) overcoat (Rwn); 2) {syn: kerkon; kevnik [2]; p'aç' II & p'aç[']ik; p'ate II; p'eȓok; p'îne; p'ot} rags; ragged, worn-out clothing: •**Mirovên geda û belengaz nikarin tiştên taze û mukum bikrin ... mirov wa dibînit cilên wan *qerpal* in** (Drş #227, 74) People who are poor beggars cannot buy new and sturdy things ... one sees that their clothes are *rags* [or, ragged]. {also: <qerpal> قـرپـال (HH)} [EP-7/K/A/IFb/HH/GF/ZF/FD]

qerp'ûz قـەرپـووز *m.(K)/f.(EP-7)* **(/-a; /-ê).** 1) {syn: saxirî (Z-1/EP-7); terkû (EP-7)} croup, crupper, rump of a quadruped: •**Dizgînê ser *qerp'ûzê*da dadixîne** (EP-7) He lowers the bridle onto the croup [of the horse]; 2) pommel *(of saddle, sword, etc.)* (PS/JJ); saddle? (EP-7). {also: [qarpouz] قرپوز (JJ)} [EP-7/K/JJ]

qerqaş قـەرقاش *adj.* snow white, bright white: **-'enîya qerqaş** (B) snow-white forehead; **-mîya qerqaş** (B) white ewe. {also: <qereqaş> قـــرقـــاش (HH)} {syn: çîl-sipî} [Ag/Kmc-2/K/IFb/B/GF//HH] <spî I>

qerqeşe قەرقەشە (IFb/FS) = commotion. See **qerqeşûn II**.

qerqeşûm قەرقەشووم (K) = lead. See **qerqeşûn I**.

qerqeşûn I قـــەرقـــەشـــوون *f.* **(;-ê).** lead (chemical element: Pb): •**Li Kebanê kanên *qerqeşûnê* hene** (A.Tîgrîs. Cografya Kurdistanê 20) In Keban there are *lead* mines. {also: qerqeşûm (K); qerşûn (IFb); [kurguschun] قورغشن (JJ)} {syn: zirêç} Chagatay qūrγāšūn قورغاشون; T kurşun; NENA qerqûshim ܩܪܩܘܫܡ (Maclean); Sor qurquşim قـوڕقـوشـم; Za qirqişun (Mal) [B/Wkt//K//IFb//JJ]

qerqeşûn II قـەرقـەشـوون *f.* **(-a;).** commotion, uproar: •**Xwe nexapînin, hûn mêr in, hûn leheng in, we gelek *qerqeşûn* derbas kirine** (Wlt 2:59, 2) Don't fool yourselves, you're men, you're heroes, you have been through a lot of *commotion*. {also: qerqeşe (IFb/FS)} Cf. Sor qerqeşe قـــەرقـــەشـــە/ xerxeşe خەرخەشە [Wlt/TF/ZF3//IFb/FS]

qerqod•e قـــەرقـــۆدە *m.* **(•ê;).** 1) skeleton: **-qerqodê mirovî** (FS) do.; 2) wreckage, fuselage *(of airplane, car, etc.)*. {also: qerqote (IFb); qerqûde (Kmc-6/TF/OK-2)} [Dh/OK/AA//Kmc-6/TF/FS//IFb] <k'ilox = qehf>

qerqote قەرقۆتە (IFb) = skeleton. See **qerqode**.

qerqûde قـــەرقـــوودە (Kmc-6/TF/OK) = skeleton. See **qerqode**.

qersel قـــەرســـەل (FS) = straw remaining after the harvest. See **qesel**.

qerşûn قەرشوون (IFb) = lead. See **qerqeşûn I**.

qert قـــەرت *adj.* 1) old, past one's prime; 2) [*m.*] five-year old male goat or ram: •**Nêrîyê çar s̲alî dibêjnê maz, û yê pênc dibêjnê *qert*** (FS) A four-year old billy goat they call 'maz', and a five-year old they call '*qert*'; **-beranê qert** (FS) five-year old ram; **-nêrîyê qert** (FS/BF) five-year old billy goat. Cf. T kart [FS/G/FD/Wkt/ZF3/BF] <beran; maz I; nêrî I>

qertaf قـــەرتـــاف *f.* **(-a;-ê).** grammatical ending; affix: •**/-ê/: Bi alîkariya vê *qertafê*, navdêr, cînavk û veqetandekên mê tên nîşandan** (TaRZ, 90) /-ê/: With help of this *ending*, feminine nouns, pronouns and possessive constructions are identified •***Qertafa* nebinavkirinê ya bêjeyên nêr '-ekî'** (TaRZ, 91) Indefinite *ending* for masculine nouns '-ekî'. [TaRZ/ZF/Wkt] <paşp'irtik; pêşp'irtik>

qertel قـەرتـەل (K/IFb/B/GF/OK) = vulture, eagle. See **xertel**.

qertik قەرتِك (CCG) = type of cucumber. See **qitik**.

qerwaş قـــــــــەرواش *f.* **(-a;-ê).** maidservant, female servant: •**Ev car *qewraşa* Axê rabû çû ser hewzê da av bibe malê** (ZZ-7, 222) This time the Agha's *maidservant* arose and went to the reservoir to bring water home •**Ya stîya Zîne, hege ez hatime oda te, tê gazî kî *qerwaşê* te** (Z-2) Lady Zîn, if it is I who has come to your room, call your *servants*. {also: qerbaş (L-Mîşo); qerweş, m. (K); qewraş (Z-3); [qaravach] قـــروش (JJ); <qerwaş> قـــرواش (HH)} {syn: carî} < T karavaş = 'female slave' [IFb/HH/GF//JJ//K] See also **qerebaşî**.

qerwelk قەروەلك (Qmş) = anecdotes. See **qirwelk**.

qerweş قەروەش, m. (K) = servant. See **qerwaş**.

qerz قەرز (K[s]/IFb/GF) = debt. See **qer**.

qerzdar قەرزدار (K[s]/GF/TF) = in debt. See **qerdar**.

qesabxane قـەسـابـخـانـە (K/IFb/B) = slaughterhouse. See **qes̲ebxane**.

qesapxane قـــەســـاپـــخـــانـــە (GF) = slaughterhouse. See **qes̲ebxane**.

qesd قـــــەســــد *f.* **(-a;-ê).** intention, plan; aim, goal, purpose: **-qesda *ft-î* kirin** (K) to make for, head for, bend one's steps toward, set out after, intend: •**Wextê bû zistan, dîsa Art̲îşî her weku caran r̄abû, çû Mûsilê, *qesda* mala dostê xo *kir*** (SK 31:279) When it was winter the Artushi rose again, as before, went to Mosul and *made for* his friend's house •**Xelkê go bê li ser kursîya zêr rûnin, *qesda* qîza wî *dikin*** (L) People who come sit on the gold chair, *are coming for* [i.e., are intending to marry] his daughter. {also: qest (B/

SK-2/JB1-A&S/GF-2/TF); [qasd] قـــصـــد (JJ); <qesd> قصد (HH)} {syn: armanc; nêt} < Ar qaṣd قصد = 'intention, object, goal' [L/K/JB3/IFb/SK/GF//B//JJ/HH]

qese قەسە (OK/Hk) = talk; bad words. See **qise**.

qeseb قەسەب (K) = oath. See **qesem**.

qesebxan•e قـەصـەبـخـانـە *f.* **(•a;•ê).** slaughterhouse; butcher shop. {also: qesabxane (K/IFb/B); qesapxane (GF); <qessabxane> قصابخانه (HH)} <Ar qaṣṣāb قـصّـاب = 'butcher' + P xāneh خـانـه = 'house'; Sor qesabxane قەسابخانە [Bw//K/IFb/B//HH//GF]

qesef قەسەف (L) = cage. See **qefes**.

qesel قـــەســـەل *m./f.(B/FS)* **(-ê/-a; /-ê).** stalks of straw remaining after the harvest: **•Wî *qesela* genimê xwe gêre kir** (FS) He threshed *the stalks of* his wheat. {also: qersel (FS-2); xesel (CCG-2); <qesel> قسل (HH)} {syn: sap} < Ar qaṣal قصل = 'chaff, husks, shucks, awns, stalks (of grain)'; Sor qeser قـــەســـەر (Arbil) [Zeb/K/A/IFb/B/HH/TF/CCG/FS] <lask>

qesem قـــەســـەم *m./f.(ZF3)* **(/-a; /-ê).** oath, vow: **•Ez *bi qesema* navê xwedê *kim*** (lotikxane.com: Bazê Qendîlê 10.v.2015) May I *swear* by the name of God. {also: qeseb (K); <qesem> قسم (HH)} {syn: sond} < Ar qasam قسم [Z-922/IFb/HH/ZF3/Wkt//K]

qesidîn قـــەسِـــدیـــن *vi.* **(-qesid-).** to consult with, seek counsel from, come to s.o. with a problem: **•Xelefê Zêbarî di çavên min de mîna çiyayekî bû. Heger ew rojekê li min *biqesidiyaya*, min dê tiştek ji bo wî texsîr nekiraya** (Wkt: E.Karahan: *Nesrîn*, Nefel.com, ix.2009) Khalaf Zebari was a mountain in my eyes. If one day he *had come to me with a problem*, I would have spared nothing to help him. < Ar qaṣada قـــصـــد = 'to head for, intend' [Wkt/K/A/IFb/ZF3]

qesir قەسِر (K/B/GF) = castle. See **qesr**.

qesîl قەسیل (IFb) = mat. See **qisîl**.

qesîs قەسیس *adj.* greedy, miserly, tightfisted [T cimri; Fr avare, radin]: **•Mirovên vî gundî ew qasî *qesîs* (destgirtî) bûne ku di nav civakê de kesî navê gundê wan bi lêv nedikir** (diyamame.com 26.iii.2015) The people of this village were so *tightfisted* that no one in society would pronounce the name of their village. {also: **xesîs** (K/A/IFb/JJ/HH/Hej/ZF/RZ/Wkt/CS/OrK); xesûs (Y. Sarılmaz)}{syn: ç'avbirçî; ç'ikûs; çirûk; devbeş; evsene} [Nsb/TF/Wkt]

qesp I قـــەســـپ *f.* **(-a;-ê).** dates, *especially light [zer], dry [hişk] and hard [ȓeq] ones*, bot. *Phoenix dactylifera*: **-liba qespê** (FS) a single date. {also: <qesp> قـسـب (HH); <qesp> قـەسـپ (Hej)} {syn: xurme} Cf. Ar qaṣab قـصـب = 'cane, reed, stalk'; Sor qesp قەسپ = kuȓkuje کورکوژه = 'Zahidi dates' [Zeb/AA/Kmc-2/CB/IFb/HH/SK/GF/OK/Hej/FS]

qesp II قـــەســـپ *adj.* solid (of a stone's interior)--the quality of a flintstone. {≠ fisfisok = kuş} [Qzl/A] <berheste>

qesr قـــەســـر *f.* **(-a;-ê).** castle, palace; stone building, mansion: **•...Her şeş serî jêkirin, ew jî bi yek serî hişt û jê qariha, ȓast çû *qesrê*** (HR 3:132) He chopped off all 6 heads, he left him with one head and left him that way, and went straight to *the palace* **•Qubad Aẍaê Zerzan o xulamêt wî w Osê w kuȓêt wî w çend xudan-silaḧêt Zerzan hemî kewtine *qesra* Qubad Aẍa. Muḧasere bon pênc şew o pênc ȓojan. Li-ser *qesrê* bo şeȓ. Hindî Herkîyan hucûm kirine *qesrê*, çi fayde nebo. Her hucûmê bîst mêr zêde li-bin *qesrê* ji Herkîyan telef dibon. Çend ȓexêt *qesrê* ji-ber cendekan dîhar nebon** (SK 40:379) Qubad Agha of the Zerzan and his men and Ose and his boys and some armed men of the Zerzan, they all assailed *the castle of* Q.A. They were besieged for 5 nights and 5 days. There was a war over *the castle*. No matter how much the Herkis attacked *the castle*, it was no use. In each attack, 20 men or more of the Herkis perished below *the castle*. Some sides *of the castle* were not visible due to the [pile of] corpses; **-qesir û qûnax** (Z-3) palace. {also: qesir (K/B/GF); [kasser] قـصـر (JJ); <qesr> قصر (HH)} < Ar qaṣr قصر < Lat castellum [K/B/GF//(A)/JB3/IFb/HH/SK//JJ]

qest قـەسـت (B/SK/JB1-A&S/GF/TF) = plan; aim. See **qesd**.

qeş•a قـەشـا *f.* **(•a;•aê/•ê).** 1) {syn: cemed} ice: **•Min ew tasa çeqilmêst a ku hîn *qeşa* wê neheliyabû ji destê wê girtibû, çend gulp jê vexwaribû** (KS, 49) I took that cup of çeqilmast--in which *the ice* had not yet melted --from her hands and drank a few gulps of it; **-qeşa girtin** (IFb/B) to freeze *(vi.)* (IF); to be covered with hoar-frost (B); 2) {syn: qiȓav; xûsî} frost, hoar-frost. {also: qişa (B); [qycha] قـشـا (JJ); <qeşa> قـشـا (HH)} Cf. T kış = 'winter' [K/A/JB3/IFb/HH/GF/TF//B/JJ] <qiȓav; zivistan>

qeşaşîr قـەشـاشـیـر *f.* **(-a;-ê).** ice cream: **•Bajarê Mereş a Bakurê Kurdistanê, bi çêkirina *qeşaşîra* xwe,**

nav û dengê xwe li cîhanê belav kiriy[e] (Rûdaw 17.ix.2017) The city of Marash of Northern Kurdistan has become famous worldwide for making *ice cream* •**Ew *qeşîrê* xweş çêdikit** (FS) She makes *ice cream* well •**Wî *qeşîr* xwar** (FS) He ate *ice cream*.. {*also*: qeşeşîr (Wkt-2); qeşîr (FS)} {syn: berfeşîr; *bestenî; *dondirme; *qerimok} <qeşa = 'ice' + şîr = 'milk' [(neol)Qzl/Wkt//FS]

qeşe قـه‌شـه *m.* **(-yê;-yî).** Christian clergyman, priest, minister: •**Kitêba *qeşeyê* îtalî Maurizio Garzoni "Grammatica e Vocabolario della Lingua Kurda" (Rêziman û ferhengoka zimanê kurdî) sala 1787ê li Romaya Îtalyayê hatiye çapkirin** (rojname.com 17.ix.2016) The book of the Italian *priest* M. Garzoni "Grammar & Vocabulary of the Kurdish Language" was printed in Rome, Italy in 1787. {also: [qacha/kasia (G)] قـشـا (JJ)} {syn: k'eşîş} <Syr qašā ܩܫܐ, contracted form of qašīšā ܩܫܝܫܐ = 'elder; ancestor; priest, presbyter'; NENA qāšā ܩܫܐ (Maclean: qâshâ) & Turoyo qāšō; cf. Ar qiss/qass قَسّ/qissīs قـسّـيـس [clq qassīs], clq Baghdadi also kišīš كشيش; P kašīš كشيش; Sor qeşe قه‌شه [K(s)/SK/OK/FS//JJ] <dêr>

qeşeşîr قه‌شه‌شير (Wkt) = ice cream. See **qeşaşîr**.

qeşirandin قـه‌شِـرانـدِن (ZF3) = to espy, catch sight of. See **qişirandin**.

qeşîr قه‌شير (FS) = ice cream. See **qeşaşîr**.

qeşmer قـه‌شـمـه‌ر *m.&f.* **(-ê/-a;-î/).** 1) {syn: qirdik; şemo} clown, buffoon, laughingstock; comedian, jokester, jester: •**Kesên ku bêhtir di dîwanxaneyên mîran de pêkenok digotin û carna weke şanogerekî bi rola xwe ve radibûn, ew "*qeşmer*" bûn** (CP, 6) People who told jokes and sometimes acted out their stories in the courts of emirs, were "*jesters*"; 2) {syn: bê îĥtiram; emekĥeram; sakol} jerk, fool; person without honor, bum, scoundrel: •**De wir de here *qeşmera* pîs** (DBgb, 14) Get over there, dirty *scoundrel* (f.) •**[K'eftar̄] fêm dike ku şêr bi hîleyên wî hesiyaye ... Şêr bang dike, dibêje: "... *Qeşmerê* teres, divê ku ez careke din te li hizûra xwe nebînim"** (Wlt 2:100, 13) [The hyena] understands that the lion has caught onto his ruses ... The lion shouts "... Worthless *bum*, I don't want to see you in my presence ever again!" {also: qeşmêr (OK-2); <qeşmer> قشمر (HH)} {qeşmer[t]î} [Bw/A/IFb/HH/GF/TF/OK]

qeşmerî قه‌شمه‌رى *f.* **(-ya;-yê).** clowning, buffoonery, being a laughingstock; comedy, joking, jesting. {also: qeşmertî (A/IFb-2)} {syn: qirdikî} [IFb/GF/TF/ZF3/Wkt//A] <qeşmer>

qeşmertî قه‌شمه‌رتى (A/IFb) = clowning. See **qeşmerî**.

qeşmêr قه‌شمێر (OK) = clown, fool. See **qeşmer**.

qeşrandin قـه‌شـرانـدِن (FK-eb-1/Rwn) = to espy, catch sight of. See **qişirandin**.

qet I قـه‌ت *adv.* 1) any; ever: •**Te îro *qe* hrî r̄ist?** (J) Have you spun *any* wool today? •**Te *qe* 'emrê xweda dîtîye ewqas bedew dinêda?** (Z-1) Have you *ever* in your life seen such a beautiful one (in the world)?; 2) [+ *neg.*] {syn: hîç} (not) at all: •**K'ê ku p'akî haj ji şivantîyê t'unebû, hew zanibû, ku ew tiştekî çetin nîne, ku şivan xwer̄a nava kulîlkada diger̄in ... û *qet* xema wana *nîne*** (Ba2:1, 203) Those who were not well acquainted with shepherding thought that it was something not very difficult, that shepherds roam among the flowers ... and they have *no* cares *at all* •**Lê kur̄ê dinê *qet* tê der*ne*xistin** (Ba) But the other boys had *not* guessed *at all* •**Merîyêd ku *qe* tiştek jî jê *ne* lazimbûya** (Ba) People who would*n't* need anything *at all* •**Tu *qe* *ne*grî** (J) *Don't* you cry *at all*; **-qet ne be/bit** (JB3) at least. {also: qe; [qat قـط/qé قـه] (JJ)} < Ar qaṭ قـط. *See AKR (p. 60-61) for detailed discussion of* ***qet***. [Ba/K/A/JB3/IFb/B/SK/GF/TF/OK/AKR//JJ]

qet II قـه‌ت *m.* **(-ê;).** piece, part *(of a whole)*: •**Ma te sêva devê sewîl dît? *Qetek* bû, ew *qet* jî mi xwaribû, *qetekî* [sic] mabû** (HR 3:228) Didn't you see the apple in the mouth of the clay jug? It was *one piece* [of it], and I ate that *piece*, *another piece* is left •***qetek* nanê cehî** (JB1-S, #206) *a piece of* barley bread. {also: [qat/qit] قـــط (JJ); <qet> قـت (HH)} {syn: ker I; kerî I; p'ar II; parî; p'erçe; şeq; telîş I} Cf. Ar √q-ṭ-' قـطـع = 'to cut' [HR/K/A/B/FJ/TF/GF/JB1-S/HH//JJ]

qetandin قه‌تاندِن *vt.* **(-qetîn-).** to tear, break, snap off, cut: •**Eger xebera te derew be, ezê şûrekî li stuyê te dim, / Serê te ji gewdê te *biqetînim*** (Z-2, 68) If what you say is a lie, I will take a sword to your neck, / I will *sever* your head from your body •**Kêr dan şerîtî, *qetandin*** (L) They took a knife to the rope, *tore/cut* it. {also: [qatandin] قطاندين (JJ); <qetandin قتاندن (diqetîne) (دقتينه)> (HH)} {syn: qut kirin [*see* qut I]} Cf. Ar qaṭa'a قـطـع = 'to cut' [L/K/A/JB3/IFb/B/HH/JB1-S/GF//JJ] <qetîn>

Qeterî قەتەری *adj.* Qatari. [Wkt/Wkp]

qetirm•e I قـەتِـرمـە *m.* **(•ê;).** carrion, carcass, dead animal corpse: **•*Qetirmê* hêstirê li çolê ma** (FS) The camel *corpse* remained in the desert. {syn: berat'e; leş} [IFb/FS/ZF3]

qet'irm•e II قـەتِـرمـە *f.* **(;•ê).** rein; bridle: **•Gêm û *qentirmên* hespa çawan in?** (Wlt 1:42, 4) How are the horses' bits and *bridles*? {also: qentirme (Wlt)} {syn: bizmîk [1]; celew I; dizgîn; gem; lixab} [F/B//Wlt] <gem>

qetîn قـەتـيـن *vi.* **(-qet-).** 1) to split, crack, break *(vi.)*, tear, rip *(vi.)*: **•Bakî tenik t'eşîê dixe, t'eşî *diqete*** (J) A light wind lifts the distaff, the distaff *breaks* **•Ezê bigerim heyanî sola min *biqete*** (L) I shall wander until my shoe *cracks*; 2) [+ **ji**] to take one's leave of s.o., part company, separate *(vi.)*: **•Q. *ji* Memê *qetîya*** (Z-1) Q. *parted from* Mem; **-ji hev qetîn** (K) to part company, take one's leave; **-ji dû neqetîn** (ZF3) to stalk s.o., pursue s.o. [lit. 'not to separate from behind]: **•*Ji dû* min *nediqet-iyan*** (R. Dildar. Kitana Spî, 33) They *kept on pursuing* me. {also: [qatiian] قـطـيـان (JJ); <qetan قـتـان (diqete) (دقته)> (HH)} Cf. Ar qaṭa'a قطع = 'to cut' [L/K/IFb/B/GF//JJ//HH] <piçan; qetandin>

qetlaz قەتلاز (SS) = rare, scarce. See **qetlazî**.

qetlazî قـەتـلازى *adj.* rare, scarce, hard to find or come by: **•Rizq û te'am qetlazî ye** (Nûr al-Dîn Birîvkanî) Food is scarce; **-bi qetlazî** (Zeb) scarcely, hardly [+ *neg*]: **•Goşt/fêqî bi qetlazî dest nakevît** (Zeb) Meat/fruit is scarcely available. {also: qetlaz (SS)} [Zeb/Nûr al-Dîn Birîvkanî (Mizûrî)/BF/FS/Ald//SS]

qevastin قەڤاستِن (ZF3/FS) = to jump. See **qevaztin**.

qevaztin قـەڤـازتِـن *vt.* **(-qevêz-)**: to jump (over), leap: **•Wî li ser keviran ra *qevast* û çû** (FS) He *leapt* over the rocks and went on; **-xwe qevaztin** (HYma) do.: **•Diya zarokên cêwî xwe di ser zikê nepixî re diavêt. *Diqevazt*** (HYma, 34) The twins' mother jumped over the bloated stomach. She *leapt* **•Sofî Teker, bi sivikayiya kêroşkekê xwe ber bi Şerîfo de *qevazt*** (HYma, 43) Sofî Teker *leapt* toward Şerîfo with the nimbleness of a rabbit. {also: qevastin (ZF3/FS)} {syn: bazdan [2]; çeng III bûn; firqas kirin; hilpekirin; lotik dan; pengizîn; qevz dan [*see* qevz II]} Cf. qevz dan [*see* qevz II] = 'to jump' & qevizîn (TF) = 'to jump over' < Ar √q-f-z قفز = 'to jump' [HYma//ZF3/FS]

qevd قـەڤد, m. (JB3/IFb/GF) = handle, haft (of sword). See **qebd**.

qevş قەڤش (B) = handful, bunch. See **qefş**.

qevz I قـەڤـز (Z-1/K/GF) = handle, haft *(of sword)*. See **qebd**.

qevz II قـەڤـز *f.* **(;-ê).** 1) {syn: banz; ç'indik; firqas; lotik} jump[ing], leap[ing], hop[ping]: **-qevz dan** (IFb/RZ) to jump, leap, hop {syn: bazdan [2]; çeng III bûn; firqas kirin; hilpekirin; lotik dan; pengizîn; qevaztin}; 2) step, pace: **•Jina te sê *qevzan* li paş te tê ... Jina Hesen deh qevzan li p[ê]şiya Hesen dimeşe** (Sadînî. Ji kelepora Kurdî pêkenok, 252) Your wife is walking [lit. 'comes'] 3 *steps* behind you ... H.'s wife is walking 10 steps in front of H.; 3) unit of length, equal to width of the palm of the hand or of the fist, about 9 cm. (B). {also: qefz (IFb-2); qewz (CS-2); <qefz> قـفـز (HH)} < Ar √q-f-z قفز = 'to jump' [Sadini/A/IFb/B/TF/RZ/ZF/CS//HH]

qewaf قەواف (Frq/A/IFb) = potter. See **qewaq**.

qewamtin قەوامتِن (Hk) = to happen. See **qewimîn**.

qewaq قـەواق *m.* **(;-î).** potter: **•Dilê *kewaq* bixwaze, dikare çimbilekî zeyde bi carê ve çêke** (L #218, 219) If *the potter* feels like it, he can add another handle to the jug [*prv.*]. {also: kewaq (L); kewax̂ (FS-2); qewaf (Frq/A/IFb); qewax II (FS-2); <qewaq> قـواق (HH)} {syn: p'irûd} Cf. Syr qūqā ܩܘܩܐ = 'water pitcher, urn' & qūqoyā ܩܘܩܝܐ = 'potter' [Frq/A/IFb//GF/HH/FS/ZF3/Kmc]

qewas قەواس = messenger. See **qewaz**.

qewat قـەوات *f.* **(-a;-ê).** strength, power: **•Ewa tu dibêjî ji *qewata* min dere** (FK-eb-1) What you're asking [lit. 'saying'] is beyond my *power* **•*Qewat* be ji teȓa** (J) More *power* to you [a greeting]. {also: qewet (B/IF/ZF); qiwet (IF-2); [qouvet] قوت (JJ); <quwwet> قوّت (HH)} {syn: birî I; ȟêl; hêz; qedûm [2]; t'aqet; zexm I [2]; zor I} < Ar quwwah قوّة --> T kuvvet [Z-1/J/F/K//B/IF/ZF//HH//JJ]

qewax I قـەواخ *f.* **(-a;-ê).** 1) {syn: evran; sipindar} poplar tree, bot. *Populus* (IF/JJ) [kawak]; 2) birch tree, bot. betula (JJ) [qavag]. {also: [qavag/kawak قواغ/ dar-a qavaghi دارا قواغى] (JJ)} < T kavak = 'poplar tree' [IFb//JJ] <pelk>

qewax II قەواخ (FS) = potter. See **qewaq**.

qewaz قـەواز *m.* **(-ê;).** 1) {syn: qasid} errand boy, courier, 'gopher'; messenger: **•Al-p'aşa gazî du *qewaza* kir** (Z-1) A.p. summoned two *couriers*; 2) bodyguard (of kings and the like) (B). {also: qewas} [Z-1/K/B/ZF3/FS] qewet قەوەت (B/IF/ZF) = strength, force. See **qewat**.

qewil قـــــــەول, f. (B) = words; agreement; hymn. See **qewl**.

qewimîn قــەومــيـن *vi.* **(-qewim-).** to happen, occur: **•Tiştek *neqewimye* heře cihê xwe!** (HR 4:25) Nothing *has happened*, go back to your place! **•Tu zanî *serê* min çi *qewmîye*** (FK-eb-1) You know what *has happened to* me [lit. 'to my head']; **-diqewime** (Z-1)/**diqewimît** (SK) maybe, perhaps {syn: dibe ku; heye ku}: **•Memê min çima îro derengî bûye, *diqewime* Memêyî bêk'êf *be*?** (Z-1) Why is my Mem late today, *could he be* upset? **•We *diqewimît* nêçîr tiştekî wekî ga yan kel yan hesp dibît. Eger nehêt ez bi-tinê neşêm bînim** (SK 6:63) It *may be* that the prey will be something like an ox or a buffalo or a horse. If he doesn't come I shan't be able to bring it myself. {also: qewamtin (Hk); qewimtin (Hk-2); [qaoumin] قومين (JJ)} Cf. NENA (m)qă-wim ܩܘܡ (Maclean) & qavam (Hetzron) & mqawo:me (Krotkoff) = 'to happen' [L/M/F/K/JB3/IFb/B/SK/GF//JJ//Hk]

qewimtin قەومتِن (Hk) = to happen. See **qewimîn**.

qewirandin I قــــەورِانــــدِن (B/IFb/ZF3) = to chase; to expel. See **qewrandin I**.

qewirandin II قــــــەورِانــــدِن (IFb/ZF3) = to fry. See **qewrandin II**.

qewitandin قـەوتـانـدِن (K/IFb/GF/Ardû) = to chase. See **qewtandin**.

qewiyatî قــــەويــــاتــــى (FS/Wkt) = recommendation; warning. See **qewîtî**.

qewî قــــەوى *adj.* 1) {syn: xurt} strong; 2) [*adv.*] {syn: gelek; p'iř II; ze'f} very, very much: **•Jin û biçûk û 'eyalê kuřêt Osê hemî çûne tekya Şêx 'Ubeydullah. Ew jî *qewî* xurt bû: kuřêt Cindî Axa gazî kirin, çar-sed lîraê 'usmanî ji wan stand, da 'eyalê kuřêt Osê** (SK 40:387) The wives and children and families of Oso's sons all went to Shaikh Ubeidullah's convent. He was *very* powerful: he summoned the sons of Jindi Agha and took 400 Ottoman pounds from them and gave them to the families of Oso's sons **•[Wellah, em nizanin ji kê derê ye Memed *qewî* xweyê mal û ĥal bûye û ji boy xwe xaneman jinûve bina kirine, û aşek ji boy xwe kirîye û niha *qewî* xoşĥal bûye]** (JR #4,24-25) By God, we don't know from where [=how] Memed became *very* wealthy and had mansions built (for himself), and had a mill built and has now become *very* happy **•Xelkê wî gundî *qewî* 'ezman-dirêj û cablos û bê-şerm in, diçine hemî cîyan, digeřyên, dixazin û eger mumkin bît didizin û distînin** (SK 12:114) The people of that village are *very* impudent and cunning and shameless, they go everywhere and wander about begging and, if possible, stealing and taking things; **-qewî zêde** (IFb) very much, greatly, extremely: **•[Ekrad jî weku Efrancan *qewî zêde* ji nexweşî û webayî û ĥalî û 'illetêd ku s̱arî ne diṯirsin û bi dûr dikevin]** (BN 178) Kurds, like Westerners, are *greatly* afraid of diseases and epidemics and conditions that are contagious, and shun them. {also: [qavi] قــــوى (JJ); <qewî> قــــوى (HH)} < Ar qawī قوي = 'strong' [BN/K/IFb/JJ/HH/SK/GF]

qewît قەويت (TF) = cake-like pastry. See **qawît**.

qewîtî قــەويــتــى *f.* **(-ya;-yê).** 1) recommendation; warning, admonishment, cautioning: **-qewîtî kirin** (K/IFb/HH/ZF) to recommend; to admonish, caution, warn: **•Tenê di vegerê de ji Rindê re *qewîtî kiribû* ku ji dêya xwe re tiştekî nebêje** (H v. 1, 83-84 [1932, 1:4]) She *had* only *warned* Rindê on the way back not to say anything to her [i.e., their] mother; 2) {syn: wes̱yet} will, last will and testament: **•Wî *qewiyatîyên* xwe kirin û paşî mir** (FS) He made his *will* and then died. {also: qewiyatî (FS/Wkt-2); [qaviti قـويـتـى/kauját/qavati قواتى] (JJ); <qewîtî> قويتى (HH)} {syn: t'emî} [H/K/A/IFb/GF/TF/JJ/HH/ZF/CS/Wkt//FS] <şîret; t'emî>

qewl قـــــەول *m./f.(B/IFb/SK/OK)* **(-ê/; /-ê).** 1) words, speech, talk[ing]; 2) agreement, contract: **-Qewl e ku…** (Bw) [One is] supposed to… ; 3) {syn: beyt [3]} an orally transmitted story told in a combination of prose and sung verse (Haz); talking in verse in Arabic or Kurdish, containing a story, praise, or love (HH); a story in verse (IF); 4) {syn: beyt [2]} a type of Yezidi religious poetry in three- to five-verse stanzas (Z-711); "The *qewls*, defined in **Êzdiyatî** ["Yezidism," by Xelîl Cindî & Pîr Xidr Silêman] as 'the texts we may not reveal to outsiders,' are sacred hymns, formerly memorised and chanted only by a special group, the *qewals*" from: Philip Kreyenbroek. "The Hymns of the Yezidis," *SIOS Newsletter*, 2 (Feb. 1993), 4: **•*qewl* û beyt'ê êzdîya** (Z-711) Yezidi *religious poems* and hymns. {also: qewil, f. (B); [qaoŭl] قـول (JJ); <qewl> قـول (HH)} < Ar qawl قـــــول = 'saying, speaking'; Sor qewl قـــــەول =

'promise' [Haz/Z-711/K/IFb/JJ/HH/SK/JB1-A/OK//B]

qewrandin I قــەوراندِن *vt.* **(-qewrîn-).** 1) {syn: qewtandin I[1]} to chase, pursue: •[**Memedî çêrî min kirî *ez qewrandim***] (JR) Memed cursed me [and] *chased me away*; 2) {syn: qewtandin I[2]} to dismiss, expel, fire (from a job), kick out, sack. {also: qewirandin I (B/IFb/ZF3); [qaoŭrandin] قوراندين (JJ)} [JR/K/JJ//B/IFb/ZF3]

qewrandin II قــەوراندِن *vt.* **(-qewrîn-).** to fry. {also: qewirandin II (IFb/ZF3); [qaoŭrandin] قـورانـديـن (JJ)} {syn: qelandin [1]} < T kavurmak = 'to roast, to fry' [K/JJ//IFb/ZF3]

qewraş قەوراش (Z-3) = servant. See **qerwaş**.

qewtandin قــەوتـانـدِن *vt.* **(-qewtîn-).** 1) {syn: qewrandin I[1]} to chase (after), rout, pursue: •**Kerr rabû syar bû hespê, çû, biřekî devayê çûř, te'zî qewrand** (***qewtand***) (FK-kk-2) Kerr mounted his horse, and went and *routed* a group of reddish, bare camels; 2) {syn: qewrandin I[2]} to expel, chase out: •**Divê em vî neyarê ola xwe ji gundê xwe *biqewitînin*** (Ardû, 57) We must *expel* this enemy of our religion from our village. {also: qewitandin (K-2/IFb/GF/Ardû); [ka'utāndin] قوتاندين (JJ)} [FK-kk-2/K//JJ//IFb/GF/Ardû]

qewz قەوز (CS) = jump; step. See **qevz II**.

qexpe قەخپە (IF) = profligate; prostitute. See **qab II**.

qey قــەى *adv.* 1) perhaps, maybe: **-qey + gotin** = It is as if; You might say that; It seems as if [cf. t'irê]: •[The villain Beko is about to get what he deserves. He is brought to Mem and Zin's open grave, and sees the smile of love on their faces] **Bek'o styê xwe dirêj kir, go: "Mîr ... *qey tê bêjî* řazane"** (Z-1) Beko craned his neck [to look], said, "Prince ... *it's as if* [lit. '*maybe you will say*'] they're asleep" •***Dibêje qey* lawê xwe ketîye avê, xeneqîye** (L) He *says* (=thinks), *maybe* his son fell into the water and drowned •**Ew [=cewikêd avê] usa lez dik'etin, mêriv *qey digot* ew hevřa k'etibûne lecê** (Ba2) They [=the brooks] came down so quickly, that *people said* (=it seemed as if) they were racing each other •**Ewî usa li min dinihêřî ku, *qey te digot* ew cara pêşin min dibîne** (B) He looked at me *as if* he were seeing me for the first time; 2) why? how come?: •**Ma *qey* tu naçî?** (IFb) *Why* aren't you going? •***Qey* ranazî** (IFb) *Why* don't you go to sleep? [K/A/JB3/IFb/B/GF/TF/OK] <maxwene>

qey•a قــەيـا *f.* **(;•aê/•ê).** cliff, crag. {also: [qaia] قـيـا (JJ)} {syn: zinar I} < T kaya = 'rock, cliff' [Ba2/K/B//JJ]

qeyd قــەيــد *f.* **(-a;-ê).** 1) fetters, chains, shackles: •***qeyda* pola** (EP-7) steel *chains*; **-qeyd kirin** (ZF3): a) to chain up: •[Al-paşa didn't want his son Mem to leave town on his steed bor, so he gave the order] **wekî Borê Memê *qeyd kin*, qeydê bidine wî** (Z-1) That they *chain up* Mem's Bor, [and] give the chains to him; b) to record (in writing or electronically) {syn: vegirtin}: •**Dengê min *qeyd kire* band** (ZF3) He *recorded* my voice on tape; **-qeyd û çîdar** = fetters and chains [lit. 'fetters and footshackles']; 2) restrictions (SK). {also: [qaïd] قـيـد (JJ); <qeyd> قـيـد (HH)} {syn: çîdar; zincîr} < Ar qayd قيد = 'chain' [Z-1/K/IFb/B/HH/SK/ZF3//JJ]

qeyik قەيك (B/FS) = boat. See **qeyk**.

qeyîk قەييك (ZF3) = boat. See **qeyk**.

qeyk قــەيــك *f.* **(-a;-ê).** boat, skiff, dinghy: •**Dya min minřa *qeykek* da çêkirin, ez şandim vira** (EH) My mother had *a boat* made for me, [and] sent me here. {also: qayik (FS); qeîq (F); qeyik (B/FS-2); qeyîk (ZF3); [qàiq] قايق (JJ)} <T kayık = 'boat, caique, skiff' [EH/K//F//B//ZF3//FS//JJ]

***qeynok** قەينۆك *m.* **(-ê;).** roasted grains of wheat [cf. T kavurga = ateşte kavrulmuş tahıl]: •**Jinik řadibe kuç'kê xwe dadide, ser sêlê *qeynokê* xwe diqelîne. Nav malê hine cî t'emiz dike, *qeynokê* xwe ser t'exte řadixe û dest pê dike dixwe** (Dzanec #12) The woman lights her stove, roasts her *qeynok* on the convex disk [sêl]. She does a little bit of cleaning around the house, [then] sets down her *qeynok* on the tray and starts to eat. [Dz] <dan II; danû>

qeynt'er قــەيــنــتــەر *f.* **(-a;-ê).** 1) yoke *(for carrying buckets)* (K); 2) steelyard *(type of scale for weighing sacks, saddlebags, etc.)*; 3) weighbridge. Cf. Ar qinṭār قنطار = 'kantar', unit of weight equal to 100 *raṭl* (in Syria = 256.4 kg) & qanṭarah قنطرة = 'arch' [HB/K/A/B/IF/ZF3] <nîr>

qeys قەيس *f.* **(-a;).** size, measurement: **-Qeysa pîyê te çend e?** (Frq) What size is your foot? {also: **qiyas** (SK); <qas> قـاس (HH)} <Ar qiyās قـيـاس = 'measurement, dimension' [Frq/IFb//SK/ZF3//HH] <qas; qiyas>

***qeyse** قەيسە**: -çi qeyse** = every, each {also: çiqeyse}: •**çi qeyse rêwî** (L) every traveler. [L]

qeysî قــەيــســى *f.* **(-ya;-yê).** apricot, bot. *Prunus armeniaca*; dried apricots (B); apricots with sweet pits (HH). {also: [qàisi] قايسى (JJ); <qeysî> قيسى (HH)} {syn: hêrûg; mişmiş; zerdelî} Cf. T kayısı [K/JB3/IFb/B/HH/GF/TF/OK/Kmc-2/FS//JJ]

qeyt'an قەيتان *f.* **(-a;-ê).** tape, ribbon, shoelace, braid, cord: **•Sala 1975-a ewî ser *qeyt'ana* magnîtafonê ev ȟk'yata û herçê din dabû nvîsarê. Me jî ji ser qeyt'anê bergirt** (HKC-5, 291-292) In 1975 he recorded this story and the others on magnetic *tape*. And we transcribed it from the tape. {also: [qĭtan/keitán (G)/kaitān (Lx)] قيطان (JJ)} {syn: şerît [2]} Cf. Ar qīṭān قيطان; Sor qeytan قەيتان = 'shoestring; cotton/silk braid or cord' [HCK/K/B/A/IFb/FJ/TF/GF/Kmc/JJ] <ben; şîrox>

qeza قەزا (JB3/IFb) = misfortune. See **qezîya**.

qezanc قەزانج (GF) = profit, gain. See **qazanc**.

Qezaxî قەزاخى (ZF3) = Kazakh. See **Qazaxî**.

qezenc قەزەنج (IFb) = profit, gain. See **qazanc**.

Qezexî قەزەخى (Wkt) = Kazakh. See **Qazaxî**.

qezî I قەزى, f. (;-yê) (B) = misfortune. See **qezîya**.

qezî II قەزى (Kg/IFb/DZK) = talk; bad words. See **qise**.

qezîya قەزيا *f.* **().** unhappy event, misfortune: **•*Qezîya* hat serê wî** (K) *A misfortune* befell him •[Mem & Zin were in an embrace when her father's men came in. She hid behind Mem, under his coat] **Bek'o dixast, wekî Memê ȓave p'îya mîr û cindîyava Zînê bivînin, wekî *qezîyake* giran bigihînine Memê û Zînê** (Z-1) Beko wanted Mem to stand up on his feet, so that the prince and his men could see Zin, to bring a great *disgrace* on Mem and Zin. {also: **qeda**; qeza (JB3/IFb); qezî I f. (;-yê) (B); [qaza] قضا (JJ)} {syn: 'ecêb [2]} Cf. Ar qaḍīyah قضية = 'question, issue' & qaḍā' قضاء = 'settlement, judgment' [Z-1/K//JB3/IFb//B] See also **qeda**.

qêmîş قێميش *m.* **().** mercy; pity: **-qêmîş nekirin/nebûn** (B) not to have the heart to do stg., not to get up the courage to do stg. [cf. T kıymamak]: **•Mêvanekî minî ze'fî 'ezîz hatîye, min *qêmîş nedikir* k'êlekê ȓabyama** (Z-1) A very honored guest of mine has come, I *haven't had the heart to* leave his side [lit. 'to get up [from his] side'] **•*Qêmîş nakim* ji xew rakim** (FS) I *don't have the heart to* wake him up. {also: [qymych] قمش (JJ)} Cf. T kıy[ma]mış *neg. past participle* = '(not) having spared (s.o.'s life)' [Z-1/K/B/GF/ZF3//JJ]

qêrîn قێرين (SF) = shouting, screaming. See **qîrîn**.

qibîn قِبين (IFb) = to coo *(of partridges)*. See **qebîn**.

Qibrisî قِبرِسى *adj.* Cypriot, Cyprian. {also: K'îprî (Wkp-2); Qiprisî (SS); Qubrisî (CS)} Sor Qibrisî قِبرِسى [GF/ZF3/Wkp//SS//CS]

qicik قِجِك *adj.* small, little. {syn: çûçik (Ad/Ks); piçûk} [Bg/Kg/IFb/ZF3]

qiçqiç قِچقِچ (A/FJ/TF/ZF3/FS) = sound of sizzling oil. See **qiçeqiç**.

qiçeqiç قِچەقِچ *f.* **(-a;-ê).** sizzling, hissing, sputtering *(sound of boiling oil)*: **•Dema ko miqilk û dohn danî ser agirî dengê *qiçeqiça* dohnî bi kizekiza kerengan re derket** (MGJiyaneka pêguhork) When she put the saucepan and the fat on the fire, the sound of *the sputtering of* the fat coincided with the sizzling of the cardoons. {also: qiçqiç (A/FJ-2/TF/ZF3/FS)} [MG/FJ//A/TF/ZF3/FS]

Qidis قِدِس (Wkt) = Jerusalem. See **Qudus**.

qidret قِدرەت (IF) = power. See **qudret**.

Qids قِدس (Wkt) = Jerusalem. See **Qudus**.

qidûm قِدووم (IFb/HH) = form, shape. See **qedûm**[4].

qifil قِفِل *f.* **(-a;-ê).** lock, padlock: **•Wî *qifil* êxist derîkî** (FS) He put *a lock* on the door; **-qifil bûn** (FS) to be locked; **-qifil dan** (GF)/**qifil kirin** (FS) to lock (a door): **•Wî derîk *qifil kir*** (FS) He *locked* the door. {also: qifl (Wkt-2); qilf, m. (Wkt); qilif (Wkt-2); qufil (RZ/ZF3); qûfle (Wkt-2); [qyfil] قفل (JJ); <qufl> قفل (HH)} <Ar qufl قفل; Sor qifił قِفڵ [GF/JJ/FS/CS//RZ/ZF3//HH//Wkt] <çilmêre; kilît; mifte>

qifl قِفل (Wkt) = padlock. See **qifil**.

qifle قِفلە (Btm/Czr) = herd *(of horses, etc.)*. See **qefle I**.

qiȟerîn قِحەرين (HR) = to be upset. See **qehirîn**.

qijak قِژاك (Wkt) = crow; magpie. See **qijik**[2] & [4].

qijik قِژك *f.* **(-a;-ê).** *term applied to several birds*: 1) {syn: tilûr} rook (bird) (K) [Rus grač грач]: **•*Qijik* penîr didize** (AB) The *rook* [or, *crow*] steals cheese; 2) {syn: qel; qiȓik II} crow, raven, genus *Corvus* (A/JJ/TF) [Fr corbeau/corneille; T kuzgun]; 3) greenish bird which is eaten, hazel grouse or ruffed grouse, zool. *Bonasa* (IFb) [T çil]; 4) {syn: keşkele} magpie (B/OK) [Rus soroka сорока; Germ Elster]. {also: qijak (Wkt-2); **qiȓik II**[2]; qjik (EH); [qyjik] قژك (JJ); <qijik> قژك (HH)} Cf. P kasak كسك/kašak كشك = 'magpie' [AB/K/A/IFb/B/JJ/HH/ TF/OK//EH] See also **qiȓik II**.

qijilandin قِژلاندِن *vt.* **(-qijilîn-).** to sizzle, fry, cook, sauté *(in butter or oil)* [di rûn de sor kirin] *(lit. &*

fig.): •**Di girarê de, divê tu berê rûnê xwe di beroşê de *biqijilînî*, dûre bi pîvan girara xwe di rûnê *qijilandî* de sor bikî** (Ardû, 138) In the girar [soup], first you must *sauté* your butter in the pot, then measuredly braise your girar in the *sautéd* butter •**Nîvro, wexta tavê îda dest pê kiribû *diqijiland*** (Ba2, 220) At noon, when the sun had begun *to cook*. {also: [qijirandin] قـژرانـدیـن (JJ); <qijilandin قژلاندن (diqijilîne) (دقژلینه)> (HH)} [Qzl/Qrj/K/IFb/B/HH/GF//JJ] <patin; sor kirin>

qijîn قِژین (Nofa) = to scream. See **qîjîn**.

qijnik قِـژنِـك *f./m.(FS)* **(/-ê;-ê/).** tick, zool. *Trichodectes*: •**Ew mîna *qijnikê* bi min ve dizeliqin** (nefel.com: E.Karahan. Qesas 14.vi.2007) They cling to me like *a tick*. {also: gijnik (RZ-2); gijnî (RZ-2); qijnîk (RZ/ZF3-2); **qirnî**} {syn: gene; qirnî} [A/IFb/FJ/GF/FS/ZF3//RZ]

qijnîk قِژنیك (RZ/ZF3) = tick *(insect)*. See **qijnik**.

qilafet قِلافەت (K) = appearance. See **qelafet**.

qilafîsk قِـلافـیـسـك (Qzl) = squatting, kneeling. See **qelefiskî**.

qilç' قِلچ = corner. See **qulç'**.

qilçik قِـلـچِـك *m.* **(-ê;).** 1) {syn: goşe; kujî; k'unc; qorzî} corner, angle; 2) tip, end (of handkerchief) (B). {also: [qiltchik] قـلـچـك (JJ)} [B/JJ/ZF3] See also **qulç'**.

qilêr قِـلـێـر *f.* **(;-ê).** 1) dirt; filth: •**Zîndana kevire sarda, nem, *qilêrê*da xew ç'e'vê Memê nedik'et** (Z-1) in the cold stone dungeon, because of the dampness and *filth*, Mem could not fall asleep; 2) [*adj.*] {syn: bi'ok; ç'epel; dijûn II; gemarî; p'îs; qirêj} dirty (Kş/IFb). {also: [qylir] قلیر (JJ)} [Z-1/K/IFb/B/Kş//JJ] <qirêj>

qilf قِلف, m. (Wkt) = padlock. See **qifil**.

qilif قِلِف (Wkt) = padlock. See **qifil**.

qilix I قِـلِـخ *m.* **(-ê;).** 1) {syn: bejnbal; dilqe; dirûv; qelafet} appearance; 2) {syn: dilqe} disguise, costume, attire: •**Roja dinê ewana *bi qilixê* dewrêşa çûne ba hersê bra** (FK-eb-1) On another day they went to the three brothers *disguised as* dervishes. < T kılık [FK-1/K/A/IF/B]

qilix II قِـلِـخ *m./f.(FS/ZF3)* **(;/-ê).** shears for shearing sheep: •**Wî hirîya mihê bi *qilixê* birî** (FS) He cut his sheep's wool with *the shears*. {also: [kŭlŭkh/ kŭrŭkh] قلخ (JJ); <qilix> قلخ (HH); [qalāgh] (RJ)} {syn: hevring} [HH/FS/ZF3//JJ//RJ]

qilîc قِلیج (GF) = little finger. See **qilîç'k**.

qilîç قِلیچ (A/IFb/HH) = little finger. See **qilîç'k**.

qilîçik قِلیچِك (ZF3) = little finger. See **qilîç'k**.

qilîç'k قِـلـیـچـك *f.* **(;-ê).** pinkie, little finger: **-tilîya qilîç'kê** (K)/~**qilîçane** (Msr)/~**qilîncekê** (IFb) do. {also: qilîc (GF); qilîç (A/IFb); qilîçik (ZF3); qilîncek (IFb-2) [(tilouia) kylitch (تـلـویـا) کـلـچ/ (tilouia) kyltchik (تلویا) کلچك] (JJ); <qilîç> قلیچ (HH)} {syn: *tilîya başikan (IF); t'ilîya ç'ûk (B); [telīye pečūk] (JJ-PS)} Cf. P kelenj کـلـنـج/kelenjak کـلـنـجـك [= angošt-e kūček انـگـشـت کـوچـك/angošt-e kehīn انـگـشـت کـهـیـن]; Za engişta qilanci (Mal); = Sor tûte تـــووتـــە [Msr//F/K/FS//ZF3//A/IFb/HH//JJ//GF] <bêç'î; tilî>

qilîncek قِلینجەك (IFb) = little finger. See **qilîç'k**.

qiloç قِلۆچ (IFb/GF) = horn *(of animal)*. See **qoç'**.

qilonç قِلۆنچ (IF) = horn *(of animal)*. See **qoç'**.

qilop قِلۆپ (Qrj) = with a crippled hand. See **qop**.

qilpik قِـلـپِـك *f.* **(-a;-ê).** 1) {syn: îsk} hiccup, hiccough: **-qulpik hatin** (F) to hiccup, have the hiccups: •***Qilpik hate wî*** (K) *He hiccupped* •***Qilpikê* min tên** [or **nasekinin**] (Haz) I have *the hiccups*; 2) belch(ing), burp(ing) (IFb/JJ/HH/GF/TF). {also: qirpik (IFb); qulpik (F/IFb-2/TF); [qylpik] قـلـپـك (JJ); <qulpik> قلپك (HH)} Sor qirp قِرپ = 'hiccup' [Haz/K/JJ/GF/FD/ZF3//F/HH/TF//IFb]

qilqal قِـلـقـال *f.* **(;-ê).** worry, care, concern: **-ketin qilqalê** (Wkt) to worry, be worried or concerned: •**Bi destpêkirina kampanya me re, YÖK û der dor[ê]n kevnperest *ketin qilqalê* û êrîşê kampanya me kirin** (Anadilde eğitim, Kürtçe Seçmeli Ders Kampanyası Dosyası, 145) At the beginning of our campaign, YÖK and conservative circles *got worried* and attacked our campaign •**Bi wan peyvên Emer Eynê jî *kete qilqalan*, di xwe derneanî** (Nofa, 93) With these words of Emer's, Eynê also *got worried*, but didn't let it show. {syn: k'eder; k'erb; k'eser; kovan; kul I; meraq; şayîş; tatêl; xem} Cf. Ar √q-l-q قـلـق = 'to be worried, uneasy' [Nofa/ZF3/Wkt]

qilqilîn قِلقِلین *vi.* **(-qilqil-).** 1) to worry (vi.), fret, be apprehensive, be upset {syn: xem xwarin}: •**Ev şeş-heft meh in, em di agirê xwe de *diqirqilin*** (Nbh 134:3) We have been stewing in our own juices [lit. '*fretting* in our own fire'] for the past 6-7 months; 2) to be nauseous, feel nauseated {syn: xelîn}: •**Dilê wî ji ber bêhna kelexî *qelqilî*/ *qilqilî*** (FS) He *felt nauseated* due to the smell of the carcass. {also: qelqilîn (FS-2); qirqilîn (Nbh)} Cf. Ar qaliqa قلق = 'to be worried, uneasy' [Nbh//Wkt/

FS]

qiltîş قِلتيش *f.* **(-a;).** trachoma: **-qiltîşa ç'e'va** (F) do. {syn: bîrova çavî} [F/SS] <ava r̄eş>

qilûz قِلووز (Qrj) = hunchbacked. See **kûz I**.

qime قِمه (B) = dagger. See **qeme**.

qimer قِمەر (B) = swarthy. See **qemer**.

qimqimok قِمقِمۆك (FJ/HH) = lizard. See **qumqumok**.

qimt قِمت (GF) = mountaintop. See **kumt**.

qinab قِناب (IFb) = type of rope. See **qirnap**.

qinap قِناپ (Kmc) = type of rope. See **qirnap**.

qineb قِنەب, m./f. (; qinêb/-ê). (HYma) = type of rope. See **qirnap**.

qinyat قِنيات (IFb/GF/TF) = satisfaction. See **qenaet**.

Qiprisî قِپرِسی (SS) = Cypriot. See **Qibrisî**.

qir̄ I قِـــر *f.* **(-a;-ê).** 1) severe cold, as in the dead of winter; 2) frost (HH/GF/TF). See **qir̄av**. {also: [kerr] (BG); <qir> قـر (HH)} [BG//A/IFb/HH/GF/TF/FS/ZF3] <serma; sur̄ I; zivistan>

qir̄ II قِـــر *f.* **(-a;-ê).** 1) death, destruction, ruin, one's end; mass destruction, massacre: **•[K'anûnê û K'anûnê, berf tête ji ezmanê, *qir̄a* 'ebd û însanê]** (BG) In December and January, snow falls from the sky, *the ruin* [also, *severe cold*] of all humanity *[proverbial saying]* {**qir̄** is a pun}: a) severe cold or frost; b) ruin: ***•Qir̄a* wan hat** (K) Their *end* has come; **-qir̄ kirin** (K/ZF3) to destroy, kill, annihilate, massacre: **•Wekî tiştek bê serê wî, zanibin, ezê we gişka *qir̄kim*** (Ba-1, #7) If anything happens to him, know that I *will destroy* you all; 2) cattle plague (JJ/B): •[qyr ketiié pezi] (JJ) A plague has befallen the sheep. {also: [qyr] قـر (JJ)} [Ba/K/JB3/IFb/B/SK/OK/ZF3//JJ] <komkujî; mirin; qelandin II>

qir̄ III قِر (Dh) = crow. See **qir̄ik II**.

qirafî قِرافی (FS) = frost. See **qir̄av**.

qiral قِــــــرال *m.* **(-ê; qirêl, vî qiralî).** king *(of non-Muslim country)*: **•Herûher bijî *qralê* hêja** (K-ça) Live forever, dear *King*. {also: qral (K-ça/K-2/IFb); <qiral> قرال (HH)} {syn: ȟakim; p'adşa} < T kıral < Serbian kral < Karl (=Charlemagne) [K-ça/IFb//K/HH/GF/TF/RZ]

qirar قِــرار *m.(LY/IS)/f.(JB3/EP-7)* **(-ê/-a;/-ê).** 1) {syn: biryar} decision: **•Li ser vê *qerarê*** (BX) As a result of this *decision*: **-qirar dan** = to decide: **•Her çiqas ku darizandinê nepejirîne jî nas kir û *qerar da* ku vê derê wekî platforma aştiyê bi kar bîne** (AW #175) Although he doesn't accept the judgement, he acknowledged it and *decided* to use this place as a peace platform; 2) order, command, decree: **•Mîr *qirar* derxist** (Z-1) The prince sent out a decree; 3) reign, rule: **•Lazim e, bi emrê rebb el 'Alemîn tu text teslîm bike; *qerarê* te temam bû!** (LY) You must, by order of the Lord of the Universe, give up your throne; your *reign* is over!; 4) condition, agreement: **•Çil şevî sebir bikin, ezê horîê eşkele bikim, bira cim'et bivîne, lê naha *qirar* heye wekî ez wê nîşanî kesekî nekim** (Ba3-3, #7) Wait forty nights, [and] I will present the houri for everyone to see, but now there is *an agreement* that I not show her to anyone [or, 'but now I am not supposed to show her to anyone'] **•Lê wexta tu Zîn xatûnê bibî, *qirara* min ewe, wekî tu min jî bi xwer̄a bibî** (FK-eb-1) But when you take Lady Zîn, my *condition* is that you take me too; 5) promise, one's word: **•Sîabend, tuyê her̄î, gerekê tu *qirarekî* ji mir̄a *bidî*, tu li k'u dimînî, li k'u dizewicî, gerek tu werî, min bibî** (IS-#110) Siyabend, you are going, you must *promise* me that wherever you are when you marry, you must come get me; 6) custom, practice (EP-7): ***•Qrara* welatê wan usa bû** (EP-7) *The custom* [or *practice*] in their country was such. {also: qerar (JB3/HH/SK/GF/LY); qrar, f. (EP-7); [qarar] قـرار (JJ); <qerar> قـرار (HH)} < Ar qarār قـرار --> T karar [Z-1/K/IFb/B//JJ//JB3/HH/SK/GF/LY] <daraz>

qirarge قِرارگه (K) = headquarters. See **qerargeh**.

qirase I قِراسه (IFb) = huge. See **qerase I**.

qirase II (IFb/BF) = crank, lever. See **qer̄ase II**.

qirat قِرات *f.* **().** unit of weight, dry measure: 20 kg., = 1 kod or 1/2 olçek. Cf. Ar qīrāṭ قـيـراط (pl. qarārīṭ قـراريـط) = 'inch; a dry measure (used in Egypt: = 1/32 of a qadaḥ = 0.064 liter); a square measure; kerat, a weight; carat (fineness of a gold alloy)' [CCG/ZF] <kod[2]; olçek>

qir̄av قِــــــراڤ *f.* **(;-ê).** frost, hoarfrost, rime: **-qir̄av girtin** (B) to be covered with hoarfrost. {also: **qir I**[2] (GF/TF); qirafî (FS); qir̄avî (K); [qyraw] قراڤ (JJ); <qir> قر (HH)} {syn: qeşa; xûsî} Cf. T kırağı & kırav [Erciş-Van] = 'hoarfrost' (DS, v. 8, p. 2826) [F/B/JJ/ZF3/FS///K//HH/GF/TF] <qeşa; xunav [1]>

qir̄avî قِراڤی (K) = frost. See **qir̄av**.

qirax قِــــراخ *f.(L)/m.(K/B)* **(-a/-ê; /qirêx, vî qiraxî).** edge, outskirts; side: **•Beyrim vegerîya *qiraxa* kona** (L) B. returned to *the outskirts of* the encampment; **-qiraxê be'rê** (B) seashore;

-**qiraxê gêlî** (B) the brink of a ravine; -**qiraxê şeher** (B) outskirts of a city; -**qiraxê xweda** (B) from [my] side, from [my] point of view. {also: qerax, m. (K/IFb-2/GF); qerex; [qarax] قـرخ (JJ)} [L/A/IFb/B//K/GF//JJ]

qirbî قِربى (B) = teapot; coffeepot. See **qirmî**.

qirç'e-qirç' [K]/**qirç'eqirç'** [B] قِرچەقِرچ *f.* **(-a;-ê).** gnashing, gritting, chattering *(of teeth)*; creaking, crackling, popping *(of bones)*: •**Siltanê Fîlan ... ji hêrsa spîsor bû û bû *qirçe qirça* qîlên wî** (SF 29) The Sultan of the elephants ... turned white with rage and you could hear him *gnashing* his tusks. {also: qirç qirç (GF)} {syn: çirke-çirk} Sor qirçe قِـرچـه = 'crackle (esp. of fire)' & qirçeqirç قِرچەقِرچ = 'sustained crackling' [SF/K/IFb/B//GF]

qirç qirç قِـرچ قِـرچ (GF) = gnashing; popping. See **qirç'e-qirç'**.

qird قِرد (B/Z-921) = mature, adult. See **qerd I**.

qirdik قِـردِك *m.&f.* **(-ê/ ;-î/).** 1) {syn: qeşmer; şemo} clown, buffoon, laughingstock; comedian, jokester, jester clown, buffoon; 2) costumed character, such as Santa Claus/Father Christmas (Kmc), or young people who dress up as clowns and go from house to house collecting candy and gifts during holidays (IFb: Mardin). Cf. Ar qird قرد = 'monkey, ape' [IFb/GF/TF/Kmc/RZ/CS/ZF]

qirdikî قِـردِكـى *f.* **(-ya;-yê).** clowning, buffoonery: •**Şanogerên Kurd, bi vê projeyê çanda *Qirdikîyê* didin jiyandin** (VoA, 30.ix.2013) Kurdish actors revive the culture of *clowning* with this project. {syn: qeşmerî} [VoA/TF/ZF]

qire-qir قِره قِر (IFb/GF)/qireqir قِرەقِر (A) = noise. See **qîreqîr̄**.

qir̄êj قِـرێـژ *adj.* 1) {syn: bi'ok; ç'epel; dijûn II; gemarî; mirdar; p'îs; qilêr} filthy, dirty; 2) {syn: qilêr} [*f.* **(-a;-ê)**] filth. {also: qirêjî (SK); [qyrich] قريش (JJ); <qirêj> قريژ (HH)} {qirêjahî; qir̄êjayî; qirêj[ît]î; <qirêjahî> قـريـژاهـى (HH)} [K/A/JB3/IFb/B/GF/TF//JJ]

qirêjahî قِرێژاهى (A/IFb/HH/GF) = filth; slovenliness. See **qir̄êjayî**.

qir̄êjayî قِـرێـژايـى *f.* **(-ya;-yê).** filth; slovenliness. {qirêjahî (A/IFb-2/GF-2); qir̄êjî II (K-2/IFb/TF); qirêjîtî (JB3/ZF3); <qirêjahî> قريژاهى (HH)} [K/B/GF//A/HH//IFb/TF//JB3/ZF3] <qir̄êj>

qirêjî I قِرێژى (SK) = filthy. See **qir̄êj**.

qir̄êjî II قِـرێـژى (K/IFb/TF) = filth; slovenliness. See **qir̄êjayî**.

qirêjîtî قِـرێـژيـتـى (JB3/ZF3) = filth; slovenliness. See **qir̄êjayî**.

Qirgizî قِرگِزى *adj.* Kirghiz. {also: Kirgîzî (BF)} [Wkp/Wkt/ZF3//BF]

qir̄ik I قِـرِك/**qirik** قِـرِك [A/IFb/TF/OK] *f.* **(-a;-ê).** throat, larynx: •**Ev kapê *qir̄ka* min te dîtîye?** (J) Have you seen the rope for my *neck*? •**Ji tîhna *qirika* min êdî ziwa bûbû** (LM, 5) My *throat* had gone dry from thirst •**Şwîrek li *qerika* wî xist** (L) He struck him in *the throat* with his sword (=He drove a sword into his throat); -**qir̄ika hev girtin** (K) = a) to grab one another by the throat; b) to quarrel, fight; c) to compete with. {also: qerik (L); qir̄k' (JB1-S); <qirik> قـرك (HH)} {syn: gewrî; ħefik; qeper} [J/K/B//A/JB3/IFb/ HH/TF/OK//JB1-S//L]

qir̄ik II قِـرِك/**qirik** قِـرِك [A/IFb/TF] *f.* **(-a;-ê).** 1) {syn: qel; qijik} crow, genus *Corvus*; 2) rook (bird) (K); 3) magpie (IFb). {also: qir̄ III (Dh); **qijik**; qirrik (GF); [qyrik] قرك (JJ); <qirik> قـرك (HH)} [HB/K//GF//A/IFb/JJ/HH/TF//Dh] See also **qijik**.

qirim قِـرِم *f.* **().** scythe, pruning hook: •**Di nav gundê te de *qirimên* ku dişibiyan nikulê leglegan ... xuyanî dibûn** (Ronî War: *Havîn*, diyarname.com vi.2007) In your village *scythes* which resembled stork beaks ... were to be seen. {also: qar̄im (Haz)} {syn: diryas; k'êlendî; melexan; şalok} [IFb/RF/RZ/ZF3/Wkt//Haz]

qirimsax قِرمساخ (ZF3) = pimp. See **qurumsax**.

qir̄k' قِرك (JB1-S) = throat. See **qir̄ik I**.

qirmî قِـرمـى *m.* **().** teapot; coffeepot: •**Gava seyda p'êp'elînga peya bû, qîzikê *qirmîk* li serê wî da** (HCK-1, 201) When the teacher descended the staircase, the girl struck his head with *a teapot*. {also: qirbî (B-2)} {syn: cimcime I} [HCK/K/B]

qirnab قِرناب (ZF3) = type of rope. See **qirnap**.

qirnap قِـرنـاپ *f.* **().** thick white rope *made of hemp, thinner than* **werîs**, *qv*: •***Qineb* kiribû şûna têla cilên şûştî û derpiyekî pîrekan li ser *qinêb* daleqandibû** (HYma, 37) He replaced the clothesline with *hemp rope* and hung a woman's underpants on the rope. {also: qinab (IFb); qinap (Kmc-2); qineb, m./f. (; qinêb/-ê) (HYma); qirnab (ZF3)} {syn: kap I; k'indir [2]; şerît [1]; werîs} < Ar qunnab/qinnab قـنّـب = 'hemp (Cannabis indica)'--> T kırnap [Uşak] = urgan = 'thick hawser, rope' (DS, v. 12, p. 4556) [Mzg/Kmc//ZF3//IFb//HYma] <ben[1]>

qirnaqoş قِرناقوش (SS) = see saw. See **qir̄neqos**.

qirnaqûz قِرناقووز (BF) = see saw. See **qir̄neqos**.

qir̄neqos قِـرنـەقـۆس *f.* **(;-ê).** see saw, teeter-totter: **•Zar̄o *qir̄neqosê dikin*** (FS) The children are *see sawing*. {also: qirnaqoş (SS); qirnaqûz (BF); qirneqot (FD-2)} {syn: zirnazîq; zîqûzir̄} [FS/ZF3/Wkt/FD//BF//SS]

qirneqot قِرنەقۆت (FD) = see saw. See **qir̄neqos**.

qirnî قِرنی/**qir̄nî** قِرنی *m./f.(B/OK)* **(; /-yê).** tick, zool. *Trichodectes*. {also: k'irin II (Bw-2); kir̄nî (FS); k'irnî (Bw); qernî (GF-2); **qijnik**; qirnû; qurnî; [qyrni] قـرنـی (JJ); <kirnî> کـرنـی (HH)} {syn: gene} Cf. Sor qir̄nû قِـرنـوو [F/K/A/IFb/JJ/GF/TF//B//HH/Bw//FS] <spî II; zûrî>

qirnû قِرنوو = tick. See **qirnî**.

qiroq قِـرۆق, m. (F) = restricted piece of land. See **qorix**.

qirpik قِرپك (IFb) = hiccup; burp. See **qilpik**.

qirqilîn قِـرقِـلـيـن (Nbh) = to worry; to be nauseous. See **qilqilîn**.

qirrik قِرِك (GF) = crow. See **qir̄ik II**.

qirş قِـرش *m.* **(-ê;).** 1) {syn: telîş I} splinters, chips, shavings; chaff and straw (HH): **•Kê ḧedd hebû ji *qirşekî* ḧetta pûşekî tiştekî bêjite wî?** (SK 36:323) Who would have dared to say anything [lit. 'from *shavings* to dry grass'] to him? **•Rabû p'ûşê hêlîna ç'ivîkê ji ç'e'vê wî derxist, hê *qirşê* wê têdane** (EP-5, #18) She removed from his eyes the dry grass of the bird nest which still had *chaff and straw* in it; 2) brushwood (B); sticks and twigs (IFb): **•Me li çolê sergîn û *qirş* berev dikirin bona dadana tendûrê** (Ba2-4, 219) We gathered dung and *brushwood* in the wilderness to light the stove; **-qirş û qal** (IFb)/**qal û qirş** (Qzl) sticks and twigs; 3) stick, switch *(for driving cattle)* (B). {also: qirşik (Qzl/GF-2/TF-2); <qiriş> قـرش (HH)} Cf. Ar qišr قـشـر = 'skin, peel, rind, crust' [K/A/IFb/B/SK/GF/TF//HH//Qzl] <pîj I>

qirşik قِرشِك (Qzl/GF/TF) = dim. of **qirş**[2].

qirûş قِـرووش (BX/ZF3) = small coin, penny. See **qurûş**.

qirwelk قِـروەلـك *pl.?* **().** anecdotes, short folkloristic narratives: ***•Qirwelka* bêje!** (Qzl) Tell *some stories*! {also: qerwelk (Qmş); qulûwîlk (Frq)} {syn: qelîbotk} [Qzl//Qmş//Frq] <çîvanok>

qisa قِسا (B) = story; talk. See **qise**.

qis•e قِسە *f.* **(•a;•ê).** 1) {syn: p'eyiv[2]; zarav[1]} talk, conversation, speaking, speech, words; **-qise kirin** (Ks/K)/**qezî kirin** (Kg/IFb) to speak {syn: axaftin; mijûl dan (Haz); p'eyivîn; şor kirin; şteẍilîn; xeber dan}; 2) promise, one's word: **•Naçar bîn--çi ji wana nehat, êdî--ser *qesa* xo man û nezivir̄-învе** (M-Zx #775) They had no alternative--there was nothing else they could do --so they stood by their *word* and did not go back on it; 3) {syn: çîr̄ok; ḧekyat} story: **•Bû *qisa* bizinê Ḧesen Ç'ermo** (Dz) It was *the story of* Hasan Chermo's goats *[proverbial expression describing conceited people]*; 4) [*pl.*] {syn: ç'êr̄; dijûn I; ne'let; nifir̄; sixêf; xeber[3]} insults, bad words, cussing, cursing: **•Cendirman jê ra *qezîyên xirab digotin* û lê dixistin** (DZK, 135) The policemen *insulted* them and beat them **•Wî *qese* gotine min** (Hk) He called me *names*. {also: qese (OK/Hk/M-Zx); qezî II (Kg/IFb/DZK); qisa (B-2); [qysé] قـصـه (JJ); <qisset> قسّت (HH)} < Ar qiṣṣah قصّة = 'story' [F/Dz/K/IFb/B/JJ/GF//HH//Kg/IFb/DZK//OK/Hk/M-Zx]

qiseker قِسەکەر *m.&f.* **(-ê/ ;).** speaker; spokesman: **•Demîrtaş duh jî weke *qiseker* beşdarî semînerekê bû** (ANF News) And yesterday D. participated in a seminar as *a speaker* **•Ne dikare bibe bîner û ne jî *qiseker*** (Nefel) He cannot be a spectator or *a speaker* **•Nûnerên Tevgera Jinên Kurd jî weke *qiseker* cihê xwe di konferansê de digirin** (ANHA) Representatives of the Kurdish Women Movement take their place in the conference as *speakers*. {syn: berdevk I; p'eyivdar} Sor qiseker قِسەکەر = 'speaker, person making a speech' [K/GF/ZF/Wkt/SS] <berdevk I>

qisîl قِسيل *f.* **(-a;-ê).** mat; mattress: **•Ew ser 'erdê sar, ser *xisîla* yanê jî, ḧalê k'ê hinekî p'ak bû, ser kulava r̄adizan** (Ba2-3, 213) They would sleep on the cold floor, on *mats*, or if they were a little better off, on rugs. {also: qesîl (IFb); xesîl (IFb-2); xisîl (Ba2)} {syn: ḧesîr} [Z-922/K/B/ZF3//IFb] <doşek>

qism قِسم (B) = lot, fate. See **qismet**.

qismet قِـسـمـەت *m.* **(-ê;).** lot, destiny; fate, fortune: **•'Evdê xwedê, helbe ez *qizmetê* teme, k'incê min bide min** (HCK-5, #8, 55) Slave of God [i.e., man], I'm certainly your *destiny* [=meant for you], give me my clothes **•Xorto, ez *qsmetê* teme ko wekî ter̄a hatim, de her̄e minr̄a hinek av bîne** (HCK-2, 187) Young man, I'm your *destiny* since I have come with you, so go bring me some water. {also: qism (B-2); qizmet (HCK-5); qsmet (HCK-2); [qismet] قـسـمـت (JJ); <qismet> قـسـمـت (HH)} {syn: bext; *çarenivîs; enînivîs; nesîb;

qeder II; yazî} < Ar qismah قسمة [HCK//K/B/IFb/JJ/HH/FJ/JB1-S/CS]

qisûr قِسوور (K/IFb/B) = defect; lack. See **qusûr**.

qişa قِشا (B) = ice. See **qeşa**.

qişirandin قِشِراندِن *vt.* **(-qişirîn-).** to make out, distinguish, espy, catch sight of *(from a distance)*: **•Qeret'ajdîn bin qap'ûtda gulîyê Zînê yek-yek *diqişirîne*** (Z-1) Q. *espies* each one of Zin's curls under the coat. {also: qeşirandin (ZF3); qeşrandin (FK-eb-1)} [Z-1/K//ZF3//FK/Rwn]

qişt قِشت *adj.* erect, straight; standing straight up: **•Gurgî got, "Mûêt min girj bûne?" Rîwî got, "Hey, beĥs neke! Hemî wekî dirêşan *qişt* r̄awestane"** (SK 6:69) The wolf said, "Have my hairs stood up?" The fox said, "Oh, don't mention it! They are all standing up as *straight* as bradawls." {syn: bel; girj [3]; qund; r̄ep} [SK]

qitê قِتێ (GF/FS) = type of cucumber. See **qitik**.

qitik قِتِك *m.* **(-ê;).** type of large cucumber, bot. *Cucumis melo* [T acur, Ar faqqūs فقّوس/faqqūṣ فقّوص]. {also: kûte (IFb-2); qertik (CCG); qitê (GF/FS); qitî (Czr); [qatí] قطى (JJ-Lx); <qetik> قتك (HH)} {syn: 'ecûr} Cf. T küte [Hozat -Tunceli; Elazığ; Malatya; Kilis -Gaziantep] = 'a type of cucumber, a wild cucumber' (DS, v. 8, p. 3053); <Arc qa/i/eṭṭayyā קטייא & Syr qa/oṭuṭā ܩܛܘܛܐ = 'cucumber, gourd'; = Sor çemîle tirozî چەمیلە ترۆزی [Dy/IFb/TF//HH//Czr//JJ//GF/FS//CCG] <xirtik I; xiyar>

qitî قِتی (Czr) = type of cucumber. See **qitik**.

qiwet قِوەت (IF) = strength, force. See **qewat**.

qiyas قِیاس *m.* **(-ê;).** 1) measure, extent: **-qiyasê** (SK) about, approximately {syn: qederê}: **•'Elî Beg *qiyasê* neh deh ser ĥeywanêt qelew ji beranan û şekan înan, dane kuştinewe** (SK 39:346) Ali Beg brought *about* 9 or 10 head of fat young rams and had them slaughtered **•Milletê Kuresinî, mêr û jin û biçûk, *qiyasê* hizar nufos, digel pêẍemberê xo çûne Xoy** (SK 32:288) The Kurasini people, men, women, and children, *about* a thousand souls, went with their prophet to Khoi **•R̄ojekî [sic] dî paşa derkewte seyranê, *qiyasê* s̱ed gustîrêt zêr̄ digel xo birin** (SK 22:200) Another day the Pasha went out on an excursion, taking *about* a hundred gold rings with him; 2) [*f.* **(-a;).**] comparison: **•Kesê bi xeberê mezinan neket û *qiyasa* gay li kerî *biket*, cezaê wî ewe ye** (SK 6:70) This is the reward of a person who does not do as the great ones tell him, and who *compares* an ox with a donkey. {also: [qiias] قیاس (JJ); <qiyas> قیاس (HH)} <Ar qiyās قیاس = 'dimension, measurement; comparison, analogy' [K/IFb/JJ/HH/SK] <qas; qeys>

qizban قِزبان (IFb) = terebinth. See **kezan**.

qizmet قِزمەت (HCK-5) = lot, fate. See **qismet**.

qî قی (Wkt) = swan. See **qû**.

qîc قیج (EŞ/GF) = showing one's teeth. See **qîç**.

qîç قیچ *adj.* 1) showing one's teeth; given to grinning stupidly or unpleasantly: **-qîç kirin/qîc kirin** (EŞ)/**diranê xwe qîj kirin** (K) to bare *(one's fangs or teeth)* {syn: sîqirandin}: **•Gava gur rivîna geş dît, xwe ji miyê bi dûr xist, xwe gij kir û diranên xwe *qîc kirin*** (EŞ,16) When the wolf saw the bright flame, it dropped the sheep, stiffened its back, and *bared* its teeth; 2) {syn: şaş I[3]} squinting, squint-eyed (OK/IFb): **-çav qîç kirin** (IFb) to blink one's eyes, squint. {also: qîc (EŞ/GF); qîj (K)} cf. <qîç> قیچ (Hej) = 'with one eye smaller than the other' [EŞ/GF//IFb/TF/OK/Hej//K] <firk III; fîq; qîl>

qîç'ik قیچِك *adj.* 1) {syn: zer I} yellow; bright yellow; 2) orange (colored) (Elk/QtrE). {also: [qytch قچ/ qytchik قچك] (JJ)} {qîç'ikayî} [F/K/IFb/B/SC/JJ/Elk/QtrE/ZF3/FS]

qîç'ika•yî قیچِکایی *f.* **(;•yê).** 1) {syn: zerî III} yellowness; 2) {syn: zerik III} jaundice. [K/B] <qîç'ik>

qîj قیژ (K) = showing one's teeth. See **qîç**.

qîjeqîj قیژەقیژ *f.* **(-a;-ê).** 1) loud, shrill cry of birds, crowing, cackling: **•*qîjqîja* mirîşka** (GF) *cackling of* chickens **•Te bo çî xew li xelkî ĥeram kirîye? Nîwşewê dest bi *qîjeqîjê* dikey, nahêlî xelk biniwît** (SK 4:50) Why have you made sleep impossible for people? You start *crowing* in the middle of the night and do not let people sleep; 2) roar of lions, panthers, etc.: **•Şêr *wê bê qîjqîja* wa, û t' ê k'evê axa pilinga da piling *wê* wilo *kine qîjqîj* û qarqar** (HR 3:137) The lions, they *will roar*, and when you enter the panthers' territory they *will* also *roar* and growl. {also: qîjqîj (HR/FJ/GF)} Sor qîjeqîj قیژەقیژ = 'continued screaming/shrieking' [HR/FJ/GF//K/B/IFb/SK] <qîjîn>

qîjiyan قیژیان (FS) = to scream. See **qîjîn**.

qîjîn قیژین *vi.* **(-qîj-).** 1) to scream, screech, shriek, shout (with fear): **•Mak hergav parêzer e. Gava berê wê kete tehlîkeyê, bi reflekseke xwezayî**

diqîje, **diqîre, xwe diperitîne, dike hawar û gazî** (R.Hazim. Ji welatê Xanî û Bateyî hawara Kurdî) A mother is always protective. When her child is in danger, as a natural reflex she *screams*, shrieks, tears at herself, screams for help; 2) [*f.* **(-a;-ê).**] scream(ing), screech(ing), shriek(ing), shout(ing with fear) {also: qîjînî (ZF3/CS)}: **•Bi *qijîna* Dîlberê re hemû malî li ber Neco daçikiyan** (Nofa, 91) When D. *screamed*, the whole house stood up **•Hema wê demê min li paş xwe *qîjîneke* bi tirs û xof a mezin bîhist** (Bîrnebûn #47, paîz 2010, 22) Just then I heard *a* great *shriek* of fear and terror behind me. {also: qijîn (Nofa); qîjiyan (FS); qîjqîjîn (FJ-2/GF-2); qîjyan (G)} Cf. Sor qîje قیژه = 'scream' & qîjandin قیژاندِن = 'to scream, shriek' [Nofa//B/IFb/FJ/GF/ZF3/FS/FD/Wkt/CS//G] <qîjeqîj; qîrîn>

qîjînî قیژینی (ZF3/CS) = scream, shriek. See **qîjîn**[2].

qîjqîj قیژقیژ (HR/FJ/GF) = crowing, roaring. See **qîjeqîj**.

qîjqîjîn قیژقیژین (FJ/GF) = to scream. See **qîjîn**.

qîjyan قیژیان (G) = to scream. See **qîjîn**.

qîl قیل *m.* **().** 1) {syn: kilb} fang, tooth of a canine: **•Heta ku *qîlên* (diran) guran neyên hilkirin û pencên wan neyê[n] qutkirin, ji kuştin û qirkirinê venagerin** (Wlt 2:71, 13) Until the wolves' *fangs* are pulled out and their claws are cut back, they will not stop killing and destroying; 2) (elephant) tusk: **•Siltanê Fîlan ... ji hêrsa spîsor bû û bû qirçe qirça *qîlên* wî** (SF 29) The Sultan of the elephants ... turned white with rage and you could hear him gnashing his *tusks*. [Wlt/F/IFb/B/GF] <didan; qîç>

qîm قیم *f.* **(-a;).** 1) sufficiency, satisfaction, having had one's fill: **•*Qîma* me bi vê nayê** (Wkt) This is not enough for us/We are not satisfied with this; **-qîma xwe pê anîn** (ZF3/FD) to make do with stg., be content or satisfied with stg.; **-qîmî ft-î kirin** (ZF3) to suffice, be enough for: **•Ev pere *qîmî* kirîna pirtûkê *nake*** (ZF3) This money *isn't sufficient* to buy the book; 2) agreement, consent (HH): **-qîma xwe anîn** (HR-I) to agree, come to an agreement {syn: sozê xwe kirin yek}: **•Me ȟemûwa *qîma xo anî*** (HR-I, 2:11) We *were* all *in agreement*; 3) wish, desire, fancy, whim: **•*Qîma* min nayê** (IFb) I don't feel like it. {also: [qim] قيم (JJ); <qîm> قیم (HH)} [HB/K(s)/A/IFb/JJ/HH/GF/TF/HR-I/ZF3/Wkt/FD]

qîmet قیمەت *m./f.(F/WM)* **(-ê/-a;).** value, worth: **•Zîna delal nîşan kirin** [sic] **bi t'ilîsmeke zêrîn, wek *qîmetê* wê xercê Cizîrê ȟevt sala bû** (Z-1) They betrothed lovely Zîn with a golden talisman, *worth* Jizîra's taxes for seven years; **-qîmet zanîn** (IFb) to value, appreciate: **•Kurd *bi qîmeta* zimanê kurdî *nizanin*** (Amûde.com) The Kurds *don't value* the Kurdish language **•Mirovê gundî pir dixebitin lê *qîmeta* keda xwe *nizanin*** (WM 1:2, 10) Peasants work a lot but they *don't know the worth of* their labor. {also: [qimet] قيمت (JJ); <qîmet> قیمت (HH)} {syn: qedir I[2]} < Ar qīmah قيمة --> T kıymet [K/JB3/IFb/B/JJ/HH/SK/GF]

qîq قیق *adj.* tall and thin. {also: <qîqbûn قیقبون (qîqdibe) (قیقدبە)> (HH)} [Qrj/IFb/HH/GF/FS/ZF3] <bejnbilind; zirav I>

qîr I قیر *f.* **(-a;-ê).** tar, pitch: **•Kîjan zilamê ku bi kincên wî ve çilkên *qîrê* hebin, wî bigrin bînin cem min** (ZZ-7, 251) Whichever man has drops *of tar* on his clothes, arrest him and bring him to me. {also: [qir] قير (JJ); <qîr> قیر (HH)} {syn: zift} Cf. Ar qīr قير [K/A/JB3/IFb/B/JJ/GF/ZF]

qîr II قیر: -qîr dan (A)/kirin (JB3) = to shout, scream. See **qîrîn**.

qîrandin قیراندِن (-qîrîn-) (SK/GF/M) = to scream. See **qîrîn** & **qûrîn**.

qîreqîr قیرەقیر/**qîre-qîr** قیرە قیر [K] *f.* **(;-ê).** 1) {syn: bar̄ebar̄; bir̄bir̄; hengame; hêwirze; hoqeboq; k'im-k'imî; qajeqaj; qalmeqal; qareqar; qerebalix; şerqîn; t'eqer̄eq} noise, din, tumult, uproar; loud and continuous shout, roar, or bellow (B): **•Her kes direvîne ber ve behrê, dengê *qîreqîr* û gotinên wan e** (L) Everyone ran toward the sea, [one could hear] the sound of their *shouts* and talking; 2) argument, quarrel (IFb/A); 3) {syn: wîqewîq} croaking *(of frog)* (IFb). {also: qire-qir (IFb/GF); qireqir (A); qîr̄e-qûr̄; [qyre-qyr] قرەقر (JJ)} Cf. Sor qir̄eqir̄ قڕەقڕ = 'cawing, croaking' [L/B//K/ZF3//A/IFb/JJ/GF] <qîrîn; qûrîn>

qîre-qûr قیرە قوور = noise. See **qîreqîr**.

qîrîn قیرین *vi.* **(-qîr-).** 1) to shout, scream, cry out: **•Rojekê şivanek diçe bajêr. Dinihêre ku yek derketîye ser minarê û *diqîre*** (LM, 11) One day a shepherd goes to town. He sees that someone comes out of the minaret and *shouts* [something]; 2) [*f.* **(-a;-ê).**] shouting, screaming, crying out: **•*qîrîna* sewta aşiq** (Z-1) *the shouting of* the singer's voice. {also: qêrîn (SF); qîr dan (A); qîr kirin (JB3); qîrandin (SK/GF/M)} [Z-1/K/IFb/B/FS//SK/GF/M//A//JB3] <kûřîn; qîjîn> See also **qûřîn**.

qît قيت (CS) = chopped firewood. See **qîtik II**.

qîtik I قيتِك (Wn) = unripe cucumber. See **kûtik**.

qîtik II قيتِك *m.* **( ).** pieces of chopped firewood: **•Ezê wê qumandê li bin guhê dîwêr bixim, *qîtik qîtikî bikim*!** (SBx, 17) I'm gonna shove that remote [control device] under the wall [lit. 'under the ear of the wall'], I'll *chop* it *to pieces*! {also: qît (CS-2); qutik II (IFb-2)} {syn: qoçik} [SBx/IFb/CS]

qîvar قـيـڤـار *f.* **(-a;-ê).** 1) type of thistle, bitter plant *which blooms in the springtime, eaten by donkeys*: **-Kero nemire buhare/ heta çêbin *qîvare*** (GF) Donkey, don't die, it is spring/ [wait] until the *thistles* come out *[prv.]*; 2) {syn: nêrik} stamen, male reproductive organ of a flower which bears the pollen (IFb/GF): **-Keleng hê hişk nebûye, *qîvarê*** [sic] **wê tê xwarin** (IFb) The cardoon isn't dry yet, and its *stamen* is [already] being eaten *[prv.]* {also: [qyvar/kīvār (Rich)] قـــــوار (JJ); <qîvar> قـيـڤـار (HH)} cf. NENA qîwârâ ܩܝܘܪܐ = 'briar, thistle, bramble' (Maclean) [Zeb/K/A/IFb/JJ/HH/GF/TF/OK] <givzonik; k'erbeş; kereng>

qîz قـيـز *f.* **(-a;-ê).** girl; daughter: **-qîza hakim** (L) princess, king's daughter; **-qîzik** = dim. of **qîz**. {also: [qyz قز/qyzé قزه] (JJ); <qîz> قـيـز (HH)} {syn: dot; keç(ik); zêrî} < T kız; *the long vowel serves to emphasize the distinction between this word and the taboo word* ***quz*** *= 'vagina'* {qîzanî; qîztî} [Kg/K/A/IFb/B/HH/GF//JJ]

qîzanî قيزانى (A/ZF3) = girlhood; virginity. See **qîztî**.

qîzap قيزاپ *f.* **(-a;-ê).** female first cousin, daughter of one's father's brother: **•Dîa min û Sûsîkê *qîzapê hev*in** (Ba2-#2, 206) My mother and Susik's mother are *first cousins* [i.e, their fathers were brothers]. {syn: dotmam} <qîz + ap = 'paternal uncle' [Ba2/F/K/A/B] <ap; dotmam; mam>

qîzhilî قيزهِلى (ZF3) = stepdaughter. See **qîzḧilî**.

qîzḧilî قيزحِلى *f.* **().** stepdaughter. {also: qîzhilî (ZF3)} {syn: nevisî; keçḧelî} [Frq//ZF3] <-ḧilî I; ziřdayîk>

qîzik قيزك = dim. of **qîz**.

qîzmet' قـيـزمـەت *f.* **(-a;-ê).** female first cousin, daughter of one's father's sister: **•Em dixwazin wekî tu û *qîzmet'a* te bextewar bin** (Ba2-#2, 207) We want you and your *cousin* to be happy [together]. {also: qîzmetî (K)} <qîz + met['] = 'paternal aunt' [Ba2/F/B/ZF3//K] <dotmam; met[']>

qîzmetî قـيـزمـەتـى (K) = father's sister's daughter, cousin. See **qîzmet'**.

qîztî قـيـزتـى *f.* **(-ya;-yê).** 1) girlhood: **•Pîrê çû bajêr, deste k'inc-rihelê qîza k'iřî, anî, Sîabend kir. Sîabend *qîztî* xemiland** (IS-#281-282) The old woman went to town, bought a suit of girl's clothes, and brought it, put it on Siyabend. She dressed Siyabend up *as a girl*; 2) virginity. {also: qîzanî (A/ZF3)} [IS/F/K/B//A/ZF3] <bik'ur; qîz>

qjik قژك (EH) = type of bird. See **qijik**.

qloç قلوّچ (IFb) = horn *(of animal)*. See **qoç'**.

qlonç قلوّنچ (IFb) = horn *(of animal)*. See **qoç'**.

qobbe قوّببه = dome. See **qube II**.

qoç' قـوّچ *m.* **(-ê;).** horn, antler *(of animal)*: **•*Qiloç'ê* pezk'ûvî dik'eve řanê Sîyabend** (Z-4) The deer's *antler* goes into Siyabend's thigh; **-qoç danan** (SK) to butt: **•Gurg kewte ber pîyêt gay. Derḧal gay *qoçek dana* gurgî** (SK 6:70) The wolf fell in front of the ox's feet. Immediately the ox *butted* the wolf. {also: qiloç (IFb-2/GF-2); qilonç (IF-2); qloç (IFb-2); qlonç (IFb-2)} {syn: strû; şax} Sor qoç قـوّچ = 'ram's horn'; Za qoç *m.* (Mal) [Ks/K/A/IFb/SK/GF/OK] <k'ol IV>

qoç'ax قـوّچـاخ *adj.* 1) {syn: xebatḧiz; xebatk'ar[2]} hardworking, diligent, industrious: **•Lê çima ew** [sic] **bûka *qoçax* ew xortê *qoçax* nestandye hatye vî xortê t'embel standye?** (Dz) But why didn't that *diligent* girl marry that *diligent* young man, [why] did this lazy young man marry her?; 2) brave, manly, dashing (B): **•Wekî tu çiqas *qoçaxî*, bavê te axê êlê bû ... tu çima, çira kurê min dikutî** (FK-kk-3) If you are so *manly*, your father was the agha [chief] of the tribe ... why oh why do you beat my son? {also: qoçax̌ (B)} Cf. T koçak = 'strong and brave (man); generous'; Sor qoçax قـوّچـاخ = 'clever, quick, smart' {qoç'ax[t]î; qoçax̌î} [Dz/F/K//B] <'egît; mêrxas>

qoç'axî قوّچاخى *f.* **(-ya;-yê).** 1) diligence; 2) bravery. {also: qoç'axtî (FS); qoçax̌î (B)} [K//FS//B] <qoç'ax>

qoç'axtî قـوّچـاخـتـى (FS) = diligence; bravery. See **qoç'axî**.

qoçax̌ قـوّچـاغ (B) = hardworking; brave; dashing. See **qoç'ax**.

qoçax̌î قوّچاغى (B) = diligence; bravery. See **qoç'axî**.

qoçik قوّچك *m./f.(Wkt)* **().** firewood, cut and ready to be burned: **•Wî *qoçik* bo şotinê înan mal** (FS) He brought *firewood* home for burning. {syn: qîtik II}

[Haz/Wkt/FS] <êzing; ĥejik; teřik II>

qodîk قۆدیك (Bw/Zx/Zeb) = mirror. See **qotî I**.

qodret قۆدرەت (L) = power. See **qudret**.

qof قۆف (A/IFb) = with a crippled hand. See **qop**.

qol I قــۆل *m.* **(-ê;).** 1) arm: **-qol-qol bûn** (Z-1) to be arm in arm; 2) wing; 3) sleeve. Cf. T kol = 'arm' [Z-1/K/B/GF] <bask; ç'epil; dest; mil; pîl I>

qol II قــۆل *m.* **(-ê;).** string with coins sewn on it *(woman's ornament, tied on the forehead)*: **•Zînê destxweda gilîyê Memê dife'mîne, / Destê řastê û ç'epê hevraz, berjêr hiltîne, / *qolêd* zêřa ji ne'tikê diqetîne** (Z-1) Zin immediately understands Mem's words, / She raises and lowers her right and left hand, / Breaks her ornamental golden coin *strings* from [her] forehead. [Z-1/K/B] <benî II; gerden[3]>

qol III قــۆل *adj.* 1) cut off, docked, amputated *(of animal's tail)*: **•Ku Pîrê dêla min nede min, bi vê dêla *qol* ezê tim bibim pêkenînê hevalan** (Z. Xamo. Hindik Rindik 2.vi.2011) If the old lady won't give me back my tail, with this *docked* tail I will always be the laughing stock of my friends; 2) tailless, having lost its tail: **-gurê qol** (GF) the tailless wolf; **-rûviyê qol** (FS) the tailless fox; **-seê qol** (B) the tailless dog. Cf. Sor kuł کــوڵ = 'with tail docked (of birds)' [Z.Xamo/K/B/IFb/GF/FS/G/FD] <kol IV>

qol IV قــۆل *f.* **().** sleigh, sled(ge) for transporting things over snow and ice: **•*Qol* û parxêl cida ne li nik me. Parxêlê havînan girê didin, didin dû gayan daku ga ji cihên dûr giya bînin nav gundî. Lê *qol* li ser berfê ye...** (M.Gür, ji Hekaryan, "Zimanê Kurdî", Rûname v.2012) *Qol* and parkhel are different for us. They tie up a parkhel [timber sledge] in the summer, and put it behind oxen so they they will transport the grass from distant places to the village. But *the qol* [sleigh] is on the snow.... {syn: taxok} [M.Gür/IFb/ZF3/Wkt/FS/CS] <parxêl>

qolenc قۆلەنج (GF) = colic; lumbago. See **qolinc II**.

qolinc I قــۆلِــنــج *f.* **(-a;-ê).** space between the shoulder blades: **•Eliyê Daman Beg ... rimê** [sic] **avête Hesê, li nêv reha *qolincê* xist bi derbekê di defa singê re avête der** (ZZ-10, 143) Ali D.B. ... threw a lance at H., struck him between *the shoulder blades* with a single blow and brought it out his chest [i.e., *out the other side*]. {also: [qōlýnǰ] قــلــنــج (JJ-PS)} Cf. Sor kołinc کــۆڵِــنــج = 'stiffness in shoulder and neck' [Qrj/K/IFb/JJ-PS]

qolinc II قــۆلِــنــج *f.* **(-a;-ê).** colic; lumbago: **•Tu řave ser pişta min veleze, belkî *qolincya* min dayne** (HCK-2, 183) You come lie on my back, maybe my *lumbago* will ease up; **-qolenciya tirkî** (GF) appendicitis; **-riha qolincê** (SK) lumbar nerve, plexus. {also: qolenc (GF-2); qolincayî (B); qolincî II (HCK/K); [qoulindj/kolénğ (G)] قــولــنــج (JJ); <qolinc> قولنج (HH)} < Ar qawlanj قولنج = 'colic' < Gr kōlikos κωλικος <kōlon κωλον/kolon κολον = 'colon' [HCK/K//IFb/FJ/TF/SK/GF/JJ/HH/ZF/FS//B]

qolincayî قۆلِنجایی (B) = colic; lumbago. See **qolinc II**.

qolincî I قۆلِنجی *adj.* suffering from colic or lumbago: **•Yeman, ez *qolincî*me, ezê velezim, tu řave ser pişta min veleze** (HCK-2, 183) Ouch, my back is bothering me [lit. 'I am *suffering from lumbago*'], I will lie down, you come lie on my back. {also: [qoulindji] قولنجی (JJ)} [HCK/K/JJ/ZF3]

qolincî II قــۆلِــنــجــی (HCK/K) = colic; lumbago. See **qolinc II**.

qoliptîn قــۆلِــپــتــیــن (-qolip-) (L) = to turn; to wither. See **qulibîn**.

qoloz قۆلۆز (JB1-A/OK) = high. See **quloz**.

qom قــــۆم *f./m.(FS)* **().** large earthenware container used for churning butter or yoghurt. *See drawing in Kmc#30, p. 1.* {also: qûm II (GF/ZF3/FS); <qûm> قــوم (HH)} [Kmc#30//GF/HH/ZF3/FS] <kûp; k'ûz II>

qomsî قۆمسی (Z-1/XF) = gossip, informer. See **qumsî**.

qonax قــۆنــاخ *f./m.(B/L)* **(-a/-ê; /qonêx).** 1) [< T konak = 'manor, guesthouse'] manor, mansion, palace: **•[Ew Meĥmed beg jî di *qonaẍeke* mezinda sakin dibûye]** (JR) This Mehmed beg lived in a large *manor*; 2) {syn: xan I} inn, place to stay overnight on a trip, room for the night; 3) {syn: menzîl [2]} a day's journey; distance, space, or interval between two overnight stops on a trip (K); leg or stage of a trip or journey; distance one can travel on foot in one day (IFb); day's march, distance between staging points, étape [Fr.] (JB1-A): **•Meşiha *qûnaẍek* hilanî û yek danî, *qûnaẍa* du řoj û di şêva meşî** (HR 3:46) He completed one day's traveling, and started out again the next morning [lit. 'He picked up *one stage* of the trip and put one down'], he walked *the distance of* two days and nights **•*Konaẍa* saetekê meşîyan** (L) They walked an hour's *distance*; 4) stage, phase: **•di vê *qonaxê*da** (Roj 1[1996]:4) at this *stage*; 5) [<Az

T qonağ = 'guest', cf. T konuk = do.] {syn: mêvan} guest (B). {also: konax̄ (L); qonax̄ (JB1-A/L); qûnax̄ (HR); [qonag] قـونـاغ (JJ); <qonax> قـــونـــاخ (HH)} [L//K/IFb/Ba2/B/HH/ GF/TF//JR/JJ/JB1-A] <hêwirîn; hêwirandin; qesr>

qonax̄ قۆناغ (JB1-A/L) = mansion; inn; day's march; guest. See **qonax**.

qonder•e قـــۆنــــدەرە *f.* **(•a;).** shoe; leather shoe *{as opposed to* **sol** *= plastic shoe}* (Rh): **•Bi du cot *qondereye* / *qonderek* jê mêraneye û yek jê qîzaneye** (Z-2) With two pairs of *shoes*, / One is a man's pair and one is a girl's. {also: kondere (F); qondre (IFb-2/GF); qundire (A/JB3); <qundere> قــنـــدره (HH)} {syn: meras; pêlav; sol} Cf. T kundura; Hau qonre *m.* = 'European type of shoe' (M4) [Z-2/Rh/K(s)/IFb//A/JB3//HH//F/GF]

qondre قۆندرە (IFb/GF) = shoe. See **qondere**.

qonêr قۆنێر (FS) = boil, abscess. See **qunêr**.

qontax قـــۆنـــتـــاخ (A) = slope; foot of mountain. See **qunt'ar**.

qop قـــۆپ/**qop'** [B] *adj.* with a crippled hand *(missing fingers, etc.),* lame: **•Ji bo vê qenciya te, bi Xwedê ez bi dil û can vê bizina xwe ya *qop* diyarî te dikim** (Nivîs: Bajarê Keran [2001]) For this good deed of yours, I gladly give you this *lame* goat. {also: qilop (Qrj); qof (A/IFb); <qop> قـوپ (HH)} {syn: goc; kulek I; kût I; şeht; şil II} [HB/K/B/HH/ZF/SS//A/IFb//Qrj] <nivîşkan I>

qopek قۆپەك (IFb) = hump. See **qopik**.

qopik قـــۆپـِـك *m.* **(-ê;).** hump, hunch *(on one's back)*: **•Jêhat ... *qopikê* pişta xwe rast kir** (SBx, 12) J. ... straightened *the hump on* his back. {also: qopek (IFb)} [SBx/ZF//IFb] <ħawid; kûz I>

qor I قۆر *m.* **(-ê;).** leg. {syn: ling} [Dêrsim/IFb/ZF]

qor̄ II قـــۆڕ *f.* **(-a;-ê).** line: **•*Qora* govendê tê û diçe** (AB) The dance *line* goes back and forth [lit. 'comes and goes']. {syn: r̄êz I; xet} [AB/K(s)/IFb/GF/ZF/FS]

qor̄ III قـــــۆڕ *adj.* skinny, thin, scrawny, emaciated, gaunt, puny *(of animals or people)*: **•Lênihêr̄î, ce'nûê 'Elî anîne – çîpxarin, *qor̄in*** (K'orox̄lî, 142) He saw that the colts that Ali brought were bow-legged and *scrawny*. {also: <qor> قـــــــور (HH)} {syn: jar I; lawaz; lex̄er; narîn; qels I; zeyf; zirav I} Sor qor قۆر [K'orox̄lî/K/A/B/FJ/GF/HH/CS]

qor̄ik قـــۆڕِك/**qorik** قـــۆرِك [FS] *f.* **(-a;-ê).** 1) small of the back; tailbone (TF): **-hestîyê qor̄ikê** (Kmc-6) ilium, hip bone; 2) {syn: k'emax} hip (IFb/Kmc-5). {also: <qorik> قـــورك (HH)} [AB/K/A/IFb/B/HH/TF/Kmc-5/FS] <kilêjî; qûn; zotik>

qorix قـــــــــۆرخ *f.* **(;-ê).** piece of land whose use is restricted, so that the grass growing on it can be harvested; a restricted area; a fenced-in pasture; a reserve: **-qorix kirin** (K/B) to restrict the use of a piece of land: **•Mêrg û çîman bax̄ û bax̄çê ax̄ê hebû. Bi ħezar û ħezara hêja bû. Ax̄ê biharê *qorix dikir*. Bi ħezar p'ale, gundî lê dixebitandin, xweyî dikir ħetanî havînê** (IS-#38-41) The agha owned meadows and gardens. They were worth thousands. In the springtime he *restricted access to them*. He put thousands of workers and peasants to work on them, to take care of them until the summer. {also: qiroq, m. (F); [qorig قـــورغ/qori قـــوری] (JJ) = 'défense, prohibition'; <qorix> قـــــورخ (HH)} {syn: p'awan II} Cf. also T koruḫ [Çayağzı *Şavşat-Artvin;*Erciş-Van] & koruk [Kars; Cenciğe-Erzincan] & korugan [Karakoyun *Iğdır-Kars] = 'field protected so that its grass can be harvested' [otunu biçmek için korunan tarla] (DS, v. 8, p. 2928) & koruk [Güneyce *İkizdere-Rize] = 'protected and cared-for field or grove' (DS, v. 12, p. 4566) & goruḫ [Bayburt *Sarıkamış-Kars; Yavaşak *Yıldızeli-Sivas] = 'field which is protected and not harvest-ed throughout the spring, in order to obtain grass from it' (DS, v. 6, p. 2106); also Erzurum T ķoruḫ = 'piles of stones for showing the boundaries' (Gemalmaz, v. 3, p. 203) & koruk = 'stones piled one on top of the other by farmers at the edge of the field, and by shepherds on hilltops' (Atılcan, p. 75); P qoroq قــــــرق = 'reserved, restricted'; Sor qorix قـۆرِخ = 'reserved (originally of public bath closed and reserved for important person)'; See: Doerfer vol. 3, #1462. qoruq قــــرق = 'reservation, taboo, something forbidden' [IS/K/B/HH//JJ//F]

qorî kirin قـۆری کِـرن (SK) = to scream. See **qîr̄în** & **qûr̄în**.

qor̄în قـــۆڕيـــن (-qor̄-) (K) = to scream. See **qîr̄în** & **qûr̄în**.

qorne قۆرنە *f.* **(-ya;-yê).** horn *of automobile, etc.*: **•Bi *qorneya* erebeyekê li xwe varqilîm** (R. Dildar. Kitana Spî, 33) I was brought to my senses by *the horn of* a car **•Nerazîbûna xwe bi tîtetîta *qorne-yê* jê re nîşan da** (Semedyan: Nefel 5.iv.2009) He showed him his displeasure with a honk of *the horn*. {also: korna (ZF3); korne (RZ)} <T korna < It corno [R.Dildar/IFb//RZ//ZF3]

qorûş قۆرووش = small coin, penny. See **qurûş**.

qorzî قـــۆرزی *f.* **(-ya;-yê).** corner: **•Carekê diya wî**

sendoqek mezin mişt terî û guhên ker û pisîkan li *qorzîkeke* hewşê dîtin (HYma, 12) Once his mother saw a big box overflowing with donkey and cat tails and ears in *a corner of* the yard; **-qorziya masê** (IFb) corner of the table; **-qorziya xênî** (IFb) corner of the house. {also: qorzîk (HYma); qozî (FJ/TF/GF-2/CS-2); qozîk (GF)} {syn: goşe; kujî; k'unc; qilçik; qulç} [HYma//A/IFb/CS//FJ/TF//GF]

qorzîk قۆرزیك (HYma) = corner. See **qorzî**.

qosik قۆسِك (ZF3) = slingshot. See **qosk**.

qosk قــۆســك *m./f.(BF)* **(-ê/; /-ê).** slingshot: **•Wî bi *qoskê* çûçikek kuşt** (FS) He killed a bird with the *slingshot* **•Zarokê biçûk ji mezinê xwe hîn bûye ku bi *qoskê* biçe nêçîra çûkan** (rojevamedya3.com 4.xii.2016) The small child has learned from his elders to go hunt sparrows with *a slingshot*; **-darkê qozkê** (Bw-->Dostkî) wooden Y-shaped part of slingshot. {also: qosik (ZF3); qozik (Bw--> Dostkî)} {syn: *bendek; *bertifk (Am); *çetal; darlastîk; *neçik} <Ar qaws قــوس = 'arch' [Bw-->Dostkî//Slv/FS/BF/Wkt//ZF3]

qoş قــــــــۆش *m./f.(B)* **(; /-ê).** 1) {syn: kejî; kolan I; navteng; teng II} saddle-girth, belly-band *(for horses)* (K/A); saddle-tie, crupper, leather loop passing under a horse's tail and buckled to the saddle (HH/JJ/DS) [qouch]: **-qoş kirin** (B/Dz) = a) to let gallop *(of horses)* (B); b) to yoke, harness *(of oxen)* (Dz) {syn: girêdan}; **•Divînin wê xortek gaê xwe t'eze girtye ku *qoşke*** (Dz) They see that the young man has just tied up his oxen *to harness* them **•Eva bûka jî jina wî xortê t'embele ku gaê xwe t'eze *qoşdikir*** (Dz) This young woman is the wife of that lazy young man who was just *harnessing* his oxen; 2) [< T koşmak = 'to run'] horse race (JJ/B) [qoch]. {also: [qouch [1]/qoch[2]] قوش (JJ); <qûş> قــــــــوش (HH)} Cf. T koskon [Andırın-Maraş]/koş [Kozan-Adana] = 'crupper' (DS, v. 8); T koş- = 'to run' [Dz/K/A/B//HH//DS]

qoşxane قۆشخانه (TF) = pot. See **qûşxane**.

qot قۆت (GF/RZ) = bare, naked. See **kot I**.

qotifîn قـۆتـفـیـن (L/K[s]) = to freeze, be terrified. See **qutifîn**.

qotik I قۆتِك (GF) = shirt. See **qutik I**.

qotik II قـۆتـِك *f.* **(-a;-ê).** pestilence, plague, epidemic, *especially affecting domestic animals (murrain)*: **•Di malbata me de, hetta di nav eşîra me de--yên ku bi destê hukmatê hatine kuştin û yên ku bi *qotikê* mirine ne tê de--kes bi ciwanî nemirîye** (LC, 10) In our family, even in our tribe--except for those who were killed by the [Turkish] government or who died from *plague*--no one has died in his youth; **-bi qotikê ketin** (Qrj) to catch a communicable disease, fall ill with or come down with the plague: **•*Bi qotikê ket* û mir** (Qrj) He *contracted the plague* and died **•Tu *bi qotikê kevî*** (Qrj) *May* you *catch the plague*! *[a curse]*. {also: qotk (GF)} {syn: pejî; şewb; teşene; weba} [Qrj/LC/IFb/TF//GF]

qotî I قــۆتــی *f.* **(-ya;-yê).** mirror: **•Li r̄ûwê xo mêzê, *qotîyê* ji ber xwe diderêxê, li r̄ûwê xwe dimêzênê kû weke deẍmekkî** (HR 3:227) He looks at his face, he takes out *a mirror* [and holds it] before himself, he looks at his face, that [appears] like a brand/stamp [on it]. {also: qodîk (Bw/Zx/Zeb)} {syn: 'eynik; hêlî; mirêk; nênik I} [Bşk//Bw/Zx/Zeb]

qot'î II قۆتی (L/TF) = box. See **qut'î**.

qotk قۆتك (GF) = plague, murrain. See **qotik II**.

qotmok قــۆتــمــۆك *f.* **(-a;).** cigarette butt. [Msr/Wkt] <cigare>

qoze قــۆزه *f.* **(-ya;-yê).** cocoon (of silkworm, etc.) [Ar šarnaqah شــرنــقــة; P pīlah پــیــلــه; T koza]: **•Piştî kurmikên *qozeyan* ji hêkê dertên bi 40 rojî, *qozeya* wê** [sic] **dimire** (dihaber16.net 4.iii.2017) 40 days after *cocoon* worms come out of the egg, its [sic] *cocoon* dies. Cf. T koza; Sor qozaxe قۆزاخه [IFb/FJ/ZF/SS]

qozik قۆزِك (Bw--> Dostkî) = slingshot. See **qosk**.

qozî قۆزی (FJ/TF/GF/CS) = corner. See **qorzî**.

qozîk قۆزیك (GF) = corner. See **qorzî**.

qral قرال (K-ça/K/IFb) = king. See **qiral**.

qrar قــرار, f. (EP-7) = decision; command; agreement; promise; custom. See **qirar**.

Qrux قروخ (Calendar) = Polar star. See **Qurix**.

qsmet قسمەت (HCK-2) = lot, fate. See **qismet**.

qub قوب (A/FJ/TF) = dome. See **qube II**.

qubbe قوببه (K) = dome. See **qube II**.

qube I قــوبــه *adj.* coarse; loud; proud. {also: qubet (K-2/CS)} Cf. T kaba = 'rough, coarse, rude' [K/B//CS]

qub•e II قوبه *f.* **(•a;•ê).** dome, cupola; arch, vault (K): **•Li Rûhayê kelayek çêkir, sêsed û şest û şeş *qube* bûn. Diço ser wan kela û *quba* tîr û kevan dihavêtine Xudê** (GShA, 227) At Urfa he built a fortress, with 666 *domes*. He climbed up that fortress and those *domes* and shot arrows at God with a bow. {also: qobbe; qub (A/FJ/TF); qubbe (K-2)} <Ar qubbah قبّة [Z-2/K/IFb/B/GF/CS//A/FJ/TF]

qubeqaz قـوبـەقـاز *f.* **().** swan: **•Li Gola Sasik Sîvaş a Kirimê *qubeqaz* ji ber rewşa tund a serma di golê de asê man** (Sputnik) In Lake Sasik Sivash of the Crimea *swans* were stuck due to the severity of the cold; **-qubeqaza lal** (Wkp) swan (qû). {also: qebeqaz (Wkt-2)}{syn: qazquling; qû} [Sputnik/ZF/Wkt/Wkp]

qubet قوبەت (K) = coarse; loud; proud. See **qube I**.

Qubrisî قوبرِسى (CS) = Cypriot. See **Qibrisî**.

Qudis قودِس (Wkt) = Jerusalem. See **Qudus**.

qudret قـــودرەت *f.* **(-a;-ê).** power, strength, might, force: **•bi *qodreta* xwedê** (L) by *the power of* God. {also: qidret (IF-2); qodret (L); [qoudret] قـــدرت (JJ); <qudret> قـــدرت (HH)} {syn: qedûm [2]; qewet} < Ar qudrah قدرة [L//K/IFb/B/SK]

Quds قودس (Wkt) = Jerusalem. See **Qudus**.

qudum قودوم (Z-1) = feet; strength; grief. See **qedûm**.

Qudus قـــودوس *f.* **(;-ê).** Jerusalem: -Bajarê Qudsê (SS) do. {also: Qidis (Wkt-2); Qids (Wkt-2); Qudis (Wkt-2); Quds (Wkt)} [IFb//Wkt/SS]

qudûm قـــودووم (K/B) = feet; strength; grief. See **qedûm**.

qufe قوفه (IFb) = basket. See **qûfik**.

qufik قوفِك (ZF3) = basket. See **qûfik**.

qufil قوفِل (RZ/ZF3) = padlock. See **qifil**.

qufilîn قوفِلين (HH) = to freeze. See **qefilîn**.

qujî قوژى (FS) = marten. See **kûşk & kûze**.

qul I قـــول *f.* **(-a;-ê).** 1) hole, opening, aperture: **•Diçe dik'eve *qula* zinêr** (J) It goes and enters *the hole in* the cliff **•Çwîkekî beytik hebû, kete *qulê*** (L-2, 20) There was a sparrow, it entered [its] *hole*; **-qul kirin** (K) to make a hole, pierce {syn: simtin}; 2) [*adj.*] having a hole, perforated: **•Tûrê virekan tim *qul e*** (AB) The liars' bag always *has a hole* in it **•Qjikê jêla nukulê xwe li cêr̄ xist, cêr̄ *qul* bû** (EH) The bird thrust its beak into the clay jug from below, and poked a hole in it [lit. 'the jug was *with-hole*']. {also: kul II (AB/L-2); [koul كـــل/ qul قـل] (JJ); <qul> قـل (HH)} {syn: qûn [3]} [L/J/K/A/JB3/IFb/B/JJ/HH/GF/TF/OK//AB] <simtin>

qul II قول (L/K/A/JB3) = grief. See **kul I**.

qulabtin قولابتِن (K) = to turn; to wither. See **qulibîn**.

qulaç/qulaç' [K] قـــولاچ *f.* **(-a;-ê).** 1) the span of the outstretched arms, a fathom [cf. Ar bāʿ بـــاع]: **•Werîsê wî çar *qulaç* e** (FS) His rope is 4 *fathoms* long; 2) corner: **•Ew xwe li *qulaçka* diveşêrît, lê ez dê her wî girim** (Wkt) He is hiding in *the corners*, but I will still catch him **•Wî tûrikê mêwîja li *qulaça* mezelê deyna** (FS) He put the bag of raisins in *the corner of* the room. {also: qulaç'k (B); qulanç (IFb-2); [qouladj] قولاج (JJ)} < T kulaç = 'fathom'; Sor qulanc قـــولانـــج = 'span' [K//A/IFb/FS/Wkt/BF//B//JJ//DS-Kars] <bost>

qulaç'k قولاچك (B) = fathom; span; corner. See **qulaç**.

qulanç قولانچ (IFb) = fathom; span; corner. See **qulaç**.

qulap قـــولاپ *f.* **(;-ê).** inhaling, puff, drag, 'hit' *(in smoking a cigarette)*: **•Vira apê Kote k'îsikê t'it'ûnê ji cêba xwe derxist, cix̄ara xwe pêç'a, vêxist--du-sê *qulap* ser hev lê xist** [sic] (Ba2-#2, 210) Here Uncle Koteh took his tobacco pouch out of his pocket, rolled his cigarette, lit it--and took two or three *drags* in a row. {also: [qoulab] قلاب (JJ)} {syn: hilm} [Ba2/K/B/ZF3/FS//JJ]

qulaptin قـــولاپـــتِـــن (IFb/GF) = to turn; to wither. See **qulibîn**.

qulç قولچ *m.* **(-ê;).** corner, angle: **•Di *qulçê* odê dane** (MC-1) They are in *the corner of* the room. {also: qilç'; qilçik[1] (B)} {syn: goşe; k'unc; kujî; qorzî} [MC-1/K/B] See also **qilçik**.

qule قـــولـــه *adj.* 1) skewbald, marked with spots and patches of white and some other color *(of an animal)* (K); mixed black- and yellow-colored horse (IF); isabel, dun- or cream-colored *(of horses)* (JJ); red grading to yellow *(of horses and mules)* (HH); 2) {syn: beza} fast-running, speedy *(horse)*. {also: [qoulé] قوله (JJ); <qulle> قلّه (HH)} Cf. T kula = 'dun colored (horse)' [EP-8/K/IFb/JJ/GF/FD//HH]

qulêr قولێر (FJ/GF/FS) = small window. See **kulêr**.

qulibîn قولِبين *vi.* **(-qulib-).** 1) {syn: wergeřîn} to turn *(vi.)*, be overturned (HH): **•Îsal heft salê te ye, *qoliptîye* sala heşta, ji bona xatirê kevnek jina te xwe xistîye vî halî** (L) It's been seven years, *going on* eight years, that you have been miserable over some old lady [Voici sept ans et plus que tu es dans cet état à cause d'une vieille femme]; 2) to wither, fade: **-řeng qulibîn** (B) to fade, become pale: ***•Rengê wî qulibî*** (B) *He turned pale*. {also: qoliptîn (-qolip-) (L); qulibtîn; qulabtin (K-2); qulaptin (IFb/GF); qulipîn (IFb-2); [qulypin] قلپين (JJ); <qulibîn قلبين (diqulibî) (دقلبى)> (HH)} < Ar qalaba قـــلـــب = 'to overturn' [L/Z-1//K/B/HH//JJ//IFb] <qelibandin>

qulibtîn قولِبتين = to turn; to wither. See **qulibîn**.

quling قـولـنـگ *m./f.(B)* **(-ê/-a; /-ê).** crane *(bird)*, zool. *Grus grus*: **•*Quling* ji berîyê hatin** (AB) *The cranes* came from the wilderness. {also: [koulink] كـولـنـك (JJ); <quling> قـلـنـگ (HH)} Cf. P kolang كلنگ; Sor quling قوڵنگ; Za kering (Lx)/kering/ quling *m.* (Mal) [AB/K/A/IF/B/HH/FS/ZF3//JJ]

qulipîn قولِپين (IFb) = to turn; to wither. See **qulibîn**.

qulix قـــولِـــخ *f.* **(-a;-ê).** 1) {syn: xulamtî} servitude, service: **•Hevalêd wî gelek-gelekî jê ĥiz dikirin** [sic], ***qulixa* wîda r̄adibûn-r̄ûdniştin** (EH) His friends loved him very much, they were always happy to serve him [lit. 'they would rise up and sit down in his *service*]; **-qulix kirin** (B) to work; to serve; 2) work: **•Ûsib dest bi *qulixa* xwe dike** (Ba-1, #22) Joseph begins his *work* [as emir]. {also: [qoulliq] قـولـلـق (JJ)} < T kulluk = 'slavery, bondage' [Z-1/K/B//JJ]

qulix û 'ezet قولِخ و عەزەت (K) = honor. See **'ezet**.

qulofîskî قولۆفیسکی (Ag) = squatting, kneeling. See **qelefîskî**.

quloz قـولـۆز *adj.* 1) {syn: berz; bilind; ≠nizm} lifted, raised up high: **-quloz bûn** (B/JJ/JB1-A) = a) to rise, climb, ascend, jump up (B/JB1-A/OK): **•Lê taê Ûsib li ser *quloz dibe*** (Ba) But the pan of the scale with Joseph [on it] *rises* (=the scales are tipped so that the pan of the scale with Joseph on it is higher, and therefore lighter, than the other one); b) to be skittish *(of horses)* (JJ). {also: qoloz (JB1-A/OK); [qoulouz] قـلـوز (JJ)} [F/K/B//JJ//JB1-A/ OK]

qulpik قولپك (F/IFb/TF) = hiccup; burp. See **qilpik**.

qulûwîlk قولووويلك (Frq) = anecdotes. See **qirwelk**.

qumandar قـــومـــانـــدار m. **(-ê; qumandêr).** (military) commander. {syn: fermandar} [L/K/B/IFb/SK] <r̄ayedar>

qumar قـــومـــار *f.* **(;-ê).** gambling, game of chance: **•Min dî xumarbaz *xumarê dilîzin*** (HCK-4, #2, 37) I saw gamblers *gambling*. {also: xumar (K-2/ IFb-2); [qoumar] قـمـار (JJ); <xumar خـمـار/qumar قـمـار> (HH)} < Ar qimār قـمـار; Sor qumar قـومـار [HCK//K/B/IFb/FJ/GF/JJ/HH]

qumarbaz قـومـاربـاز *m.* **().** gambler, one addicted to gambling: **•Çiqas *xumarbazê* şeher hebûn, k'ê anî – min lê bir** (HCK-4, #2, 37) However many *gamblers* there were in the city, whoever they brought – I beat him [in gambling]. {also: xumarbaz (K-2); [qoumar-baz] قمارباز (JJ)} Cf. P qumārbāz قـمـاربـاز; Sor qumarbaz قـومـاربـاز = 'rogue, cheat, dishonest person' & qumarçî قـومـارچـی = 'gambler, given to gambling' [HCK//K/ B/IFb/FJ/GF/JJ]

qumaş قـــومـــاش *m.* **( ).** cloth, fabric, material, textile: **•Sûk tije *qumaş* e, lê mela bêşaş e** (BX) The marketplace is full of *cloth*, but the mullah is turbanless *[prv.]*. {also: [qoumach] قـــمـــاش (JJ); <qumaş> قماش (HH)} < Ar qumāš قماش = 'cloth'; Sor qumaş قوماش [K/IFb/JJ/HH/GF] <tixarîs>

qumç•e قومچە *f.* **(•a;).** button. {also: qumçik (Srk-2/ Dy-2/Bw)} {syn: bişkoj; mêvok} [Srk/Dy/ZF3/FS//Bw]

qumçik قومچِك (Srk/Dy/Bw) = button. See **qumçe**.

qumqumok قـومـقـومۆك *f.* **(;-ê).** large lizard: **•Dinya wekî quzê *gumgumokê* ye, geh li jêr e, geh li jor** (Frq) The world is like *a lizard*'s vagina, sometimes down, sometimes up. {also: gimgimok (FJ); gumgumatik (GShA); gumgumok (IFb-2/ GF/TF); qimqimok (FJ-2); [gumgumúk] گـمـگـمـك (JJ); <qimqimok> قمقموك (HH)} [Haz/IFb//HH//FJ//GF/ TF//JJ//GShA] <mazelîlk; mazîzerk>

qumrî قـــومـــری *f.* **().** 1) {syn: tilûr} turtledove, zool. genus *Streptopelia*; 2) woman's name (A). {also: [qoumri] قـمـری (JJ); <qumrî> قـمـری (HH)} Cf. Ar qumrī قمري & T kumru [K/A/IFb/JJ/HH/GF/TF]

qumsî قـومـسـی *m.* **(-yê;).** gossip, informer; slanderer; sneak, scandalmonger: **-qomsî-nemam** (XF) informer, stool pigeon. {also: qomsî (Z-1/XF); [qoumsi] قـومـسـی (JJ); <qumsî'ûn> قـمـسـيـعـون (HH)} {syn: altax; destkîs; geveze; nemam; xwefiroş} {qumsîtî} [Z-1/XF//K/B/JJ//HH] <'ewan II; gelac; t'ewt'ewe>

qumsîtî قـومـسـيـتـی *f.* **(ya;-yê).** informing on someone, slandering, malicious gossip: **-qumsîtî kirin** (B) to inform on or against s.o., slander, tattle on, engage in malicious gossip. {also: [qoumsiti] قـومـسـيـتـی (JJ)} {syn: altaxî; 'ewanî; geveztî; şer̄ II[2]} [B/JJ] <qumsî>

qunc قونج, f. (IFb) = angle, corner. See **k'unc**.

quncik قـــونـــجِـــك (IFb/HH/GF) = angle, corner. See **k'unc**.

quncir قونجِر (TF) = cockle bur. See **quncir̄k**.

quncirik قونجِرك *f.* **(-a;).** pinch, nip, tweak: **•Panzdeh *quncrîka* li k'êlekê wênakê dixîne** (Z-3) He gives her 15 *pinches* in the side. {also: quncirîk (ZF3/Wkt); quncirok (K); quncrîk (Z-3); qurçî (IFb); qurincîk (Wkt-2); qur̄incik (FS); qurîncok I (Nsb); <quncirik> قـنـجـرك (HH)} {syn:

nuquç} [Z-3//HH//ZF3/Wkt//K//IFb//FS//Nsb]

quncirîk قـونـجـِـريـك (ZF3/Wkt) = pinch, tweak. See **quncirik**.

quncir̄k قـونـجـِـرك *f.* **(-a;-ê).** bur, cockle bur, bot. *Arctium* [T pıtrak], type of plant with small green moth-shaped stickers that stick to one's clothes. {also: kuncir̄ (Bw); quncir (TF); quncirûk (OK); quncîrok (IFb); qur̄încok II (FS-2)} [Bw//Zeb/FS//TF//OK//IFb]

quncirok قونجِرۆك (K) = pinch. See **quncirik**.

quncirûk قونجِرووك (OK) = cockle bur. See **quncir̄k**.

quncîrok قونجيرۆك (IFb) = cockle bur. See **quncir̄k**.

quncrîk قونجريك (Z-3) = pinch. See **quncirik**.

qund قـونـد *adj.* erect, sticking out: •**Her sênîyekî kilkekî kûr̄î di nawa serî biçeqînin weto ko *qund* r̄awestît** (SK 24:222) On each tray stick a kid's tail in the middle of the pile so that it stands *erect*. {syn: bel; girj[3]; qişt; r̄ep} [SK]

qundax قوِنداخ = slope; foot of mountain. See **qunt'ar**.

qundir قوندِر (L) = pumpkin. See **kundir**.

qundire قوندِرە (A/JB3) = shoe. See **qondere**.

qunêr قـونـێـر *f.* **(-a;-ê).** boil; abscess: •**Heker *qunêrê* janda, divêt bihê derkirin** (N.Shaheen. Dict. of Kurdish Verbs) If *the boil* hurts, it must be lanced •***Qonêrek* li ranê wî hatiye** (FS) *A boil* has broken out [lit. 'has come'] on his thigh. {also: kunêr (IFb-2/OK-2); kûnêr (IFb-2); kwîner (K); qonêr (FS); qûnêr (K[s]/OK)} Sor qunêr قـونـێـر = 'boil (suppurating tumor)' [Bar/Zeb/A/IFb//FS//K(s)/OK//K]

qunt'ar قـونـتـار *f.* **(-a;-ê).** slope, side of mountain, hillside; foot of mountain: •**Ez bixwe gundî me û gundê min di *quntara* çiyayekî de ye** (Wlt 1:37, 16) I myself am a villager, and my village is on *the side of* a mountain. {also: kontax; qontax (A); qundax; qûndax̄ (K); qûntar (ZF3/FS); qûntax} {syn: berwar; binat'ar; hevraz; jihelî; k'aş II; p'al; pesar; p'êş II[2]; sîng; ter̄azin} [Wlt/B/IFb/TF/Wkt//ZF3/FS//K//A] <çîya; nizar I; zinar I>

qur̄ قـوڕ *f.* **(-a;-ê).** mud: •***Qur̄a* wî germ e** (Qzl) He is a greenhorn [lit. 'His *mud* is hot'], *said of s.o. who is inexperienced and too sure of himself* •**Rêk piştî baranê *bû kur̄*** (FS) The road *turned to mud* after the rain. {also: kur̄ V (FS)} {syn: ĥer̄î; r̄itam; t'eqin} Cf. Sor qur̄ قـوڕ = 'mud' [IFb/OK/RZ/Qzl//FS] <lîç[2]; qilêr>

qurad قوراد (Wkt)/qur̄ad قوڕاد (FS) = leek. See **kurad**.

quraftin قـورافـتِـن *vt.* **(-qurêf-).** 1) to break off by twisting *(wire, etc.)*; 2) to pick *(grapes, corn, etc.)*: •**Bêvankeso tirî *quraft* qûfik tije kir** (Ardû, 78) So-and-so *picked* grapes, [and] filled the basket •***quraftina* garisan** (Ardû, 148) *picking* corn. {also: qurifandin (B-2/GF); qurfandin (FJ); qurufandin (B); <quraftin قـرافـتـن (diqurêfe) (دقريفه)> (HH)} {syn: çinîn} < Ar qarafa قرف = 'to peel, pare, bark, derind' [Ardû/K/A/IFb/TF/HH/CS//GF//FJ//B]

Quran قـوران /**Qur'an** قـورعـان [IFb/SK] *f.* **(-a;-ê).** Quran (Koran), the holy book of Islam. {also: [korán] قران (JJ)} < Ar al-Qur'ān القرآن [Z-3/K/B/GF//IFb/JJ/SK]

qurba قوربا = victim, sacrifice; my dear. See **qurban**.

qurban قـوربـان *f.* **(-a;-ê).** 1) {syn: cangorî; gorî; ĥeyran} victim, sacrifice: •**Ez *qurbana* we** (J) [May] I [be] your *sacrifice* [*a greeting, cf. P qurbān-e šomā* قربان شما]; **-qurban bûn** (B) to be sacrificed; **-qurban kirin** (B) to sacrifice; 2) my dear (Dz/K/B): •***Qurba*, ez ter̄a divêm dara mebir̄** (Dz) *My dear fellow*, I'm telling you not to cut down the trees. {also: qurba; [qourban] قربان (JJ); <qurban> قربان (HH)} < Ar/P qurbān قربان, Heb ḳorban קרבן < Arc qurban קורבן [J/K/JB3/IFb/B/JJ/HH/SK]

qurbeşe قـوربـەشـە (M-Ak) = badger; mole. See **kur̄ebeşk**.

qur̄beşk قوڕبەشك (FS) = badger; mole. See **kur̄ebeşk**.

qurbet قوربەت (K) = foreign land; exile. See **x̄urbet**.

qurcik قورجِك (GF) = angle, corner. See **k'unc**.

qurçik قورچِك (A) = angle, corner. See **k'unc**.

qurçimandin قورچِماندِن (F) = to wrinkle; to fade. See **qermiç'andin**.

qurçimîn قورچِمين (F) = to be wrinkled; to fade *(vi.)*. See **qermiç'în**.

qurçî قورچى (IFb) = pinch. tweak. See **quncirik**.

qur̄e قـوڕە *adj.* proud; boastful, arrogant, haughty: •**Ew zelamekê *qur̄e* ye** (FS) He is an *arrogant* man. {also: qur̄eh (B-2)} {syn: bitir̄ I; difnbilind; gewî; nefsmezin; pivikî; pozbilind; serbilind; serfiraz} {qur̄etî} [K/IFb/B/GF/TF/FS]

qur̄eder قـوڕەدەر (Frq/Dh) = stench, stink. See **kur̄eder**.

qur̄eh قوڕەه (B) = proud, haughty. See **qur̄e**.

qur̄emîş قـوڕەمـيـش: **-qur̄emîş kirin** = 1) to inlay, set *(jewels)* (EP-7): •**Tu zînekî usa minr̄a çêkî ... t'emamê wî lal, dur̄ û kevirê qîmetî têda *qur̄emîşkî*** (EP-7) Make for me a saddle in such a way that you *inlay* it completely with rubies, pearls, and precious stones; 2) to tune (a musical instrument) (B). {also: quřimîş (B)} <T kurmuş < kurmak = 'to set, assemble' (in various meanings) [EP-7//B]

quřetî قـورەتـى *f.* **(-ya;-yê).** haughtiness, arrogance, pride: **•*Quretîya* wî nema tê kêşan** (glosbe.com) His *arrogance* can no longer be endured. [K/JB3/IFb/B/FS/ZF3] <qu̇re[h]>

qurfandin قـورفـانـدِن (FJ) = break off, pick (fruit). See **quraftin**.

qurifandin قـورِفـانـدِن (B/GF) = break off, pick (fruit). See **quraftin**.

quřimîş قورِميش (B). See **quřemîş**.

qurim sax قورم ساخ (GF) = pimp. See **qurumsax**.

qurincîk قورنجيك (Wkt) = pinch, tweak. See **quncirik**.

qurix قـورِخ *f.* **(;-ê).** Morning star; Polar star: **•*Qrux* navê stêrek e. Li sibahan tê xwanê. Wê wextê serma dest pê dike. Xwiya kirina *Qruxê*, nî[ş]ana dawiya havînê û de[s]tpêkirina payizê ye** (Calendar) *Qrux* is the name of a star. It appears in the mornings: at that time the cold starts up. The appearance of *Qrux* signals the end of the summer and the onset of autumn. {also: Qrux (Calendar); Qurx (IFb-2/OK); [qouroug] قـورغ (JJ); <qurix> قرخ (HH); <qurix قورخ/quriẍ قورغ> (Hej)} Cf. T kuyruk = 'tail', esply in kuyruklu yıldız = 'comet [lit. 'star with a tail']' & kuyruk III [Maraş] = 'star which rises during grape season (i.e., Aug.-Sept.)' [üzüm zamanı doğan bir yıldız] (DS, v. 8, p. 3020) [Calendar//K/A/IFb/HH/Hej//OK//JJ] <gelavêj; karwankuj; stêr>

qurîncik قورينجِك (FS) = pinch. See **quncirik**.

qurîncok I قورينجۆك (Nsb) = pinch. See **quncirik**.

qurîncok II قورينجوك (FS) = cockle bur. See **quncirk**.

qurm قـورم *m./f.(Z-4)* **(-ê/-a; /-ê).** 1) tree stump; tree trunk: **-qurma darê** (Z-4)/**qurmê darê** (HYma) tree stump; 2) root (B): **•Li çar *qurmê* dinîyayê** (Z-3) in the four corners [lit. '*roots*'] of the world. {also: [qourm] قـرم (JJ); <qurm> قـرم (HH)} {syn: gilare (IFb); gonc} Cf. Ar qurmah قرمة [L/Z-4/K/IFb/B/JJ/HH/GF/TF/ZF] <dar I & II>

qurmiçandin قورمِچاندِن (IF/HH) = to wrinkle; to fade. See **qermiç'andin**.

qurmiçîn قورمِچين (IFb) = to be wrinkled; to fade *(vi.)*. See **qermiç'în**.

qurmîçong قـورمـيـچـۆنـگ (TF) = wrinkle. See **qermîçok**.

qurnî قورنى = tick. See **qirnî**.

qurs قورس *m.* **().** ingot, bar; disk: **•*qursê* zêřa** (EP-7) *bars of* gold. {also: <qurs> قـــرس (HH)} {syn: qalib} < Ar qurṣ قرص [EP-7/K/A/HH/ZF3]

qursandin قـورسـانـدِن (GF) = to cut, trim, shave. See **qusandin**.

qurt قـورت *f.* **(-a;-ê).** 1) swallow, gulp, draft: **•Hemû perdaq kir *qurtek*** (Wkt) He took the glass in *a single gulp* **•*Qurt qurt* av vexwar** (ZF3) He gulped down the water (*with a glugging sound*) **•*Qurtek* av jî nîn e** (ZF3) There isn't even *a drop of water* **•vexwarina *qurtekê* ji meyê** (B.Omerî. Rûniştina bi serxweşekî re) drinking *a gulp* of wine; 2) drag, inhaling (on a cigarette): **•Min tenê *qurtek* li cigareyê da û avêt** (Wkt) I only took *one drag* of the cigarette then threw it away. {syn: fiř I} [B.Omerî/K/A/B/IFb/TF/ZF3/Wkt/FD]

qurtal قورتال (FS/BF) = rescued. See under **qurtar**.

qurtandin قـورتـانـدِن *vt.* **(-qurtîn-).** to swallow; to sip (IFb); to gulp down (FS): **•Wî av *qurtand*** (FS) He *gulped down* the water. {syn: daqurtandin} [K/IFb/ZF3/FS]

qurtar قـورتـار *adj.* rescued, saved, freed: **-qurtar kirin** (Bw)/**qurtal kirin** (FS) to rescue, save, spare {syn: xelas kirin}: **•Wî karwan ji destê rêgiřa *qurtal kir*** (FS) He rescued the caravan from the hands of the brigands. {also: qurtal (FS/BF)} <T kurtarmak = 'to save, rescue' [Bw/OK//FS/BF] <řizgar>

qurtik قورتِك (RZ) = shirt. See **qutik I**.

qurufandin قوروفاندِن (B) = break off, pick (fruit). See **quraftin**.

qurumsax قـورومـسـاخ *m.* **(-ê;).** pimp, pander, procurer: **•*Qurumsax* 'Elî ez heřişandim** (SK 11:113) Ali, *the pimp*, knocked me to pieces. {also: qirimsax (ZF3); qurim sax (GF-2); quřumsaẍ (K)} {syn: qebrax} <Az T qurumsaq = 'pimp' [Urm/GF/SK//ZF3//K]

quřumsaẍ قوروومساغ (K) = pimp. See **qurumsax**.

quruş قوروش (K) = small coin, penny. See **qurûş**.

qurûş قـوروووش *m.* **(-ê;).** small coin, penny, cent; kurush, Groschen: **•*Bi qurûşekî* be jî nakirrim** (Wkt) Even if it's only *for a penny* I won't buy it **•Çend qurûş[a]** (L) Some money, a few pennies **•Sed *qurûş* dibin yek lîre** (Wkt) 100 *kurush* make one lira. {also: guřoş (EP-7); qirûş (BX/ZF3); qorûş; quruş (K); [qour(ou)ch] قرش (JJ); <qurûş> قـروش (HH)} < Ar qurūš قـرش, pl. of qirš قـروش; Cf. Germ Groschen < Lat denarius grossus [L/A/HH/Wkt//K//BX/ZF3//EP-7//JJ] <şayî>

Qurx قورخ (IFb/OK) = Polar star. See **Qurix**.

qusandin قوساندِن *vt.* **(-qusîn-).** 1) {syn: bi̇̄rîn I} to cut *(with a scissors)*; to trim, shave *(hair, beard)*: **•Te wextê bi ç'e'v r̄iha min k'et, dilê te bi min şewitî, û ti hatî, te r̄iha min *qusand*** (HR 3:34) When you noticed my beard, you felt sorry for me, and you came and *trimmed* my beard; 2) {syn: r̄ûç'ikandin} to tear out, pluck out: **•Teyrê go li ezmana re difirin, ez baskê wan *diqusînim*** (L) I *pluck out* the feathers [or *trim* the wings] of birds that fly in the skies. {also: qursandin (GF); [qousandin] قصاندين (JJ); <qeṣandin قصاندن (diqeṣîne) (دقصينه)> (HH)} < Ar qaṣṣa قصّ (<√q-ṣ-ṣ) = 'to cut' [L/K/A/JB3/IFb/JJ/TF//HH//GF]

qusûr قوسوور *f.* **(-a;-ê).** fault, defect, flaw, mistake, imperfection, shortcoming; deficiency, lack: **•Eger *qusûrî* ba, da hête 'efw kirin** (SK 52:563) Had it been *a mistake*, it would have been pardonable **•Eve ṣindoqa te ya li hêrê. Bi xo seḧ kê. *Qusûrîyek* lê hebît? Bêje min, da bo te dirûst kem. Ya *bê qusûrî* bît, te mûbarek bît bi xo bibe** (JB1-A #26,106) This here is your box. Examine it. Is there *a flaw* in it? [If so,] tell me, so that I can fix it for you. If it is *flawless*, may it be blessed for you, take it with you **•Ya xudê, tu li me xoş bî, *qusûra* me 'efw key** (SK 9:90) O God, forgive us and *pardon* our fault. {also: qisûr (K/IFb-2/B); qusûrî (JB1-A/SK-2); [qousour] قصور (JJ); <quṣûr> قصور (HH)} {syn: kêmasî} < Ar quṣūr قصور = 'incapability; deficiency' < √q-ṣ-r قصر = 'to be short, fall short' [SK/JB1-S/JJ//HH//K/ IFb/B//JB1-A]

qusûrî قوسووری (JB1-A/SK) = defect; lack. See **qusûr**.

qut I قوت *adj.* 1) severed, cut off, broken off: **•Mar dûvê xweyî *qut* bîr nake** (Dz #22, 389) The snake does not forget its *severed* tail *[prv.]*; **-qut bûn** (K/IFb/FJ) to be cut off: **•Destê me li vî beledê x̌erîb, bajarê Bex̌dayê *jêk qut dibe*** (JB1-S #206, 162) In this strange place, the city of Baghdad, we [lit. 'our hand'] *will be cut off from each other*; **-qut kirin** (K/B/A/IFb/JB1-S/GF/HH) to cut off, break off; to interrupt, abbreviate {syn: qetandin}: **•Ehda Xudê ez we hemûke bi carekê serê we *qut dikim*** (JB1-S #197, 160) I swear by God that I *will cut off* all your heads **•Şerîfo jî xweş zane ku nikare axaftina wî *qut bike*** (HYma, 48) And Sh. knows well that he cannot *interrupt* his talking; 2) {syn: kin} short *(of stature)* (Bw/HH/SK/TF/SS). {also: [qata kirin] قطع كرين (JJ)?; <qut> قت (HH)} Cf. Ar qaṭa'a قطع = 'to cut'; Sor qut قوت = 'erect, pointed, perked (ears)' [HYma/Bw/Dz/K/B/A/ IFb/JB1-S/GF/FJ//TF/HH/SK//JJ] <bi̇̄rîn II>

qut II قوت (Haz) = food. See **qût**.

qutabî قوتابى *m.&f.* **(-yê/-ya;).** pupil, student, schoolboy/schoolgirl: **•*Qutabîyên* pola pêncê xir serkeftin** (BF) All the 5th grade *students* passed **•Rêjeya serkeftina *qutabîyan* ev sale 20% pitir e ji par** (BF) The success rate *of students* this year is 20% higher than last year. {syn: şagird; xwendekar} < Sor qutabî قوتابى < Ar kuttāb كتّاب = 'Qur'ān school' [BF/K(s)/ZF3/Wkt]

qutan قوتان (M) = to hit. See **k'utan**.

qutas قوتاس *f.* **().** (large) tassel(s): **-gîfk û qutas** (Bw) tassels large and small. [Bw] <gûfik; gulik[2]; r̄işî I>

qutifîn قوتِفين *vi.* **(-qutif-).** to freeze *(vi., from cold or fright)*; to be terrified: **•Carkê nerî yek derket -- neûzû billah! -- qama wî bihistek e û riha wî gazek e. Gava çavê Gavdirêj lê ket, *qotifî*, di cîh de rûniṣt** (L-I, #4, 96, l.31-33) He saw someone come out -- God forbid! -- a span high with a beard a yard long. When Longstep caught sight of him, he *froze* in his place **•*Qutifî* ji tirsan** (GF) He *froze* from fright. {also: qotifîn (L/K[s]); <qutifîn> قتفين (diqutifî) (دقتفى)> (HH)} {syn: cemidîn; qefilîn[1]; qerimîn; qerisîn; qeşa girtin} [L/K(s)//IFb/ HH/GF/TF/OK]

qutik I قوتِك *m.* **(-ê;).** shirt: **•Xelîl Beg ... kujên *kurtikê* xwe xiste** [sic] **bin kembera pantorê xwe** (SBx, 8-9) X.B. ... pushed the corners of his *shirt* under the waistband of his pants. {also: kurtek (MG/IFb); kurtik (RZ-2/ZF); qotik I (GF-2); qurtik (RZ-2); [qotek] قوتك (JJ); <qutek> قتك (HH)} {syn: îşlik; kiras[1]; qemîs} [Msr/A/GF/TF/OK/ RZ//HH//JJ//ZF//MG/IFb]

qutik II قوتِك (IFb) = chopped firewood. See **qîtik II**.

qut'inî قوتِنى (B) = plush; silken material. See **qutnî**.

qut'î قوتى/qutî [K/IFb] *f.* **(-ya;-yê).** box, chest, container: **•Tuê van her dû muê laşê min bixî *qotîyek[ê]* û tuê pir mihafeze bikî** (L) (You will) put both hairs from my body in *a box*, and (you'll) take very [good] care of them; **-qut'îya dila vekirin** (XF) to open up one's heart to s.o., to speak frankly to s.o.; **-qut'îya t'itûnê** (B) tobacco box, snuff box. {also: kudîk II (JB1-A); qot'î II (L/TF); qutîk (A); qûtî (JB3/GF); [qouti] قوتى

(JJ); <qûtî> قـوتـى (HH)} {syn: qab I [2]; sindoq} Cf. T kutu; Sor qutû قوتوو = 'small box'; Za qutî *f.* (Todd); also Gr kouti κουτί [L/TF//K/IFb//B/XF//A//JB3/JJ/HH/GF//JB1-A]

qutîk قوتيك (A) = box. See **qut'î**.

qutnî قـوتـنـى *m.* **(-yê;).** plush (B); material made of a mixture of silk and cotton (IFb); a single-sided fabric whose warp is velvet and whose woof is spun cotton (HH): **•Li xwe kiribû *şal û qutnîyê* Helebî** (mirbotan.com: Dewrane [song]) She was wearing *a plush sash* from Aleppo. {also: qut'inî (B); qut'unî (B-2); <qutnî> قـتـنـى (HH)} < Ar quṭnī قطني = '(made of) cotton' [HB/K/IFb/HH//B]

qut'unî قوتونى (B) = plush; silken material. See **qutnî**.

quz قـوز *m.* **(-ê;).** vagina, vulva, 'cunt', 'pussy'. {also: [qouz قـوز/ qousi قـوسـى] (JJ); <quẕ> قـظ (HH)} {syn: virçik} Cf. Ar kuss كـس; Hau k^{w}sî *f.* = 'vulva' (M4) [Wn/Tkm/Msr/IFb/SK/GF/TF//HH//JJ] <kîr; gilik; zîlik>

quzferitî قـوزفـەڕتـى *adj.* wild in sexual matters *(of women)*. {syn: quzhar} [Msr] <kîrhar>

quzgesk قـوزگـەسـك (GF) = small biting insect. See **quzgezk**.

quzgezk قـوزگـەزك *f.* **(-a;).** small insect that bites, mole cricket, zool. *Gryllotalpa* [T danaburnu]. {also: quzgesk (GF)} < quz = 'vulva' + gez- = 'to bite' [Msr/IFb/ZF3//GF] <cobir>

quzhar قـوزهـار *adj.* wild in sexual matters *(of women)*. {syn: quzferitî} < quz = 'vulva' + har = 'rabid' [Msr] <kîrhar>

qû قوو *f./m.[F]* **(/-ê;-yê/).** swan, zool. *Cygnus*: **•Rengê pûrtê *qûyê* spî ye** (Wkp: qû) The color of *the swan*'s feathers is white. {also: qî (Wkt-2); qwî (Wkt-2); qwû (Wkt-2)} {syn: qazquling; qubeqaz} P qū قو; Sor قوو [Wkp/IFb/F/ZF/RZ/Wkt/FD/CS]

qûç' قـووچ *f./m.(ZF3)* **(;-ê/).** 1) pile, heap; 2) {syn: şkêr} {also: **kuç'**; qûrç (IFb)} heap of stones particularly in games (IFb). [K/IFb/B/Qmş/Qzl/Xrz] See also **kuç'**.

qûfik قـووفِـك *f.* **().** basket for grapes: **•Bêvankeso tirî quraft *qûfik* tije kir** (Ardû, 78) So-and-so picked grapes, [and] filled *the basket*. {also: qufe (IFb); qufik (ZF3)} {syn: sewî} Cf. Ar quffah قـفّـة = 'large basket' [Ardû//ZF3//IFb] <selik>

qûfle قووفله (Wkt) = padlock. See **qifil**.

qûl قـوول *m.* **(-ê;).** slave; slave of God, i.e., human being: **•T'u *qûl û benda* ez neditîme** (B) Not *a soul* saw me **•Xwedê *qûl* dixuliqîne rizqê jî jê re dişîne** (Nofa, 90) God creates *slaves* and sends them sustenance. {syn: bende; benî I; 'evd I; k'ole; hêsîr I; misexir; qerebaşî} <T kul = 'slave' [Nofa/A/B/IFb/GF/FJ/ZF3/FS/CS]

qûm I قـووم *f.* **(-a;-ê).** sand: **-qûma gir** (B) gravel. {also: [qoum] قـوم (JJ); <qûm> قـوم (HH)} {syn: xîz [1]} <T kum = 'sand' [F/K/IFb/B/JJ/HH]

qûm II قـووم (GF/HH/ZF3/FS) = earthenware churn. See **qom**.

qûn قـوون *f.* **(-a;-ê).** 1) {syn: qorik; poz II (Bw)} buttocks, bottom, backside, rear end, ass: **•*Qûna* wî ranebû ji wan cîya û wan 'erda** (Z-2) He wouldn't get up off his *ass*; **-zaru dan ser qûnê** (K) to make a child sit up; 2) {syn: zotik} anus; 3) {syn: qul I} hole; 4) {gindor III; lan} animal's lair, den: **•Hat, ser *kuna* marî sekinî** (KH, 34) He came and stood by the snake's *den* [hole] **•Here, çêçikêt me li *kunê* bîne derê** (M-Ak, #557) Go and fetch our cubs out of *the hole* [=lair]. {also: kun I (M-Ak/KH); k'un I (K[s]/IFb-2); kûn I (K-2/IFb-2); [koun كن/kounik كنك] (JJ); <qûn قون/kun كـن> (HH)} Cf. P kūn كـون; Sor king كِـنـگ/qing قِنگ/qûn قوون = 'arse, rump, buttocks'; Hau qinge *f.* (M4) [Z-2/K/IFb/B/HH/SK/Msr//M-Ak/KH//K(s)] <pind; zotik>

qûnalês قـوونـالـێس *m.&f.* **().** brown-nose, sycophant, ass-licker, ass-kisser. {syn: solalês} <qûn + alês- < alastin = 'to lick' [Qzl/K/Kmc]

qûnax قووناغ (HR) = mansion; inn; day's march; guest. See **qonax**.

qûndax قـوونـداغ (K) = slope; foot of mountain. See **qunt'ar**.

qûnde قـوونـده *m.* **().** *derogatory term for a* homosexual. {also: qûnder (Wkt); <qûnd[e]> قـونـد (HH)} {syn: qûnek [1]} < qûn = 'buttocks, anus' + de- = 'to give', cf. T göt veren [Msr/K/A/IF/HH/ZF3//Wkt]

qûnder قـوونـدەر (Wkt) = *derogatory term for a* homosexual. See **qûnde**.

qûnek قوونەك *m.* **().** 1) {syn: qûnde} *derogatory term for a* homosexual; 2) [*f.*] {syn: qab II; qalt'ax [3]} prostitute (Msr/K). Cf. Sor kûnî كوونى = 'catamite' {qûnekî} [Msr/K/A/IFb/GF] <forq; qab II>

qûnekî قـوونـەكـى *f.* **(-ya;).** 1) *derogatory term for* homosexuality; sodomy, "buggery"; 2) debauchery, depravity. [K/ZF3] <qûnek>

qûnêr قوونێر (K[s]/OK) = boil, abscess. See **qunêr**.

qûntar قوونتار (ZF3/FS) = slope; foot of mountain. See **qunt'ar**.

qûntax قوونتاخ = slope; foot of mountain. See **qunt'ar**.

qûrç قوورچ (IFb) = heap of stones. See **qûç'** [2].

qûr̄în قـووڕيـن *vi.* **(-qûr̄-).** 1) to scream, shout, wail, howl; 2) [*f.* **().**] screaming, shouting, wailing, howling: **-qûr̄în û gazî** (IS) screaming and shouting. {also: qîrandin (-qîrîn-) (M); qorî kirin (SK); qor̄în (-qor̄-) (K-2); [qouri قـــــــورى/qorin قورين] (JJ)} Sor qûlandin قوولاندِن (-qûlên-) = 'to wail, howl' [IS/K/IFb/GF//M//SK//JJ] <kûr̄în> See also **qîr̄în**.

qûrqûrok قوورقوورۆك *f.* **(-a;).** bullfrog. [Msr] <beq>

qûşxan قووشخان (Wkt) = pot. See **qûşxane**.

qûşxan•e قووشـخـانـه *f.* **(•[ey]a;•[ey]ê).** 1) {syn: qazik} cooking pot: **•Derxûn: ... ew tiştê ku devê *qûşxaneyê* digire** (FZT) Lid/cover: ... that thing which closes the opening of *a pot*; 2) {syn: cifnî} large metal bowl. {also: qûşxan (Wkt); qoşxane (TF)} [Msr/IFb/ZF3//TF] <beroş; lalî II; mencel; miqilk>

qût قـــــووت *m.(B/ZF3)/f.(SK)* **(-e/;).** 1) {syn: xwarin; zad} food; 2) dried foods that can be stored for the winter, including wheat, bulgur [=cracked wheat germ], flour, dried fruits and vegetables, meat, etc.; 3) {syn: lext} birdseed. {also: qut II (Haz); [qout] قوت (JJ); <qût> قوت (HH)} <Ar qūt قوت = 'food, nutriment' [Haz//K/A/IFb/B/JJ/HH/SK/GF/TF]

qûtî قووتی (JB3/GF) = box. See **qut'î**.

qûz قووز (B) = hunchbacked. See **kûz I**.

qûzayî قووزایی (B) = hunchbackedness. See **kûzayî**.

qwî قوی (Wkt) = swan. See **qû**.

qwû قووو (Wkt) = swan. See **qû**.

R/R̄ ر/ڕ

-r̄a ڕا *psp. postpositional suffix indicating motion toward (place to which), used in conjunction with prepositions, or alone*: 1) with [=**bi ...-r̄a**]: •**Jinik qîza xwe jî xwer̄a tîne** (J) The woman brings her own daughter *with* her •**Xwe*r̄a* dibe bajarê Misrê** (Ba) He takes [him] *with* him to the city (=land) of Egypt; 2) to [=**ji ...-r̄a**]: •**Aqû p'êxember wan*r̄a* go** (Ba) Jacob the prophet said *to* them; 3) for [=**ji ...-r̄a**]: •**R̄ojekê wan çend giregir û cindîyê şeherê Cizîrê hildan, hatine dîwana mîr Sêvdîn, pirsa merivatîyê danîn, seva Zîna delal bixazin Ç'ekan*r̄a*, birê Qeret'ajdîn*r̄a*** (Z-1, 46) One day they took some of the notables and noblemen of the city of Jizîr, and went to mîr Sêvdîn's court, brought the question (or-word) of family relations, to ask for [the hand of] lovely Zîn *for* Chekan, the brother of Qeretajdîn. {also: -re; <re> ره (HH)} Cf. P rā را = *marker of definite dir. obj.* [BX/J/Z-1/K/IFb/B/GF]

r̄a I ڕا, m. (A/GF/TF/RZ) = root; vein; nerve. See **r̄eh**.

r̄a II ڕا *f.* (;-ê). surrender, capitulation: **-hatin r̄aê** (EP-8/K)/**hatin rayê** (ZF3) to surrender, capitulate; to come around, give in: •**Duşmin *hate r̄aê*** (B) The enemy *surrendered* •**Kur̄ê wî *naê r̄aê*** (B) His son *won't stop making mischief* •**Xanê k'urda, *were raê* / ... Xelqê me *naê raê*** (EP-8) Khan of the Kurds, *surrender* / ... Our people *won't surrender*. [EP-8/K/B/ZF3]

r̄aber ڕابەر *prep.* 1) up toward *(motion upward)*: •**Destê xwe *raberî* xwedê kim** (BX) I reach out my hands *up to* God *[popular song]*; **-r̄aberî *fk-ê* kirin** (K/B/IF) = a) to show, present, address to (K): •**Em li jêr wê gotarê ... *raberê* xwendevanên xwe *dikin*** (Ber) Below we *present* that speech *to* our readers; b) to introduce, make known to, familiarize with (B): •**Wana hevalê xwe *r̄aberî* xweyê malê *kirin*** [sic] (B) They *introduced* their friend *to* the landlord; 2) {syn: dijber; miqabil; pêşber} facing, opposite. [BX/K/A/JB3/IFb/B/GF]

r̄abon ڕابۆن (SK) = to rise, get up. See **r̄abûn**.

r̄a•bûn ڕابوون *vi.* (**r̄a-b-**). 1) to rise, get up: •**Ez *r̄adibim*** = I *get up* •**Ez *r̄adibûm*** = I *was getting up/used to get up/would get up* •***R̄abe*!** = *Get up*! •***R̄abû*** = He *got up* •**Aqû p'êxember *r̄abû* ser xênî** (Ba) Jacob the prophet *got up* on the roof [lit. 'on the house'] •**Ûsib *r̄adive ser* t'akî mêzînê, zêr̄a jî dikine t'aê dinê** (Ba) Joseph *climbs onto* one pan of the scales, and they put gold on the other pan; **-ji xew rabûn** (L) to wake up *(vi.)*, get up [from sleep]; -[**ser**] **p'îya**[**n**] **r̄abûn** = to stand on one's [own two] feet; **-rabûn ser xwe** = to stand up straight, stand straight up: •**Lawik nerî go *rabûne ser xwe*** (L) The boy watched them stand up •**Şêr ... p'ir xeyîdî hema *rabû ser xwe*** (Dz) The lion ... was [so] furious that he *sprung up*; **-r̄abûne pîya ve** (Zeb) to stand up, rise to one's feet; 2) to begin the undertaking of some action, to commence to do stg.: •**Gur *r̄abû* herçî goştê nerm ji xwer̄a danî** (Dz) The wolf *got up and* set [aside] all the soft meat for himself •***R̄abe* tu vî goştî li me p'ar bike** (Dz) You *get up* and divide this meat between us •**Jinikê *r̄abû* tendûr dada** (Dz) The woman *got up and* lit the stove •**R̄ojekê gundîk *r̄adibe* dike her̄e cem xwedê** (Dz) One day a villager (or, peasant) is about to go to [visit] God; 3) to have an erection: •**Kîrê te *r̄adibe*?** (Msr) Do you have a hard on?; 4) [+ **ji**] to stop, cease, discontinue (doing stg.) : •[**Ker *ji* tir *rabî***] (YSZx) The donkey *stopped* farting [*prv.*] {said when an incompetent person is removed from a high position}; 5) [+ **-e** (Z-3)/**ber** (K)/**pêş** (K)] to rise up against (in attack or rebellion): •***R̄abine* Memo ... *r̄adibine* Memo çil xedem fe'n** (Z-3) *Rise up against* Mem ... 40 servants *rise up against* Mem; -[**li**] **ber ft-î r̄abûn** (Wlt/XF) to be opposed to or against stg., to object to stg.: •**Malbata min *li ber* biryara min *rabû*** (Wlt 1:36, 16) My family *was opposed* [or, *objected*] *to* my decision; **-r̄abûn r̄ûyê hev** (B) to argue (vi.); to insult one another. {also: r̄abon (SK); [ra-boun] رابون (JJ); <rabûn رابون (radibe) (رادبه)> (HH)} [K/A/JB3/IFb/B/JJ/HH/GF/TF//SK]

r̄abûn û r̄ûniştandin ڕابوون و ڕوونشتاندن (Ba2/XF) = lifestyle; manners. See **r̄abûn û r̄ûniştin**.

r̄abûn û r̄ûniştin ڕابوون و ڕوونشتن *vi.* (**r̄a-b- û r̄û-n-**). 1) to act, behave, comport oneself [lit. 'to stand up and sit down']: **•Gundî ... yanê em... em însanên rehet in, wî got. Em di nav tebîetê de ne, tekiliya me bi tebîetê re pir xurt e. Heye ku ji ber vê yekê be, em li gor daxwaziya dilê xwe *radibin û rûdinin* ... Pîvanên me jî li gor me ne. Ez nabêjim ku yên me ji yên komik û civatên din çêtir yan jî xirabtir in. Lê pîvanên me li gor me û civata me ne û em li gor wan *radibin û rûdinin*** (MUm, 57) Villagers... or we ... we are relaxed people, he said. We are close to [lit. 'inside'] nature, our connection to nature is very strong. Perhaps that is why we *act* according to our desires ... Our measures [standards?] fit us. I'm not saying that ours are better or worse than those of any other group or assembly. But our measures fit us and our group, and we *act* according to them; 2) to interact (with): **•Ez ji xwe re dixwînim. Digerim, diçim qahwê, *bi* dost û hevalan *re radibim rûdinim*. Em munaqeşe dikin, dikevin nava suhbetên dûr û dirêj** (LC, 8) I read. I wander about, I go to the café, I *interact with* friends. We have discussions, we get into long, drawn-out talks; 3) [*f.* **(-a;-ê).**] lifestyle, way of life; customs and traditions: **•Vira ew ḧemû dera digeřin, diçine gundê k'urda û çewa lazime derheqa ḧalê wana, *řabûn û řûniştina* wana pê diḧesin** (Ba2-3, 214) They go around everywhere, they go to Kurdish villages and find out what is necessary about their conditions and *way of life*; 4) {syn: şêl} behavior, conduct; manners: **•Řaste ewî mîna t'emamîya k'urdêd me nexwendî bû, lê alîyê *řabûn-řûniştandinê* û zanebûna xweva ew zaf 'eyan bû** (Ba2-4, 219) True, he was illiterate like all of us Kurds, but when it came to *behavior and manners* and knowledge he was well respected **•Şêxê 'ereba texmîna xo tê kir, *řabîn û řûniştina* wan ya maqûl bû, mirovêt 'aqil bûn** (M-Ak #640, 290) The Sheikh of the Arabs made his appraisal of them [and saw that] their *behavior* was excellent and that they were intelligent men. {also: řabûn [û] řûniştandin (Ba2/XF)} Cf. Sor hełs-u-kewt هه‌ڵس و كه‌وت/hełsan-u-danîştin هه‌ڵسان و دانیشتن = 'behaviour in society, manners; treatment, [way of] dealing with stg.' [Ba2/K/B/GF/OK/RF//XF] <'edeb I>

řa•ç'andin ڕاچاندِن *vt.* **(řa-ç'în-).** to spin, to weave; to spin *(web, of spiders)*; to create, make. {also: [ra-tchandin/rāchāndin (Rh)] ڕاچاندين (JJ)} [Bw/K/IFb/JJ/GF/TF/OK] <rêstin; tevnpîrk>

řad•e ڕاده *f.* **(•a;).** degree, level, grade: **•Gelek şagirt... bi serfirazî gihîştine *rada* bilind** (RC2. Ku heye Xwedê hiş bide gelê Kurd) Many pupils ... proudly attained a high *degree.* {syn: *derece} < Sor řade ڕاده = 'extent, point, degree, limit' [RC2/IFb/RZ/ZF/SS/CS]

řader ڕادەر *f.* **(-a;-ê).** infinitive, verbal noun:-**řaweya řader** (GF) infinitive mood. {syn: jêder [2]; mesder} [(neol)IFb/GF/TF/ZF]

radio ڕادیۆ (A) = radio. See **řadyo.**

radîo ڕادیئۆ (B)/řadîo ڕادیئۆ (K) = radio. See **řadyo.**

řadyo ڕادیۆ *f.* **(-ya;-yê).** radio. {also: radio (A); radîo (B); řadîo (K)} {syn: bihîstok (neol); pêlweş (IF)} [JB3/IF/BK//K//A//B] <îzgeh>

řaêxistin ڕائێخستِن (Bw/SK) = to hang. See **řaxistin.**

řaf ڕاف (Haz) = flock of birds. See **řef I.**

řa•gihandin ڕاگه‌هاندِن *vt.* **(řa-gihîn-).** 1) to communicate, inform, report; 2) [*f.* **(-a;-ê).**] communication. Sor řageyandin ڕاگه‌یاندِن = 'to communicate to, inform' [VoA/IFb/GF/OK/ZF3]

řa•girtin ڕاگِرتِن *vt.* **(řa-g[i]r-).** 1) to hold, keep, preserve: **•Belê, ḧetta ez têm, eger nêçîrek hingo îna, *řa-girin* da wextê hatim bişkînim** (SK 6:65) But, if you bring some prey before I return, *keep* it for me to rend when I come **•Mêr û jin û biçûk dihatin, malekî bê-ḧisab bo wî diînan** [sic], **ew awe bo tebeřuk dibirin, dixarinewe û dikirine şûşan, li malêt xo *diřagirtin*** (SK 12:119) Men, women, and children came, bringing him countless wealth, and took the water for good luck, and drank it and put it into bottles and *kept* it in their homes; 2) to keep *(animals)*: **•Ḧeywanê ho terîf, ho kirêt bo çî *řagirîn*?** (SK 25:229) Why *should we keep* such a strange and hideous animal?; 3) to hold up, prop up (SK): **•Wê carê, madam we ye, zû be, kêjikekî bo min hawêje xarê da bixom, dilê min qahîm bibît, bişêm çyay *řa-girim*** (SK 3:19) Now, since this is so, hurry up and throw down a chick for me to eat so that my heart may be strengthened and I may be able *to hold up* the mountain; 4) to hold out or up, show, wave in front of: **•Di dilê xo da hizr kir, "Ew hijîre laîq e bi dîharî bibem bo muxtarê gundî." Dana ser destê xo, bir, li pêş muxtar *řagirt*, gotê, "Min ew hijîre bo te bi dîharî înaye"** (SK 20:181) He thought to himself, "It is fitting that I take this fig as a present to the headman of the village." He placed it on his hand, took it and *held it out* before the headman, saying, "I have brought you this fig as a present"; 5) to procure, engage, get, hire, employ: **•Imamek bo pêş-niwêjîya gundî û xutbe xundinê r̄agirti-bû** (SK 17:160) He *had procured* an imam to lead the village in prayer and to recite the khutbah; 6) to hold back, restrain, stop, detain, hold, or keep in check: **•Hersêk ĥalen înane ĥuzora xelîfey, r̄agirtin** (M-Ak, #569, 258) All three were immediately brought and *held* in the presence of the caliph; 7) {syn: şidandin} to pull tight *(rope, etc.)* (B). Sor r̄a•girtin ڕاگـــرتِـــن = 'hold back, delay, observe (rule), harbor, engage or employ (servant), keep (animal), keep, maintain, take up a position' [VoA/K/A/IFb/B/JB1-S/SK/GF/TF/Kmc]

r̄a•hatin ڕاهـاتِـن *vi.* **(r̄a[t]ê-).** [+li ...] to get used to, be accustomed to: **-lê r̄ahatî** (Qzl) used to stg., accustomed to stg. {syn: 'elimîn; hîn bûn [hîn I]} Sor r̄a•hatin ڕاهـــاتِـــن = 'to become accustomed, become familiar [pê = with]' [Qzl/A/GF] <lê banîn>

r̄ahet ڕاهەت (K/JB3) = calm. See **r̄iĥet**.

r̄ahetî ڕاهەتی (K/JB3) = comfort. See **r̄eĥetî**.

r̄ahêlan ڕاهـــێـــلان (JB1-A/OK/Bw) = to pounce, leap. See **r̄ahiştin** [2].

rahin راهِن (TF) = thigh. See **r̄an**.

r̄a•hiştin ڕاهِشتِن *vt.* **(r̄a-hêl- / r̄a-hêj- [Z-2]/ r̄a-hij-).** 1) [+ *dat. constr.*] to remove, pick up, take away; to take hold of: **•Beyrim çû *rahişte* serê hût û anî** (L-5, 148, l. 12-13) Beyrim went and *picked up* the monster's head and brought it **•Ew qundir, *rahiştinê*** [sic], **danî ser refkê** (L-1, 2, l. 4-5) They *picked up* this gourd and put it on a shelf **•Hat û li ser textê xwe rûnişt û *rahişte* tembûra xwe** (L) He came and sat down on his bed and *took up* his tambur **•*Raje* [=*rahêje*] goşt dêne ber şêr, *r̄aje* r̄îşî dêne ber mehînê** (HR 3:141) *Pick up* the meat and place it before the lion, *pick up* the dried hay [and] place it before the mare; 2) [+ **ser** or *dat. constr.*] {syn: xwe avêtin} {also: r̄ahêlan (JB1-A/OK/Bw)} to pounce on, attack; to throw o.s. at, leap *(of a dog or wild beast in pursuit of prey)*; to run after, pursue: **•Gurêd birçî ji nava xilxilê kevira derdik'etin û *r̄adihiştne* ser pêz** (Ba2:1, 203) Hungry wolves came out from the rock heaps and *pounced on* the sheep **•Lê gura Ûsib dîtin** [sic], ***rahiştnê*** [sic], **ew xarin** [sic] (Ba, 314:8) But the wolves saw Joseph, *pounced on him*, [and] ate him **•Tuê *rahêjî* wî teyrî, bibî** (L) You *will pursue* this bird, and take [it] **•Wana *r̄ahişte ser* duşmin** (B) They *pounced on* the enemy **•Xezalek hat berahîyê, telismê zêr̄î stoy da. *Rahêla* xezalê, r̄evî, çû di bistanî da** (M-Zx #753) A gazelle came before him with a gold talisman round its neck. He *set off after* the gazelle, it fled and went into the garden. {also: r̄ahêlan (JB1-A/OK-2); [ra-hichtin راهـشـتـيـن/ra-hilan راهـلان] (JJ); <rahiştin راهـشـتـن (radihêle) (رادهيله)> (HH)} [K/A/IFb/B/JJ/HH/GF/TF/OK//JB1-A/Bw]

rahîbe راهـيـبـه *f.* **().** nun, sister: **•Ez bi navê hemû *rahîbeyên* li Kylemoreyê ji ber vexwendina te spas dikim** (EN) I thank you in the name of all *the nuns of* Kylemore for your invitation. {also: raxîbe (Wkt-2); rehîbe (IFb)} {syn: r̄eben II (f.)} <Ar rāhibah راهبة [EN/ZF/RZ/Wkt//IFb]

r̄ahmet ڕاهمەت (B) = mercy, pity. See **r̄eĥmet**.

r̄ahmetî ڕاهمەتی (B) = deceased. See **r̄eĥmetî**.

r̄aĥet ڕاحەت (SK/JJ/HH) = calm; comfort. See **r̄eĥetî** & **r̄iĥet**.

r̄aĥetî ڕاحەتی (SK) = comfort. See **r̄eĥetî**.

r̄a•k'etin ڕاکـەتِـن *vi.* **(r̄a-k'ev-).** to lie down, go to bed; to sleep. {also: [ra-ketin] راكـــتـــيـــن (JJ); <raketin راكتن (radikeve) (رادكفه)> (HH)} {syn: nivistin; r̄azan [1]} Za rakewnã [rakewtiş] (Srk) [K/A/IFb/B/JJ/HH/GF/TF]

r̄ak'êşan ڕاکـێـشـان (K[s]/JR) = to pull, stretch. See **r̄ak'işandin**.

r̄a•kirin ڕاکِـرِن *vt.* **(r̄a-k-).** 1) to remove, take off [Fr ôter]: **-'erd r̄akirin** (K) to plough; **-k'ok r̄akirin** (K) to uproot; 2) to do away with, repeal: **•Ev qanûn *hate rakirin*** (JB3) This law *has been repealed*; 3) to pick up, lift, raise: **-ji xewê r̄akirin** (K/B) to wake s.o. up (vt.). {also: [ra-kirin] راكـريـن (JJ); <rakirin راكـرن (radike) (رادكـه)> (HH)} [K/A/JB3/IFb/B/JJ/HH/SK/GF/TF] <r̄abûn>

r̄a•k'işandin ڕاکِـشـانـدِن *vt.* **(r̄a-k'işîn-).** to stretch, draw out, extend, pull, tighten; to pull out, extract (teeth). {also: r̄ak'êşan (K[s]/JR-2)} [JR/K/IFb/GF/Ba2/F]

r̄aman I ڕامـــــان *vi.* **(-ram-).** 1) {syn: duşirmîş bûn; fikirîn I[1]; hizir kirin; p'onijîn [2]} to think, ponder: **•Yên din *diramin*, dibêjin "qey ew tirsonek e?"** (BM, 5) The others *think* [and] say, "He's not a coward, is he?"; 2) [*f.* **(-a;-ê).**] {syn: fikar; fikir [1]; hizir; mitale; xiyal} thought, idea: **-r̄aman kirin** (IFb) to think. <Sor r̄a•man ڕامـــان

(r̄a-mên-) = 'to pause for thought, ponder, meditate'; **-man**: [Pok. 3. men- 726.] 'to think, be aroused mentally': Skt mányate = 'thinks'; Av man-yete = do.; OP maniyay = 'I think' (Kent); cf. also Lat mēns, mentis = Eng mind [(neol)BX/K/JB3/IFb/GF/OK]

R̄aman II ڕامان *f.* **().** name of a mountain just to the south of the town of Batman, in Kurdistan of Turkey.

ramedan رامەدان (RZ) = to lie down. See **r̄amedîn**.

r̄a•medîn ڕامەدين *vi.* **(r̄a-med-).** to lie down, stretch out on one's back. {also: ramedan (RZ)} {syn: p'aldan; r̄azan; xwe dirêj kirin} < ra- + Ar √m-d-d مدّ = 'to stretch out' [IFb/ZF//RZ]

r̄amedîyayî ڕامەدييايى *adj./pp.* lying down, supine: •**Gava şêr bêcan li erdê *ramediyayî* dibîne, devê tifinga xwe dide bin guhê şêrê bêcan û diteqîne** (JB2-Osman Sebrî/Rnh 14 [1943], 8-9) When he finds the lion *lying* lifeless on the ground, he points the butt of his gun beneath the lifeless lion's ear and discharges it. [Rnh/JB2/IFb]

ramîsan راميسان (A) = to kiss. See **r̄amûsan**.

r̄a•mûsan ڕامووسان *vt.* **(r̄a-mûs-/r̄a-mîs-[L]).** 1) {syn: hatin r̄ûyê fk-ê; maç' kirin; paç' kirin} to kiss: •**Ez gelikî jê memnûn im û destê wî *radimîsim*** (L) I'm very pleased with him and *kiss* his hands; 2) [*f.* **(-a;-ê).**] {syn: maç'; paç' I} a kiss: •**Te ez bi *ramûsana* xwe helandim** (Wkt) You made me melt with your *kiss*. {also: ramîsan (A/L); r̄amûsandin (IFb-2); r̄amûsin; [ra-mousan] راموسان (JJ)} [L/A//Z-2/F/K/JB3/IFb/JJ/GF]

r̄amûsandin ڕاموساندِن (IFb) = to kiss. See **r̄amûsan**.

r̄amûsin ڕامووسِن = to kiss. See **r̄amûsan**.

r̄amyarî ڕاميارى *adj.* political: •**Ji ber vê yekê jî Metîn kete nava hemû rengên gotebêjên *ramyarî*, civakî** (Wlt 2:59, 13) Therefore Metin undertook all sorts of *political* [and] social negotiations. {syn: rêzanî; siyasî} <Sor r̄amyarî ڕاميارى (K2/Hej) [(neol)Wlt/ZF3/Wkt]

r̄an ڕان *m.* **(-ê;).** thigh, haunch; thigh of humans *(cf.* ***hêt*** *= thigh of animals)* (Bw/Zx): •**Qiloç'ê pezk'ûvî dik'eve *r̄anê* Sîyabend** (Z-4) The deer's antler goes into Siyabend's *thigh* •**Qonêrek li *ranê* wî hatiye** (FS) A boil has broken out [lit. 'has come'] on his *thigh*. {also: rahin (TF); r̄ehin II (OK-2); r̄ehn (Bw/Zx/OK-2); ren (F); r̄e'n (K); [ran] ران (JJ); <ran> ران (HH)} {syn: hêt; kulîmek; tilor I} Cf. Av rāna- (Tsb2, 11); P rān ران = 'thigh'; Sor r̄an ڕان; Hau r̄an [Z-1/K//A/JB3/IFb/B/JJ/HH/SK/GF//TF//F//Bw/Zx] <k'elef I; k'emax>

r̄anî-bergûz ڕانى بەرگووز (SK) = Kurdish man's suit of clothes. See **bergûz**.

r̄a•p'elikîn ڕاپەلِكين *vi.* **(r̄a-p'elik-).** to climb up, clamber up *(a tree, etc.)*: •**"Cil ji xwe diqetin," Alfons dibêje. Bi taybetî dema mirov *radipelike* daran** (BM, 15) "Clothes get torn on their own," Alfons says. Especially when one *climbs up* trees. {also: rapellikandin (GF); raperikandin (GF-2)} {syn: hilk'işîn} [BM/K/ZF3//GF]

rapellikandin راپەللِكاندِن (GF) = to climb up. See **r̄ap'elikîn**.

raperikandin راپەرِكاندِن (GF) = to climb up. See **r̄ap'elikîn**.

rapor راپۆر *f.* **(-a; -ê).** report. {also: raport (K-2/SK-2/OK)} <T rapor <Fr rapport [Wlt/IFb/SK/GF//K/OK] <t'eblîx>

raport راپۆرت (K/SK/OK) = report. See **rapor**.

rarî kirin رارى كِرِن (Zx) = to play. See **yarî II**.

r̄aser ڕاسەر *prep.* [+ **li** or **-î**] above, over: •**Du keleh ji van kelehan *li raserî* lêva golê *ne*** (SB, 50) Two of those fortresses *overlook* the shore of the lake •**Mizgeft *raserî* gund e** (BX) The mosque is *above* the village. [BX/K/IFb/GF/TF/OK] <fêz>

r̄ast ڕاست *adj.* 1) {≠çep (=left)} right *(direction; correct)*: •**Riya *rast*, riya evîna welat e** (AB) The *right* way is the way of loving the country; **-destê r̄ast(ê)** (K) right hand; **-r̄ast hatin** (K/ZF3) to encounter, meet up with, chance upon, come across, bump into {syn: t'ûşî ft-î bûn}: •**Gele gur *r̄astî* me *hatin*** (Ba) A pack of wolves *chanced upon* us •**Merivek r̄astî wî hat go:** (Dz) A man *chanced upon* him [and] said: •**R̄êva *r̄astî* kalekî *tê*** (Dz) On the way he *comes across* an old man •**Şêrek û gurek û r̄ovîk .. bi hevr̄a çûn *r̄astî* hespekî *hatin*** (Dz) A lion, a wolf, and a fox ... traveled together and *encountered* a horse; 2) straight, direct; 3) {syn: dirust} true; correct, right; 4) {syn: *r̄êzdar I} regular: **-fêlê [ne]r̄ast** (B) [ir]regular verb; 5) [?*m.*] {also: r̄astî, f.; <rastî> راستى (HH)} {≠derew; ≠vir̄ II} truth: •***R̄ast* bêje** (L) Tell *the truth*; 6) [*f.* **(-a;-ê)**] {syn: best; deşt} plain, prairie, steppe: •**Ez îro çûme *rasta* jêrîn ravê û nêç'îrêye!** (EP-5, #2) today I went hunting in the lower *prairie*. {also: [rast] راست (JJ); <rast> راست (HH)} [Pok. I. reĝ- 855.] 'direct': Av rāštəm = 'straight'; P rāst راست; Sor r̄ast راســـــــت = 'right (opp. to left), direction, straight, level, correct, true, honest, faithful'; Hau r̄as = 'true' (M4); cf. also Lat rectus {r̄astî} [K/A/JB3/IFb/B/JJ/HH/SK/GF/TF] <çep; r̄asteqîne>

rastekî راســـتـــەكـــى (FJ/GF) = genuine, real. See **r̄asteqîne**.

rastekîn راستەكينە (CS) = genuine, real. See **r̄asteqîne**.

rasteqîn راســـتـــەقـــيـــن (ZF3) = genuine, real. See **r̄asteqîne**.

r̄asteqîne ڕاستەقينە *adj.* genuine, authentic; real, true: **•Hikûmet hertim bi çavê hevwelatiyên *rasteqîne* li mesîhiyan dinêre** (KRG 23.xi.2010) The government always regards Christians as *genuine* citizens **•Sedemên *rasteqîne* yên çalakiyên PKKê** (Welatê Me 3.xii.2009) The *real* reasons for the PKK's activities **•Şoreşa Rojava, şoreşa *rasteqîne* û rewa ya Sûriyê ye** (PYD 9.xi.2016) The Syrian Kurdish revolt is the *true* and legitimate revolt of Syria. {also: rastekî (FJ/GF); rastekîn (CS); rasteqîn (ZF3-2)} {syn: xwer̄û} < rast + Ar yaqīn يقين = 'certain, sure'; Sor r̄asteqîne ڕاستەقينە [KRG/PYD/IFb/ZF3/FD/Wkt/RZ] <r̄ast>

rastgêr راستگێر (SS) = rightist. See **r̄astgir**.

r̄astgir ڕاســـتـــگِـــر *adj.&m.* rightist, right wing: **•Nivîskarê rojnameya Cumhuriyetê Hikmet Çetinkaya di nivîsa xwe de sernavekî wiha bi kar anîbû: "Çepgirên neteweperest û *rastgirên* neteweperest"** (AW69A1) The writer for the newspaper Cumhuriyet, Hikmet Çetinkaya, used this title in his article: "Nationalist leftists and nationalist *rightists*." {also: rastgêr (SS)} [AW/VoA/ZF3/Wkt//SS]

r̄astî ڕاســـتـــى *f.* **(-ya;-yê).** 1) straightness; 2) {syn: dirustî} truth; truthfulness: **•Ez dixazim her̄ime cem xwedê, bizanibim çika *r̄astya* wî çewane?** (Dz) I want to go to God, to know what his *truth* is like [lit. 'how his truth is']; **-bi r̄astî** (K)/**birastî** (Wkt) truly, really, indeed; -[**Ya**] **r̄astî gotî** (K)/**bi rastî gotî** (AX) If truth be told, to tell you the truth. {also: r̄ast [4]; [rasti] راســـتـــى (JJ); <rastî> راستى (HH)} Cf. P rāstī راستى; Sor r̄astî ڕاستى = 'truth, straightness, straightforwardness, loyalty, really?' [K/A/JB3/IFb/B/JJ/HH/SK/TF/OK] <r̄ast>

r̄astnivîs ڕاستنِڤيس *f.* **(-a;-ê).** orthography: **•pêkanîna *rastnivîs* û rêzimaneke rast û hevgirtî** (Wlt 2:100, 2) the creation of a correct and consistent *orthography* and grammar. {also: r̄astnivîsandin (K/IFb); r̄astnivîsar (K/B); r̄astnivîsîn (OK)} [(neol)Wlt/K/IFb//B//OK]

r̄astnivîsandin ڕاستنِڤيساندِن (K/IFb) = orthography. See **r̄astnivîs**.

r̄astnivîsar ڕاســتـنِـڤـيـسـار (K/B) = orthography. See **r̄astnivîs**.

r̄astnivîsîn ڕاســتـنِـڤـيـسـيـن (OK) = orthography. See **r̄astnivîs**.

raş راش (TF) = sprinkle, light rain. See **reşêş**.

r̄a•şiqitîn ڕاشِـقِـتـيـن *vi.* **(r̄a-şiqit-).** to slip, slide, stumble: **•R̄êva lingê wî *r̄aşiqitî*** (Z-884) On the way his foot *slipped*. [Z-884/ZF3] <alîn; şiqitîn [1]>

r̄av I ڕاڤ *f.* **(-a;-ê).** 1) {syn: nêçîr[1]; seyd; şikar} hunting: **-rava kewan** (ZF3) partridge hunting; **-çûne r̄awê** (K) to go hunting: **•Qeret'ajdîn, bira û Memêva ... wê her̄in *r̄av û nêç'îrê*** (Z-1) Qeretajdin, [his] brothers and Mem ... will go out *hunting*; 2) {syn: nêçîr[2]} game, wild fowl [gibier]. {also: r̄aw (K/SK); r̄ew (B); [raw] راڤ (JJ)} Sor r̄aw ڕاو; Hau r̄awe *f.* (M4) [Z-1/IFb/JJ/GF/BF//K/SK//B]

r̄av II ڕاڤ *f.* **(-a;-ê).** stripe *(e.g., on a bee's back)*: **•*R̄avek* a lê** (Zeb) It has *stripes* (on it) **-r̄av-r̄av** (Zeb) striped. {also: <r̄av> ڕاڤ (Hej)} [Zeb/Hej/BF]

r̄ave ڕاڤە *f.* **().** explanation: **-r̄ave kirin** (K/A/IFb/GF/TF/OK) to explain {syn: îzah kirin; şîrove kirin; têgihandin}: **•Serşalyara Pakistanî gelşa Keşmîrê û herêma Himalaya û şkenandina mafên mirovatîyê ji alîyê hêzên parastina Pakistanê, bi kurtî *rave dike* ji rêberên Îran û Tirkîyê re** (VoA) The Pakistani prime minister briefly *explains* the conflict in Kashmir and the Himalaya region and the human rights violations on the part of Pakistan's security forces to the leaders of Iran and Turkey. {syn: îzah; şîrove} [VoA/K/A/IFb/GF/TF/OK]

r̄aw ڕاو (K/SK) = hunting; game. See **r̄av I**.

r̄awe ڕاوە *f.* **(-ya;).** mood, mode *(of verbs, e.g., indicative, subjunctive, etc.)*: **-r̄aweya bilanî** (IF/GF)/**~ya gerane** (IF) subjunctive or optative mood; **-r̄aweya fermanî** (K/IF/GF) imperative mood; **-r̄aweya gerînî** (K/IF/GF)/**~ya hekînî** (IF/GF) conditional mood; **-r̄aweya peşkerî** (K)/**~ya pêşker** (IF/GF) indicative mood; **-r̄aweya r̄ader** (IF/GF) infinitive mood. {syn: t'eher [2]} [(neol)K/IFb/GF/ZF3] <lêker>

r̄a•westan ڕاوەستان/**r̄a west'an** ڕا وەستان [JB1-A] *vi.* **(r̄a-west-).** 1) {syn: sekinîn} to stand, stand still, stop; to wait: **•*R̄aweste*!** (Msr) *Stop*!/*Wait*! {syn:

bisekine!}; 2) to rise up *(against)*, revolt, rebel (K[s]) [r̄awestan]; 3) [+ **li ser**] to comprehend, grasp, deal with; to study, go into, investigate, examine: **•Tu tiştekî wekî belge neketiye ber dest da meriv karibe firehtir *li ser* jiyana wî *raweste*** (CA, 67) Nothing like a document has been available so that one could *investigate* his life more fully. {also: r̄awestin (Msr/IFb-2/GF-2/TF/OK-2); r̄a west'iyan (JB1-A-2); r̄awestîn (K[s]-2); r̄awistin (A-2); [ra-westin] راڤستین (JJ); <rawestan راوستان (radiweste) (رادوسته)> (HH)} Cf. P īstādan ايستادان = 'to stand, stop'; Sor r̄a•westan ڕاوەستان = 'to stand still, halt'. For etymology see **westîn**. [Msr//K(s)/A/IFb/HH/JB1-A/SK/GF/OK//JJ/TF] <westan I; westîn>

r̄a•westandin ڕاوەستاندِن *vt.* **(r̄a-westîn-).** 1) {syn: sekinandin} to stop *(vt.)*, cause to stop or halt; to freeze: **•Ji bo vê jî divê şer *bê rawestandin*** (AW74A5) Therefore the war must *be stopped* **•Nehiştin em ji bajarekî biçin bajarekî din. Li ser riyan, li serê çiyan *em dane rawestandin*** (AW70D1) They wouldn't let us go from one city to another. On the roads, on the mountains, they *made us stop* **•Tê diyarkirin ku IMF'ê têkiliyên xwe yên bi Tirkiyeyê re heta hilbijartinê *rawestandiye*** (AW70B5) It has been stated that the IMF has *stopped* [or, *frozen*] its relations with Turkey until the elections **•Xwest, ku rayedarên ewlekariyê şîddeta xwe *rawestînin*** (CTV130) He asked the security officials *to cease* their violence; 2) [+ **li ser**] to deal with, investigate, examine, discuss, talk about, mention *[mostly used in passive]*: **•Di nûçeyê de *li ser* helwesta neyinî ya dewleta tirk jî *hatiye rawestandin*** (AW75A3) In the news item the negative attitude of the Turkish state *has been discussed* [or, *dealt with*] **•Tiştê ku zêde *li ser hatiye rawestandin* karkirina DSP û MHP'yê** (AW69A5) The thing that *was mentioned* a great deal was the working of [the political parties] DSP and MHP. Sor r̄awestandin ڕاوەستاندِن = 'to stop, put a stop to' [K(s)/IFb/GF/TF/OK/AD] <r̄awestan>

r̄awestin ڕاوەستِن (Msr/IFb/GF/OK) = to stand, stop. See **r̄awestan**.

r̄a west'iyan ڕا وەستِيان (JB1-A) = to stand, stop. See **r̄awestan**.

r̄awestîn ڕاوەستين (K[s]) = to stand, stop. See **r̄awestan**.

r̄awil ڕاوِل (ZZ-5) = small wild animal. See **r̄awir**.

r̄awir ڕاوِر *m.* **(-ê;).** 1) small wild animal, rodent and the like *(e.g., rabbit, fox, scorpion)*: **•Li ser avê serên masî û *rawirên* ecêb dixuyan** (MUm, 8) On the water the heads of fish and fabulous *creatures* appeared **•meselokên *rawilan*** (ZZ-5, 130) *animal* fables; 2) grass-eating animal *(e.g., goat, sheep, cow, rabbit)* (Zeb) [lawir̄]. {also: lawir (Kmc-10); lawir̄ (Zeb/BF/FS); r̄awil (ZZ-5); r̄ewir (Frq/Msr/F); <lawir> لاور (Hej)} [Frq/Msr/F//MUm/ IFb/B/GF/TF//ZZ-5//Kmc-10/Hej//Zeb/BF/FS] <ḧeywan; terawil>

r̄awistin ڕاوِستِن (A) = to stand, stop. See **r̄awestan**.

r̄a•xistin ڕاخِستِن *vt.* **(r̄a-x-/r̄a-xîn-).** 1) to spread stg. *(e.g., a rug)* out on the ground; to strew, scatter, spread *(e.g., grain)*: **•Ç'îya usa bedew dibû, mêriv t'irê xalîça Xur̄ustanê ser wî *r̄axistine*** [sic] (Ba2) The mountain was so beautiful [in the springtime], people thought that Khurasani rugs *had been spread out* over it **•Dostê wî jî gelek qedrê wî digirt: her tuxme t̲e'amê xoş ba, bilezet ba, ew bo wî dirust dikir … bo niwistinê jî niwînêt çak bo wî *dir̄aêxistin*…** (SK 31:274) His friend would treat him with great respect. He would prepare for him every kind of good and tasty food … He *would spread* fine bedding for him also, to sleep on **•T'êr̄a vekin, genim *r̄axin*, bira zuhyabe, xirab nebe** (Ba-1, #36) Open the sacks, *scatter* the wheat, let it dry out, lest it go bad; 2) {syn: daliqandin; hilawîstin} to hang (B); to hang up or out *(e.g., wet clothes on a line to dry), cf.* ***daliqandin & hilawîstin** = to hang up (a coat on a hook)*. {also: r̄aêxistin (Bw/SK); [ra-khystin] راخستین (JJ); <raxistin راخستن (ratêxse) (راتیخسه) [sic]> (HH)} [Ba2/K/A/JB3/IFb/B/JJ/HH/GF/BK/Msr//Bw/SK] <mehfûr; xalîçe>

raxîbe راخيبه (Wkt) = nun. See **rahîbe**.

r̄ay I ڕاى *f.* **(-a;).** opinion, point of view: ***•Bi raya min be* em neçin** (IFb) *If it's up to me*, let's not go; **-r̄aya giştî** (Wlt) public opinion; **-rayî *yekî* dan** (ZF3) to show *s.o.* stg. {syn: nîşan dan}: **•Gava dîya wî çîkolatayê *ray* wî *dide*, ew him hêrsê û him jî xeyîdîn[ê] ji bîr dike** (A. Incekan. Compact Kurdish-Kurmanji 58) When his mother *shows* him chocolate, he forgets his rage and his anger. {also: raye II (IFb-2); [reī] راى (JJ); <rayî> رايى (HH)} {syn : dîtin [4]} <Ar ra'y رأي = 'opinion' (<√r-'-y = 'to see') --> T rey = 'opinion, vote' [Wlt/K/

IFb/JB1-S/GF/TF/ZF3//JJ//HH] <dîtin>

r̄ay II رای (GF) = root; vein; nerve. See **r̄eh**.

rayber رایبەر (IF) = guide; leader. See **r̄êber**.

r̄aye I ڕایـــــــە **(-ya;-yê).** authority, delegated power; authorization; competence: **•Ew dikare mahkûmên nexweş efû bike. Em dixwazin vê *rayeya* xwe bi kar bîne** (cinarinsesi.com 26.i.2017) He can pardon sick inmates. We want him to use this *authority* of his **•Vê *rayeyê* enceq gel dikare ji min bigire** (anfkurdi.com 21.vii.2017) Only the people can take this authority from me. {syn: desthilat} Sor r̄aye ڕایـــــــە = 'scope, powers, authority, competence, entrée' [(neol)IFb/ZF3/Wkt]

raye II رایە (IFb) = opinion. See **r̄ay**.

r̄ayedar ڕایـــەدار *m.&f.* **().** person in charge, person invested with authority; an official, civil servant: **•*R̄ayedar* û fermandarên TC'ê li hev dicivin û biryar û raporekê amade dikin** (Wlt 2:71, 16) The powers that be [lit. '*people in charge* and rulers'] in the republic of Turkey convene and prepare a policy decision [lit. 'a decision and a report']. [(neol)Wlt/IFb/ZF3] <fermandar; k'arbidest; r̄aye I>

r̄az ڕاز *f.* **(-a;-ê).** a secret: **•Hemûyan zanîbû ku Benîşto *raza* xwe dernaxîne** (HYma 30) Everyone knew that B. would not betray his *secret* **•Vê *razê* ji kesî re nebêje** (Wkt) Don't tell this *secret* to anyone. {also: [raz] راز (JJ)} {syn: nepenî; sir̄ II} Cf. P rāz راز; Sor r̄az ڕاز = 'secret, mystery' [HYma/IFb/JJ/FJ/GF/CS/RZ/SS]

r̄a•zan ڕازان *vi.* **(r̄a-zê- / -r̄azê- [MK]/ r̄a-z- [B]).** 1) {syn: r̄ak'etin} to lie down; to go to bed, go to sleep; {syn: nivistin} to sleep: **•Divînin bûkek *wê* xwer̄a *r̄azaye*** (Dz) They see that the young woman is sleeping [lit. '*has gone to sleep* for herself']; 2) {syn: welidandin; zayîn} to give birth: **•Wexta jina te *r̄abizê*...** (Z-921) When your wife gives birth... **•Jina te *r̄azaye* kur̄ek *anîye*** (B) Your wife *has given birth* to a son. {also: razihan (Rnh-2:17, p.307); [ra-zan] رازان (JJ); <razan رازان (radize) (رادزە)> (HH)} [L/K/A/JB3/IF/B/JJ/HH/SK/GF/TF//Rnh] <nivistin; r̄azandin; xew>

r̄a•zandin ڕازاندِن *vt.* **(r̄a-zîn-).** 1) {syn: nivandin} to put to sleep, put to bed: **•Kevotka Memê *dane* [sic] *razandinê*** (EP-7) The doves *put* Mem *to bed* **•Dê zar̄a *r̄adizîne*** (B) The mother *puts* the children *to bed*; 2) to hospitalize: **•Çend rojan li nexweşxanê *hatiye razandin*** (Heftenameya Bas 29.viii.2017) He *was hospitalized* for a few days; 3) to spread stg. out (on the ground) (JJ); 4) to invest, deposit (money) [T yatırmak]: **•Min 10 000 euro li bankeyê *razandin*** (Wkt) I *deposited* 10,000 € in the bank. {also: [razandin] رازانـــدیـــن (JJ)} [EP-7/K/A/JB3/IFb/B/JJ/GF/TF/ZF3/Wkt] <r̄azan>

r̄azanxan•e ڕازانـــخـــانـــە *f.* **(•a;•ê).** bedroom: **•Wexta qewaza derê *r̄azanxana* Memê vekirin [sic], bala xwe danê, Memê r̄azaye bi xewa şîrin** (Z-1, 47) When the messengers opened the door of Mem's *bedroom*, they saw that M. was sleeping sweetly. [Z-1/K/CS/ZF/Wkt]

r̄azedilî ڕازەدِلی (Ba2) = consent. See **r̄azîdilî**.

razihan رازهـــان (Rnh) = to lie down, go to sleep. See **r̄azan**.

r̄azilixî ڕازِلِخی (K) = willingness. See **r̄azîlixî**.

r̄azî ڕازی *adj.* 1) {syn: qane} [+ **ji**] content, pleased, satisfied (with): **•Ez *ji* xebata te pir *razî* me** (BX) I'm very *pleased with* your work; 2) {syn: qane; qayîl} in agreement, agreeing, willing, consenting. {also: [razi] راضـــی (JJ); <razî> راظـــی (HH)} < Ar rāḍī راضـــــــي (rāḍin) (راضٍ) --> T razı {r̄azîbûn[î]; r̄azîtî} [BX/K/JB3/IFb/B/JJ/HH/JB1-A/SK/GF] <amade; r̄azî>

r̄azîbûn ڕازیـــبـــوون *f.* **(-a;-ê).** contentment, satisfaction; approval; **-cihê r̄azîbûnê** (Rûdaw) acceptable (to both sides) [lit. 'source of approval']: **•Ti edebiyatek nikare bi qasî çîrokên gelêrî û folklorî ji bo mezin û ji bo zarokan jî watedar û *cihê razîbûnê* be** (Rûdaw 3.xii.2016) No literature can be as meaningful and *acceptable* to both adults and children as folktales. {also: r̄azîbûnî (IFb)} {syn: r̄azîtî} [B/GF//IFb]

r̄azîbûnî ڕازیبوونی (IFb) = satisfaction. See **r̄azîbûn**.

r̄azîdilî ڕازیـــدِلـــی *f.* **(-[y]a-yê).** consent, agreement: **-r̄azîdilî dayîn** (B) to consent, agree to stg.: **•Me jî *r̄azedilîa xwe dida*** (Ba2:2, 208) We also *gave our consent*. {also: r̄azedilî (Ba2)} {syn: r̄azîlixî} [Ba2//B] <r̄azîlixî>

r̄azîlixî ڕازیـــلِـــخـــی *f.* **(-ya;-yê).** 1) {syn: r̄azîdilî} agreement, readiness, willingness, consent: **-r̄az[î]lixî dayîn** (B) to give one's consent, to agree; 2) gratitude, thankfulness: **•Qeret'ajdîn *razîlixîya* xwe dibêje, wekî Memê ew u hespê wîba bê xwey nehiştîye û neçûye** (FK-eb-2) Qeretajdîn expresses *gratitude* that Mem had not ridden off and left him and his horse unattended. {also: r̄azilixî (K); r̄azlixî (B-2)} <r̄azî + T -lık =

abstract noun suffix [FK-2/B//K] <r̄azî>

r̄azîtî رازیـتـی *f.* **(-ya;).** contentment, satisfaction. {also: [raziti] راضیتی (JJ)} {syn: r̄azîbûn} [JJ/ZF3] <r̄azî>

r̄azlixî رازلِخی (B) = willingness. See **r̄azîlixî**.

razyane رازیانه (IFb) = fennel. See **r̄izyane**.

-re ره *postpositional suffix*. See **-r̄a**.

r̄ebben رەببەن (B) = miserable; slave. See **r̄eben I**.

r̄eben I رەبـەن *adj.* poor, wretched, miserable, unfortunate, pitiful: •**Ew kerekî *reben* e, ez dikarim wî bikûjim** (SW) It's only a *miserable* donkey, I can kill him. {also: r̄ebben (B); [reben] ربن (JJ); <reben> ربن (HH)} {syn: belengaz; bikul; dêran II; malxirab; şerpeze; xwelîser I} [K/A/JB3/IFb/JJ/HH/GF/TF/OK//B] <kezîkurê; sêfîl>

r̄eben II رەبەن *m.&f.* **(-ê/-a;).** monk (m.); nun (f.): •**Ew *rebena* dêrê ye** (FS) She is a nun; -***rebenê* dêrê** (FS) monk. {also: [rabán] ربن (JJ)} {syn: êris} < Syr raban ܪܒܢ = 'our great one, our teacher, magister noster' [Dh/Zeb/A/JJ/GF/OK/FS] <k'eşîş; qeşe; rahîbe>

r̄ebisandin رەبِساندِن *vt.* **(-r̄ebisîn-).** to irrigate. {also: repisandin (FS-2); rewisandin (GF-2); ribisandin (FS); r̄ifsandin (Zeb/IFb/OK); <r̄ebisandin> رەبساندن (Hej)} {syn: r̄ifse kirin} < Arc rabeṣ רבץ = 'to sprinkle' & Heb ribets רבץ = 'to irrigate by sprinkling' [Zeb/IFb/OK//FS//GF/Hej/M-Zx/ZF3]

r̄ed رەد: **-r̄ed bûn** (K/B) = a) to be used up, consumed, exhausted (K/B); b) {syn: beta vebûn; r̄oda çûn; winda bûn; x̄eware bûn} to disappear, vanish (K): •**Welle, Memo çiqas jî *r̄et be* naçe malê, wê her̄e ba Zînê** (Z-3) By God, as soon as Memo *vanishes from view*, he won't go home, he'll go to Zîn; 3) *(fig.)* to perish (K); **-r̄ed kirin** (B) to use up, exhaust. {also: r̄et I bûn (Z-3)} [Z-3//K/B]

r̄ef I رەف *m.(Czr)/f.(B)* **(/-a; /-ê).** 1) {syn: t'elp} flock of birds: •**Her ṯeyrek û *refa* xwe** (FS) *appr.* Birds of a feather flock together [*prv.*]; **-r̄afik kew** (Haz) a flock of partridges; **-r̄afik mirîşk** (Haz) a flock of chickens; **-r̄afik qaz** (Haz) a flock of geese; **-r̄efa qulinga** (B) a flock of cranes; 2) *counting word for birds and other winged creatures* [cf. **fer**] (K); 3) (air force) squadron (K): •***Refên* emerîkanî ji nû ve li giravên Ponapê û Kusaiyê xistine** (RN) American *squadrons* have once again hit the islands of Ponape and Kusaie. {also: r̄af (Haz); r̄efik (A); [ref] رف (JJ); <ref> رف (HH)} [Haz//RN/K/IFb/B/JJ/HH/GF/TF/FS//A]

r̄ef II رەف *f.(L/FS)/m.(K)* **(;-ê/).** 1) shelf: •**Danî ser *refkê*** (L) [They] put [it] on *a shelf*; 2) rank (=row); file, column (K). {also: [ref] رف (JJ)} < Ar raff رَفّ = 'shelf' [L/K/A/IFb/JJ/FS]

r̄efes رەفەس *f.* **(;-ê).** kick *(of animals)*: •**Evî hespî *r̄efesek* lêda** (J) This horse gave [him] *a kick*; **-r̄efes kirin** (B/FD) to kick (of animals). {also: [refes] رفس (JJ); <refes> رفس (HH)} {syn: çivt; lotik; p'eĥîn; tîzik} < Ar rafasa رفس = 'to kick' [J/IFb/B/JJ/HH/FD/ZF3]

r̄efik رەفِك (A) = flock of birds. See **r̄ef I**.

r̄eh رەه *f.* **(-a;-ê).** 1) {syn: k'ok II} root; 2) vein: •**Wextê Dêwê Sohr lê mêzand, *r̄akî* dî jî ji dilê wî qetiha, bûne sê *r̄a*** (HR 3:107) When the Red Dev looked at him, another *vein* of his heart broke off, and became 3 *veins*; 3) nerve, sinew (SK): •**Her kesê bibiziwît dê *r̄iha* ji pişta wî kêşîn** (SK 55:636) Whosoever makes a move we shall pull *the sinews* from his back; **-r̄iha qolincê** (SK) lumbar nerve. {also: r̄a I, m. (K/GF-2/TF/RZ-2); r̄ay II (GF-2); rih II (IFb-2/SK/GF-2/FS); [reh] ره (JJ); <reh> ره (HH)} [A/IFb/JJ/HH/GF/OK/ZF3/Wkt/FD//K/TF//SK/FS]

R̄eha رەها = Urfa. See **R̄iha**.

r̄eha zer رەها زەر *f.* turmeric, bot. *Curcuma longa*. {also: riha zer (Dh/Zeb/IFb/OK-2/CB); <reha zer> رەها زەر (Hej)} = Sor zerdeçêwe زەردەچێوە [Dh/Zeb/IFb/CB//OK/Hej]

r̄ehber رەهبەر (B) = guide; leader. See **r̄êber**.

rehel رەهەل (A) = festive clothing; trousseau. See **r̄iĥal**.

r̄ehet رەهەت (IFb) = calm. See **r̄iĥet**.

rehetî رەهەتی (IFb) = comfort. See **r̄eĥetî**.

rehêl رەهێل (FS) = festive clothing; trousseau. See **r̄iĥal**.

rehilîn رەهِلین (IFb/ZF) = to quiver, tremble. See **r̄e'ilîn**.

r̄ehin I رەهِن = pledge, deposit. See **r̄ehîn**.

r̄ehin II رەهِن (OK) = thigh. See **r̄an**.

rehîbe رەهیبە (IFb) = nun. See **rahîbe**.

r̄ehîn رەهین *f.* **(-a;).** pledge, deposit; pawn; bet, wager. {also: r̄ehin I; r̄iĥîn (Z-2); [rehin] رهن (JJ); <rehn> رهن (HH)} <Ar rahn رهن & rahīnah رهينة [Z-2//K(s)/IFb//JJ] <girêv; miçilge>

r̄ehm رەهم (JB1-A)/rehm رەهم (CS) = mercy, pity. See **r̄eĥmet**.

r̄ehmet رەهمەت (B)/rehmet رەهمەت (IFb/ZF/CS) =

mercy, pity. See **r̄eḧmet**.

r̄ehmetî ڕەهمەتی (IFb) = deceased. See **r̄eḧmetî**.

r̄ehn I ڕەهن (Bw/Zx/OK) = thigh. See **r̄an.**

rehn II ڕەهن (MG) = liquid. See **r̄on II**.

rehnî ڕەهنی (Şnx) = bright; clear. See **r̄ohnî I** & **r̄on I**.

reht ڕەهت (TF/AD) = tired; worried. See **r̄e'‘t**.

rehte ڕەهتە (AD) = tired; worried. See **r̄e‘t**.

rehwan ڕەهوان (Dh/FS) = fluent. See **r̄ewan II**.

r̄eḧal ڕەحال (K) = festive clothing; trousseau. See **r̄iḧal**.

r̄eḧet ڕەحەت (B/FS) = calm; comfort. See **r̄eḧetî** & **r̄iḧet**.

r̄eḧetî ڕەحەتی *f.* **(-ya;-yê).** ease, comfort, rest, peace, tranquility: •**Nizanî, *rihetiya* canî** (L-I, #266, 224) Ignorance is bliss [lit. 'ignorance, *comfort of* the soul'] •**Dewletmendîya wan dê bîte sebebê ‘isyana wan ji dewletan. Kurdistan dê bîte cîyê şer̄ û ‘edawet û leşkirkêşîya dewlet û ‘eşîretan. Çu *r̄aḧetî* bo kes namînît** (SK 44:430) Their wealth too will be the cause of their revolting against the government. Kurdistan will become a field of battle and enmity and of manoeuvres of government and tribal armies. No *rest* will be left for anybody •**Yeqîn bizanin û bi delîl bawir biken ko meqsûd *r̄aḧet* û se‘adeta hingo ye** (SK 57:673) Know for sure and believe the evidence that their goal is your *comfort* and happiness; **-bi r̄eḧetî** (SK) in ease, at ease, peacefully: •**Eger bo me li naw Ûrosî şolekî weto çêbû, em digel milletê Kurd *bi r̄aḧetî* û serferazî li Kurdistanê r̄ûniştîn, zor baş e** (SK 48:499) If affairs are arranged for us among the Russians, so that we and the Kurdish people can settle in Kurdistan *peacefully* and with honor, well and good •**Here Îstembolê, hîç şubhe nîye ko Sultan Mecîd dê bo te me‘aşekî weto girê det ko to *bi r̄aḧetî* bijî** (SK 33:296) Go to Istanbul and without a doubt Sultan Mejid will arrange such a salary for you that you will live *in ease*. {also: r̄ahetî (K-2/JB3); r̄aḧet[î] (SK-2); rehetî (IFb); r̄eḧet (JB1-S); rihetî (L/RZ); r̄iḧetî (K); [raheti/rahatī (Rh)] راحتی (JJ); <r̄aḧet> راحەت (HH)} {syn: ḧewî} < Ar rāḥah راحة = 'rest, repose, leisure'; Sor r̄eḧetî ڕەحەتی = 'tranquility' [B/SK//IFb//JB3//L/RZ//K//JJ//HH//JB1-S] <tenahî>

r̄eḧm ڕەحم (JB1-S/JJ/HH) = mercy, pity. See **r̄eḧmet**.

r̄eḧmet ڕەحمەت *f.* **(-a;-ê).** mercy, pity, compassion; God's mercy or compassion: •**[Go carek ji cara, *reḧmet* li dê û bavê guhdara]** (PS-I, #12, 28) Once upon a time, *mercy* upon the parents of the listeners *[opening formula for folktales]* •**Hebû carek ji caran, *rehmet* li dê û bavên hazir û guhdaran, ji xeynî mar û mişkên li qulên dîwaran** (ZZ-6, 249) There was once upon a time, *mercy* upon the parents of those present and listening, except for the snakes and mice in the holes of the walls *[opening formula for folktales]*; **-çûn r̄eḧmetê** (K) to pass away, die; **-Rehmet lê be** (IFb) Mercy upon him/her *(said of one deceased)*. {also: r̄ahmet (B); r̄ehm (JB1-A)/rehm (CS-2); r̄ehmet (B-2)/rehmet (IFb/ZF/CS); r̄eḧm (JB1-S); rihme (ZZ-10); [rehm رحم/raḧmá/raḧmet رحمه] (JJ); <reḧmet رحمت/reḧm رحم> (HH)} {syn: dilovanî; dilpêvebûn; dilr̄eḧmî} <Ar raḥmah رحمة; Sor r̄eḧm ڕەحم/r̄eḧmet ڕەحمەت [PS-I/K/SK/HH//JB1-S/JJ//JB1-A//IFb/ZF/CS//B//ZZ-10]

r̄eḧmetî ڕەحمەتی *adj.* deceased, the late: •**Bavê teyî *r̄ahmetî*** (B) Your *late* father •**Ezê ... bêbextiyê li xatûna xwe ya *rihmetî* bikim** (Ardû, 172) I will ... betray my *late* wife. {also: r̄ahmetî (B); r̄ehmetî (IFb); r̄emetî (K2-Fêrîk); rihmetî (Ardû); [rahmeti] رحمتی (JJ); <reḧmetî> رحمتی (HH)} Cf. T rahmetli, Ar marḥūm مرحوم; Sor r̄eḧmetî ڕەحمەتی [K2-Fêrîk//K/HH/SK//IFb//B//JJ//Ardû] <mirin>

reḧt ڕەحت (GF/JJ/HH) = tired; worried. See **r̄e‘t**.

r̄e‘ilîn ڕەعِلین/**reilîn** ڕەئِلین [TF] *vi.* **(-re‘il-).** to quiver, shake, tremble, quake, shiver *(from fear, cold, etc.)*: •**Belê welah dora te ye! û *diri‘arê* ji tirsa** (HR 3:107) Yes, now it's your turn! and he *trembles* with fear •**Laşê wî tev ji serma *direiliya*** (DBgb, 36) His whole body *was shivering* from the cold. {also: rehilîn (IFb/ZF); ri‘arîn (HR); <re‘ilîn رعلین (dire‘ilî) (درعلی)> (HH)} {syn: ḧejîn; kil II bûn; lerzîn; r̄icifîn; r̄ikr̄ikîn} < Syr √r-‘-l ܪܥܠ = 'to vacillate, reel, quiver'; also Ar √r-h-l رهل = 'to quiver' (Hava); Sor lerîn•ewe لەرینەوە/leran•ewe لەرانەوە = 'to shake, tremble, vibrate, quiver' [HR//DBgb/TF//HH//IFb/ZF]

r̄ejî ڕەژی *f.* **(-ya;-yê).** charcoal, coal(s): **-r̄ejîya dara** (FS) do. {also: r̄ejû (K[s]-2/JB1-S/GF-2/OK); r̄eşû (GF-2); [rejou رژو/redji رجی/resciú (G)/reşú (Lx)] (JJ)} {syn: fehm II[2]}Cf. r̄eş = 'black'; Sor r̄ejû ڕەژوو = 'charcoal' [Bw/K(s)/A/IFb/GF/FS//JJ/ JB1-S/OK] <agir; p'el II; tenî>

r̄ejû ڕەژوو (K[s]/JB1-S/GF/OK) = charcoal. See **r̄ejî**.

r̄ek•e ڕەکە *f.* **(•a;•ê).** bird cage: •**Wî kew kir di**

rekehê **da** (FS) He put the partridge in the cage; -**r̄eka kewa** (Bw) cage for partridges. {also: rekeh (ZF3); rike (-ya;) (K[s]/IFb/GF-2/OK); rikew (A/IFb-2); rikke, m. (-yê;) (GF); <rikew> رکـــــــو (HH)} {syn: qefes} [Bw//K(s)/IFb/OK//A/HH//GF//ZF3/FS] <kew I>

rekeh ڕەکەھ (ZF3/FS) = bird cage. See **r̄eke**.

rekrikîn ڕەکرکین (H) = to shiver. See **r̄ikr̄ikîn**.

r̄emal ڕەمال (IFb/JJ) = fortune teller. See **r̄emildar**.

r̄emetî ڕەمەتی (K2-Fêrîk) = deceased. See **reḧmetî**.

r̄em•il ڕەمِـــل *f.* **(•la; •lê).** geomancy, fortune telling, divination: "A method of divination, widespread in the Near East. It consists of throwing cubes with designated markings [=dice] onto a board and checking the combination of marks on the cubes and on the board in a special divination book" (EP, p. 76, note 25): **•Li gor tiştê ku min di *remla* xwe de dît, boblateke mezin li pêş navçeyê me ye. Di dawîya payiza paşîn de ba û bahozek ê dest pê bike û ew ê heta sê şev û sê rojan bidome** (Ardû, 32) According to the thing that I saw in my *cubes*, a disaster is headed for our area. At the end of the fall, a powerful windstorm will start, and it will last for 3 nights and 3 days **•Rimildara *r̄imlê xwe avêtin* ... r̄imildara li r̄imlê xo mêzand** (HR 3:5-6) The fortune tellers *threw their cubes* ... they looked at their cubes [lit. 'sand']; -**r̄emlê nihêr̄în** (Z-1/EP-7) to divine, predict the future: **•Ewê jî *r̄emlê*** [sic] ***nihêr̄î bû*, wekî M. wê îro bê** (EP-7) She *divined* that M. would come today **•Wê r̄ojê Zînê *r̄emla xwe nihêr̄î*** (Z-1) On that day Zin *divined* that ... {also: r̄imil (HR); [(ilm-i) reml] علمی رمل (JJ); <remil> رمـل (HH)} < Ar raml رمـل = 'sand' --> 'ilm al-raml علـم الـرمـل = 'geomancy' [EP-7/Z-1/K/IFb/HH//JJ//HR] <fal; sêr I>

r̄emildar ڕەمِلدار/**r̄e'mildar** ڕەعمِلدار [Z-1] *m.&f.* **(-ê/;).** fortune teller, geomancer, diviner: **•Ba kire *r̄imildara*, *r̄imildara* r̄imlê xwe avêtin li dermanê çe'vê bavê wa bê ma çiye** (HR 3:5) He summoned the *fortune tellers*, they threw their cubs to find out what the cure for their father's eye would be **•Zînê *r̄e'mildar* bû** (Z-1) Zin was *a fortune teller*; -**jina r̄emildar** (K) female fortune teller. {also: r̄emal (IFb-2); remldar (Wkt); r̄imildar (HR); [remal] رمـــــال (JJ); <remildar> رملـدار (HH)} {syn: falçî; pîldar} < r̄emil + -dar = 'one who has or holds stg.', cf. Ar rammāl رمّــــال [EP-7/Z-1//K/IFb/HH/GF//Wkt//HR//JJ] <r̄emil>

remldar ڕەملدار (Wkt) = fortune teller. See **r̄emildar**.

ren ڕەن (F)/r̄e'n ڕەعن (K) = thigh. See **r̄an**.

rencber ڕەنجـبـەر (Cxn/IFb/GF/FJ) = worker, laborer. See **r̄êncber**.

r̄eng ڕەنـگ *m.* **(-ê;).** 1) {syn: gon I} color, hue; color of animal's hair or coat (B); color of person's complexion *often used as a key to one's mood*: -**hatin ser rengê xwe** (XF) to be revived, come back to life: **•Ez çawa bikim Mecrûm *bê ser rengê xwe*?** (EP-5, #19) How can I make Mejrum *come back to life*? **•*Ser rengê xwene*** (XF) They are *in good health*; -**r̄eng û r̄û** (Z-1) youth, beauty and freshness [cf. T rengübû (RTI)]; -**[bi] r̄engê ...** (K) like, similar to; 2) {syn: boyax; derman; xim} paint; dye; 3) {syn: awa; celeb I; t'eher} manner, way, fashion; 4) {syn: cins; cûr̄e; t'exlît} type, kind, sort. {also: [renk] رنـــــك (JJ); <reng> رنــگ (HH)} Cf. P rang رنــگ--> T renk; Sor r̄eng ڕەنگ = 'color, paint, form'; Za reng *m.* (Mal); Hau r̄enge *f.* (M4) [Z-1/K/A/JB3/IFb/B/HH/GF/TF//JJ] <beqem>

r̄engdêr ڕەنگدێر *f.* **(-a;-ê).** adjective, modifier: **•Çiqas ji vê *rengdêrê* hez dikin!** (nefel:H.Metê. Êş 29.vi.2005) How fond they are of this *adjective*! {syn: r̄ewş [5] (IF); xeysetnav (K/B/F)} [(neol)K(s)/JB3/IFb/GF/ZF3]

r̄engpîşe ڕەنگپیشە *f.* **(-ya;).** adverb: -**r̄engpîşên awakî** (IFb) adverbs of manner; -**~ên cihkî** (IFb) adverbs of place; -**~ên çiqasî** (IFb) adverbs of quantity; -**~ên demkî** (IF) adverbs of time; -**~ên erînî** (IFb) affirmative adverbs; -**~ên gumanî** (IFb) adverbs of doubt; -**~ên neyînî** (IFb) adverbs of negation; -**~ên pirsiyarkî** (IFb) interrogative adverbs. {syn: hoker; *nîr I[2]; zerf} [(neol)IFb/ZF3/Wkt]

r̄enî ڕەنـــــی *f.* **(-ya;-yê).** avalanche; landslide: **•Hin caran 100 leşker jî di bin *reniyê* de diman** (Wkt: A.Çiftçi. Azadiyawelat.com, xi.2009) Sometimes 100 soldiers were caught under *the avalanche*. {syn: aşît; şape I; şetele} = Sor r̄inû ڕِنـــوو [Bw/IFb/GF/OK/ZF3/Wkt/FS] <hezaz; xişîlok>

r̄enîn ڕەنین *vt.* **(-r̄en-).** to scratch, scrape; to file down; to shave, plane, level, even off, smoothe: **•Depên xwe *renîn* û maseyek jê çêkir** (Wkt) They shaved/planed/evened off their boards and made a table of them. {also: [renin] رنـيـن (JJ)} {syn: dar̄otin; t'eraştin; ver̄otin} Cf. P randīdan رنـديـدن = 'to plane, make smooth with a plane, to grate' [Bw/JJ/OK/FS/Wkt/BF/ZF3] <êge; hesûn; k'artik>

r̄ep رەپ *adj.* protruding, sticking out, erect: •**Serê gur k'ete 'erdê û dûvê wî ma *r̄ep*** (Dz) The wolf's head fell to the ground (=the wolf was knocked to the floor) and his tail remained *erect* •**Aqilê xwe ji dûwê *r̄ep* hilîna** (Dz) She learned her lesson from the *erect* tail *[prv., cf. "The lion's share"]*; **-boç'ik r̄ep bûn** (IFb) for *(an animal's)* tail to prick up; **-guh r̄ep bûn** (IFb) for one's ears to prick up. {also: <rep> رپ (HH)} {syn: bel; girj [3]; qişt; qund} Sor r̄ep رەپ = 'stiff and straight, erect' [Dz/A/IFb/HH/GF]

r̄epandin رەپاندِن *vt.* **(-r̄epîn-).** to beat up, slug (slang) (Msr); to hit, beat, strike: •***Bir̄epîne!*** (Msr) *Beat him up!* •**Min ḧebek *r̄epande*, ew tera kir 'erdê** (Msr) I *slugged him one* and knocked him to the ground. {syn: felişandin [2]; k'utan; lêdan; lêxistin} [Msr/K/IFb/B]

repisandin رەپساندِن (FS) = to irrigate. See **r̄ebisandin**.

r̄epîn رەپین *vi.* **(-r̄ep-).** to make a rapping noise, sound of hitting: •...**ku keçik bi dengê *repîna* ço hay ji wî bibe ... Piştî du sê repînên pêşîn** (Ardû, 67) ...the girl becomes aware of the *rapping sound* of the stick •***Tepîn û repîna* cendirman e bi ser gundiyan ve dikin** (Ardû, 55) It is *the hurly burly of* the soldiers on the villagers. [Ardû/K/IFb/CS]

r̄eq I رەق *m./f.(FS)* **().** 1) {syn: kûsî; şkevlatok (JB3)} turtle, zool. *Testudo*; sea turtle (Msr/HB/IF/HH) [su kaplumbağası]; 2) {syn: kevjal} *crab (Hk/K/B). {also: [raq-i âvi] رق (JJ); <req> رق (HH)} Cf. Ar raqq رَقّ = 'turtle'; also cf. Rus rak рак = 'crab' [Msr/Rh/HB/AB/A/IFb/JJ/HH/GF/TF/FS]

r̄eq II رەق *adj.* hard, solid, firm, stiff: •**Ev nan *req* bûye, nikarim bixwim** (Wkt) This bread has gotten *hard*, I can't eat it. {also: [req] رق (JJ); <req> رق (HH)} {≠nerm} [Bw/K/A/IFb/JJ/HH/SK/GF/OK/Wkt/FS] <ḧişk [2]; meḧkem>

r̄eqer̄eq رەقەرەق *f.* **(-a;-ê).** loud noise; roll of thunder, rumbling: •**Bû *r̄eqer̄eqa* wa 'ewra** (HR 3:63) *A rumbling* came from those clouds •**Wextê p'elek 'ewr wê li 'ezmana çêbê, û ji wî 'ewrî *r̄eqer̄eq* wê deng bê** (HR 3:61) When a clump of clouds appears in the sky, from those clouds [lit. 'that cloud'] *a rumbling* will be heard. {also: reqreq (A/GF/CS); <reqareq> رقارق (HH)} {syn: girmîn; gur̄e-gur̄; xumxum I[2]; xurexur} [HR/K/B/IFb//HH/A/GF/CS] <teqer̄eq>

r̄eqisîn رەقِسین *vi.* **(-r̄eqis-).** to dance: •**Mar ... r̄abû ser dûvê xwe û dest bi dîlanê kir, mar wextekî dirêj bi k'êfxweşî *r̄eqisî*** (Dz #22, 389) The snake ... got up on its tail and began dancing, the snake *danced* happily for a long time. {also: retqisîn (M); [reqysin] رقصین (JJ); <reqisîn رقسین (direqisî) (درقسی)> (HH)} {syn: govend girtin; sema kirin} < Ar √r-q-ṣ رقص = 'to dance' --> P raqṣīdan رقصیدن [Dz/K/B/IFb/JJ/HH/RZ/CS//M] <dîlan; govend; sema>

reqreq رەقرەق (A/GF/CS) = loud noise, rumble. See **r̄eqer̄eq**.

r̄esim رەسم *m./f.(K/JJ/OK)* **(-ê/-a;-î/).** 1) {syn: keval; sifat [4]; şikil; wêne} picture, photograph; drawing: •**Di wî *rismî* de Jêhat bi temenê xwe ji wê gelekî piçûktir, ciwan û bedew bû** (SBx, 21-22) In that *picture* J. was much younger in age than her, young and handsome; **-resim kirin** (Bw)/~ **çêkirin** (IFb) to draw *(a picture)*; **-resim kişandin** (IFb) to take a picture; 2) rule (SK); 3) custom, usage (JJ). {also: resm (K/IFb-2/SK/GF); risim, m. (CS); rism, m. (-ê;-î) (SBx); [resm] رسم (JJ); <resm> رسم (HH)} < Ar rasm رسم = '(a) drawing, sketch, picture, illustration, regulation, ceremony, formality'; Sor r̄esm رەسم = 'picture; formality, ceremony, fee, duty (payment)' [Bw/A/IFb/OK/RZ//K/JJ/HH/SK/GF//SBx//CS]

resm رەسم (K/IFb/JJ/HH/SK/GF) = picture; rule; custom. See **r̄esim**.

r̄esmî رەسمی *adj.* official, formal: •**Pirtûka rojnameger Nadire Mater ya bi navê "Pirtûka Memed..." li ser dîroka "*gayrî resmî* ya şer" berhemeke bêhempa ye** (AW71A2) The book of the journalist Nadire Mater called Memed's Book on the '*unofficial* history of the war' is a unique work. {syn: fermî} < Ar rasmī رسمی [K/IFb/B/SK/AD]

r̄eş رەش *adj.* 1) black: **-av[a] reş** (Hirço) coffee {syn: qawe}; **-r̄eş girêdan/wergirtin** (XF) to dress in black *(as a sign of mourning)*; to cover one's head with a black kerchief *(as a sign of mourning)*: •**Ewê û P'erî-xatûnêva *r̄eşa* Memê *girêdabûn*** (Z-1) She together with Peri-Khatun *dressed in black to mourn* Memê [young man who died prematurely]; 2) {syn: giran I; tarî} dark *(of tea, color, etc.)* (Bw); 3) black, negro; 4) [*m.* ().] {syn: qeret'û} silhouette; unclear or indistinct image, dim reflection: •***Reşek* wê ji deştê hildik'işe tê** (EP-5, #16) Something [lit. '*a black [thing]*, an unclear image'] was coming up from the plain [below]. {also: [rech] رش (JJ); <reş> رش (HH)} {r̄eşahî; r̄eşayî; r̄eşî; [rashātī] رشاتی (JJ)} Cf. P raxš رخش = 'mottled'; Sor r̄eş ڕەش = 'black, and fig. violent, disastrous, etc.' {see: **IV. Persian Etymologies** in "Varia," *Norsk Tidsskrift for Sprogvidenskap*, 12 (1942), 265} [K/A/JB3/IFb/B/JJ/HH/SK/GF/TF/Bw] <ḧemis; qemer; qer II; r̄ejî>

r̄eşad ڕەشاد *f.* **().** garden cress or garden peppergrass, bot. *Lepidium sativum*, a plant with pungent, parsley-like leaves. {also: r̄ewşat (Qzl)} {syn: dêjnik} <Ar rašād رشاد; =P šāhī شاهی & tar[reh]tîzak ترەتیزک; =Sor ter̄etîze تەڕەتیزە/ ter̄etûre تەڕەتووره [Bw/IFb/OK/CB/FS//Qzl] <kîzmas; pîz; t'ûzik>

reşahî رەشاهی (IFb/GF) = blackness. See **r̄eşayî**.

r̄eşandin ڕەشاندِن *vt.* **(-r̄eşîn-).** to sprinkle, scatter *(grain)*, sow; to sprinkle here and there in small quantities (A): **•Ewê nêzîkaya k'ûpê r̄ûn k'ulme dudu ar ser 'erdê *r̄eşand*** (Dz-anec #32) Near the butter jug she *sprinkled* on the ground a handful or two of flour **•Polîsan gaza rondikrêj li xelkê *reşand*** (Hk) The police *sprayed* tear gas on the people **•Şerîfo Teker erd û ezman bi sûndên qelew û jidil *direşandin*** (HYma 48) S.T. *sprayed* earth and heaven with thick and heartfelt oaths; **-t'op r̄eşandin** (EP-8) to spray or rain bullets. {also: [rechandin] رشاندين (JJ); <reşandin رشاندن (direşêne) (دِرشينه)> (HH)} {syn: werkirin[3]} Cf. Ar rašša رشّ = 'to spray'; *etymology of A&L (preverb *r̄e- + şandin) is incorrect* [J/M/K/A/JB3/IFb/B/JJ/HH/SK/GF/OK/ZF] <barandin>

r̄eşatî ڕەشاتی (JJ/SK) = blackness. See **r̄eşayî**.

r̄eşaẍayî ڕەشاغایی *adj.* pattern of **bergûz** material: light black (r̄eşekê vebûyî). [Bw] <bergûz>

r̄eşayî ڕەشایی *f.* **(-ya;-yê).** 1) blackness; 2) {syn: qeret'û} indistinct figure, silhouette: **•Wextê ku teyra Sîmir̄ ç'e'v bi *r̄eşaîyê* k'et kû li binê darê, go: Hebê nebê, îsal ḧeft sal e ev *r̄eşîya*** [sic] **ha ç'êlîê mi dixwê** (HR 3:246) When the Simurgh bird caught sight of *the figure* at the bottom of the tree, she said, "Say what you will, this year is 7 years that this *figure* here has been eating my chicks"; 3) {syn: bej} land, dry land, ground (K/IFb/GF). {also: r̄eşahî (IFb-2/GF-2); r̄eşatî (SK); r̄eşî (K/A/IFb-2); [rashātī] رشاتی (JJ)} [Cf. T kara = 1) 'black'; 2) 'land' (<Ar qārrah قارّة = 'continent')] [K/A/IFb/B/GF//JJ/SK] <r̄eş>

r̄eşbîn ڕەشبین *m.&f.* **().** 1) pessimist; 2) [*adj.*] pessimistic. Sor r̄eşbîn ڕەشبین {r̄eşbînî} [GF/OK/RZ/ZF3] <≠geşbîn>

r̄eşbînî ڕەشبینی *f.* **(-ya;-yê).** pessimism: **•Ev ne dema *reşbînîyê* ye** (VoA 18.iii.2011) This is no time for *pessimism*. [GF/OK/ZF3/Wkt] <r̄eşbîn>

r̄eşe ڕەشە *f./m.(CS/FS)* **(/-yê;).** 1) {syn: batirsok} scarecrow; 2) {syn: qeret'û; sawîr} ghost, spectre: **•*Reşek* ji bo dewaran çê bibû, lewra revîn** (BF) *A ghost* appeared to the cattle, so they fled. {also: reşek (FJ/GF)} [CCG/IFb/ZF/CS/Wkt/BF/FD/FS//FJ/GF]

reşek ڕەشەک (FJ/GF) = scarecrow; ghost. See **r̄eşe**.

r̄eşel ڕەشەل (F) = starling. See **r̄eşêlek**.

R̄eşemî ڕەشەمی. Sorani name [R̄eşemê ڕەشەمێ] for Persian month of *Esfend* اسفند [Pisces] (Feb. 19-March 20). See chart of Kurdish months in this volume. <Sibat; Adar>

r̄eşeve•hatin ڕەشەڤەهاتِن *vi.* **(r̄eşeve[t]ê-).** to become or get dark, blacken *(vi.)*: **•Ç'avê min *r̄eşevehatin*** (K) My eyes *got dark*/It got dark before my eyes (lit. & fig.) **•Ç'e'vê wî *r̄eşevehatin* û ew cîbicî k'et** (Z-1) It *got dark* before him and he fell over right then and there **•Ḧemû tişt ber ç'e'vê min *r̄eşevehatin*** (B) Everything *went black* before my eyes. [Z-1/K/B] <r̄eş; t'arî>

r̄eşêle ڕەشێلە (A/IFb/GF/ZF3/Wkt) = starling. See **r̄eşêlek**.

r̄eşêlek ڕەشێلەک *f.* **(;-ê).** starling, zool. *Sturnus vulgaris*: **•Paşî ko nîwa hewya Şewatê hat, *r̄eşwêle* peyda bû. Xulamek çust hat, got e mîr, "Mizgînî li mîr, *r̄eşwêle* hat, ewe bihar nêzîk bû"** (SK 29:262) After half the month of February had passed *the starling* appeared. A servant came quickly and said to the Mir, "Good news for the Mir. *The starling* has come and spring is near." {also: r̄eşel (F); r̄eşêle (A/IFb/GF/ZF3/Wkt); r̄eşhêle (K/B); r̄eşwêle (SK/FS); [rechilé رشیله/ rashwēl رشویل] (JJ); <reşêle> رشیله (HH)} {syn: alik; garanîk; zerzûr} [Wn//K/B//A/IFb/HH/GF/ZF3/Wkt//F//JJ//SK/FS]

reşêş ڕەشێش *f.* **(-a;).** sprinkle of rain, light rain, drizzle: **•Ew bayê hênik î ku piştî *reşêşkên* baranê bêhna axê jê difûriya** (SBx, 13) That light breeze, from which the smell of earth wafts after *light sprinkles of* rain. {also: raş (TF); reşêşk (SBx/CS); reşiş (Kmc-2); rişêşk (Kmc); [rechiché] رشیشه (JJ); <reşîş> رشیش (HH)} < Ar raššah رشّة = 'light drizzle' & rašāš رشاش = 'drizzle, spray, spattered liquid' [SBx/CS//A/IFb] <baran>

reşêşk رهشـێـشـك (SBx/CS) = sprinkle, light rain. See **reşêş**.

r̄eşhêle ڕهشهێله (K/B) = starling. See **r̄eşêlek**.

r̄eşik I ڕهشِـــــــك *f.* **(-a;-ê).** pupil *(of the eye)*: **-r̄eşika ç'avan** (K)/~**ç'e'va** (F) do. {syn: bibiq} [K/IFb/B/GF/TF/FS] <ç'av>

r̄eşik II ڕهشِـــــــك *f.* **(-a;).** moccasins made of animal (goat) skin. {also: [rechik/rescek (G)] رشـــك (JJ); <reşik> رشـــــــك (HH)} [Bw/IFb/JJ/HH/GF/OK/FS] <k'alik II; p'êlav; sol>

r̄eş•ik III ڕهشِـــــــك *f.* **(•ka;).** black caraway, black cumin, bot. *Nigella sativa.* {also: reşreşik (IFb-2); reşreşk (OK-2/FS); [räšík] رشـــك (JJ)} Sor r̄eşke ڕهشكه [Zeb/K/A/IFb/JJ/OK//FS] <şembelûle; zîre>

reşiş رهشِش (Kmc) = sprinkle, light rain. See **reşêş**.

r̄eşî ڕهشی (K/A/IFb) = blackness. See **r̄eşayî**.

r̄eşkot ڕهشـكـوت *m.* **().** 1) brunette (K); 2) {also: [3] Reşkotan (IFb); <reşkotan> رشـكـوتـان (HH)} a Yezidi tribe living in the province of Diyarbakır in Kurdistan of Turkey; one of the Beshiri tribes (HH). [Z-2/K//IFb/HH] <kej I>

R̄eşkotan ڕهشـكـۆتـان (IFb/HH) = Yezidi tribe living in the province of Diyarbakır in Kurdistan of Turkey. See **r̄eşkot** [3].

r̄eşmal ڕهشـمـال *f./m.(FS)* **(-a/;-ê/).** tent made of black goat hair: **•Hawînê keşkêt wan li serbanêt *r̄eşmalan* o keprokan o xanîyan dir̄ewêm, dixom** (SK 1:3) In summer I snatch their buttermilk, (drying) on the roofs of *tents* and bough-huts and houses, and eat it. {also: [rash-māl] رشــمـال (JJ-Rh)} {syn: çadir; kon; xêvet} [SK/K/JJ-Rh/GF/OK/FS/ZF3]

reşme رهشمه (GF/JJ/FS) = chain; halter. See **r̄işme**.

reşreşik رهشـرهشِـك (IFb) = black caraway. See **r̄eşik III**.

reşreşk رهشرهشك (OK/FS) = black caraway. See **r̄eşik III**.

r̄eşû ڕهشوو (GF) = charcoal. See **r̄ejî**.

r̄eşwêle ڕهشوێله (SK/FS) = starling. See **r̄eşêlek**.

r̄et I: r̄et bûn ڕهت بـــــــوون (Z-3) = to be used up; to vanish. See **r̄ed**: **-r̄ed bûn**.

r̄e't II ڕهعـت *adj.* 1) tired, weary, fatigued; "bushed," "pooped": **-r̄e't bûn** (Frq)/**r̄eḧt bûn** (HH): a) to be tired {syn: betilîn; qefilîn [2]; westîn}; b) to be worried; **-r̄eḧt kirin** (GF/HH): a) to tire s.o. out; b) to worry s.o.; 2) {syn: kovan; xemxwer; zeḧmetk'êş} worried, concerned, anxious (GF/TF). {also: reht (TF/AD); rehte (AD-2); reḧt (GF-2); [reht رحت/rehti رحتی] (JJ); <reḧt> رحت (HH)} [Frq/GF//JJ/HH//TF/AD]

retem رهتهم (FS) = mud. See **r̄iṯam**.

retim رهتِم (FS) = mud. See **r̄iṯam**.

retqisîn رهتقِسین (M) = to dance. See **r̄eqisîn**.

r̄evandin ڕهڤانـدِن *vt.* **(-r̄evîn-).** 1) to vanquish, defeat; 2) to kidnap, abduct, hijack: **•Emê hev dû *birevînin*** (L) Let's run away together [lit. 'We'll *kidnap* one another']; 3) to drive away, chase away, cause to flee, put to flight: **•Mêş dihatin e dew, çaw, difnêt Silêman. Hirçê jî baweşîn dikir o mêş *dir̄ewandin*** (SK 10:98) Flies came on Sulaiman's mouth and eyes and nose. The bear *was* fanning him and *driving away* the flies. {also: r̄ewandin (SK); [rewandin] رڤـــانــــديـــــن (JJ); <revandin رڤاندن (direvîne) (درڤينه)> (HH)} Sor r̄ewandin ڕهوانـــــدن = 'to scare away, drive away, disperse', cf. also r̄ifandin ڕِفـــانـــدِن & fir̄andin فِـڕانـدِن = 'to snatch, wrench, wrest away; kidnap' [K/A/JB3/IFb/B/JJ/HH/GF//SK]

reve رهڤه (GF) = herd of horses. See **r̄evo**.

r̄evend ڕهڤـــهنـــد *m.* **(-ê;).** nomadic "caravan," i.e., entire clan when it migrates from winter to summer pasture, or vice versa *{cf. **karwan**, which moves merchandise for business purposes}*: **•Ḧetta sala pêrar jî do nêçîrwanêt wan kerek li şûn malêt Herkî *r̄ewend* li çolî dîtinewe** [sic] (SK 25:231) For even the year before last, two of their huntsmen found a donkey in the wilderness, in the tracks of some *nomadic* Harki households. {also: r̄ewend (SK); [revend/ravénd (G/Lx)] روند (JJ)} Cf. P ravande رونــــــــــده = 'goer, wayfarer, traveler' < raftan رفـــتـــن (rav- رو) = 'to go'; Sor r̄ewend ڕهوهنـــــــــد = 'nomad(ic)' [Zeb/FS//JJ/SK] <karwan>

r̄eve-r̄ev ڕهڤه ڕهڤ/**r̄ever̄ev** ڕهڤهڕهڤ [B] *adv.* swiftly, speedily, quickly; on the double: **•Eh, çi difikire, bira ji xwer̄a bifikire, --min got û alîyê k'ûçê ç'epêr̄a *reve-rev* çûm** (K2-Fêrîk) "Oh, let him think whatever he wants!" I said and *quickly* took a left turn down the street. [K2-Fêrîk/F/K/B/ZF3] <r̄evîn; zû>

r̄evî I ڕهڤـــــی *m.* **().** fugitive, runaway; deserter. {syn: firar; qaçax} [F/K/GF/ZF3]

r̄evî II ڕهڤی (IFb/HH) = herd of horses. See **r̄evo**.

r̄evîn ڕهڤـــیـــن *vi.* **(-r̄ev-).** 1) to run, speed: **•Mirovê tirsonek weke bayê *reviya* û çû xwe di pişt**

latekî de veşart (AW69B8) The cowardly man *ran* like the wind and went and hid behind a rock; 2) to run away, flee, escape; to be defeated: **•Dema ew pisîk wekî kûçikan bihewte, ew pisîkên din wê *birevin* û wê her yek bi cihekî ve bibezin û belav bibin** (AW69B8) When that cat barks like a dog, those other cats will *scamper* and run every which way **•[Weku şeřê Rom û Îranê li deşta Aleşkerê bûyî ordûya Romê *revî* û belav bûyî]** (JR #39,120) When the Turco-Iranian war took place on the plain of Eleşkirt, the Turkish army *was routed* and dispersed. {also: [rewin] رڤـــيـــن (JJ); <revîn رڤـيـن (direve) (درڤـه)> (HH)} Cf. P ramīdan رمـــيـــدن = 'to shy (of horses)'; Sor řewîn ڕەویـن; Za remenã [remayiş] (Todd/Srk) = 'to flee, run away'; Hau řemay (řem-) *vi.* = 'to run' (M4) [K/JB3/IFb/B/JJ/HH/JB1-A/GF/RZ]

řevîvan ڕەڤیڤان (HH/GF) = horse herder. See **řevoçî**.

řevo ڕەڤـــۆ *m./f.(B)* **(-ê/; /-ê).** herd *(of horses, mules, reindeer, etc.)* left to forage in the mountains: **•'Elî bi xwe yî Celalî bû; beyt'erê şah bû, hespê şah, miĥînê, *revoê* şah dibir ber Ayẍir golê diç'êrand** (K'oroẍlî, 141) Ali was a Jalali; he was the king's veterinarian, he took the king's horses, his mares, the king's *herd of horses* to graze by Lake Ayghir. {also: reve (GF); řevî II (IFb-2); [rewou] رڤـــــو (JJ); <revo رڤو/revî رڤـى> (HH)} {syn: îrxî; qefle I} Mid P ram(ag) = 'herd, flock' (M3); P rame رمـه = 'herd, flock'; Sor řewe ڕەوە = 'flock, troop' [K/IFb/HH/B//JJ//GF] <hesp; kerî II; řef I; ẍar>

řevoçî ڕەڤـۆچـی *m.* **(-ê;).** horse herder, horseherd, one in charge of caring for a herd of horses, mules, etc.: **•Şah gazî 'Elî kir, go: --Kuřo, 'Elî, tu beyt'erê minî, dêmek tu *revoçîê* minî, tu sibê du ce'nûê t'emiz rind layqlî, hevsara têxî sêrî, ber dergê min hazirbe** (K'oroẍlî 141) The king summoned Ali and said, "Boy, Ali, you're my veterinarian, that means you're my *horseherd*. Tomorrow ready 2 fine colts, put halters on their heads, and bring them to before my gate" {also: revîvan (GF); řevovan (IFb); [rewoudji] رڤـــوجـــى (JJ); <revîvan> رڤـيـڤـان (HH)} {syn: îrxîçî; seyîs} [Z-1/EP-8/K//JJ//IFb//HH/GF] <gavan; hesp; řevo; selwan>

řevovan ڕەڤۆڤان (IFb) = horse herder. See **řevoçî**.

řew ڕەو (B) = hunting; game. See **řav I**.

řewa I ڕەوا *adj.* legitimate, lawful, licit; permissible, admissible, allowable; fair, just, equitable; suitable, befitting: **•Ger kurd bibin yek, tu kes û hêz nikare têkoşîna wan ya *rewa* û mafdar rawestîne** (AW74A3) If the Kurds unite, no person or force can stop their *legitimate* and just struggle. Cf. P revā روا = 'allowable, permissible, legal'; Sor řewa ڕەوا = 'permissible' [K/IFb/GF/TF/OK]

Řewan I ڕەوان *f.* **().** Erevan, capital of Soviet Armenia. {also: Êrêvan (Ba2); [revan] روان (JJ)} Cf. Arm Erewan Երևան, T Revan [K/A/IF/JJ//Ba2]

řewan II ڕەوان *adj.* fluent, flowing: **•Zarokên Kurdan li xerîbiyê çend pêtir bi Kurdî baxivin, Kurdiya wan dê bi hêztir bikeve û ew dê bi Kurdî *rehwantir* û zîrektir bin** (Zimanê Kurdî, E. Darvin, 24.12.2012) The more Kurdish children in the diaspora speak Kurdish, the stronger their Kurdish will become and they will be *more fluent* and more clever in Kurdish. {also: rehwan (Dh/FS = Zimanê Kurdî, E. Darvin, 24.12.2012)} Cf. Ar rahwān رهوان = 'ambler (horse)' [Dh/FS//K/GF/ZF/SS]

řewandin ڕەوانـدِن (SK) = to defeat; to kidnap; to drive away. See **řevandin**.

***řewaq** ڕەواق *f.* **(;-ê).** 1) arch, vault; 2) portico; 3) {syn: kon; xêvet} tent; 4) {syn: palkon (EP-7); telar; yazliẍ} balcony (EP-7); hipped roof; 5) penthouse: **-k'oşk û řewaq** (EP-7) do.; 6) veil; curtain; tent flap. {also: [revaq] رواق (JJ)} < Ar riwāq رواق = 'tent; tent flap; curtain' [EP-7/K/A/IFb/JJ]

řewas ڕەواس (K) = rhubarb. See **řibês**.

řewayet ڕەوایەت (K) = account, story. See **řiwayet**.

řewend ڕەوەند (SK) = caravan. See **řevend**.

řewir ڕەوِر (Frq/Msr/F) = small wild animal. See **řawir**.

rewisandin ڕەوِســــــــانـــدِن (GF) = to irrigate. See **řebisandin**.

řewişt ڕەوِشـت *f.* **(-a;-ê).** 1) {syn: exlaq; sinçî} ethics, morals; 2) {syn: 'adet; kevneşop; tîtal; t'oře} custom, usage: **•Ji *rewişt* û tîtalên Kurdewarî** (M.H. Binavî. Ji rewişt û tîtalên Kurdewarî) From traditional Kurdish *customs* and usages **•We ye xudê her tiştî dişêt biket, emma tiştê muẍayirî 'adet hemî wexta naket, da nizam o *řewişta* dunyaê têk-neçît** (SK 9:93) It is so, that God can do everything, but He does not always do extraordinary things lest the order and *course* of the world be destroyed; 3) character, temper, natural disposition. Sor řewişt ڕەوِشــــــــــــت = 'character, temper, natural disposition; behavior, conduct' [SK/K(s)/A/IFb/FJ/GF/TF/ZF/RZ/CS/FD/BF]

řewîn ڕەوین (M-Ak/SK) = to bark. See **řeyîn I**.

r̄ewş رەوش *f.* **(-a;-ê).** 1) shine, light, brightness, brilliance; 2) {syn: dest û dar; ḧal; ḧewal; kawdan} situation, condition: **•Di nav vê rewşa nebaş da** (Ber) in this bad situation; 3) {syn: awa[2]} grammatical case: **-rewşa banglêkirinê** (TaRK) vocative case; **-rewşa tewandî** (TaRK) objective case; **-rewşa xwerû** (TaRK) direct case; 4) type, style, manner (HH/JJ). {also: [revich] روش (JJ); <rewş> روش (HH)} [K/A/JB3/IFb/B/HH/ZF//JJ]

r̄ewşat رەوشات (Qzl) = garden cress. See **r̄eşad**.

r̄ewşen رەوشەن *adj.* clear, bright. {also: [raouchan] روشن (JJ)} {syn: geş; r̄on I/r̄ohnî I} < P rōšan روشن [K/A/JB3/IFb/JJ/GF/TF] <biriqok; r̄on I>

r̄ewşenbîr رەوشەنبیر m.&f. (). intellectual, scholar: **•Bi taybetî Celadet Bedirxan û gelek ronakbîrên Kurd .. roleke mezin lîstin** (Ber) Especially Djeladet Bedirkhan and several Kurdish intellectuals played a major role **•Ew bi xwe bi van çîrokên xwe, van rewşenbîran, bi awayekî îronîk rexne dike** (Wlt 1:39, 11) With these stories of his, he himself is criticizing these intellectuals in an ironic manner. {also: ronakbîr (Ber); roşinbîr (Nbh)} Cf. P rōšanfekr روشنفکر; Sor r̄oşinbîr ڕۆشنبیر = 'enlightened (EM)' {r̄ewşenbîr[t]î} [(neol)Wlt/IFb/GF/TF//Nbh//Ber]

r̄ewşenbîrî رەوشەنبیری (GF/ZF3) = intelligentsia. See **r̄ewşenbîrtî**.

r̄ewşenbîrtî رەوشەنبیرتی *f.* **(-ya;-yê).** intelligentsia; intellectuality, being an intellectual: **•Çend gotin li ser "Kevoka Spî" û *rewşenbîrtîyê*** (Wlt 1:39, 11) A few words about [the new book] "The White Dove" and *the intelligentsia*. {also: r̄ewşenbîrî (GF/ZF3)} [(neol)Wlt//GF/ZF3] <r̄ewşenbîr>

rewt رەوت (A) = wooden pole. See **r̄ot**.

r̄ex I رەخ *m.* **(-ê;).** 1) {syn: alî; hêl II; teref} side; direction: **•Ezê çim nêçîrê *r̄exê* r̄ojhelatê** (M-Zx #749, 348) I shall go hunting on the eastern *side*; 2) [*prep.*] {syn: bal I; cem; hinda I; ḧafa [*see* ḧaf]; lalê; li def (Bw); nik I} next to, beside, at the house of [Fr chez/Germ bei]: **•Were *rex* min rûne** (BX) Come sit *next to* me **•*r̄ex hev*** (BX) *side by side* **•Aşvanê te r̄abû, *rex* r̄ûvîê xwe k'et** (J) Your miller got up, went *over to* his fox **•Du r̂êwî *r̄ex* gomekê derbaz dibûn** (Dz) Two travelers were passing *by* an animal pen; **-bi rex ... ve** (FS) do.: **•Ew *bi rex* Azadî *ve* rûnişt** (FS) He sat down beside A. {also: [rekh/rakh] رخ (JJ); <rex> رخ (HH)} [Dz/BX/F/J/K/A/JB3/IFb/B/JJ/HH/JB1-A&S/SK/GF/TF/OK/FS]

r̄ex II رەخ *m./f.* **(; /-ê).** (chess) castle, rook. {also: <rex> رخ (HH)} [K/A/IFb/B/HH/ZF3] <k'işik; şetrenc>

rexder رەخدەر (ZF3) = door frame. See **r̄exderî**.

r̄exderî رەخدەری *m.(Rwn/K/ZF3)/f.(B)* **(; /-yê).** door frame, door post. {also: rexder (ZF3)} [Rwn/K/B//ZF3] <derî I; serder; sîvande>

r̄exma رەخما (JB3/ZF3) = in spite of. See **r̄eẍme**.

r̄exne رەخنە *f.* **(-ya;-yê).** criticism: **•Divê mirov ji *rexneyan* netirse. Dost *rexne* jî li hev *digrin*, çewtiyên hev jî ji hevûdin re dibêjin** (Wlt 1:20, 3) One must not be afraid of *criticism*. Friends both *criticize* one another, and tell each other about their [=the other's] mistakes **•Program û livbaziyên (lebatên) HEP'ê dikarin bibin mijarên *rexneyê*** (Wlt 1:43, 9) The programs and activities of HEP can be the subject (or, object) of *criticism*; **-r̄exne girtin** (Wlt)/~**kirin** (IFb/TF) to criticize. {also: reẍne (GF)} <Sor r̄exne ڕەخنە/ r̄eẍne ڕەغنە = 'criticism (EM)'; cf. P raxne رخنه = 'slit, crack, chink' [(neol)Wlt/K(s)/A/IFb/TF/OK/RZ/ZF//GF]

r̄exnegir رەخنەگر *m.&f.* **(-e/ ;).** critic: **•Ji destpêka nivîsandina romanê heta dawî, *rexnegirê* Kurd ... ez tenê nehîştim** (Mîr Qasimlo. Dilya & Zalar, 6) From the start of writing the novel until the end, the Kurdish *critic* ... did not abandon me **•Lê *r̄exnegir* birêz Omerî xwezî li ser van isbatên min rawestiyaba** (Nbh 125:52) But if only the *critic* Mr. O. had looked into these arguments [lit. 'proofs'] of mine. < r̄exne + -gir; Sor r̄exnegir ڕەخنەگر [Nbh/ZF/CS]

r̄ext رەخت *m./f.(B)* **(-ê/ ; /-ê).** 1) {syn: ç'ek; zirx} coat of mail, armor; 2) cartridge belt; 3) {syn: hevsar; r̄işme} harness; silver bridle-harness, an ornament hung on a horse's head (JJ); ornament put on a horse's chest (HH): **-r̄ext û r̄işme** (Z-1)/**r̄ext û t'axim** (K) harness (and bridle) of horse; 4) woman's chest ornaments consisting of silver and gold coins. {also: [rekht] رخت (JJ); <rext> رخت (HH)} [Z-1/K/A/IFb/B/JJ/HH/GF] <bejn>

r̄ex û çan رەخ و چان (Zeb) = circumference. See **ç'ar rex**.

r̄ex û çar رەخ و چار (Hk) = circumference. See **ç'ar rex**.

r̄eẍme رەغمە *prep.* in spite of, despite: **•*ji rexma* wî *re*** (ZF3) *in spite of* him **•Meşa Hewlêrê *li rexmê* astengiyan jî destpêkir** (RojNews) The Arbil

March began *in spite of* the obstacles •***Rexmê* van hemû planan jî** (amidakurd.net 18.iv.2017) *In spite of* all these plans; **-rexma ko** (JB3) although. {also: rexma (JB3/ZF3)} {syn: digel [2]; dijî [2]; gir III} < Ar raγman رغما [BX/(K)//JB3/ZF3]

reẍne رەغنە (GF) = criticism. See **r̄exne**.

reyhan رەیهان (FJ) = sweet basil. See **r̄iḧan**.

r̄eyîn I ڕەيـيـن *vi.* **(-r̄ey-).** 1) {syn: 'ewtîn; kastekast kirin} to bark *(of dogs)*: •**Seh *dir̄aye*, karwan dibihore** (Dz #1400) The dog *barks*, the caravan passes *[prv.]*; 2) [*f.* **(-a;-ê).**] {syn: bile-bil [1]; 'ewte'ewt; kastekast; kute-kut} barking (of dogs): •**Kûçik hişyar ma û berbî nîvê şevê dest bi *reyînê* kir** (hindik-rindik 4.ii.2011) The dog stayed awake and towards midnight started *barking*. {also: r̄ewîn (M-Ak/SK); riyîn (IFb-2); [réin] ريـن (JJ); <reyîn ريين (direyî) (دريى)> (HH)} [Pok. 3. rei-/rē(i)- 859.] 'to cry, roar, bark' & [Pok. I. lā-/lē- 650.] *(onomato-poetic)*: Skt rā́yati = 'barks'; O Ir *rāya- = 'to cry': Sgd rāy- = 'to weep'; Wakhi rɯy- = 'to howl'; Oss räiun/räin = 'to bark'; Sor wer̄în وەڕيـن = 'to bark'; cf. Av gāθra-rayant; Khotanese Saka rai<ndä> = 'they cry aloud'. See: M. Schwartz. "Irano-tocharica," in: *Mémorial Jean de Menasce*, ed. Ph. Gignoux & A. Tafazzoli (Louvain: Imprimerie Orientaliste : fondation Culturelle Iranienne, 1974), p. [399]. [K/JB3/IFb/HH/GF//M-Ak//JJ] <kûzkûz; lûrîn>

r̄eyîn II ڕەيين (-r̄ey-) (IFb) = to defecate. See **r̄îtin**.

r̄ez ڕەز *m.* **(-ê;-î).** vineyard, orchard: •**Dibêjin carekê sê kes çûne karwanî ... geheştine *r̄ezekî* dûr ji gundî. Dewarêt wan birsî bûbûn, ew jî mandî bûbûn ... wan her sê dewar berdane naw *rezî*, gya û zira'et dixarin û wan jî fêqî xarin** (SK 8:78) They say that three men once went on a caravan … they arrived at *an orchard* far from a village. Their beasts had become hungry, and they themselves tired … They all three set their beasts loose *in the orchard*, where they grazed on the grass and the crops, and they themselves ate the fruit. {also: r̄êzom, f. (JB3-2); [rez] رز (JJ); <rez> رز (HH)} Cf. Mid P raz = 'vine, vineyard' (M3); P raz رز = 'vineyard'; Sor r̄ez ڕەز; Za rez *m.* (Mal) [BX/K/A/JB3/IFb/B/JJ/HH/SK/JB1-A/GF/OK] <gûşî; mewîj; mêw; tirî>

R̄ezber ڕەزبـەر. A Sorani name for Persian month of *Mehr* مـهـر [Libra] (Sept. 23-Oct. 22). See chart of Kurdish months in this volume. <Îlon; Çirîya Pêşîn>

r̄ezewan ڕەزەوان (SK) = vintner, gardener. See **r̄ezvan**.

r̄ezvan ڕەزڤـان *m.* **(-ê;).** 1) wine-grower, vintner; 2) caretaker or guard of vineyard; 3) {syn: baẍvan; cenan} gardener (B). {also: r̄ezewan (SK); [rez-van] رزوان (JJ); <rezvan> رزڤـــان (HH)} Sor r̄ezewan ڕەزەوان = 'vine-dresser' [K/A/JB3/IFb/B/HH/GF//JJ//SK] <r̄ez>

r̄ê ڕێ *f.* **(r̄îya/r̄eya/r̄iya/r̄êya; r̄êyê).** way, road: •***R̄ê reya* mirinê be jî, tu her li pêş be** (BX) Even if *the road* is *the road to* death, always be first [lit. 'at the front'] *[prv.]* •***R̄êva* r̄astî kalekî tê** (Dz) *On the way* he comes across an old man •***R̄iya* rast, *riya* evîna welat e** (AB) The right *way* is *the way* of loving the country; **-bi r̄ê ve çûn/r̄ê çûn** (B) to walk, go: •**Pîrejinek di kûçeke Londrê de *bi rê ve diçû*** (Ronahî) An old woman *was walking* in a London street •**Ew ze'f zû *r̄ê diçe*** (B) He *walks* very quick-ly; **-bi r̄êvaçûna k'ûsî r̄ê çûn** (XF) to go at a snail's pace, to move very slowly; **-ne li r̄ê dîtin** (XF) to consider improper, unfair or inappropriate: •**Lê teyrine mayî ew ferman[a] ha *ne li r̄ê dîtin*** [sic] (SW-1) But other birds *considered* this order *unfair*; **-r̄ê jê dernexistin** (XF) to be unable to find a way out of a situation, not to know which way to turn: •**M. gelekî şaş û ḧeyrî ma, t'u *r̄ê jê dernexist*** (EP-7) M. was perplexed and bewildered, he *didn't know what to do next*; **-[bi] r̄ê k'etin** (Z-1/ZF3) to set out (on a trip), hit the road (See also **r̄êkk'etin**): •**Memê *wê* sibê *r̄ê k'eve*** (Z-1) Mem *will set out* tomorrow; **-r̄ê kirin** = to see s.o. off, escort; to send. See **r̄êkirin**; **-r̄îya *fk-ê, ft-î* k'işandin** (XF) to wait for s.o., stg.: •**Me gele wext *rîa* apê Şevav *k'işand*** (Ba2-4, 222) We *waited for* Uncle Shavav for a long time; **-r̄ê lê girtin**. See **r̄êlêgirtin**; **-r̄ê xweş kirin** (VoA/ZF3) to facilitate, set the stage for, prepare the way for. {also: r̄êk (SK-2); [ri] رى (JJ); <rê> رى (HH)} {syn: dirb I} [Pok. ret(h) 866.] 'to run, roll' & [Pok. roto- 866.] 'wheel': Skt ratha- *m.* = 'carriage'; Av & O P raθa- = 'wagon' & Av raiθya- = 'road'; P rāh راه; Sor r̄ê ڕێ/r̄êga ڕێگا/r̄êge ڕێگە; Za ray *f.* (Mal/Todd); Hau r̄a *f.* (M4); cf. also Lat rota = 'wheel' [F/K/A/JB3/IFb/B/HH/SK/JB1-A&S/GF/TF/OK/ZF3//JJ] <bêrê; kolan II; kûçe; zikak>

r̄êbaz ڕێبـــاز *f.* **(-a;-ê).** method; procedure; policy: •**Dewlet çi dixwaze, ew tê weşandin. Dewlet çi**

difikire, ew tê parastin. Çapemeniya ku li dijî wan *rêbazan* derkeve, li dijî rejîmê tê qebûlkirin (AW71D2) Whatever the state wants, gets published. Whatever the state thinks, gets protected. If the press comes out against those *policies*, it is considered to be against the regime **•Gelo welatên ku ji sedî yeka *rêbazên* gerdûnî yên mafên mirovan û ewlekariya canê mirovan neparastibin, dikarin xwe wekî "abîdeya demokrasiyê" nîşan bidin?** (AW72C2) Can countries which have not observed even one percent of the universal *procedures* for human rights and security call themselves "a shrine of democracy"? **•KT'ê li dijî kurdan û PKK'ê her *rêbaz* ceriband** (AW77C2) Turkey has tried every *method* against the Kurds and the PKK. Sor r̄êbaz ڕێباز = 'way through, passage, procedure, way of life; policy, principle' [(neol)AW/IFb/OK/AD/ZF3]

R̄êbendan ڕێبەندان. Sorani name for Persian month of *Bahman* بهمن [Aquarius] (Jan. 20-Feb. 18). See chart of Kurdish months in this volume. <Kanûna Paşîn; Sibat>

r̄êber ڕێبەر *m.&f.* **(-ê/ ;).** 1) {syn: beled II; r̄êzan} guide; 2) {syn: pêşeng; r̄êzan; serek; serok; serwer} leader; 3) {syn: r̄êwî} traveler (B); 4) [*f.* **(-a;-ê).**] guidebook, handbook, manual. {also: rayber (IF-2); r̄ehber (B)} Cf. P rahbar رهبر --> T rehber {r̄êberî} [K/A/JB3/IFb/GF/TF/OK/FS//B]

r̄êberî ڕێبەری *f.* **(-ya;-yê).** guidance, leadership: **•...Eger keşkele bît şarezakarê qewmî, *dê r̄êberîya* wan *ket* bo r̄êkêt helakî** (SK 4:43) If the magpie becomes the guide of a people, he *will lead* them along the roads of destruction. Sor r̄êberayetî ڕێبەرایەتی [SK/K/IFb/GF/TF/OK] <r̄êber>

r̄êbir̄ ڕێبِڕ *m.* **().** bandit, brigand, highwayman. {also: [ri-bir] ریبر (JJ); <rêbir/rêber> ریبر (HH)} {syn: ħerebaşî; k'eleş II; nijdevan} < r̄ê = 'road' + bir̄- = 'to cut' {r̄êbir̄î} [JR/K/A/JB3/IFb/B/HH/GF/OK/ZF3/BF//JJ] <diz>

r̄êbir̄î ڕێبڕی *f.* **(-ya;-yê).** brigandage, banditry, highway robbery: **•Wan zarokan ji texmîna me gelek zûtir dest bi karên *rêbirîyê...* kir** (lotikxane.com 6.viii.2010) Those children began acts of *banditry* much earlier than we expected. {also: [ribiri] ریبری (JJ)} {syn: k'eleşî; nijdevanî} [K/GF/ZF3//JJ] <r̄êbir̄>

r̄êç I ڕێچ: **-r̄êç kirin** (Slm/A) to sweep off, scrape *(snow, animal pen)*: **•Keyê gundê me ... li ser pişta xaniyê xwe berf li gel azepê xwe *rêçdikir*** (Cankurd:RN2 56[1998] 11) The head of our village ... was on the roof of his house *sweeping off* the snow with his unmarried [son]. {also: rêj kirin (Qrj); r̄êş II kirin (Krş/Mzg); [retch kirin] رچ کرین (JJ)} {syn: gêzî kirin; maliştin} [Slm/Cankurd/A//JJ/Krş/Mzg//Qrj] <verotin>

r̄êç' II ڕێچ *f.* **(-a;-ê).** 1) {syn: dews [2]; şop} trace, track: **-r̄êç'a *fk-ê/ft-î* çûyîn** (B) to follow in s.o.'s tracks or footsteps; 2) mountain path (A). {also: [ritch] ریچ (JJ); <rêç> ریچ (HH)} [Fischer&Jastrow/K/A/JB3/IFb/B/HH/GF/TF/OK//JJ] <pêgeh; ta V>

r̄ê•dan ڕێدان *vt.* **(r̄ê -d-).** 1) {syn: hiştin; îzin dan} to permit, let, allow: **•Tu *r̄ê didî* min, ez bibuhurim [biborim]** (Msr) You *allow* me to pass; **-r̄ê lê nedan** (K) to bar s.o.'s way, prevent s.o. from passing; 2) [*f.* **(-a;-ê).**] {syn: îzin} permission: **•*Rêdana* te heye ez bikevim hundur?** (Msr) May I have your *permission* to enter? {also: r̄ê dayîn (B)} [Msr/Wlt/IFb/GF/AD//B]

r̄ê dayîn ڕێ دایین (B) = to permit. See **r̄êdan.**

rêhesin ڕێهەسِن (IFb/JB3/GF/ZF) = railroad. See **r̄êħesin.**

r̄êhl ڕێهل, m. (Elk/FS) = forest. See **r̄êl.**

r̄êhtin ڕێهتِن (Bw) = to pour, spill. See **r̄êtin I.**

r̄êħesin ڕێحەسِن *f.* **(-a;-ê).** railway, railroad: **•Bombeavêjên me ên sivik ... li şargeh ... li *rêhesinên* erdê Kaparanikayê xistine** (RN) Our lightweight bombers have struck *the railways of* the land of Kaparanika from the air. {also: rêhesin (IFb/JB3/GF/ZF); rêyahesin (A); r̄iya hesin (F)} Cf. P rāh-i āhan راه آهن; Sor r̄êga-y asin ڕێگای ئاسِن [RN/JB3/IFb/GF/ZF//K//A//F] <trên>

rêj kirin ڕێژ کِرِن (Qrj) = to sweep, scrape. See **r̄êç I.**

rêjber ڕێژبەر (GF) = worker, laborer. See **r̄êncber.**

rêje ڕێژە *f.* **(-ya;-yê).** rate, percentage, proportion: **•*Rêjeya* hinardeya bajarê Amedê bilind bûye** (Rûdaw 4.iv.2018) *The rate of* exports from the city of Diyarbakir (Amed) has risen **•*Rêjeya* xwendekarên ji pola xwe derdiçin 80% e** (Wkt) *The percentage of* students who graduate from their class is 80 %; **-rêjeya bêkarîyê** (ZF3) the rate of unemployment. Sor r̄êje ڕێژە = 'ratio, rate; percentage; proportion' [(neol)Rûdaw/ZF3/Wkt/BF/FD]

r̄êk ڕێك (SK) = road, way. See **r̄ê.**

rêketin ڕێکەتِن (FS) = to agree; to occur by chance. See **r̄êkk'etin**[2].

r̄ê•kirin ڕێکِرِن *vt.* **(r̄ê-k-).** 1) {also: verêkirin} {syn: hinartin; şandin} to send, dispatch: **•Û çar-s̱ed mêran, s̱ed Şemdînan, s̱ed Girdî, s̱ed Herkî, s̱ed Mizûrî, ko ewe xo bi meħ<b>ûbêt te dizanin, digel Teto *r̄ê ke* Rezge** (SK 61:754) And *send* 400 men, 100 Shemdinan, 100 Girdi, 100

Herki, 100 Mizuri, who regard themselves as your adherents, with Tato to Razga; 2) {also: kirin r̄ê} to see s.o. off, escort: **•Dê-bavê wana û cime'ta Kilhanîê ew *r̄ê kirin* nêç'îrê** (Ba) Their parents and the people of Kilhani (=Canaan) *saw them off* [on their] hunting [trip]; 3) [*f.*] escort(ing), seeing s.o. off (K). {also: [be ri kirin] به رى كرين (JJ)} [K/A/JB3/IFb/B/SK/GF/TF//JJ] See also **verêkirin**.

r̄êkkeftin ڕێككەفتن (Zeb) = to agree. See **r̄êkk'etin**.

r̄êk•k'etin ڕێككەتن *vi.* **(r̄êk-k'ev-).** 1) to agree, come to an agreement; 2) to coincide (with), happen by chance: **•Hema hosa *rêket* ku min ew li bazar̄î dît** (FS) It just so *happened* that I saw him in the bazaar; 3) [*f.* **(-a;-ê).**] agreement: **•Heger Amerîka xwe ji wê *rêketinê* bikişîne** (rupelanu.com 9.iv.2018) If America withdraws from that *agreement*; 4) coincidence. {also: rêketin (FS); r̄êkkeftin (Zeb); r̄êkkevtin (OK/BF)} Sor r̄ê[k]kewtin ڕێككەوتن = 'to come to agreement' & r̄ê[k]kewt ڕێككەوت = 'chance happening' [Zeb//GF/FS//OK/BF] <li hev hatin> See also **[bi] r̄ê k'etin** under **r̄ê**.

r̄êkkevtin ڕێككەڤتن (OK/BF) = to agree. See **r̄êkk'etin**.

rêk û pêk ڕێك و پێك/**rêkûpêk** ڕێكوپێك [TF]/ **rêkupêk** ڕێكوپێك [OK] *adj.* regular, well arranged, methodical, systematic: *often* **bi rêk û pêk**: **•Çalakiyên ku li Frankfurtê her roja pêncşemê *bi awayekî rêkûpêk* dihatin li dar xistin, doh bidawî bûn** (CTV214) Activities which were conducted *regularly* every Thursday in Frankfurt, came to an end yesterday •...**Em demokrasiyeke *bi rêkûpêk* dixwazin û em dixwazin Kêşeya Kurd bi riyeke demokratîk çareser bibe** (AW72D2) ...We want *systematic* democracy, and we want the Kurdish issue to be resolved democratically **•Li Tehranê bi temamî jiyan *bi rêk û pêk* bû** (CTV129) In Tehran life was totally *regular*. Sor r̄êk-u-pêk ڕێك و پێك = 'well arranged, in good order' [IFb/GF/FD//TF/ZF3//OK] <ser û ber>

rêk û pêkî ڕێك و پێكى [AW]/**rêkûpêkî** ڕێكوپێكى [CTV] *f.* **(-ya;-yê).** order, good organization, regularity, methodicalness: **•*Rêkûpêkî* di hemî karan da ya başe** (Wkt) *Methodicalness* in all matters is good **•Di daxûyaniyê de ku tê diyar kirin, digel ku Tirkiye endamê neteweyên yekbûyî ye, îşkence li vî welatî *birêkûpêkî* berdewam dike** (CTV170) In the communique it is stated that although Turkey is a member of the United Nations, torture *systematically* continues in that country **•Di nava destana Siyabend û Xecê de çewtiyeke rêzimanî ku *bi rêk û pêkî* hatiye dubarekirin tevliheviya pirjimariya bi alîkariya lêkerê ye** (AW77C3) In the story of S. and Kh., a grammatical error which is *regularly* repeated is the confusion of plurals with the help of the verb. [AW/CTV/ZF3/Wkt]

r̄êk•xistin ڕێكخستن *vt.* **(r̄êk-x[în]-).** 1) to organize, arrange, set up: **•Çalakiyên edebî *rêk dixin*** (krd.riataza.com 11.vii.2018) They *organize* literary activities; 2) [*f.* **(-a;-ê).**] {also: r̄êkxistî (VoA)} organization, association: **•*Rêkxistineke* mafê mirovan li dijî rejîma Îranê û cezaya îdamê daxûyaniyekî diweşîne** (tishktvnews 17.ix.2016) A human rights *organization* publishes a statement against the Iranian regime and the death penalty. {also: rêxistin (TF/OK-2/FD)} Sor r̄êkxistin ڕێكخستن = 'to organize, arrange' & r̄êkxiraw ڕێكخراو = 'organization' [A/IFb/OK/Wkt/ZF3//TF/FD]

r̄êkxistî ڕێكخستى (VOA) = organization. See **r̄êkxistin**.

r̄êl ڕێل *f./m.(FS/Elk)* **(/-ê;-î).** a) forest, woods, copse, small grove of trees; b) large forest (Elk): **•Ew... û di pencerê r̄a li *rêhlî* nêrî** (FS) S/he ... looked at *the woods* through the window **•Gelek lawir û dehbe di nav *rêhlî* da dijîn** (FS) Many animals and beasts live in *the forest*; **-bi dehl û rêlan** (BX) through the woods. {also: lêr m. (SK); lîrê m. (F); r̄êhl, m. (Elk/FS); [rel] ريل (JJ)} {syn: daristan; dehl [2]; gorange; mêşe} [K/JB3/IFb/GF/TF/ZF3/BF//JJ//SK//F//Elk/FS] <dar I>

r̄êlêgirtin ڕێلێگرتن [Wlt]/**r̄ê lê girtin** ڕێ لێ گرتن [IFb/XF] *vt.* **(r̄ê li ... -g[i]r-).** 1) to bar, obstruct, block *(s.o.'s way)*; to stop, prevent, hinder; 2) [*f.* **(-a;-ê).**] barring, obstructing, blocking (s.o.'s way) ; stopping, prevention, hindering: **•Armanca damezrandina vê grûbê lêkolînkirin û *rêlêgirtina* wan bêmafî û sitembariyên, ku li dijî gelê Kurd çêdibin e** (Wlt 1:37, 16) The purpose of establishing this group is the investigation and *prevention of* human rights violations [lit.'injustice and tormenting'] that are being perpetrated against the Kurdish people. [Wlt/IFb/XF/BF/ZF3]

r̄êncber ڕێنجبەر *m.* **(-ê;).** worker; unskilled laborer; farmhand: **•Kur̄ik' mezin bî, bispor bî, şeş ḧeft' heyva, şolker bî, *r̄êncber* bî** (M-Zx, #759, 352) The boy grew up, he reached an age when he could look after the animals and help about the home, for 6 or 7 months he was a worker, *a laborer* •**Peyayê dewletê, *rencberê* dijminê Kurd û Ermen bû** (Cxn, 47) He was a man of the state, *a worker for* the enemies of the Kurds and Armenians. {also: rencber (Cxn/IFb-2/GF/FJ); rêjber (GF-2); [rendj-ber] رنجبر (JJ); <rêncber> رينجبر (HH)} {syn: k'arker; p'ale; xebatk'ar} Cf. P ranjbar رنجبر = 'toiler, hard worker' < ranj رنج = 'toil, hardship' + -bar بر = 'bearer' --> T rençber; Sor r̄encber ڕەنجبەر = 'toiler, laborer (esp. agricultural worker)' [M-Zx/K/B/IFb/HH//Cxn/GF/FJ/JJ] <zeĥmetk'êş>

r̄êntin ڕێنتِن (-r̄ên-) (Msr) = to watch, look at. See **nêr̄în**.

rês ریْس (A/IFb/GF/FJ) = woolen yarn. See **r̄îs**.

r̄êsî ڕێسی *f.* **(-ya;).** bunches or bales of dried grass or hay used for animal fodder: •***Rîşî* li ber şêre, goşt li ber mehînê ye. Raje [=r̄ahêje] goşt dêne ber şêr, r̄aje *r̄îşî* dêne ber mehînê** (HR 3:141) *The dried hay* is in front of the lion, the meat is in front of the mare. Pick up the meat and put it before the lion, pick up *the hay* and put it before the mare •**Zistana, herk'es coĥt dikê, ĥetta dibê bihar; kû bû bihar, dest bi aşêf û *r̄îsîya* dikin. Kû *r̄îsî* jî xelas bûn, paleyî diderkeve** (HR-I 1:42-43) In winter, everyone plows, until it is spring; when spring comes, they begin weeding and making *bales of hay*. When *the bales* are done, it's time to harvest; **-r̄êsîya giyay** (Zeb) do. {also: r̄îsî (HR-I/IFb-2); r̄îşî II (HR-3); <rîsî> ريسى (HH)} [HR-I/HH//Zeb/A/IFb/TF//HR-3]

r̄êsîn ڕێسین (IF) = to spin wool. See **r̄êstin**.

r̄êspî ڕێسپی (Rondot) = village elder. See **r̄îspî**.

r̄êstin ڕێستِن *vt.* **(-r̄ês-).** 1) to spin *(wool)* (vt.) : •**Keçik radibe ser zinêr, teşîya xwe *dirêse*** (J) The girl climbs up on the cliff, [and] *spins* [wool with] her distaff; 2) to pass, cross over, travel. {also: r̄êsîn (IF-2); r̄istin (IF-2/BK/M); [ristin] رستين (JJ); <ristin رستن (dirêse) (دريسه)> (HH)} [Pok I. rei- 857ff.] 'to scratch, tear, cut' --> [reik(h)- --> reifi-]: Skt reś- = 'to pluck, tear our'; O Ir *rais- (Tsb 40): Av raēš-/iriš- = 'to wound, damage'; Baluchi rēsag/rēsaγ = 'to spin, weave'; P ristan رستن/rištan رشتن = 'to spin (wool)' & abrīšam ابريشم = 'silk'; Sor r̄istin ڕِستِن (-r̄ês-); Za [riştiş] (Mal)/rêsenã [rêstiş] (Srk); Hau r̄êstey (r̄ês-) *vt.* (M4) [S&E/K/A/IFb/JJ/GF/BK] <hevirmiş; hirî; liva; r̄aç'andin; r̄îs; t'eşî>

rêş I ریْش (IFb) = skin irritation. See **r̄îş**.

r̄êş II: r̄êş kirin ڕێش کِرِن (Krş/Mzg) = to sweep, scrape. See **r̄êç I**.

rêşî ڕێشی (IFb/Tof) = tassel. See **r̄îşî**.

r̄êştin ڕێشتِن (JB1-S/OK/M) = to pour, spill. See **r̄êtin I**.

r̄êtin I ڕێتِن *vt.* **(-rêj-).** to pour, spill *(vt.)*; to shed (tears): •**Bes hêsirên xwe *birêje*** (Diyar. Yar nekene 4.ii.2013) Stop *shedding* tears •**Wî gilêş *r̄êt*** (FS) He *poured out* the garbage. {also: r̄êhtin (Bw); r̄êştin (JB1-S/OK-2/M-2); rihtin (FS-2); riştin (FS); [retin] ريتن (JJ); <rêtin ريتن (dirêje) (دريژه)> (HH)} {syn: r̄ijandin} [Pok leiku- 669.] 'to leave' + "root *wleik- = 'to flow, run' related by some to [this Pok root], but more likely a separate IE form" (Am Her, p. 1526): O Ir *raik- (Tsb 40): Av raēk- (pres. raēčaya) = 'to pour'; P rīxtan ريختن (-rīz-) (ريز); Sor r̄iştin ڕِشتِن (-r̄êj-) = 'to pour, apply (color), adorn, make up (face), darken w. kohl (eyes)' & r̄ijan ڕژان (-rijê-) = 'to be spilled'; Za rişyenã = 'to be spilled' & Za rijnenã [rijnayiş] (Srk)/rişnenã [rişnayiş] (Todd) = 'to spill *(vt.)*'; cf. also Lat liqueo, -ēre = 'to be fluid' [F/BX/K/JB3/IFb/B/JJ/HH/OK/M//JB1-S//FS//Bw] <r̄ijandin; r̄ijîn>

r̄êtin II ڕێتِن (IFb) = to defecate. See **r̄îtin**.

r̄êv ڕێڤ (IFb/OK/FS) = pubic hair. See **r̄ov**.

r̄êvaçûyîn ڕێڤاچوویین (B) = to walk. See **bi rê ve çûn**.

rêvas ڕێڤاس (FS) = rhubarb. See **r̄ibês**.

rêvaz ڕێڤاز (Bw) = rhubarb. See **r̄ibês**.

rêveber ڕێڤەبەر (IFb/ZF3) = director. See **r̄êvebir**.

r̄êvebir ڕێڤەبِر *m.* **(-ê;).** director, manager, person in charge: •**Hûn *rêvebirên* Komeleya Mafên Mirovan, ji bo dema pêş çi bername amade kirine** (Wlt 1:39, 16) You *directors of* the committee for Human rights, what programs have you prepared for the near future? {also: birêveber (Wkt); rêveber (IFb/ZF3)} {syn: mezin [4]; pêşeng; r̄êber; r̄êzan; serek; serk'ar [1]; serok; serwer} < Sor ber̄êweber بەڕێوەبەر = 'manager, director, person in charge' < be r̄ê'we birdin بە ڕێوە بِردِن = 'to manage, direct, lead' [(neol)Wlt//IFb/ZF3//Wkt] <bi rê ve birin; pêşeng; r̄êber>

rêvebirin ڕێڤەبِرِن (IFb) = to conduct, run. See **bi r̄ê ve birin**.

r̄êveçûn ڕێڤەچوون (K) = to walk. See **bi rê ve çûn**.

r̄êvin ڕێڤِن *adj.* covered with mud, muddy; dirty, soiled: •**Wî cilkên *rêvin* şûştin** (FS) He washed the *soiled* clothes. [Rnh/K/JB3/IFb/GF/FS/BF] <ĥerī; qur̄;

t'eqin>

r̄êvî رێڤی (Qzl) = fox. See **r̄ovî I**.

rêvîng رێڤینگ (FS) = traveler. See **r̄êwî**.

rêwas رێواس (IFb) = rhubarb. See **r̄ibês**.

rêwing رێونگ (TF) = traveler. See **r̄êwî**.

rêwingî رێونگی (TF) = journey. See **r̄êwîtî**.

r̄êwî ڕێوی *m.* **(-yê;).** traveler, wayfarer: •**Ji *rêwyan* yekî gote hevalê xwe** (Dz) One of *the travelers* said to his companion •**Herdu *rêwîyê* birçî çûne gomê** (Dz) Both of the hungry *travelers* went to the animal pen •**Gelek *rêwîngê* mîna te ji rê dadgeřîne** (EP-7) She leads many *travelers* like you astray [lit. 'from the road']. {also: rêvîng (FS); rêwing (TF); r̄êwîng (EP-7); [rewinghi] رڤنگی (JJ); <rêwî ریوی/rêwengî ریونگی> (HH)} {syn: r̄êber [3]} = Sor r̄êbwar ڕێبوار/r̄êbigar ڕێبگار [Sinneh]; Hau r̄awîer m. (M4) {r̄êwîtî; r̄êwingî} [K/IFb/B//TF//FS//HH//JJ] <r̄ê>

r̄êwîng ڕێوینگ (EP-7) = traveler. See **r̄êwî**.

r̄êwîtî ڕێویتی *f.* **(-ya;-yê).** journey, trip; travel: •**Eger dawiya vê *rêwîtiyê* nehata, ew her û her bidomiya! Lê eger vegera *rêwîtiya* min tunebûya?** (MUm, 12) What if this *trip* never came to end, but just went on and on! What if there was no return from my *trip*? {also: rêwingî (TF)} {syn: sefer} [Z-1/IFb/B/GF//TF] <r̄êwî>

r̄êx ڕێخ (K/F/B/Srk) = cow manure. See **r̄îx**.

rêxistin ڕێخستن (TF/OK/FD) = to organize. See **r̄êkxistin**.

rêyahesin رێیاهەسن (A) = railroad. See **r̄êḧesin**.

r̄êz I ڕێز *f.* **(-a;-ê).** 1) {syn: qoř II; xet} line, file, row: -**r̄êza ç'îya** (B) mountain chain; -**r̄êz kirin** (K/ZF3) to arrange in a row or line, to line up; to draw a line; to outline: •**Di nav çarçoveya qanûnên Almanya de wezîfeyên Heyva Sor wiha *tên rêzkirin*...** (Wlt 2:59, 4) Within the framework of the German legal system [lit. 'the laws of Germany'] the duties of the red Crescent *can be outlined* as follows...; 2) {syn: selef; yekîne} unit in formation (mil.). {also: [riz] ریز (JJ); <rêz> ریز (HH)} [K/A/JB3/IF/B/HH/TF/ZF3/Wkt//JJ] <r̄êzik>

r̄êz II ڕێز *f.* **(-a;).** respect, honor: -**r̄êz girtin** (GF/TF/OK) to respect, honor. {syn: giram; hurmet [3]; me'rîfet; qedir I; r̄ûmet} Sor r̄êz ڕێز = 'respect' (K2/Hej) [(IFb)/GF/TF/OK/ZF3/BF] <'erz; namûs; şeref>

r̄êzan ڕێزان *m.* **(-ê;).** guide, leader: •***Rêzanê* wan yê bi navê Cano jî xweş bi Kurdî zanîbû** (Wkp: Lawija Mesîh) And their *guide*, named Jano, knew Kurdish well. {syn: beled II; pêşeng; r̄êber [1&2]; serek; serok; serwer} <r̄ê = 'road' + zan- = 'to know' [BX/K/A/IFb/ZF3/BF/FS/Wkt]

r̄êzdar I ڕێزدار *adj.* regular, according to the rules (K/IF/TF): -**lêkera rêzdar** (IF) regular verb. {syn: r̄ast [4]; ≠bêr̄êz} [(neol)K/IF/TF] <r̄êz I>

r̄êzdar II ڕێزدار *adj.* honorable, respected; Mister: •**Hemû wêjedostên Kurd li başûrê Kurdistanê vî navî dinasin, torevanekî (wêjevanekî) *rêzdar*, birûmet û nîştimanperwer** (Wlt 2:73, 13) All Kurdish literature lovers in northern Kurdistan know this name, a *respected*, renowned, and patriotic littérateur. {syn: bir̄êz; qedirgiran} [VoA/IFb/OK/ZF3/Wkt/BF] <r̄êz II>

r̄êz•ik ڕێزك *f.* **(•ka;•ikê).** line *(of writing, poetry, etc.)*: •**Malikek ji dû-sê-çar *r̄êzkan* çêdibît** (Bw) A stanza is made up of two, three, or four *lines*. <dim. of **r̄êz I** [Bw/K/GF/TF/ZF3/BF/Wkt] <malik>

r̄êzil ڕێزل *f.* **(-a;-ê).** chain: •**Mîna xelekên *rêzilê*** (R.Barnas. Kadiz 55) Like links in a *chain*;-**rêzila asinî** (FS) iron chain. [Haz/FS/Wkt] <zincîr>

r̄êziman ڕێزمان *f.(Wlt/Metîn)/m.(K/OK)* **(-a/ ;-ê/).** grammar: •**Lê berî lîjne bihêt Îraqê daxaz ji hindek zimanzan û xemxur û zanayên Kurdan kir ku *rêzimanekê* bo zarokên devera Kurdistanê berhevken** (Metîn 77[1998], 50) But before the committee came to Iraq, it asked some Kurdish linguists and intellectuals to put together a *grammar* [book] for children of the region of Kurdistan •**pêkanîna rastnivîs û *rêzimaneke* rast û hevgirtî** (Wlt 2:100, 2) the creation of a correct and consistent orthography and *grammar*. {also: r̄êzman (IFb-2)} Sor r̄êzman ڕێزمان [(neol)Wlt/K/IFb/TF/OK/ZF3] <ziman>

r̄êzman ڕێزمان (IFb) = grammar. See **r̄êziman**.

rêzom ڕێزۆم, f. (JB3) = vineyard. See **r̄ez**.

ri'arîn رعارین (HR) = to quiver, tremble. See **r̄e'ilîn**.

rib رب (IFb/CS/Wkt) = quarter, fourth; unit of measure. See **ribik**.

r̄ibad ڕباد (SK) = decoy partridge. See **r̄ibat**.

r̄ibat ڕبات *adj. or m.* **(-ê;).** trained hunting partridge, decoy partridge: •**Dîsa Derwêş 'Elî wekî kewê *r̄ibad* qebqeb kir** (SK 60:726) Once again Dervish Ali cooed like a *decoy* partridge. {also: r̄ibad (SK); <ribaṯ> رباط (HH)} < Ar √r-b-ṭ ربط = 'to tie, bind' [SK//A/IFb/GF/TF/FS/ZF3//HH] <kew I>

ribek ربەك (CS) = quarter, fourth; unit of measure. See

ribik.

r̄ibês رِبـێـس *f.* **(;-ê).** 1) rhubarb, bot. *Rheum* [T ışkın otu/okçun otu/ravent]: **•Li hin herêman ji *Ribêsê* re dibêjin "mûzê zozanan".... Tama *Ribêsê* tirş e** (Rûdaw 31.v.2014) In some regions they call rhubard "banana of the summer pasture"... its taste is sour; 2) sorrel, dock, bot. *Rumex, Oxalis* (JJ/GF). {also: r̄ewas (K); rêvas (FS); rêvaz (Bw); rêwas (IFb-2); ribêz (GF-2); r̄ibêz (Btm [Ḧatḧatkê]); rîvas (GF-2); rîvaz (TF); [ribas] ريباس (JJ)} Cf. P rībās ريباس/rīvās ريواس = 'rhubarb; sorrel'; Sor r̄êwas رێواس = 'rhubarb' [Btm[Ḧatḧatkê]//A/IFb/GF/ZF3//K//TF//JJ//FS//Bw] <giyabend>

ribêz ربێز (GF) = rhubarb. See **r̄ibês.**

ribik ربِك *f.* **().** 1) {also: rib (IFb/CS/Wkt-2); ribek (CS): <rib> رب (HH)} quarter, fourth, 1/4; 2) {also: rib (Frq); ribi = ribî (GF); r̄ibîk (K)} unit of measure: 2.5 kg (K): **•Du kulm, *ribek* e; çar *rib*, ç'apek e** (Frq) 2 handfuls are a *rib* (dry measure), 4 *ribs* are 1 çap. <Ar rub' ربع = quarter, 1/4; Sor r̄ibe ڕبه = 'weight of about 25 kgs' [Qzl/Wkt//GF//K//Frq/HH/IFb/CS] <ç'ap I; k'ulm; olçek>

ribisandin رِبساندِن (FS) = to irrigate. See **r̄ebisandin.**

ribis رِبس (FS) = irrigated land. See **r̄ifse.**

r̄ibisî رِبسی (IFb) = irrigated land. See **r̄ifse.**

ribî ربی (GF) = unit of measure. See **ribik**[2].

r̄ibîk رِبيك (K) = unit of measure. See **ribik**[2].

r̄icaf رِجاف *f.* **(-a;-ê).** shivering, trembling. {also: r̄icif (IFb/B)} < Ar rajafa رجف = 'to tremble, to shake' (vi.) [Z-1/K/GF//IFb/B]

r̄ical رِجال *adj.* childless *(of married couple)*. {syn: warkor} [Bw]

r̄icif رِجِف (IFb/B) = shivering. See **r̄icaf.**

r̄icifandin رِجِفاندِن *vt.* **(-ricifîn-).**1) to shake stg. *(vt.)*, to agitate, cause to tremble: **•Li ber defa sîngê xwe erbaneyekê bi eşq û hunereke welê *diricifîne*** (Tof, 7) He *shakes* a tambourine in front of his chest with such passion and skill; 2) to have fever (JJ/Lx). {also: [rijifāndin] رجفاندين (JJ)} < Ar rajafa رجف = 'to tremble, to shake' (vi.) [K/A/IFb/B/JJ/GF] <r̄icifîn>

r̄icifîn رِجِفين *vi.* **(-ricif-).** to tremble, shake (vi.). {also: [redjefin] رجفين (JJ); <recifîn رجفين (direcife) (درجفه)> (HH)} {syn: ḧejîn; kil II bûn; lerzîn; r̄e'ilîn; r̄ikr̄ikîn} < Ar rajafa رجف = 'to tremble, to shake' (vi.) [F/K/IFb/B/HH/GF//JJ] <r̄icifandin>

r̄idîn رِدين (SK) = beard. See **r̄ih I.**

r̄ifsandin رِفساندِن (Zeb/IFb/OK) = to irrigate. See **r̄ebisandin.**

r̄ifs•e رِفسه *m./f.(FS)* **(;/•ê).** wet land, irrigated land: -**r̄ifse kirin** (MD-Byt) to irrigate {syn: r̄ebisandin}: **•Ezê zeviya *mi rifsê kirî* ezê bikêlim** (MD-Byt, 161) I will plough the field *that I irrigated.* {also: ribis (FS); r̄ibisî (IFb-2); <rebase> ربـاسه (HH)} < Arc rabeș רבץ = 'to sprinkle' & Heb ribets רבץ = 'to irrigate by sprinkling' [MD-Byt/IFb/GF/OK//FS] <dêm>

r̄ih I رِه *f.* **(-a;).** beard: **-r̄ih/r̄î/r̄û berdan** (IFb/K/SS)/**r̄ih hiştin/r̄ih dirêj kirin** (F) to grow a beard: **•Te wextê bi ç'e'v *r̄iha* min k'et, dilê te bi min şewitî, û ti hatî, te *r̄iha* min qusand** (HR 3:34) When you noticed my *beard*, you felt sorry for me, and you came and trimmed my *beard.* {also: r̄idîn (SK); rihdîn (BF/FS-2); r̄î (BX/IFb-2/GF-2/RZ-2); r̄îh (RZ-2); r̄û [5] (K/B/RZ-2); [réh ره/ri رى] (JJ);<rih> ره (HH)} Cf. Southern Tati dialects (all *f.*): Chali, Takestani, Eshtehardi, Xiaraji & Sagz-abadi riša *f.* (Yar-Shater); P rīš ريش; Sor r̄idên ڕدێن/r̄îş ڕيش; Za erdîş (Todd)/erdîşi/erîşe/erîşi (Mal) *f.*; Hau r̄îş *m.* (M4) [A/IFb/JB3/HH/GF/RZ/SS/FS//BX//K/B//JJ//BF//SK] <r̄û; simbêl>

rih II رِه (IFb/SK/GF/FS) = root; vein; nerve. See **r̄eh.**

rih III رِه (ZF3) = soul, spirit. See **r̄uh.**

R̄iha رِها *f.* **(-ya;-yê).** Urfa, a city in Turkish Kurdistan, according to local legend the birthplace of the prophet Abraham/Ibrahim. It is the capital of the il or vilayet (=province) of Urfa ["Şanlıurfa"], and its main administrative districts are: Birecik, Suruç, Akçakale, Viranşehir, Siverek, Hilvan, Bozova, and Halfeti. in Crusader times, it was known as *Edessa* and its language was Syriac. Today the principal languages spoken in the province are Turkish, Kurdish, Arabic, and Zaza: **-Lîwa R̄ihayê** (BX) the district/province of Urfa; **-Valîtîya Ruhayê** (BK) The governorship of Urfa. {also: R̄eha; Ruha (BK/IF-2); [urfa] ارفا (JJ)} Cf. Ar al-Rahā الرها; Arm Uṙha[y] Ուռհայ [BX//BK/IF]

rihan رِهان (L/IFb/TF/Kmc) = sweet basil. See **r̄iḧan.**

riha zer رِها زەر (Dh/Zeb/IFb/OK/CB) = turmeric. See **r̄eha zer.**

r̄ihdirêj رِهدرێژ *adj.* long-bearded: **•Baş bû yê ku li derî xist ne Perwînê, lê parsekekî kal, *rihdirêj* û pişttewiyayî bû** (KS, 39) It was good that the one who knocked on the door was not Perwin, but rather an old, *long-bearded* beggar with a bent back. {also: rûdirêj (K); [reh dirij] رەدریــــــژ (JJ)} [KS/ZF3/Wkt//JJ//K]

rihdîn رِهدين (BF/FS) = beard. See **r̄ih I**.

rihel رِهــەل (L/ZF3/Wkt) = festive clothing; trousseau. See **r̄iḧal**.

r̄ihet رِهەت (IFb/CS) = calm. See **r̄iḧet**.

rihetî رِهەتى (L/RZ) = comfort. See **r̄eḧetî**.

rihme رِهمە (ZZ-10) = mercy, pity. See **r̄eḧmet**.

rihmetî رِهمەتى (Ardû)= deceased. See **r̄eḧmetî**.

r̄ihsipî رِهسِپى (A) = village elder. See **r̄îspî**.

rihsitên رِهسِتێن (TF) = taker of souls. See **r̄uhistîn**.

r̄ihspî رِهسپى (FS) = village elder. See **r̄îspî**.

rihtin رِهتِن (FS) = to pour, spill. See **r̄êtin I**.

r̄iḧ رِح (Z-2/HH) = soul, spirit. See **r̄uh**.

r̄iḧal رِحــــــــال *f./m.(FS)* **(-a/-ê;).** 1) festive clothing, one's "Sunday best"; 2) woman's bridal trousseau (A); the things a bride needs to bring with her to her husband's house (HH): **-riḧêlê bûkê** (FS) do. {also: rehel (A); rehêl (FS-2); r̄eḧal (K); rihel (L/ZF3/Wkt); riḧêl (FS); [rihal] رحــــال (JJ); <reḧel> رحــــــــل (HH)} [Z-1/JJ//L/ZF3/Wkt//FS//K//A//HH] <cihaz; dermalî; k'inc; libs; qelen>

r̄iḧan رِحــــــــان *f.* **(-a;-ê).** sweet basil, bot. *Ocimum basilicum*: **•Ezê herim tenekak *rihan* di devê bîrekê de deynim. Her roj, yek ji we here li vê *rihanê* binere** (L-5, 134, l. 9-10) I am going to put a pot of *sweet basil* at the edge of a well. Every day, one of you should go look at this *basil*. {also: reyhan (FJ); rihan (L/IFb/TF/Kmc); rîhan (GF/K-2/TF-2); [rihan] ريحــان (JJ); <rîḧan> ريحــان (HH)} < Ar rayḥān ريحــان < rīḥah ريحــة = 'odor, smell'; Sor r̄êḧane رێحانە [L/IFb/TF/Kmc//K/B//GF/TF//JJ/HH//FJ]

r̄iḧet رِحــــــەت *adj.* 1) peaceful, calm, quiet, tranquil; comfortable: **•Ew *reḧet* e** (FS) He is *well/fine*; **-r̄ahet bûn** (K)/**r̄eḧet** ~(B)/**rehet** ~(IFb)/**rihet** ~(CS): a) to rest, relax: **•Me av vexwar, ser ç'avê xwe, lingêd xwe şûştin û r̄ûniştin, ku hinekî *r̄eḧet bin*** (Ba2, 220) We drank water, washed our faces and feet and sat down, *to rest* a bit; b) to recover, get better: **•Ç'e'vê wî *wê riḧet bibê*** (HR 3:16) His eye *will get better*; **-xwe r̄iḧet kirin** = to rest, relax; 2) easy, simple; 3) [*n.*] peace, calm (HH). {also: r̄ahet (K/JB3); r̄aḧet (SK); r̄ehet (IFb); r̄eḧet (B/FS); r̄ihet (IFb-2/CS); [rahet] راحت (JJ); <raḧet> راحت (HH)} < Ar rāḥah راحة = 'rest, repose, leisure'; Sor r̄eḧet رەحــــــــەت = 'tranquil' {r̄eḧetî} [K/JB3//IFb//B/FS//JJ/HH/SK//CS]

r̄iḧetî رِحەتى (K) = comfort. See **r̄eḧetî**.

riḧêl رِحــێــل (FS) = festive clothing; trousseau. See **r̄iḧal**.

r̄iḧîn رِحين (Z-2) = pledge, deposit. See **r̄ehîn**.

r̄iḧsivik رِحسِڤِك [GF]/**r̄ihsivik** رِهسِڤِك *adj.* likeable, amiable, affable: **•Gelê Kurd *rihsivik* e** (Wlt 2:59, 16) The Kurds are an *amiable* people. {syn: cir̄xweş; dilovan; mihrivan; xwînşîrîn} <r̄ih [r̄uh] = 'soul' + sivik = 'light (of weight)' [Wlt/GF]

riḧstên رِحستێن (GF) = taker of souls. See **r̄uhistîn**.

riḧstîn رِحستين (GF) = taker of souls. See **r̄uhistîn**.

r̄ij رِژ *adj.* plain, dry *(of rice, bulgur, etc. without fat or butter)*: **-girara rij** (FS) plain porridge. {also: r̄ijî (B)/rijî (IFb/GF/TF); rujî (IFb-2); [reji] رژى (JJ); <rijî> رژى (HH)} {syn: bêrûn; kêmrûn; t'isî [2]} [Qzl/A/FS/ZF3//B/IFb/JJ/HH/GF/TF] <çivir>

r̄ijandin رِژانــدِن *vt.* **(-rijîn-).** to spill; to pour: **•Paşa der-kewt e seyranê, qiyasê sed gustîrêt zêr̄ digel xo birin. ... Kîsikê gustîran ji berîka xo îna der, got e xulaman, "Ez *dê* wî kîsikey *r̄ijînim.* Her kesê hindî hel-girît bo wî bin. Ez dê hespê xo ẍar dem, çim e serkaniyê ḧetta hung tên." Kîsik *r̄ijand*** (SK 22:200) The Pasha went out for an excursion, taking about a hundred gold rings with him. ... He brought the bag of rings out of his pocket and said to the henchmen, "I *shall pour out* (the rings in) this bag. However many each person picks up, they are for him. I shall gallop my horse off to the spring until you come." He *poured out* the bag. {also: <rijandin رژانــــــــدن (dirijîne) (درژيــــنه)> (HH)} {syn: r̄êtin} Cf. P rīxtan ريختن (-rīz-) (ريز) [K/A/JB3/IFb/HH/SK/GF/TF/BK] <r̄êtin; r̄ijîn>

r̄ijd رِژد *adj.* 1) {syn: ç'ikûs; çirûk [2]} selfish, stingy, parsimonius, greedy, miserly; 2) insistent, bent or set *on doing stg.*, decided {also: bi rijd}: **•Kesê *li ser* boçûna xwe *rijd*, çi rast yan şaş be** (BF) Some-one *set on* his opinion, whether it is right or wrong; **-rijd bûn** (FD/BF)/**rişt bûn** (FS) to insist: **•Ew *li ser* axaftina xwe *rişt bû*** (FS) He *insisted on* what he said **•Kurd *rijd in* ku divê Kerkûk bibe parçek ji herêma federala başûrê Kurdistanê** (Wkt) The Kurds *insist* that Kirkuk must be part of the KRG **•PKK *bi rijd e* ku li Şingalê bimîne** (Rûdaw 3.iv.2017) The PKK *insists* on staying in Shingal [Sinjar]. {also: rijde (GF); r̄işt (IFb-2/Zeb/FS-2)} Mid P ruzd = 'greedy' (M3); Sor r̄ijd رِژد = 'miserly, parsimonious' {r̄ijdî} [IFb/

Wkt/FD/BF//GF//Zeb/FS]

rijde رژده (GF) = stingy. See **řijd**.

řijdî رِژدی *f.* **(-ya;-yê).** 1) {syn: tima} stinginess, greed, parsimony, miserliness; 2) insistence (Zeb/R): **•Yekgirtû di dezgehêt xo yêt ragihandinê da *rijdî* (israr) *ya* xo li ser paristina vê ezmona dîmukratî eva li Kurdistanê diyar kir** (R 15 [4/12/96] 2) In its media, Yekgirtû [an Islamic movement] has stated its *insistence* on preserving this democratic experiment in Kurdistan; **-rijdî/riştî kirin** (FS) to insist, urge: **•Wî gelek *riştî li* Behremî *kir* ku ligel wî xwarinê bixwit** (FS) He *urged* B. very much to eat a meal with him. {also: riştî (FS)} Cf. Mid P ruzdīh = 'greed' (M3) [IFb/GF/Zeb/R//FS] <řijd>

řijhan رِژهـان (-řijhê-) (M-Zx) = to be poured out. See **řijîn**.

řijiyan رِژِیان (JB3) = to be poured out. See **řijîn**.

řijî رِژی (B)/rijî رژی (IFb/GF/TF) = plain *(of food)*. See **řij**.

řijîn رِژیـن *vi.* **(-řij-).** 1) to be poured out, spilt; to pour, spill *(vi.)*: **•Çavê te *birije*!** (SW) May your eyes fall out (lit, '*be poured out*') *[curse]*; 2) {syn: xuricîn} to fall *(stars)*: **•Ew mîna steîrkeke geş bû, wekî ji 'ezmana *biřije*** (EP-7) He was like a bright star which *falls* from the heavens. {also: řijhan (-řijhê-) (M-Zx); řijiyan (JB3-2); řijyan (-řijyê-) (M/SK); řiştin (-řiş-) (Bw/M-Gul); [rejiian] رژیـان (JJ); <rijîn رژیـن (dirijî) (درژی)> (HH)} [EP-7/K/A/JB3/IFb/B/HH/GF/TF//JJ//M//Bw] <řêtin; řijandin>

řijyan رِژیـان (-řijyê-) (M/SK) = to be poured out. See **řijîn**.

řik' I رِك *f.* **(-a;-ê).** 1) {syn: serĥişkî; serk'êşî; serřeqî} obstinacy, stubbornness (K/A/HH): **•*Rika* wî *rika* mirîşkê ye** (FS) His *stubbornness* is that of a chicken, = He is as stubborn as a mule; **-rik girtin** (Zeb) to be stubborn; 2) anger (K): **•Meryê aqilsivik *t'ucara* lê *meke řik'*** (Dz-#1083) *Never make* a foolish man *angry [prv.]* **•*rik û hêrsa* kîtleyan** (Ber) the *anger of* the masses; 3) hostility, bad feelings, ill will, dislike, hatred. {also: řik'a (;-ê /řik'ê) (B); [rik رك/rikn ركـن] (JJ); <rik> رك (HH)} Sor řiq رِق = 'anger; obstinacy; spite' [Ber/K/A/JB3/IFb/JJ/HH/GF/TF//B]

řik II رِك *adj.* steep, precipitous, sheer: **•evrazekê rik** (FS) a steep incline; **-řik û řik** (Zeb) steep: **•Be<u>t</u>eneka rik û rik e** (Zeb) It is a very steep mountainside. = Sor lêj لێژ [Zeb/FS/BF]

řik'a رِكا (;-ê/řik'ê) (B) = stubbornness. See **řik'**.

rike رِكـــه (-ya;) (K[s]/IFb/GF/OK) = bird cage. See **řeke**.

rikew رِكەو (A/IFb) = bird cage. See **řeke**.

řik'êb رِكێب *f.* **(-a;-ê).** 1) {syn: zengû} stirrup: **-lingê xwe kirin řik'êba[n]** (K) to put one's foot in the stirrup; 2) spur(s) (K): **-hesp řik'êb kirin** (K) to spur on *(horse)*; 3) onslaught, onset, charge (K): **-řik'êb kirin** (K) to rush upon, charge at, throw o.s. at: **•Sîabend *rik'êv kir li* ort'a meydanê** (IS) Siyabend *rushed into* the middle of the field; 4) {syn: berêkanê; lec; pêşbazî} competition, contest (K): **-hevřa k'etin řik'êbê** (K) to compete with. {also: řik'êf (B-2); řik'êv (B); [rikib] ركـب (JJ); <rikêb> ركـيـب (HH)} < Ar rikāb ركـاب = 'stirrup' [EP-7/K/JB3/JB1-S/IFb/HH/GF/TF//JJ//B]

řik'êf رِكێف (B) = stirrup; spur; contest. See **řik'êb**.

řik'êv رِكێڤ (B) = stirrup; spur; contest. See **řik'êb**.

rikke رِككه, m. (-yê;) (GF) = bird cage. See **řeke**.

řikřikîn رِكـرِكـيـن *vi.* **(-řikřik-).** to shiver, tremble, chatter *(of teeth, from the cold)*: **•Ew ji <u>s</u>arma *dirikřikî*** (FS) He *was shivering* from the cold **•Herdu jî, ji sermayê direcifîn, diranên wan *direkrikîn*** (H v. 1, 83 [1932 1:4]) Both of them were shivering from cold, their teeth were *chattering*. {also: rekrikîn (H); <řikřikîn> رِكرِكـيـن (Hej)} {syn: lerzîn; řeʻilîn; řicifîn} = Sor çoqeçoq چۆقەچۆق = 'chattering (of teeth)' [H//K/Hej/TF/ZF/FS]

řim رِم *m./f.(B)* **(-ê/-a; /-ê).** 1) {syn: niştir; nize} spear, lance, javelin: **•Bû şîqeşîqa *riman*** (ZZ-10, 143) The crashing *of lances* could be heard; 2) unit of measure the length of a spear (SW): **•Ji jêr de du *rima* bilind û ji jor de jî *rimek* bilind** (SW) Two "*spears*" high from below and one "*spear*" high from above. {also: řimb (K[s]); [rim] رم (JJ); <rim> رم (HH)} < Ar rumḥ رمـح = 'spear' [L/SW/K/A/IFb/B/JJ/JJ/HH/GF/TF] <tîr I; xişt III; zerg>

řimb رِمب (K[s]) = spear. See **řim**.

řimil رِمِل (HR) = fortune telling. See **řemil**.

řimildar رِملدار (HR) = fortune teller. See **řemildar**.

řind رِنـد *adj.* 1) {syn: baş; çê; law [4]; qenc; xweş} extremely good: **•Ew *rind* dixwînit** (FS) She reads *beautifully* **•P'iř *řind* e!** = It's very *good*! **•Min *řind* kir xwar** (Ks) I'm glad I ate them/I'm not sorry I ate them/It's a good thing I ate them; 2) {syn: bedew; cindî; spehî} beautiful: •**Keçeka pir *rind* e** (BF) She is a *beautiful* girl. {also: [rind] رند (JJ); <rind> رند (HH)} {r̄indayî; r̄indî} Cf. P rend رند --> T rind = 'jolly, unconventional, humorous man' [K/A/JB3/IFb/B/JJ/HH/GF/ZF3/BF/FS]

r̄indayî رِندایی *f.* **(-ya;-yê).** 1) {syn: başî; qencî} goodness, kindness: •**Em *rindîya* te qe ji bîr nakin** (yekmal.com:Zoto 31) We will never forget your *kindness*; 2) {syn: bedewtî; spehîtî} beauty. {also: r̄indî (K-2/IFb/GF/Wkt); [rindi] رندی (JJ)} [K/B/ZF3//IFb/JJ/GF/Wkt] <r̄ind>

r̄indî رِندی (K/IFb/JJ/GF/Wkt) = goodness; beauty. See **r̄indayî**.

risim رِسِم, m. (CS) = picture; rule; custom. See **r̄esim**.

risîn رسین (GF) = nosebleed. See **r̄iskyan**.

riskîn رسکین (GF/FS) = nosebleed. See **r̄iskyan**.

r̄iskyan رِسکیان *vi.* **(-r̄iskyê-).** 1) {syn: ver̄estin[4]} to have a nosebleed: •**Difna wî *ya r̄iskiya*** (Zeb) = •**Xwîna bêvila wî *riskî*** (FS) His nose *is bleeding* ; 2) to become granulated *(of honey or grape molasses)*: •**Doşava me *ya r̄iskiyay*** (Zeb) Our grape molasses *has become granulated* (at the bottom of a container); 3) [*f.* **().**] nosebleed: **-difin riskyan** (OK) do. {also: risîn (GF-2); riskîn (GF/FS)} [Zeb/OK//GF/FS]

rism رسم, m. (-ê;-î) (SBx) = picture; rule; custom. See **r̄esim**.

r̄ispî رِسپی (SK) = village elder. See **r̄îspî**.

r̄ispîyatî رِسپییاتی (SK) = eldership. See **r̄îspîtî**.

r̄istik رِستِك *f./m.(Bw)* **(-a/;-ê/).** necklace, chain, string (of pearls, etc.): •**Zîvkerî *ristikeka* zîvî bo Rewşê çêkir** (FS) The silversmith made a silver *necklace* for R. {syn: benî II; gerden[3]; *menteşe; *mih̄emmedî; *stivank; t'oq; *zincîrk} [Bw/IFb/FS/ZF3/BF]

r̄istin رِستِن (IF/BK/M) = to spin wool. See **r̄êstin**.

r̄isxet رِسخەت (K) = permission. See **r̄uxset**.

rişêşk رشێشك (Kmc) = sprinkle, light rain. See **reşêş**.

r̄işk رِشك *f.* **(-a;-ê).** nit, louse larva: •***Rişka* daye serê wî** (FS) *Nits* have infested his head [i.e., hair]; **-rişka sipihê** (FS) do. {also: [richk] رشك (JJ); <rişk> رشك (HH)} Skt likşa- (Tsb2, p.61); Pashto riča <*riškā; Oss lysk'; P rešk رشك; Sor r̄işk رِشك & mêtulke مێتولكه [Hk/K/A/IFb/B/JJ/HH/GF/TF/OK/ZF3/BF/FS] <nûtik; spî II>

r̄işm•e رِشمه *m./f.(ZZ-10)* **(•ê/•a;).** 1) small silver chain as ornament on horse's bridle (JJ/FS); 2) {syn: hevsar; r̄ext} harness; halter (A): **-r̄ext û r̄işme** (Z-1) harness and bridle (of a horse). {also: reşme (GF-2/FS); [rechmé] رشمه (JJ); <reşime> رشمه (HH)} cf. Ar rašmah رشمة = 'halter' [Z-1/K/A/IFb/GF//JJ/FS//HH]

r̄işt رِشت (IFb/Zeb/FS) = selfish; insistent. See **r̄ijd**.

rişţî رِشتی (FS) = stinginess; insistence. See **r̄ijdî**.

r̄iştin رِشتِن (-r̄iş-) (FS) = to pour, spill. See **r̄êtin I**; (Bw/M-Gul) = to be poured out. See **r̄ijîn**.

rişwet رشوەت (Wkt) = bribe. See **r̄uşet**.

r̄iţam رطام/**r̄itam** رِتام [FS] *f./m.(FS)* **(-ê/ ;-ê/).** mud, mire, wet clay: •**û xwe ji axê û ji *ritamê* diweşînin** (KLw, #7, 35) and shake off soil and *mud* [Lwj: 'encumbrances']. {also: retem (FS); retim (FS-2); [ritam] رطام (JJ); <riţam> رطام (HH)} {syn: h̄er̄î; qur̄; t'eqin} Cf. Ar raţama رطم = 'to involve, implicate, drag into stg. unpleasant' [Lwj/JJ/HH//K(s)/IFb/GF/Kmc/ZF//FS]

r̄itil I رِتِل *f.* **(;-ê).** unit of weight : 2.5 kg. (K); formerly, 10 pounds [Rus funt фунт] (B); 8 kg. (IFb); 18 pounds [Fr livre: 1 livre = 1.1 lb. av.] (JJ): •**Em sê-çar *ritil* titûn li kerê xwe ê lexer bar dikin** (MB) We load three or four *rotls* of tobacco onto our decrepit donkey. {also: [ritel] رطل (JJ); <riţil> رطل (HH)} {syn: batman I[1]} Cf. Ar raţl رطل = 'rotl, a weight (Eg. 449.28 g [15 3/4 oz.], Syr. 3.202 kg. [5 lbs.], Beirut & Aleppo 2.566 kg.)' < Gr litra λιτρα; Turoyo riţlo, *m.*/raţlo, *f.* = 'appr. 8-10 kg.' (HR2); NENA riţlâ ܪܛܠܐ, *f.* = 'a pound weight' (Maclean) [MB/K/A/IFb/B/TF//JJ//HH] <batman I>

r̄itil II رِتِل *f./m.(FS)* **().** scrotum. {also: [rotl] رتل (JJ-G); <r̄itil> رتل (Hej)} [IFb/OK/Hej/ZF3/BF/FS//JJ] <batî; gun; hêlik>

rivên رِڤێن (GF) = flame. See **r̄ivîn**.

r̄ivîn رِڤین *f.* **(-a;-ê).** flame: •**Êzingê min êdî tu *rivîn* nedida** (EŞ, 16) My firewood gave no more *flames* •**Gava gur *rivîna* geş dît, xwe ji miyê bi dûr xist** (EŞ,16) When the wolf saw the bright *flame*, it distanced itself from the sheep. {also: rivên (GF-2)} {syn: agir = ar I; alav; p'êt} [EŞ/K/A/IFb/GF/TF/OK]

r̄iwayet رِوایەت *f.* **(-a;-ê).** account, narrative, story; version: **-r̄iwayet kirin** (K/JR) to tell, recount {syn: gilî kirin; kat kirin; neqil kirin; vegotin; vegêr̄an}. {also: r̄ewayet (K); [rouvaiet] روایت (JJ)} < Ar riwāyah رواية = 'narrative; novel' [K//IFb/JJ] <ç'îr̄ok; h̄ekyat; şax>

riwek روەك *f./m.(BF)* **(-a/;-ê/).** plant, vegetation:

•*Riweka* **sebrê tehl e, lê mêweya wê şîrîn e** (A. Gurdilî.Aforîzmayên feylesofan… 47) *The plant of* patience is bitter, but its fruit is sweet. {also: rowok (SS)} <Sor r̄uwek ڕووەك [(neol)ZF3/BF/Wkt//SS] <heşînatî>

riwîn ڕوین (IFb) = liquid. See **r̄on II**.

r̄ix ڕخ (Mzg/IFb) = cow manure. See **r̄îx**.

riyan ڕیان (TF) = to defecate. See **r̄îtin**.

riyîn ڕیین (IFb) = to bark. See **r̄eyîn I**.

r̄izgar ڕزگار *adj.* 1) {syn: aza I; serbest; xelas} free, freed, liberated: **-r̄izgar bûn** (IFb/CS) to be freed, be liberated; **-r̄izgar kirin** (A/IFb/FJ/GF/CS/AD) to free, liberate; 2) rid (of): **-jê rizgar bûn** (SS): to be or get rid of {syn: jê xelas bûn; yaxa xwe xilas kirin}: •**Xwe kuştiye yan jî xwe bi saxî veşartiye ji bo ku** ***rizgar bibe ji*** **van teşqele û bûyerên bêserî** (HYma 29) He has killed himself or buried himself alive in order *to be rid of* these silly problems and events. Cf. P rastegār رستگار = 'free, delivered, saved'; Sor r̄izgar ڕزگار = 'free, rescued, safe' {r̄izgarî} [HYma/A/IFb/FJ/GF/TF/CS/AD/SS] <xelas>

r̄izgarî ڕزگاری *f.* **(-ya;-yê).** 1) {syn: azadî; serbestî} freedom, liberty: •**Têkoşîna** ***rizgariyê*** **hêz divê** (Ber) Striving for *freedom* requires force; 2) {syn: felat; xelasî}liberation, deliverance: •***Rizgarîya*** **pîreka Kurd, bi ya netewa wê ve û bi taybetî jî bi ya çîna wê ve girêdayî ye** (Ber #7, 10) *The liberation of* the Kurdish woman is tied to the liberation of her nation, and especially to the liberation of her class •**Xwezî ez jî mirtib bama... Min ji xwe ra nekirana derd û kul** ***rizgarîya*** **gelê Kurd** (RC2. Ku heye Xwedê hiş bide gelê Kurd) If only I were a Roma [Gypsy] as well... I would not be worried about *the liberation of* the Kurdish people; 3) salvation. Cf. P rastegārī راستگاری = 'salvation'; Sor r̄izgarî ڕزگاری = 'freedom, liberation' [Ber/K/A/IFb/GF/TF/FJ/ZF/CS] <azadî; r̄izgar>

r̄izî ڕزی *adj. & pp.* 1) decayed, dilapidated, worn out: •**Werîsê** ***r̄izî*** **bêkêr e** (AB) A *worn-out* rope is useless; 2) {syn: petot; p'ûç' [3]} rotten: •**Ev sêva** ***ya r̄izî*** (Bw) This apple *is rotten*; **-r̄izî bûn** (JB3) to rot. {also: rizyayî (A); [rizi] رزی (JJ)} [AB/K/IFb/JJ/TF/OK//A] <r̄izîn>

r̄izîn ڕزین *vi.* **(-r̄iz-).** 1) {syn: helisîn} to decay, rot: •**Kaxetên ko min li ser wan nivîsîye, hêdî hêdî** ***dirizin*** **û kurm û mişk wan dixun** (RN) The pieces of paper I wrote them on are slowly *decaying*, and worms and mice are eating them; 2) to wear out (vi.), become dilapidated (K). {also: r̄izî bûn (JB3); [rizin] رزین (JJ); <rizîn رزین (dirizî) (درزی)> (HH)} Cf. Sor da•r̄izan داڕزان (da-r̄izê-) = 'to decompose, fall to pieces' [K/A/IFb/B/JJ/HH/OK/M/Bw] <fesidîn; ȟerimîn>

r̄izq ڕزق *m.* **(-ê;-î).** one's daily bread; food, sustenance, provision; reward: •**Ya r̄ebbî, tu r̄idînekî dirêj û pan û 'ezmanekî lûs bideye kur̄ê min, êdî hîç** ***r̄izqî*** **nede wî, bila** ***r̄izqê*** **wî li ser wî bît** (SK 12:116) O God, (if) you give my son a long and broad beard and a smooth tongue, give him no further *sustenance*, let his *sustenance* be on his own head. {also: [rizq رزق/risk رسك] (JJ); <rizq> رزق (HH)} < Ar rizq رزق <Mid P rōzīg = 'daily bread' (Jeffery, p. 142-43) & Parth rōčīk = 'food stuff; wages' (Achar, vol. 4, p.145ff.) [K/IFb/JJ/HH/JB1-A&S/SK/OK] <debirîn>

r̄izyan•e ڕزیانە *f.* **(•[ey]a;•ê).** fennel, anis, aniseed, bot. *Foeniculum vulgare*. {also: razyane (IFb-2); rizyanik (A/GF); rizyang (OK-2); rizyank (OK-2); [reziána] رزیانە (JJ-G); <rizyanik> رزیانك (HH)} P rāziyāne رازیانە = 'fennel' --> T rezene; Sor r̄azyane ڕازیانە [Bw/IFb/JJ/OK/ZF3//A/HH/GF] <heliz>

rizyang ڕزیانگ (OK) = fennel. See **r̄izyane**.

rizyanik ڕزیانك (A/GF) = fennel. See **r̄izyane**.

rizyank ڕزیانك (OK) = fennel. See **r̄izyane**.

rizyayî ڕزیایی (A) = worn out. See **r̄izî**.

r̄î ڕی (BX/IFb/GF/RZ) = beard. See **r̄ih I**.

r̄îbêz ڕیبێز (Btm[Ȟatȟatkê]) = rhubarb. See **r̄ibês**.

r̄îh ڕیه (RZ) = beard. See **r̄ih I**.

rîhan ریهان (GF/K/TF) = sweet basil. See **r̄iȟan**.

rîȟan ریحان (JJ/HH) = sweet basil. See **r̄iȟan**.

r̄în I ڕین (BX/M/K/A) = to defecate. See **r̄îtin**.

rîn II ڕین (IF) = liquid. See **r̄on II**.

r̄îs ڕیس *m.* **(-ê;).** 1) woolen yarn, woolen thread, worsted; 2) [*adj.*] made of woolen yarn: **-gorêd r̄îs** (B) woolen socks. {also: rês (A/IFb-2/GF/FJ-2); [ris] ریس (JJ); <rîs> ریس (HH)} Cf. Sor r̄ês ڕێس = 'thickness of thread, yarn, etc.' & r̄îs ڕیس = 'thread, string' [Elk/Qzl/K/IFb/B/JJ/HH/TF/FJ//A/GF] <ç'ûr I; hirî; kulk; liva; r̄êstin>

rîsipî ڕیسپی (GF) = village elder. See **r̄îspî**.

r̄îsî ڕیسی (HR-I/IFb/HH) = bale of dried hay. See **r̄êsî**.

r̄îspî ڕیسپی *m.* **(-yê;).** (white-bearded) old man; village elder; "Every lineage has a number of elders or ***rî spî*** [lit. 'white-beards'], who are supposed to advise the agha and elect his successor but have no real power" {from: Martin van Bruinessen. *Agha, shaikh and state: On the social and political organization of Kurdistan*. Doctoral dissertation (Utrecht : Rijksuniversiteit, 1978), p. 81}; "The ***rêspî***, whose name seems to be an allusion to the white hair of the old men, are men of recognized experience, revered more for their personal worth and age than for the prestige of their **bavik** [='patrilineal clan']. The entire village participates in choosing them, and the gatherings of these **rêspî** form a sort of council of elders." {from: P. Rondot. "Les tribus montagnardes de l'Asie antérieure," *Bulletin d'Études Orientales*, 6 (1936), 23}: **•Tevda mîna gotina rîspî û kalan e** (LT-Mîşo) It was all in all just as the aged and elderly had said [it would be]; **-r̄ûspîyê gund** (K) village elder. {also: r̄êspî (Rondot); rihsipî (A); r̄ihspî (FS); r̄ispî (SK); rîsipî (GF); r̄ûspî II (K); [réh-sipi رهسپی/ri-spi ریسپی] (JJ); <rêspî> ریسپی (HH)} < r̄î/r̄ih = 'beard' + s[i]pî = 'white'; Cf. P rīš sefīd ریش سفید = 'gray-beard, elder'; Sor r̄idênsipî ڕدێنسپی = do.; Za erîşsipî/sipyerdiş *m.* (Mal); Hau r̄îşçerme *m.* (M4); cf. also T aksakal = 'community elder'; NENA diqnaxwara/xwardiqna = 'old man, elder' (Garbell); cf. also Heb zaḳen זָקֵן = 'old' (bearded one), < zaḳan זקן = 'beard' (cf. Ar d̲aqn ذقن) {r̄ispîyatî; r̄ispîtî; r̄ûspîtî} [IFb/B/JJ//HH//GF//A//FS//SK//K//Rondot] <giregir; kal I; maqûl; pîr>

r̄ispîtî ڕیسپیتی *f.* **(-ya;-yê).** eldership; obligations of the village elder; carrying out of the obligations of the village elder. {also: r̄ispîyatî (SK); r̄ûspîtî (K)} [B/ZF3//SK//K] <r̄ispî>

r̄îş ڕیش *f.* **(-a;-ê).** type of skin irritation, such as oriental sore or skin cancer: **•Lê *rîşek* ku bi qasî kefa destekî hêlek rûyê wê şewitandibû** (SBx, 16) But *a skin irritation* the size of the palm of one's hand had burned a side of her face. {also: rêş I (IFb-2); [rich] ریش (JJ); <rîş> ریش (HH)} [Pok. I. rei- 857.] 'to cut, cleave'-->reis-: Av raēš- = 'to wound'; Mid P rēš = 'wound, sore' (M3); P rīš ریش = 'wound, sore'; Sor r̄êş ڕێش = 'sore' [Qzl/A/IFb/JJ/HH/GF/ZK/Qzl] <pençeşêr>

r̄îşî I ڕیشی *m.(K/F)/f.(B)* **(; /-yê).** 1) {syn: gulik [2]; gûfik} fringe, tassels; filaments (K/B): **•*Rêşiyên* li dora şahra serê wî di ser hev de pêl didin** (Tof, 7) *The tassels* around his head band hit against one another; **-gulik û r̄îşî** (Z-2) fringes and tassels; 2) short, thick noodles (B); 3) sore, pimple (K). {also: rêşî (IFb-2/Tof); [rechi رشی/richi ریشی] (JJ); <rîşî> ریشی (HH)} Cf. P rīše ریشه [Z-2/F/K/IFb/B/JJ/HH/GF/TF//Tof] <qutas>

r̄îşî II ڕیشی (HR-3) = bale of dried hay. See **r̄êsî**.

r̄îtin ڕیتِن *vt.* **(-rî-).** to defecate, have a bowel movement, shit: **•Paşî eger Meḧmûd Şewket xo bizawtiba hinde pêna da li pişta wî dem ko li-bin xo *r̄îtiba*** (SK 36:323) Then if Mahmud Shevket had budged I would have given him so many kicks in the back that he *would have fouled* himself. {also: r̄eyîn II (-r̄ey-) (IFb-2); r̄êtin II (IFb-2); riyan (TF); r̄în (BX/M/K/A); [ritin] ریتن (JJ); <rîtin ریتن (dirî) (دری)> (HH)} Cf. Mid P rīdan (riy-) (M3); P rīdan ریدن (-rīn-) (رین); Sor r̄în ڕین/r̄iyan ڕییان/r̄itin ڕیتِن (Arbil) [BX/M/K/A//IFb/JJ/HH/SK/GF//TF] <destav; gû; mîz; sergîn>

rîvas ریڤاس (GF) = rhubarb. See **r̄ibês**.

rîvaz ریڤاز (TF) = rhubarb. See **r̄ibês**.

r̄îvî I ڕیڤی (M-Ak) = fox. See **r̄ovî I**.

rîvî II ریڤی (IFb) = intestines. See **r̄ovî II**.

r̄îvîkore ڕیڤیکۆرە (IF) = blind gut, c[a]ecum. See under **r̄ovî II**.

r̄îwî ڕیوی (SK) = intestines. See **r̄ovî II**.

r̄îx ڕیخ *f.* **(-a;-ê).** the dung or manure of large domestic animals such as cows or buffaloes, in its natural (moist) state, *as opposed to **sergîn** = dried dung ready for use as kindling fuel* (Msr): **•Bîna pêz, dêwêr û *r̄êxê* t'u cara ji mala dernedik'et** (Ba2-3, 213) The smell of sheep, cattle and *dung* never left the house **•Gur̄î çû ji xwer̄a kevir anîn, ji xwer̄a xênîkekî li ber *sergoyê r̄êxê* çê kir** (Z-4) The mangie one went and took some stones, [and] made himself a house in front of *a heap of cow manure*. {also: r̄êx (K/F/B/Ba2/Srk); r̄ix (Mzg/IFb); [rikh] ریخ (JJ); <rîx> ریخ (HH)} {syn: k'erme (Ag)} Cf. P rīx ریخ = 'thin excrement in a diarrhoea' [Msr/Kş/A/JJ/HH/GF/TF/OK//K/F/B/Srk//Mzg/IFb] <deve II; dirg; k'erme; peyîn; qelax; sergîn; tepik>

r̄iya hesin ڕییا هەسِن (F) = railroad. See **r̄êḧesin**.

r̄o I ڕۆ (Ks/Ad/Kg/Ba/L/Rh/IFb) = day; sun. See **r̄oj**.

r̄o II ڕۆ *m.* **(-yê;).** river; small stream, brook (A/HH); large river (Haz): **-r̄o bûn** (B) to be spilled, poured out {syn: r̄êtin I[2]; r̄ijîn}; **-r̄o kirin** (B) to spill, pour out {syn: r̄êtin I[1]; r̄ijandin}: **•Kur̄ derê [=devê?] t'êr̄a vedikin, gênim *r̄o dikine* 'erdê** (Ba-1, #37) The boys open the sacks [lit.

'the doors (or: mouths) of the sacks'], and *spill out* the wheat onto the ground; **-řoda** = with/against the stream. See also **řoda**. {also: rû II (FS); <ro> رو (HH)} {syn: av[2]; çem; řûbar; şet} OP rautah- *n.* = 'river' (Brand); P rūd[xāne] [رود[خانه]; Sor -řo ڕۆ/-ro رۆ = 'river' (in place names) ; Za Ro = 'Euphrates river' [IF(s)/A/JB3/(B)/HH/Haz]

řoava ڕۆئاڤا (K/IF/B) = west. See **řojava**.

řobar ڕۆبار (IFb/GF/TF/OK/JJ-G) = river. See **řûbar**.

řoda ڕۆدا: **-řoda birin** (B) to carry away *(of rivers, seas, etc.)*; **-řoda çûn**: a) to be carried away by the water; b) {syn: xeřiqîn; ẍerq bûn} to drown, sink; c) {syn: beta vebûn; řed bûn[2]; winda bûn; ẍeware bûn} to disappear, vanish; to be or get lost: **•Cefê wî *řoda çû*** (B) His effort *was for nothing* **•Gustîlka t'ilîya min deřk'et, *řoda çûye*** (Z-1) The ring on [lit. 'of'] my finger came off, [and] *disappeared* (or, *fell in the river*). {also: [be roda(ni) tchouié] به رودا(نی) چویه (JJ)} [Z-1/K/B/JJ] <řo II>

řodî ڕۆدی *pl.* intestines, guts. {also: řodîk (Msr-2); [roudé] روده (JJ); <rodî> رودی (HH)} {syn: pizûr; řovî II; ûr} Cf. P rūde روده = 'intestine, gut' [Msr/IFb/JJ/HH/ZF3]

řodîk ڕۆدیك (Msr) = intestines. See **řodîk**.

rogirtî رۆگِرتی (FJ/GF) = solar eclipse. See **řojgirtin**.

řohelat ڕۆهەلات (BX) = east. See **řojhilat**.

řohilat ڕۆهِلات (K/F/B/IF) = east. See **řojhilat**.

řohilatnas ڕۆهِـــلاتـــنـــاس (K) = orientalist. See **řojhilatnas**.

řohilatnasî ڕۆهِـــلاتـــنـــاســـی (K) = orientalistics. See **řojhilatnasî**.

řohn ڕۆهن (JB3/FJ) = liquid. See **řon II**.

řohnî I ڕۆهـــنـــی *adj.* bright, brilliant, light; clear, translucent: **•Îşev hîv pir *rohnî* ye** (AB) Tonight the moon is very *bright*. {also: rehnî (Şnx); **řon I**; řonahî II; řonak (K[s]/A/JB3); řuhnî I (L/K/A); [roaník] رونـك (JJ-Lx); <ronî> رونـی (HH)} {syn: beloq; biriqok; geş; řewşen} Cf. P rōšan روشـــن; Sor řûn ڕوون & řûnak ڕوونـاك = 'light, bright'; Za roşn = 'bright, clear'; Hau řoşin = 'light, bright' (M4) {řonî I; řonîyî} [AB//K/IFb/GF//A//JB3//JJ//HH//Şnx] See also **řon I**.

řohnî II ڕۆهـنـی = (source of) light; clarity. See **řonahî I**.

řoȟ ڕۆح, f. (SK) = soul, spirit. See **řuh**.

řoj ڕۆژ *f.* **(-a;-ê).** 1) day: **•Deh *ro* di wê navê çûn** (L) Ten *days* passed in that way; **-řo nîvro** (EP-4) in broad daylight: **•Sîabend *ro nîvro* da t'erkûya xwe, revand** (EP-4, #12) *In broad daylight*, Siyabend put her on the back of his saddle [=behind himself], and abducted her; **-řoja paştir** (JB1-A) the next day, the following day {syn: dotir; řojtir}; **-řojekê** (L) one day {also: řokê (Ba)}; **-řojekê ji rojê xwedê** (L) one day, once upon a time; **-wê rojê** = [on] that day; 2) {also: řo I (IFb/B)} {syn: hûr (K); t'av (Bg)} sun: **•*Roj* çû [ser] ava** (K/[AB]) *The sun* set **•Weke *řojê* p'eřlemîş dibû** (EP-7) She shone like *the sun*; **-tava rojê** (IFb) sunlight. {also: řo I (Ks/Ad/Kg/Ba/L-2/Rh); [rouj] روژ (JJ); <roj> روژ (HH)} [Pok. leuk- 687.] 'light, brightness': Skt rocis- *n.* = 'light, brightness'; Av raočah- = 'light, bright'; O P raučah- = 'day' (Brand); Mid P rōz (M3) & rōč (Brand); P rūz روز = 'day'; Sor řoj ڕۆژ = 'day, sun'; Za roc/roj/roz *m./f.* = 'day, sun' (Mal); Hau řo *m.* = 'day' & řojîar *m.* = 'sun' (M4); cf. also Lat lux, lucis f. = 'light, lustre'; Gr leukos λευκός = 'white'; Arm luys լոյս = 'light, lustre'--see also etymology at **řon I**. [L/K/A/JB3/IFb/B/HH/SK/GF/ TF//JJ//Ks/Ad/Kg/Ba/Rh] <hîv; sibe[h]; şev; tav I>

řojava ڕۆژئاڤا/**řoj-ava** ڕۆژئـــاڤـا *f./m.* **(-ya/-yê;-ê/).** 1) west, direction in which the sun sets; occident; 2) [Řojava] Syrian Kurdistan: **•Federaliya Demokratîk a Bakûrê Sûriyê, navê perçeyekî Kurdistanê ye, ku dikeve nav sînorên Sûriyê. Paytexta Federasyona Rojavayê Qamişlo ye. Navê herêmê herwiha wek *Rojavaya* Kurdistanê, *Rojavayê* Kurdistanê an bi kurte *Rojava* tê zanîn** (Wkp) The Democratic Federation of Northern Syria (DFNS) is the name of the part of Kurdistan that lies within the borders of Syria. The capital of the Federation of Rojava is Qamishli. The region is also known as *Western* Kurdistan or *Rojava*. {also: řoava (K/IFb/B); řojawa (SK); [rou(j) awa] روژ اڤـــــــا (JJ) = 'sunset'} {syn: moẍrib [3]} < řoj = 'day, sun' + ava = 'setting (of sun)'; Sor řojawa ڕۆژاوا = 'sunset, west' [F/A/JB3/GF/TF/Wkt/ZF3//SK//K/IFb/B//JJ] <bakur; başûr; cenûb; řojhilat>

řojawa ڕۆژاوا (SK) = west. See **řojava**.

řojbûn ڕۆژبـــوون *f.* **(-a;-ê).** birthday: **•Di pasaporta min de, piştî nav û paşnav û *rojbûnê* peyva 'nivîskar' hatibû nivîsandin** (HYab, 5) In my passport, after my first and last names and *birthday*, the word 'writer' appeared [lit. 'had been written'] •***Rojbûna* te pîroz be** (FB) Happy *birthday*. {syn: sersal} [FB/CS/AD/ZF/Wkt]

r̄ojen ڕۆژەن (K[s]/JB3/BF/ZF3) = skylight; smokehole. See **r̄ojin**.

r̄ojev ڕۆژەڤ *f.* **(-a;-ê).** agenda, daily program: •**Divê pirsa Kurdan bikeve *rojeva* s[a]zgehên navneteweyî** (Wlt 1:37, 16) The Kurdish issue must get on *the agenda of* international agencies. [(neol)Wlt/IFb/ZF3/Wkt]

r̄ojgirtin ڕۆژگِرتِن *f.* **(-a;-ê).** solar eclipse, eclipse of the sun [Ar kusūf كسوف; P āftāb'giriftagī آفتاب گرفتگی; T güneş tutulması; Heb liḳui ḥamah ליקוי חמה]: •***Rojgirtina* herî mezin a dîrokê pêk tê** (rojname.com 21.viii.2017) The biggest *solar eclipse* in history is taking place. {also: girtina r̄ojê (Zeb/RF); ro[j]girtî (FJ/GF); rojgîran (IFb); cf. [rouj hatiié ghirtin] روژ هاتیه گرتین (JJ) = il y a l'éclipse du soleil}{syn: *girtina tavê (ZF); *r̄ojẍeyrîn (Bw); *xirabûna rojê (RF-2)}Sor r̄ojgîran ڕۆژگیران [rojname/BF/SS//FJ/GF//IFb//Zeb/RF] <heyvgirtin>

rojgirtî ڕۆژگِرتی (FJ/GF) = solar eclipse. See **r̄ojgirtin**.

rojgîran ڕۆژگیران (IFb) = solar eclipse. See **r̄ojgirtin**.

rojhelat ڕۆژهەلات (JB3/IFb/SK/DM) = east; sunrise. See **r̄ojhilat**.

rojhelatnas ڕۆژهەلاتناس (DM/JB3/K[s]) = orientalist. See **r̄ojhilatnas**.

r̄ojhilat ڕۆژهِلات *f.* **(-a;-ê).** 1) {syn: mişriq; şerq, f. (F)} east; orient: •**Ber bi *rohelatê* çû** (BX) He headed *east* •**Li *Rojhilatê* "birînêd reş" pirin** (BR) in the *East* [of Turkey] there are many [cases of the disease] "Black Wounds"; **-alîê r̄ohilatê** (Ba2) facing east; **-Rojhilata Navîn** (IFb/GF/TF) the Middle East; 2) sunrise; 3) [Rojhilat] Kurdistan of Iran: •***Rojhilata* Kurdistanê perçeyê Kurdistanê ye ku di nav sînorên Îranê deye** (Wkp) *Eastern* Kurdistan is the part of Kurdistan that lies within the borders of Iran. {also: r̄ohelat (BX/IFb-2); r̄ohilat (K/F/B/IFb-2); rojhelat (JB3/IFb-2/SK/DM)} < r̄oj = 'day, sun' + hil[h]at- = 'to rise' (of sun); Sor r̄ojhełat ڕۆژهەڵات [BX//A/IFb/GF/TF//F/K/B//JB3/DM/SK/ZF3/Wkt] <bakur; başûr; r̄ojava>

r̄ojhilatnas ڕۆژهِلاتناس *m.* **(-ê;).** [Western] scholar or specialist on the Middle East, orientalist. {also: r̄ohilatnas (K); rojhelatnas (DM/JB3/K[s])} [cf. Ar mustašriq مستشرق < šarq شرق = 'east, orient'] {r̄ojhilatnasî} [IFb/ZF3//DM/JB3/K(s)//K]

r̄ojhilatnasî ڕۆژهِلاتناسی *f.* **(-ya;-yê).** the scholarly study of the Middle East, Middle Eastern studies, orientalistics. {also: r̄ohilatnasî (K)} [K/IFb/ZF3] <r̄ojhilatnas>

r̄ojin ڕۆژِن *f.* **(-a;-ê).** 1) {syn: k'ulek II; p'ace} hole in the ceiling; skylight: •**Hirçê li ser xênî, di *rojinê* (kulek) ra li wan guhdarî dikir** (hindik-rindik: Qisirkeno 18.vii.2011) On the roof, the bear was listening to them through *the skylight*; 2) {syn: pixêrîk} chimney (Rh); {syn: pîpok} smokehole (A); " ... But the Kurdish peasant lives in rough houses ... A hole in the roof serves as a chimney ... " (EI[2]). {also: r̄ojen (K[s]/JB3/BF/ZF3); <rojin> روژن (HH)} Sor r̄oçnê ڕۆچنێ [S&E/A/HH/Rh//K(s)/JB3/BF/ZF3]

r̄ojî ڕۆژی *f.* **(-ya;-yê).** fast, abstention from food for religious or other reasons: •**Tu di vê *rojîya* remezanî mubarek de çawan dikarî avê vexwî?** (LM, 5) How can you drink water on this blessed *fast* of Ramadan?; **-rojî girtin** (IFb) to fast: •**Wekî her kesî Apê Leto jî *rojîyê digre*** (LM, 5) Like everyone else, Uncle Leto also *fasts*. {also: [rouji] روژی (JJ); <rojî> روژی (HH)} Cf. P rūze روزه --> T oruç; Sor r̄ojû ڕۆژوو [K/A/IFb/B/HH/GF/TF/ZF3//JJ]

r̄ojîgir ڕۆژیگِر *m.&f.* **(-ê/;).** faster, one who fasts (abstains from eating): •**Bangê fitarê: gaziya ku ji mizgeftan tê kirin ku êdî *rojîgir* dikarin bixwin û vexwin** (Wkt) The call to break the fast: the call made from mosques [saying] that *those fasting* can finally eat and drink. [Wkt/FS] <r̄ojî>

r̄ojnam•e ڕۆژنامە *f.* **(•a/•eya** [Kmc]**;•ê).** 1) newspaper, daily: •**Hela çend caran fala xwe di *rojnamê* de bixwînin êdî hûnê jî piçek be bawerîyê pê bînin** (LC, 8) Just read your fortune in *the newspaper* a few times, and you will [begin to] believe it a little bit; 2) {syn: r̄ojnîş; salname} calendar (A/B). {also: r̄ojneme; r̄ojne'me (B-2)} Cf. P rūznāme روزنامه; Sor r̄ojname ڕۆژنامە = 'daily newspaper' [Ber/K/A/JB3/IFb/B/GF/TF/OK] <ç'apemenî; kovar>

r̄ojnameger ڕۆژنامەگەر (SS/AW) = journalist. See **r̄ojnamevan** [1].

r̄ojnamegerî ڕۆژنامەگەری (OK/AW/SS) = journalism. See **r̄ojnamevanî**.

r̄ojnamenivîs ڕۆژنامەنِڤیس (K) = journalist. See **r̄ojnamevan**[1].

r̄ojnamevan ڕۆژنامەڤان *m.&f.* **(-ê/-a; rojnamevên** [Rnh]/**).** 1) {also: r̄ojnameger (SS-2/AW);

r̄ojnamenivîs (K-2)} journalist: •R.Bedirxan yekemîn *rojnamevana* Kurd bû (welateme.net) R. B. was the first Kurdish woman *journalist* **•Rojekê *rojnamevanekî* biyanî ji serekwezîrê Mecaristanê pirsî** (Rnh) One day a foreign *journalist* asked the prime minister of Hungary...; 2) newspaper seller or vendor. {r̄ojnamevanî} [Ber/K/IFb/GF/TF/OK/AD]

r̄ojnamevanî رۆژنـامـەڤـانـی *f.* **(-ya;-yê).** journalism: **•Roja *Rojnamevanîya* Kurdî li Qamişlo hat pîroz kirin** (VOA 22.iv.2015) The Day of Kurdish *Journalism* was celebrated in Qamishli. {also: r̄ojnamegerî (OK/AW/SS)} = Sor r̄ojnamegerī رۆژنامەگەری [IFb/TF/AD//OK/AW/SS] <r̄ojnamevan>

r̄ojneme رۆژنـــەمـــە/r̄ojne'me رۆژنـــەعـــمـــە (B) = newspaper; calendar. See **r̄ojname**.

r̄ojnivîs رۆژنِڤیس (K/CS) = diary. See **rojnivîsk**.

rojnivîsk رۆژنِـڤـیـسـك *f.* **(-a;-ê).** diary: **•Ji *rojnivîskên* girtiyan mirov moral û coşiya girtiyan di berxwedanê de dibîne** (ANF News 19.iv.2017) From *the diaries of* the prisoners one can see the morale and the enthusiasm of the prisoners in the resistance **•Loma min di wê *rojnivîskê* de royên Şemî û Yekşemê hindik nivîsandîye** (perxudres.blogspot.com 14.iv.2001) Therefore I wrote a little in that *diary* on Saturday and Sunday. {also: r̄ojnivîs (K/CS)} [perxudres/Wkt/ZF3/FD//K/CS]

r̄ojnîş رۆژنیش *f.* **(-a;-ê).** calendar. {syn: r̄ojname [2]; salname} [F/K/B/ZF3]

r̄ojtir رۆژتِـــر *adv.* on the next day; on the following day: **-r̄ojtira din[ê]** (B) do.: ***•R̄ojtira dinê* em r̄astî hev hatin** (B) *On the following day* we bumped into each other. {syn: dotir; r̄oja paştir} [EP-7/K/B/ZF3] <dusibe; sibetir>

r̄okirin رۆكِرِن = to pour. See **r̄o II**.

r̄ol رۆل/**rol** رۆل [B] *f.* **(-a;-ê).** rôle [or, role], part, function: **-r̄olekê leyîstin** (ZF3) to play a rôle or part: **•Bi taybetî Celadet Bedirxan û gelek ronakbîrên Kurd .. *roleke* mezin *lîstin*** [sic] (Ber) Especially Djeladet Bedirkhan and several Kurdish intellectuals *played a* major *role* **•Ew t'atronêda *rola* Memê *dilîze*** (B) He'*s playing the part of* Mem in the theater. {syn: wezîfe} < Fr rôle [Ber/IFb/B/GF/ZF3]

rolik رۆلِك (SS) = oleander. See **r̄ûl**.

R̄om رۆم *m.* **().** 1) {also: Romî (JB3/SK/GF); [roumi] رومی (JJ); <romî> رومی (HH)} {syn: T'irk} Turk {Many centuries ago, before the Turks conquered Anatolia, it was under the control of the Byzantine Greeks, the Eastern wing of the Roman Empire. The Muslims referred to them as 'Rum.' Even today, Istanbul Greeks are referred to by the same name, and their language is called 'Rumca.' A possible etymology for the name Erzurum (Armenian "Garin") is Arabic Arḍ al-Rūm أرض الـــروم (=Land of the Rum, i.e., of the Byzantine Greeks). The term 'Rom' has been preserved by the Kurds, who apply it to the current rulers of the region, the Turks}: **-Jina r̄om** (K) Turkish woman; **-welatê r̄omê** (B) Turkey{syn: T'irkiye}; **-zimanê r̄omê** (K) Turkish language; 2) {syn: Yewnan} Greek (person); 3) [*f.* **(-a;-ê).**] {also: [roum] روم (JJ)} [Ottoman] Turkey: **•[Hûn digel êlatêd xwe bar bikin û biçine sînora *Romê*]** (JR #39,120) Pack up and go with your people to the frontier of *Turkey*. [EP-8/K/IFb/B//JJ//JB3/HH/SK/GF/ZF3]

roman رۆمـــــــــــان *f.* **(-a;-ê).** novel, work of fiction: **•Dîroka *romana* Kurdî, ne gelek kevn e** (Dqg, 85) The history of the Kurdish *novel* is not very old **•Ji destpêka nivîsandina *romanê* heta dawî, rexnegirê Kurd ... ez tenê nehîştim** (Mîr Qasimlo. Dilya & Zalar, 6) From the start of writing *the novel* until the end, the Kurdish critic ... did not abandon me. < Fr roman = 'novel'; Sor r̄oman رۆمان [Dqg/IFb/FJ/GF/TF/RZ/ZF/SS/CS]

Romanî رۆمــــــــانــــــــی (Wkt/BF) = Romanian. See **R̄omanyayî**.

romannivîs رۆمان نڤیس *m.&f.* **(-ê/-a;).** novelist, novel writer: **•...û ḧeta digehe *romannivîsê* cihê mebesta me Laleş Qaşoyî** (Dqg, 85) Until it arrives at *the novelist* we mean, L.Q. < roman + nivîs-; Sor r̄omannûs رۆمـــان نـــووس [Dqg/ZF/SS/Wkt] <çîr̄oknivîs; nivîsk'ar>

R̄omanyayî رۆمـانـیـایـی *adj.* Romanian. {also: Romanî (Wkt-2/BF); Romenkî (ZF3)} Sor R̄omanyayî رۆمانیایی [Wkt//BF//ZF3]

Romenkî رۆمــــــەنــــكــــی (ZF3) = Romanian. See **R̄omanyayî**.

Romî رۆمی (JB3/HH/SK/GF) = Turk. See **R̄om**[1].

r̄on I رۆن *adj.* light, bright, brilliant (as opposed to dark): ***•Ron* dikim Elo naxwe tir dikim Welo naxwe** (ZF3) If I make it *light*, E. won't drink it; if I make it dark, W. won't drink it [*prv.*] = I'm damned if I do, and I'm damned if I don't **•Sibe *ron* bû** (K/EP-7) Morning has broken/It has become *light*. {also: **r̄ohnî I**; r̄onahî II; r̄onak

(K[s]/A/JB3); r̄uhnî I (L/K/A); <ronî> رونـــــــــــى (HH)} {r̄onî I; ronîyî (A)} [Pok. leuk- 687.] 'light, brightness': Skt rocana- = 'bright'; Av raoxšna- = 'light, bright' & raoxšnā *f.* = '(source of) light'; P rōšan روشـــن; Sor r̄oşin ڕۆشِـــن = 'bright, clear' & r̄ûn ڕوون & r̄ûnak ڕوونـــــــاك = 'light, bright'; Za roşn = 'bright, clear'; cf. also Lat luna *f.* (<lousna) = 'moon'--see also etymology at **r̄oj**. [EP-7/K/A/IFb/GF/BF//JB3//HH] See also **r̄ohnî I**.

r̄on II ڕۆن *adj.* 1) liquid, fluid; 2) [*m.*] liquid (B). {also: rehn II (MG); riwîn (IFb); rîn II (IF-2); r̄ohn (JB3/FJ); ruyn I (IFb-2); ruhn (GF); r̄ûhn (A); rûn II (GF-2); rwîn (IF-2); [roun رون/rouin رويـــن] (JJ); <ron> رون (HH)} {r̄onayî II; r̄onî II} [K/IFb/B/HH/ZF3//A//JB3/FJ//GF//MG]

r̄onahî I ڕۆنـــاهـــى *f.* **().** 1) light, brightness; light *(as opposed to darkness)*; daylight; source of light, lighting; brightness [T aydınlık]: **•Nerî go gustîlek e, anî ber *ruhnîyê*** (L) He saw it was a ring, he held it up to *the light* [lit. 'he took it before the light'] **•Avayîkî biç'ûk *r̄onkaya* wî tê xanê** (Z-922) A small house whose *light* is visible [lit. 'its light comes visible']; **-r̄onahî kirin** = to light up, illuminate; 2) clarity. {also: r̄ohnî II; r̄onayî I (K/B/IFb-2/GF-2/TF); ronak (A); r̄onî I (K/IFb/HH); r̄onîyî (A); r̄onkayî (K-2); r̄uhnayî (K-2); r̄uhnî II (K-2); r̄ûnayî (Msr); [ro(u)n رون/rounahi روناهی/rounaï رونای/rounikaï رونكای] (JJ); <ronî> رونى (HH)} Cf. P rōšanā'ī روشنائى --see etymology at **r̄on I**. [IFb/GF//K/B/TF//A/JB3// HH//JJ//Msr] <sînahî; şewq>

r̄onahî II ڕۆناهى = bright; clear. See **r̄ohnî I** & **r̄on I**.

r̄onak ڕۆنـــاك (K[s]/A/JB3) = bright; clear; light. See **r̄ohnî I** & **r̄on I** & **r̄onahî I**.

ronakbîr ڕۆناكبير (Ber) = intellectual. See **r̄ewşenbîr**.

r̄onayî I ڕۆنـــايـــى (K/B/IFb/GF/TF) = light; clarity. See **r̄onahî**.

r̄onayî II ڕۆنايى (K) = liquidity. See **r̄onî II**[1].

r̄ondik ڕۆندِك (Bw) = tears. See **r̄onî II**[2].

r̄onî I ڕۆنى (K/IFb/HH) = light, brightness; clarity. See **r̄onahî I**.

r̄onî II ڕۆنـــــــى *f.* **().** 1) liquidity, fluidity; 2) {also: r̄ondik (Bw); r̄ûndik, pl. (Zx/Bw)} {syn: hêstir I} tears (Hk): **-r̄ondikêt çava** (Bw) tears. {also: r̄onayî II (K)} [K/Hk] <r̄on II>

r̄onîyî ڕۆنيى (A) = brightness. See **r̄onî I**.

r̄onkayî ڕۆنكايى (K) = light; clarity. See **r̄onahî I**.

r̄oşinbîr ڕۆشِنبير (Nbh) = intellectual. See **r̄ewşenbîr**.

r̄ot ڕۆت *m.* **(-ê;).** straight wooden pole, rod or stick *used in reinforcing the ceilings and roofs of traditional houses.* {also: rewt (A); rotik (GF-2); [rot روت] (JJ); <rot̤> روط (HH)} Cf. Syr rawṭā ܪܘܛܐ = 'flexible thin branch, lath' [Mdt/IFb/JJ/GF/TF/ZF3/FS//A] <beşt; çilak; garîte; k'êran; max; mertak>

rotik ڕۆتِك (GF) = wooden pole. See **r̄ot**.

r̄ov ڕۆڤ *m.(ZF3)/f.(RF)* **().** pubes, pubic hair. {also: r̄êv (IFb/OK/FS); r̄ûv (IFb-2/GF/ZF3); r̄ûvik (GF-2); [row/reve (G)] روڤ (JJ) ; <rûvik> روڤـــك (HH)} [Pok. 2. reu-/reu̯ə-:rū̆- 868.] 'to rip open, dig, root up; to extract, snatch' {or perhaps [Pok. 1. reu- 867.] 'mystery, secret'}: Skt róman- = 'hair on the body of men and animals'; O Ir *rauma- (A&L p. 95-96 [XIX,2]); Bakhtiari rūmb (Vahman 1994, p.109); P rom رم/ronb رنب/ronbe رنبه; Sor r̄ûm ڕووم/r̄ûy ڕووى (Hej); Za ram-i (Mal) [A&L/A/JJ//IFb/OK/FS//GF/ZF3//HH] <pirç'[1]>

r̄ovî I ڕۆڤـــــــــى *m.* **(-yê;).** 1) fox: **•*Rovî* dijminê mirîşkan e** (AB) *The fox* is the chickens' enemy; 2) {syn: pêşkese (Zeb)} person sent to house of father of prospective bride to announce that the wedding procession will come on the following day (Ag). {also: r̄êvî (Qzl); r̄îvî I (M-Ak); r̄ûvî I (K/B/GF-2); [rōuwi] روڤـــى (JJ); <rûvî> روڤـــى (HH)} [Pok u̯lp/lup- 1179.] 'fox, wolf': Skt lopāśá- *m.* = 'jackal, fox'; Av urupi-s (<*lupi-s) = 'dog' & raopi-s = 'fox, jackal'; Mid P rōbāh (M3); Pahl rōpāh; Baluchi rōphask; Southern Tati dialects: Danesfani luās *m.* (Yar-Shater); P rūbāh روباه; Sor r̄êwî ڕێـــوى; Za lû *f.* (Todd); Hau r̄ûase *f.* (M4); cf. also Lat vulpes = 'fox' & lupus = 'wolf'; Gr alōpēx ἀλώπηξ, Mod Gr alepou ἀλεποῦ = 'fox'; Arm ałuēs աղուէս = 'fox' [AB/A/JB3/IFb/GF/Ag//K/B/HH//JJ//M-Ak//Qzl] <dolebaşî; gur̄ I; kûç'ik; torî I>

r̄ovî II ڕۆڤـــى *f.* **(-ya;-yê).** guts, entrails; intestines: **-r̄ûvîya kor** (K/B)/**r̄îvîkore** (IF) c[a]ecum, blind gut; **-r̄ûvîya qalin** (B)/**r̄îvîyê stûr** (IF) large intestine; **-r̄ûvîya r̄ast** (K) rectum; **-r̄ûvîya zirav** (K)/**r̄îvîyê barik** (IF) small intestine; **-ûr û r̄ovî** = guts, intestines {syn: **'ûr û pizûr** (Msr)/**ḧûr û p'izûr** (B)}: **•Ûr û r̄ovî ji r̄ovîra danîn** (Dz) He left the entrails for the fox [to eat]. {also: rîvî II (IFb); r̄îwî (SK); r̄ûvî II (B/K); [roŭwi] روڤـــى (JJ); <rûvî> روڤى (HH)} {syn: pizûr; r̄odî; ûr} Cf. Av urvata; P rūde روده; Sor r̄îxołe ڕیـــخـــۆڵـــه/r̄îxołeçewre ڕیخۆڵەچەورە/r̄êłexo ڕێڵەخۆ [Sinneh];

Za loqera/loqila *f.* (Mal); Hau r̄olexa *f.* (M4) [Dz/A//F/K/B/HH//JJ//IFb//SK] <dil-hinav>

rowok رۆوۆك (SS) = plant, vegetation. See **riwek**.

r̄sqet ڕسقەت (HCK) = permission. See **r̄uxset**.

r̄uçikandin ڕوچِکاندِن (SW/TF) = to pluck out. See **r̄ûç'ikandin**.

r̄uh ڕوه *m./f.(SK)* **(-ê/-a;).** soul, spirit: **•Wexta Al-p'aşayê kal û jina xweva eva gilîya derheqa Memêda bihîstin, qudum çokê wanda nema, *r̄uḧ* lê teyîrîn** (Z-1) When old Al-pasha and his wife heard these words about Mem, they felt weak, their *spirits* left them; **-r̄uh tê de neman** (ZF3)/**nebûn** = to be in bad/sad shape {syn: ḧal di ...-da neman/nebûn}: **•*R̄uḧ* Memêda *nemabû*** (Z-1) Mem *was in sad shape*. {also: rih III (ZF3); r̄iḧ (Z-2); r̄oḧ, f. (SK); r̄uḧ (Z-1/B); [rouh] روح (JJ); <riḧ> رح (HH)} < Ar rūḥ روح [Z-1/B//K/IFb//ZF3//Z-2/HH//JJ//SK]

Ruha روها (BK/IF) = Urfa. See **R̄iha**.

r̄uhistîn ڕوهِستین *m.* **(-ê;).** 1) killer, murderer, taker of souls, soul snatcher: **•şûrkêşê *ruhistîn*** (LC, 5) sword-wielding *soul snatcher* **•Zû rabe an ne ezê gazî *rühstîn*** [sic] **bikim** (GF) Get up quickly, or else I will call *the taker of souls*; 2) {syn: melk'emot} angel of death, Azrail. {also: rihsitên (TF); riḧstên (GF); riḧstîn (GF-2); ruhstên (IFb); rühstîn [sic] (GF-2); r̄uhustîn (K-2); ruḧistin (FS)} <r̄uh = 'soul' + stên-/stîn- = 'to take', cf. Ar qābiḍ al-arwāḥ قابض الأرواح = 'taker of souls' & T can alan/ruh alan [LC/K/ZF3//FS//IFb//GF//TF]

ruhn روهن (GF) = liquid. See **r̄on II**.

r̄uhnayî ڕوهنایی (K) = light; clarity. See **r̄onahî I**.

r̄uhnî I ڕوهنی (L/K/A) = bright; clear. See **r̄ohnî I** & **r̄on I**.

r̄uhnî II ڕوهنی (K) = light; clarity. See **r̄onahî I**.

ruhsat روهسات (IFb) = permission. See **r̄uxset**.

ruhstên روهستێن (IFb) = taker of souls. See **r̄uhistîn**.

r̄uhustîn ڕوهوستین (K) = taker of souls. See **r̄uhistîn**.

r̄uḧ ڕوح (Z-1/B) = soul, spirit. See **r̄uh**.

ruḧistin روحستین (FS) = taker of souls. See **r̄uhistîn**.

rujî روژی (IFb) = plain (of food). See **r̄ij**.

r̄uquç'andin ڕوقوچاندِن (Dz) = to pluck out. See **r̄ûç'ikandin**.

Rusî روسی (Wkt) = Russian. See **R̄ûsî**.

Rusyayî روسیایی (Wkt) = Russian. See **R̄ûsî**.

r̄uşet ڕوشەت *f.* **(-a;-ê).** bribe: **-r̄uşet xwerin** (K)/**xwarin** or **hildan** (B) to take a bribe. {also: rişwet (Wkt); r̄uşvet; r̄uşwet (IFb/ZF3); [reşvät] رشوت (JJ)} {syn: bertîl; bexşîş [3]} < Ar rišwah/rušwah/rašwah رشوة --> T rüşvet [F/K/B//IFb/ZF3//JJ//Wkt]

r̄uşvet ڕوشڤەت = bribe. See **r̄uşet**.

r̄uşwet ڕوشوەت (IFb/ZF3) = bribe. See **r̄uşet**.

r̄uxset ڕوخسەت *f.* **(;-ê).** leave, permission: **•Ewe 'Elî kur̄ê Xal Eḧmede. Ji mêj e min nedîtîye. Ez ew şewe *wî r̄uxset nadem*, iḧtimal e sube jî *r̄uxset nedem*** (SK 8:83) This is Ali, the son of Uncle Ahmad. I haven't seen him for a long time. I *shan't let him go* tonight, and maybe not even tomorrow **•Go: --*Rsqet heye*, em xeberdin? Go: --Heye!** (HCK-3, #2, 25) "May we speak? [lit. '*Is there permission*, that we speak?]" "Yes! [lit., There is!]" **•*Heger r̄uxset bît* ji terefê te, em dê r̄a bîn** (JB1-A, #70, 118) If we may have your permission [lit. '*if there is permission* from your side], we'll get up. {also: r̄isxet (K); r̄sqet (HCK); ruhsat (IFb)} {syn: îzin; r̄êdan} < Ar ruxṣah رخصة --> T ruhsat = 'permit, permission' [JB1-A&S/SK//IFb//K//HCK]

ruyn I روین (IFb) = liquid. See **r̄on II**.

r̄û I ڕوو *m.* **(-yê/riwê [BX];).** 1) {syn: dev û çav; dîndar I; serçav; sifet [3]; sûret I[1]} [Cf. P rū رو] face: **•Ewê nedixast *rûyê* kesekî bibîne** (Ba) She didn't want to see anyone [lit. 'anyone's *face*']; **-hatin r̄ûyê *fk-ê*** (XF/IF/B) to kiss s.o. on the cheek {syn: maç' kirin; paç' kirin; r̄amûsan}: **•Wî çaxî dîa min nêzîkî min bû, ez ḧemêz kirim, du-sê cara *hate r̄ûê min*** (Ba2-#2, 207) Then my mother approached me, hugged me, and *kissed me* two or three times; **-r̄û bi r̄û** (K/IFb/GF) face to face; 2) *(fig.)* (sense of) shame or honor: **•*R̄ûyê* wî t'une** (B) He has no *sense of shame*; **-r̄û girtin** (IFb) to be emboldened, have the nerve or courage (to do stg.): **•*R̄ûyê min girt*, min ew got** (K) *I got up the courage* to say that; **-r̄ûyê *fk-ê* nag[i]re** (XF): [cf. T yüzü tutmamak] a) to be ashamed: **•*R̄ûyê wî nagire* ter̄a bêje** (B) *He is ashamed* to tell you **•*R̄ûyê wê negirtîye*, her̄e mala bavêye/** (EP-5, #7) *She was ashamed* to return to her father's house; b) to be shy, bashful; c) not to dare (to do stg.): **•*R̄ûyê min nagire*** (K): a) I am [too] ashamed or shy (to do stg.); b) I don't dare; **-r̄û r̄eş bûn** (K) to be disgraced; **-r̄û r̄eş kirin** (K) to disgrace; **-r̄ûyê xwe spî kirin** (XF) to be justified, vindicated; to have reason to feel proud [Cf. T yüzünü ağartmak]: **•Hem *ruyê xwe*, hem ruyê me**

spî bike (Ro) Give yourself and us a reason to feel proud [lit. '*Whiten your own face* and ours']; 3) {syn: alek; gup; hinarik; lame} cheek (Bw/JB1-A&S); 4) surface: •**Gemî li ser *r̄ûyê* be'ra diçe** (Z-2, 67) The ship goes along *the surface of* the seas; 5) [cf. P rīš ریـــش] beard. See **r̄ih I**. {also: [rou رو/rouï روی] (JJ); <rû> رو (HH)} Mid P rōy = 'face' (M3); P rū رو; Sor r̄û ڕوو = 'face, front, aspect, surface, cover, top, side, form'; Hau r̄ûe *f.* = 'face' (M4) [Kg/BX/K/A/JB3/IFb/B/JJ/HH/JB1-A&S/SK/GF/TF/OK/Bw] <dêm II; t'ûş II>

rû II ڕوو (FS) = river. See **r̄o II**.

r̄ûbar ڕووبـــار *m.(Bw/K/FS)/f.(SK/JB1-A)* **(-ê/ ;).** river: •***Rûbarê* Xabîrî di Zaxo ra diborit** (FS) The Khabur *River* passes through Zakho; **-r̄ûbarê avê** (Bw) do. {also: r̄obar (IFb-2/GF-2/TF/OK-2); [roubar/robár (G)] روبار (JJ)} {syn: av[2]; çem; r̄o II; şet} OP rautah- *n.* = 'river'; Mid P rōd-bār = 'river bank' (M3); P rūdbār رودبار = 'river system'; Sor r̄o ڕۆ; Za Ro = 'Euphrates' [Bw/K/A/IFb/JJ/JB1-A/SK/GF/OK/FS//TF] <r̄o II>

r̄ûç'ikandin ڕووچِکـانـدِن *vt.* **(-r̄ûç'ikîn-).** to pluck, pluck out *(feathers)*; to pull out *(feathers or plants)* (JJ): •[The prophet Solomon commanded all the birds as follows:] **Divê hûn *xwe biruçikînin*, da ko ji bo Belkîsê nivîneke çêkin!** (SW) You must *pluck out* all your feathers to make a bed for Belkis! •**Ma ne guneh e, ko ji bona jina xwe me gişkan han *bidî ruçikandin*!** (SW) Isn't it disgraceful that you're *making* us all *pluck out* [our feathers] for the sake of your wife! •**Wek p'erçemûk *xwe* pêşda *r̄uquç'and*** (Dz) Like the bat, he was the first to *take off* [his feathers] [*prv.*]. {also: r̄uçikandin (SW); r̄uquç'andin (Dz); [rou-tchkandin] روچکاندین (JJ)} {syn: p'er̄itandin; p'ûrtikandin} [BK/K/IFb/B/JJ/GF/ZF3//SW/TF//Dz] <bask; p'er̄; p'ûrt>

rûdirêj ڕووددرێژ (K) = long-bearded. See **r̄ihdirêj**.

r̄ûhn ڕووهن (A) = liquid. See **r̄on II**.

r̄ûk'en ڕووکـــەن *adj.* smiling, genial, good-humored, with smiling face: •***Rûken be rûken be*, dilê xwe teng neke** (Kerim Sevinç: Rûken be) *Keep smiling, keep smiling*, don't let your heart be sad. {r̄ûk'enî} [K/IFb/FJ/GF/TF/ZF/FS]

r̄ûk'enî ڕووکـــەنـی *f.* **(-ya;-yê)**. smile, smiling (n.): •**Ji xortên wir F.M.S. û M.M.E. derketin pêşiya min û bi *rûkenî* û bi dilgermî destê min guvaştin** (WT, 88) From the young men there, F.M.S. and M.M.E. came out to greet me and with *smiles* and warmth they squeezed my hand. {also: cf. [rou kenin] رو كنين (JJ)} [WT/ZF/Wkt]

r̄ûl ڕوول *f.* **(-a;-ê).** oleander, bot. *Nerium oleander*; flower which grows along river banks (Dh). {also: lûrk (IFb-2/A/KZ); rolik (SS); r̄ûlk (KZ); r̄ûr (PS); <rûl> رول (HH)} {syn: jale; ziqûm (IF)} Mid P rūrag = 'medicinal plant, herb' (M3); = Sor jałe ژاڵە [IFb/HH/OK/Dh/FS/ZF3//A/KZ//SS//PS]

r̄ûlk ڕوولك (KZ) = oleander. See **r̄ûl**.

r̄ûmet ڕوومـــەت *f.* **(-a;).** 1) {syn: 'erz; hurmet [3]; qedir I; r̄êz II} honor, respect: •**Min *rûmetek* [sic] mezin didayê ku ew jî li hemberî min têkeve rewşa xezûrtiyê** (Lab, 7) I showed him a great deal of *respect*, so that he would be willing to be come my father-in-law [lit. 'so that he would enter into the status of father-in-lawhood regarding me'] ; **-r̄ûmet girtin** (K) to respect, esteem; 2) fame, renown, reputation (GF/TF). {also: r̄umet (TF); [roumt] رومت (JJ)} Cf. r̄û [2] + hurmet < Ar ḥurmah حـــرمـــة = 'sacredness, reverence; woman'; Sor r̄ûmet ڕوومـەت = 'cheek' (W&E/K2/Hej), 'honor' (Hej) [K/A/IFb/GF/OK//JJ//TF] <namûs; şeref>

r̄ûn I ڕوون *m.* **(-ê;).** butter; clarified butter, cooking oil: •**Hine *r̄ûnê* min hebû min anî ter̄a kire p'êxûn** (Dz) [If] I had a little *butter*, I would have brought [it and] made you some *poxîn* (qv.) •***Rûnê* gamêşan ji yê bizinan pirtir e** (AB) Buffalo *butter* is more plentiful than goat butter; **-r̄ûnê malê** (Msr) home-made butter; **-r̄ûnê nivîşk** (Ag) butter. {also: [roun] رون (JJ); <rûn> رون (HH)} {syn: nivîşk} [Pok. reugh-m(e)n 873.] 'cream': proto IndIr **raughan- (with -an- < *m̥n-): Av raoγna- *n.* = 'butter (ghee)' *[eaten by the blessed in paradise]*; Mid P rōγn = 'oil, butter' (M3)/Manichaean rwyyn [rōyen]; P rōγan روغـــن = 'fat, grease'; Sor r̄on ڕۆن = 'oil, clarified butter'; Za ruwen *m.* = 'oil, grease' (Todd); Hau r̄ûen *m.* = 'cooking oil, clarified butter' (M4) [L/Dz/F/K/A/IFb/B/JJ/HH/SK/GF/TF/Msr] <çivir; dew; to I>

rûn II ڕوون (GF) = liquid. See **r̄on II**.

r̄û•nandin ڕوونـانـدِن *vt.* **(r̄û-nîn-).** to seat s.o., cause s.o. to sit down: •**Piştî gavekê xweha xwe *rûnand* rex xwe** (H v. 1, 83 [1932 1:4]) After a while she seated her sister beside her. {also: rûnihandin (FS-2); rûnişkandin (IFb-2); rûniştandin (K/A/GF-2/TF/FS-2/ZF-2); rûniştikandin (Wkt-2);

<r̄ûnandin> رۆنـــانـــدِن (Hej); <rûniştandin> رونـشـتـانـدن (HH)} [H/K(s)/SS/Hej/FS/ZF/GF//K/A/TF/HH] <r̄ûniştin>

r̄ûnayî ڕوونایی (Msr) = brightness. See **r̄onahî I**.

r̄ûndik ڕووندِك, pl. (Zx/Bw) = tears. See **r̄onî II**[2].

r̄ûnerm ڕوونـەرم *adj.* gentle, mild, meek: **•Slo ... bi xeysetê xweva *r̄ûnerme*** (HCK-2, 195) Silo ... is *gentle* in his personality. {r̄ûnermî} r̄û = 'face' + nerm = 'mild, gentle' [HCK/K/IFb/FJ/GF] <nazik>

r̄ûnermî ڕوونەرمی *f.* **(-ya;-yê).** gentleness, mildness, meekness: **•Ji dilpaqijiya xelkê wî pêva, dilçakî û *r̄ûnermiya* şex jî ev hezkirina han roj bi roj zêde dikirin** [sic] (Rnh 2:17, 326) In addition to the honesty of his people, the goodheartedness and *gentleness of* the sheikh made this love [for him] increase day by day. {syn: nazikî} [Rnh/K/GF/OK]

rûnihandin روونِهاندِن (FS) = to seat. See **r̄ûnandin**.

rûnişkandin روونِشكاندِن (IFb) = to seat. See **r̄ûnandin**.

rûniştandin روونِشتاندِن (K/A/GF/TF/FS/ZF) = to seat. See **r̄ûnandin**.

rûniştikandin روونِـشـتِـكـانـدِن (Wkt) = to seat. See **r̄ûnandin**.

r̄û•niştin ڕوونِـشـتِـن *vi.* **(r̄û-n- / r̄û-nê- / r̄û-nî- / -r̄ûn-** [MK/Bw]**).** 1) to sit, sit down: **•*R̄ûne*!** = *Sit down*! **•Li ser kursîya zîv *rûdinê*** (L) He *sits* on the silver chair; 2) {syn: jîn} to dwell, live, reside *(in a place)* [cf. T oturmak]; 3) {syn: cihê xwe girtin} to become [well] entrenched, become current *(e.g., of a saying or expression)*. {also: [rou-nichtin] رونـشـتـيـن (JJ); <rûniştin رونـشـتـن (rûdine) (رودنـه)> (HH)} r̄û- <O Ir *fravata- (Tsb 74) + ni- (Tsb 72) + [Pok sed- 884.] 'to sit': Skt sad- & ni-ṣad-; Av & OP had- & ni-šad- (Brand); Mid P nišastan (nišīn-) (M3); P nešastan نـشـسـتـن (-nešīn-) (نـشـيـن); Sor da•niştin دانیشتِن (da-nîş-); Za roşenã [roniştiş] (Todd); Hau ara•nîştey (nîş-) *vi.* (M4); cf. also Lat sedeo, sedēre; Germ sitzen (sass, gesessen); Rus sidét' сидеть [K/(A)/JB3/IFb/B/JJ/HH/SK/GF] <r̄ûnandin>

r̄ûp'el ڕووپـەل *f.* **(-a;-ê).** page *(of a book)*. {also: r̄ûper̄, m. (-ê;) (Msr/OK-2); rûp'êl (K/B)} {syn: berper} =Sor lapeṙe لاپـەڕە [K/B//JB3/IFb/GF/TF/OK/ZF3] <belg [2]; k'axez; p'er̄ [3]>

r̄ûper̄ ڕووپەڕ, m. (-ê;) (Msr/OK) = page. See **r̄ûp'êl**.

rûp'êl رووپێل (K/B) = page. See **r̄ûp'êl**.

r̄ûpoş ڕووپـۆش *f.* **(-a;-ê).** mask, veil, curtain: **•Kî oldarekî ji dil e û kî minafiq e bê tirs û xof wan îfşa dike. *Rûpoşa* wan dadixîne û li ser wan dinivisîne** (A. Taş. Kevirê Namûsê, 42) Who is genuinely religious and who is a hypocrite, he exposes them without any fear. He removes their *veil* and writes about them. {also: rûpoşî (K[s]); rûpûş (IFb/FD/SS)} Sor r̄ûpoş ڕووپۆش = 'veil (worn on the face)' [ZF3/Wkt//K(s)//IFb/FD/SS] <ç'adir; ç'arik; p'erde>

rûpoşî رووپۆشی (K[s]) = mask, veil. See **r̄ûpoş**.

rûpûş رووپووش (IFb/FD/SS) = mask, veil. See **r̄ûpoş**.

r̄ûr ڕوور (PS) = oleander. See **r̄ûl**.

r̄ûr̄eş ڕووڕەش *adj.* disgraced, defamed: **•Tu min *rûreş dernexî*!** (L) You'*re not going to disgrace* me! {also: [rou-rech] رورش (JJ)} < r̄û = 'face' + r̄eş = 'black' {r̄ûr̄eşî} [L/K/IFb/B/JJ/TF/ZF3]

r̄ûr̄eşî ڕووڕەشی *f.* **(;-yê).** disgrace, defamation, scandal: **•Herdu bûk ditirsîyan ku xelk seba wê *rûreşîyê* kar û îş nedine wan** (Zerîn Tek:RN2 56[1998] 7) Both daughters-in-law were afraid that no one would give them a job because of that *scandal*. {syn: 'et'ib; 'eyb; fedî[karî]; fehêt; sosret [2]; şerm; şermezarî; xax} [K/IFb/B/GF/ZF3] <hetk; r̄ûr̄eş>

R̄ûs I ڕووس *m.* **().** Russian: **-jina r̄ûs** = Russian woman; **-zimanê r̄ûsa[n]** = Russian language {also: Ûris (F-2/K-2/JB3); [rous] روس (JJ)} [F/K/IFb/B/JJ/ZF3//JB3]

r̄ûs II ڕووس/ڕویـس [Bw] (JB1-A/SK/GF/Bw) = naked, nude; flat broke. See **r̄ût**.

rûsipî رووسِـپـی (FJ/GF/JJ) = blameless, vindicated. See **r̄ûspî I**.

R̄ûsî ڕووسی *adj.* Russian. {also: Hûrisî (Wkt-2); Rusî (Wkt-2); Rusyayî (Wkt-2); Rûsyayî (Wkt-2); Ûrisî (Wkt-2/BF-2)} Sor R̄usî ڕوسی [IFb/BF/Wkt/ZF3/SS/CS]

r̄ûspî I ڕووسـپـی *adj.* 1) blameless, unsullied, with one's reputation or honor in tact; 2) vindicated, proven right: **•Cma'et, divînî, go, ez ew jinim, ... îro jî *r̄ûspîme*** (HCK-3, #2, 29) People, you [sing.] see, I am that woman, ... today I am *vindicated*; **-r̄ûspî derk'etin** (K/B) to be vindicated, be proven right; **-r̄ûspî derxistin** (K/B)/**rûsipî kirin** (FJ/GF) to vindicate, prove s.o. right. {also: rûsipî (FJ/GF); [rou sipi] روسپی (JJ)} Cf. T akyüzlü & Ar abyaḍ al-wajh أبـيـض الـوجـه [lit. 'white of face']; Sor r̄ûsipî ڕووسِـپـی = 'honorable, of fine character, reputable' [HCK/K/IFb//FJ/GF/JJ/ZF3]

r̄ûspî II ڕووسپی (K) = village elder. See **r̄îspî**.

r̄ûspîtî ڕووسپیتی (K) = eldership. See **r̄îspîtî**.

Rûsyayî رووسیایی (Wkt) = Russian. See **R̄ûsî**.

r̄ûşandin ڕووشاندِن *vt.* **(-r̄ûşîn-).** to scrape, scratch; to graze, brush up against. Sor r̄ûşandin ڕووشـانـدِن = 'to abrade, scrape, skim past' [Bw/IFb/OK]

r̄ût ڕووت *adj.* 1) {syn: kot (JB3); tazî I; zelût} naked, nude, bare *(lit. & fig.)*: **-rût û zilût** (BZ) stark naked: **•Quling *rût û zelût dibe* û çermê wê tev didirre, xwîn jê diherike** (ZZ-3, 259) The stork *is stripped bare* and her flesh is completely torn, she is bleeding; 2) {syn: bêp'ere[2]} poor, destitute; flat broke, penniless (Bw) [r̄ûs]: •[**Babê keçê nadit ku Polo *rûse***] (JR) The girl's father won't give [her (=marry her off) to Polo] because Polo is *poor* **•Ez ê *r̄ûs* im** (Bw) I am *flat broke*/I don't have a penny to my name; 3) bare *(tree)* (JB3); barren *(land)* (IF): **-r̄ûte-tazî** (Ba2) do.: **•kevirêd *r̄ûte-tazî*** (Ba2) *bare* rocks; 4) bald (K). {also: lût (K[s]); r̄ûs II (JB1-A/SK/GF-2/Bw); [rout رت/rous روس] (JJ); <rût> روت (HH)} Sor r̄ût ڕووت; Hau r̄ût (M4) {r̄ût[ay]î} [K/A/IFb/B/JB1-S/JB3/JJ/HH/GF/TF//K(s)//JR/JB1-A/SK/Bw]

r̄ûtayî ڕووتـــايـــى *f.* **(-ya;).** nudity, nakedness. {also: r̄ûtî (K/A/IFb/TF)} {syn: tazîtî} [K/B//A/IFb/TF/ZF3] <r̄ût>

r̄ûtî ڕووتى (K/A/IF/ZF3) = nudity. See **r̄ûtayî**.

r̄ûv ڕووڤ (IFb/GF/ZF#) = pubic hair. See **r̄ov**.

r̄ûvik ڕووڤِك (GF/HH) = pubic hair. See **r̄ov**.

r̄ûvî I ڕووڤى (K/B/HH/GF) = fox. See **r̄ovî I**.

r̄ûvî II ڕووڤى (B/HH) = guts, intestines. See **r̄ovî II**.

rwîn روين (IF) = liquid. See **r̄on II**.

S س

sabat سابات (TF)/s̲abat صابات (HR) = basket; box. See **sebet**.

sabav ساباڤ/s̲abav صاباڤ (TF) = son of a dog. See **sebav**.

sabûn سابوون *f.* **(-a;-ê).** soap: -**sabûn kirin** (B/IF) to soap up; -**sabûna desta** (B) hand soap; -**sabûna k'inca** (B) laundry detergent. {also: savûn; [saboun] صابون (JJ); <s̲abûn> صابون (HH)} Cf. Ar ṣābūn صابون, T sabun [L/K/A/JB3/IFb/B/JJ/HH/GF/TF]

saçm•e ساچمه/**saç'me** [JB1-S]/**s̲açme** صاچمه *f.* **(;•ê).** 1) buckshot, small shot, BB pellets; 2) shrapnel (Zeb): •***Saçmeyek*** **vê ket** (Zeb) He was hit by a *piece of shrapnel*. {also: [satchmé] صاچمه (JJ); <s̲açme> صاچمه (HH)} <T saçma <saçmak = 'to scatter, strew'; Sor saçme ساچمه = 'small shot' [Zeb/K/IFb/B/JB1-S/GF/OK//JJ/HH]

sade ساده/**s̲ade** صاده [FS/HH] *adj.* 1) plain, simple; 2) white (Bw). {also: [sadé] ساده (JJ); <s̲ade> صاده (HH)} Cf. P sāde ساده; Sor sade ساده = 'plain, simple, artless' [Bw/K/IFb/JJ/GF/AD//HH/FS]

sadegî سادهگی (IFb/GF) = simplicity. See **sadetî**.

sadetî سادهتی *f.* **(-ya;-yê).** simplicity: •***sadetîya*** **jîyana gundîya** (Mehfel 5[2001], 7) *the simplicity of* the life of villagers. {also: sadegî (IFb/GF-2); sadeyî (GF-2/ZF3-2); [sadeti] سادهتی (JJ)} Cf. P sādegī سادگی [JJ/GF/ZF3/Wkt]

sadeyî سادهیی (GF/ZF3) = simplicity. See **sadetî**.

saet سائەت/**sa'et** ساعەت [HH/SK] *f.* **(-a;-ê).** 1) {syn: demjimêr[2]} hour; time: -**nîv saetê** = half hour; 2) {syn: demjimêr[1]} clock, timepiece, watch: •**30 sal berê *seeta* bavê min ketibû vê bîrê, min jî îro derxist** (LM, 12) 30 years ago my father's *watch* fell into this well, today I brought it out. {also: seet (LM); sehet I (K); seȟat (GF); seȟet I (B/EP-7/Z-1); siȟet (Z-1); [saat] ساعت (JJ); <sa'et> ساعت (HH)} < Ar sā'ah ساعة --> P sā'at ساعت --> T saat; Hau se'ate *f.* = 'hours, clock' (M4) [K//JB3/IFb//HH/SK//GF//B//JJ//LM]

saf ساف (IFb/GF) = clear. See **safî**.

safî سافی *adj.* clear *(in its various meanings)*; pure: -**ji hev safî kirin** (IF) to separate from each other: •**Ort'a [wana] şûr *safî dike*** (XF) [They] are at daggers with each other/[They] are on bad terms with each other [lit. 'a sword separates between them']: •**Erke ko tu qebûl nakî, were ez û te hev û din, li vir *safî bikin*, hêja ezê heřim** (Z-3) If you don't accept it, come let's you and I *part on bad terms* and I will go. {also : saf (IFb-2/GF-2); [safi] صافی (JJ); <s̲afî> صافی (HH)} <Ar ṣāfī صافی (ṣāfin) (صافٍ) [Z-3/K/IFb/B/JJ/HH/GF/XF] <sayî I>

sahî ساهی (OK)/s̲ahî صاهی (FS/HH) = clear. See **sayî I**.

sahm ساهم (Elk) = terror; awe. See **saw**.

sahmek ساهمهك (GF) = terror; awe. See **saw**.

sak ساك *m.* **(-ê;).** buffalo calf: -**sakê gamêşê** (FS) do. {also: <sak> ساك (HH)} {syn: gedek} [Haz/IFb/HH/GF/ZF3/FS] <gamêş; medek>

sakol ساكۆل *m.* **(-ê;).** good-for-nothing, worthless bum, base, low, vile, vulgar person: •[***Sakol***<ê> {سكول} **xwe bila bişînin bi xwandinê**] (Necdet. "Cotkarî," Rojî Kurd, 1913, 25) They should send their *bums* to study •[**Şewîş** (?) **nola *sakol***<ê> {ساكول} **gundî teşqelekî** [sic] **nedikir**] (F.Temo. "Çîrok," Rojî Kurd, 1913, 25) Shewish did not make problems like the village *bum*. {also: sakûl (GF); [sa-koulê] ساكله (JJ)} {syn: qeşmer; t'ewt'ewe} <s̲e = 'dog' + kolan = 'street' [Rojî Kurd/A/IFb/HH/FS//GF//JJ]

sakûl ساكوول (GF) = good-for-nothing. See **sakol**.

sal سال/**s̲al** صال [FS/HH] *f.* **(-a;-ê).** year: •**p'aê *salêyî* p'iř** (Ba2) a large part *of the year* •**Îsal heft *salê* te ye, qoliptîye *sala* heşta, ji bona xatirê kevnek jina te xwe xistîye vî halî** (L) It's been seven *years*, going on eight *years*, that you have been miserable over some old lady; -**îsal** (BX/K/A/JB3/IF/JJ/B) this year; -**sala çûyî** (A/ZF3)/**sala borî** (JB3) last year {syn: par I}. {also: [sal] سال (JJ); <s̲al> صال (HH)} [Pok. 1. k̑el- 551.] 'warm': Skt śarád- = 'autumn'; Av sarəd- = 'year'; OP θard- (Kent); P sāl سال; Sor sał ساڵ; Za serri *m.* (Todd); Hau sałe *f.* (M4) [K/A/JB3/IFb/B/JJ/SK/GF/TF/ZF3//HH/FS] <par; pêrar; sersal>

salewext سالەوەخت *f.* **(-a;-ê).** 1) twelvemonth, a year's time *(approximately 365 days)*: •**Çend řoja şûnda t'emam dibe *salewexta* kuřê min, ku ew li Moskvaê dixûne** (B) In a few days it will be *a* *full year's time* that my son has been studying in Moscow; 2) yearly salary. {also: salewextî (B-2); s̱alwext, m. (FS)} < sal = 'year' + wext = 'time' [Ber/K/B/GF/ZF3//FS]

salewextî سـالـەوەخـتـی (B) = a year's time. See **salewext**.

salik سالِك (TF) = basket. See **selik**.

salinî سالِنی (IFb) = [x] years old. See **salî**.

salix سـالِـخ *m./f.(ZF3/FS)* **(-ê/-a; sêlix/).** 1) {syn: cab [2]; xeber} *(often in pl.)* information, data; knowledge; news or information about stg. unknown: **•Kurdên Êzidî ... gehiştine welatên din bi daxwaza tenahî û aştîyê û ... heta van salên dumahîyê *saloxên* wan zor kêm ji me ra dihatin** (Metîn 6:3, Adar 1992, 49) Yezidi Kurds ... have reached other countries in search of peace and security ... these last few years we have heard little *news* of them **•Erê te çi *salox* jê seḧ nekirin?** (FS) Haven't you found out any *news* of it? [asked about stg. lost]; **-salix dayîn** (B) to report, give information; **-salix hildan** (K) to find out about, receive or get information or news about: **•Wexta Al-p'aşa *salixê* kalê *hilda*, îdî xwexa r̄abû çû pey kalê** (Z-1) when Al-pasha *received news of* the old man (=found out about), he got up and went to [lit. 'after'] him; **-salix kirin** (B) to inquire, gather information; **-salix-sûlix** (K)/**salix û sûlix** (EP-7)/**salox û silûx** (ZF3) data, information; news; 2) {syn: pênase} description; definition. {also: saliẍ (GF); saloq (FS-2); salox (A/IFb/TF/ZF3/FS); saloẍ (GF-2); [salig] سـالـگ (JJ); <saloẍ> سـالـوغ (HH)} Cf. T salık/sağlık = 'advice, inquiry or answer as to the location of a place' [Z-1/K/A/IFb/B/ZF3/FS//JJ//GF//HH]

saliẍ سالِغ (GF) = information, news. See **salix**.

salî سـالـی *adj.* ... years old: **•Tu çend *salî* [yî]?** = How old are you? **•Casimê Celîl bû 75 *salî*** (Ber) Jasim Jelil has turned 75. {also: salinî (IFb)} [Ks/Ber/K/A/ZF3//IFb] <'emir II; jî III; qulibîn>

salname سـالـنـامـە *f.* **(-ya;-yê).** 1) {syn: rojname [2]; rojnîş} calendar: **•Nûbihara ku ev çar sal e *salnameya* Kurdî diweşîne îsal jî *salnameya* xwe derxist** (FB: Bediuzzeman Seîdê Kurdî) N. which has been publishing a Kurdish *calendar* for 4 years has put out its *calendar* for this year as well; 2) yearbook, annual (Kmc). {also: salneme (K-2)}P sālnāme سالنامه; Sor sałname ساڵنامە [ZF/RZ/GF/FJ/K/IFb/CS/TF/Kmc/ZF3]

salneme سـالـنـەمـە (K) = calendar; yearbook. See **salname**.

saloq سالۆق (FS) = information, news. See **salix**.

salos سـالـۆس (A/IFb/HH/GF) = hypocritical. See **salûs**.

salox سالۆخ (A/IFb/TF/ZF3/FS) = information, news. See **salix**.

saloẍ سالۆغ (GF) = information, news. See **salix**.

salûs سـالـووس *adj.* two-faced, hypocritical: **•Ew *mirovekê salûs* e** (FS) He is *a hypocrite*. {also: salos (A/IFb-2/GF); [salous] سالوس (JJ); <salos> سـالـوس (HH)} {syn: dur̄û I} Cf. P sālūs سـالـوس [K/IFb/JJ/FS//A/HH/GF]

salvan سالڤان (FS) = camelherd. See **selwan**.

salveger̄ سـالـڤـەگـەڕ *f.* **(-a;-ê).** anniversary: **•PKK di *salvegera* damezrandina xwe de, 4 leşkerên tirk ku di êrîşan de dîl girtibû** [sic] **azad kir** [sic] (Wlt) On *the anniversary of* its establishment, the PKK set free four Turkish soldiers who had been taken prisoner in attacks. {syn: sersal [1]} [(neol)Wlt/ZF3/Wkt]

salwan سالوان (GF) = camelherd. See **selwan**.

salwanî سالوانی (GF) = camel herding. See **selwantî**.

s̱alwext صـالـوەخـت, m. (FS) = a year's time. See **salewext**.

sam سام (GF) = terror; awe. See **saw**.

s̱amal صـامـال (FS) = blue **bergûz** material. See **semayî**.

samî سـامـی *f.* **().** oxbow, the rods tied around the draft animal's neck on a yoke. {syn: guhnîr; k'ulabe} [CCG/IFb/ZF3]

sanahî ساناهی (Bw) = ease. See **asanî**.

sanayî سانایی (OK) = ease. See **asanî**.

sandiqساندِق (EH/IF) = box. See **sindoq**.

sandux ساندوخ (B) = box. See **sindoq**.

sandûq ساندووق = box. See **sindoq**.

sanik سـانِـك (ZF3) = infant boy at his circumcision ceremony. See **sanîk**.

sanîk سـانـیـك *m.* **().** infant boy being circumcised while sitting in the lap of his *kirîv*, qv.; godson. {also: sanik (ZF3)} [Ag//ZF3] <kirîv>

sansûr سـانـسـوور *f.* **(-a;-ê).** censorship, ban [Ar murāqabah مراقبة, T sıkıdenetim/sansür, P sānsūr سـانـسـور]: **•Piştî 13 salan Îranê *sansûra* li ser romana nivîskarê kurd rakir** (rudaw.net 3.vi.2017) After 13 years Iran has lifted *the ban* on the novel of a Kurdish author; **-sansûr kirin** (Wkt/ZF3)/ **sensor kirin** (IFb) to censor, ban: **•THY**

rojnameya BîrGun li hewayê *sansûr kir*! (ANFNews 13.vii.2013) Turkish Airlines *censored* the newspaper Birgün in the air. {also: sensor (IFb)} {syn: *çavdêrî} <Fr censure; Sor sansor سانسۆر [rûdaw/ZF3/Wkt//IFb]

sap ساپ *m.* **(-ê; sêp).** stalks of straw remaining after the harvest. {also: <sap> ساپ (HH)} {syn: qesel} Cf. T sap; Sor sap ساپ = 'stack of winnowed grain' [CCG/K/B/A/IFb/FJ/GF/HH/Kmc/ZF] <lask>

sapîte ساپیته, m. (SS/FS) = ceiling. See **s̲apîtke**.

sapîtk ساپیتك, m. (FS) = ceiling. See **s̲apîtke**.

s̲apîtk•e صاپیتكه *f.* (;•ê). ceiling: •**Xizmeta te jî li min xoş hat. Serak û naw *sapîtke* û kunedîwar jî min dan e te. Mala xo têda da-nê** (SK 1:5) Your service too has pleased me. I have given you the rafters and (crannies) in *the ceiling* and holes in walls. Make your home in them. {also: sapîte, m. (SS/FS); sapîtk, m. (FS-2); sapûtk (OK); sepîtk (Kmc-6282/RZ)} {syn: ar̄îk; asraq; *binban (Kmc); kuşxank (Bw); *qarçik (Kmc/RZ)} Cf. Mod Gr sofita σοφίτα; Yiddish sufit סופיט [SK//OK//RZ/Kmc-6282//SS/FS]

sapog ساپۆگ (B) = boot. See **sapok**.

sapok ساپۆك *m./f.(B)* (/-a; /-ê). boot(s): •**Kerro *sapokê* min ji nigê min bikşîne** (FK-kk-13:130) Kerro, take my *boots* off my foot •**K'esîvê te k'incê cendirmê xwe dike, *sapokê* wî p'ê dike, ...** (Z-922, 315) 'Your pauper' puts on the policeman's clothes, puts his *boots* on, ... {also: sapog (B)} {syn: p'otîn} <Rus sapog сапог [Z-922/K/A/IFb//B] <sol>

sapûtk ساپووتك (OK) = ceiling. See **s̲apîtke**.

sar سار/**s̲ar** صار [SK-2/HH/FS] *adj.* 1) cold: •**Payîz dahat, dunya pîçek *sar* bû** (SK 2:12) Autumn came and the weather became a little *cold*; 2) indifferent, reluctant, listless: -**destê *fk-ê* sar bûn** (XF) to be confused; to lose one's head; to be indifferent to stg.: •[After the deaths of Mem and Zin] ***destê* P'erî-Xatûnê ji mal û ḧala *sar bûbû*** (Z-1) Peri-Khatun had *lost interest in* her house and chores [lit. 'Peri-Khatun's hands had gotten cold from her house and condition'] {also: [sar] سار (JJ); <s̲ar> صار (HH)} {≠germ} [Pok. 1. k̂el-551.] 'warm': Skt śiśira-- = 'cold'; O Ir*sarta- (A&L p. 84 [IV,3] & p. 90 [XIII, 1]): Av sarəta- = 'cold' & sarə-δā- = 'bringing cold'; P sard سرد; Oss sald; Sor sard سارد; Za serd (Todd); Hau serd (M4). *For connection between hot and cold, see Buck, p. 1077, §15.85: "It is well known that extreme heat and cold, as in touching a red-hot iron or a piece of ice, produce the same sensations, and there is every probability that a certain group of words for 'hot' (Lat. 'calidus', etc.) and another for 'cold' are, in fact, cognate."* Eng 'cold' < [Pok. 3. gel(ə)- 365.] 'cold; to freeze', cf. Lat gelare = 'to freeze' {sarayî; sarî I; serma} [K/A/JB3/IFb/B/JJ/JB1-A/SK/GF/TF/OK//HH/FS] <qerisokî; serma; sur̄ I; t̲ezî II; zivistan>

sarayî سارایی (K) = coldness. See **sarî I**.

sarinc سارِنج *f.* **(-a;-ê).** 1) cistern: •**Ava *sarincê* s̲ar e** (FS) *Cistern* water is cold; 2) (IFb/ZF3/Wkp/Wkt) = refrigerator. See **sarincok**. {also: saring (FD-2/CS-2); sarînc (GF)} Cf. T sarnıç & Ar ṣahrīj صهريج < P sārinj سارنج = 'cistern'--> T sarnıç [K/IFb/TF/ZF3/FD/FS/CS/Wkt/Wkp//GF] <k'ûp[2]>

sarincok سارِنجۆك *f.* **(-a;-ê).** refrigerator, fridge, icebox [Ar t̲allājah ثلّاجة/barrādah برّادة; T buzdolabı; P yaxčāl يخچال]: •**Divê zêde deriyê *sarincokê* vekirî nemîne** (diyarname 28.vi.2008) The door *of the refrigerator* should not remain open too long •**Hekariyên ku di demsala havînê de pincarên ku ji serê çiyayan berhev dikin û xurekên ku hazir dikin ji bo ji germahiya havînê mihafeze bikin şikeftên heremê** [sic] **wek *sarincê* bi kar bînin** [sic = **tînin**] (kelhaamed 09.viii.2017) People from Hakkari who collect edible plants from the mountains in the summer and protect the food which they prepare from the summer heat, use the caves of the region as *refrigerators* •**Li Silopiyê termê 6 welatî li nav *sarincokê* mal û mizgeftan tên ragirtin!** (RojavaNews 03.i.2016) In Silopi the corpses of 6 citizens are being held in *the refrigerators* of homes and mosques. {also: sarinc[2] (IFb/ZF3-2/Wîkîpediya/Wkt)} {*other proposed words*: avsark; *avsarker; *cemedank; *dolaba qeşayê; *dolaba sarker; *sarker; *selace} = Sor yexçał یەخچاڵ [ZF3/RZ/Kmc/Wkt/Wîkîpediya/CS//IFb] <avsark>

saring سارِنگ (FD/CS) = cistern. See **sarinc**.

sarî I ساری *f.* **(-ya;-yê).** coldness, frigidity: •**di sariya sibehê / û hingûra êvarê de** (Wkt) in the cold of the morning / and the evening twilight. {also: sarayî (K-2); sarîtî (ZF3-2/Wkt-2)} [K/JB3/IFb/GF/TF/OK/ZF3/Wkt] <sar; serma; sur̄ I>

sarî II ساری/**s̲arî** صاری *adj.* contagious, catching *(disease)*: •[**Ekrad jî weku Efrancan qewî zêde**

ji nexweşî û webayî û ĥalî û 'illetêd ku s̱arî ne dit̲irsin û bi dûr dikevin] (BN 178) Kurds, like Westerners, are greatly afraid of diseases and epidemics and conditions that are *contagious*, and shun them. {also: [sari] سـارى (JJ)} < Ar sārin سارٍ (<√s-r-y سرى) = 'contagious (disease)' [BN//JJ/OK] <vegirtin [5]>

sarîtî ساريتى (ZF3/Wkt) = coldness. See **sarî I**.

satar ساتار *m./f.(FS)* **(/-a; vî satarî/).** heath, meadow, uncultivated patch of ground *(in a forest)*: **•Ad û qirar be, cisnê** [sic] **min di *satar* da zehf in, ku tu min berdî ezê li cinsê xwe temî bikim, ku di nava vî *satarî* de kes nêzîkî te nebe** (J2, 26) Let this be an oath and a vow, there are many of my species in *the heath*, if you let me go I will instruct all of my species that on *this heath* no one should come near you [to harm you]. [J2/IFb/GF/FS] <mêrg>

satil ساتِل *f.* **(-a;-ê).** 1) {syn: dewl I; 'elb} bucket, pail; small bucket *as opposed to* **sîtil** = *large bucket* (Wn): **•Kalo *satil* ji zêran dagirt û min kişand jorê** (ZZ-10, 149) The old man filled *the bucket* with gold pieces and I pulled it up **•*Satilek* girtîye destê xwe û dest pê kirîye ava lîçê bi wê *satilê* vala kiriye** (Bkp, xxviii) He took *a bucket* in his hand and began emptying the water of the pool with that *bucket*; 2) Aquarius *(astr.)* (Ro). {also: [sitil] ستل (JJ); <s̱atil> صاتل (HH)} Cf. Ar saṭl سطل ; W Arm sidł սիտղ; Lat situla = '(water) bucket' [Wn/JB3/IFb/OK/Ro//JJ//HH] <gadoş> See also **sîtil**.

sat[']ircem ساتِرجەم *f.* **().** (head) cold, common cold, catarrh; flu, influenza: **•Al-p'aşa û giregirava gelekî hev birin-anîn, yek go--*sat'irceme*, yek go--sermaye, yek go--tirsaye** (Z-1) Al-pasha and his entourage debated a great deal among themselves, one said it was *the flu*, one said it was a cold, one said it was out of fear. {syn: p'ersîv; sitam} Cf. setircem [Erciş-Van] = 'pleurisy' [akciğer yangısı, zatülcenp] (DS, v. 10, p. 3593); Za satilcan (Mal); NENA satirjam = ?'frozen' (Garbell) [Z-1/(K)/Wkt]

satircemî ساتِرجەمى *adj.* having a cold, having caught cold [enrhumé]: **-sat'ircemî bûn** (K) to catch cold. [K]

sat'or I ساتۆر/**s̱ator** صاتۆر [FS] *f.* **(-a;-ê).** 1) large knife for cutting meat, butcher's knife, meat cleaver: **•Wî goşt bi *s̱atorê* hûr kir** (FS) He cut up the meat with a *meat cleaver*; 2) executioner's sword: **•Gazî sat'orçîyê xo ke, / Bila sat'orekê li serê min xe** (Z-3) Call your executioner, / so that he can chop off my head with a sword/cleaver. {also: satûr (IF-2); [sator] صاطور (JJ)} {syn: sîkar} Cf. Ar/P sāṭūr ساطور = 'meat-cleaver, large chopping knife', T satır/satur [Z-3/IF/JJ/FS/ZF3] <hisan; k'êr III; şefir; şûr>

sat'orçî ساتۆرچى *m.* **(-yê;).** executioner: **•Gazî *sat'orçîyê* xo ke** (Z-3) Call your *executioner*. {syn: celat} [Z-3] <sat'or I>

satranc ساترانج (IFb) = chess. See **şetrenc**.

satranç ساترانچ (A) = chess. See **şetrenc**.

satrinc ساترنج = chess. See **şetrenc**.

satûr ساتوور (IF) = meat cleaver. See **sat'or I**.

sava ساڤا (OK/BF/Wkt)/s̱ava صاڤا (FS) = newborn. See **sawa**.

savar ساڤار/**s̱avar** صاڤار [FS] *m./f.(SK)* **(-ê/-a; savêr** [K/B]/**sêvêr** [B]/**-ê** [SK]**).** FS: *m.* when uncooked; *f.* when cooked; 1) bulgur, cracked wheat germ; wheat groats or chaff: **•Me *savarê* xwe liser tehtê kutaye** (GF) We beat our *bulgur* [*barley groats*] against the stone slab; 2) dish of cooked grain or groats (B): **•Ne dixwim *sawarê*, ne diçim hawarê** (IF/BX) Neither do I eat *savar*, nor do I respond to the call for help [cf. T Ne şeytanı gör, ne salâvat getir = 'Neither see the devil nor call on god'] *[prv.]* **•Wextê ko Smail Paşa zanî dîharîya maqûlêt Mizûrîyan kûr in, pîçek di dilê xo da sil bû. Gote pêşxizmetêt xo, "Têşta wan *s̱ewar* bît. Sênîyan tejî biken, serê wan qubbeyî biken, pişkêt qelîya goştê kûran bi r̄exêt *s̱ewarê* wenên. Her sênîyekî kilkekî kûr̄î di nawa serî biçeqînin weto ko qund r̄awestît" ... Wextê wan temaşe kir ko têşta wan *s̱ewar* --we li nik wan *s̱ewar* gelek 'eybekî mezin e bo mêwanêt mu'teber--we ser wê hindê r̄a jî kilkêt kûran li ser sênîyan çeqandine, di yêk-û-do fikirîn, destêt xo kêşane paş. Pêkwe gotin, "Paşa, me têr xar. Xudê zêde ket ..."** (SK 24:222,224) When Ismail Pasha learnt that the present of the Mizuri elders was kids, he became a little annoyed in his heart. He said to his attendants, "Let their morning meal be *of crushed wheat*. Fill the trays, pile them up like a dome and put the pieces of fried kid-meat round *the boiled wheat*. On each tray stick a kid's tail in the middle of the pile so that it stands erect." ... When they saw that their meal was *of crushed wheat*--and with them *crushed wheat* [instead of rice] was a most shameful thing for respectable guests--and that in addition the tails of kids had been stuck on top of the trays, they looked at each other and withdrew their hands. They all said together, "Pasha, we have eaten our fill. May God increase it for you" **•Zikê bixwe *sawarê* divê here hawarê** (BX) The stomach that eats [=i.e., he who eats] *savar*, must respond to a call for help [*prv.*] *This proverb alludes to the duty created by hospitality: he who has enjoyed another's hospitality is honor bound to fight, if necessary, to protect his former host.* {also: sawar, f. (;-ê) (JB3/IFb/OK-2); s̱ewar (SK); [sawar] ساڤار (JJ); <savar> ساڤار (HH)} Sor sawer ساوەر = 'wheat-meal prepared for use as kind of porridge'; Cf. W Arm cawar ձաւար = 'cracked wheat'; perhaps also NENA sare = 'barley' (Garbell) [AB/K/A/B/JJ/HH/GF/ OK/Wn//JB3/IFb/BX/ /FS//SK] <sindik>

savarok ساڤاروك *f.* **().** tiny hailstones (Wn) *[because they resemble grains of **savar** = bulgur].* {syn: xilolîk I[1]} [Wn/K/A/JB3/ZF3] <gijlok; teyrok; zîpik I>

savûn ساڤوون = soap. See **sabûn**.

saw ساو *f.* **(-a;-ê).** great fear, terror; awe; great anxiety, dread: **•*Saw* k'ete dilê wî** (K) *Fear* took hold of him [lit. 'fell into his heart'] **•*Saw* k'etye ser wî** (B)/***Sehm* a bi serê wî ketî** = ***Sehm* a bo çê bû** (Bw) do.; **-saw dayîn** (B) to terrify; **-saw k'işandin** (B) to be terrified; **-sawa xwe xistin** (Z-4) to terrify: **•*Sawa xwe xistîye ser* zar̄okê gund** (Z-4) He *terrified* the children of the village. {also: sahm (Elk); sahmek (GF-2); sam (GF-2); sehew (GF-2); sehiw (TF-2); sehm (IFb-2/SK/GF-2/TF/Bw); sehw (GF-2)} {syn: tirs} [Pok. tres- 1095.] 'to tremble'-->proto-IE *tres-mo(n)- --> proto Ir *θrah-ma(n)- --> P sahm سهم = 'terror, dread'; Sor sam سام = 'awe, dread, majesty'; Cf. NENA sahm *m.* = 'fear, dread' (Garbell); sahvē = 'fear' & sahvānā = 'dreaded, feared' (Zakho) (Sabar: Shemot, p. 156); msahowe [ms-h-w] (Amadiyah) & msahove [ms-h-v] (Zakho) = 'to be frightened' (Hoberman, pp. 150, 219) [Ba2/K/A/IFb/B/GF/OK//Elk//SK/TF/Bw] <tirs>

sawa ساوا *adj.* newborn (baby or young of an animal, or plant): **-berxê s̱ava** (FS) newborn lamb; **-golikê s̱ava** (FS) newborn calf; **-karika sawa** (ZF3) newborn kid; **-zar̄eke sawa** (Ba-1, #19)/ **zar̄okê s̱ava** (FS) a suckling infant, a babe in arms; **-zebeşê s̱ava** (FS) newly grown watermelon. {also: sava (OK/BF/Wkt)/s̱ava (FS)} {syn: şîrmêj} Cf. Sor sawa ساوا = 'very young animal, baby, small fresh shoot (plant)' [Ba-1/A/SK/ ZF3//OK/BF/Wkt/FS] <t'ifal>

sawar ساوار, f. (;-ê) (JB3/IFb/OKw) = cracked wheat germ. See **savar**.

sawêr ساوێر (A/FD/ZF) = fantasy; ghost. See **sawîr**.

sawir ساوِر (Wkt) = fantasy; ghost. See **sawîr**.

sawîlke ساویلکە *adj.* simple, naive, gullible, ignorant, unsophisticated. {also: <sawîlke> ساویلکه (Hej)} {syn: xeşîm} Sor sawîlke ساویلکە [Zeb/OK/Hej/ZF3]

sawîr ساویر *m./f.* **(-ê/-a;/-ê).** 1) fantasy, imaginings, vision; hallucination: **•Ew kete guman û *sawîra*** (FS) He started imagining the worst [lit. 'He fell to doubts and *fantasies*'] **•*Sawîrekê* xwe li serê wî da** (FS) *A fantasy* appeared in his head; 2) ghost, phantom, specter: **•Wekî *sawîrekî* kete ber çavê min** (FS) Like *a ghost* it appeared before me [lit. 'before my eye']. {also: sawêr (A/IFb/FD-2/ZF-2); sawir (Wkt)} Cf. Ar taṣawwur تصوّر = 'fantasy, idea' [A/IFb//GF/TF/FS/ZF3//Wkt] <saw>

sax ساخ *adj.* 1) {syn: p'ak; saxlem} well, healthy; alive; **-sax û selamet** (IFb) a) safe and sound: **•Wana pez ji qir̄bûne xilaz dikir yanê jî ji destê cerdê derdixist û *sax û silamet* vedigeṙande gund** (Ba2:1, 204) They rescued the sheep from destruction or snatched them from the clutches of brigands and returned them *safe and sound* to the village; b) hale and hearty; **-sax bûn** (B) to heal *(vi.)*, be cured {syn: k'ewîn; qenc bûn}: **•Aqû p'êxember wî kirasî nêzîkî ç'avê xwe dike, wî çaxî herdu ç'avê wî dest xweda *sax dibin*** (Ba-1, #37) Jacob the prophet brings this shirt close to his eyes, and both his eyes *are* immediately *cured* [of blindness] **•Dewlçî ç'evekî kor bû ... ç'evê wî *sax dibe*** (Ba) The bucket carrier was blind in one eye ... his eye *heals*; **-destê te saẍ be** (Ag) blessing said by guest to host[ess] after meal [lit. 'may your hands be well'] [reply: **loşî (lûşî) can** (Ag)/**noxşî can** (Srk)]; **-sax kirinve** (Bw) to revive, resuscitate, bring back to life {syn: vejandin}; 2) whole; intact. {also: saẍ (K); [sag] صاغ (JJ); <saẍ> ساغ (HH)} < T sağ; Sor saẍ ساغ/sax ساخ; Hau saq = 'well, fit' (M4) {sax[et]î; saẍî} [K/HH//(JB3)/JB1-A&S//JJ//IFb/A/B/SK/GF/TF/OK/Ba]

<saxesax; saxbûn>

saxbûn ســاخــبــوون *f.* **(-a;-ê).** 1) recovery, convalescence *(from an illness)*; healing *(of a wound)*: **•Bi *saxbûna* wan birînan re lerzeta jî diçû** (Wkp:Lerzeta) With *the healing of* those wounds the malaria also subsided; 2) being in good health (JJ). {also: saẍbûn (K); [sag bouin] صاغ بوين (JJ); <saẍbûn> ساغبون (HH)} [K/HH//A/JB3/(IF)/B/ZF3//JJ]

saxelem ســاخــلــەم (IFb) = healthy; reliable. See **saxlem**.

saxesax ساخەساخ *adj.* alive: **•T'enê Ûsib mirîşka xwe *saxesax* paşda [a]nî** (Ba3-1) Only Joseph brought back his chicken *alive*. {also: saẍe-saẍ (F/K)} [Ba3-1/B/ZF3//F/K] <sax>

saxetî ساخەتی (A) = wholeness; health. See **saẍî**.

saxirî ساخِری *f.* **(-ya;-yê).** croup, crupper, rump of a quadruped: **•Îsmayîl çû nava hespan, destê xwe li *saxirîya* Qirat xist** (krd.riataza.com Koroxlî û Eslan Paşa) I. went among the horses, put his hand on Q.'s *croup*. {also: [sagri] صاغری (JJ)} {syn: qerp'ûz [1] (EP-7); t'erkû (EP-7)} Cf. T sağrı = 'rump (of an animal)' [Z-1/K/ZF3//JJ]

saxî ساخی *f.* **(-ya;-yê).** 1) wholeness; 2) (good) health: **-bi saxî** (HYma) in good health, alive: **•Xwe kuştiye yan jî xwe *bi saxî* veşartiye** (HYma, 29) Did he kill himself or bury himself *alive*; 3) checking. See **saẍtî**. {also: saxetî (A); saẍî} [JB3/IFb/B/SK/GF/OK/ZF//A] <sax; saẍtî>

saxlem ساخلەم *adj.* 1) {syn: p'ak; saẍ} healthy, well; sound, unharmed; alive; 2) {syn: emîn [2]; ewlekar; merd; xudanbext} reliable, trustworthy: **•Bi mebesta ku em ji jêderên *saxlem* xwe li ser rewşa Êzîdiyan bikin xwedî zanîn me ji devê Mîrê Êzîdiyên Duhokê pirsgirêkên wan guhdarîkirin** (Wlt 2:73, 16) With the purpose of informing ourselves about the situation of the Yezidis from *reliable* sources, we have listened to their problems straight from the mouth of the Mîr of the Yezidis of Dihok. {also: saxelem (IFb); saẍlem (F/K); <saẍlem> ساغلم (HH)} <T sağlam = 'healthy, strong, trustworthy' [Bw/Wlt/A/(B)/OK//IFb//F/K/HH]

saxtî ســاخــتــی (K/ZF3) = checking, examination. See **saẍtî**.

saẍ ساغ (K/HH) = whole; healthy. See **sax**.

saẍbûn ســاغــبــوون (K/HH) = recovery, healing; good health. See **saxbûn**.

saẍe-saẍ ساغەساغ (F/K) = alive. See **saxesax**.

saẍî ساغی = wholeness; health. See **saxî**.

saẍlem ساغلەم (F/K) = healthy; reliable. See **saxlem**.

saẍtî ساغتی *f.* **(-ya;).** checking, examination, testing; search: **•Mêrik *çû saẍî* gihîşte darbiř** (Dz, anecdote #7) The man *went out to check*, and reached the woodcutter [who had been wounded by a falling tree]; **-sextîya *fk-ê* kirin** (Erg)/**saxtî kirin** (L): a) to visit, call on, look in on *(a sick person)*: •[Mem didn't come pass out coffee to the members of his father's court. His father sent two men to see why] **Du merî çûn *sêtya* Memê *kirin*** (EP-7, #9) Two men went *to look in on* Mem; b) to examine, inspect, check out {syn: seh kirin [e]}: **•Tuê hindurê vê bîrê *saxtî bikî* bê çi tê de ye** (L-1 #3, 74, l.13) You go inside this well and *check out* what is in it. {also: saxtî (K/ZF3); saẍî (Dz); sextî (Erg); *sêtî (EP-7)} *[Perhaps originally 'checking in on s.o. ill in hopes of finding him well']* [EP-7//K/ZF3//Erg] <saẍ>

saye سایە (SK) = shade, shadow. See **sî I**.

s̲ayis̲ صايِص *m.* **().** three-year-old male goat. {also: seyis II (ZF3); seyîs II (Zeb); seys II (FS); sêyîs (FS-2); [sèis] سیس (JJ)} {syn: hevûrî; kûr I} JJ compares this with Ar tays تيس = 'male goat' [Bşk//JJ/FS//ZF3//Zeb] <gîsk; hevûrî; nêrî I>

sayî I سایی *adj.* clear, bright; cloudless *(of sky)*: **•Ew vira ser piştê vedilezya nava kulîlka, li 'ezmanê *sayîyî* bê 'ewr dinihêřî û dest xweda dik'ete xwe a şirin** (Ba2:1, 202) He would sprawl on his back among the flowers, look up at the *clear*, cloudless sky, and immediately fall fast asleep **•sibeke *ç'îk-sayî*** (Ba) one fine morning. {also: sahî (OK)/s̲ahî (FS); [saï] صای / صاحی (JJ); <s̲ahî> صاهی (HH)} [Ba/K/IFb/B/GF/TF/ZF3//HH/FS//OK//JJ] <řohnî I; safî>

saz ساز *m./f.(FS/ZF3)* **(; sêz, vî sazî/-ê).** 1) saz, bağlama *[stringed musical instrument with long neck]*: **•Wextê hingo keyfa min dîîna bi gotina *saz o lawjan* min deh car hind keyfa hingo dîîna bi gotina xelatan** (SK 27:249) While you were giving me pleasure with your music and singing *songs* I was giving you ten times as much pleasure by talking of presents; **-saz û sazbend** (Z-2) saz and saz player; **-saz xistin** (B) to play the saz; 2) tune (=condition of being in tune) (A): **-saz kirin** (B): a) to tune an instrument; b) to make, found, establish {syn: damezirandin}:

•**Hinek nivîskar diyar dikin ku MHP *xwe ji nû ve saz dike* û ber bi demokratîkbûnê ve diçe** (AW69A1) Some writers declare that the MHP [Nationalist People's Party] is *re-making itself* and becoming more democratic. {also: [saz] ساز (JJ); <saz> ساز (HH)} [Z-1/K/A/JB3/IFb/B/JJ/HH/SK/GF/TF/FS] <t'embûr>

sazbend سازبەند *m.* **(-ê;).** 1) musician who plays on the saz or any stringed instrument: •**Baştirîn *sazbendê* başûrê Kurdistan bû** (avestakurd.ne 20.xii.2015) He was the best *musician* of southern [=Iraqi] Kurdistan; -**saz û sazbend** (Z-2) saz and saz player; 2) zither, dulcimer (JJ) [sas-bänd]. {also: [sas-bend/ sas-bänd] ساسبند (JJ); <sazbend> سازبند (HH)} {sazbendî} [Z-2/EP-7/K/JB3/IFb/B/HH/GF/ZF3/FS//JJ] <begzade [2]>

sazbendî سازبەندی *f.* **(-ya;-yê).** 1) occupation or profession of playing a saz or other stringed instrument (B); 2) art of playing string instruments (B). [K/B/FS] <saz; sazbend>

sazgeh سازگەه *f.* **(-a;-ê).** 1) organization: •***Sazgeha* yekemîn a Kurdan a alîkariyê, li bajarê bochumê li Almanyayê bi navê Heyva Sor (Kızılay) di 15'ê Adarê de damezirî** (Wlt 2:59, 4) The first Kurdish helping *organization*, by the name of the Red Crescent, was established in the city of Bochum in Germany on the fifteenth of March; 2) factory, plant. [(neol)Wlt/ZF3/Wkt/BF] <sazî>

sazî سازی *f.* **(-ya;-yê).** association, institution, foundation *(corporate body)*: •**Heyva Sor bi *saziya* girtiyan HEVKOMÊ re jî di têkiliyê de ye** (Wlt 2:59, 4) The Red Crescent is also in touch with HEVKOM, *the foundation for* prisoners. {syn: weqf} [(neol)Wlt/GF/TF/ZF3] <sazgeh>

se سە/**s̱e** صە [Bw/SK] *m.* **(-yê; sê).** dog, hound: -**seê avê** (B) otter, zool. genus *Lutra*; -**seyê gure** (A) sheepdog, dog adept at protecting sheep from wolves [see gurêẍ] {syn: sepandî}: •**Ḧer kerîkî pêzṟa sê-çar *seêd gurêẍ* derdik'etne çolê** (Ba2) With every flock of sheep, three or four *sheepdogs* went out to the pastures; -**seê har** (A) rabid dog. {also: seg; [seh] سه (JJ); <s̱eh> صه (HH)} {syn: k'elb; kûçik} [Pok. k̑u̯on- 632.] 'dog': Proto Ir *swan-: Median *spaka-; Southern Tati dialects: Chali asbá *m.*; Eshtehardi esbá *m.* (Yarshater); P sag سگ (<*saka- <*swa-ka-); Sor seg سەگ/s̱eg صەگ; cf. Rus sobaka собака. See A&L p. 90 [XIII, 1]. [K/A/JB3/IFb/B/JJ//SK//HH] <ḧemis>

se' kirin سەع کِرِن (Msr) = to hear; to find out; to understand. See **seh: -seh kirin**.

seb I سەب (IFb) = reason. See **sebeb**.

seb II سەب (KH) = for. See **seba**.

seba سەبا *prep.* 1) {syn: bona} for, for the sake of: •**Al-p'aşa ḧukum kir, ku aşiq k'ilameke evînîyê bêje *seva* Memê wî** (Z-1) Al-pasha ordered the singer to sing a love song *for* his [son] Mem •**Lê xwedê meke, ko tu *seb* talankirina gencîneya marî marî bikujî** (KH, 34) God forbid that you kill the snake *for the sake of* pillaging its treasure •**Paşê çû cem t'erzî, t'emî kir *seva* k'incê xwe** (Z-1) Then he went to a tailor, and gave instructions *for* his clothes; -**seba xatirê** ... = do.: •***seva xatirê* min** (Z-1) *for my* sake; -**seba çi** (A/JB3) why? what for?; 2) [*conj.*] [+ *subj.*] in order to, so that: •**Hatine dîwana mîr S. ... *seva* Zîna delal bixazin Ç'ekanṟa** (Z-1) They came to prince S.'s court ... *in order to* request [the hand of] darling zin [in marriage] for Chekan •**Lazime k'omek bidine Q., *seva* k'oçk-serê xwe çê ke** (Z-1) They should help Q. *so that* he can build his palace •**T'eme dida wan, *seva* ewana fikra M. biḧesin** (Z-1) He instructed them *to* find out M.'s opinion. {also: seb II (KH); seva (Z-1); sewa II} Cf. [seb سب/sebeb سبب] (JJ); < Ar sabab سبب = 'cause, reason' [BX/Z-1/K/A/(JB3/IFb)/B/TF//KH]

sebab I سەباب *m.* **().** 1) author, initiator; 2) culprit: •**Were hinekî hêsa be, paşê tuyê *sebaba* nas bikî** (Z-1) come rest a little, then you will meet [lit. 'know'] *the culprits*. {also: sebebk'ar (K/B)} < Ar sabbāb سبّاب [Z-1//K/B]

s̱ebab II صەباب II (SK) = son of a dog. See **s̱ebav**.

s̱ebav صەباڤ *m.* **(-ê; wî s̱ebavî).** *term of abuse*: son of a bitch, son of a dog, dirty cur: •***S̱ebav*, keç'a kûç'ik!** (HR 3:289) *Dirty cur*, daughter of a dog! •**Wî *s̱ebavî* k'êr li telya xo da bû** (HR 3:290) That *son of a bitch* stuck a knife in his finger •**Wextê ko hingo ez ji ṟispîyatî êxistim ew kîşk day-ḧîz e, ew kîşk *s̱e-bab* e dê li cîyê min ṟûnêt?** (SK #167) When you have removed me from the eldership which whoreson, which *son of a dog* is going to sit in my place? {also: sabav (TF); s̱ebab II (SK); segbav (IFb); sehbav (GF)} < se = 'dog' + bav = 'father'; Sor segbab سەگباب [HR/ZF3//TF//SK//IFb//GF] <forq; me'ṟis; p'ûşt; t'eres>

sebeb سەبەب *f.(F/K/IFb)/m.(B/JB1-A/SK)* **(-a/ ;).** cause, reason. {also: seb I (IFb-2); sevev (B-2);

[seb سبب/sebeb سبب] (JJ)} {syn: eger II; sedem I; ûşt} <Ar sabab سبب; Sor sebeb سەبەب [F/K/IFb/B/JJ/JB1-A/SK/GF]

sebebk'ar سەبەبكار (K/B) = author; culprit. See **sebab I**.

sebeq سەبەق (FS) = stanza. See **sebeqe**.

sebeq•e سەبەقە *f.* **(•a;•ê).** stanza *(of Yezidi qewls, beyts, qesîdes and du'a or 'prayers')*: **•Bi vê *sebeqê* Birahîm Xelîl soz da heke ew ji agirê mencenîqê xilas bit**... (GShA, 231) In this *stanze* Ibrahim the Friend promised that if he was released from the fire... **•Ev Qewl ... bi herfên latînî hate weşandin û ji 24 *sebeqan* pêk tê** (Kh.Omarkhali.Metodeke analîza qewlên Êzdiyan, 145) This qewl ... was published in Latin letters and consists of 24 *stanzas*. {also: sebeq (FS)}{syn: malik} [GShA/Omarkhali.Metodeke analîza qewlên Êzdiyan//FS]

sebet سەبەت *f.* **(-a;-ê).** 1) {syn: 'edil; kelik; selik} basket; large basket (B) [sebet]; 2) box, trunk, chest; small box (HH); box or case made of hide with iron trimmings (JJ) [sabat]: **•Çû ber *s̱abata* xwe, xeml û xêlê bûkanîyê li xwe kir** (HR 3:282) She went to her *chest*, put on her bridal finery. {also: sabat (TF)/s̱abat (HR); sepet (K/IFb/GF/ZF); [sebet/sabat] سبت (JJ); <sebet> سبت (HH)} <P sabad سبد --> T sepet; Sor sebete سەبەتە [F/A/B/JJ/HH//K/IFb/GF/ZF//TF/HR] <mekev; sewî; zembîl>

sebir سەبر (K/B/IFb) = patience; sneeze. See **sebr**.

sebî سەبى *m.* **(-yê;).** child, boy: **•Ezê serê te û *sebî* t'ev jêkim** (Z-3) I will behead both you and *the boy*. < Ar ṣabī صبي [Z-3/Frq/ZF3/Wkt]

sebr سەبر /**s̱ebr** صەبر [SK] *f.(L)/m.(Bw/JB1-A)* **(-a/-ê;-ê/-î).** 1) {syn: t'ebatî} patience: **-sebrî kêşan** (Bw) to be patient: **•Pêdivîya tu *sebrî bikêşî*** (Bw) You should *be patient;* **-sebr kirin** = to be patient, wait: **•*Sebirke*, lawo, xwedê řeĥme!** (J) *Be patient*, son, God is merciful!; 2) joy, pleasure, delight, fun: **-sebra dil** (K/XF) do.; **-sebrê *fk-ê* bi *fk-ê* hatin** (Bw/SK) to take delight in s.o., find s.o.'s company enjoyable [in neg. means 'to be bored']: **•Mamo, *s̱ebrê min nethat*** [=nedihat], **ejî** [=ez jî] **hatime nik te** (JB1-A #144) Uncle, *I was bored*, so I came to [see] you **•*S̱ebra min* qewî *bi* te *têt*** (SK 9:82) *I'm delighted* to have you [as a guest] **•*Sebrê* min *pê dihêt*** (Bw) I *enjoy being around him* •[**sûretê tajî û ẍezalê**] **Ferca wan xweş e, *sebra* miro *pê tê*** (L-I, #4, 108, l. 8-9) [the picture of the hound and the gazelle] The sight of them is pleasant, people *enjoy it*; **-sebra dilê *fk-ê* hatin** (XF/K) do.: **•*Sebra dilê* min bê te *nayê*** (K) *I can't enjoy myself* [or, relax] without you around; **-sebra xwe pê anîn** (ZF) to amuse o.s., derive enjoyment from: **•Ez pir aciz dibim: tiştek ji min re divê ko *ez sebra xwe pê bînim*** (SW1, 55) I am very bored: I need something *to amuse myself with*; 3) sneezing several times in a row: *the Kurds believe that sneezing several times brings bad luck; therefore, after doing so, one must wait for a few minutes before resuming whatever one was doing prior to sneezing* (K/B): **-sebr hatin** (F) to sneeze {syn: bêhnijîn; hênijîn [3]; pêkijîn}. {also: sebir (K/B/IFb-2); [sebr] صبر (JJ); <s̱ebr> صبر (HH)} < Ar ṣabr صبر = 'patience' [JJ/HH/SK//L/F/JB3/IFb/Bw//K/B] <bi sebr; t'ab>

Sebt سەبت *f.* **(;-ê).** Saturday: **-Sebtê** (Msr) on Saturday. {also: Sept (Czr)} {syn: Paşînî; Şemî} < Ar sabt سبت [Msr/Btm/K/JB3/IF/ZF3//Czr]

sed سەد/**s̱ed** صەد [SK/FS/HH] *num. m.(K)/f.(JB3).* hundred, 100: **•Zînker *sed* zêř xwest, memê dusid zêř daê** (EP-7) The saddlemaker asked for *100* gold pieces, Mem gave him 200 (gold pieces); **-dusid** = two hundred, 200 *(qv.)*. {also: sid; [sed] سد (JJ); <s̱ed> صد (HH)} [Pok ḱm̥tóm <*(d)ḱm̥tóm 192.] 'hundred' <[deḱm̥ 191.] 'ten': Skt śatám; Av satəm; Mid P sad (M3); P ṣad صد; Sor sed سەد; Za se (Todd); Hau s̱ed (M4) [BX/K/A/JB3/IFb/B/JJ/GF//HH/SK/FS] <bi sedan; sedem II>

sedem I سەدەم *f./m.* **(-a/-ê;).** 1) {syn: eger II; sebeb; ûşt} reason, cause: **•Baş e, *sedem* çi ye?** (Wlt 1:49, 16) Well then, what is *the reason*? **•Mixmixk *sedemê* gelek nexweşiyan e** (Wkp) The mosquito is *the cause of* many diseases **•*Sedemek* bi tenê heye** (Wlt 1:49, 16) There is only *one reason*; 2) [*prep.*] because of, for the sake of (JJ/GF): •[***Sedem-a* té hatim**] (JJ) I came *because of* you. {also: semed, m. (BZ/Bkp/FS-2); [sedem] سدم (JJ); <sedem> سدم (HH)} [Wlt/IFb/JJ/HH/GF/TF/ZF/FS//BZ]

sedem II سەدەم/**s̱edem** صەدەم [FS] *adj.* hundredth, 100th. {also: sedemîn (IFb/GF/Wkt-2)} Cf. P ṣadom صدم; Sor sedem[în] سەدەم[ین] [Wkt/FS//IFb/GF/ZF3] <sed>

sedemîn سەدەمین (IFb/GF/Wkt) = hundredth. See **sedem II**.

ṣedeq•e صەدەقە/**sedeqe** سەدەقە [IFb/OK] *f.* **(•a;•ê).** alms, charity: •**[Eger mirofek ji ṯayifa xwendîyan îḧsan û *sedeqeyekê* weyaxû ṯe'am û zadekî bidine feqîrekî ez dê çomaẍekî li vê deholê bidim]** (JR-2) If someone from the class of the learnèd should give *charity* or food to a poor person, I will strike a blow on this drum. {also: [sadaqa] صدقه (JJ); <ṣedeqe> صدقه (HH)}< Ar ṣadaqah صدقة = 'charitable gift, voluntary contribution of alms'; Sor sedeqe سەدەقە [JR/JJ/HH/SK//IFb/OK/ZF3] <îḧsan>

sedir سەدر *m.* **(-ê; sêdir, vî sedirî).** president: •***Sedrê* Cvata Řêspûblîka Ermenîstanêye Mletîê Babkên Arark'syan 18-ê Oktyabrê bi seredana řesmî çûye T'ûrk'îaê** (RT 22[1995] 1) *The president of* the national assembly of the Republic of Armenia, Babken Ararksyan, went to Turkey on an official visit on the 18th of October. {also: sedr (F)} {syn: serok [2]} [RT/K/B//F]

sedmêr سەدمێر *f.* **().** group of 100 soldiers, company *(mil.)*: •**Duhî tevdana kewte û *sedmêran* dom kiriye** (RN) Yesterday the movements of troops and *companies* continued. < sed = '100' + mêr = 'man' [(neol)RN/K(s)]

sedr سەدر (F) = president. See **sedir**.

sedsal سەدسال *f.* **(-a;-ê).** century, 100 years: •**Di *sedsala* XIIan de ji erebî hat wergerandin bo ibranî** (YPA, 43) In the 12th *century* it was translated from Arabic to Hebrew. {also: sedsalî (K/B/GF); [sed sal] سد سال (JJ)} {syn: ç'erx[2]} < sed = '100' + sal = 'year'; =Sor sede سەدە [IFb/JJ/RZ//K/B/GF/ZF]

sedsalî سەدسالی (K/B/GF) = century. See **sedsal**.

seet سەئەت (LM) = hour; clock. See **saet**.

sefar سەفار *m.* **(-ê;).** tinsmith, tinner. {also: seffar (FJ)} <Ar ṣaffār صفّار = 'brazier, brass worker' < ṣufr صفر = 'brass' [IFb/Wkt/ZF3//FJ] <mîsk'ar; sifir>

sefarî سەفاری *f.* **(;-yê).** tinsmithery, tinnery: •**Ew ji me jîrtir bûn ko ji destên wan dihat cildirûtî, terzîtî, *sefarî*, xeratî, koçkarî û nalbendî** (Nefel, 2008) They were more skilled than us, as they were proficient in sewing, tailoring, *tinsmithery*, carpentry, cobblery and shoeing horses. {also: sefartî (Wkp-2)} [Nefel/Wkt/ZF3/Wkp]

sefartî سەفارتی (Wkp) = tinsmithery. See **sefarî**.

sefer سەفەر *f.* **(-a;-ê).** 1) {syn: řêwîtî} trip, journey; travel: **-sefer kirin** (IFb) to take a trip, to travel; 2) {syn: şeř} battle, war, fight; holy war or campaign against infidels: **-deşta seferê** (B) battlefield, battleground {syn: qada şeř}. {also: [sefér] سفر (JJ); <sefer> سفر (HH)} < Ar safar سفر [Z-1/K/IFb/B/JJ/HH/SK/GF/ZF3]

sefî سەفی (Ba3) = stupid. See **sefîh**.

sefîh سەفیه *adj.* stupid: •**Navê wî Bênemêne, řaste ew birê meye, lê belengaze, *sefîye*, tiştekî fam nake** (Ba3-3, #37) His name is Benjamin; true, he is our brother, but he is miserable, he *is stupid*, he doesn't understand anything. {also: sefî (Ba3); [sefih] سفیه (JJ); <sefîh> سفیه (HH)} {syn: aqilsivik; bêaqil; eḧmeq; xêtik} <Ar safīh سفيه = 'stupid; insolent' [Ba3//K/JJ/HH/SK] <aqil I; aqil II>

sefîl سەفیل (JB3/IFb/JJ/ZF3/FS/Wkt) = miserable; poor; simple; ugly. See **sêfîl**.

sefîlî سەفیلی (JB3/ZF3/Wkt) = misery; poverty; powerlessness. See **sêfîlî**.

seg سەگ = dog. See **se**.

segban سەگبان (ZF3) = guard; foot soldier. See **segman**.

segbav سەگباڤ (IFb) = son of a dog. See **ṣebav**.

seglawî سەگلاوی *adj.* fine breed of horse: •**Hespê Bek'o 'esîle, *seklawîye*** (Z-3) Beko's horse is noble, a *seglawi*. {also: seklawî (Z-3); [seqlavi] صقلاوی (JJ); <seglawî> سگلاوی (HH)} according to JJ < Ar ṣaqlāwī صقلاوي, a district near Fallūjah (in Iraq), west of the Euphrates [Z-3//IFb/HH/TF//JJ]

segman سەگمان *m.* **(-ê;).** 1) watchman, guard: •***Segmanên* qesirê bêjî û peyayên wî tev de kuştî bûn û cendekê mîrê bêjî kaş kiri bûn heta ber deriyê qesirê** (Rnh 3:23, 7) The palace *guards* killed the bastard together with his men, and dragged the corpse of the bastard emir up to the gates of the palace; 2) hunter (K/GF). {also: segban (ZF3-2); segvan (TF)} Cf. P sagbān سگبان = 'dogkeeper' (hence 'hunter') [Rnh/K/IFb/GF/OK/ZF3/Wkt//TF]

segur سەگور/**ṣegur** صەگور [FS] *f.* **(-a;-ê).** 1) {syn: berbang; elind; ferec; hingûr [1]; serê sibê; siḧar; spêde; şebeq} dawn, daybreak, sunrise, early morning: •**Dinya bûbû *segur*** (DBgb, 49) The day had dawned [lit. 'the world had become *dawn*'] •***Ṣegur*: Demek e li spêdê û piştî rojava bûnê ye, gava ku dinya piçekê ṯarî dibit ku mirov ṣe û gurgî jêk cuda nakit** (FS) A time in the early morning and after sunset, when it becomes a little dark, so one cannot tell dogs [se] from wolves [gur(g)]; **-sehgura sibê** (Kmc) dawn; 2) {syn: hingûr [2]} twilight, dusk. {also: sehgur (FJ-2/GF-2/Kmc); sewgir (FJ-2); sewgur (GF-2/ZF); sewgurî (Kmc-2); sewgûr (TF) } [DBgb/FJ/GF//FS//Kmc//ZF]

segvan سـەگـڤـان (TF) = guard; foot soldier. See **segman**.

seh سـەه: **-seh kirin** = a) {syn: bihîstin; guh lê bûn (Bw)} to hear *[in Misirc/Kurtalan, province of Sêrt/Siirt, this verb completely replaces **bihîstin**]* [seh kirin]: •**[Melayî weku ev xebera ji jinê *seh kirî*, xwe sil kir]** (JR-3) When the mullah *heard* these words from the woman, he got angry •**Memê dengê Zînê *seh kir*** (EP-7) Mem *heard* Zin's voice •**Min duhu *seh kir* ku ewê here şeher** (B) I *heard* yesterday that he was going to town; b) {syn: guh dan/kirin; guhdarî kirin} to listen to; to perceive; c) {syn: pê ĥesîn} to find out: •**Erê te çi salox jê *seĥ nekirin*?** (FS) *Haven't* you *found out* any news of it? [asked about stg. lost]; d) to examine, inspect, check out (Bw/JB1-A/JJ) [sah' kirin]{syn: saxtî kirin [b]}. {also: se' kirin (Msr); seĥ kirin (JB1-A); [seh kirin سـه كـريـن/sah' kirin صـح كـريـن] (JJ); <seĥkirin سـحـكـرن (seĥdike) سحدكه> (HH)} Cf. Ar ṣaḥḥa صحّ = 'to be correct, true, right' [EP-7/K/JB3/IFb/JJ//Msr//HH/JB1-A/Bw]

sehbav سەهباڤ (GF) = son of a dog. See **s̱ebav**.

seher سـەهـەر, m. (K/CS) = dawn, early morning. See **siĥar**.

sehet I سەهەت (K) = hour; clock. See **saet**.

sehet II سـەهـەت *f.* **(-a;-ê).** health: •***Seheta* wî xirabe** (K/B) He is in bad *health* •***Seheta* wî xweşe** (B) He is in good *health* •***Seheta* we çawane** (F)/**çewane** (B) How is your *health*?/How are you?; **-Sehet be** (IF/HH) bon appétit; **-Seĥet xweş!** (B/HH/IF)/**Seĥeta te xoş** (JB1-A) bravo! good for you! {also: seĥet II (JB1-A/B); sihet (IFb-2); [sahat] صـحـت (JJ); <seĥĥet> سـحّـت (HH)} {syn: saxî} < Ar ṣiḥḥah صحّة [F/K/IFb//JB1-A/B//JJ//HH]

sehew سەهەو (GF) = terror; awe. See **saw**.

sehgur سـەهـگـور (FJ/GF/Kmc) = dawn; dusk. See **segur**.

sehiw سەهو (TF) = terror; awe. See **saw**.

sehm سـەهـم (IFb/SK/GF/TF/Bw) = terror; awe. See **saw**.

sehw سەهو (GF) = terror; awe. See **saw**.

seĥar سەحار (PS) = dawn, early morning. See **siĥar**.

seĥat سەحات (GF) = hour; clock. See **saet**.

seĥet I سەحەت (B/EP-7/Z-1) = hour; clock. See **saet**.

seĥet II سەحەت (JB1-A/B) = health. See **sehet II**.

seĥ kirin سـەح كـرن (HH/JB1-A/JJ/Bw) = to hear; to find out; to understand; to check out. See **seh: -seh kirin**.

seîyed سەييەد/سەئييەد (F) = hunter. See **seydvan**.

seke سەكە (ZF) = stake. See **sik'e.**

sekerat سـەكـەرات *f.* **(-a;-ê).** death watch, waiting at s.o.'s deathbed: •**Herçendî mirina axê bi gundiyan xweş jî bihata, ji tirs û xofa ewqas salan, diviya bû ew bihatana *sikrata* axayê xwe** (Ardû, 53) Although the agha's death pleased the villagers, after the fear and terror of so many years, they felt obliged to wait at their agha's *deathbed* •**Hinek dinalin, hinek dikalin û hinek di niqrîskê [*sekerata*] mirinê dene** (ZZ-10, 149) Some whimper, some sob and some are at death's *doorstep*. {also: sikrat (Ardû); <sekerat> سـكـرات (HH)} <Ar sakrat al-mawt سـكـرة الـمـوت = 'agony of death' [Ardû//IFb/TF/HH/ZF]

seket سەكەت (SK) = lame. See **seqet**.

sekih سەكِه (TF) = stake. See **sik'e.**

sekihîn سـەكِـهـيـن *vi.* **(-sekih-).** to be set on edge *(of teeth)*: •**Bav harsim dixwê, dranên kur *disekihin*** (BX) The father eats sour grapes, and the son's teeth *are set on edge [prv.]*. {syn: alû bûn} Cf. Heb ḳahah קהה & NENA qahe {q-h-j/0} (Garbell) = 'to be blunted, set on edge (teeth)' & qâhé ܩܗܐ/qâyî ܩܝܐ (Maclean) [BX/IFb/ZF] <alû; didan; harsim; xidok>

sekin سەكِن *f.* **(-a;-ê).** stop, stopping place; rest: **-sekin û hedan** (Msr) rest, calm: **-sekin û hedan bi *fk-ê* nak'eve** (Msr) S.o. cannot sit still: •***Sekin û hedan pê nak'eve*** (Msr) *He just can't sit still* •***Sekin û hedan bi te nak'eve*** (Msr) You *just won't sit still* (said to a naughty or overactive child). {also: sekn (GF)} [Msr/K/IFb/ZF3//GF] <hedan; nesikinî; t'ena I>

sekinandin سـەكِـنـانـدِن *vt.* **(-sekinîn-).** 1) {syn: r̄awestandin} to stop *(vt.)*, cause to stop or halt: •**Ew bazirgan *dide sekinandinê*** (Ba) He *has* the caravan *halt*; 2) to park *(a car)* (Zx). {also: [sekinandin] سكناندين (JJ); <sekinandin سكناندن (disekinîne) (دسكنينه)> (HH)} < Ar sakana سكن = 'to calm down; to reside' [K/JB3/IFb/B/JJ/HH/GF/Zx/ZF3] <sekinîn>

sekinîn سـەكِـنـيـن *vi.* **(-sekin-/-sen- [Ag/J]).** 1) {syn: r̄awestan} to stand: •**Gavan çû, ber tatê *sekinî***

(L) The cowherd went and *stood* in front of the rock; 2) to stop: •**Ez ber çem *sekinîm*** (L) I *stopped* (or, *stood*) by the river •**K'eç'ik digrî, qasekê *disene*** (J) The girl cries, *rests* for a while •[description of a wedding] **Mala berbûyêda rokî *bisene* bûkê. Řokî *disene*, qîzê gund, bûkê gund, gencê gund gi top dibin, de'at bilîzin** (Ks) At the house of the bride's sister, the bride *rests/stops*. On the day she *rests*, the girls of the village, the young women of the village, the young men of the village, all gather to dance [at] the wedding •**Wextekê *disene*, keç'ik ze'f belengaz dibe** (J) When she *stops*, the girl becomes very troubled; 3) {syn: ç'av li rê bûn; li bendî bûn/man; hêvîya ... man/bûn; p'an I} to wait for. {also: [sekinin] سـكـنـيـن (JJ); <sekinîn سـكـنـيـن (disekine) (دسـكـنـه)> (HH)} < Ar sakana سكن = 'to calm down; to reside' [K/JB3/IFb/B/JJ/HH/GF] <sekinandin>

sekitîn سەکِتین *vi.* **(-sekit-).** to die *(of ritually unclean animals, e.g., dogs; contemptuous when used of humans; for ritually clean animals,* **mirar bûn** *is used, qv.).* {also: [sekitin] سـكـتـيـن (JJ); <ṣekitîn صكتين (diṣekitî) (دصكتى)> (HH)} [Bw/F/K/IFb/B/JJ/OK//HH] <mirar; mirin>

seklawî سەکلاوی (Z-3) = breed of horse. See **seglawî**.

sekn سەکن (GF) = stopping place. See **sekin**.

sel سەل/**ṣel** صەل [HH/SK] *m.* **().** stone slab (B); broad stone, flat stone (SK): •**Vira hinda kevirekî *sel* apê Şevav em dane sekinandinê** (Ba2-4, 220) Here, near a stone *slab*, Uncle Sh. stopped us. {also: <ṣel> صـــــــل (HH)} [Ba2/K/IFb/B/GF//HH/SK] <kevir; tat I>

ṣelal صەلال (FS) = above, up[stairs]. See **silal**.

selam سەلام (EP-7/K) = greetings, regards. See **silav**.

selamet سەلامەت *adj.* 1) {syn: emîn; t'ena I} safe, secure: •**Eger wucoda wî *selamet* bît û digel bende xudan-merĥemet bît hemî dunya malê min e** (SK 22:202) So long as he is *safe* and well and kind to his servant then all the world's riches are mine •**Şukr bo xudê ku min dujminê xo telef kir û tola xo kireve, ez mam *selamet*** (SK 61:774 = ST, 30 [2nd group]) Thank God, I have finished my enemy and taken my revenge in safety [lit. 'I remained *safe*']; **-sax û selamet** (IFb) a) safe and sound; b) hale and hearty; 2) {syn: sax; saxlem} well, healthy, whole; 3) safety; health. See **selametî**. {also: silamet (B); [salamét (G)/salāmat (Rh)] (JJ); <selamet> سلامت (HH)} <Ar salāmah سلامة = 'safety, well-being': P salāmat سلامت = 'health, safety; safe, healthy'; Sor selamet سەلامەت {selametî; silametî} [K/IFb/JJ/HH/JB1-S/SK/GF/OK //B]

selametî سەلامەتی *f.* **(-ya-yê).** 1) {syn: asayîş; ewlekarî; t'enahî} safety, security; 2) {syn: saxî} health, well-being: •***Silametîya* kuřê te dixwazim** (B) I wish your son a speedy *recovery*. {also: silametî (B); [selameti] سـلامـتـى (JJ)} Cf. P salāmatī سلامتى = 'health, security'; Sor selametî سەلامەتی [K/IFb/JJ/SK/OK/ZF3//B] <selamet>

selav سەلاڤ = greetings, regards. See **silav**.

selb سەلب (Kmc/ZF3) = pannier. See **sepil**.

sele سەلە (B) = basket. See **selik**.

selef سەلەف *m.* **(-ê;).** 1) {syn: ç'avkanî; kanî} spring, source (K): •**Min sê řoj berde *selefê* van kanîyane** (Z-1) Leave me for three days [by] *the source of* these springs; 2) {syn: řêz I[2]; yekîne} group, unit (of people): **-selefê siwaran** (IFb) unit of cavalrymen; 3) percent, % (K): •**pênc *selef*** (K) five *percent*, 5%; 4) interest (accrued interest of money). {also: [seléf] سـلـف (JJ); <selef> سـلـف (HH)} [EP-7/Z-1/K/JB3/IFb/JJ/HH/GF/TF]

selik سەلِك *f.* **(-a;-ê).** basket: •***Selik* ji destên wî ketibû erdê. Kevir bela wela bûn** (HYma, 32) *The basket* fell to the ground from his hands. The stones went all over the place; **-selika gemarê** (İ.Sidar/Ş.Soreklî)/**selka gilêşî** (RZ/SS) waste basket, waste bin: •**Mamoste xwazt rûpela ku Lîna tiji nivîs kiribû biavêje *selika gemarê*, lê bêyî mebest çavên wî li hevoka "Mamosteyê hêja..." ketin** (Shahînê Soreklî FB 27.xii.2015) The teacher was about to throw into *the waste basket* the page that L. had filled with writing, but his eyes accidentally fell on the sentence "Dear teacher". {also: salik (TF); sele (B); selle (GF); sellik (GF-2); selûk (JB1-A); [selé سـلـه/ selik/salek (G)/salik (Rh) سـلـك] (JJ)} {syn: 'edil; kelik; sebet} < Ar sallah سلّة [HYma/K/IFb/JJ/RZ/SS/Kmc/CS//B//GF//JB1-A]

ṣelka mêşka صەلکا مێشکا (Bw) = beehive. See **ṣelmêşk**.

selle سەللە (GF) = basket. See **selik**.

sellik سەللِك (GF-2) = basket. See **selik**.

ṣelmêşk صەلمێشك *f.* **(-a;).** beehive: •**ṣelmêşka mêşa** (FS) do. {also: ṣelka mêşka (Bw-2)} {syn: kewar [1]; kewarmêş} [Bw/Dh/FS] <mêş [2]; xilêfe>

ṣelûk صەلووك (JB1-A) = basket. See **selik**.

selwan سەلوان *m.* **(-ê;).** camelherd; animal herder: •**Êvarekê Hakim Tey rabû cilika selwanan li xwe kir û çû ba devehan** (ZZ-10, 157) One evening H.T. put on the garb of camelherds and went over to the camels •**Serwanekî şêxê Ereba ê deva jî heye** (L) The Arab sheikh also has a camelherd. {also: salvan (FS-2); salwan (GF-2); selwan (ZZ-10/Kmc); servan (GF); serwan (L/K[s])} Cf. P sārbān ساربان = 'camel driver' {syn: heştirvan} [L/K(s)//ZZ/Kmc/FS//GF] <r̄evoçî; şivan>

selwantî سەلوانتی *f.* **(-ya;yê).** camel herding, profession of camelherd or of cameleer: •**Lawik hey li *selwantiya* devehan domand ... Hatime ku ji xwe re li cem wî selwantiyê bikim** (ZZ-10, 157) The boy continued *herding* camels ... I have come to do camel herding for him. {also: salwanî (GF)} [ZZ//GF]

sema سەما *f.* **(-ya;-yê).** dance, dancing: **-sema kirin** (FJ/CS) to dance {syn: r̄eqisîn}: •**Mar hat mîna her̄o, bi dilp'akî, *sema kir*** (Dz #22, 390) The snake came as it did every day, and *danced* with sincerity. {syn: de'wat; dîlan; govend} < Ar samā' سماع = 'hearing; fame; song, harmony' (Hava) --> P samā' سماع = 'singing; music and dance' --> T sema = 'whirling dance of Mevlevi dervishes'; Sor sema سەما = 'dancing (esp. with twisting and finger snapping)' [Dz/K[s]/IFb/FJ/GF/CS]

semaî سەمائی (Bw) = blue **bergûz** material. See **semayî**.

s̱emal صەمال (FS) = blue **bergûz** material. See **semayî**.

semalî سەمالی (Zeb) = blue **bergûz** material. See **semayî**.

semayî سەمایی *adj.* pattern of **bergûz** material: light blue (şîn). {also: s̱amal (FS); semaî (Bw-2);s̱emal (FS-2); semalî (Zeb)} [Bw//Zeb//FS] <bergûz>

semed سەمەد, m. (BZ/Bkp/FS) = reason, cause. See **sedem I**.

semen سەمەن (GF) = idol. See **senem**.

semt سەمت *m./f.(Dh/Zeb)* **(-e/-a; /-ê).** 1) {also: simt (Zeb/Dh)} {syn: alî} side, direction (K/JJ/GF/Zeb); 2) region, district, country (JJ): •**[Ekradêd *simtê* Bohtan û Ḧekariyan kêm bi ecelêd xo dimirin]** (BN 138) The Kurds of *the regions of* Bohtan and Hekkari seldom die a natural death; 3) {syn: fesal [3]} comfortable stance or position (B): •**Ewî *semt* hilda û agir kir** (B) He took a *comfortable stance* and fired [his gun]; 4) the right moment, propitious or auspicious moment (B); 5) {also: simt (IFb)} hilltop, summit, peak (IFb): •**Xecê wê siḧetê li *semtê* wê zozanê konê r̄eşî 'erebî rakir û vegirt** (IS-#360) Then Khej pitched the black Arab [=bedouin] tent on *the slope of* that summer encampment. {also: simt (IFb/Zeb/Dh); [semt] سمت (JJ)} <Ar samt سمت = 'way, road; manner, mode'; T semt = 'neighborhood' [IS/K/B/JJ/GF//IFb/Dh/Zeb]

semyan I سەمیان (Zeb/Dh/FS) = master. See **sermiyan**.

senayî سەنایی = easy. See **asan**.

sencab سەنجاب *f.* **().** squirrel. {syn: pilûr; siwûrî} < Ar sinjāb سنجاب --> T sincap; Sor sincaw سِنجاو = 'grey squirrel' [F/Ad]

sendan سەندان (GF) = anvil. See **sindyan**.

senem سەنەم *m.* **().** idol: •**Bo xatirê Azir û *senema* carek din vegerînin** (GShA, 229) For the sake of Azir and his *idols*, make him come back again •**Her kesê şirîkan bo xudê çê-ket o sicde bo *seneman* biket, wî bikujin, bila îmanê bi min biket** (SK 48:513) Every person who makes partners for god and bows down before *idols*, kill him, he should believe in me. {also: semen (GF); [sanám (G)/sanem (Rh)] صنم (JJ); <senem> صنم (HH)} < Ar ṣanam صنم [GShA/K/IFb/SK/JJ/HH//GF]

sen'et سەنعەت *f.* **(-a;-ê).** 1) {syn: hiner} art, skill; 2) profession, trade, craft; 3) {syn: p'îşesazî} industry: **-senḧeta giran** (B) heavy industry; **-senḧeta sivik** (B) light industry. {also: senḧet (B); sinet (IFb); sinhet, f.(K)/m.(JB3); [senaat] صنعت (JJ); <sin'et> سنعت (HH)} < Ar ṣan'ah صنعة = 'work(manship), art' --> T zanaat = 'craft, trade' [(Ber)//HH//K/JB3//IFb//B]

sen'etk'ar سەنعەتكار *m.* **(-ê;).** 1) {syn: pîşek'ar (Ber/JB3)} artisan, craftsman; 2) {syn: hunermend} artist. {also: senḧetçî (B-2); senḧetdar (B); senḧetk'ar (B-2); sinetkar (IFb); sin'etkar (GF); sinhetk'ar (K); [senaat-ker] صنعتكر (JJ)} [Ber//K//B//IFb//GF//JJ]

sengele سەنگەلە *m.* **().** young man: •**Îcar tu ji *sengeleyên* xwe re bibêje, bila wisan mekin, da ku siqûmatek li vir neqewime!** (ZZ-4, 180) So tell your *young men* not to do that, lest a tragedy occur here. {syn: xort} [ZZ/ZF]

senger سەنگەر *m.* **(-ê;-î).** 1) {syn: çeper I; k'ozik} fortification, rampart, bulwark; 2) {syn: çeper I; k'ozik} trench, entrenchment, ditch. {also: [sengher] سنگر (JJ)} Cf. P sangar سنگر =

'entrenchment, stronghold'; Sor senger سەنگەر = 'parapet of a trench' [Bw/K/A/IFb/JJ/GF/TF/OK]

senĥet سەنحەت (B) = art, skill; profession; industry. See **sen'et**.

senĥetçî سەنحەتچی (B) = artisan; artist. See **sen'etk'ar**.

senĥetdar سەنحەتدار (B) = artisan; artist. See **sen'etk'ar**.

senĥetk'ar سەنحەتکار (B) = artisan; artist. See **sen'etk'ar**.

sensor سەنسۆر (IFb) = censorship. See **sansûr**.

sentenet سەنتەنەت/**ṣentenet** صەنتەنەت [M-Am] *f.* **(-a;-ê).** splendor, magnificence, pomp; luxury: **•Muxabinî te, te ev qesra ava kirî û ev ṣentenete û bê jin!** (M-Am #740, 340) It's a pity for you, that you've built this palace and have all this *majesty*, but no wife! {also: <sentene> سەنتەنە (Hej)} *[Zeb/K/M-Am//Hej]*

sepandî سەپاندی *m.* (). sheepdog: **•Ji kûçikên şivanan re dibêjin *sepandî*** (Wkp: Kûçik) The dogs of shepherds are called *sheepdogs* [*sepandî*] **•Keriyê min ê ko sê şivan, serşivanek û çar *sepandiyê* wî bûn, dirêjiya salê di navbera 8 û 13 pezan de bi dev guran ve berdidan** (SW1, 26) My flock, which had 3 shepherds, a head shepherd and 4 *sheepdogs*, during the year gave away between 8 and 13 sheep into the mouths of wolves. {syn: seê gurêẍ} [SW1/IFb/ZF/CS] <k'elb; kûçik; se>

sepet سەپەت (K/IFb/GF/ZF) = basket; box. See **sebet**.

sepil سەپل *f.* **(-a;-ê).** pannier, wooden frame on donkey's packsaddle *for carrying water, stones, etc.* [Wek du kursiyan berovajî hev li ser kurtanê pişta ker û li herdû aliyan ji jorve bi 2-3 qet zincîr dighan hev û li ser pişta kerê dihat danîn û her aliyek du teneke av dihewandin]: **•Li Xirbe Zirgan mi ker bi *sepila* avê biriye mal** (Xirbe Zirgan) In Kh.Z. I took the donkey home with a *pannier* of water [on its back]. {also: selb (Kmc/ZF3); sepl (Kmc-2); seple (Xirbe Zirgan-2)} {syn: *darcêrk (Kmc); *xerek (Kmc)} Cf. Syr sbal ܣܒܠ = 'to bear, carry' [Xirbe Zirgan//Kmc/ZF3]

sepîtk سەپیتك (Kmc-6282/RZ) = ceiling. See **ṣapîtke**.

sepl سەپل (Kmc) = pannier. See **sepil**.

seple سەپلە (Xirbe Zirgan) = pannier. See **sepil**.

Sept سەپت (Czr) = Saturday. See **Sebt**.

seqa kirin سەقا کِرِن *vt.* **(seqa -k[e]-).** 1) to temper (iron, steel); to anneal; to quench (steel), cool heated steel suddenly by immersion in water [T su vermek]; 2) {syn: sûtin[2]; tûj kirin} to sharpen, whet, hone (Zeb/AId/FJ/GF/TF) {also: seqandin (A/IFb/CS)}: **•Wî das û bivir *seqa kirin*** (Zeb) He *sharpened* the sickle and the axe. {also: siqa kirin (TF/FS-2); <siqa kirin سقا کرن (siqa dike) (سقا دکه)> (HH)} <Ar saqy (al-fūlād̲) سقي (الفولاذ) = 'tempering (of steel)' [X.Saliĥ/Zeb/FJ/GF/Wkt/BF/SS/ZF/FS/AId//TF/HH//A/IFb/CS]

seqandin سەقاندِن (A/IFb/CS) = to sharpen. See **seqa kirin**[2].

seqawêl سەقاوێل (Ag) = large broom. See **siqavêl**.

seqed سەقەد (OK/JJ-Lx) = lame. See **seqet**.

seqem سەقەم *f.* **(-a;-ê).** cold (weather), frost, *especially strong or severe cold spell*: **•*Sir û seqema zêde* astengên mezin di jiyana xelkên deverê de çêdike** (RojevaKurd 24.i.2010) *Severe cold* creates big obstacles in the life of the people of the region **•Şevek sar û *seqem* bû** (Nofa, 89) It was a cold and *frosty* night. Cf. Ar saqam سقم = 'illness, weakness' [Nofa/A/IFb/FJ/TF/ZF3/Wkt/G/FS/CS] <sar; serma; sur̄ I>

seqet سەقەت *adj.* 1) crippled, lame, disabled; mutilated, maimed: **•Paşî mar hat e pêş, got, "... Jehra min gelek dijwar. Ewê nemirît eẍleb *seqet* dibît"** (SK 1:6) Then the snake came forward and said, "... My venom is very strong. He who does not die is generally *maimed*"; **-xwe seqet kirin** (M-Ak) to have o.s. emasculated: **•Çare ewe biçime lalî duxtorekî, *xo seqet bikem*** (M-Ak, #632) The remedy was for me to go to a doctor and *have myself emasculated*; 2) rude, impolite, coarse *(of speech)*: **•Axaftin *seqet* e** (Bw) The talk is *rude*. {also: seket (SK-2); seqed (OK-2); [saqat/saqád (Lx)] سقط (JJ); <seqet> سقت (HH)} <Ar saqaṭ سقط = 'any worthless thing; trash; junk'; T sakat = 'handicapped, disabled (person); unsound, defective'; Sor seqet سەقەت = 'broken down, dangerous (action, character, talk)' [SK/Bw/K/IFb/B/JJ/HH/GF/OK/ZF3]

seqevêl سەقەڤێل (F) = large broom. See **siqavêl**.

ser I سەر *m.* **(-ê;).** 1) {syn: k'elle II} head: **•Ez *[bi]* serê te kim** (Z-1) I swear *by your head* **•*Serê* min dêşe** (AB) My *head* aches/I have a headache **•*Serê* bavê we kim** (K) I swear by your father's *head [oath]*; **-Çend serê wî hene?** (XF) How dare he?/Who does he think he is? [lit. 'How many heads does he have?']: **•*Çend serê te hene*, wekî**

tu usa dikî? (Z-1) How dare you [=lit. *'how many heads do you have?'*] do such a thing?; **-serê *fk-î* anîn** = to do to s.o., to cause to befall: **•Tiştek *serê wî nanye*** (Ba) They *didn't do anything to* him; **-serê *fk-î* hatin** = to befall, happen to s.o. [cf. P sargozašt سرگذشت; T başından geçenler]: **•Wekî tiştek *bê serê* wî** (Ba) If anything *happens to* him; **-ser li 'erdê** = down, low, on the ground: **•T'aê Ûsib *ser li 'erdê* dimîne, lê t'aê zêr̄ têda bilind dibe** (Ba #16, 315) The pan of the scales with Joseph [on it] remains *on the ground*, but the scale with the gold in it rises; **-ser û ber: •Bi ser û berê xwe ve** (BX) entirely; 2) point, tip; 3) beginning, start: **•[Yazde bi Hezîranê, *serê* havînê, berê xwe bide zivistanê]** (BG) The 11th of June (Julian calendar - BG), *the start of* the summer, look toward the winter *[prv.]*; 4) end, extremity: **•Bila her çil x̱ulam, bi kur̄ê te r̄a r̄awestihin, û her̄in, her *serê* dih mitroa dido ji pey veger̄ihin** (HR 4:38) Let all 40 manservants accompany your son, and every 10 meters [lit. 'at every *end of* 10 meters'] let two of them turn back. {also: **serî**; [ser] سر (JJ); <ser> سر (HH)} [Pok. 1. k̑er- 574.] 'horn, head; with derivatives referring to horned animals, horn-shaped objects, and projecting parts': P sar سر; Sor ser سه‌ر = 'head, top, summit, hill, chief, beginning, extremity, end, tip (fingers, toes), the Arabic vowel fatḥa'; Za sere *m.* = 'head, chief, point, top, hill, ear (of corn)' (Mal); Hau sere *m.* (M4) [K/A/JB3/IFb/JJ/HH/SK/GF/TF//B] See also **serî**.

ser II سه‌ر *prep.* 1) on: **•Vê kitêbê dêne *ser* masê** (BX) Put this book *on* the table; 2) *in combination with postpositions*:

-bi ser ... de = on *(with motion)*, onto: **•Av *bi ser* wî *de* rijand** (BX) He poured water *on* him **•R̄ojekê ji rojên xwedê, *bi ser* wan *de* hatiye Eyda qurbane** (DM) One day, the Feast of Immolation (greater Bayram) came *upon* them;

-bi ser … re = over *(with motion)*: **•Refên me *bi ser* qada şerî *re* firiyane** (RN) Our squadrons flew *over* the battlefield;

-bi ser ... ve = to: **-Bi ser *ft-î* ve zêde kirin** = to add to; **-bi ser ve çûn** = to pass, elapse *(of time)*: **•Ew îrade û pişgirtin, dema çend sal *bi ser ve çûn* an sist dibe, an jî mezintir dibe** (AW72D3) This desire and support, when a couple of years *have passed*, will either weaken or become greater;

-di ser ... de = on *(location, without motion)*: **•Çwîk *di ser* hêlîna xwe *de* ye** (L) The sparrow is *in* (or, *on*) its nest;

-di ser ... re = a) above, over *(with or without motion)*: **•Xaniyên wan *di ser* hev *re* ne** (BX) Their apartments are *above* one another (or, one above the other) **•Kevir *di ser* dîwêr *re* avêt** (BX) He threw the rock *over* the wall **•Daran *di ser* xwe *re* mebire** (BX) Don't cut the trees *above* you *[prv., cf. "Don't bite the hand that feeds you"]*; b) in spite of, despite {syn: li ser ... r̄a}: ***•Di ser* bayên germ û yên sar û qerisokî *re* firîn** (EN) *In spite of* the warm and freezing cold winds, they flew;

-ji ser = from off of [cf. Rus s **(c)** + gen.]: **•R̄ojname *ji ser* kirsiyê rakir** (BX) He picked the newspaper up *off* the chair **•Wexta bira *ji ser* bîrê çûn** (Bz) When the brothers went *away from* (=left) the well;

-li ser = a) about, regarding {syn: derbare; derheqa}: **•Min kitêbek *li ser* Êzîdiyan nivîsand** (BX) I wrote a book *about* the Yezidis **•Tu gelikî diqehirî *li ser* kevnek jina** (L) You are very sad *about* (or, *over*) an old woman; b) on: ***•Li ser* kursîya zîv rûdinê** (L) He sits down *on* the silver chair; c) in consequence of, following, as a result of: ***•li ser* vê qerarê** (BX) *as a result of* this decision;

-li ser … r̄a = in spite of, despite {syn: di ser ... re}: **-li ser hindê r̄a** (Dh/Zeb) nevertheless; moreover: **•Wextê wan temaşe kir ko têşta wan s̱ewar---we li-nik wan s̱ewar gelek 'eybekî mezin e bo mêwanêt mu'teber---we *se<r> wê hindêr̄a* jî kilkêt kûran li-ser sênîyan çeqandine, di yêk-u-do fikirîn, destêt xo kêşan e paş** (SK 24:224) When they saw that their meal was of crushed wheat---and with them crushed wheat (instead of rice) was a most shameful thing for respectable guests---and that *moreover* the tails of kids had been stuck on top of the trays, they looked at each other and withdrew their hands;

-li ser ... ve = in the direction of, toward: ***•Li ser* kebab *ve* çû, *li ser* dexdexana keran *ve* bû** (BX) He went *toward* [the smell of] kebab, he arrived *at* the branding of donkeys *[prv.]*.{also: [ser] سر (JJ); <ser> سر (HH)} Cf. P sar-e سرِ [BX/K/JB3/IF/B/JJ/HH]

serabin سه‌رابِن (BF) = upside down. See **ser û bin**.

serac سەڕاج *m.* (). saddler, saddlemaker: •**Evdal ji *seracanên* Qonaxê rîca kir ku jê re taximekî xemilandî çêkin. Wan di demeke kurt de taxim çêkirin** [sic] **û ew dan** [sic] **Evdal** (M.Uzun. R. Evd. Zeyn., 108) Evdal asked *the saddlers* of Q. to make him a fancy horse tack. They made the horse tack in a short time and gave it to E. {also: seracan (Uzun); serrac (GF); [seradj] سراج (JJ); <serac> سراج (HH)} {syn: zînker} < Ar sarrāj سرّاج = 'saddlemaker'; Sor serac سەڕاج = zîndirû زیندروو [Uzun//K/IFb/FJ/JJ/HH/ZF3//GF] <zîn I>

seracan سەراجان (Uzun) = saddlemaker. See **serac**.

serad سەڕاد/**serad** سەراد [OK/TF/A] *f.* **(-a;-ê).** winnowing sieve with large holes: **-serad kirin** (K)/**serad dan** (OK) to sift. {also: serat (B/Mzg); [serrad] سرراد (JJ); <serrad> صرّاد (HH)} <Ar √s-r-d سرد = 'to pierce' & sarad سرد/misrad مسرد = 'coarse sieve'; Sor seren[d] سەرەند = 'riddle, coarse sieve' [Bw/K/A/IFb/JJ/GF/TF/OK/FS//HH//B/Mzg] <bêjing; moxil>

sera•dan سەرادان *vt.* **(sera-d[e]-).** 1) to visit, drop in on, pay a visit to: •**Dê hêm *sera* te *dem*** (Bw) I will come *visit* you •**Dê *serekî* li mala hewe jî *dem*** (Bw) I'll *drop by* your house for a little bit too •**Em dê rabîn, çîn, *sera* babê te *deyn*** (M, #692, 312) We shall rise and go and *pay a visit to* your father •**Ew sê sal bû min *sera* te *neday*** (Bw) I *haven't visited* you for three years; 2) [*f.* **(-a;-ê).**] a visit: •**Ez dê hêm nik te bo *seradanê*** (Bw) I will come pay you a *visit*. {also: serdan (K/IFb/HH/FJ/GF); seredan (SS); serlêdan (A)} [Bw//K/IFb/HH/FJ/GF//SS/A]

seranser سەرانسەر *adv.* 1) all over, from end to end, from head to toe: •**Dema dibû bihar, deşt *seranser* bi kulîlkên nêrgizan dixemiliya** (DBgb, 7) When spring came, the prairie would be adorned *all over* with daffodil flowers; 2) [*prep.*] [-ê] all over *(e.g., the world)*: •**Ne li bajêr tenê belê *li seranserê* welêt** (HYma, 52) Not only in the city, but *all over* the country. {also: seraser (K-2/A/CS-2); sertaser (Kmc-2)} Cf. P sarānsar سرانسر; Sor seranser سەرانسەر/sertaser سەرتاسەر = 'from end to end; totally, entirely, wholly' [HYma/DBgb/IFb/FJ/TF/GF//K/A/CS//Kmc]

seraser سەراسەر (K/A/CS) = all over. See **seranser**.

serast سەراست (IFb) = honest. See **serrast**.

serat سەرات (B/Mzg) = coarse sieve. See **serad**.

serban سەربان *m.* **(-ê;-î).** 1) {syn: ban II; sit'ar} roof: •**Hawînê keşkêt wan li *serbanêt* reş-malan û keprokan û xanîyan direwêm, dixom** (SK 1:3) In summer I snatch their buttermilk, (drying) on *the roofs of* tents and bough-huts and houses, and eat it; 2) terrace (K/JJ). {also: [ser-ban] سربان (JJ); <serban> سربان (HH)} [JR/Ba2/K/IFb/JB1-A/JJ/HH/SK/GF] <kuşxank; sapîtke>

serbar سەربار *m.* **(-ê;).** additional load or burden; unwelcome addition: •**Bar min naêşîne, *serbar* diêşîne** (Dz #55, 51) The burden doesn't cause me pain, *the additional load* [=the rider] causes me pain *[prv.]* •**Halê me ne besî me ye, yê te *serbarê* jûr da li ser e** (Drş #336, 100) [As if] our worries are not enough for us, yours are *an additional burden* on top of them. [Dz/Drş/K/FJ/GF/ZF]

serbaz سەرباز *m.* (). 1) {syn: esker; leşker[2]} soldier; 2) officer (JB3/IFb). Cf. P sarbāz سرباز; Sor serbaz سەرباز = 'soldier' [EP-7/K/A/JB3/IFb/GF/ZF3] <pêşmerge>

serbest سەربەست *adj.* 1) {syn: aza I; rizgar; xelas} free; 2) clear *(of a road, path, etc.)* (Bw); 3) independent (IFb/GF/OK); 4) brave, courageous (HH/GF). {also: <serbest> سربست (HH)} Cf. P sarbaste سربسته = 'closed' [lit. 'with head tied']--> T serbest = 'free'; Sor serbest سەربەست = 'free, uninhibited' {serbestî} [F/K/A/JB3/IFb/B/HH/GF/TF/OK/Bw]

serbestî سەربەستی *f.* **(-ya;-yê).** freedom, independence: •**Bi wê derecê *serbestîya* axiwtinê çak nîye** (SK 60:720) *Freedom of* speech to that degree is not good •**Wî hest dikir ev jîngehe ya dibîte hêzeka rêgir beramber viyanêt wî yêt hunerî û viyana wî bo *serbestîyê*** (Peyv 3[1996], 38) He felt that this environment was getting in the way of [lit. 'becoming a preventive force'] his artistic desires and his desire for *freedom*. {also: [ser-besiiet] سربسيت (JJ)} {syn: azadî; rizgarî} Cf. P sarbastī سربستی = 'freedom'; Sor serbestî سەربەستی [Peyv/K/A/IFb/B/SK/GF/TF//JJ]

serbijêr سەربِژێر *adv.* down, downward. {syn: berbijêr; jêr; xwar} < ser = 'head' + bi + jêr = 'under' [BX/ZF3/Wkt]

serbijor سەربِژۆر *adv.* up, upward. {syn: bala; berbijor; jor} < ser = 'head' + bi + jor = 'over' [BX/ZF3/Wkt]

serbilind سەربِلِند *adj.* 1) {syn: serfiraz} proud; dignified, self-respecting; 2) {syn: difnbilind; nefsmezin; pozbilind; qure; serfiraz} haughty, arrogant. {also: [ser-belenda (G)/ser-belínd (PS)] سربلند (JJ)} < ser = 'head' + bilind = 'high' ; Sor serbiłind سەربِڵند/serberz سەربەرز = 'eminent, excellent, proud (in good sense)' {serbilindahî; serbilindî} [K/A/JB3/IFb/GF/TF/OK/ZF//JJ]

serbilindahî سەربِلنداهی (GF) = pride. See **serbilindî**.

serbilindî سەربِلندی *f.* **(-ya;-yê).** 1) {syn: şanazî} pride, dignity; self-respect, self-esteem: **•Ji bo me *cihê serbilindîyê* bû** (FB: Kurdî-Der Sêrt) It was *a source of pride* for us **•Sedemê wê jî, çima ku em li canemergên xwe xwedî derketin û me xwest em wan bi şanazî û bi *serbilindî* bi gor bikin** (Wlt 2:59, 13) The reason for it [=the reprisal] was that we took care of our dead young ones, and that we wanted to bury them with dignity and *pride*; 2) {syn: serfirazî} haughtiness, arrogance. {also: serbilindahî (GF-2)} [Wlt/K/IFb/GF/TF/OK] <serbilind>

ser-bi-xo سەربِخۆ (SK) = independent. See **serbixwe**.

serbixwe سەربِخوە *adj.* independent; on one's own: **•Cudaxwaz, di ferhenga dijminên azadiyê de, her Kurdekî ku dixwaze û dixebite ji bo Kurdistaneke *serbixwe* û azad** (Wlt 2:73, 7) Separatist, in the lexicon of the enemies of freedom, [is] every Kurd who wants and works for an *independent* and free Kurdistan. {also: ser-bi-xo (SK)} {syn: serxwe} <ser = 'head' + bi = 'on, in, by' + xwe = 'self'. Sor serbexo سەربەخۆ = 'independent' {serbixweyî} [Wlt/K/A/IFb/GF/TF/OK//SK]

serbixweyî سەربِخوەیی *f.* **(-ya;-yê).** independence: **•Dema guncayî bo ragihandina *serbixweyîyê* kengê ye?** (rojevakurd.com 25.iv.2012) When is the appropriate time for declaring *independence*? {syn: serxwebûn; xwexwetî} [GF/OK/ZF3] <serbixwe>

Serbî سەربی (Wkp) = Serbian. See **Sirbî**.

serçav سەرچاڤ *m.* **(-ê;).** 1) {also: ser-o-çaw (SK); serûç'av (JB3/JB1-S)} {syn: dev û çav; dîndar I; r̄û I[1]; sifet [3]; sûret I[1]} face: **•Wî timî bi kefiyeke leşkerî ve *serçavê* xwe dipêça** (aramyayin-evi.net: Geliyê Zilan) He always covered his *face* with a military headdress; 2) {also: ser çavan} gladly, OK! [*indicates willingness to carry out a request*]; You're welcome. [cf. Ar 'alá 'aynī علی عینی; P čašm چشم; T baş üstüne & göz üstüne] < ser = 'head; on' + çav = 'eye(s)' [Ba2/K/IF/ZF3//JB3/JB1-S]

***serçavk** سەرچاڤك *f.* **(-a;).** any easily kindled material for lighting stoves and the like, for getting the flame going. [Qzl] <dadan; vêxistin>

serda سەردا *adv.* 1) above, to the top; [=ji serda] from above: **•Dar *serda* k'et birîndar kir** (Dz) The tree fell *down (from above)* [and] wounded [him] **•Xûna sor *serda* hat** (EP-7) Red blood came *up* [or, *out*]; 2) {syn: zêdebar[î]} in addition, moreover, into the bargain; 3) *used in verbal compliments*: **-bi serda birin** (Bw) to explain, elucidate, clarify; -**[di] serda birin** (Dh/Bw/AId) to mislead, fool, deceive, cheat, lead astray. [Dz/EP-7/K]

serdab سەرداب *f.* **(-a;-ê).** 1) {syn: padval} cellar, basement; 2) {syn: k'ar̄êz; tûn} subterranean canal; tunnel. {also: serdeb (K); [sardáb] سرداب (JJ)} < P sardāb سرداب [A/IFb/JJ/ZF3//K] <leqem>

serdan سەردان (K/IFb/HH/FJ/GF) = [to] visit. See **seradan**.

serdeb سەردەب (K) = cellar; tunnel. See **serdab**.

serdem سەردەم *f.* **(-a;-ê).** period, era, epoch: **•Ew jî *serdema* Mîrnişîna Baban e** (AW73A3) That is *the period of* the Baban Principality **•*Wê serdemê* şovenîzm li Tirkiyeyê ewqasî xurt nebûbû** (AW72C1) *In that period*, chauvinism in Turkey had not become so strong [yet]. Sor serdem سەردەم = 'moment, epoch' [IFb/GF/OK/SS/ZF3] <dem; 'esir; nîr II>

serder سەردەر *f.* **(-a;).** lintel, part above the door or entrance: **•Yê ku ḧêştira xudan bikit, divêt ku *serdera* xwe bilind bikit** (FS) He who raises camels, must make his *door lintel* high. {also: serderî (K[s]/IFb); serderk (K[s]-2)} Sor serderga سەردەرگا = 'wooden beam in wall above door' [Qzl/Frq/ZF3/FS//K(s)/IFb] <derî I; r̄exderî; sîvande>

serderî سەردەری (K[s]/IFb) = lintel of door. See **serder**.

serderk سەردەرك (K[s]) = lintel of door. See **serder**.

serdest سەردەست *adj.* 1) victorious; dominant: **•Ji aliyê mêrên xwe û civakê ve, ji aliyê *serdestan* ve dihatin perçiqandin û keda wan dihat xwarin** (Wlt 1:35, 16) [Women] were crushed and exploited by their husbands and society, by *those in power* [=*the dominant ones*]; 2) [*m.* **(-ê;).**] {syn: alt'dar} victor, winner; one who defeats, beats, wins, is victorious. [Wlt/K/A/IFb/GF/TF]

sere I سەرە *adj.* old *(of people)*, agèd, elderly, senior aged: **•Me dît jineke *sere* ber bi me tê** (X. Çaçan. Benê me qetiya, 21) We saw an *elderly* woman coming toward us. {also: [seré] سره (JJ)} {syn: kal I;

mezin[2]; navsera; pîr} [Çaçan/K/A/FJ/GF/JJ/RZ/ZF/CS]

serecam سەرەجام (TF) = result. See **serencam**.

serecem سەرەجەم *f.* **(-a;-ê).** 1) {syn: naverok} contents; 2) {syn: naverok; nêta k'itêbê (F); p'êrist} table of contents: **-serecema k'itêbê** (F) do.; 3) sum, total. [F/K/B/ZF3]

seredan سەرەدان (SS) = [to] visit. See **seradan**.

serederî سەرەدەرى *f.* **(-ya;-yê).** comprehension, understanding: **-lê serederî kirin** (K) to comprehend, interpret, give a meaning to: **•K'utasî, t'u ḧekîma û wê cime'ta dorê** ***serederî li*** **nexweşîya Memê** ***nekirin*** [sic] (Z-1) In short, *no* doctors or those around them *could comprehend* Mem's illness; **-serederî ji** ***f-kê/f-tî*** **derxistin** (B) to understand, comprehend: **•Ez** ***serederîyê ji*** **wî** ***dernaxim*** (B) I *can't understand* him. [Z-1/K/B/ZF3] <fehm kirin; seh kirin [2]>

serefraz سەرەفراز (K/IFb) = proud; excellent; conqueror. See **serfiraz**.

serefrazî سەرەفرازى (K/IFb) = victory; success; pride. See **serfirazî**.

serejêr سەرەژێر *adj.* down *(in crosswords).* {syn: stûnî} <ser- = 'head, top' + jêr = 'down' [Wlt/TF/ZF3] <çeperast; xaçepirs>

serek سەرەك *m.* **(-ê;).** leader, head, chief: **•***serekê* **pênsed xulamî** (Z-3) *the head of* 500 servant boys; 2) eldest, oldest, senior: **•Sê kuȓê mîr hene /** ***serekvanê*** **kuȓa jêȓa dibêjen** [sic] **kû Gûrgîne** (Z-3) The emir has three sons / *The eldest of* them is called Gurgin. {also: serekvan (Z-3-2); [serek] سرك (JJ)} {syn: mezin [4]; pêşeng; ȓêber; ȓêvebir; ȓêzan; serk'ar [1]; serok; serwer} Cf. Sor serak سەراك = 'leader, president' [Z-3/K/B/JJ/IFb/SK/GF] <mezin [4]; ȓêvebir>

serekvan سەرەكڤان (Z-3) = leader, chief; eldest. See **serek**.

serekwezîr سەرەكوەزیر *m.* **(-ê;).** prime minister: **•Ȓojekê rojnamevanekî biyanî ji** ***serekwezîrê*** **Mecaristanê pirsî** (Rnh) One day a foreign journalist asked *the prime minister of* Hungary... [Rnh/K/JB3/IFb/GF/ZF3]

serenav سەرەناڤ *m.* **(-ê;).** proper noun, proper name *(gram.).* [(neol)K/JB3/IFb/GF/TF/ZF3] <nav I[3]>

serencam سەرەنجام *f.* **(-a;-ê).** end, result, outcome; final outcome: **•Paşiya paşîn ez bûm zelûlê** ***serencameke*** **kirêt** (WT, 87) In the end I fell victim to an unpleasant *outcome.* {also: serecam (TF)} P sar'anjām سرانجام = 'end, conclusion'; Sor serencam سەرەنجام = 'conclusion, decision, deduction' [WT/K/FJ/GF/ZF/RZ/Wkt/SS/ZF3//TF] <encam>

seȓeq سەرەق (FS) = stubborn. See **serȓeq**.

seȓeqî سەرەقى (FS) = stubbornness. See **serȓeqî**.

serê sibehê سەرێ سِبەهێ (JB3) = dawn, early morning. See **serê sibê**.

serê sibê سەرێ سِبێ *m.* **().** 1) {syn: berbang; elind; ferec; hingûr [1]; segur; siḧar; spêde; şebeq} dawn (K/JJ); morning (JB3/JJ); 2) [*adv.*] early in the morning, at dawn: **•***Serê sibê* **emê t'emam derêne cerdê** (Z-3) *At dawn* we will all go out raiding. {also: serê sibehê (JB3); sersibe (GF); [sér-i sebéh] سر صباح (JJ)} [Z-2/K/IFb//JB3//JJ//GF]

serêş سەرێش *f.* **(-a;-ê).** headache *(lit. & fig.)*: **•Ew li mala bavê xwe ye, ne hay ji evîna mamoste Kevanot û ne jî hay ji** ***serêşa*** **bavê xwe heye** (Lab, 8) She is in her father's house, and is aware neither of Professor Kevanot's love [for her] nor of her father's *headache.* {also: [ser-eichi] سر ايشى (JJ)} [F/K/A/IFb/B/GF/TF/Msr//JJ] <êş>

serf سەرف/**s̱erf** صەرف *f.* **().** expense: **-serf kirin** (IFb/OK)/**s̱erf kirin** (HH/SK) to spend, expend (money, effort): **•Eger emr fermû, baş e, hingî** ***ȓoḧa xo dê bo*** **wê şulê** ***s̱erf kem*** (SK 54:591) If he permits, very well, then I *shall put my soul into* the affair. {syn: mezaxtin}. {also: [serf/saraf (G)] صرف (JJ); <s̱erf kirin صرف كرن (s̱erf dike) (صرف دكه)> (HH)} <Ar √ṣ-r-f صرف = 'to spend' [IFb/OK//JJ/HH/SK]

serferaz سەرفەراز (SK) = honorable, eminent. See **serfiraz**.

serferazî سەرفەرازى (SK) = honor, eminence. See **serfirazî**.

serfermandar سەرفەرماندار *m.* **(-ê;).** commander-in-chief: **•***serfermandarê* **stola emerîkanî** (RN) the *commander-in-chief* of the American navy. [(neol)RN/K/GF]

serfiraz سەرفِراز *adj.* 1) {syn: difnbilind; nefsmezin; pozbilind; quȓe; serbilind} proud; haughty, arrogant: **-Serfiraz bûm** = Pleased to meet you; 2) outstanding, honorable; prominent, eminent; 3) [*m.&f.*] vanquisher, conqueror, victor: **-serfiraz bûn** = to triumph. {also: serefraz (K/IFb-2); serferaz (SK); serfirz} {serfirazî; serefrazî} [K//JB3/IFb/GF/TF//SK]

serfirazî سەرفِرازى *f.* **(-ya;-yê).** 1) pride; haughtiness, arrogance; 2) eminence, honor; 3) {syn: alt'indarî} triumph, victory; success. {also:

serefrazî (K/IFb); serferazî (SK)} [Ber/JB3/GF/TF//SK//K/IFb] <serfiraz>

serfirz سەرفِرز = proud; excellent; conqueror. See **serfiraz**.

sergedan سەرگەدان (EH) = poor, miserable. See **sergerdan**.

serger سەرگەر (A/IF) = hilltop. See **sergir I**.

sergerdan سەرگەردان *adj.* 1) disordered, deranged, disheveled, in chaos; 2) poor; unhappy, unlucky; miserable, wretched; 3) vagrant, wandering, stray. {also: sergedan (EH); [ser-gherdan(é)] سرگردان(ه) (JJ)} [Z-1/K/XF/GF//JJ//EH]

sergerm سەرگەرم *adj.* frisky, unbridled *(animals)*: •**Dewara xo bir û anî, ḧetta kû *sergerm* bû** (HR 3:74) He let his horse run back and forth, until it became *unruly*. {also: [ser-gherm] سرگرم (JJ)} Cf. P sargarm سرگرم = 'busy, occupied'; Sor sergerm سەرگەرم = 'keen, intent' [Qzl/K/JJ/GF/TF/Ald] <≠sernerm>

sergir I سەرگِر *m.* **().** hilltop; flat area at the top of a hill. {also: serger (A/IF); [ser-ghir] سرگر (JJ)} [BK/JJ//A/IF] <semt>

sergîn سەرگین *f.(B)/m.(Dz)/pl.* **(;-ê/).** pressed dung *(used as fuel)*; dung in the form of bricks used for heating; dung dried and ready for use as kindling fuel, *as opposed to **r̄îx** = dung in its natural (moist) state* (Msr); dung of small domestic animals, such as goats and sheep [=pişkul], *as opposed to **k'erme** = dung of large domestic animals* (Ag): •**Bûka malê r̄abû mal gêzîkir, av anîn, *sergîn* anîn** (J) The bride of the house got up, swept the house, brought water and *fuel* (=*dung*); **-t'ertê sergîn** (Dz) pressed dung cake/ loaf: •**Lê pê *t'ertê sergîn* be'r tê şewitandin?** (Dz) But does the sea get ignited (=can the sea be set on fire) by *pressed dung*? {also: [serghin] سرگین (JJ); <sergîn> سرگین (HH)} {syn: tepik; t'ert[ik]} [Pok sḱer-(d-) 974.] 'to defecate; dung, excrement': Av sairya- = 'manure, dung' + gû = 'feces'; Mid P sargēn = do. (M3); P sargīn سرگين --> Ar sarqīn سرقين = 'dung, esp. dried & kept for firing'; Sor sewr[ga] سەور[گا] [Sinneh]; Hau sewro *m.* = 'cow dung' (M4) [Dz/J/F/K/IFb/B/JJ/HH/GF/TF/Ag/Msr] <axpîn; bişkul/pişkul; ç'êrt; deve II; dirg; guhûr; k'erme; keşkûr; peyîn; qelax; r̄îx; sergo; sêklot; t'epik II; t'ers; t'ert[ik]; zibil; zirîç>

sergo سەرگۆ *m.* **(-yê;).** dung heap: •**Dîk çû ser *sergo*** (AB) The rooster went on top of *the dung heap* •**Gur̄î çû ji xwer̄a kevir anîn, ji xwer̄a xênîkekî li ber *sergoyê r̄êxê* çê kir** (Z-4) The mangie one went and took some stones, [and] made himself a house in front of *a heap of cow manure*. {also: sergu (IFb-2); sergû (TF); [ser-gouwek] سرگوقك (JJ); <sergo> سرگو (HH)} {syn: axpîn; poxan; ting} *See etymology under **sergîn***; Hau sewroga *m.* = 'dunghill, midden' (M4) [AB/A/IFb/HH/GF/Msr//TF//JJ] <gû; dirg; k'erme; pesarî; sergîn; t'epik II>

sergotar سەرگۆتار *f.* **(-a;-ê).** lead article, headline *(in a newspaper, etc.)*: •**Di *sergotara* vê hejmarê de tê diyarkirin ku** ... (Wlt 2:59, 12) In *the lead article of* this issue, it is made clear that... [(neol)Wlt/ZF3/BF] <gotar>

sergovend سەرگۆڤەند *m.* **(-ê;-î).** dance leader: •***Sergovendî* govend kêşa** (FS) *The dance leader* led the dance. {also: sergovendî (B)} [K/A/IFb/GF/ZF3/FS//B] <govend>

sergovendî سەرگۆڤەندی (B) = dance leader. See **sergovend**.

sergu سەرگو (IFb) = dung heap. See **sergo**.

sergû سەرگوو (TF) = dung heap. See **sergo**.

serhatî سەرهاتی *f.* **(-ya;-yê).** 1) biography, life story, memoir: •**Wî xwexwa dest bi *serhatîya* vê hurmetê, neynesîya dînbûna wê kir** (X. Çaçan. Benê min qetiya, 22) Of his own accord he began *the story of* this woman, the reason for her insanity; 2) story, narrative: •**Eve *serhatya* Ûsivê [N]evya** (Ba3-3, #41) This is *the story [or, life story; or, adventure] of* Joseph the prophet •**Çaxê wana pez ji qir̄bûnê xilaz dikir yanê jî ji destê cerdê derdixist û sax û silamet vedigeer̄ande gund, *serhatîyêd* başqe-başqe ser wana çê dikirin** (Ba2:1, 204) When they rescued the sheep from destruction or snatched them from the clutches of brigands and returned them safe and sound to the village, they made up a variety of *stories* about them; 3) adventure; 4) event, occurrence; accident. {also: serpêhatî (TF); [ser-hati] سرهاتی (JJ)} Cf. Sor serhat سەرهات [Ba3/F/K/IFb/B/JJ/GF/OK//TF] <bûyer; ç'îr̄ok; dîrok; jînenîgarî>

serheng سەرهەنگ *m.* **(-ê;).** colonel *(military rank)* [Ar ʻaqīd عقيد; T albay]; lieutenant colonel *(military rank)* [Ar muqaddam مقدّم; T yarbay]: •**Suleymanê Ehmed jî *serheng* (albay) bû** (Nbh 133:50) S.E. was also a *colonel*. {also: serhing (K); serḧeng (B)} P sarhang سرهنگ = '(lieutenant) colonel'; Sor serheng سەرهەنگ =

'colonel' [Nbh/IFb/FJ/GF/ZF/CS/BF/Wkt/AD/Hej//B//K]

serhevda سەرھەڤدا *adv.* all in all, in toto: **•Zînê ji horîya bedewtir bû, ewqas bedew, ewqas k'emal, *serhevda* husulcemal bû** (Z-1) Zin was more beautiful than the houris, so beautiful, so perfect, *all in all* a ravishing beauty. [Z-1/K]

serhildan سەرهِلدان *f.* **(-a;-ê).** rebellion, revolt, insurrection: **•Berî *serhildana* 91'an hemû dezgehên çandî di bin destê rejîma Baas de bûn** (Wlt 2:101, 16) Before the 1991 *revolt,* all cultural institutions were controlled by the Baathist regime. {also: serîhildan} {syn: sewr; şoreş} <ser = 'head' + hildan = 'to raise, lift', cf. T başkaldırma [K/ZF/FS] <berxwedan>

serhing سەرهنگ (K) = colonel. See **serheng**.

serhişk سەرهِشك (A/IFb/HH/GF/TF/OK/RZ) = stubborn. See **serḧişk**.

serhişkî سەرهِشكى (GF/TF/OK) = stubbornness. See **serḧişkî**.

serḧeng سەرحەنگ (B) = colonel. See **serheng**.

serḧişk سەرحِشك *adj.* stubborn, obstinate; headstrong, defiant; thick-skulled. {also: serhişk (A/IFb/GF/TF/OK/RZ); <serhişk> سرهشك (HH)} {syn: serk'êş I; serr̄eq} {serhişkî; serḧişkayî; serḧişkî} [Hk/K/B//A/IFb/HH/GF/TF/OK/RZ]

serḧişkî سەرحِشكى *f.* **(-ya;-yê).** stubbornness, obstinacy; defiance; being thick-skulled. {also: serhişkî (GF/TF/OK); serḧişkayî (B-2)} {syn: r̄ik' I; serk'êşî; serr̄eqî} [K/B//GF/TF/OK/ZF3] <serḧişk>

serḧişkayî سەرحِشكايى (B) = stubbornness. See **serḧişkî**.

seridîn سەردين *vi.* **(-serid-).** to set *(bot.)*, to develop, to grow ears *(corn)*: **•Genim *seridî*** (AB) The wheat *has set/grown.* {also: serîdan (A/IF)} [AB/K/GF/TF/ZF3//A/IFb]

serik سەرك *m.(Rnh)/f.(K/B)* **(-ê/ ; /-ê).** 1) tip, end, point; 2) bowl *(of a pipe)*: **•Dema Xaneyê bi teqîna tifing û vizîna berikê ra firîna *serikê* qelûna xwe dît, bê ko bitertile an di xwe bi derxe, herwekî tu tişt ne bû be, rabû ser xwe û çû *serikeke* din anî** (Rnh 2:17, 309) When Khaneh [a woman] saw *the bowl of* her pipe fly off with the explosion of a rifle and the buzzing of a bullet, without faltering or losing composure, as if nothing had happened, she got up and went to bring another *bowl.* {also: [serik] سرك (JJ)} ser + -ik = dim. suffix [Rnh/K/A/IFb/B/JJ/GF] <qelûn>

serî سەرى *m.* **(-yê; sêrî).** 1) head: **-hatin/çûn serî** (K) to be completed or finished; to be carried out, to come to pass: **•Nêta wan *ne hate serî*** (K) Their desire *didn't come to pass*; 2) ear (of grain). {also: ser I; <serî> سرى (HH)} [Z-1/BK/K/A/IFb/B/HH/GF] See also **ser I**.

serîdan سەريدان (A/IFb) = to set *(bot.)*, grow ears *(corn)*. See **seridîn**.

serîhildan سەريهلدان = revolt. See **serhildan**.

serjê•kirin سەرژێكِرِن *vt.* **(serjê-k-).** 1) to behead, to chop s.o.'s head off, decapitate: **•Hakim *wê* serê min *jêbikê*!** (L) The king *will cut off* my head!; 2) to slaughter (cattle) (B). {also: şerjêkirin; [ser ji-kirin] سر ژيكرين (JJ)} < ser = 'head' + jê = 'from it' + kirin = 'to do, to make' [L/K/IFb/B/GF/TF//JJ] <kuştin>

serjinik سەرژِنِك *adj.* effeminate *(of a man)*; hen-pecked: **•Di gund de kesê ku dijûn nekiribûna jina xwe, an lê nedabûya, jê re digotin "*serjinik*," an jî "ji jina xwe ditirse"** (DBgb, 52) In the village, they said of anyone who didn't cuss at his wife, or beat her, that he was *effeminate/henpecked* or afraid of his wife **•Ew mêrik *yê serjink* e** (Bw) That man is *effeminate.* [Bw/A/IFb/ZF/FS]

serk'ar سەركار *m.* **(-ê;).** 1) {syn: mezin [4]; pêşeng; r̄êvebir; serek; serok; serwer} director, manager, person in charge; leader, head, chief; chairman, chief (of an office)--{but **not** a government leader}; 2) supervisor, overseer: **•*Serkarê* me ji me re gelek baş bû** (ZF3) Our supervisor was very good to us. {also: <serkar> سركار (HH)} Cf. P serkār سركار = 'chief, overseer, supervisor, superintendent'; Sor serkar سەركار = 'superintendent' {serk'ar[t]î} [F/K/IFb/B/HH/Zeb/ZF3]

serk'arî سەركارى *f.* **(-ya;-yê).** 1) {syn: serwerî} leadership, guidance, direction: **•Mîr Zeynedîn donzde hezar esker bi serkarîya Qeretajdîn dişîne şer̄** (K-dş) Prince Zeynedin sends 12,000 soldiers to war under the leadership of Qeretajdin; 2) supervision, overseeing. {also: serk'artî (K-2/B-2)} [K-dş/K/B/ZF3] <serk'ar>

serk'artî سەركارتى (K/B) = leadership; supervision. See **serk'arî**.

serk'eftin سەركەفتِن (Bw/Dh/Zeb/OK/RZ) = to succeed; to win. See **ser•k'etin**.

ser•k'etin سەركەتِن *vi.* **(ser-k'ev-).** 1) {syn: hilk'işîn} to mount, ascend, climb ; 2) to succeed; 3) to win, be victorious, beat; 4) [*f.* **(-a;-ê).**] success:

•***Serketina* we, *serketina* gelê Kurd e** (dengekurdistan.nu 2003) Your *success* is the Kurdish people's *success*; 5) victory: •***Serketina* tîmê fûtbola Kurdistan li Vêrcîniye** (VoA 14.vii.2011) *Victory* for the Kurdistan soccer team in Virginia. {also: bi ser k'etin (OK); serk'eftin (Bw/Dh/Zeb/OK-2/RZ); serk'evtin (OK-2); serkewtin (SK)} Sor serkewtin سەرکەوتِن [Bw/Dh/Zeb/RZ//K/IFb/GF/TF/OK//SK]

serk'evtin سەرکەفتِن (OK) = to succeed; to win. See **ser•k'etin**.

serkewtin سەرکەوتِن (SK) = to succeed; to win. See **ser•k'etin**.

serk'êş I سەرکێش *adj.* obstinate, headstrong, stubborn; restive, disobedient, refractory, unruly: •**[Û xwecihî jî dibêjin ku her çî zarokêd ku ji jinêd Ekradan biwelidin bê edeb û diz û *serkêş* dibin]** (BN, 100) And the locals say that what-ever children are born of Kurdish women are rude and thieving and *unruly*. {also: [ser-kich] /سرکیش سرکش (JJ)} {syn: serȟişk; serr̄eq} Cf. P sarkaš سرکش = 'restive, refractory, mutinous, arrogant'; Sor serkêş سەرکێش = 'obstinate, headstrong' {serk'êşî} [BN/K(s)/A/IFb/GF/TF//JJ]

serk'êşî سەرکێشی *f.* **(-ya;-yê).** obstinacy, stubbornness; disobedience, unruliness. {also: [ser-kechi] سرکشی (JJ)} {syn: r̄ik' I; serȟişkî; serr̄eqî} Cf. P sarkašī سرکشی = 'restiveness, mutinousness, arrogance'; Sor serkêşî سەرکێشی = 'obstinacy, rebellion' [K(s)/GF/TF//JJ] <serk'êş>

serkil سەرکِل (A/IFb/GF/FJ) = donkey dung. See **serkul**.

serkul سەرکول *m./f.(FS)* **(/-a;).** donkey dung: -**kersila kerî** (FS) do.; -**kersila hêstirê** (FS) mule dung. {also: kersil (Bw/FS); serkil (A/IFb/GF-2/FJ-2); [kersil] کرسل (JJ)} {syn: *kospil (Elk); sêklot (Msr)} =Sor qersequl قەرسەقول/tersequl تەرسەقول [Qrj/GF/FJ/ZF3//A/IFb//Bw/JJ/FS]

serleşker سەرلەشکەر (Wkt) = military commander. See **serokleşker**.

serlêdan سەرلێدان (A) = [to] visit. See **seradan**.

serma سەرما *f.* **(-ya;-yê/sermaê [B]/sermê [B]).** cold (n.), the cold weather: •**R̄ûnişt li germa, r̄abû li *serma*** (Dz-#1377) He sat around in the warmth, he got up in *the cold [prv.]*; -**serma kirin** (Ag) to be cold (of persons): •***Serma dikim*** (Ag) I*'m cold*; -**sur̄ û serma** (EP-7) do. {also: [serma] سرما (JJ)} {syn: sarî I; seqem; sur̄ I} Cf. P sarmā سرما [K/JB3/IFb/B/JJ/SK/TF/Ag] <qefilîn; qerimîn; qir I; sar; simirîn; sur̄ I; zivistan>

Sermawez سەرماوەز. A Sorani name for Persian month of *Mehr* مهر [Libra] (Sept. 23-Oct. 22) or *Āẕer* آذر [Sagittarius] (Nov. 22-Dec.21). See chart of Kurdish months in this volume. <Îlon; Çirîya Pêşîn; Çirîya Paşîn; Kanûna Pêşîn>

sermaye سەرمایە *f./m.(K/Wkt)* **(-ya/-yê;).** capital, wealth: •**Xelk mezintirîn *sermayeya* me ne** (www.citizenship.gov.on.ca) The people are our greatest *capital*. P sarmāye سرمایە --> T sermaye; Sor sermaye سەرمایە [K/IFb/FJ/GF/ZF3/RZ/Wkt/BF/FD/SS/CS] <mal II>

sermayedar سەرمایەدار *m.* **(-ê;).** capitalist, bourgeois. {also: sermiyandar; sermîyandar (DZK)} [DZK//K/IFb/GF/ZF3]

sermest سەرمەست *adj.* drunk, inebriated, intoxicated. {also: sermeste} {syn: serxweş} Cf. P sarmast سرمست {sermestî} [Z-1/K/IF/ZF3]

sermeste سەرمەستە = drunk, inebriated. See **sermest**.

sermestî سەرمەستی *f.* **(-ya;-yê).** drunkenness, inebriation, intoxication. {syn: serxweşî} [K/ZF3/Wkt] <sermest>

sermijane سەرمِژانە (GF/Hej/Zeb) = pole connecting plow beam to yoke. See **sermijank**.

sermijank سەرمِژانك *f./m.(FS)* **().** pole or shaft connecting plow beam to the yoke. {also: sermijane (GF/Zeb); <sermijane> سەرمِژانە (Hej)} [Bw/AA/OK/FS//GF/Hej/Zeb] <mijane; nîr I>

sermiyan سەرمِیان *m.* **(-ê;).** lord, master, head *(of a household)*: -**sermiyanê malê** (IFb/FS) head of household: •**Lê anuha dewsa *sermiyanê malê* girtiye û bi kevnepîra diya xwe ve di binê maxên xaniyekî de dijîn** (Ardû, 114) But he is *the master of the house* now, and lives under one roof with his old mother •***semyanê mala* babê min** (Zeb/Dh) *the master of* my father's *house*. {also: semyan I (Zeb/Dh/FS-2); sermîyan (K)} {syn: malxwê; xwedî}. [Zeb/Dh//Ardû/A/IFb/GF/FS//K]

sermiyandar سەرمِیاندار = capitalist. See **sermayedar**.

sermîyan سەرمییان (K) = master. See **sermiyan**.

sermîyandar سەرمییاندار (DZK) = capitalist. See **sermayedar**.

sernerm سەرنەرم *adj.* docile, quiet *(animals)*. {also: [ser-nerm] سرنرم (JJ)} Sor sernerm سەرنەرم = 'quiet (esp. horse)' [Qzl/K/A/JJ/GF/TF] <kedî; ≠sergerm>

sernivîs سەرنڤیس *f.* **(-a;-ê).** headline *(in newspaper)*;

title. {also: sernivîsar I [2]} [(neol)K/IFb/B/(GF)/OK/ZF3] <sergotar>

sernivîsar I سەرنڤیسار *f.* **(-a;-ê).** 1) lead article (in newspaper); 2) headline. See **sernivîs.** [(neol)K/IFb/B/OK/ZF3] <sergotar>

sernivîsar II سەرنِڤیسار (Hej) = editor-in-chief. See **sernivîsk'ar.**

sernivîser سەرنِڤیسەر (OK) = editor-in-chief. See **sernivîsk'ar.**

sernivîsk'ar سەرنڤیسکار *m.&f.* **(-ê/-a;).** editor-in-chief, chief editor; chief writer. {also: sernivîsar II (Hej); sernivîser (OK); sernivîsyar (GF)} Sor serek nûser سەرەك نووسەر (Hej) [(neol)IFb/ZF3//Hej//OK//GF] <nivîsk'ar>

sernivîsyar سەرنِڤیسیار (GF) = editor-in-chief. See **sernivîsk'ar.**

ser-o-çaw سەر ۆ چاو (SK) = face. See **serçav**[1].

serok سەرۆك *m.* **(-ê;).** 1) {syn: mezin [4]; pêşeng; r̄êber; r̄êvebir; r̄êzan; serek; serk'ar [1]; serwer} leader, head, chief: •**Divê serokên ku ji alî gel ve têne hilbijartin, bi hemû pirsgirêkên gel ve têkildar bibin** (Wlt 1:49, 16) *Leaders* who are elected by the people should be involved in all of the problems of the people; 2) {syn: sedir} president. Sor serok سەرۆك = 'chieftain, headman, leader, chief' (EM) [Wlt/K(s)/IFb/GF/ZF3] <mezin[4]; r̄êvebir>

serokleşker سەرۆکلەشکەر *m.* **().** commander-in-chief, military commander: •**Te yê bigota qey hember *serokleşkerekî* rawestiyaye** (HYma, 31) It was as if she was facing *a military commander.* {also: serleşker (Wkt)} Cf. Sor serleşkir سەرلەشکِر = 'division commander' [HYma//Wkt]

serp'ê سەرپێ (K/B) = sheep trotters. See **ser û pê.**

serpêhatî سەرپێهاتی (TF) = adventure; story. See **serhatî.**

serpişik سەرپِشِك *adj.* favored, first: •**Pirsa aştîyê armanca *serpişk* e** (Zeb) The issue of peace is the *first* priority [lit. 'first goal']. {also: serpişk (OK); <serpişk> سەرپشك (Hej)} [Zeb//OK/Hej]

serpişk سەرپشك (OK) = favored, first. See **serpişik.**

serqot سەرقۆت *adj.* bareheaded, with head uncovered, not wearing a hat [cf. Ar faṣ'ān فصعان, clq Palestinian Ar mfarri' مفرّع]. {also: [ser-qot] سرقوط (JJ)} {syn: kot I} [K/A/IF/B/JJ/GF/TF/BK/Mzg/ZF3]

serrac سەڕاج (GF) = saddlemaker. See **ser̄ac.**

ser̄ast سەڕاست *adj.* honest, trustworthy: **-serrast bûn** (Bw) to be over *(of a pregnancy, either by the mother's successfully giving birth or by her miscarrying or aborting the foetus)*, to no longer be pregnant *(of a woman)*; **-ser̄ast kirin** (K/IFb/B/RZ/ZF3) to correct {syn: 'edilandin [3]}. {also: serast (IFb-2)} Sor ser̄ast سەڕاست [Bw/K/IFb/B/GF/OK/RZ/AId/ZF3]

ser̄eq سەڕەق *adj.* stubborn, obstinate, hardheaded, willful: •**Ew kur̄ekê *ser̄eq* e** (FS) He is a *stubborn* boy •**Wî gelek *xwe ser̄eq* kir** (FS) He *was* very *obstinate.* {also: ser̄eq (FS)} {syn: serĥişk; serk'êş I} Sor ser̄eq سەڕەق [GF/RZ/SS/Wkt//FS]

ser̄eqî سەڕەقی *f.* **(-ya;-yê).** stubbornness, obstinacy, hardheadedness, willfulness {also: ser̄eqî (FS)} {syn: r̄ik I; serĥişkî; serk'êşî} Sor ser̄eqî سەڕەقی [GF/BF//FS]

sersal سەرسال *f.* **(-a;-ê).** 1) {syn: salveger} anniversary: •***Sersala* te pîroz be** (AB) happy anniversary / happy birthday [lit. 'may your *anniversary* be blessed']; 2) {syn: cejna zayînê (IF); r̄ojbûn} birthday; 3) New Year's day (IFb/TF/GF); 4) food donation given as alms on the first anniversary of s.o.'s death (HH). {also: sersalî (K); [ser-sal] سرسال (JJ); <sers̱al> سرصال (HH)} [AB/A/JB3/IFb/B/JJ/GF/TF//HH//K]

sersalî سەرسالی (K) = anniversary; birthday. See **sersal.**

sersar سەرسار *adj.* insensitive; empty-headed, dull, obtuse; slow-witted: •**Tu zilamekî p'ir̄ *sersar* î** (Msr) You are a very *insensitive* [*thick-skulled*] person. {also: sersax̄ (B)} {sersarî; sersax̄î} [Msr/K/GF/ZF3//B] <p'arsû-qalim>

sersarî سەرساری *f.* **(-ya;-yê).** insensitivity; empty-headedness, dullness, obtuseness; slow-wittedness. {also: sersax̄î (B)} [Msr/GF/ZF3//B] <sersar>

sersax̄ سەرساغ (B) = insensitive; slow-witted. See **sersar.**

sersax̄î سەرساغی (B) = insensitivity; slow-wittedness. See **sersarî.**

sersed سەرسەد *f.* **(-a;-ê).** furrow's end, end of a row in a field: •**Ji bo roja din, zevî lat da; li *sersedê* gayên xwe rawestandin** (DBgb, 7) He measured ¼ of dönüm of the field for the next day; he placed his oxen at *the end of the furrow* •**Yek ji herdu dizan xwe dixe nav dahleke nêzî cotarî û yek jî diçe li *serseda* cotê wî rûdine** (ZZ-3, 148) One of the two thieves goes to a grove of trees near the farmer and the other goes and sits down at *the end of the furrow*. < ser + sed [DBgb/ZZ/FJ/TF/GF/Kmc/ZF3]

sersibe سەرسِبە (GF) = dawn. See **serê sibê**.

serstûm سەرستووم (FS) = clay butter churn. See **sirsûm**[2].

serşo سەرشۆ *f.* **(-a;-ê).** 1) {also: [ser-chou] سرشو (JJ)} female bath attendant (JJ/JB1-A): •***Serşoa* min jî carîya mine** (EH) My *bath attendant* is also my maidservant; 2) {also: serşok (A/IFb/K-2); <serşû> سرشو (HH)} bath, bathing room; bathroom, toilet (IFb); 3) washing of the head (K/B). < ser = 'head' + şo- = 'wash' See JB1, note #20, p. 198. [EH/K/B/JB1-A//A/IFb//JJ/HH] <delak>

serşok سەرشۆك (A/IFb/K) = bath. See **serşo** [2].

sertaser سەرتاسەر (Kmc) = all over. See **seranser**.

sertaş سەرتاش *m.* **(-ê;).** barber; hairdresser. {also: sert'eřaş (K); sertiraş (GF); [ser-trásc] سرتراش (JJ-G)} {syn: berber I; delak} < ser = 'head' + P/T traş = 'shave'; Cf. P sartarāš سرتراش = 'barber' [K(s)/IFb/ZF3//K//JJ-G/GF] <kuř IV>

sert'eřaş سەرتەڕاش (K) = barber. See **sertaş**.

sertiraş سەرتِراش (GF/JJ-G) = barber. See **sertaş**.

ser û ber/serûber سەر و بەر *adj.* neat, tidy, orderly, in order: **-ser û ber kirin** (IFb/FJ/GF/ZF) to put in order, tidy up {syn: lêkdan[2]}: •**Min odeya xwe *serûber kir*** (IC, 70) I *tidied up* my room. {also: [sar-u-bar] سروبر (JJ-Rh) = prêt, i.e., ready} [IC/IFb/FJ/GF/JJ/ZF/BF] <bê ser û ber; řêk û pêk>

ser û bin/serûbin سەر و بِن *adj.* upside down, reversed, messed up: **-ser û bin kirin** (IFb/FJ/GF/TF/ZF/FS) to turn upside down, turn on its head, overturn, knock over, bowl over, upset; to mess up, wreck: •**Fîlmekê dokumenter yê Swêdî Îtalya *serûbin dike*** (Bloga Zinar 3.ix.2009) A Swedish documentary film *turns* Italy *on its head* •**Pêşmerge li Başîkê tunelên DAIŞê *serûbin dike*** (Rûdaw Kurdî, YouTube, 10.xi.2016) Peshmerga in Ba'shiqa *wrecks* the tunnels of ISIS. {also: serabin (BF); [ser ou bin] سروبن (JJ)} [BlogaZinar/K/IFb/FJ/GF/TF/JJ/ZF/FS//BF]

serûç'av سەرووچاڤ (JB3/JB1-S) = face. See **serçav** [1].

ser û pê سەر وپێ [GF]/**serûpê** سەرووپێ [A/IFb/TF/ZF3] *pl./f.(B)/m.(ZF3)* sheep trotters [lit. 'head and feet'] prepared as a dish. {also: serp'ê (K/B)} {syn: k'elle paçe} [Bw/GF//A/IFb/TF/ZF3//K/B]

servan سەرڤان (GF) = camelherd. See **selwan**.

serwa سەروا *f.* **(-ya;-yê).** rhyme: •***Serwa* di şûna peyva qafiyeyê de tê bikaranîn û ji aliyê etîmolojiyê ve têkiliya wan bi hev re heye** (Adak, 358) *Serwa* is used instead of the word 'qafiye' [=rhyme], and from the point of view of etymology, they are related to each other. {syn: beşavend; paşbend; qafiye} Sor serwa سەروا [Adak/SS]

serwan سەروان (L/K[s]) = camelherd. See **selwan**.

serwer سەروەر *m.* **(-ê;).** 1) {syn: mezin [4]; pêşeng; řêber; řêvebir; řêzan; serek; serok; serk'ar [1]; serwer} leader, head, chief, commander, person in charge, authority figure; tribal chief[tain] (HH): •***Serwerên* kovara kurdî "Řoja Nu"** (Cxn-5 [Kurdoev's intro]) The heads of the Kurdish journal Roja Nu [=new day]; 2) owner, master, lord: **-serwêrê malê** (B) master of the house; landlord. {also: serwêr (B); [servir] سرور (JJ); <serwer> سرور (HH)} P sarvar سرور; Sor serwer سەروەر = 'lord, master' {serwerî; serwêr[t]î} [F/K/IFb/HH/GF/TF/ZF3//B//JJ]

serwerî سەروەری *f.* **(-ya;-yê).** 1) {syn: serk'arî [1]} leadership, command, direction, guidance: **-serwerî kirin** (K) to govern, lead: •...**Ew *serwerî li* şeherê Cizîra botan bi temî û wesyetêd giregirêd xwe *dike*** (K-dş) He *governs* of the city of Jezira bohtan by the orders of his nobles; 2) hegemony, sovereignty, dominance; 3) thrift, economy, good housekeeping (B). {also: serwêrî (B); serwêrtî (B)} [K-dş/K/IFb/GF/TF/ZF3//B] <serwer>

serwext سەروەخت *adj.* 1) {syn: aqil I; jîr} intelligent, bright; clever, sharp, quick[-witted], smart: •**Kuřo, *serwextê* min k'anê?**/ (Ba3-3, #20) Boys, where is my *genius*?; 2) {syn: agahdar; haydar} aware *(of a situation)*, updated, informed, having noticed or realized stg.: •**Carekê gundîyek diçe li malekê dibe mêvan. Kebanîya malê jê re şorbê tîne datîne ber, lê kevçî ji bîr ve dike. Mêvan dinihêre ku kebanî *serwext nabe*** (LM, 7) Once a villager is a guest at a house. The lady of the house brings him soup and sets it down before him, but she forgets [to bring] a spoon. The guest sees that the lady of the house *doesn't notice* [or *realize*]; **-serwext kirin** (ZF) to cause s.o. to realize; to bring s.o. up to date, brief s.o., inform s.o.: •**Wezîrê Karên Hundirîn ê Komara Tirkîyê wan dixûne huzûra xwe, da ku di heqê wezîfa wan da dîrektîf bide wan û wan *serwext***

bike (Bkp, 16) The Minister of Internal Affairs of the Republic of Turkey summons them to his presence, in order to give directives regarding their duty and *to bring them up to date.* {also: [ser-veqt] سروقت (JJ)} {serwextî} [Ba3/K/IFb/B/GF/TF/ZF//JJ]

serwextî سەروەختی *f.* **(-ya;-yê).** intelligence, brightness; cleverness, sharpness. [B/ZF3/Wkt] <serwext>

serwêr سەروێر (B) = leader; master. See **serwer.**

serwêrî سەروێری (B) = leadership. See **serwerî.**

serwêrtî سەروێرتی (B) = leadership. See **serwerî.**

serxes سەرخەس *f./m.(AD)* **(;-ê/).** fern, bot. *Filices* [Ar & P sarxas سرخس, Ar *also* xinšār خنشار; T eğrelti otu]. {also: sexes (ZF3)} {syn: *geyî xirçe; tilîpeř} Sor serxes سەرخەس [Wkt/AD/SS//ZF3]

Serxet سەرخەت *f.* **(-a;-ê).** Kurdistan of Turkey, which lies "above (or on) the line" (referring to the railroad which forms the border between Turkey and Syria): **•Êdî nikare li ber xwe bide, dîsa direve *Serxetê*, li gundê Nisêbînê Weysîkê dest bi şivantiyê dike** (Nbh 132:13) He can't stand it any more, once again he flees *above the line* (*=to Turkey*), and begins to be a shepherd in the village of Weysik near Nusaybin **•Piştî Sorgonê vedigere *serxetê*, gundê Çalê** (Wkp) After Sorgon he returns to *Turkey (above the line)*, to the village of Chalê. [Nbh/Wkp] <Binxet>

serxoş سەرخۆش (IFb/JJ/SK) = drunk, inebriated. See **serxweş.**

serxwe سەرخوە *adj.* independent: **-serxwe bûn** = to be or become independent; **-serxwe řabûn** (IFb/GF) to revolt. {syn: serxwebûyî; xweser} [K/IFb/GF/TF/ZF3]

serxwebûn سەرخوەبوون *f.* **(-a;-ê).** independence: **•Li dijî têkoşerên serxwebûna Kurdistanê şerekî gemarî dimeşîne** (Wlt 1:36, 1) It is carrying out a dirty war against those fighting for the independence of Kurdistan. {also: serxwebûnî (IFb-2)} {syn: serbixweyî; xwexwetî} [K/IFb/GF/TF/ZF3]

serxwebûnî سەرخوەبوونی (IFb) = independence. See **serxwebûn.**

serxwebûyî سەرخوەبوویی *adj.* independent: **•Me Kurdistanek yekbûyî, *serxwebûyî* û demokratîk divê** (Ber) We need a united, *independent*, and democratic Kurdistan. {syn: serxwe} [Ber/ZF3]

serxweda سەرخوەدا**: -serxweda hatin**: a) to come to one's senses, regain consciousness; b) to get well, recover, recuperate. [EP-7/K]

serxweş سەرخوەش *adj.* 1) {syn: sermest} drunk, tipsy, inebriated, intoxicated: **-serxweş bûn** (B) to get drunk; **-serxweş kirin** (B) to make drunk, inebriate; 2) merry, free of restraint, unrestrained. {also: serxoş (IFb-2/SK); [ser-xoš] سرخوش (JJ); <serxuweş> سرخوش (HH)} Cf. P sarxōš سرخوش --> T sarhoş = 'drunk'; Hau serweş (M4) {serxoşî; serxweşî; serx[w]eştî} [Z-1/K/A/JB3/IFb/B/GF/TF//JJ/SK//HH]

serxweşî سەرخوەشی *f.* **(-ya;-yê).** 1) drunkenness, inebriation, intoxication: **•Marî xwe berda *serxweşiya* semayê** (Dz #22, 389) The snake abandoned itself to *the intoxication of* the dance; 2) {syn: behî; tazîye [1]} condolence, comforting (upon s.o.'s death) {Cf. T başsağlığı} (Wlt/IFb). {also: serxoşî (SK); serx[w]eştî (A)} {syn: sermestî} [K/JB3/IFb/GF/TF//A//SK] <serxweş>

serx[w]eştî سەرخوەشتی (A) = drunkenness, inebriation. See **serxweşî.**

sesê سەسێ = three. See **sê** & **sisê.**

setrenc سەترەنج, m. (K/IFb/JJ/ZF) = chess. See **şetrenc.**

seûd سەئوود (L) = good luck. See **siûd.**

seva سەڤا (Z-1) = for. See **seba.**

sevev سەڤەڤ (B) = reason. See **sebeb.**

sevî سەڤی (A/GF/Zeb/BF)/sevî صەڤی (HH) = basket. See **sewî.**

sewa I سەوا**: -sewa ... sewa** *conj.* whether ... or: **•*Sewa* xatirê Ûsib *sewa* bedewya wî** (Ba) *Whether* because of Joseph *or* his beauty. Cf. Ar sawā' سواء [Ba]

sewa II سەوا = for. See **seba.**

sewal I سەوال *m.* **(-ê;).** domestic animals such as sheep and goats; livestock: **•Eme kehniya mezin, bexçe û bistanê gund ĥemû, av didê; heft a[ş]a digeřênê, û *sewalê* gund û xerîba ĥemû jê divexun** (HR-I, 2:51) But the big spring provides water for the gardens and plots of the entire village; it turns seven mills, and all *the livestock*, both of the village and of strangers, drink from it. [Frq/Msr/GF/TF/HR-I/ZF3] <dewar; ĥeywan; pez>

sewal II سەوال (EP-8) = question. See **sual.**

sewalî سەوالی, f. (K) = question. See **sual.**

sewar صەوار (SK) = cracked wheat germ. See **savar.**

sewax سەواخ *f.* **(-a;-ê).** plaster: **-sewax kirin** (Wlt/JJ)/ **sewax kirin** (B)/**sîwax kirin** (K) [+bi] to coat, daub, plaster (with) {syn: dûtin; seyandin}: **•Li**

Kurdistanê, qelaxan ji kerme, sergîn û pesariyan çêdikin û bi rêxê *sewax dikin* ku bi wê rêxê ji berf û baranê bête parastin (Wlt 1:37, 13) In Kurdistan, they make piles of pressed dung patties from [various types of dried manure], then *coat* them with moist dung so that they will be protected from rain and snow. {also: sewax̂ (B); siwax (OK/B-2); sîwax (F/K); suwax (IFb); [savakh/suwākh (Rh)] صـواخ (JJ)} {syn: gec} <T sıva --> clq Ar ṣuwāḥ صـــــــواح = 'plaster'. For another example of a Turkish word in -a which becomes -ax/-ax̂ in Kurdish, See **boyax**. [Wlt/ZF3//JJ//B//OK//F/K//IFb]

sewax̂ سەواغ (B) = plaster. See **sewax**.

sewda سەودا/**s̱ewda** صەودا [FS] *m.* **(-yê;).** 1) passion, passionate love; melancholy (JJ) [séuda]; 2) {syn: aqil; ḧiş} sense, (capacity for) reason: •**Zelîxe bûbû maşoqa Ûsib, *sewda* lê nemabû, hiş lê çûbû** (Ba) Zalikha fell in love with Joseph, her *sense* left her [lit. 'sense did not remain for her, reason went from her'] •**Malxirav, aqil, *sewda* sêrîda t'unîne** (Z-1) You wretch, there's no sense or *reason* in your head. {also: [seoŭda/séuda] سودا (JJ)} < Ar sawdā' ســوداء = 'black (f.); black bile, melancholy' --> T sevda = 'passion, melancholy' [Ba/K/IFb/GF//JJ//FS]

sewgir سەوگر (FJ) = dawn; dusk. See **segur**.

sewgur سەوگور (GF/ZF) = dawn; dusk. See **segur**.

sewgurî سەوگورى (Kmc) = dawn; dusk. See **segur**.

sewgûr سەوگوور (TF) = dawn; dusk. See **segur**.

sewik سەوِك/**s̱ewik'** صەوِك *f.(Bw)/m.(Zeb/Dh/ZF3)* **(-a/-ê;-ê/).** type of home-made bread (flat, round, thick, often with sesame seeds) (Zeb/Dh); type of cake called in Turkish 'kavut' (=dish made of roasted wheat ground with dried wild pears) (JJ): -**s̱ewk'êt hêka** (JB1-A) omelettes {syn: hêkerûn}. {also: [seviq] سويق (JJ)} [IFb/ZF3//Bw/Zeb/Dh/JB1-A/FS//JJ] <kilor; kuloç'>

sewir سەور (K) = revolution. See **sewr**.

sewî سەوى *f.* **(-ya;-yê).** 1) {syn: qûfik} basket for grapes and other fruits; 2) large water jug (IFb). See **sewîl**. {also: sevî (A/GF/Zeb/BF); [sevi] سوى (JJ); <s̱evî> صـڤـى (HH)} Cf. Sor sewî سـەوى = 'pannier, large wicker basket' [IFb/JJ/SK/ZF3//A/GF/Zeb/BF//HH] <'edil; mekev; sebet; tirî; zembîl>

sewîl سەويل *m.* **(-ê;).** earthenware water jug: •**Sofîk hebû: *sewîlê* xwe bir û çû serê kaniyê, da ko destmêj bigirê** (Rnh 3:22, 426) There was a sufi: He took his *clay jug* to the spring, to wash his hands [=to do his ritual ablutions]. {also: sewî [2] (IFb-2); sewîlk (GF-2); [sevil سويل/saoul /سـول ساول] (JJ); <sewîl> ســويـل (HH)} {syn: şerbik} [Rnh/A/IFb/JJ/HH/GF/TF/FS/ZF3] <cer; hincan; lîn>

sewîlk سەويلك (GF) = earthenware jug. See **sewîl**.

sewr سـەور *f.* **(-a;).** uprising, insurrection; revolution: -**Sewra Azadî** (Cxn-2) Freedom revolution *(title of Cigerxwîn's second collection of poems [dîwan])*. {also: sewir (K); sewre} {syn: serhil-dan; şoreş} <Ar ṯawrah ثورة = 'revolt, riot' [Cxn-2/IFb//K]

sewre سەوره = revolution. See **sewr**.

sewt ســەوت *f./m.(B)* **(-a/ê;-ê/).** 1) {syn: deng} voice: •**qîrîna *sewta* aşiq** (Z-1) the shouting of the singer's *voice*; 2) sound (B): -**sewt dayîn** (B) to sound, make a sound; 3) cry, shout (B): -**sewtê qulinga** (B) cries of the cranes. < Ar ṣawt صوت = 'voice' [Ad/Z-1/K/B]

sexbêr سەخبێر *m.&f.* **().** caretaker; monitor: -**sexbêra *fk-î* kirin** (JB1-A) to take care of: •**Gelek ji xelkî ji ber tengîya hizr û bîrêt xo wesa hizir diken ku jinê çi rolê xo nîne di avakirina civakê da û ev role bitinê yê zelamî ye çunkî rolê jinê girêdiden bi çarçuvê *sexbêr kirina* malê û perwerdekirina zaroka** (R 15 [4/xii/96] 5) Because of narrowmindedness, many people think that women have no role in building society, and that that role belongs solely to men, because they tie the women's role to *taking care of* the house and raising the children •**Min çu jin nevên ... bes, lazim bo te êkê bînî da *sexbêra* me jî *biket*** (JB1-A, #136) I don't want a wife ... but you should find one for you, so that she can *care for* us as well. {also: sexbîr (OK); <sexbîr> ســەخــبــيــر (Hej)} <NENA [m]sakhbir ܡܣܟܒܪ = 'to visit, go and see' & sakhbûr ܣܟܒܘܪ = 'careful (adj.); care, attention (n.)', cf. khâbir ܚܒܪ = 'to find out, discover' (Maclean) < Arc s + √ḥ-b-r {sexbêrî} [Zeb/Dh/JB1-A/ZF3//Hej/OK]

sexbêrî ســەخــبێــرى *f.* **(-ya;-yê).** care; supervision. {also: sexbîrî (OK-2/RZ); sex̂bîrî (GF)} [Dh/Zeb/Elk/OK/ZF3//RZ//GF] <miqatî; sexbêr; t'îmar>

sexbîr ســەخــبــيــر (OK/Hej) = caretaker; monitor. See **sexbêr**.

sexbîrî ســەخــبــيــرى (OK/RZ) = care; supervision. See **sexbêrî**.

sexes سەخەس (ZF3) = fern. See **serxes**.

sexmaret ســەخــمــارەت (Zeb) = because of; for the sake

of. See **sexmerat**.

sexmerat سەخمەرات *prep.* 1) {syn: pêxemet} because of, for the sake of [-î or -a]: **•Azad ji ber te hatiye vêrê, anku ser xatira te, *sexmeratî te* hatiye** (FS) A. has come here because of you, i.e., *for your sake* he has come **•Ew *sexmerata* rizgarkirina welatî gelek xebitî** (FS) He has worked a lot *for* the liberation of the homeland **•Ew *se[x]merata* Zoroyî ket di wê gelşê da** (FS) He has gotten into that mess *thanks to* Z. **•*sexmaretî* te** (Zeb) *for* your *sake* (Ar min ša'nika من شأنك); 2) [*conj.*] in order to, so that: **•Li çerxê nozdê da Ingilîza çend peymanên ramyarî û leşkerî mor kirin ligel şêxên wê devera kendavî *ji bo sexmeratîya* wan biparêzin, û destê xo dana liser hemî deverê** (Metîn 62[1997]:27) In the 19th century, the English signed several political and military treaties with the sheikhs of the gulf region *in order to* protect them, and to take control of the entire region. {also: sexmaret (Zeb); sexmeratî (Hej)} {syn: bi xêra; dewlet serê; pêxemet} [Zeb//Metîn/FS/BF//Hej] <pêxemet>

sexmeratî سەخمەراتى (Hej) = because of; for the sake of. See **sexmerat**.

sextî سەختى (Erg) = checking, examination. See **saxtî**.

seẍbîrî سەغبيرى (GF) = care; supervision. See **sexbêrî**.

sexlet سەخلەت (). trait, characteristic, feature: **•Ev yarîye wekî sê kêlanê ye di gele *sexletêt* xweda, di gelek tişta jî da cudayî ya hey** (YK 12) This game is like "sê kêlanê" in many of its *characteristics*, [but] in many things there is a difference **•Hesenê Metê jî bi awayekê pir zelal, informatîv û têkel bi tecrubeya xwe wek novelnivîs li ser novelê (kurteçîrokê) rawestiya, ew çû ser behsa *sexletên* taybet yên hunerê novelê û ferqiya wê ji romanê** (Nefel) H.M. discussed the short story in a very clear and informative manner linked to his experience as a short story writer, he went into the issue of specific *traits* of the art of the short story and its difference from the novel **•Kultura dema peydabûna civaka si'netî (pîşesaziyê) rengek dî yê jiyan û danûstandina civakî xuliqand ku *sexletên* cuda ji kultura fiyodalî hebûn** (Kulturname) The culture of the period of the appearance of the industrial society created a different type of life and social relations which had different *characteristics* from feudal culture **•Serhengî daxwaz ji Qazî Mihemed kir, ... eger di şiyan de hebe bo wî bahsê hinek *sexletên* (taybetên) Mela Mistefayê Barzanî bike** (Wkp: Gotûbêja bikarhêner: Sipan Silwaneyi) The general asked Qazi Mihemed ... if he could to discuss some of *the characteristics of* Mulla Mustafa Barzani. {syn: t'aybetmendî; tebî'et; xeyset} [YK/Nefel/Wkp/ Kulturname]

seyandin سەياندن *vt.* **(-seyîn-).** 1) {syn: dûtin; sewax kirin} to coat, daub, plaster, smear *(with plaster, clay, mud, etc.)*: **•Keçelok emrî ser xûlama kir, devê çel çewalê qîr vekirin, li kanîya avê xistin û pê *seyandin*** (L) Kechelok [=Bald boy] gave the servants the order, [and] they opened the forty sacks of tar, poured them into the springs of water, and *coated* them with it (=the tar); 2) to close up, block, cork up. {also: <s̠eyandin صياندن (dis̠eyîne) (دصيينه)> (HH)} <Ar sayya' II سيّع = 'to plaster (wall) with mud and straw' [L/K(s)/A/IFb/ GF/FS//HH] <sewax>

seyasetî سەياسەتى (-ya;) (B) = politics. See **siyaset**.

seyd سەيد *f./m.(K)* **(-a/ ;-ê/).** hunting: **-seyda teyra** (L) bird hunting. {also: [sēd] صيد (JJ) = 'hunting dog'} {syn: nêçîr; r̄av I; şikar} < Ar ṣayd صيد [L/ K/IFb/ZF3]

seyda سەيدا *m.* **(-yê;).** teacher, professor; religious teacher: **•Êdî *seydayê* min ji bavê min re got: "Gerek ev gede here cihê din li medresa bixwîne"** (Wlt 2:66, 2) Finally my *teacher* said to my father, "This child should go somewhere else and study in the [big] schools" **•*Seyda*, lê te çawa şer̄ avîte min, te çû go: 'Xelq derîkîr̄a diçe, derîkîr̄a tê'** (HCK-1, 210) *Teacher*, how could you slander me [like that], you went and said, 'People go in one door and come out another door' *[describing woman as whore]*.{also: [seïd سيد/ seïda سيدا] (JJ); <seyda> سيدا (HH)} <Ar sayyid سيّد = 'master, lord, mister, title for descendants of the Prophet Muhammad' [Wlt/K/A/IFb/JJ/HH/SK/GF/TF/ OK] <dersdar; feqî; mamosta>

seydevan سەيدەڤان (K) = hunter. See **seydvan**.

seydvan سەيدڤان *m.* **(-ê;).** hunter. {also: seîyed (F); seydevan (K); seyyîd (K-2); [se'id-vār̄] صيدوار (JJ)} {syn: nêçîrvan; şikarçî} Cf. Ar ṣayyād صيّاد [IFb/ZF3//F//K//JJ] <seyd>

seyis I سەيس (GF) = horse groomer. See **seyîs I**.

seyis II سەيِس (ZF3) = three-year-old male goat. See

sayis.

seyîs I سەیس *m.* **(-ê;).** (horse) groom, stableman. {also: seyis I (GF); seys I (EP-7); [sèis] سایس (JJ)} {syn: r̄evoçî} < Ar sā'is سائس, cf. also Heb sus סוס & NENA sûsî ܣܘܣܐ (Maclean) & suse (Garbell); sisyo (Ṭūrōyo: Ritter) = 'horse' [EP-7/JJ//GF//K/ZF3] <r̄evo; stewl; t'ewle>

seyîs II سەییس (Zeb) = three-year-old male goat. See sayis.

seyr سەیر *adj.* strange, odd, peculiar; remarkable, incredible: •**Nas bike ka bê çi dunyayeke *seyr* e** (Epl 24) Recognize what a *strange* world it is. {syn: 'ecêb [3,4]} < Sor seyr سەیر = 'strange, incredible, remarkable' [Epl/A/SS]

seyran سەیران *f.* **(-a;-ê).** 1) {syn: seyrange} walk, stroll, promenade: •**Ew derk'etne *seyranê*** (B) They went for *a walk*; 2) picnic, outing; •**ji *seyrana* r̄ojê westîyayî** (Z-1) tired from the day's *outing*. {also: "sahrane"; [serián/séirán] سیران (JJ); <seyran> سیران (HH)} Cf. T seyran & clq Syrian Ar sērān سیران = 'picnic, outing' < Ar sār (سير) سار = 'to set out (on a trip)' [Z-1/K/A/IFb/B/JJ/HH/GF/TF]

seyrang•e سەیرانگە *f.* **(•a;•ê).** 1) place for taking a walk; 2) {syn: seyran} walk, stroll, promenade: •**Ew diçin li dinyayê digerin, ji vê rêwîtiyê re dibêjin "*seyranga* dinê" û "dewra dinê"** (R. Alakom. Folklor û jinên Kurd 13) They go travel around the world, they call this trip "world *promenade*" & "world tour";-**seyrange kirin** = to take a walk, stroll. {also: seyrangeh (IFb); [seïran-gah] سیرانگاه (JJ)} [EP-7/K/B//IFb/GF//JJ] <seyran>

seyrangeh سەیرانگەه (IFb) = place for strolling; stroll, walk. See **seyrange**.

seyranger سەیرانگەر (IFb/CS) = picnicker. See **seyranî**.

seyranî سەیرانی *m.&f.* **().** picnicker: •**Belê Mih̄emedî nezanî ew hevalê wî ye û hizir dikir *seyranî* ne[;] ji birsa da ma li hîviya *seyraniya* ta ku biçin ... îna piştî çûyn[,] Mih̄emed çû cihê *seyraniya*** (M. Bamernî. Dîtin hizarê, 38) But M. did not know that it was his friend, and he thought they were *picnickers*; famished, he waited for the *picnickers* to go away ... after they went, M. went to the place *of the picnickers*. {also: seyranger (IFb/CS)} [Bamernî/SS//IFb/CS/BF]

seys I سەیس (EP-7) = horse groomer. See **seyîs I**.

seys II سەیس (FS) = three-year-old male goat. See sayis.

seyyîd سەیید (K) = hunter. See **seydvan**.

sê I سێ *num.* three, 3: ,"sisê" is used independently (free form), while "sê" is immediately followed by a dependent noun (bound form), Cf. didû vs. du I *(in Behdinan, **sê** alone is used both as free form and as bound form).* {also: sesê; **sisê** (BX-2/K-2); sêsê (A); [si] سی (JJ); <sê سی/sis[s]ê سسی> (HH)} [Pok trei- 1090.] 'three': Skt tráyaḥ *m.*/trī[ṇi] *n.*/tisráḥ *f.*; O Ir *θrayah; Av θrayō/θrayas *m.*/θri *n.*/tisrō *f.*; Mid P sē̆ (M3); P se سه; Sor sê سێ; Za hîrê (Todd); Gurani yare (M4); cf. also Lat tres (m. & f.)/tria (n.); Gr treis τρεῖς *(m. & f.)*/tria τρία *(n.)*; Rus tri три; Germ drei [BX/K/JB3/IFb/B/HH/SK/GF/TF//A//JJ] <didû; du I; sêkî; sêzdeh; sisê; sî II>

sê II سێ = shade, shadow. See **sî I**.

sê III سێ (JB1-A) = third. See **sisîya**.

sêanî سێئانی (K) = third. See **sisîya**.

sêbahî سێباهی (Wn) = swimming. See **sobahî**.

sêbanî سێبانی (Qzl) = swimming. See **sobahî**.

sêber سێبەر *f.* **(-a;-ê).** shade, shadow: •**Ez dareka mazinim: havînê wextê germê mirovek dê hêtin li r̄êkê, dê hête bin *sêbera* min, dê r̄û nêt** (M-Ak, #548) I am a big tree: in summer when it is hot a man will come along the road, he will come under my *shade* and sit down •**Xelkê wê dirkê hemî dijîn di kepra ve. [Di]çine çiyay, tiştekî tînin--dibênê çulî--dihavêne ser kepra, dibîte *sîber* û gelek xoş dibin** (M-Am #721, 332) The people there all live in bough shelters. They go to the mountains and bring something called 'chuli' [young, leafy branches of oak] and put them on top of the shelters and it makes a *shade* and they are very pleasant. {also: sîber (K/GF/JB1-A/M-Am); [sibéri] سیبری (JJ)} {syn: sî I} Cf. Sor sêber سێبەر [M-Ak/SK/OK//K/GF/JB1-A/M-Am//JJ]

sêdar•e سێدارە *f.* **(;•ê).** gallows: •**Min û sêpêkê jivan e / Min û *sêdarê* jivan e** (from poem by Muayyid Tayyib of Dihok) I have a rendezvous with the gallows, / I have a rendezvous with *the gibbet*. {syn: daraxaç; sêp'î} Sor sêdare سێدارە [Bw/A/GF/OK/ZF3]

sêê سێئێ (M-Am&Bar&Shn) = third. See **sisîya**.

sêfîl سێفیل *adj.* 1) {syn: belengaz; bikul; malxerab; r̄eben I; şerpeze} miserable, wretched: -**sêfîl û sergedan** [sic] (EH) do.; 2) {syn: feqîr; xizan} poor. {also: sefîl (JB3/IFb/ZF3/FS-2); [sefil] سفیل (JJ)} < Ar safīl سفيل {sefîlî; sêfîlî} [K/B/GF/FS//JB3/

IFb/JJ/ZF3/Wkt]

sêfîlî سێفیلی *f.* **(-ya;-yê).** 1) misery: **•Û ji bona wan hilqeysê teb û *sêfîlî* min dît** (L) [After] I experienced [lit. 'saw'] so much torment and *misery* for their sake; 2) {syn: feqîrî; xizanî; zivarî} poverty; 3) powerlessness. {also: sefîlî (JB3/ZF3)} < Ar safīl سفيل [L/K/A//JB3/ZF3/Wkt] <sêfîl>

Sêgav سێگاڤ (ZF3) = *name of Kurdish folk dance.* See **Sêgavî**.

Sêgavî سێگاڤی *f.* **(;-yê).** Sêgavî, name of a Kurdish folk dance: **•Bi giranîyê dest pê dikir û *sêgavîyê*, şarxoş barî û hewayê din berdewam dikir** (Bîrnebûn #45, bihar [2010], 45) He began with Giranî [slow dance], and continued with *Sêgavî*, Sharkhosh Bari and other tunes. {also: sêgav (ZF3); sêgavkî (Wkp)} [Hezex/Çandname.com/IKP//Wkp//ZF3] <govend>

Sêgavkî سێگاڤکی (Wkp) = *name of Kurdish folk dance.* See **Sêgavî**.

sêgeh سێگه‌ه (A/IFb) = pitchfork. See **sêguh I**.

sêgoş سێگۆش (OK) = triangle. See **sêguh II**.

sêgoşe سێگۆشه (F/K/B/GF/FS) = triangle. See **sêguh II**.

sêguh I سێگوه *m./f.(FS)* **(;/-ê).** three-tonged pitchfork: **•Wî bi *sêguhê* qirş lêkda** (FS) He gathered the brushwood with *the pitchfork*. {also: sêgeh (A/IFb); sêgulî (TF); <sêguh> سیگه (HH)} [Bw/HH/GF/OK/FS//A/IFb//TF]

sêguh II سێگوه *f.* **().** 1) triangle; 2) [*adj.*] triangular. {also: sêgoş (OK-2); sêgoşe (F/K/B/GF-2/FS); sêgûşe (OK-2)} <sê = three + guh = 'ear' or goşe = 'corner'. *For another example of ears being equated with triangles, compare the triangular pastry made by Jews on Purim, called in Heb **ozne haman** אזני המן ='the ears of Haman (the villain)'.* [IFb/GF/OK//F/K/B/FS]

sêgulî سێگولی (TF) = pitchfork. See **sêguh I**.

sêgûşe سێگووشه (OK) = triangle. See **sêguh II**.

sêhem سێهه‌م (IFb/Wkt) = third. See **sêyem**.

sêhemîn سێهه‌مین (IFb/Wkt) = third. See **sêyem**.

sêhil سێهل (Bw) = metal disk for baking bread. See **sêl**.

sêhl سێهل (FS) = metal disk for baking bread. See **sêl**.

sêhwane سێهوانه (FS) = umbrella. See **sîwan**.

sêk سێك (IFb/HH/FD/BF/FS) = vinegar. See **sihik I**.

sêkî سێکی *f.* **(-ya;-yê).** a third, 1/3: **•*Sêkîya* gundê xo min firot** (AR, 287) I sold *a third of* my village. {also: sêyek (K/IFb/GF/BK/CT); siseyek (BX); cf. [ji siian iek] ژ سیان یك (JJ)} Sor sê-yek سێیه‌ك/سی یه‌ك [Zeb/AR//K/IFb/GF/BK/CT//BX]

sêklot سێکلۆت *m.* **(-ê;).** donkey dung: **-sêklotê k'era** (Msr) do. {syn: serkul} [Msr] <dirg; peyîn; r̄ix; sergîn; t'epik II>

sêl سێل *f.* **(-a;-ê).** large convex (bowl-shaped) metal disk upon which bread is baked, and in which meat (K) or kernels of grain (B) are roasted {=Jewish NENA of Zx: dōqā}: **•Jinik r̄adibe kuç'kê xwe dadide, ser *sêlê* qeynokê xwe diqelîne** (Dz-anec #12) The woman lights her stove, roasts her qeynok on *the convex disk* [sêl]; **-nanê sêlê** (Wkp) fresh bread baked on a *sêl*. {also: sêhil (Bw-2); sêhl (FS); [seil] سیل (JJ); <sêl> سیل (HH)} JJ's etymology "formed from Ar sāj ساج with the help of the suffix -l, before which the -j has been suppressed" is unlikely. Cf. Sor sêle سێله = 'flat stone used as griddle' [Bw/Zx/K/A/IFb/B/JJ/HH/GF/TF/OK//FS] <nan; tîrok; xanik>

sêlav سێلاڤ *f.* **(-a;-ê).** 1) {syn: şîp} torrent, stream; 2) {syn: lêmişt; t[']ofan} flood, inundation. {also: [seil-aw] سیلاو (JJ)} <Ar sayl سيل = 'flood' + av = 'water'; cf. P seylāb سيلاب [F/K/B/JJ/GF/ZF3] <avr̄abûn; lehî; şirav; şîp>

sêlim سێلِم, f. (Erh/IFb/HH/TF) = ladder. See **silim**.

sêmir̄ سێمر *m.* **().** 1) simurgh, roc, fabulous bird in Persian and Kurdish (i.e., Iranian) folklore: **-teyrê sêmir** (L-2) do. {also: teyrê sîmir̄ (K/B)}; 2) large bird whose flesh is not eaten (IFb/HH) [sîmir]; eagle (B); red vulture, zool. *Gypus vulvus* [T kızıl akbaba] (IFb) [sîmerx]. {also: sîmerx (IFb-2/FS); sîmir (IFb/GF/TF/FS); sîmir̄ (K/B); [sīmer] سيمر (JJ); <sîmir> سيمر (HH)} Cf. P sīmorγ سيمرغ; Sor sîmurẍ سیمورغ/sîmirẍ سیمِرغ [L//K/IFb/B/HH/GF/TF/FS//JJ//FS] <mirîşk>

sênc سێنج *f./m.(FS)* **(-a/-ê;).** hedge, fence made of brush; hedge of thorny plants around a garden or vineyard: **•Rabûn çûn ber bi / *sênca* rezekî** (Rnh 214, 2[242]) They got up and went towards *the hedge of* a vineyard: **-sênc danîn** (GF)/~ **kirin** (A) to surround with a hedge. {also: <sênc> سنج (HH)} {syn: çeper; k'ozik; p'ercan; tan} < Ar siyāj سياج = 'fence' [Rnh/A/FJ/GF/HH/TF/RZ/CS]

sênî سێنی *f.* **(-ya;-yê).** 1) {syn: berkeş; lengerî; mecme'; mersef} tray, platter (K/A); large tray (IF); tray on which to put plates (JJ); round copper pan in which food is served (B): **•Qawekê**

ji mîrê xweřa bik'elîno / Tu têxe du ḧeb fincanê ferfûrî û dayne ser *sênîya* zêrîno (Z-2) Boil coffee for your emir / pour it into two china cups and put them on a golden *tray*; 2) dish, plate (K/GF). {also: sinî (B); sînî (IFb-2); [sini] سينى (JJ)} Cf. Ar ṣīnīyah صينية = 'tray with high lip in which food is cooked' < Ar ṣīnī صينى = 'chinese porcelain'; Sor sînî سينى = 'tray'; Hau sînî m. (M4) [Z-2/K(s)/A/IFb/JJ/SK/GF/TF//B] <berkeş; lengerî; tiryan>

sênîk سێنيك *f.* **(-a;-ê).** plate, dish; small platter: •**Her êk kire d[i] *sênîk'ekê*** [sic] **ferfûrîda dane d[i] mecma'êda, bir dane ser mêzey mabeyna her duk'a** (JB1-A #78) He put each one on a porcelain *plate* which he put on a tray, and he put them on the table between the two of them •**Kuřik' zivirî, ... k'ut'ilik'a xalê xwe *sênîk'ê* îna derê, kir di *sênîk'a* dayk'a xweda, k'ut'ilik'a dayk'a xwe kir di *sênîk'a* xalê xweda** (M-Zx, #769, 354) The boy turned round, ... took his uncle's kutilk off his *plate*, and put it in his mother's *plate*, he put his mother's kutilk in his uncle's *plate*. {also: sihnîk (Bw); [sehni صحنى/sini سينى] (JJ)} < Ar ṣīnī صينى = 'chinese porcelain' + -k; also cf. Ar ṣaḥn صحن = 'plate'; cf. Sor sînî سينى = 'tray' [Bw//JB1-A/OK/RZ/FS//JJ] <aman; firaq>

sênzdeh سێنزده (B) = thirteen. See **sêzdeh**.

sêpê سێپێ (IFb/HH/TF/OK) = tripod; gallows. See **sêp'î**.

sêp'î سێپى *f.* **(-ya;-yê).** 1) {syn: dûstan; kuçʼik II[2]} trivet, tripod *(on a which a pot is placed while cooking* [<sêpê> سيپى (HH)]; *on which a yoghurt churn is placed* [<sêpik> سيپك (HH)]); 2) {syn: daraxaç; sêdare} gallows: •**Dîsa şêx, avêtibûn kindirê *sêpê* da** (Ah) Once again they hanged [lit. 'threw'] the sheikh on the *gallows* rope. {also: sêpê (IFb-2/TF/OK); [si-peï] سى پى (JJ); <sêpê سيپى/sêpik سيپك> (HH)} P seh´pā سه‌پا = 'three-legged' & seh´pāye سه‌پايه = 'tripod, trivot'--> T sehpa = 'tripod; coffee table; easel; gallows'; Sor sêpa سێپا/sêpê سێپێ = 'tripod' [Ah/HH/TF/OK//K/A/IFb/B//JJ]

sêr I سێر *f.* **(-a;-ê).** magic, sorcery; magic trick (B): •**Ewî ismê *sêrê* li xwe xwend** (L) He recited *magic* spell to himself •**Me *sêr avêtiye* ser çavên Abidê Şkeftê** (ZZ-7, 197) We *cast a spell* on the eyes of A.S. {also: sihir I (IFb); sihr (IFb-2/GF); [sihir] سحر (JJ); <sihrî> سهرى (HH)} {syn: efsûnî} < Ar siḥr سحر --> T sihir [L/K/B/ZF//IFb//GF//JJ//HH] <îsm; řemil; t'ilism>

Sêrek سێرك (Ber) = Siverek. See **Sêwreg**.

sêsed سێسه‌د/**sêsed** سێصه‌د [SK] *num.* three hundred, 300. {also: sêsid (B)} Skt triśatā-; Av θrisata- & tišrō sata; P sēṣad سيصد; Sor sêsed سێسه‌د [K//SK//B]

sêsê سێسێ (A) = three. See **sê** & **sisê**.

sêsid سێسِد (B) = three hundred. See **sêsed**.

Sêşem سێشه‌م *f.* **(-a;-ê).** Tuesday. {also: Sêşemb (JB3/IFb/TF); Sêşembe (GF-2); Sêşemî (K/GF/Erg); [sichem] سيشم (JJ)} Cf. P seh šanbe سه‌شنبه; Sor Sêşem[m]e سێشه‌ممه/Sêşemû سێشه‌موو; Za Sêşeme (Todd) [F/B/Rh//JJ//K/GF//JB3/IFb/TF]

Sêşemb سێشه‌مب (JB3/IFb/TF) = Tuesday. See **Sêşem**.

Sêşembe سێشه‌مبه (GF) = Tuesday. See **Sêşem**.

Sêşemî سێشه‌مى (K/GF/Erg) = Tuesday. See **Sêşem**.

*sêtî سێتى (EP-7) = checking, examination. See **saxtî**.

sêv سێڤ *f.* **(-a;-ê).** apple: •***Sêvna* bîne** (BK) Bring *some apples*; **-sêva bin 'erdê/bin'erd** (B) Jerusalem artichoke. {also: sîv (Rh); [siw] سيڤ (JJ); <sîv> سيڤ (HH)} Mid P sēb (M3); Southern Tati dialects (all *f.*): Takestani & Ebrahim-abadi asifa; Eshtehardi siva; Sagz-abadi asua (Yar-Shater); P sīb سيب; Sor sêw سێو; Za sa *f.* (Todd); Hau sawî *f.*(M4) [AB/K/A/JB3/IFb/B/GF/TF/OK/BK//JJ/HH/Rh]

sêvang•e سێڤانگه, f. (;•ê) (B) = umbrella. See **sîwan**.

sêvil سێڤِل (GF) = field mouse. See **sêvle**.

sêvle سێڤله *m.* **().** field mouse, zool. *Microtus arvalis & Microtus agrestis*. {also: sêvil (GF); sêvlo (FS); sêvole (GF-2); sîvle (A); sîvlore (Bw); <s[ê]vle> سيڤله (HH)} {syn: mişkê teřezinê} [Bw//A//IFb/HH/Hej//GF//FS] <cird; mişk>

sêvlo سێڤلۆ (FS) = field mouse. See **sêvle**.

sêvole سێڤۆله (GF) = field mouse. See **sêvle**.

sêvsêvok سێڤسێڤۆك *f.* **(-a;).** kneecap, anat. *Patella*: **-sêvsêvoka çokî** (Bw) do. [Bw] <çok>

sêwemîn سێوه‌مين (K) = third. See **sêyem**.

Sêwereg سێوه‌ره‌گ (Wkp) = Siverek. See **Sêwreg**.

sêwirandin سێوراندِن *vt.* **(-sêwirî-).** 1) {syn: xiyal kirin} to imagine, picture in one's mind; to think, ponder, deliberate: •**Mîrze Mihemed xwe bi xwe *sêwirî*, lê tu çare nedît** (ZZ-7, 192) M.M. *deliberated* with himself, but he could find no solution •**Şerdîn bîstikek *sêwirî* û devê xwe vekir, got** ... (ZZ-7, 259) Sh. *thought* for a moment and opened his mouth and said ... •**Wî di hizra xwe da *sêwirandibû* ku Zoro gelek bihêz e**

(FS) In his mind he *had imagined* that Z. was very strong **•Wî di serê xwe da *sêwirandibû* ka xaniyê xwe çawa dê ava bikit** (FS) In his head he *had pictured* how he would build his house; 2) {syn: vehûnan[2]} to compose (e.g., poems): **•Mijarên ku ez dê di rojên pêş de binivîsim min ew di serê xwe de *sêwirandine*** (ZF3) I *have been composing* in my head the topics that I will write about in days to come **•Tevî helbestê usan jî miqam hatye *sêwirandin*** (Wkt:Eskerê Boyîk: Cegerxwîn û folklora kurdî) Together with such poems he *composed* songs [maqams] as well. {also: sêwirîn (ZZ-7); sêwrandin (FJ)} [ZZ-7//ZF3/Wkt/FS/FD///FJ]

sêwirîn سـێـوِریـن (ZZ) = to imagine; to think. See **sêwirandin**.

sêwî سێوی *m.&f.* **(-yê/-ya; /-yê).** orphan; child whose mother is dead, but whose father is still alive (Bw/JB1-A/GF); child whose mother is dead, or whose both parents are dead (TF): **•Derew *sêwî* ye** (BX) Lies are *orphans* [lit. 'the lie is (an) *orphan*'] *[prv.]* **•Wê zar û zêçên me *sêwî* bihêlin** (Ber) They will leave our women and children [widows and] *orphans*; **-êt'îm û sêwî** (Bw) child orphaned of both parents. {also: [sivi] سـيـوى (JJ); <sêwî> سيوى (HH)} {syn: êt'îm} {sêwîtî} [K/A/JB3/IFb/B/HH/JB1-A/GF/TF/OK//JJ] <bî I>

sêwîtî سێویتی *f.* **(-ya;-yê).** orphanhood, particularly loss of the mother. {syn: êt'îm[t]î} [K/A/IFb/GF/TF/ZF3] <sêwî>

sêwîxane سـێـویـخـانـه *f.* **(-ya;-yê).** orphanage: **•Emerîkayê li Qersê *sêwîxane* vekiriye, zarokên bê dê û bav berhev dikin, dibin xwedî dikin** (KO, 39) America has opened *an orphanage* in Kars, they gather children without parents, they take them and care for them. {syn: êt'îmxane} < sêwî + xane [KO/K/IFb/FJ/GF/ZF/CS/BF/Wkt]

sêwrandin سـێـوراندِن (FJ) = to imagine; to compose. See **sêwirandin**.

Sêwreg سـێـورهگ *f.* **(-a;-ê).** Siverek, a town in the northeast corner of the province of Urfa (Riha), where both Kurmancî and Zaza (Dimilî) are spoken: **•*Siwêreg* her çiqas girêdayî Rihayê be jî, di hêla dîrokî û erdnigarî de zêdetir girêdayê Amedê ye** (Wkp) Although *S.* is linked to Urfa, it is more closely tied to Diyarbakir [Amed] both historically and geographically. {also: Sêrek (Ber); Sêwereg (Wkp-2); Siwêreg (Wkp-2); Swêrek (A/G)} Za Soyreg (Todd) [Ber//A/G//Wkp]

sêyek سێیەك (K/IFb/GF/BK/CT) = a third. See **sêkî**.

sêyem سێیەم *adj.* third, 3rd. {also: sêhem (IFb/Wkt-2); sêhemîn (IFb-2/Wkt-2); sêwemîn (K); sêyemîn (CT-2/ZF-2/TF/GF-2/Wkt-2); **sisîya**} Cf. P sevvom سوّم; Sor sêhem[în] سێـهـهمـین [A/CT/GF/ZF/Wkt//IFb//TF//K] <sê I; sisê>

sêyemîn سـێـیـهمـین (CT/ZF/TF/GF/Wkt) = third. See **sêyem**.

sêyê سێیێ (M-Sur&Ak) = third. See **sisîya**.

sêyîs سـێـیـیـس (FS) = three-year-old male goat. See **s̱ayis̱**.

sêzde سـێـزده (K/IFb/SK/JB1-A&S/GF/M/Rh) = thirteen. See **sêzdeh**.

sêzdeh سێزدهه *num.* thirteen, 13. {also: sênzdeh (B); sêzde (K/IFb/SK/JB1-A&S/GF/M/Rh); [sezdeh سيزده/douhousi دهوسى] (JJ)} Skt tráyodaśa; Av θridasa = thirteenth; Mid P sēzdah (M3); P sīzdah سيزده; Sor sêzde سێزده/siyanze سِيانزه; Za hîrês/desuhîrê (Todd); Hau sênze (M4) [F/SC/JJ//K/IFb/SK/JB1-A&S/GF/M/Rh//B] <sê I; sisê; sî II>

sêzdehem سـێـزدههـهم *adj.* thirteenth, 13th. {also: sêzdehemîn (CT-2/ZF-2/Wkt-2); sêzdem (Wkt-2); sêzdemîn (IFb/Wkt-2); sêzdeyem (Wkt-2); ; sêzdeyemîn (Wkt-2)} Cf. P sīzdahom سيزدهم; Sor siyanzehem سِيانزههم/siyanzemîn سِيانزهمين [CT/ZF/Wkt//IFb] <sêzdeh>

sêzdehemîn سـێـزدههـهمـین (CT/ZF/Wkt) = thirteenth. See **sêzdehem**.

sêzdem سێزدهم (Wkt) = thirteenth. See **sêzdehem**.

sêzdemîn سـێـزدهمـیـن (IFb/Wkt) = thirteenth. See **sêzdehem**.

sêzdeyem سێزدهیهم (Wkt) = thirteenth. See **sêzdehem**.

sêzdeyemîn سـێـزدهیـهمـیـن (Wkt) = thirteenth. See **sêzdehem**.

siba سِبا (B) = tomorrow. See **sibe** [2].

Sibat سِبات *f.* **(;-ê).** February: **•Deynê *Şibatê* li Adarê ye** (L-1, #95, 202) *February's* debt is due in March **•[*Sibat* e, çi şer̄ e û çi şewat e, xwezî nîv mehada nehata]** (BG) *February*, what struggling and what devastation, I wish there were no such month [lit. 'that it did not come among the months'] *[prv.]*. {also: Sivat; Şibat (GF-2/OK-2); Şivat (F); [choubat] شباط (JJ); <s̱ibaṯ> صباط (HH); [çabatt] (BG)} Syr švoṭ/švaṭ ܫܒܛ [NA Išwaṭ/Ishwâṭ (Maclean)/sh'vutt (Oraham); Heb ševaṭ שבט --> Ar šubāṭ شـبـاط --> T Şubat; corresponds to last part of R̄êbendan رێـبـهنـدان (P bahman بـهـمـن) [Aquarius] & 1st part of R̄eşemê رهشـهمـێ/Polan

پۆلان (P esfand اسفند) [Pisces] [K/JB3/IFb/B/GF/OK//HH//F//JJ//BG]

sib•e سِـبـه *f.* **(•a;•ê).** 1) {also: sibeh; sibih (HR); sive; s̲ube (FS)} morning: **•*Siba* te bi xêr!** (K) Good morning! *[greeting]* **•*Sibe* r̄on bû** (EP-7/K) *Morning* has broken/It has become light; **-dusibe** = the day after tomorrow; **-sibe-sibe** (B) in the mornings; **-sibetir** = the day after tomorrow; **-sibetira dî/dine** = a) three days from now; b) on the next or following day; **-sibezû** (JB3) a) early in the morning; b) early morning; **-sibê** = a) in the morning; b) tomorrow {also: sibehê; subahê (Zx)}; **-sibê şebeqê** (Dz) = a) tomorrow morning; b) early the next morning {also: sibehê şibaqê (L)}; 2) [*adv.*] {also: siba (B); sibehê; sibê (A); subahê (Zx)} tomorrow. {also: [sabahh/sabāh' صباح/subé صبح] (JJ); <s̲ibhî> صبهى (HH)} < Ar ṣabāḥ صباح & ṣubḥ صبح = 'morning'; Sor siba سِبا = 'early morning' & sibey[nê] سِبەینێ/sibḧey[nê] سِبحەینێ = tomorrow; Hau se'b *m.* = 'morning' & seway = 'tomorrow' (M4) [BX/A/JB3/IF/B//JJ//HH/ZF//HR] <spêde>

sibeh سِبەه = morning. See **sibe**[1].

sibehê سِبەهێ = tomorrow. See **sibe**[2].

siberoj سِـبـەرۆژ *f.* **(-a;-ê).** the future, tomorrow: **•Gelekan ji wan tevahiya şevê diyarî ji bo jinên xwe yên *siberojê* amade kirin** (EN) Many of them prepared gifts for their *future* wives all night long **•*Siberoja* Kurdistana me ya ezîz di metirsiyê de ye!** (EN) *The future of* our beloved Kurdistan is in danger! {syn: paşeroj} [EN/ZF/Wkt]

sibê سِبێ (A) = tomorrow. See **sibe**[2].

sibih سِبِه (HR) = morning. See **sibe**[1].

sibit سِبِت (Dh/FS) = dill. See **şiwît**.

siboq سِبۆق (Zx) = paint. See **s̲ibẍe**.

sibox سِبۆخ (Wkt) = paint. See **s̲ibẍe**.

sibore سِبۆرە (Hk) = squirrel. See **siwûrî**.

s̲ibẍ•e صِـبـغـه *f.* **(•a;).** paint: **-siboq kirin** (Zx) to shine, polish (shoes); **-s̲ibẍa dîwara** (Bw) wall paint; **-s̲ibẍa nînoka** (Bw) nail polish. {also: siboq (Zx); sibox (Wkt)} {syn: boyax kirin} <Ar √ṣ-b-γ صبغ = 'to paint, dye' [Bw//Zx//Wkt] <boyax>

sid سِد = hundred. See **sed**.

sifar سِفار (DZK) = copper. See **sifir**.

sifet سِـفـەت *m.* **(-ê;).** 1) quality, attribute, trait, characteristic; personality (HH); 2) outward appearance, aspect; 3) {syn: r̄û I[1]; serçav; sûret I[1]} face: **•*Sifetê* wê bedew e** (B) She has a pretty *face*; 4) {syn: r̄esim; sûret I[4]; şikil; wêne} picture, image: **-sifet k'işandin** (B) to draw a picture. {also: [sifet] صفت (JJ); <s̲ifet> صفت (HH)} < Ar ṣifah صفة = 'description' (√w-ṣ-f وصف)--> P ṣifat صفت; --> T sıfat [K/IFb/B/HH/JJ]

sifir سِـفِـر *f./m.(B)* **(/-ê;).** 1) {syn: mîs} copper; **-sifirê sor** (B) do.; **-sifirê zer** (B) brass; 2) copper vessel. {also: sifar (DZK); sifr (SK); [sifyr] صفر (JJ); <s̲ifir> صفر (HH)} < Ar ṣufr صفر = 'brass', cf. aṣfar أصفر = 'yellow' [Z-1/K/IFb/B/JJ/GF/TF/BF//SK//HH] <birinc II; sefar>

siforî سِفۆرى (IF/HH) = squirrel. See **siwûrî**.

sifr سِفر (SK) = copper. See **sifir**.

sifr•e سِـفـرە *f.(K/B/SK)/m.(EP-7)* **(•a/•ê;•ê/).** 1) dinner table, table which has a meal laid out on it *[pan-Mid Eastern concept: laid table, place where food is laid out, rather than physical table]*: According to E. W. lane: "The thing [whatever it be] upon which one eats ..."; leather tablecloth, serving as table for meals (B): **•Tu dibînî ku ez tu carî narim ser *sifra* wî û nanê wî jî naxwim** (ZZ-10, 159) You see that I never go to his *table*, and I won't eat his food; 2) tablecloth. {also: sivir (Ba3); [súfra] سفره (JJ)} Cf. Ar sufrah سفرة, P sofre سفره, T sofra [EP-7/K/IFb/B/SK/GF/ZF/FS//JJ//Ba3]

sift سِـفـت *adj.* first. {also: sifte (ZF3); sifteh (IFb)} {syn: 'ewil; pêşîn; yekem[în]} Cf. T siftah = 'first sale of the day'; Za sifte = first (adv.) (Todd); < Ar istiftāḥ استفتاح = 'first sale of the day' [Ad//ZF3//IFb] <sifte>

sifte سِفتە *adv.* 1) at first; 2) (ZF3) = first. See **sift**. Za sifte = first (adv.) (Todd) [K/B/ZF3] <sift>

sifteh سِفتەه (IFb) = first. See **sift**.

sih I سِه (JB3/GF) = shade, shadow. See **sî I**.

sih II سِه (BX/JB3/JB1-S) = thirty. See **sî II**.

sih III سِه (IFb) = angry. See **sil**.

sihar سِهار (Wkt) = dawn, early morning. See **siḧar**.

sihbet سِهبەت (IFb) = conversation, talk. See **s̲uḧbet**.

sihem سِهەم (Wkt) = thirtieth. See **sîhem**.

sihemîn سِهەمین (TF/Wkt) = thirtieth. See **sîhem**.

siher سِهەر, f. (K) = dawn, early morning. See **siḧar**.

sihet سِهەت (IFb) = health. See **sehet II**.

sihik I سِـهـك *f.* **(-a;-ê).** vinegar: **•Wî *t̲irşîya sihikê* çê kir** (FS) He made *pickled vegetables* [lit. 'vinegar pickles']. {also: sêk (IFb-2/FD/BF/FS-2); sihink (TF); sihir II (A); silk'e (; silk'ê) (B/K-2); sirk'e; [sirké سركه/siké سيكه/sik سيك] (JJ); <sihik سهك/sirke سركه/sêk سيك> (HH)} Cf. P sirke سركه-->

T sirke [K/JB3/IFb/HH/GF/ZF3/FS/Wkt//A//B//JJ//FD/BF//TF]

sihik II سِهِك *f.* **().** shade, shadow [dim. of sî I/sih I] Cf. P sāye سايه; < sî/sih = 'shade' + -ik [dim. ending] [K]

sihink سِهنك (TF) = vinegar. See **sihik I**.

sihir I سِهِر (IFb) = magic. See **sêr I**.

sihir II سِهِر (A) = vinegar. See **sihik I**.

sihî سِهى (SK) = thirty. See **sî II**.

sihnîk سِهنيك (Bw) = plate. See **sênîk**.

sihor سِهۆر (Wkp) = squirrel. See **siwûrî**.

sihr سِهر (IFb/GF) = magic. See **sêr I**.

sihûd سِهوود (IFb) = good luck. See **siûd**.

siḧar سِحار *f.* **(-a;-ê).** dawn, daybreak, early morning: **•Subahî *siḧarê* ji qebrê xwe derk'et', ço ligel kiçik'ê** (M-Zx, #757, 350) *Early* next morning he came out of his grave and went with the girl **•[Subahî rabû *seḧarê*]** (PS #33, 95, l. 3) He got up *early* the next morning. {also: seher, m. (K/CS); sihar (Wkt-2); siher, f. (K-2); [saḥārē] سحار (PS)} {syn: berbang; elind; ferec; hingûr [1]; segur; serê sibê; spêde; şebeq} < Ar saḥar سحر = 'time before daybreak, early morning, dawn' [M-Zx/Wkt//PS//K/CS]

siḧet سِحەت (Z-1) = hour; clock. See **saet**.

siḧûd سِحوود (Z-2) = good luck. See **siûd**.

sik I سِك *adj.* ugly: **•Sofî Mihemed merivekî wisa *sik* ê bêmirêz bû** (ZZ-7, 162) S.M. was an *ugly* and bitter person.{also: <sik> سك (HH)} {syn: bi'ok; k'irêt} [ZZ/K(s)/IFb/FJ/GF/HH/ZF/RZ/SS]

sik II سِك (BK/HB) = stomach; inside. See **zik**.

sik' III سِك = stake. See **sik'e**.

sik'•e سِكه *f.* **(•a;•ê).** stake, pale, sharp stick: **•P'erîşan-xanim berva vek'işîya, sik'ek nav ç'e'vê Xeloda lêda** (Z-15, 230) P. came forward, drove a stake into Khelo's eye. {also: seke (ZF); sekih (TF); sik' III; <sikkeh> سكه (HH)} {syn: çîxin; qazux; sing I} < Ar sikkah سكّة = '(minting) die; coin; road' [Z/K/A/B/IFb//HH//TF//ZF]

sikir سِكِر *f./m.(FS/Wkt)* **(/-ê;).** 1) {syn: bend I[1]} dam, weir: **•Em li serê *sukur* ava dikin, jê derdixin elektrîka rohnî, a wek zêr** (AB) We build *a dam* at the top, from which [lit. 'from it'] we get electricity, [which is valuable] like gold: **•*Sikrê* rûbarî qayim e** (FS) The river *dam* is sturdy; 2) barrier. {also: sukur I (AB); <sikir> سكر (HH)} < Ar sikr سكر = 'dam'; Cf. Arc sokhara סוכרא & Syr skārā ܣܟܪܐ = 'dam, lock, barrier' [AB//K/JB3/IF/HH/FS/ZF3/Wkt]

sikrat سِكرات (Ardû) = death watch. See **sekerat**.

sil سِل *adj.* 1) {syn: zîz II} angry, mad, annoyed: **-ji *fk-ê* sil bûn** (K/IFb) to get angry or mad at: **•[Îcarî mela Bazîd *sil bûye*, gote jina xwe]** (JR-3) Then mullah Bazîd *got angry* [and] said to his wife...; **-xwe sil kirin** (JR) to get angry or mad: **•[Melayî weku ev xebera ji jinê seh kirî, *xwe sil kir*]** (JR-3) When the mullah heard these words from the woman, *he got angry*; 2) touchy, sensitive, easily offended (B); fearing the consequences of an offence one has committed (IFb/HH). {also: sih III (IFb-2); [sil] سل (JJ); <sil> سل (HH)} [JR/K/IFb/B/JJ/HH/SK/GF]

silaḧ سِلاح (SK/JB1-S) = weapon(s). See **sîleh I**.

silal سِلال/**ṣilal** صِلال [JB1-A] *adv.* above, upstairs, up: **•[Çûme *silal*]** (JJ-G) I went *upstairs* **•Ji *ṣelal* hat xwar** (FS) He came down from *upstairs* [or, from *above*] **•[Were *silal*]** (JJ-G) Come on *up*! {also: ṣelal (FS); [salál] سلال (JJ-G); [salāl] (RJ)} {syn: hevraz; jor; ≠xwar} [Bw//JB1-A//JJ-G/RJ//FS] <fêz; hevraz; jêla; jor>

silam سِلام = greetings, regards. See **silav**.

silamet سِلامەت (B) = safe; healthy. See **selamet**.

silametî سِلامەتى (B) = safety; health. See **selametî**.

silav سِلاڤ *f.* **(-a;-ê).** greeting(s), regards: **-li *fk-ê* silava kirin/dan** = to greet, send greetings to: **•Birê te ... *silava li* te *dike*** (L) Your brother ... *sends* you his *regards*; **-silav dayîn/lêkirin/vedan** (B) to greet s.o.; **-silav û k'ilav** (B) greeting and gift; **-silav [û] k'ilav şandin** (B) to send one's best wishes; **-silav vegirtin** (K) to return s.o.'s greeting. {also: selam (EP-7/K-2); selav; silam; silaw (SK); slav (FK-eb-2); [silaw سلاڤ/selam سلام] (JJ); <silav سلاڤ/silam سلام> (HH)} < Ar salām سلام = 'peace' (used in greetings); Sor siław سِلاو = 'peace, greeting' [L/K/A/JB3/IFb/B/JJ/HH/TF//SK]

silaw سِلاو (SK) = greetings, regards. See **silav**.

sileh سِلەه (JB3) = weapon(s). See **sîleh I**.

silim سِلِم *m.* **(-ê;).** ladder. {also: sêlim, f. (Erh/IFb/TF); <sêlim> سيلم (HH)} {syn: nerdewan; pêlegan; pêpelîng[3]; pêstirk} < Ar sullam سلّم = 'ladder'--> T sülüm (Maraş, Gaziantep) [Haz//Erh/IFb/HH/TF] <derenc>

silk سِلك (A/HH/TF/Rh) = beet. See **silq**.

silk'e سِلكه (; silk'ê) (B/K) = vinegar. See **sihik I**.

Silovakî سِلۆڤاكى (BF) = Slovak. See **Slovakî**.

Silovênî سِلۆڤێنى (BF) = Slovene. See **Slovenî**.

silq سِلق *f.* **(-a;-ê).** beet, bot. *Beta*. {also: silk (A/TF/Rh); silx (Erg); [selq/selk (G)/silk (Lx/Rh)] سلق & [silqok] سلقوك (JJ); <silk> سلك (HH)} Cf. Ar salq/silq سلق = 'type of chard'; Sor siłq سِلْق = 'spinach-beet' [Qzl/K/IFb/B/GF//JJ//A/HH/TF/Rh//Erg] <şêlim>

silt'an سِلتان *m.* **(-ê; silt'ên, vî silt'anî).** sultan, monarch, (absolute) ruler: **•Rêyekê bibîne û me bigihîne *Siltên*** (SF 2) Find a way to get us to *the Sultan*. {also: sult'an (B)/sultan (SK/GF/IFb-2); [sultán] سلطان (JJ)} < Ar sulṭān سلطان = 'power, reign, authority; sultan, absolute ruler' [SF/K/IFb//B/SK/GF//JJ] <p'adşa>

silx سِلخ (Erg) = beet. See **silq**.

sim سِم *f.* **(;-ê).** 1) hoof [*pl.* hooves]: *IFb distinguishes between **sim** = hoof of solid-hoofed animals, such as that of the horse, and **ç'im** = hoof of even-toed (split-hoofed) ruminants, such as that of sheep and cows*: **•*Sim* - *simê* k'erê ne, fêl - fêlê P'erê ne** (Dz-#32, 401) *The hooves* are donkey *hooves*, but the deeds are [the thief] Para's deeds *[prv.]*; 2) horseshoe. {also: [sim] سم (JJ); <sim> سم (HH)} Cf. Mid P sumb (M3); P som سم/sonb سنب; Sor sim سِم; Hau sum; Za sim *m.* (Mal) [S&E/K/A/JB3/IFb/B/JJ/HH/GF/TF/OK] <ç'im I; hesp; neynûk>

simaq سِماق *f.* **(-a;-ê).** sumac[h], bot. *Rhus*; a tree which grows in hot climates, whose bark is used for medicinal purposes, and whose lentil-like seeds are pounded to yield a sour-flavored spice (TF): **-simaqa hêrayî** (DBgb) ground sumac; **-Yê simaqê difroşît** (Bw) He is angry, but is holding it inside [lit. 'He is selling sumac': *expression which implies that one looks angry, because when one eats something sour-tasting (like sumac), one knits one's brow*]. {also: <simaq> سماق (HH)} <Arc samōq סמוק = 'red': Ar summāq سمّاق; T sumak; P somāq سماق; Sor simaq سِماق [Bw/A/IFb/HH/GF/TF/OK/ZF]

simbêl سِمبێل *f./m.(B/ZF3)/pl.(JJ)* **(/-ê;).** moustache, whiskers: **-simêl badan** (B/JJ) to twirl one's moustache;

-simbêlê *fk-ê* melûl bûn (Z-2) to get angry: **•Mîr Zêydîn *simbêlê wî melûl bûn*** (Z-2) M.Z. *got angry* [lit. 'his *whiskers became gloomy*']. {also: simêl (K/GF-2); sinbêl (JB3/IFb-2); [sinbil] سنبل (JJ); <simbêl> سمبیل (HH)} Cf. P sebīl سبیل & Ar sabalah سبلة (pl. sibāl سبال); Sor simêł سِمێڵ; Za zimḗli (Lx)/zimêl[-i] (Mal); Hau simêłê *pl.* (M4) [A/IFb/HH/GF//K/B//JB3//JJ] <r̄ih; r̄û>

simbêlreş سِمبێلرەش (ZF3) = with black whiskers. See **simêlr̄eş**.

simbil I سِمبِل *f./m.(B)* **(-a/;).** 1) {syn: liqat} ear, spike *(of wheat or corn)*: **-simbila genim** (ZF3) spike of wheat; 2) Virgo *(astr.) by analogy with T başak, which has both meanings 1) & 2) shown here; this is because in ancient Babylonia this sign of the zodiac featured a cornmaiden, a goddess associated with the harvest season, often depicted holding a spike of wheat*. {also: simbûl II (K[s]); simil (K/B); sinbil I (JB3/IFb-2); [sounbul] سنبل (JJ); <simbil> سمبل (HH)} < Ar sunbul سنبل [HB/F/A/IFb/HH/GF/TF//B/K//JJ//K(s)] <genim; liqat>

simbil II سِمبِل (IFb) = hyacinth. See **sunbul**.

simbûl I سِمبوول, f. (B) = hyacinth. See **sunbul**.

simbûl II سِمبوول (K[s]) = ear of corn. See **simbil I**.

simêl سِمێل (K/GF) = moustache. See **simbêl**.

simêlr̄eş سِمێلڕەش *adj.* 1) with black whiskers, with black moustache(s); 2) angry, annoyed, mad. {also: simbêlreş (ZF3)} < sim[b]êl = 'moustache' + r̄eş = 'black' [B//ZF3]

simil سِمِل (K/B) = ear of corn. See **simbil I**.

simirîn سِمِرین *vi.* **(-simir-).** to be numb; to freeze: **•Dît marek yê di nav befrêda, yê *simirî* li serma** (M-Ak, #544) He saw a snake in the snow, frozen [or, numb] with cold. [M-Ak/OK] <cemidîn; qerimîn>

simolek سِمۆلەك (IF) = squirrel. See **siwûrî**.

simore سِمۆره = squirrel. See **siwûrî**.

simsîyark سِمسییارك (FS) = vulture. See **sîsalk**.

simt سِمت (IFb/Zeb/Dh) = hilltop. See **semt** [4].

simtin سِمتِن/**s̲imtin** صِمتِن [Bw/FS] *vt.* **(-sim-/-s̲im-** [Bw]**).** to bore, pierce *(pipes, tunnels, round things)*: **•Berê tivingê sînga Baram *simtiye*** (GF) The rifle bullet *pierced* Baram's chest **•Wî dar bi mikarê *s̲imt*** (FS) He *made a hole in* the wood [or tree] with a chisel. {also: *simtîn (GF); <simtin سمتن (disime) (دسمه)> (HH); JJ has erroneous *[sontin] سونتين]} {syn: qul kirin} P softan سفتن (-sonb-) (سنب); Sor simîn سِمین (-sim-) = 'to bore, pierce' [Bw/FS//HH/OK/M/ZF3//(GF)]

*simtîn سِمتین (GF) = to pierce. See **simtin**.

sinbêl سِنبێل (JB3/IFb) = moustache. See **simbêl**.

sinbil I سِنبِل (JB3/IFb) = ear of corn. See **simbil I**.

sinbil II سِنبِل (IFb) = hyacinth. See **sunbul**.

sinc I سِنج *f.* **(;-ê).** oleaster, wild olive tree, Russian olive, bot. *Elaeagnus angustifolia* [T iğde ağacı];

its fruit is sour, but edible; buckthorn, jujube tree, Chinese date, bot. genus *Zizyphus* [P senjed سنجد] (JJ): **•Dara *sincê* bê esl e. Lewra kêran jê çênabin, martak jê dernakin, textik jê çênabin û bê kêr e** (ZZ-7, 265) The *oleaster* tree is baseless. That's why crossbeams aren't made of it, they don't make rafters of it, boards aren't made of it and it is useless. {also: *sincû; [sinjov] سنجو (JJ); <sincî> سنجی (HH)} {syn: gûsinc (IF)} Cf. P senjed سنجد = 'buckthorn or jujube tree'; Sor sincû سِنجوو = 'oleaster' [HB/K/A/IFb/B/TF/FS//JJ//HH]

sinc II سِنج (ZF/FS/BF) = ethics. See **sinçî**.

sincêrî سِنجێری *f.*(). or *adj.* round, sweet grapes, yellow with a slight blue tinge (Msr); type of grape from which dims, aqit or mot [T pekmez] is made: **-tirîyê sincêrî** (FS) do. {also: <sincêrî> سنجیری (HH)} < Sincar [Şingal] (mountain in Kurdistan of Iraq) [Msr/A/IFb/HH/GF/TF/ZF3/Wkt/FS] <tirî>

sincirandin سِنجِراندِن *vt.* **(-sincirîn-).** to heat up an oven, *as for baking bread*; to fire a kiln, *as for baking clay pots*: **•Wê tenûr *sincirand*** (FS) She *heated up* the oven.{also: <sincirandin سنجراندن (disincirîne) (دسنجرينه)> (HH)} [A/IFb/HH/GF/Wkt/FS] <sincirîn>

sincirî سِنجِری *adj.* piping hot, red hot: **•Ze'f sincírî ye** (Erh) It's very hot. [Erh/A/TF/ZF3] <germ>

sincirîn سِنجِرین *vi.* **(-sincir-).** to be heated up, heat up *(vi.)*; to melt (HR-I): **•Ew jî dibê kevç'îyê hesinî, di nav girara germ da *disincirê*; ji wê yekê kevç'îyê darî qîmetlitir e** (HR-I, 1:40) They also say that iron spoons [lit. 'the iron spoon'] *melt* [or, *heat up*] in hot porridge; for this reason wooden spoons are [lit. 'the wooden spoon is'] more valuable. {also: <sincirîn سنجرین (disincirê) (دسنجری)> (HH)} [A/HH/TF/HR-I/ZF3/FS]

sincoq سِنجۆق *m./f.(ZF3)* **(-ê/;).** 1) large intestine of animals; 2) food, such as sausage, made from animal intestines. {also: sincûq (ZF3); <sincoq> سنجوق (HH)} cf. T sucuk = 'sausage' [Frq/(A)/IFb/HH//ZF3] <r̄ovî II; 'ûr>

*sincû سِنجوو = oleaster. See **sinc I**.

sinçî سِنچی *m.* **().** morals, ethics: **•Wî *sincekê* ciwan heye** (FS) He has good *morals*. {also: sinc II (ZF/FS/BF)} {syn: exlaq; r̄ewişt} cf. Ar sajīyah سجيّة = 'natural disposition, temper' [(neol)RN/IFb//ZF/FS/BF]

sind سِند (L. Shepherd. Kurmanji in use) = finely ground wheat meal, semolina. See **sindik**.

sindan سِندان (A/IFb/FJ/TF/Kmc)/s̱indan صِندان (FS) = anvil. See **sindyan**.

sindik سِندِك *m.(ZF3)/f.(FS)* **(;/-ê).** finely ground wheat meal (more finely ground than **danhêrk**), semolina: **•Savar û xwarinên ku ji *sindikê* çê dibin, weke girar** (Rûdaw 23.x.2016) Bulghur and foods made of *sindik*, such as 'girar' [buttermilk and cooked barley groat porridge]. {also: sind (L. Shepherd. Kurmanji in use); <sindik> سندك (HH)} {syn: savarê hûr; *simîd} [Shepherd/ZF/MS//IFb/FJ/GF/HH/Kmc] <dan II; danhêrk; savar>

sindirîk سِندِریك *f.* **(-a;-ê).** 1) coffin: **-sindirîka mirî** (FS) do; 2) box or chest for storing things: ***•Wî bacanşork kirin di sindirîkê da*** (FS) He put the eggplants in *the box*; **-sindirûka cilan** (ZF3) clothes chest. {also: sindirûk (GF/ZF3); sindûrek (GF-2); [sandrúk] (JJ-G)} [Bw/FS/BF//GF/ZF3//JJ] <darbest; gor̄ I; sindoq>

sindirûk سِندرووك (GF/ZF3) = coffin; box. See **sindirîk**.

sindiyan سِندیان (FJ/SWI) = anvil. See **sindyan**.

sindîyan سِندییان (K) = anvil. See **sindyan**.

sindoq سِندۆق/**s̱indoq** صِندۆق [JB1-A/SK] *f./m.(JB1-A)* **(-a/;-ê/).** box, chest, coffer: **-sindoqa piştê** (Bw) trunk, boot (of a car), rear compartment. {also: sandiq (EH/IF-2); sandux (B); sandûq; sendûq (F/K/IF-2); [syndouq/sandrúk (G)/sandúx (Lx)/sanduk (Rh)] صندوق (JJ)} {syn: qab I[2]; qut'î} Cf. P/Ar ṣandūq صندوق; T sandık; Sor sindûq سِندووق; Hau sin[n]oq *m.* (M4); cf. also Rus sunduk сундук [EH//K(s)/A/IF/JB1-A/SK//B//F/K//JJ] <sindirîk>

sindûrek سِندوورەك (GF) = coffin. See **sindirîk**.

sindyan سِندیان *m.* **(-ê; sindiyên, wî sindyanî).** anvil: **•Asingerî asin li ser *s̱indanî* quta** (FS) The ironsmith beat the iron against *the anvil* **•Heger sindiyanê te şikest, tu yê ji minre tîr û kevanek jê çêkî?** (SWI, 56) If your anvil breaks, will you make me a bow and arrow from it? {also: sendan (GF-2); sindan (A/IFb/FJ/TF/Kmc)/s̱indan (FS); sindiyan (FJ-2/SWI); sindîyan (K-2); sndyan (HCK); [sindan] سندان (JJ); <sindan> سندان (HH)} < Ar sandān/sindān سندان; Sor sidan سِدان [HCK//K/GF//A/IFb/FJ/TF/Kmc/JJ/HH//FS]

sinet سِنەت (IFb) = art, skill; profession; industry. See **sen'et**.

sinetkar سِنەتكار (IFb)/sin'etkar سِنعەتكار (GF) = artisan; artist. See **sen'etk'ar**.

sing I سِنگ/**s̲ing** صِنگ [Bw/JB1-A/FS] *m.* **(-ê;).** (tent) stake, spike, pile, post: **•Bira *singê* çadira hil kin** (Z-3) They should pull up the tent *stakes* (i.e., break camp, pack up to leave); **-sing k'utan** (K) to hammer stakes. {also: [sink] سنك (JJ); <s̲ink> صنك (JJ)} {syn: çîxin (Bw)} Sor sind سِند/ sing سِنگ = 'peg, short stake' [Z-3/F/K/A/IFb/B/SK/GF/TF/OK//Bw/JB1-A/FS//JJ//HH] <çadir; kon; pîj I>

sing II سِنگ (JB3/HH/Rnh/TF) = chest; mountain slope. See **sîng**.

singdan سِنگدان (Z-2) = prison, dungeon. See **zindan**.

singiw سِنگو = bayonet. See **singo**.

singî سِنگی = bayonet. See **singo**.

singo سِنگۆ/**s̲ingo** صِنگۆ [FS] *f./m.(FS)* **(/-yê;).** bayonet: **•Li gora vê fermana hukumetê, divê hun gule bernedin wan, lê belê wan bidin ber *singûyan*!** (Bkp, 5) According to this government order, you must not shoot bullets at them, but rather stab them with *bayonets*. {also: singiw; singî; singû (K/ZF)} < T süngü [HB/A/IFb/GF//FS//K/ZF]

singû سِنگوو (K/ZF) = bayonet. See **singo**.

sinhet سِنهەت, f.(K)/m.(JB3) = art, skill; profession; industry. See **sen'et**.

sinhetk'ar سِنهەتکار (K) = artisan; artist. See **sen'etk'ar**.

sinif سِنِف *f.* **(-a;-ê).** 1) {syn: pol III} class *(in school)*: **-sinifa yekemîn** (ZF) first grade; 2) {syn: ç'în[2]} social class: **-sinifa gundîya** (B) peasant class; **-sinifa k'arkeran** (ZF)/~ **p'ala** (B) working or workers' class; **-sinifên leşkerî** (Kmc) military classes; **-sinifa şerkar** (Kmc) warring or warriors' class; **-sinifa xizmetkar** (Kmc) service class. < Ar şinf صنف = 'kind, sort, genus, class; sex' --> T sınıf = 'class (1 & 2)' [B/IFb/RZ/Kmc/ZF/CS] <dersxane>

sinî سِنی (B) = tray. See **sênî**.

sinûr سِنوور (BF) = border, limit. See **sînor**.

sior سِئۆر (TF)/s̲i'or صِعۆر (HR) = squirrel. See **siwûrî**.

sipartin I سِپارتِن (L/IFb/BK/JJ) = to entrust, commit. See **spartin**.

sipartin II سِپارتِن (B/JJ/CS) = to lean, support. See **p'esartin**.

sipas سِپاس (K/A/IFb/GF/TF/OK) = thanks. See **spas**.

sipasdar سِپاسدار (TF) = grateful. See **spasdar**.

sipehî سِپەهی (IFb/TF) = pretty, beautiful. See **spehî**.

sipehîtî سِپەهیتی (IFb/JJ/TF) = beauty. See **spehîtî**.

sipeyî سِپەیی (IFb/JJ) = pretty, beautiful. See **spehî**.

sipêde سِپێدە (IFb/GF) = dawn. See **spêde**.

sipêne سِپێنە *f.(Zeb)/m.(OK)* **().** wedge; wooden splint put around bottom of pillar or column to ensure that it sticks straight up (Zeb). {also: sipîn (GF); sipne (OK-2); spêne (Zeb/IFb-2/ZF3)} Cf. Ar isfīn إسفين = 'wedge' [Zeb/IFb/ZF3//OK//GF]

sipih سِپِه (IFb/TF) = louse (pl. lice). See **spî II**.

sipindar سِپِندار *f.* **(-a;-ê).** poplar tree, bot. *Populus*; white poplar tree, tall tree with white bark (HH): **-dara sipindar** (F) do. {also: sipîdar (GF); sipîndar (IFb/TF); spêhîdar (A); spîdar (A); spindar (GF-2); spîndar (A/IFb-2/SK/ZF3/FS); [spīdār سپيدار/spindār سپيندار] (JJ); <spîndar> سپيندار (HH)} {syn: evran; qewax} Cf. P safīdār سفيدار/ sapīdār سپيدار = 'aspen, white poplar tree'; Sor sipî[n]dar سِپیندار = 'white poplar' [F/K/B//A/JJ/HH/SK/ZF3/FS//IFb/TF//GF] <pelk>

siping سِپِنگ *f./m.(Mzg)* **(/-ê;-ê/).** yellow goatsbeard, meadow salsify, bot. *Tragopogon pratensis* or *Tragopogon porrifolius* (T yemlik), *a springtime plant which is eaten raw.* {also: sipink (Mzg); sping (A/IFb-2/OK/FS); spink (EŞ); spînk (GF); <sip[i]nk> سپنك (HH); <siping> سپنگ (Hej)} = Sor şing شِنگ = 'salsify, purple goat's-beard' [EŞ//Mzg/HH//K/IFb/ B/Hej//A/OK/FS//GF] <gêzbelok>

sipink سِپِنك (Mzg/HH) = meadow salsify. See **siping**.

sipî I سِپی (AB/A/B/F/JJ/HH/GF/TF) = white. See **spî I**.

sipî II سِپی (A/B) = louse (pl. lice). See **spî II**.

sipîçal/sipîç'al [F/K/B] سِپیچال *f.* **(;-ê).** sheet, bedsheet: **•Eva hersê zeveşa tîne dixe negerîke t'emiz, *spîç'alekê* davêje ser ... P'adşa tîne tê *spîç'alê* vedike, gazî cima'eta xwe dike zeveşa bixun** (HCK-3, #16, 180) He brings the 3 watermelons and puts them on a clean tray, throws *a sheet* over them ... The king comes and uncovers *the sheet*, calls his retinue to eat the watermelons. {also: spîç'al (K-2/HCK/ZF3)} {syn: çarşev [3]} [F/K/B//HCK/ZF3]

sipîçik سِپیچِك (IFb) = egg white. See **spîlik I**.

sipîçolk سِپیچۆلك (A/GF) = pale. See **spîç'olkî**.

sipîç'olkî سِپیچۆلكی (B/F) = pale. See **spîç'olkî**.

sipîdar سِپیدار (GF) = poplar. See **sipindar**.

sipîk سِپیك (OK/GF/JJ) = egg white. See **spîlik I**.

sipîlik سِپیلِك (GF) = egg white. See **spîlik I**.

sipîlk سِپیلك (GF) = egg white. See **spîlik I**.

sipîn سِپین (GF) = wedge. See **sipêne**.

sipîndar سِپیندار (IFb/TF) = poplar tree. See **sipindar**.

sipîtî سپيتى (TF) = whiteness. See **spîtayî**.
sipîyatî سپيياتى (BF) = whiteness. See **spîtayî**.
sipne سپنه (OK) = wedge. See **sipêne**.
siqa kirin سقا كرن (TF/FS/HH) = to temper (steel); to quench (steel); to sharpen. See **seqa kirin**.
siqavêl سقاڤێل *f.* **(;-ê).** large broom used for sweeping out stables (Kp/Ag): **-seqawêl kirin** (Ag) to sweep out (a stable). {also: seqawêl (Ag); seqevêl (F); siqawêl (ZF3)} {syn: avlêk; cerîvk (Bw); gêzî; k'inoşe; melk'es; serge (Ad); sivnik; şirt I} Cf. Arm awel աւել = 'broom'; T sahavél [Ağın-Elâzığ]/ sahavül [Bahçebaşı-Tokat; Ağın-Elâzığ]/sahayluk [Bayburt]/ sahbil [Hozat-Tunceli]/sahovu [Arapkir-Malatya]/sakavel (Bayburt; Yusufeli-Artvin]/sakavil [Yusufeli-Artvin; Narman-Erzurum; Tercan-Erzincan, etc.]/sakavul [Erzurum; Erzincan]/ sakgavul [Çıldır, Sarıkamış, Selim-Kars]/sakkavul [Kars; Erzurum; Erzincan; Kayseri]/sakkol [Ergân-Erzincan] (DS, v. 10, p. 3515) [K/Kp//F//Ag//ZF3] <gêzî; maliştin>
siqawêl سقاوێل (ZF3) = large broom. See **siqavêl**.
siqêf سقێف (A) = curse. See **sixêf**.
siqûmat سقوومات *f.* **(-a;-ê).** tragedy, disaster, misfortune: **•Di bingeha çîrokê de, gelek *siqûmat* û bûyerên mezin hene ku bi serê hin kesan ve hatine** (Rojevakurd: Bingeha Çîroka Folklorî) In the basis of the story, there are many *misfortunes* and big events which have befallen some people **•Kirîv di şîn û şahiyan de bi ser hev de diçin û tên, di *siqûmat* û serpêhatîyên xirab de alîkarîya hev dikin** (Wkp: Kirîvatî) Kirîvs [Fictive kin/godpar-ents, etc.] come and go in times of sorrow and joy, they help one another in *disasters* and bad episodes; **-bela û sqûmat** (fax from Zeynela-bidîn Zinar) calamities and tragedies. {also: sqûmat (ZZ)} {syn: bela; bêt'ar; boblat; gosirmet; qeda; şetele; t'ifaq} [ZZ//Rojevakurd/Wkp]
sir I سر/**sir̄** سڕ [IFb-2] *f.* **(-a;).** 1) dry cold, nip in the air; 2) cool breeze or draft: **•Li her du 'aliyên riya kanîyê sipîndar, darên sêva, erûga û încasa hebûn. Gişt rêz bûbûn. Pelên wan bi *sira* bayê, yekser dixuşîyan, û li vî alî, li wî alî dihejîyan** (MB-Meyro) On both sides of the road to the well there were poplars, apple trees, and plum trees, all in a row. Their leaves rustled in the cool evening breeze [lit. 'in *the breeze of* the wind'], tilting this way and that. {also: **sur̄ I**[2] (GF-2); [ser] سر (JJ); <sir> سر (HH)} [MB/IFb/HH/ GF/TF//JJ] <sar; seqem; serma>
sir̄ II سڕ *f.* **(-a;-ê).** secret: **•*Sur̄a* wê dîhar bû** (Z-1) Her *secret* was revealed. {also: sur̄ II (K/B); [syr] سر (JJ)} {syn: nepenî; r̄az} < Ar sirr سرّ [Z-1/IFb/JJ/ K/B]
sir•a سرا, f. (;•ê) (B) = (one's) turn. See **sirê**.
Sirbî سربی *adj.* Serbian. {also: Serbî (Wkp)} Sor Sirbî سربی [ZF3/Wkt/BF/SS//Wkp]
sire سره (IFb) = (one's) turn. See **sirê**.
sir•ê سرێ *f.* **(•îya** [EP-8]**;•ê).** (one's) turn *(in a game, in line, etc.)*: **-bi sirê** (EP-7) by turns: **•Ewana *bi sirê* k'ilam avîtne ser M.** (EP-7) They took turns singing to M. [lit. 'They threw songs on M. *by turn*'] {also: sir•a (;•ê) (B); sire (IFb)} {syn: dor; ger̄ II[3]; nobet} Cf. T sıra & Mod Gr seirá σειρά [EP-7/EP-8/K//IFb//B]
sirge سرگه *f.* **().** broom. {also: sivirge (Wkt)} {syn: avlêk; cerîvk (Bw); gêzî; k'inoşe; melk'es; siqavêl; sivnik; sizik; şicing; şirt I} < T süpürge = 'broom' [Ad/RZ//Wkt] <gêzî; maliştin>
sirgûn سرگوون *f.* **(-a;-ê).** exile, banishment: **-sirgûn kirin** (K/B/GF)/**surgûn kirin** (SK) to exile, banish: **•Wextê mezinêt wan dikuştin, *surgûn dikirin*, nedigotin** [sic], **"Da milletê dî yê feqîr bi-xudan bikeyn û r̄eh̄mê bi h̄alê wan bikeyn." Weto dihêlan** (SK 56:643) When they *were* killing and *exiling* their leaders they did not say, "Let us take care of this poor nation and have mercy on them." They simply left them. {also: surgûn (SK); [sourgoun] سورگون (JJ)} {syn: k'oçberî; ẍurbet} < T sürgün [K/IFb/B/GF//SK//JJ]
sirişk سرشك *f.* **().** tears *(of sorrow, joy, etc.)*: **•*Sirişk-ên* wî hatin xwar** (FS) His *tears* came down. {also: sirîşk (ZF3)} {syn: hêstir I; r̄onî II} MidP srešk (M3) --> P sirišk سرشك [S&E/K/IFb/FD/FS//ZF3]
siriştء سرشت (Wkt) = nature. See **siruşt**.
sirîşk سريشك (ZF3) = tears (of sorrow). See **sirişk**.
sirk'e سركه (JJ/HH) = vinegar. See **sihik I**.
sirnî سرنی/**sir̄nî** سڕنی [K] *m.(K/B)/f.(ZF)* **(-yê/ ; /-yê).** axle or axletree, esp. of plough or wagon: **-sirnîyê erebê** (IFb) wagon axle. {also: surnî (RZ/ Nbh-2)} [Nbh_124:32/K/A/B/IFb/Kmc/ZF//RZ] <mijane>
sirsûm سرسووم *f.* **(-a;-ê).** 1) wooden butter churn, *as opposed to **meşk** = (butter) churner made of animal skin*; 2) {also: serstûm (FS-2)} clay butter churn (FS): **•Wê *serstûm* ka** (FS) She rocked *the butter churn*. {also: sursûm (Wn)} [Wn//K/A/IFb/B/GF/ FS] <h̄îz; k'il III; meşk; p'ost [4]; xinûsî>
siruşt سروشت *f./m.* **(-a/-ê;-ê/).** nature: **•Hozanvanê jêhatî û şehreza di vehandina hozan û**

helbestan da, desthel û pisporê lêkînana peyivan, evîndarê ciwanîya *siruştê* Kurdistanê bi çiya û gelî û dol û rûbarên xo ve (Nisret Hacî. "Feqê Teyran û Çîrokên Binavkirina Wî," Peyam 5-6 [1996], 2) The poet skilled and expert at composing poems and verses, handy and clever at putting words together, enamored of the Kurdistan's natural beauty with its mountains, valleys, ravines, and rivers. {also: sirişt (Wkt); sirûşt (IFb/SS/ZF3); surişt (GF); suruşt (K[s]/TF)} {syn: tebî'et; xweza} Sor sirişt سِرِشت/siruşt سِروشت [Nisret Hacî//IFb/SS/ZF3//K(s)/TF//GF//Wkt]

sirûşt سِروووشت (IFb/SS/ZF3) = nature. See **siruşt**.

Siryanî سِریانی (Wkt) = Syriac. See **Suryanî**.

siseyan سِسەیان (BX) = third. See **sisîya**.

siseyek سِسەیەك (BX) = a third. See **sêkî**.

sisê سِسێ *num.* three, 3: ,"sisê" is used independently (free form), while "sê" is immediately followed by a dependent noun (bound form), Cf. didû vs. du. My theory: 'sisê' was invented to distinguish **sê** (3) from **sî/sih** (30). {also: sesê; sisê (BX-2/K-2); sêsê (A); [si] سی (JJ); <sê سی/sis[s]ê سسی> (HH)} Cf. P se سه; Sor sê سێ; Za hîrê (Todd) [BX/K/JB3/IFb/B/HH/GF//A//JJ] <didû; du; sê I; sêkî; sêzdeh; sî II>

sisiyê سِسِیێ (JB1-S) = third. See **sisîya**.

sisîya سِسییا *adj.* third, 3rd. {also: sê III (JB1-A); sêanî (K); sêê (M-Am&Bar&Shn); sêwemîn (K-2); **sêyem**; sêyê (M-sur&Ak); siseyan (BX); sisiyê (JB1-S); sisya (B); sîsîya[n] (K-2); [sii] سیی (JJ)} Cf. P sevvom سوّم; Sor sêhem[în] سێهەمین; Za hîrin/hîreyin (Todd) [F//JB1-A//K//M-Am&Bar &Shn//M-Sur&Ak//BX//JB1-S//B//JJ] <sê I; sisê>

sist سِست/**sist** صِصت [Bw]/**sist** سِسط [FS] *adj.* 1) {syn: lawaz [2]; qels I[1]; zeyf [2]} weak, powerless, limp: •[**Xûnê ser û çavêd Behramî peçavt û ew jî îdî weku berê nemayî *sist bûyî* û qeme ji destan ket**] (JR) Blood covered Behram's face [lit. 'head and eyes'], and he was no longer as before, he *became weak* and the dagger fell from [his] hands; 2) loose, slipshod, slack: •**girêka** ***sist*** (FS) *loose* knot; **-sist kirin** (Bw) to loosen, unscrew {syn: vekirin [3]}. {also: [sist] سست (JJ); <sist> سست (HH)} {sistayî; sistî} [JR/Ba2/F/K/IFb/B/JJ/HH/SK/GF//Bw//FS] <nemêr>

sistahî سِستاهی (ZF3) = weakness; laziness. See **sistî**.

sistayî سِستایی (K/B/ZF3) = weakness; laziness. See **sistî**.

sistî سِستی *f.* (;-yê). 1) {syn: qelsî [1]} weakness; impotence; powerlessness, limpness; 2) laziness, indolence, slackness. {also: sistahî (ZF3-2); sistayî (K-2/B-2/ZF3-2); [sisti] سستی (JJ)} [K/IFb/B/JJ/GF/ZF3] <sist>

sisya سِسیا (B) = third. See **sisîya**.

sitam سِتام *f.* (;-ê). the common cold, head cold, catarrh: **-bi stamê ketin** (ZF3) to catch a cold. {also: stam (RZ/ZF3-2)} {syn: p'ersîv; sat'ircem} [ZF3/RZ//Wkt]

sit'ar سِتار *f.* (-a;-ê). 1) {syn: ban II; serban} roof: •**ser** ***sit'arê*** (EP-7) on *the roof*; 2) {syn: nivan} refuge, shelter: •**Bira, çend zaroyên min hene, *sitara* min li cem wan tune, ji mêvanan ra çawan î?** (J2, 21) Brother, I have several children, none of them will give me *refuge*. How do you feel about [taking in] guests? •[**Mişkê**] **got: "Ê, bira ez te berdim, tu ê heyfa me ji Rûvî hildî? *Sitara* me di destê Rûvî da tune"** (J2, 23) [The mouse] Said, "Well, let's say I let you go, will you take revenge on Fox for us? We have no *refuge* from Fox's hand; 3) belongings, goods and chattels, particularly those of the poor (B); clothes (HH). {also: star (ZF3); <sitar> ستار (HH)} < Ar sitār ستار [EP-7/K/IFb/B/HH//ZF3]

sitewil سِتەوِل (IFb) = horse stable. See **stewl**.

sitêl سِتێل (L) = worthy, deserving. See **stêl**.

sitêrik سِتێرِك (TF) = star. See **stêr I**.

sitêrnas سِتێرناس (FJ/TF) = astronomer; astrologer. See **stêrnas**.

sitirandin سِترِاندِن (TF) = to sing. See **stiran I**.

sitirih سِترِه (IFb/TF) = animal horn. See **strû**.

sitirihan سِترِهان (TF) = to knead. See **stiran II**.

sitirihandin سِترِهاندِن (TF) = to knead. See **stiran II**.

sitirî سِترِی (IFb) = thorn. See **stirî I**.

sitûn سِتوون (F) = column; pole. See **stûn**.

sitûr سِتوور (TF) = thick. See **stûr**.

siûd سِئوود *f.* (-a;). 1) {syn: bext; îqbal} good luck, good fortune; chance; success: •**Go seûda te hebe, tu li ser beranê spî kevî, wê te bi rû dinyaya gewrik xîne. Go *seûda te tune be*, tuê li ser beranê reş kevî. W[ê] gavê, heft tebeqê erdê wê te daxe, wê te bavêje welatê cina** (L-I, #4, 108, l. 18-21) If *you're lucky*, you'll fall on the white ram, and he'll bring you to the white world. If *you're unlucky*, you'll fall on the black ram. In that case, he'll take you down seven layers under the earth, and throw you into the land of the Jinn

•**Heke îşê wî çû serî, dibêjin ko *siûda* wî a baş bû** (BX) If his affair goes over well, they say that he had good *luck*; **-siḧûd û îqbal** (Z-2) do.; 2) {syn: menfa'et} advantage, benefit. {also: seûd (L); sihûd (IFb); siḧûd (Z-2)} <Ar su'ūd سعود, pl. of sa'd سعد = 'good luck'; Za siḧud *m.* (Todd) [Z-2//IFb//K(s)/TF/ZF3//L]

sivande سِڤانده (IFb) = eaves. See **sîvande**.

Sivat سِڤات = February. See **Sibat**.

sivde سِڤده (GF/HH) = eaves. See **sîvande**.

sivder سِڤدەر *f.* **(-a;-ê).** entrance hall, vestibule (lit. & fig.); brink; corridor: •**Iraq li ber *sivdera* şerê navxweyî ye** (Netkurd.com, ix.2006) Iraq is on *the brink of* civil war. [Ag/Ptn/K/B/ZF3/FS/Wkt]

sive سِڤه = morning. See **sibe**[1].

sivêrnek سِڤێرنەك (Frq) = eaves. See **sîvande**.

sivik سِڤِك *adj.* 1) {syn: bêtên [2]; ≠giran} light *(weight)*, not heavy; 2) {syn: asan; ≠dijwar} easy: •**Ezê şerdekî *sivik* ji tere bêjim** (L) I'll give [lit. 'tell'] you an *easy* task; **-sivik-sivik** = ever so slightly: •***Sivik-sivik* rabû ji berda** (EP-7) [The prince] rose *ever so slightly* [as a sign of respect]; 3) {syn: vebûyî; zer I} light *(of tea)* (Bw). {also: siwik (SK); [siwik] سفك (JJ); <sivik> سڤك (HH)} Cf. P sabuk سبك; Sor sûk سووك {sivikayî; sivikahî; sivikî; siviktî} [L/K/A/JB3/IFb/B/JJ/HH/GF/TF/OK/Bw//SK]

sivikahî سِڤِكاهى (BX/K/JB3/IFb/GF/OK) = easiness; lightness. See **sivikayî**.

sivikayî سِڤِكايى *f.* **(-ya;-yê).** 1) lightness *(of weight)*; 2) ease, easiness: **-bi sivikayî** = with ease, easily. {also: sivikahî (BX/K-2/JB3/IFb/GF-2/OK-2); sivikî (K-2/A-2/TF/OK); siviktî (K-2); [siwikaï] سفكاى (JJ)} [K/A/B/JJ/GF//BX/JB3/IFb//TF/OK] <sivik>

sivikî سِڤِكى (K/A/TF/OK) = easiness; lightness. See **sivikayî**.

siviktî سِڤِكتى (K) = easiness; lightness. See **sivikayî**.

sivir سِڤِر (Ba3) = tablecloth. See **sifre**.

sivirge سِڤِرگه (Wkt) = broom. See **sirge**.

sivî سِڤى *f.* **(-ya;-yê).** bran: **-gerka sivîyê** (Zeb) bran dust. {also: [sevî] سفى (JJ); <sivî> سڤى (Hej)} = Sor serhêłek سەرهێڵەك & kepek کەپەك [Zeb/OK/Hej/AA/ZF3//JJ]

sivîng سِڤينگ (IFb) = eaves. See **sîvande**.

sivîrnek سِڤيرنەك (Haz) = eaves. See **sîvande**.

sivnik سِڤنِك *f./m.(FS)* **(-a/;-ê/).** broom made from the broom plant, used for wiping the backs of oxen: •**Zeyno *sivnik* di destê xwe da hejand** (FS) Z. waved *the broom* in her hand. {also: [sywnik] سفنيك (JJ); <sivnik> سڤنك (HH)} {syn: avlêk; cerîvk (Bw); gêzî; k'inoşe; melk'es; sirge (Ad); siqavêl; sizik; şicing (Krs); şirt I} [IFb/JB3/JJ/HH/OK/Mtk/Frq/MB/FS] <gêzî; maliştin>

sivor سِڤۆر (ZF/Wkt) = squirrel. See **siwûrî**.

sivore سِڤۆره (Slv/ZF/FS) = squirrel. See **siwûrî**.

siwande سِوانده (SK) = eaves. See **sîvande**.

siwar سِوار *m.* **().** rider, horseman; knight: •**Lawik *siwarekî* baş e** (AB) The boy is a good *rider*; **-li *ft-î* siwar bûn** = a) to mount, ride *(an animal)*: •***Li* hespê *swar bûm*** (K) I *got on* (or, *mounted*) the horse; b) to get on/in *(a vehicle)*: •**Ez *li* trênê *siwar bûm*** (JB3) I *boarded* the train; **-siwar kirin** = to cause to ride, mount *(vt.)*: •**Hakim qîza xwe *suwar kir*** (L) The king *had* his daughter *mount* [a steed]; **-li hev siwar kirin** = to assemble, put together: •**Vê tifingê ji min re *li hev siwar bike*** = *Assemble* this rifle for me •**Ev du gotin *li hev siwar na bin*** (JB3) These two words *contradict each other* [lit. '*cannot ride together*']. {also: sîyar (F/K/Z-1/Bw); soyar (Ba2); suyar (B); suwar (L/IFb-2/GF); sûwar (Z-3/SK); swar (A/K-2); syar (Ad); [souvar] سوار (JJ); <suwar> سوار (HH)} <O P asa-bāra-: asa- = 'horse' + bāra- = 'to ride; to be carried': P savār سوار --> Ar sawārī سواري; --> T süvari; Sor suwar سووار; Za espar *m.* (Mal); Hau sûar = 'mounted, horseman' (M4) [AB/JB3/IFb/TF//Ba2//L/HH/GF//Ad//F/K/Bw//A//B//JJ//Z-3/SK] <hesp>

siwax سِواخ (OK/B) = plaster. See **sewax**.

Siwêç سِوێچ (K) = Sweden. See **Swêd**.

Siwêdî سِوێدى (BF) = Swedish. See **Swêdî**.

Siwêreg سِوێرەگ (Wkp) = Siverek. See **Sêwreg**.

Siwîsrî سِويسرى (BF) = Swiss. See **Swîsreyî**.

siwûrî سِووورى *f.(K/ZF3)/m.(FS)* **().** squirrel, zool. *Sciurus vulgaris*: •***Siwûrî* ji darê diket, go: "Qentarek goşt ji min çû!"** (L[1937]) *The squirrel* fell from the tree and said, "I have lost a kantar [in Syria 1 kantar = 256.4 kg] of flesh!" *[prv.]*. {also: sibore (Hk); sihor (Wkp); simore; sior (TF)/s̱i'or (HR); sivor (ZF/Wkt); sivore (Slv/ZF-2/FS); <siforî> سفورى (HH)} {syn: pilûr; sencab} Cf. Sor simore سِمۆره [K/JB3/IFb/L(1937)//HH/TF/HR//Wkp//Slv/FS//ZF/Wkt]

sixêf سِخێف *f./pl.* **(;-ê).** curse, verbal abuse: •**M. mêzand va ḧûtek hat, *sxêf kirnêda*, go, "Sebav, keç'a kûç'ik! Ji êvarê ve bela va zarowê te frotye mi"** (HR 3:288-9) M. saw that an ogre came, *cursed her*, saying, “Dirty cur, daughter of a dog! Your children have been causing me trouble since the evening” **•*Sixêfên* kirêt ji herdu aliyan bilind dibûn** (HYma 43) Ugly *curses* were rising from both sides. {also: siqêf (A); sixêv (FS); sxêf (HR)} {syn: ç’êr̄; dijûn I; ne‘let; nifir̄; qise[3]; xeber[3]} [HR//HYma/FJ/GF/AD/Wkt//FS//A]

sixêv سِخێڤ (FS) = curse. See **sixêf**.

sixlet سِخلەت *f.* **(-a;-ê).** crowd, multitude, crush, throng, plurality: **•Stêrka livbaz di nav mital û fikarên min de ji ber çavên min winda bûbû. Ketibû nav *sixleta* stêrkan. Her çendî lê gerîm jî min nedît** (Nofa, 29) I lost sight of the moving star in my thoughts. It had fallen in among *the multitude of* stars. No matter how much I looked for it, I couldn't find it. {also: sixletî (G)}{syn: qerebalix; t’op I; ferc} [Nofa/IFb/ZF3//G]

sixletî سِخلەتی (G) = crowd. See **sixlet**.

siyaset سِیاسەت *f.* **(-a;-ê).** politics. {also: seyasetî (-ya;) (B); sîasetî (B-2); sîyaset (K); sîyasetî (K/B-2)} {syn: r̄êzanî} < Ar siyāsah سیاسة --> T siyaset [K//JB3/IFb/ZF//B]

siyasetmedar سِیاسەتمەدار (AW/CTV) = politician. See **siyasetvan**.

siyasetvan سِیاسەتڤان *m.* **(-ê;).** politician: **•Îcar heqê *siyasetvanan* tuneye ku ber li hunermendan bigire, hunermendan têxe nava tarîqata xwe** (Nûdem 30 [1999], 27) So *politicians* have no right to obstruct artists, to force artists into their camp **•Ji berdêla ku *siyasetvanên* me rê li ber hunermendan vekin, wan bi pêş de bibin, ew ji bo propogandaya xwe dikirin alet** (Nûdem 30 [1999], 27) Instead of our *politicians* encouraging artists and promoting them, they made use of them for their own propaganda. {also: siyasetmedar (AW/CTV); siyasetzan (RZ/ZF)} Cf. P siyāsatmadār سیاستمدار; Sor siyasetmedar سِیاسەتمەدار [VoA/Nûdem/Wkt//RZ/ZF//AW/CTV]

siyasetzan سِیاسەتزان (RZ/ZF) = politician. See **siyasetvan**.

siyasî سِیاسی *adj.* political: **•Di dewra K.P. da li Tirkîyê girtîyên *sîyasî* tunebûn** (Bkp, 4) During the era of K.P, there were no *political* prisoners in Turkey. {also: sîyasî (K)} {syn: r̄êzanî; r̄amyarî} < Ar siyāsī سياسي [BX/ZF/RZ//K]

sizik سِزِك *f.* **(-a;).** broom. {also: sizing (ZF3-2)} {syn: avlêk; cerîvk (Bw); gêzî; k’inoşe; melk’es; sirge (Ad); siqavêl; sivnik; şicing (Krs); şirt I} [Krç/Mlt/RZ/ZF3]

sizing سِزنگ (ZF3) = broom. See **sizik**.

sî I سی *f.* **(-ya;-yê).** shade; shadow: **•Dar *sî* dide ser me** (AB) Trees give us *shade* [lit. 'The tree gives *shade* on us'] **•Feqî li *sîya* darê razaye** (AB) The theologian lay down in *the shade of* the tree; **-sîya darê** (B) shade of a tree. {also: saye (SK); sê II; sih I (JB3/GF-2); [sê سە/si سی (JJ); <sih> سە (HH)} {syn: sêber (SK)} [Pok. sḱāi-, sḱəi-:sḱī- 917.] 'to gleam; reflection' & [Pok. sḱii̯ā- 917.] 'shadow': Skt chhāyā *f.*; O Ir *sḱhāyā- *f.*: Av *saiia- *in* a-saiia = 'shadowless'; P sāyeh سایه; Sor sa سا/sê[ber] سێبەر; Za sersey *f.* (Todd); Hau seye *f.* (M4); cf. also Gr skia σκιά = 'shadow' [F/K/A/IFb/B/JJ/GF//HH/JB3/Hk/Rh] <sihik [2]; sîwan>

sî II سی *num.* thirty, 30. {also: sih II (BX-2/JB3/JB1-S); sihî (SK-2); sîh II (A/IFb-2/SK); su (Rh); [sii] سیی (JJ); <sih> سه (HH)} Skt triṃśát-; Av θrisatəm [*acc.*]; Mid P sīh (M3); P sī سی; Sor sî سی; Za hîris (Todd); Hau sî (M4) [BX/K/IFb/B/GF//A/SK//JB3/HH//JJ//SK//Rh] <sîhem>

sî III سی (OK/ZF3) = lung. See **sîh I**.

sîasetî سیئاسەتی (B) = politics. See **siyaset**.

sîber سیبەر (K/GF/JB1-A/M-Am) = shade, shadow. See **sêber**.

sîç سیچ (Bw) = fault; offense. See **sûc**.

sîgarêt سیگارێت, f. (F) = cigarette. See **cigare**.

sîh I سیه *f.* **(-a;).** lung. {syn: cegera spî; k’ezeba sipî; mêlak[a sor]; pişa spî} {also: sî III (OK/ZF3)} = Sor sêpelak سێپەلاك [Hk//OK/ZF3] <dil; fateřeşk; hinav; zirav II>

sîh II سیه (A/IFb/SK) = thirty. See **sî II**.

sîhem سیهەم *adj.* thirtieth, 30th. {also: sihem (Wkt); sihemîn (TF/Wkt-2); sîhemîn (IFb-2/Wkt-2); sîyem (GF/Wkt-2); sîyemîn (GF-2/Wkt-2)} Cf. P. sī'om سی ام; Sor sîyem[în] سییەم[ین] [A/IFb//Wkt//TF//GF] <sî II>

sîhemîn سیهەمین (IFb/Wkt) = thirtieth. See **sîhem**.

sîkar سیکار *f.* **(-a;-ê).** meat cleaver, butcher's knife: **•*Sîkar* vi ȟefka wî dikevît û r̄iha ȟefkê lê diqetînît** (X. Saliȟ. Hindek serhatiyên Kurdî, 89) *The knife* enters his throat and cuts his jugular vein. {also: sîkard (IFb/Wkt/SS)} {syn: sat’or I} Sor sîkard سیکارد = 'cleaver' (P kārd کارد = 'knife') [X.Saliȟ/Hej//IFb/Wkt/SS] <k’êr III>

sîkard سیکارد (IFb/Wkt/SS) = cleaver. See **sîkar**.

sîl•e سیلە *f.* **(•a;•ê).** slap, smack, cuff, box *(with the hand)*: **-sîle li *fk-ê* dan/xistin** (K)/**sîle kirin** (IF/B) to slap, smack s.o.: **•Ew milê Ûsiv digire *sîleke* usa *lê dixe*, wekî ji ç'avê wî pirîsk dipekin** (Ba3-3, #25) He grabs Joseph's arm and *slaps* him so hard that sparks fly out his eyes. {also: sîleh II (B-2); [silé] سيله (JJ)} {syn: şimaq; t'ep II} P sīlī سيلى --> T sille [Msr/F/K/IFb/B/JJ/OK]

sîleh I سيلهه *f.* **(-a;-ê).** weapon(s), arms: **•Bikaranîna *vê sîlehê* di dema şerrên koloniyal de belav bû** (Le Monde diplomatique kurdî xii.2010, 6) The use of *this weapon* during the colonial wars was common. {also: islah; isleh; îslah; îsleh; îslêh (L); silaḧ (SK/JB1-S); sileh (JB3); sîlḧe (B); sîliḧ (F/SC); [silah] سلاح (JJ); <sileḧ> سلح (HH)} {syn: ç'ek [3]} < Ar silāḥ سلاح [L//K/IFb/ZF3/Wkt//JB3//HH//JJ//B//F/SC//SK/JB1-S] <cebirxane>

sîleh II سيلهه (B) = slap. See **sîle**.

sîlḧe سيلحه (B) = weapon(s). See **sîleh I**.

sîliḧ سيلح (F/SC) = weapon(s). See **sîleh I**.

sîm•e سيمه *m.* **(•ê;).** 1) (iron) fence; 2) silver wire (IFb/OK). *See etymology at* **zîv**. [Bw/IFb/OK/Wkt/BF] <k'ozik I; p'ercan; tan>

sîmerx سيمەرخ (IFb/FS) = Simurgh; red vulture, zool. *Gypus vulvus*. See **sêmir̄**.

sîmir̄ سيمِڕ (K/B)/sîmir سيمِر (IFb/HH/GF/TF/FS) = simurgh. See **sêmir̄**.

sînahî سيناهى *f.* **(-ya;-yê).** glimmer (of light), weak light, dim light, as that which shines through an opening in a door: **•Di şkefteka tarî da *sînahîyeka* piçûk bes e** (Zeb) In a dark cave, a little *glimmer* of light is enough **•Yê ḧutm e--xo *sînahîyekê* nabînît** (Zeb) He is blind--he can't even see *a dim light*. {also: sînayî (OK)} [Zeb/FS/BF//OK] <pêjin; qeret'û; r̄onahî I>

sînak سيناك (Elk) = clubs (in card games). See **sînek**.

sînayî سينايى (OK) = dim light. See **sînahî**.

sînd سيند (Bw) = oath. See **sond**.

sînek سينەك *f.* **(;-ê).** clubs *(suit of playing cards)*. {also: sînak (Elk); <sînek> سينەك (Hej)} {syn: îspatî} cf. T sinek = 'fly (insect); clubs (playing cards)' [Bw/Qzl/Hej//Elk]

sîng سينگ *m.(Ba2/JB3)/f.(W/HR)* **(-ê/-a;).** 1) chest, bosom: **•Her̄e pê li *singa* wê bike** (HR 3:142) Go step on her *chest*; **-depa sîng** (Wn)/**depê sîngî** (Bw/Elk)/**defa sing** (K)/**defa sîngê** (Qzl/Qrj)/ **derfa sing** (IS) thorax, chest, area between the neck and the diaphragm; 2) {syn: berwar; hevraz; jihelî; p'al; pesar; p'êş II[2]; qunt'ar; ter̄azin} slope *(of mountain)*: **-sîngê ç'îyê** (B) do.: **•Ser *sîngê* Dûmanlûê cîcîna xulexula cewikêd avê bû** (Ba2:1, 202) On *the slope of* [Mount] Dumanlu here and there was the babbling of brooks (of water); 3) front, forward part *(e.g., the front seat of a car)* (Bw). {also: sing II (JB3/Rnh/TF); [sing] سينگ (JJ); <sing> سنگ (HH)} Cf. P sīne سينه --> T sine; Hau sîne *m.* (M4) [Ba2/K/A/IFb/B/JJ/GF/OK/ZF//JB3/HH/TF] <memik>

sînî سينى (IFb/JJ) = tray. See **sênî**.

sînor سينۆر *m./f.(JR)* **(-ê/-a;).** border, limit, frontier: **•[Hûn digel êlatêd xwe bar bikin û biçine *sînora* Romê]** (JR #39,120) Pack up and go with your people to *the frontier of* Turkey **•Sefewiyan jî ji bo parastina *sînorê* dewleta xwe li hemberî împaratoriya berfireh a Osmaniyan şîetî wekî mezhebekî dînî û fermî ... dan** [sic] **xuyakirin** (Zend 2:3[1997], 56) And the Safavids, in order to protect *the border of* their state against the expansive Ottoman Empire, declared Shiism their official religious sect. {also: sinûr (BF); sînûr (JB3); [sinor] سنور (JJ); <sînor> سينور (HH)} {syn: t'ixûb} < Gr synoro(n) συνορο(ν) [syn-συν-= 'with, co-' + ὅρος horos = 'boundary'] --> T sınır; Za sînor *m.* (Todd) [F/K/A/IFb/B/HH/GF/OK//JB3//JJ/BF] <bêsînor>

sînot سينۆت *f.* **(-a;).** the members of a ruler's entourage or court: **•Usa jî *sînota* dîwana bavê wî** (Z-1) So also *the members of* his father's court **•*Sînota* p'adşê êvarê beladibe diçe** (Z-921) The king's *court* adjourns (or, disperses, dissolves) in the evening. < Gr synodos συνοδος [Z-1] <giregir>

sînûr سينوور (JB3) = border, limit. See **sînor**.

sîqandin سيقاندن (TF/ZF) = to bare one's teeth. See **sîqirandin**.

sîqirandin سيقِراندن *vt.* **(-sîqirîn-).** to gnash or grind one's teeth, bare one's teeth: **•Bêhna wî bi dijûnan tenê fireh nebûbû, didanên xwe jî *disîqirandin*** (DBgb, 44) Not only did he content himself with curses, he also *bared* his teeth **•Hema pisîk xwe gelemozî dike, gij dike, diranên xwe *disîqirîne*, devê xwe qîç û mûç dike û xwe diheleqe nav ser û çavên rovî** (ZZ-3, 244) The cat ... puffs himself up, *bares* his teeth, grimaces something awful and lunges at the fox's face. {also: sîqandin (TF/ZF)} {syn: qîç kirin} =Sor dan lê cîr̄ kirdn•ewe دان لىٚ جيڕ كِردنەوە = 'to show displeasure by baring one's teeth' [ZZ/DBgb//TF/ZF] sîq-û-sir سیق و سیر (Qilaban)/sîqûsir سیقووسیر (Şnx) = see saw. See **zîqûziř.**

sîr سـیـر *f.* **(-a;-ê).** garlic, bot. *Allium sativum*: **•Te li ber *sîrê* destê xo bi devê xove na, da bên nehête min?** (M-Ak #609, 276) Was it on account of *the garlic* then that you put your hand over your mouth, so that the smell should not reach me? {also: [sir] سـیـر (JJ); <sîr> سـیـر (HH)} Cf. OP θāigarci-/θāigraci- = 'third month, May-June, possibly orig. 'Garlic-collecting month' (Kent/ Justi, ZDMG 51:243); P sīr سیر; Sor sîr سیر [F/K/A/JB3/IFb/B/JJ/HH/GF/TF/RZ/FS/BF] <pîvaz>

sîravik سیراڤِك (IFb) = saltwater. See **sûravk**.

sîrdim سیردِم (A/GF) = wild garlic. See **sîrim**.

sîrik I سیرِك (IFb/B/GF/TF/Hk/HH) = wild garlic. See **sîrim**.

sîrik II سـیـرِك *f.* **(;-ê).** dandruff, scurf: **•*Sîrikê* serê min qîza p'adşê ç'e'v pê k'evin, wê serê min bihe'řişînin** (HCK-3, #16, 180) If the princess [lit. 'king's daughter'] notices *the dandruff on* my head, they will scratch my head. {syn: keletor; nemes} [HCK/B]

sîrim سـیـرِم *f.* **(-a;-ê).** wild garlic *used as a spice in home made cheese*; a) chives, bot. *Allium schoeno-prasum* (IFb); b) bot. *Allium rotuntum* [T kömüren]. {also: sîrdim (A/GF-2); sîrik I (IFb-2/ B-2/GF/TF/Hk); sîrme (B); sîrmî (K); sîrmok (GF-2); sîrmûk (K-2); <sîrik> سـیـرك (HH)} Cf. P mūsīr موسیر/sīrmū سیرمو = 'shallot, ashkelonian garlic'; Sor sîrmoke سـیـرمـۆکـە = 'wild garlic' [Frq/ IFb/FS//A//HH/GF/TF/Hk//B//K] <sîr>

sîrkut سـیـرکـوت *m.* **(-ê;).** wooden garlic press. {also: sîrkutik (IFb/TF); sîrkutk (A); <sîrkut> سـیـرکـت (HH)} [Qrj/HH/GF/ZF3//IFb/TF//A]

sîrkutik سـیـسرکـوتِك (IFb/TF) = wooden garlic press. See **sîrkut**.

sîrkutk سـیـرکـوتـك (A) = wooden garlic press. See **sîrkut**.

sîrme سیرمە (B) = wild garlic. See **sîrim**.

sîrmî سیرمی (K) = wild garlic. See **sîrim**.

sîrmok سیرمۆك (GF) = wild garlic. See **sîrim**.

sîrmûk سیرمووك (K) = wild garlic. See **sîrim**.

sîs I سـیـس *adj.* pure white: **-mîya sîs** (Rwn) white sheep. {also: [sis] سـیـس (JJ)} {syn: s[i]pî I} cf. 'dark purple color' (A); 'black' (JJ) [Kg/Rwn/K/IFb/GF]

sîs II سیس *adj.* 1) {syn: beqem} faded, withered: **-sîs bûn** (Bw) to fade; to wither {syn: beyîn}; 2) weak, faint (IFb/OK). [Bw/K(s)/IFb/OK] <[1] beyîn; [2]sist>

sîsalek سیسالەك (FJ) = vulture. See **sîsalk**.

sîsalk سـیـسـالـك *f.* **(-a;-ê).** vulture. {also: simsîyark (FS); sîsalek (FJ); sîsarîk (TF); sîsark (IFb/GF-2/ FJ-2); sîsik II (GF-2); sîsyarik (GF-2); sîsyarok (Btm); sîsolek (IFb-2); [sisālik سـیـسـالـك (Lx)/ sürsiārik سـرسـیـارك/simsiyār (PS)] (JJ); <simsiyarik> سمسیارك (HH)} {syn: kurt II} Sor sîsarg سیسارگ /sîsargekeçełe سیسارگەکەچەڵە [Qrj/ GF//JJ-Lx//FJ//IFb//TF//Btm//HH//FS] <başok; elîh; xertel>

sîsarîk سیساریك (TF) = vulture. See **sîsalk**.

sîsark سیسارك (IFb/GF/FJ) = vulture. See **sîsalk**.

sîsik I سـیـسِـك *f.* **(-a;).** pip, stone, pit *(of raisins, terebinth, dates, apples, peaches, apricots)*. {also: sîsk (GF)} {syn: dendik} [Krb/IFb/TF//GF] <dendik>

sîsik II سیسِك (GF) = vulture. See **sîsalk**.

sîsin سیسِن (FS) = lily. See **sosin**.

sîsiřk سیسِرك *f.(FS)/m.* **(-a/-ê;).** 1) {syn: kirîstik; kulî I} cricket, zool. *Gryllus*: **•"*Sîsirkê* Hesinî" berhemeke Selîm Berekat e** (krd.riataza.com 20.ii.2018) "The Iron Grasshopper" is a work of Salim Barakat's; 2) cockroach, zool. *Blattidae* (Bw). {also: sûsirk (IFb-2)} Sor sîsirk سیسِرك [Bw/IFb/GF/ TF/OK/FS]

sîsîya[n] سیسییا[ن] (K) = third. See **sisîya**.

sîsk سیسك (GF) = pip, pit (of fruit). See **sîsik I**.

sîsolek سیسۆلەك (IFb) = vulture. See **sîsalk**.

sîsyarik سیسیارِك (GF) = vulture. See **sîsalk**.

sîsyarok سیسیارۆك (Btm) = vulture. See **sîsalk**.

sîtavk سیتاڤك *f.* **(;-ê).** umbrella; parasol. {also: sîte'vk (B)} {syn: sîwan; şemse} [F/K//B]

sît•e سیتە/سویتە *f.* **(•a;•ê).** trap for catching partridges, consisting of a hole dug in the ground covered with a wooden trapdoor: **-sîta kewan** (Zeb) do.: **•Dar û dû ben / êxistine têda / bûne řeben [*sîta kewa*]** (AZ #18, 34) Wood and two strings / were put in it / they became pitiful (or, a monk/nun) *[rdl.: ans.: partridge trap]* {also: sût I (AA-2/FS); sûte, m. (OK/AA); <sût> سوت (HH); <sîte سیتە/ sût سـوت> (Hej)} Cf. GF sûtal/sûtar = 'trap' [Zeb/ Hej/AZ//OK/AA//HH/FS] <dav I; telhe; tepik I; xefik>

sîte'vk سیتەعڤك (B) = umbrella. See **sîtavk**.

sîtil سـیـتِـل *f.* **(-a;-ê).** 1) {syn: dewl I; 'elb; helgîn (Krş)} bucket, pail: large bucket, *as opposed to* ***satil*** *= small bucket* (Wn); copper bucket; 2) {syn: mencel} large cauldron; copper kettle (HH); copper cauldron (JJ). {also: [sitil] سـتـل (JJ); <sîtil> سیتل (HH)} Cf. Ar saṭl سطل [J/F/K/A/IFb/B/JJ/

HH/GF/Wn] <den I; mencelok; satil; zerik [2]>

sîv سيڤ (Rh/HH) = apple. See **sêv**.

sîvan سيڤان (Haz/GF/OK) = umbrella. See **sîwan**.

sîvand•e سيڤانده *f.* **(•a;).** eaves of roof (Bw/IFb/GF/SK); awning (GF/HH); gutter on roof (OK). {also: sivande (IFb); sivde (GF-2); sivêrnek (Frq); sivîng (IFb-2); sivîrnek (Haz); siwande (SK); sonder (Erh); <sivde سڤده/selende صلنده/suwander صوانذر> (HH)} Sor [gwê-/gö-]suwane گوێ سووانه (W&E) & suwan[d]e سووانده (Hej) = 'eaves' [Bw/GF/OK//IFb//SK//HH//Haz//Frq//Erh]

sîvle سيڤله (A) = field mouse. See **sêvle**.

sîvlore سيڤلۆره (Bw) = field mouse. See **sêvle**.

sîwan سيوان *f.* **(-a;-ê).** umbrella, parasol. {also: sêhwane (FS); sêvang•e f. (;•ê) (B); sîvan (Haz/GF-2/OK-2); [seivan] سيوان (JJ); <sîwan> سيوان (HH)} {syn: sîtavk; şemse} cf. P sāyebān سايهبان = 'shade formed by an arbor, etc.; canopy; parasol'; Sor seywan سهيوان = 'large tent; hut, arbor' [Haz//A/IFb/HH/GF/TF/OK//JJ//FS//B] <baran; sî I>

sîwax سيواخ (F/K) = plaster. See **sewax**.

sîxuř سيخوڕ *m.* **(-ê;).** 1) porcupine; 2) {syn: *casûs; destkîs} spy, mole; traitor. {also: [sikór (G)/sīχúr (Lx)] سيخور (JJ); <sîxur> سيخر (HH)} Cf. "P and Pamiric words for 'porcupine, hedgehog' cognate with Av sukurəna- (? < *suk- wṛHna- 'having prickly wool' with root-stem *suk- 'pricking, piercing', to Av sūkā, P sūzan 'needle'," from M. Schwartz. "On some Iranian secret vocabularies," in: *Trends in Iranian and Persian linguistics* (Berlin: DeGruyter, 2018), p. 77, 2.5 (18). P sīxūl سيخول/ sīxūr سيخور = 'porcupine, hedgehog'; Sor sîxuř سيخوڕ [Qrj/A/IFb/JJ/HH/GF/TF/FJ/FS] <jûjî>

sîyar سيار (F/K/Z-1/Bw) = rider. See **siwar**.

sîyaset سياسەت (K) = politics. See **siyaset**.

sîyasetî سياسەتى (K/B) = politics. See **siyaset**.

sîyasî سياسى (K) = political. See **siyasî**.

sîyem سيیەم (GF/Wkt) = thirtieth. See **sîhem**.

sîyemîn سيیەمين (GF-2/Wkt) = thirtieth. See **sîhem**.

Skoçî سكۆچى (IFb/ZF3/Wkt) = Scottish. See **Skotlendî**.

Skoçyayî سكۆچيايى (Wkt) = Scottish. See **Skotlendî**.

Skotî سكۆتى (Wkt) = Scottish. See **Skotlendî**.

Skotlandayî سكۆتلاندايى (Wkt) = Scottish. See **Skotlendî**.

Skotlandî سكۆتلاندى (Wkt) = Scottish. See **Skotlendî**.

Skotlendî سكۆتلەندى *adj.* Scottish. {also: Îskoçî (Wkt-2); Îskoçyayî (Wkt-2); Skoçî (IFb/ZF3/Wkt-2); Skoçyayî (Wkt-2); Skotî (Wkt); Skotlandayî (Wkt-2); Skotlandî (Wkt-2)} Sor 'Uskutlendî ئوسكوتلەندى [SS/Wkp//Wkt//IFb/ZF3]

slav سلاڤ (FK-eb-2) = greetings, regards. See **silav**.

Slovakî سلۆڤاكى *adj.* Slovak. {also: Silovakî (BF)} Sor Slovakî سلۆڤاكى [Wkt/ZF3/SS//BF]

Slovenî سلۆڤەنى *adj.* Slovene. {also: Silovênî (BF)} Sor Slovînî سلۆڤينى [Wkt/ZF3//BF]

sndyan سنديان (HCK) = anvil. See **sindyan**.

sobahî سۆباهى *f.* **(-ya;-yê).** swimming: **-sobahî kirin** = to swim. {also: sêbahî (Wn); sêbanî (Qzl-2); sobaî (JB3); sobanî (Qzl); sobayî (K/GF/TF/Bt-2); sobehî (A); sobek'arî (K-2/B); sobelan[î] (Qmş); soberî (Xrz); some[karî] (QtrE); sovek'arî (F/Rwn); [sobàï سباى/sobàïti سبايتى] (JJ); <sûbahî> سوباهى (HH)} {syn: ajnê; avjenî; melevanî} Cf. Ar sabaḥa سبح = 'to swim'; = Sor mele مەلە [IFb/Bt//HH/K/GF/TF//A//JB3/JJ//B//Wn//Qzl//Qmş//Xrz//QtrE//F/Rwn]

sobahîker سۆباهيكەر (A) = swimmer. See **sobek'ar**.

sobaî سۆبائى (JB3) = swimming. See **sobahî**.

sobanek سۆبانەك (A) = swimmer. See **sobek'ar**.

sobanî سۆبانى (Qzl) = swimming. See **sobahî**.

sobarbeř سۆباربەڕ (Msr) = swimmer. See **sobek'ar**.

sobayî سۆبايى (K/GF/TF/Bt) = swimming. See **sobahî**.

sobehî سۆبەهى (A) = swimming. See **sobahî**.

sobek'ar سۆبەكار *m.&f.* **(-ê/-a;).** swimmer. {also: sobahîker (A); sobanek (A-2); sobarbeř (Msr); sovekar (F); [soba] سوبا (JJ); <sûba> سوبا (HH)} {syn: avjen; melevan} < Ar sabaḥa سبح = 'to swim' & sabbāḥ سبّاح = 'swimmer' [Msr//K/B/ZF3/FS//A//F//JJ//HH] <sobahî>

sobek'arî سۆبەكارى (K/B) = swimming. See **sobahî**.

sobelan[î] سۆبەلانى (Qmş) = swimming. See **sobahî**.

soberî سۆبەرى (Xrz) = swimming. See **sobahî**.

sode سۆده *f.* **().** type of small pastry, round, glazed. [Am] <k'ade>

sofî I سۆفى *m.* **(-yê;).** 1) Sufi, member of one of several mystical dervish orders: **•Ya *sofîyê* delal** (L) My dear old man [lit. 'O dear *sufi*'] [cher vieillard]; 2) someone who obeys closely all laws and rules, a 'stickler' (JJ). {also: [sofi] صوفى (JJ); <sofî> صوفى (HH)} < Ar ṣūfī صوفي --> T sofu [L/K/IF/B/JJ/HH/ZF3]

sofî II سۆفى *m.* **(-yê;).** side of knucklebone (k'ap II) that sticks out (hildayî) [T yüz üstü - âşık kemiğinin çukur tarafının yere gelmesi hali]. {syn: pik (Qzl/A/GF/TF)} {≠çik} [Wn/ZF3] <k'ap

II>

sohbet سـوّهـبـهت (K/B) = conversation, talk. See **s̲uḧbet**.

s̲ohr صوّهر (HR-I) = red. See **sor**.

s̲ohratî صوّهراتى (FS) = redness. See **sorayî**.

sohrik سوّهرك (TF) = measles. See **sorik**.

sohtin سوّهتِن (A) = to burn (vt.). See **sotin**.

s̲oḧbet صـوّحـبـهت (JB1-A) = conversation, talk. See **s̲uḧbet**.

sol سوّل/**s̲ol** صوّل [SK-2/HH/FS-2] *f.* **(-a;-ê).** 1) {syn: meras; pêlav; qondere} shoe(s); plastic shoe *{as opposed to **qondere** = leather shoe}* (Rh); boot(s): **•Bo min du zengilan bînin. Dê bi serê *sola* xo we dirûm da deng bihêt, mêrû biḧelên, pîyê min nekewîte ser wan** (SK 38:337) Bring me two bells and I shall sew them onto my *shoes* so that they ring, the ants run away and my foot may not fall on them **•Paşî Derwêş ʻAlî jî hat. Wextê hate jor, *solêt* xo helgirtin, înane naw meclisê, li ber xo danan. Xelkê ḧazir bûn gotine** [sic] **Derwêş ʻAlî, "ʻAlî, ewe çi ye? Te bo çî ewe kir? Li ḧuzora cenabê muctahid *sol* danan li ber xo şolekî munasib nîye." Derwêş ʻAlî got, "Belê, ez jî dizanim kirêt e, bê edebî ye, muxalifî ʻadetê cê ye, emma çi bikem? Çare nîye, dibît bikem, çûnkû zemanê Muḧemmed xelkî *solêt* xo dibirine mizgewtê, li ber xo didanan, ji tirsa Şîʻan da nedizin"** (SK 60:717) Then Dervish Ali came. When he entered, he picked up his *shoes* and brought them into the assembly, and put them down. The assembled group said to Dervish Ali, "Ali, what is this? Why did you do that? To put one's *shoes* down in the presence of the Jurisprudent is not proper." Dervish Ali said, "Yes, I too know it is ugly, disrespectful, and contrary to local custom, but what can I do? I have no choice, I must do it, because in the time of Muhammad, people brought their *shoes* into the mosque and put them down, lest the Shiites steal them"; 2) horseshoe (B/JJ/GF). {also: [sol] سـول (JJ); <s̲ol> صـول (HH)} Cf. NENA ṣâ-wiltâ ܨܐܘܠܬܐ = 'shoe' (Maclean); sole = 'pair of shoes' (Christian Urmi: my informant) & Heb sulyah סוליה = 'sole (of shoe)' [Ks/K/A/JB3/IFb/B/JJ/SK/GF/TF/OK/Rh/FS//HH] <çarox = k'alik II; kelêj I; sapok; şekal; şîrox>

solalês سـوّلالـێـس *m.* **().** bootlicker, brown-nose, yes man: **•Em bi serokeşîran ra rûnanin, vana kesên *solalês* in, em gotinên *solalêsan* cidî nagrin** (Z. Xamo. Hindik rindik, blog 28.iv.2010) We won't sit with tribal chieftains, they are *bootlickers*, we don't take the words of *bootlickers* seriously. {also: sol-alîs (FS)} {syn: qûnalês} <sol = 'shoe' + alês- = 'to lick' [Z.Xamo/Qzl//FS] <salûs>

sol-alîs سوّل ئاليێس (FS) = bootlicker. See **solalês** .

solbend سوّلبەند/**s̲olbend** صوّلبەند [FS] *m.* **(-ê;-î).** 1) {syn: nalbend} blacksmith, one who shoes horses; 2) {syn: k'oşk'ar; soldirû} bootmaker, cobbler, shoemaker: **•*Solbendî* s̲olek ji wî r̄a çêkir** (FS) *The cobbler* made a pair of shoes for him. {also: [sol-bend] سولبند (JJ)} {solbendî} [Bw/K/B/JJ/GF/OK/RZ//FS]

solbendî سـوّلـبـەنـدى *f.* **(;-yê).** 1) {syn: nalbendî} profession of a blacksmith, shoeing horses; 2) {syn: k'oşk'arî} profession of a cobbler. [B/GF/ZF3/BF] <solbend>

soldir سوّلدِر (Wkt/ZF3) = shoemaker. See **soldirû**.

soldirû سـوّلـدِروو/**s̲oldirû** صـوّلـدِروو [FS] *m.* **(;-yî).** shoemaker, cobbler: **•*Soldirû* pêxwasin, cildirû bê kirasin** (kurdipedia.org) *The cobblers* are barefoot, the tailors are shirtless *[prv.]*. {also: soldir (Wkt-2 /ZF3-2); soldrû (IFb); soldur (K-2)} {syn: k'oşk'ar; solbend} <sol- = 'shoe' + dirû- = 'to sew' [kurdipedia/K/A/B/Wkt/ZF3//FS//IFb]

soldrû سوّلدروو (IFb) = shoemaker. See **soldirû**.

soldur سوّلدور (K) = shoemaker. See **soldirû**.

s̲olîn I صـوّلـين *f.* **(-a;-ê).** subterranean clay water pipe or conduit: **-ava solînê** (FS) *water from such a conduit.* {also: solîne I (FS); [solína] سولينا (JJ)} <Arc silon סילון & Syr sīlōnā ܣܝܠܘܢܐ = 'gutter, duct, pipe, tube, channel' <Gr sōlēn σωλήν = 'channel, gutter, pipe' [Bw/JJ/ZF3/BF/FD//FS] <k'ar̄êz>

solîn II سوّلين/**s̲olîn** صوّلين [Bw/FS] *f.* **(-a;).** 1) flower bud on the verge of blooming *{phase of development between **bişkoj** [bud] and **gul** [flower]; cf. **balete** for a similar concept regarding fruit}* (Bw): **-s̲olîna gulê** (FS) do.; 2) field of flowers. {also: solîne II (IFb/OK)} [Bw/FS/ /IFb/TF/OK/FD/BF] <bişkoj [2]; gul>

solîne I سوّلينه (FS) = underground conduit. See **s̲olîn I**.

solîne II سوّلينه (IFb/OK) = flower bud. See **solîn II**.

some سوّمه (QtrE) = swimming. See **sobahî**.

somekarî سوّمەكارى (QtrE) = swimming. See **sobahî**.

somer سـوّمـەر *f.* **().** unit of measure: Turkish measure for grain (JJ); 16 kods = 1 somer (JJ); unit of weight equal to 10-12 Russian poods (1 pood =

16.38 kg. or appr. 36 lb. avoirdupois), equal to the load of a beast of burden (K). {also: [somar] سـومـار (JJ)} Cf. T somar [Amasya; Trabzon; Rize; Artvin; Kars; Erzincan; Erzurum] = 'grain measure equal to 16 kilograms' (DS, v. 10) [K/B/ZF3//JJ] <kod>

sond سۆند *f.* **(-a;-ê).** oath, vow: **•Ez te bi xudê *didem e sûndê* ko ji şolêt min bi te kirî gerdena min aza ke** (SK 9:89) I *conjure* you by God to pardon me for everything I have done to you **•Te bi serê mîrê Şeqlawê *sûndê*, wê carê bê-edebîya me bibexşe** (SK 13:127) *We conjure you* by the head of the Mir of Shaqlawa, forgive our rudeness this time; **-sond xwarin** = to swear, take an oath [cf. P sogand xordan سوگند خوردن; T and içmek]:**•Bira *sond xar*, ku tiştek serê Ûsib naê** (Ba) The brothers *swore* that nothing would happen to Joseph **•Diçin e-naw besta beran, çawêt xo dimiçînin, pêş paş diçin, panîya pîyê wan geheşt e kîşk berî dê înin, bi terazîyê kêşin, çend der-kewt *dê sûndekî* [sic] mezin û kirêt *xot* ko, "Ħetta bi-qeder giranîya wî berey pare-y zêr̄ yan zîw neînim nahêmewe"** (SK 12:117) They go to the vale of stones, shut their eyes, go back and forth and, whichever stone the heel of their foot touches, they will bring it and weigh it in a balance and, however much it turns out, *they will swear a* mighty and ugly *oath* that, "I shall not return until I bring the weight of this stone in gold or silver." {also: sînd (Bw); sund (JB3); sûnd (A/SK); [sond] سـونـد (JJ); <s̱ond> صـونـد (HH)} {syn: qesem} [Pok. kau-/kĕu-/kū- 535.] 'to howl; to cry (of birds)'--words beginning with palatal, p. 535-36, as supplemented by M. Schwartz: Indo-Iranian and Baltic *k̑euk- = 'to call out, proclaim': Proto Ir *saukanta-; Av *saokənta- = 'oath' (<√sauk); Sgd swk'nt [sōkand]; Khwarezmian sknt; Mid P sōgand (M3); Baluchi sauγan/sogind; P sōgand سـوگـنـد; Sor swênd [sönd] سـوێـنـد; Za suánd (Lx)/suwend *m.* (Mal). See: M. Schwartz. "Pers. saugand Xurdan, etc. 'to take an Oath' (Not *'to drink sulphur')," in: *Études Irano-Aryennes offertes à Gilbert Lazard* (Paris: Association pour l'avancement des études iraniennes, 1989), pp. 293-95. [F/K/IFb/B/JJ/GF//HH//Bw//A/SK//JB3]

sond•e سـۆنـده *f.* **(•a;).** water hose: **-sonda avê** (Dh) do. {syn: marpîç} Sor sonde سـۆنـده (HG) [Dh/OK/AA/Wkt]

sonder سۆندەر (Erh) = eaves. See **sîvande**.

sondxwarî سـۆنـدخـوارى *m.* **(-yê;).** 1) {syn: hevalbend} ally; 2) [*pl.*] the Allies (during World War II): **•Mêla hikûmeta we ji kê re çêtir heye, ji elemanan re an ji sondxwariyan re?** (Rnh) Who is your government in favor of, the Germans or the Allies? {also: sondxwerî (K); sundxwarî (JB3)} [Rnh/ZF3//K//JB3]

sondxwerî سۆندخوەرى (K) = ally. See **sondxwarî**.

sone سۆنە/**s̱one** صۆنە [SK] *m.&f.* **().** drake (m.), duck (f.): **•Çûn ħetta geştine gomekê. Dîtin** [sic] ***s̱oneyek* di gomê da melewanî diket** (SK 4:39) They went until they came to a pond. They saw *a drake* swimming in the pond. {also: sûne, f. (FS); [sona] سـونـه (JJ)} {syn: miravî; werdek} Cf. T süne = 'drake'; Sor sone سۆنە = 'duck, drake' [K/A/IFb/GF//SK//JJ//FS]

sor سۆر/**s̱or** صـۆر [FS/HH] *adj.* 1) red: **-sor kirin** = a) to heat up, make red hot: **•şîşêd *sorkirî*** (Dz) *red-hot* skewers; b) to roast: **•Berxek şerjêkirin ... avêtin hindurê firnê, qenc *sor kirin* û anîn ji B. re** (L) They slaughtered a lamb ... threw it in the oven, *roasted* it well, and brought it to B; c) to incite, provoke. See **lê sor kirin**; 2) hot, spicy *(regardless of color)* (Dy): **-backê sor** (Dy) hot pepper. {also: s̱ohr (HR-I); [sor] سـور (JJ); <s̱or> صـور (HH)} Cf. Southern Tati dialects: Chali sur; P sorx سرخ; Sor sûr سوور = 'red, burnt (bricks)'; Hau sûr (M4) {sorahî; soranî III; sorayî; sorî; <s̱orahî> صـوراهـى (HH)} [K/A/JB3/IFb/B/JJ/SK/GF/Dy//HH/FS//HR-I] <gevez; qijilandin>

sorahî سۆراهى (K) = redness. See **sorayî**.

Soranî I سـۆرانـى *f.* **().** central dialect of Kurdish, spoken in Iraq and Iran. In Iranian Kurdistan (Rojhilat), the northern sub-dialects, spoken in the Mukriyan region centered around Mehabad (Sablax), are called Mukrî; the southern sub-dialects, in historical Ardalan, are spoken in Sanandaj (Sineh). The intervening area includes Baneh, Merîwan, Saqqiz and Kelar. In Iraqi Kurdistan ("Başûr" [the South, relative to Turkey, although this is central Kurdistan]), Sorani is spoken in Sulaimaniyah (Silêmanî), Kirkûk, & Arbil (Hewlêr). Soran is a small region near Arbil, famous for its swords. [K/A/IFb/BF]

soranî II سـۆرانـى *f.* **(-ya;-yê).** 1) {syn: şûr} sword: **•Lê ewî bin qap'ûtê xweda *soranîya* xwe veşartibû** (Z-1) But he had hidden his *sword* underneath his overcoat; 2) type of dagger.

[Z-1/K/A/JB3/IFb/B/FS]

soranî III سۆرانی (K) = redness. See **sorayî**.

Soranîaxêf سۆرانی ئاخێف (Wkt) = Sorani-speaking. See **Soranîaxêv**.

Soranîaxêv سـۆرانـی ئـاخـێـڤ *m.&f.* **().** 1) Sorani speaker; 2) [*adj.*] Sorani-speaking: **•Komara Kurdistanê jî ku jiyê wê yazde meh bûn, li Mukiryana *soranîaxêv* hat damezrandin** (Kulturname: Emîr Hesenpûr) The Kurdish Republic, which lasted 11 months, was established in *Sorani -speaking* Mukriyan. {also: Soranîaxêf (Wkt-2); Soranîaxif (Wkt-2); Soranîaxiv (Wkt)} [ZF//Wkt]

Soranîaxif سۆرانی ئاخِف (Wkt) = Sorani-speaking. See **Soranîaxêv**.

Soranîaxiv سۆرانی ئاخِڤ (Wkt) = Sorani-speaking. See **Soranîaxêv**.

sorat سۆرات (Wkt) = surah of the Quran. See **sûret II**.

s̱oratî صۆراتی (FS) = redness. See **sorayî**.

sorayî سـۆرایـی *f.* **(-ya;-yê).** redness: **•*S̱oratîya* xwînê li ser befrê diyar e** (FS) *The redness of* the blood is visible on the snow. {also: s̱ohratî (FS); sorahî (K); soranî III (K-2); s̱oratî (FS); sorî (K-2/GF); <s̱orahî> صوراهی (HH)} [K/B/ZF3//HH//FS] <sor>

sore سۆره (SK) = surah of the Quran. See **sûret II**.

s̱oret I صۆرەت (SK) = face. See **sûret I**.

soret II سـۆرەت (Wkt) = surah of the Quran. See **sûret II**.

sorgul I سـۆرگـول *m./f.(ZF3)* **().** type of wheat, very good for making bulgur (cracked wheat germ) [ji savar re gelek baş e]. {also: <surguł> سـورگـوڵ (Hej)} [Qzl/A/IFb/ZF3//Hej] <genim>

sorik سـۆرِك/**s̱orik** صـۆرِك [FS/HH] *f./pl.* **(;-ê).** measles: **•*Sorikên* zar̄okî çûn** (FS) The child's *measles* have gone; **-sorik derxistin** (B) to come down with the measles; **-sorika k'etin** (B) do. {also: sohrik (TF); sorîk (Ak); surik II (IFb-2); [sorik] سـورك (JJ); <s̱orik> صـورك (HH)} {syn: bîrov} [K/A/JB3/IFb/B/JJ/GF//HH/FS//Ak//TF]

soring سـۆرِنـگ/**s̱oring** صـۆرِنـگ *f.* **(;-ê).** plant and dye on the back of sheep and goats after they have been shorn, madder, bot. *Rubia tinctorum*: **•beranê soringkirî** (Qzl) ram dyed with madder **•Gelek xûn ji leşê wî çûbû û berfa ku ew li ser dirêj bûbû, mîna *soringê* xweya dikir** (Cankurd: RN2 56 [1998]12) He had lost a lot of blood, and the snow he was lying on resembled *red madder*. {also: sorink (GF-2); [sorink] سـوريـنـك (JJ); <soring> سـۆرنـگ (Hej)} = Sor r̄onyas ڕۆنـیـاس [RN2/Qzl/A/IFb/GF/Hej/ZF3//JJ//FS] <batov>

sorink سۆرِنك (GF/JJ) = madder. See **soring**.

sorişk سۆرِشك (AA/OK) = esophagus. See **sorîçk**.

sorî سۆری (K/GF) = redness. See **sorayî**.

sorîçik سـۆریـچِـك (A)/s̱orîçik صـۆریـچِـك (HH) = esophagus. See **sorîçk**.

sorîçk سـۆریـچـك/**s̱orîçk** صـۆریـچـك [FS] *f.* **(-a;-ê).** esophagus, gullet. {also: sorişk (AA/OK); sorîçik (A); sorsorik (GF/OK-2/Kmc-7); sorsork (AA-2/A-2)/s̱ors̱ork (FS-2); sûrîçk (K); <s̱orîçik> صوریچك (HH)} {syn: zengelûk [3]} Sor sûrênçik سووریێنچك/sûrêne سوورێنه [Zeb/IFb/BF/FS//AA/OK//RF]

sorîk سۆریك (Ak) = measles. See **sorik**.

sorsorik سـۆرسـۆرِك (GF/OK/Kmc-7) = esophagus. See **sorîçk**.

sorsork سۆرسۆرك (AA/A)/s̱ors̱ork صۆرصۆرك (FS) = esophagus. See **sorîçk**.

soryas سـۆریـاس *f.* **(-a;-ê).** *type of plant*: asphodel [T çiriş] (Prw), has head like an onion, is sticky [çir̄], glue is made from it (Zeb); wild garlic (CB/Hej); mountain garlic (GF); haemanthus hybridus [Ar başal al-ḥanš بصل الحنش] (AA); edible plant put in rice or bulgur [savar] (Dh/Hej). {also: soryaz (IFb/GF/OK/CB/AA); suryaz (CB-2); <s̱oryaz> صـوریـاز (HH/FS); <sorpaz سـۆرپـاز/soryas سۆریاس/soryaz سۆریاز> (Hej)} {syn: gûlik} [Bw/Dh/Zeb/Hej//Prw/IFb/GF/OK/CB/AA//HH/FS] <sîr; şîrêz>

soryaz سۆریاز (IFb/GF/OK/CB/AA)/s̱oryaz صۆریاز (HH/FS) = asphodel. See **soryas**.

sosin سـۆسِـن *f.* **(-a;-ê).** 1) lily, bot. *Lilium*; blue fragrant flower (HH); 2) *woman's name*. {also: sîsin (FS); [sosin] سـوسـن (JJ); <sûsin> سـوسـن (HH)} < Ar sawsan سـوسـن = 'lily of the valley'; Sor sosen سۆسەن = 'autumn crocus' [Z-1/K/A/IFb/B/JJ/GF/TF//HH//FS] <gul; kulîlk>

sosiret سـۆسِـرەت (Z-2) = marvel, wonder; shame, disgrace. See **sosret**.

sosret سـۆسـرەت *f.* **(-a;).** 1) {syn: 'ecêb} marvel, wonder, strange and wondrous thing (IF/JJ); a person or thing whose appearance is ridiculous or peculiar (IFb): **•Vê 'ecêba giran, *sosireta* mezin bi ç'e'vê xwe dibîne** (Z-2) He sees that marvel, great *wonder* with his own eyes--*(in context, what he saw could also have been a great disgrace, see **[2]**)*; 2) {also: sosretî (B)} {syn: 'et'ib; 'eyb; fedî; fehêt; gosirmet; r̄ûr̄eşî; şerm; şermezarî; xax} shame, disgrace (K): **•Îcar piştê wê *sosreta* mezin ku rovî bi qulingê dike, quling dibêje: ...**

-Ma ev t[i]ştê ku te bi min kir, karê dostan e? (ZZ-3, 259) After that great *shame* that the fox does to the stork, the stork says, ... "Is this thing that you did to me, a deed of friends?"; 3) [*adj.*] shameful, disgraceful (B); 4) strange, unusual: **•Şolêd zor *sosret* û 'ecêb dikin** (FS) They do very *strange* and amazing things. {also: sosiret (Z-2); [sosret] سوسرت (JJ); [2] sosretî (B)} [Z-2//K/IFb/B/JJ/GF/TF/FS]

sosretî سۆسرەتی (B) = shame, disgrace. See **sosret** [2].

sotin سۆتِن/**s̱otin** صۆتِن [M/SK-2/FS] *vt.* **(-soj-/-so-[B]).** 1) {syn: şewitandin} to burn *(vt.) (lit. & fig.)*: **•Agir-alavê dil-ḧinavê Q. birava *disotin*** (Z-1) The fire and flames *burnt* (fig.) the hearts of Q. [and] his brothers **•Agirî cilkên wî *s̱otin*** (FS) The fire burned his clothes; 2) {syn: şewitîn} *in southern dialects, often has intransitive meaning 'to be burnt', also fig. 'to undergo an unpleasant experience (and to have been burnt as a consequence)'*: **•Agir ber-da menzila mêşan, xanîyê wî nîwek *sot*, mêşêt wî, ko zirkête bûn, *sotin*** (SK 35:321) He set fire to the room with the bees. Half of his house *was burnt* and his bees (which were wasps) *were burnt* **•Erê Lorîn, bi mehan e bi vî agirî *disojim*** (K.Bîlen. Meşa jiyanê 96) Yes L., I *have been burning* with this fire [of love for you] for months **•Rojek[ê] kotir gelek xemgîr bo ji-ber kêjikêt xo. ... r̄a-bû, çû nik qelê, ...kotirê got, "Tu nizanî cawa çergê min bo bicûkêt xo *disojît*"** (SK 3:20) One day the pigeon was very sad about her chicks. ...She got up and went to see the crow, ...The pigeon said, "You don't know how my heart *burns* for my chicks"; 3) to be ruined, be lost: **•Ew zû nehat, lewra ger̄a wî *s̱ot*** (FS) He didn't come early, so he lost his turn [lit. 'His turn *(was) burned*']; 4) {syn: biraştin} to roast, broil; 5) {syn: daẍ kirin} to brand (with a branding iron) (IFb). {also: sohtin (A)/s̱ohtin (FS-2); sûtin [3] (A-2); [sotin] سوتن (JJ); <s̱ohtin صوهتن (dis̱oje) (دصوژه)> (HH)} [Pok. k̑ēu-; k̑əu-; k̑ū- 595.] 'to ignite, kindle, burn down' (cf. Gr kaiō καίω = 'to burn') & [Pok. k̑euk- 597.] 'to shine; to glow; to be bright or white' (cf. Skt √śuc [śōcati] = 'to shine, flame, gleam, glow, burn' & śōka- *m.* = 'sorrow, anguish, pain'): O Ir *sauk- (Tsb 40): Av saok- (*pres.* saoča-); Sgd *pres. stem* sōc-; P sūxtan سوختن (-sūz-) (سوز) = 'to burn' (vi.) but (vt.) in Afghanistan; Sor sûtan سووتان = 'to burn (vi.)' & sûtandin سووتاندِن = 'to burn, eliminate (vt.)'; SoK suzanın (Fat 565); Hau sotey (soç-) *vi.* (M4); cf. also Mid P sōg (M3) = 'burning, combustion' & P sūg سوگ = 'sorrow, grief' [BX/Z-1/K/JB3/IFb/B/JJ/SK/GF/BK//M/FS//A//HH] <kuzirandin; sûtin; şewitîn>

sovekar سۆڤەکار (F) = swimmer. See **sobek'ar**.

sovek'arî سۆڤەکاری (F/Rwn) = swimming. See **sobahî**.

sovet سۆڤەت (EP-7) = (soviet) advice, counsel. See **sovêt**.

sovêt سۆڤێت *f.* **(-a;-ê).** (soviet) advice, counsel: **-T'ifaqa Sovêtê** (B) Soviet Union. {also: sovet (EP-7); sovît; sovîyêt; sovyat; sowyet (IFb)} < Rus sovet совет [EP-7/K/B//IFb] <şîret>

Sovêtîstan سۆڤێتیستان *f.* **(-a;-ê).** USSR, the Soviet Union: **•*Sovêtistana* berê** (AAA-Cankurd.jpg 13.vii.2010) The former Soviet Union. {also: Sovîyêtîstan; Sovyetistan; Sowyetistan (IFb)} {syn: T'ifaqa Sovêtê} [K/JB3//IFb]

sovît سۆڤیت = (soviet) advice, counsel. See **sovêt**.

sovîyêt سۆڤییێت = (soviet) advice, counsel. See **sovêt**.

Sovîyêtîstan سۆڤییێتیستان = Soviet Union. See **Sovêtîstan**.

sovyat سۆڤیات = (soviet) advice, counsel. See **sovêt**.

Sovyetistan سۆڤیەتِستان = Soviet Union. See **Sovêtîstan**.

sowyet سۆویەت (IFb) = (soviet) advice, counsel. See **sovêt**.

Sowyetistan سۆویەتِستان (IFb) = Soviet Union. See **Sovêtîstan**.

soxte سۆختە (IFb) = religious student. See **suxte**.

soyar سۆیار (Ba2) = rider. See **siwar**.

soz سۆز *m./f.(Zeb/Hk)* **(-ê/-a;).** promise, one's word: **-soz dan** = to give one's word, to promise: **•Lê Memê t'u *soz nedida* hevalêd xwe** (Z-1) But Mem *didn't promise* his friends anything **•Mîr S. *sozê* Zînê jî *da* Ç'ekan** (Z-1) Prince S. *promised* Zin *to* Chekan [in marriage]; **-sozê xwe kirin yek** (K) to agree, be of one mind {syn: qîma xwe anîn}. {also: [souz] سوز (JJ); <soz> سوز (HH)} < T söz = 'word, utterance; promise' [Z-1/K/IFb/B/HH/GF/TF//JJ]

Spanî سپانی *adj.* Spanish. {also: Espanî (Wkt-2); Espanyayî (Wkt-2); Ispanî (Wkt-2); Ispanyayî (Wkt-2); Îspanî (IFb/SS)} Sor Îspanî ئیسپانی [Wkt/BF//IFb/SS]

spartek سـپـارتـەك *f.* **(-a;-ê).** homework, assignment: **•Îro** ***spartekên*** **me gelek in** (Fêrkera Kurdî, Asta destpêkê, 13) Today we have a lot of *homework* **•Ji kerema xwe re binihêrin … ka zaroka we** ***spartekên*** **xwe hemû çêkirine an na!** (Schule- Informationen für Eltern/Dibistan - Agahî ji bo dê û bavan, 44) Please look and see … whether or not your child has done all of his/her *homework.* [(neol)ZF/Wkt]

spartin I سـپـارتـن *vt.* **(-spêr-/-sipêr-[B]).** to entrust, commit, hand over, deliver (s.o./stg. to s.o.): **•Min** ***tu sipartî*** **xwedê** (L) I *have entrusted you* to God *[parting formula]* [cf. T alla[ha]ısmarladık] {also: sipartin (L/IFb/GF/BK); [sipartin] سـپـارتـیـن (JJ); <spartin سپارتن (dispîre) (دسپیره)> (HH)} Cf. P sepordan سـپـردن (-sepār-) (سـپـار); Sor sipardin سِپاردِن (-sipêr-) [K/A/JB3//L/IFb/B/JJ/GF/BK]

spartin II سـپـارتـن (B/JJ/CS) = to lean, support. See **p'esartin**.

spas سـپـاس *f.* **(-a;).** thanks: **-spas kirin** (K/IFb/GF)/ **spasîya (yekî) kirin** (ZF3) to thank: **•Ez spasiya we dikim = Ez we spas dikim** (Wkt) I thank you **•Ez** ***supasa te dikim*** **ku te harîkariya min kir** (FS) I *thank you* for helping me; **-spas xweş** (Wkt/ memrise/tirşik.net) You're welcome. {also: sipas (K-2/ A/IFb-2/GF/TF/OK-2); spasî (ZF3-2/WKt-2); supas (BF/FS)} <P sepās سپاس = 'thanks(giving); praise'; Sor sipas سِپاس/supas سوپاس; not related to Rus spasibo спасибо (cf. спасти spasti = 'to rescue') [(neol)K/IFb/OK/ZF3/ Wkt//A/GF/TF//BF/FS]

spasdar سپاسدار *adj.* grateful, thankful: **•Xisûsî** ***ji*** **we re gelekî** ***spasdar*** **im, ku hûn bi Welat riya me ya azadî û serxwebûnê ronahî dikin** (Wlt 2:59, 2) I am especially *grateful to* you for lighting our way to freedom and independence through Welat [the newspaper]. {also: sipasdar (TF); supasdar (BF)} {syn: minetdar} <P sepāsdār سـپـاسـدار; Sor sipaskar سِپاسکار/sipasguzar سِپاسگوزار {spasdarî} [(neol)Wlt/OK//TF//BF] <bê nan û xwê; spas>

spasdarî سـپـاسـداری *f.* **(-ya;-yê).** gratefulness, gratitude, thankfulness: **•Ez** ***spasdarîya*** **xwe ya bê hed û hesab didime we hemûyan** (hekar.net 24.v.2017) I give you all my boundless *gratitude.* Sor sipasdarî سِپاسداری [IFb/OK/ZF3] <spasdar>

spasî سپاسی (ZF3/Wkt) = thanks. See **spas**.

spehî سـپـەهی *adj.* pretty, beautiful, handsome: **•Wî serê xo şûşt û xwe** ***speḧî*** **kir** (FS) He took a shower and made himself look *handsome.* {also: espehî (L); sipehî (IFb-2/TF); sipeyî (IFb-2); speḧî (FS); [sipehi] سـپـهـی (JJ); <speḧî> سـپـحـی (HH)} {syn: bedew; cindî; gurcî; k'eleş III; xweşik} Cf. Ar ṣabīḥ صـبـیـح = 'handsome', pl. ṣibāḥ صـبـاح; Cf. NENA spaj [spāy] (Urmia - Polotsky) = 'well, good' & spáhīn (Zakho - Polotsky) = 'beautiful, handsome' {spehîtî; [sipehiti] سپهیتی (JJ)} [L//BX/K/A/JB3/IFb/GF//JJ/TF//HH/ FS] <delal>

spehîtî سـپـەهـیـتـی *f.* **(-ya;-yê).** beauty. {also: sipehîtî (IFb/TF); [sipehiti] سـپـهـیـتـی (JJ)} {syn: bedewtî; xweşikî} [K/JB3//IFb/JJ/TF] <spehî>

speḧî سپەحی (FS/HH) = beautiful. See **spehî**.

spenax سپەناخ (Wkt) = spinach. See **spînax**.

spêd•e سپێدە *f.* **(;•ê).** (early) morning; sunrise, dawn: **•*Spêde* baş!** (Bw) Good *morning*! **•*spêdê*** (JB1-A) the following *morning* **•S̲ubahî** ***sipêdê*** **wextê em biçîne ser şolî, ew k'esê ewwilî bêt, di wêrê r̄a biborit, emê girîn** (M-Zx #774) Tomorrow *at dawn*, when we go to work, we shall seize the first person who comes along and passes by there. {also: sipêde (IFb-2/GF-2); [spēda] سـپـیـدا (JJ)} {syn: berbang; elind; ferec; hingûr [1]; segur; serê sibê; siḧar; şebeq} Cf. P sefīde-dem سـفـیـده‌دم/ sepīde-dem سپیده‌دم = 'dawn'; Sor sipîde سِپیده = 'first glow of dawn' [Bw/K/IFb/(JB1-A)/SK/GF/OK//JJ] <sibeh; spî I>

spêhîdar سپێهیدار (A) = poplar tree. See **sipindar**.

spênax̂ سپێناغ (FS) = spinach. See **spînax**.

spêne سپێنە (Zeb/IFb/ZF3) = wedge. See **sipêne**.

spêtirk سپێترك (Snd) = ladder; stairs. See **pêstirk**.

spih سپە (JB3/IFb) = louse (pl. lice). See **spî II**.

spinax سپناخ (GF) = spinach. See **spînax**.

spindar سپندار (GF) = poplar. See **sipindar**.

sping سـپـنـگ (A/IFb/OK/FS) = meadow salsify. See **siping**.

spink سپنك (EŞ) = meadow salsify. See **siping**.

spî I سـپـی *adj.* white: **-spî kirin** (Bw) to peel *(e.g., a banana)* {syn: ji qelp kirin}. {also: sipî I (AB/A/ B/F/GF/TF); [sipi سـپـی/ispi اسـپـی] (JJ); <sipî> سـپـی (HH)} {syn: sîs [1]} [Pok. 3. k̑u̯ei- 628.] 'white; to shine': Skt śveta- ; Proto Ir *su̯aita-: Av spaēta-; Sgd sp'yt [spēt]; Pahl spēt; P sefīd سـفـیـد/ sepīd سپید; Sor sipî سپی; Za sıpe/sıpe (Todd/Mal); cf. also Arm spitak (W: sbidag) սպիտակ (<Pahl/ Mid P); Old Eng hwīt --> Eng white {spîtayî; spîtî; [spīyātī سـپـیـاتـی/sipitàï سپیتای] (JJ); <sipîtahî> سـپـیـتـاهـی (HH)} [K/JB3/IFb/SK//AB/F/A/B/JJ/HH/GF/TF] <ç'al I; çîl-sipî; qerqaş>

spî II سپی *f.* **(-a;-yê).** louse (pl. lice), zool. *Pediculus*. {also: sipih (IFb-2/TF); sipî II (A/B); spih (JB3/IFb); [sipi سپی/ispi اسپی] (JJ); <siph> سپه (HH)} Cf. Southern Tati dialects (all *f.*): Chali, Takestani, Eshtehardi, & Xiaraji espeja; Sagz-abadi esbeja (Yar-shater); P šepeš شپش; Sor espê ئەسپێ; Za işpij *f.* (Todd)/espici & espiji & ispide *f.* (Mal); Hau heşpişî *f.* (M4) [K/Msr//A/B/JJ//JB3/IFb//HH//TF] <gene; kêç'; nûtik; r̄işk>

spîç'al سپیچال (K/HCK/ZF3) = bedsheet. See **sipîçal**.

spîçik سپیچك (IFb) = egg white. See **spîlik I**.

spîçok سپیچۆك (IFb) = egg white. See **spîlik I**.

spîç'olekî سپیچۆلەکی (K2-Fêrîk) = pale. See **spîç'olkî**.

spîç'olkî سپیچۆلکی *adj.* pale, faded: **•Li r̄ûê Nûrê *spîç'olekî* dinihêr̄im** (K2-Fêrîk) I look at Nur's *pale* face; **-spîç'olkî bûn** (K/F/B) to pale, fade (vi.). {also: sipîçolk (A/GF); sipîç'olkî (B/F); spîç'olekî (K2-Fêrîk)} [K2-Fêrîk//K//A/GF//F/B]

spîdar سپیدار (A/JJ) = poplar tree. See **sipindar**.

spîk سپیك (K) = egg white. See **spîlik I**.

spîlik I سپیلِك *f.* **(-a;).** albumen, egg white, white *(of egg)*: **-spîlka hêke** (Dh) do. {also: s[i]pîçik (IFb); sipîk (OK/GF-2); sipîl[i]k (GF); spîçok (IFb-2); spîk (K); [sipik] سپیك (JJ); <spîlik> سپیلك (Hej)} Sor sipêne سپێنە [Bw/Dh/Hej/BF//GF//IFb//OK/JJ//K] <hêk; zerik II>

spîlik II سپیلِك *f.* **(-a;).** white meat *(of poultry)*: **•*spîlka* mirîşkê** (FS) white meat of chicken. {also: <spîlik> سپیلك (Hej)} [Bw/Hej/FS] <goşt; mirîşk>

spîndar سپیندار (A/IFb/JJ/HH/SK/ZF3/FS) = poplar tree. See **sipindar**.

spînax سپیناخ *f.* **(-a;-ê).** spinach, bot. *Spinacia oleracea*: **•*Spînax* rêgirî li nesaxîyên penceşêrê dike** (waarmedia 02.ii.2017) *Spinach* prevents cancer. {also: espanax (IFb); espenaq (A); êspenax (Wkt-2); îspanax (Kmc); îspenax (K/ZF/G/CS/Wkt-2); îspînax (Wkt-2); spenax (Wkt-2); spênax̄ (FS); spinax (GF); spînax̄ (Şingal); spînok (FS-2); [ispanak اسپانك/spink سپنك] (JJ)} Ar sabānix سبانخ; T ispanak; P isfināj اسفناج; Sor sipênax سپێناخ/sipînax̄ سپیناغ [Şng//FS//RZ/Wkt/SS//K/ZF/G/CS//Kmc//IFb//A]

spînax̄ سپیناغ (Şng) = spinach. See **spînax**.

spînk سپینك (GF) = meadow salsify. See **siping**.

spînok سپینۆك (FS) = spinach. See **spînax**.

spîtayî سپیتایی *f.* **(-ya;).** whiteness: **•*Spîyatîya* befrê ciwan e** (FS) The whiteness of the snow is lovely. {also: sipîtî (TF); sipîyatî (BF); spîtî (K); spîyatî (GF/FS); [spīyātī سپیاتی/sipitàï سپیتای] (JJ); <sipîtahî> سپیتاهی (HH)} [K//JJ/GF/FS//HH//TF] <spî I>

spîtî سپیتی (K) = whiteness. See **spîtayî**.

spîyatî سپیاتی (GF/JJ/FS) = whiteness. See **spîtayî**.

sqûmat سقوومات (ZZ) = misfortune. See **siqûmat**.

stam ستام (RZ/ZF3) = the common cold. See **sitam**.

stambûlî ستامبوولی (Qzl-->Nsb) = tomato. See **stembolî**.

standin ستاندِن *vt.* **(-stîn- / -stên-).** 1) {syn: girtin} to take by force, seize, grab: **•Mamê R̄ezgo çend tiştêt ji lawê namerd *standibûn*, hemî dane wî** (SK 37:333) Mam Razgo gave the cowardly youth all the things which he *had taken* from him **•*Wê* qîza te îja ji te *bistîne*** (L) He *will take* your daughter from you this time **•Xelkê wî gundî qewî 'ezman-dirêj û cablos û bê-şerm in, diçine hemî cîyan, diger̄yên, dixazin û eger mumkin bît didizin û *distînin*** (SK 12:114) The people of that village are very impudent and cunning and shameless, they go everywhere and wander about begging and, if possible, stealing and *taking things*; **-jin standin** = to marry a woman *(said of a man)* {syn: jin anîn}; **-tol standin** (K/JJ/GF/OK) [+**ji**]: a) to take revenge (on), avenge o.s. (on), pay (s.o.) back for: **•[Û belku ez dê vê *tolê* bi izna Xwedê *ji* Zeman Xanê Ayrûmî *bistînim*]** (JR #39,120) And perhaps with God's permission I *will take revenge on* Zeman Khan the Ayrumi; 2) {syn: wergirtin} to obtain, get, receive; 3) {syn: k'ir̄în} to buy. {also: stendin (A/B); [istandin استاندین/sitandin ستاندین] (JJ); <standin سطاندن (distîne) (دسطینه)> (HH)} Cf. P setādan ستادن (-setān-) (ستان); Sor sanḍin ساندِن (-sên-)/ estandin ئەستاندِن (-estên-); SoK sin-/sand-, etc. = 'to buy' (Fat 356); Hau esay (esan-) *vt.* = 'to take, buy' (M4). *The basic meaning is 'to take by force', but the other meanings are under influence of T almak = 'to take, obtain, buy'* [K/JB3/IFb/SK/JB1-S/GF//HH//A/B//JJ]

stang ستانگ (GF/Hej) = hornet. See **stêng**.

star ستار (ZF3) = roof; shelter. See **sit'ar**.

steîrk ستەئیرك = star. See **stêr I**.

stekan ستەکان (B/GF) = tea glass. See **îstekan**.

stembolî ستەمبۆلی *f.* **().** tomato. {also: stambûlî (Qzl-->Nsb)} {syn: bacanê sor; firingî; şamik} < İstanbul [Nsb//Xurs (between Qzl & Mardin)] stendin ستەنڎِن (A/B) = to take; to receive; to buy. See **standin**.

stewil ستەوِل, f. (JB3) = horse stable. See **stewl**.

stewir ستەوِر *adj.* sterile, infertile, barren (of animals): **•ç'êleka *stewr*** (B) *sterile* cow. {also: stewr (JB3/IFb/B/RZ); stuwîr (Zeb); [isteour] استور (JJ)} {syn: bêber} {stewrayî; stewrî; [isteouri] استوری (JJ)} [K/A//JB3/IFb/B/RZ//JJ] <bêweç; bêzuřet; xirş>

stewl ستەول *m.(K)/f.(JB3)* **(-ê/ ;).** stable *(for horses)*. {also: sitewil (IFb); stewil, f. (JB3)} {syn: pange [1]; t'ewlexane} Cf. Ar iṣṭabl إسطبل [K/GF//JB3//IFb] <extexane; naxir>

stewr ستەور (JB3/IFb/B/RZ) = sterile. See **stewir**.

stewrayî ستەورایی (B) = sterility. See **stewrî**.

stewrî ستەوری *f.* **(-ya;).** sterility, barrenness, infertility (of animals). {also: stewrayî (B); [isteouri] استوری (JJ)} [K/IFb//B//JJ] <stewir>

steyr ستەیر (K) = star. See **stêr I**.

steyrk ستەیرك (B) = star. See **stêr I**.

steyrnas ستەیرناس (HCK/K) = astronomer; astrologer. See **stêrnas**.

steyrnasî ستەیرناسی (HCK/K) = astronomy; astrology. See **stêrnasî**.

stêng ستێنگ *m.* **().** hornet: **•Tijî şkeftekî / hespêt enî çal in [*Stêng*]** (AZ 61:20) A cave full of / horses with dented foreheads *[rdl.; ans.: hornets]*. {also: stang (GF); [stenk] ستنك (JJ); <stang ستانگ/steng ستەنگ/stîng ستینگ> (Hej)} {syn: moz I} [AZ/IFb/OK//JJ//GF/Hej] <zilketk>

stêr I ستێر *f.* **(-a;-ê).** star: **•Ezman bi *stêran* dixemile** (AB) The sky is adorned with *stars* **•Ḧesabê tav û teyrê çolê û *steyrkê* 'ezmana hene, ḧesabê minara t'une** (EP-7:7:186) One could count the beasts and birds of the wilderness and *the stars* in the heavens, but one could not count the minarets **•*steîrkeke* geş** (EP-7) a bright *star*; **-stêra gerok** (SS) = planet. See **gerestêr**. {also: estere; estêr (A-2); estîr(e); hesterik (MK); sitêrik (TF); steîrk; steyr (K); steyrk (B); stêrk I; stêwêrk (FK-kk-13); [istirk] استرك (JJ); <stêr> ستیر (HH)} [Pok 2. stĕr- 1027.] 'star': Skt tṛ́/stṛ́; Av *acc. sg.* stārəm, *gen.* stārō; Mid P stārag (M3); Southern Tati dialects (all *f.*): Chali sāri; Takestani āstāria; Eshtehardi esdāra; Ebrahim-abadi & Sagz-abadi estāria (Yar-shater); P setāreh ستاره; Sor estêre ئەستێرە; Za istare *m.* (Todd); Hau hesare *m.* (M4); cf. also Lat stella; Gr astēr ἀστήρ; Arm astł աստղ [AB/A/JB3/IFb/HH/SK/GF//K//B//JJ//FK-kk-13] <hîv; kadiz; Qurix; řoj; şev I>

stêř II ستێر *m./f.(ZF)* **().** bedding arranged in a pile and covered with a carpet [cf. T yüklük]; "Every Yezidi home must have a *stêr*. Generally installed in the living room, facing east, the *stêr* is a pile of mattresses and blankets placed on rocks or on a box-mattress. It is covered with a carpet or a sheet which is removed at night. Open from sunset to sunrise, the *stêr* "replaces the sun in its absence" … The *stêr* is hallowed. It is at once a visual representation of the home and a protector of its property. The Yezidis hide valuable items in the *stêr*," from: Estelle Amy de la Bretèque. *Paroles mélodisées : récits épiques et lamentations chez les Yézidis d'Arménie* (Paris: Classiques Garnier, [2013]), p. 159 (photos of *stêr* on p. 160): **•Şîrqîn ji 'ezmîn hat, birûskê li 'erdê xist. … Lênihêřî p'erçe ḧesinê wa. Eva ḧesina kire hevana xwe … derxist da jina xwe … Jinê ḧesin hilda, avîte binê t'êřê, da bin *stêř*, bira bisekine** (K'oroxlî, 141) A noise came from the sky, lightning struck the earth. … He saw a piece of iron there. He put this iron in his sack … took it out and gave it to his wife … The woman picked up the iron, threw it under the saddlebag, put it under the *stêr*, so that it should stay there. [AmydelaBretèque/K'oroxlî/K/B/ZF] <kulîn II>

stêrenas ستێرەناس (IFb) = astronomer; astrologer. See **stêrnas**.

stêrenasî ستێرەناسی (IFb) = astronomy; astrology. See **stêrnasî**.

stêrik ستێرك (Haz) = tears. See **hêstir I**.

stêrk I ستێرك = star. See **stêr I**.

stêrk II ستێرك (Msr) = tears. See **hêstir I**.

stêrnas ستێرناس *m.* **().** 1) astronomer; 2) astrologer: **•Brê *steyrnas*, go: -- Carkê steyrka qîzapa me binêře k'a çawane?** (HCK-5, #41, 232) Hey, *astrologer*: "Why don't you look at our [female] cousin's star, and see how she will fare?". {also: sitêrnas (FJ/TF); steyrnas (HCK/K); stêrenas (IFb); [istirk-chinas] استرك شناس (JJ)} Cf. P sitāre´šinās ستارهشناس = 'astronomer; astrologer'; Sor estêrenas ئەستێرەناس = 'astronomer' & estêrejmêr ئەستێرەژمێر = 'astrologer' {stêrnasî} [HCK/K//GF/SS//FJ/TF//IFb]

stêrnasî ستێرناسی *f.* **(-ya;-yê).** 1) astronomy; 2) astrology. {also: steyrnasî (HCK/K); stêrenasî

(IFb)} Cf. P sitāre'šināsī ســـتـــارەشـــنـــاســـى = 'astronomy; astrology'; Sor estêrenasî ئـەســتـێـرەنـاسـى = 'astronomy' [HCK/K//GF/SS//IFB] <stêrnas>

stêwêrk ستێوێرك (FK-kk-13) = star. See **stêr I**.

stiran I ستِران *vt.* **(-stirê- / -stir-** [JB3/B]**/-stêr-**[IF]**).** 1) {syn: k'ilam gotin; lêlandin} to sing: •**Ew zef baş *distirê*** (F) He *sings* very well •**Ji xwe re li tembûrê dixe û *distirê*** (L) He plays to himself on the tambour and *sings*; 2) [*f.***(-a;-ê).**] {syn: k'ilam} song (Bw): -**stranan gotin** (Bw) to sing. {also: sitirandin (TF); stirandin; stirîn (-stir-[JB3]/-stêr-[IFb]) (JB3/IFb); stran I (-strê-) (K/GF/Bw); [istiran استران/istirin استرين] (JJ); <sitran> ستران (HH)} [Pok. 1. ḱleu- 605.] 'to hear': Av *pres. stem* srāwaiia- = 'to proclaim, recite'; P sorūdan سرودن; Sor sitran سِـتـران = 'lay, ballad, song'. For other examples of str- from original *sr- See **stirî I** & **strû**. [L/F/A/B//JB3/IFb//JJ//K/GF/Bw//HH//TF] <k'ilam; mûzîk>

stiran II ستِران *vt.* **(-stirê-).** to knead *(dough)*: •**Hevîr çiqasî *bistirêyî*, nanê wê te'm dibe** (Dz-#664) The more you *knead* the dough, the tastier the bread will be *[prv.]* •**Memê, eva heye Cizîra Botane, / hevîrtirşkê xwe ji xûnê *strane*** (EP-7) Mem, this is Jizirah of Bohtan, / [Its inhabitants] *knead[ed]* their dough with blood. {also: histiran (BK); sitirihan[din] (TF); stirhandin (GF-2); stran II (K/EP-7); strandin (IFb/GF)} {syn: hevîr kirin; şêlan [1]} [B//EP-7/K//IFb/GF//TF//BK] <hevîr; hevîrtirş>

stiranbêj ستِرانبێژ *m.* **(-ê;).** singer. {syn: şaîr [2]} {also: stiranvan (A); stranbêj (K/IFb/GF/ZF); stranvan (GF-2)} [K/IFb/GF/ZF//A]

stirandin ستِراندِن = to sing. See **stiran I**.

stiranvan ستِرانڤان (A) = singer. See **stiranbêj**.

stirhandin ستِرهاندِن (GF) = to knead. See **stiran II**.

stirih ستِرِه (GF) = animal horn. See **strû**.

stirî I ستِرى *f.(K)/m.(B/JB3)* **().** 1) {syn: dirî; k[']elem II; şewk[3]} thorn; thornbush: •[ẖwîna bákō awân de-bû dä qabrê mámu u zīnê dârki istrî] (HM) Báko Awân's blood became a thornbush on the grave of Mámu and Zînê; -**sturî dayîn** (B) to take ill (of cattle); 2) {syn: dirik; dirîmok (Haz); tûreşk} bramble, blackberry, bot. *Rubus fruticosus* [T böğürtlen] (IF/JJ) [sturî/strî]; 3) {syn: dasî [1]} fishbone (Bw). {also: istrî (HM); sitirî (IF-2); strî I (K/JB3/IF-2); stroh; sturî I (B/IF-2); sturu I; [istiri استرى/stiri سترى] (JJ); <sitrî> سترى (HH)} [Pok. 1. ḱer- 574.] 'horn, head; with derivatives referring to horned animals, horn-shaped objects, and projecting parts': Sor estirî ئـەسـتِـرى/hestirî هـەسـتِـرى = *name applied to varieties of thistles and thorny shrubs. For another example of str- from original *sr- See **stiran I**.* See: Alan J. Nussbaum. *Head and Horn in Indo-European* (Berlin: W. de Gruyter, 1986), 305 p. [A/IFb/Bw//HM//K/JB3//B//HH] See also **strû**.

stirî II ستِرى (K) = animal horn. See **strû**.

stirîn ستِرین (-stir-[JB3]/-stêr-[IFb]) (JB3/IFb) = to sing. See **stiran I**.

stirû ستِروو (GF) = animal horn. See **strû**.

stî ستى *f.* **(-ya;-yê).** 1) lady, madam: -**Stîya Zîn** (Z-2) Lady Zîn, in the folk romance Mem û Zîn; 2) wife of a priest or imam (K); wife or daughter of a nobleman (beg) or religious personage (B); 3) a *woman's name* (K); Zîn's sister in some versions of the folk romance Mem û Zîn (IFb). {also: [siti] ستى (JJ)} < clq Ar sittī ستّي = 'my lady' [Z-2/K/JB3/IFb//B/JJ]

sto ستۆ (JB3/IFb/OK)/s̱to صطۆ (M-Zx/JB1-A) = nape, neck. See **stû**.

stol ستۆل *f.* **(-a;).** navy, fleet *(of ships)*: •**serfermandarê *stola* emerîkanî** (RN) the commander-in-chief of the American *navy*. < Ar usṭūl أسطول = 'fleet' < Gr stolos στόλος = 'navy, fleet' [RN/K/GF] <cengkeştî; gemî; keşt[î]>

stow ستۆو = nape, neck. See **stû**.

stran I ستران (-strê-) (K/GF/Bw) = to sing; song. See **stiran I**.

stran II ستران (K/EP-7) = to knead (dough) . See **stiran II**.

stranbêj سترانبێژ (K/IFb/GF/ZF) = singer. See **stiranbêj**.

strandin ستراندِن (IFb/GF) = to knead. See **stiran II**.

stranvan سترانڤان (GF) = singer. See **stiranbêj**.

strî I سترى (K/JB3/IFb) = thorn. See **stirî I**.

strî II سترى (K) = animal horn. See **strû**.

strîtêl ستریتێل *pl.* **(-ên;-an).** barbed wire: •**Neco deh deqeyan şûnde wekî marekî teyar di nava tepink û *strîtêlên* sînor re xwe gihandibû wî alî** (Nofa, 91) 10 minutes later, like a snake N. got himself to the other side despite the mines and *barbed wire* •**Salên 80yî li ser sînorê Nisêbîn û Qamişloyê.. Kurdên ku xizmên hevdu ne û ji ber *strîtêlan* nekariye werin cem hev** (Kürtçe Soru ve Bilgi Sayfası-FB 17.vii.2015) In the 1980's on the border of Nusaybin and Qamishli, Kurds could not reach their relatives [on the other side] because of *the barbed wire.* < st[i]rî = 'thorn' + t'êl = 'wire' [Nofa/ Kürtçe Soru ve Bilgi Sayfası]

stroh ستڕۆھ = thorn. See **stirî I**.

stru سترو = animal horn. See **strû**.

strû ستروو *m.* **(-[y]ê;).** horn *(of an animal)*, antler: •**Ezê jî *strûê* xwe tûjkim** (J) As for me, I will sharpen my *horns* •**[Zanî ku mar kûvîyek dabeland lê *strûyên*** [sterène] **wî neçûne xwarê û mane li gewrîya wî da û jê aciz bû]** (BG, 25) He understood that the snake had swallowed a wild animal, but its *horns* had not gone down and had stayed in his throat and he was suffering from this; -**ḧeywanetê sturî** (B) horned animals. {also: sitirih (IFb-2/TF); stirih (GF-2); stirî II; stirû (GF); strî II (K); stru; sture (F); sturî II (B); sturu II; ûstûrî; [oustouri] استوری (JJ); <stroh> سطروه (HH); [stero] (BG)} {syn: qoç'} [Pok. 1. ḱer-574.] 'horn, head; with derivatives referring to horned animals, horn-shaped objects, and projecting parts': Skt śṛṅga- *n.*; Av srū-/sruuā- *f.* = 'fingernail; horn'; Mid P srū = 'horn, nail, prong'; P sarū/surū سرو/sarūn سرون; Za istre *m.* (Todd)/ istere & istrî & iştirîm. (Mal); cf. also Lat cornu *n.*; Gr keras κέρας (*gen.* keratos κέρατος); Germ Horn. for another example of str- from original *sr- See **stiran I**. See: Alan J. Nussbaum. *Head and Horn in Indo-European* (Berlin: W. de Gruyter, 1986), 305 p. [J/JB3/IFb/OK//GF//K//F//B//JJ//HH/ /TF] See also **stirî I**. <k'ol IV>

strû-şkestî ستروو شکەستی *adj.* with a broken horn *(of animals)*. [EP-4] <strû>

stu ستو (K/L/B) = nape, neck. See **stû**.

stukir ستوکِر (K/SK/OK) = nape of neck. See **stukur**.

stukur ستوکور *f.* **(-a;-ê).** nape of neck: •**Des[t] di *sukirê* werand ku dê maçî ket** (M-Ak #534, 242) He put his arm around 'her' *neck*, intending to kiss 'her' •**Marî jî xo li *stukira* r̄îwî aland** (SK 2:11) And the snake wound itself round the fox's *neck*. {also: histukur (IFb-2); stukir (K-2/SK/OK); stûkurk (IFb-2/Kmc-6); sukir (M-Ak); sukur II (Ak); [oustoukour] استوکور (JJ)} {syn: paştû; p'ate I} [Ak//M-Ak//K/IFb/B//Kmc-6//SK/OK//JJ] <stû>

sture ستوره (F) = animal horn. See **strû**.

sturî I ستوری (B/IF) = thorn. See **stirî I**.

sturî II ستوری (B) = animal horn. See **strû**.

sturu I ستورو = thorn. See **stirî I**.

sturu II ستورو = animal horn. See **strû**.

stuwîr ستوویر (Zeb) = sterile. See **stewir**.

stuxar ستوخار = miserable, unhappy. See **stûxwar**.

stuxwar ستوخوار (K) = miserable, unhappy. See **stûxwar**.

stuxwarî ستوخواری (K) = misery, unhappiness, distress. See **stûxwarî**.

stû ستوو *m.* **(-[y]ê;).** neck, nape of the neck: •**Keçelok pişta *stuê* xwe xorand û hat** (L) Kechelok scratched the back of his head [lit. '*neck*'] [in bewilderment] and came; -**stûyê xwe dirêj kirin** = to crane one's neck to see stg. [lit. 'to stretch out one's neck']: •[The villain Beko is about to get what he deserves. He is brought to Mem and Zin's open grave, and sees the smile of love on their faces] **Bek'o *styê xwe dirêj kir*, go: "Mîr ... qey tê bêjî r̄azane"** (Z-1) Beko *craned his neck* [to look], said, "Prince ... it's as if [lit. 'maybe you would say'] they're asleep." {also: sto (JB3/IFb-2/OK-2)/sto (M-Zx/JB1-A); stow; stu (K/L/B); stûh (JB1-S-2/OK-2); ustî (Kg); ûstî; ûstû (JR); [oustou] استو (JJ); <stû> سطو (HH)} Sor esto ئەستۆ [IFb/JB1-S/OK//L/K/B//JB3//M-Zx/JB1-A//HH/ /Kg//JJ]

stûh ستووھ (JB1-S/OK) = nape, neck. See **stû**.

stûkurk ستووکورك (IFb/Kmc-6) = nape of neck. See **stukur**.

stûn ستوون *f.* **(-a;-ê).** column, pillar; pole, post: •***Stûneke* pêşyêye / *stûna* pêşin zîvîye** (EP-5, #2, #3) There is a *pole* in front / the front *pole* is silver. {also: sitûn (F); [istoun استون/stún ستون (G)] (JJ)} [Pok. st(h)āu-:st(h)ū- 1008.] 'to stand, place': Skt sthūṇa- = 'column, pillar'; O Ir stūnā- (Ras, p.131): Av stūna- /stunā-; OP stūnā- ; Mid P stūn; P sotūn ستون --> T sütun; Sor sitûn سِتوون/ estûn ئەستوون/hesûn ھەسوون [EP-5/K/IFb/B/SK/GF/OK/ /F//JJ]

stûnî ستوونی *adj.* 1) vertical; 2) {syn: serejêr} down *(in crossword puzzles)*. [Bw/GF/AD] <≠ berwar = çeperast; xaçepirs = xaçerêz>

stûr ستوور *adj.* 1) thick, stout; thick *of round things only* (MK): •...**Lix̄awekî asin dû gez dirêj, gezek pan, bi qeder zenda destî *stûr* bide çêkirin** (SK 33:297) Go and get an iron bridle made, two yards long, a yard wide, and as *thick* as a man's wrist •**Zincîrekî** [sic] **asin, gelek *stûr*, wekî taze ji kûrê înaye der sor bû** (SK 11:108) A very *thick* iron chain, red and sparking as if it had just been brought out of the furnace; 2) thick *(fig.)*, coarse, rough; rude, common, vulgar (JJ): **•...Wextê x̱îret û ḧemîyetê demara me Kurdan gelek *stûr* e ... em Kurd mirina xo ixtiyar dikeyn, nawê kirêt û bê-x̱îretî qebûl nakeyn** (SK 54:624) When we Kurds are full of zeal and indignation our rancor is very *strong* ... We Kurds choose our own death rather than accepting a bad name and dishonor; 3) heavy *(rain, snow)*: **•barîna befreka *stûr*** (Zeb) *heavy* snowfall. {also: sitûr (TF); [oustour استور/stour ستور] (JJ); <stûr> ستور (HH)} [Pok. st-eu-/st-eu̯ə- 1009.] 'massive, firm, thick, broad' <[Pok. stā-:stə- 1004. ff.] 'to stand, to put': Skt sthūrá-/sthūlá- = 'thick'; Av stūra- = 'massive, strong, solid'; P setorg سترگ = 'huge'; Sor estûr ئەستوور {estûrî; êsturayî; stûr[t]î; [oustouri] استورى (JJ)} [K/A/JB3/IFb/HH/JJ/SK/GF/OK/Zeb//TF]

stûrî ستووری *f.* **(-ya;-yê).** 1) thickness: **•Li çiyayê *stûrîya* berfê jî gihêşt 15 santîmetroyê** (trtnuce.com 12.ii.2012) On the mountain *the thickness of* the snow reached 15 cm.; 2) rudeness, coarseness. {also: estûrayî (A); êsturî (A); stûrtî (A); [oustouri] استورى (JJ)} [K/IFb//A//JJ] <stûr>

stûrtî ستوورتی (A) = thickness; coarseness. See **stûrî**.

stûxar ستووخار (Z-1/IFb) = miserable, unhappy. See **stûxwar**.

stûxwar ستووخوار *adj.* 1) miserable, unhappy, distressed: **•Tu çima wa serê me dikî, me *stûxar* dihêlî?** (Z-1) Why do you do this to us [lit. 'to our heads'], make [lit. 'leave'] us *miserable*?; 2) suffering from torticollis or wryneck (JJ). {also: stuxar; stuxwar (K); stûxar (Z-1); [oustou-khar] استوخوار (JJ)} < stû = 'neck' + xwar = 'bent' {stuxwarî; stûxwarî} [Z-1/IFb//GF//K//JJ]

stûxwarî ستووخواری *f.* **(-ya;-yê).** misery, unhappiness, distress. {also: stuxwarî (K)} [K/ZF3//GF] <stûxwar>

su سو (Rh) = thirty. See **sî II**.

sual سوئال *f./m.(K)* **().** question: **•Emê *sualekê* lê bikin** (L) We will ask him [lit. 'We will put *a question* to him']. {also: sewal II (EP-8); sewalî, f. (K-2); suwal, m. (K/SK-2)} {syn: pirs; ≠ bersîv; cab} Cf. [souvala kirin] سوالا كرين (JJ) = 'to buy (books)', 'to ask for information'; < Ar su'āl سؤال --> T sual [L/SK//K//EP-8]

subahê سوباهێ (Zx) = tomorrow. See **sibe** [2].

s̱ube صوبه (FS) = morning. See **sibe**[1].

subḧet سوبحەت (MC-1) = conversation, talk. See **s̱uḧbet**.

suhbet سوهبەت (K) = conversation, talk. See **s̱uḧbet**.

s̱uḧbet صوحبەت *f.* **(-a;-ê).** conversation, chat, talk: **•...R̄ûniş[t]ne xarê, şîva xo xar, dest havête *s̱oḧbetê*, gotê: 'Hey, mêhvanê baş, tu ji k'îve têy? Tu xelkê k'îrey? Tu çi k'es î?'** (JB1-A #17,102) They sat down, ate their supper, and started *talking*: [the old woman] said to him, 'O good guest, where are you coming from? Where do you hail from? Who are you?' **•Tu vê *s̱oḧbetê* tbêjî, ewey r̄oja Xodê kirime r̄izqê te û ḧeta nuhu te çu cara ev tiştêt hos̱a nekirine û negotine** (JB1-A #14,102) These things [lit. 'this *talk*'] you are saying, ever since the day God gave me to you, you have never acted or spoken like this; **-s̱uḧbet kirin** (SK) to converse, chat, keep company: **•Wextê çûne mala wî, Xace 'Alî ji k'êfa wî gelek hat û gelek qedrê wa girt. R̄ûniştine xarê, qehwa xo vexar, *s̱oḧbeta xo kir*** (JB1-A #3,98) When they went to his house, Hadji Ali was delighted and treated them very well. They sat down, drank their coffee, and *had a nice chat*. {also: sihbet (IFb); sohbet (K/B); s̱oḧbet (JB1-A); subḧet (MC-1); suhbet (K-2); <s̱iḧbet> صحبت (HH)} Cf. T sohbet & P sohbat صحبت = 'conversation, chat' <Ar ṣuḥbah صحبة = 'friendship, accompaniment' [SK//JB1-A//K/B//HH//IFb//MC-1]

sukir سوکِر (M-Ak) = nape of neck. See **stukur**.

sukur I سوکور (AB) = dam, weir. See **sikir**.

sukur II سوکور (Ak) = nape of neck. See **stukur**.

sult'an (B)/sultan سولتان (SK/GF/IFb) = sultan. See **silt'an**.

sumbul سومبول (IFb) = hyacinth. See **sunbul**.

sunbul سونبول *m.(F)/f.(B)* **(; /-ê).** hyacinth, bot. *Hyacinthus orientalis*; blue, fragrant flower (HH). {also: simbil II (IFb-2); simbûl I, f. (B); sinbil II (IFb-2); sumbul (IFb); [sunbul] سنبل (JJ); <sunbul> سنبل (HH)} Cf. T sünbül/sümbül; Sor simił سِمِڵ [F/JJ/HH//IFb/B]

sund سوند (JB3) = oath, vow. See **sond**.

sundxwarî سوندخواری (JB3) = ally. See **sondxwarî**.

supas سوپاس (BF/FS) = thanks. See **spas**.

supasdar سوپاسدار (BF) = grateful. See **spasdar**.

sur̄ I سوڕ *f.* **(-a;-ê).** 1) {syn: sarî I; serma} cold, cold weather: **-sur̄ û serma** (EP-7) do.: **•Ḧetanî êvarê wana ber tavê, *sur̄ê û sermê*, bin baranê û**

teyrokê... pez diç'êrand (Ba2:1, 204) They would graze the sheep until evening in sunlight and *cold*, under rain and hail; 2) cool breeze. See **sir I**. {also: [ser] سر (JJ); <sir> سر (HH)} [Ba2/EP-7/K/B//HH] <qir I; sar; seqem; serma; sir I; zivistan>

sur̄ II سوڕ (K/B) = secret. See **sir̄ II**.

suravk سوراڤك (TF) = saltwater. See **sûravk**.

sur̄dar سوڕدار *f.* **(-a;).** confidante. [EH]

surgûn سورگوون (SK) = exile. See **sirgûn**.

sur•ik I سورِك *f.* **(•ka;).** 1) gutter (on roof of house); 2) {syn: vizik II} stream, jet (of water) (SK): **•Dibêjin carekê muroekî** *[=mirovekî]* **Paweyî hate layê S̱omayê û Biradost û Kuresinîyan, xo kiribû şêx ... her gundê diçûyê, li pêş çawêt xelkî tizbîyêt xo li bin huçikê 'ebay li hindawê şerbikê aw-xarinewê digiwişî, aw bi *suruk* jê dihate xar, xelk hemî muteḧeyyir dibûn** ... (SK 12:118) [118] They say that a Pawai man came to Somay and Biradost and the Kurasinis and made himself out to be a Shaikh ... in every village that he visited he would, in full view of the people, squeeze his rosary, under the sleeve of his cloak, over a water pot. Water would flow in a *stream* out of it. The people were all amazed ... {also: suruk (SK); **şir̄ik**} [Zeb//SK/Hk] <şir̄ik; şîp>

surik II سورك (IFb) = measles. See **sorik**.

surişt سورِشت (GF) = nature. See **siruşt**.

surnî سورنى (RZ/Nbh) = axle. See **sirnî**.

sursûm سورسووم (Wn) = wooden butter churner. See **sirsûm**.

suruk سورووك (SK) = gutter; stream of water. See **surik I** .

suruşt سورووشت (K[s]/TF) = nature. See **siruşt**.

Suryanî سوريانى *m.&f.* **().** 1) Syriac Christians (Assyrians, Chaldeans): **•Ḧeta rojên îroyîn gelek jin û qîzên êzdîya û *suryanîya* hê destên çetên Daesh-danin** (EzidxanNews 3.ii.2016) Even these days many Yezidi and *Syriac* women and girls are still in the hands of groups of Daesh **•Ne Rahib û keşşê dêra Za'feranê, û ne *suryanîyê* derdora Midyatê nikarî bûn di hewara wan da bihatina** (MGC Haber 25.i.2012) Neither the monks and priest of the Za'feran monastery nor the *Syriac Christians* around Midyat could come to their aid;

2) [*f.* **(-ya;).**] Syriac language: **•Ev bû sedema ku zimanê *Suryanî* dîsa xwedî hêz bibe û were bi karanîn** (Wkp: Suryanî) This was the reason that the Syriac language regained strength and came back into use. {also: Siryanî (Wkt-2); Sûriyanî (SS)} [Wkp/Ezidxan/IFb/ZF3/Kmc//Wkt//SS] <Aramî II; file; mexîn>

suryaz سورياز (CB) = asphodel. See **soryas**.

suwal سووال, m. (K/SK) = question. See **sual**.

suwar سووار (L/IFb/HH/GF) = rider. See **siwar**.

suwax سوواخ (IFb) = plaster. See **sewax**.

suxre سوخره *f.* **().** corvée, forced labor: **•Hesam Axa, hem çend şkeftên wî hebûn, hem bi *suxre* koçkek ji kevirên necirandî bi gundiyan dabû avakirin** (DBgb, 6) Hesam Agha both owned some caves and by *forced labor* had a mansion of carved stones built by the villagers. {also: [soukhré] سخره (JJ); <suxre> سخره (HH)} {syn: olam [2]} < Ar suxrah سخرة = 'corvée, statute labor, forced labor'; Syr šūḥārā ܫܘܚܪܐ = 'forced labor'; Sor suxre سوخره [DBgb/IFb/FJ/TF/GF/JJ/HH/Kmc/CS]

suxte سوخته *m.* **().** Muslim religious student in a traditional medreseh *(higher than feqî, lower than muste'î)*: **•Bila me ji serbor û şarezayîya xo bêbehr neken û me bi *suxte* û şagirdên xo bihejmêrin** (A.Xalid. Perlemanê mişkan, 7) Let them not deprive us of their experience and expertise and [=but rather] count us among their *students* and disciples **•Mele ji *suxteyan* pirsî** (LM, 15) The mullah asked *the students*. {also: soxte (IFb-2); [soukhté] سوخته (JJ); <suxte> سخته (HH)} < P sūxte سوخته = 'burnt, scorched' --> T softa = 'Muslim theological student (as a taper lit by his teacher [Redhouse])'; Sor soxte سۆخته = 'theological student (more advanced than feqê)' [LM/A.Xalid/IFb/FJ/GF/TF/JJ/HH/ZF/Wkt/CS] <feqî; mirîd; şagird; xwendekar>

suyar سويار (B) = rider. See **siwar**.

sûc سووج *m./f.(SK/M-Ak)* **(-ê/-a;).** 1) {syn: binas; gune II; t'awan I} fault; guilt, culpability: ***•Sûcê* min nîne** (B) It's not my *fault*; **-bêsûc** = innocent; 2) offense, crime: **•Ka *sûca* kur̄ê min çiye?** (M-Ak #675, 304) What is my son's *crime*?; **-sûc kirin** (B/IFb) to commit an offense, to transgress. {also: sîç (Bw); sûç (A/JB3/SK/GF/OK); [soutch] سوچ (JJ); <sûç> سوچ (HH)} < T suç; Sor sûç سووچ = 'fault, transgression'; Za şûj *m.* (Todd) [Z-1/K/IFb/B//A/JB3/JJ/HH/SK/GF/OK//Bw]

sûcdar سووجدار *adj.* guilty. {also: sûck'ar (B); sûçdar (JB3/GF)} {syn: t'awanbar} [K/IFb//JB3//B]

<sûc>

sûck'ar سووجكار (B) = guilty. See **sûcdar**.

sûç سووچ (A/JB3/JJ/HH/SK/GF/OK) = fault; offense. See **sûc**.

sûçdar سووچدار (JB3/GF) = guilty. See **sûcdar**.

Sûdanî سوودانى *adj.* Sudanese. Sor Sudanî سودانى [BF/Wkt/SS/Wkp]

sûk سووك *f.* **(;-ê).** market, marketplace: •**Kurê pîrê daket *sûkê*** (L) The old woman's son went (down) to *the market* •***Sûk* tije qumaş e, lê mela bêşaş e** (BX) *The marketplace* is full of cloth, but the mullah is turbanless *[prv.]*. {also: sûke (B); [souq] سوق (JJ); <sûk> سوك (HH)} {syn: bazar} < Ar sūq سوق; Cf. Za sûk *f.* = 'large town' [L/K/JB3/IFb/HH/TF//B//JJ] <bajar; şeher>

sûke سووكه (B) = market(place). See **sûk**.

sûlav سوولاڤ *f.* **(;-ê).** waterfall: •**Ne weke barîna baranê û weke herikîna ava bi ser *sûlavan* de biçe** (MG. Tavê ew dît) It goes, not like the falling of rain nor like the flowing of water over waterfalls. {syn: şilêr; şirav; şîp} Sor sûlav سوولاڤ/solav سۆلاڤ = tavge تاڤگه [MG/IFb/FJ/CS/AD/RZ/SS]

sûn سوون (IF) = to rub together; to whet, hone; to light, kindle. See **hesûn** & **sûtin**.

sûnd سووند (A/SK) = oath, vow. See **sond**.

sûne سوونه, f. (FS) = drake, duck. See **sone**.

sûr I سوور *f.* **(-a;-ê).** 1) {syn: beden I; şûre I} city wall, rampart: •**Dengek ji serê *sûrehê* seh kir, got, bigire** (Rnh 2:17, 307) He heard a voice from the top of *the city wall*, it said, 'catch!'; 2) fence (B). {also: sûreh (Rnh); sûrih (HR); [sour] سور (JJ); <sûr> سور (HH)} < Ar sūr سور [Z-1/K/A/IFb/B/JJ/HH/GF/ZF//Rnh//HR]

sûr II سوور (Bw/Krs/SK/OK) = salty. See **şoř III**.

sûrat سوورات (Wkt) = surah of the Quran. See **sûret II**.

sûravk سووراڤك *f.* **(-a;-ê).** saltwater, (pickling) brine. {also: sîravik (IFb-2); suravk (TF); swîravk (Qrj-2); şorav (IFb/GF/FJ); şořav (K/B); [chouraw] شوراڤ (JJ); <şorav> شوراڤ (HH)} Cf. P šūrāb شوراب/šūrābe شورابه; Sor şorawk شۆراوك [Qrj/A//TF//IFb/HH/GF/FJ//K/B//JJ]

sûre سووره, f. (K/IFb) = surah of the Quran. See **sûret II**.

sûreh سوورەه (Rnh 2:17, 307) = city wall. See **sûr I**.

sûret I سوورەت *m.* **(-ê;).** 1) {syn: řû I[1]; serçav; sifet[3]} face, countenance: •**Hêstirek ji ç'a'vê Xecê k'ete ser *sûretê* Sîabend** (IS-#342) A tear from Khej's eye fell on Siyabend's *face*; 2) {syn: gup; hinarik; lame} cheek; 3) outward appearance: •**Vana *sûretê* wa û şikletê wa 'eynî d tişbihne hev** (HR 4:9) These [two in] their *appearance* and form resemble one another; 4) {syn: sifet[4]; wêne} image, picture, portrait; photograph. {also: soret I (SK); [souret] صورت (JJ); <sûret> صورت (HH)} < Ar ṣūrah صورة = 'image, picture' --> P ṣūrat صورت; --> T suret/surat [EP-7/K/IFb/B/GF//JJ/HH/ZF//SK] <dêm II>

sûret II سوورەت *m.* **(-ê;).** *surah*, chapter (of the Quran): •**Çend ayet dibin *sûretek* û di Qur'anê de 114 *sûret* hene** (Wkt) Several verses [together] make [lit. 'become'] a *surah* (=chapter), and in the Quran there are 114 *surahs* •***sûretê* Yasîn** (Wkt) the Yāsīn *surah* (of the Quran). {also: sorat (Wkt-2); sore (SK); soret II (Wkt-2); sûrat (Wkt-2); sûre, f. (K/IFb); <sûret> (HH)} < Ar sūrah سورة [Wkt/HH//K/IFb//SK]

sûrih سوورِه (HR) = city wall. See **sûr I**.

sûrikîn سووركين *vi.* **(-sûrik-).** to creep, crawl on one's belly (JJ); to steal away, slink away, sneak away (A): •[**Dûmo şeşxaneyê digrite destê xo û bi çarlepî devarûyî wekû kelban *disûrike***] (JR #27, 80) Dumo takes his revolver into his hand and *crawls* on all fours like a dog [lit. 'like dogs']. {also: [sourikin] سوركين (JJ)} {syn: şûlikîn} [JR/A/JJ/(GF)] See also **şûlikîn**.

Sûriyanî سووريانى (SS) = Syriac. See **Suryanî**.

Sûriyeyî سووريەيى (Wkt) = Syrian. See **Sûrî II**[2].

sûrî I سوورى *m.* **(-yê;).** (large) flock or herd of sheep: •[*surâjä* dôstē mámu alân tuníno/] (HM-1) Mámu Alan does not have *a herd of* lovers *{*If my understanding of this passage is correct}*; **-kerî-sûrî** (F) flock, herd: •**Awqa mal, zêr, zîvê te heye, *kerî sûrîyê* te heye** (FK-kk-1) You have so much wealth--gold and silver, so many *herds*. {also: [surâ-] (HM)} {syn: col; kerî II; xar II} <T sürü = 'herd, flock' [HM//FK-kk-1/F//K/B] <biř I[4]; mî I; pez>

Sûrî II سوورى *f.* **().** 1) Syria; 2) *[adj.]* {also: Sûriyeyî (Wkt-2)} Syrian. Sor Surî سورى [IFb/Wkt/BF/Wkp/SS/CS]

sûrîçk سووريچك (K) = esophagus. See **sorîçk**.

sûsirk سووسِرك (IFb) = cricket. See **sîsirk**.

sût I سووت (AA/HH/FS) = trap. See **sîte**.

sût II سووت *adj.* blue, navy blue: •**ç'e'vê *sût*** (B) *blue* eyes. {syn: heşîn [1]} [Elîfba Ezdîkî/K/B]

sûte سووته, m. (OK/AA) = trap. See **sîte**.

sûtin سووتِن *vt.* **(-sû- / -so-).** 1) to rub together *(to cause friction in order to light a fire and the like)*; 2) {syn: seqa kirin; tûj kirin} to whet, hone, sharpen *(knife)*; 3) to light, kindle, set fire to. See **sotin**. {also: **hesûn**; sûn (IF-2); sûyîn (IF-2); [hesoun] هسون (JJ); <sûtin سوتن (disû) (دسو)> (HH)} [Pok. ḱē(i)-: ḱō(i)-: ḱə(i)- 541-2.] 'to sharpen, whet'--*probably extension of* aḱ- = 'sharp': Skt śi-śā-ti/śy-áti = 'sharpens, whets'; O Ir *su-/*sav-: Av saēni- = 'tip, point'; P sūdan سودن (-sāy-) (ساى) & sōhān سوهان = 'file (tool)'; Sor s[u]wan سووان = 'file; to be rubbed' & sûn سوون = 'to rub'; Za sawenã [sawitiş] = 'to rub, sharpen' (Mal/Srk) [K/A/IFb/HH//JJ] <êge; k'artik; sotin> See also **hesûn**.

sûwar سووار (Z-3/SK) = rider. See **siwar**.

sûyîn سوويين (IF) = to rub together; to whet, hone; to light, kindle. See **sûtin**.

sûxar سووخار\سويخار (Zeb) = hoarfrost. See **xûsî**.

Svêçistan سڤێچستان, f. (JB3) = Sweden. See **Swêd**.

swar سوار (A/K) = rider. See **siwar**.

Swêd سوێد *f.* **(;-ê).** Sweden. {also: siwêç (K); Svêçistan, f. (JB3); Şvêsîa (Ba2)} < Fr Suède --> Ar swēd سويد [Ber/IFb//Ba2//K//JB3]

Swêdî سوێدى *adj.* Swedish. {also: Siwêdî (BF)} Sor Swîdî سويدى [IFb/Wkt/ZF3/BF/SS/CS//BF]

Swêrek سوێرەك (A/G) = Siverek, a town near Urfa. See **Sêwreg**.

Swisî سوسى (SS) = Swiss. See **Swîsreyî**.

Swîçreyî سويچرەيى (Wkt/ZF3) = Swiss. See **Swîsreyî**.

swîravk سويراڤك (Qrj) = saltwater. See **sûravk**.

Swîsrayî سويسرايى (BF) = Swiss. See **Swîsreyî**.

Swîsreyî سويسرەيى *adj.* Swiss. {also: Siwîsrî (BF-2); Swisî (SS); Swîçreyî (Wkt-2/ZF3-2); Swîsrayî (BF); Swîsrî (Wkt-2)} Sor Swîsrî سويسرى [Wkt/ZF3/Wkp//BF//SS]

Swîsrî سويسرى (Wkt) = Swiss. See **Swîsreyî**.

sxêf سخێف (HR) = curse. See **sixêf**.

syar سيار (Ad) = rider. See **siwar**.

Ş ش

şa شـا *adj.* happy, glad: **•Em ze'f *şane*, ku tu hatî** (B) We are very *happy* that you came **•Ewî xeberê *şa* bihîstine** (B) He heard some *good* news; **-şa bûn** (K/A/JB3) to be happy, rejoice *{Used particularly in concluding formulas in folktales, cf. " They lived happily ever after," T " Onlar ermiş muradına"}*: **•Ev bi miradê xwe *şa bûn*, em bi miradê xwe *şa* bibin** (L) They *were happy* with their desire, *may* we *be happy* with ours *[concluding formula]* **•Ew çûn mirazê xwe *şabûn*, hûn jî heřin mirazê xwe *şabin*** (J) They went [and] *rejoiced* with their desire, you too go *rejoice* with yours *[concluding formula]* **•Xêr û silamet ew çû mirazê xwe *şabû*, em jî mirazê xwe *şabin*** (J) Safe and sound [lit. 'goodness and health'], he went [and] *rejoiced* in his desire, may we also *rejoice* in ours *[concluding formula]*; **-şa kirin** (K/A/JB3) to make s.o. happy, to cause s.o. to rejoice. {also: şad I (IFb-2/OK-2/BF/FS); [cha] شا (JJ)} {şadî; şahî; şayî I} Av šāta- *passive pp. of* šā-/šyā- = 'to rejoice' (Tsb2, p.61): P šād شـاد; Sor şad شـاد = 'glad, happy, cheerful'; Za şa/şad (Mal) [K/JB3/IFb/B/JJ/GF/TF/OK//BF/FS]

şabaş شـابـاش *f.* **().** 1) showering bride and groom with money *(at their wedding)* (K); *during the folk dancing at a wedding celebration, a musician goes from person to person collecting money for the bride and groom* (Msr); 2) tip, monetary gift to the wedding musicians; **-şavaş dan** (K): a) to give money to the musicians *(at a wedding)*; b) to waste in vain *(money)*; c) exclamation used to congratulate the bride and groom at their wedding (K); exclama-tion of the hired musicians at a wedding, urging people to give them gifts (B); **•Bengzade *şabaş kir*, go: "*Şabaş* ser serê Sîabendê Silîvî--Xeca zerînřa, malî ava, zêřek daye!"** (EP-4) The gypsy musician *exclaimed*, "*Hurray* for Siyabendê Silîvî and Kheja Zerîn, may they prosper, they've given a gold piece!"; 3) praise, extolling (A). {also: şavaş (K); şebaş; [chabach] شـابـاش (JJ); <şabaş> شـابـاش (HH)} [Msr/EP-4/A/IFb/JB3/B/JJ/HH/GF/TF/ZF3/FS/BF//K]

şabûn شـابـوون *f.* **(-a;-ê).** rejoicing; joy. {also: şabûnî (JB3/IFb); <şabûn> شابون (HH)} {syn: şayî} [EP-7/K/B/HH//JB3/IFb]

şabûnî شـابوونی (JB3/IF) = joy. See **şabûn**.

şad I شاد (IFb/OK/BF/FS) = happy. See **şa**.

şad II شاد (IFb) = witness. See **şade**.

şade شـــاده *m.* **(-yê;).** witness: **-şahad-şihûd** (B)/**şad û şihûd** (IFb) all possible witnesses, every imaginable witness; **-tilîya şadê** (Msr) index finger, pointer. {syn: t[']ilîya nîşanê}. {also: şad II (IFb-2); şahad (B); şahid (IFb/SK/Wkt); şe'de (FK-eb-1); şehde (K-2); [chahid] شـاهـد (JJ); <şehde> شـهـده (HH)} < Ar šāhid شـاهـد {şahad[t]î; şe'detî; [chehdeï] شـهـدهی (JJ)} [Z-/K/ZF3//B//IFb/JJ/SK/Wkt//HH//FK-eb-1]

şadetî شـــادهتـــی *f.* **(-ya;-yê).** witnessing, testimony, bearing witness: **•Bûyerên van rojên dawî, ku ji Şengalê tên, hema *şadetîya* vê yekê didin** (avestakurd.net 6.viii.2014) The events of these past few days, which come from Sinjar/Shingal, bear *witness* to this. {also: şahadî (B); şahadtî (B-2); şahidî (SK/Wkt); şe'detî (B-2); [chehdeï] شـهـدهی (JJ)} [B//JJ//SK/Wkt//ZF3] <şade>

şadirvan شادِرڤان (IFb) = fountain. See **şadîrewan**.

şadî شـادی (K[s]/A/IFb/GF/OK) = happiness. See **şayî I**.

şadîrewan شـادیـرهوان *f.* **(;-ê).** fountain adorned with water-jets, situated at center of mosque courtyard used for ritual ablutions. {also: şadirvan (IFb); şadrewan (K); şehderewan (TF); [chadirevan شادروان/chazirevan شاذروان] (JJ)} Cf. P šādrevān شـادروان --> Ar šāḏirwān شـاذروان; --> T şadırvan [EP-7/JJ//IFb//K//TF]

şadrewan شادرهوان (K) = fountain. See **şadîrewan**.

şa'er شاعر (JB1-S) = poet; singer. See **şayîr**.

şafiř I شـــافِـــر *m./f.(BF)* **(-ê/;-î/).** ditch reed, bot. *Phragmites communis*, green plant eaten by animals [nav bîstanê, cihêt avî şîn dibît--cihêt dêm ne--giyayê wî yê dirêj e, belgê wî dirêj e û piçekî zivir--destêt mirovî dibiřît eger mirov dest bavêjtê; binê wî zor yê qahîm e = it grows in gardens and irrigated places--not ones watered by rainfall alone--its grass is long, its leaf is long and a little rough--it cuts one's hand if one touches it;

its underside (root?) is very strong]: •**Zevîya me ya tejî *şafir* bûy** (Bw) Our field was full of *ditch reed*; -**gominkê şafirî** (Bw) clump of **şafir**. cf. şavêr̄ (AA) = 'sweet vernal grass' [Bw/Qrj/GF/FJ/FS/Wkt/BF]

şagird شـــاگِــــرد *m.&f.* **(-ê/-a; /-ê).** 1) {syn: qutabî; xwendek'ar} pupil, student; 2) disciple, follower:: •**Me bi suxte û *şagirdên* xo bihejmêrin** (A.Xalid. Perlemanê mişkan, 7) Let them count us among their students and *disciples*; 3) {syn: *berhosta} apprentice: •**Ew *şagirdê* asingerî ye** (FS) He is the iron-smith's *apprentice*; -**şagirdê ḧedadî** (JB1-A) blacksmith's apprentice. {also: şagirt (K/A/B/IFb/FJ/GF/HH/RZ/ZF/CS); şahgirt (JB1-S); [chaghird] شاگرد (JJ); <şagirt> شاگرت (HH)} < P šāgird شـاگِـرد = 'apprentice; pupil, student'; Sor şagird شـاگِـرد [A.Xalid/JJ/SS/JB1-A/FS/BF//K/A/B/IFb/FJ/GF/HH/RZ/ZF/CS//JB1-S] <feqî; suxte>

şagirt شـاگِـرت (K/A/B/IFb/FJ/GF/HH/RZ/ZF/CS) = student; apprentice. See **şagird**.

şagul شـاگـول (CCG) = plumb line; type of trap. See **şaqûl**.

şahad شاهاد (B) = witness. See **şade**.

şahadî شاهادى (B) = testimony. See **şadetî**.

şahadtî شاهادتى (B) = testimony. See **şadetî**.

şaheng شـاهـەنـگ *f.* **(-a;-ê).** queen bee: •***Şaheng* hêk berdide çavikê** (Yumpu: Mêşhingiv çawa çêdibin) *The queen bee* deposits an egg in the cell. <şa[h] = 'king' + heng = 'bee' cf. hingiv = 'honey'; Sor şaheng شاهەنگ [Yumpu/IFb/GF/ZF3/Wkt/FD/BF/CS] <mêşa hingiv>

şaheser شـاهـەسـەر *f.* **(-a;-ê).** masterpiece: •**"Mem û Zîn" *şahesera* Ehmedê Xanî ye, lê wî hin pirtûkên din jî nivîsîne** (Wkt) "Mem û Zîn" is Ahmedê Khani's masterpiece, but he also wrote some other books. cf. P šāh'asar شـاهاثـر [IFb/GF/ZF3/Wkt]

şahgirt شـاهـگِـرت (JB1-S) = student; apprentice. See **şagird**.

şahid شاهِد (IFb/SK/JJ/Wkt) = witness. See **şade**.

şahidî شاهِدى (SK/Wkt) = testimony. See **şadetî**.

şahir شاهِر (JB3/IFb/GF) = poet; singer. See **şayîr**.

şahî شاهى (IFb/JB1-S/OK/ZF)= happiness. See **şayî I**.

şahîk شـاهـيـك (IFb/TF/Kmc) = smooth; slippery. See **şayik**.

şahnazî شاهنازى (TF/OK) = pride. See **şanazî**.

şahr شاهر (Tof) = head band. See **şar I**.

ş[a]hreza شاهرەزا (A) = expert. See **şareza**.

şahrezayî شاهرەزايى (A) = expertise. See **şarezayî**.

şair شـائِـر (ZF)/şa'ir شـاعِـر (SK) = poet; singer. See **şayîr**.

şaîr شائير (B) = poet; singer. See **şayîr**.

şaîş شائيش (EH) = worry. See **şayîş**.

şaîşî شائيشى (B) = worry. See **şayîş**.

şak شاك (GF) = two-year-old ram. See **şek**.

şal I شـال *m.* **(-ê; şêl).** 1) {syn: şalvar} pants, trousers; wide-bottomed trousers characteristic of the Kurds; baggy trousers made of woven wool (HH): •**Şivîn p'otê xwe êxist, *şe'lê* xwe êxist** (HCK-1, 205) The shepherd took off his overcoat, took off his *pants*; -**şal û şapik** (AB/M/FS)/**şel û şepik** (FS-2)/**şelûşapik** (Wkt) Kurdish man's suit of clothes {syn: peşme w bergûz (M-Ak); r̄anî-bergûz (SK)}: "in Badinan the material is normally coloured, striped or pure white, and may have a colourful woven pattern in addition. Finally, the tailor embroiders the finished suit lavishly (nowadays with a sewing-machine) in a contrasting colour. The trousers have wide bottoms, and are always named first, the suit being known as [r̄anî w berbûz] in [Rewanduz], [peşme w bergûz] in Akre, and [şal ô şap'ik'] in Zakho" [M, v. 2, p. 376, note 720]: •***Şal û şapikê* bavê min dirîyan** (AB) My father's *pants and breeches (=suit)* tore; 2) type of cloth (IF); type of thin woolen cloth and sash (A). {also: şe'l IV (B); [chal] شـال (JJ); <şal> شـال (HH)} [AB/M/K/A/IFb/JJ/HH/TF/Dy/FS//B//Wkt] <bergûz; p'antol; şapik; şûtik>

şal II شال (GF) = large saddlebag. See **şel II**.

şal III شـال (FS) = cloth for wrapping bundles. See **şalik II**[2].

şalik I شـالِـك *f.* **(;-ê).** apron: •**P'erîşan-xanim r̄abû çû sik'a hespa Xelîl-begê derxist, anî hat kire bin *şalikê*** (Z-15, 230) P. went and took out Kh.'s horse's stake, then came and put it under her *apron*. {also: şe'lik (B)} {syn : berdilk [4]; berk'oş; bermalk; bervank; melîtk; mêzer [4]} [Z/K/CS//B]

şalik II شالِك *f.* **(-a;-ê).** 1) a cloak made of virgin wool [tiftik], similar to Arab *'aba*, but without embroidery [ji keja bizinan (tiftik) wek 'ebayê 'ereban lê bê neqşê destan] (Qzl/A/TF); 2) {also: şal III (FS)} square cloth in which to wrap items for a trip (cf. buxçik) [perçekevnikê mezin yê çargoşe ku wek buxçikeke mezin bi kar tînin] (Qzl): •**Ez te bi *şalika* li pişta xwe kim jî, t'ê bêjî**

'Ay, qûna min dêşe' (Qzl) If I carry you on my back in my *pack*, you'll say "Ouch, my bottom hurts". [Qzl/A/TF//FS] <buxçik>

şalîl شاليل (FS) = blackbird. See **şalûl**.

şalo شـــالـــۆ (OK/FS) = scythe-like implement. See **şalok**.

şalok شـــالـــۆك *f.* **(-a;-ê).** scythe-like implement for cutting down grass (Bw) or for picking fruit (OK); pruning hook: **•Wî giya bi *şalokê* dirû** (FS) He cut down the grass with *the pruning hook*. {also: şalo (OK/FS-2); şalûk (IFb-2)} {syn: diryas} [Bw/Elk/IFb/FS//OK] <das>

şalûk شـــالـــووك (IFb) = scythe-like implement. See **şalok**. şalîl (FS); şalûr (FS) = blackbird. See **şalûl**.

şalûl شـــالـــوول *m./f.(FS)* **().** *type of small bird*: a) bee eater, zool. *Merops apiaster* [T arı kuşu] (IFb/RF); b) blackbird, thrush, zool. *Turdus* [Ar šaḥrūr شـــحـــرور] (GF/AA): **•dengê *şalûl* û bilbilan** (Alkan, 71) the sound of *bee eaters* and nightingales. {also: şalîl (FS); şalûr (FS-2); şehlûl (AA/OK); [sciálulá] شـــالـــوله (JJ)} Cf. Ar šaḥrūr شحرور = 'blackbird, thrush' [Alkan/K/A/IFb/GF/RF/BF//JJ//OK/AA//FS]

şalûr شالوور (FS) = blackbird. See **şalûl**.

şalvar شـــالـــڤار *m./pl.(SK)* **(-ê;).** baggy trousers. {also: şalwar (IFb/ZF3); şelwal (JB1-A/SK/OK/Bw/FS); şelwar (A/IFb-2/GF); şerval (Çnr/OK-2); şerwal (OK-2); [chelvar] شـــلـــوار (JJ)} Cf. Ar sirwāl سروال/širwāl شروال = 'trousers'; P šalvār شلوار--> T şalvar; Sor şełwar شـــەڵـــوار; Za şilwalî = 'long underwear' *pl.* (Todd); cf. also Heb šarvul שרוול = 'sleeve' [K/Kp/Dy//IFb/ZF3//A/JJ/GF//JB1-A/SK/OK/Bw/FS] <deling; doxîn; navr̄an; şal I>

şalwar شالوار (IFb/ZF3) = baggy trousers. See **şalvar**.

şalyar شـــالـــيـــار *m.&f.* **(-ê/-a;).** government minister: **-şalyarê berevanîyê** (BF) minister of defense; **-şalyarê derve** (BF) foreign affairs minister; **-şalyara ragehandin** (BF) (female) minister of communications. {syn: wezîr} Cf. P šahriyār شـــهـــريـــار = 'monarch, king'; Sor şaryar شـــاريـــار/şalyar شـــالـــيـــار = 'monarch' {şalyarî} [(neol)VoA/A/IFb/TF/ZF3/BF/Wkt]

şalyarî شـــالـــيـــارى *f.* **(-ya;-yê).** government ministry. {syn: wezîrî} [(neol)A/IFb/TF/ZF3/BF] <şalyar>

şamdank شامدانك (ZF3)= candlestick. See **şemdan**.

şamik شـــامِـــك *f.* **(-a;-ê).** 1) {syn: bacanê sor; firingî; stembolî} tomato; 2) vine leaf disease (Haz). < Ar al-šām الـــشـــام = 'Damascus, Syria'; cf. Sor bayincanî şam بايِنجانى شام = 'tomato' & Za şamik *f.* = 'tomato' (Todd) [Ad/Srk/Haz/Klk/IFb/RZ/Kmc-2/ZF3/Wkt]

şamî شـــامـــى *m.&f.* **(/-ya;).** turkey (fowl), zool. *Meleagris gallopavo*. {syn: bûqelemûn; coqcoq; culûx̄; ‘elok; kûr̄kûr̄} [AB/IFb/OK/ZF3/BF]

şan شـــان *f./m.(ZF3)* **(-a/;).** honeycomb: **•Mêşhingiv hingiv û kirmên xwe di *şaneyan* da didane** (BF) Bees place their honey and larva [lit. 'worms'] in honeycombs; **-şe‘na hingiv** (Msr)/**şaneyekî hingûnî** (SK) do. {also: şane (Bw/SK/GF/OK/FS/BF); şehn (GF-2); şe‘n (Msr); şe‘nik (Msr-2); [scián-a enghivín] شان (JJ); <şan> شان (HH)} Cf. P šān(-e asal) (عسل) شان; Sor şane hengwîn شانه هەنگوين; Za şa’n (Mal) [Msr//K(s)/A/IFb/JJ/HH//Bw/SK/GF/OK/FS/BF] <movane; şeh; şema [3]>

şanazî شانازى *f.* **(-ya;-yê).** pride, dignity; self-esteem, self-respect: **•Amerîka *şanazîyê bi* piştevanî-kirina pêşmerge *dike*** (Rojname 12.ii.2017) America *is proud of* supporting the peshmergas **•Hûn duh sêwîyê ommetê bûn, hûn îro bûn *fexr û şanazîya* ommetê** (Îlkha.com 19.iv. 2015) Yesterday you were an orphan, today you are the people's *pride* **•Mihemed Kerkûkî *cihê şanazîya* gelê Kurdistanê ye** (Rojname 27.ii.2017) M.K. is *a source of pride* for the people of Kurdistan **•Sedemê wê jî, çima ku em li canemergên xwe xwedî derketin û me xwest em wan *bi şanazî* û bi serbilindî bi gor bikin** (Wlt 2:59, 13) The reason for it [=the reprisal] was that we took care of our dead young ones, and that we wanted to bury them *with dignity* and pride **•Zimanê Kurdî qedr û qîmet û *şanazîya* gelê Kurd e** (Dengê Kurdistan 20.ii.2018) The Kurdish language is the dignity and *pride of* the Kurdish people. {also: şahnazî (TF/OK-2)} {syn: serbilindî} Sor şanazî شـــانـــازى = 'proper pride' [Wlt/IFb/OK/ZF3//TF]

şand•e شانده *f.* **(•[ey]a;).** delegation, mission: **•Li Amed a Bakurê Kurdistanê ger û seredanên *şanda* DBP, HDP û KCDê ya ji bo 'yekîtiya netewî' û 'giştpirsiya pergala serokomariyê' berdewam dike** [sic] **... Mesûd Tek jî di her dû waran de rexne li *şandeya* navborî girt** (Rûdaw, 14.ii.2017) In Diyarbakir of North Kurdistan the tours of the DBP, HDP and KCD *delegation* for national unity and the referendum for the presidential system continues ... M.T. criticized the aforementioned *delegation* in both fields. <şandin = 'to send' [Rûdaw/Wkt/ZF3/FD]

şandin شاندِن *vt.* **(-şîn-/-şên-** [Msr]**).** to send, dispatch: **•Te çawa** ***ez şandibûm,*** **min jî** ***tu şandî*** **wê** (HCK-2, 179) Just as you *had sent me*, I also *sent you* there **•Xwedê** ***ez şandime*** **bal te** (Dz) God *has sent me* to you; **-dû** ***fk-ê*** **şandin** (L) to send for/after s.o.: **•Hakim** ***şand dû*** **kurê pîrê** (L-2 22) The king *sent for* the "old woman's boy." {also: şiyandin (IFb-2/TF/FJ-2); şîyandin; [chandin شاندین/chehandin شهاندین] (JJ); <şandin شاندن/ şiyandin شیاندن (dişîne) (دشینه)> (HH)} {syn: hinartin; [ve]rêkirin} [K/A/JB3/IFb/B/JJ/HH/FJ/GF/Msr/ZF3// TF] <çûn>

şane شانه (Bw/SK/GF/OK/FS/BF) = honeycomb. See **şan**.

şaneşîn شانەشین *f./m.(Z-1)* **(-a/-ê;-ê/).** 1) royal court, royal residence; 2) balcony; 3) [*adj.*] beautiful, splendid (B). {also: şanişîn (BF); şehnişîn; [chanichin] شانشین (JJ)} < P šāhnešīn شاهنشین [Z-1/K/B/ ZF3/Wkt//JJ/BF] <dîwan>

şaneyekî hingûnî شانەیەکی هِنگوونی (SK) = honeycomb. See **şan**.

şanişîn شانِشین (BF/JJ) = royal court; balcony. See **şaneşîn**.

şanî dan شانی دان (L/EŞ) = to show; to teach. See **nîşan dan** under: **nîşan**.

şano شانۆ *f.* **(-ya;-yê).** stage, theater; drama, play: **•Nivîserê** ***vê şanoyê*** **Murathan Mungan e** (tigrishaber.com 14.i.2014) The author of this *play* is M.Mungan. < Sor şano شانۆ < T şano < It scena? [Deng(journal)/IFb/GF/TF/FJ/CS/ZF/BF]

şanoger شانۆگەر *m.&f.* **(-ê/ ;).** actor, thespian: **•Kesên ku bêhtir di dîwanxaneyên mîran de pêkenok digotin û carna weke** ***şanogerekî*** **bi rola xwe ve radibûn, ew "qeşmer" bûn** (CP, 6) People who told jokes and sometimes acted out their stories [lit. 'as *an actor* carried out their role'] in the courts of emirs, were "jesters" **•*Şanogerên* Kurd, bi vê projeyê çanda Qirdikîyê didin jiyandin** (VoA, 30.ix.2013) Kurdish *actors* revive the culture of clowning with this project. [(neol.)CP/TF/RZ/ZF] <lîstikvan>

şanzde شانزده (K/B/JB1-A&S/GF/M-Ak & Am & Bar & Shn) = sixteen. See **şanzdeh**.

şanzdeh شانزده *num.* sixteen, 16. {also: şanzde (K/ B-2/JB1-A&S/GF/M-Ak & Am & Bar & Shn); şazde (A/M-sur); şa̱zde (M-Zx & gul); [chanzdeh شانزده/dehouchech دهوشش] (JJ)} Skt ṣóḍaśa (<*ṣazḍaśa); Av xšvaš-dasa; Mid P šāzdah (M3); P šānzdah شانزده; Sor şazde شازده/şanze شانزه; Za şîyês/desuşeş (Todd); Hau şanze (M4) [F/IFb/B/ JJ/ SC//K/JB1-A&S/GF/M-Ak & Am & Bar & Shn//A/M-Sur//M-Zx & Gul] <şeş; şêst>

şanzdehem شانزدەهەم *adj.* sixteenth, 16th. {also: şanzdehemîn (GF/Wkt-2); şanzdemîn (IFb); şanzdeyem (Wkt-2); şanzdeyemîn (Wkt-2); şazdehem (CT/ZF/Wkt); şazdehemîn (Wkt-2); şazdeyem (Wkt-2); şazdeyemîn (Wkt-2)} Cf. P šānzdahom شانزدهم; Sor şanzehem[în] شانزەهەم[ین]/şanzemîn شانزەمین [CT/GF/ZF//IFb//A/ Wkt] <şanzdeh>

şanzdehemîn شانزدەهەمین (GF/Wkt) = sixteenth. See **şanzdehem**.

şanzdemîn شانزدەمین (IFb) = sixteenth. See **şanzdehem**.

şanzdeyem شانزدەیەم (Wkt) = sixteenth. See **şanzdehem**.

şanzdeyemîn شانزدەیەمین (Wkt) = sixteenth. See **şanzdehem**.

şap I شاپ (TF/OK/GF) = avalanche. See **şape I**.

şap II شاپ (GF/TF) = flood. See **şape II**.

şap•e I شاپە *f.* **(•a;•ê).** 1) {syn: aşît; r̄enî; şetele} avalanche: **•Wekî** ***şapê*** **ji jorve tême xwarê/...** (from poem by Syrian poet Keleş) Like *an avalanche* I come down from on high; **-şapa befrê** (Zeb)/**şapa berfê** (GF) do.; 2) snow-drift (K/B). {also: şap I (TF/OK-2/GF-2); şepa; şepe (K/RZ)/şep'e (B); [chapé شاپه/chepé شپه] (JJ); <şape> شاپه (HH); <şape شاپه/şap شاپ> (Hej)} [Zeb/Keleş//A/IFb/JJ/HH/GF/ FS/OK//K/B/RZ//TF] <berf; hezaz; xişîlok>

şape II شاپە *f.* **(-ya;-yê).** flood, inundation: **•Dîroka bobelata** ***şapeyê*** **ya bi rabûna bendavê re pêkhatî ku di Qur'anê de tê vegotin...** (mucizeyenqurane.com: Gelê Sebe û şapeya bendavê) The history of the *flooding* disaster consisting of the collapse of the dam which is told in the Quran.... {also: şap II (GF/TF)} {syn: lehî; lêmişt} [Mdt//GF/TF/ZF3]

şapik شاپِك *m.* **(-ê;).** jacket of Kurdish traditional men's garb; short embroidered jacket with full sleeves [çepken] unique to the Kurds (A/IF); garment made of woven wool which doesn't go beyond the navel (HH); overcoat without lining, with goat hairs in the fabric (JJ): **-şal û şapik** (AB/M) Kurdish man's suit of clothes. See under **şal** I: **•Şekl û rengên** ***şal û şapikê*** **li gor herêm, ol û civak diguhêre** (Wkp) The shapes and colors of *the shal û shapik* vary according to region, religion and social group. {also: [sciápék] شـــاپـــك (JJ); <şabik> شابك (HH)} Cf. W Arm šabig/E Arm šapik շապիկ < WMIr šāpīk, Mid P šabīg [špyk'] = '(Mazdean's ritual) under-shirt' (M3); P šabī شبی; [AB/M/K/A/IF/JJ/Dy//HH] <şal I; şalvar>

şapînoz شاپینۆز *adj.* fake, false, made up, counterfeit, phony: **•Bi çend strîtêl û tepinkan alîyên *şapînoz* û derewîn çêkiribûn** (Nofa, 91) With some barbed wire and mines, they had made some *fake* places [to discourage smugglers] **•Romana "*Şapînoz*" (ev peyva nadir tenê carekê di romanê de derbas dibe) bi teknîkeke kemilî, bi bûyerên watedar, bi saloxdaneke bêalî û bi zimanekî dewlemend hatiye hûnandin** (H. Muhammed. Nefel 9.ix.2011) The novel "*Shapinoz*" (this rare word only occurs once in the novel) has been crafted with a fine technique, with meaningful events, from an unbiased standpoint and with a rich [use of] language. [Nofa/ZF3/Wkt] <derewîn; xapînok>

şapqe شاپقه (GF) = hat. See **şewqe**.

şaqis شـــاقِـــس *adj.* amazed, frightened, in awe: -**şaqis man** (Z-2)/**şaqiz man** (GF) to be amazed: **•Tirs û saw û hêbeteke giran k'ete dilê wane,/ Herdu ji xwer̄a li hev û dinê *şaqis mane*** (Z-2) Fear and terror and awe entered their hearts,/ The two of them *were in awe of* each other. {also: şaqiz (GF/ZF3)} [Z-2//GF/ZF3]

şaqiz شاقِز (GF/ZF3) = amazed. See **şaqis**.

şaqol شاقۆل (GF/SS) = plumb line; type of trap. See **şaqûl**.

şaqûl شـــاقـــوول *f./m.(ZF)* **(/-ê; /-î).** 1) plumb line, pendulum: **•*Şaqûl* bi serê benkî va ye, ji bo ku qorê dîwara rast bên em di lêkirina dîwara da dişixulînin** (M.Mukrîyanî. Ebando, 50) *The plumb line* is at the end of a string, we use it in building walls so that the walls line up straight **•Vizik û *şaqûlên* hevdû direvandin** (SBx, 8) They would steal each other's spinning tops and plumb lines; -**benê şaqolî** (SS) do.; 2) bird and mouse trap (A/IFb/FJ/GF/TF/HH). {also: şagul (CCG); şaqol (GF); <şaqûl> شاقول (HH)} Cf. Ar šāqūl شاقول [SBx/A/B/IFb/FJ/HH/ZF/CS/Kmc//TF//GF/SS//CCG]

şar I شار *f.* **(-a;-ê).** headband, turban (K); black-silver headdress worn by women (A/HH); black cloth wrapped around a woman's headdress (IFb/Haz); large black silken kerchief (B): **•Rêşiyên li dora *şahra* serê wî di ser hev de pêl didin** (Tof, 7) The tassels around his head band hit against one another; -**şar-şemaq** (EP-7) silk neck kerchief. {also: şahr (Tof); şehr I (GF-2); şe'r III (B); <şe'r> شـــعـــر (HH)} [EP-7/K/A/IFb/GF/Haz//B/HH//Tof] <k'ofî>

şar II شار (IFb/GF/SK) = city. See **şeher**.

şaran شـــاران *m.* **(-ê;).** string of dried fruit (raisins, figs, walnuts), for winter use: -**şaranê gûzan** (Xrz) string of walnuts; -**şaranê mewîjan** (Xrz) string of raisins. {syn: gelwaz; xarûz} <Arm šar շար = 'string, file' [Xrz/Wn/GF/FJ] <benî II[1]; meşlûr>

şarandin شـــارانـدِن *vt.* **(-şarîn-).** 1) {syn: sincirandin} to heat stg. up *(to the point of turning red)*, to smelt; to brand (IFb); to cauterize (IFb): **•Wê t̲enûr *şarand*** (FS) She *heated up* the oven; 2) {syn: lê sor kirin; nav tê dan} to incite, provoke. [Zeb/IFb/OK/ZF/FS] <azirandin; germ>

şaraza شارازا (B) = expert. See **şareza**.

şarazatî شارازاتی (B) = expertise. See **şarezayî**.

şareza شـــارەزا *adj.* 1) knowing the way, knowing one's way around, familiar with the area: **•'Eskerê Fazil Paşa li naw dolê şaş bûn, nezanîn kêwe bih̄elên. Leşkirê 'eşîretan ku digel 'eskerê Fazil Paşa hatibûn hindek şareza bûn, ser kewtine çiyan, xo xilas kirin** (SK 48:488) Fazil Pasha's troops went astray in the middle of the canyon, not knowing whither to flee. Some of the tribal force which had come with Fazil Pasha's troops *knew the country* and climbed up into the hills and so saved themselves; 2) acquainted or familiar with or expert in a subject: **•Her şkeftekê çend dergehek hene. Ko *mirovekî şareza* wan dergehan dibîne, di cihê xwe de şaş dimîne** (SB, 50) Each cave has several doors. When *an expert person* sees those doors, he becomes baffled **•S̲ubeya da digel xo bete dikanê da mi'amilê nîşê det ... *şarezay* mi'amila bajerî *bû*** (M-Ak #651, 294) In the mornings he would take him to the shop and show him the business ... he *became acquainted with* the business of the market; 3) [*m.&f.* ().]{ syn: p'ispor} expert; specialist: **•Ew bo çêkirina tirimbêla *şareza* ye** (FS) He is *an expert at* building cars. {also: şahreza (A); şaraza (B-2); şehreza (K-2/IFb-2/GF-2/TF/FS-s); şe'reza (B); [sciárazá (G)/shārāza (Rh)] شـــارازه (JJ); <şehreza> شهرزا (HH)} <Sor şar - "city" + -e- + za = 'born', 'born in (& familiar with) the city: Sor

şareza شارەزا = 'well-informed, proficient, expert' {şahrezayî; şarazatî; şarezahî; şarezayî; şehrezayî; şe'rezatî} [SB/K/IFb/SK/GF/OK//HH/TF/FS//A//B//JJ]

şarezahî شارەزاهی (OK) = expertise. See **şarezayî.**

şarezayî شارەزایی *f.* **(-ya;-yê).** 1) familiarity with a subject or area; expertise, expert knowledge, specializa-tion: **•Wî *şarezayîyeka* baş di bazirganîyê da heye** (FS) He has good *familiarity* with com-merce; 2) experience. {also: şahrezayî (A); şarazatî (B-2); şarezahî (OK-2); şehrezayî (K/GF/ TF/FS-2); şe'rezatî (B); [sciárazáia (G)] شارازی (JJ)} Sor şarezayî شارەزایی = 'proficiency, expert knowledge' [IFb/SK/GF/OK/FS//HH/TF//A//B//JJ] <şareza>

şarge شارگه (K[s]) = sky. See **şargeh.**

***şargeh** شارگەه **().** sky, air: **•Bombeavêjên me ên sivik ... li *şargeh* ... li rêhesinên erdê Kaparanikayê xistine** (RN) Our lightweight bombers have struck the railways of the land of Kaparanika from *the air*. {also: şarge (K[s])} {syn: 'ezman I} [RN/IF//K(s)]

şaristan شارستان (IF) = civilization; city center. See **şaristanî.**

şaristanetî شارستانەتی (K) = civilization. See **şaristanî.**

şaristanî شارستانی *f.* **(-ya;).** civilization: **•Aramê Dîkran nûnerekî payebilind yê *şaristaniya* Rojhilatê bû** (mediakurd.com 8.viii.2010) A. Dikran was a first rate representative of *the civilization of* the East. {also: şaristanetî (K); şarsanîyet (Haz/ZF3) şarsanîyetî (JB3)} {syn: medenîyet; temedon} Sor şaristanîyetî شارستانییەتی [(neol)Haz/ZF3//K//A/IFb/Wkt/BF//JB3]

şarsanîyet شارسانییەت (Haz/ZF3) = civilization. See **şaristanî.**

şarsanîyetî شارسانییەتی (JB3) = civilization. See **şaristanî.**

şaş I شاش *adj.* 1) crooked, bent; 2) {syn: ç'ewt; xelet [2]} wrong, mistaken; doing the opposite of what one wants or intends (HH): **-şaş bûn** = to be mistaken, wrong; **-şaş man** = to be puzzled, confused: **•Ûsib ha hevraz nihêřî ha berjêr nihêřî û *şaşmayî* gote bavê** (Ba #5, 313) Joseph looked now up, now down, and *puzzled*, said to his father ...; **-şaş û ȟeyrî** (EP-7) confused, puzzled, bewildered; **-xwe şaş kirin** = to be wrong, to make a mistake: **•Careke dinê *xwe şaş nekin*** (J) Next time *don't make* [such] *a mistake*; 3) {syn: qîç} squint-eyed, cross-eyed. {also: [chach] شاش (JJ); <şaş> شاش (HH)} <T şaşmak = 'to be amazed; to deviate; to make a mistake; to lose one's way' [K/(A)/JB3/IFb/B/JJ/HH/GF/TF]

şaş II شاش *f.* **().** turban: **•Sûk tije qumaş e, lê mela *bêşaş* e** (BX) The marketplace is full of cloth, but the mullah is *turbanless [prv.]*. {also: şaşik, f. (JB3/IFb/SK/TF); [chach] شاش (JJ); <şaş> شاش (HH)} [BX/A/JJ/HH/GF/FS//JB3/IFb/SK/TF] <k'ofî>

şaşik شاشِك, f. (JB3/IFb/SK/TF) = turban. See **şaş II.**

şaşî شاشی *f.* **(;-yê).** error, mistake: **•Ev bêje û hevokên şaş ên ku min yek bi yek li jor rêz kirine, ne *şaşiyên* daktîlo û yên çapê ne** (AW73C2) These incorrect words and sentences which I have laid out above are not typographical *errors* **•Împeryalîzm di vir de *di şaşiyê de* ye, xwe dixapîne** (AW77C2) Imperialism is *in error* here, it is fooling itself. {syn: ç'ewtî; xelet} [K/IFb/B/TF/AD]

şaşmayî شاشمایی *p.p./adj.* astounded, surprised, dumbfounded, perplexed, confused: **•Bênams *şaşmayî* li bavê dinihêře** (Ba #36, 319) *Dumb-founded*, B. looks at Father. {syn: 'ecêbmayî; ȟeyrî; ȟêbetî; mendehoş; met'elmayî} [Ba/K/FJ/GF/AD/CS] <şaş I>

şavaş شاڤاش (K) = gift of money to musicians at a wedding. See **şabaş.**

şax شاخ *f./m.(SK)* **(-a/;-ê/).** 1) {syn: ç'iq[il]; çirpî; gulî II; ta VI} branch; 2) {syn: qoç'; strû} horn *(of animal)*; antler *(of deer)*; 3) cliff, precipice, mountain slope; 4) part, section, chapter, division; 5) line, track; furrow; 6) {syn: guharto [1]; şov I [6]} version. {also: şax̆; [chakh] شاخ (JJ)} Cf. P šāx شاخ = 'branch; horn, antler'; Sor şax شاخ = 'mountain; horn' [K/A/JB3/IFb/B/JJ/JB1-S/SK/GF]

şaxab شاخاب (FJ) = drill. See **şixab.**

şaxmat شاخمات *f.* **(;-ê).** chess: **-şaxmat lîstin** (B) to play chess. {syn: k'işik [1]; şetrenc} [F/B]

şax̆ شاغ = branch; horn. See **şax.**

şayes شایەس *f.* **(-a;).** explanation, description, definition: **•Ehmedê Xanî jî li ser vê taybetmendiya bajarê Cizîrê beşek ji mesnewiya xwe ... bi hûrdekarî *şayesa* baxçeyê navborî *dike*** (Z. Ergün. Di Peydabûna Edebîyata Kurdî ya li Cizîra Botan de Karîgerîya Bajarvanîyê) Regarding this characteristic of the city of Cizre, Ahmedê Khani *describes* in detail the aforementioned garden in part of his masnavi **•Lehengên nivîskar ên di**

berhemên Ahmet Mithat de *şayesa* nivîskarên bêqisur in (Axaftina Nobelê Û KêmNivîskarî) The heroic writers in the works of Ahmet Mithat are *the definition* of perfect writers. [Wkp/Wkt/ZF]

şayik شايِك *adj.* 1) {syn: hilû I} smooth, soft: **-şayik bûn** (ZF) to be or become smooth or soft: **•Birûyên wî bela wela bûbûn û *şayîkbûna* xwe winda kiribûn** [sic] (SBx, 13) His eyebrows became disheveled and lost their *smoothness*; **-şahîk kirin** (TF)/**şayik kirin** (FJ) to smooth out stg., soften; 2) slippery, slick. {also: şahîk (IFb/TF/Kmc); şayîk (SBx)} [SBx//FJ/GF/ZF//IFb/TF/Kmc]

şayiş شايِش (GF) = worry. See **şayîş**.

şayî I شايى *f.* **(-ya; şayê).** 1) happiness, joy; 2) banquet, feast, celebration; 3) *woman's name.* {also: şadî (K[s]/A/IFb/GF/OK-2); şahî (IFb-2/JB1-S/OK/ZF); [chaï] شاى (JJ)} Av šāti-; O P šiyāti- = 'joy' (Tsb2, p.61); Sor şadî شادى = 'pleasure' & şayî شايى = 'merrymaking, festivity (esp. wedding)'; Hau şadî (M4) [B/JJ//K(s)/A/IFb/GF//JB1-S/OK/ZF] <şa>

şayîk شاييك (SBx) = smooth; slippery. See **şayik**.

şayîr شايير *m.* **(-ê;).** 1) {syn: biwêj I; helbestvan; hozanvan} poet; 2) {syn: stiranbêj} singer. {also: şa'er (JB1-S); şahir (JB3/IFb/GF); şair (ZF); şa'ir (SK); şaîr (B-2); [scăr] شاعر (JJ)} < Ar šā'ir شاعر = 'poet' [K/B//JB3/IFb/GF//JJ//ZF//SK//JB1-S] <helbest; k'ilam; stiran I; şêr II>

şayîş شاييش *f./pl.* **(;-ê/).** worry, concern, anxiety: **-şayîş kirin** (K/B)/**şayîş[a(n)] k'işandin** (K/B/XF) to worry: **•Tu qe *şayîşa nek'işîne*, ez hatime, wekî te îro xilazkim** (XF) *Do not be* at all *worried*, I have come to rescue you today. {also: şaîş (EH); şaîşî (B); şayiş (GF)} {syn: cefa; fikar; k'eder; k'erb; k'eser; kovan; kul I; qilqal; t'alaş; tatêl; xem; xiyal [2]} [EH//B//K/XF//GF] <şik>

şazde شازده (A/M-Sur)/şazde شاظده (M-Zx & Gul) = sixteen. See **şanzdeh**.

şazdehem شازدهه‌م (CT/ZF/Wkt) = sixteenth. See **şanzdehem**.

şazdehemîn شازدهه‌مين (Wkt) = sixteenth. See **şanzdehem**.

şazdeyem شازديه‌م (Wkt) = sixteenth. See **şanzdehem**.

şazdeyemîn شازديه‌مين (Wkt) = sixteenth. See **şanzdehem**.

şe I شه (-yê; şê) (K/B/IFb/GF/BK/JB1-A/JJ/Ks/Bw) = comb. See **şeh**.

şe II شه: **-şe kirin** (Ad/RZ/ZF) to be able to, can; to succeed in: **•Ez *şe nakim*** (Ad) I *cannot.* {syn: karîn; pê ç'êbûn; şiyan} [Ad/RZ/ZF]

şeb شه‌ب *f.* **(-a;-ê).** alum, vitriol: **•Ewê, ko li şekir hat li *şebê* ĥesilî** (Z-3) She who came for sugar got *alum*; **-şeva [hê]şîn** (K/B) blue alum/vitriol; **-şeva sipî** (K/B) white alum/vitriol. {also: şev II (K/B); [chab] شاب (JJ); <şeb> شب (HH)} <Ar šabb شبّ --> P šāb شاب --> T şap; W Arm šip' շիփ/šab շապ; Sor şaf شاف [Z-3/HH/TF//K/B//JJ]

şebak شه‌باك (A) = dawn. See **şebeq**.

şebaş شه‌باش = gift of money to musicians at a wedding. See **şabaş**.

şebek شه‌به‌ك = dawn. See **şebeq**.

şebeq شه‌به‌ق *f.* **(-a;-ê).** dawn, daybreak: **-şeveqa sibêȓa** (B) at daybreak; **-sibehê şibaqê** (L)/**sibê şebeqê** (Dz) tomorrow at daybreak. {also: şebak (A); şebek; şefeq (IFb/GF-2); şeveq (B); şewaq; şeweq (GF); şibaq I (L); şivaq (GF-2)} {syn: berbang; elind; ferec; hingûr [1]; segur; serê sibê; siĥar; spêde} Cf. Ar šafaq شفق --> T şafak [L//A//K/Dz//GF//B//Ba/F//IFb]

şebeş شه‌به‌ش (Btm/Czr/Grc) = watermelon. See **zebeş**.

şebeyxûn شه‌به‌يخوون *f.* **(;-ê).** surprise night attack, camisado: **•[Ekradêd simtê Ĥekariyan ekserî şerî û de'wayî bi şev dikin û zaf *şebeyxûnê* didine dijminan]** (BN 136) The Kurds of the Hekkari region mostly fight and do battle at night and carry out many *surprise night attacks* on their enemies. {also: şebxûn (K); şevxûn (GF); [cheb-khoun] شبخون (JJ); <şebeyxûn> شه‌به‌يخوون (Hej)} Cf. P šabīxūn شبيخون; Sor şebeyxûn شه‌به‌يخوون [BN/IFb/Hej//K/JJ//GF] <êrîş>

şebh شه‌به *f.* **().** doubt; suspicion. {also: şibhe (K-2/IFb); şubhe (SK); [chubhé] شبهه (JJ)} {syn: guman; ĥeseĥes; şik} < Ar šubhah شبهة --> T şüphe [Rh/K//IFb//JR/JJ/SK] <ĥeseĥes>

şebqe شه‌بقه (GF) = hat. See **şewqe**.

şebxûn شه‌بخوون (K) = surprise night attack. See **şebeyxûn**.

şe'de شه‌عده (FK-eb-1) = witness. See **şade**.

şe'detî شه‌عده‌تى (B) = testimony. See **şadetî**.

şe'etîn شه‌عه‌تين (Gz) = to decline, deteriorate. See **şihitîn**.

şefeq شه‌فه‌ق (IFb/GF) = dawn. See **şebeq**.

şef•ir شه‌فِر *f.* **(;•rê).** a large knife: **•Ka şefrê bîne** (Bw) Bring [me] a large knife. < Ar šafrah شفرة

= 'large knife; blade' [Bw/Wkt] <hisan; k'êr III; sat'or I>

şefqe شەفقە (K/A/IFb/GF/CS) = hat. See **şewqe**.

şeh شـــەه *m.* **(-ê; şê** [BK/B]**).** 1) comb: **-şeh kirin** = to comb {also: şkinîn}; **-şehê dîk** = cock's comb; **-şeyê mar** (Msr) centipede; 2) the five digits of the hand or foot (Bw/Zx): **-şeyê dest** (Bw) five fingers of the hand ['comb of the hand']; **-şeyê pê** (Bw)/**şehê pî** (Zx) five toes of the foot ['comb of the foot']. {also: şe I (-yê; şê) (K/B/IFb-2/GF-2/BK/JB1-A-2/Ks); [chè] شـه (JJ); <şeh> شـه (HH)} Cf. P šāne شانە; Sor şane شانە/şe شـه [A/JB3/IFb/JB1-A/HH/GF/TF/Zx//K/B/JJ/BK/Ks/Bw] <p'oř III; şan>

şehde شەهدە (K/HH) = witness. See **şade**.

şehderewan شـــــەهـــــدەرەوان (TF) = fountain. See **şadîrewan**.

şeher شـــەهـــەر *m.* **(-ê;).** city, town: •**Zemanê Sultan 'Ebdulḧemîd Xan ... Rizwan Paşa hebû, walî<yê> *şehrê* Istembolê bû** (SK 52:559) In the time of Sultan AbdulHamid Khan ...there was (a certain) Rizvan Pasha, governor of *the city of* Istanbul. {also: şar II (IFb/GF-2/SK); şehr II (IFb-2/GF/SK-2); [шегерь/shahr] شـهـر (JJ)} {syn: bajar} [Pok. kþē(i)-/kþə(i)- 626.] 'to obtain, acquire, take control of' (Kent: proto IE *qþei-) [cf. **şiyan**]: Av xšaθra- = 'dominion, empire'; Mid P šahr [štr'] = 'land, country; city' (M3); P šahr شـهـر ='city' --> T şehir; Sor şar شـار [Z-1/K/B//JJ//GF//IFb/SK]

şehitîn شـەهِتين (Wkt/FS) = to decline, deteriorate. See **şihitîn**.

şehîn شـــەهـــيـــن (K[s]/A/IFb/HH/GF/TF/Kmc-9/FS) = scales. See **şihîn**.

şehîre شەهيرە (Wkt) = noodles. See **şiîre**.

şehlûl شەهلوول (AA/OK) = blackbird. See **şalûl**.

şehn شەهن (GF) = honeycomb. See **şan**.

şehnişîn شەهنشين = royal court; balcony. See **şaneşîn**.

şehr I شەهر (GF) = head band. See **şar I**.

şehr II شەهر (IFb/GF/SK) = city. See **şeher**.

şehreza شـەهـرەزا (K/IFb/GF/TF/HH/FS) = expert. See **şareza**.

şehrezayî شـەهـرەزايـى (K/GF/TF/FS) = expertise. See **şarezayî**.

şehriye شەهريە (IFb) = noodles. See **şiîre**.

şeht شـــەهـــت *adj.* paralyzed, crippled, lame, disabled *(e.g., hand)*: •**Ev reben keça *şeht*, çi delal e, çi şêrîn e ... Hema xwezî ev keçik tuneba ma ne gunehe Xwedê ew hewqas spehî çêkir û piştre ew *şeht* kir** (AI, 63) This poor *crippled* girl, how lovely, how sweet she is ... I wish this girl didn't exist--isn't it a pity that God made her so pretty, and then made her *crippled*! {also: <şeḧt> شـحـت (HH)} {syn: goc; kulek I; kût I; qop; şil II} {*şehtî} [AI/IFb/GF/TF//HH] <nivîşkan I>

şek شـــــــــەك *m.* **(-ê;).** two-year-old ram, male sheep (Zeb/GF/Hej/FS/BF); three-year-old ram (IFb/SK): •**'Elî Beg qiyasê neh deh ser ḧeywanêt qelew ji beranan û *şekan* înan, dane kuştinewe** (SK 39:346) Ali Beg brought about nine or ten head of fat young rams and had them slaughtered. {also: şak (GF); <şek> شـــــــــەك (Hej)} {syn: berindir} cf. P šāk شـاك = 'he-goat'; Sor şek شـەك = 'yearling lamb' [Zeb/K(s)/IFb/SK/OK/Hej/FS/BF//GF] <beran; berdîr; mî I; xirt>

şekal شـــەكـــال *m./f.(Nbh)* **(-ê/-a;).** 1) old, worn-out shoe: •[A man sees a pretty young girl and says to himself] **Ez xort bûma, minê quz li wê bikira *şikal*** (Msr) If I were young, I'd make her cunt an old shoe (i.e., from much use) •**Hingê min *şekala* xwe deranî** (Nbh 128:38) Then I took off my worn out shoe; 2) {syn: qondere; p'êlav; sol} shoe (Haz/TF/OK). {also: lekaş (IFb-2); şikal (Haz/Msr); [chekal] شكال (JJ); <şekal> شكال (HH)} Cf. Sor kełaş كـەڵاش = 'shoe with rag sole'. *For other examples of special words for old things see **kalûme**.* [IFb/JJ/HH/JB1-A/GF/TF/OK/Srk/Klk/Nbh//Haz/Msr] <kelêj I; p'êlav; sol>

şek'er شەكەر = sugar. See **şekir**.

şekil شەكِل (JJ/ZF) = form; picture. See **şikil**.

şekir شـــەكِـــر *m./f.(SK)* **(-ê/ ; şêkir, vî şekirî/).** sugar: **-şekirî şkandin** (Zeb) to break the ice, start a friendly conversation. {also: şek'er; [chekir] شـكـر (JJ); <şekir> شكر (HH)} <Prakrit & Pali sakkharā < Skt śarkarā = 'gravel, grit; later sugar' (Laufer, p.584); Sor şekir شـەكِـر; Za şeker *m.* (Todd); Hau şekir *m.* = qen (M4) [Z-3/F/K/A/IFb/B/JJ/HH/SK/GF/TF/OK/Zeb]

şekirdan شـــەكِـــردان (K/B/GF/BF) = sugar bowl. See **şekirdank**.

şekirdang شـەكِـردانـگ (F/K/B/TF) = sugar bowl. See **şekirdank**.

şekirdank شەكِردانك *f.* **(-a;-ê).** sugar bowl: •**Wê şekir kir *şekirdankê*** (FS) She put sugar in *the sugar bowl.* {also: şekirdan (K/B/GF/BF); şekirdang (F/K-2/B-2/TF)} Sor şekirdan شـەكِـردان [Bw/Zx/IFb/OK/FS//K/B/GF/BF//F/TF]

şekirî شـەكِـرى *adj. pattern of **bergûz** material*: off-white. [Bw] <bergûz>

şekirok I شـەكِـرۆك (A/GF/HH/IFb) = type of globe thistle. See **şekrok**.

şekirok II شـەكِـرۆك *f.* **(-a;-ê).** candy, sweetmeat: **•Îcar zarûkên wî bo şekirokan li berîkên saqoyê wî digerin** (ZZ-4, 172) So his children search the pockets of his coat for candies. {syn: şîranî} [ZZ/SS/FS]

şekîyat شەكيیات = complaint. See **şikyat**.

şekok شـەكـۆك *f.* **(-a;-ê).** wild pear, bot. *Pyrus pyraster* [T ahlat]. {also: şekûke (Ad); şelqoq (A); şikoke (GF); <şkok> شكوك (HH)} {syn: kirosik} [IFb/RF/CB/ZF3/BF/FS//HH//GF//Ad//A] <hermê; încas [1]; karçîn>

şekrok شـەكـرۆك *f.* **().** type of globe thistle, bot. *Echinops sphaerocephalus*. {also: şekirok I (A/GF/IFb); <şekirok> شكروك (HH)} {syn: *serteşî (Bw/Wn)} [Qrj/FJ/FS//A/HH/GF/IFb]

şekûke شەكووكە (Ad) = wild pear. See **şekok**.

şel I شەل (IFb/GF/HH) = paralyzed. See **şil II**.

şel II شـەل *f.* **(;-ê).** 1) very large saddlebag *loaded on the back of a camel, filled with stocks of grain [gidîş] to transport to threshing floor [bênder]*; 2) action of transporting stocks of grain [gidîş] to the threshing floor [bênder]: **-şel kişandin** (Qzl) to transport grain to the threshing floor: **•Em *şela dikişînin*** (Qzl) We are dragging saddlebags, i.e., We are transporting grain to the threshing floor. {also: şal II (GF-2); şele (GF)} Cf. Sor şeĺte شـەڵـتـە = 'kind of saddle-bag' [Qzl/ZF3//GF] <şixre; t'er̄ III>

şel III شـەل *m.* **(-ê;).** lump, chunk, piece *(of ice, rock, snow, coal, etc.)*, clod *(of earth or mud)*: **-şelê berfê** (B) lump of snow; **-şelê bûz** (GF) chunk of ice: **•Hêta min şkestîye, minê *şele* bûz daye ser** (HCK-2, 91) My hip is broken, I have put *a chunk of* ice on it; **-şelê xwelîyê** (B) heap of ashes. {syn: loq I} [HCK/K/B/FJ/GF/TF/Kmc/ZF3/FS] <p'erçe>

şe'l IV شەعل (B) = trousers. See **şal I**.

şelandin شـەلانـدِن *vt.* **(-şelîn-).** 1) {syn: şiqitandin} to undress, strip, take off *(s.o.'s clothes)*, strip *(vt.)*: **-xwe şêlandin** (K/IFb): to undress (o.s.), take one's clothes off, strip *(vi.)*: **•[Ew her sê mirof hatine devê çemekî û *xwe şelandin* ku ji avê derbaz bibin]** (JR) Those three men came to the edge of a river and *stripped*, so that they could cross the water; 2) to plunder, rob: **•Karwanekî Şêxê Barzanê diçû Akrê. Nijda Sûrçîyan hat, karwan *şeland* û deh muro kuştin** (SK 50:533) A caravan of the Shaikh of Barzan was going to Akre. A Surchi raiding party came, *plundered* the caravan, and killed ten men. {also: şêlandin (K/IFb/B); [chelandin] شلاندين (JJ); <şelandin شلاندن (dişelîne) (دشلينه)> (HH)} [JR/JJ/HH/SK/GF/TF//K/IFb/B]

şelbik شەلبِك (Ba2/HCK) = water pitcher. See **şerbik**.

şele شەلە (GF) = large saddlebag. See **şel II**.

şelengo شەلەنگۆ *f.* **().** type of round cucumber. {also : şelengok (ZF3); şiling (GF)} {syn : *ecûr; *êmidî} Cf. Sor şiling شِـلـنـگ = kalyar كـالـيـار = 'type of large cucumber' [Qzl/Kmc//ZF3//GF] <kûtik; xiyar>

şelengok شـەلـەنـگـۆك (ZF3) = round cucumber. See **şelengo**.

şelifîn شـەلِـفـيـن *vi.* **(-şelif-).** to stumble, trip: **•Jiyana min tu xwe ragire *tu car neşelife*!** (M. Çobanoğlu. Jiyana min neşelife) Life of mine, keep yourself together and *never stumble*! {also: şelipîn (FD/IFb-2); <ş[e]l[i]pîn شـلـپـيـن (dişelipî) (دشـلـپـى)> (HH)} {syn: alîn; lik'umîn; tehisîn} Cf. NENA shâlip ܫܠܦ = 'to be dislocated, be out of joint' (Maclean) [M.Çobanoğlu/A/IFb/ZF3//HH/FD]

şe'lik شەعلِك (B) = apron. See **şalik I**.

şelipîn شەلِپين (FD/IFb/HH) = to stumble. See **şelifîn**.

şelît شەليت (HR) = rope; string. See **şerît** [1].

şelmaq شەلماق (K/B) = smack, slap. See **şimaq**.

şelqoq شەلقۆق (A) = wild pear. See **şekok**.

şelûf شـەلـووف *m.* **(-ê;).** cockerel, young rooster. {also: şelûfk (ZF3); şelûvk (Kmc-9); <şelûf> شـلـوف (HH); <şelûf> شـەلـوف (Hej)} {syn: ç'êt} [Kmc-9//A/IFb/HH/GF/Hej/FS//ZF3] <dîk>

şelûfk شەلووفك (ZF3) = young rooster. See **şelûf**.

şel û şepik (FS) شـەل و شـەپِـك/**şelûşapik** (Wkt) شـەلـووشـەپِـك = Kurdish men's outfit. See **şal û şapik** under **şal I**.

şelût شەلووت (RZ) = naked. See **zelût**.

şelûvk شەلووڤك (Kmc-9) = young rooster. See **şelûf**.

şelwal شـەلـوال (JB1-A/SK/OK/Bw/FS) = baggy trousers. See **şalvar**.

şelwar شـەلـوار (A/IFb/GF) = baggy trousers. See **şalvar**.

şem شەم (K) = wax. See **şema**.

şema شـەمـە *f.* **(;-ê, şimê [B]).** 1) {syn: mûm [1]} wax; 2) {syn: find; mûm [2]; şemal[k]} wax candle: **•Wextê jin çûn, *şemala şemaê* birine** [sic] **hindav gay, dîtin** [sic] **ko ga mirar bûy** (SK

30:273) When the women went and held *a wax candle* over the ox they saw that it had died; 3) new, light honeycomb wax (Zeb) as opposed to **movane**, qv. {also: şem (K-2); şima (K/A/IFb-2/B/TF/OK-2); [chima] شـمـع (JJ); <şima> شـمـا (HH)} < Ar šam' شـمـع = 'wax, wax candle'; Sor şem شـهـم [Zeb/IFb/SK/OK/FS//K/A/B/JJ/HH/TF] <[3] movane; şan>

şemal شەمال *f.* **(-a;-ê).** 1) brightness, brilliance, shine: -**şemala tîrêjna te'vê** (B) the brilliance of rays of sunshine; 2) [? < Ar miš'āl مشعال = 'torch'; Cf. P šamālah شـمـالـه = 'candle'] {syn: r̄onahî} light, lighting (IFb/B); 3) {also: şemalk (Bw/BF/FD); [chemal] شـمـال (JJ)} {syn: çira I: fanos; find} lamp; candle: •**Wextê jin çûn, *şemala* şemaê birin** [sic] **e-hindaw gay, dîtin** [sic] **ko ga mirar bûy. Pîçek şemal wêwetir birin** [sic]**, dîtin** [sic] **ker kuştîyewe** (SK 30:273) When the women went and took a wax *candle* to [view] the ox they saw that it had died of itself. They took *the candle* a little to one side and saw that the donkey was slaughtered; -**şemal dayîn** (B) to light up, illuminate; 4) [< Ar šamāl شـمـال] {also: şimal (F); [chimal] شمال (JJ)} {syn: bakur; mifriq} north; 5) north wind. [EP-7/K/A/IFb/B/JJ/SK/GF/FS//Bw/BF/FD//F]

şemalk شەمالك (Bw/BF/FD) = candle. See **şemal**[3].

şemam شـەمـام (K/B) = type of fragrant melon. See **şimamok**.

şemamik شـەمـامِك (IFb) = type of fragrant melon. See **şimamok**.

şemaq I شەماق *f.* **().** woman's head kerchief; woman's kerchief with white dots on it (B): -**şar-şemaq** (EP-7) silk neck kerchief. {also: şemaqî, f. (K/B/ZF3)} {syn: şar I} [EP-7//K/B/ZF3] <k'ofî>

şemaq II شەماق = smack, slap. See **şimaq**.

şemaqî شـەمـاقـى, f. (K/B/ZF3) = woman's head kerchief. See **şemaq I**.

şematok شەماتۆك (A/GF/FJ) = slippery. See **şematokî**.

şematokî شـەمـاتۆكـى adj. slippery: •**Lê belê qeraxên wê (bîrê) gelikî *şematokî* bûn** (FS) But the sides of that (well) were very *slippery*; -**'erdê şematokî** (Qzl) slippery ground. {also: şematok (A/GF/FJ); şemitok (IFb/ZF3/BF); şemitokî (Qrj); şimitokî (K/B); [chemitouk] شـمـتـوك (JJ)} {syn: *teĥesok} [Qzl/FS//A/GF/FJ//IFb/ZF3/BF/JJ//K/B]

şembelîlk I شـەمـبـەلـيـلـك *f.* **(-a;).** icicle: •***Şembilîl* bi kevirê** [!] **çê bûne** (FS) *Icicles* formed on the rock. {also: bizmilûg (IFb-2); şembilîl (FS); zembelik (TF); zembelîlk (GF-2); <şembelîlk> شمبليلك (HH)} *For another example of initial ş-/z- alternation see **zebeş**.* [Frq/Haz/Erh/IFb/GF/ZF3//TF//FS]

şembelîlk II شـەمـبـەلـيـلـك (GF/Wkt) = fenugreek. See **şembelûle**.

şembelûl•e شـەمـبـەلـوولـە *f.* **(;•ê).** fenugreek, bot. *Trigonella foenumgraecum*. {also: şembelîlk II (GF/Wkt); şembelûlk (IFb/OK/AD); <şembelîl[i]k> شـمـبـلـيـلـك (HH)} Cf. P šanbalīle شَنبليله; Sor şimlî شِملّی [Zeb/Dh//IFb/OK/AD//HH/GF/Wkt] <r̄eşik III>

şembelûlk شەمبەلوولك (IFb/OK/AD) = fenugreek. See **şembelûle**.

şembilîl شەمبِليل (FS) = icicle. See **şembelîlk I**.

Şembî شەمبی (K/JB3/JJ/SK) = Saturday. See **Şemî**.

şemdan شـەمـدان *f.* **(-a;).** candlestick, candelabrum. {also: şamdank (ZF3); şemhedan (GF); şimadank (IFb-2); [chemadan/scamadán (G)] شـمـعـدان (JJ)} {syn: findank} Cf. P šam'dān شـمـعـدان < Ar šam' شـمـع = 'wax; candles'+ -dān دان --> T şamdan [HCK/K/IFb//GF//JJ//ZF3]

Şeme شەمە (A) = Saturday. See **Şemî**.

şememok شـەمـەۆك (Rh) = type of fragrant melon. See **şimamok**.

şemetîn شەمەتين (A) = to slip. See **şemitîn**.

şemhedan شەمهەدان (GF) = candlestick. See **şemdan**.

şemil شـەمِل *f.* **(-a;).** Kurdish man's headdress. {syn: cemedanî; dersok; kevîng; p'oşî} <Ar šamlah شملة = 'turban' [Wn] <egal>

şemilk شەمِلك (FS) = prayer rug. See **şemlik**.

şemirandin شـەمِـرانـدِن *vt.* **(-şemirîn-).** 1) {syn: t'erk dan/kirin; t'erkandin} to abandon, leave, give up: •**Û me ji tiştû malê dever *şemirand*** (Lwj #24, 37) And we *have given up* worldly things and possessions; 2) {syn: hildan; hilk'işandin; hilmiştin; vedan; vemaliştin} to roll up *(sleeves)*: •**Hingê Çorçîl rabûye, çîpên xwe heta çokan û zendên xwe heta enîşkan *şemirandine*** (Bkp, xxviii) Then Churchill *rolled up* his pants legs to the knees and his sleeves to the elbows. {also : [chemirandin] شـمـرانـديـن (JJ); <şemirandin شمراندن (dişemirîne) (دشمرينه)> (HH)} < Syr š-m-r ܫܡܪ (šmar) = 'to dismiss, let go; to let loose' [Bkp/Lwj/K/A/IFb/FJ/GF/JJ/HH/CS/Kmc/ZF]

şemitandin شـەمِـتـانـدِن *vt.* **(-şemitîn-).** to cause to slip, cause to slide. {also: şimitandin (K/B); <şemitandin شـمـطـانـدن (dişemitîne) (دشـمـطـيـنـه)> (HH)} {syn: teĥisandin} [A/IFb/GF//K/B//HH]

<lik'umandin; şemitîn>

şemitîn شەمِتین *vi.* **(-şemit-).** to slip, slide: **•Beyrim li ser devê çalê *şemitî*** (L) Beyrim *slipped* over the mouth of the pit. {also: şemetîn (A); şimitîn (K/B); [chemitin] شمتین (JJ); <şemiṯîn شمطین (dişemiṯî) (دشمطی)> (HH)} {syn: şiqitîn; teĥisîn} < Arc šmaṭ שמט/šmeṭ שמיט = 'to loosen, detach, break loose, take away; to slip off, glide; to be released, rest, lie fallow' & Syr √š-m-ṭ ܫܡܛ = 'to draw, unsheath; to pluck, tear out (hair, feathers); to pull off (shoes)' [L/JB3/IFb/JJ/GF//HH//K/B//A] <şemitandin>

şemitok شەمِتۆك (IFb/ZF3/BF) = slippery. See **şematokî**.

şemitokî شەمتۆكی (Qrj) = slippery. See **şematokî**.

Şemî شەمی *f.* **(-ya;-yê).** Saturday. {also: Şembî (K/JB3/SK); Şeme (A); [chembi] شمبی (JJ); <şemî> شمی (HH)} {syn: Paşînî; Sebt} Cf. P šanbe شنبه; Sor şemû شەموو; Za şeme *m.* (Todd) [F/IFb/B/HH/GF/TF//K/JB3/JJ/SK//A]

şemlik شەملِك *f.* **(-a;-ê).** prayer rug: **•Cihê min û *şemlika* min bibe mezelka mina nivistinê** (Çîvanoka gayê sor, 2006, 9) Take my bedding and my prayer rug to my bedroom **•Wî li ser *şemilkê* nivêj kir** (FS) He prayed on *the rug*. {also: şemilk (FS); <şemlik> شەملك (Hej); <şemlik> شملك (MJ)} [Çîvanoka gayê sor/Hej/MJ//FS]

şemo شەمۆ *m.* **().** clown, laughingstock, buffoon, jester; ugly and ridiculous, apelike. {syn: qeşmer; qirdik} [Hk/Zeb/TF/ZF3]

şems•e شەمسە *f.* **(•a;).** umbrella, parasol. {also: şemsiye (K/IFb-2); şemşe (IFb); [chemsiié] شمسیه (JJ)} {syn: sîtavk; sîwan} < Ar šamsīyah شمسية [< šams شمس = 'sun'] --> T şemsiye [Krç//K/JJ//IFb]

şemsiye شەمسِیە (K/IFb/JJ) = umbrella. See **şemse**.

şemşe شەمشە (IFb) = umbrella. See **şemse**.

şe'n شەعن (Msr) = honeycomb. See **şan**.

şengal شەنگال (IFb) = terebinth. See **şengêl**.

şengebî شەنگەبی (FJ/GF/Kmc) = weeping willow. See **bîşeng**.

şengêl شەنگێل *f.* **(-a;-ê).** (wild) terebinth, bot. *Pistacia terebinthus* (IFb); nettle tree, bot. *Celtis australis* (ZF3). {also: şengal (IFb); şînok (A)} {syn: kezan} [Frq/ZF3//IFb//A] <bêmk>

şengiste شەنگستە *m.* **(-yê;).** foundation *(of house, etc.)*, basis: **•Me *şengiste* danane dê dîwarekî ava keyn** (BF) We have laid *the foundation*, we will build a wall **•Ziman *şengisteyê* neteweyî ye** (X.M.Yûsif. Zimanê neteweyî di tevera rizgarîxwaza Kurdî da, 26) Language is the national *foundation* [i.e., the basis of nationhood]. {syn: binat'ar [2]; bingeh; binî; esas; ĥîm} [Yûsif/BF/RZ/ZF3]

şe'nik شەعنِك (Msr) = honeycomb. See **şan**.

şepa شەپا = avalanche. See **şape I**.

şep'al شەپال *adj.* handsome, beautiful, graceful: **•Wext dibuhure, kurik mezin dibe û xortekî *şepal* jê derdikeve** (Ardû, 26) Time passes, the boy grows up and a becomes a handsome young man [lit. 'a handsome young man comes out of him']. {also: şepel (A)} {syn: xweşik} cf. Sor şepał شەپاڵ = 'lion cub' [Ardû/K/B/IFb/FJ/GF/HH/Kmc/CS/FS//A]

şepe شەپە (K/RZ)/şep'e (B) = avalanche. See **şape I**.

şepel شەپەل (A) = handsome, beautiful. See **şep'al**.

şepirze شەپرزە (Zeb/GF/TF) = miserable; hurried. See **şerpeze**.

şepirzetî شەپرزەتی (TF) = misery. See **şerpezeyî**.

şepqe شەپقە (RZ) = hat. See **şewqe**.

şeq شەق *m./f.(B)* **(-ê/ ;-a/-ê).** 1) side, direction: **•bi *şeqê* çepê** (IF) on the left *(side)*; 2) {syn: ker I; kerî I; p'ar II; parî; p'erçe; şeq; qet II; telîş I} piece, slice: **•Sêv kire du *şeqane*** (Z-2) He split the apple into two *pieces*; 3) inner side of thigh, from the hip bone to the foot (B/IFb); 4) {syn: dugulî; navřan} crotch. {also: şeqe (K[s]); <şeq> شق (HH)} < Ar šiqq شقّ = 'side, portion' & šaqq شقّ = 'crack' [Z-2/IFb/A/B/HH/TF/Qzl//K(s)]

şeqal شەقال (K) = jackal. See **çeqel**.

şeqam شەقام (IFb/GF/TF) = smack, slap. See **şimaq**.

şeqe شەقە (K[s]) = side; piece; leg. See **şeq**.

şeqil شەقِل *f.* **(-a;-ê).** wooden seal or marker *put on grain husks on threshing floor at night to prevent theft*: **•Wî *şeqla* xwe li cêza genimî da** (FS) He put his *seal* on the stack of wheat. {also: şeql (GF); <şeql> شقل (HH)} [Qzl/IFb/TF/ZF3/Wkt/FD/FS//GF/HH]

şeqitandin شەقِتاندِن (IFb/HH/GF/TF/OK) = to strip; to split. See **şiqitandin**.

şeqitîn شەقِتین (IFb/HH/GF) = to slip; to climb down; to be split. See **şiqitîn**.

şeql شەقل (GF/HH) = seal on grain husks. See **şeqil**.

şeř I شەڕ *m.* **(-ê; şêř, vî şeřî).** 1) {syn: ceng} war, battle; fight: **•Ezê dakevim *şerê* te** (L) I will take you on (in *battle*) **•*Şerê* min tera *şere*** (J) This means war! [lit. 'My *war* with you is *war*']; 2) argument, quarrel, fight: **-şeř bûn** = to quarrel, argue: **•Xizêma poz, qaş, qerefîl, guharê zêř xala sûretřa *şeřbûn*** (Ba) [Her] noserings ... [and] golden earrings *quarreled* with the birthmark [on her neck]; **-şeř kirin** = a) to battle, fight; b) to beat, vanquish, subdue, defeat: **•Tu kes nikare *şerê* wî *bike*** (L) Nobody can *vanquish* him; 3) type of song in which a battle is portrayed (e.g., between two tribes) (Msr): **-k'ilamên şeř** (Hamelink) war songs. {also: [cher] شر (JJ)} Cf. Ar šarr شرّ = 'bad, evil'; Sor şeř شەڕ = 'fight, quarrel, war' [F/K/A/JB3/IFb/B/JJ/SK/GF/TF/Msr/ZF]

şeř II شەڕ *m.* **().** 1) evil, wickedness; 2) {syn: altaxî; 'ewanî; geveztî; qumsîtî} slander: **•Mîrê min, şixul bi *şeřa* nabe** (Ba3-3, #30) My emir, this matter should not be accomplished through *slander* [lit. 'the work does not happen with *slanders*']; **-şeř avîtin (ser) *fk-ê*** (K/B/XF) to slander, calumniate, denounce {syn: lomandin}: **•Ew diçe cem mîr, *şeřa davê* Ûsiv** (Ba3-3, #29) He goes to the emir [and] *denounces* Joseph **•Seyda, lê te çawa *şeř avîte* min, te çû go: 'Xelq derîkîřa diçe, derîkîřa tê'** (HCK-1, 210) Teacher, how could you *slander* me [like that], you went and said, 'People go in one door and come out another door' *[describing woman as whore]*. < Ar šarr شرّ = 'bad, evil' [Ba3/K/B/SK/XF] <'ewan; nemam>

şe'r III شەعر (B) = scarf; turban. See **şar I**.

şerab شەراب *f.* **(-a;-ê).** wine: **•Mestî *şeraba* 'alema lahût û serxoşî cemala bezma melekût e** (SK 4:36) He is drunk with *the wine of* the divine world and intoxicated by the beauty of the assembly of angels; **-şerava tirîya** (B) grape wine. {also: şerav (F/B); [шерапь/šeräb] شراب (JJ); <şerab> شراب (HH)} {syn: mey} < Ar šarāb شراب (√š-r-b شرب = 'to drink') --> T şarap; Cf. Sor şerab شەراب [K/IFb/HH/JJ/SK/GF//B/F]

şerav شەراڤ (F/B) = wine. See **şerab**.

şerbet شەربەت *f.* **(-a;-ê).** sherbet, a sweet beverage made of sugar and water or fruit syrup; lemonade (JJ): **•Lê her ku kevçiyê *şerbetê* yan jî liba derman nêzîkî devê xwe dikir, dikir ku vereşe** (HYma, 34) But whenever he brought a spoonful *of syrup* or a pill near his mouth, he almost threw up **-Şerbet be!** (B) *formula said when a glass of wine, water, or the like is brought in, and also in answer to a toast.* {also: [cherbet] شربت (JJ); <şerbet> شربت (HH)} < Ar šariba شرب = 'to drink' [EP-7/K/IFb/B/JJ/HH/GF/TF/ZF] <şîranî>

şerbik شەربِك *m.(SK/Wlt/FS)/f.(K)* **(-ê/ ;-î/).** water-pot, water pitcher, tankard: **•Hat, *şelbik* hilda avê bixwe** (HCK-3, #2, 26) He came, picked up *the water pitcher* to drink water **•Min di vê şikêra hanê de *şerbikek* zêr hilandiye (veşartiye)** (Wlt 2:59, 15) I have hidden *a pot of* gold in this pile of stones **•Sibê zû em ji xewê řakirin, danê me ȟer yekî kerî nanê tendûrê û *şelbikekî* mezin şîrê mîa** (Ba2, 220) They woke us early in the morning, gave us each a piece of freshly baked bread and a big *pitcher of* sheep's milk. {also: şelbik (Ba2/HCK); [cherbik] شربك (JJ); <şerbik> شربك (HH)} {syn: sewîl} [Wlt/K/IFb/JJ/HH/SK/GF/TF/FS//Ba2/HCK]

şerd شەرد (L) = condition; bet; task. See **şert**.

şeřdar شەڕدار (B) = warrior. See **şeřvan**.

şeředev شەڕەدەڤ *f.* **(-a;).** war of words, verbal sparring, argument: **•Dihî *şeředeva* wan bû** (FS) They had a *war of words* yesterday. [Dh/Zeb/FS]

şeref شەرەف *f.* **(-a;).** honor: **•Ev, go zilamekî diz bûna [sic] ... wê *şerefa* me bişkenandana** (L) If this man were a thief, he would have ruined our *honor* (=disgraced us). {syn: namûs; řûmet} < Ar šaraf شرف --> T şeref [K/IFb/SK/GF/ZF] <'erz; namûs; řêz II>

şeřenîx شەڕەنیخ (Zeb) = battle, fight. See **cerenîx**.

şerenqe شەرەنقە (FS) = syringe, shot. See **şirînqe**.

şeřevan شەڕەڤان (K/TF) = warrior. See **şeřvan**.

şe'reza شەعرەزا (B) = expert. See **şareza**.

şe'rezatî شەعرەزاتی (B) = expertise. See **şarezayî**.

şerite شەرِتە, f. (K) = line. See **şerît** [2].

şerîet شەریئەت *f.* **(-a;-ê).** the Shari'ah, the Islamic code of law; justice: **•Em hatine cem te *şerîetê*** (ZZ-6, 126) We have come to you for *justice*. {also: şirî'et (EP-7); [cheriiet] شريعت (JJ)} < Ar al-šarī'ah الشريعة [EP-7//K/JJ/ZF] <neşerî>

şerît شەریت *f.* **(-a;-ê).** 1) {also: şelît (HR); şirît (IFb/B); [chirid] شريد (JJ)} {syn: kap I; k'indir [2]; qirnap; werîs} rope (L/B); thick string or twine (B): **•Braê wî řabû *şelît* avêtne [sic] noqa wî û kşandin** (HR 3:190) His brother[s] threw *the rope* around his waist and pulled **•Êdîka *şerît* bi newqa wî ve girêda** (L) Slowly (or, gently) he tied *the rope* around his waist; **-şirît û k'indîr** (Z-2) rope and twine; 2) {syn: qeyt'an} ribbon, tape (JJ); 3) {also: şerite, f. (K); şilît (GF); şirît

(IFb/B); [cherité] شریطه/[chirid] شرید (JJ)} line, row, file (K). < Ar šarīṭ شـــریــــط = 'ribbon' --> T şerit [L/A/JB3/ZF3//K//IFb/B//JJ//GF//HR]

şerjêkirin شەرژێکِرن = to behead. See **serjêkirin**.

şerkar شەرکار (IFb) = warrior. See **şeřvan**.

şerker شەرکەر (GF) = warrior. See **şeřvan**.

şerm شـــەرم *f./m.(JB1-A)* **(-a/ ;-ê/).** shame, disgrace: **•Ewî** ***şerma*** **řûyê xwe unda kirîye** (B) He overcame his *disgrace* **•[Ji] minřa** ***şerme*** (B) I am ashamed **•*Şerm* teřa!** (B) *Shame* on you!; **-şerm kirin** = a) to feel ashamed: **•Tu** ***şerm nakî*** = *Aren't* you *ashamed*?, *also:* You are brave!; b) to be shy, be bashful: **•Sûsîk hinekî dûrî mêra řûniştibû, ewê ji me** ***şerm dikir*** (Ba2:2, 206) Susik sat a ways from us men, she *was shy*. {also: [cherm] شرم (JJ); <şerm> شرم (HH)} {syn: 'et'ib; 'eyb; fedî; fehêt; řûřeşî; sosret [2]; şermezarî; xax} [Pok. ḱormo- 615.] 'pain, shame': O Ir *fšarma- (Tsb2, p.50, 62; Ras, 212): Av fšarəma-; P šarm شـرم; Sor şerm شـەرم; Za şermi *m.* (Todd) [Z-1/K/A/JB3/IFb/B/JJ/HH/JB1-A/SK/GF/ TF/OK]

şermesar شـــەرمـــەســار (K) = ashamed; bashful. See **şermezar**.

şermezar شـــەرمـــەزار *adj.* 1) {syn: fedîkar; fehêtkar} ashamed: **-şermezar bûn** (IFb) to be ashamed: **•Tu li mala min, çu li te nehatîye, ez** ***da şermizar bim*** (JB1-A #81,122) You are at my house, nothing has happened to you, [if it had] I *would be ashamed*; 2) {also: fehêtok; şermoke} bashful. {also: şermesar (K-2); şermizar (JB1-A); şermsar (K/GF)} Cf. P šarmsār شـــرمـــســار = 'ashamed, disgraced, abashed, confused'; Sor şermezar شەرمەزار/şermesar شـەرمـەسـار = 'ashamed' [Zeb/ K(s)/IFb/TF/ZF]

şermezarî شـەرمـەزاری *f.* **(-ya;-yê).** shame, disgrace: **•Madem te dizanî eto dê çî, te bo çî ez mare kirim, te ev** ***şermuzarîye*** **îna řêka babê min?** (M-Ak #645, 292) Since you knew that you would go, why did you marry me and so bring this *shame* on my father? {also: şermsarî (K/GF); şermuzarî (M-Ak)} {syn: 'et'ib; 'eyb; fedî; fehêt; gosirmet; řûřeşî; sosret [2]; şerm; xax} Sor şermezarî شـەرمـەزاری/şermesarî شـەرمـەساری [Zeb/ ZF//M-Ak//K/GF]

şermizar شـــەرمِـــزار (JB1-A) = ashamed; bashful. See **şermezar**.

şermînok شەرمینۆك (BF) = shy, timid. See **şermoke.**

şermok شـەرمۆك (K/IFb/GF/Wkt/RZ/ZF) = shy, timid. See **şermoke.**

şermoke شـەرمۆکە *adj.* shy, timid, bashful, diffident: **•Ji mêvanê xwe** ***şermoke*** **bû** (FS) She was *bashful* around her guest **•Zamoyê ku** ***şermoke*** **û asê dihat naskirin** ... (EN) Zamo, who was known as *shy* and aloof ... {also: şermînok (BF); şermok (K-2/IFb/GF/Wkt-2/RZ-2/ZF-2); [chermouk] شرموك (JJ)} {syn: fedîkar; fehêtkar; fehêtok; şermezar} = Sor şermin شـەرمِـن [EN/K/BF/ FS/ZF/Wkt//IFb/GF//JJ//BF]

şermokî شـــەرمـــــۆکـــی *f.* **().** shyness, timidity, bashfulness, diffidence; shame: ***•Bi çaw-şorî û şermokî*** **çûne nik Cindî Axa** (SK 40:363) Hanging their heads *in shame* they went to Jindi Agha. {also: şermokîtî (Wkt)} [SK/ZF//Wkt]

şermokîtî شـەرمـۆکـیـتـی (Wkt) = shyness; shame. See **şermokî**.

şermsar شـەرمـسـار (K/GF) = ashamed; bashful. See **şermezar**.

şermsarî شـــەرمـــســـاری (K/GF) = disgrace. See **şermezarî**.

şermuzarî شـــەرمـــوزاری (M-Ak) = disgrace. See **şermezarî**.

şerpeze شـەرپـەزە *adj.* 1) {syn: belengaz; bikul; dêran II; malxirab; řeben I; xwelîser I} miserable, wretched; in a bad way (IFb): **•Rewşa wî** ***şepirze*** **ye** (FS) He is in a *wretched* state **•Tu çire wilo** ***şerpeze bûyî*** (SW) Why *are* you so *miserable*?; 2) broken off, interrupted, suspended, halted (K); broken, disturbed *(silence, peace, sleep)* (K); 3) hurried, in a rush (Zeb); 4) [*f.* **(; şerpezê)**] interference, hindrance (B). {also: şepirze (Zeb/ GF-2/TF)} {şerpezeyî} [SW/K/IFb/B/GF//Zeb/TF]

şerpezetî شەرپەزەتی (Wkt) = misery. See **şerpezeyî.**

şerpezeyî شـەرپـەزەیی *f.* **(-ya;-yê).** 1) misery; 2) being broken off or interrupted. {also: şepirzetî (TF); şerpezetî (Wkt)} [IFb/ZF3//Wkt//TF] <şerpeze>

şerq شـــەرق *f.* **(;-ê).** 1) east; 2) the East, the "Orient" (JJ). {also: [cherq] شـرق (JJ)} {syn: mişriq, f. (F); řojhilat} < Ar šarq شرق [F/K/B/JJ]

şerqîn شـەرقـیـن *f.* **(-a;).** noise, shrill sound; knock, thump, crash (B); thundering (ZF/IFb): **•Min dî** ***şirqîn*** **ji tatê hat** (L) I sensed a *noise* coming [lit. 'came'] from the boulder **•*Şirqîn*** **ji 'ezmîn hat, birûskê li 'erdê xist** (K'oroxlî, 141) *A noise* came from the sky, lightning struck the earth. {also: çerqîn (L-2); şirqîn (L-2/B); şirqînî (B-2); şirqîn (K'oroxlî/ZF)} {syn: galegûrt; galigal[4];

hêwirze; hose; k'im-k'imî; qajeqaj; qalmeqal; qareqar; qerebalix; qîr̄eqîr̄; t'eqer̄eq} Cf. [tcherkin] چركين (JJ) = 'ugly'; P čerkīn چركين = 'filthy'; T çirkin = 'ugly' [L/K//B//K'oroxlî/ZF/IFb]

şer̄agirtin شەڕراگرتِن *f.* **(;-ê).** cease-fire, truce, armistice. {syn: şer̄awestin} [(neol)OK/ZF3]

şer̄awestin شەڕراوەستِن *f.* **(;-ê).** cease-fire, truce, armistice: **•Ji destpêka *şerrawestinê* ta roja 24'ê gulanê, pêvajoya 40 rojan, tevî hemû êrîşên hêzên dewletê gerîlayên ARGK'ê ji bo ku *şerrawestin* ji aliyê wan ve neyê îhlalkirin bêdeng diman** (Wlt 2:67, 1) From the start of *the cease-fire* until the 24th of May, a period of 40 days, in spite of all the attacks of the govern-ment forces, the ARGK guerrillas remained silent, lest *the cease-fire* be broken from their side. {syn: şer̄agirtin} [(neol)Wlt/ZF3]

şert شەرت *m./f.(JB3)* **(-ê/ ;).** 1) {syn: merc I} condition, stipulation, terms *(of an agreement)*: **•Ez jî dê bêm lê *bi şertê ku* em bi tirimpêlê biçin** (Wkt) I will come too but *on condition that* we go by car; **-şert girê dan** (B) to make an agreement; 2) {syn: merc I; miçilge} bet, wager (IFb/B): **-şert girtin** (B) to bet, wager; 3) task, test, ordeal [épreuve] (L): **•Hakim qîza xwe na de bi pera, dide bi *şerda*** (L) The king doesn't give his daughter [in exchange] for money, he gives her [in exchange] for *tasks* **•Ezê *şerdekî* sivik ji te re bêjim** (L) I'll assign you an easy *task*; **-şert anîn** = to complete, carry out, accomplish a task: **•*Şerdê* go min jê re gotîye ni kare bîne** (L) He can't complete *the task* I gave [lit. 'told'] him **•Min *şerdê* te anî** (L) I completed your *task*; **-şert avêtin** = to assign, propose a task: **•Ezê *şerdekî* bavêjim te** (L) I will *assign a task* to you **•*Şerda* davêje ser wan** (L) He *assigns* them *tasks*. {also: şerd (L); şird (L-2); şirt II (Z-3); [chert] شرط (JJ); <şerṭ> شرط (HH)} < Ar šarṭ شرط [L//K/JB3/IFb/B/JJ/SK/GF//HH]

şerûd شەڕوود (GF)/şer̄ûd شەڕوود (K) = hostile. See **şerût**.

şer̄ûde شەڕوودە (K) = hostile. See **şerût**.

şerût شەرووت *adj.* hostile, evil: **•Û gur bi çavên xwe yên tûj û *şerût* li min dinêrî û xwe kar dikir bête min** (EŞ, 16) And the wolf looked at me with its sharp and *hostile* eyes, and got ready to pounce on me. {also: şerûd (GF-2); şer̄ûd (K); şer̄ûde (K-2)} Cf. şer̄ I = 'war' & şer̄ II = 'evil' [EŞ/GF//K]

şerval شەرڤال (Çnr/OK) = baggy trousers. See **şalvar**.

şer̄van شەڕڤان *m.* **(-ê;).** warrior, fighter; combatant, militant: **•Ji ber ku piraniya gelê Keşmîrê misilman e, dewleta Pakistanê piştevaniya *şervanên* Keşmîrê dike** (AW77A5) Because the majority of the Kashmiri people are Muslims, the Pakistani government supports the Kashmiri *fighters*; **-şer̄vanê 'edilayê** (B) peace advocate; **-şer̄darê azayê** (B) freedom fighter. {also: şer̄dar (B-2); şer̄evan (K/TF); şerkar (IFb-2); şerker (GF-2); şerwan (A); [cher-ker] شركر (JJ); <şerker> شركر (HH)} [EP-8/B/IFb/GF//K/TF//A//JJ/HH]

şerwal شەروال (OK) = baggy trousers. See **şalvar**.

şerwan شەروان (A) = warrior. See **şer̄van**.

şesid شەسِد (EH/B/F) = six hundred. See **şeşsed**.

şeş شەش *num.* six, 6. {also: [chech] شش (JJ); <şeş> شش (HH)} [Pok sųeḱs/seḱs/kseḱs/ksųeḱs/ųeks(:uḱs) 1044.] 'six': Skr ṣáṭ (<saṭṣ); Av xšvaš-; Mid P šaš (M3); P šeš (*colloquial* šīš) شش; Sor şeş شەش; Za şeş (Todd); Hau şiş (M4); cf. also Lat sex; Gr hex ἕξ; Rus šest' шесть; Germ sechs; cf. also Heb šeš שש [F/K/IF/B/JJ/HH/JB1-S] <nîvdest; şanzdeh; şêst; şeşêk>

şeşa شەشا *adj.* sixth, 6th. {also: şeşan (K-2/BX/IFb); **şeşem**; şeşê (JB1-A/SK); şeşyê (JB1-S); [chechi] ششى (JJ)} Cf. P šešom ششم; Sor şeşem[în] شەشەمين; Za şeşin (Todd) [F/K/B//BX/IFb//JB1-A/SK//JB1-S//JJ] <şeş>

şeşagir شەشاگِر (A/IFb/HH) = pistol. See **şeşar**.

şeşan شەشان (K/BX/IFb) = sixth. See **şeşa**.

şeşar شەشار *f.* **(-a;-ê).** sixshooter pistol, revolver. {also: şeşagir (A/IFb-2); <şeş agir> شش اكر (HH)} {syn: debançe; şeşderb} [K/IFb/ZF3//A/HH]

şeşderb شەشدەرب *f.* **(-a;-ê).** 1) {syn: debançe; şeşar; şeşxane} sixshooter pistol, revolver; 2) six-chamber rifle (B). [A/IFb/B/ZF3/FS]

şeşem شەشەم *adj.* sixth, 6th. {also: **şeşa**; şeşemîn (TF/IFb-2/GF-2/CT-2/ZF-2/Wkt-2)} Cf. P šešom ششم; Sor şeşem[în] شەشەمين [A/IFb/GF/CT/ZF/Wkt//TF] <şeş>

şeşemîn شەشەمين (TF/IFb/GF/CT/ZF/Wkt) = sixth. See **şeşem**.

şeşê شەشێ (JB1-A/SK) = sixth. See **şeşa**.

şeşêk شەشێك *f.* **(-a;).** a sixth, 1/6: **•Wî *şeşêka* parên xwe dan kur̄ê xwe** (FS) He gave his son *one sixth of* his money. {also: şeşyek (K); şeşyêk (A); <şeşêk شەشيك/şeşyek ششيك> (HH)} Sor şeşyek شەشيێك (Sulaimania & Kerkuk) /şeş-yêk شەشيێك

(Arbil) [Zeb/AR/HH/FS//A//K]

şeşpê شەشپێ *adj.* six-footed: **•Li navçeya Sariqamişê kesên ku nogina *şeşpê* dibînin ecêbmayî dimînin** (tigrishaber.com 12.viii.2014) In the Sarıkamış district, people who see a *six-footed* heifer are amazed. <şeş = pê [tigrishaber/SS/Wkt]

şeşsed شەشسەد/**şeşṣed** شەشصەد (SK) *num.* six hundred, 600. {also: şesid (EH/B/F)} Av xšvaš satāiš [*obl.*]; Sor şeşsed شەشسەد; Za şeş sey [EH/B/F//K/SK] <şeş>

şeşxan شەشخان (FS) = six-chamber rifle; sixshooter. See **şeşxane**.

şeşxan•e شەشخانە *f.* **(•a;•ê).** 1) {syn: şeşderb; t'ifing} six-chamber rifle; 2) {syn: şeşderb} sixshooter pistol, revolver (B). {also: şeşxan (FS); [chech-khané] ششخانه (JJ); <şeşxane> ششخانه (HH)} [K/A/B/JJ/HH/BF//FS]

şeşyek شەشیەك (K/HH) = a sixth. See **şeşêk**.

şeşyê شەشیێ (JB1-S) = sixth. See **şeşa**.

şeşyêk شەشیێك (A) = a sixth. See **şeşêk**.

şet شەت *m.* **(-ê;).** river, particularly the Tigris. {also: [sciahht] شط (JJ); <şeṯ> شط (HH)} {syn: av [2]; çem; r̄o II; r̄ûbar} < Ar šaṭṭ شطّ [MC-1/K//JJ//HH]

şetele شەتەلە *f.* **(-ya;-yê).** 1) avalanche {syn: aşît; r̄enî; şape I}; 2) calamity, misfortune, disaster {syn: bela I; bêt'ar; boblat; gosirmet; siqûmat}: **•Rebî jin û zarokên me ji *şeteleyan* biparêzî ku *şetele-ya* hera mezin bêkesî ye, ya duyem bêmalî ye û ya sêyem bêwelatî ye** (Umid Demirhan-FB 18.v.2018) Lord, protect our wives and children from *misfortunes*, of which the greatest *misfor-tune* is loneliness, the second is homelessness and the third is statelessness. [Wkt/ZF3/FD]

şetrenc شەترەنج *f.* **(-a;-ê).** chess. {also: satranc (IFb-2); satranç (A); satrinc; setrenc, m. (K/IFb/ZF); [setrendj] سطرنج (JJ); <siṯrinc> سطرنج (HH)} {syn: k'işik[1]; şaxmat (F)} <Skt catúr aṅga = 'comprising four parts [of the army], viz. elephants, chariots, cavalry & infantry': Ar/P šaṭranj/šiṭranj شطرنج; Sor şetrenc شەترەنج/şetrinc شەترِنج/setrinc سەترِنج [K/IFb/JJ/ZF//A//HH//GF/SS/Kmc/Wkt/BF/FS] <ferzîn = 'queen'; fêris = 'knight' (Z-1); fîl = 'bishop'; k'erkedan = ?'knight'; peyak = 'pawn'; r̄ex II = 'castle, rook'>

şev I شەڤ *f.* **(-a;-ê).** night: **-îşev** = tonight; **-nîvê şevê** = midnight; **-şeva baranê** = rainy night [lit. 'night of rain']; **-şeva dî** (Bw) night before last, two nights ago {as opposed to **şivêdî** = 'last night'}; **-şevê** (B) at night; **-şevêdî** (qv.)/**şivêdî** = last night; **-şevtir** = night before last [l'autre nuit]; **-şevtira dî** = three nights ago. {also: şew (SK); şêv (HR); [chew] شف (JJ); <şev شڤ/şêv شیڤ> (HH)} [Pok. kᵘsep-(?) 649.] and similar words for 'dark': Skt kṣáp/kṣapā́- = 'night'; Av xšap- = 'darkness; night' (M, v.1, p.220); P šab شب; Sor şew شەو; Za şew *f.* (Todd); Hau şewe *f.* (M4) [K/A/JB3/IFb/B/JJ/HH/GF/TF/ZF//SK//HR] <êvar; hîv; r̄oj; şevêdî; şîv>

şev II شەڤ (K/B) = alum. See **şeb.**

şeva din شەڤا دِن (IFb) = last night. See **şevêdî**.

şevadî شەڤادی (K) = last night. See **şevêdî**.

şeva dû شەڤا دوو (OK) = last night. See **şevêdî**.

şevar̄ê شەڤارێ (Btm) = country road, rough path. See **şiver̄ê**.

şevbêrî شەڤبێری (K/FS) = evening entertainment. See **şevbuhêrk**.

şevbêrk شەڤبێرك (Frq) = evening entertainment. See **şevbuhêrk**.

şevbihêrî شەڤبِهێری (B) = evening entertainment. See **şevbuhêrk**.

şevborî شەڤبۆری (IFb) = evening entertainment. See **şevbuhêrk**.

şevbuhêrk شەڤبوهێرك *f.* **(-a;-ê).** evening or nightly entertainments *(conversations, games, storytelling, etc.)*, evening get-together, soirée [Cf. Ar musāmarah مسامرة]: **-şevbêrî kirin** (K)/**şevbihêrî** ~(B)/**şevbuhêrk derbaz** ~(IFb/Haz) to pass [or, spend] the night *(partaking of such entertainments)*: **•*Şevbêrîya* me xoş bû** (FS) Our evening get-together was pleasant **•*Şevbuhêrka* xwe li vir derbaz kirin** [sic] (IFb) They passed the night here. {also: şevbêrî (K/FS); şevbêrk (Frq); şevbihêrî (B); şevborî (IFb-2); şevbuhurî (B-2); şevbûwar (TF); şevbûwêrk (Haz-2); şevêrk (Frq-2)} Sor şewb[u]wêr kirdin شەوبووێر کِردِن = 'to pass the night with entertainments' [Haz/IFb/GF//K/FS//Frq//B//TF]

şevbuhurî شەڤبوهوری (B) = evening entertainment. See **şevbuhêrk**.

şevbûwar شەڤبووار (TF) = evening entertainment. See **şevbuhêrk**.

şevbûwêrk شەڤبووێرك (Haz) = evening entertainment. See **şevbuhêrk**.

şevder شەڤدەر (A/HH/GF) = spending the night out. See **şeveder**.

şeveder شەڤەدەر *adj.* spending the night outside;

camping out; staying out all night *(of young men)* (Hk): **•Cihû mecidîyek nezr kir ku kur̄ê wî *şeveder nebît.* Piştî ku kurê wî *şeveder bû* jî, du mecidî nezr kirin da ku venegeri̇̄te mal** (Hk) The Jew pledged 1 cent that his son *would not stay out late* at night. After his son *started staying out late*, he pledged 2 cents so that he would not return home. {also: şevder (A/GF); [chewe der màin] شڤه در ماين (JJ); <şevder> شڤدر (HH)} Cf. NENA šavadar *in:* hāl ʼımma, ula šōqıt yāla šavadar (YSZx #56) = 'Give a hundred (coins), and do not let (your) child spend the night in the streets' [Hk/K/JJ/TF/FS//A/HH/GF]

şeveq شەڤەق (B) = dawn. See **şebeq**.

şevê din شەڤێ دِن (L) = last night. See **şevêdî**.

şevêdî شەڤێدی *adv.* last night, yesterday night: **•Gavan got-ê, ey bira tu çira bê kêf î? Şivan got, min *şevêdî* xewnek diye lewre ez bê kêf im** (Rnh 2:17, 306) The cowherd said to him, "Brother, why are you so unhappy?" The shepherd answered, "*Last night* I had a dream, that's why I'm unhappy" **•*Şevê din,* min agirek dî** (L-5, 142, l. 21-22) *Last night*, I saw a fire. {also: şeva din (IFb); şevadî (K); şeva dû (OK); şevê din (L); şevêdû (OK-2); şivêdî (Bw); [chew-a douhouni] شـا دهـنـی (JJ)} Note that for Bw, **şeva dî** = 'night before last, two nights ago' *{as opposed to şivêdî = 'last night'}* [Rnh//IFb//K//OK//Bw//JJ//L] <şev I>

şevêdû شەڤێدوو (OK) = last night. See **şevêdî**.

şevêrk شەڤێرك (Frq) = evening entertainment. See **şevbuhêrk**.

şevîn شەڤین *f.* **(-a;-ê).** night feeding *(of animals)*; night grazing *(of animals)* (A/HH): **•Çaxa *şevînê* jî pif dikim bilûrê** (AB) At the time of *the night feeding (or, pasturing)* I blow on my flute **•Şivanî pez rakir *şevînê*** (FS) The shepherd took the sheep out for *the night feeding*. {also: şevînî (IF-2); [chewin] شڤين (JJ); <şevînî> شڤينی (HH)} {syn: palîn} *For a description of the entire milking cycle among Kurdish nomads, see*: B. Nikitine. *Les Kurdes: étude sociologique et historique* (Paris: Imprimerie nationale : Librairie C. Klincksieck, 1956), p. 50, note 1. [AB/K/A/IFb/JJ/GF//HH] <ç'êrîn; dotin; hevêz = hevşî; palîn I; şev I>

şevînî شەڤینی (IF/HH) = night feeding or grazing of animals. See **şevîn**.

şevkor شەڤکۆر *adj.* 1) suffering from night-blindness, night-blind, nyctalopic [cf. Ar a'šá أعشى] (K/A/IF/HH/Bw); 2) near-sighted, weak-sighted, myopic (K/JJ); 3) short-sighted (K). {also: şevkûrhe (FS-2); [chew-kor] شڤكور (JJ); <şevkor> شڤكور (HH)} {şevkorî} [JR/K/A/IFb/JJ/HH/GF/TF/Bw/BF/FS]

şevkorî شەڤکۆری *f.* **(;-yê).** 1) night-blindness; 2) myopia, near-sightedness. [K/IFb/GF/TF/BF] <şevkor>

şevkûrhe شەڤكوورهە (FS) = night-blind. See **şevkor**.

şevqe شەڤقە (TF) = hat. See **şewqe**.

şevrevînk شەڤرەڤینك *m./f.(ZF3/Wkt)* **().** bat, zool. *Chiroptera*. {also: <şevrevînk> شڤ رڤينك (HH)} {syn: barç'imok; çekçekîle; çil II; pîrçemek; şevşevok} [Bw/IFb/HH/GF/OK/RZ/BF/FS/ZF3]

şevşevik شەڤشەڤِك (IFb) = bat *(zool.)*. See **şevşevok**.

şevşevok شەڤشەڤۆك *m.* **(-ê;).** bat, zool. *Chiroptera*. {also: şevşevik (IFb)} {syn: barç'imok; çekçekîle; çil II; pîrçemek; şevrevînk} [Haz/GF/RZ/FS//IFb]

şevxûn شەڤخوون (GF) = surprise night attack. See **şebeyxûn**.

şew شەو (SK) = night. See **şev I**.

şewaq شەواق = dawn. See **şebeq**.

şewat شەوات *f.* **(-a;-ê).** 1) {also: şewate (IFb)} {syn: agir; ar I} flame, fire: **-Sala Şewatê** (Bkp) the Year of Fire (1925): **•Ew qetlîama barbar̄kî ya ku Kemal Paşa di sala 1925'an da piştê şikandina bizava Şêx Seîd li Kurdistanê kir, di dîroka gelê Kurd da bûye nuqteyeka kifşkirî ... Li Kurdistana Jorîn di nava gelê Kurd da navê sala 1925'an bûye "*Sala Şewatê*"** (Bkp, 77, #66) That barbaric massacre which K.P. carried out in 1925 after the defeat of the Sheikh Sa'id rebellion in Kurdistan, has become a specific point in the history of the Kurdish people ... In Upper [Northern] Kurdistan, among the Kurds the name of the year 1925 is "*the Year of Fire*"; 2) {also: şewate (IFb)} fuel for heating an oven or furnace (B); 3) passion, ardor, heat: -[**bi**] **k'el û şewat** (Z-1) passion(ately); 4) burn, scald(ing), wound from being burnt; pain: **•Birîna ser destê wî ji *şewatê*ye** (B) The wound on his hand is from *a burn*; **-şewata dil** (B) heartache, emotional pain; 5) damage, devastation (OK): **•[Sibat e, çi şer̄ e û çi *şewat* e, xwezî nîv mehada nehata]** (BG) February, what struggling and what *devastation*, I wish there were no such month [lit., that it did not come among the months] *[prv.]*. {also: [chevat شوات /chevaté شواته/chevati شواتی] (JJ); <şewat>

شواط (HH); [chouat] (BG)} Cf. Ar šawá شوى = 'to broil, grill, roast' [Z-1/K/A/IFb/B/JJ/OK//HH//BG] <sotin; şewitandin; şewitîn>

şewate شەواتە (IFb) = flame; fuel. See **şewat**.

şewb شەوب *f.* **(-a;-ê).** epidemic, contagion, infectious disease, plague *(lit. & fig.)*: **•Ev *şewba* neteweperestiyê Jon Tirkan ji Ewrûpiyan vegirtibûn** [sic] (R. Sorgul. Gurxenêq, 61) The Young Turks caught this *epidemic of* nationalism from the Europeans **•Vê *şovê* ew girtiye** (FS) This *contagion* has spread to him/her; **-şewba çivîkan** (FD) a disease of birds (dimşînk, nikilreş). {also: şob (Wkt-2/ZF3-2); şof (SS); şov II (RZ/FS)} {syn: pejî; qotik II; teşene; weba} [R.Sorgul/A/IFb/TF/Wkt/ZF3//RZ/FS//SS] <nesaxî; nexweşî>

şeweq شەوەق = dawn. See **şebeq**.

şewitandin شەوتاندِن *vt.* **(-şewitîn-).** 1) to set on fire, light, kindle, ignite: **•Ezê he̅rim be'rê *bişewtînim*** (Dz) I will go *set* the sea *on fire* **•Lê pê t'ertê sergîn be'r *tê şewitandin*?** (Dz) But does the sea *get ignited* (=can the sea be set on fire) by pressed dung?; 2) {syn: sotin} to burn *(vt.)*: **•Îsotê devê min *şewitand*** (AB) The pepper *burned* my mouth. {also: şewtandin; [chevitandin] شوتاندين (JJ); <şewiṯandin شـوطـاندن (dişewiṯîne) (دشوطينه)> (HH)} [K/A/JB3/IFb/B/JJ/GF/BK] <sotin; sûtin; şewat; şewitîn>

şewitîn شەوتين *vi.* **(-şewit-).** 1) to burn *(vi.)*, be on fire: **•Dilê wî *bi* gavan *şewitî*** (L) He *felt sorry for* the cowherd [lit. 'His heart *burned for* the cowherd'] **•Dilê wî ser xebata wî *dişewite*** (B) He's worried sick about his work [lit. 'His heart *burns* over his work']; **-[ji] serma şewitîn** (B) to be numb with cold; 2) to decline, deteriorate. See **şihitîn**. {also: [chevitin] شوتين (JJ); <şewiṯîn شوطين (dişewiṯî) (دشوطى)> (HH)} [K/A/JB3/IFb/B/JJ/GF//HH] <sotin; sûtin; şewat; şewitandin>

şewk شەوك *f.* **(-a;).** 1) fishing rod, fish hook: **•Berî ku tor derkevin, girtina masiyan bi *şewk* û şebekeyan bû; masîgiran êvaran kêvjal, an jî masiyên piçûk bi serên *şewkan* ve dikirin diavêtin gêrê** (DBgb, 5-6) Before the nets came out, the fishing was with *hooks* and sharp sticks; in the evenings fishermen would spear crabs, or small fish, with *fish hooks*, and would throw them into the pool **•Masîgirek çobû masiya bigrit; *şoka* wî di sindoqê aliya sindoq kêşa** (GShA, 226) A fisherman had gone to catch fish; his *fish hook* got caught on the box and it pulled the box up; 2) {syn: çengel I; ç'iqil; nîk} hook; 3) {syn: dirī; kelem II; stirî I} thorn; 4) {syn: ç'iq[il]; çirpî; şax} thin branch (SK): **-şokêt bîyê** (SK) osiers, willow branches: **•Here, hindek *şokêt bîyê* bîne, li-pêş çawêt xelkî sê çar xilêfan çê-ke** (SK 35:314) Go and bring some *osiers* and make three or four hive-baskets in the sight of people. {also : şok (GShA/SK); [cheouk/sciúk (G)/šōk (PS)] شوك (JJ)} < Ar šawk شوك = 'thorns; forks' [DBgb/K(s)/IFb/FJ/GF/JJ/CS//GShA/SK/PS] <masî; t'or̄ I>

şewq شەوق *f.* **(-a;-ê).** shine, brilliance, luster; light: **•Bi bedewtîya Ûsib, bi *şewqa* dîndara wî ç'evê wî sax dibe** (Ba) From Joseph's beauty, from *the lustre of* his countenance, his (=Jacob's) eyes become whole (or, well) **•Li ber *şewqa* rojê dibiriqîn** (Alkan, 70) They were shining from *the brilliance of* the sun. {also: [cheoŭq] شوق (JJ); <şewq> شوق (HH)} According to Redhouse, T şavk [شوق] = 'light' < şafak < Ar šafaq شفق = 'twilight, dusk' rather than Ar šawq شوق = 'desire' [Ba/K/A/IFb/B/JJ/HH/GF/Msr] <r̄onahî I>

şewqe شەوقە *f.* **(-ya;-yê).** hat, cap: **•Kofî *şewqeya* jinan ya kevneşopî ye** (tirsik.net:perxudres 26.ii.2014) The kofî is the women's traditional *hat*. {also: şapqe (GF-2); şebqe (GF); şefqe (K/A/IFb-2/GF-2/CS); şepqe (RZ); şevqe (TF)} {syn: kulav [4]; k'um[ik]} < T şapka < Rus šapka шапка; Sor şepqe شەپقە [SBx/IFb/ZF//K/A/CS//TF//GF//RZ]

şewtandin شەوتاندِن = to ignite, light; to burn *(vt.)*. See **şewitandin**.

şexsiyet شەخسِيەت (IFb/Wkt) = personality; identity. See **şexsîyet**.

şexsîyet شەخسيەت *f.* **(-a;-ê).** 1) {syn: kesanetî} personality: **•Ev helwest nahêle ku HEP bibe xwedî *şexsiyet*** (Wlt 1:43) This attitude does not allow HEP to have *a personality* of its own; 2) {syn: nasname} identity. {also: şexsiyet (IFb/Wkt)} < Ar šaxṣīyah شخصية [Ber//IFb/Wkt]

şex̄re شەغرە (GF) = transporting grain. See **şix̄re**.

şeyî شەيى *m.* **().** shayi, a petty coin [USSR]; five-kopeck coin (B); Persian coin, 1/200 of a tuman (Lopat, p. 11, note #1). Cf. NA šai [Urmia] (Garbell) [Z-922/K/B] <kapêk; manat; p'ere I>

şeylo شەيلۆ (K[s]) = turbid, cloudy. See **şêlo**.

şeytan/şeyt'an [B] شەيتان *m.* **(-ê; şeytên).** 1) devil, satan *(lit. & fig.)* [a taboo word among the Yezidis]: **•Daimî xiyala *şeytanî* ew e, welîyan û**

şofîyan û tobekaran ji r̄êka behêştê û necatê derêxît û bibete ser r̄êka cehennemê û helakî (SK 4:42) The *devil's* thoughts are always directed toward leading holy and pious and repentant men astray from the road to paradise and salvation and setting them on the road to hell and destruction •...**û nifir li *şeytanê* pîs dibarandin** (HYma 37) and he showered the dirty *devil* with curses [lit., showered curses on the dirty *devil*] •***Şeytan* pêl kir/şeytan pê k'enî** (Msr) He had a wet dream or nocturnal emission •***Şeytan* pê li min kir** (Msr) I had a wet dream; 2) [*adj.*] cunning, wily, clever, shrewd, crafty: •**Lawik gelikî *şeytan* bû** (L) The boy was quite *cunning* •**Şêx û beg û axa zor bo halê xo û menfe'etê zatîyê xo zana û *şeytan* in, emma r̄e'îyet zor bêçare û nezan û wehşî ne** (SK 56:655) The shaikhs and begs and aghas are very wise and *cunning* in looking after their own case and their personal profit, but the peasantry are quite hapless and rude and ignorant. {also: [cheïtan] شيطان (JJ); <şeytan> شيطان (HH)} < Ar šayṭān شـيـطـان {şeytanî; şeytantî} [K/JB3/IFb/B/JJ/HH/SK/GF/TF] <cin; dêw; ferhît; ji me çêtir>

şeytanî شـەيـتـانـى *f.* **(-ya;-yê).** devilishness, devilry. {also: şeytantî (K-2)} [K/IFb/TF/ZF3/BF] <şeytan>

şeytanok شەيطانوك/شەيتانوك**/şeytanok** شەيطانوك [FS] *m./f.(FS/ZF3)* **(-ê/-a;/-ê).** snail. {syn: guhşeytan; hiseynok} [L/A/JB3/IFb/GF/TF/ZF3//FS]

şeytantî شەيتانتى (K) = devilishness. See **şeytanî**.

şez شەز (Wkt) = forest fly. See **şêz**.

şê شـــــــى *adj. word denoting the coloring of horses*: 1) light brown, reddish; chestnut *(of horse)* [Fr alezan] (K/JJ); yellowish *(of horse or mule)* (IF); isabel, dun *(coloring of a horse)* (B); roan, sorrel *(of a horse)* [Ar ašqar أشـــقـر] (HH): •**Hespê me hersêka *şêne*** (Z-1) All three of our horses are *chestnut colored* (or-white on the forehead and on three legs); 2) with a white forehead and three white legs *(of horse)* (A); 3) {syn: çûr̄ II; kej} blond(e), fair-haired (B). {also: [chi] شـــــى (JJ); <şê> شـــى (HH)} <proto Ir *(a-)xšaita-; cf. Arm ašxēt աշխէտ = 'sorrel or chestnut (color)' [Z-1/K/A/IFb/B/HH/GF//JJ] <qule>

şêf شێف (M2) = furrow. See **şov I**.

şêl شـێـل *f.* **(-a;-ê).** 1) {syn: r̄abûn û r̄ûniştin; t'evger̄} behavior, conduct [T davranış]; 2) attitude, stance, state, condition [T tavır, durum, hal] (TF): •**Bi baweri-ya min ev *şêleke* siyasî ye û dibê kurd sebebê vê şêla Zubêr Aydar jê bipirsin** (Zinarê Xamo: Hindik Rindik) In my opinion this is a political *stance* and the Kurds should ask Z.A. about this stance of his. {syn: helwest} [Wlt/TF/ZF/CS/FS]

şêlan شـێـلان *vt.* **(-şêl-).** 1) {syn: hevîr kirin; stiran II} to knead (K[s]/OK/M); 2) to stir *(for solid things made liquid by stirring)* (Zeb). [Zeb/K(s)/OK/M]

şêlandin شـێـلانـدِن (K/IFb/B) = to strip; to plunder, rob. See **şelandin**.

şêlav شێلاڤ (FS) = pancreas; rennet bag. See **şîlav**.

şêlavk شێلاڤك (Bw) = pancreas; rennet bag. See **şîlav**.

şêlig شێلِگ (IFb) = volley. See **şêlik**.

şêlik شــــێــــلِــــك *f.(Zeb/FS)/m.(SK)* **(-a/;-ê/).** volley, fusillade: •**Selîm Beg sê-sed mêrêt bijare digel xo r̄akirin, nîw-sa'et berî spêdê hawête ser Binawokê: *şêlikêt* tifengan li dû yêk kirine gundî** (SK 41:400) Selim Beg took 300 chosen men with him and half an hour before dawn flung them against Binawok: they fired *volleys* one after the other on the village •**Wextê li Sofî 'Ebdullah r̄ast hatin, *şêlikekî* tifengan kirine muroêt şêxî, sê kuştin, yêk birîndar kirin** [sic] (SK 48:508) When they came up to Sofi Abdullah, they fired a rifle *volley* at the Shaikh's men, killing three and wounding one; -**dane ber şêligê tifinga** (IFb) to fire on (a place) in volleys. {also: şêlig (IFb)} Cf. P šalīk/šellīk شـلـيـك = 'volley, discharge, report (of gun)'; Sor şêlig شـێـلِـگ [Zeb/SK/FS/BF/ZF3//IFb] <derb; gulebaran>

şêlim شـێـلِم *f.* **(;-ê).** turnip, bot. *Brassica rapa*. {also: [chilim] شـلـم (JJ); <şelim> شـلـم (HH)} {syn: bin'erdk [1]} Cf. P šalγam شـلـغـم --> T şalgam;--> Ar saljam سلجم; Sor şêlim شێلِم [F/K/IFb/B/GF/TF/BF/Wkt//JJ//HH] <silq; tivir>

şêlî شێلى (FS/BF) = turbid, cloudy. See **şêlo**.

şêlo شێلۆ *adj.* turbid, muddy, cloudy, roiled *(of water)*: -**ava şêlû** (B) turbid water. {also: şeylo (K[s]); şêlî (FS/BF); şêlû (F/K/B/GF); şîlo (Msr); şwêlî (SK); [chilou] شـلـو (JJ); <şîlo> شـيـلـو (HH)} {≠ber̄aq; ≠zelal} Cf. Sor şilûq شِـلـووق/şiloq شِـلۆق = 'disturbed, confused' [Msr/HH//A/JB3/IFb//F/K/B/GF//JJ//K(s)//SK//FS/BF] <tîr II>

şêlû شێلوو (F/K/B/GF) = turbid, cloudy. See **şêlo**.

şêmik شێمِك (GF) = threshold. See **şêmîk**.

şêmî شـێـمـى (IFb/FJ/GF/RZ/FS/Wkt) = raspberry. See **t'ûşêmî**.

şêmîk شـێـمـيـك *f.* **(-a;-ê).** threshold: •**P'îyê hespê *şêmîka* dêrî k'et, Werdeka dê pê hesîya** (FK-kk-13:125) The horse's foot caught on *the threshold of* the door, [and] Mother Werdek heard it [lit. 'became aware of it']. {also: şêmik (GF); şêmûg (IFb); [chimik] شـمـيـك (JJ)} {syn: derç'ik; şîpane} [JR/JJ//K/B/Ba2/F/XF//GF//IFb] <r̄exderî>

şêmûg شێمووگ (IFb) = threshold. See **şêmîk**.

şên شـێـن *adj.* 1) {syn: ava} flourishing, blossoming, blooming, thriving; cultivated (land); inhabited, well-populated; prosperous: **•Xwedê bedena te *şên* bike** (Qzl) May God give you children [lit. 'make your body flourish'] **•Xwedê warê te *şên* bike** (Frq) May your house prosper [or, continue]; **-şên bûn** (B) to prosper: **•Gundêd me *şên dibin*** (B) Our villages *are prospering*; 2) abundant, rich; well-equipped: **-mala şên** (B) a house with all the modern conveniences; 3) happy, lively (A/IFb): **•Civat ker̄ bû, lê Alîşêr hat, civat *şên kir*** (Qzl) The assembly was quiet, but Alisher came and *livened it up*. Cf. O Ir šayana- (Av šaiiana-) = 'a dwelling'; Arm šinel շինել = 'to build' & šēnk' շէնք = 'building' ; Geo a-šen-eb აშენებ = 'to build'; T şen = 'merry, well-populated and prosperous, flourishing, thriving'; some link this with [**he**]**şîn** = 'green' {şênahî; şênayî; şînahî; şînayî; şînkayî} [Ba3/K/A/IFb/B/GF/TF/Qzl/Frq]

şênahî شـێـنـاهـی *f.* **(-ya;-yê).** 1) prosperity; 2) cheerfulness, gaiety, merriment. {also: şênayî (K/A/ZF3); şînahî (K-2); şînayî (K-2); şînkayî (K-2)} [K/A/ZF3//JB3/IFb/Wkt] <heşînatî; şên; şênî>

şênayî شێنایی (K/A/ZF3) = prosperity; merriment. See **şênahî**.

şênî شـێـنـی *f.* **(-ya;-yê).** 1) {syn: war; zome[1]} populated area; settled area, encampment: **•Lawik siwar bû, çû û li nava êlan gerriya, pirsa *şêniya* Hakim Tey kir. Geriya negeriya *şênîya* H.T. nedît** (ZZ-10, 156) The boy rode off, went and roamed among the tribes, looking for H.T.'s *encampment*. No matter how hard he looked, he didn't find H.T.'s *encampment*; 2) [*pl.*] population, inhabitants, townspeople, people of (a place): **•Ew gazên jahrê, gazên firmîsk rijandinê, li ser *şêniyên* Nisêbinê diavêjin** (Wlt 2:59, 13) They cast poisonous gases, tear gas, over *the population (or, populated areas) of* Nusaybin **•Ji çar sed û bîst *şêniyên* gundê me bi kêmanî heşt kesên wan har, dehê wan dîn, bîstê wan cinî** ... (Lab, 68) Of the 420 *inhabitants* of our village, at least 8 of them are rabid, 10 of them crazy, 20 of them possessed by the jinn. {also: [chini] شـيـنـی (JJ)} [Wlt/K/IFb/GF/FS/ZF3//JJ] <avan; heyşet; şên; şênahî>

şêr I شێر *m.* **(-ê;).** 1) lion: **•*Şêr şêr* e, çi mê ye çi nêr e** (AB) *A lion* is *a lion*, whether it is female or male *[prv.]*; 2) Leo *(astr.)*; 3) *personal name*. {also: [chir] شـيـر (JJ); <şêr> شـيـر (HH)} Cf. Skt siṁha- *m.*; Khwarezmian srγ; Sgd šrγw [šarγ-u-]; Pahl & Mid P šagr (M3); Southern Tati dialects: Eshtehardi šir *m.* (Yar-shater); P šīr (*originally* šēr) شـيـر; Sor şêr شێر; Za şêr *m./f.* (Todd). *For a theory about alternating n/r before X* [e.g., **serγ/*senγ], See W. B. Henning, "A Grain of Mustard," *Annali dell'Istituto universitario Orientale di Napoli, sezione linguistica*, 6 (1965), 29-47. [F/K/A/IFb/ B/HH/SK/GF/TF/OK//JJ] <piling; p'isîk; weşeq>

şêr II شـێـر *f.* **(-a;-ê).** poetry; poem. {also: şiîr (IFb); şiîr (Nbh); şi'r (SK/OK); [cheâr] شـعـر (JJ)} {syn: helbest; hozan I} <Ar ši'r شعر [F/K/B//IFb//SK/(GF)/OK//JJ//Nbh]

şêrîn شێرین (L/A/IFb/HH/OK) = sweet. See **şîrin**.

şêrînahî شـێـریـنـاهـی (M.Uzun) = candy, sweetmeats; betrothal. See **şîranî**.

şêrînî شێرینی (A/IFb/OK) = sweetness. See **şîrînî**.

Şêrkoh شـێـرکـۆه *m.* **().** *man's name* [lit. 'lion of the mountains']. < şêr = 'lion' + koh = 'mountain,' cf. P kūh کوه = 'mountain' [Haz]

şêrpence شێرپەنجە (SS) = cancer. See **penceşêr**.

şêst شـێـسـت *num.* sixty, 60. {also: şêşt (IF-2); [chest] شـسـت (JJ); <şêst> شـيـسـت (HH)} Skt ṣaṣṭáy-; Av xšvaštīm [*acc.*]; Mid P šast (M3); P šaṣt شـصـت; Sor şest شەست; Za şestî (Todd); Hau şes̱ (M4) [BX/Z-1/EP-7/K/A/JB3/IFb/B/HH/GF/TF//JJ] <şeş; şêstem>

şêstem شێستەم *adj.* sixtieth, 60th. {also: şêstemîn (IFb/TF/GF-2/Wkt-2)} Cf. P šaṣtom شـصـتـم; Sor şestem[în] شەستەم[ین] [GF/Wkt//IFb/TF] <şêst>

şêstemîn شـێـسـتـەمـیـن (IFb/TF/GF/Wkt) = sixtieth. See **şêstem**.

şêşt شێشت (IF) = sixty. See **şêst**.

şêt شـێـت *adj.* crazy, mad, insane. {syn: dîn II; neh̄iş} < Arc šēḏā שידא = 'devil'--*The insane were thought to be possessed by a devil, or a jinn*, cf. Arab majnūn مجنون = 'possessed by *jinn* جنّ'; also P šeydā شيدا = 'passionate, frenzied'; Sor şêt شێت = 'crazy; Hau şêt (M4) {şêtî} [K(s)/A/IFb/SK/GF/OK/BF]

şêtî شێتی *f.* **().** madness, insanity. {syn: dînayî; ne'işî} [IFb/GF/OK/ZF3/BF] <şêt>

şêv شێڤ (HR/HH) = night. See **şev I**.

şêwerdar شـێـوەرەدار (HR) = adviser, counsellor. See **şêwirdar**.

şêw•ir شـێـوِر *f.* **(•ra;•rê).** 1) {syn: şîret [1]} advice: **•bi *şêwra* wana** (EP-7) on their *advice* **•*şêwra* qencîyê** (B) good *advice*; **-şêwr dayîn** (B) to give advise; 2) deliberation, parley. {also: şêwr (IF/B); [chivir] شـور (JJ); <şêwir> شـيـور (HH)} < Ar šāwara III شـاور = 'to consult' [EP-7/IFb/B/GF/TF/ /K/HH/ /JJ]

şêwirdar شـێـوِردار *m.* **(-ê;).** adviser, counsellor: **•...r̄ihsipîyê wî, û *şêwirdarê* wî li hev gihane hevdû** (HR 4:37) His village elders and *advisers* got together [i.e., held a meeting]. {also : şêwerdar (HR-2); şêwrdar (B)} {syn: şîretk'ar} < Ar šāwara III شـاور = 'to consult' [HR/K/IFb/FJ/GF/ TF/CS//B] <şêwirîn>

şêwirîn شـێـوِرين *vi.* **(-şêwir-).** to ask or seek s.o.'s advice, to consult (with) s.o.: **•Çaxê pez anî cem çem, *li hev şêwirîn*, kî çi bike!** (FS: Çîroka Fêro û Porsor/ Q) When they brought the sheep to the river, *they consulted together*, [to see] who would do what!; **-lev (=li hev) şêwirîn** (K/EP-7) to take counsel, deliberate, consult with one another. {also: şêwirtin (IF-2); şêwrîn (EP-7); [chivirin] شـورين (JJ)} < Ar šāwara III شـاور = 'to consult' [L/K/IFb/B/ FS//EP-7//JJ]

şêwirtin شـێـوِرتِن (IF) = to consult with s.o. See **şêwirîn**.

şêwr شێور (IF/B) = advice; deliberation. See **şêwir**.

şêwrdar شـێـوردار (B) = adviser, counsellor. See **şêwirdar**.

şêwrîn شـێـورين (EP-7) = to consult with s.o. See **şêwirîn**.

şêx شێخ *m.* **(-ê;).** shaikh, spiritual leader: "There are several ways in which a person may derive political and economic leverage from association with the Divine. This is done most successfully in Kurdistan by the *shaikhs* … these popular saints and religious leaders … their primary roles … are that of holy man, object of popular devotion, and that of leader-instructor in mystical brotherhoods (dervish or sufi orders) … Because of the respect they enjoy they are ideal mediators in conflicts, which in turn gives them political leverage … in Kurdistan only two [dervish orders] are present: the Qadiri and Naqshbandi orders. All *shaikhs* belong to either of these." [from: Martin van Bruinessen. *Agha, Shaikh and State: The Social and Political Structures of Kurdistan* (London: Zed Books, 1992), pp. 205 & 210; see entire chapter for full discussion of the ***shaikh***]: **•Her *şêxek* û her aẍayek û her begek nabît padşahek bît, û çawa ḧez biket weto digel r̄e'îyeta bêçare biket** (SK 56:654) Every *shaikh* and agha and beg cannot be a king and do as he pleases with the hapleş peasantry **•*Şêx* û beg û aẍa zor bo ḧalê xo û menfe'etê zatîyê xo zana û şeytan in, emma r̄e'îyet zor bêçare û nezan û weḧşî ne** (SK 56:655) *The shaikhs* and begs and aghas are very wise and cunning in looking after their own case and their personal profit, but the peasantry are quite hapleş and rude and ignorant. {also: [chékh] شيخ (JJ); <şêx> شيخ (HH)} < Ar šayx شيخ; Sor şêx شـێـخ = 'sheikh, title of spiritual guide in mystical dervish order' {şêxetî; şêxînî; şêxîtî} [K/ IFb/B/JJ/HH/SK/GF/TF] <aẍa; beg; mela>

Şêxanî شـێـخـانی *f.* **(-ya;-yê).** Sheikhani, name of a Kurdish folk dance and the accompanying song: **•Ew *Şêxanîyê* dikin** (FS) They are dancing *Sheikhani.* [IFb/ZF3/FD/FS/BF] <govend>

şêxetî شێخەتی *f.* **(;-yê).** title, rank, position, or calling of shaikh; shaikhhood: **•Bab û bapîrêt Şêx 'Ebdulqadir postnişîn bûne, r̄e'îsêt r̄oḧanî bûne. Wezîfa wan irşad e û *şêxetî* ye, dibît ew 'elaqey şola siyasî neken** (SK 53:571) The ancestors of Shaikh Abdulqadir have been Sufis and spiritual leaders. Their duty is teaching and following *the calling of Shaikh.* They should not concern themselves with political matters **•Bû xelîfe û ji teref Şêx 'Usman izna *şêxînîyê* wergirt. Bû şêx, hatewe bo naw 'eşîreta Balikan** (SK 45:434) He became a Khalifa and received the licence *to teach as a shaikh* from Shaikh Usman. He became a shaikh and came back among the Balik tribe **•Her tiştê xudê biket kes neşêt men' biket. Xudê melatî û seydatî û xelîfetî daye min. Li nik wî senayî ye *şêxetî* jî bidete min** (SK 46:448) No man can prevent what God does. God gave me my position as Mullah and Teacher and Khalifa. It is easy for him to give me *the position of Shaikh* also. {also: şêxînî (SK-2/ZF3-2); şêxîtî (TF/ZF3)} *Note: in SK, MacKenzie glosses **şêxetî** as 'rank of shaikh' and **şêxînî** as 'shaikhhood'*; Sor şêxêtî شێخێتی = 'status of sheikh' [IFb/SK//TF/ZF3] <şêx>

şêxînî شێخینی (SK/ZF3) = shaikhhood. See **şêxetî**.

şêxîtî شێخیتی (TF/ZF3) = shaikhhood. See **şêxetî**.

şêz شێز *f.* **().** 1) forest fly, zool. *Hippobosca equina* [T at sineği]; 2) tick found on goats (A/IFb/FD). {also: şez (Wkt)} [Kmc/A/IFb/ZF3/FD/FS/G//Wkt]

şib شِب *m.(OK)/f.(Zeb/Dh)* **().** bronze, fake gold. {syn: birinc II; mefreq} [Zeb/Dh/OK] <mîs; sifir I>

şibak شِباك *f.* **(-a;-ê).** window. {also: şibaq II (IF-2); [chebak] شباك (JJ); <şebak> شباك (HH)} {syn: akoşke; p'encere} < Ar šubbāk شبّاك [L/K/IFb/ZF3//JJ/HH]

şibandin شبباندِن *vt.* **(-şibîn-).** to liken stg. to, cause to resemble; to mistake stg. [*dir. obj.*] for stg. else [*dat. constr.*]: •**Min ew *şibande* xezalê** (ZF3) I *mistook* him/her *for* a gazelle •**Min *tu şibandî* kesekî din** (Msr) I thought you were s.o. else/I mistook you for s.o. else [lit. 'I *likened you to* s.o. else']. {also: şibihandin (K[s]); [chebihandin شبهاندين/shibandin شباندين (Rh)] (JJ)} <Ar šabiha شبه = 'to resemble'; Sor şibhandin شِبهاندِن (-şibhên-) = 'to liken (pê = to)' [Msr/IFb/ZF3/Wkt//K(s)/JJ] <şibîn>

şibaq I شِباق (L) = dawn. See **şebeq**.

şibaq II شِباق (IF) = window. See **şibak**.

Şibat شِبات (GF/OK) = February. See **Sibat**.

şibet' شِبەت (JB1-A) = like, similar to. See **şitî II**.

şibet'î شِبەتی (JB1-A/M-Am) = like, similar to. See **şitî II**.

şibhe شِبهە (K/IFb) = doubt; suspicion. See **şebh**.

şibihîn شِبهین (K[s]) = to resemble. See **şibîn**.

şibihandin شِبهاندِن (K[s]) = to liken to. See **şibandin**.

şibit شِبت (Bw) = dill. See **şiwît**.

şibîn شِبین *vi.* **(-şib-).** [+ dat. constr.] to resemble, look like: •**Herdu jî *dişibên* [sic] *hev*** (IFb) They *look alike* •**Tu *dişibî* bavê xwe** (Msr) You *resemble* your father. {also: şibihîn (K[s]); [chibehin شبهين/chibéin شبين] (JJ)} {syn: man [4]} <Ar √š-b-h: šabiha شبه = 'to resemble'; Sor şibhan شِبهان (-şibhê-) pê = 'to resemble' [Msr/IFb/ZF3/Wkt//K(s)/JJ] <şibandin; şitî II>

şicing شِجِنگ *f.* **(-a;-ê).** broom. {also: şijing (Wkt)} {syn: avlêk; cerîvk (Bw); gêzî; k'inoşe; melk'es; sirge (Ad); siqavêl; sivnik; sizik; şirt I} [Krs/ZF3//Wkt]

şidandin شِداندِن *vt.* **(-şidîn-).** 1) squeeze, press: •**Destê wî girt û *şidand* [givaşt]** (BF) He grabbed his hand and *squeezed* it •**Heta ku wî li filan kesî *neşidand*, parên wî nedanê** (FS) Until he *pressed /squeezed* so-and-so, he wouldn't give him his money •**Sola min piyê min *dişidîne*** (ZF3) My shoe is *squeezing/pinching* my foot; 2) to bind tightly, tighten (K); to saddle up *(vt.)*: •**Ezê rabim, hespê xwe *bişidînim* û suwar bibim** (L) I will get up, *saddle up* my horse and mount it •**Stîya 'Ereb, de r̄abe dergûşa kur̄î li ber p'êsîra xwe *bişidîne*, / Ji ber min bir̄eve û bilezîne** (Z-2, 85) Lady Ereb, get up and *fasten* the infant['s cradle] to your garment [like a papoose], / Then quickly flee before me; **-teng şidandin** (B) to tighten the saddle-girth; 3) to strengthen, reinforce: **-xwe şidandin** (IFb) to get ready to strike or attack: •**Ev gur giha serê mêrgê û *xwe şidand* û berê xwe da mihê** (SW) This wolf reached the meadow, *got himself all geared up* and headed for the sheep; 4) to stress, emphasize, accentuate; 5) {syn: badan [4]} to screw in, tighten: •**Wî birẍî *şidand*** (FS) He tightened in the screw; 6) [*f.* **(-a;-ê).**] stress, emphasis, accent: **-şidandina dengan** (Wkt) accentuation. {also: jidandin (HR); [chidandin] شداندين (JJ); <şidandin شداندن (dişidîne) (دشدينه)> (HH)} < Ar šadda شدّ = 'to pull' [L/K/JB3/IFb/B/JJ/HH/GF/Bw/ZF/Wkt/FS/BF//HR] <[4]: dernefîs>

şiddet شِددەت (Wkt) = violence. See **şidet**.

şidet شِدەت *f.* **(-a;-ê).** 1) intensity, vehemence: •**R̄omî *bi şiddet* li-dû wî diger̄yan** (SK 48:515) The Turks were *intensively* searching for him; 2) violence {syn: t'undî; t'undûtîjî}: •**Awa û tebeqeyên cihêreng ên *şideta* li ser jina kurd** (Lolav M. Hassan Alhamid. Kurdish Studies 6:1 [2018]) The various forms and layers of *violence* imposed on Kurdish women. {also: şiddet (Wkt-2); [chidet] شدت (JJ)} <Ar šiddah شدّة = 'force, intensity, violence' --> T şiddet = 'violence' [Alhamid/K/JJ/RZ/ZF3/Wkt/Kmc//SK]

şifte شِفتە *f.* **().** grilled ground beef or lamb with onion, parsley, and spices. {also: <şifte> شفتە (Hej)} Sor şifte شِفتە [Zeb/Hej/OK/Wkt]

şiftik شِفتِك (HH) = grape vine branches. See **şirtik**.

şiftî شِفتی *m./f.(BF/ZF3)* **().** watermelon, bot. *Citrullus vulgaris*. {also: şitî I (Bw); şimtî (Zeb); şivtî (K[s]/OK-2/AA); [chiwti/chouwti] شڤتی (JJ)} {syn: k'al III; zebeş} Cf. Sor şûtî شووتی (Arb. şiftî شِفتی) [IFb/GF/OK/M/BF/FS/ZF3//JJ//K(s)/AA//Bw//Zeb]

şihitîn شِهتین *vi.* **(-şihit-).** to weaken *(vi.)*, (go into) decline; to decay, deteriorate, degenerate, collapse; to be spoiled, be ruined, to fail: •**Gava**

ku mala êkî dişewiṯit, dibêjin: Filan kes *şehitiye* (FS) When someone's house burns down, they say: So-and-so *has been ruined* **•Hilşandina sîstema sovyetê, gelê me di nava wan welatên mezin de belav kir. Gelek jê, ji warê xwe yê berê *şihitîn*, halê wan ê aborî jî xerab bû** (Wlt 2:59, 16) The collapse of the soviet system dispersed our people among those large countries. Many of them *did not do well* in their previous place, their economic situation was also bad. {also: şe'etîn (Gz); şehitîn (Wkt/FS); şewitîn [2] (M); şiḧitîn (-şiḧit-) (B)} {syn: hilweşîn} Cf. Arc šḥaṭ שחט = 'to be spoilt' & Syr šeḥaṭ ܫܚܛ = 'to harm, abuse, violate' [Wlt/K/ZF3//B//Gz//Wkt/FS//M] <belengaz; şeht; şerpeze>

şihîn شِهين *f.* **(-a;-ê).** scales, balance: **•Dikandarî mêwîj bi *şehînê* kêşan** (FS) The shopkeeper weighed the raisins on *the scales*. {also: şehîn (K[s]/A/IFb-2/GF/TF/Kmc-9-2/FS); [chin شين/ chihin شهين] (JJ); <şehîn> شهين (HH)} {syn: mêzîn; t'erazî} Cf. P šāhīn شاهين = 'beam of a balance, pointer of a scale' [Şnx/Kmc-9/IFb/JJ/OK//K(s)/A/HH/GF/TF/FS]

şiḧitîn شِحِتين (-şiḧit-) (B) = to decline, deteriorate. See **şihitîn**.

şiîr شِئير (IFb) = poetry. See **şêr II**.

şiîre شِئيره *f.* **().** noodles: **•Dema *şiîre* çêdikirin** (DBgb, 8) While they were making *noodles*. {also: şehîre (Wkt); şehriye (IFb)} Cf. T şehriye < Ar šaʻīrīyah شعيرية = 'vermicelli' [DBgb/TF//Wkt//IFb]

şijing شِژنگ (Wkt) = broom. See **şicing**.

şijûn شِژوون (B) = large needle. See **şûjin**.

şik شِك *f.* **(-a;-ê).** doubt; suspicion: **-bê şik** (B) doubtless, undoubtedly; **-k'etin şika** (Ba2) to be in doubt, have one's doubts: **•Birê min, çimkî tu *dik'evî şika*, were em keriyê pêz vira bihêlin, heṟne qiraxê xilxile** (Ba2:2, 205) My brother, because you *are having doubts*, come let's leave the flock of sheep here and go to the edge of the mountain-ridge; **-ser *fk-ê* k'etin şikê** (B) to suspect s.o. *(of stg.)*; **-şik birin** = a) to doubt: **•Aqû p'êxember dibîne, ku jin *şikê dibe ser* wî** (Ba) Jacob the prophet sees that [his] wife *doubts* him; b) to suspect: **•Aqûb, tu *şikê neve ser* gura, zeda Ûsiv destê birane** (Ba3-3, #22) Jacob, *do not suspect* the wolves, whatever happened to Joseph was at the hands of his brothers; **-şik kirin** (JB3) to suspect; **-şik pêşda anîn** (B) to arouse or excite suspicion; **-şik û şa[y]îş** (B) doubts, suspicions; worries: **•Ez *k'etme şik û şayîşa*, lê apê Kotê ber xwe nedik'et** (Ba2-#2, 205) I *began to get worried*, but uncle K. was not perturbed. {also: [chek] شك (JJ); <şik> شك (HH)} {syn: şebh} < Ar šakk شكّ [Ba/K/JB3/IFb/B/HH/GF/TF/OK//JJ] <ḧeseḧes; şayîş>

şikaêt شِكائێت (SK) = complaint. See **şikyat**.

şikal شِكال (Haz/Msr) = (old) shoe. See **şekal**.

şikandin شِكاندِن (JJ/GF/TF/OK) = to break. See **şkênandin**.

şikar شِكار *f.* **(;-ê).** 1) {syn: nêçîr; ṟav I; seyd} hunting, the chase: **-çûn şikarê** (K) to go hunting; 2) game, quarry. {also: [šekār] شكار (JJ-Khurasan)} [Pok. 3. (s)ker- (933. &) 935.] 'to turn, bend; to move, return': O Ir *skăr- (Ras, p.132): Av skar- = 'to chase' in skārayaṯ-raθa = 'chariot-chasing'; P šikār شكار = 'hunt, chase' [K/IFb/OK//JJ]

***şikarçî** شِكارچى *m.* **().** hunter, huntsman. {syn: nêçîrvan; seydvan} [SS] <şikar>

şikayet شِكايەت (IFb/ZF) = complaint. See **şikyat**.

şikeft شِكەفت (K/IFb/TF/BK) = cave. See **şkeft**.

şikestin شِكەستِن (K/JJ/GF/TF/OK) = to break *(vi.)*. See **şkestin**.

şiket شِكەت (BK) = cave. See **şkeft**.

şikev شِكەڤ *f.* **(-a;-ê).** 1) {syn: bot [1]} (wooden) trough; 2) {syn: legan; t'eşt} tub, wash basin; basin *(for dough)* (B); 3) {syn: varîl} barrel; 4) small boat [T tekne] (Wkt): **•*Şikeva* plastîk a ku 28 penaber tê de bûn ... li zinaran xist û binav bû** (Wkt: Aa.com.tr/kk xi.2015) The plastic *boat* in which there were 28 refugees ... hit the rocks and sank. {also: şkef (A-2); şkev (K-2/B/GF-2); [chikew] شكڤ (JJ); <şkev> شكڤ (HH)} [K/A/JB3/IFb/JJ/GF/BF//B/HH/Wkt] <afiṟ>

şikeva شِكەڤا (TF/RF/FJ) = unleavened. See **şkeva**.

şikênandin شِكێناندِن (TF) = to break. See **şkênandin**.

şikêr شِكێر (TF/Wlt/Wkt) = pile of stones. See **şkêr**.

şik•il شِكِل *m.* **(•lê;).** 1) {syn: t'eşe; teva I} form, shape; aspect, appearance: **•Heywanek heye di binê behrê de, di *şiklê* hespan e** (L) There is an animal at the bottom of the sea, in *the shape of* a horse; **-şeklê *fkî* dan** (Bw) to look like, resemble: **•Ez *şeklê* wî *didem*** (Bw) I *look like* him [=**Ez şitî** (or **wekî) wî me**]; 2) {syn: keval; ṟesim; sifat [4]; wêne} picture, drawing, painting, image (K/B): -

şikil kirin/k'işandin (K/B) = a) to draw, depict, paint; b) to take a picture of, photograph; 3) photograph (K/B). {also: şekil (ZF); şikl (SK/GF); şiklet (HR); [chekil] شكل (JJ); <şikl> شكل (HH)} < Ar šakl شكل --> T şekil; Sor şikł شكڵ = 'form'; Za şikil *m.* = 'picture' [L/HH/SK/GF//F/K/B/IFb/JB1-A//JJ/ZF//HR]

şikinandin شِكِناندِن (FD) = to comb; to card. See **şkinîn**.

şikinîn شِكِنين (K/JJ) = to comb; to card. See **şkinîn**.

şikir شِكِر (K/IFb/B/HH/GF) = gratitude. See **şikirîn** [1].

şikirîn شِكِرين *f.* **(-a;-ê).** 1) gratitude, thankfulness, thanks: **-şikirîna xwe anîn** (K) to express one's gratitude: **•*Şikrî[n]ê* ji řebbê xweřa *tîne*** (Z-2) He *expresses his thanks* to God; 2) Thank God: **•*Şikir [xwedêřa]* tu sax û silametî** (B) *Thank God* you're safe and sound; **-şikir xwedêřa** (B) do. {also: şikir (K-2/IFb/B/GF); [choukr] شكر (JJ); <şikir> شكر (HH)} < Ar šukr شكر [EP-7/K//IFb/B/HH/GF//JJ]

şikl شِكل (SK/HH/GF) = form; picture. See **şikil**.

şiklet شِكلەت (HR) = form; picture. See **şikil**.

şikoke شِكۆكە (GF) = wild pear. See **şekok**.

şikyat شِكيات *m./f.(GShA)* **(/-a;).** 1) {syn: gazin; gilî I[2]} complaint: **-şikyat kirin** (B) to complain: **•Xelq *şikyata* kurê te *dikin*** (GShA, 226) People *are complaining about* your son; 2) {syn: gazin} legal suit, law suit. {also: şekîyat; şikaêt (SK); şikayet (IFb/ZF); şikyet; şkat; şkîyat; şkyat; [cheka شكا/ chikaiet شكايت] (JJ)} < Ar šikāyah شكاية--> P šekāyat شكايت --> T şikâyet; Sor şkat شكات & sikałe سِكاڵە [K/B//IFb/ZF//SK//JJ]

şikyatçî شِكياتچى *m.* **(-yê;).** complainer; litigant, plaintiff: **•*Şikyatçîyê* we kaxez nivîsîne** (kagiz.org :Ĥecîyê Cindî 14.vi.2016) Your *plaintiff* has written letters. {also: şikyatker (K); şkatker; [chkat-ker] شكاتكر (JJ)[Sor]} [Z-1/EP-7//K//JJ]

şikyatker شِكياتكەر (K) = complainer; litigant. See **şikyatçî**.

şikyet شِكيەت = complaint. See **şikyat**.

şil I شِل *adj.* wet *(of living things, e.g., earth [alive for Kurds], hair, lips; whereas* **ter** *[qv.] is wet of inanimate things)*; damp; moist {≠ ziwa}: **-şil bûn** (K/A/JB3) to become wet; **-şil kirin** (K/A/JB3) to wet, moisten, dampen (vt.) : **•Dikeve avê, *şil* nabê [sih]** (L) It falls into the water, [but] it doesn't get *wet [rdl.; ans.: a shadow]*. {also: [chil] شل (JJ); <şil> شل (HH)} {syn: nem; teř; ≠ĥişk; ≠ziwa} {şilatî; şilitî; şilî} [F/K/A/JB3/IFb/B/JJ/HH/Ag]

şil II شِل *adj.* paralyzed, lame, limp *(of hand)*: **•Ez ne j[î] t'opalim, ji p'îya / ne kerrim, ji guha / ne *şilim*, ji desta** (FK-kk-13:124) I am neither lame in the feet / nor deaf in the ears / nor *limp* in the hands. {also: şel I (IFb/GF); [chill] شل (JJ); <şel> شل (HH)} {syn: goc; qop; şeht} < Ar ašall أشلّ (√š-l-l) = 'paralyzed, lame'; Sor şel شەل [FK-kk-13/K/B/JJ/SK//IFb/HH/GF] <kulek I; kût I; leng; nivîşkan I>

şilatî شِلاتى (K) = wetness, moisture. See **şilî** [1].

şilavik شِلاڤك (IFb) = pancreas; rennet bag. See **şîlav**.

şilêl شِلێل *m.* **(;-î).** rye, bot. *Secale cereale*: **-nanê şilêlî** (Wkt) rye bread. {also: şilîl (K); [chilil/shilēl/shilīl (Rh)] شليل (JJ); <şilêl> شليل (HH); <şilêl> شلێل (Hej)} {syn: aç'ar II} [Kmc-6/IFb/HH/GF/Hej/ZF3/FS/Wkt//K/JJ]

şilêr شِلێر *f.* **(-a;).** small waterfall, cascade. {also: [chiler] شيلر (JJ-Chodzko [Sulaimania])} {{syn : sûlav; şirav; şîp} [Bw//JJ] <sêlav; şîp [2]>

şilf شِلف *f.* **(-a;-ê).** blade, (sharp) edge: **•Tu *şilfa* şûr derxe** (Z-922) Take off the sword's *blade*. {also: [chilw] شلف (JJ); <şilf> شلف (HH)} {syn: dev [4]; tî I} Cf. Ar šilfah شلفة = '(rasor) blade'; W Arm šełp շեղբ [Z-922/K/A/IFb/HH/GF/TF//JJ]

şilfî tazî شِلفى تازى (Qzl) = stark naked. See **şilf tazî**.

şilf tazî شِلف تازى/**şilftazî** شِلفتازى [Wkt] *adj.* stark naked: **•Ji ciyê xwe radibe, wî xeftanî ji nav milên wê dide alî û keçik *şilf tazî* li pêş wî ye** (Epl, 42) He gets up from his place, throws aside that caftan on her shoulders and the girl is standing *stark naked* before him. {also: şilfî tazî (Qzl); şilf û tazî (IFb)} {syn: řût; zelût} Cf. NENA shülkhâ-yâ ܫܠܟܚܐ = 'naked' & shâlikh ܫܠܟ = 'to strip, vi.' (Maclean) [Qzl//Epl/ZF3/Wkt//IFb]

şilf û tazî شِلف و تازى (IFb) = stark naked. See **şilf tazî**.

şilh شِلە (GF/TF) = swarm of bees. See **şilxe**.

şilik شِلك (TF/CS) = pancake, crêpe. See **şilikî**.

şilikî شِلكى *f.* **(;-yê).** pancake, crêpe [T bazlama, gözleme]: **•*şilikî*/nanê avê: li hin deveran, bi hêk û rûn, li hin deveran, tenê bi rûn, li hin deveran jî bi şîr, hêk û rûn tê çêkirin** (CCG, 138) *shiliki*: in some regions it is made with eggs and oil, in some regions only with oil, and in some regions with milk, eggs and oil. {also: şilik (TF/CS)} < şil I = 'wet' [CCG/ZF3/Kmc/GF//TF/CS] şiling شِلِنگ (GF) = round cucumber. See **şelengo**.

şilitî شِلِتی (A) = wetness, moisture. See **şilî** [1].

şilî شِـلـی *f.* **(-ya;-yê).** 1) {also: şilatî (K-2); şilitî (A); [chilli] شـلـی (JJ)} wetness, moisture: **•*Şilî* şayî ye** (Haz) *Wetness* is rejoicing, said when water is spilt accidentally; 2) {syn: baran} rain (Kg/Mzg/Mş): **•*Şilî* dibare** (Mş) It's raining [lit. '*Rain* is raining']; 3) rainy weather; precipitation: **•Dinya *şilî* ye** (Haz) It's *rainy* outside. [Kg/Haz/Ag/K/A/IFb/B/TF//JJ] <şil I>

şilîl شِليل (K) = rye. See **şilêl**.

şilît شِليت (GF) = rope; ribbon. See **şerît**.

şilop'•e شِـلـۆپـه *f.* **(;•ê).** 1) {syn: xilolîk I[2]} snow mixed with rain (Ag/Wn); 2) {syn: lêlav} slush (K/B); wet, melting snow: **•Legleg jî zû têt, wextê hatina wê hêşta befr û *şilowe* ye, serma ye, bihar nîye** (SK 29:263) The stork also comes early. When it comes there is still snow and *slush* and it is cold, it is not spring. {also: şilove I (IFb-2/GF-2); şilowe (SK)} Cf. Sor şîlêwe شيلێوه = 'snow mixed with rain' [Ag/Wn/K/IFb/B/GF/ZF3//SK] <baran; berf; şilî; zivistan>

şilopil شِلۆپِل *adj.* soaking wet, drenched, sopping wet. {also: şilpil (ZF3)} {syn: şil} [Wn//ZF3]

şilor شِـلـۆر *f.* **(;-ê).** type of sour plum, black plum [T kara erik]: **-dara şilorê** (B) plum tree. {also: [chilour] شـلـر (JJ); <şilor> شـلـور (HH)} Cf. Arm salor սալոր [K/A/IFb/B/JJ/HH/GF/ZF3] <alûçe; dembûl; hêrûg [1]; ĥûlîreşk; încas>

şilove I شِـلـۆڤـه (IFb/GF) = melting snow. See **şilop'e** [3].

şilove II شِـلـۆڤـه: şilove kirin (ʻEbdulla) = to explain, interpret. See **şîrove**.

şilowe شِلۆوه (SK) = melting snow. See **şilop'e**.

şiloxe شِلۆخه (IFb/OK/Zeb) = shoelace. See **şîrox**.

şilpil شِلپِل (ZF3) = soaking wet. See **şilopil**.

şilqan شِلقان (FS) = to splash *(vi.)*. See **ç'eliqîn**.

şilqandin شِـلـقـانـدِن (FS/BF) = to shake; to splash. See **ç'eliqandin**.

şilqiyan شِلقِيان (FS) = to splash *(vi.)*. See **ç'eliqîn**.

şiltaqî شِلتاقی (GF) = slander. See **şilt'ax**.

şilt'ax شِـلـتـاخ *f.* **().** slander, libel, calumny: **•[Eger xwecihî lê bidin û mirovekî Ekradan bikujin, êdî ĥetta qiyametê şeř û *şiltaẍêd* Ekradan xilas nabin]** (BN, 101) If the local inhabitants beat them or kill one of the Kurds' men, the battles and squabbles [lit., '*slanders*'] of the Kurds won't end until Judgement Day **•Wî *şiltaxî bi* Behremî *ve na*** (FS) He *smeared* B. *with slander*: **-şiltax kirin** (GF) to slander, accuse: **•Wî *şiltaxî li* Behremî *kir*** (FS) He *slandered* B. {also: şiltaqî (GF-2); şiltaxî (TF/FS); <şiltaẍ> شـلـتـاغ (BN)} {syn: altaxî; ʻewanî} Cf. Clq Iraqi Ar šaltaɣ شـلـتـغ = 'to deceive, cheat, lie'; P šeltāq شـلـتـاق = 'dishonest dealing, dispute, tumult'; T şıltak [şiltık] = 'slander, blaming' [suç atma, karalama] (DS, v. 10, p. 3768) [BN//K/GF//TF/FS]

şiltaxî شِلتاخی (TF/FS) = slander. See **şilt'ax**.

şilx شِلخ (GF) = swarm of bees. See **şilxe**.

şilx•e شِلخه *f.* **(•a;).** swarm of bees *(after splitting off from main hive, in search of new nest)*: **•Ma tu nizanî li-naw hemî Kurdistanê ew mesele meşhûr e, "Hingî mêşêt hingûnî zêde dibin, *şilxan diden* û hingûnê çak diken ko xudanê mêşan mêşekî bikiřît û yêkî bixazît û yêkî bidizît"?** (SK 35:315) Don't you know that all over Kurdistan this saying is famous: "Bees increase and *swarm* and make good honey when their owner buys a bee, begs one and steals one"?; **-şilxa mêşên hingivînî** (FS)/**şulxa mêşê** (Zeb) do. {also: şilh (GF-2/TF); şilx (GF-2); şulhe (GF); şulxe (Zeb)} {syn: bars} [Zeb//IFb/SK/OK/BF/FS//GF//TF]

şima شِما (K/A/IFb/B/TF/OK) = wax. See **şema**.

şimadank شِمادانك (IFb) = candlestick. See **şemdan**.

şimal شِمال (F) = north. See **şemal** [5].

şimam شِمام = type of fragrant melon. See **şimamok**.

şimamok شِـمـامـۆك *f.* **(-a;-ê).** small, yellow fragrant melon (Kp/B). {also: şemam (K/B); şemamik (IFb-2); şememok (Rh); şimam; [chemamouk/ šimamōk] شـمـامـوك (JJ); <şimamok> شـمـامـوك (HH)} Cf. Ar šammām شـمّـام = 'muskmelon, cantaloupe' < šamma شمّ = 'to smell, to sniff' [Kp/A/IFb/HH//JJ//K/B//Rh] <zebeş>

şimaq شِـمـاق *f.* **(-a;-ê).** smack, slap, blow, cuff: **•...ji wê *şimaqa* ku me xwariye ji kekê xwe** (pirtukxane.blogspot.com 8.iv.2006) ... from that *smack* which we got from our older brother. {also: şelmaq (K/B); şemaq II; şeqam (IFb/GF/TF); şiqam (IFb-2/GF-2); [sciákkám] شـكـام (JJ); <şiqam شقـام/şimaq شـمـاق> (HH)} {syn: sîle; t'ep II} [K/B//A/HH//IFb/GF/TF]

şimik شِـمِـك *f.* **(-a;-ê).** slipper(s), in the shape of wooden-soled sandals for the bath and the home; type of footwear worn by women and sheikhs: **•Wî *şimik* kir piyê xwe** (FS) He put *slippers* on his feet; **-ji şimikê ta kumikê** (BF) from head to toe [lit. 'from the slippers to the hat']. {also: [chimik] شمك (JJ); <şimik> شمك (HH)} [J/K/A/JB3/IFb/B/JJ/HH/GF/TF/BF/FS] <sol>

şimitandin شِمِتاندِن (K/B) = to cause to slip. See **şemitandin**.

şimitîn شِمِتين (K/B) = to slip. See **şemitîn**.

şimitokî شِمِتۆکی (K/B) = slippery. See **şematokî**.

şimtî شِمتی (Zeb) = watermelon. See **şiftî**.

şindilîn شِندِلین (FS) = to dangle, hang down. See **şingilîn**.

şingên شِنگێن (TF) = rattling, clanking. See **şingîn**.

şingênî شِنگێنی = rattling, clanking. See **şingîn**.

şingilîn شِنگِلین *vi.* **(-şingil-).** to dangle, hang down (vi.): **•Kuřo rûvî, ew çiye bi devê te ve *şindilîye*** (FS) My dear fox, what is that *hanging* from your mouth? **•Li cem her kesekî bi awayekî, reng û şêweyekî cihê *şingilîme*, pev ketime** (C. Kulek. Nameyek ji Xwedê re, 131) I *have been left hanging*, I have clashed with everyone in different ways, shapes and forms. {also: şindilîn (FS)} [C.Kulek/Wkt/ZF3//FS]

şingîn شِنگین *f.* **(-a;-ê).** rattling, clanking, sound, noise: **•*şingîna* suwara** (MC-1) *the sound of* horsemen **•Rojekê di banga sibê da Kulik bi *şingîna* bazirganekî ji xwe şiyar bû** (ZZ-7, 165) One day with the morning call to prayer K. awoke to *the sound of* a caravan; **-şingîna zengil** (B) tinkling of a bell. {also: şingên (TF); şingênî; şingînî; zingîn (F)} [MC-1/K/B/GF//TF//F]

şingînî شِنگینی = rattling, clanking. See **şingîn**.

şipiya شِپِیا (SS) = standing up. See **şipîya**.

şipîya شِپییا *adj./adv.* upright, standing on one's feet: **•Li ser bêndera cem mala xwe *şipyakî* mir, piştî çend rojan ku biyaniyan destê xwe danîn ser erdê hawîrdora gund** (HYma, 30) She died *standing up* on the threshing floor beside her house, a few days after strangers had grabbed the land around the village; **-řabûn şipîya** (K) to stand on one's (own) feet: **•*Yê şipya* bila rûnin û yê rûniştî bila *rabin şipya*** (GF) *Those standing up* should sit down, and those who are seated should *stand up on their feet.* {also: şipiya (ş); şipîyakî (CS-2); şipya (GF); şipyakî (HYma)} <ji pîya[n] < p'ê II = 'foot' [HYma//K/CS//GF//SS]

şipîyakî شِپییاکی (CS) = standing up. See **şipîya**.

şipya شِپیا (GF) = standing up. See **şipîya**.

şipyakî شِپیاکی (HYma) = standing up. See **şipîya**.

şiqab شِقاب (GF) = drill. See **şixab**.

şiqam شِقام (IFb/HH/GF) = smack, slap. See **şimaq**.

şiqitandin شِقِتاندِن *vt.* **(-şiqitîn-).** 1) {syn: şelandin} to remove, strip, take off (clothing) : **•Wana libasê kewotka ji Zînê *şiqitandin*** [sic] (Z-1) They *took* the dove garb *off* Zin [a girl]; 2) to split, cleave in two (vt.) (IFb/HH/GF/TF); 3) to cause to climb down (B). {also: şeqitandin (IFb-2/GF/TF/OK-2); <şeqitandin شقتاندن (dişeqitîne) (دشقتينه)> (HH)} [Z-1/K/IFb/B/OK//HH/GF/TF] <şiqitîn>

şiqitîn شِقِتین *vi.* **(-şiqit-).** 1) {syn: řaşiqitîn; teĥisîn} to slide, slip; 2) to climb down (B); 3) to fall off *(e.g., a button off a shirt)*: **•Hêratîya serê wê *şiqitî* bû** (Zerîn Tek:RN2 56[1998] 6) Her headscarf *had fallen off*; 4) to split *(vi.)*, be split or cleft in half (HH/GF). {also: şeqitîn (IFb); <şeqitîn شقتين (dişeqitî) (دشقتى)> (HH)} [Ks/K/B//IFb/HH/GF] <alîn; şiqitandin>

şi'r شِعر (SK/OK) = poetry. See **şêr II**.

şirav شِراڤ *f.* **(-a;).** small waterfall, cascade. {also: çirav[2] (ZF3/RZ); çireav (RZ-2)}{syn: sûlav; şilêr; şîp} [Haz//ZF3/RZ] <sêlav; şîp [2]>

şird شِرد (L) = condition; bet; task. See **şert**.

şirenqe شِرەنقە (BF/FS) = syringe, shot. See **şirînqe**.

şiře-şiř kirin شِرەشِر کِرِن (K/B) = to babble, murmur *(of water)*. See **şirşiřandin**.

şirêz شِرێز (IFb/JB1-S) = resin; concentrated juice; resin; must. See **şîrêz**.

şiřik شِرِك/**şirik** شِرِك *f.* **(-a;-ê).** 1) {syn: vizik II} stream, spurt, jet, downpour (of water): **•Ji ber *şirikê* çû ber mezrîbê** (ANHA, Hawarnews.com/Drş, #426, 121) From the pot into the kettle (lit. 'From *the stream of water* he went to the gutter') *[prv.]* **•Me ji ber baranê bazda em çûne ber *şirikê*** (Nasname.com) We fled the rain, we ended up under the [heavy] *downpour [prv.]*; 2) downspout, drainpipe, gutter (pipe to carry off rainwater from roof): **•*Şiřka* serbanê wan diçit kolanê** (FS) *The downspout from* their roof goes [i.e, empties] into the street. {*also*: çiranek (Kmc-2); çirik III (IFb-2/FJ-2/RZ-2); çirîk (Kmc); çironek (IFb-2); çirûnek (FS-2); çirtik (RZ-2); **surik I** (SK); şirînek (A/RZ-2); şirrik (AD); şořeke (FS-2); şurik (FJ-2/SS-2/CS-2); şurrik (GF-2); şûrik II (Kmc-2); [chourik/šorrýk (S)] شرك (JJ); <şirik> شرك (HH)} Cf. Sor çirûnek چِروونەك = pilûsk پلووسك = 'gargoyle; gutter' [K/B/FS/AD//FJ/GF/TF/HH/BF/Wkt/ZF/SS/CS/RZ//IFb//A//JJ] <surik I>

şiringe شِرِنگە (IFb) = syringe, shot. See **şirînqe**.

şiringe شِرنقه (GF/RZ) = syringe, shot. See **şirînqe**.

şirî'et شِريعهت (EP-7) = shari'ah. See **şerîet**.

şirîk شِـريـك *m.* **(-ê;).** partner; companion: **•Her kesê *şirîkan* bo xudê çê-ket o sicde bo seneman biket, wî bikujin, bila îmanê bi min biket** (SK 48:513) Every person who makes *partners* for god and bows down before idols, kill him, he should believe in me **•Me qesd kir biçîne hewara *şirîkê* xo** (SK 37:331) We intended to go to the help of our *comrade* **•Xwest ku êşa *şirîkê* xwe sivik bike** (HYma 51) He wanted to ease his *companion's* pain. {also: [chirik/scirík & sciarík (G)] شـريـك (JJ); <şirîk> شـريـك (HH)} {syn : hevk'ar; hevp'ar[2]} < Ar šarīk شَـريـك; Sor şerîk شەريك [HYma/K/B/IFb/JJ/HH/SK/CS]

şirîn I شِرين (JB1-A&S/SK/OK) = sweet. See **şîrin**.

şir̄în II شِـــريــــن *vi.* **(-şir̄-).** 1) to murmur, purl *(of running water)*; 2) [*f.* **(-a;)**] murmuring, purling *(of running water)*: **•Dengê *şirîna* avê dibihîst êdî** (MB-Meyro) She could already hear *the splashing of* the water. {also: [chourin] شـريـن (JJ)} Cf. P šārīdan شـاريـدن = 'to flow with noise'; Sor şir̄e شِرِه/şir̄eşir̄ شِرِشِر = 'murmur (especially of running water)' [MB/K/FS//JJ] <xulîn> See also **şirşir̄andin**. <gujeguj>

şirînek شِـريـنـهك (A/RZ) = jet of water; drainpipe. See **şir̄ik**.

şirînî I شِرينى (SK) = sweetmeat, candy. See **şîranî**.

şirînî II شِرينى (OK) = sweetness. See **şîrînî**.

şirînqe شِـريـنقـه *f.* **(;-yê).** syringe, hypodermic needle, shot: **•Noşdarî *şirînqek* li nesaxî da** (FS) The doctor gave the patient *a shot*. {also: şerenqe (FS-2); şirenqe (BF/FS-2); şiringe (IFb); şirinqe (GF/RZ)} <Gr syrinx σῦριγξ = 'musical pipe' --> Eng syringe: T şırınga; Sor şirînqe شِرينقه [Bw/OK/FS//BF//GF/RZ//IFb] <derzî>

şirît شِريت (IFb/B) = rope; string. See **şerît** [1].

şiro شِـــرۆ: -şiro kirin (K/B) to explain, interpret. See **şîrove**.

şirove شِـــرۆڤـــه (GF/BF/FS/SS) = explanation. See **şîrove**.

şiroxe شِرۆخه (FS) = shoelace. See **şîrox**.

şirqîn شِرقين (L/B) = noise. See **şerqîn**.

şirqînî شِرقينى (B) = noise. See **şerqîn**.

şirrik شِررك (AD) = jet of water; drainpipe. See **şir̄ik**.

şirşir̄andin شِـــرشِـــرانـــدِن *vt.* **(-şirşir̄în-).** to cause to babble, murmur, purl *(of water)*. {cf. also: şir̄e-şir̄ kirin (K/B); cf. <şirşir> شـرشـر (HH)} [Haz/(A)/ZF3//K//HH] <xulexul; xulîn> See also **şir̄în II**.

şirt I شِـــــــرت *f.* **(-a;-ê).**1) {syn: avlêk; cerîvk (Bw); gêzî; k'inoşe; melk'es; sirge (Ad); siqavêl; sivnik; sizik; şicing} broom (Erg/Qrj): **-şirt kirin** (Qrj) to sweep; 2) young (oak) tree that does not bear fruit (IFb). [Erg/Qrj/IFb/GF/ZF3] <gêzî; malişt in>

şirt II شِرت (Z-3) = condition; bet. See **şert**.

şirtik شِرتِك *f.* **(-a;-ê).** branch, bough (B); branches of grape vines and the like, used in making baskets. {also: <şirtik شِرتك/şiftik شفتك> (HH)} [A/IFb/B/HH/GF] <ç'iq[il]; çirpî; şax>

şirûxe شِرووخه (FS) = shoelace. See **şîrox**.

şiştin شِشتِن (PB) = to wash. See **şûştin**.

şitil شِـتِـل *f.(Z-3)/m.(B)* **(-a** or **şitla/ ;)** sapling, young tree; young plant: **-şitilê k'elema** (B) cabbage seedling; **-şitla bîyê** (Z-3) young willow tree *[used figuratively to describe a tall person]*; **-Wekî *şitla* tihokê** (ZF3) tall and slender (like a hackberry tree *sapling*). {also: şet'el (K[s]); şetil; [scetel] شـتـل (JJ); <şitil> شـتـل (HH)} < Arc štal שתל/štēl שתיל & Heb šatal שתל= 'to plant (trees)'; Syr šetlā ܫܬܠܐ & NENA shitla ܫܬܠܐ = 'plant' (Maclean) & šatalta/štilta = 'grove of planted trees' (Oraham); cf. also Ar šatlah شـتـلة = 'nursery plant' [Z-3/IFb/B/HH/GF/TF/ZF3//K(s)/JJ] <dar I; xilp>

şitî I شِتى (Bw) = watermelon. See **şiftî**.

şitî II شِتى [Bw]/**şit'î** [JB1-A] *prep.* 1) like, similar to, resembling, as: **•Çonev bajêrekî *şibet'î* Mûsilê** (M-Am #737) They went … to a city *like* Mosul **•Çu carêt dî k'es *şibet'* min neket** (JB1-A #18) No one should ever again act *like* me [=as I did] **•Em *şitî* bivirê melay ne** (Bw) We are strong, robust; We are untouched (not subject to wear and tear) [lit. 'We are *like* the mullah's hatchet'] **•Ez *ştî* wî me** (Bw) I *look like* him [=**Ez wekî wî me/Ez şeklê wî didem**] **•Ma beyna heyvekê wî qesrek li wê dana, yanî *şibet'î* wê qesrê çi çi 'erda nebo** (M-Am #738) Within a month he had built a palace there, such a palace as had no *like* anywhere at all **•Tilêt desta ne *şitî* êk in** (Bw) The fingers of the hand are not all *alike [prv.]*; 2) [*conj.*] As if: **•*Şibet'î* sê mrova hatine ber çavê wî** (JB1-A #43) *As if* three men had come into view [lit. 'had come before his eyes']. {also: şibet' (JB1-A-2); şibet'î (JB1-A-2/M-Am); ştî (Bw-2); [sibi] شبى (JJ)} {syn: mîna; nola; wek} <Ar √š-b-h: šabiha شـبـه = 'to resemble' [Bw/JB1-A/FS/M-Am//JJ] <şibîn>

şitû شِـتـوو *f.* **().** small, tart pear (Şnx) which ripens in the winter (HH/GF). {also: <şitû> شـتـو (HH); <şitu> شـتـو (Hej)} [Şnx/IFb/HH/GF/Hej/FS/ZF3] <hermê; karçîn>

şiv شِـڤ *f.* **(-a;-ê).** 1) {syn: ço; çogan; gopal; kevezan; metreq; şivdar} stick, club, cudgel: **•T'asêd xwe digirtne destêd xwe, pê *şiva* li wan dixistin, wekî bi wî dengî gura bitirsînin** (Ba2:1, 203) They would take their bowls and bang on them with their *staffs*, so as to scare away the wolves with this noise; **-şivik** (Ad/A/IFb) = dim. of **şiv**; 2) strike or blow with a stick, club, or cudgel: **•De ka ez binêrim bê te çend ço xwarine, tu mêrekî çawa ye! ... Lê na-- ez bawer nakim ku te tew *şivek* jî bi xwe kiri be** (Ardû, 117) Let me see how many times you've been hit with their stick, let me see what kind of man you are! ... But no-- I don't think you got even *a single blow*; 3) {syn: ç'iq[il; çirpî; gulî II; şax; şirtik; ta VI} branch, bough (B/GF); 4) stripe *(cloth pattern)*; 5) pipe (JJ/GF-Îikak). {also: [chiw] شڤ (JJ)} [Ad/K/A/IFb/B/JJ/JB1-S/GF/TF/OK]

şivan شِـڤـان *m.* **(-ê; şivên/şivîn** [B-2], **vî şivanî).** shepherd, herdsman: **•Şuxulê *şivana* zaf çetin bû, lê heqê xebata wana gelekî kêm bû** (Ba2:1, 204) The *shepherds*' job was very hard, but their earnings were very small [lit. 'few']; **-darê şivên** = the shepherd's rod or staff. {also: şwan (SK); [chiwan] شـڤـان (JJ); <şivan> شـڤـان (HH)} {syn: serwan} < O Ir *fšu- (*zero grade of* *pasu-) = 'sheep' + pāna- = 'guard, protector': **fšu-/pasu-**: [Pok. 2. peḱ- 797.] 'wealth, movable property': cf. **pez**; + **-pāna**: [Pok. pā- 787.] 'to feed; to protect'. Mid P šubān; P čūpān چـوپـان --> T çoban; Southern Tati dialects (all *f.*): Chali cupun; Ebrahim-abadi cupēn; Esfarvini copon; Sagz-abadi cāppun = 'shepherd' (Yar-shater); Sor şiwan شِـوان/şuwan شـووان; Za şwane *m./f.* (Todd); Hau şûane *m.* (M4) {şivan[t]î; şivanîtî} [K/A/JB3/IFb/B/JJ/HH/JB1-S/GF/TF/OK//SK] <berxvan; bizin; çêrandin; mî I; naxirvan; pez; selwan>

şivanî شِـڤـانـی (K/IFb/GF/OK) = sheep herding. See **şivantî**.

şivanîtî شِڤانيتی (OK) = sheep herding. See **şivantî**.

şivantî شِـڤـانـتـی *f.* **(-ya;-yê).** sheep herding, profession of being a shepherd, shepherding: **•K'ê ku p'akî haj ji *şivantîyê* t'unebû, hew zanibû, ku ew tiştekî çetin nîne** (Ba2:1, 203) Those who were not well acquainted with *shepherding* thought that it was something not very difficult. {also: şivanî (K-2/IFb/GF-2/OK); şivanîtî (OK-2); şwanî (SK)} [K/B/GF/TF//IFb/OK//SK] <berxvanî; şivan>

şivaq شِڤاق (GF) = dawn. See **şebeq**.

Şivat شِڤات (F) = February. See **Sibat**.

şivdar شِـڤـدار *f.* **(-a;-ê).** wooden stick, club, cudgel, staff: **•Min *şivdara* xwe bilind kir û ser wî da ḧejand** (Ba2:2, 206) I raised my *staff* and waved it at him; **-dan ber şivdara** (Dz) to club, beat with a stick: **•Çaxê ew nêzîkaya malê dibe ji k'erê peya dibe û k'era xwe *dide ber şivdara*** (Dz-anec #15) when he gets near the house, he gets down off his donkey and *gives it a beating*. {also: şivder (GF); şivedar (B-2)} {syn: ço; çogan; çomax̌; gopal; kevezan; metreq; şiv} [Dz/F/K/B//GF]

şivder شِڤدەر (GF) = cudgel. See **şivdar**.

şivedar شِڤەدار (B) = cudgel. See **şivdar**.

şiveȓ•ê شِـڤـەڕی *f.* **(•îya;).** rural road, country road; rough path; narrow path, trail: **•Ȓokê bazirganekî giran tê *şiveȓîya* ber bîrêȓa derbaz dibe** (Ba) One day a large caravan passes by the well on *a path (or, country road)*. {also: şevaȓê (Btm); şivêle, f. (JB3); şivîle (K-2/A); [chiw-a ri] شـڤـارى (JJ); <şivarê> شـڤـارى (HH)} Cf. Arc švīlā שבילא = 'road, path' & NENA shwîlâ ܫܒܝܠܐ = 'highway' (Maclean). *If the form **şiverê** is indeed of Aramaic provenance, the final syllable -lā was identified by Kurds as **ȓê** (f.), the Kurdish word for 'road' (cf. Persian rāh راه). This would also account for the feminine gender in Kurdish, whereas the posited original Aramaic word is masculine. Cf. **doşav** for another example of the identification of the final part of a foreign word (in this case -av) with a native word.* [Ba/K/IFb/B//JJ/HH//Btm//JB3//A] <pêgeh; ȓê>

şivêdî شِڤێدی (Bw) = last night. See **şevêdî**.

şivêle شِـڤـێـلـە, f. (JB3) = country road, rough path. See **şiveȓê**.

şivik شِڤِك (Ad/A/IF) = dim. of **şiv**.

şivin شِڤِن (FS) = deer. See **şivir**.

şivir شِـڤِـر *m.&f.* **(-ê/-a;).** *type of deer*: 1) red deer (OK); 2) stag (GF): **-şivira mê** (IFb/OK) female deer, doe; **-şivira mos** (IFb/OK) type of large deer, zool. *Alcus americane*; **-şivirê kedî** (IFb/OK) reindeer, zool. *Rangifer*. {also: şivin (FS-2); şivr (GF-2)} Cf. Sor şûr شـوور/şûl شـوول = 'roe-deer, fallow deer, wild goat' (K2) [IFb/GF/OK/FS/ZF3] <ask; gak'ûvî; mambiz; pezk'ûvî; xezal I>

şivîle شِـڤـيـلـه (K/A) = country road, rough path. See **şiverê**.

şivr شِڤر (GF) = deer. See **şivir**.

şivtî شِڤتی (K[s]/OK/AA) = watermelon. See **şiftî**.

şiwît شِـويـت *f.* **(-a;).** dill, bot. *Anethum graveolens.* {also: sibit (Dh/FS); şibit (Bw); şwit (CB)} Ar šibitt شِبِتّ; P šavīd شِويد; Sor şiwît شِـويـت [Bw//IFb/GF/OK/RF/ Kmc-3//CB//Dh/FS]

şixab شِـخـاب *f.* **(;-ê).** drill, drilling machine, borer: **•Darteraşî dar bi *şixabê* kun kir** (FS) The carpenter made a hole in the tree with *a drill.* {also : şaxab (FJ); şiqab (GF-2); şixav (GF/SS-2/FJ-2); şiẍab (FS-2); xerşeb (GF-2); xeşeb (Kmc/RZ-2); [chikhab] شخاب (JJ); <şiẍab> شغاب (HH)} <Arm šałap' շաղափ [IFb/SS/RZ/JJ//HH/FS//Kmc//FJ//GF] <burẍî; mikare>

şixav شِخاڤ (GF/SS/FJ) = drill. See **şixab**.

şixre شِـخـره (A/IFb/HH/TF/AD/FS) = transporting grain or tool for transporting grain. See **şiẍre**.

şixrevan شِـخـرەڤان (A/IFb/FS) = one who transports grain. See **şiẍrevan**.

şixul شِخول (K/IFb/PS/B) = work. See **şuxul.**

şixulîn شِـخـولـيـن *vi.* **(-şixul-).** to work *(lit. & fig.)*: **•Li me bû bû nîvê şevê û cihetnima jî *nema dişixulî*** (Rnh 1:11, 196) It was already past midnight and the compass *stopped working* [=no longer worked]. {also: şiẍulîn (Rnh); şuxulîn (IFb-2); şuẍulîn (Ad); şûlîn (OK-2); şûẍilîn (-şûẍil-) (JB1-S); [choukhoulin شخولين/chougoulin شغولين] (JJ); cf. also <şiẍil kirin> شغل كرن (HH)} {syn: k'ar [II] kirin; xebitîn} <Ar šuɣl شـغـل = 'work' [Ad//Rnh//K/IFb/OK//JJ//JB1-S] <şuxul>

şiẍab شِغاب (FS) = drill. See **şixab**.

şiẍare شِـغـاره (FS) = transporting grain or tool for transporting grain. See **şiẍre**.

şiẍr•e شِـغـره *f.* **(;•ê).** 1) transporting grain from the field to the threshing floor loaded on the back of a beast of burden *(donkey, horse, or camel)* [bi keran (yan bi beygîran, hêştiran) veguhastina zad ji zevîyê ḧeta bênderê]; 2) utensil or tool *(such as net [GF/AD] or wood [HH])* for transporting grain from the field to the threshing floor (HH/GF/TF/AD). {also: şeẍre (GF); şixre (A/IFb/TF/AD/FS); şiẍare (FS-2); xişre (FS-2); <şixre> شخره (HH)} Cf. Syr šūḥrā ܫܘܚܪܐ = 'forced labor' [Qzl//GF//A/IFb/HH/TF/AD/FS] <*darşiẍre; şel II>

şiẍrevan شِـغـرەڤان *m.* **(;-î).** one who transports grain from the field to the threshing floor loaded on the back of a beast of burden: **•*Şixrevanî* ceh ji firêzê kêşa coxînê** (FS) *The grain transporter* dragged the barley from the field of stubble to the threshing floor; **-bi şopa şiẍrevana ketin** (Qzl) to get a free ride, get a free lunch, eat on someone else's dime, to try to profit from s.o. else's labor. {also: şixrevan (A/IFb/FS)} [Qzl//A/IFb/FS/ZF3] <şiẍre>

şiẍul شِغول = work. See **şuxul.**

şiẍulîn شِغولين (Rnh) = to work. See **şixulîn**.

şiyan شِـيـان *vt.(M/SK)/vi.(K[s]/Bw)* **(-şê-;** *neg.* **ne-).** 1) {syn: karîn; pê ç'êbûn; şe kirin [şe II]} to be able to, can *(in southern Kurmanji [Behdînî] dialects, this verb replaces **karîn**)*: **•Ez *neşêm*** (Bw) I *cannot* **•Dibêjin di nihalekîda r̄îwîek hebû. ... bazeberek hebû, r̄îwî lê derbaz dibû her wextê ḧez kiriba. ... Marek jî di wê nihalêda hebû. *Nedişya* li bazeberî derbaz bibît** (SK 2:9) They say that there was a fox (living) in a ravine. ... There were stepping-stones and the fox crossed over whenever he liked. ... There was also a snake in that ravine. He *could not* cross over the stepping-stones; 2) [+ *dat. constr.*] to be stronger than s.o., prevail over s.o., be able to defeat s.o.; [+ *neg.*] be no match for s.o.: **•Hung *neşêne* hêtîmekî?** (M-Ak #537) Are you (pl.) *unable to defeat* an orphan?; 3) {also: şîyan (TF)] [*f.* **(-a; -ê).**] power, strength, ability, capability: **•li dûv *şiyan û pêçêbûna* xo** (R 15 [4/12/96] 2) to the best of one's *ability* **•Me pêkolkiriye, ku *li dwîv şiyanan* di şilovekirina hozanên wanda babetî bîn** ('Ebdulla, B.Y. Hozana afretan di edebê Kurdîda, 6) We have strived, *as much as possible* to be objective in interpreting their poems. {also: şîyîn, vi. (-şê) (K[s]); şyan, vt. (-şê-) (M/SK); [chiin] شـيـيـن (JJ); shiān (RJ)} [Pok. kþē(i)-/kþə(i)- 626.] 'to obtain, acquire, take control of' (Kent: proto IE *qþei-): Skt kṣáyati = 'possesses, controls'; O Ir *xšā(y)- (Tsb 43): Av xšā(y)- = 'to prevail, have dominion over'; OP xšay- = 'to rule' (Kent); Mid P šāyistan (šāy-) = 'to rule, have power, be able' (Boyce); 'to be appropriate' (M. Schwartz); 'to be worthy' (M3); P šāyad شايد = 'perhaps, it can be' & šāyeste شايسته = 'appropriate, fitting'; Sor şiyan شِيان (-şê-/-şiyê-/-şî-) = 'to be suitable, be appropriate, be permissible'; Za şenā [şyayiş; *past:* şa] = 'to be able' (Todd/Srk); Hau eşiay = 'must, ought' (M4)

[IFb/JB1-A/OK/ RZ/RJ//M/SK//TF//K(s)//JJ]

şiyandin شِيـــانـــدِن (IFb/HH/TF/FJ) = to send. See **şandin**.

şiyar شِيار = awake; aware. See **ĥişyar**.

şîhr شيهر (M-Am) = wall. See **şûre I**.

şîîr شيئير (Nbh) = poetry. See **şêr II**.

şîlaf شيلاف (GF) = pancreas; rennet bag. See **şîlav**.

şîlan I شـــيــلان *f.* **(;-ê).** 1) dogrose, bot. *Rosa canina*, wild rose with simple, rather than double, flowers [Rus šipovnik шиповник], a type of thornbush planted around vineyards: **-dara şîlanê/k'ola şîlanê** (B) dogrose bush: **•Ĥer dera *k'olêd şîlanê* hêşîn dibin** (Ba2) Everywhere *dogrose* bushes blossom; 2) hawthorn, whitethorn [Fr aubépine] (JJ). {also: şîlane (FS-2); şîlank (FS-2); [chilan] شيلان (JJ); <şîlan> شيلان (HH)} [Ba2/K/A/IFb/B/JJ/HH/TF/FS] <gîjok>

şîlan II شـــيــلان *f.* **(-a;-ê).** (royal) banquet, feast; "The meal offered by a prince. Koranic tradition imposes zakāt, legal alms. In the Ottoman Empire, the Sultan offered meals to the poor on the occasion of public holidays, the most important of which was the one marking the end of [the fast of] Ramadan. Well-to-do believers made donations for this purpose" (JB1-A, 200): **•Kurê Şerîfê Mekêhê ew p'are nîvek hediye kirin bo *şîlana* Soltanî û nîva dî l[i] pişt'a ĥemala kirin** (JB1-A #100) The son of the Sherif of Mecca donated half of the money for the Sultan's *feast* [for the poor], and the other half for the backs of the porters. {also: [chilan] شـــيــــلان (JJ)} <P šīlān شـــيـــلان = 'royal entertainment or feast'; T şölen. [JB1-A/JJ/OK/FS]

şîlane شيلانه (FS) = dogrose. See **şîlan I**.

şîlank شيلانك (FS) = dogrose. See **şîlan I**.

şîlav شـــيـــلاڤ *f.* **(;-ê).** 1) pancreas; 2) rennet bag, abomasum particularly one used for curdling milk. {also: şêlav (FS); şêlavk (Bw); şilavik (IFb); şîlaf (GF); şîlavk (Elk); [chilaw] شـيـلاڤ (JJ)} Sor şîlawuk شـيـلاووك = 'sweetbread, pancreas' [Qzl/K/IFb/B/JJ//Elk//FS//Bw//GF]

şîlavk شيلاڤك (Elk) = pancreas; rennet bag. See **şîlav**.

şîlo شيلو (Msr/HH) = turbid, cloudy. See **şêlo**.

şîn I شـــيـــن *f.* **(-a;-ê).** mourning, grief *(for someone deceased)*: **•Bila kêfa we kêfa me, *şîna* we jî *şîna* me be** (Nbh 129:4) May your joy be ours, may your *grief* be ours as well **•Şeherê Cizîrê wê řojê t'emam *nava şînêda* bû** (Z-1) On that day the whole city of Jezir was *in mourning*; **-şîn kirin** (B) to mourn; to dress in black; **-k'incê şînê xwe kirin/wergirtin** (B) to dress in black, for mourning. {also: [chin] شـــيــن (JJ); <şîn> شـيــن (HH)} <O Ir *xšaiwan-: Sgd 'γš'ywn; Mid P šēwan = 'lament' (M3); Sor şîn شـيـن = 'mourning, lamentation'; Hau şîwen *m.* (M4); cf. also Arm šivank' շիվանք [Z-1/BX/K/A/JB3/IF/B/JJ/HH] <behî; lûbandin; serxweşî; zêmar>

şîn II شين (ZF3) = green; blue. See **heşîn**.

şînahî شيناهى (K) = prosperity; merriment. See **şênahî**.

şînayî شينايى (K) = prosperity; merriment. See **şênahî**.

şînkatî شـيـنـكـاتـى (Bw) = verdure; vegetation. See **heşînatî**.

şînkayî شـيـنـكـايـى (K) = prosperity; merriment. See **şênahî**.

şînok شينوك (A) = terebinth. See **şengêl**.

şîp شـــيـــپ *f./m.(B)* **(-a/;).** 1) fast-moving stream or current; jet, stream, current, torrent: **•Liber *şîpa avê* de çû** (GF) He was swept away by *the current* **•Min dît ko sal mîna *şîpa avê* diherikin** (RN) I saw that the years moved by like a [fast- moving] *water current*; 2) {syn : sûlav; şilêr; şirav} waterfall, cascade; 3) gutter, trough, chute, small ditch (on a mill, through which water flows to the millstone) (B/JJ). {also: [chip شيپ/sip سيپ] (JJ); <şîp> شـــيــپ (HH)} [RN/K(s)/A/JB3/IFb/B/JJ/HH/GF/TF] <av; sêlav; şilêr; şirav; vizik II>

şîpande شيپانده (K) = threshhold. See **şîpane**.

şîpan•e شـيـپـانـه *f./m.(FS)* **(•a/•ê;).** threshold, door frame: **-şîpana derî** (ZF3) door frame; **-şîpanê pencerê** (FS) window frame. {also: şîpande (K); [chipané] شپانه (JJ); <şîpane> شيپانه (HH)} {syn: derç'ik; şêmîk} Sor şîpan شيپان [A/IFb/JJ/HH/TF/FS//K] <řexderî>

şîqeşîq شيقهشيق (ZF) = crashing, cracking. See **şîqşîq**.

şîqşîq شـيـقـشـيـق *f.* **(-a;-ê).** *various loud noises*: crashing, cracking; crackling; rattling, clicking, jingling; clanking; popping: **•Bes bike *şîqe şîq*, eyb e ji te re eyb, dengê te dihere xelkê!** (SBx, 18) Quit making *such a racket*, shame on you, everyone can hear you! **•Bû şîqeşîqa riman** (ZZ-10, 143) *The crashing of* lances could be heard **•*şîqşîqa* birûskan** (DBgb, 20) *the crack of* the thunderbolts. {also : şîqeşîq (ZF); şîrqeşîrq (K/B); cf. also [chaqa-chaq] شقاشق (JJ)} [DBgb/FJ//ZF//K/B]

şîr I شـــيـــر *m.* **(-ê;).** milk: **-ji şîr biřîn** (B) to wean *(a* *child)*; **-şîrê dê** (B) mother's milk; **-Şîrê min li te ḧelal be!** (B) May my milk be to your health, *expression said by a mother when praising a good child.* {also: [chir] شـيـر (JJ); <şîr> شـيـر (HH)} [Pok. su̯ēid- 1043.] = 'milk': Skt √ksviḍ [kṣviḍyati] = 'be wet'; Av xšvīd- *m.* = 'milk'; < *xšīra-: P šīr شـيـر; Sor şîr شـيـر; < *xšvipta-: Za şid/şit *m.* (Todd); Hau şot *m.* (M4) {See: G. S. Asatrian. "O rannyx armenizmax v kurdskom" [=On early Armenianisms in Kurdish], Patma-banasirakan handes = Istoriko-filologičeskij Žurnal, 113, (1986), p. 172, note 15} [J/F/K/A/JB3/IFb/B/ JJ/HH/ JB1-S/SK/GF/ TF/OK] <mast; to I>

şîr II شير (JR/JJ/HH/SK/OK) = sword. See **şûr I**.

şîranî شـيـرانـى *f.* **(-ya;-yê).** 1) {syn: şekirok II} candy, sweetmeat, sweets; 2) {syn: paşîv} dessert: **•Şilikî navê *şîraniyeke* kurdan e û ji *pêjgeha* Rihayê ye** (Wkp) Shiliki is the name of a Kurdish *dessert* and is from the cuisine of Urfa; 3) refreshment drunk on the occasion of a wedding engagement, in the home of the bride's father; the betrothal ceremony in which family of the bride and family of the groom drink a sweet beverage together: "Engagement ceremonies consist of a reception in which refreshments are served. When one says: 'to drink sorbet', one means 'to betroth'" (JR, p. 35, note 2); **-şîranî xwarin** (B)/**şîranî vexwarin** (JR) to betroth, engage one's daughter in marriage: **•Bi vî awayî, Evdal û Gulê Bengîn û Meyro kirin destgirtî û kincên nû li wan kirin û ji çavên wan maç kirin. Şeveke xweş a havînê, ew li meydana gund civiyan û *şêrînahiya* B. û M. *xwarin*** [sic] (M.Uzun R. Evd. Zeynikê, 11) In this way, E. & G. betrothed B. & M., and put new clothes on them and kissed them on their eyes. On a pleasant summer night, they gathered in the village square and drank B. & M.'s sorbet **•[Kurekî xweyî mal ḧal hebûye navê Şemas, ew kur mirofan verêdike û Barnîkê ji boy xwe dixwaze û babê Barnîkê jî keçê dide Şemasê û *şîranî vedixwin*]** (JR, 32) There was a wealthy boy named Shemas, who sent men to ask for [the hand of] Barnîk [in marriage], and Barnîk's father gives the girl to him and they drink sorbet **•R̄okê nişkêva bavê min gazî min kire bal xwe, got, wekî siba ew û dîya min wê her̄ne mala Mîloê bavê Sûsîkê, ku *şîranya min û wê bixun*** (Ba2:2, 207) One day suddenly my father called me to him and said that the following day he and my mother would go to the house of Milo, Susik's father, *to drink shirani* [= to engage me to her]. {also: şêrînahî (M.Uzun); şirînî I (SK)} [K/IFb/B/TF/OK/ZF3/BF//M.Uzun] <şerbet; şîrînî>

şîre شـيـره (B) = resin; concentrated juice; resin; must. See **şîrêz**.

şîret شـيـرهت *f.* **(-a;-ê).** 1) {syn: şêwir} (piece of) advice, counsel, recommendation: **•Eva wer̄a *şîret*** (J) This is [my] *advice* to you **•Her roj piştî nimêja êvarê, şêx *şîretên dînî* li mirîdên xwe dikirin** (Rnh 2:17, 340) Every day after the evening prayer, the sheikh would give *religious advice* to his disciples [or, would advise his disciples on religion]; **-dan pey şîretên yekî** (JB3) to follow s.o.'s advice; **-şîret kirin** = a) to advise; b) to exhort, admonish, warn: **•Maka wan *şîret dike*** (J) Their mother *warns* them; **-şîreta *fk-ê* hildan** (IS) to heed or follow s.o.'s advice: **•Sîabend *şîreta* pîrê *hilda*** (IS-#295) Siyabend *heeded* the old woman's *advice*; 2) warning, exhortation. {also: [chiret] شـيـرت (JJ); <şîret> شـيـرت (HH)} < Ar √š-w-r: šāra شـار (u) = 'to advise' [J/F/K/A/JB3/IFb/B/JJ/HH/GF/TF/OK] <şîretk'ar>

şîretçî شيرهتچى (B) = adviser. See **şîretk'ar**.

şîretdar شيرهتدار (B) = adviser. See **şîretk'ar**.

şîretgêr شيرهتگير (IFb) = adviser. See **şîretk'ar**.

şîretk'ar شيرهتكار *m.* **().** adviser/advisor, counsellor; instructor; consultant: **•Ew bo Azadî *şîretkarekê* baş e** (FS) He is a good adviser for A. {also: şîretçî (B-2); şîretdar (B); şîretgêr (IFb); şîretker (K-2/JB3/IFb-2/GF/OK); [chiret-ker] شيرتكر (JJ)} {syn: şêwirdar} [Z-2/F/K//IFb//JB3/JJ/GF/OK//B] <şîret>

şîretker شـيـرهتـكـهر (K/JB3/IFb/JJ/GF/OK) = adviser. See **şîretk'ar**.

şîrêj شـيـريَژ *f.(Bw)/m.(OK)* **(-a/ ;).** curds; what is left after the whey is drained off. {also: [chir-i rizi] شيرى رزى (JJ)} {syn: giv[î]} Sor şîrêj شيريَژ = 'a dish prepared from [boiled] *do [dew, i.e., yoghurt drink].' Glossed as 'whey' by JJ [petit-lait] and OK [Molke]* [Bw/K(s)/OK/FS//JJ] <dew I; keşk>

şîrêz شيريَز *f.* **(-a;-ê).** 1) concentrated juice *(of grapes or other fruits)*; 2) {syn: benîşt; debûş} resin: **•Helva ji *şîrêzê* çênabe** (BX) Halvah is not made of *resin [prv.]*; 3) must, unfermented wine; grape juice prior to becoming wine; 4) (shoemaker's) paste, glue: **•Ziman, wekî mîraseka qedîm, milkekî muşterek û çîmento yan jî ew *şîrêza***

jiyanî ya bihevrebûna xelkekî ye (zazaki.net:R.Lezgîn 1.viii.2009) Language, as an ancient legacy, is the common property and cement, or the vital *glue* that keeps a people together. {also: şirêz (IFb-2/JB1-S); şîre (B-2); [chiré شـيـره / šīv شـيـو] (JJ); <şîle> شـيـلـه (HH)} Cf. P šīre شـيـره = 'grape molasses' {=T pekmez} [BX/K/A/IFb/B/TF/BF/G/FD//JB1-S//JJ//HH] <dims; gûlik; mot; soryas>

şîrharamî شـيـرهـارامـى (TF) = dishonesty, baseness of character. See **şîrĥeramî**.

şîrhe شيرهه (BF) = wall. See **şûre I**.

şîrheram شـيـەهـورام (K/A/IFb/ZF3) = dishonest. See **şîrĥeram**.

şîrheramî شيرهەرامي (K/ZF3) = dishonesty, baseness of character. See **şîrĥeramî**.

şîrĥeram شيرحەرام *adj.* dishonest, no good, base *(of character)*, bad natured, dastardly: **•Yên ziman qedexe dikin *şîrheram* in** (yuksekovahaber.com.tr 20.ii.2010) Those who ban a language are *rotten to the core*. {also: şîrheram (K/A/IFb/ZF3)} [B//K/A/IFb/ZF3]

şîrĥeramî شـيـرحـەرامـى *f.* **(-ya;-yê).** dishonesty, bad nature, baseness *(of character)*, dastardliness: **-şîrĥeramî kirin** (B) to act unethically, act badly: **•Go min *şîrĥeramî kir*** (HCK-3, #2, 27) He said, "I *acted badly*". {also: şîrheramî (K/ZF3); şîrharamî (TF)} [HCK/B//K/ZF3//TF]

şîrikî شيركى (IFb) = purple. See **şîrkî**.

şîrin شـــيـــرِن *adj.* 1) sweet: **-ber dilê *fk-î* şîrîn kirin** (Zeb) to make stg. seem desirable to s.o., promote stg.; **-xwe şîrîn kirin** (Zeb) to flatter s.o., butter s.o. up, ingratiate o.s. with s.o.; 2) soft, gentle: **•Bi dengê sazî *şîrin* ... M. ji xewê ç'e'vê xwe vekir** (Z-1) From the *soft* sound of the saz ... M. awoke and opened his eyes. {also: şêrîn (L/A-2/IFb-2/OK-2); şirîn I (JB1-A&S/SK/OK); şîrîn (A/JB3/IFb/GF/Zeb); [chirin] شـيـريـن (JJ); <şêrîn> شـيـريـن (HH)} Cf. P šīrīn شيرين; Sor şîrîn شيرين = 'sweet, amiable'; Za şırın (Mal) {şêrînî; şîrinayî; şirînî; şîrînî; şîrnayî; [chirini شـيـريـنـى/chirinàï شـيـريـنـاى] (JJ); <şêranî> شـيـرانـى (HH)} [Z-1/K/B//A/JB3/IFb/JJ/Zeb//L/HH]

şîrinayî شيرِنايى (B) = sweetness. See **şîrînî**.

şîrîkî شيريكى (A) = purple. See **şîrkî**.

şîrîn شيرين (A/JB3/IFb/JJ/GF/Zeb) = sweet. See **şîrin**.

şîrînî شـيـريـنـى *f.* **(-ya;-yê).** 1) sweetness; 2) softness, gentleness; 3) betrothal. See **şîranî**. {also: şêrînî (A/IFb-2/OK-2); şirînî II (OK); şîrinayî (B); şîrnayî (K-2); [chirini شـيـريـنـى/chirinàï شـيـريـناى] (JJ); <şêranî> شـيـرانـى (HH)} [K/IFb/JJ/TF/ZF//OK//B//A//HH] <şîranî; şîrin>

şîrker شيركەر (BN) = swordsmith. See **şûrger**.

şîrkî شـيـركـى *adj.* purple, violet: **•Ez ji rengê *şîrkî* hez dikim** (D.EbdulFettah. Ameda Paytext û Konfiransê Zimanê Kurdî 30.xi-5.xii.2004) I love the color *purple*. {also: şîrikî (IFb); şîrîkî (A)} {syn: binefşî; erẍewanî; mor I} [Kk/ZF3/Wkt//IFb//A]

şîrmêj شـيـرمـيـژ *adj. or m./f.* **(;/-ê).** suckling infant, babe in arms: **•Di paş xwe re jin û kurê xwe ê *şîrmêj* Hevind, yê ko hêj di landikê de bû hişti bûn** (Rnh 3:23, 5) He left behind his wife and *suckling infant* H., who was still in the cradle; **-zaṙokê şîrmêj/şîrmij** (FS) do. {also: şîrmij (K/GF-2/OK-2/FS-2/ZF3); [chir-myj] شـيـرمـژ (JJ)} {syn: sawa} <şîr = 'milk' + mêj- = 'to suck' [Rnh/IFb/GF/OK/FS//K/JJ/ZF3] <dergûş; landik; sawa>

şîrmij شـــيـــرمـــژ (K/GF/OK/FS/ZF3) = infant. See **şîrmêj**.

şîrnayî شيرنايى (K) = sweetness. See **şîrînî**.

şîrov•e شـيـرۆڤـه *f.* **(•a;•ê).** explanation, interpretation (also of dreams): **•Ji bo vê nûçeyê pêdivî bi *şîrovê* tune ye** (orient-news.net 22.iv.2016) There is no need for *an explanation* of this report **•Li pey vê *şîrova* li ser navdêrên "bilxwir/bilgur/sawarê"** (CCG, 82) According to this *explanation* about the nouns "*bilxwir/bilgur/sawarê*" **•*Şîrova* Qur'anê** (FS) *Interpretation of* the Quran **•Wî *şîrova* xewna Behremî da** (FS) He gave *an interpretation of* B.'s dream; **-şîrove kirin** (ZF3/Wkt)/**şirove kirin** (K/B/GF/BF/FS/SS)/**şiro kirin** (K-2/B-2)/**şilove kirin** ('Ebdulla) to explain, clarify, interpret (also dreams) {syn: ĥel kirin; îzah kirin; ṙave kirin; têgihandin}: **•Gerekê tu gazî wî xortî bikî, ewê xewna te ji teṙa *şirovebike*** (Ba3) You should call that youth: he *will explain* your dream to you **•Me pêkolkiriye, ku li dwîv şiyanan di *şilovekirina* hozanên wanda babetî bîn** ('Ebdulla, B.Y. Hozana afretan di edebê Kurdîda, 6) We have strived, as much as possible to be objective in *interpreting* their poems **•Seyda rewşa welatî ji mera *şirove kir*** (BF) The teacher *explained* the condition of the country to us.{also: şirove (GF/BF/FS/SS)} {syn: îzah; ṙave} Cf. Ar šarḥ شــــــرح = 'explanation'; = Sor şî•kirdinewe شيكردنەوە = 'to analyze, examine, reason out' [Ba3/K/B/GF/BF/FS/SS//IFb/FJ/TF/Wkt/ZF/RF/CS/Wkt] <îzah>

şîrox شيرۆخ *f.* **(-a;).** shoe string, shoelace; strings for tying sandals to ankle: •**Xerboqa *şiroxa pêlava wî* vebû** (FS) The knot of *his shoelace* came undone. {also: şiloxe (IFb/OK/Zeb); şiroxe (FS-2); şirûxe (FS); <şiluxe> شـلـوخـه (Hej)} {syn: ben [3]} < NENA širyōxa (Sabar: Dict)/shiryûkhâ ܫܪܝܘܟܐ (Maclean) = 'shoe-string, sandal-cord by which shoes and sandals are tied to the ankle', cf. Arc serakh סרך = 'to interweave, twist; to clutch, hold fast' & Syr √s-r-k ܣܪܟ = 'to adhere, stick'; cf. also Heb serokh שרוך & Ar širāk شـــراك = 'shoelace' [Bw//FS//IFb/OK/Zeb//Hej] <çarox; p'êlav; qeyt'an; sol>

şîrqeşîrq شيرقەشيرق (K/B) = crashing, cracking. See **şîqşîq**.

şîrqîn شيرقين (K'oroxlî/ZF/IFb) = noise. See **şerqîn**.

şîş شـيـش *f.* **(-a;-ê).** (iron) rod, skewer, spit: •**Şivan[a] ... bi *şîşêd* sorkirî k'erê xwe daẍ dikin** (Dz) The shepherds are branding their donkeys with red-hot *skewers* •***Şîşek* li wî milê wî da, yê r̄astê da, yê çepê derêxist, hilawîst bi xanî ve** (M-Zx #750) He stuck *a spit* through his right shoulder, bringing it out at the left, and hung him up in the house; **-şîşa birûskê** (Z-4) thunderbolt, bolt of lightning. {also: [chich] شـيـش (JJ); <şîş> شـيـش (HH)} {syn: bist I; caẍ} [Dz/F/K/A/IFb/B/JJ/HH/GF]

şîtik شيتِك (Bw) = cummerbund. See **şûtik**.

şîv شيڤ *f.* **(-a;-ê).** dinner, supper, evening meal: •**Bû *wexta şîvê*** (L) It was *dinnertime* •***Şîva* me goşt û savar e** (AB) Our *dinner* is meat and bulghur. {also: şîw (SK); [chiw] شـيـڤ (JJ); <şîv> شـيـڤ (HH)} Av *xšāfnya- = 'evening meal, dinner' (Ras, p.142); Mid P & P šām شام; Sor şêw شێو; Za şamî *f.* (Todd); Hau şam (M4) [L/F/K/A/JB3/IFb/B/JJ/HH/JB1-A&S/ GF/TF/OK/Msr//SK] <firavîn; şev; taştê>

şîw شيو (SK) = evening meal. See **şîv**.

şîyan شييان (TF)] = strength. See **şiyan**[3].

şîyandin شييانِدن = to send. See **şandin**.

şîyar شييار (L) = awake; aware. See **ĥişyar**.

şîyîn شـيـيـين, vi. (-şê) (K[s]) = to be able to, can. See **şiyan**.

şk'andin شـكـانـدِن (-şk'ên-) (JB1-A)/şkandin (-şkîn-) (SK/OK/Qrj/Ad/Wn) = to break. See **şkênandin**.

şkat شكات = complaint. See **şikyat**.

şkatker شكاتكەر = complainer; litigant. See **şikyatçî**.

şkef شكەف (A) = trough; tub; basin; barrel. See **şikev**.

şkeft شكەفت *f.* **(-a;-ê).** cave, cavern; naturally formed cave, *as opposed to* ***miẍare*** *(qv.), a man-made cave* (Haz): •**Qasoyê Nêçîrvan û mar çûn ketin *şkeftekê. Şkeft* tije mar bûn** [sic] (ZZ-7, 241) Q.N. and the snake went and entered *a cave. The cave* was full of snakes. {also: eş[kev]t (A-2); şikeft (K-2/IFb/TF/BK); şiket (BK-2); şkevd; şkevt (Ba2/K/B); [chikewt] شـكـفـت (JJ); <şkeft> شكەفت (HH)} {syn: miẍare; t'ûn [2]} [Pok. (s)kĕp-/(s)kŏp-/(s)kăp- & (s)kĕb(h)-/(s)kŏb(h)-/(s)kab(h)- 930-1.] 'to cut with sharp tool, split, cleave' & [skab(h)-ro-] 'sharp' & [skapā] 'gegrabenes' & [skopelo-] 'rock, cliff' + [C. *forms in* -p]: P šekāftan شكافتن = 'to split, cleave' & šekaft شكفت = 'cave'; Sor eşkewt ئـەشـكـەوت [Ba2/K/B/HH//A/JB3/GF//IFb/TF/BK//JJ]

şkenandin شكەناندِن (Qzl) = to break. See **şkênandin**.

şkenc شكەنج (GF) = torture. See **îşkence**.

şkence شكەنجە (K[s]/GF) = torture. See **îşkence**.

şkestin شـكـەسـتِـن/**şk'est'in** [JB1-A] *vi.* **(-ş[i]kê-/ *-şkest- [IF]).** 1) to break *(vi.)*, be broken: •**Ezê bigerim heyanî ... gopalê min *bişkê*** (L) I shall wander until ... my stick *breaks*; 2) to be ruined, sullied *(s.o.'s honor or reputation)*: •**Ez îslehê wan ji wan bidizim, *wê* namûsa wan *bişkê*, guneh e** (L) If I steal (or, stole) their weapons from them, their honor *will be ruined*, it would be a shame. {also: şikestin (K/GF/TF/OK-2); şkîn (Qrj); şkyan (Qrj-2); [chikestin] شـكـسـتـيـن (JJ); <şkestin شـكـسـتـن (dişkê) (دشـكـى)> (HH)} [Pok. (s)k(h)ed- 918.] 'to split, scatter' *extended form of* [Pok. 2. sĕk- 895. & sken-(d)- 929.] 'to cut': O Ir *skad-na- (Tsb 44): Av skand-, sčandayeiti = 'breaks, ruins'; OP *ska[d]-nā-tiy = 'breaks'; Mid P škastan (šken[n]-); P šekastan شـكـسـتـن (-šekan-) (شـكـن); Sor şikan شِـكـان (-şikê-); Za şikyenã [şikyayiş] (Todd) [K/JJ/GF/TF//A/JB3/IFb/B/HH/ SK/OK/Ad/ Qzl/Xrz//JB1-A//Qrj] <şkênandin>

şkev شـكـەڤ (K/B/HH/GF) = trough; tub; basin; barrel. See **şikev**.

şkeva شـكـەڤـا *adj.* unleavened *(bread)*: **-cejna şkeva** (Frq) Passover, feast of unleavened bread; **-nanê şkeva** (RF) unleavened bread, matzoh. {also: şikeva (TF/RF/FJ); şkevale (FS-2); şkiva (FS-2)} [Frq/A/IFb/GF/FS//TF/RF/FJ]

şkevale شكەڤالە (FS) = unleavened. See **şkeva**.

şkevd شكەڤد = cave. See **şkeft**.

şkevik شـكـەڤِك: **-şkevik kirin** (Zeb/Dh) to sort out the stones and dirt from grain or rice; to separate *(wheat from chaff)*. [Zeb/Dh] <vavartin>

şkevt شكەڤت (Ba2/K/B) = cave. See **şkeft**.

şkênandin شكێنانِدِن/**şk'ênandin** [JB1-S] *vt.* **(-şkên-/-şkênîn-/-şk'ênîn-** [JB1-S]**).** 1) to break *(vt.)*: **-ç'av şkênandin** (GF) to embarrass; to insult; **-dil şkênandin** (JB3) to hurt s.o.'s feelings, to break s.o.'s heart: **•Te çire *dilê wî şkênand*?** (JB3) Why *did* you *hurt his feelings*?; **-taştê şkênandin** (JB3) to break bread, have a bite to eat, snack; 2) to ruin, sully *(s.o.'s honor)*: **•Ev, go zilamekî diz bûna ... *wê* şerefa me *bişkenandana*** (L) If this man were a thief, he *would have ruined* our honor (=disgraced us); 3) to cut *(cards in a card game)* (Qzl). {also: şikandin (GF/TF/OK-2); şikênandin (TF-2); şk'andin (-şk'ên-) (JB1-A)/şkandin (-şkîn-) (SK/OK-2/Qrj/Ad/Wn); şkenandin (Qzl); [chikandin شكاندين/chikinandin شكناندين] (JJ); <şkênandin شكيناندن (dişkêne) (دشكينه)> (HH)} See etymology under **şkestin**. Sor şikandin شِكاندِن (-şikên-); SoK šıkândın (Fat 564); Za şiknenã [şiktiş] (Todd/Srk) [L/K/A/JB3/IFb/B/HH/OK/Qmş/Rwn/Slm//JB1-S//Qzl//JJ/GF/TF//JB1-A/SK/Qrj/Ad/Wn] <şkestin>

şkêr̄ شكێر *f.* **(-a;-ê).** pile of stones: **•Min di vê *şikêra* hanê de şerbikek zêr hilandiye (veşart-iye)** (Wlt 2:59, 15) I have hidden a pot of gold in this *pile of stones*; **-şkêr̄a bera** (FS) do. {also: şikêr (TF/Wlt/Wkt); [škēr] شكير (JJ); <şkêr> شكير (HH)} {syn: qûç' [2]} [Wlt/TF/Wkt//A/IFb/JJ/HH/SK/GF/OK/FS/ZF3] <ber III; k'elek II; kevir>

şkinandin شكِناندِن (Qzl) = to comb; to card. See **şkinîn**.

şkinîn شكِنين *vt.* **(-şkin-).** 1) to comb (hair) {syn: şeh kirin}: **•Wî pirça serê xwe *şkinî*** (FS) He *combed* his hair; **-por şkinandin** (Qzl) do.; 2) to card (wool) {syn: jendin}. {also: şikinandin (FD); şikinîn (K); şkinandin (Qzl); [chekinin] شكنين (JJ)} [Qzl//FD//K/JJ//FS]

şkiva شكِڤا (FS) = unleavened. See **şkeva**.

şkîn شكين (Qrj) = to break *(vi.)*. See **şkestin**.

şkîyat شكييات = complaint. See **şikyat**.

şkû شكوو *interrog.* how? {syn: çawa} < ji = 'from' + ku = 'where' [Msr]

şkyan شكيان (Qrj) = to break *(vi.)*. See **şkestin**.

şkyat شكيات = complaint. See **şikyat**.

şob شۆب (Wkt/ZF3) = epidemic. See **şewb**.

şof شۆف (SS) = epidemic. See **şewb**.

şok شۆك (GShA/SK) = fish hook; hook; thorn; branch. See **şewk**.

şokil شۆكِل (Wkt) = vetch, wild bean. See **şolik**.

şol شۆل (M/JR/IFb/JB1-A/PS/HH) = work. See **şuxul**.

şolik شۆلِك *m.(Qzl)/f.(B/ZF)/pl.(K)* **(-ê/-a; /-ê).** wild bean or pea, type of vetch, similar to lentil, eaten by cattle: **-şolikê ga/~ gê** (Qzl) do. {also: şokil (Wkt-2); şoqil (K[s]/A/IFb/FJ-2/GF-2/TF-2/Wkt/ZF-2; [šōqýl] شوقل (JJ-PS); <şûlik> شولك & <şoqil> شوقل (HH)} *The form **şoqil** is common in Mardin.* [Ah/Qzl/Rwn/K/A/B/GF/TF/FJ/SS/ZF//HH//A/IFb/Wkt/JJ-PS] <kizin; maş; polik II>

şonik شۆنِك (IFb/GF) = washing paddle. See **şûnik**.

şop شۆپ *f.* **(-a;).** track, trace; step, footstep: **•Gelek şayîrên me yên hêja jî, li dû *şopa* wî çûne û diçin** (Rwş #2, 15) Many of our finest poets also have followed in his *footsteps* and continue to [lit. 'they went after his tracks and they go'] **•Min *da ser şopa wî* û ez çûm** (ZZ-10, 165) I *followed in his tracks* and went [after him]. {syn: dews [2]; r̄êç' II} Cf. NENA shôpâ ܫܘܦܐ = 'footprint, mark, trace' (Syr 'friction, rubbing') [Rwş/K/A/IFb/GF/TF/ZF] <gav; kevneşop>

şopandin شۆپاندِن *vt.* **(-şopîn-).** to follow (lit. & fig.); to watch, observe: **•Min pir şer *şopandin* lê ti şervanên egît û wêrek wek van jin û mêrên Kurd, ku dijî DAIŞ şer dikin, nedîtin** (M. Çiviroğlu) I *covered/followed* many wars, but I never before saw such brave and courageous warriors as these Kurdish men and women, who are fighting against ISIS. {syn: dan dû; dan pey; dû çûn; dû hatin; dû k'etin; pey hatin} < şop = T iz = 'tracks, footsteps' --> T izlemek = 'to follow' [M. Çiviroğlu/ZF/TF/CS]

şoqil شۆقِل (K[s]/A/IFb/FJ/GF/TF/Wkt/ZF/JJ-PS/HH) = vetch, wild bean. See **şolik**.

şor I شۆر *f.* **(-a;-ê).** word: **-şor kirin** (IFb) to speak, talk {syn: axaftin; p'eyivîn; mijûl dan; qise kirin; ştaẍilîn; xeber dan}: **•Di salên min ên zarotî ... di nav mala me de bi Zazakî û Kurmancî *dihat şorkirin*** (Ber) In my childhood years ... Zaza and Kurmanji *were spoken* at home (=We grew up hearing both languages). {syn: gilî; p'eyiv; pirs [2]; xeber} [Ber/K/JB3/IFb/ZF3/FS] <gilî>

şor̄ II شۆڕ *adj.* hanging down or out, loose, dangling, droopy: **-şor bûn** (ZF3/Wkt/BF) to hang down, dangle {syn: şingilîn}: **•Kezîyêt wê kiçikê *şor bibîn* di kelşa p'irê r̄a** (M-Zx #776) The girl's braids *were hanging down* through a crack in the bridge **•Porê wê yê dirêj *şor bûbû* û ketibû ser milên wê** (ZF3) Her long hair *hung down* and fell on her shoulders; **-şor kirin** (SK) to hang low, dangle *(vt.)*: **•Şewekî** [sic] **we qewimî**

řîwîyek hat e serbanê oda ximî, serê xo di kulekêda *şor kir*, bêna mirîşkan li difna wî da (SK 4:28) One night it so happened that a fox came onto the roof of the dye-house and *lowered* his head down through the skylight, when the smell of chickens assailed his nose. {also: şûr III (IFb-2); [scióra] شـــــور (JJ-G)} Sor şoř شــۆڕ = 'hanging down, drooping' [Bw/K(s)/A/IFb/SK/GF/FS/BF//JJ-G] <darda>

şoř III شــۆڕ *adj.* salty, briny, brackish: **-ava şoř** (FS) salty water, saltwater; **-xwarina şoř** (FS) salty food. {also: sûr II (Bw/Krs/SK/OK-2); [chour] شــور (JJ); <şor> شــور (HH)} {syn: t'êrxwê} Cf. Mid P sōr (M3); P šūr شـور; Sor swêr [sör] سوێر/ şor شــۆر [Mzg/Srk/F/K/A/IFb/B/HH/GF/TF/OK/FS//JJ//Bw/Krs/SK] <kelî II; xwê>

şorav شـــۆراڤ (IFb/GF/FJ)/ şořav شـــۆڕاڤ (K/B) = saltwater. See **sûravk**.

şorbanîsk شۆربانیسك (GF) = See **şorbenîsk**.

şorbawe شۆرباوه (SK) = soup. See **şorbe**.

şorb•e شۆربه/**şořb•e** شۆڕبه [FS] *f.* **(•[ey]a;•ê).** soup: **•Kebanîya malê jê re *şorbê* tîne datîne ber** (LM, 7) The lady of the house brings him *soup* and sets it down before him; **-şorba nîska** (IFb) See **şorbenîsk**; **-şorbeya birincê** (BF) rice soup. {also: şorbawe (SK); [chorbé] شــــــوربــــه (JJ); <şorbe> شــوربــه (HH)} P šorbā شــوربـا; clq Ar šor[a]ba شــوربــه; T çorba; Sor şorba شــۆربـا; Za şorba *f.* (Mal) [F/K/A/IFb/B/JJ/HH/GF//FS//SK]

şorbeçî شۆربەچی *m.* **().** cook, soup chef: **•Evê te ber destê *şorbeçî* dixevite ĥetanî meha wî t'emam dive** (HCK-5, #41, 230) This person of yours is working for *the cook* until his month is up. {syn: aşpêj} < şorbe + -çî [HCK/K]

şorbenîsk شــۆربـەنـیـسـك *f.* **(-a;-ê).** lentil soup. {also: şorbanîsk (GF); şorba nîska (IFb)} [Wkp//GF//IFb]

şoř•e شــۆڕه [K/B]/**şore** شــۆره *f.* **(;•ê).** saltpeter, niter, potassium nitrate. {also: şûre II (ZF3); [chouré] شــوره (JJ); <şûre> شــوره (HH)} Cf. P šūre شــوره; Sor şore شۆره [K/B//A/IFb//JJ/HH/ZF3] <axzûtî>

şorecî شۆرەجی *m.* **().** saltpeter manufacturer: **•[Illa ji Ekradan barûtpêj û *şorecî* û beyṯar heyn]** (BN 134) [Of professions] there are only gunpowder and *saltpeter manufacturers* and veterinarians from the Kurds. Cf. P šūreger شورەگر [BN] <şoře>

şořeke شــــۆڕەکــــه (FS) = jet of water; drainpipe. See **şiřik**.

şoreş شــــۆرەش *f.* **(-a;-ê).** revolt, rebellion; revolution: **•Piştî şikestina *şoreşa* Berzanî, min û Kak Îqbal Hacî, me grûbeke muzîka Kurdî ava kir** (Wlt 1:37=38, 16) After the defeat of Barzani's *revolt*, brother Iqbal Haji and I [=Nasir Rezazî] formed a Kurdish music group; **-şoreşa p'îşesazîyê** (ZF3) industrial revolution: **•Pêwîste êdî em fêhm bikin, cîvaka kû *şoreşa pîşesazîyê* ava kiribu di paş de maye** (civakademokratik.com 1.iii.2018) We must understand by now that the society which had created the industrial revolution has fallen behind. {also: şoriş (A/GF-2); şûriş (JB3)} {syn: serhildan; sewr} Sor şoriş[t] شۆڕشت [Ber/Wlt/IFb/GF/TF/ZF3//A//JB3] <têkoşîn>

şoreşgeř شــۆرەشــگــەڕ *m.* **().** a revolutionary; rebel: **•Ji ber ku wan hêzên xwefiroş, planê împeryalîzmê bi cih anîn** [sic] **û bi alîkariya artêşa tirk êrîş anîne ser hêzên *şoreşgerên* gelên me** (Wlt 1:37=38, 6) Because those mercenary forces have brought the imperialistic plan into place and have mounted attacks against the revolutionary forces of our people [lit. 'the forces of the *revolutionaries* of our peoples ']. {also: şoreşgêř (IFb)} <Sor şoriş[t]gêř شۆڕشتگێڕ = 'rebel; revolutionary' (K2) [(neol)Wlt/TF/ZF3//IFb]

şoreşgeřî I شــۆرەشــگــەڕی *adj.* revolutionary: **•Min li radyoyê du marşên *şoreşgerî* tomar (qeyd) kirin** (Wlt 1:37=38, 16) I recorded two *revolutionary* marches for the radio. [(neol)Wlt]

şoreşgêř شـــۆرەشـــگـــێـــڕ (IFb) = revolutionary. See **şoreşgeř**.

şoriş شۆڕش (A/GF) = revolt. See **şoreş**.

şoşban شۆشبان (IFb/GF) = best man. See **şoşman**.

şoşbîn شۆشبین (IFb) = best man. See **şoşman**.

şoşman شـــۆشـــمـــان *m.* **(-ê;).** 'best man' at a wedding (Mzg/Srk); *(at traditional Kurdish weddings)* friend of the bridegroom's, during the wedding together with the groom throws an apple at the bride: **•Niha jî ji min xwast ku ez li mehra wî ya li Londonê de bibim *şoşbanê* wî** (nêrbazgeh 12.vi.2018) And now he has asked me to be his *best man* at his wedding in London.**-şoşmîne de'atê** (QtrE) do. {also: şoşban (IFb-2/GF); şoşbîn (IFb); şoşmîn (QtrE); şoşpan (IFb-2); [chouch-bin] شوشبین (JJ)} Cf. Assyrian susabinu (Delitzsch, p. 506); Heb šošvin שושבין & Arc šošvina/šušvina שושבינא = 'best man; king's friend, counsellor' (M. Jastrow); Syr šošvēnā ܫܘܫܒܝܢܐ = 'bridegroom's friend, groomsman; bridesmaid; godparent, sponsor'; NENA shushe-bey-na (Oraham); Ar išbīn إشبين = 'godfather; best man' [Mzg/Srk//GF//IFb//JJ//QtrE] <bûk I; cejin; de'wat; zava>

şoşmîn شۆشمين (QtrE) = best man. See **şoşman**.

şoşpan شۆشپان (IFb) = best man. See **şoşman**.

şov I شـــۆڤ *f.* **(-a;-ê).** 1) {syn: xet [2]} furrow: **-şov kirin** (B) to leave a furrow or wake behind one, to plow; 2) (garden) bed; 3) plowed field (JJ/HH); 4) fallow land (IFb): **•*Şûva* me îsal tune** (AB) This year we have no *fallow land*; 5) plowing, tillage; first plowing (M); 6) {syn: guharto [1]; şax [6]} version; variant: **•Derheqa *şovêd* "Mem û Zîna" zargotî û *şova* "Mem û Zîna" Eĥmedê Xanî** (K-dş) About the folkloristic *versions of* Mem û Zîn and *the version of* Mem û Zîn of Ahmed-i Khani [*name of article by Kurdoev*]. {also: şêf (M2); şuw [şöw]; şûv (IFb); [chow] شـوف (JJ); <şov> شـوڤ (HH)} Cf. P šoxm شـخـم; Sor şêf شـێـف/şow شـۆو/şom شـۆم = 'land after first plowing' [AB/K/A/B/JJ/HH//IFb//M2] <beyar; qarix>

şov II شۆڤ (RZ/FS) = epidemic. See **şewb**.

şqelp kirin شـقـەلـپ كـرن (Bw) = to peel. See **-ji qelp kirin** under **qelp II**.

ştaẍilîn شتاغِلين *vi.* **(-ştaẍil-).** to speak, talk: **•Nerîn go qundir *ştaẍilî*** (L) Suddenly the gourd spoke [lit. 'They saw that the gourd *spoke*'] **•Ûsufşa jî ne şteẍilî** (HR 3:27) U. did not even speak. {also: ştexilîn (-ştexil-) (K/IFb/GF); şteẍilîn (HR)} {syn: axaftin; deng çûn; gotin; k'êlimîn; mijûl dan (Haz); p'eyivîn; qise kirin; şor kirin} < Ar ištaγala VIII اشتغل = 'to work'; cf. also Turoyo √j-ğ-l/ş-ğ-l = 'to speak' [L//K/IFb/GF//HR] <mijûl>

ştexilîn شتەخِلين (-ştexil-) (K/IFb/GF) = to speak. See **ştaẍilîn**.

şteẍilîn شتەغِلين (HR) = to speak. See **ştaẍilîn**.

ştî شتى (Bw) = like, similar to. See **şitî II**.

şubhe شوبهه (JJ/SK) = doubt. See **şebh**.

şulhe شولهه (GF) = swarm of bees. See **şilxe**.

şulxe شولخه (Zeb) = swarm of bees. See **şilxe**.

şund شوند (IFb) = place. See **şûn**.

şunda شوندا (IFb) = after[ward]. See **şûnda**.

şurik شـورِك (FJ/SS/CS)/şurrik شـوررِك (GF) = jet of water; drainpipe. See **şiȓik**.

şuştin شـوشـتِـن (IFb/BK/JB3/JB1-S/M/GF/OK) = to wash. See **şûştin**.

şuw شوو [şöw] = furrow. See **şov I**.

şuxul شوخول *m./f.* **(-ê/ ;).** 1) {syn: îş; k'ar II; xebat} work, labor; job: **•Vê carê *şolê* wî we 'emelê wî bî nêçîr** (M-Zx #756, 350) Then his *work* and livelihood became hunting **•*Şuxulê* şivana zaf çetin bû, lê heqê xebata wana gelekî kêm bû** (Ba2:1, 204) The shepherds' *job* was very hard, but their earnings were very small [lit. 'few']; 2) affair, deal, matter, concern, issue: **•*Şixulê* min bal te heye** (B) I have *a matter* to discuss with you. {also: şixul (K/IFb/B/GF/PS); şiẍul; şol (M/JR/IFb-2/JB1-A/TF/PS-2); şuẍul (PS); şûl, f. (IFb-2/JB1-S/OK-2); şûẍil, f. (JB1-S); [choukhoul شـخـول/choul شـول] (JJ); <şuẍil شـغـل/şol شـول> (HH)} < Ar šuγl شغل = 'work' [F/Ba2/JJ/OK//K/IFb/B/GF/PS//M/JB1-A/TF//JB1-S//HH]

şuxulîn شوخولين (IFb) = to work. See **şixulîn**.

şuẍul شوغول (PS) = work. See **şuxul**.

şuẍulîn شوغولين (Ad) = to work. See **şixulîn**.

şû شـــوى/شـــوو *m.* **(-yê;).** husband: **•Demê *şûyê* wê hatiye = Ew li *şûya* ye** (FS) It is time for her to be married off; **-şû dan** (GF) to marry off *(a daughter)*; **-şû kirin** (JB1-A/A/IFb) to get married *(said of a woman)*: **•Ew Zîn hêj *şû nekiriye* / kesek bi çavê xwe nedîtiye** (PS-II, #1, 74, ll.8-9) That Zin *has not* yet *been married off* / no one has laid eyes on her [or, she has not laid eyes on anyone]. {also: [chou] شـــو (JJ)} {syn: mêr} Cf. Mid P šōy (M3); P šōhar شـوهـر = 'husband'; Sor şû شـوو = 'husband' & şû [pê] kirdin شـوو پـێ كـردِن = 'to take a husband, get married (of a woman)' [PS-II/JB1-A/A/IFb/JJ/GF/OK/FS] <malxwê>

şûhr شووهر (M-Am) = wall. See **şûre I**.

şûjin شـــووژن *f.* **(-a;-ê).** large needle, pack(ing)-needle, bodkin: **•Rewşê têȓ bi *şûjinê* dirû** (FS) R. sewed the saddle bag with *a pack needle*. {also: şijûn (B); [choujin] شـــوژن (JJ); <şûjin شـــوژن/bijûjin بـــژوژن> (HH)} {syn: derzî} <O Ir *s(a)učina- (A&L p. 89 [XI, 2]): P sūzan سـوزن = 'needle'; Sor sûjin ســووژِن = 'packing needle, bodkin' [F/K/A/IFb/JJ/HH/GF/(TF)/Mzg//B] <derzî>

şûl شوول, f. (IFb/JB1-S/OK) = work. See **şuxul**.

şûlikîn شوولِكين *vi.* **(-şûlik-).** to crawl, creep; to sneak up on: **•Gelek çû, hindik, Memê nizane, lê Bor nola bê *dişûlike*** (Z-1) Mem cannot tell if he covered much ground or little, it seems that Bor *is crawling* **•Ser sîngê Dûmanlûê cîcîna xulexula cewikêd avê bû, êd ku mînanî mara jorda *dişûlikîn*** (Ba2:1, 202) On the slope of [Mount] Dumanlu here and there was the babbling of brooks (of water), those which *were creeping* from above like snakes. {syn: sûrikîn} [Z-1/K/B/ZF3] See also **sûrikîn**.

şûlîn شوولین (OK) = to work. See **şixulîn**.

şûm شـــووم *adj.* 1) naughty, restless *(of children)*: •**Wî kur̄ekê *şûm* heye** (FS) He has an *ill-behaved* son; 2) bellicose *(of adults)*: •**Zelamê *şûm*: yê ku şer̄ê xelkî dikit û gelşa bo wan çê dikit** (FS) A *bellicose* man: one who fights with people and conflicts with them. {also: şwîm (BF-2); [choum/ sciúma] شــــــوم (JJ); <şom> شــــــوم (HH)} {syn: nesekinî} <Ar šu'm شـؤم = 'bad luck, misfortune, evil omen' [Bw/K/JJ/FS/BF//HH]

şûn شـــوون *f.* **(-a;-ê).** place, spot, stead: •***Şûna* xweda r̄ûnî** (B) Sit in your *place* •***şwîna* ningê wan** (L) *the place of* their feet (=the place where their feet are); **-di şûna *fk-ê/ft-î* de** (ZF)/**li şûna *fk-ê/ft-î*** (BX) instead of, in place of: •***li şûna* wî** = *instead of* him, *in* his *place*: •**Serwa *di şûna* peyva qafiyeyê *de* tê bikaranîn** (Adak, 358) 'Serwa' is used *instead of* the word 'qafiye' [=rhyme]; **-li şûna ko** [+ *subj.*] = instead of ...-ing; **-şûna *fk-î* girtin** = to replace, substitute for. {also: şund (IFb-2); şûnd (IFb-2); şwîn (L); [choun] شون (JJ); <şûn> شــــــون (HH)} {syn: cî [1]; der I; dever I; dews I; êrdim; yêr} Sor şwên [şön] شــوێــن; Hau şonî *f.* = 'track, trail, trace' (M4) [L//K/A/JB3/IFb/B/JJ/HH/SK/GF/TF/ZF]

şûnd شووند (IFb) = place. See **şûn**.

şûnda شــــــووندا *adv.* after (time), afterward, then {referring to the future}; **-ji *ft-î* şûnda** (K) after *(prep.)*: •***Ji* wan gilya *şûnda* mîr Ûsiv davêje ḧevsê** (Ba3-3, #31) *After* those words, the emir throws Joseph into prison •***Ji wê şûnda* min ew ne dît** (K) *After that* I never saw him. {also: şunda (IFb); şûnde (GF)} {syn: dûr̄a; hingê, etc.; paşê; (di) pişt re; ≠pêşda} Cf. T sonra = 'after' [K/A/JB3/B//GF//IFb]

şûnde شوونده (GF) = after[ward]. See **şûnda**.

şûnik شـوينِك/شـوونِـك *m.* **(-ê;).** 1) wooden paddle for beating clothes clean: **-şûnkê cilka** (Zeb) do.; **-şûnkê serbanî** (Czr) harrow, roller {syn: t'apan}; 2) tadpole (Bw). {also: şonik (IFb-2/GF-2); <şûnik> شونك (HH)} [Bw/Zeb//A/IFb/HH/GF/TF]

şûr I شـــــوور *m.* **(-ê;).** 1) sword: •**kalûmekî şûran** = old, rusty sword •***Şîrekî* gelek kewn hebû, kalwanê wî zîw bû, destikê wî zêr̄ bû, qaşêt elmas û pîroze hatibûne têgirtin, tîyê wî kerman bû** (SK 26:234) There was a very ancient *sword* with a silver scabbard, its hilt of gold inlaid with gems of diamond and turquoise, and its blade of Kermani steel •***Şûrê* vî zemanî qelem e** (AB) *The sword of* this language (or, time) is the pen; **-şûr k'işandin** = to draw or unsheath a sword: •**B. *şwîrê xwe kişand*** (L) B. *drew his sword*; **-şûrê cot/~ kotanê** (Kmc) plow beam *or* co[u]lter of a plow; 2) blow with a sword: •**Eger xebera te derew be, ezê *şûrekî* li stuyê te dim, / Serê te ji gewdê te biqetînim** (Z-2, 68) If what you say is a lie, I will take a sword to your neck [lit. 'I will give *a blow with a sword* to your neck'], / I will sever your head from your body. {also: şîr II (JR/ SK/OK-2); şwîr (L/HM); [chour شـور/chir شـیـر] (JJ); <şûr شور/şîr شیر> (HH)} [Pok. kes- 585.] 'to scratch, to comb': Skt kṣura- *m.* = 'blade'; P šamšīr شمشیر; Sor şîr شیر; Za şemşêr m. (Todd); cf. also Gr xyron ξυρόν *n.* = 'razor' [K/A/JB3/IFb/B/JJ/HH/JB1-S/ GF/TF/OK/BK//JR/SK//L/HM] <kalan; kalûme; k'ose II; qebd; şilf>

şûr II شوور (M-Ak) = wall. See **şûre I**.

şûr III شــــوور (IFb) = dangling, hanging down. See **şor II**.

şûr•e I شـــــووره *f.* **(•a;).** 1) {syn: beden I; sûr I} wall, fortification wall, curtain wall of a town: •**Amêdîê ya li serê girekî, ya ḧisar-kirîye. Domendorêt wê *şîhr*in, hemî *şîhr*in, di bilindin, bejna do kîlomêtra di bilindin** (M-Am, 718) Amadiye is on the top of a hill and is walled round. All round it there are *walls*, all *walls*, high, to a height of two kilometers •**Xulase ker o xudanê kerî her do ji *şûra* rezî wajî kirin** (SK, 80) In short he tipped both the donkey and its owner over *the wall of* the (terraced) orchard; 2) wooden fence surrounding a field or a garden (IFb). {also: şîhr (M-Am); şîrhe (BF); şûhr (M-Am-2); şûr II (M-Ak); şûrhe (M-Zx/FS); [chour شـور/sour سـور] (JJ)} <Arc šūr(ā) (א)שור & Syr šūrā ܫܘܪܐ = 'city wall, fortification'; Sor şûre شــــــووره [Rewandiz: See M, v. 2, p. 376, note 718]; cf. Ar sūr سـور [M-Am//IFb/SK//M-Ak/JJ//M-Zx/ FS//BF]

şûre II شووره (ZF3/JJ/HH) = saltpeter, niter. See **şor̄e**.

şûrger شـــــوورگـــر *m.* **().** swordsmith: •[***Şîrker* û hesinger û solger û xeyyat û zerger û neccar evene jî ji Filan heyn ji Ekradan tunenin**] (BN 134-135) *Swordsmiths* and ironmongers and cobblers and tailors and goldsmiths and carpenters--there are all of these among the

Christians (Armenians), but not among the Kurds. {also: şûrker (ZF3); [chir-gher] شـيـرگـر (JJ); <şîrker> شيركر (BN)} [BN//ZF3//JJ//GF] <şûr I>

şûrhe شوورهه (M-Zx/FS) = wall. See **şûre I**.

şûrik I شـــوورك *m.* **(-ê;).** plow-beam, wooden front part of plow. [Btm/IFb/GF/TF/FS] <gîsin; halet; hincar; k'otan II>

şûrik II شـــوورك (Kmc) = jet of water; drainpipe. See **şiřik**.

şûriş شوورش (JB3) = revolt. See **şoreş**.

şûrker شووركەر (ZF3) = swordsmith. See **şûrger**.

şûrk'êş شـــووركـێش *m.* **(-ê;).** sword-bearer, sword wielder: **•*şûrkêşê* ruhistîn** (LC, 5) *sword-wielding* soul snatcher. <şûr = 'sword' + k'êş- = 'to pull, unsheathe'; [LC/K/IFb/B/GF/ZF3]

şûş•e شـــووشـــه *f.* **(•a;•ê).** 1) {syn: cam} glass *(material)*: **-feraqa şûşe** (B) glass plates or dishes; **-Şûşa dilê min şkestîye** (K) My heart is broken; **-şûşa p'encerê** (K/B) window pane; **-şûşe kirin** (B) to glaze, fit with glass; 2) bottle, flask: **-şûşa avê** (K) water bottle, canteen; **-şûşa şeravê** (K) wine bottle, decanter; 3) {syn: îstekan; p'eyale} small vase-shaped glass in which tea is served (Msr/Bw). {also: [chouché] شـوشـه (JJ); <şûşe> شـوشـه (HH)} Cf. Mid P šīšag = 'bottle, flask' (M3); P šīše شيشه = 'glass, bottle' --> T şişe; Az T şüşə; Sor şûşe شووشه; Za şûşa *f.* (Todd) [F/K/A/IFb/B/JJ/HH/SK/GF/TF/Msr/Bw] <dîndoq>

şûştin شـووشـتـن/**şûşt'in** [JB1-A/M-Gul] *vt.* **(-şo-).** to wash: **•Celaçî kefen û sabûn anîn ji bona go B. bikujin û laşê wî *bişon* û kefen bikin** (L) The executioners brought a shroud and soap, in order to kill B. and *wash* his corpse and enshroud it. {also: şiştin (PB); şuştin (IFb/BK/JB3/JB1-S/M/GF/OK); [chouchtin] ششتين (JJ); <şûştin شوشتن (dişo) (دشـو)> (HH)} Cf. Mid P šustan (šōy-) [HLLWN-tn] (M3); P šostan شستن (-šūr-) (شور); Sor şitin شِتِن/şiştin شِشتِن (-şo-); Za şiwenã [şitiş/şutiş] (Mal/Srk); Hau şitey (şor-) *vt.* (M4) [F/K/B/HH//M-Gul/JB1-A//JB3/IFb/JB1-S/M/BK/JJ/GF/OK//PB] <veşûştin>

şûtik شـويـتـك/شـووتِـك *f.* **(-a;-ê).** cummerbund which Kurdish men wrap around their waists *(part of traditional folk costume)*: **•"Gullê şînikê ji birîna min bîne der, paşî loma min bike." Wextê Eĥmed *şûtika* wî kirewe birîna biraê xo dît** (SK 18:173) "Come and take the musket ball out of my wound and chide me afterward." When Ahmad undid his *cummerbund* he saw his brother's wound. {also: şîtik (Bw); [shutik] شـوتـك (JJ-Rh); <şûtik> شـوتـك (HH)} [Bw//IFb/JJ-Rh/HH/SK/GF/OK] <bergûz; şal I>

şûv شووڤ (IFb) = furrow. See **şov I**.

şûxil شووغِل, f. (JB1-S) = work. See **şuxul**.

şûxilîn شـــووغِـلـيـن (-şûxil-) (JB1-S) = to work. See **şixulîn**.

Şvêsîa شڤێسيا (Ba2) = Sweden. See **Swêd**.

şwan شوان (SK) = shepherd. See **şivan**.

şwanî شـــوانـــی (SK) = shepherding. See **şivantî**.

şwêlî شوێلی (SK) = turbid, cloudy. See **şêlo**.

şwit شوِت (CB) = dill. See **şiwît**.

şwîm شويم (BF) = naughty. See **şûm**.

şwîn شوين (L) = place. See **şûn**.

şwîr شوير (L/HM) = sword. See **şûr I**.

şyan شـيـان, vt./vi. (-şê) (M/SK) = to be able to, can. See **şiyan**.

T/T' ت

ta I تا/ **ṯa** طا [Hk/SK] *m.* **(-ê; tê, vî tayî).** 1) thread, string: **•Ew** ***taê*** **bi tenêye (K)/Ew** ***takî*** **t'enêye** (B) He is one of a kind; **-ta û derzîk** (Am) needle and thread; 2) strand *(of hair)*: **•Bi navê "*Tayek* porê sipî" kurteçîrokeke Qedrî Can heye** (LC, 5) Qedri Jan has a short story called "*A single* white hair." {also: tayîk (Msr); [ta] تا (JJ); <ṯa> طا (HH)} {syn: dezî; t'êl [2]} [K/A/JB3/IFb/B/JJ/TF/OK//HH/SK/Hk//Msr] <derzî; gulok>

t'a II تا *m.* **(-ê;).** scale, dish, pan *(of weighing scales)*: **•K'ulme xwelî bavêje** ***t'aê*** **zêȓa** (Ba) Throw a handful of dirt onto *the scale* [containing] the gold **•*T'aê* Ûsib ser li 'erdê dimîne** (Ba) *The scale with* Joseph [in it] remains on the ground **•Ûsib ȓadive ser** ***t'akî*** **mêzînê, zêȓa jî dikine** ***t'aê dinê*** (Ba) Joseph gets onto *one pan of* the scales, and they put gold on *the other pan*; **-taê mêzînê** = do. {syn: *kasa terezûya} [Ba/GF] <mêzîn; şihîn; terazî>

t'a III تا *f.* **(-ya;-ê).** 1) fever: **•Ȓojekê** ***ta*** **hate Smaîl, me'da wî pîçek nexoş bû** (SK 34:307) One day Ismail was unwell [lit. '*fever* came to Ismail'] and his stomach was a little upset; 2) malaria: **-ta û lerz** (GF) malaria {syn: lerzeta}. {also: [ta] تا (JJ); <ta> تا (HH)} Cf. Mid P tab (M3); P tab تب; Sor ta تا [K/A/JB3/IFb/B/JJ/HH/SK/GF/TF/OK]

t'a IV تا *prep.* 1) until, till, up to: **•li vir** ***ta*** **gund** (IFb) from here *to* the village **•*ta bi* şevê** (BX) *until* nighttime; 2) [*conj.*] until: **•Bisekin** ***ta ko*** **ez hatim** (IFb) Wait *until* I come **•*T'a* ew** ***neê*****, em naçin** (B) *Until* he comes, we won't go; 3) so that, in order that. {also: heta[nî]; heya[nî]; ḧetanî (B-2); ḧeya (B-2); ḧeyanî (B-2); [ta] تا (JJ)} Cf. Mid P tā = 'until, so that' (M3); P tā تا [BX/K/IFb/B/JJ/SK/GF/TF/OK] See also **ḧeta**.

ta V تا *m.* **(-yê;).** animal tracks, animal footprints: **•Wê şaxê Sîp'anê-Xelatê** ***tayê*** **karê kar-xezala digeȓîne** (EP-4, #30) He is on the peak of Mount Suphan following *the tracks of* young gazelles. {also: [ta] تا (JJ)} [EP-4/JJ] <ȓêç'>

ṯa VI طا [M-Ak/SK-2/Bw]/**ta** تا *m.* **(-[y]ê;).** branch, bough: **•Ev** ***ṯaê*** **hanê yê başe bo hincar** (M-Ak, #548) This *bough* here is a good one for a plough-beam; **-ṯayê darê** (Bw) tree branch. {syn: ç'iq[il]; çirpî; gulî II; şax [1]} Cf. Mid P tāg (M3) [M-Ak/Bw/SK/GF/OK]

t'ab تاب *f.* **(-a;-ê).** 1) patience, endurance; by extension, joy, fun [cf. sebr]: **•Tu û M.va ḧeta êvarê ȓûdinên, çewa** ***t'aba*** **we tê?** (Z-1) You and M. sit together [every day] until the evening; how do you amuse yourselves? [lit. 'how does your *patience* come?']; **-tab dayîn/kirin** (B) to stand, endure, bear, withstand, put up with: **•Ji ber ku êdî** ***nikare*** **li ber heqaret û lêxistinê** ***tab bike*****, rojekê dîsa direve** (Nbh 132:12) Because he *can't stand* the insults and beatings anymore, one day he runs away again; 2) {syn: îza} torment, suffering, pains: **•*Taba* min ber telef neçe** (L) [So that] my *pains* won't go to waste **•Û ji bona wan hilqeysê** ***tab*** **û sêfîlî min dît** (L) [After] I experienced [lit. 'saw'] so much *torment* and misfortune for their sake. {also: t'eb; tehb (ZF)} Cf. < Ar ta'b تعب [L/Z-1/K/A/JB3/B//ZF]

tab•e تابه *f./m.(B)* **().** beast *(of prey)*, wild animal: **•Eva xilxilê kevira cîyê gura, ȓûvîya û** ***tabêd*** **dinê bû** (Ba2:1, 203) That heap of rocks was the place of wolves, foxes, and other *wild beasts*; **-baẍê teva** (F) zoo, zoological gardens; **-tav û teyr** (EP-7) beasts and birds, wildlife, fauna, 'the birds and the bees'. {also: dehbe (IFb/GF-2/TF/OK-2); tav II (EP-7); teba (JB3/GF/OK); tebe (GF-2); te'be (B); teva II (F/K-2)} {syn: canewar; diȓende; terawil} Cf. Ar dābbah دابّة = 'beast, animal' [Ba2/K//EP-7//JB3/GF/OK//B// F//IFb/TF] <ḧeywan; k'ûvî>

tabiyet تابیعت (IFb) = nature; characteristic. See **ṯebî'et**.

tabok تابۆك (Wkt) = brick. See **tabûq**.

taboq تابۆق (HR) = brick. See **tabûq**.

tabûk تابووك (Wkt) = brick. See **tabûq**.

tabûq تابووق *f.* **().** brick: **•Cêryê xwe bi** ***taboqê*** **qesrêda berda û qisda bexçe kir** (HR 3:119) The maidservants let themselves down [i.e., climbed down] *the bricks of* the castle and headed for the garden. {also: tabok (Wkt); taboq (HR); tabûk (Wkt-2)} {syn: k'elpîç; xişt II} Cf. Iraqi Ar ṭābūq

طابوق [HR//FJ/GF//Wkt]

t'abûr تـابـوور *f.* **(-a;-ê).** squadron, batallion: **•*tabûrek* esker** (L) *a squadron of* soldiers. {also: [tabour] طابور (JJ)} Cf. Ar ṭābūr طابور; Sor tabûr تـابـوور [L/K/IFb/GF/ZF3]

t'ac تـــــــاج *m.(K/B/SK)/f.(JB3/IFb)* **(-ê/-a; t'êc/).** 1) crown: **•Ew çi *tanc* e te danaye serê xo?** (SK 4:51) What *crown* is that you have put on your head?; **-t'acê ȓeş** (B) I swear! [lit. 'black crown']; 2) hat worn by sheikhs and dervishes (B/HH). {also: taç (A); tanc (SK/GF-2); [tadj] تـــاج (JJ); <tac> تـاج (HH)} < Ar/P tāj تـاج, Arc taga תגא; Sor tanc تـــانـــج [Z-921/K/JB3/IFb/B/JJ/HH/GF//A//SK] <text [2]; zerazeng>

Tacikî تاجِكى (Wkt) = Tajik. See **T'acîkî.**

t'acir تاجِر (RZ/HH) = merchant. See **t'ucar II**.

T'acîkî تاجيكى *adj.* Tajik. {also: Tacikî (Wkt-2); Tajîkî (BF)} [Wkp/Wkt//BF]

taç تاچ (A) = crown. See **t'ac**.

t'ada (K/IF)/tada (IFb/GF) تـــــادا = violence; injustice; oppression. See **te'darî.**

t'adarî تادارى (K) = oppression. See **te'darî.**

tadayî تادايى (IFb/OK) = oppression. See **te'darî.**

t'ade تاده (L) = oppression. See **te'darî.**

tafilê تـــافـــيـــلـــێ (Frq/ZF3) = immediately, at once. See **t'avilê.**

taharet تاهارەت (IFb) = ritual purity. See **ṯaret**.

tahfîl تاهفيل (ZZ-1) = bathing after sex. See **teȟfîl.**

tahîk تاهيك (Wkt) = hackberry tree. See **tihok.**

tahlik تاهلِك (A) = unripe melon. See **talik.**

taht تاهت = boulder; cliff. See **tat I.**

tajî تـاژى/**ṯajî** طـاژى [FS/HH] *f.(K)/m.(B/JB3)* **(-ya/ ;).** greyhound, hunting dog: **•Nêç'îrvanekî *te'jî* berda k'êwrûşkê** (Dz) A hunter set [a] *hound* after [a] rabbit **•Nêç'îra min tê, gûyê *te'jîya* min tê** (Ag) *proverb used when one is about to do something, but something suddenly comes up to prevent it* [lit.: '(Just when) my hunt/game/quarry comes, my *greyhound* has to relieve himself']. {also: te'jî II (F/B/Dz/Ag); tehjî (IFb-2); [taji] تـــازى (JJ); <ṯajî> طـاژى (HH)} Cf. Mid P tāzīg = 'swift, fast' (M3); P tāzī تـــازى --> T tazı; Sor tancî تـانـجـى = 'gazelle-hound'; Hau tancî; Za tanzi *m.*/tanzî *f.* (Mal) [AB/K/A/JB3/IFb/JJ/GF/TF/OK//HH/FS//Dz/F/B/Ag] <kûçik>

Tajîkî تاژيكى (BF) = Tajik. See **T'acîkî.**

t'akekes تـــاكـــەكـــەس *m.* **(-ê;).** individual: **•Divêt desthilata siyasî jî balansê bixe navbera *takekes* û civakê de** (nefel 20.viii.2008) The political authorities should strike a balance between *the individual* and society **•Li Tirkiyê û Îraqê û Sûriyê û Îranê sitemkarî û bindestiya dirêj hîştiye ko *takekesê* kurd ji xwe aciz bibe û baweriya xwe bi xwe wenda bike** (nefel 20.viii.2008) In Turkey, Iraq, Syria, and Iran long standing oppression and subordination has let the Kurdish *individual* be dissatisfied with himself and to lose faith in himself. {syn: nefer} Sor takekes تاكەكەس/taqekes تاقەكەس [(neol)ZF3/Wkt]

t'aksî تــــاكـــســــى *f.* **(-ya;-yê).** taxi cab: **•Li bajarê Hesekê ... motorsîklêtan cihê *taksiyan* girtiye** (Rûdaw 26.vii.2015) In the city of Heseke ... motorcycles have replaced *taxis* **•Wextê *texsî* xuya bû gişa bazdan ser rê** (SBx, 15) When *the taxi* appeared, everyone ran out to the road. {also: taqsî (TF); teksî (SS); teqsî (SS-2); texsî (SBx/ZF)} < Eng taxi [SBx/ZF//IFb/FJ/RZ/Kmc//TF//SS] <cemse; p'îqab; trimbêl>

tal I تـــال/**ṯal** طـال [FS] *adj.* bitter *(lit. & fig.)*: **•bextê *te'l*** (B) *bitter* fate **•dermanê *te'l*** (B) *bitter* medicine **•Evîniya her du aşiqan *a tehil*** (SW) The *bitter* romance of the two lovers. {also: tehil (SW/TF); teȟil (FS-2); tehl (JB3-2/IFb-2/RZ); te'l (B/JB1-S); [tal] تـــال (JJ); <te'l> تـعـل (HH)} Cf. Mid P taxl (M3); P talx تـلـخ; Sor tał تـاڵ = 'bitter, acid, tannin'; Hau tał (M4); Za ta'l (Mal) {talî I; tehlî; te'layî} [SW/TF//FS//RZ//K/A/JB3/IFb/JJ/GF//B/HH/JB1-S] <tirş>

tal II تال (IFb) = spleen. See **teȟêl.**

t'alan تـــــــالان *m.(K)/f.(OK)* **(-ê/ ; t'alên/t'êlên/).** 1) {syn: cerd [2]} robbery, burglary, pillage, looting, plundering: **•Sê çar salan weto dujminatî kêşa, daimî mêr ji yêk-u-do dikuştin û *talan dibirin*** (SK 41:390) For three or four years enmity dragged on in this way and they were constantly killing and *plundering* men from each other's sides; **-t'alan kirin** = a) to rob, pillage, loot, plunder: **•Dê hucûm keyne welatê Zerzan ... û ji ẍeyrî gundêt Felan, hemîyan *dê talan keyn* û sojîn** (SK 40:377) We shall attack the Zarzan country ... and except for the Christian villages, *we shall plunder* and burn them all; b) to confiscate; to capture: **•Diqewimî usa jî, wekî cerdê pez *t'alan dikir*** (Ba2:1, 203) It would happen also that bandits *would capture* some sheep **•Lê xwedê meke, ko tu seb *talankirina***

gencîneya marî marî bikujî (KH, 34) God forbid that you kill the snake in order *to pillage* its treasure; 2) {syn: cerd I [4]} booty, spoils, loot, plunder; 3) (war) indemnity; 4) confiscation, seizure; capture; 5) cattle (HR): **•Wextê kû ti weȓê, kevir, *talan*, çilo, ‘erd, ḧeywanat, mar, tupişk, mişk ... wê bê** [=**bêje**]: **haaat û hat** (HR 3:143) When you come, the stones, *the cattle*, the branches, the earth, the animals, the snakes, scorpions, mice ... will say: "He's back!". {also: talanî (A); [talan] تـالان (JJ); <talan> تـالان (HH)} < T talan; Sor tałan تاڵان = 'loot(ing), booty' [Ba2/K/JB3/IFb/B/JJ/HH/SK/GF/TF/OK//A] <nijde; şelandin>

talanî تالانى (A) = pillage; booty. See **t’alan**.

t’alaş تـالاش *f.* **(-a;-ê).** worry, care, concern, anxiety: **•Carna bi strandin an bi fîkandin, bê tirs û *telaş*, wek pez kuviya, ji tehteke me xwe davête tehteke din** (SW: E.Şemo. Şivanê Kurd, 43-44) Sometimes with singing or whistling, without fear or *worry*, they would leap from one rock to another like mountain goats **•*T’alaşa* wî nîne** (K) He hasn’t *a care* in the world; **-t’alaşa dînî** (JJ) religious fanaticism; **-t’alaş k’işandin** (K) to worry {syn: xem xwarin}: **•To *t’alaşê mek’şîn*** (HCK-2, 180) *Don't worry*! {also: t’elaş II (K-2/GF); telaşe (IFb); [talach/telach] تـلاش (JJ)} {syn: cefa; fikar; k’eder; k’erb; k’eser; kovan; kul I; qilqal; şayîş; tatêl; xem; xiyal [2]} Cf. P talāš تـلاش --> T telâş; Sor telaş تەلاش = ‘flurry, frantic/last minute effort’ [HCK/K/B] <tasewas>

talaz تالاز *f.* **(;-ê).** whirlwind, tornado, cyclone, strong windstorm; dust devil: **•Dû ra quliband, kir bahoz, hecac û *talîzok* rabû, berberî asîmanan bû** (Z. Xamo. Hindik rindik) Then he turned it around, made it into a storm, a gale and *whirlwind* arose and headed for the sky **•Û bi wê va bereber ba û *talazek* rabîye** (Bîrnebûn/Wkt) And with that it arose with a *windstorm* {also: talîzok (Wkt-2); talozek (Wkt-2)} {syn: babelîsk} [GF/Kmc/FS/FD/G/Wkt/ZF3] <hecac>

talde تـالده (K/IFb/JJ/GF/FS) = shelter; cover, concealment. See **te‘lde**.

ṯale طـالـه/**tale** تـالـه [OK] *f.* **().** sorghum; millet. {also: teḧle, m. (Bw/FS); [taala (G)/tāla (Rh)] طـالـه (JJ)} [SK/JJ/OK/AA//Bw/FS] <garis; gilgil>

talik تـالِك/**ṯalik** طـالِك [FS] *m./f.(ZF3)* **(-ê/;).** unripe melon: **•Cara dawîn min *talik* û zebeş ji bistan didan hev ta ku wan di xurcikê xînim** (HYma, 12) The last time, I gathered *unripe melons* and watermelons from the garden to put in the saddlebag. {also: tahlik (A); tehlik (TF); teḧlik (FS-2); te’lik II (GF)} < tal I = 'bitter' [HYma/Qzl/Qmş/ZF3//FS//A//TF//GF] <k’al II & III>

talî I تـالـى *f.* **(-ya;-yê).** bitterness: **•*Teḧlatîya* qehwê xoş e** (FS) Coffee's *bitterness* is pleasant. {also: tehlî (K/JB3); teḧlatî (FS); teḧlî (FS-2); te‘layî (B); [tali] تالى (JJ)} [K/IFb/JJ//JB3//B//FS] <tal I>

talî II تـالـى *f.* **(-ya;).** 1) {syn: dawî; dûmahî} end; result; 2) [*adv.*] {also: taxlî (Z-922)} finally (K/JB3): **•P’erê xwe distine, *taxlî* nava bazarê dive** (Z-922) He gets his money, *then* [*finally*] he takes [it] to the marketplace. Cf. Ar tālī تالى (tālin) (تالٍ) = 'next' [K/A/JB3/IFb/GF/TF]

talîşk تـالـيـشـك *f.* **(-a;).** 1) chicory; 2) milkweed (?), type of tall weed (Bw). {also: teḧlîşk (Bw/FS)} Sor tałîşk تـاڵـیـشـك/tałg تـاڵـگ = '*plant similar to dandelion*' [Bw/FS//K(s)/IFb/GF/OK/ZF3]

talîzok تاليزۆك (Wkt) = whirlwind. See **talaz**.

taloq I تـالـۆق *f.* **(;-ê).** postponement, delay: **•Civat ne wek mahkemê ye. Heqê xweparastinê nade te, ... *Bê taloq* û bê ku lêbikole, di celsa pêşî de te mahkum dike** (LC, 15) Society is not like a court. It doesn't give you the right to defend yourself ... *Without delay* and without doing any research, it condemns you at the first session; **-taloq kirin** (Wlt/RN2) to postpone, delay, put off: **•Diyar e ku hemû kes guhertinê dixwaze. Baş e, guhertin wê kîngê çê bibe? Divê guhertin ji bo dema pêş *neyê taloqkirin* û divê heqê guhertinê ji bo enstituyê hebe** (RN2 14:80 [#37], 8) It is obvious that everyone wants change. Fine! When will change occur? Change must *not be put off* for the future, and the institute must have the right [to effect] change **•Mehkemeya doza Welat ji ber tunebûna wergêrê Kurdî *hate taloq kirin*** (Wlt 2:103, 8) The trial for the case against Welat [the Kurdish newspaper] *was post-poned* due to the lack of a Kurdish translator. [Wlt/RN2/ZF3]

***taloq II** تـالـۆق *m.* **().** relative by marriage: **•Em *taloqê* hevdu ne** (Qzl) We're *related by marriage* **•zava û taloq** (Drk) son-in-law and relative by marriage. {syn: xinamî; xizm} {taloqtî} [Qzl]

***taloqtî** تـالـۆقـتـى *f.* **(-ya;).** being related by marriage, affinity, having in-laws: **•Ger ez jina xwe berdim, *taloqtîya* min diqede, [yan] ez ji *taloqtîya* wan derdikevim** (Qzl) If I divorce my wife, I will no longer have *in-laws*, [or] I will be relieved of my *in-laws*. {syn: xinamîtî} [Qzl] <taloq II>

talozek تالۆزەك (Wkt) = whirlwind. See **talaz**.

taluke تالوکە (JB3) = danger. See **talûke**.

talûk•e/t'alûke [K(s)] تالووکە *f.* **(;•ê).** danger, hazard, peril: **•Emê li hember vê *talûkê* çi bikin?!** (RN) What are we going to do about this *hazard*? **•Wê ji bona te û wî *tehlûkeke* mezin hebe** (BX ¶286) There will be great *danger* for you and him. {also: taluke (JB3); tehlûke (BX); <tehluke> تهلکە (HH)} {syn: metirsî; xeter} Sor tałûke تاڵووکە = 'urgency; urgent' & talûke تالووکە = 'jeopardy, danger' cf. T tehlike = 'danger' < P tahleke تهلکە = 'perdition' < Ar tahlikah تهلكة [RN/K(s)/IFb//JB3//BX//HH] <tengavî>

ta'm تاعم/**tam** تام [K/JB3/IFb/GF/TF] *m.(K)/f.(B/JB3)* **(-ê/ ; /-ê).** 1) taste, sense of taste: **•Tê wî çaxî *te'mê* min bibînî** (J) Then you'll see *my taste* (=how tasty I am): **-ta'm kirin** = to taste; 2) tasty food, delicacy: **•Dostê wî jî gelek qedrê wî digirt: her tuxme *te'amê* xoş ba, bi-lezet ba, ew bo wî dirust dikir: xarina bajerîya, ku şirînî, pilaw, goşt, êprax, şorbawa bi dermanêt bên-xoş û tiştêt wekî wan e, bo wî didanane ser sifrê** (SK 31:274) His friend would treat him with great respect. He would prepare for him every kind of good and *tasty food*: He would set on the tablecloth townsmen's food, which is sweetmeats, pilaf, meat, stuffed grape leaves, soup with fragrant spices and other such things **•[Eger mirofek ji tayfa xwendîyan...*tiam û zadekî* bidine feqîrekî]** (JR) If a learned person should give *food* to a poor man... **•Baxçakî wî hakimî heye, çiqeysê darê *tiamê* go li dinyaê hene, timam di nav baxçê wî de ye** (L-5) This prince has a garden, in which every kind of fruit tree in the world can be found [lit. 'every *food* tree there is in the world, all are in his garden']; 3) tasting, sampling *(of food or drink)*. {also: te'am (SK/HR); tem (F); te'm (B/J/Ba2); tiam, f. (L); [tam] طعم (JJ); <tam> طام (HH)} < Ar ṭa'm طعم = 'taste' & ṭa'ām طعام = 'food'; Sor tam تام = 'taste' [L/JR//SK/HR//K/JB3/IFb/GF/TF//B/J/Ba2//F]

tamandin تامانْدِن *vt.* **(-tamîn-).** 1) to coat, plate, gild *(a base metal with gold or silver)*: **•Dawî emir da xulaman û koçer birin** [sic] **sûkê; ji wî û zarokên wî ra gelek cil û kinc kirîn û şûr û tifingeke *bi zîv tamandî* jî danê û koçer bi rê kirin** [sic] (JB2-Osman Sebrî/Rnh 14 [1943], 8-9) In the end he ordered his servants to take the nomad to the marketplace, where they bought many clothes for him and his children, and gave him a *silver-plated* sword and rifle, then sent him on his way; 2) to vaccinate; 3) {syn: patrome kirin} to graft *(branch of one tree onto the trunk of another)*. {also: tamdan (GF-2); <tamdan> طامدان (HH)} <Ar ṭa''am II طعّم = 'to vaccinate; to engrave' [Rhn/JB2/A/IFb/GF/TF/OK//HH] <deqandin [2]>

tamar تامار (B/K/GF/FS) = vein. See **t'emar**.

tamdan تامدان (GF/HH) = to engrave; to vaccinate. See **tamandin**.

tamîş تامیش *adj.* firm, stable, steady (B): **-tamîş bûn** (K) /~ **kirin** (K/B) = a) to bear, endure, suffer, [with]stand; b) to be patient, wait patiently. {also: teyamîş (K/B)} ? < T dayanmış = 'having withstood' [Ks/Krç//K/B]

tan طان/**tan** تان *m.* **(-ê;).** wooden fence; reed fence, hedge (OK). {also: <tan> طان (HH)} {syn: çeper; k'ozik; p'ercan; sênc} Sor tan تان = 'warp (loom); pole, shaft; partition, room divider' [Bw/HH/FS//A/IFb/OK] <çeper; k'ozik I; sîme>

tanc تانج (SK/GF) = crown. See **t'ac**.

tanî تانی (TF) = soot. See **tenî**.

tap I تاپ (GF) = epilepsy. See **tep I**.

tap II تاپ (TF) = slap. See **t'ep II**.

t'apan تاپان *f.* **(-a;-ê).** harrow, roller: **•Wî *tapan* di ser zeviya xo ȓa anî û bir ku kêstekên axê hûr bibin** (FS) He passed [lit. 'brought and took'] *the harrow* over his field so that the clods of earth would be broken up [lit. 'become tiny']. {also: topan (Wn/Xrz)/topan (Twn); [tapan] تاپان (JJ)} {syn: şûnkê serbanî (Czr)} Cf. T taban = 'roller'; W Arm dap'an տափան [Ag/Ml/K/B/JJ/FS//Wn/Xrz] <bagirdan; lox>

taq تاق *adj.* with white or speckled (spotted) ears *(of goats)*: **•Ka bizina *taq*?** (Ardû, 115) Where is the *white-eared* [or, *speckle-eared*] goat? [Ardû/IFb] <bel; kever; k'ol IV; qer II; xez>

t'aqet تاقەت/**taqet** طاقەت [SK/JJ/HH] *f.* **(-a;-ê).** strength, power, might; endurance: **•Min *taqet* nemaye** (IFb) My *strength* is waning **•*T'aqeta* min t'une** (K) I am powerless [lit. 'My *power* does not exist'] **•To çawa munasib dizanî, ji xeberê te der-nakewîn, emma em dê mehw bîn. Me *taqeta* Horemarîyan nîye** (SK 61:731)

Whatever you deem proper, we will not run counter to it, but we will be annihilated. We *are no match for* the Horemaris; **-ji t'aqetê k'etin** (B) to lose strength or power; to grow weak. {also: [taqet] طاقت (JJ); <taqet> طاقت (HH)} {syn: birî I; ḧêl; hêz; qedûm [2]; qewat; zexm I [2]; zor I} < Ar ṭāqah طاقة = 'ability, faculty, power'; Sor taqet تاقەت = 'ability to endure; mood' [HCK/K/B/IFb/FJ/GF/Kmc//SK/JJ/HH] <karîn; şiyan>

taqim تاقِم (FJ/GF) = set; horse tack; group, team. See **t'axim**.

taqsî تاقسی (TF) = taxi cab. See **t'aksî**.

tar تار (TF) = wet; fresh. See **ter̄**.

tarat تارات (HCK) = ritual purity. See **ṯaret**.

ṯaret طارەت/**t'aret** تارەت [IFb] *f.* **().** cleanliness, purity, ritual ablution or purification *(for prayer, or after defecation)*: •**Derê derva, *taratek* dudu nimêj bike, paşê were r̄azê ḧeta sivê** (HCK-1, 207) Go outside, purify yourself and pray [lit. 'pray *an ablution* or two'], then come to bed until morning •**Ez dê çim-e ser awê, *tehareteki*** [sic] **girim o hêm** (SK 8:84) I shall go to the water to make my *ablutions* and then come. {also: taharet (IFb-2); tarat (HCK); teharet (SK); <teharet> طهارت (HH)} < Ar ṭahārah طهارة = 'cleanliness, purity' [HCK//IFb//SK]

t'arêq تارێق (B) = date; history. See **t'arîx**.

t'ariş/tariş [K] تارِش *m.* **(-ê; t'êriş).** cattle, large domestic animals, grazing livestock: •**Çarde *t'ariş* hatine xware** (Ba3-3, #33) Fourteen [heads of] *cattle* came down •**Îsal pûtê *terşê* me bese** (Haz) This year we have enough winter fodder for our *cattle* [lit. 'this year the fodder of our cattle is enough']. {also: terş (Haz/K-2/A/GF/OK); [tarich] طرش (JJ); <terş> ترش (HH)} {syn: çavrî; gar̄eş} Cf. clq. Syrian Ar ṭarš طرش = 'herd (of cattle), flock (of sheep)' [Ba3/B/K/JJ//Haz/A/HH/GF/OK] <dewar; ga; gar̄an; naxir>

tarî تاری/**ṯarî** طاری [Bw/SK/HH] *adj.* 1) dark, obscure: •**Êvar hat, bû *tarî*** (AB) Evening came, it became *dark* •**Ç'e'vekî min ma p'encerê, yek bû *te'rî*** (Z-1) One of my eyes stayed [glued] to the window, one got *dark*; 2) {syn: giran I; r̄eş} dark *(of tea, color, etc.)* (Bw); 3) [*f.* **(-ya;-yê).**] {syn: tarîban} darkness: •**Wexta ko *tarî* dikeve erdê** (JB3) When it becomes dark [lit. 'when *darkness* falls on the land']. {also: tarîk; te'rî II (Z-1/B); [tari/tarí] تاری (JJ); <ṯarî> طاری (HH)} Cf. P tārīk تاریك; Sor tarîk تاریك = 'dark'; Hau tarîk (M4) {tarîk[ay]î; tarî[tî]} [AB/K/A/JB3/IFb/JJ/OK//HH/SK/GF/Bw//Z-1/B]

tarîban تاریبان *f.* **(-a;-ê).** darkness: •***tarîbara* serê sibê** (Z-3) *the darkness of* daybreak. {also: tarîbar (Z-3); te'rîban (B); te'rîbar (B)} {syn: tarî [2]; tarîtî} [Z-3//K//B]

tarîbar تاریبار (Z-3) = darkness. See **tarîban**.

tarîk تاریك = dark. See **tarî**.

tarîkayî تاریکایی (K[s]) = darkness. See **tarîtî**.

tarîkî تاریکی (K) = darkness. See **tarîtî**.

t'arîq تاریق (B) = date; history. See **t'arîx**.

tarîtî تاریتی *f.* **(-ya;-yê).** darkness. {also: tarî [3]; tarîkayî (K[s]); tarîkî (K); [tariti] تاریتی (JJ)} {syn: tarîban} [K/JB3/IFb/JJ/GF//K(s)]

t'arîx تاریخ *f.* **(-a;-ê).** 1) (calendrical) date, date of an event (e.g., March 21, 2003): •**Newroz di *tarîxa* 21'ê Adarê da tê pîrozkirin** (BZ, v. 1, 290) Newroz is celebrated on *the date of* March 21st •**Nûçenama Kurdî ya pêşîn Kurdistan, di *tarîxa* 22'yê Nîsana 1898'an da dest bi derketinê kirîye** (BZ, v. 1, 290) The first Kurdish newspaper, Kurdistan, began publication on *the date of* April 22, 1898; **-r̄oj û tarîx** (RZ) date; 2) {syn: dîrok I} history. {also: t'arêq (B); t'arîq (B-2); [tarikh] تاریخ (JJ)} < Ar ta'rīx تأريخ = 'date; history'; Sor tarîx تاریخ = 'date; history' & mêjû مێژوو = 'history' [BZ/K/IFb/JJ/RZ/CS//B] <berwar>

tarûmar تارووومار *adj.* 1) destroyed, ruined, wrecked, ravaged, razed: **-tarûmar kirin** (IFb/TF/ZF) to wreck, ruin, destroy, ravage: •**Te ez kirim dîn û har / *kirim tarûmar*** (*from* Tarûmar [song]) You made me crazy and rabid / you *ruined me*; 2) in disarray; strewn, scattered. {also: [tar-ou-mar] تارومار (JJ) = désarroi = disarray} Tur tarumar = 'confused, jumbled, topsy-turvy'; Sor tarumar تارومار = 'widely scattered' [Nbh/K/IFb/FJ/GF/TF/ZF/CS/SS/Wkt]

t'as تاس *f.* **(-a;-ê).** 1) basin, bowl; round, shallow drinking cup with handle: •**Du *tas* dewê hênik dianî datanî ber me** (Alkan, 71) She would bring two *cups of* cool buttermilk and place them before us •**Min ew *tasa* çeqilmêst a ku hîn qeşa wê neheliyabû ji destê wê girtibû, çend gulp jê vexwaribû** (KS, 49) I took that *cup of* çeqilmast -- in which the ice had not yet melted--from her hands and drank a few gulps of it •***Tas* tijî ava zelal e** (AB) *The bowl* is full of clear water •***T'asêd* xwe digirtne destêd xwe, pê şiva li wan

dixistin, wekî bi wî dengî gura bitirsînin (Bs2:1, 203) They would take their *bowls* and bang on them with their staffs, so as to scare away the wolves with this noise; 2) unit of weight, about 6 liters (JB1-A). {also: [tas] طاس (JJ); <ṯas> طاس (HH)} Cf. Ar ṭās طاس/ṭāsah طاسة --> T tas; Sor tas تاس = 'metal bowl' [AB/K/IFb/B/JJ/JB1-A/GF/OK//HH] <fîncan; k'asik>

tasewas تاسەواس *f.* **(-a;-ê).** apprehension, anxiety, misgiving: **•Dilê Biharê bi *tasewas* bû** (SBx, 21) B.'s heart was full of *apprehension*; **-bêyî tirs û tasewas** (Wkt) unwincingly, unflinchingly. {also: taswasî (FJ)} {syn: cefa; tatêl; xem û xîyal} [SBx/ZF/Wkt//FJ] < kovan; şayîş; t'alaş>

taswasî تاسواسی (FJ) = anxiety. See **tasewas**.

tasyan تاسیان (SK) = to slip. See **teĥisîn**.

taşt•ê تاشتێ *f.* **(•îya;•îyê).** 1) breakfast: **•Keçikê ji bavê xwe ra *taştê* bir** (AB) The girl took her father *breakfast* **•*Taştiya* min nan û mast e** (AB) My *breakfast* is bread and yoghurt; **-taştê kirin** (B): a) to feed or give s.o. breakfast; b) to have breakfast; **-taştê xwarin** (B) to have or eat breakfast; **-taştîya mîranî** (IFb) late breakfast; **-taştîya pale** (IFb) early breakfast; 2) mid-morning coffee break (Ad); second breakfast, taken between 8 and 9 o'clock (JB1-A&S/OK); 3) lunch (Hk/TF). {also: te'ştê (B); têşt (OK-2/SK/Bw); t'êşt' (JB1-A); [tacht تاشت/tachti تاشتی (JJ); <ṯaştê> طاشتی (HH)} Cf. P čāšt چاشت = 'morning; dawn; breakfast'; Sor çêşt چێشت = 'meal'; Za taştî *f.* = 'meal eaten before noon' (Mal); Hau çaştî *f.* = 'meal, (any boiled) food' (M4) [Ad/AB/K/A/IFb/TF/OK/Msr//B//HH//JJ//JB1-A/SK/Bw]

tat I تات/**ta't** تاعت *f.* **(-a;-ê).** 1) boulder, large rock (L); cliff, crag, precipice (K); mountain ridge made of massive boulders (IFb): **•Carna bi strandin an bi fîkandin, bê tirs û telaş, wek pez kuviya, ji *tehteke* me xwe davête *tehteke* din** (SW: Erebê Şemo. Şivanê Kurd, 43-44) Sometimes with singing or whistling, without fear or worry, they would leap from *one rock to another* like mountain goats **•Li hindav û nêzî Wanê û Gola Wanê kelehên mezin û dîrokî hene, du keleh ji van kelehan li raserî lêva golê ne, herdu jî li ser *tatên* pan û mezin hatine nijandin** (SB, 50) Above and beside Van and Lake Van there are large and historic fortresses, [and] two of those fortresses overlook the shore of the lake, both of them have been built on flat and large *cliffs*; 2) {also: tet II (B)} stone slab (K[s]/B/GF): **•Me savarê xwe liser *tehtê* kutaye** (GF) We beat our bulgur [barley groats] against *the stone slab*. {also: taht; teht (IFb-2/K-2/GF-2/TF/RN/SW); <teĥt> تحت (HH)} [L/K/IFb/GF//RN/SW/TF//HH//B] <ĥelan; neĥît; sel>

tatêl تاتێل *f.* **(-a;-ê).** worry, care, concern, anxiety: **•Di dilê Meyro da germayî û kêfxweşî ya ku qasekî berê hebû, êdî nemabû. Şûna wê tirs, êş û *tatêl* girtibû** (MB, 65) Gone were the feelings of warmth and happiness which Meyro had been relishing a short while before. In their stead came fear, pain, and *worry*. {syn: cefa; fikar; k'eder; k'erb; k'eser; kovan; kul I; qilqal; şayîş; t'alaş; xem; xiyal [2]} [MB/Ag/Erzurum/ZF3] <tasewas>

ṯatî طاطی/**tatî** تاتی [IFb] *m.* **(-yê;).** felt rug: **•Ĥurmet, r̄abe, *tatîyê* bi bisk, gul-gul, ĥazir bike bo niwîna mêwanî û *tatîyekî* jî lûl de, bike balge** (SK 31:277) Wife, go and bring an embroidered and fringed *felt rug* for our guest's bedding, and roll up another *rug* and make it into a cushion. {also: <ṯatî> طاتی (HH)} {syn: kulav [3]} Sor tatî تاتی [SK//HH//IFb] <kulav>

tav I تاڤ *f.* **(-a;-ê).** 1) {syn: hûr; r̄oj [2]} sun, sunlight *{as source of warmth, not the physical star itself}*: **•Hela *tavê* nedabû ĥeç'êd ç'îya** (Ba2:1, 204) The *sunlight* had not yet touched the mountain peaks **•Îro *tav* germ e** (AB) Today *the sun* is warm; **-ber te'vê germ bûn** (B) to sunbathe, warm o.s. in the sun; **-ber te'vê velezyan** (B) to lie in the sun; 2) light, daylight, sunlight: **-tava heyvê** (IFb)/~ **hîvê** (Ag) moonlight; full moon; **-tava rojê** (IFb) sunlight. {also: hetaw (SK); taw (SK-2); te'v II (B); [taw] تاو/تاڤ (JJ); <ṯav> طاڤ (HH)} [Pok. tep- 1069] 'to be warm': Skt tápas- *n.* = 'heat'; Av tāpaiti = 'is warm'; cf. Mid P taftan (tab-) = 'to grow hot, shine' & tāftan (tāb-) = 'to heat, burn, shine' (M3); P āftāb آفتاب = 'sun' & tābestan تابستن = 'summer'; Sor hetaw هەتاو = 'sun'; cf. also Lat tepidus = 'warm'; Rus tëplyĭ тёплый = 'warm' [Kg/Ag/K/A/JB3/IFb/JJ/GF/TF/OK//B//HH//SK] <tavehîv; tîrêj>

tav II تاڤ (EP-7) = wild animal, beast. See **tabe**.

ṯav III طاڤ (Zeb)/tav تاڤ (TF/OK/Hej) = cloudburst. See **tavî**.

tavaheyv تاڤاهەیڤ (TF) = moonlight. See **tavehîv**.

tavehîv تاڤەهیڤ *f.* **(;-ê).** moonlight: **•Li ber *tavehîvê* çavên wê yên gir û reş dibiriqîn** (MB-Meyro) Her large, black eyes twinkled in *the moonlight*

•**Şevek ji şevên havînê bû. *Tavehîv* bû** (MB-Meyro) It was a summer night. The moon was shining [lit. '*moonlight* was']. {also: tavaheyv (TF); tava heyvê (JB3); tavheyîv (K); tavheyv (GF); [taw-a hiwi] تـاڤا هـيـڤـى (JJ); <taveheyv> طاڤهيڤ (HH)} {syn: hîveron[1]} [MB//TF//JB3//K//GF//JJ//HH] <tav I>

tavheyîv تاڤهەييڤ (K) = moonlight. See **tavehîv**.

tavheyv تاڤهەيڤ (GF) = moonlight. See **tavehîv**.

t'avilê تاڤِلى *adv.* immediately, at once: •**Bawer dikim ku roja ez vî camêrî bibînim ezê *tafilê* wî bikujim** (Frq) I think that the day I see that fine fellow, I will kill him *at once* •**Lê bêyî ku ez vê sar û şermê li xwe bidime der *tavilê* dibêjim:-- Pirtûkên çi? Min pirtûk ne nivisandine ku... Ez nanivisinim, keko** (Epl, 18) But without manifesting this coldness, I say *at once*, "What books? I haven't written any books ... I don't write, my friend" •**Van hevalan *tavilê*, dotira rojê dest bi xebatê kir û xebata xwe bêwestan û rawestan bir serî** (AW73A3) These comrades *immediately* on the following day began working and carried out their work without stopping. {also: tafilê (Frq/ZF3)} [Epl/AW//Frq/ZF3]

tavî تاڤى/**tavî** طاڤى [Bw/HH]/**ta'vî** تاعڤى [K/OK-2] *f.* **(-ya;-yê).** cloudburst, sudden downpour: •[***Tavîya* Nîsanê, hêjaya malê Xuristanê**] (BG) An April *cloudburst* is worth all the riches of the universe *[prv.]*. {also: tav III (Zeb)/tav (TF/OK-2/Hej); tehvî (GF); te'vî II (B); [tawi] تـاڤـى (JJ); <tavî> طـاڤـى (HH); [tavi] (BG)} Cf. Sor tafaw تـافـاو = 'torrent' & tafetaf تـافـەتـاف = '(sound of) rushing water' & taw-u-tof تاو و تۆف = 'storm' [Bw/HH//IFb/JJ/GF/OK//K//B//TF/Hej//Zeb] <baran>

tavrik تاڤرِك (FJ) = small hatchet. See **tevrik I**.

taw طاو (SK) = sun. See **tav I**.

t'awan I تـاوان *f.* **(-a;-ê).** 1) {syn: gune II; sûc} guilt; 2) {syn: sûc} crime; 3) {syn: gune II} sin. {also: <tawan> تـاوان (Hej)} Cf. Mid P tāwān = 'compensation, obligation' (M3); P tāvān تـاوان = 'indemnity, damage; compensation; penalty'; Sor tawan تـاوان = 'guilt, offense, crime, gross violation of the law; sin, wrong' [VoA/K(s)/A/IFb/FJ/GF/TF/OK/RF/Hej/ZF/Kmc] <binas>

t'awan II تاوان (K) = frying pan. See **t'awe**.

t'awanbar تاوانبار *adj.* 1) {syn: gunehbar} accused, suspected; **-t'awanbar kirin** (RZ/Kmc) to accuse: •**Hûn hemû, hema Xurşoyê xwelîser *tawanbar dikin*, belkî ne ji wî be** (DBgb, 12) You all *accuse* poor old Khursho, maybe it's not from him [=maybe he didn't do it]; 2) {syn: sûcdar} guilty. Sor tawanbar تـاوانـبـار = 'guilty, culpable; culprit' [DBgb/IFb/FJ/GF/TF/RZ/Kmc/ZF]

tawaş تـاواش (Haz) = oil products used in cooking. See **tewaş**.

t'aw•e تـاوه *f.* **(•a;•ê).** pan, saucepan, frying pan. {also: t'awan II (K-2); tewe (IFb-2); tewik (AD); [tavé] تـاوه (JJ); <tawe> تـاوه (HH)} {syn: miqilk} Cf. Mid P tābag (M3); P tābe تـابـه; Sor tawe تـاوه [Frq/K/IFb/B/HH/GF//JJ//AD]

t'awet تاوەت (K/B) = patience; calm, rest. See **t'ebatî**.

tawik تاوك (GF) = hackberry tree. See **tihok**.

tawlaz تـاولاز (TF) = womanizer, profligate, adulterer. See **tolaz**.

tawûg تاووگ (IFb) = sleigh. See **taxok**.

t'ax I تاخ *f.* **(-a;-ê).** 1) {syn: mihel} district, quarter *(of city)*, neighborhood: •**Min li mizgefta *taxê* bang da** (HYma, 44) I made the call to prayer from the *neighborhood* mosque •***t'aẍa* jorîn** (Dyd) the upper *quarter* (of a city); 2) district, region (K/B). {also: taxe I (IFb-2); t'aẍ (K/Dyd); [tag] تـاغ (JJ); <tax> تـاخ (HH)} < Arm t'ał թաղ = 'district, quarter of town, ward' [A/IFb/B/HH/ZF//K/JJ/Dyd]

tax II تاخ (FS) = stack; bundle. See **t'exe**.

taxe I تاخه (IFb) = district. See **t'ax**.

taxe II تـاخـه, m. (IFb/HH/GF/OK) = stack; bundle. See **t'exe**.

t'axim تـاخِـم *f.* **(;-ê).** 1) set *(of cooking utensils, dishes, tools, etc.)*; 2) [takhoum-i hespi (JJ)] horse tack, equestrian equipment, accessories (saddles, stirrups, bridles, halters, reins, bits, harnesses, etc.): •**Evdal ji seracanên Qonaxê rîca kir ku jê re *taximekî* xemilandî çêkin. Wan di demeke kurt de *taxim* çêkirin** [sic] **û ew dan** [sic] **Evdal. *Taxim* bêkusûr bû: bi rengên kesk, sor û zer hatibû şixulandin û xemilandin. Zengû, zexme, rikêb û hesinê lîwanê hespê mîna tîrêjên tavê diçirûsîn** (M.Uzun. R. Evd. Zeyn., 108) Evdal asked the saddlers of Q. to make him a fancy *horse tack*. They made *the horse tack* in a short time and gave it to E. *The horse tack* was flawless: it had been worked and adorned in green, red and yellow. The stirrup and its strap, the spurs and the iron of the horse's bridle glistened like rays of the sun •[**Min hespekî ki'êl qewî spehî bi sê hezar qurûşî istandîye, bilanî *taxum bikin* û bînin, tu lê siwar**

bibe kanê begen dikî] (JR, 38) I bought a really gorgeous bay horse for 3,000 piasters-- let them *outfit it* [*tack it up*] and bring it, you mount it and see if you like it •**[Xelîl Bek emrê x̱ulaman dike ku filan hespî *taxum* û zîn *bikin*, bilanî Ḧesen Bek li hespî siwar bîtin, kanê begen dike, îcarî hespî zîn û *taxum dikin*, Ḧesen Bek lê siwar dibî]** (JR, 38) Khalil Beg orders the servants *to tack up* and saddle such and such a horse, so that Hasan Beg can mount it and see if he likes it, so they saddle and *tack up* the horse, and H.B. mounts it; 3) group, team, crew. {also: taqim (FJ/GF-2); [taxum] تـاخـوم (JR); [takhoum] طـاخـم (JJ); <taxim> تـاخـم (HH)} < T takım --> Ar ṭaqm طقم = 'set, complement, series, harness'; Sor taqim تـاقِم = 'set, group, platoon' [JR/JJ//K/B/A/IFb/GF/HH/CS//FJ]

taxlî تاخلی (Z-922) = finally. See **talî II** [2].

taxok تاخۆك *f.* **(-a;-ê).** sleigh, sled(ge) for transporting things over snow and ice: •**Wî çilî bi *taxokê* îna mal** (FS) He brought the winter sheep fodder [tree branches] home on *a sleigh.* {also: tawûg (IFb); taxor (FS-2); taxork (SS/FS-2/ZF3-2); taxurk (GF-2/CS-2); taxûk (A/FD); taxûrk (CS-2); <taxûk> تـاخـوك (HH)} {syn: qol IV} [FS/GF/TF/ZF3/Wkt/CS//SS//A/FD/HH//IFb]

taxor تاخۆر (FS) = sleigh. See **taxok**.

taxork تاخۆرك (SS/FS/ZF3) = sleigh. See **taxok**.

taxurk تاخورك (GF/CS) = sleigh. See **taxok**.

taxûk تاخووك (A/FD/HH) = sleigh. See **taxok**.

taxûrk تاخوورك (CS) = sleigh. See **taxok**.

t'ax̱ تاغ (K/JJ/Dyd) = district. See **t'ax**.

taybet تایبەت (ZF) = special, specific. See **t'aybetî**.

t'aybetî تایبەتی *adj.* special, particular: •**Derheqa kar de zanîna xwe ya *taybetî* heye** (IFb) He has his own *special* knowledge about work •**Rojnameya *taybetî* ya Enstîtuya Kurdî ya Parîsê** (Kmc) the *special* newspaper of the Kurdish Institute of Paris; -[**bi**] **taybetî** (K/IF) specifically, especially {syn: îlahî; nemaze}: •***bi taybetî* Celadet Bedirxan û gelek ronakbîrên Kurd** (Ber) *especially* Djeladet Bedirkhan and many Kurdish intellectuals; -**taybet** [**bi... ve**] = peculiar to, specific to: •**Pêdaçûnek li ser hindek belgenamên *taybet bi* Kurdan *ve*** (*title of book by* Selaẖ M.S. Hirurî, 2006) A study of some documents *specific to* the Kurds. {also: taybet (ZF); teybetî (A)} {syn: xas} <Ar ṭabī'ah طبيعة = 'nature' [Ber/K/JB3/IFb/OK/RZ//ZF//A]

t'aybetmendî تایبەتمەندی *f.* **(-ya;-yê).** characteristic, trait: •**Şerefxan Cizîrî di nivîsa xwe ya bi sernavê "Edebiyat an jî kultur" de digel *taybetmendiyên* wêjeya devkî, têkilî û cudatiya wê ya ji wêjeya nivîskî jî li ber çavan radixe** (AW72B5) Sheref Khan Jiziri presents *the characteristics of* oral literature, its relationship to and difference from written literature in his article entitled "Literature or culture". {syn: sexlet; xeyset} [AW/ZF3]

tayf تایف (ZF3) = type of grape. See **tayfî**.

ṯayf•e طایفه *f.* **(•a;•ê).** 1) tribe, small tribe: "a) Ashiré, large tribe, b) Qabilé, medium-sized tribe, c) Tàifé, small tribe....however the word tàifé is often taken in the general sense, signifying any tribe, whether ashiré, qabilé, or tàifé. The large tribes, ashirés, are composed of qabilés and of tàifés or simply of tàifés. There are a large number of qabilés and tàifés which do not depend on an ashiré; such a tribe is normally called طـايـفـه يـى مـتـفـرقـه [tayfeyê mutafarriqa], isolated tàifé." (JR, p. 1, note 2); 2) group; caste (B): •**[mirofek ji *tayfa* xwendîyan]** (JR) a learned person [lit., 'a man from the *group/caste of* learned ones']; 3) splinter groups within a tribe (B). {also: teîfe (F); t'eyfe (B/Ba2-2); [tàifé] طايفه (JJ)} < Ar ṭā'ifah طائفة [Ba2/K/A/JB3//IFb//F//B//JJ] <azbat; berek; binemal; 'eşîret; îcax; obe; qebîle>

tayfî تایفی/**ṯayfî** طایفی *m.* **().** purple, tart type of grape. {also: tayifî (TF); tayf (ZF3); teyfî (FD/BF)} [Msr/GF//FS//TF//ZF3//FD/BF] <tirî>

tayifî تایِفی (TF) = type of grape. See **tayfî**.

tayî تایی (Kmc) = hackberry tree. See **tihok**.

tayîk تاییك (Msr) = thread. See **ta I**.

t'aze تازه *adj.* 1) {syn: teř [2]} fresh, green: •**Te çima dewsa kevezanê destê xwe ew çiqê *t'eze* şînbûyî biřî?** (Abbasian #6:144) Why have you cut that *green* branch in place of [=to replace] the stick [you carry in] your hand?; 2) {syn: nû} new, recent: -**Ṟîya T'eze** = The New Way, name of a Kurdish newspaper originally published in Erevan in Cyrillic script, now on line in Latin script; 3) fine, excellent (HH/JB1-A); 4) [*adv.*] {syn: niha} now, just now (Ad/Dz/K): •**Divînin wê xortek gaê xwe *t'eze* girtye ku qoşke** (Dz) They see that the young man has *just barely* taken his bull(s) to tie them to the plough {describes him as lazy [taze = ?just barely]} •**Eva bûka jî jina wî xortê t'embele, ku gaê xwe *t'eze* qoşdikir** (Dz) This young woman is the wife of that lazy young man who was *just barely* ploughing with his oxen. {also: tazî II/ta'zî II (JB1-S); t'eze (Dz/K/B/A-2/IF-2); [tazé] تازه (JJ); <taze> تازه (HH)} Cf. P tāze تازه --> T taze; Sor taze تازه = 'recent, new, fresh, recently' {tazetî; tezetî} [Ad/A/JB3/IFb/HH/JB1-A//Dz/K/B]

ṯazin طازِن (-ṯaz-) (JB1-A) = to go numb. See **tevizîn**.

taziye تازِیە (IFb/SK) = condolence. See **t'azîye**.

tazî I تازی/**ta'zî I** تاعزی [JB1-S] *adj.* 1) {syn: r̄ût; zelût} naked, nude, bare: **-r̄ûte-tazî** (Ba2) do.: **•kevirêd *r̄ûte-tazî*** (Ba2) *bare* rocks; 2) drawn (sword) : **•Q., şûrê wînakê *tazî*, bi pey dik'eve** (Z-3) Q., his sword *drawn*, pursues her. {also: tezî I; te'zî (B); [tazi] تازی (JJ); <ṯazî> طازی (HH)} {tazîtî; te'zîtî} [AB/AJ/F/K/A/JB3/IFb/JB1-S/JJ/GF/TF//HH//B] <şilf tazî>

tazî II تازی/ta'zî II تاعزی (JB1-S) = fresh; new. See **t'aze**.

t'azî III تازی (Bw/JJ-Rh) = condolence. See **t'azîye**.

tazîtî تازیتی *f.* **(-ya;-yê).** nakedness, nudity. {also: te'zîtî (B)} {syn: r̄ûtayî} [K/IFb/TF//B] <tazî I>

t'azîy•e تازییە *f.* **(;•ê).** 1) {syn: behî; serxweşî [2]} condolence, comforting *(upon s.o.'s death)*; 2) (Shiite) passion play (SK): **•Hung sunnî gelek bê-insafin. Qelbê hingo gelek r̄eqe. Hung qet *taziyê* bo Imam Ĥuseynî mezlom, şehîdê Kerbelaê, naken, xo nakutin, nagirîn** (SK 60:709) You Sunnis are very unjust. Your hearts are very hard. You never perform *a passion-play* for the oppressed Imam Hussein, the martyr of Kerbela, you do not beat yourselves, you do not weep. {also: taziye (IFb/SK); t'azî III (Bw); t'ezî'yî (K); [teaziié/tahhzí (G)/tāzī (Rh)] تعزیه (JJ)} <Ar ta'ziyah تعزية, verbal noun of √'-z-y II عزّى = 'to condole, give comfort, express one's sympathy'--> P ta'ziyeh تعزیه = 'passion play, condolence' & ta'ziyat تعزیت = 'condolence'; T taziye [Bw/JJ-Rh//OK//IFb/SK//JJ//K]

te تە *prn.* {oblique case of **tu I**} 1) you *(sing.)*, thou, thee: **•Ez *te* dibînim** = I see *you* [*thee*] **•Te ez dîtim** = *You* saw [*Thou saw(e)st*] me; 2) your, thy: **•hevala *te*** = your (girl)friend. {also: [té] تە (JJ); <te> تە (HH)} [BX/K/JB3/IFb/B/JJ/HH/SK/GF/TF]

ṯe'am طەعام (SK/HR) = tasty food. See **ta'm**.

t'eb تەب = patience; suffering. See **t'ab**.

teba تەبا (JB3/GF/OK) = wild animal, beast. See **tabe**.

tebaq تەباق (IFb) = hoof and mouth disease. See **tebeq I**.

tebat تەبات (K/IFb/FJ/TF/RZ/AD/JJ/HH) = patience; calm, rest. See **t'ebatî**.

t'ebatî تەباتی *f.* **(-ya;-yê).** patience, endurance; calm, rest, peace: **•Dibêjin, *tebatiya* Birahîm Xelîl *nedihat*, destê xo havête dîwarê zêndanê** (GShA, 231) They say that Ibrahim *found no rest*, he hit the prison wall with his hand **•Gurpegurpa dilê mêrik e lêdide û *bê tewatî* li bendî gotinên rîsipî ye** (Ardû, 19) The man's heart is pounding and he *impatiently* awaits the pronouncements of the village elder •[Tebat-a min naï] = ***Tebata* min naê** (JJ) I feel impatient/I have no *peace*. {also: t'awet (K-2/B); tebat (K-2/IFb/FJ/TF/RZ/AD); t'ewat (K-2/B-2/GF); tewatî (Ardû); [tebat تبات/tabet تبت] (JJ); <tebat> تبات (HH)} {syn: bînfirehî; sebr} Cf. Ar ṯabāt ثبات = 'firmness, steadiness' [GShA/A//IFb/FJ/TF/RZ/AD/JJ/HH//GF//Ardû//K/B]

Ṯebax I طەباخ/**T'ebax** تەباخ [K/B] *f.* **(-a;-ê).** August *(month)*: •[**Temûz û *Tebaxê*, agir digirite axê, dû dirabite ji şaxê**] (BG) In July and *August*, fire takes hold of the soil [i.e., the soil catches fire], smoke rises from the horns (of animals) *[prv.]*; **-meha Tebaxê** = do. {also: T'ebaẍ III (B-2); [tebakh طباخ/tebag طباغ] (JJ); <tebax> تباخ (HH)} according to HH < Ar ṭabbāx طبّاخ (ṭabaxa طبخ = 'to cook'--> 'to ripen'], *because during this month fruits ripen*; corresponds to last part of Xermanan خەرمانان (P murdād مرداد) [Leo] & 1st part of Gelawêj گەلاویژ/Berewpayîz بەرەوپاییز (P šahrīvar شهریور) [Virgo] [F/K/A/JB3/IFb/B/JJ/HH/GF/TF/OK]

t'ebax II تەباخ *m.(B)/f.(K/JJ/JB1-S)* **(/-a;).** 1) {syn: belg; p'el I} sheet, leaf (of paper) : **•Me *t'ebaxe* k'aẍez kirye bin xalîçê** (Ba3-1) We put *a sheet of* paper under the carpet; 2) layer, stratum. {also: t'ebaẍ II (B-2); tebeq II (JB1-A/SK/GF); t'ebeq (JB1-S); t'evax (Ba3-1); [tabaq] طبق (JJ)} <Ar ṭabaq طبق = 'layer'; Sor tebeq تەبەق [Ba3-1/K/B//JJ//SK/GF]

tebaẍ I تەباغ (B) = hoof and mouth disease. See **tebeq I**.

t'ebaẍ II تەباغ (B) = sheet *(of paper)*; layer. See **t'ebax II**.

T'ebaẍ III تەباغ (B) = August. See **Ṯebax I**.

tebe تەبە (GF)/te'be تەعبە (B) = wild animal, beast. See **tabe**.

tebek تەبەك (GF/Elk)/ṯebek طەبەك (FS) = hoof and

mouth disease. See **tebeq I**.

t'ebel تەبەل *f.* **(-a;).** marble, small glass balls that boys like to play with: **•Ew bi *t'ebelan* dileyzit** (FS) He plays with *marbles*. {syn: dîndoq; mat I; ẍar III} [Bw/FS/Wkt]

tebeq I تەبەق *f.* **(;-ê).** foot and mouth disease, hoof and mouth disease (of cattle): **•*Tebek* lê ketiye** (GF) [The animal] has come down with *hoof and mouth disease*. {also: debaẍ (K/B); tebaq (IFb); tebaẍ I (B); tebek (GF/Elk); t̲ebek (FS); tebexe (K-2); teweg (IFb-2); <t̲ebeq> طبق (HH)} {syn: mazber; *şebek} Cf. T tabak; Sor tebeq تەبەق [A//HH//GF/Elk//FS//K/B//IFb] <kam II>

tebeq II تەبەق (JB1-A/SK/GF)/t'ebeq (JB1-S) = sheet *(of paper)*; layer. See **t'ebax II**.

tebeřuk تەبەڕوك (SK) = talisman. See **t'iberk**.

tebesî تەبەسی *adj.* turquoise, light blue. {syn: pîroze} [Elk/FJ] <heşîn>

tebexe تەبەخە (K) = hoof and mouth disease. See **tebeq I**.

t'ebitîn تەبِتین *vi.* **(-t'ebit-).** to calm down, become tranquil: **•Sewê heta nîv saetekê pa, nîv saeteke şûn ve tu deng ji sînor nehat. Dilê Sewê *tebitî*** (Nofa, 91) S. waited for half an hour, after half an hour there was no sound from the border. S. calmed down [lit. 'S.'s heart *calmed down*']. {syn: ȟewhan} <Ar √t̲-b-t ثبت = 'to stand firm' [Nofa/K/IFb/GF/TF/ZF3/Wkt/FD/CS/FS]

t̲ebî'et طەبیعەت/**t'ebî'et** [K] تەبیعەت *f.(K)/m.(SK/Z-2)* **(-a/-ê;-ê/).** 1) {syn: siruşt; xweza} nature *(lit. & fig.)*; essence; 2) {syn: t'aybetmendî; sexlet; xeyset} characteristic, property, quality, trait; character, disposition, temper. {also: tabiyet (IFb); t'eb[î]yet (B); t'ibîȟet, m. (Z-2); [tabiãt] طبيعت (JJ); <tebî'et طبيعت/teb'et طبعت> (HH)} <Ar ṭabī'ah طبيعة = 'nature' [Z-2//K/SK//B//IFb//JJ//HH] <t'aybetî>

t'ebîyet تەبییەت (B) = nature; characteristic. See **t̲ebî'et**.

teblî تەبلی (GF) = ashtray. See **t̲eblîk**.

t̲eblîk طەبلیك *f.* **(-a;).** ashtray: **-t̲eblîka cigara** (FS) do. {also: teblî (GF)} {syn: xwelîdank} [Wkt/FS//GF]

t'eblîx تەبلیخ *f.* **().** notification, announcement, communiqué, paper; report: **•*Teblîx* û axaftinên di vê sempozyumê de hatin pêşkêşkirin bi naverok û mijarên xwe balkêş û xurt bûn** (Nbh 125:6) *The papers* and talks which were presented in this symposium were interesting and strong in their content and topics. {also: t'eblîẍ, m. (K)} < Ar tablīɣ تبليغ < ballaɣa II بلّغ = 'to convey, transmit, report, communicate' [Nbh/ZF//K] <řagihandin; řapor>

t'eblîẍ تەبلیغ, m. (K) = notification; report. See **t'eblîx**.

tebûr تەبوور *f.* **(-a;-ê).** wooden pitchfork for winnowing grain: **•Wî coxîn bi *tebûrê* da bayî** (FS) He winnowed the threshing floor with *a pitchfork*. {also: <tebûr> تبور (HH)} {syn: k'arêc; milêb} [A/IFb/HH/ZF3/FS] <kunore; sêguh I>

t'ebyet تەبیەت (B) = nature; characteristic. See **t̲ebî'et**.

teda تەدا (K)/te'da تەعدا (GF) = oppression. See **te'darî**.

t'edarek تەدارەك (K) = preparations; repair. See **t'edarik**.

t'edarik تەدارِك *m./f.(HR)* **(-ê/-a;).** 1) {syn: k'ar II} preparations, gathering together the necessary articles *(for a journey)*: **•Wê keç'kê jî çiqa mala wê *tidarika* wê hebû, berê xwe bar kir û bi Ûsufşa řa hat** (HR 3:155) That girl loaded up whatever goods, whatever *preparations* she had, and came with U.; **-t'edarik kirin** (K) to make preparations, get ready *(for a journey)*; 2) correction, repair (K). {also: t'edarek (K); tedaruk (SK); tidarik (HR); t'ivdarek (B/F/K-2); [tedarik] تدارك (JJ); <tedarik> تدارك (HH)} < Ar tadāruk تدارك --> T tedarik = 'preparations' [JR/IFb/JJ/HH//SK//K//F/B//HR]

te'darî تەعداری *f.* **(-ya;-yê).** oppression, injustice, persecution; disturbance, bothering, torment[ing], torture; violence, robbery, assault: **•Çu zemanan deh sal li-dû-yêk neçûne ku li cîyekî mezinekî Kurdan ji zulm û *te'eddîya* 'Usmanîyan neçar nebûbît bi eşqîyatîyê yan ȟelatinê bo-naw dewletkî dî yan bi şeř kirinê ȟetta meȟw bûy** (SK 56:639) At no time have ten years on end gone by without some Kurdish leader in some place having been obliged, by the tyranny and *oppression* of the Ottomans, to take either to rebellion or flight to another state or fighting to the death **•Sûto û kuřêt wî û birayêt wî û hemî mezinêt ocaẍa wî gelek zulm û *te'eddîyê* li Řêkanîyan kirin** [sic] (SK 61:730/ST, 15) Suto, with his sons, his brothers, and the elders of his clan visited many persecutions and *impositions* upon the Rekani; **-te'darî lê kirin** (Bw)/**tadayî** ~ (IFb) to bother, torment, disturb, harass; torture, cause discomfort: **•Çel keleş ... gelikî *tadeyê li***

xelkê *dikin* (L) Forty brigands ... greatly *harass* the people •**Kesekî *tade li* te *ne kirîye*** (L) *No*body *has done* you any *harm* •***Te'darî li* min *neke*** (Bw) *Don't torment* me! {also: t'ada (K-2/IF)/tada (IFb-2/GF); t'adarî (K); tadayî (IFb/OK); t'ade (L); teda (K-2); te'da (GF-2); te'eddî (SK); [tadoiī] تـــداى (JJ-Rh); <te'edda تـــعـــدّا/te'edahî تـعـداهـى> (HH); <te'eda> تـەعـەدا (Hej)} <Ar ta'addá V تـــعـــدّى & verbal noun ta'addī تـــعـــدّي (ta'add[in] تـــعــدٍّ) (√'-d-w عـدو, e.g., 'adūw عـــدوّ = 'enemy'): *Forms in -darî [with -r-] perhaps by identification with such words as* ***z̤ordarî*** [L//Bw/Hk//K//IFb/OK//HH//SK//Hej//GF] <destdirêjî>

tedaruk تەداروك (SK) = preparations. See **t'edarik**.

tedbîr تـــەدبـــيـــر (SK/IFb/OK/JJ/HH) = plan, plot. See **t'evdîr**.

te'eddî تەعەددى (SK) = oppression. See **te'darî**.

t'efandin تـــەفـــانـــدِن *vt.* **(-t'efîn-).** 1) {syn: mirandin; temirandin; vekuştin; vemirandin; vêsandin} to extinguish, put out *(fire, lights)*; 2) {syn: qiř kirin} to destroy, ruin: •**Em çewa bikin, evî zalimî mêrg û çîman, baẍ û baẍçê me *t'efand û xirab kir*** (IS-#53) What should we do? this tyrant has *ruined* our meadows and gardens! {also: [tefandin] طفاندين (JJ); <t̲efandin طفاندن (dit̲efîne) (دطفينه)> (HH)} <Ar ṭafi'a طَـفِـئَ = 'to be extinguished' [IS/K/IFb/OK//JJ/HH] <t'efîn>

t'efekûrî تـــەفـــەكـــوورى *f.* **(-ya;-yê).** 1) worry, concern, care: •**Ser vê xeberê Qeret'ajdîn gelek *t'efekûrî k'işand*** (FK-eb-1, 282) After hearing this, Qeretajdîn *became mournful* •**T'enê *t'efekûrîya* kuřê xweyî Bênamsda bû** (Ba-1, #34) His only *concern* was for his son Benams; 2) [*adj.*] sad, gloomy, mournful (B): **-t'efekûrî bûn** (B) to be sad; **-t'efekûrî kirin** (B) to sadden, make mournful. <Ar tafakkur تـــفـــكّـــر = 'contemplation, reflection, meditation' [Ba-1/FK-eb-1/K/B]

t'efîn تەفين *vi.* **(-tef-).** to be extinguished, go out (fire, lights): •**Ji ber ku tenê komên dildar mudaxileyî şewatê dikin, şewat *natefe*** (mezopotamyaajansi.com 23.viii.2018) Because on volunteer/amateur groups are interfering with the conflagration, the fire *is not being extinguished.* {also: [tefiian] طفيان (JJ); <t̲efan طـــفـــان (dit̲efe) (دطـــفـــه)> (HH)} {syn: temirîn; vemirîn; vêsîn} <Ar ṭafi'a طَـــفِـــئَ = 'to be extinguished' [IFb/OK//JJ/HH] <t'efandin>

tefşî (OK) تەفشى = adze. See **t'evşo**.

t̲eharet طەھارەت (SK/HH) = ritual purity. See **t̲aret**.

tehb تەھب (ZF) = patience; suffering. See **t'ab**.

tehel تەھەل (OK) = spleen. See **teḧêl**.

t'eher تـــەهـــەر *m.* **(-ê;-î).** 1) {syn: awa; celeb I; cûře} way, manner, method: •**Min k'esek nedît *teherê vî xanî*** (Z-1) I haven't seen anyone *who fits the description of* this khan; **-bi vî t'eherî** (Ba) in this way; 2) {syn: řawe} mood, mode *(of verb, e.g., indicative, subjunctive, etc.)*: **-t'eherê fermanîyê** (B/F) imperative mood; **-t'eherê şertî** (B) conditional mood. [Ba/F/K/IFb/B/GF]

tehewî تەهەوى (GF) = hackberry tree. See **tihok**.

tehil تەهِل (SW/TF) = bitter. See **tal I**.

tehisandin تـــەهِـــســـانـــدِن (IFb) = to cause to slip. See **teḧisandin**.

tehisîn تەهِسين (RZ) = to slip. See **teḧisîn**.

tehjî تەهژى (IFb) = greyhound. See **tajî**.

tehl تەهل (JB3/IFb/RZ) = bitter. See **tal I**.

tehlik تەهلِك (TF) = unripe melon. See **talik**.

tehlî تەهلى (K/JB3) = bitterness. See **talî I**.

tehlûke تەهلووكە (BX) = danger. See **talûke**.

tehn تەهن (GF) = energy, power. See **tên**.

teht تەهت (RN/IFb/GF/TF/K/SW) = boulder; cliff. See **tat I**.

tehvî تەهڤى (GF) = cloudburst. See **tavî**.

tehwî تەهوى (Wkt) = hackberry tree. See **tihok**.

t̲eḧêl طـەحێـل *f.* **(-a;).** spleen. {also: tal II (IFb); tehel (OK); tihe'l [sic] (GF); tihêl (TF); [tahhel طـحـل (JJ-G)} {syn: dêdik; fateřeşk; xalxalk} < Ar ṭiḥāl طحال (*pl.* ṭuḥul طـحـل) = 'spleen, milt'; = Sor sipił سپڵ [Bw//IFb//OK//GF//TF//JJ-G]

teḧfîl تـەحفيل *f.* **( ).** cleansing or bathing seven times, to purify o.s. after sex; washing a bowl seven times after a dog licked it (FS): **-xwe tahfîl kirin** (ZZ-I) to bathe after sex: •**Mêrê min paşa ye û mêrê wê gavan e! Her sibe ew *xwe* li ser kanîyê *tahfîl dike*, û ez ancax heftîyek yan deh rojan carekê *xwe tahfîl dikim*!** (ZZ-I, 110) My husband is a pasha, and her husband is a cowherd! Every morning she *bathes* [=purifies herself] at the spring, and I only *bathe* [=purify myself] once every week to ten days •**Şirînê qazana ku seyî devê xwe kirî têda, *teḧfîl kir*** (FS) Sh. *cleaned seven times* the pot which the dog had put its mouth on. {also: tahfîl (ZZ-1); <teḧfîl> تـحـفـيـل (HH)} Cf. Ar √ḥ-f-l حـفـل = 'to celebrate' [ZZ-1//HH/GF/FS]

teḧil تەحِل (FS) = bitter. See **tal I**.

teḧisandin تەحِساندِن *vt.* **(-teḧisîn-).** to cause to slip or trip. {also: tehisandin (IFb)} {syn: lik'umandin; şemitandin} [Bw/FS//IFb] <teḧisîn>

teḧisîn تەحِسین *vi.* **(-teḧis-).** to slip, slide; to trip and fall, stumble. {also: tasyan (SK); tehisîn (RZ); <teḧisîn> تحسين (HH)} {syn: alîn [2]; hilîngiftin; hilpekîn; lik'umîn; şelifîn} [Zx/M/HH/FS//RZ//SK] <[r̄a]şiqitîn>

teḧlatî تەحلاتی (FS) = bitterness. See **talî I**.

teḧle تەحلە, m. (Bw/FS) = sorghum. See **t̲ale**.

teḧlik تەحلِك (FS) = unripe melon. See **talik**.

teḧlî تەحلی (FS) = bitterness. See **talî I**.

teḧlîşk تەحلیشك (Bw/FS) = type of weed. See **talîşk**.

teîfe تەئیفە (F) = tribe. See **t̲ayfe**.

teîr تەئیر (F/J) = bird. See **teyr**.

teîrok تەئیرۆك (F) = hail[stones]. See **teyrok**.

te'îtawûk تەعیتاووك (Kmc) = hackberry tree. See **tihok**.

***tej I** تەژ *f.* **().** unit of measure equal to one-fourth (1/4) of a dönüm, or 250 square meters (IF) [cf. T evlek] {syn: lat [2]} [IFb]

tej II تەژ *m./f.(ZF3/Wkt/FS)* **(; têj/-ê).** 1) type of thin, napless carpet; long thin napless carpet or kilim: **•Ew li ser *tejê* rûnişt û pala xwe da berpalî, û di pencerê r̄a li rêhlî nêrî** (FS) S/he sat on *the carpet* and reclined on the bolster, and regarded the woods through the window; 2) tent strip made of black goathair (A/B). [K/A/IFb/B/GF/ZF3/Wk/FSt] <tejik I>

tejik I تەژِك *m.* **().** 1) kilim, flat-weave pileless carpet; 2) garment made of flax (HH). {also: <t̲ejik> طژك (HH)} {syn: ber̄ IV; cacim; cil II; gelt; k'ilîm; merş} [K/A//HH] <tej II>

tejik II تەژِك (Dz) = young of animal, cub. See **têjik**.

tejî I تەژی (JB3/IFb/JJ/HH/SK) = full. See **t'ijî**.

te'jî II تەعژی (F/B/Dz/Ag) = greyhound. See **tajî**.

t'ek تەك *f.* **().** 1) {syn: fer I; kit} one of a pair; unit; item: **•*t'eke* çarix** (B) *one* slipper **•*t'eke* gore** (B) *one* sock; 2) coin equivalent to 2 1/2 kurushes (HH); 3) [*adj.*] {syn: t'enê} sole, alone, single; 4) [*adv.*] only, just: **•Ew jî dihate meydanê, wekî *t'ek* dîndara Ûsib bibîne** (Ba) He came to the square *just* to see Joseph's countenance. {also: [teké] تكه (JJ); <tek> تك (HH)} Cf. Mid P tāg = 'item, unit; alone, single' (M3); P tak تك --> T tek; Sor tek تەك = 'one of a pair, single thing' {t'ektî} [Ba/K/IFb/B/HH/GF//JJ] <cot; ḧeb; kit>

t'eker تەكەر *f.* **(-a;-ê).** wheel; tire [Br. tyre]: **•Wê *tekerên* te di nav heriyê de bimînin. Û *tekerên* min wê biteqin eger em di vê rewşê de man** (HYma 48) Your *tires* will remain in the mud. And my *tires* will burst if we stay in this condition. {also: t'ekere (B); t'ekerek (K/RZ-2); [tekeré] تكره (JJ); <tekelek> تكلك (HH)} {syn: çerx} <T tekerlek [HYma/IFb/RZ//B/JJ//K//HH]

t'ekere تەكەرە (B/JJ) = wheel, tire. See **t'eker**.

t'ekerek تەكەرەك (K/RZ) = wheel, tire. See **t'eker**.

tekoz تەكۆز (FS) = complete, perfect. See **t'ekûz**.

teksî تەكسی (SS) = taxi cab. See **t'aksî**.

t'ektî تەكتی *f.* **(;-yê).** solitude, loneliness. [K/B/ZF3] <t'ek>

tekuz تەكوز (TF) = complete. See **t'ekûz**.

t'ekûz تەكووز *adj.* complete, perfect, of high quality, fine: **•Ev goharto ji gişan *tekûztir* e** (DM) This version is *the most complete* of all. {also: tekoz (FS); tekuz (TF)} [DM/K(s)/GF/ZF3//TF//FS]

te'l تەعل (B/HH/JB1-S) = bitter. See **tal I**.

telandin تەلاندِن *vt.* **(-telîn-).** to hide *(vt.)*, conceal: **-xwe telandin** = to hide *(vi.)* {syn: telîn; xwe veşartin; xwe xef kirin}. {syn: veşartin} Cf. Turoyo t-l-y = 'to be removed' [Z-1/K/B] <telîn>

telar تەلار *f.* **().** balcony. {syn: behwe; palkon; r̄ewaq [4]; yazlix̧} Cf. P tālār تالار = 'hall, parlor' [IFb/OK/ZF3/Wkt]

telaş I تەلاش (; telêş) (A/IFb/B/JJ/HH) = wood chips, filings, sawdust. See **telîş**.

t'elaş II تەلاش (K/GF) = worry, concern. See **t'alaş**.

telaşe تەلاشە (IFb) = worry, concern. See **t'alaş**.

te'layî تەعلایی (B) = bitterness. See **talî I**.

te'ld•e تەعلدە *m.(K/B)/f.(JB3)* **(•ê/;).** 1) cover, concealment, camouflage: **•Melle ... ber *te'ldê* landikê rûnişt** (Dz) The mollah ... sat down under *the concealment of* the cradle [=hid behind the cradle]; 3) [*adj.*] secluded: **•cîyê te'lde** (B) secluded place **•Heryek diçe cîkî te'lde** (Ba) Each one goes to a secluded place; 2) shelter. {also: talde (K/IFb/GF/FS); [taldé] تالده (JJ)} [Ba/A/JB3/B//K/IFb/JJ/GF/FS]

t'elef تەلەف *f.* **().** loss, perdition, destruction: **-ber telef çûn** (L) to go to waste, be wasted: **•Taba min *ber telef neçe*** (L) [So that] my pains *won't go to waste*; **-t'elef kirin** (IFb/SK/OK) to destroy: **•Şukr bo xudê ku min dujminê xo *telef kir* û tola xo kireve, ez mam selamet** (SK 61:774 = ST, 30 [2nd group]) Thank God, I *have finished off* my enemy and taken my revenge in safety [lit. 'I remained safe']. {also: [telef] تلف (JJ)} < Ar talaf تلف [L/K/IFb/JJ/SK/OK]

t'elefon تەلەفۆن *f.* **(-a;-ê).** telephone, phone: **-t'elefonî *fk-î* kirin** (ZF) to telephone, ring up, call s.o. up [on the phone]: **•*Telefonî* min *bikin* sibe** (tatoeba.org) *Call* me tomorrow. {also: t'êlêfon (B)} {syn: bihîstok[2]} < Gr tēl- τηλ- = 'far, distant' + phōnē φώνη = 'voice' [K/A/IFB/TF/RZ/ZF/SS/CS//B]

t'elegraf تـەلـەگـراف (K) = telegram; telegraph. See **t'êlgraf**.

telep تەلەپ (BK) = group. See **t'elp**.

teletel تـەلـەتـەل/**tele-tel** تـەلـە تـەل [K/F] *adv.* sneakily, secretly, surreptitiously; unnoticed; silently, without a sound: **•Em *teletel* çûne hundurê malê** (B) We *secretly* went inside the house **•Vira Aqûb *teletel diçe* ber hewz** (Ba3-3, #5) Here Jacob *sneaks* over to the pool. {syn: ker̄eker̄} [Ba3/F/K/B/GF] <ber xweda; telîn>

televizyon تـەلـەڤِـزيـۆن (SBx/SS) = television. See **t'elevîzyon**.

t'elevîzyon تەلەڤیزیۆن *f.* **(-a;-ê).** television, TV: **•Her serê saetekê li xeberên *televîzyonê* guhdarî kirin** [sic] (SBx, 16) At the start of each hour they listened to the *TV* news **•Ma niha ev çi hime hima vê *televizyonê* ye bi ser me de ji bona Xwedê?** (SBx, 17) Now what is this booming of this *television* over our heads, for heaven's sake? **•Serokê PKKê ... di *Televizyona* MEDê de dijûn bi hin kesan kirine** (Z. Zinar, introd.) The leader of the PKK ... cursed some people on MED *TV* **•Xelîl Beg bi qumanda di destê xwe de dengê *televizyonê* hebekî kêm kir** (SBx, 17) Kh.B. turned down the sound of the *TV* a little bit with the remote in his hand. {also: televizyon (SBx-2/SS); telewîzyon (IFb/CS)} < Eng television < Gr tēl- τηλ- = 'far, distant' + Lat vision- = 'vision, sight' (visum = 'seen' < videre = 'to see') [SBx/RZ/ZF//SS//IFb/CS]

telewîzyon تـەلـەویـزیـۆن (IFb/CS) = television. See **t'elevîzyon**.

telexraf تـەلـەخـراف (IFb) = telegram; telegraph. See **t'êlgraf**.

telgiraf تەلگِراف (FJ/TF/CS) = telegram; telegraph. See **t'êlgraf**.

telgraf تـەلـگـراف (A/ZF) = telegram; telegraph. See **t'êlgraf**.

telh•e تەلهە [IFb/Hej]/**ṯelh•e** طەلهە [Bw/FS] *f.* **(•a;•ê).** trap or snare for catching big animals (bear, wolf, deer, fox, sheep): **•Rûvî gelek lebat kir ku xwe ji *ṯelhê* bînit der** (FS) The fox thrashed about a lot to get itself out of *the trap*; **-ṯelha ravê/~ nêçîra** (Bw) do. {also: ṯelik I (Hk); telî II (Zeb); <telhe> تـەلـهـە (Hej)} <O Ir *tanθra- = 'stretched', cf. P tār تـار = 'string'; Mid P talag (M3); P tale تـلـه; Sor tełe تەڵە [Bw/FS/IFb/Hej//Hk//Zeb] <dav I; sîte; tepik I; xefik>

ṯelik I طەلِك (Hk) = trap. See **telhe**.

te'lik II تەعلِك (GF) = unripe melon. See **talik**.

t'eliqîn تـەلِـقـيـن *vi.* **(-t'eliq-).** to give birth to pups *(of dogs)*: **•Em dibêjin jinê welidand; kûçik *teliqî*, mih/bizin/çêlek za** (kulturname-Amîdabad 2.ix.2012) We say that a woman gave birth; a dog *had puppies*, a sheep/goat/cow brought forth its young. {also: deliqîn (IFb-2/OK-2); ter̄ikîn II (Bt/B)} Sor terekîn تـەرەكـيـن = 'to whelp, produce pups' [Qzl/K/IFb/OK/FJ//Bt/B] <avis; welidîn; zayîn>

ṯelism طەلِسم (M-Zx) = talisman, charm. See **t'ilism**.

telî I تەلی (HR-I) = finger. See **t'ilî I**.

telî تەلی (Zeb) = trap. See **telhe**.

telîn تەلین *vi.* **(-tel-).** to hide (vi.) , conceal o.s.: **•Zînê k'etibû bin qap'ûtê Memê, *telîya bû*** (Z-1) Zin got under Mem's coat, she *hid*. {syn: xwe telandin; xwe veşartin; xwe xef kirin} Cf. Turoyo t-l-y = 'to be removed' [Z-1/K/A/B] <telandin>

t'elîs تـەلـيـس *m.* **(-ê;).** sack made of hemp: **•*T'elîsek* arvan li ser pişta wîye** (Z-2, 74) *A sack of* flour on his back... {also: <telîs> تـلـيـس (HH)} {syn: ç'ewal; ferde; gûnîk; mêşok; t'êr̄ III} [Z-2/A/IFb/HH/GF/Bw/ZF3]

telîş I تەلیش *m.* **().** 1) {syn: qirş} (wood) splinter, chip (S&E/K); filings, sawdust; 2) {syn: ker I; kerî I; p'ar II; parî; p'erçe; qet II; şeq} slice, piece (A). {also: telaş I (; telêş) (A/IFb/B); t'eraş I; tilîş (S&E-2/K); [telach] تـلاش (JJ); <ṯelaş> طـلاش (HH)} Cf. T t[ı]raş = 'shave, shaving' & talaş = 'wood shavings, sawdust'; Sor tełaş تـەڵاش = 'shavings' [S&E//K//A/IFb/B/JJ//HH] <teraştin>

telîş II تەلیش (GF) = bandage. See **ter̄îş**.

t'elp تـەلـپ *m.* **(-ê;).** 1) a thick group of clouds (IFb); thick fog or smoke (K); storm cloud (K): **•*telpek* ewrî reş** (IFb) *a mass of* black clouds **•*telpek* avê** (IFb) *a mass of* water; 2) herd or flock *(of birds or animals)*: **•*telpek* têr** (IFb) *a flock of* birds; 3) group *(of soldiers)* (IF); group *(of men or horsemen)* (BK): **•*telpê* êsker** (IFb) *troop of* soldiers. {also: telep (BK)} [K/IFb//BK] <[1] ewr; p'elte; [2] kerî II; r̄evo; [3] cêrge; lek>

t'elqe تەلقە (Elk) = pulling, yanking. See **t'eqil**.

telẍraf تـەلـەغـراف (SK) = telegram; telegraph. See **t'êlgraf**.

tem تـەم (F)/te'm تـەعـم (B/J/Ba2) = taste; tasty food; tasting. See **ta'm**.

temah تەماھ (IFb) = greedy; greed. See **tima**.

t'emam تـەمـام *adj.* 1) {syn: gişk; her; ḧemû} all *[generally follows the word it modifies]*: **•Ezê vê qesrê û malê têde *timam* teslîmê te bikim** (L) I will hand over to you this palace and *all* the property in it **•Teyr *t'emam* bin destê Silêman-p'êxemberda bûn** (Z-828) The birds were *all* under the control [lit. 'hand'] of Solomon the prophet; 2) whole, entire, complete *[generally precedes the word it modifies]*: ***•timam* libsê wan sor** (L) their *whole* garb--red [=they (are) entirely clad in red]. {also: timam (L); [temam] تـمـام (JJ); <temam> تمام (HH)} < Ar tamām تمام; Sor tewaw تەواو {t'emamî} [L/K/JB3/IFb/B/JJ/HH]

t'emamî تـەمـامـی *f.* **(-ya;-yê).** 1) entirety; sum total, aggregate: **-bi temamî** (SK) entirely; 2) the whole, the entire: ***•T'emamîa* cim'etê bi ḧewask'arî Meyanê diniḧêre** (Ba3-3, #9) The entire group [lit. '*the entirety of* the group'] looked at Meyaneh with interest ***•t'emamîya* dunîyaê** (B) *the whole* world ***•temamiya* gund** (IF) *the whole* village ***•t'emamîya* welêt** (B) *the whole* country. [Ba3/K/IF/B/SK] <t'emam>

t'emar تـەمـار/**te'mar** تـەعـمـار [B] *f.* **(-a;-ê).** 1) vein; 2) nerve(s). {also: damar (K/IFb-2/JB3); demar (FS-2); tamar (B-2/K-2/GF-2/FS); [tamar] طـمـر (JJ); <ṯemar> طـمـار (HH)} < T damar = 'vein'; Sor demar دەمار = 'vein, nerve'; Za damari/tamar *f.* (Mal) [F/IFb/GF//B//HH//K/JB3//FS//JJ] <betan[1]; xwîn>

temaşa تـەمـاشـا (A/JB3/JJ/HH/GF) = spectacle, show. See **t'emaşe**.

t'emaş•e تـەمـاشـە *f.* **(•a;•ê).** sight, spectacle, show: **-li *ft-î* temaşe kirin / temaşa *ft-î* kirin** = to observe, watch, look at: **•Ev e nîv saeta min qedîya, ez ji xwe re *li* te *temaşe bikim*** (L) I'*ve been watching* you for half an hour **•Wele, wekî ez bimirim jî, ezê xweȓa rabim, *li* Memê *t'emaşekim.* Xulam çû dîwanêda sekinî û *t'emaşa* Memê *kir*** (EP-7) By God, even if I were dying, I'd get up *to have a look at* Mem. They boy went and stood in the divan and *looked at* Mem. {also: temaşa (A/JB3/GF); [temásca] تماشا (JJ); <temaşa> تماشا (HH)} < P temāšā تماشا (of Arabic origin) [L/K/B/IFb//A/JB3/JJ/HH/GF]

t'embe تەمبە = instructions; warning; order. See **t'emî**.

t'embel تەمبەل adj. lazy. {also: t'emel (GF-2); t'enbel; [tenbel] تنبل (JJ)} {syn: t'iȓal} Cf. P tanbal تنبل -> T tembel; Hau temeł (M4) {t'embel[t]î; t'enbel[t]î} [Dz/F/K/B/GF//JJ]

t'embelî تـەمـبـەلـی *f.* **(-ya;-yê).** laziness: **•Tedbîr bi-senaî ye, emma ḧetta noke me ji *tembelî* nekiriye** (SK 19:177) The remedy is easy, but up till now we have not applied it out of *laziness*. {also: t'embeltî (K/B); t'enbelî (K); t'enbeltî (K)} {syn: t'iȓalî} [K/B/SK/GF] <t'embel>

t'embeltî تەمبەلتی (K/B) = laziness. See **t'embelî**.

t'emberî تـەمـبـەری *f.* **(-ya;-yê).** forelock, curl falling on the forehead, bangs (of men's hair). {also: t'emborî (K-2/GF-2/Kmc); temelî (Kmc-2); t'emerî (K-2/Kmc-2); t'emorî (K-2/B); temorîk (Kmc-2); [temerou تـمـرو/temelí تـمـلـی (Lx)/yäk tämbari (PS)/temouri تـمـوری] (JJ); <tenbûrî> تـنـبـوری (HH)} {syn: t'ûncik} [Qzl/A/FJ/IFb/GF//Kmc//B//HH//JJ] <bisk; çiẍ; gulî I; kezî; poȓ III>

tembih تـەمبِە = instructions; warning; order. See **t'emî**.

t'embî تـەمـبـی (B) = instructions; warning; order. See **t'emî**.

t'emborî تـەمـبـۆری (K/GF/Kmc) = forelock. See **t'emberî**.

t'embûr تـەمـبـوور *f.* **(-a;-ê).** tambur, Kurdish musical string instrument, identical with Turkish saz/ bağlama: **•Li *tembûra* xwe dixe** (L) He plays his *tambur* ***•Tembûra* xwe danî ser çoga xwe** (L) He put his *tambur* on his knee **•Û ji xwe re li *tembûrê* dixe** (L) And he plays to himself on the *tambur*. {also: t'embûre (B-2); [tambúr] تـنـبـور (JJ)} [L/K/JB3/IFb/B/JJ/GF]

t'embûre تـەمـبـووره (B) = musical string instrument. See **t'embûr**.

teme I تەمە (F/JJ) = checkers. See **dame**.

t'eme II تـەمـە (Z-1) = instructions; warning; order. See **t'emî**.

temeh تـەمـەھ (IFb) = instructions; warning; order. See **t'emî**.

t'emel تەمەل (GF) = lazy. See **t'embel**.

temelî تەمەلی (Kmc) = forelock. See **t'emberî**.

t'emen تەمەن *m.* **(-ê;).** age, years (of person): **•Evîn-darî *temenê* mirov dirêj dike** (Rûdaw 17.ii.2018) Love lengthens *the span of one's life* **•Navê jina wî Xemê bû ew pênc sal bûn anîbû, dema anî jî *temenê* wî ji sihan derbas bûbû** (DBgb, 7) His wife's name was Khemê, he had married her 5 years before, when he married her his *age* was over thirty •***Temenê* te çend e?** (Wkt/BF) How old are you? [lit. 'How much is your *age*?']. {syn: 'emir II; jî III} < Sor temen تەمەن [(neol)Rûdaw/DBgb/IFb/FJ/GF/TF/Kmc/RZ/IFb/Wkt/ZF3/BF/FD//CS/SS]

t'emerî تەمەری (K/Kmc) = forelock. See **t'emberî**.

temesî تەمەسی (GF/HH) = woman's silk head scarf. See **t'emezî**.

t'emet تەمەت *prep*. the same size or age as (in comparisons): •**Azad *temet* Behremî ye** (FS) A. is *the same size (or age) as* B. •**Ev kevre *temet* xanîyekî ye** (BF) This rock is *the size of* a house •**Ez ew *temet êk* în** (BF) He and I are *the same size* •**Ez ne *temetî* wî dirêj im (Ew ji min dirêjtir e)** (Wkt) I'm not as tall as him (He is taller than me). [FS/Wkt/ZF3/BF]

t'emezî تەمەزی *f.* **(-ya;-yê).** woman's silk head scarf; transparent head kerchief (Haz): •**Piştre çû *temeziya* li ser ruyê wê hilda ruyê rastê maçî kir û derket çû** (ZZ-&, 248) Afterwards he went and lifted *the kerchief* from her face and kissed her right cheek and went out. {also: temesî (GF-2); [temezi] تمزی (JJ); <temezî تمزی/ temesî تمسی> (HH)} {syn: k'itan} [Haz/K/A/IFb/B/JJ/HH/GF] <hêratî; ĥibrî; k'ofî; laç'ik; p'oşî; xavik>

temirandin تەمِراندِن/**ṯemirandin** طەمِراندِن [M-Zx] *vt.* **(-temirîn-/-ṯemirîn-**[M-Zx]**).** to extinguish, put out *(a fire)*; to turn off *(lights, radio, etc.)*: •**Min ç'ira *temirand*** (B) I *extinguished* the lamp. {also: [temirandin] طمراندين (JJ)} {syn: damirandin; mirandin; t'efandin; vekuştin; vemirandin; vêsandin; ≠dadan} [F/K/A/IFb/B/OK//JJ/M-Zx] <temirîn>

temirîn تەمِرین/**ṯemirîn** طەمِرین [Bw] *vi.* **(-temir-/-ṯemir-**[Bw]**).** 1) {syn: t'efîn; vemirîn; vêsîn} to be extinguished, go out *(a fire, the lights)*: •**Newroz bûye nîşana şoreşa Kawayên hemdemî, pêt û şûleya agirê wê daye hemû cîhanê û *natemire*** (Wlt 2:61, 13) Newroz has become the symbol of the struggle of the modern Kawas, it has lit the entire world with its flames and *will not be extinguished*; 2) to stall *(automobile)* (Bw); 3) to die (JJ); to croak, die *(of animals; contemptuously of people)* (IFb/HH). {also: [temirin] طمرين (JJ); <ṯemirîn طمرين (diṯemirî) (دطمری)> (HH)} [Bw/JJ/HH//Wlt/F/K/A/IFb/B/OK] <hilkirin [2]; temirandin>

t'emiz تەمِز *adj.* 1) {syn: p'ak [1]; p'aqij} clean, pure: •**Şivan xwer̄a nava kulîlkada diger̄in, bîna hewa ç'îyaye *t'emiz* dik'işînin** (Ba2:1, 203) Shepherds roam among the flowers, breathing in *pure* mountain air; 2) [*adv.*] thoroughly, properly: •**Evê vêcarê kurkê meĥbûb .. *t'emiz* pêç'a** (EP-7) Then she *thoroughly* swaddled the dear child. {also: temîs (SK); temîz (IFb/SK-2); [temiz] تميز (JJ); <temîz> تميز (HH)} Cf. P tamīz تميز --> T temiz; Sor temîz تەمیز = 'clean' {t'emizayî; t'emiz[t]î} [EP-7/K/B/GF//IFb/JJ/HH/OK//SK]

t'emizayî تەمِزایی (B) = cleanliness. See **t'emizî**.

t'emizî تەمِزی *f.* **().** cleanliness. {also: t'emizayî (B); t'emiztî (K); temîzî (OK)} [K//B//OK] <t'emiz>

t'emiztî تەمِزتی (K) = cleanliness. See **t'emizî**.

t'emî تەمی *f.* **(-ya;-yê).** 1) instruction(s), directive(s); 2) admonition, warning: •**Eva *t'emîya* min wer̄a** (Ba) This is my *warning* to you •***Tenbîha* min li te be** (L) Let me warn you [lit. 'May my *warning* be on you']; **-t'emî dan *fk-î*** (K) to advise, admonish, warn: •**Dibe ku te *t'emî dane* Ûsib** (Ba) Perhaps you *warned* Joseph (=tipped Joseph off); 3) order; commandment. {also: t'embe; tembih; t'embî (B); t'eme II (Z-1); temeh (IFb); tenbih (IFb-2); t'enbî; t'enbîh (-a;) (L); [tenbíh] تنبه (JJ); <tenbe[h]> تنبه (HH)} < Ar tanbīh تنبيه [Ba/K//B//Z-1//L//IFb//JJ//HH] <qewîtî>

temîs تەمیس (SK) = clean. See **t'emiz**.

temîz تەمیز (IFb/JJ/HH/OK) = clean. See **t'emiz**.

temîzî تەمیزی (OK) = cleanliness. See **t'emizî**.

t'emorî تەمۆری (K/B) = forelock. See **t'emberî**.

temorîk تەمۆریك (Kmc) = forelock. See **t'emberî**.

T'emûz تەمووز *f.* **(-a;-ê).** July: •[***T'emûz* û T'ebaxê, agir digirite axê, dû dirabite ji şaxê**] (BG) In *July* and August, fire takes hold of the soil [i.e., the soil catches fire], smoke rises from the horns (of animals) *[prv.]*. {also: [temouz] تموز (JJ); <temûz> تموز (HH); [tamouze] (BG)} {syn: Tîrmeh} Syr Tamūz ܬܡܘܙ --> Ar tammūz تمّوز -->T Temmuz; corresponds to last part of Germaciman گەرماجمان/Pûşper̄ پووشپەڕ (P tīr تیر) [Cancer] & 1st part of Xermanan خەرمانان (P murdād مرداد) [Leo] [BG//K/IFb/B/JJ/HH/GF/OK]

te'n تەعن *f.(Msr/B)/m.(K)/pl.(Msr)* **(;-ê/).** 1) scolding, criticism; reproach, reproof; blame, censure; mockery, ridicule; 2) threat, threatening action (B): **-te'n dayîn** (B) to threaten *(with words or gestures)*;

3) sharp pain (B): •**te'na birînê** (B) sharp pain from a wound. {also: tene II (F); [tan dàin] طعن داين (JJ) = 'to censure' [Fr censurer]} < Ar ṭa'n طعن = 'piercing; slandering' --> P ṭa'n طعن = 'taunting; wounding with words; reproaching' & ṭa'neh طعنه = 'sarcasm; bitter taunt; jeer' [Msr/K/B//JJ//F]

t'ena I تەنا *adj.* calm, tranquil, quiet, peaceful; safe, secure: •**Êdî bi hev re bo yekgirtinê û jîneka *tena*** (BH, 60) Let's all together [go] for unity and a *tranquil* life. {also: [taná] تنا (JJ); <tena> تەنا (Hej)} {syn: emîn; selamet} Cf. Jewish NENA tana = 'quiet, at ease' (YS) {t'enahî[1]} [BH/Bw/JJ/Hej/FS]

t'ena II تەنا (A/JB3/IFb) = alone; only. See **t'enê**.

t'enahî تەناهى *f.* **(-ya;-yê).** 1) {syn: asayîş; ewlekarî; selametî} safety; security; tranquility, calm, stability, repose (VoA/Bw/Hej): •**Emerîka pêwîste herêma *t'enahiyê* ji Kurdan re wek xwe bihêle** (VoA) America must leave the safe haven [lit. 'area of *security*'] for Kurds as it is •**Her çende welatên mezin pûte û bihayekê fer didene wê deverê ji demekê mêje, belê ta noke neşiyayne *tenahîyeka* berdewam li deverê peyda biken** (Metîn 62[1997]:25) Although the major powers have long given attention and critical importance to that region, up till now thay have not been able to bring permanent *stability* to it •***Tenahî* bi zar̄okê ket** (FS) The child fell silent [lit. 'calm fell on the child']; -**Civata t'enahiyê** (VoA) security council; 2) solitude; loneliness (JB3/IFb). See **t'enêtî**. {also: tenayî (BF); [tanāyī] تناى (JJ); <tenahî> تەناهى (Hej)} [VoA/Bw/Hej/JB3/IFb/RZ/FS//JJ-Rh] <dişliq; ewlekarî; t'ena I>

tenayî تەنايى (BF) = safety; security; calm. See **t'enahî**.

t'enbel تەنبەل = lazy. See **t'embel**.

t'enbelî تەنبەلى (K) = laziness. See **t'embelî**.

t'enbeltî تەنبەلتى (K) = laziness. See **t'embelî**.

tenbih تەنبِه (IFb) = instructions; warning; order. See **t'emî**.

t'enbî تەنبى = instructions; warning; order. See **t'emî**.

t'enbîh تەنبيه (-a;) (L) = instructions; warning; order. See **t'emî**.

t̠endûr طەندوور/**tendûr** [B]/**t'endûr** [K] تەندوور *f.* **(-a; -ê).** oven *(for baking bread)*: •**Jinikê r̄abû *tendûr* dada** (Dz) The woman got up and lit *the oven*; -**nanê t̠enûrê** = oven-baked bread. {also: tenûr (A/JB3/IFb-2/GF-2)/t̠enûr (FS); [tenour تنور/tendour تندور] (JJ); <tenûr تنور/tendûr تندور/t̠enûr طنور> (HH)} {syn: fir̄ne [2]} < Ar tannūr تنّور = 'oven'; Heb tanur תנור; Sor tenûr تەنوور/tendûr تەندوور [Dz/K//IFb/B/JJ/HH/GF//A/JB3//FS] <fir̄ne; kuçik II; t̠enûrvan; t'ifik>

tene I تەنە *f./m.(FS/ZF3)* **(/-yê;).** cereal, grain: -**paliya tenan** (Ardû, 148) grain harvest •***Tene* hîna kal e** (Ardû, 149) *The grain* is still unripe. {syn: dexl; zad} [Ardû/IFb/Kmc/AD/FS/ZF3]

tene II تەنە (F) = reproach. See **te'n**.

t'enê تەنێ *adj.* 1) alone: -**bi tenê** = alone, by oneself: •**Qîza hakim *bi tenê* ma li mix̄arê** (L) The king's daughter remained *alone* in the cave; 2) [*adv.*] only: •**Ewê *t'enê* Ûsib ḧiz dikir** (Ba) She *only* loved Joseph. {also: t'ena II (A-2/JB3/IFb-2); tenya (IF-2); [tenha] تنها (JJ); <tenê تنى/tenha تنها> (HH)} Cf. P tanhā تنها--> T tenha; Sor tenya تەنیا/tenê تەنێ = 'lone, alone' {t'enahî[2]; t'enêtî; t'enhayî} [L/K/A/JB3/IFb/B/HH/TF//JJ] <t'ek>

t'enêtî تەنێتى *f.* **(-ya;-yê).** solitude; loneliness: •**Bidû vegera wî da *tenêtiyê* ew bêhtir dorpêçkiribû** (HYma, 30) After his return, *solitude* surrounded him even more. {also: t'enahî[2] (JB3/IFb); t'enhayî (K[s])} [K/B/TF//JB3/IFb//K(s)] <t'enê>

teng I تەنگ/**t̠eng** طەنگ [FS/HH] *adj.* narrow; tight: -**bêna *fk-ê* teng bûn** (L) to be sad, upset, distressed: •***Bêna* min *teng e*** (L) I am sad, upset, distressed [lit. 'My *breath is narrow*']. {also: [tenk] تنگ (JJ); <t̠eng> طنگ (HH)} [Pok. tengh-1067] 'to pull, stretch': cf. Av θang- = 'to pull, tighten a bow'; Mid P tang = 'narrow, tight' (M3); P tang تنگ; Sor teng تەنگ = 'tight, narrow, defile, gorge'; Hau teng (M4) {tengasî; tengavî; tengayî; tengî} [Z-1/L/K/A/JB3/IFb/B/JJ/GF/OK//HH/FS] <berteng>

teng II تەنگ/**t̠eng** طەنگ [Bw/FS/HH] *m./f.(Bw)* **(-ê/-a; têng/).** saddle-girth, belly-band, band or strap *that encircles animal's body to fasten pack-saddle on its back*: -**t̠eng lê helçinîn** (Zeb) to put constraints on s.o. {also: navteng; tenge (IFb); [tenk] تنگ (JJ); <t̠eng> طنگ (HH)} {syn: kejî; kolan I; navteng; qoş [1]} Sor tenge تەنگە = 'strait, leather girth (saddlery)'; Hau teng *m.* (M4) [K/A/B/JJ/GF//IFb//HH/Bw/Zeb] <berṯeng II; hesp; k'urtan; zîn>

tenganî تەنگانى (GF) = narrowness; trouble. See **tengavî**.

tengasî تەنگاسى (K) = narrowness; trouble. See **tengavî**.

tengav تەنگاڤ/**t̠engav** طەنگاڤ [FS/HH] *adj.* 1) hard-pressed, desperate, in dire straits; 2) urgently needing to relieve o.s., badly in need of going to the bathroom. {also: tengaw (SK); [tán´gháv]

تنگاف (JJ); <tengav> طنگاف (HH)} Sor tengaw تەنگاو = 'worried' {tengavî; tengawî} [Zx/K/A/IFb/ JJ/ GF/OK//HH/FS//SK] <aciz; asê; bêgav; qehirîn>

tengavî تەنگاڤی/**tengavî** طەنگاڤی [FS] *f.* **(-ya;-yê).** 1) narrowness; 2) straits, trouble, bad situation, crisis, distress: •**Řefîqê dirust ewe ye li xoşî û *tengawîyê* řefîq bit, ne li xoşîyê bi-tinê** (SK 29:269) A true companion is one who is a companion in pleasant times and in *difficulty*, not just in pleasant times •**Roja go tuê ketî *tengîyekê* ...** (L) [If] someday you are in *trouble* [lit. 'fall into *straits*'] •**Vê mehê tu di *tengasîyê* de yî** (LC, 8) This month you are in *dire straits*. {also: tenganî (GF-2); tengasî (K-2/IFb-2/B-2/GF-2/OK-2); tengawî/tengawî (SK); tengayî (K-2/A/IFb-2/B); tengî (K-2/A-2/IFb-2/B-2/OK-2); [tenghawi تنگاڤی/tenghi تنگی] (JJ)} [L//K/IFb/GF/OK//FS//SK//A/B] <teng I; tengav>

tengaw تەنگاو (SK) = desperate. See **tengav**.

tengawî طەنگاوی/tengawî تەنگاوی (SK) = narrowness; trouble. See **tengavî**.

tengayî تەنگایی (K/A/IFb/B) = narrowness; trouble. See **tengavî**.

tenge تەنگە (IFb) = saddle-girth, bellyband. See **teng II**.

tengî تەنگی (K/A/IFb/B/JJ/OK) = narrowness; trouble. See **tengavî**.

t'enhayî تەنهایی (K[s]) = solitude; loneliness. See **t'enêtî**.

tenik تەنِك/**tenik** طەنِك [FS/HH] *adj.* 1) thin (of clothes); 2) delicate, gentle, light; fine: •**Bakî *tenik* t'eşîê dixe** (J) A *light* wind drops the spindle; 3) {syn: meyav[1]; ≠k'ûr III} shallow. {also: [tenik تنك (JJ); <tenik> طنك (HH)} Mid P tanuk = 'thin, shallow' (M3); P tonok تنك = 'sparse, shallow'; Sor tenik تەنِك = 'thin, shallow' {tenikahî; tenikayî; tenikî} [Ad/K/A/IFb/B/JJ/JB1-S/OK/ /HH/FS]

tenikahî تەنِكاهی (IFb) = thinness; shallowness. See **tenikayî**.

tenikayî تەنِكایی *f.* **(-ya;).** 1) thinness: •***tenikîya* peřokê** (FS) *thinness* of the cloth; 2) delicateness, gentleness, softness; 3) shallowness. {also: tenikahî (IFb); tenikî (K-2)/tenikî (FS)} [K/B//FS/ /IFb] <tenik>

tenikî تەنِكی (K)/tenikî طەنِكی (FS) = thinness; shallowness. See **tenikayî**.

tenişt تەنِشت/**tenişt** طەنِشت [SK/HH/FS] *f.* **(-a;-ê).** side, flank. {also: [tenicht] تنشت (JJ); <tenişt> طنشت (HH)} {syn: alî; hêl II; k'êlek} [K/A/JB3/IFb/B/ JJ/OK/ /HH/SK]

tenişta تەنِشتا/**t'enişta** طەنِشتا [FS] *prep.* near, beside, alongside, next to: •**Were *tenişta* min rûne** (L) Come sit *beside* me; **-li tenişta** (L/FS) do.: •**Lawik anî, *li tenişta* xwe danî** (L) She brought the child [and] set him down *beside* her •**Pezê şivanî *li tenişta* gundî bû** (FS) The shepherd's sheep were *beside* the village; -[**di**] **tenişta yekî de** (JB3) beside, next to s.o. < *ezafeh of* **tenişt** [L/K/ JB3/IFb/JB1-A//FS]

tenî تەنی/**tenî** طەنی [FS/HH] *f.* **(-ya;).** soot, thick layer of soot [T kurum]: •**Nêçîrvanêt me řûyřeşin / řûy *tenûyne*** (Bw) Our hunters are black-faced [=disgraced] / *soot*-faced. {also: tanî (TF) = tenî; tenû (Bw); [teni] تنی (JJ); <tenî> طنی (HH)} {syn: dû IV[2]} Za teney *f.* (Mal); ?<Arc tenan[a] [תננ[א/tanna תננא & Syr tinanā ܬܢܢܐ = 'smoke'; NENA tin-nâ ܬܢܢܐ/tinâ ܬܢܐ/tinâ = 'smoke' (Maclean) [Bw//K/A/IFb/JJ//HH/FS//TF] <dû IV; dûk'el; p'el II; řejî>

tenîrvan طەنیرڤان (M-Am) = baker. See **tenûrvan**.

tenû تەنوو (Bw) = soot. See **tenî**.

tenûr تەنوور (A/JB3/IFb/JJ/HH/GF)/tenûr طەنوور (FS) = oven. See **tendûr**.

tenûrvan طەنوورڤان *m.* **().** baker, bread maker; one who maintains a bread-baking oven *(tendûr)*: •**Balîl řabo, ço nik hinde xebaza, nik hindek *tenîrvana*, nan k'iřî** (M-Am, #707A, 326) B. got up, went to a few *bakers* and bought bread •**Balîl sê *tenûrvan* girt'in, nan bo peĥt** (M-Am, #707, 322) B. got 3 *bakers* to bake bread for him. {also: tenîrvan (M-Am-2)} {syn: nanpêj} Sor tenûr[e]wan تەنوورەوان (GMK) [M-Am] <tendûr>

tenya تەنیا (IF) = alone; only. See **t'enê**.

tep I طەپ [Dh]/**tep** تەپ *f.* **().** epilepsy [Ar ṣar' صرع, T sara]: •***Tep* a hatîyê/girtîyê** (Dh) He or she had an epileptic fit. {also: tap I (GF-2); <tep> تەپ (Hej)} {syn: 'edro} < Ar ṭab' طبع = 'natural disposition, temper, character'?; = Sor fê فێ [Dh/ /IFb/GF/OK/AA/Hej]

t'ep II تەپ/**tep** طەپ [SK] *f.* **(;-ê).** slap *(in the face)*, cuff, box: •**Dê *t'epek* li sêrî xist** (HCK-1, 208) The mother gave him *a slap* on the head •**Dê *t'epek* da nav ç'e'va** (HCK-1, 203) The mother gave him *a slap* between the eyes •**Wextê Eĥmed şûtika wî kirewe birîna biraê xo dît. Hat e serê**

xo bi çepelan o hat e r̄anêt xo bi *ṯepan* o tejî ser serê xo ax kir (SK 18:173) When Ahmad undid his cummerbund he saw his brother's wound. He began to slap his head and *beat* his thighs and pour earth on his head. {also: tap II (TF)} {syn: sîle; şimaq} Sor tep تەپ = 'slap, downward blow (with foot or palm of hand)' [HCK/K/B/A/IFb/TF/CS//SK]

ṯepançe طەپانچە (SK) = pistol. See **debançe**.

tepelik تەپەلِك (IFb) = drum. See **t'epliq**.

tepeser تەپەسەر: **-tepeser kirin** (AId) to oppress, suppress, repress. {syn: berṯeng kirin; p'erçiqandin} [VoA/GF/AId/ZF3]

ṯepik I طەپك [Bw/Zeb/Hk/HH/SK/FS]/**tepik** تەپك [A/IFb/JJ/GF/OK/Hej/AA] *f.* **(;-ê).** type of trap for catching birds (Bw) or mice (SK) consisting of a ditch or hole: **•Kewek ket *ṯepikê*** (FS) The partridge fell into *the trap* **•Paşî mişk hate pêş, got ... bo girtin û kuştina min kitikan bi xudan diken û *ṯepikan* dikir̄in** (SK 1:7) The the mouse came forward and said, ... to catch and kill me they keep cats and buy *traps*; **-tepikê li ber fk-î danan** (Zeb) to set or lay a trap. {also: tapik (IFb-2); [tapk] تپك (JJ-Rh); <ṯepik> طپك (HH); <tepik> تەپك (Hej)} Sor tepke تەپكە [Bw/Zeb/Hk/HH/SK/FS//A/IFb/JJ/GF/OK/Hej/AA] <dav I; sîte; telhe; xefik>

t'epik II تەپك *pl./m.(B)* pressed dung *(used as fuel)* (K); dung which has been pressed against a wall or other solid place to dry (IF): **-t'epik lê dan** (K)/ **lêxistin** (B) to press dung into 'cakes'. {also: [tepik] تپك (JJ)} {syn: k'erme; sergîn; t'ert[ik]} Cf. P tāpe تاپە = 'cow-dung' ; Sor tepałe تەپاڵە = 'cow-dung (made into cakes and dried for fuel)' [F/K/A/IFb/B/JJ/GF] <deve II; dirg; qelax; r̄îx; t'ert[ik]; zibil>

ṯepik III طەپك (FS) = ball. See **top II**.

tepilk تەپلك (GF) = drum. See **t'epliq**.

t'episandin تەپسانِدن *vt.* **(-t'episîn-).** to crush, crumple, mash, trample. {syn: dan ber lingan; dewisandin; 'eciqandin; her̄işandin; p'ekandin; p'elaxtin; p'erçiqandin; pêpes kirin} [F/K/B/GF]

tepînk تەپینك *f.* **(-a;-ê).** mine *(hidden explosive)*. {syn: leqem [2]} [IFb/OK/ZF3]

ṯepk طەپك (Bw) = ball. See **top II**.

teplik تەپلِك (IFb) = drum. See **t'epliq**.

t'epliq تەپلِق *f.* **(-a;).** hand drum, small drum: **•bi merzîqa ve û *tepliqa* ve** (L) with music and *drums*. {also: tepelik (IFb); tepilk (GF); teplik (IFb-2); <ṯepelik> طپلك (HH)} Cf. Ar ṭabl طبل & ṭablah طبلة; Sor tepł تەپڵ = 'kettle drum' [L/K//IFb/HH//GF] <def; dehol>

teqan تەقان (HH) = to split, burst; to explode. See **t'eqîn**.

t'eqandin تەقاندِن *vt.* **(-t'eqîn-).** 1) to split, crack *(vt.)*, cause to split or crack; 2) to fire or shoot *(a gun)*: **•Devançe *diteqînin*** (HM) They *shoot off* the pistol; **-tifing teqandin** (IF) to shoot off a rifle. [HM/K/A/JB3/IFb/B/GF/TF] <p'eqîn; t'eqîn>

t'eqer̄eq تەقەڕەق *f.* **(-a;-ê).** noise, tumult, clamor, uproar: **•Dema ku *teqe reqê* Hecî Sadûn ji xew rakir, nîvê mirîşkan biribûn** [sic] (HYma 49) When *the noise* roused H.S. from sleep, he had carried off half of the chickens. {also: teqûreq (GF)} {syn: galegûrt; galigal; hêwirze; hose; k'im-k'imî; qajeqaj; qerebalix; şerqîn} Sor teqe-w-r̄eqe تەقە و ڕەقە = 'noisy disturbance, fuss' [HYma/K//GF] <r̄eqer̄eq>

teqes تەقەس (GF) = for sure. See **t'eqez**.

t'eqez تەقەز *adv.* absolutely, without fail, for sure: **•*Teqez* ezê bêm** (IF) I'll *certainly* come **•*T'eqez* tu jêr̄a bibêjî** (Srk) Be *sure* to tell him. {also: teqes (GF-2)} {syn: 'ese; helbet [2]; miqîm (F); mitleq (F)} [Srk/K/IFb/GF/TF/Kmc-6936]

t'eqil تەقِل:**-teqil lêdan** (Z-2/Elk) to [cause to] move, pull, yank *(at a rope)*: **•Stîya Zîn û qerwaşa bi şerîtê girt û *t'eqil lêda*** (Z-2:89) Lady Zîn and her servants took hold of the rope and *pulled* it **•Tu tiştekê girêdidî û di nişkê da telqekê anjî *teqlekê lêdidî* û ji cih dilivînî** (Elk) You tie something up and then suddenly you *give it a yank* and make it move.{also: t'elqe (Elk-2)} [Z-2/Elk/ZF3]

t'eq•in تەقِن *f.* **(•na;•nê).** mud; clay: **•Piyê wî di *teqnê* r̄a daçika** (FS) His foot got stuck in *the mud*; **-teqn û ḧer̄î** (Zx) mud. {also: t'eqn (Zx); <teqn> تقن (HH)} {syn: ḧer̄î; qur̄; r̄iṯam} [Zx/FS//HH/FS] <ax>

teqiyan تەقِيان (JB3) = to split, burst; to explode. See **t'eqîn**.

t'eqîn تەقین *vi.* **(-t'eq-).** 1) to split, burst, crack open *(vi.)*: **•Bor dîna xwe daê, Memê *wê* ji k'erba *bit'eqe*** (EP-7) Bor saw that Mem *was about to burst* with grief **•Nerî go qundir *teqîqa* [?=*teqîya*], xortek jê derket** (L) Suddenly the gourd *split open*, [and] a young man came out of it; 2) {syn: terikîn I} to explode; to go off *(gun)*. {also: teqiyan (JB3); teqîyan (F); [teqiian تقيان/

teqin تقين] (JJ); <teqan> تقان (HH)} [L/F/K/A/JB3/IFb/B/JJ/GF/TF//HH] <t'eqandin>

teqîyan تـهقـيـان (F) = to split, burst; to explode. See **t'eqîn**.

teql تهقل (TF/HH) = weight. See **t'eqil**.

t'eqn (Zx/HH) = mud. See **t'eqin**.

teqsî تهقسی (SS) = taxi cab. See **t'aksî**.

teqsîr تهقسیر (ZF3) = negligence; sparing. See **t'exsîr**.

teqûreq تهقووڕهق (GF) = noise, clamor. See **t'eqer̄eq**.

ter̄ تـهڕ *adj.* 1) {syn: nem; şil I} wet, moist, damp *(of inanimate things, e.g., trees, plants; whereas şil I [qv.] is wet of living things)* {≠ĥişk}: •**Li ba yên hişk, *ter* jî dişewitin** (IFb) Beside the dry, *the wet* also burn [*prv.*]; -**ter̄ û telîs** (Zeb) soaking wet; 2) {syn: t'aze} fresh; young, new: -**Destê te ter̄ be** (Haz) greeting said to anyone who does stg. for you, e.g., serves you tea [lit. 'May your hand be fresh'] {cf. T eline sağlık, Ar sallim 'idēk سلّم إيديك, P dast-at dard nakonad دستت درد نکند}; 3) flexible, pliant, lithe. {also: tar (TF); [ter] تر (JJ); <ṯer> طر (HH)} [Pok. 3. ter- ... teru- : treu- 1071 ff.] 'to rub, turn, pierce': Skt táruṇa- = 'young, tender'; Av tauruna- = 'young'; Mid P tarr = 'moist, fresh' (M3); P tar تـر = 'wet, moist, fresh, green'; Sor ter̄ تـهڕ = 'wet, moist, damp, fresh'; Za tern = 'wet, fresh' (Mal); Hau ter̄ (M4) [F/K/A/IFb/B/JJ/JB1-A/SK/GF/OK//HH//TF]

tera تـهڕا: -**tera bûn** (Msr/HH/A/GF) to fall, drop *(from on high)*: •**Cewer Beg *tera* erdê *bû*** (ZZ-5, 81) J.B. *dropped/fell to* the ground; -**tera kirin** (Msr/HH) to throw, drop or knock onto the ground *(by accident or on purpose)* {syn: li 'erdê dan}: •**Min ĥebek r̄epande, ew *tera kir* 'erdê** (Msr) I slugged him one, and *knocked* him *to* the ground. {also: <ṯerabûn طـرابـون (ṯeradibe) (طرادبـه)> & <ṯerakirin طـراكـرن (ṯeradike) (طرادكه)> (HH)} [Msr/A/ZF//HH]

terakî تهراکی (A) = type of peach. See **teraqî**.

teral تهرال (LM/AD) = lazy. See **t'ir̄al**.

teralî تهرالی (LM/AD) = laziness. See **t'ir̄alî**.

terane تهرانه (A/IFb/HH/SK) = joke. See **t'ir̄ane**.

teraqî تـهراقـی *f.* (**-ya; **). nectarine; type of peach without fuzz, which grows in the area of Nusaybin. {also: terakî (A); tereqî (Bw/Kmc-2/ZF3)} Cf. Syr Ar durrāq درّاق = 'peach' [A//Bw/Kmc-2/ZF3] <xox>

t'eraş I تـهراش = wood chips, filings, sawdust. See **telîş**.

t'er̄aş II تـهڕاش/**teraş** تـهراش [OK] *m.(K/SK?)/f.(Bw/OK)* (**/-a; /-ê**). 1) {syn: devî; kem; k'ol III; t'ûm} bush, shrub: •**Ne şiv li *ter̄aşê* ye, ne ga li gar̄anê ye** (Zeb) It has nothing to do with me [lit. 'Neither the stick is in *the bush*, nor is the bull in the herd']; 2) thicket (K/SK/OK). {also: t'ir̄aş (Bw)} <Syr ṭarāšā ܛܪܫܐ/ṭarīšā ܛܪܝܫܐ = 'bush, shrub; barren oak' [Bw/AA//K/SK/OK]

teraş kirin تـهراش كِرِن (A/IFb)/t'er̄aş kirin تـهڕاش كِرِن (K) = to sharpen; to shave. See **teraştin**.

teraştin تـهراشتِن/**t'er̄aştin** [K] تـهڕاشتِن *vt.* (**-terêş-/-t'er̄êş-** [K]). 1) {syn: necirandin} to hew, whittle, sharpen, carve; 2) to shave; to trim, shave off, clip. {also: t'eraş kirin (K/A/IFb); **t'er̄işandin**; [terachin] تراشين (JJ); <ṯeraştin طراشتن (diṯerîşe) (دطريشه)> (HH)} Sor taşîn تـاشين (taş-) = 'to cut, shave, work (wood, stone, etc.)'; Hau taşay (taş-) *vt.* = 'to shave' (M4) [S&E/TF//HH//JJ//K/A/IFb] <telîş>

terawil تـهراوِل *m.* (). wild animal, beast: •**'Emir kir ku ĥemû *terawilê* welatê wî berevbin cem wî** (Ba3-1) He ordered all *the wild animals* in his kingdom to assemble before him. {also: terewil (K)} {syn: canewar; dir̄ende; tabe} [Ba3-1/B/IFb//K] <ĥeywan; r̄awir>

t'eraz تهراز = scale. See **terazî**.

ter̄azin تـهڕازِن *f.* (**;-ê**). slope, hillside *(pointing northward)*: -**mişkê ter̄ezinê** (K) fieldmouse. {also: ter̄ezin (Z-828); [terazin] ترازين (JJ)} {syn: berwar; hevraz; jihelî; p'al; pesar; p'ês II[2]; qunt'ar; sîng} [Z-828//K/IFb/B/JJ] <ber̄oj; berwar; hevraz; zinar [2]>

terazî تـهرازی/**ṯerazî** طـهرازی [FS/SK] *f.* (**-ya;-yê**). 1) {syn: mêzîn; şihîn} pair of scales *(for weighing)*: •***Tirazî* 'eyn e** (Bw) *The scales* are balanced or equal •**Wextê diçin e seferê ji r̄êwe diçin e-naw besta beran, çawêt xo dimiçînin, pês paş diçin, panîa pîê wan geheşt e kîşk berî dê înin, bi *ṯerazîyê* kêşin** (SK 12:117) When they go on a journey they go first of all to the vale of stones, shut their eyes, go back and forth and, whichever stone the heel of their foot touches, they will bring it and weigh it in *a balance* •**Wî sêv bi *ṯeraziyê* kêşan** (FS) He weighed the apples on *the scale*; 2) equilibrium, balance (K); 3) Libra (astrology). {also: t'eraz; t'erazû (K-2/SK-2/GF-2/OK/RZ); t'erezî (B); t'erezû (F); tirazî (Bw); [terazou/tarazú] ترازو (JJ)} Cf. Mid P tarāzūg (M3); P terāzū ترازو --> T terazi; Sor terazû تـهرازوو [K/

IFb/GF//FS/SK//JJ/OK/RZ//B//F//Bw] <‘eyn; t’a II>

terazû (GF/OK/RZ/JJ)/t’erazû تـەرازوو (K)/ṯerazû طەرازوو (SK) = scale. See **terazî**.

terciman تەرجمان (IFb) = translator. See **t’ercimeçî**.

t’ercim•e تـەرجـمـە *f.* **(;•ê).** translation; interpretation: **-t’ercime kirin** (F/K/B/JJ/SC) to translate {syn: paçve kirin; wergeřandin [3]}; to interpret. {also: t’ercme (B-2/SC); tercume (SK); [terdjumé] ترجمه (JJ)} {syn: p’açve; wergeř I} < Ar tarjamah ترجمة = 'translation' --> P tarjume ترجمه = id.--> T tercüme = id.; Cf. Heb tirgem תרגם = 'to translate' & tirgum תרגום = 'translation', & Arc targum תרגום = 'translation of the Bible'; E Arm t‘argmanel/W Arm t‘arkmanel թարգմանել = 'to translate'. *Possibly of Hittite origin* [F/K/B//JJ/SK//SC] <wergeřandin[3]>

t’ercimeçî تـەرجـمـەچـى *m.* **().** translator; interpreter. {also: terciman (IFb); t’ercimedar (B-2); t’ercmeçî (B-2); t’ercmedar (B-2); <terceman> تـرجـمـان (HH)} {syn: p’açveker; wergêř} Cf. Sor tercuman تەرجومان [F/K/B//SC//IFb//HH] <t’ercime>

t’ercimedar تـەرجِـمـەدار (B) = translator. See **t’ercimeçî**.

t’ercme تەرجمە (B/SC) = translation. See **t’ercime**.

t’ercmeçî تەرجمەچى (B) = translator. See **t’ercimeçî**.

t’ercmedar تەرجمەدار (B) = translator. See **t’ercimeçî**.

tercume تەرجومە (SK/JJ) = translation. See **t’ercime**.

teref/t’eref [K/B] تەرەف/**ṯeref** طەرەف [JJ/HH/SK] *m.* **(-ê;).** side, direction: **-ji terefê** (SK) by (agent) {syn: ji alîyê ... -ve; bi destê ...}: **•Û *ji terefê* ḧukometê jî emrekî xusosî bo muḧafeza te dê dem e teḧsîl kirin** (SK 61:743) And I will have a special order promulgated *by* the government for your protection. {also: [teref] طـرف (JJ); <ṯeref> طــرف (HH)} {syn: alî; hêl II; řex I} < Ar ṭaraf طرف = 'side, direction' [IFb/GF/SK//K/B//JJ/HH]

terembêl تەرەمبێل (HYma) = automobile. See **trimbêl**.

tereqî تـــەرەقـى (Bw/Kmc-2/ZF3) = nectarine. See **teraqî**.

t’eres/teres [JB1-A] تـــــــەرەس *adj.* 1) unfaithful, disloyal; untrustworthy, unreliable, flaky: **•Herseta wan *teresê* birê min** (L) Sorrow over (or, longing for) those *good-for-nothing* brothers of mine **•[K’eftař] fêm dike ku şêr bi hîleyên wî hesiyaye ... Şêr bang dike, dibêje: "... Qeşmerê *teres*, divê ku ez careke din te li hizûra xwe nebînim"** (Wlt 2:100, 13) [The hyena] understands that the lion has caught onto his ruses ... The lion shouts "... *Worthless* bum, I don't want to see you in my presence ever again!"; 2) [*m.*] scoundrel, bastard, son of a bitch (S.O.B.); 3) cuckold (SK/GF). {also: <ter[e]s> تــــرس (HH)} ***T’eres** is a grave insult.* [L/K/A/IFb/JB1-A/SK/GF/TF/OK//HH]

terewil تەرەول (K) = beast. See **terawil**.

teřezin تەرەزن (Z-828) = hillside. See **teřazin**.

t’erezî تەرەزى (B) = scale. See **terazî**.

t’erezû تەرەزوو (F) = scale. See **terazî**.

tergijok تەرگژۆك (Zeb) = hail[stones]. See **teyrok**.

terh تەرە *f.* **(-a;-ê).** young shoot, bud, sprout; tendril: **•Marî xwe berda serxweşiya semayê; mîna levenekî di avêda, weke *terhekê* li ber bayî xwe diḧejand** (Dz #22, 389) The snake surrendered itself to the intoxication of the dance; it shook itself like a reed in the water, like *a young shoot* in the wind; **-terḧa salê** (Kmc) yearly sprout. {also: terḧ (GF-2); terhik (FJ-2/GF-2); tirh (TF/GF-2); tirhik (TF-2)} {syn: aj; bişkoj gupik III; zîl} Cf. Sor terḧ تەرح = 'unripe (watermelon)' & terz تەرز = 'tendril' [Dz/A/GF/FJ/ZF3//TF]

terhik تەرهِك (FJ/GF) = young shoot, bud. See **terh**.

terhî تـــەرهـى (A/IFb) = Kurdish woman's headdress. See **terḧî**.

terḧ تەرح (GF) = young shoot, bud. See **terh**.

terḧî تـــەرحـى *f.* **(-ya;).** type of fine muslin or gauze, which Kurdish women tie around their heads to make a headdress. {also: terhî (A/IFb); <terḧî> تــرحــى (HH)} {syn: ç’arik (Haz-valley); laç’ik; meles (Srk); t’emezî} <Ar ṭarḥah طـــرحـــة = '(embroidered) veil worn by Arab women as headcloth' [Haz/HH/GF/FS//A/IFb] <k’itan; k’ofî>

t’erḧîl تـەرحيل**:-t’erḧîl kirin** (Bw) to deport, forcibly relocate. <Ar tarḥīl ترحيل ='emigration, exodus' [Bw]

t’eřibandin تـەرِبـانـدِن *vt.* **(-t’eřibîn-).** to interrupt *(s.o.'s work)*; to hinder, prevent; to disturb, break *(silence, sleep, etc.)*: **•Berî gişka ew Zelîxe ji mal derdixe, ku ew şixulê wî *net’eřibîne*** (Ba-1, #23) First of all he drove Zulaikha out of the house, lest she *hinder* his work. <Ar tarraba II تـرّب = 'to soil or cover with dust, to kick or sprinkle dust on stg.' [Ba-1/K/B/GF]

terik I تەرك (B) = crack; cracked. See **terk**.

teřik II تـــەرك *m.* **().** 1) wet firewood; 2) {syn: çûçik I[3] (Msr) = baby boy's; ‘ewîc; hêlik [2]; kîr; xir I} penis (slang). {also: <ṯeřik> طـرّك (HH)} < teř = 'wet' [Msr/A/IFb/GF/OK/RF//HH] <êzing>

t'erikandin II تەرِكاندِن (K/JB3/IFb/JJ/HH) = to leave, abandon; to cease. See **t'erkandin**.

terikî I تەرِكى *adj.* cracked, split. {also: terk (A-2)} [K/A/(JB3)/TF]

teȓikî II تەڕِكى *adj.* huge, vast, enormous: **•Hema wî çaxî me dît çewa gurekî *teȓikî*, tiştekî dêvda nava kevirada ç'ivana dide, ḧevraz diȓeve** (Ba2:2, 205) At that very moment we saw a *huge* wolf with something in its mouth winding its way [lit. 'it gives twists'] through the rocks, running upward **•kevirê *teȓikî*** (B) *huge* rock **•Wexta mêriv li wan zinarêd *teȓikî* dinihêȓî, 'ecêb dima** (Ba2:1, 203) When one looked at those *huge* crags, one was astounded. {syn: girs; gumreh; qerase I} [Ba2/K/B/QtrE]

terikîn I تـەرِكـيـن *vi.* **(-terik-).** to split, crack, burst *(vi.)*. {also: [terekin] تـركـيـن (JJ); <terikîn تـركـين (diterikî) (دتـركـى)> (HH)} {syn: t'eqîn} [K/A/JB3/B/HH//JJ]

teȓikîn II تـەڕكـيـن (Bt/B) = to give birth (of dogs). See **t'eliqîn**.

t'eȓişandin تـەڕِشـانـدِن (K[s]/B)/**terişandin** تـەرِشـانـدِن (IFb) *vt.* **(-t'eȓişîn-).** to trim, cut off, prune, clip, shave off: **•Hikûmeta AKP-ê jî ji bo xurtkirina desthilata xwe heroj bi awayekî per û baskên hêzên eskerî *diterişîne* û Kemalîzmê û mîlîtarîzmê bêqudret dike** (A.Zêrevan. Dewleta tirkan bi quweta kurdan li ser lingan dimîne, iv.2007) Every day the AKP government *clips* the wings of the military forces so to speak to strengthen its own authority and renders Kemalism and militarism powerless. {also: teraştin; terşandin (FJ)} {syn: çipilandin; k'ezaxtin; pejikandin} [CCG/K(s)/B/IFb/Wkt//FJ//TF]

teȓî I تـــەڕى *(K/B)*/**terî** تـــەرى *f.* **(-ya;-yê).** 1) {syn: boç'[ik]; dêl II; k'ilk; kurî I (Bw); qemç[ik]} tail of an animal *(dog, goat, sheep, donkey, or horse)*: **•Ez bûm meriv, lê *terriya* kûçikan bi min ve ma** (ZZ-10, 154) I have become a human being, but the dog's *tail* has stayed with/on me **•*Terîya* hespê wî di bin çîyê de ma; kêr daê, terîya hespê xwe jêkir** (L) His horse's *tail* remained [=was caught] under the mountain; he took a knife to it, and cut off his horse's tail; 2) {syn: dûv I} fattail. {also: [teri] ترى (JJ); <ṯerî طرى> (HH)} [L/IFb/JJ/GF/ZF/FS//K/B//HH] <t'erkû>

te'rî II تەعرى (Z-1/B) = dark. See **tarî**.

te'rîban تەعريبان (B) = darkness. See **tarîban**.

te'rîbar تەعريبار (B) = darkness. See **tarîban**.

terîş تـەريش *m.* (). bandage, long cut piece of muslin, piece of cloth: **•Ji xwe re *terîş* anî, li serê xwe gerand, xwe kir wek hecîkî** (RN 30/7/45) He took a *bandage*, wrapped it around his head, and made himself into a hadj [=Muslim pilgrim]. {also: telîş II (GF-2); tîroş (Qzl-2); tîş II (GF-2)} [RN/A/IFb/GF/Qzl]

terk I تەرك *f.* (;-ê). 1) {syn: derz; kelş; qelîştek; tîş I} cleft, crack, fissure (in a stone, rock, etc.); 2) [adj.] cracked, split. {also: terik I (B); <terk> تـــــــــرك (HH)} [Haz/K/A/IFb/HH//B] <terikîn>

t'erk II تـــەرك *f.* **(-a;).** abandonment: **-t'erk dan** (K/HH)/~ **dayîn** (B)/~ **kirin** (K/IFb/B/JJ/HH/SK/RZ) to leave, abandon, quit {syn: şemirandin; t'erkandin}: **•Ew deqekê *t'erka* min *nake/nade*** (B) He *won't leave* me *alone* for a minute **•Ew nikare *t'erka* ciẍarê *bike/bide*** (B) He can't *quit* smoking **•Lê herçî eskerên Vîşiyê, *terka* Şamê *didan*** [sic] **û bajar vala dikirin** [sic] (H2 9:31, 775) But as for the soldiers of Vichy, they *were abandoning* Damascus and leaving the city empty **•Madem to ho bo min muxlis bî, digel min were: ez jî *terka* te *nakem*** (SK 2:10) Since you have become so devoted to me, come with me: I *won't leave* you either; **-t'erka dunîyaê dan** (K) to depart from this world, die, expire; **-t'erka edet dan** (K)/~ **kirin** (SK) to break a habit, abandon a custom: **•Wextê Nadir Şah ew ḧukme kir, li her cîyekî ew *'adet hate terk kirin*** (SK 11:104) When Nadir Shah made this command, the custom *was abandoned* everywhere. {also: [terk kirin] (JJ); <terk kirin ترك كرن (terkdike تركدكه) & terkdan تـركـدان (terkdide تركددە)> (HH)} {syn: berdan; dev jê berdan; hiştin; t'erkandin} < Ar √t-r-k ترك = 'to abandon, leave' [H2/K/IFb/B/JJ/HH/SK/RZ]

t'erkandin تـــەركـــانـــدِن *vt.* **(-t'erkîn-).** 1) {syn: şemirandin; t'erk dan/kirin} to leave, abandon: **•Min mal û ḧalê xwe, bavê xwe *t'erkandye*** (EP-7) I *have left* my home and my folks [lit. 'father']; 2) {syn: dest jê k'işandin; dev jê berdan; hiştin; ji ... rabûn; qeran} to cease, stop, quit: **•Ewî ciẍare *t'erikandîye*** (B) He *quit* smoking. {also: t'erikandin II (K-2/JB3/IFb); [terikandin] تـركـانـديـن (JJ); <terikandin تـركـانـدن (diterikîne) (دتركينه)> (HH)} < Ar taraka ترك [EP-7/K//JB3/IFb/B/JJ/HH] <berdan>

t'erkî تـــەركـى (B/IFb/GF) = rump; rear part of saddle. See **t'erkû**.

t'erkû تەركوو *f.* **(-ya;-yê).** 1) {syn: qerp'ûz [1]; saxirî (Z-1)} croup, crupper, rump of a quadruped; 2) rear part of saddle. Cf. T terki = 'croup; back part of saddle' {also: t'erkî (B/IFb/GF)} [EP-7/K//B/IFb/GF] <boç'[ik]; teřî I>

ṯerm طەرم/**term** تەرم *m.* **(-ê;).** dead body, corpse, cadaver *(human or animal)*: •**Ewcar rîwî ṯermê marî dirêj kir** (SK 2:16) Then the fox stretched out the snake's *corpse*; **-termê adem** (GF)/**termê nihê** (OK) the Little Bear, Ursa Minor *(star constellation)*; *The Great Bear according to Zeb & M [KDS-I, ¶267 (B), p.164]*. {also: [tärm] ترم (JJ-PS); <ṯerm> طرم (HH)} {syn: berat'e [2]; cendek; cinyaz; k'eleş I; leş; meyt'} Sor term تەرم = 'human corpse' [Wn/K(s)/A/IFb/JJ-PS/GF/TF/OK//HH/SK/Zeb]

t'ers تەرس *m./f.(K/FS)* **(/-a;).** cattle or horse dung: **-tersa hespî** (FS) horse manure. {also: [ters] ترس (JJ)} {syn: dirg; k'erme; peyîn; řîx} Sor ters تەرس = 'dung of horse, mule' [/K/B/F/IFb/GF/OK/JJ/ZF3/FD/FS]

terş تەرش (Haz/K/A/GF/HH/OK) = cattle. See **t'ariş**.

terşandin تەرشاندِن (FJ) = to trim. See **t'eřişandin**.

t'ert/tert [B] تەرت *m.* **(-ê;).** lump of dried manure used as fuel (A): •**Carekê pîrek *t'erte sergîn* nift dike** (Dz) Once an old woman poured kerosene on *a pressed dung cake* •**Pîrê, lê pê *t'ertê sergîn* be'r tê şewitandin?** (Dz) Old woman, but can the sea be set on fire with *a pressed dung cake*? {also: tert (B); tertik (A); <tert> ترت (HH)} {syn: k'erme; sergîn; t'epik II} [Dz//B/IFb/HH/GF//A] <deve II; dirg; t'ers>

tertik تەرتِك (A) = dried manure used as fuel. See **t'ert**.

t'ertilîn تەرتِلين *vi.* **(-tertil-).** to start, jump with fright; to waiver, falter, be unsteady: •**Dema Xaneyê bi teqîna tifing û vizîna berikê ra firîna serikê qelûna xwe dît, *bê ko bitertile* an di xwe bi derxe, herwekî tu tişt ne bû be, rabû ser xwe û çû serikeke din anî** (Rnh 2:17, 309) When Khaneh [a woman] saw the bowl of her pipe fly off with the explosion of a rifle and the buzzing of a bullet, *without faltering* or losing composure, as if nothing had happened, she got up and went to bring another bowl. {also: [tertilin] ترتلين (JJ)} [Rnh/JJ/GF]

t'erzî تەرزى *m.* **(-yê;).** tailor: •***T'erzî* řabûye deste k'inc dirûye, lêkirîye** (HCK-5, #41, 236) *The tailor* sewed a set of clothes, [and] put them on her. {also: [derzi/darzī درزى (Rh)/ terzī ترزى (Lx)] (JJ); <terzî> ترزى (HH)} {syn: cildirû; k'incdirû; xeyat} Cf. P darzī درزى --> T terzi; Sor derzî دەرزى = bergdirû بەرگدِروو {t'erzîtî} [HCK/K/B/FJ/TF/GF/JJ/HH]

t'erzîtî تەرزيتى *f.* **(;-yê).** tailoring, sewing, couture; the profession and the handiwork of a tailor: •**Ew ji me jîrtir bûn ko ji destên wan dihat cildirûtî, *terzîtî*, sefarî, xeratî, koçkarî û nalbendî** (Nefel, 2008) They were more skilled than us, as they were proficient in sewing, *tailoring*, tinsmithery, carpentry, cobblery and shoeing horses. {syn: cildirûtî} [Nefel/K/B/FJ/ZF/Wkt] <t'erzî>

t'esbih تەسبِه = prayer beads. See **t'izbî**.

t'esbîh تەسبيه (K) = prayer beads. See **t'izbî**.

t'esele تەسەلە : •**Dengek *li* min *t'esele bû*** (EP-7) I *heard* (or, *noticed, perceived*) a voice. [EP-7]

t'eselî تەسەلى *f.* **(-ya;-yê).** 1) [according to JJ < clq Ar tasalli <tasā'al VI تساءل < √s-'-l سأل = 'to ask'] look, check, control, revision: **-t'eselî kirin** (B): a) to supervise, look in on, check up on; to test: •**Heře oda Memo, ko ji bona em *t'eselîya* biratîya wî *bikin*** (Z-3) Go to Memo's room, so that we can *test* his brotherhood; b) to console, comfort: •***Teseliya me kirin*** [sic] (KO, 40) They *consoled* us; 2) {also: dilmînî; ȟewî} consolation, comfort, solace. {also: [teseli] (JJ)} ? < Ar tasallī تسلّي (tasallin) (تسلٍّ) = 'diversion, entertainment' [EP-7//K/B/IFb/JJ/FS]

t'esîr تەسير/**te'sîr** تەئسير [SK] *f.* **(;-ê).** 1) {syn: bandûř; eger II} influence, effect; **-k'etin bin t'esîrê** (K) to come or fall under s.o.'s influence; **-tesîr[ê] kirin** (IFb/SK) to influence, have an effect, leave an impression: •**Gava ku min xwend *tesîreke* pir mezin *li* min *kir*** (LC, 5) When I read it, it *had* quite *an effect on* me [or, made quite an impression on me] •**Wextê Şêxê Bicîlê ho axiwt *te'sîr kir* di qelbê Şêx Muȟemmed Siddîq** (SK 50:541) When the Shaikh of Bijil spoke in this way, it *had its effect on* Shaikh Muhammad Siddiq; 2) impression. < Ar ta'ṯīr تأثير = 'influence' (√'-ṯ-r أثر) [LC/K/IFb//SK]

t'eslîm تەسليم *m.* **(-ê;).** handing over, delivering, entrusting, committing; surrender, submission: **-t'eslîm bûn** (B) to surrender {syn: hatin řaê}: •**Ew *t'eslîmî* duşmin *nebû*** (B) He *did not surrender to* the enemy; **-t'eslîm kirin** (B) to hand over, deliver, entrust {syn: spartin I}: •**Ezê vê qesrê û malê têde timam *teslîmê* te *bikim*** (L) I will completely *hand over to* you this palace and the property in it. {also: [teslim/teslím] تسليم (JJ); <teslîm> تسليم (HH)} < Ar taslīm تسليم (√s-l-m سلم) [L/K/B/IFb/JJ/HH/SK]

t'eşe تەشە *f.(Ber/ZF)/m.* **(-ya/;).** shape, form. {syn: şikil[1]; teva I} [(neol)Ber/IFb/TF/RF/ZF/RZ/FS]

teşene تەشەنە *f.* **().** 1) infection; contagion, spreading (of a disease) (IFb/OK); inflammation (K): -**teşene kirin** (OK) to spread *(of a disease)*; 2) [*adj.*] sore, inflamed, irritated (lit. & fig.). {also: t'eşenek (K); [techenek] تشنك (JJ) = gangrène, inflammation} *according to JJ* <P teš < ātеš آتش = 'fire' [Zeb/Bar/IFb/OK//K/JJ] <kul I; pejî; şewb; weba>

t'eşenek تەشەنەك (K/JJ) = infection; inflamed. See **teşene**.

t'eşî تەشى *f./m.(OK)* **(-ya/;-yê/).** spindle, distaff: •**Ewa tê kûz dibe, *t'eşîê* hiltîne** (J) She comes [and] stoops over, [and] picks up *the distaff* •**Keç'ik řadibe ser zinêr, *teşîya* xwe diřêse** (J) The girl climbs up on the cliff, [and] spins [wool with] her *distaff* •**Keç'ik *t'eşîyê* û hrîê hildide** (J) The girl picks up *the spindle* and wool •**Nîka *teşîya* min jê derket** (AB) The point [or hook] of my *distaff* came out. {also: teşû (OK-2); têşî[k'] (JB1-A); [techi] تشى (JJ); <teşî> تشى (HH)} --> T teşi (Erzurum); Sor teşî تەشى [J/K/A/IFb/B/JJ/HH/GF/TF/OK//JB1-A] <hirî; liva; řêstin>

teşîřêsk تەشيرێسك (FS) = dragonfly. See **teşîrok**.

teşîrok تەشيرۆك *f.* **().** dragonfly. {also: teşîřêsk (FS)} {syn: ħespa bûkê; ħespa gihîyê} [Msr//FS]

t'eşk تەشك *f./m.(FS)* **(/-ê;-ê/).** shin (K/B); part of the foot between the heel and the hip (HH). {also: [tech(i)k] تشك (JJ); <teşk> تشك (HH)} {syn: çîp} [K/A/JB3/IFb/B/JJ/HH/GF/OK/FS] <hêt; řan>

t'eşkele تەشكەلە (B) = cheating; problem. See **t'eşqele**.

t'eşqel•e تەشقەلە *f.* **(;•ê).** cheating, fraud; problem, obstacle, misfortune: •**Muroek hebû ji 'eşîreta Sûrçîyan ... nawê wî 'Elî bû. Gelek dewletmend bû ... her tişt hebû, emma daimî tund û tebî'et-nexoş bû. Eger ħisab digel kesekî heba dikir e *teşqele*, şeř û 'edawet *dikir*. Nawê wî meşhûr bo, digotin ê 'Elî *Teşqelan*** (SK 14:135) There was once a man of the Surchi tribe… whose name was Ali. He was very rich, …having everything, but he was always fierce and bad-tempered. If ever he had an account to settle with anyone he *would cheat* and cause quarrelling and enmity. His name became notorious---they called him Ali '*Cheat*' •**Xwe kuştiye yan jî xwe bi saxî veşartiye ji bo ku rizgar bibe ji van *teşqele* û bûyerên bêserî** (HYma, 29) He has killed himself or buried himself alive in order to be rid of these silly *problems* and events. {also: t'eşkele (B); teşxele (GF-2); [techqalé/téskala (GF)] تشقلە (JJ); <teşqele> تشقلە (HH)} Sor teşqełe تەشقەڵە = 'false claim' [K/A/IFb/HH/SK/GF//JJ//B] <alozî; arêşe; pirsgirêk>

t'eşt تەشت *f.* **(-a;-ê).** basin, tub, metal or brass vessel *(for washing clothes or dishes, or kneading dough)*: •**Va ez ê legana (*teşt*) xwe bibim û herim** (ZZ-10, 154) I will take my *basin* and leave. {also: [techt] تشت (JJ); <teşt> تشت (HH)}{syn: legan; şikev} Cf. Ar ṭišt/ṭašt طشت; T teşt; Sor teşt تەشت = 'large shallow copper/aluminium basin (often used for washing laundry)' [ZZ/K/B/A/IFb/FJ/GFTF/JJ/HH/ZF/Kmc/CS]

te'ştê تەعشتێ (B) = breakfast; mid-morning coffee break. See **taştê**.

teşû تەشوو (OK) = spindle. See **t'eşî**.

teşxele تەشخەلە (GF) = cheating; problem. See **t'eşqele**.

tet I تەت (IFb) = hand (in baby talk). See **t'etik**.

tet II تەت (B) = stone slab. See **tat I**[2].

t'etik تەتِك *m.* **().** 1) {syn: pepik} little hand; hand *in babytalk*; 2) {syn: lepik} [*f.* **(;-ê).**] glove (A/B/HH). {also: tet I (IFb-2); <tetik> تتك (HH)} [K/A/IFb/B/HH] <dest>

tetirxanî تەترخانى *adj.* suffering from indigestion, stomachache or diarrhea; upset: -**tetirxanî bûn** (ZF/G) to have or suffer from indigestion, etc. *(lit. & fig.)*; to be upset: •**Ji bo dijmin biqehirin û *tetirxanî bibin*, her tiştî ji nû ve ava dikin** (ANHA 5.xi.2015) In order that the enemy be upset and *distressed*, they are rebuilding everything; -**tetirxanî kirin** (G) to give s.o. indigestion, etc. *(lit. & fig.)*; to upset s.o.: •**De ka em binihêrin meriv çima merivan *tetirxanî dikin*?** (Nusaybinim 24.viii.2015) Let's look at why people *give* other people *a hard time*. [Frq/ZF/FD/G/PF] <navêş; zikçûn>

t'ev I تەڤ *adv.* 1) together (with): •***T'ev* hevala çû geřê** (B) He went for a walk *with* his friends; -**tevde** (A/JB3) do. {syn: bihevřa; pêkve}; 2) all, everyone; everything; •**Berx hatin nava pêz, dilê *tevan* dibijî şîr, pir dibijî** (AB) The lambs came in among the sheep, the hearts of *all* yearn for milk, very much yearn for it •**Cînarê me *teva* ê mî şerjêkirîye** (J) Our neighbors *all* slaughtered a sheep; 3) [*prep.*] with, together with; **-tev bi** = do. {also: têk; [3] tevî I; [tew] تـــڤ (JJ) = 'ingérance, mélange'; <tev تـڤ/tevda تـڤـدا> (HH)} < di + hev [BX/K/(A)/(JB3)/IFb/B/JJ/HH/GF/TF]

te'v II تەعڤ (B) = sun; sunbeam; sunlight. See **tav I**.

teva I تـــەڤـا *m.* **().** shape, form: •... **Ev çi*teva*ye?** (J/K) What is this thing?/What in the world is this? {syn: şikil[1]; t'eşe} [K/A/JB3/IFb]

teva II تەڤا (F/K) = wild animal, beast. See **tabe**.

t'evahî تـــەڤـاهـى *f.* **(-ya;).** entirety, totality; the whole, the entire; sum total: •**Ji 165 nûnêran, ku *tevahiya* nûnêran di meclîsê de ne, 60-70 bi destnivîsên (îmzeyên) xwe alîgirîya me dikin** (Wlt 1:37, 16) Out of 165 representatives, which is *the total number of* representatives in the assembly, 60-70 support us with their signatures •***tevahiya* vê ferhengê** (IFb) this *entire* dictionary/ *the whole of* this dictionary/this dictionary *in its entirety*. {also: t'evayî (K/IFb-2)} {syn: t'omerî} [Wlt/IFb//K]

t'evax تـــــەڤـــــاخ (Ba3-1) = sheet (of paper); layer. See **t'ebax II**.

t'evayî تەڤايى (K/IFb) = entirety. See **t'evahî**.

t'evdan تـــــەڤــــــدان *f.* **(-a;).** 1) confusion, disorder, disarray (K); 2) ado, ruckus, commotion, rumpus (K); 3) movement (JB3): •**Duhî *tevdana* kewte û sedmêran dom kiriye** (RN) Yesterday the *movements* [or: *confusion*?] of troops and companies continued. [RN/K/JB3/IFb/GF]

tevdêr تەڤدێر (IFb) = plan, plot. See **t'evdîr**.

t'evdîr تەڤدير *f.* **(-a;-ê).** 1) plan, plot, scheme: •**Memê wa bi *t'ivdîra* xwe rêwîtîya xwe bû** (Z-1) This is how Mem's trip should be according to his *plan* •**Řastî, ewe *tedbîrekî* çak e. Hindî mulaĥeze dikem ji wê çêtir nahête xiyala min** (SK33:294) Truly this is a good *idea*. However much I consider it I can think of nothing better; 2) {syn: t'ivdarek} preparations (B). {also: tedbîr (SK/IFb/OK); tevdêr (IFb-2); t'ivdîr (Z-1); [tedbir تـدبـيـر/ tebdir تبدير (G)] (JJ); <tedbîr> تدبير (HH)} < Ar tadbīr تـــدبـــيـــر (√d-b-r II دبّـــر) = 'planning, organization, management' [Z-1//K/B/GF/TF//IFb/JJ/HH/SK/OK]

t'evgeř تەڤگەڕ *f.* **(-a;-ê).** 1) movement *(pol.)*: •**Ew di wê baweriyê de bûn ku *tevgera* kurdî parçekirîye** (AW 1:36, 8) They believed that the Kurdish *movement* was divided; 2) {syn: şêl} behavior, conduct: •**Vê *tevgera* wê baweriyeke xurt da min û ez gelek pê kêfxweş bûm** (Ardû, 171) This *behavior* of hers has convinced me [lit. 'given me a strong belief'] and I am very happy about it. [(neol)Wlt/IFb/GF/TF/OK/ZF/RZ]

tevin تەڤن (OK/IFb) = loom; web. See **t'evn**.

tevinpîrk تەڤنپيرك (OK) = spider. See **t'evnpîrk**[1].

tevir تەڤر/**t̲evir** طەڤر [FS/HH] *m.(K/FS)/f.(B)* **(-ê/ ;-î/ -ê).** 1) {syn: balt'e; bivir} hatchet, axe: •**Goşt-firoşî hestî bi *t̲evirî* şkand** (FS) The meatseller broke the bone with *the hatchet*; 2) {syn: k'uling} pick, pickaxe; 3) {syn: meř II; metirke [2]} spade: •**Wî bi *t̲evirî* ax kola** (FS) He dug the earth with *the spade*; 4) {syn: kulbe} hoe: **-tevir dan/kirin** (ZF) to hoe. {also: tevr I (IFb-2/GF-2); [tewir تڤر/ tefer تفر]] (JJ); <t̲evr طەڤر/tever تڤر> (HH)} Cf. P tabar تبر; Sor tewr تەور = 'axe'; Hau tewer [Z-2/K/A/ IFb/B/JJ/GF/OK/ZF//HH/FS] <bêr; k'uling; meř II; metirke; tevirzîn; t'evşo>

tevirzîn تـەڤـرزيـن/**t̲evirzîn** طـەڤـرزيـن [FS] *m.* **(-ê;).** doubled-headed hatchet or axe *used in war*. {also: tevirzîr (K)} Cf. P tabar تبر; Sor tewrzîn تەورزين = ' battle-axe' [BX/IFb/OK//FS//K] <bivir; tevir>

tevirzîr تـەڤـرزيـر (K) = doubled-headed hatchet. See **tevirzîn**.

teviz I تـــــــەڤِــــز *f.* **(;-ê).** 1) chill, shudder, tremor, trembling: •***Tevz* canê minra çû** (K) *A shudder* went through me •**Aqû ku dengê Ûsib dibihê *teviz* bedena wîřa diçin** (Ba3) When Jacob hears Joseph's voice, *shudders* run through his body; 2) spasm; 3) stretching: **-teviz dayîn xwe** (B) to stretch o.s. {also: tevz (K)} [Ba3/B//K] <firk I; girîzok>

tevizîn تەڤزين/**t̲evizîn** طەڤزين [Haz/HH] *vi.* **(-teviz-/ -t̲eviz- [Haz]).** 1) to be or go numb, prickle, tingle, "go to sleep" *(of hand or foot)*: •**Destên min *tevizîn*** (IFb) My hands have *gone to sleep*; **-tevizîna zivistanê** (IFb) hibernation: •**Hinek heywan zivistanê *ditevizin*** (IFb) Some animals *hibernate* in winter; 2) to freeze up, become stiff, stiffen. {also: tazin (-taz-) (JB1-A); tevzîn (GF); tezîn (OK); tezîn (M-Am & Zx); [tewzin تـڤـزيـن/ tezin تـزيـن] (JJ); <t̲evizîn طـڤـزيـن (dit̲evizî) (دطڤزى)/t̲ezîn طزين (dit̲ezî) (دطزى)> (HH)} [Haz/ HH//F/K/IFb/B//GF/JJ//OK//M-Am&Zx//JB1-A] <cemidîn; qefilîn [1]>

tevî I تەڤى = together with. See **t'ev I**[3].
te'vî II تەعڤى (B) = cloudburst. See **tavî**.
t'evlihev تـەڤـلِـهـەڤ *adj.* all mixed up, confused: **-t'evlihev kirin** (IFb) to mix up, confuse. {also: tevluhev (TF)} {syn: belawela; bê ser û ber} [IFb/GF//TF]
tevluhev تەڤلوهەڤ (TF) = confused. See **t'evlihev**.
t'evn تـــەڤـــن *m.(Bw/SK/OK)/f.(K/B)* **(-ê/-a; /-ê).** 1) loom, carpet loom; 2) tissue, fabric; 3) {also: t'evnik (A/IFb/TF)} {syn: t'evnpîrk [2]} cobweb, spider's web: **-tevnê pîrkê** (Bw)/**tevnka pîrê** (A)/ **tevnepîrk** (GF)/**tewnê dapîroşkê** (SK) do. {also: tevin (OK/IFb-2); tewn (SK); <tevn> تـڤـن (HH)} Sor tewn تەون = 'loom; warp (of fabric)' [Bw/K/A/IFb/B/HH/GF/TF//OK//SK] <befş; dezgeh; hepik; pîjik I; r̄aç'andin; xanût>
tevnepîr تەڤنەپیر (IFb) = spider. See **t'evnpîrk**[1].
tevne pîre تەڤنە پیرە (GF) = spider. See **t'evnpîrk**[1].
tevnepîrk تەڤنەپیرك (GF) = cobweb. See **t'evnpîrk**[2].
t'evnik تەڤنِك (A/IFb/TF) = cobweb. See **t'evn**[3].
t'evnpîrk تـەڤنپیرك *f.* **(-a;-ê).** 1) spider{also: tevinpîrk (OK); tevnepîr (IFb); tevne pîre (GF)} {syn: dapîroşk; pêrtevînk; p'indepîr; pîr [4]; pîrhevok; pîrik [3]}; 2) spider's web, cobweb{also: pêrtevînk; tevnepîrk (GF); tevnê pîrkê (Bw); tevnka pîrê (A)} {syn: t'evn[ik] [3]}. [Bw//OK//IFb//GF//A]
tevr I تەڤر (IFb/GF) = hatchet; pickaxe. See **tevir**.
tevr II تەڤر (SS) = radish. See **tivir**.
tevrik I تەڤرِك *m.* **(-ê;).** small hatchet or axe [dim. of **tevir**]: **•*Tevrikê* xwe hilgirt û çûbû wan** (HYma, 30) He picked up his *hatchet* and went to them. {also: tavrik (FJ)} [HYma/IFb/GF/Kmc/CS//FJ]
tevrik II تەڤرِك (Kmc) = radish. See **tivir**.
tevrî تـــەڤـــرى *f.* **(-ya;-yê).** *type of tree*: 1) short tree found in summer pastures (Bw); 2) tree similar to morello, small bitter cherry [morello = Sor bełałok بەلاڵۆك] (Hej); 3) Daphne acuminata. [Bw/Hej/Elk]
tevşî تەڤشى (K/Kmc-13) = adze. See **t'evşo**.
t'evşo/tevşo [B] تـەڤـشـۆ *m.* **(-yê; t'êvşo, vî t'evşoyî).** adze: **•Mam Tal bi keyfxoşî *tewşî* îna, sindoq şkand** (SK 28:257) Mam Tal, very pleased, brought an *adze* and broke open the chest. {also: tefşî (OK); tevşî (K-2/Kmc-13-2); tevşû (Kmc-13-2); tewşî (SK); [tewchou تـڤـشـو /tevchi توشى] (JJ); <t̠efşû> طـفـشـو (HH)} Cf. P taš تش/ tīše تیشه = 'adze'; Sor teşwê تەشوێ; Hau tirêşte/ tereşte (M4) [SK/JJ//K/A/IFb/B/Kmc-13//HH//OK] <bivir; tevir>
tevşû تەڤشوو (Kmc-13) = adze. See **t'evşo**.
tevz تەڤز (K) = shudder, tremor; spasm. See **teviz I**.
tevzîn تەڤزین (GF) = to go numb. See **tevizîn**.
tew I تـەو/**t̠ew** طـەو [FS/HH] *f./m.(FS)* **(-a/-ê;).** fold, pleat *(in a garment)*: **-tew girtin** (Msr) to fall into place, be appropriate or suitable: **•*Tewa* xwe *girt*** (Msr) It fell into place/It was fitting or appropriate/It fit or matched perfectly. {also: <t̠ew> طـو (HH)} < Ar ṭawá طـوى = 'to fold' [Msr/GF//HH/FS]
t'ew II تـــــەو *adv.* [+ *neg.*] not at all, not in the least: **•Lê xort dinêre ku ev barê wî yê ewqas giran, *tew* jî bala keçikê nakişîne … Keçik her bi eşêfa xwe daketiye û *tew* bala xwe nade xort û barê wî yê pir** (Ardû, 67) But the young man sees that his extremely heavy load *doesn't even* attract the girl's attention in the least … The girl is into her weeding and *doesn't* notice the young man and his great load *at all*. {syn: qet [2]} [Ardû/A/IFb/FJ/TF/GF/CS] <hew; t'u II>
tewaf تـــــــەواف/**t̠ewaf** طـــــــــەواف [SK] *f.* **(-a;).** circumambulation of the Kaabah and other holy sites (as part of the Islamic pilgrimage ceremonies): **•Em ji Silêmanîyê hatîne bo *t̠ewafa* merqedê mubarekî Ĥezretê Imam Ĥuseyn** (SK 11:106) We have come from Sulaimaniya to perform *the circumambulation of* the blessed tomb of the great Imam Husain **•Min divê, ez her̄im û mala Xwedê *t'ewaf bikim*** (Dz #22, 389) I want to go and *circumambulate* the house of God [i.e., make the pilgrimage to Mecca]. {also: <t̠ewaf> طواف (HH)} < Ar ṭawāf طواف; Sor tewaf تەواف [Dz/IFb/GF/CS//SK/HH] <ĥec; ĥecî>
t'ewakel تـــــەواكـــــەل (B) = reckless; frivolous. See **t'ewekel**.
t̠ewal طــــــــــەوال *m./f.* **().** bird, fowl: **•Baz *t̠ewalekê* nêçîrvan e** (FS) The falcon is a predatory/hunting *bird*; **-teyr û tewal** (ZF3) birds (of all sizes): **•Bila bibe xurê *teyr û tewalan*** (ZF3) Let it be food for *the birds*. [FS/BF/FD] <çûk I; lorî I; teyr>
t̠ewan طەوان (FS/HH) = to bend (vi.). See **tewîn**.
tewandin تـــەوانـــدِن/**t̠ewandin** طــەوانــدِن [FS/HH] *vt.* **(-tewîn-).** 1) to bend *(vt.)*, incline, bow *(vt.)*: **•Em serê xwe *natewînin*** (Wlt 2:66, 2) We *won't bow* our head[s] (as sign of submission); **-xwe tewandin** = to bow down (vi.): **•Min *xwe* ji qrêl re *tewand*** (K-ça) I *bowed down* before the king;

2) to decline *(nouns in grammar)*. {also: <ṯewandin طواندن (diṯewîne) (دطوينه)> (HH)} < Ar ṭawá طوى = 'to fold' [Wlt/F/K/IFb/B/GF/OK//HH/FS] <tewîn>

tewang تەوانگ/**ṯewang** طەوانگ [FS] *f.* **(-a;-ê).** declension *(of nouns and pronouns)*; inflection: **•Di kurmancî de *tewang* bi du awayan pêk tê** (TaRK, 90) In Kurmanji, *declension* occurs in 2 ways **•*tewanga* qertafên nebinavkirinê** (TaRK, 91) *declension of* indefinite endings [e.g., -ekî in hevalekî]. [TaRK/IFb/FJ/GF/Kmc//FS] <tewandin>

t'ewaqet تەواقەت (;-ê) (B/F) = request. See **t'eweqe**.

t'ewaqetî تەواقەتی (B) = request. See **t'eweqe**.

tewaş تەواش *m.* **().** oil products used in cooking: cooking oil, olive oil, shortening, grease, fat, butter, margarine, tallow. {also: tawaş (Haz); <ṯewaş> طواش (HH)} [K(s)/A/IFb/GF//HH//Haz] <azûxe [2]; bez I; çivir; r̄ûn>

t'ewat تەوات (K/B/GF) = patience; calm, rest. See **t'ebatî**.

tewatî تەواتی (Ardû) = patience; calm, rest. See **t'ebatî**.

tewbe تەوبە (SK) = repentance. See **t'obe**.

tewbeker تەوبەکەر (SK) = penitent. See **t'obekar**.

tewe تەوە (IFb) = frying pan. See **t'awe**.

teweg تەوەگ (IFb) = hoof and mouth disease. See **tebeq I**.

t'ewekel/t'ewek'el [EH] تەوەکەل *adj. all-purpose negative adjective*: reckless, loose, wild, dissolute, debauched; disorganized, disorderly; careless, unconcerned, carefree; frivolous, light-witted; risky, dangerous; useless: **•Îskender lao, tu t'eze bûyî p'adşa, ser t'extê min r̄ûniştîy, gerek glîê aqil bikî, ne ku *t'ewek'elbî*** (EH) Iskender my boy, you have recently become king and sat on my throne, you must make wise pronouncements, [and] not *be frivolous* **•Mêvanê Gulp'erîyê mêvanekî usa *t'ewekelî* nîne wekî bide pey xulamekî û bê mala wan** (FK-eb-2) Gulperî's guest is not so *frivolous* as to follow a servant boy to their house. {also: t'ewakel (B)} [FK-2/EH/K//B]

t'eweq•e تەوەقە *f.* **(•a;).** request, prayer: **-jê t'ewaqe[t] kirin** (Ba)/**t'ewaqa *fk-ê* kirin** (Z-1/GF)/**t'eweqe kirin** (K) to beg, entreat s.o.; to request, ask for: **•Evana diçine cem bavê, *t'ewaqet* jê *dikin*** (Ba) They go to their father, [and] *entreat* him **•Ew jî ji bavê *t'ewaqet dike*** (Ba) he also *begs* his father **•Herd xûşkê çûk *t'eweqa* xûşka mezin *kirin* [sic], go ...** (Z-1) Both younger sisters *asked* their older sister to ... {also: tewaqe (GF); t'ewaqet (;-ê) (B/F); t'ewaqetî (B-2); t'eweqetî; [tika] تکا (JJ)} {syn: hêvî [3]; lavahî; limêj} <Ar tawaqqu' توقّع = 'expectation' -->P tavaqqo' توقّع = 'expectation; request, wish'; Az T təvəggə etmək = 'to request'; Sor tika تِکا = 'request' [Ba/K//F/B]

t'eweqetî تەوەقەتی = request. See **t'eweqe**.

tewik تەوک (AD) = frying pan. See **t'awe**.

tewiz تەوز (GF) = joke. See **tewz**.

tewî تەوی (BK) = very much; most. See **t'ewrî**.

tewîn تەوین/**ṯewîn** طەوین *vi.* **(-tew-).** to bend *(vi.)*, bow down, stoop: **•Di sala 1988'an de ez dîsa hatim girtin û min gelek lêdan û îşkenceyên dijmin dîtin û ez çar meh li Girtîgeha Batmanê mam ... lê ez *netewiyam*** (Wlt 2:66, 2) In 1988 I was arrested again, and I was beaten and tortured a great deal by the enemy, and I spent four months in Batman prison ... but I *did not bow down* [=give in]. {also: ṯewan (FS); ṯewhan (FS-2); tewîyan (F); <ṯewan طوان (diṯewe) (دطوه)> (HH)} < Ar ṭawá طوى = 'to fold' [Wlt/K/A/IFb/B/OK//F//HH/FS] <tewandin>

tewîyan تەوییان (F) = to bow down. See **tewîn**.

tewl تەول (GF)//ṯewl طەول (FS) = horse stable. See **ṯewle**.

ṯewle طەولە [FS/JJ]/**tewl•e** تەولە/**t'ewle** تەولە [K] *f.* **(;•ê).** horse stable: **•Wana mirîşk birin, yekî li *tewlê* şerjê kir, yekî li gomê şerjê kir** (Ba3-1) They took the chickens, one slaughtered [his] in *the stable*, one slaughtered [his] in the sheepfold. {also: tewl (GF-2)/ṯewl (FS-2); ṯewlexan (FS-2); tewlexane; [taoûlé] طوله (JJ)} {syn: borxane; pange [1]; stewl} Sor tewîle تەویلە [JR//Wn/K/IFb/JJ/GF] <extexane; naxir>

ṯewlexan طەولەخان (FS) = horse or cow stable. See **ṯewle**.

tewlexane تەولەخانە = horse or cow stable. See **ṯewle**.

tewn تەون (SK) = loom; web. See **t'evn**.

tewok تەوۆك (SS) = hackberry tree. See **tihok**.

t'ewrî تەوری *adv.* very, very much (K); most, -est, *used in forming superlative adjectives* (K/BK): **•gundê *t'ewrî dûr*** (B) *the furthest/farthest* village **•hevalê *t'ewrî baş*** (B) *the best* friend **•*t'ewrî mezin*** (K) *the biggest* **•*yê tew[r]î biçûk*** (BK) *the smallest one*. {also: tewî (BK-2)} [BK/K/JB3/B] <here I; ji hemû -tir; -tirîn>

t'ewş تـەوش *adj.* worthless, good for nothing, useless; unprofitable; in vain: •**Lê çûbûn ku? Ji xwedê pê ve kesî ne dizanî. Me dest pê kir em li gundên hawirdor gerîyan. Gund bi gund me pirsî. Lê *tewşbû.* Me tu salox ji wan negirtin** (MB-Zava yê dehsalî) But where had they gone? Only God knew for sure. We began to look in the surrounding villages. We asked in every last village. But *it was no use*. We could find no trace of them anywhere. [MB/K/GF/TF/OK] <badîhewa; bêkêr; t'ewt'ewe>

tewşî تەوشى (SK) = adze. See **t'evşo**.

t'ewt'ewe تـەوتـەوە *adj.* good for nothing, worthless *(person)* (HR-1); busybody, nosy, gossip (IFb): •**Dih jî vî wextî dido weke te hatin, go: 'eqlê mi ji wa her duwa negirt. Ne ti camêr bûn, *t'ewt'ewe* bûn** (HR-I, 3:31) Yesterday at about this time two [fellows] like you came, but I didn't like them. They were not well-mannered <camêr>, they were *good-for-nothings.* {syn: emekḧeram; qeşmer} [HR-I/A/IFb/GF/RF] <'ewan; qumsî; sakol; t'ewş>

tewz تـەوز *f./m.(FS)* **(-a/-ê;).** joke; derision, scorn, mockery: **-tewza xwe lê kirin** (Glosbe)/**tewzê xwe pê kirin** (FS) to tease, make fun of, mock: •**Ew *tewzê xwe bi* Zoroyî *dikit*** (FS) He *teases* Z. {also: tewiz (GF); <ṭevz> طـڤـز (HH)} {syn: ḧenek; qerf; tinaz; t'iřane; yarî II} Cf. P ṭanz طنز = 'ridicule'; Sor tewze تـەوزە = 'mockery' [Ad/JB3/IFb/TF/OK/ZF3/FS//GF//HH] <me'na; pêk'enok; qerf>

t'ex•e تـەخـە *f.* **(•a;).** 1) (orderly) stack *(e.g., of grape leaves neatly piled one on top of the next; cf.* ***kom*** *= pile, heap--haphazard, no particular order)*; 2) small bundle, as of tobacco leaves (HH): •**texa tûtinî** (FS) bundle or stack of tobacco leaves. {also: tax II (FS-2); taxe II, m. (IFb/GF-2/OK); tûx (FS-2); <taxe> تاخه (HH)} [Bw/GF/FS//IFb/HH/OK]

texlîd تەخليد (ZF3) = kind, sort, type. See **t'exlît**.

t'exlît تەخليت *m.* **(-ê;-î).** kind, sort, type: •**4-5 *texlîtên* kewan hene ko 'kew sîs' jî yek ji wan e** (MG) There are 4-5 *types* of partridge, of which 'kew sîs' is one •**Ev herdu peřok *texlîtek* in** (FS) These two cloths are of *one kind* (i.e., the same) •**kaxizên ji her *texlîdî*** (ZF3) papers of every *kind* •**Wî peřok ji *texlîtê* peřokê te kiřî** (FS) He bought a cloth of *the type that* your cloth [is]. {also: texlîd (ZF3); <texlît> تـخـلـيـت (HH)} {syn: cins; cûře; řeng} < Ar taqlīd تـقـلـيـد = 'imitation' [T taklit] (or taxlīṭ تـخـلـيـط = 'mixture' [T tahlit]); Sor texlît تەخليت [MG/K/IFb/FJ/GF/TF/HH/Kmc/FS//ZF3]

t'exmîn تـەخـمـيـن *f.* **(-a;-ê).** 1) supposition, guess, assumption; **-bi t'exmîna min** (B) in my opinion; **-t'exmîn kirin** = a) to suppose, guess, presume, assume: •**M. û Z.va *t'exmîn kirin*** [sic], **wekî sîyar îdî ji şeher dûr k'etine** (Z-1) M. and Z. *supposed* that the horsemen were by now far away from the city •**Mîr got, "Her kesê mizgînîya ṯeyrî bo min bînît ez dê xelatekî bi keyfa wî dem ê." Xelkî jî weto *texmîn kirin*** [sic] **mîr beḧsê mizgînîya ṯeyrê biharê ye** (SK 29:261) The Mir said, "Whoever brings me the good news of the bird I shall give him a present which will please him." People *imagined* that the Mir was talking of the good news of the coming of the bird of spring; b) to think; c) to estimate; 2) estimate. {also: [takhmin] تـخـمـيـن (JJ); <texmîn> تـخـمـيـن (HH)} < Ar taxmīn تخمين --> T tahmin (√x-m-n II خمّن) [Z-1/K/JB3/IFb/B/JJ/HH/SK]

texsî تەخسى (SBx/ZF) = taxi cab. See **t'aksî**.

t'exsîr تـەخـسـيـر *f.* **(-a;-ê).** negligence, being remiss: **-t'exsîr kirin** (B/Z-1) to be negligent or remiss; [in *neg.*] not to spare (effort): •**Xelefê Zêbarî di çavên min de mîna çiyayekî bû. Heger ew rojekê li min biqesidiyaya, min dê tiştek ji bo wî *texsîr nekiraya*** (Wkt:E.Karahan: *Nesrîn*, Nefel.com, ix.2009) Khalaf Zebari was a mountain in my eyes. If one day he had come to me with a problem, I *would have spared nothing* [to help him] •**Zînê cahil bû, usa jî Memê, evînî usa ew biribûn, wekî gilîyê Bek'oyê qomsî *t'exsîr nekirin*** (Z-1) Zin was naive, so was Mem; love brought them to the point where they *didn't spare* [their love], just as Beko the troublemaker [didn't spare] his complaining. {also: teqsîr (ZF3-2); texstîr (B-2); [taksír] تـقـصـيـر (JJ) = ménagement} < Ar taqṣīr تقصير --> P taqṣīr تقصير --> T taksir (√q-ṣ-r II قصّر) [Z-1/IFb/B/TF/OK/ZF3//JJ] <hêvşandin>

texstîr تەخستير (B) = negligence; sparing. See **t'exsîr**.

text/t'ext [B] تـەخـت *m.* **(-ê;).** 1) {syn: cî [2]; nivîn} bed *(outside on the roof, in summer; cf.* ***cî****, indoor bed)*; 2) throne: **-text û t'ac/text-t'ac**, *m.* = throne and crown (=sovereign power): •[A childless king complains as follows] **Gelo xwedê, wekî ez bimirim, *t'ext û t'acê* minê bêxayî bimîne** (Z-921) Oh God, when I die, my *throne and crown* will have no owner; **-t'extê p'adşê** (B) the royal throne. {also: [tekht] تخت (JJ); <text> تخت (HH)} < Ar/P taxt تخت [L/K/A/JB3/IFb/B/JJ/HH/SK/GF/TF]

t'exte تەختە *m.* **(-yê;).** 1) board, plank; 2) game board: **-texteyê şetrencê** (Ag) chessboard. {also: [takhta/tekhté] تختە (JJ); <texte> تەختە (HH)} {syn: dep; keval} Cf. P taxte تخته --> T tahta [EP-7/K/IFb/B/JJ/HH/GF/Qmş/Ag]

t'extik تەختِك = dim. of **t'exte**.

teyamîş تەيامیش (K/B) = firm, steady. See **tamîş**.

teyar•e تەیارە/طەیارە **t̰eyare** طەیارە *f.* **(;•ê).** airplane. {syn: balafiȓ; fiȓoke} < Ar ṭayyārah طيّارة = 'airplane' (√ṭ-y-r طير = 'to fly') [EP-7/K/IFb/B]

t'eyax/teyax [K/B] تەیاخ *adj.* strong, firm, solid, stable, steady, hardy: **-teyax da[yî]n/kirin** (B) to bear *(a burden)*; to endure, stand, withstand, bear: **•Hineka ji wana nikarbû ber qeweta avê *teyax bida*, avê ew berjêr dibirin** (Ba2-3, 216) Some of them could not *withstand* the force of the water, the water pulled them under **•T'alana, dizîyê, ȓuşeta, girtinê, mêrkuştinê, bêzakonîyê gundîyêd belengaz gihîyandibûne xezebê, wana îda nikaribû *teyax bida*** (Ba2-3, 214) Depredations, stealing, brivery, arrests, murder, lawlessness had made the miserable villagers [so] angry that they could no longer *endure it* **•Vira me îda *teyax neda*, dest pê kir hevȓa kire qîȓîn û gazî** (Ba2-4, 222) We *could no longer hold it in*, [and] all together began to scream and yell. <T dayak & Az T dayag = 'prop, support' [Ba2/K/B/GF] <meḧkem; zexm>

teybetî تەیبەتی (A) = specific characteristic. See **t'aybetî**.

t'eyfe تەیفە (B/Ba2) = tribe. See **t̰ayfe**.

teyfik تەیفِك *f.* **(-a;-ê).** dish, plate: **•*Teyfika xwe* heta serî tijî dike** (S.Yalsizûçanlar. Cam û Almast, 42) He fills his *plate* to the limit. {syn: dewrî; firaq} [Frq/Kmc-7004/IFb/ZF/RZ] <aman>

teyfî تەیفی (FD/BF) = type of grape. See **tayfî**.

teyisandin تەیِساندِن/طەیِساندِن **t̰eyisandin** [FS] *vt.* **(-teyisîn-).** to shine *(vt.)*, polish, cause to shine or glisten: **•Wî 'eyne hind paqij kir, heta ku *t̰eyisand*** (FS) He cleaned the mirror so well that he *made* it *shine*. {syn: biriqandin; çirûsandin} [Dh/IFb/GF/TF/OK//FS] <teyisîn>

teyisîn تەیِسین/طەیِسین **t̰eyisîn** [FS] *vi.* **(-teyis-).** to shine *(vi.)*, glisten, glimmer, gleam, glitter, sparkle. {also: teysîn (K/GF); t̰eysîn (M-Zx); [teïsin] تیسین (JJ)} {syn: biriqîn; birûs[k]în; çirûsîn; teys dan} [K/GF/JJ//M-Zx//FS//IFb/TF/OK] <teyisandin>

teyîrîn تەیرین *vi.* **(-teyîr-).** to fly: **•Ȓuḧ lê teyîrîn** (Z-1) Their hearts sunk [lit. 'Souls flew from it']. {syn: fiȓîn} < Ar ṭāra طار (yaṭīru) (يطير) [Z-1]

***teyk** تەیك **().** low-quality raisins that have fallen onto the ground from the vine. {syn: bistaq (Msr/HH)} [Klk] <mewîj>

teyr تەیر/**t̰eyr** طەیر [FS/JJ/HH] *m.* **(-ê;-î).** 1) bird; large bird (B): **•Wana *teyrek* kuşt** (Ba) They killed *a bird* **•Tuê *wî teyrî* bibî ji hakim re** (L) You will take *that bird* to the prince **•Xûna *teyr*** (Ba) The *bird*'s blood; **-tav û teyr** (EP-7) beast and birds, wildlife, fauna, 'the birds and the bees'; **-teyrê bazî** (K) eagle; **-teyrê et'meçe** (B) falcon; **-teyrê sîmiȓ** (B) simurgh; **-teyr û tû/teyrtû** (K) = birds, fowl, winged creatures: **•*Ne teyre, ne tîye*, ne cote, ne cotk'arî** (Z-1) It is *neither bird, nor fowl*, nor plow, nor farmer; 2) {syn: elîh} eagle (J). {also: teîr (F/J); têr II (IF-2); [teïr] طير (JJ); <t̰eyr> طير (HH)} {syn: ç'ûk I; teyare [2]} < Ar ṭā'ir طائر = 'bird'; Sor teyr تەیر [Ba/L/K/JB3/IFb/B/GF//JJ/HH/F//J]

teyred•e تەیردە *pl.* **(;•a).** birds, particularly large, wild birds. {syn: teyr û tû} [Z-828/K/B]

teyrik I تەیرِك/طەیرِك **t̰eyrik** [JJ] *m.* **(-ê;-î).** small bird [*dim. of* **teyr**]: **•Ewî doxtir sê dest derman nvîsî** [sic], **kire k'aẍezêda, p'eȓê *wî teyrikî* va dirût, *teyrik* berda** (HCK-5, #41, 233) That doctor wrote 3 cures [prescriptions], put them down on paper, sewed them to the the feathers *of that little bird*, and let *the bird* go. {also: [teirik] طيرك (JJ)} [HCK/JJ/ZF3]

teyrik II تەیرِك (GF) = hail[stones]. See **teyrok**.

teyrok تەیرۆك/طەیرۆك **t̰eyrok** [FS] *f.* **(-a;-ê).** 1) {syn: gijlok; zîpik I} hail[stones] *(precipitation)*: **•Ḧetanî êvarê wana ber tavê, suȓê û sermê, bin baranê û *teyrokê*, carna t'î û birçî pez diç'êrand** (Ba2:1, 204) They would graze the sheep until evening in sunlight and cold, under rain and *hail*, sometimes [even] hungry and thirsty **•*Teyrok* tê/dibare** = It's hailing **•*Teyrok* zerareke mezin didin sebze û mêweyên nû** (Wkp) *Hail-stones* bring great harm to new [young] vegetables and fruits; 2) {syn: girmîn} thunder(storm). {also: teîrok (F); tergijok (Zeb); teyrik II (GF-2); tîrî (IFb-2); [teirik تيرك/teirouk تيروك] (JJ); <t̰eyrok> طيروك (HH)} Cf. Southern Tati dialects (all *f.*):

Chali & Sagz-abadi tiarsa; Takestani terezga; Eshtehardi tiarga (Yar-shater); P tegarg تگرگ; Sor terze تەرزە; Za torg *f.* (Todd). *Note the form tergijok (Zeb) [cf.* ***gijlok*** *=* ***teyrok]*** [K/A/IFb/B/GF/RZ//JJ//HH/FS//Zeb] <baran; berf; şilî; *types of hail*: savarok & xilolîk [1] = 'tiny hailstones'>

teyrtû تەیرتوو (K) = birds. See under **teyr**.

teys تەیس: **-teys dan** (EP-7) to sparkle, twinkle, glitter, shine {syn: teyisîn}: **•Kuř mîna şemalekê *teys da*** (EP-7) The boy *sparkled* like a light. [EP-7]

teysîn تەیسین (K/GF/JJ)/ţeysîn طەیسین (M-Zx) = to sparkle. See **teyisîn**.

tezbêh تەزبێه (OK) = prayer beads. See **t'izbî**.

t'eze تەزە (Dz/K/B/A/IFb) = fresh; new. See **t'aze**.

tezî I تەزی/te'zî تەعزی (B) = naked. See **tazî I**.

ţezî II طەزی [Bw/FS]/**tezî** تەزی [GF/RZ] *adj.* cold *(of water)*: **•Wî bi ava *tezî* serê xo şûşt** (FS) He showered with *cold* water. {syn: sar} [Bw/FS//GF/RZ] <cemidîn; qefilîn [1]>

ţezîlank طەزیلانك (FS) = numbness. See **ţezţezînk**.

tezîn تەزین (OK)/ţezîn طەزین (M-Am & Zx/HH) = to go numb. See **tevizîn**.

te'zîtî تەعزیتی (B) = nudity. See **tazîtî**.

t'ezî'yî تەزیعیی (K) = condolence. See **t'azîye**.

ţezţezînk طەزطەزینك *f.* (;-ê). numbness, "falling asleep" of hand or foot: **-teztezînk girtin** (Bw) to be numb, go to sleep of hand or foot {syn: tevizîn}: **•Destê min *ţezţezînkê girt*** (Bw) My hand *fell asleep*. cf. ţezîn (M-Am & Zx) = to go numb. {also: ţezîlank (FS-2)} [Bw/FS] <tevizîn>

têbînî تێبینی *f.* **(-ya;-yê).** 1) comment, remark: **•Zoroyî *têbînîya* wî pejirand** (FS) Z. accepted his *remark*; 2) {syn: jêrenot} note, footnote (IFb/TF). Sor têbînî تێبینی = 'careful consideration, deliberation, caution' [(neol)voA/K(s)/IFb/GF/TF/OK/FS]

têda تێدا *adv.* in it, therein, there; inside: **-têda hatin** (BK) to be stricken suddenly with a fatal disease; to suffer a stroke; to have a heart attack: ***•têda hato*** (BK) *said to a person you wish would be stricken suddenly with a fatal disease or would suffer a stroke [curse]*; **-tê de man** (IFb) to be stuck, not to know what to do; to fail: **•Mamosta ji min pirsî, ez *têde mam*** (IF)b The professor asked me, [and] I *was stuck*. {also: têde/tê de (IFb); [tida] تیدا (JJ)} < di + wî/wê + da = 'in it'; Sor têda تێدا/tya تیا [BK//IF//JJ]

tê•dan تێدان *vt.* **(tê-d-/-de- [Bw]).** to spread *(e.g., butter on bread)*, smear: **•Min divêt hinde(k) teĥînê *di* nanê xo *bidem*** (Bw) I want *to spread* some tahina [=sesame sauce] on my bread **•Min kerî nan hilda řûn *têda* û xwar** (B) I took a piece of bread, *spread* butter [on it] and ate [it] **•Qesir p'aqij kirin u hinik ĥeřî *têdan*, dûtin ...** (JB1-S, #197) They tidied up the castle and *spread* some mud and coated [the floor with it]. {also: [ti-dan تیدان/ti-dàin تیداین] (JJ)} [Bw/K/B/JB1-A&S/GF/TF/OK/ZF3/FS//JJ] <dûtin; seyandin>

têde تێدە/tê de تێ دە (IFb) = in it; inside. See **têda**.

têderxistinok تێدەرخستنۆك *f.* **(-a;-ê).** riddle: **•Şêx bi cûre *têderxistinokê* pirse dide Aqûb** (www.pen-kurd.org:E.Boyîk.Qewlê Şêx û Aqûb) The sheikh questions Jacob with a type of *riddle*. {syn: apik; mamik; tiştanok (Z); tiştik} [IFb/ZF3] <xaçerêz>

têgeh تێگەه (Helbest) = meaning; concept. See **têgih**.

têgehandin تێگەهاندن (SK) = to clarify. See **têgihandin**.

têgeheştin تێگەهەشتن (Bw) = to comprehend. See **têgihan**.

têgehîştin تێگەهیشتن = to comprehend. See **têgihan**.

têgeyan تێگەیان (A) = to comprehend. See **têgihan**.

têgeyîştin تێگەییشتن (A) = to comprehend. See **têgihan**.

têgih تێگِه *f./m.(Helbest)* **(/-ê;).** 1) {syn: me'na; wate} meaning, sense; 2) term, concept: ***•Têgehê*** **neteweperweriyê di gelek biyavan da dihêt bikarînan** (Helbest 9 [2013], 7) *The term* 'nationalist' is used in many fields. {also: têgeh (Helbest)} [(neol)Wlt/ZF/CS//Helbest]

tê•gihan تێ گِهان *vi.* **(tê-gihê-).** 1) to realize, comprehend: **•Ez *têgiham* ku ez kurdekî asîmîlekirî me** (Ber) I *realized* that I was an assimilated Kurd; 2) {syn: fehm kirin} to understand (Bw): ***•Di* êk û dû *digihen*** (Bw) They *understand* each other **•Eger xelet ez *tê negeheşt-im*** (Bw) If I understood correctly [lit. 'If I *didn't understand* incorrectly'] **•Mîr got, "Her kesê mizgînîya ţeyrî bo min bînît ez dê xelatekî bi keyfa wî dem ê." Xelkî jî weto texmîn kirin** [sic] **mîr beĥsê mizgînîya ţeyrê biharê ye. Meqseda mîr *tê-negeştin* çi ye** (SK 29:261) The Mir said, "Whoever brings me the good news of the bird I shall give him a present which will please him." People imagined that the Mir was talking of the good news of the coming of the bird of spring. They *did not understand* the Mir's meaning. {also: têgeheştin (Bw); têgehîştin;

têgeyan (A); têgeyîştin (A); têgihaştin (IFb-2); têgihîn (IFb-2); têgihîştin (tê-gihîj-) (K/IFb)} Cf. Sor têgeyştin تێ گەیشتِن = 'to understand' [Ber//K/IFb//A//Bw]

têgihandin تـێ گِـهـانـدِن *vt.* **(tê-gihîn-).** to clarify, explain, give to understand: **•Û neferatêt quşonî ket-ket *tê-bigehînin* ko ser-bi-xo r̄e'îyetê 'aciz neken we milletî dil-xoş biken** (SK 56:658) And they should *give* the personnel of the army *to understand*, one by one, that they should not independently annoy the populace, and they should placate the people **•Wextê ko şêx ew xebere digot xulaman dizanî çi ye dibêjît, çonko di pêşda *tê-gehandibûn*** (SK 50:529) When the Shaikh said this the henchmen knew what he was implying because he had previously *given* them *to understand* [=*had explained* it to them]. {also: têgehandin (SK)} {syn: îzah kirin; r̄ave kirin; şîrove kirin} Sor têgeyandin تێ گەیاندِن [Bw/IFb/GF/OK//SK] <şîrove kirin; têgihan>

têgihaştin تـێـگِـهـاشـتِـن (IFb) = to comprehend. See **têgihan**.

têgihîn تێگِهین (IFb) = to comprehend. See **têgihan**.

têgihîştin تـێـگِـهـیـشـتِـن (tê-gihîj-) (K/IFb) = to comprehend. See **têgihan**.

têhelandin تـێـهەلانـدِن (tê-helîn-) (OK) = to dip (bread into food). See **têhilandin**.

tê•hilandin تێ هِلاندِن *vt.* **(tê-hilîn-).** to dip, e.g., one's folded piece of bread into food, using the bread in place of a fork or spoon; to dip into water (FS): **•Wî tirar *di* kanîyê *hiland*** (FS) He *dipped* the copper cup into the well. {also: têhelandin (tê-helîn-) (OK)} [Bw/GF/FS//OK]

têhn تێهن (Zeb/FS) = energy, power. See **tên**.

têhnî تێهنی (Bw/JB1-A) = thirsty. See **tî III**.

têje تێژە, m. (K) = young of animal, cub. See **têjik**.

têj•ik تـێـژك *f.* **(•ka;•ikê).** cub, whelp, young of animal: **•*Tejikê* mara ji mara p'îstirin** (Dz #1493) The snakes' *young* are worse [lit. 'dirtier'] than the snakes *[prv.]*; **-têjka [têşka] biznê** (Bw) kid; **-têjka kitkê** (Bw) kitten; **-têjka mirîşkê** (Bw) chick {syn: *çîçelok}; **-têjka şêrî** (Bw) lion cub {syn: ferxeşêr}: **•*Têjka şêrî* her şêr e** (Bw) *A lion cub* is still a lion *[prv.]*. {also: **ç'êjik**; tejik II (Dz); têje, m. (K); <têjik> تـيـژك (HH); <têjik> تێژك (Hej)} [Dz//IFb/B/HH/Hej/Bw//K] <ç'elîk>

têk تـێـك *adv.* together. {also: t'ev I; [tikda] تـكـدا (JJ)} < di + êk [BX/K(s)/IFb//JJ]

têkçon تێكچۆن (SK) = to be ruined. See **têkçûn**.

têk•çûn تێكچوون *vi.* **(têk-ç-).** 1) to be spoiled, ruined, destroyed; to fail: **•We ye xudê her tiştî dişêt biket, emma tiştê muxayirî 'adet hemî wexta naket, *da* nizam o r̄ewişta dunyaê *têk-neçît*** (SK 9:93) It is so, that God can do everything, but He does not always do extraordinary things *lest* the order and course of the world *be destroyed*; 2) to shrink *(of clothes)* (Dh/BF); 3) to be angry (SK): **•Ilyasof got, "Baş e, bipirse," emma pîçek *têkço*, li wî xoş nehat** (SK 54:591) Ilyasof said, "Okay, ask," but *he was* a little *angry*, he didn't like it; 4) [*f.* **(-a;-ê).**] failure, foiled attempt; argument, quarrel: **•Dewleta tirk, tevî hemû *têkçûnên* polîtîkayên xwe yên pişaftinê (asîmîlasyonê) dev ji van kirinên xwe bernade** (Wlt 1:35, 5) The Turkish state, in spite of all its political *failures* at assimilation, will not give up those activities. {also: têkçon (SK); têkçûyin (TF)} [K(s)/A/JB3/IFb/Dh/FJ/GF/ZF/BF//SK//TF]

têkçûyin تێكچووين (TF) = to be ruined. See **têkçûn**.

têk•dan تـێـكـدان *vt.* **(têk-d[e]-).** 1) to upset, ruin, mess up, spoil: **•Meydana şerî bi carekê wekî topeke agirî lê hat û terr û hişk hemî *têkda*** (Çandname: Destana Dimdim ya Çîrokî 10.x.2017) The battlefield suddenly became like a fireball and *destroyed* everything, both wet and dry; 2) {syn: lê sor kirin; nav tê dan} to provoke, stir up, incite (IFb/OK/RF/CS); 3) to mix, stir (HH/ZF/GF/FJ): **•Savarê xwe *têkda*** (GF) He *mixed/stirred* his bulghur. {also: <têkdan تـيـكـدان (têkdide) (تـيـكـدده)> (HH)} [Zeb/K/A/IFb/OK/RF/Hej/GF/FJ/HH/ZF/SS/CS]

têkel تێكەل (MUs/K[s]/IFb) = mixed up. See **têkil**.

têkelî تـێـكـەلـی (IFb/SK) = mixture; interference. See **têkilî**.

tê•k'etin تـێ كـەتِـن *vi.* **(tê-k'ev-).** to enter, go into: **•Daristaneke weha ye ku piling *têkevê* nema dikare ji nav derkeve** (SF 19) It is such a [dense] forest that if a tiger *enters it*, he can't get back out **•Emê derbas bibin, em*ê* *têkevin nava* bajêr** (L) We will pass [through the gates], we *will enter* the city **•Ezê lê suwar bibim, *têkevim* vê tatê** (L) I will mount it [=the magic flying cauldron] and *enter* the boulder **•[Ji] tirsa gura kesekî dil nedikir *têk'eve nava* wan kevira** (Ba2:2, 205) For fear of wolves no one dared *go between* those boulders. {syn: k'etin [2]} [L/K/GF/TF/Ba2]

têkil تێكِل *adj.* mixed up: **•Lê, tişt, cîh û wextên *têkel***

bi ser wî re tên (MUs, 8) But *mixed up* things, places, and times pass by him; **-têkil kirin** (GF/OK)/**têkel kirin** (IFb) to mix, mix up, stir up; **-xwe têkil fk-î/ft-î kirin** (Hk) to get involved with: •**Xwe *têkil* ṣa *neke*** (Hk) *Don't get involved with* dogs = Stay away from dogs. {also: têkel (MUs/K[s]/IFb)} Cf. [tikil] تــكــل (JJ) = trouble, mélange & [teklavé kirin] تكلاوه كرين = 'to mix' & <têklihevkirin> تـيـكـلـهـڤـكـرن (HH) = 'to mix two things together'; *according to BX* < di + êk + li [BX/Hk/K/GF/OK//MUs/K(s)/IFb] See also **têkilî**.

têkildar تـێـكِـلدار *adj.* [+**bi** ... **ve**] involved (in/with): •**Divê serokên ku ji alî gel ve têne hilbijartin, *bi* hemû pirsgirêkên gel *ve têkildar* bibin** (Wlt 1:49, 16) Leaders who are elected by the people should be *involved in* all of the problems of the people. [(neol)Wlt/ZF3/Wkt] <girêdayî; têkilî>

têkilî تێكِلى *f.* **(-ya;-yê).** 1) mixture, mixing, blending: •***têkilîya* zaravayan** (Ber) *mixing of* dialects; 2) interference, intervention; involvement: **-têkilî bûn** (K/JB3) a) to be mixed (K[s]/JB3); b) to interfere (K[s]); **-xwe têkilî kirin** = a) to interfere in/with (K[s]); b) to participate, take part in (JB3); 3) {syn: peywendî} connection, relation(ship): •**Ev mînak di heman demê de *têkiliya* di navbera folklor û edebiyatê de jî şanî me dide** (YPA, 41) This example at the same time also shows us *the connection* between folklore and literature •***Têkilya* min pê nîne** (GF) I have nothing to do with it/I have no *connection* to it; **-k'etin têkilîyê** (RN2) to get in touch with, contact: •**Berîya ku civîn bê organizekirin, berpirsiyarên Enstîtuya Kurdî bi berpirsiyarên kovar, rojname, weşanxaneyan û bi nivîskarên Kurd re *ketin têkiliyê*** (RN2 14:80 [#37], 3) Before the meeting was organized, those in charge of [lit. 'responsible for'] the Kurdish Institute *got in touch* with the heads of Kurdish journals, newspapers, publishing houses, and with Kurdish writers. {also: têkelî (IFb/SK); têkîlî; têklî (K[s]); [tikil] تــكــل (JJ)} Sor têkeł تـێـكـەڵـى/têkeławî تـێـكـەڵاوى = 'intermixture, complexity, intimacy, close friendship' [Ber/[GF]/TF/OK//IFb/SK//K(s)//JJ] <hatin û çûn>

tê•kirin تێ كِرِن *vt.* **(tê-k-).** 1) to put, place, set (K); 2) to insert, put in, stick in; to load; to fill up; 3) to pour into *(e.g., tea into a glass, sugar into a glass full of tea)*: •**"Çawêt min sor bûne?" Rîwî got, "Helbet. Dibêjî dermanê qirmizî *hatîye têkirin*"** (SK 6:68) "Have my eyes become red?""The fox said, "Certainly, you'd think red dye *had been poured* into them" •**Çayekê bo min *tê ke*** (Bw) *Pour* me a glass of tea. {also: têr̄a kirin (B); [ti kirin] تـى كـريـن (JJ)} Sor tê•kirdin تـێ كِـردِن = 'to pour out (into)' [Z-1/K/JB3/GF/Bw//JJ//B]

têkîlî تێكيلى = mixture; interference. See **têkilî**.

têklî تێكلى (K[s]) = mixture; interference. See **têkilî**.

têkoşer تـێـكـۆشـەر *m.&f.* **(-ê/-a;).** fighter *(for a cause or an ideal)*, s.o. willing to struggle *(for stg.)*, defender; combatant, warrior; struggler: •**Li dijî *têkoşerên* serxwebûna Kurdistanê şerekî gemarî dimeşîne** (Wlt 1:36, 1) It is carrying out a dirty war against *those fighting for* the independence of Kurdistan. Sor têkoşer تێكۆشەر = 'one who strives; warrior' [(neol)Wlt/IFb/GF/TF] <têkoşîn>

tê•koşîn تـێ كـۆشـين *vi.* **(tê-koş-).** 1) to try, attempt; to exert o.s., strive; 2) to struggle, fight; 3) [*f.* **(-a;-ê).**] striving (for), aspiration (to); struggle, fight: •***Têkoşîna* rizgariyê hêz divê** (Ber) *Striving for* freedom requires force. {also: têkûşan; têkûşîn (JB3)} Cf. Sor têkoşan تـێ كـۆشـان/têkoşîn تـێ كۆشين = 'to strive' [Ber/K/IFb/GF/TF//JB3]

têkûşan تـێ كـووشـان = to strive; to struggle; striving; activity. See **têkoşîn**.

têkûşîn تـێ كـووشـيـن (JB3) = to strive; to struggle; striving; activity. See **têkoşîn**.

t'êl تـێـل *f./m.(B)* **(-a/ê;-ê/).** 1) wire; string of musical instrument (guitar, fiddle, etc.) ; 2) {syn: dezî; ta I} thread: **-t'êlê r̄îs** (B) yarn; 3) string (K); 4) telegram; telegraph. {also: [tel] تـل (JJ)} *Bailey's etymology*: [Pok. 3. ter- 1071.] 'to rub, turn; to bore': O Ir *taryrya-: Khotanese ttīla- = 'string, wire of musical instrument'; Oss tel = 'wire'; Sor tel تەل = '(metal) wire'; *both* T tel *and* Arm t'el թել are loans. For detailed etymology see: H. W. Bailey. "A Range of Iranica" in: *W. B. Henning Memorial Volume* (London : Lund Humphries, 1970), pp. 30-33 [under **7. tēl**]. [F/K/(A)/IFb/B/JB1-S/GF/SC//JJ] <[2] derzî; gulok>

t'êlegraf تـێـلـەگـراف (B) = telegram; telegraph. See **t'êlgraf**.

t'êlêfon تێلێفون (B) = telephone. See **t'elefon**.

t'êlgiraf تـێـلـگِـراف (K) = telegram; telegraph. See **t'êlgraf**.

t'êlgraf تێلگراف *f.* **(-a;-ê).** telegraph; telegram, wire, cable: **•Gelek muro ji her doyan hatin e kuştin, belê mala Şêxê Bicîlê digotin nîw milyon lîre zerer hat ê. Şêxê Bicîlê 'erzi-ĥal dan e walîyê Mûsilê.** ***Telẍraf*** **kêşan e meqamêt 'aliye** (SK 50:535) Many men were killed on both sides but it was said that the Shaikh of Bijil's family suffered a loss of half a million lire. The Shaikh of Bijil sent petitions to the Governor of Mosul. *Telegrams* were sent to higher authorities **•Ji K.P. ra** ***têlgraf*** **şandîye û daye zanîn ku ew heval-bendê wî … ye** (Bkp, 29) He sent *a telegram* to K.P. and let him know that he was … his ally. {also: t'elegraf (K-2); telexraf (IFb); telgiraf (FJ/TF/CS); telgraf (A/ZF); telẍraf (SK); t'êlegraf (B); t'êlgiraf (K)} {syn: *birqî} < Gr telegraph- (tēl- = 'far, remote' + graph = 'writing') --> T telgraf & Ar tiliɣrāf تلغراف [Bkp//K//B//IFb//FJ/TF/CS//A/ZF//SK]

t'êlk'êş تـيـلـكـيـش **().** quiver; sheath: **•Ji ber xwe hilk'işand** ***t'êlk'êş*** **Zilfeqare** (EP-7) He unsheathed his Zulfikar {name of Ali ibn Abi Talib's sword, used metaphorically to denote any fine sword}. {also: [tirkech] تيركش (JJ)} [EP-7//JJ] <tûj>

tên تێن *f.(Zeb/IFb)/m.(OK)* **(-a/ ;).** 1) energy; power; effect of heat or warmth *(of fire or other source of energy)*: **•Lê her ku roj bilind dibû … zelaliya wê** ***tîna*** **xwe bi ser siyê ve hildiweşand** (Alkan, 70) But as the sun rose higher … the purity of its *warmth* overcame the shade; **-hêz û têhn** (Zeb) energy, power; **-tîna agirî** (IFb)/**têhna agirî** (FS) heat of the flame; **-tîna tavê** (IFb) heat of the sun, solar energy; 2) thirst (SK). See **tîn II**. {also: tehn (GF-2); têhn (Zeb-2/FS); tihn II (IFb-2); tîn I (K[s]/IFb-2/GF); <tîn> تين (Hej)} [Zeb/A/IFb/OK//K(s)/GF/Hej//FS] <birî I>

tênî تێنی (Bw/SK/OK) = thirsty. See **tî III**.

tênîtî تێنیتی (OK) = thirst. See **tîn II**.

t'êr I تـێـر *adj.* 1) {syn: zikt'êr} full, sated, satisfied, having had one's fill: **•B. çend roja li wê derê ma, xwe rihet kir,** ***têr*** **li nav bajarê wan** ***gerîya*** (L) B. stayed there a few days, relaxed, *had his fill of walking around* their town **•Em** ***têra*** **xwe ne** (L) We *can take care of* ourselves **•Emê vira bimînin,** ***t'êr*** **hevr̄a xeverdin** (Z-1) We will stay here, and *have our fill of* speaking together **•Gişk tên li Ûsib dinihêrin,** ***ji*** **bedewtîya wî** ***t'êr nabin*** (Ba) Everyone comes [and] looks at Joseph; they *can't have enough of* his beauty **•Herekê me gepeke, lê wekî tu me biçêrînî, her yekê me** ***t'êra*** **rojekêye** (J) Each one of us is [only] a bite, but if you take us to pasture, each one of us will [provide] a day's *satiety* (=will provide enough meat for a whole day's worth of eating) **•Xulamêt Eĥmed Aẍayê eslî dest dane metreqan, r̄abûne mutirban,** ***têr kutan*****, kirine der** (SK 27:251) The real Ahmad Agha's henchmen laid hold of their sticks and went for the Gypsy musicians, *gave them a thorough beating*, and drove them out **•Zikê** ***t'êr*** **haj zikê birçî t'une** (K) A *full* stomach doesn't comprehend a hungry one [lit. 'hungry stomach'] *[prv.]*; **-t'êr xwarin** = to eat one's fill, be satiated: **•Min** ***t'êr xwar*** = I'*ve had enough to eat*/I'm full; 2) [*pr. mod. & f.* **(-a;).**] enough (for + *ezafeh*), a fair amount: **•Azoqeyê me** ***têra*** **du mehane** (BF) Our provisions are *enough for* 2 months **•Go** ***t'êr*** **xwê mi kirîye tilya xwede** (HR 3:281) He said, I put *a fair amount of* salt on my finger; **-t'êra** ***ft-î*** **kirin** (B) to be enough, suffice: **•Ewî heqî** ***t'êra*** **xerc û xer̄acêd malêd wana** ***nedikir*** (Ba2:1, 204) Those wages *were not enough* to cover the expenses of their households **•Va ava** ***t'êra*** **du r̄oja** ***nake*** (B) This water *won't last for* two days [or, *won't be enough for* two days]; **-t'êra xwe** = enough: **•Ez** ***t'êra xwe*** **naxwim** = I don't eat *enough*/I don't eat until I'm full. {also: [tir] تير (JJ); <têr> تير (HH)} Cf. P sīr سير; Sor têr تێر {t'êrayî; têretî; t'êr[t]î} [F/K/A/JB3/IFb/B/HH/SK/JB1-A&S/GF/TF//JJ]

têr II تێر (IF) = bird. See **teyr**.

t'êr̄ III تـێـڕ *f.* **(;-ê).** (large) saddle bag; large sack: **•Behremî genim kir di** ***têr̄ê*** **da** (FS) B. put the wheat in *the sack* **•Herin** ***t'êr̄ê*** **mêvana bi genimê r̄ind dagirin** (Ba-1, #32) Come fill the guests' *sacks* with fine wheat **•Rewşê** ***têr̄*** **bi şûjinê dirû** (FS) R. sewed *the saddle bag* with a pack needle. {also: têr̄e (IFb-2); <têr> تـيـر (HH)} {syn: t'elîs; xaşî (IF); xerar (IF)} Sor têr̄ تێڕ [Z/K/IFb/B/GF/TF//HH] <şel II>

têr̄a kirin تێڕا کرن (B) = to put; to insert; to pour. See **têkirin**.

t'êrber تـێـربـەر *adj.* fruitful, fertile, productive: **•Ev navçeya bedew ku ji çar aliyên wê bi çol, beyar û çiyan ve hatiye dorpêçkirin, xwedî mexereke** ***têrber*** **e** (Gundê Avadorê [blogspot]) This lovely area [Kerboran] which is surrounded by wilderness, barren land and mountains, is on [lit. 'possessed of'] a *fertile* plain **•Zevîya wî têrber e** (FS) His field is *fertile*. {syn: bijûn[2]} < t'êr I + ber V [GundêAvadorê/IFb/Wkt/FS] <bêber>

têr̄e تێره (IFb) = large bag or sack. See **t'êr̄ III**.

Têrmeh تێرمەھ (IFb) = July. See **Tîrmeh**.

t'êrxew تێرخەو *adj.* well-rested, *having slept enough that one is no longer tired*: **•Birazîyê min berêvarkî çend seetkî raza, niha rabû dibêje: "Ez *têrxew* bûm, niha nikarim razim, xwezî ez *têrxew* nebûma"** (tirşik.net) My nephew slept for a few hours in the late afternoon, now he has gotten up and says, "I have slept [so much that] I can no longer sleep, if only I were not [so] *well-rested*" **•Tu têrxew bûyî?** (Şmd) Did you sleep well?/Are you well-rested? < t'êr I + xew [Şmd/tirşik.net/Wkt]

t'êrxwê تێرخوێ *adj.* salty, salted. {syn: şor̄ II} [Wkt/Hej]

têsik تێسِك (SS) = kicking (of donkeys). See **tîzik**.

têşî[k'] [ك]تێشی (JB1-A) = spindle. See **t'eşî**.

têşt (OK/SK/Bw)/t'êşt' (JB1-A) تێشت = breakfast; mid-morning coffee break. See **taştê**.

têştexew تێشتەخەو *f.* **(-a;).** sleeping late, sleeping in, waking up late in the morning: **•Dawud her ro *têştexewa diket*** (Bw) Every day Dawud *sleeps until late* **•Min *têştexeweka* xweş *kir*** (Bw) I *had a* good, *long sleep*/I slept in. [Bw/FS]

têtî تێتی *f.* **().** lark, zool. *Alaudidae*: **•Rabû *têtî* hêlîna xwe li tenişta gevizka fîl çêkir** (RN) *The lark* built her nest next to the elephant's scratching ground. {also: tîtî I (ZF/SS/CS/FS)} [RN//ZF/SS/CS/FS]

têvel تێڤەل *adj.* 1) various, varied: **•Ev hemû sedem jê re bûne alîkar ku zimanê wan zengîn be û *têvel* û rengîn be** (Nbh 133:40) All of these reasons came together [lit. 'were helpful to him'] so that their language was rich and *varied* and colorful; 2) different, distinct: **•Şev û roj *têvel* in** (Wkt) Night and day are *different* (from each other). [Nbh/IFb/FJ/GF/TF/ZF/Wkt/Kmc40/CS/SS]

tê•werandin تێ وەراندِن = to envelop, enfold, surround. See **werandin I**.

têwerkirin تێ وەركِرِن = to pelt, shower. See **werkirin**.

t'êx تێخ *f.* **(;-ê).** heap of unwinnowed grain (after threshing); **-t'êx kirin** (K)/**t'êẍ kirin** (B) to rake *unwinnowed grain* into a heap. {also: t'êẍ (B)} [CCG/K/IFb//B] <gêre I; sap>

tê•xistin تێ خِستِن *vt.* **(têx-).** 1) to insert, put into, add to: **•Çiqeyse êzingê we ... *têxin* filan çalê** (L) Everyone *put* your firewood in a certain ditch/pit **•Devê xwe *têxî* qula tatê** (L) *Put* your mouth *up to* the hole in the rock **•Qawekê ji mîrê xwer̄a bik'elîno / Tu *têxe* du ḧeb fincanê ferfûrî û dayne ser sênîya zêr̄îno** (Z-2) Boil coffee for your emir / *pour* it into two china cups and put them on a golden tray **•Ya dê, şîva min *têxe* bin textê min** (L) O mother, *put* my dinner under my bed; 2) to introduce, present (BX). [BX/K/A/JB3/IFb/GF/TF]

t'êẍ تێغ (B) = unwinnowed grain. See **t'êx**.

t'êz تێز *f.* **(-a;).** gunpowder. {also: <têz> تيز (HH)} {syn: barût} [Bw/A/IFb/HH/OK/ZF3/FS/BF]

têzav تێزاڤ (BF) = acid. See **tîjav**.

ti I تِ (Wkt) = you, thou. See **tu I**.

t'i II تِ (Z-3) = no, none. See **t'u II**.

tiam تِئام, f. (L) = taste; tasty food; tasting. See **ta'm**.

t'ibarek تِبارەك (K) = talisman. See **t'iberk**.

t'ibark تِبارك (K) = talisman. See **t'iberk**.

t'iberk تِبەرك *f.* **().** 1) {syn: nivişt; t'ilism} talisman, amulet (JB2/K/OK): **•Ḧeve xwel̄îya bin k'oka darê hilda nav desmalekêda girêda, kire ber pişta xwe çawa *t'iberk*** (JB2-Şamilov) She took a piece of dirt from under the tree [lit. 'under the root of the tree'] and wrapped it in a handkerchief, putting it in her belt as *a talisman*; 2) good omen, blessing (SK) [tebeṟuk]; 3) [*m.* **().**] flat cake given to the faithful on religious festivals *(among the Yezidis)* (B/HH). {also: tebeṟuk (SK); t'ibarek (K-2); t'ibark (K); <teberik> تبرك (HH)} <Ar tabarraka V تبرّك = 'to bode well' (<√b-r-k برك = 'blessing') [Bw/JB2/B/OK//K//HH//SK] <berbejn; sêr I>

t'ib•il تِبِل (•la) (Bw) = finger. See **t'ilî I**.

t'ibîḧet تِبیحەت, m. (Z-2) = nature; characteristic. See **tebî'et**.

t'icar تجار (IFb/JB1-A&S) = merchant. See **t'ucar II**.

t'icaret تِجارەت *f.* **(-a;-ê).** business, commerce, trade: **•Beyrim dest bi *tucaretiya* pez kir** (L-5, 182, l. 12-13) B. began *to trade* in sheep **•Bo min s̱ed bareka jî dirûst ke ji tişt'ê faxir, ez û tu dê çîne *t'icaretê*** (JB1-A, #61, 116) Make up 100 loads of precious things for me as well, you and I are going to do *business* **•Ew sale çak e biçim e kûstanêt Ert̲ûşîyan, hem ziyaret, hem *ticaret*** (SK 31:275) This year it would be good for me to go to the Artushi highlands both for a visit and for *business* **•Go mi *ticaretiya* xwe dikir** (HR 3:269) He said,

"I was doing *business* for myself". {also: t'icaretî (HR/JB1-A-2); t'icarî (K-2); t'îcaret (M-Am); t'ucaretî (K/L); t'ucarî (K-2/B); [tidjaret] تـجـارت (JJ)} {syn: bazirganî} < Ar tijārah تـجـارة [HR//M/JB1-A/SK/JJ//M-Am//K/L] <t'ucar II>

t'icaretî تِـجـارەتـی (HR/JB1-A) = business, trade. See **t'icaret**.

t'icarî تِجاری (K) = business, trade. See **t'icaret**.

tidarik تِـــــــــدارِك (HR) = preparations; repair. See **t'edarik**.

t'if تِـــف *f.* **().** saliva, spittle, sputum: **-t'if kirin** (K/A/IFb/HH/SK/GF) to spit, expectorate. {also: t'ûf (K-2); [tiw/touw] تـف (JJ); <tif> تـف (HH)} {syn: ava dev; girêz; t'ûk II} Cf. Ar taffa تـفّ = 'to spit'; P tof تـف; Sor tif تـف [K/A/IFb/HH/JB1-A/SK//JJ] See **t'û II** & **t'ûk II**.

t'ifal/tifal تِـفـال *f./m.(B)* **(;-ê/tifêl).** 1) {syn: kuř II; law; mindal; zaro} child; 2) greenhorn, inexperienced person (IFb). {also: [tufāli] طـفـالـی (JJ)} < Ar ṭifl طفل [EP-7/K/A/IFb/B//JJ]

t'ifaq تِـفـاق *f.* **().** 1) occurrence, event; 2) {syn: bela I; bêt'ar; boblat; gosirmet; oyîn; qeda; siqûmat; şetele} accident, disaster: **•Xwedê derê *tifaqa* bigre** (Haz) *greeting used when wishing someone who has been in an accident or the like 'a speedy recovery'* [Cf. Ar al-ḥamdu lillāh 'alá al-salāmah الـحـمـد لله عـلـى الـسـلامـة, T geçmiş olsun; lit. 'may God close the door of *accidents*']. {also: <tifaq> تـفـاق (HH)} < Ar ittifāq اتّـفـاق = 'accident, chance occurrence, coincidence', *verbal noun of* ittafaqa VIII اتّفق (√w-f-q وفق) [Haz/HH/GF] <bûyer; t'ifiqîn>

tifek تِفەك (GF/HH) = rifle. See **t'ifing**.

tifeng تِفەنگ (SK) = rifle. See **t'ifing**.

tiffik تِففِك (GF) = oven. See **t'ifik**.

t'ifik تِفِك *f.* **(-a;-ê).** oven, furnace; fireplace; any place where a fire has been lit for cooking, etc. {also: tiffik (GF); <tifik> تـفـك (HH)} {syn: kuçik II} [Haz/Frq/A/IFb/HH/TF//GF] <fiřne; tendûr>

t'ifing تِـفِـنـگ *f.* **(-a;-ê).** rifle, gun: **•Ji kûr tê, ji dûr tê, vedirêşê, xwîn tê [*tifing*]** (L) It comes from something deep, it comes from afar, it vomits, and blood flows *[rdl.; ans.: a rifle]*; **-tifing berdan** (IFb/ZF3) to fire at, shoot at s.o.: **•Emer *tifing* bera Efo *daye*** (H. Akyol. Zava ker in, 9) Emer *shot at* Efo; **-t'ifing teqandin** (IF) to shoot off a rifle. {also: tifek (GF-2); tifeng (SK); t'ivek (M-Zx); tiving (GF-2); t'iving (F/B); [toufek/tifek تـفـك/ tifenk تفنك] (JJ); <tifek> تفك (HH)} {syn: şeşderb; şeşxane} Cf. P tofang تـفـنـگ; T tüfek; Sor tifeng تِفەنگ; Za tifang *m.* (Mal); Hau tifeng *m.* (M4) [K/JB3/IFb/GF/TF//F/B//SK//JJ//HH//M-Zx] <aẍzûtî; berik II; debançe; gule; sîleh; şeşar>

t'ifiqîn تِـفِـقـیـن *vi.* **(-t'ifiq-).** 1) to appear, show up, come to light: **•Wekî cara duda tu li vira *t'ivqîî*, emê p'iřtkê teyî mezin guhê te bêhêlin** [sic] (EP-7) If you *show up* here again, we will fix it so that the largest piece of you is your ear!; 2) to be born *(of animals)*: **•Memê *t'iviqye* ji damnê dê** (EP-7) Mem *appeared* from (=was born out of) [his] mother's lap. {also: t'iviqîn (EP-7); [tifeqin] تفقين (JJ); <tifiqîn تفقين (ditifiqe) (دتفقه)> (HH)} < Ar ittafaqa VIII اتّـفـق (√w-f-q وفـق) = 'to agree; to occur' [EP-7//K/JJ/HH] <t'ifaq I>

tihe'l تِهەعل [sic] (GF) = spleen. See **teȟêl**.

tihêl تِهێل (TF) = spleen. See **teȟêl**.

tihn I تِهن (JB3/HH/GF) = thirsty. See **tî III**.

tihn II تِهن (IFb) = energy, power. See **tên**.

tihnayî تِهنایی (A) = thirst. See **tîn II**.

tihok تِـهـۆك *f.* **(-a;-ê).** European hackberry tree, bot. *Celtis tournefortii* [T dağdağan/dardağan]: **-Wekî şitla *tihokê*** (ZF3) tall and slender (like a *hackberry tree* sapling). {also: tahîk (Wkt-2); tawik (GF); tayî (Kmc-2); tehewî (GF-2); tehwî (Wkt-2); te'îtawûk (Kmc-2); tewok (SS); tiȟo (G); ti'ok (Kmc-2); tu'ok (Kmc-2)} [IFb/ZF3/FD/Wkt/Kmc//G//GF//SS]

tihtavik تِهتاڤِك *f.* **(-a;-ê).** mint, bot. *Mentha aquatica*: **•Pûjan (nane, *tihtavika* hişk a biharatî)** (KWkp: Şorbeya Gurgumê) Mint (dried mint used as a spice). {also: تهتاڤك <tihtavik> (HH)} {syn: pûjan; pûng} [KWkp/IFb/HH/FS/ZF3]

tiȟo تِحۆ (G) = hackberry tree. See **tihok**.

t'ije تِژە (GF) = full. See **t'ijî**.

t'ijî تِـــــژی *adj.* full *(of)*: **•Afir *tijî* ka ye** (AB) The trough is *full of* straw **•Firaq *tijî* savar e** (AB) The bowl is *full of* bulghur **•Qelûna bavê min *tijî* titûn e** (AB) My father's pipe is *full of* tobacco **•Sûk *tije* qumaş e, lê mela bêşaş e** (BX) The marketplace is *full of* cloth, but the mullah is turbanless *[prv.]* **•Tas *tijî* ava zelal e** (AB) The bowl is *full of* clear water **•*Tije* av bû** (L) It became *full of* water/It filled itself with water [s'emplit d'eau] **•*T'ijî* ye ji mirova** (Zeb/Dh) It is *full of* people (i.e., crowded); **-t'ijî kirin** = to fill {syn: dagirtin}: **•Sîtila xwe *tijî* av *dike*** (J) *She fills up* her bucket with water. {also: tejî I (JB3/

IFb-2); tije (GF); [teji] تــژى (JJ); <tejî تــژى/tejî طــژى> (HH)} {≠vala} {*tijetî; *t'ijîtî} [K/A/IFb/B/JB1-S/TF/OK//JB3/JJ/HH/SK//GF] <mişt II>

til I تِـــل *f.* **().** abdomen. {also: <til> تــل (Hej)} [Kmc-5/IFb/OK/Hej/ZF3] <zik>

til II تِل (-a;) (Bşk/Zx) = finger. See **t'ilî I**.

tilh تِلھ (ZF3) = lump; boil. See **tulḧ**.

tilih تِلِه (PB) = finger, toe. See **t'ilî I**.

t'ilism تِـلِسم *f./m.(M-Zx)* **(-a/-ê;-ê/).** talisman, charm, amulet: **•Nebî tu p'înê me bilind ç'iqlê darêva girêdî, ḧeta ji te tê, tu nimz girêde, nêzîkî k'okê girêde çimko *t'ilizma* darê ji k'okêye** (JB2-Íamilov) Don't tie our rag high up on a tree branch: do your best [lit. 'as far as it comes from you'] to tie it low, tie it near the root, because the tree's *charm* is from the root; **-t'ulusma zêrîn** (FK-eb-2) golden amulet: **•Xezalek hat berahîyê, telismê zêrî stoy da** (M-Zx #753) A gazelle came before him with *a gold talisman* round its neck. {also: telism (M-Zx); t'ilismat (K-2); tilizim (OK); t'ilîsm (Z-1); tilsim (GF); t'ulusm; t'ulusme} {syn: nivişt; t'iberk} < Ar ṭilasm طلسم --> T tılsım; Sor telîsm تەلیسم; Za tılsım *m.* (Mal) [Z-1//K/IFb/ZF//GF//OK] <berbejn; îsm; sêr I>

t'ilismat تِلسمات (K) = talisman, charm. See **t'ilism**.

tilizim تِلزِم (OK) = talisman, charm. See **t'ilism**.

t'ilî I/tilî [K] تِلى *f.* **(-ya;-yê).** 1) {syn: bêç'î II} finger; toe: **•K'îjan *t'ilyê* jêkî, je'na ḧemya yeke** (Dz #778, 164) Whichever *finger* you cut off, they all hurt just the same [lit. 'the pain of all is one'] **•*T'ilyê* desta ḧemû ne yekin** (Dz #1546, 276) *The fingers of* the hand are not all the same [*prv.*]; **-serê tipla** (Ak) fingertips;

-t'ilîya beranî (K/F/B)/**tiliya girdikê** (ZF)/~**gir[(d)ik]** (RZ)/**t'ilîya mezin** (F/K/B) thumb {syn: beranek; girdik};

-t'ilîya ç'ûk (B)/**tilîya qilîçane** (Msr)/~**qilîç'kê** (K)/~**qilîncekê** (IF)/~**başikan** (IF)/[telīye pečûk] (JJ-PS) pinky, little finger;

-t'ilîya gustilê (B/Msr)/~**gustilkê** (B/IF)/~**gustîlkirinê** (K)/~**hinglîskê** (IF)/~**bênav** (K) ring finger;

-t'ilîya nîşanê (F/B)/~**nîşandekê** (IF)/~**nîşankirinê** (K)/~**şadê** (Msr) index finger, forefinger, pointer;

-t'ilîya ort'ê (F/K/B)/**tilîya navê** (K)/~**navîn** (IF)/~**nêvî** (Msr) middle finger; 2) fingertip(s) (Klk). {also: telî I (HR-I); t'ib•il (•la) (Bw); til II (-a;) (Bşk/Zx); tilih (PB); tillî (GF); tipil (Ak); tuli (Klk); tulî (Hk); [tilou] تــلو (JJ); <tilî> تــلى (HH)} =Sor emust ئەموست/[h]engust ھەنگوست; kilik کِلِك; pence پەنجە; pîlk پیلك; qemik قەمِك; = Za engişt *f.* (Mal) [Z-1/F/K/JB3/IF/Çnr/Czr/Kp/Msr/Rh/Tkm/Wn//B//JJ//PB//GF//Bw//Ak//Bşk/Zx//Klk//Hk//HR-I] <beranek; gumik; neynûk; p'ê II; qilîç'k>

tilî II تِــلى *f.* **(-ya;).** a single grape: **-tilîya tirî** (Bw) do.: **•Cana min ê *tilîya tirî* / çi zû xastî û çi zû birî** (song of Tehsîn Taha) My soul [=beloved] is *a single grape* / how quickly is she desired, how quickly is she taken [=no sooner is she desired than she is taken away]. [Bw/Zx] <tirî>

tilîk تِليك **().** boiled raisin: **•Ezê *tilîka* dixom** (Bw) I am eating *boiled raisins* **•Me *tilîk* yêt çêkirîn** (Bw) We have made [=prepared] *boiled raisins*. [Bw] <mewîj; tilî II>

tilîlî تِليلى *f.* **(-ya;).** shrill, trilling cries of joy uttered by women at weddings; ululation {Ar zaγrūdah زغــرودة}: **•Çaxê ku bûk ji mala babê derxistin** [sic]**, jinka da ber *tilîlîya*** (FS) When they took the bride from her father's house, the women met her with ululations; **-tilîlî vedan** (Bw) to ululate, utter shrill and trilling cries of joy (of women at weddings): **•*Tilîlî vedana* te ya xoş bû!** (Bw) Your *ululations* were really something! {also: <tilîlî> تليلى (HH/Hej)} Sor tilîlîl تِلیلیلی = helhele ھەلھەلە = 'shrill and sustained cries of joy (women)' [Bw/A/IFb/HH/GF/Hej]

t'ilîpeř تِلیپەڕ *f./m.(Wkp)* **(/-ê;).** fern, bot. *Filices* [Ar & P sarxas سرخس, Ar *also* xinšār خنشار; T eğrelti otu]: **•Li ser çiyaçolan û di nav Andenê perdeya mij (daristana hîdrofîlîk) hene, li ku ji bo nimûne, *tilîperê darokî* (bi spanî Helecho arborescente) hêşin dibe** (Wkp:Şîle) On the high deserts and in the Andes, there are rain forests, where for example *tree ferns* grow. {syn: *geyî xirçe; serxes} = Sor serxes سەرخەس [IFb/ZF3/CS]

t'ilî pindk تِــلى پِــنــدك *f.* **().** children's game in which players stick their fingers up the anus of one player. {also: tilîping (Qzl); tillîpink (GF)} [Msr//Qzl//GF]

tilîping تِــلــيــپِــنــگ (Qzl) = children's game. See **t'ilî pindk**.

t'ilîsm تِليسم (Z-1) = talisman, charm. See **t'ilism**.

tilîş تِليش (S&E/K) = wood chips, filings, sawdust. See **telîş**.

tillî تِللى (GF) = finger. See **t'ilî I**.

tillîpink تِلليپنك (GF) = children's game. See **t'ilî pindk**.

tilm تِــلم *f.* **().** unit of weight, dry measure: 80 or 100 kg. = 2 *olçeks* (CCG); 23 kg. in Urfa (IFb); **-nîv tilm** (IFb) 11.5 kg. [CCG/IFb/Wkp/ZF3] <kêl III; olçek>

tilor I تـلـۆر *m./f.(ZF3)* **(-ê/;).** thigh, haunch. {also: tîlor (Mzg-2)} {syn: hêt; kulîmek; řan} [Mzg/IFb/ZF3]

tilor II تلۆر (Bw) = type of bird. See **tilûr**.

tilsim تِلسِم (GF) = talisman, charm. See **t'ilism**.

tilûr تـلـوور *m.* **().** *type of bird*: 1) {syn: qumrî} turtledove [Ar turɣul تـرغـل] (GF): **•Em dibezîn ser avê, ku wan *tilûrên* hîn birîndar mane serjêbikin** (Cankurd: RN2 56[1998] 10) We used to run down to the water, to slaughter the wounded *birds*; 2) {syn: qijik} rook [Rus grač грач] (K); 3) {syn: qijik; qiřik II} crow [Rus vorona ворона] (K). {also: tilor II (Bw); tilûrî (TF); turlî (GF-2); <tilûr> تـلـور (Hej)} [Cankurd/K/IFb/GF/Hej/FS//TF//Bw] <teyr>

t'im تـم *adv.* 1) {syn: her [2]; hergav; hert'im} always; **-tim û daim** (JB3) continuously, eternally; **-tim û tim** (IF) endlessly, ceaselessly; 2) often, frequently (B): **•Ew *t'imê* wan gilîya diwek'ilîne** (B) He *often* repeats those words. {also: t'imê (K/Z-1); [tim تـم/témi تـمـى] (JJ)} < t'emam = 'all' [K/B//A/JB3/IFb/JJ/GF/TF] <misêwa>

tima تـمـا *adj.* 1) {syn: çikûs; çirûk [2]; řijd} greedy, miserly, stingy; 2) [*f.*] {syn: řijdî} avarice, greed, miserliness, stinginess. {also: temah (IFb); [tama] طمع (JJ); <ṯima> طما (HH)} < Ar ṭama' طمع = 'greed' [JR/K/F/B/Ba2/TG2//IFb]

timam تِمام (L) = all; whole. See **t'emam**.

t'imê تِمێ (K/Z-1) = always; often. See **t'im**.

tinaz تـنـاز *m.* **(-ê; tinêz).** 1) {syn: ȟenek; qerf; tewz; t'iřane; yarî II} joke, joking; 2) ridicule, mockery, scoffing. {also: <ṯinaz> طناز (HH)} Cf. Ar/P ṭanz طنز [Msr/K/A/IFb/B/GF/TF//HH] <pêk'enok>

tindûtîjî تِندوتيژى (Wkt) = violence. See **tund û tîjî**.

t'ine تِنه (Wkt) = there is not. See **t'une**.

ting تـنـگ *m./f.(ZF3)* **(-ê/;).** dung heap, dung hill, garbage dump: **•... ziblê dewêr wê li milê wî ye û wê** [sic] **davête ser *ting*** (HR 3:171) [Carrying] cow dung on his shoulder, and he was throwing it onto *the dung heap*. {syn: axpîn; poxan; sergo} [HR/GF(Botan)/TF/FJ/SS/ZF3]

ti'ok تِعۆك (Kmc) = hackberry tree. See **tihok**.

tipil تِپِل (Ak) = finger. See **t'ilî I**.

-tir تـر *suffix designating the comparative degree of adjectives*: cf. English '-er' (happier, bigger) and 'more' (more spacious, more capable) [+ **ji** ژ = than]: **•Ew îrade û pişgirtin, dema çend sal bi ser ve çûn an sist dibe, an jî *mezintir* dibe** (AW72D3) This desire and support, when a couple of years have passed, will either weaken or become *greater* **•*Ji* pêncî carî *bêhtir* gotina "mist " di şûna gotina "mizdanê "de, bi çewtî hatiye bikaranîn** (AW73C2) *More than* 50 times the word "mist" was incorrectly used instead of the word "mizdan" **•Me gotibû hilbijartinên herêmî *ji* ya parlamentoyê *girîngtir* in** (AW72D2) We had said that regional elections are *more important than* the parliamentary one **•Paşî mar hat e pêş, got, "Zerera min *mezintir* e. Dibît xelatê min *çêtir* bît"** (SK 1:6) Then the snake came forward and said, "The damage I do is *greater*. My reward ought to be *better*" **•Perên ku didane me ne pir bin jî, dîsa jî *ji* meaşên hemû karmend û karkerên wan *zêdetir* bûn** (AW72B3) Even if the money they gave us was not a lot, it was still *more than* the wages of all their workers **•Zînê *ji* horîya *bedewtir* bû, ewqas bedew, ewqas k'emal, serhevda husulcemal bû** (Z-1, 45) Zîn was *more beautiful than* the houris--so beautiful, so perfect, all in all a ravishing beauty; **-ji hemû** (K)/**ji gişka** (K)/**ji hemîyan -tir** = the most, -est {syn: here I; t'ewrî; -tirîn}: **•Paşî mişk hat e pêş, got, "Xizmeta min *ji hemîyan zêdetir* e, bes lazim e xelatê min ji yê hemîyan çêtir bît"** (SK 1:7) Then the mouse came forward and said, "My service is *greatest of* all, so my reward must needs be better than everybody's [=the best]" **•Selam li-ser te, ey *cwantir ji hemî* ṯeyran û *maqûltir ji wan*** (SK 4:40) Peace be upon you, O *most handsome* and *most honoured* of birds. {also: [ter] تر (JJ)} Cf. P -tar تر; Sor -tir تر [K/IFb/B/OK//JJ]

tiř تـڕ/ **ṯiř** طـڕ [SK/HH/FS] *f.* **(-a;).** flatulence, (intestinal) gas, fart; audible fart, *as opposed to* ***fis*** *= silent fart or "silent but deadly" {SBD}*: •[**Ker ji *tir* rabî**] (YSZx) The donkey stopped *farting [prv.] {said when an inferior (=incompetent person) is removed from a high position}* **•*Tiřek* ji wî nayêt** (FS) He is ineffective/never gets anything done [lit. 'Not even a fart comes from him']; **-tiř kirin** (K) to fart, break wind: **•Wî *ṯiř kir* = *Ṯiřa* wî hat** (FS) He *broke wind*. {also: [tyr] تـر (JJ); <ṯir> طر (HH)} {syn: piv I} Cf. Sor tiř تِڕ; W Arm dēř տէր [YSZx/K/A/IFb/JJ/GF/TF/OK//HH/SK/FS] <fis; k'uş II>

tirabêlk تِرابێلك *f.* **(-a;-ê).** fine dust, speck of dust: **•Ba û bablîsok toz û *tirabêlk*** (Cigerxwîn. Halê gundiya) Wind and dustdevils, powder and *dust.* {syn: gerik I; t'oz; xubar} cf. Ar tirāb تـــراب = 'dust, earth, dirt' [JB2/FJ/Kmc/ZF]

tiraf تِـــــــراف *f.* **(-a;-ê).** embers, ashes with glowing coals. {also: traf (IFb-2)} {syn: bizot; helemor; k'ozir} [A/IFb/ZF3]

t'iral تِـرال *adj. & m.* lazy, idle: **•Hersê mehên payîzê / Ma bê kar û ma *tiral*** (Cxn-KE: Rencberê Bi rûmet) All three months of the fall / he remained without work and *idle* **•*Teralek* pişta wî dixure, lê ji teralî û tembelîyê nikare pişta xwe bixurîne, hema hundurê destê xwe dixurîne û diavêje paş xwe!** (LM, 15) The back of *a lazybones* itches, but out of laziness he can't scratch his back, so he scratches the palm of his hand and throws it behind himself. {also: teral (LM/AD); [tyral] تـرال (JJ); <ṯeral طرال/ tilar تلار> (HH)} {syn: t'embel} [Cxn-KE/K/IFb/B/JJ/GF/TF//HH/OK//LM/AD]

t'iraletî تِرالەتى (B) = laziness. See **t'iralî.**

t'iralî تِــــرالـــى *f.* **(-ya;-yê).** laziness: **•ji ber *tiralîya* rojnamegeran di warê fêrbûna nivîsandina bi zimanekî Kurdî yê dirust** (ccsdsyria.org: Rênîşandera Hemwelatiyê Rojnameger 15) due to the *laziness/ disinclination of* journalists in the realm of learning to write in a correct Kurdish. {also: teralî (LM/AD); t'iraletî (B-2)} {syn: t'embelî} [LM/AD/ /K/IFb/B/ZF3] <t'iral>

tirambêl ترامبێل (IFb) = automobile. See **trimbêl.**

tirancek ترانجەك (Haz) = steps, staircase. See **derenc.**

t'iran•e/tirane تِــرانـــە *f.* **(•a;).** 1) {syn: ḧenek; qerf; tewz; tinaz; yarî II} joke: **•'Elî Beg jî, çûnkû xoş-meşreb bû, ḧej *tirane* û suḧbetan dikir** (SK 39:345) Now Ali Beg, being merry-natured, liked *jokes* **•Ez *tiranan* bi te *dikem*** (Dh) I'*m kidding* you **•Tu micit î yan *bi tirane* we dibêjî?** (SK 2:13) Are you serious, or do you say this *as a joke*?; 2) {syn: lîstik; yarî II} game: **•Qel çû gundekî, du se dîtin li naw ḧewşekî *tirane dikirin*** (SK 4:53) The crow went to a village and saw two dogs *romping* in a courtyard. {also: terane (A/IFb/SK-2); [tirané] تـرانـه (JJ) = 'clown, jokester'; <terane> ترانه (HH)} Cf. P tarāne ترانه = 'song, melody'; Sor terane تەرانە = 'melody' [Dh/ K/JJ/SK//A/IFb/HH]

t'irar تِـــرار *m.* **(-ê;-î).** copper water cup or bowl: **•Vî t'irarî bişo** (Dh) Wash this cup **•Wî *tirar* di kanîyê hiland** (FS) He dipped *the copper cup* into the well; **-t'irarê avê** (Dh) do. {also: trar (GF-2); [trár (G)/trār (Rh)] تـرار (JJ); <tirar> تـرار (Hej)} [Dh/IFb/JJ/GF/OK/RZ/Hej/FS]

t'iraş تِراش (Bw) = shrub. See **t'eraş II.**

tirazî ترازى (Bw) = scale. See **terazî.**

t'irb تِرب *f.* **(-a;-ê).** 1) {syn: gor I; meẍber; mezel [3]; qebr} tomb, grave: **•Weke tê zanîn *tirba* Ehmedê Xanî li Bazîdê ye û weke ziyaretgeha xelkê herêmê ye** (Wlt 1:37, 3) As is known, *the tomb of* Ahmed-i Khani is in [Doğu]Bayazit, and is like a shrine for the people of the region; **-kevirê ser t'irbê** (K)/**kevirê t'irbê** (B) tombstone;
2) cemetery, graveyard (JJ) [tyrb]. {also: [tyrb/ tirb تـرب/tourbé تـربـه] (JJ); <tirb> تـرب (HH)} < Ar turbah تـربـة --> T türbe; --> P torbat تـربـت [EP-7/F/K/A/IFb/B/JJ/HH/GF/TF]

tiren ترەن (TF) = train. See **trên.**

t'irê تِـــرێ *v.* [+ **ji** / + *obl.*] It seems to {me, you, him, etc.}, to think or be under the impression that ...: **•Ç'îya usa bedew dibû, *mêriv t'irê* xalîça Xuṙustanê ser wî ṙaxistine** (Ba2:1, 202) The mountain was so beautiful, *people thought* that Khurasani rugs had been spread out over it **•*Ewî t'irê*, Zîna delal p'aşlêdane** (Z-1) *He thought (or, was under the impression)* that darling Zin was in his embrace **•*Ji me t'irê ne* sê roje, *me t'irê* ev gave û ev seḧete** (EP-7) *It doesn't seem like* three days to us, it seems to us like a moment or an hour **•*Ji wan tirê* ew roje** (EP-7) *It seemed to them* it was a day [that had passed, when in fact it was 3 days] **•Ma *ji te wetrê* ku wisan e?** (ZF3) *Do you think* it is so? {also: wetrê (ZF3-2)} [EP-7/Z-1/K/B/ZF3]

tirên ترێن (TF)/t'irên تِرێن (K) = train. See **trên.**

tirh تِره (TF/GF) = young shoot, bud. See **terh.**

tirhik ترهك (TF) = young shoot, bud. See **terh.**

tirih تِره (TF/HH) = grapes. See **tirî.**

tirimbêl ترمبێل (TF) = automobile. See **trimbêl.**

tirî تـــرى *m.(K/JB1-A)/f.(B)* **(-yê/ ; /-yê).** grapes, bot. *Vitis*: **•Wan stirî çandin, xiyala wan ew bû dê *tirî* çinin. Nezanîn** [sic] **berê stirî stirî ye, *tirî* nîye** (SK 48:511) They planted thorns, thinking to reap *grapes.* They did not know that a thornbush bears thorns, not *grapes.* {also: tirih (TF); [tiri] ترى (JJ); <tirih تره/tirî ترى> (HH)} {syn: mewîj [2]} Sor tirê تِـــرێ. *For a list of types of grapes, see: Salih Omerî. "Navên Tirîyan bi Kurdî," RN2 52 & 53 (1998)* [K/A/IFb/B/JJ/HH/JB1-A/SK/GF/OK//TF]

<harsim; k'işmîş; mewîj; mêw; r̄ez; sewî [1]; tilî II; *types of grapes*: binête'tî; gozane; işqir; mezrona; misebq; sincêrî; tayfî; torane; xanoq>

tirîj تریژ (IFb) = sunbeam, ray. See **tîrêj**.

-tirîn ترین *pr. mod. suffix designating the superlative degree of adjectives*: cf. English 'the -est' (the happiest, the biggest) and 'the most' (the most spacious, the most capable): **•Belediyeya Hudingenê, ku yek ji *girîngtirîn* bajarên derdora Stokholmê ye** (AW72A2) The municipality of Hudingen, which is one of *the most important* cities around Stockholm **•Îro Partiya Çep, yek ji *mezintirîn* partiyên Ewrûpayê ye** (AW72A2) Today the Leftist Party is one of Europe's *largest* parties **•Kiarostamî wekî yek ji *baştirîn* derhênerên cîhanê tê binavkirin** (AW70B4) Kiarostami is being called [or, is known as] one of the world's *best* producers. {syn: here I; ji hemû -tir; t'ewrî} *recent (1992) borrowing from Sorani and Persian*; Cf. P -tarīn ترین; Sor -tirîn ترین [IFb/OK/ZF3]

tirîşke تریشکه (IFb/ZF3) = lightning. See **trûsk**.

T'irk ترك *m.* **().** Turk: **-jina T'irk** (K)/**k'ulfeta T'irk** (B) Turkish woman; **-zimanê T'irka[n]** (K) Turkish language. {also: [turk] ترك (JJ)} {syn: r̄om} [Ad/K/A/IFb/B//JJ/GF]

T'irkiye ترکیه *f.* **(;-yê).** [Republic of] Turkey: **•der heqê têkiliyên *Tirkiye* û welatên cîhanê de** (AW69A1) about relations [between] *Turkey* and the [other] countries of the world. {also: Tirkyê (AD); T'ûrkî (K)} [AW/IFb//AD//K]

t'irkî ترکی *adj.* Turkish. {also: [tyrki] ترکی (JJ)} {t'irkîtî} [K/A/IFb/B/JJ]

t'irkîtî ترکیتی *f.* **(-ya;-yê).** turkishness, being a Turk. [A/ZF3] <t'irk[î]>

T'irkmanî ترکمانی *adj.* Turkmen, Turcoman. {also: Turkmenistanî (BF-2); Turkmenî (BF)} Sor Turkmanî تورکمانی [Wkp/Wkt/ZF3]

Tirkyê ترکیێ (AD) = Turkey. See **T'irkiye**.

tirp ترپ, m. (AD/Wkt) = radish. See **tivir**.

tirs ترس *f.* **(-a;-ê).** fear, fright: **•*Tirsa min* dawîyê serê min biêşe** (L) *I'm afraid that* later I'll have troubles [lit. 'my head will ache']; **-ji tirsa [re]** / **tirsa** (B)/ **tirsar̄a** = out of fear, for fear: **•Hema *ji tirsa re*, xew wî naye** (L) *Due to fear* (or, *Out of fear*) he couldn't fall asleep **•Mîz kir *ji tirsa re*** (L) He pissed *out of fear*. {also: [tyrs] ترس (JJ); <ṯirs> طرس (HH)} {syn: saw} Cf. P tars ترس; Sor tirs ترس = 'fear, danger(ous)'; Hau tersî *f.* (M4) [K/A/JB3/IFb/B/JJ/SK/GF/TF//HH] <tirsandin; tirsîn>

tirsan ترسان (K/A/SK/OK) = to fear. See **tirsîn**.

tirsandin ترساندن *vt.* **(-tirsîn-).** 1) to frighten, scare, terrify: **•Êrîşa gur, pez *ditirsîne*** (AB) The wolf's attack *frightens* the sheep **•T'asêd xwe digirtne destêd xwe, pê şiva li wan dixistin, wekî bi wî dengî gura *bitirsînin*** (Bs2:1, 203) They would take their bowls and bang on them with their staffs, so as *to scare away* the wolves with this noise; 2) to spur or goad on *(a horse)*: **•Bi zengûya rastê min *bitirsîne*** (EP-7) *Spur* me *on* with the right spur [as opposed to the left spur] **•Bi zengûya Bor *tirsand*** (EP-7) *He spurred on* Bor with [his] spurs. {also: [tyrsandin] ترساندین (JJ); <ṯirsandin طرساندن (diṯirsîne) (دطرسینه)> (HH)} Cf. P tarsāndan ترساندن; Sor tirsandin ترساندِن; Za tersanenã [tersanayiş] (Todd) [K/A/JB3/IFb/B/JJ/GF/TF//HH] <tirsîn>

tirsek ترسەك (B) = coward. See **tirsonek**.

tirsî ترسی (JB1-A/OK/BF/FS) = stale (of bread); plain (of bread). See **t'isî**[1].

tirsîn ترسین *vi.* **(-tirs-).** [+ **ji**] to fear, be afraid or frightened of: **•*Ditirsyam*, ku pey çûyîna min r̄a nişkêva gur xwe bavêjne ser kerîyê pêz** (Ba2:2, 205) *I was afraid* that after I left [lit. 'my going'] the wolves would suddenly pounce on the flock of sheep **•Ew gavan gelikî *tirsîya*** (L) That cowherd *was* very much *afraid* **•Tu ji xwedê *natirsî*** (L) You *don't fear* God. {also: tirsan (K/A/SK/OK-2); tirsyan (M/SK-2); [tyrsin ترسین/tyrsiian ترسیان] (JJ); <ṯirsan طرسان (diṯirse) (دطرسه)> (HH)} [Pok. tres-/ters- (*teres) 1095.] 'to tremble': Skt trásati = 'he trembles'; O Ir *tṛs- (Tsb 45) < Proto IE *tṛs-sḱe- (Kent): Av tərəsaiti; OP θrah- (*pres.* tarsatiy) [+ hacā + ablative]; P tarsīdan ترسیدن; Sor tirsan ترسان (-tirsê-); Za tersenã [tersayiş] (Todd); Hau tersay (ters-) *vi.* (M4); cf. also Gr treō τρέω = 'I tremble'; Lat terreo, -ēre = 'to frighten'; Rus triasti трясти = 'to shake' (vi.) [F/JB3/IFb/B/JJ/JB1-A&S/GF/TF/OK//K/A/SK//HH]

tirsok ترسۆك (K/A/IFb/GF) = coward. See **tirsonek**.

tirsonek ترسۆنەك *m.* **().** coward, 'scaredy-cat': **•*Tirsonek* tim li paş in** (AB) *The cowards* are always at the rear (or, always in back). {also: tirsek (B); tirsok (K-2/A/IFb-2/GF-2); [tersounek ترسونك/tersók ترسوك] (JJ); <ṯirsonek> طرسونك (HH)} {syn: bizdonek; newêrek} Sor tirsnok

تِرسـنـۆك = 'coward'; Za tersnok (Todd) {tirsokî; tirsonek[t]î} [AB/K/JB3/IFb/GF/TF/ZF//JJ//HH//A//B]

tirsonekî تِـرسـۆنـەكـى *f.* **(-ya;-yê).** cowardliness, cowardice. {also: tirsonektî (K)} {syn: newêrekî} [K/JB3/B/TF/ZF] <tirsonek>

tirsonektî تِرسۆنەكتى (K) = cowardice. See **tirsonekî**.

tirsyan تِرسيان (M/SK) = to fear. See **tirsîn**.

tirş تِـرش/**ṯirş** طِـرش [HH/SK] *adj.* sour: **-madê xwe tirş kirin** (XF) to frown, make a face, be dissatisfied. {also: [tyrch] تـرش (JJ); <ṯirş> طـرش (HH)} Cf. [Pok. (s)ter-/(s)terə:(s)trē- 1022 ff.] 'stiff': 3. (s)terp-: *tṛfša-: Mid P tru(f)š (M3); P torš تـــرش; Sor tirş تِـــرش = 'sour, acid, [*n.*] sumac' {tirşayî; tirşî} [F/K/A/JB3/IFb/B/JJ/ GF/TF//HH/SK] <miz II; tal>

tirşayî تِرشـايـى *f.* **().** sourness. {also: tirşî (K-2/A/IFb/TF); tirşîtî (GF)} [K/B//A/IFb/TF//GF] <tirş>

tirşik تِرشِك *f.* **(-a;-ê).** type of vegetable stew: **-tirşika kutilka** (CB) type of food made with *danhêrk* (type of wheat flour) consisting of patties stuffed with ground meat and minced onions, in a sour sauce [in the region between Cizîra Bohtan and Dihok]. {also: <ṯirşik> طـرشـك (HH)} [Bw/CB/K/A/IFb/GF/TF/OK//HH] <k'utilk>

tirşî تِرشى (K/A/IFb/TF) = sourness. See **tirşayî**.

tirşîtî تِرشيتى (GF) = sourness. See **tirşayî**.

tirşo تِـرشـۆ *m.* **(-ê/tirşê** [B-2]**;).** sorrel, bot. *Rumex*, any of various plants with sour (tirş) juice; sour plant with wide leaves (HH). {also: tirşok (IFb); [terchouk] تـرشـوك (JJ); <ṯirşok> طـرشـوك (HH)} Cf. tirş = 'sour' [Ba2/K/A/B//IFb//JJ//HH]

tirşok تِرشۆك (IFb) = sorrel. See **tirşo**.

tiryan تِـريـان *m./f.(Zeb/BF)* **(/-a;-î/).** wicker tray *(on which dry, folded bread is laid and sprinkled with water before being eaten)* (SK): **•Du nanêt kuloregenim jî danê ser *tiryanî*, bo şîwa mêwanî bîne** (SK 31:277) Put two wheaten loaves on *the tray* and bring them for our guest's supper **•*Tiryanka* nanî ji biçûkan ra, dîha çilî ji gîskan ra** (BF) *A wicker bread tray* for the children, a pile of tree branches for the goats. {also: tiryank, f. (Zeb); <tiryan تريان/tiryane تريانه> (Hej) = 'small fruit basket'} [SK/Hej/BF//Zeb] <berkeş; lengerî; mecme'; sênî>

tiryank تِريانك, f. (Zeb) = wicker tray. See **tiryan**.

t'isî تِـسـى *adj.* 1) {also: tirsî (JB1-A/OK/BF)} stale *(of bread)*: **•Were, em nanê xwe *t'isî* bi şîrê xamberdîra bixun** (EP-7) Come, let's eat our *stale* bread with the milk of three-year-old barren sheep; 2) {also: tirsî (Wkt); tissî (GF); tursî (Wkt-2); tusî (Wkt-2)} plain, without condiment *(of bread, food)*: **•Wî nanê *tisî* xwar** (FS) He ate *plain* bread; 3) poor, indigent (JJ). {also: [tisi] تسى (JJ); <tisî> تسى (HH)} {t'isîtî} [EP-7/K/IFb/JJ/HH/TF/FS/ZF3/G//GF//JB1-A/OK/BF/Wkt]

t'isîtî تِـسـيـتـى *f.* **().** staleness *(of bread)*. {also: [tisiti] تسيتى (JJ)} [K/JJ] <t'isî>

tisqîtî تِسقيتى *f.* **().** meanness, meanspiritedness, nastiness: **•Heta nha t'u rewşenbîrekî ermenî îzn nedaye xwe bi *tisqîtî*, dijminayîke ha derheqa cimeta me, rewşenbîrêd wêda xeberde** (E.Serdar. Cinê nav me, 4.i.2014) Up till now no Armenian intellectual has allowed himself to speak *nastily*, with enmity about our society, or the intellectuals of that place **•Vê *tisqîtî* û neheqîya Xudo sebra Eto êdî anî serê pozê wî** (W. Eşo. Sîber, 47) This *nastiness* and injustice of Kh.'s was the last straw for E. [W.Eşo/E.Serdar]

tissî تِسسى (GF) = plain (of food). See **t'isî**[2].

tişt تِـشـت *m.(K/B)/f.(W/MC-1/Hk)* **(-ê/-a;-î/-ê).** 1) thing: **•Tuê here ji mi re li van pera *tişta* bikire!** (L) Go buy me *some things* with this money; **-tiştî** (Dz) once, as soon as: **•Jinik, teř̄a yek nîne, *tiştî* ez tu hev nabînin, yan Mûşê, yan ber dara dergûşê?** (Dz) Woman, does it matter to you, *once* we are out of each other's sight, whether I'm in mush or under an infant's cradle? *[prv.]*; 2) [+ *neg.*] nothing, not anything: **•Merîyêd ku qe *tiştek* jî jê nelazimbûya** (Ba) People who didn't need *anything* at all **•Nikare *tiştekî* bike** (Ba) He can't do *anything* **•*Tiştek* serê wî nanye** (Ba) They didn't do *anything* to him [lit. 'They didn't bring anything to his head']. {also: [tycht] تـشـت (JJ); <tişt> تـشـت (HH)} Cf. Mid P čiš/tis (M3); P čīz چيز; Sor şit شِت/çişt چِشت; Za çî (Todd/Mal)/çîy (Mal) *m.*; Hau çêw *m.* (M4) [K/A/JB3/IFb/B/JJ/HH/SK/JB1-A&S/GF/TF]

tiştanok تِـشـتـانـۆك *f.* **(-a;).** riddle: **•Ew *tiştanoka* meşhûr jî ev e; mamikê mino mamanî, tiştek heye heta qonaxekî li ser çar lingan diçe, qonaxa dî li ser du lingan û qonaxa dîtir jî li ser sê linga diçe [insan e]** (www.tirşik.net:Oedipus) And that famous *riddle* is: ... There is something that for one stage goes on 4 legs, another stage on 2 legs and yet another stage on 3 legs [ans.: man]. {also: tiştonek (Wlt)} {syn: apik (Kg); mamik; têderxistinok; tiştik (IF); xacerêz (IF)} [Z/Qzl/ZF3//Wlt] tiştîr تِشـتـيـر (K/IFb/CG/B/GF) = young female goat. See **tuştîr**.

tiştonek تِشتونەك (Wlt) = riddle. See **tiştanok**.

titin تِتِن (JB3/HH) = tobacco. See **t'itûn**.

t'itûn تِـتـــوون *f.* **(-a;-ê).** tobacco: •**Li kevir dixim, naşkê, li avê dixim, dişkê [Pelê *titinê*]** (L) I throw it onto a rock, it doesn't break, I throw it onto the water, it breaks [rdl.; ans.: *cigarette* paper] •**Li pêş mezinekî xwe nabe ku em *titûnê* bikêşin** (Epl, 23) In front of an elder it is not all right for us to smoke *tobacco* •**Qelûna bavê min tijî *titûn* e** (AB) My father's pipe is full of *tobacco*. {also: titin (JB3); tutin (TF); t'ûtin (M-Zx); [toutoun توتون/toutin توتن] (JJ); <titin> تتن (HH)} Cf. Ar tutun تـتـن, T tütün [AB/K/IFb/B/GF//JJ//TF//M-Zx//JB3/HH] <kamaş>

t'ivdarek تِـڤـدارەك (B/F/K) = preparations; repair. See **t'edarik**.

t'ivdîr تِڤدير (Z-1) = plan; preparations. See **t'evdîr**.

t'ivek تِڤەك (M-Zx) = rifle. See **t'ifing**.

tiving (GF)/t'iving (F/B) تِڤنگ = rifle. See **t'ifing**.

t'iviqîn تِـڤِـقـيـن (EP-7) = to appear; to be born (of animals). See **t'ifiqîn**.

tivir تِڤِر/**ṯivir** طِڤِر [FS-2/HH] *f./m.(AD/Wkt/SS)* **(-a/-ê; -ê/).** radish, *bot. Raphanus sativus*: **-tivira tûj** (B)/**tevrê tûj** (SS) horseradish; **-tivrika sor** (RZ) radish. {also: tevr II (SS); tevrik II (Kmc-2); tirp, m. (AD-2/Wkt-2); tivr (B-2/TF/GF-2/Wkt-2); [tiwir/tover (G)] تـڤـر (JJ); <ṯivir> طـڤـر (HH)} P turb تـرب --> T turp; Sor tûr توور [K/IFb/B/GF/HH/Kmc/ZF/CS/AD/FS/BF//HH//TF//SS] <şêlim>

tivr تِڤر (B/TF/GF/Wkt) = radish. See **tivir**.

tixandin تِـخـانـدِن *vt.* **(-tixîn-).** to cause (a camel) to kneel down: •**Rast ço pêşiya wê hermetê û bi serê delûla wê girt û *tixand*** (GShA, 132) She went directly to that woman, grabbed hold of the head [or reins] of her [she-]camel and *made it kneel*. {syn: nixandin; xiya kirin} Cf. Ar nayyaxa II نيّخ [GShA/Şng]

tixarîs تِـخـاريـس *f.* **(-a;).** piece of material used in sewing garments: one starts with a rectangular piece of material which is cut diagonally into two pieces, then the straight, long outside edges are sewn together in such a way that the diagonal sides form a trapezoid, one end of which is narrow, the opposite end of which is wide: •**Wê *tixarîseka* biçûk xist kirasê xwe** (FS) She added a small *tikharis* to her dress. [Qzl/GF/FS]

t'ixûb تِــخـــووب *m./f.(Dz)* **(-ê/-a;).** border, limit, boundary: •**Esker-leşkerê gran, ji *t'xûbê* benî adem derk'etin, ghîştin cîkî usa, wekî r̄eşk-tarî bû, nêzîkî p'er̄ê 'ezman bûn** (EH) The great army passed beyond *the boundary of* human beings, and reached a place which was dark, near the edge (or, "wings") of the sky •***T'ixûba* xorta t'uneye** (Dz) There is no *limit for* young men (=the young think they can do everything) *[prv.]*. {also: t'xûb (EH); [tokóbi] تخوبى (JJ-G); [t'khob] (JJ-Rh); <tuxûb> تـخـوب (HH)} {syn: sînor} <Arc [& Heb] teḥum תחום = 'dominion, area, district, border, limits', (originally a surrounded, marked place, cf. Heb ḥomah חומה = 'city wall'); Syr tḥūmā ܬܚܘܡܐ = 'border, limit; precept, regulation, penalty'; NENA tikhûb ܬܚܘܒ (Maclean), from the K form; Sor tixûb تِـخـووب = 'boundary, frontier' [EH//K/IFb/SK/GF//HH//JJ-G//JJ-Rh]

t'izbih تِزبِه = prayer beads. See **t'izbî**.

t'izbî تِـزبـى *m./f.(Rh)* (**/-ya;**). rosary, prayer beads, chaplet; worry beads: •**Her kesê peşkekê ji awa *tizbîyêt* min wexotewe, cendekê wî agirê cehennemê nabînît** (SK 12:119) Whoever drinks a drop of the water from my *rosary*, his body will not see the fire of Hell. {also: t'esbih; t'esbîh (K-2); tezbêh (OK-2); t'izbih; tizbîh (F); tizbîk (OK); [tizbi تـزبـى/tezbikh تـزبـخ] (JJ); <tizbe تزبه/tizbî تزبى/tizbîḧ تزبيح> (HH)} <Ar tasbīḥ تسبيح = 'glorification of God' (done while passing prayer beads [misbaḥah مسبحة] through one's fingers); --> P tasbīḥ تسبيح = 'prayer beads' --> T tespih; Sor tezbêḧ تـەزبـێـح = 'rosary, gen. of 99 round beads (denik), two flattened beads (îmame) dividing them into 3 parts of 33 (but sometimes of 33 beads only), and larger elongated bead (şawuł شـاوولّ) where the two ends are brought together' (W&E, p. 146); JJ distinguishes between rosaries for Muslims [tizbi تـزبـى/tezbikh تـزبـخ] and those for Christians [msbahh مـسـبـح]. [K/IFb/B/JJ/HH/SK/GF/Srk/Kş/ Rh//F//OK]

tizbîh تِزبيه (F) = prayer beads. See **t'izbî**.

tizbîk تِزبيك (OK) = prayer beads. See **t'izbî**.

tizûrig تِزوورگ (IFb) = leech. See **zûrî**.

tî I تـى *m.* **(-yê;).** 1) {syn: kevî I} sharp edge *(e.g., of table, shovel, etc.)* (Bw); 2) {syn: dev [4]; şilf} blade (SK/JJ-G): •**Şîrekî gelek kewn hebû, kalwanê wî zîw bû, destikê wî zêr̄ bû, qaşêt elmas û pîroze hatibûne tê-girtin, *tîyê* wî**

kerman bû (SK 26:234) There was a very ancient sword with a silver scabbard, its hilt of gold inlaid with gems of diamond and turquoise, and its *blade* of Kermani steel; 3) layer, crust: **-tîyê 'erdî** (Zeb) the earth's crust. {also: [tí] تـــــــــى (JJ-G)} [Pok. (s)teig- 1016] 'to stick; pointed': Av taeγa-; Mid P tēx = 'sharp edge, ridge; ray' (M3); P tīγ تـــيــغ = 'sword, razor'; Sor tîx تـــيــغ = 'blade, razor, side-arms' [Bw/JJ-G/SK/Zeb]

t'î II تـــــــى *m.* **(-yê;).** brother-in-law [pl. brothers-in-law], (a married woman's) husband's brother: **•*T'îyê* min îro çûye bajêr** (Haz) My brother-in-law went to town today. {also: t'îy (HB/A/IFb-2/ Haz); [ti] تى (JJ); <tî> تى (HH)} [HB/A/Haz//F/K/IFb/B/ JJ/HH/GF/TF/OK/Bw/FS] <birajin; bûra; diş; jint'î II; t'îza>

tî III/t'î [K/B] تـــى *adj.* thirsty: **•Her ħeft jî mane *t'î*** (Dz) All seven of them remained *thirsty*; **-t'î-birçî** (J) hungry and thirsty. {also: têhnî (Bw/JB1-A); tênî (SK/OK/Bw-2); tihn I (JB3/GF-2); tîhn I (A); [ti] تى (JJ); <tihn تـهن /tîn تـين/tî تـى> (HH)} [Pok. ters- 1078.] 'to dry, to feel thirst': Skt tṛṣṇā *f.* = 'thirst'; O Ir *tṛšna- (Ras, p.134): Av taršna-; Mid P tišn[agīh] = 'thirst' & tišnag = 'thirsty'; P tešne تشنه = 'thirsty'; Sor tînû تـينـوو; Za teyşan (Todd); also Germ Durst; Eng thirst {tênîtî; tihnayî; t'în II; t'îhn II; t'îtî; [titi] تـيـتـى (JJ)} [K/IFb/B/JJ/HH/GF/TF//Bw/ JB1-A//SK/OK//A//JB3] <birçî; tîn II>

T'îbetî تیبەتی *adj.* Tibetan. Sor Tîbitî تیبتی [Wkt/SS]

t'îbûn تيبوون (B) = thirst. See **tîn II**.

t'îcar تيجار (M-Am) = merchant. See **t'ucar II**.

t'îcaret تـــيـــجـــارەت (M-Am) = business, trade. See **t'icaret**.

tîhn I تيهن (A) = thirsty. See **tî III**.

t'îhn II تيهن (K) = thirst. See **tîn II**.

tîj تيژ (HB/Bw/SK/GF) = sharp; hot, spicy. See **tûj**.

tîjav تيژاڤ *f.* **(;-ê).** acid: **•*Têzava* patiriya tirombêlê ya kêm bûy** (BF) The car's battery *acid* has run out. {also: têzav (BF); tîzav (ZF3); [tizaw] تـيـزاڤ (JJ)} Cf. P tīzāb تيزاب = 'acid'; Sor têzab تێزاب = 'aquafortis, nitric acid' [Zeb/K(s)//JJ/ZF3//BF]

tîlor تيلۆر (Mzg) = thigh. See **tilor I**.

t'îmar تـــيـــمـــار *f.* **(-a;-ê).** 1) {syn: miqatî; sexbêrî} nursing, tending, looking after, caring for, treatment: **-t'îmar kirin** (B) = a) to nurse, tend, care for, treat; b) to groom (horse); 2) grooming, combing (horse). {also: [timar kirin] تيمار كرين (JJ); <tîmar> تيمار (HH)} Cf. T tımar [EP-7/K/A/IFb/ B/JJ/HH/GF]

tîmsah تـــيـــمـــســـاه (IFb) = crocodile, alligator. See **t'îmseh**.

t'îmseh تـــيـــمـــســـەه *m./f.(ZF3)* **(-ê/;/-ê).** crocodile; alligator: **•Jina mirovekî zengîn ji mêrê xwe cotek solên ji çermê *tîmsehan* xwest** (LM, 26) The wife of a rich man asked her husband for a pair of shoes of *alligator* skin. {also: tîmsah (IFb)} < Ar timsāḥ تـمـساح --> T timsah [LM/ZF3// IFb]

tîn I تين (K[s]/IFb-2/GF/Hej) = energy, power. See **tên**.

tîn II تـــيـــن *f.* **().** thirst: **•Lêvên min *ji tînan* ziwa bûn** (AB) My lips became dry *from thirst*. {also: tên[2] (SK); tênîtî (OK); tihnayî (A); t'îbûn (B); t'îhn II (K); tînî[tî] (GF); t'îtî (K); [titi] تـيـتـى (JJ)} Za teyş *m.* (Mal); Hau tejne *m.* (M4) [K//A//B//GF//OK//SK//JJ] <birçîtî; tî III>

tînî تينى (GF) = thirst. See **tîn II**.

tînîtî تينيتى (GF) = thirst. See **tîn II**.

tîp تـــــيـــــپ *f.* **(-a;-ê).** letter *of the alphabet*: **•Tê xuyakirin ku, nemir du *tîp* ji alfabeya xwe avêtine, ew herdu *tîp* ev in: Ḧ - Ẍ** (Wlt 1:42, 10) It seems that the dearly departed [=Celadet Bedirxan] removed two *letters* from his alphabet; those two *letters* are Ḧ and Ẍ **•*Tîpa* (V) deng dide weke *tîpa* (W) ya Kurdî** (Wlt 1:42, 10) The *letter* 'V' sounds like the Kurdish *letter* 'W'. {also: pît II (A)} <Fr type; Sor tîp تـيـپ/pît پـيـت [Wlt/K/IFb/GF/ OK/ZF/RZ//A] <alfabe>

tîpguhêzî تـيـپـگـوهـێـزى *f.* **(-ya;-yê).** transcription, transcribing: **•Lewra di karê *tîpguhêzî* û edîsyonê de xeletî jî "biqasê" biryarên rast normal in** (Nbh 125:51) That's because in the work of *transcribing* and editing, errors are as normal as correct decisions. [Nbh/ZF/Wkt]

tîr I تـيـر *f.* **(-a;-ê).** 1) arrow: **•Lê *tîra* min bi şaşî çû li wî marê delal ket û dûvê wî qut kir** (ZZ-7, 241) But my *arrow* went by mistake into that nice snake and cut off his tail; **-tîr avêtin** (K/JB3) to shoot an arrow; 2) {syn: mijane; morsele} part of the plow connecting the yoke to the main body of the plow: beam: **-tîra cot** (CCG) do. {also: [tir] تـيـر (JJ); <tîr> تـيـر (HH)} [Pok steig- 1016.] 'to stick; pointed': Av tiγra- = 'sharp, pointed' & tiγri- = 'arrow'; OP tigra- = 'sharp, pointed'; Mid P tigr = 'arrow' (M3); Pashto tērə = 'sharp, pointed' (<*taigra-); P tīr تـــيـــر; Sor tîr تـــيـــر; Za tirı *f.* = 'arrow; rolling-pin' (Mal); Hau tîre *f.* (M4) [K/A/JB3/

IFb/B/JJ/HH/GF/TF/CCG] <kevan; nêçîr; zerg>

tîr II تـیـر *adj.* dense, thick *(of liquids)*: •**Xwarina me *tîr* e** (GF) Our food is *thick*; -**dewê tîr** (IFb) thick dew [=drink of yoghurt and water]; -**qatixê tîr** (B) thick yoghurt; -**şîrê tîr** (K) thick milk; -**tîr bûn** (A/B/IFb) to thicken (vi.), be or become dense or thick; -**tîr kirin** (B/IFb/JJ) to thicken *(vt.)*, make dense or thick, condense. {also: [tir] تیر (JJ); <tîr> تیر (HH)} [Bw/K/A/IFb/B/JJ/HH/GF/TF/OK] <şêlo>

tîravêj تیراڤێژ/**tîr-avêj** تـیـرئـاڤـێـژ *m.* (**-ê;-î**). archer, bowman, one who shoots arrows from a bow: •***Tîr-avêjî* tîrek berda kewî** (FS) *The archer* shot an arrow at the partridge. {also: tîrvan (A); [tir-awij] تـیـراڤـیـژ (JJ)} Sor tîr[h]awêj تـیـرهـاوێـژ = 'archer; bowshot' {tîravêjî} [K/IFb/GF/ZF3/FS//JJ//A] <tîr; kevan; ṇêçîr>

tîravêjî تیراڤێژی *f.* (;**-yê**). archery, the art of shooting an arrow from a bow: •**Mem li pêşîyê te'lîm û terbîyeta xwe li cem dayê distand, paşê li cem lele cure-cure 'ulim hîn bûye, ew hînî suwarîyê, *tîravêjîyê* dikirin** [sic] (K-dş, 88) Mem received his first education and training from his mother, then he learned various sciences from his pedagogue; they taught him horseback riding [and] *archery*. [K-dş/ZF3] <tîravêj>

tîrêj تیرێژ *f.* (**-a;-ê**). 1) ray, beam *(of light)*; sunbeam; sunlight entering through an opening; ray of light; gleam, *lit. & fig.*; light [tîrêj]: •**Lê *tîrojên tavê* dijwar bûn** (MG.Tavê ew dît) But the *sunbeams* were harsh; -**tîrêja tavê** (Z-2) sunbeam; -**tîrêjnêd tavê** (Ba2) sun's rays; 2) radiation, emanation; shining [tîrêjn]; 3) long, thin object *(e.g., field, carpet)*, shaft (Qzl). {also: tirîj (IFb-2); tîrêjn (Ba2/K-2/A/B); tîrênc (K-2); tîrênj (B-2); tîroj (MG); [teïrij] تـیـرژ (JJ); <tîroj> تـیـروژ (HH)} Sor tîşk تـیـشـك [Z-2/K/A/IFb/GF/TF/OK/Qzl//JJ//Ba2/A/B//HH] <r̄oj; r̄onahî; r̄onî I; tav>

tîrêjn تیرێژن (Ba2/K/A/B) = sunbeam, ray. See **tîrêj**.

tîrênc تیرێنج (K) = sunbeam, ray. See **tîrêj**.

tîrênj تیرێنژ (B) = sunbeam, ray. See **tîrêj**.

tîrik تیرك (IFb/TF/CB) = rolling pin. See **tîrok**.

tîrî تیری (IFb) = hail[stones]. See **teyrok**.

Tîrm•e تیرمه (;•ê) (K/B) = July. See **Tîrmeh**.

Tîrmeh تـیـرمـەه *f.* (;**-ê**). July. {also: Têrmeh (IFb-2); Tîrm•e (;•ê) (K/B-2); [tirmé] تـیـرمـه (JJ); [tirmeh] (BG)} {syn: T'emûz} Cf. P tīr[māh] تـیـر[مـاه]; corresponds to last part of Germaciman گەرماجمان/Pûşper̄ پووشپەڕ (P tīr تیر) [Cancer] & 1st part of Xermanan خەرمانان (P murdād مرداد) [Leo] [K/JJ//JB3/IFb/B/GF/OK/BG]

tîroj تیرۆژ (MG/HH) = sunbeam, ray. See **tîrêj**.

tîrok تـیـرۆك *f.(Bw)/m.(OK)* (**-a/ ;-ê/**). long, thin rolling pin for making bread: •**Xwanik: depê pehn û gilovirr yê ku nan bi *tîrokê* li ser tê belavkirin berî ku bikeve ser sêlê yan jî di tenûrê de** (Wkt) X[w]anik: a low, round board on which bread is rolled out with a *tîrok* [rolling pin] before it is placed on a sêl [qv.] or in the oven. {also: tîrik (IFb/TF/CB)} <tîr = 'arrow' + -ik = diminutive suffix. Sor tîrok تـیـرۆك = 'thin kind of rolling pin' [BW/K(s)/OK/Wkt//IFb/TF/CB] <nan; sêl; xanik>

tîroş تیرۆش (Qzl) = bandage. See **ter̄îş**.

tîrvan تیرڤان (A) = archer. See **tîravêj**.

tîsk تیسك (HYma) = kicking (of donkeys). See **tîzik**.

tîş I تـیـش *f.* (). crack, split, fissure: •**Welle li wê taxê *tîşek* bi 'ewrekî ketîye, çûye bi hev ve bidirû, ewê nuka were!** (LM, 21) In that part of town a cloud developed *a crack*, he went to sew it back together, and he'll be coming any minute. {also: tîşk (Ag)} {syn: derz; kelş; terk} [LM/AD//Ag]

tîş II تیش (GF) = bandage. See **ter̄îş**.

tîşk تیشك (Ag) = crack. See **tîş I**.

tîtal تـیـتـال *f./m.(FS), often pl.* (**/-ê;**). custom, usage: •**Ev *tîtale* niho pîçe guhar̄tin tê bi serda hatîn û wekî berê nemane** (M.H.Binavî. Ji rewişt û tîtalên Kurdewarî, 155) Now these *customs* have undergone some changes and have not stayed as [they were] before. {syn: 'adet; kevneşop; r̄ewişt; t'or̄e} [Binavî/Wkt/FS]

tîtik تیتك (BF) = unripe cucumber. See **tûtik II**.

tîtilk تیتلك *f.* (). clitoris. {syn: gilik; zîlik} [FS/Wkt/BF]

tîtî I تیتی (ZF/SS/CS/FS) = lark. See **têtî**.

t'îtî II تیتی (K/JJ) = thirst. See **tîn II**.

tîvil تـیـڤـل *m./f.(JJ)* (**/-a;**). skin *(of fruit)*, peel, shell, rind: -**tîvil kirin** (IFb/OK) to peel. {also: tofil (TF); tovil (IFb-2/OK-2); [towil] تـوڤـل (JJ); <ṭovil> طـوڤـل (HH); <tîvil> تـیـڤـل (Hej)} {syn: qalik; qaşil; qelp II} = Sor twêkił [tökił] تـوێـکـڵ/tokił تـۆکـڵ/têkuł تـێـکـوڵ; Hau tokił *m.* (M4) [Bw/IFb/OK/Hej/AA//JJ//HH//TF]

t'îy تیی (HB/A/IF/Haz) = brother-in-law. See **t'î II**.

t'îza تـیـزا *m.&f.* (**-yê/-ya;**). child of one's husband's brother (from the woman's perspective), nephew or niece (of one's husband). <t'î II = 'brother-in-law' + -za = 'offspring'; = Sor hêwerza هـێـوەرزا

[Bw] <brazî; xwarzî>

tîzav تيزاڤ (ZF3/JJ) = acid. See **tîjav**.

tîzik تـيـزِك *f.* **(-a;).** kicking with both hind legs *(of donkeys)*: **-tîzik lê dan** (SS)/~ **lê xistin** (RZ) to kick {syn: hilavêtin[2] }: **•...pirr li kerê xwe agahdar bûm, hetanî ku vê dawiyê ez ji hinek kirinên wî tirsiyam. Yek caran *tîsk didan.* Min sedem di cî de naskir. Yên ziktêr tenê *tîskan didin*** (HYma 12) I paid attention to my donkey, until recently I was frightened by some of his actions. Sometimes he *would kick with both hind legs*. I immediately recognized the cause. Only those with full bellies *kick*. {also: têsik (SS-2); tîsk (HYma); zîtik (RZ-2/SS-2); zîtirk (FJ-2); zîtok (CS-2)} {syn: çivt; lotik; p'eȟîn; r̄efes} [HYma//IFb/FJ/GF/CS/RZ/SS] <lotik>

to I تــو *m.* **(-[y]ê;).** 1) thin layer, film, skin *(on milk, etc.)*; layer of cream on top of yoghurt; 2) {syn: toxavk} cream; clotted cream; soured or cultured cream: **•Kevanîya malê şîv tîne datîne ber mêvanê xwe. Nan, penêr, *to*, qat'ix, de çi xwedê kiribû qismet tîne datîne ser t'exte** (Z-842) The lady of the house brings dinner and places it before her guest. Bread, cheese, *cream*, yoghurt, in short whatever happened to be there, she places on the board **•Şîrê min bira çê be--*toê* minê p'ak be** (Dz) Let my milk be good, [and] my *cream* will be fine *[prv.]*. {also: tû III (A); [to] تــو (JJ); <t̠o> طـو (HH)} Cf. Southern Tati dialects: Chali, Eshtehardi, & Xiaraji tu *m.*; Takestani túya *f.* = 'cream' (Yar-shater); P to تـو = 'skin formed on the surface of milk'; Sor twêj تـوێـژ = 'thin layer, film, skin on liquid' & twêjał تـوێـژاڵ = 'cream' [Msr/F/K/B/IFb/OK//HH//A/JJ] <mast; qat'ix; şîr; toraq; xavik>

to II تۆ (SK/JB1-A) = you (sing.), thou. See **tu I**.

t'ob•e تـۆبـە *f.* **(;•ê).** repentance: **-t'obe kirin** (IFb/B/JJ/SK/OK) to repent {syn: li xwe zivir̄în}. {also: tewbe (SK-2); t'obet (K-2); [tobé] تــوبــه (JJ); <tobe> توبه (HH)} <Ar tawbah توبة (<Syr √t-w-b ܬܘܒ = 'to return, repent'); Sor tobe تـۆبـە [RN/K/A/IFb/B/JJ/HH/SK/GF/OK]

t'obedar تۆبەدار (RN) = penitent. See **t'obekar**.

t'obekar تۆبـەكـار *adj.* penitent, having mended one's ways: **•Daimî xiyala şeytanî ew e, welîyan û sofîyan û *tobekaran* ji r̄êka beȟeştê û necatê derêxît** (SK 4:42) The devil's thoughts are always directed toward leading holy and pious and *repentant men* astray from the road to paradise and salvation. {also: tewbeker (SK-2); t'obedar (RN); [tobekár] تــوبــەكــار (JJ-G)} Sor tobekar تۆبەكار [RN/K/A/IFb/B/JJ/HH/SK/GF/OK] <t'obe>

t'obet تۆبەت (K) = repentance. See **t'obe**.

tofan/t'ofan [K/JB1-A] تــۆفــان *f.* **(-a;-ê).** 1) {syn: lêmişt; sêlav [2]} flood, inundation, deluge: **•Belkî *tofanek* bazirganê te r̄abe, t'emama xerq bike** (Ba3-3, #25) Perhaps *a flood* will engulf your caravan, [and] drown everyone; 2) {syn: bager; bahoz; bap'eşk; barove; firtone; hureba} storm. {also: [toufan] طوفان (JJ); <t̠ofan> طوفان (HH)} <Ar ṭūfān طـوفـان (<√ṭ-w-f طـوف = 'to overflow its banks'); T tufan; cf. Sor tof تــۆف = 'storm' [Ba3/K/IFb/B/HH/JB1-A/TF//JJ] <avr̄abûn; lehî; sêlav; şîp>

tofil تۆڤِل (TF) = peel, shell. See **tîvil**.

tohv تۆهڤ (TF) = seed, grain. See **tov**.

tok تۆك (EP-7) = hoop; necklace. See **t'oq**.

tol I تــۆل *m&f.* **().** 1) profligate, libertine (K); adulterer (m.), adultress, whore (f.); 2) {syn: xort} young man, youth (HH); 3) *[adj.]* {syn: tolaz} idle, out of work, unemployed (Haz). {also: [tol] تـول (JJ); <t̠ol> طـول (HH)} {tolayî} [Haz/K/A/IFb/B/JJ/GF//HH] <zinêk'ar>

t'ol II تــۆل *f.* **(-a;-ê).** 1) {syn: 'evdîn; ȟeyf[1]} revenge, vengeance: **•[Û dayim Herkî li *tola* xûna Terlan Aẍayî digeřiyan]** (JR #27,83) And the Herkis [a tribe] are always seeking to *avenge* the blood of Terlan Agha; **-tol [bi]deranîn** (JR)/ **~girtin** (GF/OK)/~ **hilanîn** (K)/**~a xwe hildan** (K)/**~a xwe rakirin** (OK)/~ **standin** (K/JJ/GF/OK)/**~vekirin** (K/SK/GF/OK/Bw) [+**ji**]: a) to take revenge (on), avenge o.s. (on), pay (s.o.) back for: **•[Ewî daîm ... her guhdar bû da rojekê derfetê bîne û ewê *tolê ji* Zeman Xanî *biderîne*]** (JR #39,120) He was always listening ... so that one day he would have the chance *to take revenge on* Zeman Khan; b) to avenge s.o.'s death; **-tol vebûn** (M-Zx) to be avenged: **•Ez jî çûm, min ew k'afir kuşt, *tola* birayêt min *vebî*** (M-Zx #756) I too went and killed the monster and my brothers *were avenged*; 2) fine, mulct (SK/Zeb): **•Şêx Muȟemmed S̱iddîq got, "Fi-l-ȟeqîqe 'adetê 'eşîretî weto ye, emma 'edaweta hingo do cihet hene. Yêk 'eşîretî ye, bila ew 'eşîretî bît. Yêk şexsî ye, bila ew *bi tole* bît"** (SK 50:542) Shaikh Muhammad Siddiq said, "Certainly this is the tribal custom, but your enmity has two causes.

One is tribal, let that be settled tribally. One is personal and that must be (settled) *by a fine*." {also: tole II (A/SK/OK-2); [tol] تـــــــــول (JJ)} According to JJ, <Arc & Syr √t-b-' ܬܒܥ = 'to require, claim, avenge' & tva'tā ܬܒܥܬܐ [Maclean twâthâ] & NENA tûlâ ܬܘܠܐ/ܬܘܥܠܐ = 'revenge' (note ' ;) & ṭôlâ ܛܘܠܐ = 'penalty': in NENA, from the original root √t-b-': b--> w & ' --> ø; the -l of Kurdish **t'ol** could come from the prep. li (= 'to'), or from the -th- of twâthâ becoming -l- (*twâlâ: a standard vowel shift in Jewish 'qīman' dialects of Iranian Kurdistan, e.g., -ūthā --> -ūlā) [JR/K/IFb/JJ/GF/TF/OK/Bw//A/SK]

tolayî تۆلایی *f.* **().** adultery. {syn: tolazî} [K/B] <tol I>

tolaz تۆلاز *m.* **().** 1) womanizer, casanova, lady's man; profligate, libertine; adulterer; 2) idler, loafer [used only of men]; rascal; 3) youth, young man: **•Rojekê *çend tolazek* ji cûan çûne-pêş derê qesra S̲adiq Beg, gazî kirin** [sic] (SK 26:237) One day *some* Jewish *youths* went to the door of Sadiq Beg's palace and called. {also: tawlaz (TF); tolaze (K); [tolaz] تـــولاز (JJ); <t̲olaz> طـــولاز (HH)} {syn: tol I} Cf. Turoyo ṭaulâz/ṭōlâz = 'frivolous, vagabond, adulterer' (Ritter) {tolazî} [Haz/A/JB3/IFb/JJ/SK/GF/TF//HH//K//TF] <çavlider; gef̄ok; zinêk'ar>

tolaze تـــۆلازه (K) = womanizer, profligate, adulterer. See **tolaz**.

tolazî تـــــۆلازى *f.* **(-a;-ê).** adultery, debauchery: **•Di encama vê *tolazîyê* de jinikek 20 salan jê biçûktir dikeve xefik û kemîna wî** (lotikxane 28.vii.2006) As a result of this *debauchery*, a woman 20 years younger than him falls into his trap and ambush. {syn: tolayî} [K/A/Haz/ZF3] <qûnekî; tolaz>

tole I تۆله (IFb) = hunting dog. See **t'ûle**.

tole II تۆله (A/SK/OK) = revenge. See **t'ol II**.

tolek تۆلەك (OK) = mallow. See **tolik**.

tolg تۆلگ (AA) = mallow. See **tolik**.

t̲ol•ik طۆلِك [Zeb/Dh/Hk/HH]/**tolik** تۆلِك *f.* **(•ka;•ikê).** mallow, bot. *Malva sylvestris*, an edible plant [T ebegümeci, Ar xubbāz خـبّـاز/xubbayz خـبّـيـز, P panīrak پـنـيـرك]. {also: tolek (OK); tolg (AA); [tolk] تـــولـك (JJ-G); <t̲olik> طـولـك (HH)} Sor tołeke تۆڵەکە [Dh/Zeb/Qzl/HH//K/A/IFb/B/GF/TF/CB//OK//JJ-G//AA]

t'omerî تـومـەرى *f.* **(-ya;-yê).** 1) entirety, all; totality: **•bi *t'omerîya* cindîyê Cizîrêva** (Z-1) with *all* (=*the totality of*) the nobles of Jezirah; -[**bi**] **t'omerî** (K) wholly, entirely, completely; 2) sum, total; result; 3) generality, universality. Cf. Ar tumm تمّ = 'whole' [Z-1/K/B/ZF3] <lap; t'evahî>

Tonisî تۆنِسى (BF) = Tunisian. See **T'ûnisî**.

t'op I تـــۆپ *f.* **().** mob, crowd, gathering: **-t'op bûn** = to gather, assemble *(vi.)* {syn: berhev bûn; civîn; k'om bûn; xir̄ ve bûn}; **-t'op kirin** (B/ZF3) to gather, assemble *(vt.)*, round up {syn: berhev kirin; civandin; k'om kirin; xir̄ ve kirin}: **•Ç'êleka wê dêwêr *t'opî* ser hev *dike*** (J) Her cow *gathers* the cattle together. Cf. T toplamak = 'to gather, to collect' {syn: ferc; k'om; qerebalix; sixlet} [F/J/K/JB3/IFb/B/GF/ZF3]

top II تـــۆپ/**t'op** [K/B]/**t̲op** طـــۆپ [SK] *f.* **(-a;-ê).** 1) {syn: gog[1]; hol I} ball: **-t̲epkê li 'erdê dan** (Bw) to bounce/dribble a ball; 2) cannon. {also: t̲epik (FS); t̲epk (Bw); [top] تـــــوپ (JJ); <t[o]p> تـوپ (HH)} Cf. T top = 'ball'; Sor top تـۆپ = 'ball, roll, bale, total, gun'; Hau tope *f.* (M4) [K/A/JB3/IFb/B/JJ/GF/HH/ZF3//SK//Bw//FS]

t'op III تـــــــۆپ *m.* **().** hill(ock): **•Çû, çû derk'ete *t'opekî*, vegerya, dî kerî pezî wêye** (HCK-3, #2, 20) He went and went, climbed up *a hill*, came back, saw a flock of sheep there. {syn: banî II; dîyar II; gir II; kuç'[3]; zûr} Cf. P tapeh تپه = 'hill, mound' [HCK/K/B]

t'opal تۆپال *adj.* lame, cripple: **•Ez ne j[î] *t'opalim*, ji p'îya / ne kerrim, ji guha / ne şilim, ji desta** (FK-kk-13:124) I am neither *lame* in the feet / nor deaf in the ears / nor limp in the hands **•Min boxekî strû-şkestî, ç'e'vekî kor, lingekî *t'opal* dît** (EP-4) I have seen a bull with one broken horn, blind in one eye, *lame* in one foot. {also: [topal] طـوپـال (JJ)} {syn: leng} < T topal = 'lame' {t'opalî} [K/B/JJ]

t'opalî تۆپالی *f.* **(;-yê).** lameness. [K/B] <t'opal>

topan تـۆپـان (Wn/Xrz)/t̲opan طـۆپـان (Twn) = harrow. See **t'apan**.

topavêj/t'opavêj [K] تـۆپـاڤـێـژ *m.* **(-ê;).** artillerist, artillery gunner, cannoneer. {syn: topçî} [K/IFb/GF/ZF3]

topçî/t'opçî [K/B] تۆپچی/**t̲opçî** طۆپچی [SK] *m.* **(-yê;).** artillerist, artillery gunner, cannoneer. {also: [toptchi] طوپچی (JJ)} {syn: topavêj} < T topçu = 'cannoneer' [K/B//JJ/SK]

t'oq تـــۆق *m.* **().** 1) hoop, circle; 2) {benî II; gerden[3]; r̄istik} necklace, chain: **-tok û benî** (EP-7) neckchain, woman's adornment made of silver coins; 3) iron ring encircling wheel of traditional plow (Kmc/Nbh 124:32). {also: tok (EP-7); [tok] طوق (JJ)} < Ar ṭawq طوق = 'circle, hoop' [EP-7//K/JJ/GF/FJ/TF/Kmc/ZF/Nbh]

t'oř I تۆڕ *f.(B/JJ/JB3)/m.(K)* **(/-a; /-ê).** fishnet, fisherman's net: •[rōeke tárğī báḥrä tā̊r davitin tárğiā bädär xístin ğo'ānīkī báḥre] (LC-1) One day fishermen threw their nets into the sea, and brought out a sea colt •**Îro, torvanan *tora* xwe avêtine behrê bi çend ciyan e, / Ketiye nava *torê* tiştekî girane** (LT) Today the fishermen cast their *nets* into the sea in a few places, / There fell into *the net* something heavy •**Bi k'otek *t'ořa* xwe k'işandin, ko vaye ce'nûekî hespa di t'ořêdaye** (Z-2) They pulled in *the net* with great force, and lo and behold there was a horse's foal in it. {also: [tor] تور (JJ); [tā̊r] تار (LC)} {syn: merat} Cf. Pashto & Wakhi tor = 'net'; P tōr تور = 'net'; T tor = 'fine-meshed net(ting)'; Sor toř تۆڕ = 'net'. According to G. Doerfer, this is a loanword from Chagatay. See his "Ein altosmanisches Lautgesetz im Kurdischen," *Wiener Zeitschrift für die Kunde des Morgenlandes*, 62 (1969), 258-59 & 261. [DM/K/JB3/IFb/B/JJ/GF//LC] <masî; t'ořvan>

t'oř II تۆڕ *adj.* wild, savage: •**Tu *tor* bûyî?** (Msr) Have you gone *mad*? {also: t'ořî II (K)} {syn: ç'olî I; k'ûvî; weĥş [3]} < Ar ṭūrī طوري = 'wild' (< ṭūr طور = 'mountain', cf. P kūhī كوهى = 'wild' [cf. K k'ûvî] < kūh كوه = 'mountain'); Sor toř تۆڕ = 'unbroken (horse), untrained, undisciplined' [Msr//K/ZF3] <hov>

torak تۆراك (Kg/TF) = curds, creamy cheese, strained yoghurt. See **toraq**.

***torane** تۆرانە **().** type of small, white grape which ripens at the end of the season, in November. [Msr] <tirî>

toraq تۆراق *f.* **(-a;-ê).** type of creamy cheese, strained yoghurt [T çökelek, Rus tvorog творог] made of yoghurt or ***dew*** [qv.] [Rus paxtan'e пахтанье] (B); low-quality cheese as opposed to high-quality cheese (HH) [cf. Ar labane لبنة/laban muṣaffá لبن مصفّى, T süzme yoğurt]; ***toraq** is moist, whereas **ç'ortan** is dry*: •**Xurekê wanî ĥert'imî nanê t'isî û hine *toraq* bû** (Ba2-3, 213) Their daily food was stale bread and some *toraq*. {also: torak (Kg/TF); t'oraẍ (K[s]); [toraq] طوراق (JJ); <tûraq> توراق (HH)} {syn: jajî} Cf. Rus tvorog творог = 'curds, cottage cheese' [Kg/TF//K/IFb/B/JJ/GF/Krç//HH] <ç'olik II; ç'ortan; lorik; to I>

t'oraẍ تۆراغ (K[s]) = curds, creamy cheese, strained yoghurt. See **toraq**.

t'ořçî تۆڕچى (K/B/Z-2) = fisherman. See **t'ořvan**.

t'oře تۆڕە [Wkt] *f.* **(-ya;).** 1) {syn: 'adet; kevneşop; řewişt; tîtal} custom, practice, tradition, usage: •**Li gora *toreyên* Kurdan, biçûk destên mezinan, mezin jî çavên biçûkan radimîsin yan maç dikin** (BZ, v. 1, 407) According to Kurdish *customs*, children kiss their elders' hands, and adults kiss the children's eyes; 2) {syn: edebiyat; wêje} literature; the arts: •**Di dîroka *toreya* klasîka Kurdî de, gelek berperên zêrîn hene** (Dqg, 5) In the history of Kurdish classical *literature*, there are many golden pages; 3) {syn: ç'and} culture; high culture, education. {also: torre (Wkt)} Cf. T töre = 'custom, accepted practice; ethics'; Sor tûre تووره = 'literature' [BZ/BF/FJ/GF/Kmc/SS//Wkt] <t'ořevan I>

t'ořevan I تۆڕەڤان *m.* **().** man of letters, littérateur; writer; scholar: •**Hemû wêjedostên Kurd li başûrê Kurdistanê vî navî dinasin, *torevanekî* (wêjevanekî) rêzdar, birûmet û nîştimanperwer** (Wlt 2:73, 13) All Kurdish literature lovers in northern Kurdistan know this name, a respected, renowned, and patriotic *littérateur*. {syn: wêjevan} [(neol)Wlt/IFb/GF/OK] <nivîsk'ar>

torevan II تۆڕەڤان (IFb) = fisherman. See **t'ořvan**.

torim تۆرم *m.&f.* **(/-a;).** young camel: •**Hiş û aqilê arwane jî li ser *torima* wê ya ku li pey xwe hîştibû. Lema derdê wê jî zû ji vê rêwîtiyê zû vegere û bi *torima* xwe şîr bide û pê şa bibe** (Hindik Rindik 4.xii.2016) As for the she-camel, all she could think about was her *baby* that she had left behind. Therefore her goal [lit. 'pain'] was to return as soon as possible from this journey and give milk to her *baby* and rejoice in it. {also: torin I (GF)/tořin I (FS); torm[ik] (IFb)} {syn: k'oçek [4]; kûdik [3]} Cf. T torum/türün [Urfa +] = 'young camel' (DS, v. 10, p. 3970) [Qzl//IFb//GF] <deve; ĥêştir; lok' II>

torin I تۆرن (GF)//tořin I تۆڕن (FS) = young camel. See **torim**.

t'ořin II تۆڕن *m.* **().** 1) man of noble descent, nobleman, gentleman, member of the gentry: •**Seva xatirê min--*t'ořin*, nazik Zînêyî** (Z-1) For my sake, *noble*, delicate Zin; 2) {syn: b[i]razî} nephew, son of one's brother; 3) [*adj.*] noble; 4) picky, fussy. {also: t'oȓind; [torin] تـورين (JJ)} Cf. T torun = 'grandchild' & Arm t'oȓn թոռն = 'grandchild' [Z-1/K/JB3/IF/B/JJ]

t'oȓind تۆرِند = noble; fussy; nephew. See **t'oȓin II**.

torî I تــۆرى/**t'oȓî** تــۆڕى [K] *m.(OK)/f.(K)* **().** jackal, zool. *Canis aureus*: •**Çu kes ne ma li gunda, û bê xudan bûbûn, û *torîya* û bûma ji xwe ra mesken kiribûn** (BG, 13) There was no one left in the villages, and the jackals and owls had inhabited them. {also: torîk (IFb/GF-2); tûrik (Zeb); tûrî (Dh); [turí] تورى (JJ-G); <ṯorî> طورى (HH)} {syn: ç'eqel; wawîk} Cf. P tūre تــوره; Sor toȓik تۆڕك (Hej)/tûrg تووورگ (Arbil) [BG/K/A/GF/OK//JJ-G//HH//IFb//Zeb//Dh] <kûçik; guȓ I; ȓovî I>

t'oȓî II تۆڕى (K) = wild. See **t'oȓ II**.

torîk تۆريك (IFb/GF) = jackal. See **torî I**.

torm تۆرم (IFb) = young camel. See **torim**.

tormik تۆرمِك (IFb) = young camel. See **torim**.

torre تــــــــۆڕه (Wkt) = culture; custom; literature. See **t'oȓe**.

t'oȓvan تــۆڕڤـان *m.* **().** fisherman, angler: •**Dît ku tevî *torvanan* pir meriyan destên xwe avêtine benê torane** (LT) He saw that together with the *fishermen* many men had grabbed the ropes of the nets. {also: t'oȓçî (K-2/B/Z-2); torevan II (IFb); [tárğî] تــــارجــــى (LC)} {syn: masîgîr} [DM/K//IF//B//LC-1] <masî; t'oȓ I>

toşbî تۆشبى (ZF3/FD) = gland. See **toşpî**.

toşpî تۆشپى *f.* **(-ya;-yê).** gland [T salgı bezi; Ar γuddah غدّة]: •**Hirmî ji ber ku *toşpîya* tifa dev û avzêyên (îfrazat) rûvikan zêde dike, ... jibo nexweşên şekir bê xisar e** (zanistuteknoloji.blogspot.com ii.2011) Pears are not harmful to diabetics because they increase the secretions of the oral salivary *gland* and intestines. {also: toşbî (ZF3/FD)} Sor toşp تـۆشـپ [IFb/FJ/FS/Wkt/RZ/CS//ZF3/FD]

tot تــۆت: **-tot bûn** (K/B) to roll *(vi.)*, to come rolling down; to fall down, collapse: •**Wekî ew [zinarêd teȓikî] nişkêva ji cîêd xwe bileqyana, ewê ȓast *tot bibûyana* ser gundê me** (Ba2) If they [the huge rocks] were suddenly to budge from their place, they *would come rolling* straight at our village; **-tot kirin** (B) to throw down, bring down. {also: toto bûn (K)} [Ba2/B/ZF3//K]

totik I تـۆتِـك *f.* **(;-ê).** cookie, biscuit: •**Wexta k'ulfeta sibê em-zaȓ berevî ser hev dikirin, ȟer yekî me *totikek* didanê** [sic] (Ba2-4, 219) When the women of the family gathered us children in the morning, they gave each one of us *a cookie*. {also: bîskuwît} [Rwn/QtrE/Slm/Ba2/K/B/GF]

totik II تۆتِك (A/IFb) = type of bird. See **tûtik I**.

toto bûn تۆتۆ بوون (K) = to roll. See **tot**: **-tot bûn**.

tov تــۆڤ/**ṯov** طــۆڤ [FS/HH] *m.* **(-ê;).** 1) seed; grain: •**Cotyarê *ṯovê* xwe avêt şovê** (FS) The lady farmer threw her *seeds* into the furrows; 2) {syn: dol I} sperm: •--**Xwedê *tovê* mêran biqelîne ...** --**Xwelîserê, ma ku *tovê* mêran biqele vêca emê çawa bikin?** (DBgb, 13) "May God destroy the *sperm* of men" "You poor thing, if men's *sperm* is destroyed, then what will we do?" {also: tohv (TF); **t'oxim**; [tow] توڤ (JJ); <ṯov> طوڤ (HH)} [Pok. teuk- 1085.] 'seed, progeny': Skt túc & toká- *n.* = 'offspring, children' & tókman- *m.* = 'young blade of corn, barley, etc.'; O Ir *tauxma-: Av taoxman- *n.* = 'seed; *pl.* relatives'; O P taumā- *f.* = 'clan, family, race'; Mid P tōm = 'seed, family' & tōhmag = 'seed; stock, family' (M3); P toxm تـخـم--> T tohum = 'seed' & P toxme تـخـمـه = 'seed; stock, family' & -dom in mardom مــــــــــردم = 'mankind, people' (Mid P mardō[h]m (M3) <O Ir *martiya- + *tauxma-); Sor tow تۆو & tuxm تـوخم; Hau tom *m.* (M4). *Perhaps the -x- in P toxm(e) is a borrowing from some non-Persic dialect.* [AB/K/A/JB3/IFb/B/JJ/GF//HH/FS//TF] See also **t'oxim**. <dan II; dendik; tovik>

ṯovik طــۆڤِــك *m./f.(FS)* **(/-a;).** seed(s), *as sunflower seeds, pumpkin seeds, and other edible seeds*: **-ṯovkêt şitî** (Bw) watermelon seeds. [Bw/FS] <dendik; tov>

tovil تــۆڤِـل (IFb/OK/JJ)/tovil (HH) = peel, shell. See **tîvil**.

toxavk تــۆخــاڤـك *f./m.(FS)* **(-a/ ; -ê/).** cream; clotted cream; soured or cultured cream. {also: toẍavk (F/B); [tou-khaw تـوخـاڤ/tou khaf تـوخـاف] (JJ)} {syn: to I} [K/ZF3//F/B//JJ] <to>

t'oxim تـــۆخِـــم *m.* **(-ê;).** 1) seed; grain: •**Daê, xelq *t'oxim* diȓêşîne** (J) Mom, people are sowing *grain*; 2) {syn: dol I} sperm; 3) {also: tuxm (IFb); <tuxm> تـخـم (HH)} lineage, genealogical descent (HH). < P toxm تـخـم --> T tohum--for etymology see **tov**. [J/K/B/GF//IFb/HH] <dol I> See also **tov**.

toẍavk تۆغاڤك (F/B) = cream. See **toxavk**.

t'oz تۆز *f.* **(-a;-ê).** dust; powder; dirt: **-t'oz û xubar**, f. (Z-1/B) dust. {also: [toz] طــوز (JJ); <tûz> تــــوز (HH)} {syn: gerik I; tirabêlk; xubar} < T toz; Sor

toz تۆز = 'dust' [Z-1/L/K/A/JB3/IFb/B/JJ/GF/TF/ZF3//HH]
traf تراف (IFb) = embers. See **tiraf**.
trambêl ترامبێل (IFb) = automobile. See **trimbêl**.
trar ترار (GF/JJ) = copper water cup. See **t'irar**.
trembêl ترەمبێل (ZF3) = automobile. See **trimbêl**.
tren ترەن (ZF) = train. See **trên**.
trên ترێن/**t'r̄ên** ترێن [K] *f.* **(-a;-ê).** train (rail transport): **•*Trêneke* Sibêryayê. Ûris li van *trênan* ji fabrîkên Rohelê tang û her texlît hacetên cengê siwar dikin** (Rnh 2:14, 247) A Siberian *train*. The Russian load tanks and every sort of war materiel onto these *trains* from the factories of the East; **-ji trenê man** (ZF) to miss the train; **-k'etin t'ir̄ênê** (K) to board the train. {also: tiren (TF); tirên (TF-2); t'ir̄ên (K-2); tren (ZF)} {syn: ç'îman II} < Eng train & Fr train [Rnh/IFb/RZ/CS//K//TF//ZF] <r̄êḧesin>
trimbêl ترمبێل *f.* **(-a;-ê).** automobile, car: **•Û berî şar'êt Beẍdayê ne wek nuha d fireh bûn, *trimbêl* nebûn, t'eyara nebûn** (JB1-S #215) And before, the streets of Baghdad were not wide like they are now, there were no *cars*, no planes. {also: terembêl (HYma); t[i]rambêl (IFb); tirimbêl (TF); trembêl (ZF3); trumpêl (Zeb/JB1-S-2); trûmbêl (K)}< automobile < Gr auto = '(by) itself' + Lat mobilis = 'moving, mobile' [JB1-S//IFb//TF//Zeb//K//ZF3//HYma] <cemse; p'îqab; t'aksî; wesayît>
trumpêl ترومپێل (Zeb/JB1-S) = automobile. See **trimbêl**.
trûmbêl تروومبێل (K) = automobile. See **trimbêl**.
trûsk ترووسك *f.* **(-a;-ê).** lightning bolt; flash of lightning. {also: tirîşke (IFb/ZF3)} Sor tirîşqe تِریشقە = 'stroke of lightning' [Wn/GF//IFb/ZF3] <birûsk>
tu I تو *prn.* **(te).** you *(sing.)*, thou; thee: **•Pismam, ez a tbînim *eto* pîte p min nakey, *eto* yê çûye bajera, bîladêt mazin, *ete* jinêt cwan yêt dîtîn, noke *te* ez nevêm** (M-Ak #633) Cousin, I see that *you* are not interested in me, *you* have been to towns and great countries and seen beautiful women, now *you* do not want me. {also: eto (M-Ak/SK-2); ti I (Wkt-2); to II (SK/JB1-A-2); [tou] تو (JJ); <tû> تو (HH)} [Pok tu-, *gen.* t(e)u̯e, *dat.* toi/tebh(e)i, *acc.* te 1097.] 'second person singular pronoun' [Kent: *tuu̯om *and not* *tû]: Skt tuvám; O Ir *tuvam (*gen.* *tava) (Tsb 19): Av tvəm (Old Av)/tum (Young Av)/*tuvəm; OP tuvam (*acc.* θuvām, *gen.* [-]taiy) (Kent); Mid P tō (M3); P tō تو; Sor to تۆ/eto ئەتۆ; Za ti (*obl.:* to) (Todd) [BX/K/JB3/IFb/B/JJ/JB1-A&S/GF/TF/OK/Wkt//HH//SK//M-Ak] <cenab>
t'u II تو *neg. prep. mod.* 1) [+ *neg.*] {syn: hîç [2]} none, not any, no: **•Dibêjin di nihalekîda r̄îwîek hebû. ... bazeberek hebû, r̄îwî lê derbaz dibû her wextê ḧez kiriba. ... Marek jî di wê nihalêda hebû. Nedişya li bazeberî derbaz bibît. Zor ḧez dikir ew jî wekî r̄îwî hat-u-çonê biket, *çu* çare nedît** (SK 2:9) They say that there was a fox (living) in a ravine. ... There were stepping-stones and the fox crossed over whenever he liked. ... There was also a snake in that ravine. He could not cross over the stepping-stones. He very much wanted to come and go like the fox, but could see *no* solution; **-t'u car** = never {also: ç'ucar}; **-t'u çax** = never; **-t'u kes** (K/JB3) no one, nobody {also: ç'ukes}; **-t'une** [pl. **t'unene**] = there is (are) not [≠ heye, pl. hene] {also: ç'une} (see listing below); **-t'utişt** (K) nothing {also: ç'utişt}; **-t'u wext** = never; 2) any: **•bêî *tu* dişwariyê** (BX) without *any* difficulty **•*T'u* lawê te hene?** = Do you have *any* children? {also: ç'u (Zx/JB1-A&S/SK/OK-2); t'i II (Z-3); [tou تو/ciú چو] (JJ)} [K/(A)/JB3/IFb/B/JJ/GF/OK//Zx/JB1-A&S/SK]
t'ucar I توجار = never. See **t'u car** under **t'u II.**
t'ucar II توجار *m.* **(-ê; t'ucêr).** merchant, businessman: **•Ez r̄abûm digel *tucara*, min ticareta xo dagirt** (M-Ak, #631, 286) I got up with *the merchants*, arranged my merchandise **•Rojekê *t'îcarêt* Beẍda r̄abûn, k'arê xo kir da çine t'îcaretê li Besra** (M-Am, #704, 322) One day *the merchants of* Baghdad got up and made themselves ready to go and trade in Basra **•[Yûsif bûye *ticar* li Mêrdînê]** (PS-I, #6, 13, 1.13) Joseph became *a merchant* in Mardin. {also: t'acir (RZ-2); t'icar (IFb-2/JB1-A&S); t'îcar (M-Am); [teğār تجار/tējir تاجر] (JJ); <tacir> تاجر (HH)} {syn: bazirgan} < Ar tujjār تجّار, pl. of tājir تاجر = 'merchant' {t'icaret} [HR/K/B/IFb//JB1-A&S/JJ//M-Am//HH]
t'ucaretî توجارەتی (K/L) = business, trade. See **t'icaret**.
t'ucarî توجاری (K/B) = business, trade. See **t'icaret**.
tul' تولع (Qzl) = lump. See **tulḧ**.
tulḧ تولح *f.* **().** lump, swelling node, rounded protuberance; boil. {also: tilh (ZF3); tul' (Qzl)} [Qrj/G//ZF3//Qzl] <çene; girê>

tuli تولِ (Klk) = fingertip. See **t'ilî I**[2].

tulî تولی (Hk) = finger. See **t'ilî I**.

t'ulusm[e] [ە]تولوسم = talisman, charm. See **t'ilism**.

tuncik تونجِك (Rwş) = lock of hair. See **t'ûncik**.

t'und تـونـد *adj.* sharp, violent, fierce, vehement: **•Muroek** [=mirovek] **hebû ji 'eşîreta Sûrçîyan, daxili qeza Akrê, nawê wî 'Elî bû: gelek dewletmend bû ... emma daimî *tund* û tebî'et-nexoş bû** (SK 14:135) ... **Dayka Eĥmed jî, "Esmer" digotinê** [sic], **çûnku digel 'Elî Teşqelan r̄a-baribû, ew jî wekî wî *tund* û tîj bû** (SK 14:143) There was once a man of the Surchi tribe, in the district of Akre, whose name was Ali: he was very rich ... but he was always *fierce* and bad-tempered (135) ... Ahmad's mother, who was called "Asmar," because she had lived with Ali the Cheat, was also *fierce* and sharp like him (143) **•Tahir Ax̄a zor *tund* e, emma em weto texmîn dikeyn ku bo zatê hingo çu gotinan naket, belku dê memnûn bît** (SK 42:406) Tahir Agha is very *fierce*, but we consider that he will not say anything about you, rather he will be grateful. {also: [tound] تند (JJ)} {syn: dir̄ I; xurt} Cf. Mid P tund = 'sharp, violent' (M3); P tund تـنـد = 'swift; pungent, acrid, sharp, hot'; Sor tund تـونـد = 'tight, firm, strong, violent, harsh, peppery, severe, angry, swift'; Za tun = 'hot, spicy (of peppers)' (Mal) [K(s)/IFb/JJ/SK/TF]

t'undî تـونـدى *f.* **(-ya;-yê).** sharpness, violence, fierceness, vehemence: **•Ew şole *bi tundî* çê nabît: bi tedbîr û ĥekîmane dê mumkin bît** (SK 61:737) This job cannot be done *with violence* [or, *force*], it would only be possible with stratagem and cunning. {syn: şidet; xurtî} Cf. P tundī تـنـدى; Sor tundî توندى [K(s)/IFb/SK/TF] <t'undûtîjî>

tund û tijî تـونـد و تِـژى (Dengê Kurdistan/RojevaKurd/RojaWelat) = violence. See **t'undûtîjî**.

t'undûtîjî توندوتیژى/**t'und û tîjî** توند و تیژى *f.* **(-ya; -yê).** violence: **•Ji bona çareser kirina pirsa Kurd siyaseta dewletê, siyaseta *tundûtijiyê* girte ber** (Dengê Kurdistan 30.v.2012) In order to solve the Kurdish question he adopted the politics of the state, the politics of *violence* **•Ji dîktatorên navçe dixwaze guhê xwe bidine daxwazên gel û *tund û tijî* bi kar neynin** (RojevaKurd 29.iii.2011) He asks the dictators of the region to listen to the people's demands and not use *violence* **•Kêşeyê Kurd ne pirsa *tund û tijî* ye û ne jî bi tenê pirsa demokrasiyê ye, pirseka netewî ye** (RojaWelat 10.v. 2015) The Kurdish issue is not a question of *violence*, nor is it only a question of democracy, it is a national question ***•Tundûtûjiya* dijî afretan ber bi zêdebûnê ye** (Wkt) *Violence* against women is on the rise. {also: tindûtîjî (Wkt-2); tund û tijî (Dengê Kurdistan/RojevaKurd/RojaWelat); tund û tûjî (ZF/Wkt-2)} {syn: k'otek; şidet; t'undî; zor I} <Sor tund û tîjî تـونـد و تـیـژى [Dengê Kurdistan/RojevaKurd/RojaWelat//Wkt//ZF] <tundî>

tund û tûjî تـونـد و تـووژى (ZF/Wkt) = violence. See **tund û tîjî**.

t'une تـونـه (*pl.* **t'unene**). there is (are) not [past tense: **t'unebû**, *pl.* **t'unebûn**]. {also: çunîne (Başkale & Behdînî); t'ine (Wkt); [touné تـونـه/touniné تـونـيـنـه] (JJ); <tine تنه/tinne تنّه> (HH)} {≠heye [pl. hene]} [K/A/IF/B/JJ/ZF3//HH//Wkt] <t'u II>

tu'ok توعۆك (Kmc) = hackberry tree. See **tihok**.

ture توره (GF) = grapevine branches. See **tûreh**.

turiş/t'uriş [B] تورش *m.* **().** risk; daring: **-t'uriş kirin** (B)/**turuş kirin** (K) to dare, risk {syn: wêrîn}: **•Eskerê ku 'ecele dihat, nişkêva cîyê xweda 'edilî, *kesî turiş nekir* pêşda bê** (H.Cindî. Hewarî, 151) The army that was quickly advancing, suddenly stopped in its tracks, *no one dared* to advance. {also: turuş (K/CS)} Sor turuş تـوروش = 'daring, boldness; pluck' [Tsab/B//K/CS]

Turkmenistanî تـورکـمـەنِـسـتـانـى (BF) = Turkmen. See **T'irkmanî**.

Turkmenî تورکمەنى (BF) = Turkmen. See **T'irkmanî**.

tursî تورسى (Wkt) = plain (of food). See **t'isî**[2].

turuş توروش (K/CS) = risk; daring. See **turiş**.

tusî توسى (Wkt) = plain (of food). See **t'isî**[2].

tuştîr توشتير *f.* **(-a;-ê).** one-year-old female goat (IFb/CG/Ag/HH/JJ) [tychtour]; two-year-old female goat (K/Haz/JJ) [tishtūr]; three-year-old female goat (K); young female goat (up to the first time it bears young) (B): ***•tiştîra* Îsa û nêriyê Mihemed** (ZZ-1, 181) Jesus' *nanny goat* and Muhammad's billy goat. {also: tiştîr (K/IFb-2/CG/B/GF-2); [tychtour/tishtūr] تـشـتـور (JJ); <teştîr> تشتير (HH)} Sor tiştîr تِشتير/tuştîr توشتير/twêştîr تـوێـشـتـيـر = 'one- to two-year-old female goat' & çiştîr چِـشـتـيـر = 'young she-goat that has been covered' [A/GF/Haz/Bsk/Ag//CG/K/IFb/B//JJ//HH] <bizin>

tutin توتِن (TF) = tobacco. See **t'itûn**.

t'utişt توتِشت/**t'u tişt** تو تِشت [B/GF] nothing. {also: [tu-tuštī] توتشتى (JJ)} {syn: hîç [3]} < t'u = 'not' +

tişt = 'thing' [K/IFb/B/GF//JJ] <t'u II>

tuxm توخم (IF/HH) = lineage. See **t'oxim**.

tû I/t'û [K] تـــــوو *f.* **(-ya;-yê).** mulberry, bot. *Morus*: **•Tûna bîne** (BK) Bring some (mul)berries; 2) mulberry tree (IFb): **-dartû** (IFb)/**dara t'ûtê** (K) mulberry tree. {also: t'ût (;-ê) (K/B); [tou] تو (JJ); <tû> تـــو (HH)} Skt tūda & tūla (Laufer, 582) --> Ar tūt تـوت --> T dut; Sor tû تـوو = 'mulberry' [BK/A/JB3/IFb/JJ/HH/TF/OK/AA//K/B]

t'û II تـوو: **-t'û kirin** (K) to spit, expectorate: **•Hevraz *t'ûkim* - simêle, berjêr *t'ûkim* - r̄ûye** (Dz - #665) If I *spit* upward, there's my moustache, if I *spit* downward, there's my beard *[prv.]* (i.e., damned if I do, damned if I don't: cf. T Aşağı tükürsem sakal, yukarı tükürsem bıyık). {also: tif kirin (A/IF); t'ûf kirin (K-2); [tiw/touw kirin] تف كرين (JJ); <tifkirin تفكرن (tifdike) (تفدكه)> (HH)} [Dz/K/B//IFb/A/HH/GF//JJ] See also **t'if** & **t'ûk II**.

tû III توو (A) = skin (on milk); cream. See **to**.

***tûdya** تـــــوودیـــا **().** plant which ripens in the fall, containing yellow powder used as cure for eye disorders. Cf. T tutya [Nizip -Gaziantep] = 'a remedy for eyeaches, spread on the eye like collyrium [sürme]' (DS, v.10, p. 4002). [Bşk]

t'ûf تووف (K) = saliva. See **t'if** & **t'û II**.

tûfirengî تـــووفِـرەنــگـــی *f.* **(-ya;-yê).** strawberry, bot. *Fragaria vesca*: **•Sebze, fêkiyên wek tû, *tûfirengî*, tirî hwd. û hinek cureyên fêkiyan ji bo we baş in** (www.diabetes.no) Vegetables, fruits like mulberries, *strawberries*, grapes etc. and some [other] types of fruits are good for you. {also: tûfiringî (Wkt); tûfrengî (IFb/ZF3/Kmc/CS); tûtfirengî (RZ/Kmc-2)} Cf. Ar tūt ifranjī توت إفرنجي [BF/FD//IFb/ZF3/Kmc/CS//Wkt//RZ]

tûfiringî تووفِرِنگی (Wkt) = strawberry. See **tûfirengî**.

tûfrengî تـووفـرەنـگـی (IFb/ZF3/Kmc/CS) = strawberry. See **tûfirengî**.

tûj تـــووژ *adj.* 1) sharp *(knife)*: **-tûj kirin** (IFb/ZF) to sharpen, whet, hone {syn: seqa kirin; sûtin}: **•Guro, tu diranê xwe *tûjke*** (J) Wolf, *sharpen* your teeth!; 2) {syn: dijwar [3]} hot, spicy *(onions, jajî on its way to going bad, etc.: cf.* ***dijwar****, of peppers, tobacco, karî II [qv.])* (Bw); 3) severe: **•Şovenîzm li Kurdistanê her çûye *tûjtir* bûye** (Ber) Chauvinism in Kurdistan has become increasingly *more severe*. {also: tîj (HB/Bw/SK/GF-2); [touj] توژ (JJ); <tûj> توژ (HH)} Cf. Mid P tēz = 'quick; sharp' (M3); P tīz تـیـز; Sor tund-u-tîj توند و تیژ = 'hot, spicy, peppery'; =Za tûn; Hau têj (M4) {tûjahî; tûjayî; tûjî} [K/A/JB3/IFb/B/JJ/HH/GF//HB/Bw/SK]

tûjahî تووژاهی (K) = sharpness; spiciness. See **tûjî**.

tûjayî تووژایی (K/B) = sharpness; spiciness. See **tûjî**.

tûjî تـــــووژی *f.* **(-ya;-yê).** 1) sharpness; 2) spiciness. {also: tûjahî (K-2); tûjayî (K-2/B)} [K/IF/GF/ZF3//B] <tûj>

t'ûk I تـــــــــــووك *f.* **(-a;-ê).** 1) {syn: pirç'} hair *(of animals)*, fur; hair of the body *{as opposed to hair of the head}* (Bşk): **•Dîna xwe daê, Borê wî dîsa mîna berê anede doxme bûye, *t'ûka* sipî dewsa brîna şîn bûye** (EP-7) He looked and saw that Bor (=his horse) was as good as new [T anadan doğma], that white *hair* was growing over the wound; 2) down, fluff; feather(s) (HB/K); 3) soft, fluffy hair (K/A). {also: [touk] تـــوك (JJ); <tûk> توك (HH)} Cf. T tüy = 'hair, feather'. *According to G. Doerfer, T tüy is from older T tûk < tû + the diminutive suffix -k: hence Kurdish preserves the older form. See his* "Ein altosmanisches Lautgesetz im Kurdischen," *Wiener Zeitschrift für die Kunde des Morgenlandes*, 62 (1969), 259 & 261. [HB/EP-7/MC-1/K/A/IFb/B/JJ/ HH/GF/Bşk] <p'or̄ III>

t'ûk II تـــووك *f.* **(-a;-ê).** saliva, spit, spittle, sputum: **-t'ûk kirin**: a) to spit, expectorate (K/B/JJ); b) to poo-poo stg., treat with contempt (B). {also: tû II; [tou تو/touk توك] (JJ); <tûk> توك (HH)} {syn: ava dev; girêz; t'if} Cf. T tükürük = 'saliva, spit(tle)' [F/K/IF/B/JJ/HH/GF] See also **t'if** & **t'û II**.

t'ûl•e تـــوولــه *m.* **(•ê;•ê).** puppy, young dog (Wn/K); small hunting dog; hairless dog (IF). {also: tole I (IFb); [toulé] توله (JJ); <tûle> توله (HH)} [Wn/F/K/A/B/JJ/HH//IFb] <kûçik; se>

t'ûm تـــووم *m.* **(-ê;).** bush, shrub; a thorny bush which grows on mountainsides, whose thick branches are cut and burnt as firewood (Ig): **•Mûsa hilkişiya li ser çiyayê Horeb, ku pezêd wî biçêrin. Li wir ewî *tûmê* agirpêketî dît** (wol.jw.org Serhatî 30) Moses climbed up mount Horeb, so that his sheep could graze. He saw the burning *bush* there **•Xwe da ber *tûmekî*** (L) He hid behind *a bush*. {syn: devî; kem; k'ol III; t'er̄aş II} [L/F/K/A/B/ZF3]

t'ûncik تـوونـجِـك *f./m.(ZF3)* **(-a/;-ê/).** lock of hair, tuft of hair *(hanging down over forehead)*, forelock: **•Anku bes e ku bibêjin Kurd dabaşa (bahsa)**

biskan, çavan û xiyala guliyan û *tuncikên* xweşik bikin (Rwş #2, 15) In other words, enough of saying that Kurds investigate [only] curls of hair, eyes, and imaginings of beautiful bangs and *locks*. {also: tuncik (Rwş); [toumdjik] تـومـجـك (JJ); <tûncik> تـونـجـك (HH)} {syn: t'emberî} [Rwş//F/K/IFb/B/HH/ZF3//JJ] <bisk; gulî I; kezî; mû; ne'tik; p'or̄ I>

T'ûnisî تووِنسى *adj.* Tunisian. {also: Tonisî (BF)} [Wkp/SS//BF]

tûr I توور *m.* **(-ê;).** bag, sack; small sack (HH): **•Ez û tu rahêjin *tûrê* parsê û herin weke aşiq û mitirban ji xwe re li nava eşîr û ebrê bigerrin** (ZZ-10, 136) Let's you and I pick up a beggar's *sack* and go as bards and singers and wander among the tribes and clans **•*Tûrê* virekan tim qul e** (AB) The liars' *bag* always has a hole in it; **-tûr şandin** (IFb) to send gifts [in a sack] at the occasion of a wedding, engagement, circumcision, etc. {also: [tour تـور/tourik تـورك] (JJ); <tûr> تـور (HH)} {syn: cendik (M-Ak/OK)} [AB/K/A/IFb/B/JJ/HH/GF/Kş/ZF]

tûrav تووراڤ (FS) = grapevine branches. See **tûreh.**

tûre تـووره (FJ/JJ/HH/ZF3) = grapevine branches. See **tûreh.**

tûreh تـوورهه *f.* **().** grapevine branches which have been cut from the vine: **•Wî mêw dikezixandin, wê jî *tûrhên* wan yên hatîn birîn ji nav rez paqij dikirin** (DBgb, 51) He would trim the vines, and she would remove their cut-off *branches*. {also: ture (GF); tûrav (FS); tûre (FJ/ZF3); tûrhe (FS-2); [touré] تـوره (JJ); <tûre> تـوره (HH)} [DBgb//FJ/JJ/HH/ZF3//GF//FS] <lem; mêw; r̄ez; tirî>

tûr̄eşk تـووڕهشـك *f.* **(-a;-ê).** blackberry, bramble, bot. *Rubus fruticosus*. {syn: dirik; stirî I} [IFb/OK/ZF3/FS]

tûrhe توورهه (FS) = grapevine branches. See **tûreh.**

tûrik تووِرك/تويرك (Zeb) = jackal. See **torî I**.

tûrî توورى/تويرى (Dh) = jackal. See **torî I**.

T'ûrkî توورکى (K) = Turkey. See **T'irkiye**.

t'ûs تـووس *m.* **(-ê;).** in a game, anything with which the **gog** [ball, puck, etc.] is hit, such as a stick, Ping-Pong paddle, baseball or cricket bat, tennis racket. [Bw/FS] <gog>

t'ûş I تـووش *f.* **().** 1) glade, clearing; 2) hollow, depression (geog.). [EP-7/K]

t'ûş II تـووش**: -t'ûşî *ft-î* bûn** (Bw)/**tûşî yekî bûn** (IFb): to encounter stg. or s.o., face stg. or s.o., come across stg. or s.o., be faced with stg., undergo stg. {syn: r̄ast hatin} **•Di vê rewşê de bêje *tûşî* hinek guherînan *dibin*** (TaRK, 90) In this situation, nouns *undergo* some changes **•Ew *tûşî* nesaxiyeke giran *bû*** (Zx) He *was faced with* a serious illness **•[Harold] Pinter di piçûkiya xwe de *tûşî* êrîş û piçûkxistinên antîsemîtîk *bû*** (Tirej.com, x.2005) In his childhood, [Harold] Pinter *encountered* antisemitic attacks and humiliation. {syn: r̄û bi r̄û} Sor tûş bûn تـووش بـوون = 'to encounter, come upon, meet, face' [Bw/TaRK/IFb/FJ/GF/Wkt]

tûşemb تووشهمب (BF) = raspberry. See **tûşêmî.**

tûşembî تووشهمبى (FS) = raspberry. See **tûşêmî.**

tûşêmî تـووشـێـمـى *f.* **(-ya;-yê).** raspberry, bot. *Rubus idaeus*: **•Di bijîşkiya gelêrî ya kurd de sûd ji *tûşêmiyê* tê girtin** (Wkp) In Kurdish folk medicine *raspberries* are used. {also: şêmî (IFb/FJ/GF/RZ/FS-2/Wkt-2); tûşemb (BF); tûşembî (FS); tûşmî (ZF3-2)} Cf. Ar tūt šāmī تـوت شـامـي = 'mulberry' [Wkp/ZF3/Wkt//FS//BF//IFb/FJ/GF/RZ]

***tûşk** تووشك/تويشك *m.* **(-ê;).** rice husk: **-tûşkê birincî** (Zeb) do. [Zeb] <birinc I; ç'eltûk; p'ûşk>

tûşmî تووشمى (ZF3) = raspberry. See **tûşêmî**.

t'ût تووت (;-ê) (K/B) = mulberry. See **tû I**.

tûtfirengî تـووتـفِـرهنـگـى (RZ/Kmc) = strawberry. See **tûfirengî**.

tût•ik I تـووتـِك *f.* **(•ka/•ika;•ikê).** *word designating different types of bird*: 1) {syn: mirîşk} chicken (Msr/Frq): **•Qaso dît ku *tûtika* wî li ser poxanê kîsikekî** [sic] **xist serê nikulê xwe** (ZZ-7, 243) Q. saw his *chicken* on the dung heap putting a pouch on the tip of its beak; 2) {syn: qumrî} turtledove (HH). {also: totik II (A/IFb); <ṯûṯak> طـوطـك (HH)} [Msr/ZF/RZ//A/IFb//HH]

tûtik II تـووتِك *m./f.(BF)* **(-ê/-a;-î/-ê).** unripe zucchini, cucumber, etc.: **•Eger xiyar e, ji *tûtikî* diyar e** (Bw)/**Eger xiyar e, bi *tûtkê* diyar e = Xiyar e, ji *tîtkî* diyar e** (Wkt) If it's a cucumber, it will be apparent in its *early stages* [*prv.*]. {also: tîtik (BF)} {syn: kûtik; xirtik I} [Bw/Elk/Wkt/FS/ZF3//BF] <arû; xiyar>

t'ûtin تووتِن (M-Zx) = tobacco. See **t'itûn.**

tûx تووخ (FS) = stack; bundle. See **t'exe.**

t'ûzik تـووزك *f.* **(-a;-ê).** *plant with pungent leaves used in salads that grows on banks of river*: watercress, bot. *Nasturtium officinale*. {also: <tûzik> تـووزك (HH)} {syn: kîzmas; pîz}

[Btm(Ĥatĥatkê)/IFb/HH/GF/Qzl/FS/ZF3] <dêjnik; r̄eşad>

t'ẍûb تغووب (EH) = border. See **t'ixûb**.

U و /ئو

‘ufare عوفاره (Qzl) = chaff; unpicked fruit. See **‘efare**.

Ukraynayî وكرايناييى (Wkt) = Ukrainian. See **Ûkraynî**.

Ukraynî وكراينى (Wkt) = Ukrainian. See **Ûkraynî**.

ulm ولم/**’ulm** ئولم *m.* **(-ê;).** 1) {syn: zanîn [3]; zanyarî} knowledge; 2) {syn: zanist} science; -ology; 3) subject (of study), (scholarly) discipline. {also: ‘ilm (SK); [ilm] علم (JJ); <‘ilm> علم (HH)} < Ar ‘ilm علم --> T ilim [F/K/B//HH/SK//JJ]

ulmdar ولمدار/**’ulmdar** ئولمدار *m.* **(-ê;).** scholar; scientist: **•Lomonosov *ulmdarê* ûřisayî mezine** (B) Lomonosov is a great Russian *scholar*. {syn: zana} {ulmdar[t]î} [K2-Fêrîk/F/K/B] <ulm>

ulmdarî ولمدارى/**’ulmdarî** ئولمدارى *f.* **(;-yê).** learning, erudition, scholarship. {also: ulmdartî (B-2)} [F/B/K] <ulmdar>

ulmdartî ولمدارتى/’ulmdartî ئولمدارتى (B) = erudition. See **ulmdarî**.

‘Umanî عومانى *adj.* Omani. {also: Omanî (Wkp)} [Wkt//Wkp]

’ummet ئوممەت (SK/HH) = community of Islam. See **omet**.

uncûz ونجووز/’uncûz ئونجووز (EP-7) = wild plant. See **incûz**.

unda وندا (B) = lost. See **winda**.

Urdinî وردنى (Wkt/CS) = Jordanian. See **’Urdunî**.

’Urdunî ئوردونى *adj.* Jordanian. {also: Erdenî (BF/Wkp-2); Urdinî (Wkt/CS)} Sor ’Urdunî ئوردونى [IFb/SS/Wkp//Wkt/CS//BF]

urz ورز (IFb/AA/OK) = cedar. See **wurz**.

usa وسا (B) = thus, so. See **wisa**.

ussa وسسا (B/IS) = thus, so. See **wisa**.

ussan وسسان (IS) = thus, so. See **wisa**.

utî وتى (OK) = [flat]iron. See **ût’î**.

Uzbekî وزبەكى (ZF3/Wkt) = Uzbek. See **Ûzbekî**.

Û ئوو

û ئوو/وو/ و conj. and. Cf. P ō / va و [K/JB3/ZF3/BF/FS]

ûcax ئـــووجـــاخ (ZZ-10) = oven; furnace; hearth; family; shrine. See **ocax**.

Ûkranyayî ئووكرانيايى (ZF3) = Ukrainian. See **Ûkraynî**.

Ûkraynayî ئووكراينايى (Wkp) = Ukrainian. See **Ûkraynî**.

Ûkraynî ئـووكـرايـنـى *adj.* Ukrainian. {also: Ukrayn[ay]î (Wkt); Ûkranyayî (ZF3); Ûkraynayî (Wkp-2)} Sor Okranî ئۆكرانى [Wkp/BF//ZF3//Wkt]

ûlo ئوولۆ (L/K) = so, thus. See **wilo**.

ûmûd ئووموود, f. (K) = hope. See **omîd**.

ûn ئوون (Z-2/F) = you. See **hûn.**

ûnîvêrsîte ئـوونـيـڤـێـرسـيـتـه (GF) = university. See **ûnîvêrsîtê**.

ûnîvêrsîtê ئوونيڤێرسيتێ *f.* **().** university. {also: ûnîvêrsîte (GF); ûnîvêrsîtêt (B)} {syn: zanîngeh; zanko} [F/K//GF//B]

ûnîvêrsîtêt ئـوونـيـڤـێـرسـيـتـێـت (B) = university. See **ûnîvêrsîtê**.

ûr ئـــوور/**'ûr** عـــوور [GF/Msr/FS] *m.* **(-ê;).** bowels, entrails, intestines, guts: **-'ûr û pizûr** (Msr)/**ḧûr û p'izûr** (B)/**ûr û r̄ovî** (Dz) entrails, tripe, organs situated in the abdominal cavity: **• ... û *ûr û r̄ovî* ji r̄ovîra danîn** (Dz) ... and he left *the entrails* for the fox **•*'Ûr û pizûr*, para xezûr, ser û pepik, para metik** (Msr) *Intestines and undesirable parts* [are] the father-in-law's portion, the head and trotters are the maternal aunt's portion *(this is part of a folk poem which indicates how the parts of a slaughtered goat or sheep are divided among family members).* {also: hûr II (A); ḧûr (B); [hour] هـــور (JJ); [uhhr] اور (JJ-G); <'ûr> عـــور (HH)} {syn: pizûr; r̄odî; r̄ovî II} [Dz//A/JJ//B//HH/GF/Msr/FS] <r̄ovî II>

Ûr̄is ئوورِس (F/K/JB3) = Russian (person). See **R̄ûs I**.

Ûrisî (Wkt/BF) ئوورِسى = Russian. See **R̄ûsî**.

ûstî ئووستى = nape, neck. See **stû**.

ûstû ئووستوو (JR) = nape, neck. See **stû**.

ûşî ئـــووشـــى (JB3/IFb/GF/Bw) = bunch of grapes. See **gûşî**.

ûşt ئـــووشـــت *f.* **(-a;).** cause, reason: **•Gotina "bêpar kirin" yan jî "maf ji dest girtin" bi gelek *ûştan* ve girêdayî ye** (Ber 5/86, 15) The [use of] the term "to deprive" or "to remove one's rights" may depend on several things [lit. '*causes*']. {also: ûşte (OK)} {syn: eger II; sebeb; sedem I} [(neol)Ber/IFb//OK/ZF3/Wkt]

ûşte ئووشته (OK) = reason. See **ûşt**.

ûtêl ئـووتـێـل *f.* **(-a;-ê).** hotel: **•Ezê *ûtêlekê* tê de çêkim** (L) I'll make *a hotel* out of it [lit. 'in it']. {also: otel (ZF3); otêl (K-2/JB3/Wkt)} [L/K/BF//JB3/Wkt//ZF3]

ût'î ئـــووتـــى *f.* **(-ya;-yê).** iron, flatiron: **-ûtîya kehrebê** (FS) electric iron; **-ûtî kirin** (FS?BF/ZF3)/**ût'o kirin** (K)/**ût'u/ût'û kirin** (B) to iron, press: **•Wî kincên xwe *ûtî kirin*** (FS) He *ironed* his clothes. {also: otî (IFb-2/OK); utî (OK-2); ût'o (K); ût'u (B-2); ût'û (B)} < T ütü, cf. Rus utiug утюг [IFb/GF/FS/BF/ZF3//OK//K//B]

ût'o ئووتۆ (K) = [flat]iron. See **ût'î**.

ût'u ئووتو (B) = [flat]iron. See **ût'î**.

ût'û ئووتوو (B) = [flat]iron. See **ût'î**.

Ûzbekî ئـووزبـه‌كـى *adj.* Uzbek. {also: Ozbekî (Wkt-2/BF/SS); Ozbekistanî (BF-2); Uzbekî (ZF3/Wkt-2)} Sor 'Uzbêkî ئوزبێكى [Wkp/Wkt//BF/SS//ZF3]

ڤ V

-va ڤا (Z-1) = prepositional suffix. See **-ve**.

va I ڤـا . here! (presentative) [voici; voilà]: •***Vame* ez diçim ber çêm** (AB) *Here I am* going to the river; -**vaye** (K) here he/she/it is!: •***Vaye*, xortekî gelikî espehî hatîye** (L) *Here* a very handsome youth has come •***Vaye* min ji te re goşt anî** (L) *Here* I've brought you some meat. {also: vaê (IF); vaye (B/GF); [vaya/wé] ڤه (JJ); <va> ڤا (HH)} [K/HH//IFb//B/GF//JJ]

va II ڤا (Ad) = this, these. See **ev**.

vaê ڤائێ (IF) = here! See **va I**.

vajê ڤاژێ (B) = backward. See **vajî**.

vajî ڤـاژى *adj.* backward, inverted, reversed; upside down; inside out: -**vajî kirin** (K) to turn inside out, flip: •**Ḧûrê karê derxist şûşt, ... ḧûr *vajî kir*, kir serê xwe, bû forma k'eçelokekî û çû** (HCK-3, #2, 21) She took out the goat's intestines and washed them, ... she *turned* the intestines *inside out*, put it on her head, took on the form of a bald boy, and went. {also: vajê (B); wajî (SK); [wàji ڤـاژى/vaji واژى] (JJ); <vajî> ڤـاژى (HH)} P važūn واژون/vāžgūn واژگـون = 'upside down, inverted, upset'; Sor awejû ئـاوهژوو = 'reversed, back to front' [Frq/F/K/(A)/IFb/JJ/HH/GF/TF//B//SK]

vala ڤـالا *adj.* 1) {syn: betal; boş I; ≠t'ijî} empty, vacant; 2) useless, futile: •**Vî merivî dîna xwe dayê *vala* ye, got, "Merivek hatiye /pêşîya min, bila hema bizinek jê ra be". Bizinek da wî** (J2, 37-8) This man saw that it was *futile* [to protest], he said "A man came before me, one of the goats should go to him." He gave him a goat; 3) {syn: betal} idle, free, off (of work): •**Vêca rojên ku ez *vala* me jî, ez naxwazim wisa be. Ez dixwazim qet nebe van rojan dereng razêm** (tirşik.net 20.iv.2014) So on days that I am *off* [work], I don't want it to be like that. At least on these days I want to sleep late. {also: [wala ڤـالا/vala والا] (JJ); <vale> ڤـاله (HH)} {valahî; valayî; [walati] ڤالاتى (JJ) ; <valehî> ڤالهى (HH)} [K/A/JB3/IFb/B/JJ/GF/TF//HH]

valahî ڤالاهى (Ber/JB3/IFb/GF) = emptiness; idleness. See **valayî**.

vala•yî ڤـالايـى *f.* **(•ya;•yê).** 1) emptiness; vacancy; 2) idleness (JJ). {also: valahî (Ber/JB3/IFb/GF-2); [walati] ڤـالاتـى (JJ) ; <valehî> ڤـالـهـى (HH)} [K/A/B/GF/TF//Ber/JB3/IFb//JJ//HH] <vala>

valîtî ڤـالـيـتـى (BK) = province; governorship. See **walîtî**.

vaȓik ڤارِك/**varik** ڤارك [FS] *f.* **(-a;-ê).** 1) {syn: cûcik; ç'elîk; çîçik III; ferx} chick, young of chicken; 2) female chicken, hen (IFb/HH/SK). {also: <varik> ڤارك (HH)} [K/A/IFb/B/HH/SK/GF/FS/ZF3]

varîl ڤـاريـل *f.* **(-a;-ê).** barrel, cask: •**[Seyyid Eḧmed Paşa li tebeqa jorî ye, tu vê *varîlê* bibe di bin oteya wîda]** (JR) S.A.P. is on the upper floor, you take this barrel to below his room. {also: warîl (IFb-2/ZF); [varîl] ڤـاريـل (JR); [varil] واريـل (JJ)} {syn: şikev[3]} Cf. Mod Gr vareli βαρέλι [JR/IFb/ RZ//JJ/ZF]

varqilîn ڤارقِلين *vi.* **(-varqil-).** to come to one's senses, become aware of, realize: •**Bi pêşveçûna zanyarîya xwe ya sîyasî ve, ez *li* realîta xwe *varqilîm*** (Ber #7, 9) As my political knowledge progressed, I *became aware of* my reality •**Meyro bi dengê mêrê xwe ra *li xwe v'arqilî* û destê xwe di ber xwe ra ber da** (MB-Meyro) At her husband's voice, Meyro *came to her senses*, and she put her hand down. {also: vearqilîn (ZF3)} [(neol)Ber/MB//ZF3]

vatinî ڤـاتِـنـى *f.* **(-ya;-yê).** duty, obligation; service *(military)*: •**Cîyê *vatinîya* min a leşkerî Mûş bû** (Ber #7, 9) The place of my military *service* was mush •**Wan *vatiniya* xwe bi cih neanî** (Wkt) They did not carry out their *obligation*. [(neol)Ber/IFb/TF/Wkt/ZF3] <peywir; wezîfe>

vavartin ڤـاڤـارتِـن *vt.* **(-vavêr-).** to sort out, separate *(good from bad, large from small, etc.)*: •**... Lê divê em vekolîna li ser bikeyn û baş û xiraban ji yek *vavêrîn*** (Bêhnişk, 5) But we must do research on them and *sort out* the good from the bad •**Pêkolek bo *vavartina* zimanê nivîsînê** (Peyiv 1 [1993], 17) An effort *to sort out* the written language •**Wan pezê xwe ji hev *vavart*** (FS) They *sorted out* their sheep. [Peyiv/Bêhnişk/Zeb/Dh/BF/FS] <bijartin I; *gogirandin; şkevik kirin>

vaye ڤايه (B/GF) = here! See **va I**.

-ve ڤـه *psp. postpositional suffix indicating*

association (together with), used in conjunction with prepositions, or alone in certain dialects: 1) with, accompanied by *(an animate being)* [e.g., **bi...-*ve***]: •***Bi*** **jina xwe *ve* hat** (GF) He came *together with [accompanied by]* his wife •**Řojekê Zîna delal *bi* k'oma carîya*va* Xas-baẍçê bavê xweda gelekî geřîyan** (Z-1, 46) One day Lovely Zîn *with* a group of her maidservants took a long stroll in her father's private gardens; -**bi gund ve** (Bw) out and about, visiting around the village: •**Ez nemame *bi* gund *ve* = Ez neçûme derve (li nav gund)** = I didn't stay out late/I came home early; -**pêkve** [=*bi* êk *ve*] (Bw/Dh/Zeb/GF) together; 2) and [**û ...-*ve***]: •**Al-p'aşa dîwanê giregirê dîwanê*va* şêwirîn bona zewaca Memê** (Z-1, 48) Al-pasha *and* the noblemen of his diwan deliberated about the marriage of Mem •**Em Al-p'aşa, pîrejina wî *û* Memê delal*va* bihêlin şeherê Muxurzemînêda** (Z-1, 45) Let us leave Al-pasha, his old wife *and* dear Memê in the city of Mukhurzemîn; 3) with *(showing the manner in which stg. is done)*: •**Û *bi* van xeberêd evînîyê*va* herda hevdu ȟemêz kirin û xewřa çûn** (Z-1, 47) And *with* these words of love they embraced and went to sleep; 4) from [= **ji...-*ve***]: -**dûrva** (K/B)/ **ji dûrve** (BX/GF) from afar, in the distance: •**Memê gelekî ji cotk'arî dûr k'etibû, dîna xwe da, *dûrva* sîyarekî wê daye pey kareke xezala** (Z-1, 52) When Mem had gotten very far from the farmer, he looked and saw *in the distance* someone mounted on a horse pursuing a fawn. {also: -va (Z-1)} Sor -ewe ـەوە [BX/GF/OK//Z-1]

vearqilîn ڤـەئـارقـلـیـن (ZF3) = to come to one's senses. See **varqilîn**.

ve•behîn ڤـەبـەهین *vi.* **(ve-beh-).** to lose control of o.s., and to fall (bêdestî); to be startled. {also: [we-bihin] ڤهبهین (JJ)} {syn: *helbehîn (Zeb)} [Dh//JJ]

ve•bûn ڤـەبوون *vi.* **(ve-b-).** 1) to open *(vi.)*, be opened: •**Derî *vebû*** (B) The door *opened*; -**beta vebûn** (K) to vanish, disappear {syn: ji ber winda bûn; řed bûn; řoda çûn}: •**Kalê li ber p'adşê *beta vedibe*** (Z-921) The old man *vanishes* from the king's midst; 2) to bloom, blossom, open up *(flowers)*: •**Bahar hat, gul *vebûn*** (B) Spring has come, the flowers *have bloomed.* {also: [we-boun] ڤـه بـون (JJ); <vebûn ڤبون (vedibe) (ڤدبه)> (HH)} [Z-921/K/A/JB3/IFb/B/JJ/HH/GF/TF/FS] <vekirin I>

vebûyî ڤـەبـوویـی *adj./pp.* 1) open(ed); 2) open *(of flowers)*, in bloom; 3) {syn: sivik; zer I} light *(of tea)* (Bw); light *(of color)*. {also: [we-bouï] ڤه بوی (JJ)} cf. T açık = 'open; light (of tea)' [Bw/JJ/GF] <vebûn>

ve•ciniqandin ڤـەجِـنِـقـانـدِن *vt.* **(ve-ciniqîn-).** to startle, frighten, spook: •**Lê bi şev xewnine bi tirs *ez vediciqandim*** (WT, 88) But at night bad dreams *would startle me*. {also: vecniqandin (FJ); [we-djenekandin] ڤـەجـنـكـانـديـن (JJ); <veciniqandin ڤجنقاندن (vediceniqîne) (ڤدجنقینه)> (HH)} [WT/K/A/B/IFb/GF/TF/HH/Wkt//FJ//JJ] <veciniqîn>

ve•ciniqîn ڤـەجِنِقین *vi.* **(ve-ciniq-).** 1) {syn: t'ertilîn} to start with surprise, be startled; to shudder; to be alarmed, frightened; to be disturbed or upset *(animals)*: •[**Weku hêstir nêzûkî min bûyin hêj şev û tarî bû ji min *veciniqîn* û ticarê ku li ser barekî suwar bû ji hêstirî kete 'erdê**] (JR) When the mules approached me it was already dark [lit. 'night and dark'], they *were startled* by me, and the merchant who was seated atop a load fell off his mule onto the ground; 2) to rouse o.s., wake up suddenly *(vi.)*, wake with a start: •[in a version of the epic of Dimdim, a fly exits through a sleeping shepherd's nostril, flies about, then re-enters his nostril] **Şivan *veciniqî*, serê xwe bilind kir û ȟişyar bû** (EP-8) The shepherd *started*, raised his head and woke up. {also: [we-djenekin] ڤـەجـنـكـين (JJ); <vecineqîn ڤـجـنـقـيـن (vediceniqî) (ڤـدجـنـقـى)> (HH)} [EP-8/JR/K/A/JB3/IFb/B/GF/TF//HH//JJ] <veciniqandin>

vecniqandin ڤـــەجــنِــقـــانــــدِن (FJ) = to startle. See **veciniqandin**.

ve•çinîn ڤـەچِـنـیـن *vt.* **(ve-çin-).** to darn, mend *(socks)*. {also: <veçinîn ڤچنین (vediçinî) (ڤدچنى)> (HH)} Sor çinîn•ewe چنینەوە [Zeb/K/IFb/HH/GF/TF/FS]

ve•dan ڤەدان *vt.* **(ve-d-).** 1) [+ **bi**] to bite, sting, attack: •**Birê min razaî ne, tavilê ev mar tê *bi* wan *vebide*** (L) My brothers are asleep, this snake could come *bite* them •**Çavê te li min be, tu mar bi min *venedin*** (L) Keep your eyes on me, [so that] no snakes *bite* me •**Marî *pê ve da*** (IF) The snake *struck*; 2) {syn: k'olan III} to dig; to scratch (the soil): •**Meẍberê Memê *vedan*** [sic] (Z-1) They *dug up* Mem's grave; 3) {syn: vegirtin [3]; wergirtin} to return *(a greeting)*: •**Gava Memê çû derda / selam da mîr bi serda / Mîr selam 'elêk' *veda*** (EP-7) When Mem entered / he greeted the prince first / the prince *returned* his greeting; 4) to carry, resonate, sound *(of sound, voices)*: **-deng vedan** (Bw/Wlt) to echo, resound, make waves: **•Meşa YRWK'ê [=Yekîtiya Rewşenbîrên Welatparêzên Kurdistanê] li Ewrûpayê *deng veda*** (Wlt) The parade of the union of patriotic intellectuals of Kurdistan *made waves* in Europe; 5) to set, lay *(trap)*; {syn: vegirtin [2]} to pitch, set up *(tent)* (IF/JJ/HH): **•[Li deşta Geverê konêd xwe *vedabûn*]** (JR #27, 79) They *had pitched* their tents in the plain of Gewer [=T Yüksekova] **•Telhek *veda*** (BF) He *set* a trap; 6) to cease, stop, let up *(rain, snow)*: **•*Baranê veda* em herin** (IFb) It *has stopped raining*, let's go; 7) {syn: hildan; hilk'işandin; hilmiştin; şemirandin; vemaliştin} to roll up one's sleeves. {also: [we-dan] ڤـه دان (JJ); <vedan ڤدان (vedide) (ڤدده)> (HH)} [K/A/JB3/IFb/B/JJ/HH/GF/TF/BF]

veder ڤـەدەر *adj.* 1) abroad, outside: **-ji bajarê veder** (GF) outside the city; 2) {syn: xewle} isolated: **•Ew ji hevalan *veder* rûnişt** (FS) He sat *apart* from his friends **•Ma me ev xebat ji bo çi pêk anî? Ji bo ku em hesta lêqewimîn (mağdur) û *vederbûnê*** [=T dışlanma] **a kurdan ji holê rakin** (AW75A2) Why did we do this? In order to get rid of the Kurds' feeling of misery and *isolation*; **-veder kirin** (Zeb) to isolate. Sor derewe دەرەوە [AW/Zeb(VoA)/GF/FS/BF] <averê>

ve•dîtin ڤـەدیتِن *vt.* **(ve-bîn-).** to find, discover: **•Ji bo dermankirina nexweşiya Crohnê stratejiyeke nû *vedît*** (rewsenbir.com 1.xi.2017) He *discovered* a new strategy for treating Crohn's disease **•Nizanim tedbîr çîye. Hung rêkek[ê] bo wê şolê *webînin*** (SK 42:406) I do not know what to do. You *discover* some way for this affair. {also: wedîtin (SK); wedîtinewe (SK-2)} {syn: dîtin [2]; p'eyda kirin} Sor (Arbil) dîtinewe دیتِنەوە = 'to find' [Dh/Bar/ZF3/Wkt//SK]

vegeȓ ڤـەگەڕ *f.* **(-a;-ê).** return, coming back: **•Ezê ji te re roja *vegera* xwe bidim zanîn** (BX) I will let you know the date of my *return* **•Lê eger *vegera* rêwîtiya min tunebûya?** (MUm, 12) What if there was no *return from* my trip? **•Roja *vegeȓa* ḧeciyan hatî bû** (Dz-anec #22) The day of the hadjis' [=pilgrims'] *return* had arrived. {also: [va´ghár] ڤـەگـار (JJ-G)} [BX/Dz/K/A/IFb/B/GF/TF//JJ-G] <vegeȓîn>

vegeȓan ڤـەگـەڕان (FS) = to return, come back. See **vegeȓîn**.

ve•geȓandin ڤـەگـەڕانـدِن *vt.* **(ve-geȓîn-).** 1) {syn: ziviȓandin} to return *(vt.)*, give back; to cause to return: **•Wî kaviȓê ku kiȓî bû, *vegeȓand*** (FS) He *returned* the ram that he had bought; 2) [+ **li**] {syn: bersivdan; cab dan} to reply, answer: **•Rojekê wezîrên wî jê re qala ziwacê kirin** [sic]**. Mîr *li* wan *venegerand* û xwe ker kir** (SW) One day his viziers broached the subject of marriage. The emir *didn't answer* them, and kept quiet **•Serekwezîr *lê vegerand* û got** (Rnh) The prime minister *replied to* him [as follows…]; 3) to annul: **-xwazgînî vegeȓandin** (IFb) to annul a wedding engagement. {also: [we-gherandin] ڤەگراندين (JJ)} [SW/K/A/JB3/IFb/B/JJ/GF/TF] <vegeȓîn>

vegeriyan ڤـەگـەریـیـان (JB3/IFb/JJ) = to return, come back. See **vegeȓîn**.

ve•geȓîn ڤـەگـەڕیـن *vi.* **(ve-geȓ-).** 1) {syn: fetilîn [1]; ziviȓîn} to return *(vi.)*, come or go back: **•*Vedigere* cem bavê xwe** (Ba) [He] *goes back* to his father (=to where his father is) **•*Vegeȓyane* mal** (Ba) They *returned* home; 2) *often in the neg.*: to turn back (from), i.e., to stop, cease doing stg. [+ **ji**]: **•Heta ku qîlên (diran) guran neyên hilkirin û pencên wan neyê[n] qutkirin, *ji* kuştin û qirkirinê *venagerin*** (Wlt 2:71, 13) Until the wolves' fangs are pulled out and their claws are cut back, they *will not stop* killing and destroying. {also: vegeȓan (FS) ; vegeriyan (JB3/IFb-2); [we-gheriian] ڤەگریان (JJ)} Sor geȓan•ewe گـەڕانـەوە (-geȓê-ewe); Za a•geyrenã [ageyrayiş] (Srk) [K/A/IFb/B/GF/TF//JB3/JJ//FS] <vegeȓandin>

ve•gevizandin ڤـەگەڤِزاندِن *vt.* **(ve-gevizîn-).** 1) to tear to pieces, to tear limb from limb, to devour: **•Wana [=seêd şivana] gurek yanê dudu digirtin, *vedigevizandin*** (Ba2:1, 203) They [=the shepherds' dogs] seized a wolf or two [and] *tore them to pieces*; 2) to gnaw; to nibble (B). [Ba2/K/B/GF] <keritandin>

ve•gêȓan ڤەگێڕان *vt.* **(ve-gêȓ-).** 1) {syn: gilî kirin; kat kirin; neqil kirin; ȓiwayet kirin; vegotin} to narrate, tell, recount, relate *(a story)*: **•Di serdema berê de, di nav mirovên nexwendewar de ya belav bû, niha jî sax e û berdewam *dête vegêȓan*** (Dqg, 5) Previously it was widespread among unlettered folk, and it *is* still alive and continually *being told* **•Gundekî Têlî dibêjin ê, ji 'eşîreta Mizûrîyan ... Dibêjin zemanê berê gelek bê-aqil û bê-mêjî bûn. Gelek terze ḧekayetêt seyr**

û suhbet laîqi pê-kenînê ji wan *digêrînewe* (SK 19:175) A village they call Teli, of the Mizuri tribe … They say that in former times the people were very stupid and brainless. They *tell* many kinds of entertaining stories about them **•Kotirê jî ehwalê xo w řîwî bi temamî bo qelê *gêřawe*** (SK 3:20) The pigeon then *told* the crow the whole story of herself and the fox; 2) [*f.* **(-a;-ê).**] narrating, (story)telling, relating: **•Ew hinde caran bi teknîka kevn ve girêdaye û rengê *vegêranê* bi kar anîye** (Dqg, 129) Sometimes he is attached to the old technique and has used that type of *narration.* {also: gêřanewe (SK); vegêrîn (CS)} {syn: kat I kirin; vegotin} Sor gêřan•ewe گێڕانەوە [Dqg/RZ/SS/Zeb//CS//SK]

vegêrîn ڤەگێرین (CS) = to tell (a story). See **vegêřan**.

ve•girtin ڤەگِرتِن *vt.* **(ve-gir-).** 1) to seize, capture, take, occupy; to win back, reconquer: **•Mîr ew welat bi qeweta şûrê xwe *vegirti bû*** (Rnh 3:23, 5) The emir *had taken* that kingdom by the force of his sword; 2) {syn: vedan [5]} to pitch, set up *(a tent)*: **•Konê xwe *vegirt*** (L) He pitched his tent; 3) {syn: vedan [3]} to return *(a greeting)*: **-silav vegirtin** (K) to return s.o.'s greeting; 4) {syn: vekirin} to open the mouth of *(lit. & fig.)* (IFb/TF): **•Çalî *vegire* em tijî kin** (IF) *Open* the sack, let's fill it up **•Devê xwe *vegire* şekir têxim** (IF) *Open* your mouth, I'll put sugar in it **•Dê ko hat çêlik devê xwe *vedigirin*** (IFb) When their mother comes the chicks *open* their mouths **•Parsekî destê xwe li ber wî *vegirt* ku para biditê** (FS) The beggar *opened* his hand *wide* before him to give him money; 5) {syn: derxistin [5]} to be spread by contagion *(disease)* (A); to catch *(disease)* (Bw): **•Wî persîv ji Zoroyî *vegirt*** (FS) He *caught* a cold from Z.; 6) to include, comprise (Bw/Zeb); 7) to preserve *in various senses*: a) to pickle {syn: kesidandin}; b) to record, tape *(voice)* {syn: qeyd kirin}; c) to save up, amass (wealth): **•Wî gelek pare bo xwe *vegirtin* û paşî tirimbêlek pê kiřî** (FS) He *saved up* a lot of money and then bought a car with it. {also: [we-ghirtin] ڤەگرتین (JJ)} Sor girtin•ewe گرتنەوە = 'take back, catch (ball in air), hold open (hands, receptacle), mix, compound (medicines), set (bone), cast (horoscope), reach, include, comprise, cover, engulf' [L/K/A/IFb/B/JJ/JB1-S/GF/TF/OK/FS] <[5] sarî II>

ve•gotin ڤەگۆتِن *vt.* **(ve-bêj-).** 1) {syn: gilî kirin; kat kirin; neqil kirin; řiwayet kirin; vegêřan} to tell, narrate, recount, relate, describe: **•Bi řê ve hêdî hêdî serpêhatiya xwe *vegot*** (FS) On the way he very slowly *related* his story (or, experience) **•Edîbê me Elî Herîrî, ev hîkayeya menzûm, li ser bingeha "planê bûyerî" *vegotiye*** (Nbh 135:40) Our scholar Ali Hariri *recounted* this verse story, on the basis of an "event plan(?)" **•Me hemûyan nivîsên bi bandor û gelek balkêş nivîsîn. Me ji mirovên ku nizanin re *vegot*** (İstenmeyen çocuklar, 13) All of us wrote influential and interesting articles. We *told* them to people who didn't know; 2) [*f.* **(-a;-ê).**] telling, recounting, relating, narration, describing (an event): **•Ji alîyê *vegotina* bûyeran ve serkeftina nivîskar hinekî qels e** (Nbh 135:57) As far as *describing* events, the writer's success is somewhat lacking (lit. a little weak). [Nbh/ZF/Wkt/FS/CS/FJ/GF] <ç'êl III>

ve•guhastin ڤەگوهاستِن *vt.* **(ve-guhêz-).** 1) to convey, transport, transfer; to exchange (JJ); 2) [*f.* **(-a;-ê).**] transportation: **•Me got qey îro roja *veguhastina* bûkê ye!** (N. Mayî. Hêvîya Welêt 99) We said today must be the day the bride *is being transferred* [to the groom's house]. {also: veguhêrandin (K/B-2); [we-gouhastin ڤەگهاستین/we-gouhourandin ڤەگهوراندین] (JJ)} {syn: neqil kirin} Sor guwastin•ewe گوواستنەوە/gwêzan•ewe [gözan•ewe] گوێزانەوە = 'to transport, transfer (vt.); to move, change position (vi.) ' [Dh/IFb/OK/RF] <guhastin>

veguhêrandin ڤەگوهێراندِن (K/B) = to transport. See **veguhastin**.

vehandin ڤەهاندِن (ve-hîn) (Bw) = to weave; to compose. See **vehûnan**.

vehesan ڤەهەسان (FS) = to rest. See **vehesîn**.

ve•hesîn ڤەهەسین *vi.* **(ve-hes-).** 1) {syn: bêna xwe vedan; hêsa bûn; vês girtin} to rest, relax, take a break: **•Çak e lêre bêna xo bideyn, pîçek *we-hisêyn*, paşî biçîn** (SK 8:78) We had better *take a rest* here, relax a little and then go on **•Emê heřin li bin wî konî rûnin emê nankê bixwin, qehwakî vexwin, em*ê vehesin*, bîhna xwe biderxînin** (FS) We will go sit under that tent, we'll have something to eat, we'll drink coffee, we'*ll rest*, catch our breath **•Ji mêj e ez řû-niştî me. Demekî ĥez dikem bigeřyêm da pîçek ji xawî der-kewim, *we-hisêmewe*** (SK 6:65) I have been sitting down for a long time. I'd like to wander about for a while to relieve the boredom a little and *relax*; 2) {syn: jê xelas bûn} to be or get rid of: **•Em *ê* kengê *ji* van zaliman *vehesin*?** (ZF3) When *will* we *be rid of* these tyrants? {also: vehesan (FS); vehisîn (RZ); vehistin (FJ); vehisyan (M); vesihîn (SS); vesîn (SS-2); vêsihîn (RZ-2); vêsîn[2] (IFb-2/RZ-2); wehisyan(ewe) (SK)} [ZF3/Kmc/Wkt/FD//FS//RZ//FJ//M//SK//SS]

vehisîn (RZ) = to rest. See **vehesîn**.

vehistin ڤەهستِن (FJ) = to rest. See **vehesîn**.

vehisyan ڤەهِسیان (M) = to rest. See **vehesîn**.

vehonandin ڤەهۆنانـدِن (ZF) = to weave; to compose. See **vehûnan**.

ve•hûnan ڤەهوونان *vt.* **(ve-hûn-).** 1) {syn: hûnan} to twist, braid, plait, weave; 2) to compose poetry (Ar √n-ẓ-m نظم): **•Min helbestek *ya* bi te *vehûnay*!!** (Helbest 9 [2013], 68) I *have composed* a poem for/about you! **•Hozanvanê jêhatî û şehreza di *vehandina* hozan û helbestan da, desthel û pisporê lêkînana peyivan, evîndarê ciwanîya siruştê Kurdistanê bi çiya û gelî û dol û rûbarên xo ve** (Nisret Hacî. "Feqê Teyran û Çîrokên Binavkirina Wî", Peyam 5-6 [1996], 2) The poet skilled and expert at *composing* poems and verses, handy and clever at putting words together, enamored of the Kurdistan's natural beauty with its mountains, valleys, ravines and rivers {also: vehandin (ve-hîn) (Bw); vehonandin (ZF); [we-hounan] ڤەهونان (JJ)} [Bw//Helbest/JJ/JB1-A/CS//ZF]

ve•jandin ڤەژاندِن *vt.* **(ve-jîn- / -vejîn-** [JB3] **/ ve-jên- / ve-jin** [B]**).** 1) {syn: sax kirinve (Bw)} to revive, resuscitate, bring back to life: **•Qenatê Kurdo gelek çîrokên Kurdî *vejandine*** (FS) Q.K. *has revived* many Kurdish tales; 2) to scutch, swingle, separate the woody fibers by beating (flax, hemp, etc.) (B). [K/JB3/IFb/B/GF/ZF/FS] <vejîn>

ve•jîn ڤـەژیـن *vi.* **(ve-jî-).** 1) to come back to life, be revived: **•Ax bi avê vedijî** (AB) Soil is revived by water; 2) [*f.* **(-a;-ê).**] rebirth; renaissance: **•Newroz roja *vejînê* ye** (nasname.com 20.iii.2017) Newroz is the day *of rebirth*. {syn: hatin ser r̄engê xwe} [AB/GF/ZF/FS] <vejandin>

ve•k'etin ڤەکەتِن *vi.* **(ve-k'ev-).** 1) to lie down, stretch out: **•Sûsîk hinekî dûrî mêra r̄ûniştibû, ewê ji me şerm dikir, Gurzo jî bal wê *vek'etibû*** (Ba2-#2, 206) Susik [a girl] sat apart from the men, she was shy (of us), [but] Gurzo [a dog] *lay down* beside her; 2) to loaf around, idle (B); 3) to lie in wait (TF). [Ba2/K/B/GF/TF/OK]

vek'êşan ڤـەکێـشـان (Bw/FS/BF/Wkt) = to withdraw; to pull back; to last. See **vek'işandin**.

vekêşiyan ڤـەکێـشِـیان (Wkt) = to withdraw; to last. See **vek'işîn**.

vekêşîn ڤەکێشین (IFb/FD/Wkt) = to withdraw; to last. See **vek'işîn**.

ve•kirin I ڤـەکِـرِن *vt.* **(ve-k-).** 1) {≠girtin [2]} to open *(vt.)*: **•Herin, devê xizna min *vekin*** (L) Go *open* the gate of my treasury; 2) to undo, unfasten, unbutton, unhook; 3) {syn: s̲is̲t kirin (sist [2])} to unscrew, loosen; 4) to take off, remove [+ **ji** or **li**]: **•Te ev teyr-teyrede berev kirine, tu p'ûrta wan *lê vekî*, sibê tave teyroke t'emam wê bimire, dinîya teyrede nebe** (Z-828, v. 2, 189) You have gathered these birds, so that you *can remove* their plumage, tomorrow there will be storms and hail and they will all die, there will be no birds left in the world **•Wî wêne *ji* dîwarî *vekir*** (FS) He *removed* the picture *from* the wall; 5) *various idioms*: **•Hinekan dikenînim, hinekan jî *bi girî vedikim*** (D.Kelogirî. Doxînsist-îzm, 5) I make some people laugh, and I *bring* some people *to tears*. {also: [we-kirin] ڤـەکـریـن (JJ); <vekirin ڤـکـرن (vedike) (ڤدکه)> (HH)} Cf. P vā kardan وا کردن/vāz kardan واز کـردن/ bāz kardan بـاز کـردن = 'to open'; Sor kirdn•ewe کِردِنەوە {kirdin + -ewe}; Za a•kenã {a- + kenã} (Todd) [K/A/IFb/B/JJ/HH/GF/TF/OK/FS] <vebûn; vekirî>

vekirin II ڤەکِرِن (Czr) = to look at. See **fikirîn II**.

vekirî ڤەکِری *adj./pp.* 1) {≠girtî} open *(adj.)*, opened; 2) undone, unfastened, unbuttoned (B/HH). {also: [we-kiri] ڤـەکـری (JJ); <vekirî> ڤـکـری (HH)} Cf. Sor kira•we کِـــــــراوە [K/A/IFb/B/JJ/HH/GF/TF/OK/ZF3] <vekirin I>

vekişan ڤـــەکِــــشـــان (FS) = to withdraw; to last. See **vek'işîn**.

ve•k'işandin ڤەکِشاندِن *vt.* **(ve-k'işîn-).** 1) to withdraw, retract stg.: **•Danimark hêza xwe ya taybet ji Iraqê *vedikişîne*** (rudaw.net 18.v.2018) Denmark *is withdrawing* its special forces from Iraq; 2) to pull stg. back, cause stg. to move back or recede, draw stg. back: **•Têlê zêde *venekişîne* tu dê biqetînî** (ZF3) *Don't pull* the string *back* too far, you might break it; 3) {syn: ajotin; domîn; k'işandin; k'udandin; vek'işîn} to last, take (of time): ***•Dê vek'êşît*** (Bw) It *will take/last* [a long time]

•Nesaxiya wî deh roja *vekêşa* (FS) His illness *lasted* 10 days **•Şolê me deh roja *vekêşa*** (FS) Our work *lasted* 10 days. {also: vek'êşan (Bw/FS/BF/Wkt)} [Bw/FS/BF/Wkt//ZF3/G/GF/CS] <vek'işîn>

vekişiyan ڤەکِشِاین (FS/Wkt) = to withdraw; to last. See **vek'işîn**.

ve•k'işîn ڤەکِشین *vi.* **(ve-k'iş-).** 1) to withdraw (from), retreat (from), draw back (from) {syn: xwe dane paş}: **•Bi qirewira zarokan re *ji* xeyalên xwe *vekişiya*** (Nofa, 89) He *retreated* [or, awoke] *from* his reverie at the screaming of the children **•Leşkerê Israîlê ji Libnanê *vekêşiye*** (Wkt) The Israeli army *has withdrawn* from Lebanon; 2) to last, take (time) {syn: ajotin[2]; dirêj kirin[c]; domîn[2]; k'işandin[6]; k'udandin[2]}: **•Ev semînar *dê* 2 seetan *vekêşe* (dirêjiya dema dewama wê dê 2 seet be)** (Wkt) This seminar *will last* 2 hours. {also: vekêşiyan (Wkt-2); vekêşîn (IFb/FD/Wkt-2); vekişan (FS-2); vekişiyan (FS/Wkt-2); vek'işyan (B)} Sor kişan-ewe کِشانەوە = 'to recede, fall back, withdraw' [Nofa/GF/ZF3/Wkt/CS//FS//B//IFb/FD] <vek'işandin>

vek'işyan ڤەکِشیان (B) = to withdraw; to last. See **vek'işîn**.

vek'olan ڤەکۆلان (K/B/AD/FS/BF) = to dig up; to research. See **vek'olîn**.

vek'olandin ڤەکۆلاندِن (B) = to dig up; to research. See **vek'olîn**.

ve•k'olîn ڤەکۆلین *vt.* **(ve-k'ol-).** 1) {syn: k'olan III; vedan [2]} to dig up, unearth; to excavate: **•Ber derê mala xwe *vekola*** (BF) He *dug around* before his front door [in search of stg.]; 2) {syn: lêkolîn} to research, investigate, study, examine: **•Ev gotar astengên li ber zanyariya civakî, siyasî û medyayê li Kurdistana Iraqê ... *vedikole*** (KSJ) This article *examines* obstacles to social science, politics and media in Iraqi Kurdistan; 3) [*f.* **(-a; -ê).**] excavation; 4) research, investigation, study, examination: **-vekolîn kirin** (CS/ZF) to research, investigate, study, examine. {also: vek'olan (K/B/AD/FS/BF-w); vek'olandin (B-2)} Sor kołînewe کۆڵینەوە = 'to dig up' & lêkołînewe لێکۆڵینەوە = 'to examine, pursue and observe carefully' [KSJ/IFb/RZ/ZF/CS/Kmc/BF//K/B/AD/FS] <k'olan III>

ve•kuştin ڤەکوشتِن *vt.* **(ve-kuj-).** 1) to slaughter *(sheep, cow, chicken)*: **•Şofî Şêx, zû ȓabe. Gaê me wê di bi ȓoȟê da. Eger zû nagiheyê dê mirar bît. Mixabin e. *Wekuje*, her nebît çermê wî xesar nabît** (SK 30:271) Sofi Shaikh! Our ox is at the point of death. If you do not reach it soon it will (die of itself and) become carrion. It is a pity. *Slaughter* it, at least do not let the hide be wasted; 2) {syn: mirandin; t'efandin; temirandin; vemirandin; vêsandin} to extinguish, put out (light, flame). {also: wekuştin[ewe] (SK); [we-kouchtin] ڤەکشتین (JJ); <v[e]kuştin ڤکشتن (vedikuje) (ڤدکژە)> (HH)} cf. Sor kujandinewe کوژاندِنەوە = 'to extinguish, obliterate' [Zeb/K/IFb/JJ/HH/GF/OK//SK]

ve•lezandin ڤەلەزاندِن *vt.* **(ve-lezîn-).** 1) to stretch stg. out, cause to stretch; 2) {syn: nivandin; ȓazandin} to cause to lie down or stretch out, put to bed: **-xwe vezelandin** (CS) to stretch o.s. out, lie down: **•Ji ber ku pir westabû, *xwe* bêhnekê *vezeland*** (DBgb, 7) Because he was very tired, he *lay down* for a spell. {also: vezelandin (DBgb/FJ/GF/CS); vezilandin (TF)} [DBgb/FJ/GF/CS//K/B//TF] <velezîn>

ve•lezîn ڤەلەزین *vi.* **(ve-lez-).** to lounge, sprawl out, lie down, stretch out: **•Ew vira ser piştê *vedilezya* nava kulîlka, li 'ezmanê sayîyî bê 'ewr dinihêȓî û dest xweda dik'ete xewa şîrin** (Ba2:1, 202) He *would sprawl* on his back among the flowers, look up at the clear, cloudless sky, and immediately fall fast asleep; **-ber te'vê velezyan** (B) to lie in the sun. {also: velezyan (B); vezilîn (TF)} [Ba2/K//B//TF] <velezandin>

velezyan ڤەلەزیان (B) = to lie down. See **velezîn**.

ve•maliştin ڤەمالِشتِن *vt.* **(ve-mal-).** 1) to clean, wipe, dust off: **•Ser sûretê sorda hêsra *vedmale*** (EP-7) She *wipes* the tears from [lit. 'on'] her red face; 2) {syn: hildan; hilk'işandin; hilmiştin; şemirandin; vedan} to roll up *(one's sleeves)*. {also: vemiştin (K[s]-2); [we-michtin] ڤە مشتین (JJ)} [EP-7/K(s)/JB1-S//JJ] <maliştin>

ve•man ڤەمان *vi.* **(ve-mîn-).** to stay behind, be left behind. {also: vemayîn (FD)} {syn: paȓa man; paşda man} [Kmc/FJ/ZF3/BF//FD] <paşdamayî>

vemayîn ڤەمایین (FD) = to stay behind. See **veman**.

ve•mirandin ڤەمِراندِن *vt.* **(ve-mirîn-).** to put out, extinguish *(fire)*: **•Lê vegera wî ya ji nişka ve agirê van gotinan tev de *vemirand*** (HYma, 29) But his sudden return *extinguished* the fire of those rumors. {also: wemirandin (SK); [we-mirandin] ڤە مراندین (JJ); <vemirandin ڤمراندن (vedimirîne) (ڤدمرینە)> (HH)} {syn: damirandin;

mirandin; t'efandin; temirandin; vekuştin; vêsandin} [Z-1/K/A/JB3/IFb/B/JJ/HH/JB1-A&S/GF/TF/OK//SK] <vemirîn>

ve•mirîn ڤەمِرین *vi.* **(ve-mir-).** to be extinguished, go out *(fire, also fig.)*: **•Agirê ku li erdê vêketibû, wî jî xwe li nava agirî diavêt erdê. Agir *vemirî bû*, ew jî xedar birîn bûbû** (AW69B1) He jumped through the fire which had broken out on the ground. [When] the fire *had gone out*, he had been severely burned **•Serjimara (nifûs) bajarên kurdan zêde bû, bi vê yekê tekîliyên feodalî *vemirîn*** (AW79A5) The population of Kurdish cities increased, and with this, feudal relations *were extinguished.* {also: [we-mirin] ڤـەمـریـن (JJ); <vemirîn ڤمرين (vedimrî) (ڤدمرى)> (HH)} {syn: t'efîn; temirîn; vêsîn} [AW/K/A/IFb/B/JJ/HH/GF/TF] <vemirandin>

ve•mistin ڤەمِستِن *vi.* **(ve-miz-).** to emanate, come out, shoot out of: **•Hepowê xwe wer dişuxuland ku tiliyên wê *ji* gûmikên xwe qey agir *vedimistin*** (H v. 1, 83-84 [1932, 1:4]) She used her metal weaving comb in such a way that it was as if fire *was emanating from* the tips of her fingers. {also: vemiztin (FJ/GF)} [H/K(s)/Wkt/FS/SS//FJ/GF]

vemiştin ڤـەمِـشـتِـن (K[s]/JJ) = to clean; to roll up (sleeves). See **vemaliştin**.

vemiztin ڤەمِزتِن (FJ/GF) = to emanate. See **vemistin**.

venan ڤەنان (JB1-S) = to perch, land. See **veniştin**.

ve•niştin ڤـەنِـشـتِـن *vi.* **(ve-niş-).** to perch, alight, land, settle *(birds, aircraft, etc.)*: **•Jana ku li ser serpêhatiyên me, xatirên me û bîranînên me *veniştiye*, pir, pir, pir kevn e** (MUm, 60) The pain that *has settled* on our experiences, our memories, is very, very, very old. {also: venan (JB1-S); veniyan (JB1-S-2)} {syn: dadan; danîn} Sor nîştin•ewe نـیـشـتِـنـەوە = 'to fall, abate, subside (flood, anger, tumult, battle, etc.), perch, alight, land (birds, aircraft)' [MUm/K(s)/IFb/GF//JB1-S]

veniyan ڤەنِیان (JB1-S) = to perch, land. See **veniştin**.

ve•qetandin ڤـەقـەتـانـدِن *vt.* **(ve-qetîn-).** 1) to separate, divide; to sort out *(e.g., cattle upon returning from pasture)* (vt.) : **•Dema tu êvarê vedigerî, wek mafê qamçûrê, wê çaxê tu ê çar bizinan ji me re *veqetînî*** (Ardû, 114-5) When you return in the evening, as [fulfillment of] the duty of the animal tax, you can *pick out* four goats for us then **•Her yekê dewarên xwe *veqetandin*** (AB) Each one (f.) *separated* (=claimed) her cattle; **-pezê xwe ji hev veqetandin** (IFb) to sort out the sheep; 2) to distinguish, tell apart; 3) to reserve *(a place)*: **-cih veqetandin** (Şnx) do. {also: [we-qatandin] ڤـە قـطـانـديـن (JJ); <veqetandin ڤقـتـانـدن (vediqetîne) (ڤـدقـتـيـنـه)> (HH)} [AB/K/A/IFb/B/HH/GF/TF/OK//JJ] <veqetîn>

ve•qetîn ڤەقەتین *vi.* **(ve-qet-).** 1) to break away from, to be separated from: **•Bizinek *ji* nava pêz *vediqete*** (J) A goat *breaks away from* the flock; 2) [+ **ji**] to part company, take one's leave: **•Herdu bra *ji*hev *veqetîn*** (IFb) The two brothers *separated* (or, *parted company*) **•Mêrik bi awakî bêhêvî û dilşikestî *ji* rîsipî *vediqete*, berê xwe dide mala xwe û diçe** (Ardû, 19) Disappointed and brokenhearted, the fellow *takes his leave of* the old man and heads for home; 3) to disperse, return to one's home *(e.g., cattle returning from pasture)* (B). {also: veqetyan (B-2); [we-qatiian] ڤه قطيان (JJ)} [J/K/IFb/B/GF/TF/OK//JJ] <veqetandin>

veqetyan ڤـەقـەتـیـان (B) = to be separated from. See **veqetîn**.

verenik ڤـەرەنِـك (OK) = rice at bottom of pot. See **veřenk**.

veřenk ڤەڕەنك *f.* **(-a;).** (burnt) rice at bottom of the pot *(considered a delicacy)* [P tahdīg تهديگ]: **•Wî *veřenka* binê qazanê ya şîrî xwar** (FS) He ate the *verenk* at the bottom of the milk cauldron. {also: verenik (OK); veřesk (Bw-2)} {syn: binê beroşê (Qmş)} =Sor binkiř بنکِڕ [Am/Bw/FS//OK] <veřinîn>

veřesk ڤـەڕەسـك (Bw) = rice at bottom of pot. See **veřenk**.

ve•řestin ڤـەڕەسـتِـن *vi.* **(ve-res-).** 1) to be rescued, released, set free; to escape from [+ **ji**]: **•Ew vê carê jî *ji* mirinê *veřest*** (FS) He *escaped* death this time as well **•Kew *ji* rekehê *veřest*** (FS) The partridge *was set free* [or, *escaped*] *from* the cage; 2) to slip, drop; to become detached or uncoupled from [+ **ji**]: **•*Ji* destê min veresya** (Hk) It *dropped from* my hand (by accident); 3){syn: pijiqîn} to gush, spurt, squirt: **•Ava wî *veřest*** (FS) He took a piss [lit. 'His water spurted']; 4) {syn: řiskiyan} to bleed (of the nose): **•Difna wî *veřest*** (FS) He had a nosebleed [lit. 'His nose gushed']. {also: veřesyan (Hk); veřistin (FS-2); veřis[y]an (FS-2); [we-resiian ڤـەرسـيـان/we-resin ڤـەرسـيـن] (JJ); <veřisan ڤەڕسان/veřisîn ڤەڕسين/veřistin ڤەڕستِن> (Hej)} [Dh/FS/BF/Wkt/FD//Hk/JJ//Hej]

veřesyan ڤەڕەسیـان (Hk/JJ) = to be set free; to drop; to

gush. See **veȓestin**.

veȓeşan ڤەڕەشان (IF/HH) = to vomit. See **veȓeşîn**.

ve•ȓeşandin ڤـەڕەشـانـدِن *vt.* **(ve-ȓeşîn-).** to cause to vomit; to make nauseous. [K/IFb] <veȓeşîn>

vereşî ڤـەرەشـی *f.* **(-ya;-yê).** vomit, barf, puke; nausea: **•Zarok û xanima min ji *vereşî* û rêwîtiyê westiyabûn** (N.Mîro.Gava mirî biaxife, 34) My wife and children were tired from *being nauseous* and from the trip; **-verşîya *fk-î* hatin** (G) to be nauseous, to have an upset stomach. {also: verşî (G)} [N.Mîro/Wkt/ZF3//G] <veȓeşîn>

ve•ȓeşîn ڤـەڕەشـيـن *vi.* **(ve-ȓeş/ve-ȓeşyê- [M]/ve-rêş- [L]).** 1) {syn: hilavêtin[4]} to vomit, throw up: **•Ji kûr tê, ji dûr tê, *vedirêşê*, xwîn tê [tifing]** (L) It comes from something deep, it comes from afar, it *vomits*, and blood flows *[rdl.; ans.: a rifle]* **•Lê her ku kevçiyê şerbetê yan jî liba derman nêzîkî devê xwe dikir, *dikir ku vereşe*** (HYma, 34) But whenever he brought a spoonful of syrup or a pill near his mouth, *he almost threw up*; 2) to feel nauseous or dizzy (K). {also: veȓeşan (IF-2); veȓeşîyan (F); veȓeşyan (ve-ȓeşyê-) (M); [we-rechiian ڤەڕشيان/we-rechin ڤەڕشين] (JJ); <vereşan ڤرشـان/vereşandin ڤرشـانـدن (vedireşe) (ڤـدرشـه)> (HH)} Cf. Sor ȓişan•ewe ڕِشـانـەوە [L//K/IFb/B/JJ/GF//HH//F//M] <ȓeşandin; veȓeşandin>

veȓeşîyan ڤەڕەشییان (F) = to vomit. See **veȓeşîn**.

veȓeşyan ڤـەڕەشـيـان (ve-ȓeşyê-) (M) = to vomit. See **veȓeşîn**.

veȓê kirin ڤـەڕێ کِرِن *vt.* **(veȓê -k-).** 1) {syn: hinartin; şandin} to send, dispatch: **•[Min ji dûrve mirofek *verê kir* û Memed gazî nik xwe kirî]** (JR) I *sent* a man from afar and called [=had him call] Memed to me **•Paşê *em* bi vagonan *verêyî* Sêwîxaneya Gumriyê *kirin*** (KO, 39) Later they *sent us to* the Gumru Orphanage by wagon; 2) to accompany, escort, see off (B): **•Herin t'êrê mêvana bi genimê ȓind dagirin û wana *veȓêkin*** (Ba, #32, 318) Go fill the guests' sacks with the high quality wheat and *send* them *on their way* **•Hine wext apê minî Ȟesê K'eleş *em veȓê kirin*** (Ba2, #4, 220) For a while my uncle Hese Kelesh *accompanied us on our way*. {also: **ȓêkirin**; [we-ri-kirin] ڤـه ريـكـريـن (JJ); <verêkirin ڤـريـكـرن (verêdike) (ڤـريـدكـه)> (HH)} [JR/K/IFb/B/HH/GF//B] See also **ȓêkirin**.

veȓisan ڤـەڕِسـان (FS/Hej) = to be set free; to drop; to gush. See **veȓestin**.

veȓisîn ڤـەڕِسين (Hej) = to be set free; to drop; to gush. See **veȓestin**.

veȓistin ڤـەڕِسـتِن (FS/Hej) = to be set free; to drop; to gush. See **veȓestin**.

veȓisyan ڤـەڕِسـيـان (FS) = to be set free; to drop; to gush. See **veȓestin**.

ve•ȓotin ڤـەڕۆتِـن *vt.* **(ve-ȓoj-).** 1) to scrape; {syn: daȓotin} to plane; 2) to gouge, hollow out. {also: [we-routin] ڤه روتين (JJ)} [S&E/K/B/GF//JJ] <ȓêç kirin [ȓêç I]>

verşî ڤەرشی (G) = vomit; nausea. See **vereşî**.

vesihîn ڤەسِهين (SS) = to rest. See **vehesîn**.

vesîn ڤەسين (SS) = to rest. See **vehesîn**.

veşarîn ڤەشارين (IFb) = to hide. See **veşartin**.

ve•şartin ڤـەشـارتِـن *vt.* **(ve-şêr-/ve-şêrîn- [IFb-2]).** 1) {syn: telandin} to hide, conceal *(vt.)*: **-pereyê xwe veşartin** (IFb) to hide (or bury) one's money: **•Wî *parên xwe veşartin*** (FS) He *hid his money*; **-sûcê xwe veşartin** (IFb) to hide one's guilt or crime; **-xwe veşartin** = to hide *(vi.)* {syn: telîn; xwe xef kirin}: **•Lawik kete bin textekî û *xwe veşart*** (L) The boy slid beneath a bed and *hid* **•Heryekî ji me *xwe* cîkî *veşart*** (Ba) Each one of us *hid (himself)* somewhere; 2) {syn: binax kirin} to bury: **•Yekî got ku *hatiye* kuştin û *veşartin* li çolan** (HYma, 29) Someone said that he *had been* killed and *buried* in the wilderness: **-cenaze veşartin** (IFb) to bury a corpse. {also: veşarîn (IFb-2); veşêrîn (IFb-2); weşarin (SK); [we-chartin ڤه شارتين/ we-chirin ڤه سرين] (JJ) {*note: [we-chirin ڤـه سـريـن = *'se cacher', i.e., 'to hide (oneself) (vi.)'*} ; <veşartin ڤـشـارتـن (vedişêre) (ڤـدشـيـره)> (HH)} Cf. Sor şardin•ewe شـاردِنـەوە {şardin + -ewe}; Hau ewe•şaray (şar- ewe) *vt.* (M4) [L/K/A/JB3/IFb/B/JJ/HH/JB1-A/GF/TF/OK//SK] <veşartok>

veşartkanê شـارتـكـانـێ (Bw) = hide-and-seek. See **veşartok**.

veşartok ڤـەشـارتـۆك *f.* **(-a;-ê).** hide-and-seek *(game)*: **•Zarûk bi hev ra *veşartokê* dilîzin** (AB) The children are playing *hide-and-seek* (with each other). {also: veşartkanê (Bw)} {syn: *pîtros (IFb)} [AB/A/IFb/BF/Wkt//Bw] <veşartin>

veşêrîn ڤەشێرين (IFb) = to hide. See **veşartin**.

ve•şûştin ڤەشووشتِن *vt.* **(ve-şo-).** to wash thoroughly, scrub: **-xwe veşûştin** (B) to wash o.s. thoroughly, scrub o.s.: **•Xwe dişo *vedişo*** (SBx, 16) She washes and *scrubs* [herself]. Cf. Sor şitin•ewe

شِتِنەوە = ‘to rinse, wash (cereals/greens to remove impurities)’ [SBx/B/ZF/FS] <şûştin>

ve•weşandin ڤەوەشاندِن *vt.* **(ve-weşîn-).** [+ *dat. constr.*] 1) to shake, shake off or out; to rock, swing: **•Lê Pawlos mar *veweşand* nav êgir û tu ziyan nedît** (Mizginiya Kurdî: Acts 28:5) But Paul *shook* the snake into the fire and was not harmed **•Rahişt maşikê, heta jê hat *veweşandê*** (DBgb, 46) She picked up the fire tongs, and *shook* them with all her might; 2) to wave stg. menacingly, brandish: **•Min şîrê xwe *veweşande* serokê zalim** (Wkt) I *brandished* my sword *at* the unjust leader;**-ço veweşandin yekî** (IFb) to shake a stick at s.o.; 3) to throw at, fling at, sling, send (a stone, stick, etc.) flying: **•Wî berek *veweşand* çêlê** (FS) He *threw* a stone *at* the cow **•Wî destê xwe avêt xw[ê]danka xwe û kevirek jê derxist û bi berkanî *veweşand*, li eniya Golyat xist** (Dawud û Golyat: 1 Samuel 17:49) He reached into his bag, took out a stone and *slung* it with his catapult, striking Goliath on the forehead. {also: vewşandin (IFb-2)} {syn: ḧejandin} Cf. Sor weşandin وەشاندِن = ‘to shake, wave, motion (with the hands); to sow seed’ [DBgb/K/FJ/GF/CS/Wkt//IFb]

vewşandin ڤەوشاندِن (IFb) = to shake. See **veweşandin**.

vexwandin ڤەخواندِن (ve-xwîn-) (OK/FS) = to invite. See **vexwendin**.

vexwandî ڤەخواندی (FS) = invited (guest). See **vexwendî**.

ve•xwarin ڤەخوارِن *vt.* **(ve-xw- / ve-xu- [K/B]).** 1) {syn: xwarin} to drink: **-şîranî vexwarin** (JR) to betroth, make an engagement or marriage agreement. See under **şîranî**; **-t'êr vexwarin** (K) to have enough to drink; 2) {syn: k'işandin [3]} to smoke (cigarettes). {also: vexwerin (K); [we-kharin/we-khourin] ڤە خورین (JJ); <vexwarin ڤەخوارن (vedixwe) (ڤەدخوە)> (HH)} Cf. Sor xwardin•ewe خواردِنەوە [K//A/JB3/IFb/B/HH/GF/TF//JJ] <şîrînî>

ve•xwendin ڤەخوەندِن *vt.* **(ve-xwîn [K(s)/OK]/ve-xûn [K(s)]/ve-xîn [IFb]).** to invite; to summon: **•Wî Azad bo ser dawetê *vexwand*** (FS) He *invited* A. to the wedding. {also: vexwandin (ve-xwîn-) (OK/FS)} {syn: dawet kirin; ‘ezimandin; gazî kirin} [K(s)/IFb/GF/TF//OK/FS] <mêvan>

vexwendî ڤەخوەندی *adj./pp.* invited: **•Daweta keça min û R̄asto ye. Gelê me hemû *vexwendî* ne** (Wlt 2:59, 15) My daughter is marrying Rasto. All of our people are *invited*. {also: vexwandî (FS)} [Wlt/K(s)/IFb/GF/TF//FS] <mêvan>

vexwerin ڤەخوەرِن (K) = to drink. See **vexwarin**.

veytûn ڤەیتوون (GF) = limekiln. See **hêtûn**.

vezelandin ڤەزەلاندِن (DBgb/FJ/GF/CS) = to stretch out, cause to lie down. See **velezandin**.

vezilandin ڤەزلاندِن (TF) = to stretch out, cause to lie down. See **velezandin**.

vezilîn ڤەزلین (TF) = to lie down. See **velezîn**.

vêhs ڤێهس (CS) = rest, break. See **vês**.

vêk ڤێک *adv./adj.* 1) together *{according to BX, an eastern form}*: **-vêk re** (IFb) do.; 2) on good terms, reconciled: **•Azad û Behrem *vêk* in** (FS) A. and B. are *on good terms*. {also: pêk; [we-kira] ڤەکرا (JJ); <vêk> ڤیک (HH)} {syn: p'ev (W)} < bi + êk [BX/(K)/(IFb)/(HH)/FS//JJ] See also **pêk**.

vêkeftin ڤێ کەفتِن (Bw) = to find one's way. See **vêk'etin**.

vê•k'etin ڤێکەتِن/ڤێ کەتِن *vi.* **(vê-k'ev-).** 1) to catch fire, flare up: **•Çira *vê ket*** (AB) The lamp *flared up*; 2) to find one’s way (Bw/BF). {also: vêkeftin (Bw); vêkevtin (BF); [we-ketin] ڤە کتین (JJ); <vêketin ڤیکتن (vêdikeve) (ڤیدکڤە)> (HH)} [AB/K/A/IFb/B/HH/GF//JJ//Bw//BF] <vêxistin>

vêkevtin ڤێ کەڤتِن (BF) = to find one's way. See **vêk'etin**.

vêl ڤێل *adj.* 1) oblique, slanted, at an angle: **-xêza vêl** (Qzl) slanted line, oblique line; 2) shallow (of dishes): **-sênîka *vêl*** (FS) *shallow* dish. [Qzl/IFb/ZF3/FS/Wkt] <lêç; tenik>

vên ڤێن (BX/GF) = must; to need; to want; to love. See **viyan**.

vêne ڤێنە = picture. See **wêne**.

vês ڤێس *f.* **(-a;).** rest, break, pause: **•Piştî *vês* û bêhnvedaneke kurt** (Nbh 125:20) After a brief *break* and rest; **-vês girtin** (Ad/ZF)/**~a xwe girtin** (ZF)/**~a xwe dan** (IFb) to rest, take a rest, take a break {syn: bîna xwe vedan; hêsa bûn}. {also: vêhs (CS-2)} Cf. Sor wêst وێست = ‘stop, short break/pause/interval’ [Ad/Nbh/IFb/ZF/CS]

vê•sandin ڤێساندِن/ڤێ ساندِن *vt.* **(vê-sîn-).** 1) {syn: damirandin; mirandin; t'efandin; temirandin; vekuştin; vemirandin} to put out, extinguish *(fire)*: **•Gişk pê diḧesin ku mala Qeretajdîn dişewite, ber bi malê diȓevin ku agir *vêsînin*** (FS: Memê Alan) Everyone realizes that Q.'s house is on fire, they run to the house *to put out* the fire; 2) to cause to rest, make s.o. take a break (IFb/OK). [Z-1/K/IFb/B/OK/Wkt/FS/ZF3] <vêsîn I>

vêsihîn ڤێسِهین (RZ) = to rest. See **vehesîn**.

vêsiyan ڤێسِیان (FS) = to be extinguished. See **vêsîn**.

vê•sîn ڤێسین/ڤێ سین *vi.* **(vê-s-).** {syn: t'efîn; temirîn; vemirîn} to be extinguished, go out *(fire)*: •**Agir *vêsiya*** (FS) The fire *went out*; 2) = to rest (IFb/SS). See **vehesîn**. {also: vêsiyan (FS)} [Z-1/K/IFb/B/SS/ZF3//FS] <vêsandin>

vêtin ڤێتِن (BX) = must; to need; to want; to love. See **viyan**.

vê•xistin ڤێخِستِن/ڤێ خِستِن *vt.* **(vê-x-).** to light, ignite, kindle; to turn on (lights): •**Wî agir *vêxist*** (FS) He *lit* the fire; **-cixara xwe vêxistin** (IFb) to light one's cigarette. {also: **pêxistin**; [we-khystin] ڤه خستن (JJ); <vêxistin ڤیخستن (vêtêxe) (ڤیتیخه)> (HH)} {syn: dadan; hilkirin [2]} [K/A/JB3/IFb/B/HH/JB1-S/GF/ZF3/BF/FS//JJ] <serçavk; vêk'etin> See also **pêxistin**.

vine-vin ڤِنەڤِن (K) = buzzing; sobbing; grumbling; screaming. See **vinge-ving**.

vinge-ving ڤِنگەڤِنگ *f.* **(-a;-ê).** 1) buzzing: **-vingeving kirin** (B) to buzz, hum; **-vingevinga moza** (Ba2) the buzzing of bees; 2) whimpering, sniveling; sobbing; 3) grumbling; muffled speech; 4) screaming, squealing. {also: vine-vin (K)} [Ba2/IFb/B/GF//K]

vir I ڤِر *adv.* here: **-ji vir[a]** (B) from here, hence; **-ji vir bi şûn ve** = from now on: •**Ez dê hewl bidim, ku *ji vir bi şûn ve* alîkariya wê bikim** (AW69A3) I will try to help her *from now on*; **-li vir re** (L) = a) here.: •**Te zilamek û jinek ne dîne *li vir re* çûn?** (L) Did you [lit. 'didn't you'] see a man and a woman pass *this way* (or, *through here*)?; b) hence, henceforth; **-li vir** (IFb) here; **-vir[a] hada/vir[a] wêda** (B) thenceforth, henceforth, from now on; **-virda** (K) hither, here (motion toward), this way. {also: vira (B-2); [wir] ڤر (JJ); <vir> ڤر (HH)} {≠wir; wê derê} [K/A/JB3/IFb/B/JJ/HH/GF/TF]

vir̄ II ڤِڕ *f.* **(-a;-ê).** lie, fib, falsehood: •***Vir̄* ne baş e** (AB) *Lies* are not good [lit. '*The lie* is not good'] •**Vir̄a wî *aşkira bû*** (FS) His lie *came to light*; **-vir̄ kirin** (K/B) to lie, tell lies. {also: [wyr] ڤر (JJ); <vir> ڤر (HH)} {syn: derew} [AB/K/A/JB3/IFb/B/JJ/HH/GF/TF/ZF3/FS] <vir̄ek>

vira ڤِرا (B) = here. See **vir I**.

virçik ڤِرچِك *f.* **(-a;-ê).** vagina, vulva, 'cunt', 'pussy'. {also: <virçik> ڤرچك (HH)} {syn: quz} [A/HH/GF/ZF3]

vir̄ek ڤِڕەك *m.* **(-ê;).** liar: •**Tûrê *virekan* tim qul e** (AB) The *liars'* bag always has a hole in it. {also: vir̄ker (JB3/IFb-2); [wyrek ڤرك/wyre-ker ڤرکر] (JJ)} {syn: derew[ç]în; derewker} {vir̄ek[t]î} [K/IFb/B/JJ/GF/FS//JB3] <vir̄ II>

vir̄ekî ڤِڕەکی *f.* **(-ya;-yê).** being a liar, lying, fibbing *(as an avocation)*. {also: vir̄ektî (B-2/ZF3)} [K/B/Wkt//ZF3] <vir̄ek>

vir̄ektî ڤِڕەکتی (B/ZF3) = lying, fibbing. See **vir̄ekî**.

vir̄ker ڤِڕکەر (JB3/IFb/JJ) = liar. See **vir̄ek**.

virnî ڤِرنی/**vir̄nî** ڤِڕنی [B] *adj.* 1) born late *(of animals, who are thin and puny as a result, cf. ḧilî = born early)*: •**Berxên *virnî*--berx (yan kar)ên ku dereng çêdibin, buharê çêdibin, ne wek yên ḧilî girs in** (Qzl) "*Virnî*" [*late-born*] lambs--lambs (or kids) which are born late, are born in the springtime, are not plump like "hilî" [early-born] lambs; 2) harvested late *(of crops) (fig.)*: •**Gava buhar bi şilî derbaz be, û zevî dereng bêne çinîn yan dirûn, zad *virnî dikeve*** (Qzl) When the spring is wet, and the fields are harvested or reaped late, the crop *is less than ideal* •**Min ḧilî çand, lê *virnî ket*** (Qzl) I planted early, but [the crop] *came up late*, i.e., I married early, but my children didn't come until (much) later [Min zû jin anî, lê zarokên min dereng çêbûn]. {also: <virnî> ڤرنی (HH)}--<O Ir *a-pṛna-āyu(ka-) (A&L p. 82 [I]): [Qzl/QtrE/K/IFb/HH/GF/FJ//B] <ḧilî I>

virvirandin ڤِرڤِراندِن *vt.* **(-virvirîn-).** 1) to scatter, sprinkle, throw up in the air, winnow; 2) to hurl, throw with great force: •**Û heta ku birî di milên wî de heye, bi qaydê koçerane kevir davêje ... Û heta ku biriya wî heye, kevir *divirvirîne*** (ZZ-4, 171) And with all the strength in his arms, he throws the stone as nomads would ... And with all his might, he hurls the stone. [ZZ-4/ZF3/FD/BF/Wkt] <virvirîn>

virvirîn ڤِرڤِرین *vi.* **(-virvir-).** to be scattered, roll all over the place *(e.g., of round objects that fall out of a receptacle that has accidently been dropped)*: •**Nan di destek** [sic] **wî dabû, xiyar jî di destê din. Dema nêzîkî li se kir, lingê wî li singekî dewara likumî. Xwe ra negirt û bi ser dev ket erdê. Bi ketinê ra, nan û xiyar jî [j]i destên wî *virvirîn*** (MB, 11) He had bread in one hand, and a cucumber in the other. When he got near the dog, his foot tripped on a cattle post. He lost his balance and fell down, flat on his face. As he fell, the bread and cucumber *rolled out* of his hands. [MB/GF/ZF3/Wkt] <gindirîn>

virxûn ڤِرخوون (Nbh) = horse-drawn cart. See **firxûn**.

viyan ڤِـيـان *vt.* **(-vê-;** *neg. pres.* **nevêt** [Bw/M]**).** 1) {syn: gerek; lazim; pêdivî; p'êwîst} [+ *subj.*] to be necessary, obligatory; must [falloir] {impersonal verb}: •**Belê** ***diviya bû*** **jin bikira da ko warê wî kor nemînit** (SW) Yes, he *should* get married so that his family line doesn't die out [lit. 'remain blind']; 2) [+ *obl. prn.*] to need, require: •***Me*** **Kurdistanek** [sic] **yekbûyî, serxwebûyî û demokratîk** ***divê*** (Ber) *We need* [or, *want*] a united, independent, and democratic Kurdistan •***Min*** **tifingek** ***divê(t)*** (BX) = a) *I need* a rifle; b) *I want* a rifle •**Têkoşîna rizgariyê hêz** ***divê*** (Ber) Striving for freedom *requires* force •**We piştmêr** ***diviya bûn*** (BX) You *needed* [or, *wanted*] body guards; 3) {syn: xwestin} [+ *obl. prn.*] to want *{this is a standard feature of Southern Kurmanji: in the north,* ***xwestin*** *= 'to want' & 'to request', whereas it only means 'to request' in the South, 'to want' being expressed by* ***viyan****}* (Zx/Bw/JB1-A&S/HH); 4) {syn: jê ĥez kirin} to love: •**Pismam, ... eto yê çûye bajera, bîladêt mazin, ete jinêt cwan yêt dîtîn, noke** ***te ez nevêm*** (M-Ak #633, 286) Cousin, ... you have been to towns and great countries and seen beautiful women, now *you do not want me* [or, *do not love me*] •**Xwesîya te** ***tu divêyî*** (Bw) Your mother-in-law *loves you*; 5) [*f.* **(-a;-ê).**] desire, wish, will: •**Ez** ***bi viyana xwe ve*** **hatim** (IFb) I came *of my own free will* •**Wî hest dikir ev jîngehe ya dibîte hêzeka rêgir beramber** ***viyanêt*** **wî yêt hunerî û viyana wî bo serbestîyê** (Peyv 3[1996], 38) He felt that this environment was getting in the way of [lit. 'becoming a preventive force'] his artistic *desires* and his desire for freedom. {also: vên (BX-2/GF-2); vêtin (BX-2); vîn (BX/IFb-2); vîyan (TF); vyan (M); wyan (-wê-) (SK); [wàin] ڤـايـن (JJ); <van ڤـان (divê) (دڤـى)> (HH)} Cf. Sor wîstin ويـسـتِـن = 'to want' & [d]ebê[t] دەبـێـت = 'it is necessary' (< bûn بـوون = 'to be') [BX (#214)//IFb/JB1-A&S/GF/OK/Bw//TF//JJ//HH//SK] <bivê-nevê>

vizik I ڤِـزِك *f.* **(;-ê).** 1) {syn: mis'ar; ziviřok; zîzok} spinning top *(child's toy)* (AB); 2) gnat, mosquito. [Kg/AB/K/IFb/ZF3/Wkt/FD/Kmc]

vizik II ڤِـزِك *f.* **(-a;).** jet of water (or other liquid), spurt, stream or gush of water: •***Vizika*** **ava kunî dûr çû** (FS) The gush of water from the hole went far •**Zařokî** ***vizika*** **xwe dûr avêt** (FS) The child sent its *stream* [of urine] far afield. {syn: surik I; şiřik; şîp} [FS/Kmc] <pijiqîn>

vîje ڤيژە (IFb) = literature. See **wêje**.

vîn ڤين (BX/IFb) = must; to need; to want; to love. See **viyan**.

vîyan ڤييان (TF) = must; to need; to want; to love. See **viyan**.

vyan ڤـيـان (M) = must; to need; to want; to love. See **viyan**.

W و

waaz وائاز (IFb) = sermon. See **we'z**.
wade واده (K/IFb/GF) = time. See **we'de**.
wahş واهش (AB) = wild animal; pig; wild. See **weḧş**.
wahşî واهشى (K) = wildness. See **wehşî**.
wajî واژى (SK) = backward. See **vajî**.
wale واله (IF) = by God! See **wellah**.
Walesî والسى (Wkp) = Welsh. See **Wêlzî**.

walî والـــى *m.* **().** provincial governor. {also: <walî> والـى (HH)} < Ar wālī والـي (wālin والٍ) --> T vali {valîtî; walîlik; walîtî} [K/IFb/HH/GF]

walîlik واليـلـِك, f. (K) = province; governorship. See **walîtî**.

walîtî واليـتـى *f.* **(-ya;).** 1) province, district (governed by a walî) ; 2) governorship: **-valîtîya R̄uhayê** (BK) governorship of Urfa. {also: valîtî (BK); walîlik, f. (K)} [K/JR//BK] <walî>

wan I وان *prn.* 1) a) they *{As logical subject of past tense transitive verb (vt.)}*: **•*Wan* ez nedîtim** = *They* didn't see me **•*Wana* wisa jî kir** (Ba) They did just that (=that very thing); b) them *{As logical dir. obj. of non-past transitive verb (vt.)}*: **•Ez *wan* nabînim** = I don't see *them* **•Herin *wana* cîkî wisa şerjêkin, li k'u xwêde t'unebe** (Ba) Go slaughter *them* in (such) a place where there is no God; c) their *{obl. of ew [pl.]}*: **•Mala *wan* nêzîk e** = *Their* house is nearby; 2) those. {also: ewan I (B-2); ewana (B); wana (Ba/IF-2); [van وان/evan اوان] (JJ); <wan> وان (HH)} = Sor -yan يـان [Bx/K/A/IF/JJ/HH//Ba//B] <ew>

Wan II وان *f.* **(-a;-ê).** Van *(city and lake in Kurdistan of Turkey)*: **•Were em biçin bajarê Wanê** (AB) Come let's go to the city of van. [AB/K/IF/Wkp]

wana وانا (Ba/IF) = they; them; their. See **wan I**.

war وار *m.* **(-ê; wêr, vî warî).** 1) {syn: şênî; zome [1]} encampment, abode *(of a nomadic tribe)*; stopping place, halting place: **•Bo̱xekî jar dewsa *wara* dimîne** (J) A lean bull stays in the place of *the encampment* (=campsite); **-çûn waran** (IFb) to go to mountain pastures *(in summer, of nomadic tribes)*; 2) progeny, posterity, descendants [cf. ocax]: **•Belê diviya bû jin bikira da ko *warê* wî kor nemînit** (SW) Yes, he should get married so that his *family line* doesn't die out [lit. 'remain blind']; 3) {syn: aqar} homeland, native land; native place (Bw): **•Binavî *warê* min e** (Bw) Binavî [village near Dihok] is my *native place*; 4) {syn: biyav} field or area of study: **•Xemsarîyê di vî *warî* de nakin** (BH, 60) They are not neglectful in this *field* [of pursuit]. {also: [var] وار (JJ); <war> وار (HH)} Cf. Arm vayr վայր (var վար in compounds) = 'place' [J/Sw/K/A/JB3/IFb/B/JJ/HH/SK/GF/TF/OK] <zozan>

warge وارگه f.(B)/m.(K) = native place, home; camp. See **wargeh**.

wargeh وارگـــــه *f./m.(Wkt)* **(-a/ ;-ê/).** 1) native place, abode, home, cradle, stomping ground: **•Xortek delodîn im ha Urmiye *wargeha min* e** (INK361: Ayhan) I am a crazy young man, Urmiyah is my *home*; 2) camp *(e.g., of refugees)*: **•8'ê Adarê Roja Jinên Kedkar ên Cîhanê li *wargeha* Mexmûrê ji aliyê bi hezaran jin û xwendekaran ve bi coşeke mezin hate pîrozkirin** (ANF News 8.iii.2018) March 8, International Working Women's Day was celebrated with great enthusiasm by thousands of women in Makhmur *camp*; 3) (military) position. {also: warge f.(B)/m.(K)} <war + -geh [IFb/FJ/TF/GF/Kmc/ZF/BF/Wkt//K/B]

waris I وارِس = rope. See **werîs**.
waris II وارِس (K/IFb/SK/CS) = heir. See **wêris**.
warîl واريل (IFb/JJ/ZF) = barrel. See **varîl**.

warkor واركــــــــۆر *adj.* childless *(of married couple)*. {also: korewar (BF-2); warkore (FS)} {syn: r̄ical (Bw)} [Bw/K/GF/TF/ZF3/BF//FS]

warkore واركۆره (FS) = childless. See **warkor**.
wasêtî واسێتى (TF) = will, testament. See **wesyet**.
wasiyet واسِيەت (IFb) = will, testament. See **wesyet**.

wate واتــه *f.* **(-ya;-yê).** meaning, significance: **•--Ew *wateya* ayatan dizane. –Ma ku ez jî xwe fêrî *wateya* wan bikim, dîsa nabe? –Nabe lewre her kesê *wateya* wan bizanibe, nabe mela** (DBgb, 11) "He knows *the meaning of* the ayahs (Koranic verses)" "If I learn their *meaning*, wouldn't it be okay then?" "No, because everyone who knows their *meaning* cannot be a mullah"; **-hatin wateyê** = to mean: **•Bê ku bizanibe ka gotina wê *tê çi wateyê*, Sosin nêrîna xwe diyar kir** (DBgb, 13)

Without knowing what her words *would mean*, S. declared her opinion. {syn: me'na; têgih} Sor wate واته/wata واتا = 'i.e.; meaning' < Hau watey = 'to say' [(neol)Wlt/DBgb/IFb/FJ/TF/CS]

watedar واتەدار *adj.* meaningful, significant; important: **•Hin gotinên *watedar* ku bi peyvika XACIRGATî tên gotin** (Z. Zinar. Gotinên Watedar, 216) Some *significant* sayings [i.e., idioms] which are said using the word XACIRGAT **•Romana "Şapînoz" ... bi teknîkeke kemilî, bi bûyerên *watedar*, bi saloxdaneke bêalî û bi zimanekî dewlemend hatiye hûnandin** (H. Muhammed. Nefel 9.ix.2011) The novel "Shapinoz" ... has been crafted with a fine technique, with *meaningful* events, from an unbiased standpoint and with a rich [use of] language. [(neol)Nofa/ZF3/FD/Wkt] <berkeftî; giring>

wawik واوك (ZF/Wkt) = jackal. See **wawîk**.

wawî واوی (FJ/GF/ZF) = jackal. See **wawîk**.

wawîk واویك *m./f.(K/B)* **(; /ê).** jackal: **•Kûzekûza rovî û *wawîkan*, zarezara pezkoviyan e deng** (Nbh 135:26) The whimpering of foxes and *jackals*, the wailing of mountain goats, are sounds. {also: wawik (ZF/Wkt); wawî (FJ/GF/ZF-2); wawk (Wkt-2)} {syn: ç'eqel; torî I} < Clq Ar wāwī واوي, cf. Ar ibn āwá ابن آوى [Nbh/K/B/IFb/TF/Kmc/FS//ZF/Wkt//FJ/GF]

wawk واوك (Wkt) = jackal. See **wawîk**.

way وای *interj.* alas! woe! *(exclamation of grief)*: **•way li min** (B/IF)/**way li mino bavo** (AB) woe is me. {also: waylo!; wey I (IFb-2); [veï] وی (JJ); <way> وای (HH)} [AB/K/A/IFb/B/HH//JJ]

waylo وایلۆ = alas! woe!. See **way**.

waz واز (Wkt) = sermon. See **we'z**.

we وه *prn.* {*obl. of* **hûn**} 1) you (pl.): **•Ez *we* dibînim** = I see *you* **•*We* ez dîtim** = *You* saw me; 2) your: **•mala *we*** = *your* house. {also: hewe (Botan/Bw/OK-2/FS-2); hingo (SK); [vè] وه (JJ)} Sor êwe ئێوه = 'you (pl.)' *Although some use this as a polite form for one person, as T siz & Fr vous, my informants agree that this usage is foreign influence, and **hûn/we** should only be used for 2 or more per-sons; **tu/te** is used in addressing any individual, regardless of class or status.* [K/A/JB3/IF/B/JJ/OK/FS//Bw//SK] <hûn>

weba وەبا *f.* **(-ya;-yê).** plague, pestilence, epidemic: **•[Ekrad jî weku Efrancan qewî zêde ji nexweşî û *webayê* û ȟalî û 'illetêd ku s̱arî ne di̱tirsin û bi dûr dikevin]** (BN 178) Kurds, like Westerners, are greatly afraid of diseases and *epidemics* and conditions that are contagious, and shun them. {also: [veba] وبا (JJ)} {syn: pejî; qotik II; şewb; teşene} < Ar waba' وبأ/wabā' وباء = 'infectious disease, epidemic'; Sor weba وەبا = 'plague' [BN/IFb/JJ/OK/ZF3/Wkt]

we'd•e وەعدە *m.* **(•ê;).** 1) appointed time, term: **•Memê ... çil rojî *we'de* kifşkir** (EP-7) Mem ... set a forty day *term*; **-we'dê *fk-î* bûn** = for s.o. or stg.'s time to come, s.o. or stg.'s time to be ripe *(for stg.)*: **•Wexta M. mezin bû, îdî *we'dê* wî zewacê bû** (Z-1) When Mem grew up, it was (now) *time for* him to marry **•Z. îdî gihîştî bû, *we'dê* mêra bû** (Z-1) Z. had now matured, it was *time for* her to [to take] a husband [lit. 'her time for husbands was']; 2) time (B): **•*We'dê* min tune, ez nikarim bêm** (B) I don't have *time*, I can't come **•Destebirakê xweȓa *wadê* xwe derbaz dike** (Ba3-3, #4) He spends his time with his ***destbira*** [≈ bloodbrother]. {also: wade (K/IFb/GF); [vaâdé] وعده (JJ)} < Ar wa'd وعد, also maw'id موعد [Z-1/B/JJ//K/IFb/GF] <wext>

wedîtin وەدیتن (SK) = to find. See **vedîtin**.

wedîtinewe وەدیتنەوە (SK) = to find. See **vedîtin**.

wefat وەفات *f.* **(-a;-ê).** {syn: mirin} death: **-wefat bûn** (K/B)/**~kirin** (IFb/SK/ZF3) to die, pass away {syn: alîjiyan bûn; çûn ber dilovanîya xwedê; mirin}: **•Derbaz divin çend meh, Dawid *wefat dive*, dewsa wî Aqûb dive p'êxember** (Ba3-3, #4) A few months pass, David *passes away*, [and] Jacob becomes prophet in his stead. {also: [vefat] وفات (JJ); <wefat-> وفات (HH)} < Ar wafāh وفاة --> T vefat [Z-1/K/IFb/B/JJ/HH/SK/ZF3/Wkt]

weha وەها (IFb/TF) = thus. See **wiha**.

wehe وەهە (Z-922/K) = thus. See **wiha**.

wehisyan(ewe) وەهسیانەوە (SK) = to rest. See **vehesîn**.

wehş وەهش (K/IFb/ZF3/G) = wild animal; pig; wild. See **weȟş**.

wehşî وەهشی *f.* **(-ya;-yê).** wildness; savagery. {also: wahşî (K-2); wehşîtî (K-2/ZF3)} {syn: hovîtî} [K//ZF3]

wehşîtî وەهشیتی (K/ZF3) = wildness. See **wehşî**.

weȟş وەحش *f.* **(-a;-ê).** 1) wild animal; 2) {syn: beraz; domiz (Mzg); xinzîr (Haz: erudite)} pig: **•*Wahş* pîvazan dievîne** (AB) *The pig* loves onions; 3) [*adj.*] {syn: ç'olî I; hov; k'ûvî; t'oȓ II} wild. {also: wahş (AB); wehş (K/IFb/ZF3/G); [waš وش/ vehchi وحشی] (JJ)} < Ar waḥš وحش = 'wild' {wahşî; wehşî; wehşîtî} [AB//K/IFb/ZF3/G//Haz//JJ]

weiz وهیز (Wkt) = sermon. See **we'z**.

wek وهك *prep.* as, like, similar to: •**'Erd *weke* k'axaza cigarê bilind bûye** (Ba) The ground has risen *like* (=by the width of) a cigarette paper •**Lê îro ji nişka ve *wekî* piştevanên demokratîkbûnê derdikevin holê** (AW70D2) But today they suddenly appear on the scene *as* supporters of democratization •**Mala xwe kir *wek* a îsana** (L) He made his house *like* everyone else's [lit. 'like that of the people']; -**wek hev** = alike, like each other; -**wek /wekî/weke te** = like you. {also: weke (K/B/JB3-2); wekî [4]; wey II; [vek وك/vekou وكو/veki وكى] (JJ); <wek وك/ wekî وكى> (HH)} {syn: mîna; nola; şitî II} Sor wek وهك = 'like, as, when' [Bx/A/JB3/IFb/JJ/HH/GF//K/B]

weke وهكه (K/B/JB3) = like, as. See **wek**.

wekehev وهكههەڤ (IFb/TF)/weke hev (K/B) = equal; similar. See **wekhev**.

wekehevî وهكههەڤى (K/TF) = equality. See **wekhevî**.

wekhev وهكهەڤ *adj.* 1) equal: •**Li gorî vê, ev komar, yeke ku gelê kurd û tirk bi hev re *wekhev* tê de dijîn, bi temamî cumhuriyeteke demokratîk e** (AW75C1) According to this, this republic, one in which the Kurdish and Turkish people live together *equally* [=in equality], is entirely a democratic republic •**Ji derî van hersê grûbên zimanan, mafên yên din *wekhev* in** (AW69A3) Outside of these three groups of languages, all the rest have equal rights [lit. 'the rights of the others are equal']; 2) similar, alike. {also: wekehev (IFb-2/TF)/weke hev (K/B)} Cf. Sor wek yek وهك يهك = 'alike' {wek[e]hevî} [AW/A/IFb/GF//K/B/TF]

wekhevî وهكهەڤى *f.* **(-ya;-yê).** equality: •**Komara Tirkiyê ne weke berê ye. Îro pêşketin, *wekhevî* heye, dadmendî (edalet) heye** (Wlt 2:59, 13) The Turkish republic is not like before. Nowadays there is progress [and] *equality*, there is justice. {also: wekehevî (K/TF)} <wek hev = 'alike'; Cf. Sor wekyekî وهكيهكى = 'similarity' [(neol)Wlt/A/IFb/GF/OK//K/TF]

wek'ilandin وهكلاندن *vt.* **(-wek'ilîn-).** to repeat, say again: •**Ev e 30-40 sal e, ku ew van xebera *diwekilîne*, kî dizane hela ew *dê* çendik-çend salên dî jî van xebera *biwekilîne*** (X. Çaçan. Benê me qetiya, 22) It's been 30-40 years that she'*s been repeating* these words, who knows how many more years she *will repeat* these words. {syn: dubare kirin; ducar kirin} [Çaçan/K/F/ZF/CS/FS]

wekî وهكى *conj.* 1) [+ *indc.*] {syn: ko} that *(conj.)*: •**Jinê jî zanibû, *wekî* Ûsibî ze'f aqile** (Ba) The woman also knew *that* Joseph was [lit. 'is'] very smart •**Diqewimî, *wekî* gura mîk-dudu birîndar dikirin yanê jî dikuştin** (Ba2) It happened *that* the wolves wounded a sheep or two, or even killed [them]; 2) [+ *subj.*] {syn: bila; bona [2]; da II; deqene; ḧeta ko [5]} so that, in order to: •**Dibe ku te t'emî dane Ûsib, *wekî* ew mirîşkê şerjê *ne*ke, paşda bîne?** (Ba) Perhaps you warned Joseph (=tipped Joseph off) *not to* slaughter the chicken, [but rather] to bring it back? •**Ezê usa bikim, *wekî* zîanê bidim mêşê** (Dz) I will act in such a way *as to* bring harm to the forest •**Gelo nave, *wekî* em evê qîza nazik bigihînine ewî xortê tu bêjî** (Z-1) Shouldn't we unite this fine girl with this youth you're talking about [lit. 'about [whom] you speak']?; 3) {syn: eger I} if: •***Wekî* hûn Ûsibê min xweřa dibin, gerekê hûn řind miqatî wî bin** (Ba) *If* you take my Joseph with you, you must take good care of him •***Wekî* tiştek bê serê wî, zanibin, ezê we gişka qiřkim** (Ba) *If* anything happens to him, know that I will kill you all •***Wekî* em gakî şerjêkin** (J) *If* we slaughter a [or, one] cow; 4) prep. like, as. See **wek**. {also: [veki] وكى (JJ)} [K/IFb/B/JJ/GF] <wek>

wekîl/wek'îl [K/B] وهكيل *m.* **(-ê;).** agent, advocate: •***Wekîlê* silava be** (Zeb/Bw) Send my regards to the folks at home [lit. 'be *the agent of* greetings'] •***wekîlê* xo yê 'am** (M-Ak 685) his own general *agent*. {also: [vekil/vakíl (G)/vakīl (Rh)] وكيل (JJ); <wekîl> وكيل (HH)} < Ar wakīl وكيل = 'agent' [Zeb/Bw/IFb/JJ/HH/JB1-A&S/SK/OK//K/B]

wekuştin[ewe] وهكوشتن[هوه] (SK) = to slaughter. See **vekuştin**.

welat وهلات *m.* **(-ê; welêt, vî welatî).** homeland, fatherland, country: •***Welatê* min mezin e û xweş e** (AB) My *country* is big and pleasant. {also: [vilat ولات /vilàiet ولايت] (JJ)} < Ar wilāyah ولاية = 'state, province' --> T vilayet; Sor wiłat وڵات/ wułat ووڵات = 'country, native land' [K/A/JB3/IFb/B/GF/TF//JJ] <niştîman>

welatp'arêz وهلاتپارێز *m.* **(-ê;).** defender of the motherland; patriot: •***Welatparêzên* Kurdistanê yek bin!** (Ber) Kurdish *patriots* unite! [Ber/K/IFb/GF/FS] <niştîman; p'arastin; welat>

welçek وەلچەك (CCG) = unit of weight for measuring grain. See **olçek**.

wele وەلە (K/B) = By God! See **wellah**.

weleh وەلەه (B) = By God! See **wellah**.

welgeřan وەلگەڕان (FS) = to overturn (vi.); to go astray. See **wergeřîn**.

welgeřîn وەلگەڕین (B) = to overturn (vi.); to go astray. See **wergeřîn**.

welidandin وەلِدانِدن *vt.* **(-welidîn-).** 1) to assist at a birth; 2) {syn: řazan [2]; zayîn} to give birth: **•Em dibêjin jinê *welidand*; kûçik teliqî, mih/bizin/çêlek za** (kulturname-Amîdabad 2.ix.2012) We say that a woman gave birth; a dog had puppies, a sheep/goat/cow brought forth its young **•Çiqas xayîn *welidand* vî 'erdî, Xwedê** (RiaTaza 30.x.2017) How many traitors has this earth *brought forth*, O God. {also: [weledāndin] ولداندین (JJ)} < Ar walada ولد = 'to give birth' [K/B/ZF3/Wkt//JJ] <welidîn>

welidîn وەلِدین *vi.* **(-welid-).** 1) {syn: ji dayk bûn; hatin dinê} to be born; 2) [*vt.*] to bear offspring, give birth to *{in Ag, this verb is used for women, and **zayîn** is used for animals}*: **•Pey wîřa Meyane *diwelide*, Ûsivê nevîa tîne** (Ba3-3, #15) After him Meyaneh *gives birth* [again], she brings out Joseph the prophet. {also: [velidin] ولدين (JJ)} < Ar walada ولد = 'to give birth' [K/JB3/IFb/B/JJ/Ag/Rh] <avis; t'eliqîn>

wellah وەللاه interj. By God! By Jove! {also: wale (IF-2); wele (K-2/B-2); weleh (B-2); wellahî (L/K/IFb-2); welle (K-2/B-2); welleh (B); [vallah] والله (JJ)} < Ar wallāhī والله [IFb//L/K//B//JJ]

wellahî وەللاهی (L/K/IFb) = By God! See **wellah**.

welle وەللە (K/B) = By God! See **wellah**.

welleh وەللەه (B) = By God! See **wellah**.

wemirandin وەمِراندِن (SK) = to extinguish. See **vemirandin**.

wenda وەندا (GF) = lost, missing. See **winda**.

weqf وەقف *f.* **(-a;-ê).** fund, foundation, endowment, charity *(for benevolent purpose)*: **-Weqfa Mezopotamyayê** (www.tirşik.net) Mesopotamia Foundation. {also: [vaqouf] وقف (JJ)} {syn: sazî} <Ar waqf وقف; Sor weqf وەقف [Wkt/ZF3/FD//JJ]

weqî وەقی *f.* **(-ya;).** oka, ounce, unit of weight: **•Lipê teyrokê weke *weqî* ye** (HR 3:61) Hailstones weighing [lit. 'like'] *an oka* **•Petatên ku *weqîya* (kîloya) wan bi pênc qirûşan e, mêrik yek tenê bi milyonek Euro firot** (lotikxane 9.ii.2016) Potatoes are 5 piastres for *a kilo/oka*, [but] the man sold only one for a million Euros **•Wî *weqîyeka* pincařî kiřî** (FS) He bought *an oka* of greens. {also: [veki وقی/vakie وقی/hoqa هوقه] (JJ); <weqî> وقی (HH)} {syn: ḧuqe} < Ar 'uqqah أقّة/ 'ūqīyah أوقية/wiqīyah وقية = 'oka' <Lat uncia & Gr oungia οὐγκία -->T okka; Sor hoqe هۆقە/weqe وەقە [HR/IFb/FJ/GF/TF/JJ/HH/ZF/CS/FS]

wer وەر *adv.* thus, so. {also: were I (A/IFb-2); werge (IFb-2)} {syn: wiha; wilo; wisa} [L/Bx/K/JB3/IFb/Tkm//A]

weran وەران (FS) = to fall out. See **werîn II**.

werandin I وەراندِن *vt.* **(-werîn-).** 1) [tê: di ... werandin] to envelop, wrap [one's arms] around, enfold: **•Des[t] *di* sukirê *werand* ku dê maçî ket** (M-Ak #534, 242) He *put* his arm *around* 'her' neck, intending to kiss 'her'; 2) [tê: di ...werandin] to surround (JB1-A/IFb). [M-Ak/M/K/IFb/JB1-A/ZF3] See also **weranîn**.

weřandin II وەڕاندِن *vt.* **(-weřîn-).** to cause to fall off, cause to drop off; to chop off: **•Daran pelên xwe *werandibûn* û mabûn tazî** (ZF3) The trees had lost their leaves and were bare [lit. 'The trees *had caused* their leaves *to drop off*'] **•Destêt wî jê *weřandine* wê dirkê û nehiş û nehişyar bû k'afir** (M-Am #745, 342) He *chopped off* his [=monster's] hands there and the monster became unconscious. [M-Am/IFb/ZF3] <werîn II>

wer•anîn وەرئانین/وەرانین *vt.* **(wer[t]în-).** 1) {syn: çar rexî *ft-î* girtin; di rex û çana *ft-î* ziviřîn; dorgirtin; dorpêç kirin; werandin I; lê or tê wer hatin} to envelop, surround, encircle: **•Go, tu qap'ûtê hêşîn serê xwe *werîne*** (EP-7) He said, *wrap* a green overcoat about your head; 2) {syn: anîn} to bring: **•Mifirdî tawankar *weranî* dadgehê** (FS) The deputy *brought* the criminal to court; **-xwe weranîn** (EP-7) to betake o.s., to go: **•*Xwe* li nerdwana *jorda wertîne*** (EP-7) She *descends* the staircase. {also: **werandin I**; [ver-anin] ورانين (JJ)} [EP-7/K/IFb/JJ/GF/FS]

weřar وەڕار/**werar** وەرار [FS] *f.* **(-a;-ê).** development, growth, progress: **•*Werara* wî baş e** (FS) His *progress* is good/He is progressing (said of recovering patient); **-werar kirin** (Zeb/SB2) to develop, progress, improve *(vi.)*: **•Filan bajêrî gelek *weřar kiriye*** (Zeb) Such-and-such a city *has developed* a great deal **•Îsal rezê me, fabrîqa şekirê me *werar nekirin*** [sic], **bê werar in** (SB2,

71) This year our vineyard, our sugar factory, *have not developed* **•Rewşa aborî li welatî roj bi roj *werarê dike*** (BF) Economic conditions in the country *are improving* day by day. [Zeb/SB2/ZF/FS/BF] <pêşveçûn>

wer•bûn وەربـــــــوون *vi.* **(wer-b-).** 1) to fall down, roll down, go down: **•Berf li erdê hebû, mehîn likumî û lawik di bîrekê *werbû*** (ZZ-10, 163) There was snow on the ground, the mare stumbled and the boy *rolled down* into a well; 2) to set, go down *(of the sun)*: **•Roj *wer bû*** (ZF) The sun *set.* [ZZ/FJ/GF/TF/ZF/CS/FS]

werdek وەردەك *f.* **(-a;-ê).** duck *(bird)*, zool. *Anatidae*: **-werdeka nêr** (K) drake, male duck. {also: ordek (A); [verdek] وردك (JJ)} Cf. Southern Tati dialects: Chali ördak *m.* & ördaka *f.* (Yar-shater); P ordak اردك < T ördek [F/K/JB3/IFb/B/JJ/GF//A] <bet; miravî; qaz; sone>

were I وەرە (A/IFb) = thus, so. See **wer**.

were II وەرە = Come! See under **hatin**.

werge وەرگە (IFb) = thus, so. See **wer**.

wergeř I وەرگـــــــــــــەڕ *f.* **(-a;-ê).** translation: **•Di *wergeřê*da xwedîyên k'itêbê xwestine** [sic] **ku ji me'nayê meselan û met'elokan dûr nek'evin** (Dz, 41) In *the translation* the proprietors of the book wanted to stay close to [lit. 'not go far from'] the meaning of the sayings and proverbs. {syn: paçve; t'ercime} [Dz/Kmc/CS/ZF3] <wergêř>

werger II وەرگەر (K[s]/IFb) = translator. See **wergêř**.

wergeřan وەرگـــەڕان (A/FS/BF) = to overturn (vi.); to go astray. See **wergeřîn**.

wer•geřandin وەرگـــەڕانـــدِن *vt.* **(wer-geřîn-).** 1) to turn; 2) to overturn, upset, turn upside down: **-bar wergeřandin** (IFb) to knock over a load *(e.g., from on a camel's back)*; 3) {syn: p'açve kirin; t'ercime kirin} to translate: **•Di sedsala XIIan de ji erebî *hat wergerandin* bo ibranî** (YPA, 43) In the 12th century it *was translated* from Arabic to Hebrew **•Wexta mirov bixwaze wan *wergerîne* zimanekî din çênabe** (Wlt 1:37, 2) When one wants *to translate* them into another language, it doesn't work. {also: [ver-gherandin] ورگـرانـديـن (JJ); <wergerandin ورگـــرانـــدن (werdigerîne) (وردگرينه)> (HH)} Cf. Sor wergêřan وەرگێڕان = 'to turn; to translate' [K/A/JB3/IFb/JJ/HH/GF/TF] <t'ercime; wergêř>

wer•geřîn وەرگـەڕيـن *vi.* **(wer-geř-).** 1) {syn: qulibîn} to turn around, overturn, capsize, turn upside down: **•Li Hekariyê wesayîta eskerî *wergeriya*** (trtnuce.com 28.viii.2018) In Hakkari a military vehicle *overturned*; 2) to turn away, go astray: **•Şêx 'Ebdusselam û mirîdêt wî dêwane ne, *wergeřyayne*, dû şeytanî kewtîne** (SK 46:449) Sheikh Abdusselam and his disciples are madmen, they *have gone astray*, they have taken after the devil; 3) {syn: xelyan} to be twisted or sprained *(ankle)*: **•Lingê wî ket di çalê da û *wergeřa*** (FS) His foot fell into a ditch and *was sprained.* {also: welgeřan (FS-2); welgeřîn (B); wergeřan (A/FS/BF); wergeřyan (SK/G); [wer-gerīān] ورگـــريـــان (JJ); <wergeran ورگــــران (werdigere) (وردگـــره)> (HH)} Sor wergeřan وەرگـــــەڕان = 'to overturn (a vehicle); twist (ankle)' [trtnuce/JJ//SK/G//IFb/GF/ZF3/FD//A/HH/FS/BF//B] <wergeřandin>

wergeřyan وەرگەڕيان (SK/G) = to overturn (vi.); to go astray. See **wergeřîn**.

wergêř وەرگــــــــــێـــــڕ *m.&f.* **(-ê/-a;-î/-ê).** translator, interpreter: **•Mehkemeya doza Welat ji ber tunebûna *wergêrê* Kurdî hate taloq kirin** (Wlt 2:103, 8) The trial for the case against Welat [the Kurdish newspaper] was postponed due to the lack of a Kurdish *translator*. {also: werger II (K[s]/IFb-2); wergîr (OK)} {syn: paçveker; t'ercimeçî} Cf. Sor wergêř وەرگـێـڕ [Wlt/IFb/Kmc/CS/ZF3/BF//OK//K(s)] <wergeř I>

wer•girtin وەرگِـرتِـن *vt.* **(wer-gr-).** 1) {syn: standin} to receive, accept; to get, obtain; to take: **•Bû xelîfe û ji teref Şêx 'Usman izna şêxînîyê *wergirt*** (SK 45:434) He became a Khalifa and *received* the licence to teach as a shaikh from Shaikh Usman **•Xulase ṣed lîre *wergirt*, hate mala xo** (SK 28:260) In short, he *took* 100 lire and went home; 2) to acknowledge, return, accept *(a greeting)*: **•Řîwî ... silaw li kelekokî kir. Kelekokî silaw jê *wergirt*** (SK 4:30) The fox ... saluted the cock. The cock *acknowledged* his salute; 3) to wear, put on *(clothing)*: **•Sol bi tenê zivistana dikarîn *wergirin*** (MB, 61) As for shoes, only in wintertime could they *wear* any [because they were so poor]; **-cilên xwe wergirtin** (IFb) to get dressed, put one's clothes on. {also: [ver-ghirtin] ورگـرتـيـن (JJ); <wergirtin ورگـرتـن (werdigre) (وردگــــــــره)> (HH)} Sor wer•girtin وەرگِرتِن = 'to receive' [K/A/IFb/B/JJ/HH/SK/JB1-S/GF/TF]

wergîl وەرگيل (HR) = ring, hook. See **werqîl**.

werihan وەرِهان (GF/FS) = to fall out. See **werîn II**.

werimandin وەرِمـــــانـــدِن *vt.* **(-werimîn-).** 1) {syn: êvitandin; nep'ixandin; p'erçifandin} to cause to swell *(vt.)*, to puff up, inflate; 2) to praise to excess (B); **-xwe werimandin** (B) = a) to puff o.s. up *(of roosters)*; b) to put on airs, be conceited. {also: wermandin (A); [verimandin] ورمـانـديـن (JJ)} < Ar warima ورم = 'to swell up' [K/JB3/IFb/B/JJ/GF/OK//A] <werimîn>

werimîn وەرِمـيـن *vi.* **(-werim-).** to swell (up) *(lit. & fig.)*: •**Serê wî *werimî*** (J) His head *swelled up*. {also: werimtin (BF-2/FS-2); [verimin] ورمـيـن (JJ)} {syn: êvitîn; nep'ixîn; p'erçifîn} < Ar warima ورم = 'to swell up' [J/F/K/(A)/JB3/IFb/B/JJ/OK/BF/FS]

werimtin وەرِمـتِـن (BF/FS) = to swell (up). See **werimîn**.

weris وەرِس (K/IFb/B) = rope. See **werîs**.

werîn I وەریـن *vi.* **(-wer-).** 1) {syn: hatin} to come: •***Were!*** = *Come!* Occurs only in subjunctive and imperative. [BX/BF] See also **hatin**.

werîn II وەریـن *vi.* **(-wer-).** to fall *(of leaves)*; to fall out *(of hair)*: •**Pirça min *diwerit*** (Bşk) My hair *is falling out*. {also: weran (FS); werihan (GF-2/FS-2); [veriian] وريـان (JJ)} {syn: weşîn} [Bşk/K/A/GF//JJ//FS] <wer̄andin II>

werîs وەریـس *m.* **(-ê; wêris [B]).** rope; long, thick woolen twine, used for pitching tents, securing saddlebags to oxen, etc. (B); hemp rope (HH): •**Ka vî *werisî* li noqa xwe bipêçe. Ezê te berdime bîrê, avê ji me re derîne** (Wlt 2:59, 15) Tie this *rope* around your waist. I will let you down into the well, bring up water for us. {also: waris I; weris (K/IFb/B); [veris] وريـس (JJ); <werîs> وريـس (HH)} {syn: kap I; k'indir [2]; qirnap; şerît [1]} Mid P arwēs = 'rope' (M3); Sor gurês گوريّس/ gurîs گـوريـس; Hau werêse *f.* = 'woollen rope (for tying load on mule, etc.)' (M4) [AB/JB3/JJ/HH/GF//K/IFb/B/FS] <ben; dav II>

wer•kirin وەرکِـرِن *vt.* **(wer-k-).** 1) {syn: nixamtin; pêçavtin; weranîn} to cover: •**Kurkê *xwe* li serê xwe *werkir*** (L) He *covered himself* with his fur coat; 2) to put on, throw on (clothes) (B); 3) to throw, lob, cast; to pelt or shower (with); to sprinkle, scatter, sow, broadcast: **-ber tê werkirin** (FKS) to stone, pelt with stones: •**Polîsan gaza rondikrêj li xelkê reşand. Xelkê jî *bi beran pê* (koma polîsan) *wer kir*** (Hk) The police sprayed tear gas on the people. The people *pelted* the police *with rocks*. [L/Hk//K/B/FJ/GF/TF/ZF/JB1-A/Kmc/FKS]

wermandin وەرمـــانـــدِن (A) = to inflate. See **werimandin**.

wer•pixandin وەرپِـخـانـدِن *vt.* **(wer-pixîn-).** to exaggerate, inflate, overstate, make a big deal out of stg.: •**Ev kitêbên min tevek jî, ne karê *werpixandinê* ne û ne jî bi naveroka xwe *hatine werpixandin*** (Z.Zinar. Fermana 33 Rewşenbîran, 153) These books of min as a whole are not a work of *overstatement*, nor *have* they *been overstated* in their content •**Ev mesele bi zanîn** tê werpixandin (Z. Zinar: www.netkurd.info) This issue *is being exaggerated* on purpose. {syn: nep'ixandin} [Z.Zinar/ZF3]

werqîl وەرقيل *f.* **(;-ê).** wooden ring or hook through which a rope passes in fastening a load onto a pack saddle or the like; wooden hook used for tying down bales of wheat to transport them from field to threshing floor (Qzl): •**Û qant'ir jêr̄a berda *wergîl* lê kirin** (HR 3:213) And he let the mule out for him and put pack saddle *rings* on him [i.e., prepared him to be loaded up]. {also: wergîl (HR)} {syn: heçî I} [HR//Qzl/K[s]/FJ/GF/ZF3/FS/FD] <*darşix̄re; p'aldûm>

werşaq وەرشاق (GF/FS) = lynx. See **weşeq**.

werşek وەرشەك (IFb/OK/FS) = lynx. See **weşeq**.

werşeq وەرشەق (Wlt) = lynx. See **weşeq**.

werz وەرز *m.* **(-ê;).** 1) {syn: p'arêz I} field, patch, or bed in which melons and the like are grown: **-werzê gindora** (Bw) melon patch: •***Werzekê* gundura yê hey, gundurêt xo hemî bi bera ve dan, ev êt hindeyêt mezin perçiqandin, ev êt biçûk'oke yê didanîte ser** (JB1-A #189) He has a melon *patch*, he has thrown all his melons against the rocks, those that were this big he smashed, and those that were small he put on top; 2) {syn: demsal; nîr II} season *(of the year)*: •**Çar *werzên* salê; bihar, havîn, payîz û zivistan** (BF) The 4 seasons of the year: spring, summer, autumn/fall and winter. {also: <werz> ورز (HH)} Cf. P varzīdan ورزيـدن = 'to cultivate, sow' & kešāvarz كـشـاورز = 'farmer'; Sor werz وەرز = 'agricultural year, agriculture' [Bw/K/A/IFb/HH/JB1-A/GF/TF/OK/ZF3/BF] <mişar I>

werziş وەرزِش *f./m.(FS)* **(;-ê/-î).** 1) sports: •**Pîrek dikarin beşdarî çalakiyên *werzişê* bibin** (Fetwayên Kurdî) Women can participate in *sports* activities; 2) physical exercise, athletics, training. {also:

werzişt (IFb/FD/Wkt-2); werzîş (ZF3/Wkt-2)} < P varziš ورزش = 'gymnastic exercise; sports; training'; Sor werziş[t] وەرزِشت [A/BF/FS/Wkt//IFb/FD//ZF3]

werzişt وەرزِشت (IFb/FD/Wkt) = sports; exercise. See **werziş**.

werzîş وەرزيش (ZF3/Wkt) = sports; exercise. See **werziş**.

wesaît وەسائيت (ZF3) = vehicle. See **wesayît**.

wesandin وەساندِن *vt.* **(-wesîn-).** to instruct, bequeath, stipulate in one's will: **•Ma Bengî axa *ne wesandibû* ku bila Gefo bixwîne, mezin bibe, evdîna bav û welatiyên xwe veke û di rêya felata welatê xwe de bixebite?** (H v. 1, 83 [1932, 1:4]) *Didn't* Bengi Agha *stipulate in his will* that Gefo should study, and when he grows up, [that he should] take revenge for his father and compatriots, and work for the deliverance/liberation of his country? < Ar waṣṣá II وصّى = 'to order, recommend, urge' cf. also waṣīyah وصية = 'last will and testament' [H/K/ZF/CS] <we<u>s</u>yet>

wesayit وەسايِت (Wkt) = vehicle. See **wesayît**.

wesayît وەسايیت *f.* **(-a;-ê).** vehicle (car, truck, bus): **•Li Hekariyê *wesayîta* eskerî wergeriya** (trtnuce.com 28.viii.2018) In Hakkari a military *vehicle* overturned. {also: wesaît (ZF3); wesayit (Wkt)} < Ar wasā'iṭ وسائط/wasāyiṭ وسايط, pl. of wāsiṭah واسطة = 'means, medium' [trtnuce/G//ZF3//Wkt] <otobûs; p'îqab; trimbêl>

wesiyet وەسِيەت (GF) = will, testament. See **we<u>s</u>yet**.

wesîyet وەسییەت (K/B) = will, testament. See **we<u>s</u>yet**.

westabûn وەستابوون, f. (K/JB3) = fatigue. See **westan I**.

westan I وەستان *f.* **(-a;-ê).** {syn: qefilî (Kg)} fatigue, weariness, tiredness: **•Dixebitin em her gav, nizanin çi ye *westan*** (AB) We work all the time, we don't know what *fatigue* is. {also: westabûn, f. (K-2/JB3); westîyan (B); <we<u>s</u>tan> وصطان (HH)} [AB/K/(A)/IFb//B//HH] <westandin; westîn>

westan II وەستان (A/IFb/SK/OK)/west'an (JB1-A)/ we<u>s</u>tan وەسطان (FS) = to be tired; to stop. See **westîn**.

westandin وەستاندِن/**we<u>s</u>tandin** وەسطاندِن [FS] *vt.* **(-westîn-).** to tire s.o. out, exhaust, wear out: **•Box̂ k'uta, nav garanê gef̄and, *westand*** (J) He beat the bull, made it run among the cattle, *tired it out* **•Wî Behrem bi şolî ve *we<u>s</u>tand*** (FS) He *wore* B. *out* with work. {also: <we<u>s</u>tandin وصطاندن (diwe<u>s</u>tîne) (دوصطينه)> (HH)} {syn: f̄eĥt kirin} *For etymo-logy see **westîn**.* [J/K/A/JB3/IFb/B/GF/OK//FS//HH] <westan; westîn>

westiyan وەستِيان (JB3/OK)/west'iyan (JB1-A) = to be tired. See **westîn**.

westîn وەستین *vi.* **(-west- / -westa-).** 1) {syn: betilîn; qefilîn [2]; f̄e't bûn} to be tired, weary: **•Ew zû *diweste*** (B) He *tires/gets tired* easily **•Fêrîk lawo, miqatî Sûsîkê be, ewe hela biç'ûke, dibe *biweste*, paşda bimîne, bixalife, tu jê dûr nek'eve, alî wê bike** (Ba2-#2, 206) Ferik my son, take care of Susik, she is still small, perhaps she *will get tired*, fall behind, [or] get lost; you stay close to her [lit. 'don't fall far from her'], help her **•*Westîme*** = I'm tired [lit. 'I *have become tired*']; 2) to stop (SK/OK): **•Gulle li f̄exê çepî nawikê *westa*, dernekewt** (SK 18:170) The bullet *stopped* on the left side of his navel and did not come out **•Pişt-û-pişt kewt, ĥetta binê minarê *newesta*** (SK 15:150) He fell down backward and *did not stop* until he reached the bottom of the minaret. {also: wastan/wastîn (TF) = we<u>s</u>tan/we<u>s</u>tîn?; westan II (A/IFb-2/SK/OK-2)/west'an (JB1-A-2)/ we<u>s</u>tan (FS); westiyan (JB3/OK)/west'iyan (JB1-A); <we<u>s</u>tan> وصطان (HH)} [Pok. stā-:stə- 1004.] 'to stand': Skt sthā- [tiṣṭhati]; O Ir stā- (Ras, p.131): Av stā- [hištaiti] = 'to stand'; O P stā- [a-ištata *3.sing. impf.*]; Mid P ēstādan (ēst-) = 'to stand, be, continue' (M3); P īstādan ايستادن = 'to stand'; Sor westan وەستان = 'to stand'; SoK wɪs-/wɪs[y]â-, etc. (Fat 418) [Ad/K/IFb/B/GF/OK//A//FS//HH//JB3] <qefilî; westan; westandin>

westîyan وەستییان (B) = fatigue. See **westan I**.

we<u>s</u>yet وەصیەت [SK]/**wesyet** وەسیەت [B/AD] *f.* **(-a; -ê).** last will and testament: **•Wextê ez biçûk min ji babê xo bihîst, got, "Wê berxê gelek cûn dan e min. Se û şwan ĥazir bûn, neşyam tola xo wekem." *We<u>s</u>yet* li me ewladê xo kiriye, gotiye, 'Her cîyê hung wê berxê bibînin tola min weken.' Bo wihê te cewab nîye, elbette tola babê xo nahêlim, *we<u>s</u>yeta* babê xo be<u>tt</u>al nakem"** (SK 5:57) When I was small I heard my father say, "That lamb abused me greatly. The shepherd and his dog were present so I could not take my revenge." His *last words* to us his children were, 'Avenge me on that lamb whenever you may see him.' You have no answer to that. Certainly I shall not fail to avenge my father nor betray his *last words*" **•Wextê te maye bîst deqîqe. Kifinê xo**

ḧazir ke, ***weṣyetêt* xo bike û destûrîyê ji mal û ‘eyalê xo bixaze** (SK 40:361) You have twenty minutes left. Get your shroud ready, make your *testament* and take leave of your wife and family. {also: wasêtî (TF); wasiyet (IFb); wesiyet (GF); wesîyet (K/B-2); [vesiiet] وصيت (JJ); <weṣiyyet> وصـــيـــت (HH)} {syn: qewîtî[2]} < Ar waṣīyah وصـــيّـــة = 'will, testament, bequest, legacy' --> T vasiyet; Sor wesyet[name] وەسیەت[نامە]/wesêt وەسێت [SK/B/AD//GF//HH//JJ//IFb//TF] <wesandin>

weş وەش *f.* **(;-ê).** 1) shaking, trembling; 2) swinging, swaying, rocking; 3) hit, blow, strike: •**Behremî *weşek* li serê yê dî da û ew bi wê *weşê* ket** (FS) B. gave a *blow* to the other one's head, and that one was knocked down [lit. 'fell'] by that *blow*. {also: [vech] وش (JJ)} [AB/K/A/JJ/GF/FS/ZF3]

weşan I وەشان (IFb/HH/FS) = to fall out. See **weşîn**.

weşan II وەشـان *f.* **(-a;-ê).** publication: •**105 sal bi ser *weşana* yekem Rojnameya Kurdî dibihore** (pdk-xoybun.com) 105 years have passed since *the publication of* the first Kurdish newspaper •**Di meha Cotmehê de dest bi *weşana* xwe kiriye** (Nbh 125:3) In the month of October it began *publication*; **-Weşanên Roja Nû** = [lit. 'new day publications'] *series published by the Roja Nû publishing house in Stockholm, Sweden.* [(neol)IFb/TF/ZF/Wkt] <ç’ap II; neşir>

weşandin وەشاندِن *vt.* **(-weşîn-).** 1) to shake, shake out *(vt.)*; to throw about violently; 2) {syn: peresandin} to publicize, spread, diffuse; to publish. {also: [vechandin] وشـانـدنـيـن (JJ)} Sor weşandin وەشـانـدِن = 'to wave, shake, broadcast (seed)' [K/A/IFb/B/JJ/BK/GF/TF] <daw[e]şandin>

weşanxane وەشـانـخـانـە *f.* **(-ya;-yê).** publisher, publishing house: •**Heta niha vê *weşanxaneyê* 32 kitêbên kurdîya zazakî weşandine** (zazakî.net 10.xi.2009) Until now this *publisher* has published 32 books in Zaza. [IFb/Pencînar/ZF3/BF/FD/Wkt] <ç’apxane>

weşarin وەشارِن (SK) = to hide. See **veşartin**.

weşek وەشەك (IFb/OK/ZF3) = lynx. See **weşeq**.

weşeq وەشـەق *f./m.(FS)* **(-a/;-ê/).** lynx, zool. *Lynx lynx*: •**Şêr ji keftaran qet hez nakin. Lê ji *werşeqê* (*werşeq-weşeq* kûviyeke ku postê wê pirr rind e) zehf hez dikin** (Wlt 2:100, 13) Lions don't like hyenas at all. But they very much like *the lynx* (*the lynx* is a wild animal with a very nice pelt). {also: werşaq (GF/FS-2); werşek (IFb-2/OK-2/FS); werşeq (Wlt-2); weşek (IFb/OK/ZF3); weyşek (FS-2); [vachaq] وشـــــاق (JJ)} *Pahl varsnagān (JJ); Ar wašaq وشـق --> T vaşak; Sor weşek وەشـــەك [Wlt//JJ//IFb/OK/ZF3//GF//FS] <piling; p’isîk; weşeq>

weşiyan وەشِیان (JB3) = to fall out. See **weşîn**.

weşîn وەشـيـن *vi.* **(-weş-).** to fall out *(hair)*; to fall *(leaves)*: •**Payizan pel ji daran *diweşin*** (AB) in the fall, leaves *fall* from the trees. {also: weşan I (IFb-2/FS); weşiyan (JB3-2); [vechiian] وشـيـان (JJ); <weşan وشان (diweşe) (دوشه)> (HH)} {syn: werîn [2]} [K/JB3/IFb/B//HH/FS//JJ] <k’etin>

weşînek وەشینەك *f.* **(-a;-ê).** broadcast(ing): **-weşîneka k’urdî** (GF) Kurdish broadcasting. [(neol)IFb/GF/ZF3/Wkt]

wetrê وەترێ (ZF3) = it seems to (me, you, him, etc.). See **t’irê**.

wext وەخـت *m.(K/SK)/f.(W)* **(-ê/-a; /-ê).** time: **-t’u wext** = never {syn: t’ucar; t’u çax}; **-wextê çîroka** (L) story time; **-wextekê** (L) once (upon a time). {also: [vaqit] وقـت (JJ)} {syn: çax; gav; we‘de} < Ar waqt وقـت --> P vaqt وقـت; --> T vakit [Bx/K/JB3/IFb/B/SK//JJ] <wexta; xêl>

wexta [ko] [كو] وەختا *conj.* when ... : •**Dařbiř *wexta* çû mêşe ...** (Dz) *When* the woodcutter went to the forest ... •**Tê bîra te, *wexta* go em hatin ber wê avê?** (L) Do you remember *when* we went to that river? •***wexta* bû êvar** (L) *when* it was evening. {also: wextê (K/B-2/SK); [vaqt-a kou] وقـتـا كـو (JJ)} {syn: çaxê [*see* çax]; gava [ko]} < *ezafeh of* **wext** [L/Dz/IF/B//K//JJ]

wextê وەختێ (K/B/SK) = when. See **wexta [ko]**.

wex̄er وەغەر (M-Ak) = luck. See **ox̄ir**.

wey I وەی (IFb) = alas! woe! See **way**.

wey II وەی = like, as. See **wek**.

weyşek وەیشەك (FS) = lynx. See **weşeq**.

we‘z وەعز *f.* **(-a;-ê).** [Islamic] sermon: •**[Mela Bazîd ekserî *we‘z* û şîret didaye Ekradan û li mizgevtê nesîḧet dikirin û di *we‘zê* da digot…]** (JR-3) Most of the time Mullah Bazid gave *sermons* and admonitions to the Kurds and advised them in the mosque, and in his *sermons* he would say…. {also: waaz (IFb); waz (Wkt-2); weiz (Wkt); [<waaz>] وعظ (JR)} < Ar wa‘ẓ وعظ = 'admonition, warning, sermon' [JR/IFb//K//Wkt] <gotar>

wezaret وەزارەت *f.* **(-a;-ê).** government ministry: •**Berdevkê *wezareta* karê derve ya Emerîka James Rubin** (CTV7) American State

Department [=foreign *ministry*] spokesman James Rubin. {syn: şalyarî; wezîrî} < Ar wizārah وزارة [K/IFb/GF/ZF3]

wezîfe وەزیـفـە *f.* **(-ya;-yê).** 1){syn: peywir; vatinî} duty, obligation: **•Di encamê de ji bo hilgirtina van peywiran (*wezîfeyan*) ev endam hatin hilbijartin** (Wlt 1:36, 5) In the end, these members were elected to carry out these *duties*; 2) {syn: rol} role, function: ***•Wezîfeya* vê peyvê di hevokê de çi ye?** (Wkt) What is *the role of* this word in the sentence? <Ar waẓīfah وظـيـفـة; Sor wezîfe وەزیـفـە/wełîfet وەڵیـفـەت = 'duty, official appointment' [Wlt/F/K/IFb/JJ/SK/ZF3/Wkt] <vatinî>

wezîr وەزیـر *m.* **(-ê;).** vizier, government minister. {also: [vezír] وزیـر (JJ); <wezîr> وزیـر (HH)} {syn: şalyar} < Ar wazīr وزير; Sor wezîr وەزیر = 'minister, queen (chess)' {wezaret; wezîr[t]î} [K/A/JB3/IFb/B/JJ/HH/GF/TF/OK]

wezîrî وەزیـــــــری *f.* **(-ya;-yê).** office of vizier or minister; government ministry: **•Ege[r] tu fam dikî bike, eger tu nekî, ez ê te ji *wezîrtiyê* bavêjim** (ZZ-7, 262) If you can figure it out, do so, if you can't, I will kick you out of your *viziership*. {also: wezîrî (K/A/TF); wezîrtî (K-2)} {syn: şalyarî; wezaret} [K/A/TF//IFb/GF/OK] <wezîr>

wezîrtî وەزیرتی (K) = ministry. See **wezîrî**.

wê I وێ *prn. f.* 1) she, it; her, it; her, its; 2) that (f.) *{obl. of **ew** [sing. f.]}*: **-li wê (derê)** = there. [Bx/K/A/IFb/B/TF]

wê II وێ 1) [+ *subj.*] *future tense marker {also **dê**, often shortened to **-ê**, e.g., **ez wê**--> **ezê**, **em wê**--> **emê**}*: **•Her yanzdeh kuřê mine dinê *wê* jêra *xulamtîê bikin*** (Ba) All my other eleven sons *will serve* him; 2) [+ *(pres./past) indc.*] (present/past) continuous tense marking : **•Divînin bûkek *wê* xweřa řazaye** (Dz) They see that the young woman has fallen asleep **•Divînin *wê* xortek gaê xwe t'eze girtye ku qoşke** (Dz) They see that the young man has recenty taken his bull(s) to tie them to the plough {describes him as lazy} **•Dinhêřin *wê* bûkeke cahil şuxulê xwe xilas kirye û nanê mêrê xweî cotk'ar girêdaye** (Dz) They see that the young woman has finished her work and has tied up her husband the farmer's food [into a bundle]. {also: dê II; -ê} [K/IFb/GF/ZF3]

wêda وێـدا *interj.* 1) Get away! Scram! Scat! Get out!: ***•Wêda* heře!** (B) Get out of here!; **-wêda bûn** (K) to be pushed aside; **-wêda dan/kirin** (K) to push aside: **•Min boxekî strû-şkestî, ç'e'vekî kor, lingekî t'opal dît, wê ḧeft boxê qizil *wêda kirye*** [sic] (EP-4, #16) I saw a bull [or male deer] with a broken horn, blind in one eye, lame in one foot *pushing aside* [or, *keeping at bay*] seven red males; 2) [*adv.*] {syn: wê derê} there: **-virda wêda** = here and there. {also: wêde (TF/ZF3)} [EP-4/K/B//TF/ZF3] <wêve>

wêde وێدە (TF/ZF3) = there. See **wêda**.

wêdetir وێدەتر (KS) = on that side; rather. See **wêvetir**.

wêje وێـــژە *f.* **(-ya;-yê).** literature: **•Dema ku mirov li ser *wêjeya* Kurdî difikire, tê dîtin, ku gelek taybetmendî di vê *wêjeyê* de hene, ku ne dinya pê dizane, ne jî Kurd** (www.kobanikurd.com 12.vii.2011) When one thinks of Kurdish *literature*, it can be seen that there are many traits in this *literature* which neither the world nor the Kurds are aware of. <Sor wêje وێـــژە (K2) {also: vîje (IFb-2); wîje (IFb-2)} {syn: edebiyat; t'oře[2]} [(neol)Wlt/K(s)/A/IFb/GF/TF/OK/ZF3/Wkt/BF]

wêjevan وێـژەڤـان *m.* **(-ê;).** littérateur, man of letters; writer: **•Hemû wêjedostên Kurd li başûrê Kurdistanê vî navî dinasin, torevanekî (*wêjevanekî*) rêzdar, birûmet û nîştimanperwer** (Wlt 2:73, 13) All Kurdish literature lovers in northern Kurdistan know this name, a respected, renowned, and patriotic *littérateur*. {also: wêjewan (K[s]); wîjekar (IFb)} {syn: t'ořevan I} Sor wêjewan وێـــــژەوان = 'man of letters/culture, person versed in the humanities' [(neol)Wlt/GF/ZF3/Wkt//K(s)//IFb] <nivîsk'ar>

wêjewan وێژەوان (K[s]) = writer. See **wêjevan**.

wêjeyî وێـژەیـی *adj.* literary: **•Ahmad Abdulla Zero dibêjit li sala 2010 ê romana û vekolînên *wêjeyî* werar kir** (VoA 20.xii.2010) A.A.Z. says that in 2010, novels and *literary* research flourished. {syn: edebî} [(neol)Wlt/GF/TF/ZF3/Wkt] <wêje>

Wêlsî وێلسی (Wkt) = Welsh. See **Wêlzî**.

Wêlzî وێـلـزی *adj.* Welsh. {also: Walesî (Wkp); Wêlsî (Wkt)} Sor Wêłzî وێڵزی [Wkt//CS//Wkp]

wên•e وێـنـە *f./m.(Şnx/ZF3/FS/BF)* **(•eya/•[ey]ê;•ê/•eyî).** picture; portrait; photograph: ***•Weneyê* xo bi dîwarî ve hilawîst** (BF) He hung his *photograph* on the wall; **-wêne girtin** (GF/ZF3)/~ **k'işandin** (ZF3) to take pictures, photograph: **•Wî *wênê* Azad bi kamîrê girt** (FS) He took *a picture of* A. with a camera. {also: vêne; wîne (K[s])} {syn: keval; řesim; sifet [4]; şikil} <Sor wêne وێـنـە =

'example, reflection, picture' [A/JB3/IFb/GF/TF/OK/FS/ZF3/Wkt/FD//K(s)] <dîmen>

wênegir وێنەگِر (FS) = photographer. See **wênek'êş**.

wênek'ar وێنەکار *m.&f.* **(-ê/;).** 1) artist, painter: **•*Wênekar* Fevzî Bîlge, di tabloyên xwe de bi giştî jina Kurd bi awayekî folklorîk bi kar tîne** (Wlt 2:71, 6) The *artist* Fevzi Bilge generally presents [lit. 'uses'] the Kurdish woman in a folkloric manner in his paintings; 2) photographer (ZF3/Wkt). {also: wêneker (A); wênevan (IFb/GF)} [(neol)Wlt/OK/Wkt/ZF3//A//IFb/GF]

wêneker وێنەکەر (A) = artist. See **wênek'ar**.

wênek'êş وێنەکێش *m.&f.* **(-ê/-a;/-ê).** photographer, picture taker. {also: wênegir (FS)} Sor wênegir وێنەگِر [(neol)IFb/OK//FS]

wênevan وێنەڤان (IFb/GF) = artist. See **wênek'ar**.

wêran I وێران *adj.* destroyed, annihilated, in ruins, laid waste: **-wêran kirin** (B) to destroy, annihilate, lay waste, raze to the ground: **•Eskeran ji bo vê yekê gundê Qereqoyunê *wêran kir*** (Ber) Troups *destroyed* the village of Karakoyun for that reason. {also: [virané] ويرانه (JJ); <wêran> ويران (HH)} {syn: kavil; xirab [2]; ≠ava; ≠şên} Cf. P veyrān ويران; Sor wêran وێران = 'ruined, desolate' [Ber/K/A/JB3/IFb/B/HH/GF/TF//JJ]

wêran II وێران (JB3/IFb/JJ/SK/GF/TF/Bw) = to dare. See **wêrîn**.

wêris وێرِس *m.&f.* **().** heir, inheritor: **•Eve jî dewletserê hindek binemal û kes û *wêrisên* leheng û qehremanan** (Nbh 125:11) And this is thanks to (or, due to) some families and individuals and relatives/*heirs* of heroes and champions. {also: waris II (K/IFb/SK/CS); [varis/veris] وارث (JJ)} {syn: mîratgir} < Ar wāriṯ وارث = 'heir' [Nbh/ZF//K/IFb/JJ/SK/CS]

wêrîn وێرین *vt.* **(-wêr-:** *neg.* **ne-).** to dare: **•Ez *newêrim*** (Bw) I *don't dare* **•Hema *ne wêrin* rabin** (L) But they *don't dare* get up **•Tu *ne wêrî* li vê derê razê** (L) You *don't dare* sleep here **•Wîşîê tirî li hindawê r̄êkan ȟetta nêzîkî zistanê dima. Kes *nediwêra* dest biket ê** (SK 51:554) Bunches of grapes would remain (hanging) above the roads until nearly winter. Nobody *dared* to touch them. {also: wêran II (JB3/IFb-2/GF-2/Bw); [vērān] ويران (JJ); <wêrîn> ويرين (HH)} {syn: t'uriş kirin} Cf. Sor wêran وێران [L/K/A/IFb/GF/HH//JB3/JJ/SK/TF/Bw]

wêve وێڤە *adv.* on *or* to that side, that direction, thither, beyond: **•Ew *wêve* çû** (FS) He went *that way* **•Hirve ber û *wêve* ber / yê di nîvê da Mîr 'Umer [cuhnî/cûnî]** (AZ #3, 73) Stone on this side and stone on *that* / what's in the middle is Prince Omar *[rdl.: ans.: mortar]*; **-ji *ft-î* wêve** (Bw) the other side of, beyond [T -den öte; clq Ar min … u-la-γad ولغد … من]: **•*ji* cisrî *wêve*** (Bw) *the other side of* the bridge/*beyond* the bridge **•ji êrwe *wêwe*** (SK) from here *to there*. {also: wêwe (SK)} [Bw/OK/FS//SK] <hêrve; wêvetir>

wêvetir وێڤەتِر *adv.* 1) on *or* to that side, that direction, thither, beyond; 2) rather: **•Kincên wê ji yên jinekê *wêdetir* weke yên mêrekî bûn** (KS, 39) Her clothes, *rather* than being like those of a woman, were [more] like those of a man. {also: wêdetir (KS)} [Bw//KS] <wêve>

wêwe وێوە (SK) = on that side. See **wêve**.

wicdan وِجدان *f.* **(-a;).** conscience: **•Teȟqîqa madde dê ȟewale-y *wicdan* o inṣafa te keyn, emma ez gelek te'eccubê dikem, bo çî ewan muroêt hingo şahidîyê diden li-ser hingo** (SK 54:611) We shall continue the inquiry in the light of your *conscience* and sense of justice, but I wonder very much why these your own men bear witness against you **•*Wijdana* wî negirt ku teşqelê li Zoroyî bikit** (FS) His *conscience* didn't allow him make problems for Z. {also: wijdan (K/GF/ZF3/FS); wîcdan (Nbh); wîjdan (OK-2)} < Ar wijdān وجدان; Sor wîcdan ویجدان/wîjdan ویژدان [SK/IFb/OK//K/GF/ZF3/FS//Nbh] <îsaf>

wiha وها *adv.* thus, in this way, so: **•P'adşa û wezîr r̄adibin dik'evine dilqê dewrêşa, *wehekê* jî nava şeher diger̄in** (Z-922) The king and vizier go disguise themselves (or, dress up) as dervishes, and *in that way* they wander about the city **•*Wiha* binivîse** (FS) Write it this way/Write it like this. {also: weha (IFb-2/TF); wehe (Z-922/K); [vouha] وها (JJ); <wiha> وها (HH)} {syn: wer; wisa; wilo} [Z-922/K//IFb/HH/GF/ZF3/FS//JJ//TF]

wijdan وِژدان (K/GF/ZF3/FS) = conscience. See **wicdan**.

wila وِلا = so, thus. See **wilo**.

wilayet وِلایەت (SK/ZF) = province. See **wîlayet**.

wilo وِلۆ *adv.* so, such, in that way, thus: **•Gava qundir *wilo* ji bavê xwe re got** (L) When the gourd said *that* [lit. '*thus*'] to its father **•Ne *wilo* ye?** (IFb) Isn't that *so*? {also: ûlo; wila; [vülő] ولو (JJ)} {syn: wer; wiha; wisa} [K/A/JB3/IFb/JJ/GF/TF/ZF3]

winda وِنـــــدا *adj.* lost, missing: **•Wî golikê xwe yê *hinda* dît** (FS) He found his *lost* calf; -**[ji ber] winda bûn** (L) to disappear, vanish {syn: beta vebûn; r̄ed bûn; r̄oda çûn; x̄eware bûn}: **•Lê zivistanê, / wexta berf dik'et, mal bi carekêva bin berfêda *unda dibûn* ... gund bi carekêva *ber ç'ava unda dibû*** (Ba2-3, 213-214) But in winter, when it would snow, the houses *would* completely *disappear* under the snow ... the village *would* completely *vanish from sight*; -**winda bûn** (B): a) to disappear, vanish: **•Heyv di nav 'ewra r̄a *hinda bû*** (FS) The moon *got lost* amid the clouds; b) to be or get lost, go astray, lose one's way: **•Şev tarî bû lewre em *winda bûn*** (Wkt) The night was dark, therefore we *lost our way*; -**winda kirin** (B) to lose, misplace *(vt.)*. {also: hinda II (Z-2/Msr/Snd); unda (B); wenda (GF-2); wunda; [vynda] ونـدا (JJ)} {syn: berza} Cf. Mid P wany = 'lost, destroyed' (M3); Sor wun وون/win ون (=bizir بـزر) = 'mislaid, lost, absent'; Za vinî = 'lost' [K/A/JB3/IFb/JJ/GF/TF//B//Z-2/Msr]

wir وِر *adv.* there: -**li wir** (GF) do. {also: wira (B)} {syn: li wê (derê); ≠ vir I} [K/GF/ZF3//B]

wira وِرا (B) = there. See **wir**.

wirqwirq وِرقورِق (SS) = croaking. See **wîqewîq**.

wisa وِســــــا *adv.* thus, so, in such a way: **•Ezê *usa* bikim, wekî zîanê bidim mêşê** (Dz) I will act *in such a way* as to bring harm to the forest **•Herin wana cîkî *wisa* şerjêkin, li k'u xwêde t'unebe** (Ba) Go slaughter them in (*such*) a place where there is no God **•Tu ne di sindoqê de bûyî? Nemrûd gotê: Belê, *hosa*ye** (GShA, 227) Were you not in a box? Nemrud said "Yes, it is *so* [i.e., that is right]" **•Wana wisa jî kir** (Ba) They did just that (=that very thing). {also: hosa (GShA); usa (B-2); ussa (B-2/IS); ussan (IS); wisan (K/BX-2); wîsa (IFb-2); [vousa وسـا/vousan وســان] (JJ); <wisan> وصـــــــان (HH)} {syn: wer; wiha; wilo} [Ba/A/JB3/IFb/JJ/BX//K//B//HH//GShA]

wisan وِسان (K/BX) = thus, so. See **wisa**.

wî وى *prn. m.* 1) he, it; him, it; his, its; 2) that (m.) *{obl. of **ew** [sing. m.]}*. {also: wîna (GF-2); [vi وى/evi اوى] (JJ)} [Bx/K/JB3/IFb/JJ/SK/GF/TF]

wîcdan ويجدان (Nbh) = conscience. See **wicdan**.

wîjdan ويژدان (OK) = conscience. See **wicdan**.

wîje ويژه (IFb) = literature. See **wêje**.

wîjekar ويژهكار (IFb) = writer. See **wêjevan**.

wîlayet ويــلايــهت *f.* **(-a;-ê).** province, governorate, state: **•Gundek heye li-naw 'eşîreta Sûrçîyan, daxili qeza Akrê ji *wilayeta* Mûsilê, Bicîl dibêjin ê** (SK 50:520) There is a village amid the Surchi tribe, within the district of Akre of *the province of* Mosul, they call it Bijîl **•Mêrdîn *wîlayeta* herî paşdemayî ya Kurdistanê ye** (Nbh 132:12) Mardin is the most backward *province* in Kurdistan. {also: wilayet (SK/ZF); [vilàiet/volaiàt (G). ولايت/vilat ولات] (JJ)} < Ar wilāyah ولاية --> T vilayet [Nbh/K/IFb/Kmc/CS//SK/ZF//JJ] <welat>

wîn وين (Ad) = to be; to become. See **bûn**.

wîna وينا (GF) = him, his, it[s]. See **wî**.

wîne وينه (K[s]) = picture. See **wêne**.

wîqewîq ويقهويق *f.* **(-a;).** croaking *(of frogs)*: **•Beqa *wîqwîq kir*/Beqa *kir wîqwîq*** (FS) The frogs *croaked* **•*Wîqewîq* ji malzarokê bilind dibû** (HYma, 33) *A croaking sound* rose from the womb. {also: wirqwirq (SS); wîqwîq (FJ/FS); wîrqwîrq (GF)} {syn: qîr̄eqîr̄[3]} Sor waqwîq واقــويــق = 'wailing (children), croaking (frogs)' [HYma/K//FJ/FS//GF//SS]

wîqwîq ويقويق (FJ/FS) = croaking. See **wîqewîq**.

wîrqwîrq ويرقويرق (GF) = croaking. See **wîqewîq**.

wîsa ويسا (IFb) = thus, so. See **wisa**.

wîşî ويشى (SK) = bunch of grapes. See **gûşî**.

wîtewît ويــتــهويــت *f.* **(-a;-ê).** chirping, twittering *(of birds)*: **•Wê rojê hewa pir honik bû; li milekî *wîtwîta* şehlûl û bilbilan; li milekî dengê qebqeba kewan bû** (DBgb, 7) That day the weather was very cool; on one side there was *the chirping of* blackbirds and nightingales; on the other side, the sound of cooing doves. {also: wîtwît (DBgb/Wkt/FS)} {syn: ç'ivte-ç'ivt} [DBgb/Wkt/FS//K/CS]

wîtwît ويــتــويــت (DBgb/Wkt/FS) = chirping. See **wîtewît**.

wunda ووندا = lost. See **winda**.

wurz وورز *f.* **().** cedar (tree), bot. *Cedrus*. {also: erz II (F/GF/Wkt); urz (IFb-2/AA/OK)} Cf. Ar arz أرز [IFb/RF/ZF3//OK/AA//F/GF/Wkt]

wuşar ووشار (SS) = pressure. See **fişar**.

wyan ويــــان (-wê-) (SK) = must; to need; to want; to love. See **viyan**.

X خ

xacirgan خاجِرگان, f. (ZF3/Kmc) = iron grill over fire. See **xaçirgan**.

xacirgat خـاجِـرگـات (GW) = iron grill over fire. See **xaçirgan**.

xacîgat خـاجـيـگـات (Kmc) = iron grill over fire. See **xaçirgan**.

xaç/xaç' [K] خــــاچ *m./f.(Zeb/FS/BF)* **(-ê/-a; xêç/-ê).** cross: **-Xaça Sor** (OK) Red Cross. {also: [khatch] خاچ (JJ); <xaç> خاچ (HH)} < Arm xač' խաչ --> T haç [F/A/IFb/B/JJ/HH/OK/Zeb/BF/FSWkt//K]

xaçepirs خاچەپرس *f.* **(-a;-ê).** crossword puzzle. {syn: xaçerêz} [Wlt/RF/RN2/ZF3/BF/FD] <çeperast; serejêr>

xaçerêz خـاچـەرێـز *f.* **(-a;-ê).** crossword puzzle: •**[kovar] pênGAVa 7ê derket... û di dawiyê de jî bi *xaçerêza* xwe ya zext û zor ve hate xemilandin** (kurdigeh.com 28.ii.2012) Issue 7 of [the journal] pênGAV has come out ... and finally it is adorned with its difficult *crossword puzzle*. {also: xaçerêzk (TF)} {syn: xaçepirs} [IFb/ZF3/BF/FD//TF] <apik; mamik>

xaçerêzk خـاچـەرێـزك (TF) = crossword puzzle. See **xaçerêz**.

xaçiran خـاچِـران (GF) = iron grill over fire. See **xaçirgan**.

xaçirgan خاچِرگان *f.(B/ZF3)/m.(FS)* **(;-ê/).** iron grill, often in form of three-legged trivet, on which cooking pots are placed while fire is burning in hearth below: •**Dista goşt giran bû *xaçirgan* hat tewandin** (Wkt) The cauldron of meat grew [so] heavy that *the iron grill* it was on was bent •**Şirînê *xaçirgan* deyna ser kuçikî û mencel deyna ser** (FS) Sh. put *the iron grill* over the fire and placed the cauldron on top of it •***Xaçr̄anê* kuçikî dirêj e** (FS) *The iron grill of* the hearth is long. {also: xacirgan, f. (ZF3/Kmc-2); xacirgat (GW); xacîgat (Kmc); xaçiran (GF); xaçr̄an, m. (FS); xaçringan (ZF3-2); xarcigan (K); xarcigat (K-2); xarcîgat, f. (B)} Cf. T hecirget & haçırget [Iğdır]/haçırkat [Bitlis]/ haçirdek [Ahlat, Bitlis]/hatırcek [Kurtkale, Kars; Pasinler, Erzurum; Erzincan]/haticek [Erzurum]/hatircek [Erzurum; Erzincan; Sivas]/ḥeçirdek [Erciş, Van; Ahlat, Bitlis]/hetircek [Kars; Erzurum; Erzincan; Van] = 'iron grill in various shapes, for putting pots on while cooking over a fire' [tandır üzerine tencere koymaya yarayan, çeşitli biçimde olan demir ızgara] (DS, v. 7, p. 2325) [GW//Wkt/FD/IFb/A/FJ/HH/TF//ZF3//GF//FS/ /Kmc//K//B] <dûstan; kuçik II; sêp'î>

xaçr̄an خـاچـڕان, m. (FS) = iron grill over fire. See **xaçirgan**.

xaçringan خـاچِـرنـگـان (ZF3) = iron grill over fire. See **xaçirgan**.

xadê خادێ (EP-7) = God. See **xwedê**.

xadim خـادِم *f.* **().** 1) {also: [khoudamk] خـدامـك (JJ); <xadim خـادِم/xidam خـدام> (HH)} {syn: carî} female servant, maidservant; 2) [*m.*] {also: [khadim] خـادم (JJ)} eunuch. {also: xedem (Z-3); xidam; xiddam} < Ar xādim خادم = 'servant' --> T hadım = 'eunuch' [Z-3//K/IF/JJ/HH/Wkt/ZF3] <xizmetk'ar>

xag خاگ (IFb) = unripe; naïve. See **xam**.

xaîn خائين (F/B/SK) = traitor. See **xayîn**.

xaînî خائينى (F/B/JJ) = treachery. See **xayîntî**.

xaîntî خائينتى (B) = treachery. See **xayîntî**.

xal I خــــال *m.* **(-ê;-ê** [B]**).** maternal uncle, mother's brother {T dayı; P dā'ī دائـى}. {also: xwal (Bx); [khal] خال (JJ); <xal> خال (HH)} < Ar xāl خال; Sor xał خاڵ; Za xal m. (Todd) {xaltî II} [F/K/A/JB3/ IFb/B/JJ/HH/SK/Rh//Bx] <ap; jinxal; mam; pîlik; xalojn; xaltî; xwarzî>

xal II خـــــال *f.* **(-a;-ê).** 1) {syn: deq[1]; kekmek} birthmark; freckle; beauty spot: •***Xaleka* liser rûyê wî** (BF) *A birthmark* on his face; **-xala sûret** (Ba) do.; 2) {syn: niqitk [2]} point *(in several meanings)*, dot: •**Ez dikarim armanca me di çend *xalan* de şîrove bikim** (Wlt 1:37, 16) I can explain our goals in a couple of points; 3) period, full stop *(punctuation mark: [.])*. {also: xalî I (IF-2); [khal] خال (JJ)} < Ar xāl خال; Sor xał خاڵ [Ba/F/K/A/B/IFb/JJ/JB1-A/GF/TF/Wkt/BF] <nîşan[5]>

xalbendî خـالـبـەنـدى *f.* **(-ya;-yê).** punctuation: •**Wê demê nivîskarekî baş grîngiya *xalbendiyê* jî dizane** (H.H.Denîz. Rêkên rastkirin û pêşvebirina nivîsandinê) Then a good writer knows the importance of punctuation. Sor xałbendî خاڵبەندى [RR/IFb/ZF/Wkt/SS] <bendik II; bêhnok; xal II[3]; xalecot; xalepirs; xêzik>

xalecot خـالـەجـۆت *f.* **(;-ê).** colon *(punctuation mark [:])*: **•Hevok û ravekirina hevokê bi *xalecotê* tên cudakirin** (tirsik.net) The sentence and its explanation are separated by a *colon*. {also: cote xal (SS); cotxal (RZ)} <xal II[2] + cot = 'pair, couple'; Cf. Sor cûtexał جووتەخاڵ *Other proposed terms: duxal; niqtecot.* [tirsik.net/SelîmBiçûk/ZF/Wkt]

xalendor خـالـەنـدۆر (Wkt) = Smyrnium olusatrum. See **xelendor II**.

xalepirs خـالـەپـرس *f.* **().** question mark *(punctuation mark: [?])*: **•Li vir jî wek *xalepirsekê* tête serê mirov ku gelo çawa ev gotin li her derekê ji van deran rastî hev hatine!** (Nbh 133:41) Here too like *a question mark* the question presents itself [lit. 'it comes to one's mind'] how in the world these words have come together from each one of these places! Cf. Sor xałepirsî خـاڵـەپـرسـی *Other proposed terms: nîşandeka pirsê (IFb/ZF); pirsnîşan (ZF/RZ)* [Nbh/SelîmBiçûk]

xalet خالەت (Bsk) = maternal aunt. See **xaltî I**.

xalifîn خـالِـفـیـن *vi.* **(-xalif-).** to err, get lost, go astray, lose one's way: **•Fêrîk lawo, miqatî Sûsîkê be, ewe hela biç'ûke, dibe biweste, paşda bimîne, *bixalife*, tu jê dûr nek'eve, alî wê bike** (Ba2:2, 206) Ferik my son, take care of Susik, she is still small, perhaps she will get tired, fall behind, [or] *get lost*; you stay close to her [lit. 'don't fall far from her'], help her. {also: xelifîn (IFb); [khalifin] خالفين (JJ)} {syn: r̄ê winda kirin} < Ar √x-l-f خلف = 'to be left behind' [Ba2/K/B/JJ//IFb]

xalî I خالی (IF) = freckle. See **xal II**.

xalî II خالی (IFb/B) = carpet. See **xalîçe**.

xalî III خالی = ash(es); soil, dirt. See **xwelî**.

xalîç•e خـالـیـچـە/**xalîç'e** [B] *f.* **(•a;•ê).** carpet, rug; shaggy carpet (JJ) [khalitché]: **•Ewana t'evaxek k'aẍez danîne** [sic] **bin *xalîçê*** (Ba3-1) They put a sheet of paper underneath *the carpet* **•Ç'îya usa bedew dibû, mêriv t'irê *xalîça* Xur̄ustanê ser wî r̄axistine** (Ba2:1, 202) The mountain was so beautiful, people thought that Khurasani *rugs* had been spread out over it. {also: xalî II (IFb-2/B); [khalitché خاليچه/qalitché قاليچه] (JJ); <xalîçe> خـالـیـچـە (HH)} {syn: mehfûr} Cf. P qālī[če] [قالی[چه--> T halı; Sor qałî قاڵی = 'carpet' & qałîçe قاڵیچە = 'rug'; Za xalî *f.* (Todd); Hau qałie *f.* (M4) [F/K/A/JB3/IFb/B/JJ/HH/GF/OK/Ag] <kombar; kulav [3]; r̄axistin; t̲atî>

xalîle خالیله (Ah) = finger cymbal. See **xelîl**.

xalîtî خالیتی (ZF3) = unclehood. See **xaltî II**.

xaloj خالۆژ (IF) = aunt. See **xalojn**.

xalojin خالۆژِن (ZF3/FD) = aunt. See **xalojn**.

xalojn خـالـۆژن *f.* **(-a;-ê).** wife of maternal uncle, aunt: **•Çakêtê xalê min ê şîn bi rastî jî pir lê tê; lê *xalojina* min jê hez nake** (Xalbêhnok çi ye?) My uncle's blue jacket really suits him; but my *aunt* doesn't like it. {also: xaloj (IF); xalojin (ZF3/FD)} {syn: jinxal; pîlik (A/IF)} Cf. Sor xałojin خـاڵـۆژِن; < xal = 'maternal uncle' + jin 'wife' [IF//K/B//ZF3/FD] <amojin; xal I>

xaltî I خـالـتـی *f.* **(-ya;-yê).** maternal aunt, mother's sister. {also: xalet (Bsk); xaltîk (A/K-2); xat; xatî (F/K/B/Wn/Bt/Mş); [khalet] خـالـت(JJ); <xalet> خالت (HH)} <Ar xālah خالة = 'maternal aunt' --> P xāle خـالـه --> T hala = 'paternal aunt'; Za xal f. (Todd); =Sor pûr پـوور [F/K/IF/Rh//Bsk/JJ/HH//A//F/K/ B/ Wn/Bt/Mş] <xal I; xalojn/jinxal/pîlik>

xaltî II خـالـتـی *f.* **(;-yê).** relationship of kinship between a child and his mother's brother, unclehood. {also: xalîtî (ZF3)} [K/B//ZF3] <xal l; xarzî II; xwarzî>

xaltîk خالتیك (A/K) = maternal aunt. See **xaltî I**.

xalxalk خـالـخـالـك *f.(Bw)* **(-a;).** spleen. {syn: dêdik; fater̄eşk; t̲eh̄êl} = Sor sipił سپڵ [Bw/IFb/OK/ZF3/BF/FS]

xalxalok خـالـخـالـۆك *f.* **(-a;-ê).** ladybug, ladybird, lady beetle, zool. *Coccinella*. {also: <xalxalok> خالخالوك (HH)} Sor xałxałoke خاڵخاڵۆکە [Dh/IFb/HH/ GF/OK/ZF3/FS/Wkt]

xam خـام *adj.* 1) {syn: k'al II} unripe, immature *(of melons, tobacco, etc.)* [xang II]; 2) {syn: cahil; naşî; nestêl; nezan; ≠dinyadîtî} naïve, inexperienced, 'greenhorn' [xam/xav]: **•Ûsibî *xame*** (Ba) Joseph is *inexperienced*; 3) untouched, virgin *(fig.)*; 4) raw, uncooked (A/B/Haz); undercooked (B) [xav]: **•goştê *xav*** (B) = a) *raw* meat; b) *undercooked* meat **•nanê *xav*** (B) *underbaked* bread; 5) crude, coarse, rude; indelicate, unbreakable, sturdy [xam]; 6) uncultivated, untilled (land) (B) [xam/xav]; untreated, unprocessed (B) [xav]: **-p'ostê xav/ ç'ermê xav** (B) rawhide, untreated leather. {also: xag (IFb-2); xang II (F-2/IFb-2); xav I (K-2/A/ JB3/B-2/IFb-2/GF-2); xavî (K-2); xaw; [khaw خـاڤ/kham خـام] (JJ); <xav خـاڤ/ xang خـانـگ> (HH)} Cf. Ar/P xām خـام; Sor xam خـام/xaw خـاو; Za xaẍ (Todd) {xam[t]î} [Ba/F/K/IFb/B/JJ/GF//A/JB3/HH/ Haz]<firîk>

xamberdîr خامبەردیر *f.* **(;-ê).** three-year-old barren or dry sheep; ewe which has given birth for the first time (JJ). {also: xemberdîr (FS); [kham beryndyr] خام برندیر (JJ)} < xam + berdîr [EP-8/K/B/ZF3//FS//JJ] <berdîr; mî I>

xame خامە *f./m.(BF)* **(-ya/-yê;).** pen, reed pen, *writing implement*: **-bi xameya** = written by: **•105 sal bi ser weşana yekem Rojnameya Kurdî dibihore ... ku *bi xameya* babê rojnamevaniya Kurdî Miqdad Midhet Bedirxan hatibû dest pê kirin** (pdk-xoybun.com) 105 years have passed since the publication of the first Kurdish newspaper ... which had been started *by* [lit. *'with the pen of'*] Miqdad Midhet Bedirxan, the father of Kurdish journalism. {also: [khamé] (JJ)} {syn: pênûs; qelem} Cf. P xāme خامە = 'pen; stylus; reed'; Sor xame خامە = '(reed) pen' [pdk-xoybûn/K/IFb/JJ/ZF3/BF/FD]

xamî خامی (K/A) = immaturity; naïveté; sturdiness. See **xamtî**.

xamîtî خامیتی (ZF3) = immaturity; naïveté; sturdiness. See **xamtî**.

xamtî خامتی *f.* **(-ya;-yê).** 1) immaturity; 2) inexperience, innocence, naïveté (K/B); 3) sturdiness (of metal) . {also: xamî (K/A); xamîtî (ZF3-2)} [B/ZF3//K/A] <xam>

xan I خان *f.* **(-a;-ê).** inn, coaching inn, khan, caravanserai. {also: [khan] خان (JJ); <xan> خان (HH)} {syn: qonax [2]} Cf. Ar/P xān خان, T han = 'inn'; Sor xan خان [Ba2/JR/K/IFb/B/JJ/HH/GF] <ûtêl>

xan II خان (JB1-A) = house. See **xanî**.

xandin خانِدِن (M-Zx/Bw) = to read. See **xwendin**.

xandingeh خانِدِنگەه (BF) = school. See **xwendegeh**.

xanê خانێ *adj.* visible; apparent, evident, clear, obvious: **-hatin xanê** (XF) to be visible, apparent, evident, to appear: **•T'une cîkî, wekî xwedê *neê xanê*** (BA-1, #3) There is no place in which God *does not appear. The following expressions are made with this construction*: **-'Erdêva naê xanê** (XF) He is very short (of stature) [lit. 'he is not to be seen on earth']; **-Serî-binî naê xanê** (XF) It goes on forever, is endless [lit. 'its head and end are not to be seen'] {also: xwanî (GF); xwuyanê (F)} {syn: aşkere; berç'av II; diyar; k'ifş; xuya} [Ad/Z-1/K//GF//F] <xuyan I>

xang I خانگ (Bg) = sister. See **xûşk**.

xang II خانگ (F/IFb/JJ) = unripe; naïve. See **xam**.

xanik خانِك *m./f.(Dh/Wkt)* **(-ê/-a;).** small, low round table used for rolling dough to make bread: **•Şirînê hevîr li ser *xwanikê* peȟn kir** (FS) Sh. flattened the dough on *the little table*; **-xanka nanî** (Dh) do. {also: xwanik (Wkt/FS)} {syn: xonçe} Sor xuwan خووان = 'table (esp. table, tray or mat spread for meal)' [=Kurm sifre]; = Sor pine پِنە & derxon دەرخۆن (Kerkûk) [Bw/GF/OK//Wkt/FS] <nan; sêl; tîrok>

xanim خانِم *f.* **(-a;-ê).** lady, madam; Mrs. *(refers to a married woman, whereas **xatûn** is used for an unmarried woman)* (Zeb); wife of an agha, beg, etc.: **•Gote jina xo, "*xanim*." *Xanimê* got, "Belê, ez qurban"** (SK 23:217) He said to his wife, "*My lady*." *The lady* said, "Yes, at your service." {also: xanum (F); [khanoum] خانم (JJ); <xanim> خانم (HH)} Cf. P xānum خانم (of Tatar origin); Sor xanim خانِم [FT/K/A/IFb/B/HH/SK/GF/TF//F/JJ] <jin; xatûn>

xanî خانی *m.* **(-yê; xênî).** 1) house; dwelling; building--*this word is used for the physical structure, whereas **mal** = home, the mental concept (home)*: **•Aqû p'êxember ȓabû ser *xênî*** (Ba) Jacob the prophet got up on the roof [lit. 'rose to the top *of the house*'] **•*Xanî* bê karîte ava na be** (BF) *A house* without beams cannot stand **•Zava çû ser *xênî*** (AB) The groom went up on top *of the house* [i.e., to the roof]; 2) roof (BK). {also: xan II (JB1-A); [khani] خانی (JJ); <xanî> خانی (HH)} Cf. P xāne خانە; Sor xane خانە & xanû خانوو; Hau yane *m.* (M4). [BK/K/A/JB3/IFb/B/JJ/HH/SK/GF/TF] <mal I; mendele; qonax>

xan-man خان مان/**xanman** خانمان [K] *m.* **(-ê; xên-mên [B]).** 1) houses, buildings; residence: **•Borî bimbareke k'ûçe-k'ûçe Memê digeȓîne, der *xan-manê* Qeret'ajdînva dertîne** (EP-7) Blessed Bor smoothly transports Mem, brings him to *the residence of* Qeretajdin; 2) house and home; family, household. {also: xanûman (IFb/GF)} Sor xan-u-man خان و مان [EP-7/B//K//IFb/GF] <xanî>

xanoq خانۆق **().** type of black grape. [Msr] <tirî>

xanot خانۆت (M-Ak) = loom. See **xanût**.

xanum خانوم (F) = lady. See **xanim**.

xanûman خان و مان (IFb/GF) = residence; household. See **xan-man**.

xanût خانووت *f./m.(FS)* **(-a-ê;-ê/).** weaver's loom; weaver's shop (Bw): **•Cû û cot, Kurmanc û *xanût*, 'Ereb û rîvaz** (Zeb) Jews and plows, Kurds and *looms*, Arabs and rhubarb *[adage regarding ethnic identity]* **•Ew çû maleka cûa, gotê, 'Min veşêrin.' Cûa gotê, 'Were, here di**

korka *xanotê* da' (M-Ak #673, 304) He went to a household of Jews and said to them, 'Hide me'. The Jews said to him, 'Come and get into the pit *of the loom*' •**Wê *xanûtê* xwe danî** (FS) She set up her *loom*. {also: xanot (M-Ak)} {syn: t'evn} < NENA khânûtâ ܚܢܘܬܐ = 'loom' (Maclean) < Arc ḥanūṯā חנותא = 'tent, esp. tradesman's shop' & Syr ḥānūṯā ܚܢܘܬܐ = 'arched chamber, cell, stall, booth' [Zeb/IFb/GF/OK/FS//M-Ak]

xap خـــاپ *f.* **(-a;-ê).** 1) deceit, cheating, fraud, trick: •**Bi vê *xapê* me zêdetir zirar ji yên din dît** (www.amidakurd.net 7.xii.2008) Due to this *trick* we suffered more damage [lit. 'saw more harm'] than the others •***Xapa* wî sergirt** (FS) His *deceit* was successful [or, had an effect]; 2) {syn: motik} dummy egg in a chicken coop, to keep hens laying eggs, decoy. [Qrj/K/IFb/GF/TF/AD/FS/BS/Wkt/G/FD]

xapan خـــاپـــان (FS) = to be fooled; to be wrong. See **xapîn**.

xapandin خـــاپـــانـــدِن *vt.* **(-xapîn-).** to trick, fool, cheat, deceive: •**Melle, te *ez xapandim*** (Dz) Mullah, you *tricked me* •**Wî Behrem bi axaftinên xweş *xapand*** (FS) He *fooled* B. with nice words; **-xwe tiştekîda xapandin** (XF) to pretend to be busy doing stg., to soldier: •**Hema wî wextî Bek'o qesta *xwe* tengê hespa xwe*da dixapand*** (Z-1) At the same time, Beko *pretended to be busy with* his horse's saddle girth. {also: [khapandin] خـپـانـدیـن (JJ); <xapandin خـاپـانـدن (dixapîne) (دخـاپـیـنـه)> (HH)} {syn: lêbandin} Cf. W Arm xapel խաբել = 'to deceive' [Dz/F/K/A/JB3/IFb/B/JJ/HH/GF/TF/BF/FS/FD] <delk'; xapîn>

xapiyan خـــاپـــیـــان (JB3/JJ/FS) = to be fooled; to be wrong. See **xapîn**.

xapîn خـــاپـــیـــن *vi.* **(-xap-).** to be fooled, tricked, deceived, cheated: •**Baram *bi* axaftinên Zoroyî *xapa*** (FS) B. *was fooled by* Z.'s words •**...Gur çawa *xapya*** (J) ... How the wolf *was tricked.* {also: xapan (FS); xapiyan (JB3/FS-2); [khapiian] خـپـیـان (JJ)} {syn: lêbyan (SK)} Cf. W Arm xapel խաբել = 'to deceive' [F/K/IFb/B/GF/TF/BF/FD//JB3/JJ//FS] <xapandin>

xapînok خـاپـیـنـۆك *m.&f.* **(-ê/ ;).** 1) {syn: k'ose I[2]} trickster, cheat, swindler: **-xapînokê jinan** (ZF) hunter of women, lothario; 2) [*adj.*] deceitful: **-Roviyê xapînok** (SW1, #7, 24) The deceitful fox. {syn: xapok (FJ-2); xapxapok (B-2); [khapkhapouk] خپخپوك (JJ)} [SW1/K/B/IFb/FJ/GF/TF/ZF/CS//JJ]

xapok خاپۆك (FJ) = trickster; deceitful. See **xapînok**.

xapxapok خـــاپـــخـــاپـــۆك (B) = trickster; deceitful. See **xapînok**.

xar I خـــــار (K/Z-1/SK/JJ) = down; low; crooked. See **xwar**.

xar II خار (DM) = flock, herd. See **ẍar II**.

xar III خار (IFb) = gallop. See **ẍar I**.

xar IV خار (IFb/TF) = marble ball. See **ẍar III**.

xar̄andin خـــاڕانـــدِن (Z-2) = to urge on, spur on. See **xurandin**[2].

xarayî خارایی (B) = crookedness; slope. See **xwarayî**.

xarcigan خـــارجِـــگـــان (K) = iron grill over fire. See **xaçirgan**.

xarcigat خـــارجِـــگـــات (K) = iron grill over fire. See **xaçirgan**.

xarcîgat خـارجـیـگـات, f. (B) = iron grill over fire. See **xaçirgan**.

xarin خارِن (Ba/J/Ag) = to eat; food. See **xwarin**.

xaringe[h] خـــارِنـــگـــه[ه] (Zx) = restaurant. See **xwaringeh** [2].

xarî خاری (SK) = crookedness; slope. See **xwarayî**.

xarnup خارنوپ (Ah) = carob. See **xernûf**.

xaromar خارۆمار (K) = crooked. See **xwaro-maro**.

xaro maro خـــارۆ مـــارۆ (IFb) = crooked. See **xwaro-maro**.

xarovar (Zeb/Dh) خـــارۆڤـــار = crooked. See **xwaro-maro**.

xarûz خـــاروز *m./f.(ZF3)* **().** string of dried nuts, for winter use: •**Wê *xarûzekê* gûza çêkir** (FS) She made a string of nuts. {also: <xarûz> خـــــاروز (HH)} {syn: gelwaz; şaran} < Arc ḥaraz חרז = 'to string beads' & Syr ḥaraz ܚܪܙ = 'to string, perforate for stringing together, as pearls for a necklace', & NENA x-r-z/γ-r-z = 'to string (beads) (Sabar:Dict) [Btm/Grc/HH/GF/ZF3/FS/FD] <benî II[2]; meşlûr>

xarz خارز (B) = nephew or niece. See **xwarzî**.

xarza خارزا (SK) = nephew or niece. See **xwarzî**.

Xarzan خارزان. region of Sason and Ḧazo (Kozluk) in the northern part of the province of Batman, Kurdistan of Turkey: •***Xerzan* him navê rûbarekê, him navê herêmekê û him jî navê xelkê li herêma *Xerzan* rûdinin e** (Wkp) *Xerzan [Garzan]* is both the name of a river and the name of a region, as well as the name of the people who live in the *Xerzan* region. {also: Xerzan (IF/Wkp)} [Haz//IF/Wkp] <Xarzî III>

xarzî I خارزی (IF) = nephew or niece. See **xwarzî**.

xarzî II خـارزی (B) = relationship between a child and his or her mother's brother. See **xwarzîtî**.

Xarzî III خـــــــــــارزی **().** name of a Kurdish tribe inhabiting the region of Sason and Ḧazo (Kozluk) in the northern part of the province of Batman (formerly part of Sêrt [Siirt]), Kurdistan of Turkey. {also: Xerzî (Wkp)} [Haz//Wkp] <Xarzan>

xarztî خـارزتـی (B) = relationship between nephew or niece and maternal uncle. See **xwarzîtî**.

xas خـــــاس *adj.* 1) {syn: t'aybetî} special, particular: **•Birahîm mirovekî *xas* e** (GShA, 230) Ibrahim is a *special* (holy) person; **-xas û am** (K) the masses, hoi polloi; 2) {syn: *bihadar; binerx; bi qîmet} precious, high-quality: **•Ezê gemîê we t'ijî malê *xas* bikim ... lêkir zêr̄ û zîv, çiqa malê *xas*** ... (HCK-2, 182) I will fill your ship with *precious* possessions ... he put in gold and silver, and many *precious* possessions; 3) choice, select. {also: [khas] خــاص (JJ)} < Ar xāṣṣ خــاصّ = 'special, private'; Sor xas خـــاس = 'good' [HCK/GShA/K/B/A/IFb/GF/JJ/SK/CS]

xasî خاسی (F/K) = mother-in-law. See **xesû**.

xasok خاسۆك (FS/Wkt) = shrewd. See **xasûk**.

xasokî خاسۆكی (Wkt) = shrewdness. See **xasûktî**.

xastin خـاسـتِـن (-xaz-) (SK) = to want; to request. See **xwestin**.

xasûk خـــاســـووك *adj.* shrewd, cunning, sly: **•Eger heftêsalî be, wê mîna roviyan *xasûk* be** (ZZ-7, 268) If he is 70 years old, he will be *sly* like a fox [lit. foxes] **•Ew zelamekê *xasok* e** (FS) He is a *shrewd* fellow. {also: xasok (FS/Wkt)} {xasûk[t]î} [ZZ/IFb/GF/Kmc/ZF//FS/Wkt]

xasûkî خـــاســـووكـــی (Kmc/ZF) = shrewdness. See **xasûktî**.

xasûktî خـاسـووكـتـی *f.* **(-ya;).** shrewdness, cunning, slyness: **•Lêbelê dema ko rovî wê *xasûktiya* zilam dibîne** ... (ZZ-3, 149) But when the fox sees that cunning of man ... {also: xasokî (Wkt); xasûkî (Kmc/ZF)} [ZZ//Kmc/ZF//Wkt]

xat خات = maternal aunt. See **xaltî I**.

xatir/xat'ir [JB1-S] خـــاتِـر *m.(K/B)/f.(JB1-A&S/SK)* **(-ê/-a; xêtir/).** 1) good will, benevolence; favor: **-xatir xwestin** = to take one's leave: **•Hakim suwar bû û *xatir ji* mala xwe û ji mijlisa xwe *xwest*** (L) The ruler mounted [his horse] and *took his leave of* his family and friends; **-bi xatirê te** (IFb)/**bi xatira te** (JB1-A)/**xatira te** (SK) good bye {said by a guest to signal his intention to leave, to which the host responds by saying **oxir be**, qv. [cf. T Alla[h'a ı]smarladık, to which the reply is Güle güle & Ar bi-xāṭirkum بـخـاطـركـم, to which the reply is ma'a al-salāmah [مـع الـسـلامـة]}; 2) respect, honor (B); 3) remembrance; sake (SK): **-bo xatira** (SK) for the sake of. {also: [khatir] خاطر (JJ); <xatir> خاطر (HH)} < Ar xāṭir خاطر = 'idea, desire, sake'; Sor xatir خـاتِـر [K/JB3/IFb/B/JJ/HH/JB1-A&S/SK/GF/TF]

xatî خـــاتـــی (F/K/B/Wn/Bt/Mş) = maternal aunt. See **xaltî I**.

xatûn خـاتـوون *f.* **(-a;-ê).** (noble) woman, lady; Miss, *used largely for unmarried women, whereas **xanim** refers to married women* (Zeb): **•Ya *xatûna* delal** (L) My dear lady [maîtresse]. {also: [khatun] خـاتـون (JJ); <xatûn> خـاتـون (HH)} Cf. P xātūn خاتون; T hatun; Sor xatû خاتوو (title)/xatûn خـــاتـــوون [F/K/A/JB3/IFb/B/JJ/HH/JB1-A&S/GF/TF] <jin; xanim>

xav I خـــاڤ (K/A/JB3/B/IFb/JJ/HH/GF/Haz) = unripe; naïve. See **xam**.

xav II خاڤ (GF) = woman's head scarf. See **xavik**.

xavik خـاڤِـك *f.* **(-a;-ê).** 1) woman's head scarf, *made of thin gauze*: **•Ezê bi *xavika* sipî, dersoka sipî, bême daweta te jî, gidîyano** (FS:Miḧemed 'Arifê Cizîrî "Gidî, gidîyano") I will come to your wedding too, in a white *head scarf*, a white kerchief **•Jinikê *xavik* bi destê xwe yê çepê bir ber devê xwe** (MG/Şnx) With her left hand, the woman brought *the scarf* before her mouth; 2) thin layer, membrane, film, rind, skin: **-xavika penêr** (Wkt) rind on cheese; **-xavika şîr** (Wkt) skin on milk. {also: xav II (GF-2); [khaw] خـــاڤ (JJ); <xavik> خـــاڤـك (HH)} [MG/A/IFb/GF/HH/ZF/Hej/FS/Wkt/G/CS//JJ] <[1] hêratî; ḧibrî; k'ofî; laç'ik; p'oşî; t'emezî; [2] to I>

xavî خاڤی (K) = unripe; naïve. See **xam**.

xavlî خاڤلی (IFb) = towel. See **xawlî**.

xavlû خاڤلوو (IFb) = towel. See **xawlî**.

xaw خاو = unripe; naïve. See **xam**.

xawlî خـاولـی *f.* **(-ya;-yê).** towel: **•Wî bi *xawlîyê* leşê xwe zuha kir** (FS) He dried his body with a towel. {also: xavlî (IFb-2); xavlû (IFb); xewlî (Wkt-2)} {syn: p'êjgîr} < T havlu; Sor xawlî خاولی [Bw/K(s)/OK/SS/FS/Wkt/FD/G//IFb] <mêzer>

xax خـاخ *f.* **().** 1) {syn: 'et'ib; 'eyb; fedî; fehêt; r̄ûr̄eşî; sosret [2]; şerm; şermezarî} disgrace, scandal: **-kirin xax** (IFb) to disgrace: **•Ew dêlika çawa peran ji te digirê! ... Bi xwedê, ku ez ji nava**

van nivînan rabim, ezê wê *bikime xax*! (Ardû, 13) How can that bitch take money from you! … By God, when I get up from this bed, I *will make* her *a disgrace*; 2) {syn: bela I; gosirmet} [*m.* **(-ê;).**] trouble, misfortune: **•Serê wî k'ete *xaxê* giran** (K/ZF3/FS) He got into big *trouble*. [Ardû/K/IFb/CS/ZF3/FS/FD/G] <hetk>

xay I خاى (Z-1) = owner, master. See **xwedî**.

xay II خاى (FS) = salt. See **xwê**.

xayin خاين (IFb/JJ/HH) = traitor. See **xayîn**.

xayî خايى = owner, master. See **xwedî**.

xayîn خايين *m.* **(-ê;).** traitor: **•"De lêxin, lêxin birano lêxin, *xayînê* mezin axa û şêxin"** (song of Hozan Dilgeş, 1980) "Beat them, beat them brothers, the aghas and sheikhs are the big[gest] *traitors*". {also: xaîn (F/B-2/SK); xayin (IFb); [khàin] خاين (JJ); <xayin> خاين (HH)} {syn: mixenet} <Ar xā'in خائن; Sor ẍayen غاين = 'perfidious'; 'traitor' (K2) {xaînî; xa[y]în[t]î; xiyanet}[Wlt/K/B//F/SK//IFb/JJ/HH] <xwefiroş>

xayînî خايينى (K/B/Wkt) = treachery. See **xayîntî**.

xayîntî خايينتى *f.* **(-ya;-yê).** treachery, deceit, perfidy. {also: xaînî (F/B-2); xaîntî (B-2); xayînî (K-2/B-2/Wkt); [khàini] خاينى (JJ)} {syn: mixenetî; xiyanet} [K/B/ZF3//F/JJ//Wkt] <xayîn>

xazginçî خازگِنچى (Ag) = matchmaker; marriage broker, go-between. See **xwazgîn**.

xazgîn خازگين = matchmaker; marriage broker, go-between. See **xwazgîn**.

xazgînî خازگينى (Z-2) = asking for a girl's hand in marriage. See **xwezgînî I**.

xazik خازِك (ZZ-7) = spit, saliva. See **xwezî II**.

xazil خازِل (F) = if only! See **xwezî I**.

xazî خازى (IFb) = spit, saliva. See **xwezî II**.

xazok خازۆك (Bw) = beggar. See **xwazok**.

xazoqe خازۆقه (FS) = stake, stick. See **qazux**.

xebat خەبات *f.* **(-a;-ê).** 1) {syn: îş; şuxul} work, labor: **•Li salên 1957-58 min dest bi *xebata* hunerî kir** (WM 1:4, 16) In the years 1957-58 I began my artistic *work*; 2) {syn: k'eft û left; p'êk'ol} struggle: **•Wî *xebateka* dûr û dirêj dijî zordarîyê *kir*** (FS) He *struggled* long and hard against oppression; 3) effort, activity. {also: xevat; [khebat] خباط (JJ); <xebat> خبات (HH)} *For etymology see* ***xebitîn***. Sor xebat خەبات= 'effort' [F/K/A/JB3/IFb/B/JJ/HH/SK/GF/TF/FS] <pale; xebatker; xebitandin; xebitîn>

xebatçî خەباتچى (K) = worker. See **xebatk'ar**.

xebathez خەباتهەز (ZF3) = diligent. See **xebatĥiz**.

xebatĥiz خەباتحِز *adj.* diligent, industrious, hard working: **•Slo … gelekî [x]ebatĥizî ĥelale** (HCK-2, 195) Silo … is extremely industrious. {also: xebathez (ZF3)} {syn: qoçax; xebatk'ar[2]} xebat + ĥiz/ĥez [HCK/B//ZF3]

xebatîn خەباتين (A) = to work. See **xebitîn**.

xebatk'ar خەباتكار *m.* **(-ê;).** 1) {syn: k'arker; p'ale; r̄encber} worker, workman, laborer; 2) [*adj.*] {syn: qoçax; xebatĥiz} diligent, hard working. {also: xebatçî (K-2); xebatker ([1] K/A; [2] JB3/JJ); xevatçî (B-2); xevatk'ar (B-2); [khebat-kar خباط كار/ khebat-ker خباطكر] (JJ); <xebatker> خباتكر (HH)} {xebatk'arî (K)} [Haz/K/A/IFb/B/GF/FS//JB3/JJ/HH] <îş; şuxul; xebat; xebitîn; xebitandin>

xebatker خەباتكەر (K/A) = worker; (JB3/JJ) =diligent. See **xebatk'ar**.

xeber خەبەر *f.(F/K/B)/m.(JB1-A)* **(-a/;-ê/).** 1) {syn: cab; nûçe (neol)} (piece of) news, information; 2) {syn: gilî I[1]; gotin; p'eyiv; soz; şor} spoken words: **•Eger *xebera* te derew be, ezê şûrekî li stuyê te dim, / Serê te ji gewdê te biqetînim** (Z-2, 68) If *what you say* is a lie, I will take a sword to your neck, / I will sever your head from your body; **-ji xebera *fk-ê* derk'etin** (XF) to disobey; **-xeber dan** = a) to talk, speak {syn: axaftin; mijûl dan; p'eyivîn; qise kirin (Ks); şteẍilîn}; b) to scold, bawl out: **•Bavê wî *jê re xeber dan*** (L) His father *scolded him* [lit. 'said words to him']; **-Xebera teye** (K)/**Xeberî te ye** (Bw/Bar) You are right or correct: **•R̄ast *xebera teye*** (J) do. **•Wellah, *xebera wî ye*** (L) By God, *he's right* **•Wellahî, *xebera* mêvanê me *ye*** (L) By God, our guest *is right*; **-Xeber were ve** (Zeb) Let's pretend I never said anything [lit. 'may the words return (to me)']; 3) [*pl.*] {syn: ç'êr̄; dijûn I; ne'let; nifir̄; qise[3]; sixêf} verbal abuse, swearing, cuss words, insult; dirty words (Bw). {also: [khaber] خبر (JJ); <xeber> خبر (HH)} < Ar xabar خبر --> T haber = 'piece of news'; Sor xeber خەبەر = 'information, news, message' [F/K/JB3/IFb/B/HH/JB1-A/SK/GF/OK//JJ] <bêje; lavz; pirs>

xebernam•e خەبەرنامە *f.* **(•a;•ê).** dictionary. {also: xeberneme} {syn: ferheng} [F/K/B/SC]

xeberneme خەبەرنەمە = dictionary. See **xebername**.

xebitandin خەبِتاندِن *vt.* **(-xebitîn-).** 1) {syn: bi kar anîn; 'emilandin} to use, make use of, employ; 2) to cause to work. {also: xevitandin; [khabitandin]

خبطاندين (JJ); <xebitandin خبتاندن (dixebitîne) (دخبتينه)> (HH)} [K/JB3/IFb/B/JJ/HH/GF/TF//F] <xebitîn>

xebitîn خەبتين *vi.* **(-xebit-).** 1) to work: **•"Daê, k'î *xebitî*?" go: "Lawo, ez *xebitîm*, tu *xebitî*!"** (J) "Mom, who *worked* [today]?" she said: "My son, I *worked*, [and] you *worked*!" **•*Dixebitin* em her gav** (AB) *We work* all the time **•Seȟeta min *naxebite*** (B) My clock *doesn't work*; 2) to struggle. {syn: k'ar [II] kirin; şixulîn} {also: xebatîn (A); xevitîn; [khabetin] خبطين (JJ); <xebitîn خبتين (dixebite) (دخبته)> (HH)} <Syr √ḥ-p-ṭ: ḥpēṭ ܚܦܛ = 'diligent, assiduous, painstaking' & eṯḥapaṭ ܐܬܚܦܛ = 'to take pains, endeavor, be diligent; to work in'; NENA khpaa-taa ܚܦܛܐ = 'to urge on; to be diligent' (Oraham); Za xeftyenã [xeftyayiş] = 'to work' (Todd) [F/K/JB3/IFb/B/HH/*SK/GF/TF//A//JJ] <îş; p'ale; şuxul; xebat; xebitandin>

xebînet خەبينەت *f.* **(-a;-ê).** 1) regrettable cirumstance or condition, a pity, a shame; 2) *interj.* What a pity! What a shame!: **•*Heyf û xebînet e*! Va roviyek li vir miriye!** (ZZ-4, 203) *What a crying shame*! There's a fox here who has died! {syn: ȟeyf [2]; mixabin} Cf. Ar γabīnah غبينة = 'deceit, imposition' (Hava) [ZZ/GF/TF/RZ/FS]

xebîs خەبيس (CB/JJ/HH) = type of helva. See **xebûs**.

xebûs خەبووس/خەبويس *f.* **(-a;-ê).** type of helva, a sweet pastry [T cevizli helva]. {also: xebîs (CB); [khabis] خبيص (JJ); <xebîs> خبيس (HH)} Cf. Ar xabīṣah خبيصة = 'jelly-like sweet'. *For recipe, see CB, p. 94* [Hk//JJ/HH/CB] <arxavk; helva>

xecxecok I خەجخەجۆك *m./f.(FS)* **().** newt, small salamander, zool. *Triturus*; with round yellow and black spots (Zeb). {also: <xecxecok> خەجخەجۆك (Hej)} [Zeb/IFb/OK/Hej/FS]

xedar خەدار *adj.* 1) cruel; ferocious; harsh: **-xedar kirin** = a) to be cruel to, torture: **•Ȟeta hûn Memê birîndar kin, / Ezê sedî bikujim, dusidî *xedar kim*** (Z-1) If you harm Mem, I'll kill 100 [and] torture 200; ?b) to destroy, lay waste to; 2) dangerous, incurable, deadly, mortal: **-birîndarê xedar** (ZF3) severely or mortally wounded; 3) treacherous, traitorous (K). {also: xeddar (IFb); xeder (K); xidar (Z-2)} Cf. Ar γaddār غدّار = 'deceitful' {xedarî} [Z-1/JB3/B//ZF3/K//Z-2//IFb]

xedarî خەدارى *f.* **(-ya;-yê).** 1) harshness; ferocity; cruelty; 2) {syn: metirsî; talûke; xeter} danger. {also: xeddarî (IFb)} [B/GF/ZF3/Wkt//IFb] <xedar>

xeddar خەددار (IFb) = cruel; dangerous. See **xedar**.

xeddarî خەددارى (IFb) = cruelty; danger. See **xedarî**.

xedem خەدەم (Z-3) = maidservant; eunuch. See **xadim**.

xeder خەدەر (K) = cruel; dangerous. See **xedar**.

xef خەف *adj.* secret, covert: **•Ji te *xef* dibê, ji Xudê *xef* nabê** (HR 4:5) It is *hidden* from you, it cannot be *hidden* from God; **-[bi] xef** (K/JR) secretly, covertly {syn: bi dizî; dizîka}; **-xwe xef kirin** (Rnh) to hide o.s. *(vi.)* {syn: telîn; xwe veşartin}: **•Li nav dara gula de *xwe xef bike*** (Rnh 2:17, 308) *Hide* behind the rosebush. {also: [khef] خف (JJ); <xef> خف (HH)} <Ar √x-f-y خفى = 'to hide, conceal' [JR/K/IFb/JJ/HH/GF/ZF]

xef•ik خەفِك *f.* **(•ka; •[i]kê).** trap, snare *(for small animals and birds)*: **•Çûçik ket *xefkê*** (FS) The sparrow fell *into the trap*; **-xefka mişkan** (Bw) mouse trap: **•Wî mişkek bi *xefkê* girt** (FS) He caught a mouse in *the trap*. {also: xefk (TF/GF); xepik I (Zeb-2/AA); <xefik> خفك (HH)} Cf. Ar faxx فخّ = 'trap' [Bw/Zeb/K/A/IFb/B/HH/ZF3/BF/FS//GF/TF//AA] <dav I; sîte; telhe; tepik I>

xefk خەفك (TF/GF) = trap. See **xefik**.

xeftan خەفتان *m.* **(-ê;).** caftan, kind of women's dress worn over shalvar (baggy pants) [Cf. T üçetek]; garment worn over the shirt and held in place with a belt; outer garment with full-length sleeves [Ar qabā' قباء] (HH): **•*Xeftanê* wê s̱or e** (FS) Her *caftan* is red. {also: [h'aftān] خفتان (JJ); <xiftan> خفتان (HH)} [HM/K/A/IFb/JJ/GF/PS/FS//HH]

xeîdîn خەئيدين (F) = to be furious. See **xeyidîn**.

xeîset خەئيسەت (F) = character[istic]; habit. See **xeyset**.

xeîsetnav خەئيسەتناڤ (F) = adjective. See **xeysetnav**.

xela خەلا *f.* **(-ya;-yê).** famine, hunger, starvation; shortage, dearth *(of food, etc.)*: **•Kuȓê wî jî bêma'rîfet bûn, wana şeherê bavê xwe gihyandine *xelayê*** (Ba3) His sons were rude, they brought *famine* upon their father's city **•Vir bû *xelayîke* ussa, ku dê weledê xwe davît** (Ba3) There was such a [great] *famine* here, that mothers threw their children (=miscarried). {also: xelayî (K/B); ẍela (JB1-S); [khelaï] خلاى (JJ); <ẍela> غلا (HH)} Cf. Ar γalā' غلاء = 'high cost, high price' [Ba3/A/JB3/IFb/GF/TF//K/B/JJ//HH/JB1-S] <birçîtî; nêz I>

xelamûr خەلاموور, m. (GF/FJ) = glowing ashes. See **helemor**.

xelan I خەلان (IFb) = to be upset (stomach). See **ẍelîn**.

xelan II خەلان (IFb/HH) = to be sprained. See **xelyan**.

xelandin خەلاندِن *vt.* **(-xelîn-).** to sprain, dislocate, twist *(ankle, etc.)*: **•Û heke bi lengê êkî girtiba, lengê wî *dixeland*** (GShA, 226) And when he got hold of someone's leg, he *would sprain* it. {also: <xelandin> خلاندن (HH)} Cf. Ar xala'a خلع = 'to wrench, dislocate (a joint)' [GShA/IFb/GF/TF/HH/SS] <xelyan>

xelas خەلاس *adj.* 1) {syn: aza I; rizgar; serbest} free, exempt: **-ji *fk-ê/ft-î* xelas bûn** (IFb): a) to get rid of, be done with {syn: vehesîn[2]}: **•Bela hakim serê min jêbike, ez *ji* vî halî *xelas bibim*!** (L) Let the prince chop off my head, [just so long as] I'*m done with* this business!; b) to be saved, rescued; **-xelas kirin** (IFb/ZF): a) to finish **•Bûkeke cahil şuxulê xwe *xilas kirye*** (Dz) A young woman *finished* [doing] her work; b) to rescue, save {syn: qurtar kirin}: **•Vê neqlê jî te *ez* ji ḧalê wî ḧûtî *xilas kirim*, û ez ji dareke wî xilas bûm** (HR 3:79) This time you *have rescued me* from the situation of that monster, and I have been saved from his pestering; **-yaxa xwe [ji] *kesekî* xilas kirin** (K)/**xwe jê xlaz kirin** (HCK) to get rid of: **•Belki boẍ lêxe bikuje, *yaxa* pîrê *jê xilasbe*** (J) Maybe the bull will strike him and kill him, [so that] the old woman *will be rid of him* [lit. 'the collar of the old woman will be rid of him'] **•K'eçkê kir nekir, *xwe jê xlaz nekir*** (HCK-3, #2, 20) No matter what the girl did, she *couldn't get rid of him* [or, free herself of him]; 2) finished, over, terminated (JB1-A&S). {also: xilas (Dz/SK); xilaz (B/Z-1); xlaz (HCK); [khelas] خلاص (JJ); <xelas-> خلاص (HH)} < Ar xalāṣ خلاص = 'rescue, also clq finishing, getting rid of'; Sor xelas خەلاس = 'finished; freed' [L/K/JB3/IFb/JB1-A&S/GF/ZF//JJ/HH//Dz/SK//B/Z-1]

xelasî خەلاسى *f.* **(-ya;-yê).** 1) end; termination, conclusion, ending; 2) {syn: felat; rizgarî} rescue, deliverance, riddance, salvation: ***•Xelasîya* te ji destê min tune** (L) You can't get rid of me [lit. 'There is no *salvation* for you from my hand']. {also: xelazî; xilasî (Wkt)} {syn: felat} [L/K/ZF3//Wkt]

xelat/xelat' [JB1-S] خەلات *f./m.(SK/JB1-S)* **(-a/;-ê/).** 1) { syn: perû [1]} reward: **•Her kesê mizgînîya teyrî bo min bînît ez dê *xelatekî* bi keyfa wî dem ê** (SK 29:261) Whoever brings me the good news of the bird I shall give him *a reward* [or, present] which will please him; 2) { syn: dayîn II; diyarî; perû [2]; pêşk'êş} gift, present (K/A/JB3/Kp): **-xelatê pinyanişî** (Hk/Zeb) a gift which the giver takes back (cf. 'Indian giver'); 3) robe of honor (HH); coat (JJ/JB1-S). {also: [khelat/khalāt] خلات (JJ); <xelat> خلات (HH)} < Ar xil'ah خلعة = 'robe of honor' --> P xal'at خلعت; Sor xełat خەڵات = 'gift, reward (to inferior)' [J/FK-eb/A/JB3/IFb/B/JJ/HH/ SK/GF/TF/Kp//JB1-S]

xelayî خەلايى (K/B) = famine; shortage. See **xela**.

xelazî خەلازى = end; rescue. See **xelasî**.

xelboqe خەلبۆقە (Kmc) = slipknot. See **xerboqe**.

xelek خەلەك *f.* **(-a;-ê).** ring, hoop, loop; circle; curl; arc: **•Ji Stembolê min guhark'ekê kirîye guhî ji batmanekê, *xeleqa* wê du min e, nala asênî** (JB1-A, #139) In Istanbul I put in his ear an earring that weighed a batman, *the hoop of* which is two maunds, shaped like a horseshoe **•Wextê hingo nêçîr îna, eger tiştekî mezin bît, wekî ga, min 'adetek heye hingî ez dişkînim ko çawêt min sor bibin û simbêlêt min bel bibin û mûêt min girj bibin û kilka min bibît e *xeleke* li-ser pişta min** (SK 6:64) When you bring some prey, if it should be something big like an ox, I am accustomed to rend it only when my eyes become red and my whiskers bristle and my hair rises and my tail becomes *an arc* above my back. {also: xeleke (SK-2/K[s]); xeleq (K)} {syn: olk I} [SK/A/IFb/B/JB1-A/GF/TF/OK//K]

xeleke خەلەكە (SK/K[s]) = ring. See **xelek**.

xelendor I خەلەندۆر *m.* **().** beestings, colostrum, first milk: **•Berxvan dixwin *zak û firo*, *xelendor*** (FS) Lambherds eat/drink *beestings*. {also: xelindo (B); xelindor (K/Kmc); xilindor I (A/FJ/GF/Wkt/FD); [khylindour] خلندور (JJ)} {syn: firo; firşik II; xîç' I; zak} [Özalp/FS//K/Kmc//B//A/FJ/GF/Wkt/JJ/FD]

xelendor II خەلەندۆر *f.* **(;-ê).** horse-parsley, Alexanders, bot. Smyrnium olusatrum, *a sweet-tasting plant eaten by the Kurds*. {also: xalendor (Wkt-2); xelendûr (B); xilindor II (A/Kmc/Wkt-2); <xelendûr> خلندور (HH)} {syn: *benî III} Sor gindor̄ گِندۆڕ/qelendor قەلەندور [IFb/FJ/GF/Wkt/FS//B/HH//A/Kmc]

xelendûr خەلەندوور (B/HH) = Smyrnium olusatrum. See **xelendor II**.

xeleq خەلەق (K) = ring. See **xelek**.

xelet خەلەت *f./m.(Dh)* **().** 1) {syn: ç'ewtî} mistake, error: **-bi xeletî ve** (Dh) by mistake; **-xelet kirin**

(SK) to make a mistake: •**Xiyala wî ew bû ko imam *xelet kir* yan nezanî** (SK 17:164) He thought that the imam *made a mistake*, or just did not know; 2) [*adj.*] {syn: ç'ewt; şaş I[2]} wrong, incorrect, mistaken: -**xelet bûn** (Bw) to be wrong. {also: qelet (F/K-2); ẍelet (K); [galet غـلـط/xálät خـلـط] (JJ)} <Ar γalaṭ غـلـط = 'mistake'; cf. Sor xełetan خەڵەتان = 'to be deceived' [IFb/JB1-A/SK/GF/Bw//F//K//JJ]

xelifîn خەلِفین (IFb) = to err, go astray. See **xalifîn**.

xelindo خەلِندۆ (B) = first milk. See **xelendor I**.

xelindor خـەلِـنـدۆر (K/Kmc) = first milk. See **xelendor I**.

xeliqandin خـــەلِـــقـــانـــدِن (SK/JJ) = to create. See **xuliqandin**.

xelî خەلی = veil. See **xêlî I**.

xelîl خەلیل *f.* **().** finger cymbal, small cymbal used like a castanet (e.g., by a belly dancer). {also: xalîle (Ah); xelîle (ZF3)} [Ah//K//ZF3]

xelîle خەلیله (ZF3) = finger cymbal. See **xelîl**.

xelîn خەلین (TF/SS) = to be sprained. See **xelyan**.

xelk خەلك (IFb/JB1-A&S/SK) = people, nation; others. See **xelq**.

xelq خـــەلـــق *m.* **(-ê;-ê** [B/IFb]**).** 1) {syn: ebadile; gel; net'ewe} people, nation, folk; 2) inhabitants, population, tribe (JB1-S): •**Tu *xelkê* k'îrey?** (JB1-A) Where are you from? [lit. 'you are *the people of* where?']; 3) others, the other person; strangers, people who are not relatives: •**gaê *xelkê*** (IFb) *another's* or *someone else's* ox •**mala *xelkê*** (IFb) *another's* or *a stranger's* house •***Xelk* nizanî tu çi dikî** (IFb) *Others* don't know what you are doing •***Xelk* ketîye Kurdistanê** (IFb) *Strangers* have taken Kurdistan. {also: xelk (IFb/JB1-A&S/SK-2); [khelqi] خلقی (JJ); <xel خل/xelk خلك/xelq خلق> (HH)} < Ar xalq خـلـق (√x-l-q = 'to create')--> T halk; Sor xełk خـەڵـك = 'people' [F/K/JB3/B/HH/SK//IFb/JB1-A&S//JJ] <mexulqet>

xelwe خـــەلـــوە (GF/SK) = private conversation. See **xewle II**.

xelyan خەلیان *vi.* **(-xelyê-).** to be sprained, dislocated *(wrist, etc.)*: •**Destê min *ê xelyay*** (Zeb) My hand (i.e., wrist) *has been sprained.* {also: xelan II (IFb); xelîn (TF/SS); <xelan خلان (dixele) (دخله)> (HH)} {syn: wergerîn[3]} Cf. Ar xala'a خلع = 'to wrench, dislocate (a joint)' [Zeb/GF/M//TF/SS//IFb/HH] <xelandin>

xem خـــــــــەم *f.* **(-a;-ê).** grief, sorrow, distress; worry, concern: •**K'ê ku p'akî haj ji şivantîyê t'unebû, hew zanibû, ku ew tiştekî çetin nîne, ku şivan xweřa nava kulîlkada digeřin ... û qet *xema* wana nîne** (Ba2:1, 203) Those who were not well acquainted with shepherding thought that it was something not very difficult, that shepherds roam among the flowers ... and they have no *cares* at all; -**k'etin xeman** (JB3) to worry; -**xem kirin** = a) to grieve, be sad; b) to worry; -**xem k'işandin** = a) to grieve, be sad: •**Memê minî delal, tu *mek'şîne t'u xemane*** (Z-1) My dandy Mem, *do not grieve* at all; b) to worry, be concerned, care: •**Pey mirina birê me Ûsibřa ew kor bîye, ji mal dernak'eve û *xema me nak'işîne*** (Ba3) After the death of our brother Joseph he became blind [and] he doesn't leave the house or *care for us*; -**xem û xiyal** (ZF3) apprehension, anxiety; -**xem verevandin** (Zeb) to allay one's fears or concerns, -**xem xwarin** = a) {syn: k'eribîn} to grieve, be sad; b) to worry. {also: ẍemm (SK-2); [ghem] غـم (JJ); <xem خم/ẍem غم> (HH)} {syn: cefa; fikar; k'eder; k'erb; k'eser; kovan; kul I; qilqal; şayîş; t'alaş; tatêl; xiyal [2]} < Ar γamm غـمّ; Sor xem خــــــەم [L/K/A/JB3/IFb/B/HH/SK/JB1-A&S/GF/TF//JJ] <xax; xemgîn>

xemberdîr خەمبەردیر (FS) = three-year-old sheep. See **xamberdîr**.

xemçûr خەمچوور (IF) = animal tax. See **qamçûř**.

xemegur خـەمـەگـور (BF)/xemeguř خـەمـەگـوڕ (FS) = chameleon. See **xemegurî**.

xemegurî خــــەمـــــەگـــــوری *f.* **(-ya;).** land lizard; chameleon. {also: xemegur (BF)/xemeguř (FS); <xemegiřo> خـــەمـــەگِـــڕۆ (Hej)} Sor xemegurî خەمەگوری [Zeb/OK//Hej//BF//FS]

xemgir خەمگِر (K) = sad, troubled. See **xemgîn**.

xemgîn خـــەمـــگـــیـــن *adj.* sad, sorrowful; troubled, worried: •**Bazirgan te'eccub kir. Got, "Subĥanellah, madam ewe kok bît bes noke yêt nekok di çawa ne?" Gelek *xemgîr* bû, bê-hîwî geřyawe** (SK 16:159) The merchant was amazed and said, "Praise be to God, if this one is satisfied, then what will the dissatisfied be like?" He was very *depressed* and turned back in despair •**Çelebî *xemgîr* hat mala xwe** (Rnh 2:17, 308) Chelebi came home *troubled* •**Ew ji ber mirina babê xo *xemgîn* e** (FS) He is *sad* because of his father's death. {also: xemgir (K-2); xemgîr (Rnh/IFb-2/SK-2/GF-2); ẍemgîr (Rnh-2); [ghemkin] غـمـگـیـن

(JJ); <xemgîr خـمـگـیـر/ẍemgîn غـمـگـیـن/ẍemgîr غمگیر> (HH)} {syn: bikul} <P γamgīn غمگین = 'sad, sorrowful'; Sor xemgîn خـەمـگـیـن/xemîn خـەمـیـن/xemnak خـەمـنـاك = 'grieved' {xemgînî; ẍemgînî; ẍemgîrî} [Rnh/HH//K/A/IFb/SK/GF/TF/OK//JJ] <xem>

xemgînî خەمگینی *f.* **(-ya;-yê).** sadness, sorrow: **•Heta derengî piştî nîvro jî vê *xemgînîyê* ez bernedam** (Lab, 10) Even late in the afternoon this *sadness* did not leave me **•Vanessa Redgrave ji ber *xemgînîya* mirina Alanê Kurdî yê sê salî, bi kurê xwe, Carlo Nero ve, rewşa penaberan anîne** [sic] **ser ekrana sînemayê** (Rûpela Nû 23.11. 2017) V. Redgrave, because of her *sorrow at* the death of the 3 year-old Alan Kurdi, has brought the plight of refugees to the movie screen, with her son C. Nero. {also: ẍemgînî (RF); ẍemgîrî (RF-2)} {syn: melûlî; zelûlî} Cf. P γamgīnī غـمـگـیـنـی [Lab/IFb/TF/RZ/BF/ZF3//RF] <derd; hesret; xemgîn>

xemgîr خەمگیر (Rnh/IFb/SK/GF/HH) = sad, troubled. See **xemgîn**.

xem•il خـەمِـل *f.* **(•la;-ê).** adornment, ornament, decoration: **•Por *xemla* keçan e** (AB) Hair is *the ornament of* girls **•Zarok *xemla* malê ne** (IFb) Children make a house a home [lit. 'children are *the ornament of* the house']; **-xeml û xêl** (HR/ZF)/ **xeml û xêz** (GF/ZF) finery: **• …û çû ber s̱abata xwe, *xeml û xêlê* bûkanîyê li xwe kir, xwe wilo zeynand** (HR 3:282) She went to her chest, put on her bridal *finery*, adorned herself. {also: xeml (JB3/IFb-2/ZF); [khemil] خميل (JJ); <xeml> خمل (HH)} Cf. Sor xemł خەمڵ = 'appraisal; decoration' [AB/K/A/IFb/B/JB1-S//JB3/HH/ZF//JJ] <xemilandin; xemilîn>

xemilandin خـەمِـلانـدِن *vt.* **(-xemilîn-).** to adorn, decorate, embellish, beautify: **•Wan bûk *xemiland*** (FS) They *adorned* the bride **•Wan mala xo bi gula *xemiland*** (FS) They *decorated* their home with flowers. {also: [khemilandin] خملاندين (JJ); <xemilandin خملاندن (dixemilîne) (دخملينه)> (HH)} Cf. Sor xemłandin خەمڵاندِن [Z-1/K/A/JB3/IFb/B/JJ/HH/SK/JB1-A&S/GF/TF/OK/FS] <xemil; xemilîn>

xemilî خەمِلی *adj./pp.* ornate, fancy, elegant, adorned, decorated; well-dressed. {also: [khemili] خـمـلـی (JJ)} [Ba2/K/A/B/JJ] <xemil; xemilîn>

xemilîn خـەمِـلـیـن *vi.* **(-xemil-).** [+ **bi**] to be adorned, decorated *(with)*: **•Deşt û çiyayên Kurdistanê li biharê *bi* gul û giya *dixemilin*** (FS) The prairies and mountains of Kurdistan *are adorned with* flowers and plants in the springtime **•Ezman *bi* stêran *dixemile*** (AB) The sky *is adorned with* stars **•Ser Dûmanlûê t'u mêşe t'unebûn, vira dar jî hêşîn nedibûn, lê wexta bahar dihat, ew ji xewa giran ḧişyar dibû û bi ḧemû r̄engava *dixemilî*** (Ba2:1, 202) On [Mount] Dumanlu there were no forests, trees did not even grow here, but when springtime came, it awoke from a great sleep and became colorfully *adorned.* {also: [khemilin] خملين (JJ); <xemilîn خملين (dixemilî) (دخملى)> (HH)} Cf. Sor xemłan خەملآن (-xemłê-) /xemłîn خەمڵین (-xemł-) [AB/K/A/IFb/B/JJ/HH/GF/TF/FS]

xemirî خەمِری (Dh) = dark purple. See **xemrî**.

xeml خەمل (JB3/IFb/HH/ZF) = decoration. See **xemil**.

xemrî خـەمـری *adj.* dark purple, burgundy (color). {also: xemirî (Dh); xumrî (K/GF); <xumrî> خمرى (HH)} < Ar xamr خمر = 'wine' [Dh//Şnx/IFb/TF/OK/ZF3/ BF//K/HH/GF] <binefşî; mor I>

xemsar خـەمـسـار/**xems̱ar** خـەمـصـار [Bw/FS] *adj.* negligent, neglectful *(of one's studies)*, shirking *(of responsibility)*, careless, lazy, apathetic; indifferent; unenthusiastic; carefree, thoughtless: **•Ew bo şolî *xems̱ar* e** (FS) He doesn't care about his work [lit. 'he is *neglectful* of his work']. {syn: bêxîret} {xemsarî/xems̱arî} [Bw/FS//IFb/OK/BF] <destgiran; pûte>

xemsarî خەمساری/**xems̱arî** خەمصاری [Bw] *f.* **(-ya; -yê).** negligence, neglect[fulness], carelessness, laziness, indifference: **-Xemsarîyê di vî warî de nakin** (BH, 60) They are not neglectful in this field [of pursuit]. [Bw//A/IFb/OK/BF] <pûte; xemsar>

xemxor خـەمـخـۆر (CS) = worried, concerned. See **xemxwer**.

xemxur خـەمـخـور (B/ZF) = worried, concerned. See **xemxwer**.

xemxwar خـەمـخـوار (A/IFb/ZF) = worried, concerned. See **xemxwer**.

xemxwer خـەمـخـوەر *adj.* 1) {syn: kovan; r̄e't II; zeḧmetk'êş} worrying, worried, concerned, troubled; 2) [*m.&f.* **(-e/ ;).**] one who cares deeply about stg.: **•Z.A.A. ji zehmetkêş û *xemxwerên* edebiyata Kurdî ye** (Nbh 125:11) Z.A.A. is one of the hard workers who care deeply [lit. 'and *carers*'] about Kurdish literature. {also: xemxor (CS); xemxur (B/ZF); xemxwar (A/IFb/ZF-2);

xemxwûr (Nbh-2)} Cf. P γamx[v]ār غمخوار = 'sharing another's sorrows, compassionate'; Sor xemxor خەمخۆر/xemxwar خەمخوار = 'solicitous, concerned, mindful' [Nbh/K/FJ/GF/TF//A/IFb//B/ZF//CS] <xem>

xemxwûr خەمخووور (Nbh) = worried, concerned. See **xemxwer**.

xena خەنا (FS) = henna. See **ḧene**.

xencel خەنجەل (B) = dagger. See **xencer**.

xencer خەنجەر *f.* **(-a;-ê).** dagger; short, curved dagger worn in front (JJ-G): •**'Ezîz jî** ***xencera deban*** **helkêşa, hate pêşîya 'Ebdî** (SK 18:170) Aziz, for his part, drew *a damask dagger* and confronted Abdi. {also: xencel (B-2); xencêr (JB1-A); xençel (B); xençer (B-2/TF); [khendjer] خنجر (JJ); <xencer> خنجر (HH)} {syn: deban; kahûr (IF); qeme} < Ar/P xanjar خنجر --> T hançer; Sor xencer خەنجەر; Za xençerî *f.* (Todd) [HM/K/A/JB3/IFb/JJ/HH/SK/JB1-S/GF//B//JB1-A//TF] <deban; k'êr; sîleḧ>

xencêr خەنجێر (JB1-A) = dagger. See **xencer**.

xençel خەنچەل (B) = dagger. See **xencer**.

xençer خەنچەر (B/TF) = dagger. See **xencer**.

xendiqandin خەندِقاندِن (SK/FS/BF/ZF3) = to drown *(vt.)*; to strangle; to hang. See **xeniqandin**.

xendiqîn خەندِقین (BF/FS/ZF3) = to choke *(vi.)*; to drown. See **xeniqîn**.

xendiqok خەندِقۆك (FS) = whooping cough. See **xendxendok**.

xendxendok خەندخەندۆك *f.* **().** whooping cough, pertussis. {also: xendiqok (FS); xeneqûtk (B); <xendxenduk> خەندخەندوك (Hej)} [Zeb//Hej//FS//B] <kuxîn>

xene خەنە (OK) = henna. See **ḧene**.

xeneqandin خەنەقاندِن (-xeneqîn-) (JB1-S) = to sink *(vt.)*; to strangle; to hang. See **xeniqandin**.

xeneqîn خەنەقین (L) = to choke *(vi.)*; to drown. See **xeniqîn**.

xeneqûtk خەنەقووتك (B) = whooping cough. See **xendxendok**.

xenha خەنها (Bw) = henna. See **ḧene**.

xeniqandin خەنِقاندِن *vt.* **(-xeniqîn-).** 1) {syn: fetisandin} to choke, strangle, smother *(vt.)*: •**Wî mar** ***xendiqand*** (FS) He *strangled* the snake; 2) to hang *(a person)*, execute by hanging: •**Xunkariyê xebatkarek** ***xendiqand*** (FS) The government *hanged* a worker; 3) to cause to drown or sink: •**Avê ew** ***xendiqand*** (FS) The water *drowned* him [i.e., He drowned in the water]. {also: xendiqandin (SK/FS/BF/ZF3-2); xeneqandin (-xeneqîn-) (JB1-S); [khenyqandin] خنقاندين (JJ); <xeniqandin خنقاندن (dixeniqîne) (دخنقينه)> (HH)} < Ar xanaqa خنق = 'to choke, strangle'; Sor xinkandin خِنکاندِن = 'to execute by hanging' [L/K/JB3/IFb/B/JJ/HH/GF/TF/Wkt/ZF3//SK/FS/BF//JB1-S] <xeniqîn>

xeniqîn خەنِقین *vi.* **(-xeniq-).** 1) to choke, be strangled *(vi.)*; 2) {syn: r̄oda çûn; xer̄iqîn} to drown, sink *(vi.)*: •**Gelê me ... di dema şahê gorbigor da di nav nezanîke mezin da** ***dixeniqî*** (Ber) Our people ... during the time of the accursed shah *was* (or, *were*) *drowning* in a great [deal of] ignorance. {also: xendiqîn (BF/FS/ZF3-2); xeneqîn (L); [khenyqin] خنقين (JJ); <xeniqîn خنقين (dixeniqe) (دخنقه)> (HH)} < Ar xanaqa خنق; Sor xinkan خِنکان (-xinkê-)/xenikîn خەنِکین [L//K/JB3/IFb/B/JJ/HH/GF/TF/Wkt/ZF3//BF/FS] <xeniqandin; xeriqîn>

xenîke خەنیکە *f./m.(FS)* **().** straps (Hej) or wooden sticks (Zeb) which go on either side of the neck of an ox, to fasten the yoke [***nîr***] to the ox; hame (and trace). {also: xenoke (FS-2); <xenîke> خەنیکە (Hej)} <Arc ḥanāqā חנקא/ḥanēqā חניקא = 'ropes or chains around the neck' (M. Jastrow) & Syr ḥanāqā ܚܢܩܐ = 'bands, collar of a yoke, or strings with which it is tied to the neck' <√ḥ-n-q = 'to strangle'; NENA khânîqâ ܚܢܝܩܐ = 'the band of a yoke, the rope which goes under the chin of an ox' (Maclean) [Zeb/Hej/Kmc-8/FS] <cot; halet; hincar; k'ulabe; nîr I>

xenoke خەنۆکە (FS) = straps or wooden sticks to fasten yoke to plow-pulling ox. See **xenîke**.

xenzîr خەنزیر (G) = pig. See **xinzîr**.

xenzûr خەنزوور = father-in-law. See **xezûr**.

xep خەپ *f.* **().** on a traditional plow, the pins that connect the beam [***mijane***] to the body of the plow [***cot***], and are fastened in place with washers [***berxep***]. {also: xepe (AA/FS); xepik II (AA-2)} cf. NENA khâpâ ܚܦܐ/ khâptâ ܚܦܬܐ = 'wooden peg in a plough, keeping the bôṣâ [ring-like washer = berxep] fixed to the beam' (Maclean), possibly <Arc ḥāf חף = '[rim, ridge], ward of a lock; bit of a key (corresponding to ward); pivot of a door' (M. Jastrow) [Zeb//AA/FS] <berxep; nîr I>

xepar خەپار *f.* **(-a;).** hoeing, lightly digging beneath a plant in order to soften up the soil and remove weeds: •**Behrem çû** ***xepara*** **xiyara** (FS) B. went *to hoe* the cucumbers •**Demê** ***xepara*** **bîstanî ye**

(FS) It's time *to hoe* the garden; **-ade û xepare** (Bw) weeding and lightly digging (beneath plants); **-xepare kirin** (FS) to hoe, lightly dig to remove weeds. {also: xepare (Bw/FS); <xepar> خپار (HH); <xepar> خەپار (Hej)} <NA khâpir ܚܦܪ = 'to dig, esp. vineyards dug a spade's depth' (Maclean) <Arc √ḥ-f-r חפר = 'to dig' [Bw/FS//A/IFb/HH/TF/Hej] <ade I; aşêf>

xepare خەپارە (Bw/FS) = digging beneath a plant. See **xepar**.

xepe خەپە (AA/FS) = plow pin connecting the beam to the plow body. See **xep**.

xepik I خەپك (Zeb/AA) = trap. See **xefik**.

xepik II خەپك (AA) = plow pin connecting the beam to the plow body. See **xep**.

xerab خەراب (IFb/JJ/ZF3) = bad; ruined. See **xirab**.

xerabî خەرابى (K/A/ZF) = badness. See **xirabî**.

xerac خەراج *m.* **(-ê;).** 1) {syn: bac; bêş; olam [1]; xûk} tax; poll-tax; tribute *(paid by tributary state)*: **-xerc û xerac** (K/B) a) (all different kinds of) expenses, costs; b) various types of taxes and tributes: **•Ewî heqî t'êra *xerc û xeřacêd* malêd wana nedikir** (Ba2:1, 204) Those wages were not enough to cover *the expenses of* their households; 2) {syn: mesref} expenses, expenditures (K/B). {also: ȟerac I (F); xeřec (Z-2); [kharadj] خراج (JJ); <xerac خراج/xerc خرج> (HH)} < Ar xarāj خراج = 'tax, land tax' [Z-2//K/IFb/B/HH/GF//JJ//F] <qamçûř> See also **xerc**.

xerar خەرار *m.* **(-ê;-î).** large sack; woolen or goat-hair sack (JJ-G): **•Wî ka kir *xirarî*** (FS) He put the straw *into the sack*. {also: xirar (Bw/ZF3/FS); [karár] خرار (JJ-G); <xirar> خرار (HH)} {syn: mêşok; t'elîs; t'êř III} [IFb//HH/Bw/ZF3/FS//JJ-G]

xerat خەرات/**xeřat** خەڕات [B] *m.* **(-ê;).** 1) carpenter, joiner: **•Apê te jî *xerate* / pir silavên min lêke / wê tabûta min bê heq / Ew ji kîsê xwe çêke** (Cxn-KE: rencberê bi rûmet) Your paternal uncle is *a carpenter* / give him my regards / My coffin for free / he will make [paying] from his own purse **•Me kursiyek bi *xerat* da çêkirin** (Wkt) We had **the carpenter** make a chair; 2) lather, turner (K/B). {also: xeřatçî (K/B-2); xirat (ZF3); [kherat] خراط (JJ); <xerat> خرات (HH)} <Ar xarrāṭ خرّاط = 'turner, lather'; Sor xeřat خەڕات = 'itinerant turner' [Cxn-KE/A/IFb/B/JJ/HH/GF/TF/Wkt//K//ZF3]

xeřatçî خەڕاتچى (K/B) = carpenter; lather. See **xerat**.

xeratî خەراتى/**xeřatî** خەڕاتى [B] *f.* **(;-yê).** carpentry: **•Ew ji me jîrtir bûn ko ji destên wan dihat cildirûtî, terzîtî, sefarî, *xeratî*, koçkarî û nalbendî** (Nefel, 2008) They were more skilled than us, as they were proficient in sewing, tailoring, tinsmithery, *carpentry*, cobblery and shoeing horses. {also: xeřattî (B-2)} [Nefel/A/B/FJ/TF/ZF/Wkt] <xerat>

xeřattî خەڕاتتى (B) = carpentry. See **xeratî**.

xerbok خەربۆك (K) = slipknot. See **xerboqe**.

xerboq•e خەربۆقە *f.* **(•a;•ê).** easily undone knot, slipknot: **•Wê devê şeřjêke, qefesa wê veke, benekî bigre têke *xerboqe* bigre destê xwe** (HCK-1, 77) Slaughter that camel, open its cage, take a rope and make *a slipknot* in it, hold it in your hand **•*Xerboqa* şiroxa pêlava wî vebû** (FS) *The knot of* his shoelace came undone. {also: herboqe (FS-2); xelboqe (Kmc); xerbok (K-2); xirboqî (FJ/GF/Kmc-2); [kher-boga] خربوغه (JJ)} {syn: xilf} Cf. NENA x-r-b-q = 'to be(come) entangled' (Sabar: Dict2) [HCK/K/B/FS//Kmc//JJ//FJ/GF] <girê>

xerc خەرج *m./f.(SK)* **().** 1) {syn: mesref; xerac} expenses, expenditure, outlay: **-xerc û xerac** (K/B): a) (all different kinds of) expenses; b) various types of taxes and tributes; 2) {syn: bac; bêş; olam [1]} tax, duty; tribute (K/B/CG); 3) payment (K); 4) (legal) damages, compensation for loss or damage (B). {also: [kherdj] خرج (JJ); <xerc> خەرج (CG); <xercî> خرجى (HH)} < Ar xarj خرج --> T harç; Sor xerc خەرج = 'expenditure' [Z-2/K/A/IFb/B/JJ/JB1-S/GF/CG/SK] See also **xerac**.

xeřec خەڕەج (Z-2) = tax; expense. See **xerac**.

xerifîn خەرِفین/**xeřifîn** خەڕفین [K] *vi.* **(-xerif-/-xeřif-[K]).** 1) to become or go senile, become feeble-minded: **•Hayqar pîr bûye, li ser piyê qebrê ye, *xurufî* ye, peyvên wî yên hêja nemane** (Qzl) Ahikar has grown old, he is on the edge of the grave, he's *going senile*, his precious words are gone [lit. 'have not remained']; 2) to lose one's mind, go nuts, go crazy: **•Pir ne maye ku cîranê me *bixerife*...ku xatûna yekî nola min, heta çar heftan jî nehêle ez nêzîk biçim, wê çaxê ..., ez ê jî *bixerifim*** (Ardû, 12) Our neighbor is about to *lose his mind* ... if the wife of one like me were not to let me come near her for 4 weeks, then ... I *would lose my mind* as well. {also: xirifîn (IFb); xurifîn (FJ/TF/GF/ZF-2); xurufîn (Qzl); <xurifîn خرفین (dixurife) (دخرفه)> (HH)} < Ar √x-r-f

خـــــــرف = ‘to be senile or feeble-minded’; Sor xerefan خەرەفان/xerefîn خەرەفین/xełefan خەڵەفان = ‘become feeble-minded from old age’ [Qzl//FJ/TF/GF/HH//Ardû/ZF//K//IFb] <herfî>

xeriqîn خەرِقین/**xeriqîn** خەرقین [IFb] *vi.* **(-xeriq-).** 1) {syn: roda çûn [1]; xeniqîn; xerq bûn} to sink, drown; 2) {syn: bêhiş k'etin; nehiş k'etin; xewirîn} to faint, swoon (B): **•Ew cîda xeriqî û k'et** (EP-7) He fainted on the spot; **-dilê** ***fk-ê*** **xeriqî** (XF) S.o. fainted, lost consciousness. {also: [ghereqin] غـــرقـــين (JJ); <xeriqîn غرقين (dixeriqî) (دغـرقـى)> (HH)} < Ar γaraqa غرق = 'to sink' [EP-7/K/B//IFb//JJ/HH] <xerq>

xerîb خـــەريـــب *m.* **().** 1) stranger, foreigner; 2) [*adj.*] strange, foreign: **-ji** ***fk-î*** **xerîb bûn** (Bw) to miss s.o., long for s.o. {syn: bêrîya fk-î kirin}: **•Em** ***ji*** **te** ***xerîb bûyn*** (Bw) We *have missed* you; **-xerîba** ***fk-î*** **kirin** (Bşk) to miss, long for stg. {also: xerîb (JB1-A&S); [gharíb] غـريـب (JJ); <xerîb> غـريـب (HH)} < Ar γarīb غريب = 'strange, foreign' [F/K/IFb/B/JB1-A/Bw/Bşk//JJ/HH] <xerîbstan; xurbet>

xerîbistan خـەريبِستـان (B/ZF3) = foreign country. See **xerîbstan**.

xerîbstan خـــەريـــبـــســـتـــان *f.* **(-a;-ê).** foreign land or country. {also: xerîbistan (B-2/ZF3)} {syn: xurbet} [F/K/B//ZF3]

xerman خـــەرمـــان *m./f.(ZF3/BF)* **(-ê/-a;).** 1) harvest, reaping; threshing. 2) stack, rick (agricultural) (K); 3) {syn: coxîn} threshing floor. {also: خَرْمان (JJ)} Cf. T harman [K/IFb/JJ/GF/ZF3/BF] <gêre I; hol III}

xernof خەرنۆف (BF) = carob. See **xernûf**.

xernûf خـەرنـووف *f.* **(-a;-ê).** carob (fruit and tree), St. John's bread, bot. *Ceratonia siliqua*. {also: xarnup (Ah); xernof (BF-2); xerûb (Wkt); xirnîf (FS); xirnûf (GF); xurnîfk (Dh/BF); xurnîk (Zeb/BF-2); [herob] حـــروب (JJ)} <Ar xarrūb خـــرّوب/xurnūb خرنـوب = 'carob' --> P xarnūb خرنـوب; T harnup [Ah//A/IFb/ZF3//GF//Wkt//JJ//Dh/BF//Zeb]

xerq خەرق (Ba3-3/IF) = sinking. See **xerq**.

xerşeb خەرشەب (GF) = drill. See **şixab**.

xertel خـەرتـەل *m.* **().** *large bird of prey*: vulture, kite, hawk, eagle: **•Romî** ***xertel*** **in, xoşîya wan ew e keleş mişe bin** (SK 61:740) Turks are *vultures*, their pleasure is in being full of carrion. {also: qertel (K-2/IFb/B/GF/OK-2); [qartāl] قـرتـال (JJ)} <T kartal = 'eagle' [SK/K/OK//IFb/Q/GF//JJ] <başok; elîh; kurt II; sîsalk>

xerûb خەرووب (Wkt) = carob. See **xernûf**.

xerz خـــــــەرز *m.* **(-ê;).** fish eggs, fish roe, spawn: **-xerzê masî** (Bw/Zx)/**xerzê me'sîya** (B) do. {also: xirz (GF/OK)} [Bw/Zx/K/IFb/B//GF/OK] <masî>

Xerzan خـــــــەرزان (IF/Wkp) = region in Batman province. See **Xarzan**.

Xerzî خەرزى (Wkp) = from the region of Xarzan. See **Xarzî**.

xesandin خـــەســـانـــدِن *vt.* **(-xesîn-).** to castrate, geld, emasculate: **•Beranekî** ***xesandî*** **qelew jî bi dîharî bo axaê xo dîina** (SK 14:142) He would bring a fat *gelded* ram too as a present for the agha **•Ji 1ê îlonê ve dewlet alîkarîyê dide cotkaran da ku berya** ***xesandina*** **berazan ew bên bêhişkirin** (Radyoya Swêdê) Since Sept. 1, the state is helping farmers to anesthetize pigs before they are *castrated* [lit. 'so that before *the castrating of* pigs, they be anesthetized']. {also: [khesandin] خصاندين (JJ); <xesandin خساندن (dixesîne) (دخسينه)>} < Ar xaṣá (i) () خـــصـــى = 'to castrate'; Sor xesandin خەساندِن [K/B/A/IFb/FJ/GF/TF/HH/BF/SK/ZF/CS/M/FS//JJ]

xesar خـــەســـار *f.* **(-a;-ê).** harm, damage, hurt; loss: **•Çivîka wîtwîtanî: kesê ku bi nezaniya xwe him xwe him dora xwe dide** ***xesarê*** (Kmc 23:254) "Chirping bird": someone who causes harm to himself and to those around him through his ignorance (cf. someone who spills the beans, or lets the cat out of the bag); **-xesar dan** (ZF/RZ/CS) to harm, damage: **•Xesar nedin gundîyan ... em xesar nadin tu kesî** (C. Yıldırım. Mîrê çiyayan, Koçero, 80) Don't harm the villagers ... we won't harm anyone; **-xesar kirin** (SK) to loose, let off, fire (gun): **•Wextê Heyo ho got, Teto derê martînî da laê Heyo, fîşekek li wî** ***xesar kir,*** **li wê-derê Heyo kuşt** (SK 61:732) When H. said that, T. aimed his rifle at H., *let off* a cartridge at him, and killed H. right there. {also: xesaret (SK-2); xisar (K-2/IFb-2/Wkt-2/CS-2); [khesar خـســار/khesaret خـــســـارت] (JJ); <xesaret> خـــســـارت (HH)} {syn: zirar; zîyan} <Ar xisārah خـــســـارة = 'loss, lack' [C.Yıldırım/K/IFb/GF/FD/G/RZ/JJ/SK//HH]

xesaret خەسارەت (SK/HH/JJ) = harm; loss. See **xesar**.

xesel خـــــەســـەل (CCG) = straw remaining after the harvest. See **qesel**.

xesî خەسى (IFb) = mother-in-law. See **xesû**.

xesîl خەسيل (IFb) = mat. See **qisîl**.

xesîs خـــەســـيـــس *adj.* stingy, miserly, selfish, greedy, parsimonious: •**Rojekê du rêvî li daristanekê li hev rast hatin; yek *xesûs* yek jî comer[d] bû** (Y. Sarılmaz. Çavê li rê, *back cover*) One day 2 travelers met in a forest; one was *stingy* and one was generous. {also: **qesîs** (Nsb/TF/Wkt-2); xesûs (Y. Sarılmaz); <xesîs> خەسیس (Hej); [khesis] خسيس (JJ); <xesîs> خسيس (HH)} {syn: çavbirçî; ç'ikûs; çirûk; devbeş; evsene; řijd} Cf. P xasīs خسيس [Sarılmaz//K/A/IFb/JJ/HH/Hej/ZF/RZ/Wkt/CS/OrK//Nsb/TF]

xesîyet خەسییەت = character[istic]; habit. See **xeyset**.

xest'in خەستِن (-xaz-) (JB1-A) = to want; to request. See **xwestin**.

xes•û خەسوو *f.* **(•îya;•îyê).** mother-in-law [pl. mothers-in-law]: •***Xesîya* te ji te p'iř ȟez dike** (Dyd) = ***Xesîyê* te li te pir ȟez dikîye** (Ad) = ***Xesîya* te tu divêy** (Bw) Your *mother-in-law* loves you *[prv.]*. {also: xasî (F/K); xesî (IF-2); xwesî (B); xwesû (Bx); [khosi خوسى/khesou خسو] (JJ); <xesû> خسو (HH)} [Pok. sụekrū́- 1043.] 'mother-in-law': Skt śvaśrū́-; Av *hwasrū-; Pamir dialects: Ormuri syūγ/xušūi/syɔγ/xwɔ̄šiē; Parachi xuš; Yidgha x^u^šo; Sanglechi xoš; Wakhi xušdōman/ x̌aš; Shughni xīṣ̌ (Morg); P xušū خشو (Afghani); Sor xesû خەسوو; Za vıstırû *f.* (Mal); Hau hesirûe *f.* (M4); cf. also Lat socrus, *gen.* -ūs f.; Rus svekrov' свекровь; Germ Schwieger-mutter; Gr hekyra ἑκυρά; Arm skēsur սկեսուր (W Arm gesur կեսուր) [Ad/F/K//A/JB3/IFb/JJ/HH/TF//B//Bx] <xezûr>

xesûs خەسووس (Y. Sarılmaz) = stingy, miserly, greedy. See **xesîs**.

***xeşab** خەشاب *f.* **().** magazine of a gun, ammunition clip: •**Ji nişka ve çardexur derxiste rastê, berika pêşîn hajot ber devê wê, dirêjî ser kerê kir û tavilê *xeşabek* tê de vala kir** (Ardû, 134) Suddenly he brought out a browning pistol, loaded the first bullet into its mouth, then aimed it at the donkey and immediately emptied the clip into it. [Ardû]

xeşeb خەشەب (Kmc/RZ) = drill. See **şixab**.

xeşîm خەشیم *adj.* naïve, gullible, ignorant; simple, unsophisticated. {also: xişîm (BF); x̌eşîm (K-2/ OK-2); [khechim خشيم/ghascim (G) غشيم] (JJ); <xeşîm> غشيم (HH)} {syn: sawîlke} < Ar γašīm غشيم = 'naive'; Sor xeşîm خەشیم/x̌eşîm غەشیم = 'inexpert, awkward' {xeşîmî} [K/A/IFb/JJ/HH/GF/TF/OK/ /BF]

xeşîmî خەشیمی *f.* **(-ya;-yê).** naïveté, gullibility, ignorance. {also: xeşîmîtî (ZF3-2); xişîmî (Wkt)} [K/TF/ZF3//Wkt] <xeşîm>

xeşîmîtî خەشیمیتی (ZF3) = naïveté. See **xeşîmî**.

xet خەت *f./m.(SK)* **(-a/-ê;-ê/).** 1) {syn: řêz I} line: **-binê xet** (Kp) "below the line": *Syrian Kurds refer to themselves as the Kurds "below the line," referring to the line drawn on the map, i.e., the railway line, arbitrarily separating Syria and Turkey*; 2) {syn: şov [1]} furrow: •**weka *xeta* kotanê** (L) like a plow *furrow* (track); 3) [*pl.*] handwriting; script: •***Xetê* wî neřindin** (B) His *handwriting* is messy. {also: [khet/khat] خط (JJ); <xet> خت (HH)} < Ar xaṭṭ خط; Sor xet خەت = 'line, handwriting' [AB/F/K/B/IFb/JJ/HH/SK/GF/TF]

xeter خەتەر *f.* **(-a;-ê).** danger, peril: •**Ev yek jî *xetereya* li ser tenduristiya Öcalan zêdetir dike** (AW70A1) This increases *the danger* to Ocalan's health •**Rewşa wî ya tenduristî hînê *di xeterê de* ye** (CTV199) The condition of his health is still *in danger*. {also: xeder (K); xetere (AW/ZF3)} {syn: metirsî; talûke} < Ar xaṭar خطر = 'danger'; Sor xeter خەتەر [IFb/TF//AW/ZF3//K]

xetere خەتەرە (AW/ZF3) = danger. See **xeter**.

xetimandin خەتِماندِن (GF/HH) to plug up. See **xitimandin**.

xetîr•e خەتیرە *f.* **(•a;•ê).** torch, flambeau: •**Bayî *xetîra* wî temirand** (FS) The wind *extinguished* his torch •**Ew li ber ronahîya *xetîrê* çû** (FS) He went by the light of *the torch* •***Xetîra* şoreşê helkir** (Teĥsîn Taha) He lit *the torch of* revolution. {also: xitêre (IFb); <xetîre> ختيره (HH); <xetîre> خەتیرە (Hej)} cf. Arc ḥuṭrā חוטרא = 'staff, rod, stick'; = Sor çołeçira چۆڵەچِرا [Bw/Zeb/OK/Hej/ZF3/FS/ /IFb] <gurz I>

xevat خەڤات = work; struggle. See **xebat**.

xevatçî خەڤاتچی (B) = worker. See **xebatk'ar**.

xevatk'ar خەڤاتکار (B) = worker. See **xebatk'ar**.

xevitandin خەڤِتاندِن = to use. See **xebitandin**.

xevitîn خەڤِتین = to work. See **xebitîn**.

xew خەو *f.* **(-a;-ê).** sleep, slumber: •**Bi dengê sazî şîrin ... M. ji *xewê* ç'e'vê xwe vekir** (Z-1) From the sweet sound of the saz ... M. awoke and opened his eyes [lit. 'M. opened his eyes from *sleep*'] •**M. razaye *bi xewa şîrin*** (Z-1) M. was sound asleep [lit. 'went to sleep *with sweet slumber*']; **-ji xew[ê] řabûn** (L) to wake up [lit. 'get up from sleep']; **-k'etin xewê** = to go to sleep, fall asleep; **-xewa *fk-î* hatin** = to fall asleep; to be sleepy: •**Lawo, *xewa min tê*** (L) Son, *I'm* *sleepy* •**Xewa wî nayê** (L) He *can't fall asleep* [lit. 'His sleep doesn't come']; -**xewr̄a çûn** = to go to sleep, fall asleep. {also: [kheoŭ] خــو (JJ); <xew> خـــو (HH)} [Pok. su̯ep-/sup- 1048.] 'to sleep' & [Pok. su̯épōr, *gen.* *supnés, *thence* su̯epno-s/ su̯opno-s/supno-s 1048.] 'sleep': Skt svap- = 'to sleep' & svápna *m.* = 'sleep, dream'; Av x^vap- = 'to sleep'; Mid P xwamr/xwamn = 'sleep, dream' (M4) & xwāb = 'sleep' (M3); P x^vāb خــواب = 'dream' & x^vābīdan خوابيدن = 'to sleep'; Baluchi wāb/whāv; Sor xew خــه‌و/xewn خــه‌ون = 'sleep, dream' & xewtin خــه‌وتِــن (xew) = 'to sleep' (Kerkuk); Za hewn *m.* = 'sleep, dream' (Todd); Hau werm *m.* (M4); cf. also Lat somnus; Rus son сон = 'sleep' & spat' спать = 'to sleep'; Gr hypnos ὕπνος; Arm k'un քուն [F/K/A/JB3/IFb/B/JJ/HH/SK/JB1-A&S/GF/TF] <nivistin; r̄azan; t'êrxew; xewn; xilmaş>

xewar خــه‌وار *m.* **().** & *adj.* sleepyhead, s.o. who loves to sleep: •**Behrem kur̄ekê *xewar* e** (FS) B. is a *sleepyhead.* {also: <xewar> خــوار (HH)} [Wn/Qzl/Slm/Xrz/Elk/K/A/IFb/B/HH/GF/BF/ZF3/FS]

xeware خه‌واره (SS). See **ẍeware**.

xewin خه‌وِن (Rnh) = dream. See **xewn**.

xewinrok خــــه‌ونــــرۆك (Wlt) = daydream. See **xewnerojk**.

xewirîn خــه‌وِرين *vi.* **(-xewir-).** to faint: •**Tew nabîne ku pelhîtek ji kuderê de hat û li paş serê wî ket. Mêrik di nava xwînê de deverû diçe erdê. Jê û pêve jî tiştek nayête bîra wî û *dixewire*** (Ardû, 50) He doesn't see where a blow came from and fell at the back of his head. The man falls down flat on in face in a pool of blood. He can't remember anything else and he *faints*. {syn: bêĥiş bûn/k'etin/man; neĥiş k'etin; xer̄iqîn} < xew = 'sleep' [Ardû/CS/RZ/ZF3]

xewle I خــــه‌ولــه *adj.* 1) solitary, secluded; isolated; lonely: -**cîyê xewle** (B/F) secluded (or secret) place: •**Kur̄ ji malê derdik'evin, diçin *cîkî xewle*, hevdu dişêwirin** (Ba3-3, #19) The boys leave the house, go to *a secluded place*, and deliberate; 2) secret, hidden, concealed; 3) underhanded, sneaky. {cf. also: [khelveti] خلوتی (JJ) = 'isolated, set back'; <xilwe> خــلــوه (HH) = 'deserted place'} <Ar xalwah خــلــوة = 'privacy, seclusion' & see **xewle II**. [Ba3/F/K/A/IFb/B/GF] <dûr; t'enê; veder>

xewle II خــــه‌ولــه *f.* **().** private conversation, secret gathering; deserted place: -**xewle kirin** (IFb/Kmc/CS)/**xelwe kirin** (GF/SK) to meet in private, have a private talk, gather in secret: •**Berî ku ew bi rê kevin, Meyro, Bengîn *xewle kir*, ew bir hundir, bi girî, ew hembêz kir û ramûsî** (M. Uzun. R. Evdalê Zeynikê, 125) Before they set out, M. took B. aside, *brought him inside* and, in tears, hugged and kissed him •**Lê mamostê wî yê îlim û felsefê bi derdê wî hesiya û ji rabûn û rûniştina wî derxist ku birîna Çeto birîna dilan bû. Rojekê, mamoste Çeto *xewle kir*, qise anî ser qisê û jê re got** (Uzun, 117) But his [Çeto's] science and philosophy teacher noticed his pain and from his behavior he deduced that Ç.'s pain was a pain of the heart. One day, the teacher *met privately with* Ç., broached the subject and told him … •**Wextê ew r̄a-za, hêşta neniwistî, em *dê xelweyekî keyn*, ho bêjîn, weto ko ew bibihêt, "Werin, da têla şurêt wî muroey bidizîn…"** (SK #254) When he lies down but is not yet asleep, we *shall gather together secretly* and say, in a way that he can hear, "Come, let's steal this man's bag of goods…". {also: xelwe (GF/SK); [khelvet] خلوت (JJ); <xilwe> خــلــوه (HH)} <Ar xalwah خــلــوة = 'privacy, seclusion'; T halvet = 'withdrawing, seclusion; secluded retreat'; Sor xełwet خــه‌ڵوه‌ت = 'privacy, solitude'; Za xelwe/xewle = 'deserted, isolated; secluded retreat' (Mal) [Uzun/IFb/Kmc/CS//SK/GF//JJ]

xewlî خه‌ولى (Wkt) = towel. See **xawlî**.

xewn خــــه‌ون *f.* **(-a;-ê).** dream; vision: •**Ya Memo û Zînê *xewna* şevane** (EP-7) That [thing] of Mem and Zin is a nighttime *dream*; -**xewn dîtin** = to dream, have a dream; -**xewna giran** (B) deep sleep; -**xewna şeva** (JB1-S) nighttime dream (the deepest sleep). {also: xewin (Rnh); [khev(i)n] خــون (JJ); <xewn> خــون (HH)} [Pok. su̯ep-/sup- 1048.] 'to sleep' & [Pok. su̯op-ni̯o-m 1048.] 'dream': Skt svap- = 'to sleep' & svápna *m.* = 'sleep, dream'; Av x^vafna- *m.* = 'sleep, dream'; Mid P xwamn = 'sleep, dream' (M3); P x^vāb خــواب = 'dream' & x^vābīdan خــوابيدن = 'to sleep'; Sor xew خــه‌و/xewn خــه‌ون = 'sleep, dream'; Za hewn *m.* = 'sleep, dream' (Todd) [Z-1/F/K/A/JB3/IFb/B/JJ/HH/SK/JB1-S/GF/TF//Rnh] <xew>

xewneroj خــــه‌ونــــه‌رۆژ (GF) = daydream. See **xewnerojk**.

xewnerojk خــه‌ونــه‌رۆژك *f.* **().** daydream, reverie: •**Belê dewleta Tirk *xewinroka* ji xwe re bîne**

(Wlt 2:59, 7) Let the Turkish state dream on [lit. 'bring *daydreams* to itself']. {also: xewinrok (Wlt); xewneroj (GF); xewneroşk (ZF3-2)} [Wlt//IFb/TF/ZF3// GF] <xewn>

xewneroşk خـەونـەرۆشـك (ZF3) = daydream. See **xewnerojk**.

xeyal خەیال (K/IFb/GF/TF/ZF3) = thought; worry. See **xiyal**.

xeyalşkestî خـەیـالـشـكـەسـتـى = disillusioned. See **xiyalşkestî**.

xeyar خەیار (TF) = cucumber. See **xiyar**.

xeyat خەیات *m.* **(;-î).** tailor: **•*Xeyatî* dukana xo girt û hate nik me** (X. Salih. Hindek serhatiyên Kurdî, 89) *The tailor* closed his shop and came to our house. {also: [kheiat] خیاط (JJ)} {syn: cildirû; k'incdirû; t'erzî} < Ar xayyāṭ خیّاط = 'tailor' < xayṭ خیط = 'thread' [X.Salih/Wkt/JJ]

xeyb خەیب *f.* **(-a;-ê).** slander, libel; talking about s.o. behind his/her back, gossip, backbiting: **•Careke din *xeyba* wê *kir*, go, "Fêlê wê mixtaȓin"** (HCK-3:2, 17) Once more she *slandered* her, saying "Her actions are dirty". {also: xeybet (K-2/ B); [gaībet/ġhaibét (G)] غیبت (JJ); <ẍeybet> غیبت (HH)} {syn: paşgotinî} < Ar γībah غـيـبـة = 'slander, calumny' < √γ-y-b غيب = 'to be absent, hidden'; Sor ẍeybet غـەیـبـەت = 'slander behind one's back' [HCK/K/ZF//B//JJ-G/HH] <gotgotk; kurt û pist>

xeybet خەیبەت (K/B) = slander, gossip. See **xeyb**.

xeydîn خـەیـدیـن (-xeyd-) (K/B) = to be furious. See **xeyidîn**.

xeyidîn خەیِدین *vi.* **(-xeyid-).** 1) {syn: erinîn; hêrs bûn; k'eribîn; ẍezibîn} [+ **ji**] to be(come) furious or very angry (at), to rage, fume: **•Em *ji* qedera xwe *xeyidîn*** (IFb) We *cursed* our fate **•Şêr *ji* vê p'arkirinê p'iȓ *xeyîdî*** (Dz) The lion *was furious at* this division [of the spoils]; 2) to be offended, insulted. {also: xeîdîn (F); xeydîn (-xeyd-) (K/B); xeyîdîn (Dz); [kheidin] خـیـدین (JJ)} Cf. Ar γayẓ غیظ = 'fury, anger' [Dz//F//K/B/JJ//A/JB3/IFb/GF/TF]

xeyîdîn خەییدین (Dz) = to be furious. See **xeyidîn**.

xeyl خەیل (Wkp) = veil. See **xêlî I**.

xeylî خەیلی (JB1-S/OK) = veil. See **xêlî I**.

xeyna خەینا: -ji xeyna = except. See **xêncî**.

xeynî خەینی: -ji xeynî (Bx/JB3) = except. See **xêncî**.

xeyr I خەیر: -xeyr ji (IFb) = except. See **xêncî**.

xeyr II خەیر (SK) = goodness. See **xêr I**.

xeyrî خەیری: -j xeyrî (JB1-A) = except. See **xêncî**.

xeyset خـەیـسـەت *m.* **(-ê;).** 1) {syn: t'aybetmendî; ṯebî'et} characteristic, trait: **•Ew** [sic = **wî**] ***xeysetê* Memê dê û bavê wî t'imê nava neȓeḧetîyêda dihîştin** (Z-1, 45) This *trait of* Mem's kept his mother and father in a state of constant anxiety; 2) character, temperament: **•*Xeysetê* wî xirabe** (B) His *character* is bad; 3) habit; tendency. {also: xeîset (F); xesîyet; <xaṯsîyet> خاصیت (HH)} < Ar xāṣṣīyah خـاصّـيـة --> T hasiyet; Sor xasîyet خاسییەت = 'special quality' [Z-1/K/B/GF/TF//F]

xeysetnav خەیسەتناڤ *m.* **().** adjective. {also: xeîsetnav (F)} {syn: ȓengdêr} [K/B//F]

xez خـەز *adj.* (of goats) having reddish-yellow coloring around the mouth, nose, eyes, and tail **•Bizina *xez* jî ew bizin e ku dora dev, poz, çav, û heşa ji cenabê te, dora boça wê bi rengekî sorê zer, kej an jî qehweyî be, em jê re dibêjin bizina *xez*** (Hesenê Metê) = "Bizina *xez*" is a goat who has a reddish-yellow, blonde, or brownish color around its mouth, nose, eyes, and--no offense to you--around its tail]: **•Kurê min, di çav min de çend bizinê te ne xuyane. Ka... ka bizina taq? Bizina *xez* û ya bel jî ne xuyaye** (Ardu, 115) My son, it looks to me like some of your goats are not here. Where... where is the speckle-eared goat? I don't see the one *with red spots* or the one with the pointy ears either. [Ardu/Wkp] <bel; kever; k'ol IV; qer II; taq>

xezal I خـەزال *f.* **(-a;-ê).** gazelle; deer, fallow deer: **•Ezê insanekî ênim ku bi şîrê *ẍizala* mezin bû bê** (HR 3:270) I will bring a person who has been raised on the milk *of gazelles* **•*Xezal* li çîya diçêrin** (AB) *Gazelles* graze in the mountains; **-karê xezala** (K) fawn, young of deer. {also: ẍizal (HR); [gazal] غـزال (JJ); <xezal> خـزال (HH)} {syn: ask; gak'ûvî; mambiz; şivir} < Ar γazāl غـزال; Sor xezeł خـەزەڵ = 'goat with yellowish forelegs'; Za xezal *f.* = 'deer, antelope, gazelle' (Todd) [F/K/A/JB3/IFb/B/HH/TF/ZF//JJ//HR] <xifş>

xezal II خـەزال *f.* **().** yellow leaves of autumn which have fallen to the ground: **•Ha şivano, payîz hat û *xezal* weryan** (Zeb) O shepherd, fall has come and *the leaves* have fallen. {also: [gazel غـزل/ qazel قزل] (JJ)} Cf. P xazān خزان = 'autumn'; Sor xezeł خـەزەڵ = 'yellow leaves of autumn' (Hej) [Zeb/IFb//JJ] <belg; payîz>

xezalî خـەزالـى *adj.* pattern of **bergûz** material: monochrome brown (êkreng). {syn: piştpez} [Bw] xezan خەزان (A) = poor. See **xizan**.

xezanî خەزانی (A) = poverty. See **xizanî**.

xezeb خـەزەب *f.* **(;-ê).** anger, wrath, fury, ire: -**hatin xezebê** = to fly into a rage: **•P'adşa çewa mîna tiştekê me** ***hatîye xezevê*** (Z-922) It seems that the king *is* a little *angry* at us. {also: xezev; ẍezeb (SK); [khazab] خـضـاب (JJ)} {syn: hêrs} < Ar γaḍab غـضـب; Sor ẍezeb غـەزەب [Z-922/F/K/IFb/B//SK//JJ] <ẍezibîn>

xezev خەزەڤ = anger. See **xezeb**.

xezibîn خەزبین (JB3/IF) = to be angry. See **ẍezibîn**.

xezirîn خـەزريـن *vi.* **(-xezir-).** to be pigheaded, be stubborn, to refuse to budge *(of a pig)*: **•Beraz** ***yê xezirî*** (Zeb) The pig *won't budge*. {also: <xezirîn> خـەزريـن (Hej) = 'to be furious; to strike'} cf. NENA khzûrâ ܚܙܘܪܐ = 'pig, hog' [Zeb/Hej] <beraz; erinîn; serr̄eq>

xezîne خەزینە (K/IF/JJ/HH) = treasure. See **xizne**.

xezne خەزنە (F) = treasure. See **xizne**.

xezûr خـەزوور *m.* **(-ê;).** 1) father-in-law [pl. fathers-in-law]; 2) {syn: bacinax; hevling} husband of wife's sister, brother-in-law (Efr) [xezür]. {also: xenzûr; ẍezûr (Krç); [khozir خزير/khezour خزور] (JJ); <xezûr> خـزور (HH)} [Pok. su̯ékuro- (*dissimilated from* *su̯ekruro-) 1043.] 'father-in-law': Skt śváśura-; Av *x^{V}asura-; Pamir dialects: Yidgha xis(s)ur; Shughni x^{W}esor (Morg); Southern Tati dialects: Chali xösurā *m.* = 'husband's father' (Yar-Shater); P xosūr خـسـور/ xosor خـسـر *(rare)*; Sor xezûr خـەزوور; Za vistewre m. (Todd/Mal); cf. also Lat socer; Rus svëkor свёкор; Germ Schwäher; Gk hekyros ἑκυρός; Arm skēsrayr սկեսրայր (W Arm gēsrayr կէսրայր) {xezûrtî} [F/K/A/JB3/IFb/B/JJ/HH/SK/GF/TF/OK/Efr/ZF//Krç] <xesû>

xezûrî خـەزووری (Wkt) = father-in-lawhood. See **xezûrtî**.

xezûrtî خـەزوورتـی *f.* **(-ya;-yê).** being a father-in-law, father-in-lawhood: **•Min rûmetek** [sic] **mezin didayê ku ew jî li hemberî min têkeve rewşa** ***xezûrtiyê*** (Lab, 7) I showed him a great deal of respect, so that he would be willing to be come my father-in-law [lit. 'so that he would enter into the status of *father-in-lawhood* regarding me']. {also: xezûrî (Wkt)} [Lab/ZF3//Wkt] <xezûr>

xê خێ (SK/OK/Bw) = salt. See **xwê**.

xêbet خێبەت (B) = tent. See **xêvet**.

xêl I خـێـل *f.* **(;-ê).** short period of time, short while: -**wê xêlê** (B) then, at that time; -**xêlekê** (K/B) for a while, for a short time: **•Emê** ***xêlekê*** **vira bijîn** (B) We'll live here *for a while* **•'Eynê** ***xêlekê*** **ajotîye** (EP-5, #7) Ayneh rode on *for a while*; -**xêlekê şûnda** (K/B) a while later. [EP-5/K/B/ZF3] <bîstek; gav; heyam; wext>

xêl II خێل (IFb/HH) = wedding procession. See **xêlî II**.

xêlî I خـێـلـی *f./m.(OK)* **(-ya/;-yê/).** (bridal) veil, veil covering a woman's head and face: **•*Xêlîya*** **bûkê sor û zer e** (AB) The bride's *veil* is red and yellow. {also: xelî; xeyl (Wkp); xeylî (JB1-S/OK-2); [kheili] خـيـلـی (JJ); <xêlî> خـيـلـی (HH)} {syn: hêzar[1]; pêça bûkê} [AB/K/IFb/B/JJ/HH/GF/OK/ZF3/BF/FS//JB1-S//Wkp] <ç'adir[1]; ç'arik[2]; ç'arşev[1]; doẍe>

xêlî II خێلی *f.* **().** wedding procession, those who go to bring the bride to the groom's house: **•[Weku** ***xêlî*** **tête wê deştê bi emrê xudê ba rûpekê ji rûyê Lalî Xanê direvîne]** (JR, #12) When *the wedding procession* comes to that plain, by God's command the wind causes the veil to fly off Lali Khan's face **•*Xêlên*** **bûkê hatin** (FS) The bride's *escorts* have come. {also: xêl II (IFb); [kheili] خـيـلـی (JJ); <xêl> خـيـل (HH)} Cf. Ar xayl خـيـل = 'horse(s)' *(on which the bride rides)* [JR/A/JJ/TF/ZF3//IFb/HH] <bûk I; zava; mehir; zewac>

xênc خێنج (GF)= except. See **xêncî**.

xêncî خـێـنـجـی *prep.* besides, except (for), apart from, none but; other than: **•Ewê nedixast r̄ûyê kesekî bibîne,** ***xêncî*** **ḧizkirîyê xwe** (Ba) She didn't want to see the face of anyone *but* her beloved **•Hebûye tunebûye,** ***xêncî*** **xwedê kes tunebûye** (Ks) Once upon a time [lit. 'there was, there was not, *other than* God there was no one'] *[traditional introductory formula for folktales, cf. P & Azerbaijani]* **•Vira** ***xêncî*** **min du kurmancê dinê jî dixûnin** (B) There are two other Kurds *besides* me studying here **•*Xeyr ji*** **min kes nehat** (IF) Nobody came *but* me **•*xêncî*** **wê yekê** (B) *besides* that; -**ji xeynî wî** (JB3) besides, moreover: **•*Ji ẍeyna*** **ẍulamê wî pêve kû nema** (HR 4:39) *Except* for his servant, no one was left. {also: (ji) xeyna; (ji) xeynî (Bx/JB3); xeyr ji (IFb); (j) xeyrî (JB1-A); xênc (GF); xên ji (K-2); xênî (F); xênîji (F); [bi ẍeyr ji] (JR); ẍeyna; (j) ẍeynî (JB1-S); ji ẍeyri (SK); [gair غـيـر/be-gair بـغـيـر] (JJ); <ẍeyn> غـيـن (HH)} {syn: bezîji (F); bê I[2]; ji ... pê ve; ji bilî; meger [3]; pêştir [+ji]} < Ar γayr غير = 'other (than)' + ji [Ks/K/B//GF//Bx/JB3//IFb//JB1-A//F//JB1-S//SK//JJ//HH] <xeyrî>

xênî خێنی (F) = except. See **xêncî**.

xênîji خێنیژِ (F) = except. See **xêncî**.

xên ji خێن ژِ (K) = except. See **xêncî**.

xêr I خـێـر *f.* **(-a;-ê).** goodness: **•Fêrîk ku dît em *xêra* wana dixwazin ... ewî dilê xwe ber me vekir** (Ba2:2, 206) When Ferik saw that we meant them no harm [lit. 'that we want their goodness'] ... he opened his heart to us **•Te *xêr* e?** (IFb) What's up with you?/Is there something wrong? **•Tu bi *xêr* hatî** (IF) *Wel*come; **-bi xêra *fk-î*** (Frq)/**xêra rûyê *fk-î*** (K) because of, thanks to {syn: dewlet serê; pêxemet; sexmerat}: **•*Xêra rûyê wî* ew şixul qewimî** (K) *Because of him* that thing happened; **-xêr û bêr** (AB)/**xêrbêr** (K) profit, gain: **•Ax pir *bi xêr û bêr* e** (AB) The soil is very *productive* (or, profitable). {also: xeyr II (SK-2); [kheir] خير (JJ); <xêr> خـيـر (HH)} {syn: ç'akî; qencî} < Ar xayr خير; Sor xêr خێر [F/K/IFb/B/JJ/HH/JB1-A&S/SK/GF/OK]

xêratxane خـێـراتـخـانـه (ZF3) = soup kitchen. See **xêretxane**.

xêretxan•e خـێـرەتـخـانـه *f.* **(•eya;•ê).** soup kitchen, home for the poor: **•Were *xêretxanê*, nanê xwe bixwe ... Lênihêrî şivan hat, hat *xêretxanê* nan xar, av xar, axîna wî jî hat** (HCK-3, #2, 26) Come to the *soup kitchen*, eat something [lit. 'your bread'] ... He saw that the shepherd came to *the soup kitchen* and had something to eat and drink, and he sighed as well. {also: xêratxane (ZF3)} [HCK/IFb//ZF3]

xêrxaz خێرخاز (SK) = well-meaning. See **xêrxwaz**.

xêrxazî خێرخازی (SK) = good will. See **xêrxwazî**.

xêrxwaz خـێـرخـواز *m.&f.* **(-ê/;).** 1) {syn: xudanxêr} well-wisher; benefactor; 2) {syn: dildar [2]} volunteer [T gönüllü/fahri; Ar mutaṭawwi' متطوّع; P dāvṭalab داوطلب; Sor xobexş خـۆبـەخـش]: **•Bi tonan erzaqên ku bi alîkariya *xêrxwazan* hatin berhevkirin [j]i Mislimanên Arakanî re tên belavkirin** (cinarinsesi. com 13.x.2017) Tons of supplies which have been collected by *volunteers* are being distributed to the Muslims of Arakani [Rohingyas]; 3) [*adj.*] well-meaning: **•Eger sa'eteke pêştir hung nexoşîya xo bi ḧakîmêt ḧaziq û *xêrxaz* derman neken, mikrobê cehaletê û ṣefrayê sefahetê ... pîçek maye hingo bikujît** (SK 57:660) If you do not have skilled and *well-meaning* physicians treat your disease within the hour, then the microbe of ignorance and the bile of stupidity ... will kill you within a short while. {also: xêrxaz (SK); xêrxwez (F/K)} {xêrx[w]azî; xêrxwez[t]î} [B/IFb/GF/OK/FS//F/K//SK]

xêrxwazî خـێـرخـوازی *f.* **(-[y]a;-yê).** good will, well-wishing: **•Sebebê muweffeqîyetê her wextekî ittifaq e û *xêrxazîya* hewalê xo ye** (SK 53:578) At all times the cause of success is harmony and *consideration* for one's companions. {also: xêrxazî (SK); xêrxwez[t]î (K)} [B/IFb/GF/OK/ZF3//K//SK] <xêrxwaz>

xêrxwez خێرخوەز (F/K) = well wisher. See **xêrxwaz**.

xêrxwezî خێرخوەزی (K) = good will. See **xêrxwazî**.

xêrxweztî خێرخوەزتی (K) = good will. See **xêrxwazî**.

xêt خێت (FS) = stupid. See **xêtik**.

xêtik خـێـتِـك *adj.* stupid, foolish, simpleminded: **•Lê wezîrekî wî yê pir xêtik hebû** (ZZ-7, 261) But he had a very simpleminded vizier. {also: xêt (FS)} {syn: aqilsivik; bêaqil; eḧmeq; sefîh} [ZZ/ZF//FS]

xêvat خێڤات = tent. See **xêvet**.

xêvet خێڤەت *f.* **(-a;-ê).** tent; white canvas tent (JJ/JB1-S): **•Bavo, çiqas steyrin li 'ezmana, / çiqas xîzê devê behra, / Ewqas *xêvet* dor me girtine** (EP-7) Dad, as many stars as there are in the sky / as much sand as there is on the seashore / That's how many *tents* are surrounding us. {also: xêbet (B); xêvat; xîv (JB1-S); xîvet (JB3/IFb-2); [khiwet] خـيـڤـت (JJ)} {syn: ç'adir[2]; kon; r̄eşmal} <Ar xaymah خيمة; Sor xêwet خێوەت [EP-7/K/A/IFb//JB3/JJ//B//JB1-S] <sing I>

xêzek خێزەك (GF) = small line; dash. See **xêzik**.

xêzik خـــێـــزِك *f.* **(-a;-ê).** 1) small line; 2) dash, *punctuation mark* (--): **•Gava ku *xêzik* di navbera reqeman da dihê danîn, ... divê ku berî *xêzikê* û piştî wê navber tune be** (RR 29.1. d)5)) When *a dash* is placed between numerals, ... there must be no space before and after *the dash*. {also: xêzek (GF); xêzk (A)} Cf. Sor xêz خـێـز = 'stroke, stripe; hyphen' & kiştek کِـشـتـەك = 'dash' [RR/IFb/G/ZF/Wkt/RZ//GF//A] <bendik II; xalbendî>

xêzk خێزك (A) = small line; dash. See **xêzik**.

xiç خِج (A/JJ) = colostrum. See **xîç' I**.

xidam خِدام = maidservant; eunuch. See **xadim**.

xidar خِدار (Z-2) = cruel; dangerous. See **xedar**.

xiddam خِددام = maidservant; eunuch. See **xadim**.

xidmet خِدمەت (SK) = service. See **xizmet**.

xidmetçî خِدمەتچی (SK) = servant. See **xizmetk'ar**.

xifş خِـــفـــش *f.* **(-a;).** the young of a gazelle, fawn:

•Gavê ko Memo ji xewa şîrin şîyar dibe, berê wî dik'eve devê dêrî, dirêne ya ħekmetek ji navê xudê *ximşeke xizala*, horîyeke cinetê, li devê derî sekinîye ji p'êye (Z-3, 92) When Memo awakes from a deep sleep, he looks over at the door and sees by divine providence *a young gazelle*, a houri from paradise, standing in the doorway; **-xifşa ẍezalê** (Zeb) do. {also: ximş (Z-3)} {syn: kara xezal} Cf. Ar xišf خـشـف = 'newborn young of a gazelle' [Zeb/GF/ZF3//Z-3] <xezal I>

xilas خِلاس (Dz/SK) = free; finished. See **xelas**.

xilasî خِلاسی (Wkt) = end; rescue. See **xelasî**.

xilaz خِلاز (B/Z-1) = free; finished. See **xelas**.

***xilbilîk** خِلبِليك **().** evil spirits that are believed [by the people of Urmiyah and environs] to appear at sundown in the guise of real people, and who wreak havoc on their victims: safety pins are considered useful in warding them off (MK3, p. 181 [khilbileek]) [MK3]

xilç خِـلـچ *m.* **(-ê;-î).** long wooden stick with sharp tip *for uprooting thorny plants, such as* ***kereng*** (qv.) [amûra derhênana kengirê; = T kazgıç]; also used in children's game (FS). {also: gilç (Şnx/FS); ẍilç (IFb-2)} {syn: adûde} [A/IFb/FJ/ZF//Şnx/FS] <bist I>

xilêf خِـلـێـف (SK/Hej/FS) = man-made beehive. See **xilêfe**.

xilêf•e خِـلـێـفـه *f.* **(•a;•ê).** type of man-made beehive; basket used as a bee-hive: **•Jinê got, "Here, hindek şokêt bîyê bîne, li pêş çawêt xelkî sê car *xilêfan* çêke. Her kesê ji te bipirsît, 'Ew *xilêfan*** [sic] **bo çine?' bêje, 'Min sê çar mêş li naw lêrî dîtine, dê çim, girim, keme *xilêfan*'"** (SK 35:314) His wife said, "Go and bring some osiers and make three or four *hive-baskets* in the sight of people. Tell anybody who asks you what *the baskets* are for, 'I have seen three or four bees in the forest. I shall go and catch them and put them in *the baskets*'." {also: xilêf (SK/FS); xilêfk (OK/AA/FS-2); <xilêf> خـلـێـف (Hej)} NENA khilîpâ ܚܠܝܦܐ = 'beehive made of osier' (Maclean) [Zeb//SK/Hej/FS//OK/AA] <kewar[mêş]; selmêşk>

xilêfk خِـلـێـفـك (OK/AA/FS) = man-made beehive. See **xilêfe**.

xilf خِـلف *f.* **(-a;).** easily undone knot, slipknot (a knot made so that it can readily be untied by pulling one free end), *as in the drawstring [**doxîn**] of a man's trousers [**şalvar**]; as opposed to **girê**, a knot which is hard to untie*: **•Wî *xilfa* şaroxa kalikê vekir** (FS) He undid the *knot* on the shoelace of the slipper. {also: xilfe (Zeb); xulfe (Zeb-2)} {syn: xerboqe} [Bw/Kmc-17/FS/ZF3//Zeb] <doxîn; girê>

xilfe خِلفه (Zeb) = easily undone knot. See **xilf**.

xilindor I خِـلِـنـدۆر (A/FJ/GF/Wkt/FD) = first milk. See **xelendor I**.

xilindor II خِـلِـنـدۆر (A/Kmc/Wkt) = Smyrnium olusatrum. See **xelendor II**.

xilîlok خِليلۆك (Msr) = hail. See **xilolîk I**[1].

xilmaş خِـلـمـاش *f.* **(-a;-ê).** drowsiness, dozing off: **•*Xilmaşa* xewê hatiye wî** (FS) He dozed off [lit. '*drowsiness of* sleep came to him']; **-xilmaş bûn** (KS) to drop off to sleep: **•Hema ku ez *xilmaş bûm* dengê xişxişekê hate min** (KS, 58) Just as I *was about to drop off to sleep*, I heard a rustling sound [lit. 'the voice of a rustling came to me']. {also: xirmaş (Frq); xurmaş (Rwn); [khil-mach] خلماش (JJ); <xilmaş> خلماش (Hej)} Cf. NENA khilmâ/khülma ܚܠܡܐ = 'dream' (Maclean) < Arc ḥelmā חלמא/ḥīlmā חילמא [KS/K(s)/IFb/JJ/GF/Hej/ZF3/FS//Frq//Rwn] <nivistin; xew; xewar>

xilmeçî خِلمەچی (JB1-A) = servant. See **xizmetk'ar**.

xilmet خِلمەت (JB1-A&S) = service. See **xizmet**.

xilmetk'ar خِـلـمـەتـكـار (JB1-A) = servant. See **xizmetk'ar**.

xilolîk I خِـلـۆلـيـك *f.* **(-a;).** 1) {also: xilîlok (Msr); xilorîg (IFb); xilorîk II (Wkp); [kheloulik] خلولك (JJ); <xilûlîk> خلوليك (HH)} {syn: savarok} small grains of hail, tiny hailstones: **•*Xilolîkên* hêsirên çavên mêrik di ser riwê wî yê nekurkirî de gêr dibûn ser çena wî û paşê dinuqutîn erdê** (KS, 10) *The tiny hailstones of* the man's tears rolled down his unshaven face onto his chin and then dripped onto the ground **•Zîpika ku libên wê hûr in, jê re dibêjin gijlok an jî *xilorîk*** (Wkp) Hailstones that are tiny are called gijlok or *xilorîk*; 2) {syn: şilop'e [1]} snow mixed with rain. Cf. Sor xilêre خِلێره = 'round bullet' [Msr//A/ZF3/FS//JJ/HH//IFb//Wkp] <gijlok; teyrok; zîpik I>

xilolîk II خِـلـۆلـيـك (CB) = dish of ground meat and bulgur wheat. See **kilorîk**.

xilorîg خِلۆریگ (IFb) = hail. See **xilolîk I**[1].

xilorîk I خِلۆریك (Qzl/Qrj) = dish of ground meat and bulgur wheat. See **kilorîk**.

xilorîk II خِلۆریك (Wkp) = hail. See **xilolîk I**[1].

xilp خِـلـپ *f.* **(-a;).** young tree, sapling, tree over one year old, not yet full grown: **-xilpa darê** (Zeb) do. Cf. NA khélâpâ ܚܠܦܐ = 'willow' (Maclean) < Syr ḥalpā/ḥelāpā ܚܠܦܐ = ' reed, willow' & Arc ḥilfā חלפא = 'willow, young shoot'; Sor xełf خەڵف = 'shoot, young branch' [Zeb] <dar I; şitil>

xilxal خِلخال (IFb/GF/JJ/TF/OK/Mtk/Qzl) = anklet. See **xirxal**.

xilxil•e خِلخِله *m.* (**•ê;•ê**). 1) heap, pile: **•Me pez hinekî ji *xilxilê* kevira dûr xist** (Ba2:2, 205) We chased the sheep a little bit away from *the pile of* rocks; 2) obstruction, blockage *(made by pile of rocks)*: -**'erdê xilxile** (FS) ground full of holes (such as mouseholes) and thus hard to walk through; 3) mountain-ridge: **•Birê min, çimkî tu dik'evî şika, were em keriyê pêz vira bihêlin, hef̄ne qiraxê *xilxile*** (Ba2:2, 205) My brother, because you are having doubts, come let's leave the flock of sheep here and go to the edge of *the mountain ridge*. {also: [khylkhylé] خلخله (JJ)} [Ba2/K/B/JJ/ZF3/FS/BF]

xim خِم *m.* (;-î). dye: **•Li hindawê cer̄ikêt *ximî* qaydeye kulek bo r̄onaîyê dibît** (SK 4:28) It is customary for there to be a skylight above the *dye* vats for the light to get in. {also: ximb, f. (FS)} {syn: boyax; derman; r̄eng} Sor xum خوم = 'dye, indigo' [SK//FS]

ximam خِمام (Nofa) = fog. See **xumam**.

ximb خِمب, f. (FS) = dye. See **xim**.

ximdar خِمدار *m.&f.* (). dyer, one whose profession is to color cloth with dye: **•Dibêjin *ximdarek* hebû, şeş ḧevt mirîşkêt qelew hebûn. Şevê di oda ximî da lîs dibûn** (SK) They say there was one *a dyer* who had six or seven fat chickens. At night they used to roost in the dye-house. {also: ximder (IFb/OK)} Sor xumxaneçî خومخانەچی = 'dyer' [SK//IFb/OK] <boyax>

ximder خِمدەر (IFb/OK) = dyer. See **ximdar**.

ximş خِمش (Z-3) = young gazelle. See **xifş**.

ximxim I خِمخِم (IFb/GF) = nostril. See **ximximk**.

ximxim II خِمخِم (AD) = murmur; buzzing. See **xumxum I**.

ximximk خِمخِمك *f.* (**-a;-ê**). nostril: **•S̲armayê li min daye û *ximximkên* min hatine girtin** (FS) The cold has hit me [or, I've caught a cold] and my *nostrils* have gotten stopped up. {also: ximxim I (IFb/GF); xinxink (GF-2)} {syn: bêvil [1]; difn [2]; firn[ik]; kepî[2]; kulfik I (Wn)} [Bşk/Bw/OK//IFb/GF/FS/ZF3] <difn; poz I>

xinamî خِنامی *m.&f.* (). 1) relative by marriage; son-in-law's/daughter-in-law's father, "in-law" [cf. T dünür; Yiddish mekhutn מחותן]: -**bûn xinamîyê hev** (K) to become related through marriage; 2) [*f.* (;-**yê**).] son-in-law's/daughter-in-law's mother [cf. Yiddish mekheteneste מחותנתטע]. {also: xnamî (SC)} < Arm xnami խնամի {xinamîtî} [K/A/IFb/B/ZF3//SC] <taloq II>

xinamîtî خِنامیتی *f.* (**-ya;-yê**). affinity, relationship by marriage, particularly between parents of the bride and groom. {also: xinamtî (ZZ-4)} [B/ZF3//ZZ-4] <taloqtî; xinamî>

xinamtî خِنامتی (ZZ-4) = relationship by marriage. See **xinamîtî**.

xinûsî خِنووسی *f.* (). churn; round, earthenware vessel with an opening in the center of the top, used as a (butter) churner. Cf. Arm xnocʻi խնոցի = 'clay or wooden churn'; also possibly the adjectival form of **Xinûs** (T Hınıs), a town near Erzurum [IFb/ZF3] <ḧîz; meşk; p'ost; sirsûm>

xinxink خِنخِنك (GF) = nostril. See **ximximk**.

xinzîr خِنزیر *f./m.(B/G)* (**-a/ ; **). pig; swine; hog (Haz: erudite) : -**goştê xinzîr** (B) pork; -**Xûna xinzîr-be!** (XF) There is no trace of him. {also: xenzîr (G); xiznîr (IFb); [khynzir] خنزير (JJ)} {syn: beraz; domiz (Mzg); weḧ̄ş [2]} < Ar xinzīr خنزير = 'pig' [F/K/B/JJ/Haz//G//IFb]

xir I خِر/**xir̄** خِڕ [K] *m.* (). 1) {syn: çûçik (1[3]) (Msr) = baby boy's; 'ewîc; hêlik [2], m. (Msr); kîr; ter̄ik [2]} penis; 2) rod, switch (K). {also: [khyr] خر (JJ)} [Msr/A/IFb/G/ZF3/FD//K]

xir̄ II خِڕ: -**xir̄ û xalî** (K/Z-2)/**xir û xalî** (B)/**xir̄e-xalî** (FK-eb-2) deserted, depopulated, devoid of people, empty, barren: **•Ew dajo diçe, deşteke *xir̄e-xalîr̄*a derbaz dibe** (FK-eb-2) He rides off, passing through a *barren* plain. [Z-2/K/ZF3//B]

***xira I** خِرا: -**xira bûn** (Msr) to ejaculate, 'cum/come'. [Msr] <avik>

xira II خِرا = bad; ruined. See **xirab**.

xirab خِراب *adj.* 1) {syn: nebaş; nexweş [2]; ≠baş; ≠xweş; ≠r̄ind; ≠çê} bad: **•Bertîl tiştekî *xerab* e** (ZF3) A bribe is a *bad* thing **•Ew kur̄ekê *xirab* e** (FS) He is a *bad* boy; 2) {syn: kavil; wêran I} ruined, destroyed: -**xirab kirin** = to wreck, ruin, destroy: **•Ev qundir *wê* mala min *xerab bike*** (L) This gourd *will ruin* my home! [Cf. malxirab] **•Kur̄o, darbir̄, çima ... vî mêşeî bedew *xirav dikî?*** (Dz) Boy, woodcutter, why ... *are you ruining* this beautiful forest? {also: xerab (IFb-2/ZF3); xira II; xirav (Dz); [kherab] خراب (JJ); <xirab> خراب (HH)} < Ar xarāb خراب = 'ruins';

Sor xirap خراپ/xirab خراب/xiraw خراو; Za xirav (Todd) {xerabî; xirabî; xiravî} [K/(A)/JB3/IFb/B/HH/SK/JB1-A&S/GF/FS//JJ/ZF3//Dz]

xirabî خرابی *f.* **(-ya;-yê).** badness, evil; wicked deed; harm, injury: **•Çiqas *xirabyê* bikî, agir be'rê nak'ewe** (Dz) No matter how much *evil* you do, the sea won't catch on fire **•Ez dixazim *xirabya* xwe mêşeř̄a bicêřbînim** (Dz) I want to make the forest feel my *evil* (or, I want to test out my evil on the forest) **•Fikra min heye ku ez *xirabiyekê* bigehînimê** (ZZ-10, 157) I have the idea to do *something bad* to him **•Min çu *xirabî* digel te nekiriye, min çakî kiriye** (SK 2:13) I have done you no *harm*. Rather have I acted well **•Min *xirabîya* te nevêt** (Zeb) I mean you no *harm*. {also: xerabî (K-2/A/ZF); xiravî (B-2); [kherabi] خرابی (JJ)} [Dz/F/K/IFb/B/SK/FS//A/JJ/ZF] <xirab>

xirabtir خرابتر *adj.* worse: **•Li gorî dîtina min, tabloya îro ji tabloya berê ne *xirabtir* e** (AW72A3) In my opinion, today's scenario is no *worse* than the former scenario. {also: [karábtera] (JJ-G} Sor xiraptir خراپتر [AW/IFb//JJ-G]

xirar خرار (Bw/HH/ZF3/FS) = large sack. See **xerar**.

xirat خرات (ZF3) = carpenter; turner. See **xerat**.

xirav خراڤ (Dz) = bad; ruined. See **xirab**.

xiravî خراڤی (B) = badness. See **xirabî**.

xirboqî خربۆقی (FJ/GF/Kmc) = slipknot. See **xerboqe**.

xircir خرجر (IFb/CS) = argument. See **xirecir**.

xirecir خرەجر *f.* **(-a;-ê).** argument, quarrel: **•Dev ji *xirecirê* berdin!** (EN) Quit *arguing*! **•Kurê min, tu li *xirecirê* rast hat[î], lê raneweste, çunkî ji *xirecirê* mirin dertê** (Qzl) My son, if you encounter a *quarrel* [i.e., people shouting at each other], don't stop there, because death can result from a *quarrel*. {also: xircir (IFb-2/CS); xirocir (FJ); xiřucir̄ (FS); xirûcir (IFb/TF/FJ-2/GF)} {syn: cerenîx; cuře; de'w II; doz; k'eft û left; k'eşmek'eş; k'êşe; mişt û mir̄} [Qzl/ZF3//IFb/TF/GF//FS//FJ//CS]

xiře-xalî خرە خالی (FK-eb-2) = desolate, barren. See **xiř II**.

xirexir خرەخر (ZF/GF)/xiřexiř خرەخر (K/B/SK) = knocking; cracking; rattling; snoring. See **xurexur**.

xirêf خریێف *f.* **(-a;).** banquet, feast: **•Sibetirê Ĥemedoyê Birho tevî peyayên wî vexwande mala xwe û jê ra *xirêfeke* (ziyafet) bi semt çêkir** (Rnh 2:17, 309) The next day he invited Hemedoyê Birho together with his men to his house and made a *sumptuous feast* for him. {also: xirêfek (ZF3)} [Rnh/GF/CS//ZF3]

xirifîn خرفین (IFb) = to go senile; to lose one's mind. See **xerifîn**.

xirmaş خرماش (Frq) = dozing off. See **xilmaş**.

xirmîn خرمین (IF) = thunder; crash. See **girmîn**.

xirnaq خرناق *m.&f.* **(/-a;).** rabbit cub, young hare, leveret: **-xiřnika kêvrîşkê** (FS) do. {also: xirneq (A/IFb); xirnik (GF/AA/Qzl)/xiřnik (FS); xirniq (Wkt)} Cf. Ar xirniq خرنق = 'young hare, leveret' [Btm/Grc/TF//A/IFb//GF/AA/Qzl//FS//Wkt] <k'erguh>

xirneq خرنەق (A/IFb) = rabbit cub. See **xirnaq**.

xirnik خرنك (GF/AA/Qzl)/xiřnik خرنك (FS) = rabbit cub. See **xirnaq**.

xirniq خرنق (Wkt) = rabbit cub. See **xirnaq**.

xiřnîf خرنیف (FS) = carob. See **xernûf**.

xirnûf خرنووف (GF) = carob. See **xernûf**.

xiro خرۆ (SK) = durra. See **xirovî**.

xirocir خرۆجر (FJ) = argument. See **xirecir**.

xirovî خرۆڤی *f.* **().** durra, guinea corn, Indian millet. {also: xiro (SK); xurobî, m. (Bw)} [SK//OK/AA//Bw] <genim; herzin; lazût>

xirş خرش *adj.* barren, sterile, fruitless (of trees and plants): **•Bahîva nav rezê me ya *xirş*e** (BF) The almond tree in our garden is *barren*; **-dara xirş** (Zeb/FS) barren tree. {also: <xirş> خرش (Hej)} {syn: bêber} [Bw/Zeb/IFb/OK/Hej/ZF3/BF/FS] <bêweç; bêzuřet; stewir>

xirt خرت *m.* **().** three-year-old ram, male sheep (Zeb); four-year-old ram (IFb/OK); four-year-old sheep (FS): **-miha xirt** (FS) do. {also: <xirt> خرت (Hej)} {syn: hogiç} Sor xirt خرت = 'yearling; round, yearly cycle, year in life of sheep, goats, and domestic fowls' [Zeb/IFb/OK/Hej/FS] <beran; mî I; şek>

xirtik I خرتك *f.(Qzl)/m.(Elk/FS)* **(/-ê;).** unripe zucchini, cucumber, etc.: **•Pîrê bûbû mîna *xirtikekî* mezin. Werimî û şîn** (HYma, 18) The old woman became like a big *unripe cucumber*. Swollen and blue-green. {also: <xirtik خرتك/xirçe خرچە> (Hej)} {syn: kûtik; tûtik II} [Qzl/Qrj/A/GF/FJ/Hej/FS] <kundir; qitik; xiyar>

xiřucir̄ خروجر (FS) = argument. See **xirecir**.

xirûcir خرووجر (IFb/TF/FJ/GF/FS) = argument. See **xirecir**.

Xirvatkî خرڤاتكی (ZF3) = Croatian. See **Kirwatî**.

xiř ve خر ڤە: **-xiř ve bûn** (Zeb/Dh) to gather *(vi.)*, assemble *(vi.)* {also: xiř̂ bûnewe (SK)} {syn: berhev bûn; civîn; k'om bûn; t'op bûn}: •**Ewcar ji her layekîwe xulamêt paşa *xiř bûnewe*, dest bi şeřî kirin** [sic] (SK 24:225) Then the pasha's men *gathered* from all sides and began to fight; -**xir ve kirin** (IFb) to gather *(vt.)*, assemble *(vt.)*, collect *(vt.)* (IFb) {syn: berhev kirin; civandin; k'om kirin; t'op kirin}: •**Kelepor û fulklorê Kurdî hêşta bi nîvî nehatiye komkirin û *xirve kirin*** (Bêhnîşk [2006], 5) Half of Kurdish folklore has not yet been gathered and *collected* •**Şivanî pez *xiřve* kir** (FS) The shepherd *gathered* the sheep. Sor xiř bûnewe خِـڕ بـوونـەوە = 'to gather, come together' [Zeb/Dh/IFb/BF/FS//SK]

Xirwatî خِرواتى (Wkt/Wkp) = Croatian. See **Kirwatî**.

xirxal خِـرخـال *m.(K/EP-4/Qzl)/f.(B/Mtk)* **(-ê/ ; /-ê).** anklet, legband worn by women: •**Xecê *xirxalekî* lingê xweyî zêrîn girt, avît, go "Bira, *xirxalê* lingê min ser zerê maye"** (EP-4, #34) Khej took one of her golden *legbands*, threw it [over the precipice and] said, "Brothers, my *legband* has remained behind in the canyon." {also: xilxal (IFb-2/GF-2/TF/OK-2/Mtk/Qzl); [khylkhal خلخال/khyrkhal خرخال] (JJ)} <Ar xalxāl خلخال; --> T halhal; Sor xirxał خِـرخـاڵ [EP-4/K/IFb/B/JJ/GF] <bazin; xişir; xizêm>

xirxir خِـرخِـر (A/GF) = knocking; cracking; rattling; snoring. See **xurexur**.

xirz خِرز (GF/OK) = fish eggs. See **xerz**.

xisar خِسار (K/IFb/Wkt/CS) = harm. See **xesar**.

xisîl خِسيل (Ba2) = mat. See **qisîl**.

xistin/xist'in [JB1-A] خِـسـتِـن *vt.* **(-x- / -xîn- / -xin- [JB1-S]).** 1) to drop, let fall *(lit. & fig.)*: •**Qîza min, çima te *xwe xistîye* vî halî?** (L) My daughter, why have you *put yourself* in this state? (=what happened to you?); -**li 'erdê xistin** (K) to drop stg. on the floor or ground; -**li hev xistin** = a) to stir, to mix: •**Xatûn P'erî wê bi k'evgîrê emek *li hev dixe*** (EP-7) Khatun Peri *is stirring* the food with a ladle; b) to confuse, mix up; 2) to forcibly insert, thrust, drive into, cause to enter: •**Bizina kûvî strûê xwe tûj li zikê wî *dixe*** (J) The powerful (or, wild) goat *drives* her horns into his belly •**Destê xwe *xist* qula çwîkî** (L) He *thrust* his hand into the sparrow's hole (=nest) •**Heger şerdê wî nanîn, wan digire, *dixe* hebsê** (L) If they don't complete his [assigned] tasks, he arrests them and *throws* them in prison •**Mele kefen dike û tîne, *dixe* bin erdê** (L) The mollah enshrouds [the corpse] and brings it, buries it [lit. '*puts* it underground'] •**Şwîrek li qerika wî *xist*** (L) He struck him in the throat with his sword [lit. 'he *drove* a sword into his throat'] •**Tuê van herdû muê laşê min *bixî* qotîyekê** (L) You will *put* both these hairs of mine [lit. 'of my body'] in a box •**Wana teyrek kuşt, xûna teyr kirasê Ûsib *xist*** (Ba) They killed a bird, [and] *dipped* Joseph's shirt in the bird's blood; -**bi dest xistin** (IFb/GF/RZ) to obtain, procure, get, acquire; 3) to take off, remove *(clothing)* {also: êxistin}: •**Vira ewî kirasê xwe *êxist*** (Ba #32, 318) Here he *took off* his shirt; 4) to beat, strike [+ **li**] (B/JB1-S). See **lêxistin**: -**dêrî xistin** (B) to knock on the door. {also: êxistin (-êx-) (SK); [khystin خـسـتـيـن/ eïkhystin ايخستين] (JJ)} Cf. P xastan خستن = 'to wound'; Sor xistin خِـسـتِـن (-xe-: 3rd pers. sing. -xa[t]); SoK xa-/xıs(t)- = 'to throw' (Fat 357) [K/JB3/IFb/B/JJ/JB1-S/GF/TF/ZF//SK//JB1-S] <k'etin>

xişikîn خِشِكين (GF) = to slide, glide. See **xuşikîn**.

xiş•ir خِـشِـر *m./f.(JB3)* **(•rê/ ;).** (woman's) valuables, jewels; women's gold, silver, or brass ornaments: •**Ḧeyştê bar *xişrê* wê bû** (Ba) She had eighty loads of *valuables* (or, her jewels amounted to eighty loads). {also: xişr, f. (JB3/IFb-2/SK/GF); [khychir] خشير (JJ); <xişr> خشر (HH)} Cf. Sor xişł خِشڵ [Ba/F/K/A/IFb/B/JJ//JB3/HH/SK/GF] <xizêm>

***xişîlok** خِشيلۆك *f.* **().** small avalanche. [Bw] <aşît; berf; řenî; şape>

xişîm خِشيم (BF) = naïve. See **xeşîm**.

xişîmî خِشيمى (Wkt) = naïveté. See **xeşîmî**.

xişîn خِشين (IFb/JJ) = to rustle. See **xuşîn**.

xişkxişk خِـشـكـخِـشـك (A) = small bell or coin. See **xişxişk**.

xişr خِشر, f. (JB3/IFb/SK/GF) = jewels. See **xişir**.

xişre خِـشـره (FS) = transporting grain or tool for transporting grain. See **şixre**.

xişt I خِـشـت *adj.* even, on the same level, of the same length: •**Min ev bizin bi deh dînarên *xişt* kiřî** (FS) I bought this goat for ten dinars *even*. Sor xişt خِشت [Zeb/Hej/FS]

xişt II خِـشـت *m./f.(ZF3/Wkt)* **(-ê/;).** sun-dried brick. {syn: k'elpîç; tabûq} [Pok. idh- 12.] 'to burn, fire' + *-s + *-to --> *i(dh)-s-to-: Skt iṣṭakā; O Ir *išti- (Ras, p.136): Av ištya-; O P išti- = 'sun-dried brick' (Kent); P xešt خشت; Sor xişt خِشت [Zeb/K(s)/IFb/GF/TF/OK/ZF3/Wkt] <êzing; k'elpîç>

xişt III خِـشـت *f.* **(;-ê).** 1) {syn: zerg} sharp metal point or tip of a lance: **•Serê bizmarê kir *xişt*** (Bw) He made the nail's head into *a sharp point*; **-xişt kirin** (Bw) to sharpen into a point; 2) skewer with sharp tip. {also: [khecht] خشت (JJ); <xişt> خشت (HH)} P xešt خشت = 'javelin; mace, staff'; Ar xušt خشت = 'javelin' [Zeb/K(s)/IFb/GF/TF/OK/FS/ZF3] <nikil [2]>

xişxiş خِشخِش (A/FJ/GF/HH/AD) = rustling, splashing. See **xuşexuş**.

xişxişk خِشخِشك *f.* **(-a;).** 1) small bells (ZF) or coins (A/IFb), hung on a tambourine; 2) rattle, child's toy (FJ/GF/ZF/FS). {also: xişkxişk (A)} Cf. Ar xišxēša خشخيشة = 'rattle' [SBx/IFb/FJ/GF/ZF/FS//A]

xitêre خِتێره (IFb) = torch. See **xetîre**.

xitimandin خِتِماندِن *vt.* **(-xitimîn-).** to stop up, plug up; to cork; to seal: **•Çû gundê ku ava wan *xitimandî*** (Wlt 2:59, 15) He went to the village whose water *was sealed off* **•Hersêka bîr bi keviran *xitimandin*** [sic] (Wlt 2:59, 15) The three of them *plugged up* the well with rocks. {also: xetimandin (GF); [khetemandin] ختماندين (JJ); <xetimandin ختماندن (dixetimîne) (دختمينه)> (HH)} {syn: pengandin} <Ar √x-t-m ختم = 'to seal' [Wlt/K/IFb/B/OK//HH/GF//JJ]

xiya خِيا *adj.* kneeling (of camels): **•Ḧêştirvanî ḧêştira *xiya* rakir** (FS) The camelherd had the *kneeling* camel get up; **-xiya bûn** (Qzl/Qrj/GF) to kneel down, sit (of camels) {syn: nixan}; **-xiya kirin** (GF) to cause to kneel or sit (of camels) {syn: nixandin; tixandin}. {also: <xiya> خيا (Hej)} Cf. Ar nayyax II نيّخ [Qzl/Qrj/GF/Hej/FS] <deve I; ḧêştir; mexel kirin>

xiyal خِيال *f.* **(-a;-ê).** 1) {syn: aşop; fikir; hizir; mitale; r̄aman I} thought, idea; imagination: **•Daimî *xiyala* şeytanî ew e, welîyan û s̱ofîyan û tobekaran ji r̄êka beḧeştê û necatê derêxît û bibete ser r̄êka cehennemê û helakî** (SK 4:42) The devil's *thoughts* are always directed toward leading holy and pious and repentant men astray from the road to paradise and salvation and setting them on the road to hell and destruction **•*Xiyala* me dirust derkewt** (SK 32:286) Our *idea* turned out to be right **•*Xiyala* wî ew bû ko imam xelet kir yan nezanî** (SK 17:164) He thought [lit. 'it was his *thought*'] that the imam had made a mistake, or just did not know; **-hatine xiyala *fk-î*** (SK) to come to mind, to think of: **•R̄astî, ewe tedbîrekî çak e. Hindî mulaḧeze dikem ji wê çêtir *nahête xiyala* min** (SK 33:294) Truly this is a good idea. However much I consider it I *can think of* nothing better; **-xeyal kirin** (K)/**xiyal kirin** (SK/OK) to think, imagine: **•Xudanê kerî jî weto *xiyal dikir* ko her do hewalêt wî dê harî wî ken, nedizanî ko r̄ezewanî her do lêbandine** (SK 8:80) The owner of the donkey *thought* that his two companions would help him, not knowing that the gardener had deceived them; 2) {syn: cefa; fikar; k'eder; k'erb; k'eser; kovan; kul I; şayîş; t'alaş; tatêl; xem} care, worry, concern, grief (TF). {also: xeyal (K/IFb/GF/TF/ZF3); [khyial/xayāl (Lx)/kajál (G)] خيال (JJ)} < Ar xayāl خيال = 'ghost, phantom; imagination' --> T hayal = 'imagined thing, image; imagination'; Sor xeyał خەیاڵ = 'imagination, idea' [SK/JJ/OK/FS//K/IFb/GF/TF/ZF3] <bêxîyal>

xiyalşkestî خِيالشكستى *adj.* disillusioned, disappointed. {also: xeyalşkestî} Cf. T hayalkırıklığı = 'disappointment' [Hk]

xiyanet خِيانەت *f.* **(-a;-ê).** betrayal, deceit, treachery, perfidy, disloyalty: **•Ev cepha ku, bi dijminê Kurdan ên herî mezin ... re bûye yek ... ji aliyê gelê Kurd ve wek "Cepha *xiyanetê*" tê binavkirin** (Wlt 1:36, 1) This front which has united with the Kurds' greatest enemy ... is called "the front *of betrayal*" by the Kurdish people. {also: xiyanetî (B); [khyianet] خيانت (JJ); <xiyanet> خيانت (HH)} {syn: mixenetî; xayîntî} <Ar xiyānah خيانة; Sor xiyanet خِيانەت [Wlt/K/IFb/JJ/HH/SK/ZF3//B] <'ewanî; geveztî; mixenet; xapandin>

xiyanetî خِيانەتى (B) = betrayal. See **xiyanet**.

xiyar خِيار *m./f.(ZF3/Wkt)* **(-ê/-a; xiyêr/).** cucumber: **•Eger *xiyar* e, bi tûtkê diyar e = *Xiyar* e, ji tîtkî diyar e** (Wkt) If it's a *cucumber*, it will be apparent in its early stages [*prv.*]. {also: xeyar (TF); xîyar (F); [khiiar] خيار (JJ); <xiyar> خيار (HH)} {syn: arû} < Ar/P xiyār خيار --> T hiyar; Sor xeyar خەیار; Za xeyar *m.* (Todd) [EP-7/K/A/JB3/IFb/B/JJ/HH/JB1-A/GF/FS/BF/Wkt//F//TF] <kûtik; qitik; tûtik II; xirtik I>

xizan خِزان *adj.* 1) {syn: feqîr; sêfîl [2]} poor: **•Zikê *xizanan* tim birçîye** (AB) The stomachs *of the poor* are always empty [lit. 'The stomach *of the poor* is always hungry']; 2) naïve. {also: xezan (A); xîzan (JB3); [khyzan] خزان (JJ); <xîzan> خيزان (HH)} {xezanî; xizanî; xîzanî} [K/IFb/JJ/GF/

ZF3//A//JB3/HH]

xizanî خِـــزانـــى *f.* **(-ya;-yê).** poverty: •**Ji *xizanîyê* netirse, timatîyê bi comertiyê ve rake** (Wkp:Mele Xelîlê Sêrtî) Do not fear *poverty*, replace stinginess with kindness. {also: xezanî (A); xîzanî (JB3)} {syn: feqîrî; sêfîlî; zivarî} [K/IFb/GF/ZF3//A//JB3] <xizan>

xizem خِزەم (IFb) = nose-ring. See **xizêm**.

xizêm خـــزێـــم *f.* **(-a;-ê).** nose-ring; golden women's ornaments (with an inlay) in the shape of camomile flowers, worn in the nose (Ba): **-xizêma poz** = do.: •**Guharê guhê te me / *xizêma pozê* te me** (Mtk) I am the earring in your ear / I am the *nose-ring in* your nose. {also: xizem (IFb-2); xizme (TF); [khezim] خـزيـم (JJ); <xezîm> خـزيـم (HH)} < Ar xizām خـزام/xizāmah خـزامـة --> T hızma; Sor xezêm خـەزێـم = 'nose ring' [Ba/K/A/B/IFb/GF/OK/Mtk/Qzl//JJ/HH//TF] <xişir>

xizim خِزِم (A) = relative, kin. See **xizm**.

xizm خِـــــزم *m.* **(-ê;).** 1) relative, kin: •**Du muro hebûn ji ‘eşîreta Mizûrî Jorî ... her du ji ocaẍek[ê] bûn ... her du *xizmêt yêk* jî bûn. ‘Ebdî kuřê meta ‘Ezîz bû, ‘Ezîz kuřê xalê ‘Ebdî bû** (SK 18:166) There were two men of the Upper Mizuri tribe … they were both of one clan … Moreover they were r*elated to each other*. Abdi was the son of Aziz's paternal aunt, Aziz was the son of Abdi's maternal uncle; 2) {syn: xinamî} in-laws, affiances; 3) {syn: birajin; bûra} brother of a man's wife, a man's brother-in-law [birayê kebanîya mirovî] (Bw). {also: xizim (A); [khyzm/khūzm (Rh)] خـــزم (JJ)} <Ar xaşm خـــصـــم = ‘adversary, opponent’ --> T hısım = ‘relative, kin’; Sor xizm خِزم = ‘relative’ [Bw/K/IFb/B/JJ/SK/GF/Kmc-12//A]

xizme خِزمە (TF) = nose-ring. See **xizêm**.

xizmet خِـزمـەت *f.* **(-a;-ê).** service; work: •***Xizmeta* xo û zerera xo der-ḧeqq benî-ademî bo min beyan ken, da xelatê her kesekî bi-qeder *xizmeta* wî bihête dan** (SK 1:2) Tell me of your *service* and of your injuries to mankind, so that each may be rewarded according to his *service*; **-xizmet kirin** (K/B/JJ/SK)/**xilmet kirin** (JB1-A) to serve; to work: •**Kî yê wek te *xizmeta* min bike?** (K-ça) Who will *serve* me as you do? {also: xidmet (SK-2); xilmet (JB1-A&S); [khydmet خـــدمـــت/khyzmet (xizmet-Lx) خـــزمـــت] (JJ); <xizmet> خزمت (HH)} {syn: karguzarî} < Ar xidmah خدمة --> P xedmat خـدمـت & T hizmet = 'service'; Sor xizmet خِزمەت. *Perhaps the form **xilmet** is due to influence from **xulam** = 'servant boy'. See also note on Jewish 'qīman' dialects of NENA under **tol II**.* [K-ça/K/IFb/B/JJ/HH/SK/GF/ZF//JB1-A&S]

xizmetçî خِزمەتچى (B) = servant. See **xizmetk’ar**.

xizmetk’ar خِـــزمـــەتـــكـــار *m.* **(-ê;).** servant: •**Ew *xizmetkarê* mala Behremî ye** (FS) He is the servant of B.'s household. {also: xidmetçî (SK); xilmeçî (JB1-A); xilmetk’ar (JB1-A); xizmetçî (B-2); [khyzme-kar] خـــذمـــكـــار (JJ); <xizmetkar> خـــزمـــتـــكـــار (HH)} {syn: pêşxizmet; xulam} Cf. P xidmatkār خدمتكار --> T hizmetkâr; Sor xizmetkar خِزمەتكار; Za xizmkar (Todd) [L/K/IFb/B/HH/FS//JJ//JB1-A//SK] <carî; xadim>

xizn•e خِزنە *f.* **(•a;•ê).** treasure; treasury: •**Herin, devê *xizna* min vekin** (L) Go, open the gate of my *treasury*; **-xizne-defîne** (Z-1) do. {also: xezîne (K/IF); xezne (F); [kheziné] خـــزيـــنـــه (JJ); <xezîne> خزينه (HH)} {syn: defîne; gencîne} < Ar xaznah خزنة/ xazīnah خزينة; Sor xezne خەزنە [Z-1/L/A//F//K/IFb/B/JJ/HH/SK]

xiznîr خِزنير (IFb) = pig. See **xinzîr**.

xîç’ I خيچ *m.* **().** *& adj.* colostrum, beestings, first milk of mammals: **-şîrê xîç** (ZF3) do.: •**Heçîka hûn mirovin we *şîrê xîç* vexwariye** (ZZ-7, 242) As for you humans, you have drunk *colostrum milk* [i.e., you are mammals] •**Şirînê *şîrê xîç* kir firo** (FS) Sh. made the *beestings* into 'firo' [i.e., she boiled it]. {also: xiç (A); [khytch] خـــچ (JJ); <xîç> خـــيـــچ (HH)} {syn: firo; firşik II; xelendor I; zak} [ZZ/IFb/B/GF/HH/ZF/FS//A/JJ] <şîr I>

xîç’ II خيچ (B/SC)= gravel; pebble. See **xîç’ik**.

xîç’ik خـــيـــچـــك *m.* (). gravel; pebble. {also: xîç’ II (B/SC); xîz [2]; <xîçik> خيچك (HH)} {syn: bixûr; zuẍr} < Arm xič խիճ = 'pebble, gravel' [Msr/A/IFb/HH/GF//B/SC] <xîz>

xîm خـــيـــم (Msr/Hk/A/FJ/GF/Kmc/Tsab) = basis, foundation. See **ḧîm**.

xîn خين (SK/Bw/Mzg) = blood. See **xwîn**.

xîret خيرەت *f.* **(-a;-ê).** 1) zeal, fervor, ardor; diligence, industry, aşiduousneş, penchant for work: •**Bi himmeta bab û bapîran wê carê ḧeşrekî weto dê bi ‘eskerê Fuzol Paşa keyn ku bibîte ‘ibret di guhêt hemî xelkî da, û Daẍistanî û Çerkes û Arnahod jî cesaret û *xîreta* milletê kurd ... bi dirustî bizanin** (SK 48:485) By the grace of (my) ancestors we shall cause such a commotion among the troops of Fuzol ('Meddlesome') Pasha that it will be a warning (reaching) the ears of all people, and the Daghistanis and Circassians and Albanians will learn of the bravery and *zeal of* the Kurdish people **•K'î ne ji *xîretêye*, ne ji ometêye** (Dz, #17:384) He who doesn't show *zeal* (or concern) is not part of the community *[prv.]*; 2) self-respect, pride; no tolerance for insults: "If the good name of the family is threatened or stained in some way, the family members are responsible for restoring it. A woman's virtue is the concern of the entire family, and if it is lost, family members will punish her. For example, if a girl loses her virginity before she is married, her brothers or father are responsible for restoring the family's honor by ostracizing or killing her" (Sweetnam, 133); *for an example of **xîret**, see anecdote #39 in JR:* **•[Ew terze şuca'et û *x̃îreta* Suleyman Ax̃ayê Sîpkî niha jî li Kurdistanê tête gotin]** (JR #39,121) That type of bravery and *pride* of Suleyman Agha of the Sipkis is told even today in Kurdistan **•Gava ti hatî, vî lawkî bi xwer̄a bîne, / Li nîvê r̄ê serê wî ji gewdê wî biqetîne, / Mi sozek pêr̄a da, ko ew bi saxî bigihîje vir, ê li ber ç'e'vê te r̄amûsanekê ji r̄ûyê min bistîne, / Ê *xîret* û namûsa Memê Ala ji dinîayê hilîne** (Z-2 87-88) When you come, bring this boy with you, / And on the way sever his head from his body, / I have promised him, that when he returns here safely, he can have a kiss from me before your eyes, / Which would wipe Memê Alan's *pride* and honor off the face of the earth **•Teto taze cah̄êl bû, muroekî gelek cesûr bû, di naw ax̃aêt R̄êkanîyan da kesek wekî wî peyda nebûbû. Çî dî *x̃îreta* wî teh̄emmula zulma Horemarîyan nekir** (SK 61:731) Teto, yet a youth, was a man of much courage, the like of whom had never been seen among the Rekani Aghas, and now his *pride (self-respect)* could no longer brook the misrule of the Horamari; 3) disposition, inclination, tendency, propensity, penchant (for): **-xîret kirin** (B/HH/Bw)/ **~k'işandin** (B) to be disposed, inclined to, feel like doing stg.: **•Ez *xîret dikem* erkê [wacibê] xo çêkem** (Bw) I *feel like* doing my work **•Ez *xîret nakem*** (Bw) I *don't feel like it* **•Tu gemşo yî, tu *xîret nakey* çu bikey** (Bw) You're lazy, you *don't feel like* doing anything. {also: x̃îret (SK); [ghiret] غيرت (JJ); <x̃eyret> غيرت (HH)} < Ar ɣīrah غيرة = 'jealousy; zeal, fervor; sense of honor, self-respect' --> T gayret = 'zeal, ardor; energy, effort; protectiveness'; Sor x̃îret غيرەت = 'zeal' [Dz/K/IFb/B/TF//JJ/SK//HH] <bêxîret>

xîtab خيتاب *f.* **().** direct address; **-xîtab kirin** (ZF) to address s.o., speak directly to s.o.: **•Çawa ku Nûbihar *xîtabî* van du dunyayan *dike*, xebata Nûbiharê jî di bu qisman cihê dibe** (Nbh 125:4) Just as Nûbihar *speaks to* both of these worlds, so can the work of N. be divided into 2 parts. < Ar xiṭāb خطاب < xāṭaba III خاطب = 'to address, speak, direct one's words to' [Nbh/ZF/Wkt]

xîv خيڤ (JB1-S) = tent. See **xêvet**.

xîvet خيڤەت (JB3/IFb) = tent. See **xêvet**.

***Xîy** خيى **().** Kurdish tribe inhabiting the region between Sason (in the province of Batman, formerly Siirt) and Kulp (in the province of Diyarbakır) in Kurdistan of Turkey. [Haz]

Xîyan خييان (). region between Sason (in the province of Batman, formerly Siirt) and Kulp (in the province of Diyarbakır) in Kurdistan of Turkey. [Haz]

xîyar خيار (F) = cucumber. See **xiyar**.

xîz خيز *m./f.(ZF3)* **(-ê/-a;).** 1) {syn: qûm} sand: **•Bavo, çiqas steyrin li 'ezmana, / çiqas *xîzê* devê behra, / Ewqas xêvet dor me girtine** (EP-7) Dad, as many stars as there are in the sky / as much *sand* as there is on the seashore / That's how many tents are surrounding us **•Ev tişt wekî *xîzê* çema ye** (FS) This thing is like *the sand of* the rivers, i.e., it is too numerous to be counted; 2) gravel; pebble. See **xîç'ik**. {also: zîx II (A-2); [khīz] خيز (JJ) = sablonneux} Cf. Southern Tati dialects (all *f.*): Chali & Eshtehardi xöza; Takestani xoz(z)a (Yar-Shater); Sor zîx زيخ = 'gravel'; Cf. Arm xič խիճ = 'pebble, 'gravel' [K/A/JB3/IFb/JJ/SK/GF/Bw/ZF3/FS]

xîzan خيزان (JB3) = poor. See **xizan**.

xîzanî خيزانى (JB3) = poverty. See **xizanî**.

xlaz خلاز (HCK) = free; finished. See **xelas**.

xnamî خنامى (SC) = in-law; relative by marriage. See **xinamî**.

xo خۆ (SK/JB1-A&S) = oneself, -self. See **xwe**.

xo-dan-e-paş خۆ دانه پاش (SK) = reluctance. See **xwe-dane-paş**.

xodê خۆدێ (JB1-A) = God. See **xwedê**.

xof خوف *f.* **(-a;-ê).** fear, terror: **-xof kirin** (K): = a) to fear, be afraid {syn: tirsîn}; b) to frighten:

•R̄eng û r̄ûyê Memê meriv *xof dike* lê binhêre (K) Mem's appearance *makes* people *afraid* to look at him. {also: xov (B-2); [khaw خـاف/khouf خـوف] (JJ)} {syn: saw; tirs} < Ar xawf خـوف [Z-1/K/IFb/B/JJ/JB1-S/TF/ZF3]

xoh خۆھ (JB1-A) = oneself, -self. See **xwe**.

xohing خۆهِنگ (JB1-A) = sister. See **xûşk**.

xolam خۆلام (JB1-A) = servant boy. See **xulam**.

xolî خـۆلـی (JB1-A/SK/OK) = ash(es); soil, dirt. See **xwelî**.

xolîdank خۆليدانك (OK) = ashtray. See **xwelîdank**.

xonçe خۆنـچـه *f./m.(ZF3)* **(-ya/;).** low, round table *for eating or making bread on.* {also: xwançe (Wkt); [khountché] خونـچـه (JJ)} {syn: xanik} Cf. P xvān خـوان = 'table' ; Sor xuwançe خـوانـچـه = 'small table' [Kg/IFb/ZF3//JJ//Wkt]

xong خۆنگ (JB1-A) = sister. See **xûşk**.

xop'an خۆپان *m.* **(-ê;).** 1) barren, uninhabited, ruined place; place devoid of people: **•Çûme Bedlîsê, *xopanê* di kortê da/ hatim Bedlîsê, *xopanê* di kortê da** (Ah) I went to Bitlis, *ruins* in a pit/ I came to Bitlis, *ruins* in a pit *[from a famous elegy]*; 2) [*adj.*] deserted, dilapidated, run-down, in a state of collapse, ruined (house, garden, place, etc.) : **•Cezîra *xopan*** (IF) *ruined* Jezirah [T Cizre]; 3) vile, foul; accursed, damned (K/DS). {also: خـوپـان (JJ); <xopan> خـوپـان (HH)} K-->T hopan = 'neglected garden, vineyard, house, etc.' [Van; *Pütürge -Malatya]; 'vineyard with few grapes' [Urfa]; 'a curse meaning may it/he be ruined ' [Van] (DS, v.7, p. 2405) [Ah/K/A/IFb/B/JJ/HH/GF]

xorak خۆراك (SK/IF) = food. See **xurek**.

xorandin خۆراندِن (L/JJ) = to scratch. See **xurandin**.

xorc خۆرج (JB1-A) = saddlebag. See **xurc**.

xorcik' خۆرجِك (JB1-A) = saddlebag. See **xurc**.

xore خۆره (Zeb) = gluttonous. See **xure**.

xorim خـۆڕِم *f.* **(-a;).** large bale or sheaf *(of hay)*. {also: xorom (B); xorum (Wn)} [Qrj/Kmc-8/IFb//B/Wn] <gîşe; gurz II>

xorom خۆرۆم (B) = bale *(of hay)*. See **xorim**.

xort خـۆرت *adj.* 1) young; 2) [*m.* **(-ê;-î).**] {syn: sengele} young man, youth: **•Eva bûka, jina wî *xortîye*** (Dz) This young woman is that *young man's* wife **•Wext dibuhure, kurik mezin dibe û *xortekî* şepal jê derdikeve** (Ardû, 26) Time passes, the boy grows up and a becomes a handsome *young man.* {also: [xōrt] خـورت (JJ)} {xortanî; xortayî; xort[t]î} [K/A/JB3/IFb/B/JJ/GF/TF/ZF] <naşî>

xortanî خـۆرتـانـی *f.* **(-ya;-yê).** youth, adolescence; youthfulness: **•Di dema xwe ya *xortaniya* xwe de û li vî welatê pêşk[e]tî, ji xwendin û pêşveçûnê bêpar dimênin** (Wlt 5/86, 15) During the period fo their *youth* and in this progressive country, they are being deprived of learning and advancement. {also: xortayî (A); xortî (K-2/B/GF-2); xorttî (B-2)} [Ber/K/JB3/IFb/GF/TF//B//A] <xort>

xortayî خۆرتايی (A) = youth. See **xortanî**.

xortî خۆرتی (K/B/GF) = youth. See **xortanî**.

xorttî خۆرتتی (B) = youth. See **xortanî**.

xorum خۆروم (Wn) = bale *(of hay)*. See **xorim**.

xoş خـۆش (JJ/JB1-A/SK/GF/Bw) = pleasant; good; tasty; fast. See **xweş**.

xoşdivî خۆشدِڤی (BF) = dear. See **xweşdivî**.

xoşî خۆشی (SK/JJ/HR) = pleasantness. See **xweşî**.

xoş-meşreb خۆش مـەشرەب *adj.* good-natured, merry: **•'Elî Beg jî, çûnkû *xoş-meşreb* bû, ħej tirane û ṣuħbetan dikir** (SK 39:345) Now Ali Beg, being *merry-natured*, liked jokes. Cf. P xoš-mašrab خـوش مـشـرب = 'sociable, good-natured' [SK] <dilr̄eħm>

xoştivî خۆشتِڤی (Zx) = dear. See **xweşdivî**.

xov خۆڤ (B) = fear. See **xof**.

xox خـۆخ *f.* **(-a;-ê).** peach, bot. Prunus persica: **•Bawerî bi dendika *xoxê* bîne, bi qeweta xwe ewle be** (Ber 5/86, 20) Believe that *the peach* has a pit, and you'll believe in your own strength. {also: [khokh] خـوخ (JJ); <x[o]x> خـوخ (HH)} < Ar xawx [clq. xōx] خـوخ = 'peach, plum'; Sor qox قـۆخ; Za xewxı/xowxı (Mal) [Frq/Haz/K/A/IFb/JJ/HH/TF/OK/AA] <teraqî>

xoy خۆی (Kg) = salt. See **xwê**.

xoya خۆيا (JB1-A) = visible, obvious. See **xuya**.

xozan خـۆزان *f./m.(FS)* **(/-ê;).** fallow land, stubble field; unplowed field: **•Cotyarê *xozanê* pişta gundî kêla** (FS) The farmer plowed *the stubble field* behind the village **•Ne reze, ne mêrgezerê / Ew şûva du sal berê / Giha lê bû wek çeperê / Bûye kilamoka dîlberê! *[xozan]*** (CCG, 21) It is neither vineyard nor yellow meadow / That plowed field of 2 years ago / Whose grass was like a barricade / Has become a song of those in love *[Riddle; Answer: A stubble field]* **•Zevî îṣal xozan ma** (FS) The field has remained fallow this year. {syn: beyar} [CCG/K/B/IFb/ZF/FS/CS] <gort II; şov>

xozî خۆزی (JB1-A/SK) = if only! See **xwezî I**.
xu خو (-a;) (Z-3) = sister. See **xûşk**.
xubar خوبار *f.* **(-a;-ê).** dust: •***Xubarê* xwe avîtibû dev û lêvê Memêye nazik** (Z-1) *Dust* had jumped into delicate Mem's mouth and lips; **-t'oz û xubar** (Z-1) do. {also: [goubar] غبـار (JJ)} {syn: gerik I; tirabêlk; t'oz} < Ar γubār غبار [Z-1/K/JB3/IFb/B//JJ]
xuda خودا (SK) = God. See **xwedê**.
xudan I خـــــــــــودان (IFb/B) = to perspire, sweat. See **xûdan**.
xudan II خـــودان (SK/JB1-A&S) = owner, master. See **xwedî**.
xudanbext خـــودانـــبـــهخـــت *adj.* 1) {syn: emîn [2]; ewlekar; ît'bar; saxlem} trustworthy, reliable; honest: •**Li wextê berê, di heyamên kevin de mîrek hebû. Mîrekî ciwan, çeleng, *xudanbext* û bi destê xwe mêr** (Rnh 3:23, 5) In former times, in the old days there was an emir. A young, gallant, *honest*, and independent; 2) lucky; happy. {also: xwedîbext (IFb/TF/OK); [¨qodánbext] (JJ-G)} [Rnh/K/GF//JJ-G//IFb/TF/OK]
xudanî xêr خـــودانـــی خـــێـــر (Z-2) = benefactor. See **xudanxêr**.
xudanxêr خـــودانـــخـــێـــر *m.* **().** benefactor; well-wisher: •**gelî *xudanî xêr*** (Z-2) O *well-wishers*. {also: xudanî xêr (Z-2); xuyî xêr (Z-2); [qodam keira/ keirát] (JJ-G)} {syn: xêrxwaz} [Z-2//K/B//JJ]
xudê خودێ (SK/JB1-S/HH) = God. See **xwedê**.
xudênas خـــــودێـــــنـــــاس (GShA) = God-fearing. See **xwedênas**.
xudkar خودکار (FJ) = ruler, king. See **xûndkar**.
xuhdan خـــــوهـــــدان (JB1-S) = to perspire, sweat. See **xûdan**.
xuk خوك (-a;) (Z-3) = sister. See **xûşk**.
xukî خوکی (K) = tax. See **xûk**.
xulam خـــــــــولام *m.* **(-ê; xulêm/xulîm [B], vî xulamî).** valet, servant boy: •**Rabû Mecdumelek ba kire *x̱ulamê* xwe** (HR 4:23) M. called for his *servant boy*; **-Ez xolam** (JB1-A) At your service. {also: xolam (JB1-A); x̱ulam (JB1-S/SK-2/OK-2); x̱ûlam (L); [goulam] غـــلام (JJ); <xulam خـلام/ x̱ulam غـلام> (HH)} {syn: pêşxizmet; xizmetk'ar} < Ar γulām غــــــلام = 'boy, youth; slave; servant' {xulamîtî; xulam[t]î} [L//EP-7/K/A/JB3/IFb/B/HH/SK/GF/ TF/OK//JB1-A//JJ/JB1-S] <benî I; carî; qerwaş; xizmetk'ar>
xulamî خولالمی (K/IFb) = servitude. See **xulamtî**.
xulamîtî خولامیتی (KH/GF) = servitude. See **xulamtî**.
xulamk'ole خولامکۆله *m.&f.* **().** child of a servant or slave: •**Her du zarokan pismîr û *xulamkole* ji yek guhanî şîr dimêtin** (Rnh 3:23, 5) Both infants, the emir's son and *the servant's child*, sucked milk from the same breast [lit. 'nipple']. < Ar γulām غـلام = 'boy, youth; slave; servant' + T köle = 'slave' [Rnh/GF]
xulamtî خـــولامـــتـــی *f.* **(-ya;-yê).** servitude; slavery: **-xulamtîya *fk-î* kirin** = to serve s.o., be s.o.'s slave: •**Ez ê heya kengî *xulamîtîya* wî marî *bikim*?** (KH, 34) How long [lit. 'until when'] shall I *be a slave to* that snake? •**Her yanzdeh kuřê mine dinê *wê* jêra *xulamtîê bikin*** (Ba) All my other eleven sons *will serve* him. {also: xulamî (K-2/IFb-2); xulamîtî (KH/GF); x̱ulamtî (HR); [goulami] غلامی (JJ)} {syn: qulix} [Ba/K/A/IFb/B/TF/ /KH/GF//HR//JJ] <xulam>
xulbet خولبهت (Z-2) = foreign land; exile. See **x̱urbet**.
***xulbok** خـــولـــبـــۆك *f.* **(-a;).** buttonhole. {also: xulboq (Msr-2)} {syn: bişkov [2]} [Msr] <bişkoj>
xulboq خولبۆق (Msr) = buttonhole. See **xulbok**.
xulexul خولهخول/**xule-xul** خوله خول [IFb] *f.* **(-a;-ê).** sound of water flowing in a river; babbling, murmuring, rumbling, purling *(of water)*: •**Ser sîngê Dûmanlûê cîcîna *xulexula* cewikêd avê bû** (Ba2:1, 202) On the slope of {Mount} Dumanlu here and there was *the babbling of* brooks (of water). {syn: xulîn} Cf. Sor xulexul خـولـهخـول = 'spinning' [Ba2/K/B//IFb] <şirşiřandin>
xulfe خولفه (Zeb) = easily undone knot. See **xilf**.
xuliqandin خولِقاندِن *vt.* **(-xuliqîn-).** to create, make: •**Ji her te'amê Xudê ti'ala *xuliqandî*** (HR 3:116) From every food [fruit] *created* by God •**Wezîfa min jî pê-we-dan e. Xudê lewa *ez xeliqandime* da bi řoẖtuberî we-dem** (SK 2:12) My duty, moreover, is to strike [or bite]. God *has created me* for that reason to strike (other) living creatures. {also: xeliqandin (SK); xuluqandin (CS); [kheliqandin] خلقاندين (JJ)} {syn: afirandin; çêkirin} < Ar xalaqa خـــلـــق = 'to create, shape, originate'; Sor xułqandin خولّقاندِن [HR/K/B/IFb/ZF/RZ/ /CS//JJ/SK]
xulîn خولین *f.* **(-a;).** purling *(of water)*; the sound of a rising river flowing (K): •***Xulîna* pêlê be'rê bû** (EH) There was the sound of the waves of the sea. {syn: xulexul} [EH/K/ZF3] <şiřîn II; şirşiřandin>
xulîreng خولیرهنگ (FJ) = gray, ashen. See **xwelîreng**.
xuluqandin خـــولـــوقـــانـــدِن (CS) = to create. See

xuliqandin.

xumam خـومـام *f.* (;-ê). fog, mist: •**Mij û** ***ximameke*** **gewr girtibû ser bajarê Rihayê** (Nofa, 91) A grey mist and *fog* lay over the city of Urfa. {also: ximam (H.Nehsan)}{syn: dûman; mij} < Ar γamām غمام = 'clouds' [JB3/IFb/OK//Nofa]

xumar خومار (K/IFb/HH) = gambling. See **qumar**.

xumarbaz خومارباز (K) = gambler. See **qumarbaz**.

xume-xum خومه خوم (K)/xumexum خومهخوم (ZF) = murmur; buzzing. See **xumxum I**.

xumrî خومری (K/GF/HH) = dark purple. See **xemrî**.

xumxum I خـومـخـوم *f.* **(-a;).** 1) {syn: xurexur} purl, murmur, rushing *(of water)* (K/FJ/GF/JJ/ZF): •***Xumxuma*** **baranê hat** (K) It was pouring rain; -**xumxuma avê** (GF) rushing *(of water)*; 2) {syn: r̄eqer̄eq; xurexur} roll of thunder (GF/AD): -**xumxuma ewran** (GF) do.; 3) {syn: himehim} buzzing, humming *(of flies)* (HR/TF/ZF): •**Havîn e û mêş û moran de lê dibin e k'om û ẍumẍuma mêşa e** (HR 3:207) It is summertime, and the flies and ants swarm around him, and there is the buzzing of flies. {also: ximxim II (AD); xume-xum (K-2)/xumexum (ZF-2); ẍumẍum (HR); [xumāxumā] خماخما (JJ)} [HR//K/FJ/GF/TF/ZF/FS//JJ//AD]

xumxum II** خـومـخـوم *m.* **().** Yezidi priest: •**Hûn bişînin Birahîm bînin / Keşîş û** ***xumxuma **liber deyînin** (GShA, 229) Send for Ibrahim and bring him here / Confront him with priests and *clergy* •***Xumxum*** **(kahin) hebûn gotine Nemrûd: Êk dê rabit hukmê te ji destê te dê girit** (GShA, 227) There were *priests* who told Nemrud, "One will come who will take the power away from you". {syn: *kahin} [GShA]

xunaf خوناف (TF) = dew; drizzle. See **xunav**.

xunav خـونـاڤ *f.* **(-a;-ê).** 1) {syn: avî II} dew: •***Xunav*** **ketiye ser pelên gula** (FS) Dew fell on the leaves of the flowers •***Xunavê*** **giya girtiye** (FS) Dew has fallen on [lit. 'has taken'] the grass; 2) moisture; 3) drizzling rain: •***Xunava*** **hûr bî ne agirekî gur bî** (ZF3) Be a light *drizzle*, don't be a roaring fire [*prv.*]. {also: xunaf (TF); xûnav (JB3/IFb-2); [khounaw] خوناڤ (JJ); <xunav> خناڤ (HH)} cf. Arm xonaw խոնաւ = 'moist, humid'; Sor xunaw خوناو/xunawke خوناوکه = 'dew' [K/A/IFb/HH/GF/ZF3/FS//JB3/JJ//TF] <qir̄av; xûsî>

xundekar خـونـدهکـار (FJ/CS) = ruler, king. See **xûndkar**.

xundevan خوندهڤان (K) = student. See **xwendek'ar**.

xundin خـونـدِن (-xûn-) (SK) = to read; to recite; to study. See **xwendin**.

xundkar خوندکار (Kmc) = ruler, king. See **xûndkar**.

xuneda خـونـهدا *m.* **().** a literate, educated, hence cultured, refined person: •**Ne tu** ***xunedayî*** (EH) You aren't *a cultured person* •**Tu merîkî** ***xwendîyî*** (B) You are a l*iterate (educated)* man. {also: xunede; xwanda (FS); xwende (ZF3); xwendeh (IFb); xwendî (B); [khoundi خـونـدی/khoundiié خـونـديـه/khoundaié خـونـدايـه] (JJ)} Cf. P x^{V}ānde خوانده [EH/K//B//JJ//FS//ZF3//IFb] <xwendin>

xunede خـونـهده = educated, refined person. See **xuneda**.

xunkar خونكار (A/IFb) = ruler, king. See **xûndkar**.

xunkarî خونكارى (A/FS) = kingship. See **xûndkarî**.

xuran خوران = to itch. See **xurîn I**.

xurandin خـورانـدِن *vt.* **(-xurîn-).** 1) to scratch *(an itch)*: •**Keçelok pişta stuê xwe** ***xorand*** **û hat** (L) Kechelok *scratched* the back of his head [lit. 'neck'] [in bewilderment] and came •**Teralek pişta wî dixure, lê ji teralî û tembelîyê nikare pişta xwe** ***bixurîne*****, hema hundurê destê xwe** ***dixurîne*** **û diavêje paş xwe!** (LM, 15) The back of a lazybones itches, but out of laziness he can't *scratch* his back, so he *scratches* the palm of his hand and throws it behind himself; 2) {syn: tirsandin (EP-7)} to drive on, urge on, spur on, goad, whip up (an animal): •**Eva çend r̄oje zengîya ser zengîya min** ***duxurînî*** (Z-1) For several days now you *have been jabbing* the stirrups into my stirrup-bone. {also: xar̄andin (Z-2); xorandin (L); xwurandin (F); [khorandin] خوراندين (JJ); <xuwerandin خوراندن (dixwerîne) (دخورينه)> (HH)} Sor xurandin خـورانـدِن = 'to scratch to relieve itch'; Hau wurnay (wurn-) (M4) [L/JJ//K/A/IFb/B/GF//F//HH] <xurîn I; xur̄în III>

xurbet خـوربـهت (IFb) = foreign land; exile. See **ẍurbet**.

xurc خـورج *f./m.(FS)* **(-a/-ê;-ê/-î).** saddlebag: •**Siyarî nanê xo kir di** ***xurcî*** **da** (FS) The rider put his food in *the saddlebag* •***Xurcek*** **t'ijî zêr̄ê findiqî kir** (EP-7) He filled *a saddlebag* with gold findiqs [type of coin]. {also: xorc (JB1-A); xorcik' (JB1-A-2); xurcik (B-2); xurcîn; xwircik (CCG); [khourdj] خرج (JJ); <xurc خرج/xurcik خرجك> (HH)} {syn: heqîb; xurcezîn} < Ar xurj خرج ?< P xorjīn خرجين --> T hurç = 'saddlebag'; cf. Arm xorg խուրջ/k'urj քուրձ = 'sack-cloth, haircloth' [EP-7/K/A/IFb/B/JJ/HH/SK/GF/TF/FS//JB1-A]

xurcezîn خـــورجـــەزيـــن *f./m.(HR/FS)* **(/-ê;/-î).** saddlebag: •**T'êra xwe p'are, bê çi ji wa r̄a lazim bû, kirine *xurcezînê* xwe de** (HR 3:8) They put plenty of money, whatever they needed, in their *saddlebag*. {syn: heqîb; xurc} [Z-2/A/IFb/GF/ZF3/FS]

xurcik خورجِك (B) = saddlebag. See **xurc**.

xurcilîn خـورجِـلـيـن *vt.* **(-xurcil-).** to dawdle, tarry, be slow *(to do stg.)*: •**Zîne avîte zîndanê şrîta spîye, / avîte nav Memê Alaye, / Memê *xurcilîye*** (FK-eb-1) Zîn lowered a white rope into the dungeon, / she threw it to Memê Alan, / Mem *was slow to move*. {also: [khourdjilin] خـورجـلـيـن (JJ)} [FK-1/K/JJ/SS] <hêdî>

xurcîn خورجين = saddlebag. See **xurc**.

xure خـــــوره *adj.* gluttonous, voracious, eating too much: •**Gelek *xure* ye, lê çi giyana nagrît** (Zeb) He's *voracious*, but he doesn't gain any weight. {also: xore (Zeb); xwara (GF); xwere (TF); [khoura خــورا/khouraï خــوراى] (JJ); <xuwera> خورا (HH)} {syn: çil III} [Ag/A/ZF3//JJ//Zeb//HH//TF//GF]

xurek خـــــورەك *m./f.(ZF3/BF)* **(-ê/-a;/-ê).** 1) {syn: xwarin [3]} food: •***Xurekê* wanî ȟert'imî nanê t'isî û hine toraq bû** (Ba2-3, 213) Their daily *food* was stale bread and some toraq [creamy cheese]; 2) glutton, gourmand (B). {also: xorak (SK/IF); xwarek (IF-2); [khourek] خورك (JJ)} Cf. Sor xorak خــــــۆراك [Ba2/K/IFb/B/JJ/ZF3/BF//SK/IF] <xwarin>

xurexur خـــــورەخـــــور *f.* **(-a;-ê).** *various sounds*: unpleasantly loud knocking sound, bumping; cracking, crashing, popping, rumbling *(thunder)*, report *(of gun)*; snoring, snorting; light plashing; rustling; death rattle: •**'Da biçim, temaşe kem kanê ga çawan e.' Ço helê, guhê xo da ê, *xir̄exir̄a* gay bihîst, zanî ko di bi r̄oȟêda ye** (SK 30:271) "I ought to go and see how the ox is." She went to the stall and listened, heard *the rattling breathing of* the ox and realized that it was at the point of death •***xurxura* ewran** (DBgb, 20) *the crashing of* the clouds/*roll of* thunder. {also: xirexir (ZF-2/GF); xir̄exir̄ (K/B/SK); xirxir (A/GF-2); xurxur (DBgb); [khyr-khyr خـرخـر /khyre-khyr خرەخر] (JJ)} Cf. P xarāxar خراخر & xerxer خـرخـر = 'snoring, rattling'; Sor xir̄[e] [ە]خِڕ = 'rattle, sharp clattering/scraping sound' & xir̄exir̄ خِڕەخِڕ = 'continued rattling sound' [DBgb// ZF/IFb//K/B/SK//GF/JJ//A] <r̄eqer̄eq; xumxum I>

xurhan خورهان (Bw) = to itch. See **xurîn I**.

xuricîn خورِجين/**xur̄icîn** خوڕجين [FS] *vi.* **(-xuric-).** to fall *(shooting star)*: •**Stêrik li esmanê welêt *xuricî*** (Frq) The star *fell* from the skies of the nation [*euphemism designating the death of a national hero and the like*] {syn: r̄ijîn} [Frq/TF//FS] <stêr>

xurifîn خـورِفـيـن (FJ/TF/GF/ZF/HH) = to go senile; to lose one's mind. See **xerifîn**.

xuristan خورِستان (OK) = universe. See **Xur̄ustan**.

xurî I خورى (SK) = wool. See **hirî**.

xurî II خورى (A/IFb/B/GF/TF) = smallpox. See **xurîk**.

xurîk خـــوريـــك *f.* **(;-ê).** smallpox, variola [T çiçek hastalığı, Ar judarī جـــــدري]: •***Xurîk* li wî hatine** (FS) He has come down with *smallpox* [lit. 'the pox have come to him']; **-xurî derxistin/ xurîya k'etin** (B) to come down with smallpox, suffer from smallpox. {also: xurî II (A/IFb/B/GF/TF); xurîke (OK-2/AA/FS-2); [khourik] خــوريــك (JJ); <xurî> خرى (HH)} Cf. P xōre خوره = 'gangrene, cancre'; Sor xurîke خوريكه/xurîlke خـوريلكه = awłe ئاوڵه = 'smallpox'; cf. xurîn I = 'to itch' [Zeb/Dh/K/JJ/OK/FS//AA//A/IFb/B/HH/GF/TF]

xurîke خوريكه (OK/AA/FS) = smallpox. See **xurîk**.

xurîn I خورين *vi.* **(-xur[î]-).** 1) to itch: •**Teralek pişta wî *dixure*, lê ji teralî û tembelîyê nikare pişta xwe bixurîne, hema hundurê destê xwe dixurîne û diavêje paş xwe!** (LM, 15) The back of a lazybones *itches*, but out of laziness he can't scratch his back, so he scratches the palm of his hand and throws it behind himself; 2) *(of smart alecks)* to ask for it, incur s.o.'s wrath (IFb). {also: xuran; xurhan (Bw); xuryan (M); xwurîyan (F); [khoriian] خــوريــان (JJ); <xuweran خــوران (dixewere) (دخوره)> (HH)} Cf. Sor xuran خوران; Hau wurîay (wurîe-) vi. (M4) [K/JB3/IFb/B//F//JJ//HH//M//Bw] <xurandin>

xurîn II خـــوريـــن (SK) = to attack, curse. See **xur̄în III**[2].

xur̄în III خورين *vt.* **().** 1) [+ **li**] to drive, urge on, spur on, goad, whip up *(an animal)*: •**Memê delal wexta *zengû li* Bor *xur̄îya*** (Z-1) When dandy Mem *spurred* Bor [his horse] on; 2) [+ **li**] to attack, abuse, revile (SK); to curse (K). {also: xurîn II (SK)} [Z-1/EP-7/K//SK] <azirandin>

xurmaş خورماش (Rwn) = dozing off. See **xilmaş**.

xurm•e خورمه *f.* **(•a;•ê).** date(s), especially dark [r̄eş] and soft [nerm] ones, bot. *Phoenix dactylifera*.

{also: [khourma] خرما (JJ); <xurme> خرمه (HH)} {syn: qesp I} Cf. P xormā خرما --> T hurma; Sor xurma خورما [Zeb/AA/Kmc-2/CB/K/A/IFb/B/HH/GF/TF/FS//JJ]

xuř̄nîfk خوڕنيفك (Dh/BF) = carob. See **xernûf**.

xuř̄nîk خوڕنيك (Zeb/BF) = carob. See **xernûf**.

xurobî خوروٚبى, m. (Bw) = durra. See **xirovî**.

xurt خـــــورت *adj.* 1) {syn: bihêz; diř̄ I; qewî; t'und} strong, sturdy; vigorous; powerful, despotic (SK): **•Cotê me *xurt* e** (AB) Our plow (or pair of oxen) is *sturdy* **•Di navbera folklor û edebiyatê de pêwendiyeke *xurt* heye** (YPA, 11) There is a *strong* connection between folklore and literature **•Gerek baweriya te bi Xwedê *xurt* be** (HYma, 51) Your belief in God must be *strong* **•Jin û biçûk û 'eyalê kuř̄êt Osê hemî çûne tekya Şêx 'Ubeydullah. Ew jî qewî *xurt* bû: kuř̄êt Cindî Aẍa gazî kirin, çar-sed lîraê 'usmanî ji wan stand, da 'eyalê kuř̄êt Osê** (SK 40:387) The wives and children and families of Oso's sons all went to Shaikh Ubeidullah's convent. He was very *powerful*: he summoned the sons of Jindi Agha and took 400 Ottoman pounds from them and gave them to the families of Oso's sons; 2) hard, forceful *(of rain)*: **•Li derve baran *xurt* dibariya** (KS, 8) Outside it was raining *hard*; 3) {≠qels} fat (Msr/B/HH): **-xurt bûn** (Msr): a) to become fat; b) to become rich; 4) {syn: dewlemend; dewletî; maldar} rich, wealthy (Msr/B/HH). {also: [khourt] خــورت (JJ); <xurt> خــرت (HH)} Cf. Sor xurt خـــــــــورت = 'capable; vigorous' {xurtayî; xurt[t]î} [AB/K/A/JB3/IFb/B/JJ/HH/SK/GF/TF/Msr/ZF]

xurtayî خورتايى (B) = strength. See **xurtî**.

xurtî خــــورتــــى *f.* **(-ya;-yê).** 1) strength; force: **•Ewî *xurtî* li filan kesî kir heta ku parên xwe jê s̲tandin** (FS) He exerted *force* on so-and-so until he got his money from him; 2) sturdiness; 3) oppression (SK). {also: xurtayî (B-2); xurttî (B-2)} [K/A/JB3/IFb/B/TF/ZF3/FS] <t'undî; xurt>

xurttî خورتتى (B) = strength. See **xurtî**.

xurufîn خــوروفــيـن (Qzl) = to go senile; to lose one's mind. See **xerifîn**.

Xuř̄ustan خوڕوستان *f.* **(;-ê).** *place proverbially used in depicting wealth and beauty*; universe, cosmos (BG/OK): **•Ser wî kulîlkêd ħemû ř̄enga û cuř̄a hêşîn dibûn, ç'îa usa bedew dibû, mêriv t'irê xalîça *Xuř̄ustanê* ser wî ř̄axistine** (Ba2-I) Flowers of all colors and varieties grew on it; the mountain was so beautiful one would have thought that a carpet of *Khurustan* had been spread out on it **•[Tavîya Nîsanê, hêjaya malê *Xuristanê*]** (BG) An April cloudburst is worth all the riches of *Khuristan [prv.]*. {also: xuristan (OK); [khourastan-] (BG)} [Ba2//BG//OK]

xurû خوروو (GF) = simple; genuine. See **xweř̄û**.

xurxur خـــورخـــور (DBgb) = knocking; cracking; rattling; snoring. See **xurexur**.

xuryan خوريان (M) = to itch. See **xurîn I**.

xusar خوسار (IFb) = hoarfrost. See **xûsî**.

xuşexuş خـوشـهـخـوش *f.* **(-a;-ê).** rustle, rustling sound; splash, splashing sound; swishing sound of: moving water (K/B/AD); of paper, grass, trees (IFb); of clothing and jewelry (GF/HH); of snakes (K): **•Şev e, xweş şev e, baran e dibare, *xuşe xuş* e** (M.Uzun. R. Evd. Zeyn., 73) Night, sweet night, rain is falling, *splash splash*. {also: xişxiş (A/FJ/GF-2/AD); xuşxuş (A-2/GF/CS); <xişxiş> خـشـخـش (HH)} Sor xuşe خـوشـه = 'swishing sound (liquid streaming out, milk from cow's udder)' & xuşexuş خوشهخوش = 'continued swish' [Uzun/K/B/IFb//GF/CS//A/FJ/HH/AD] <xuşîn>

xuşikîn خـوشِـكـيـن *vi.* **(-xuşik-).** to slide, glide, gently descend; to skate: **•Çû ser pêlpêlikên *dixuşikin* û ber bi jêr ve *xuşikî*** (MG) He went onto the *sliding* staircase [i.e., escalator] and *slid* downward **•Gopalê wî di teħîsankê da *xuşikî* û çû xwar** (FS) His cane *slid* on the slippery spot and went down. {also: xişikîn (GF-2); [khechikin] خـشـكـيـن (JJ)} Cf. Sor xişan خِـشـان = 'to drag/creep/crawl slowly (with rustling sound)' [MG/Şnx/GF/ZF/FS/G//JJ]

xuşîn خـوشـيـن *vi.* **(-xuş-).** 1) to rustle *(leaves, etc.)*; to splash gently *(water, etc.)*: **•Li her du aliyên riya kanîyê sipîndar, darên sêva, erûga û încasa hebûn. Gişt rêz bûbûn. Pelên wan bi sira bayê, yekser *dixuşîyan*, û li vî alî, li wî alî dihejîyan** (MB-Meyro) On both sides of the road to the well there were poplars, apples trees, and plum trees, all in a row. Their leaves *rustled* in the cool evening breeze, tilting this way and that; 2) to slither (of snakes); 3) [*f.* **(-a;-ê).**] rustling; gentle splashing sound: ***•xuşîna* daran** (IFb) *the rustling of* the trees ***•xuşîna* giya** (GF) *the rustling of* the grass; 4) slithering *(of snakes)*. {also: xişîn (IFb-2); xwişîn (Alkan); [khychin] خـشـيـن (JJ)} Sor xişan خِـشـان = 'to drag/creep/crawl slowly (with rustling sound)' [MB/K/IFb/B/GF/TF/SS//JJ//Alkan] <xuşexuş>

xuşk خوشك (AB/IFb/GF) = sister. See **xûşk**.

xuşxuş خـوشـخـوش (A/GF/CS) = rustling, splashing. See **xuşexuş**.

xuw خوو (-a;) (Z-3) = sister. See **xûşk**.

xuya خـويـا *adj.* visible, apparent, obvious: **•Ya xortê delal, tu zilamekî ẍerîb *xwîya* ye** (L) O dandy youth, you *appear to be* a stranger [in these parts]; **-xuya bûn** (A/JB3/IFb-2) to appear, be seen: **•Kes *xuyan nabe (nake)*** (B) There is no one *to be seen*; **-xuya kirin** (A): = a) to show, reveal {syn: mewcûd kirin; peyda kirin}; b) to seem. See **xuyan I**. {also: xoya (JB1-A); xuyan II (B); xûya; xweya (JB1-S); xweyan I (K-2/A-2); xwîya (L); [khouia] خويا (JJ); <xuweya-> خويا (HH)} {syn: aşkere; berç'av II; diyar; k'ifş; xanê} < Arc ḥawwē חוי/aḥawē אחוי = 'to show; to tell'; NENA maxwo:ye (Krotkoff) & Turoyo máḥwe = 'to show; to look (vi.), appear' [L//K/A/JB3/IFb/JJ//B//HH//JB1-A//JB1-S]

xuyan I خـويـان *vi.* **(-xwên-/-xwey-** [Msr]**).** 1) to appear, seem, look to be: **•Tu piȓ civan *dixweyî*** (Msr) you *look* very young; 2) to make one's appearance, show up; to come to light, be discovered, show *(vi.)*, reveal o.s., manifest o.s., be seen. {also: xweyan II (-xwey-) (Msr); xwîngiyan (IFb-2); xwîngîn (-xwîngê) (IFb); xwîyan (K-2); xwuyan (F); <xuweyan خـويـان (dixweye) (دخـويـه)> (HH)} Cf. NA maxwo:ye (Zakho; Aradhin) & máḥwe (Turoyo) = 'to show; to look (vi.), appear' < Arc ḥawwē חוי/aḥawē אחוי = 'to show; to tell' [K//HH//Msr//IF] <xanê>

xuyan II خويان (B) = visible, obvious. See **xuya**.

xuyî xêr خويى خێر (Z-2) = benefactor. See **xudanxêr**.

xuzî خوزى (HR-7) = spit, saliva. See **xwezî II**.

xûdan خـوودان *vi.* **(-xûd-).** 1) to sweat, perspire; 2) [*f.* **(-a;-ê).**] sweat, perspiration: **•Dîsan bi destmala xwe ya kaxizî *xwêdana* ser çavê xwe û ya eniya xwe ya rût pakij kir** (KS, 37) He again wiped the *sweat* from his naked face and forehead with his paper handkerchief **•Min xwêdan da** (Msr) I perspired. {also: xudan I (IFb/B); xuhdan (JB1-S); xweydan (K-2); xwêdan I (F/Msr); xwîdan (K-2); [khou-dan خـودان/khou-dain خـودايـن] (JJ); <xwêhdan خـويـهـدان (xw[ê]hdide) (خـويـهـدده)> (HH)} [Pok. 2. sụeid- 1043.] 'to sweat': Skt √svid [svedate]; Av √x^{V}aēd, pres. stem x^{V}īsa- = 'to break out in a sweat' & x^{V}aēδa- *m.* = 'sweat'; Mid P xwistan = 'to sweat' & xwē̆y = 'sweat'; P xuy خـوى = 'sweat, perspiration'; cf. also Arm k'irt (W: k'ird) քիրտ (<*swe/idra); Lat sudor; Germ Schweiss [Z-1/K/JJ//IFb/B//F/Msr//HH//JB1-S]

xûgî خووگى (IFb/GF) = tax. See **xûk**.

xûk خـــــــووك *f.* **(-a;-ê).** tax(es), tribute: **•Evsale me hêşta *xwîka* xo newergirtîye. Tu gund ber gund here *xwîkê* kom bike, *xwîka* evsale hemî bo te** (X.Salih. Hindek serhatîyên Kurdî, 130) This year we haven't received our *taxes* [=tribute]. You, go collect *the taxes* village by village, [and] this year's *taxes* are all for you. {also: xukî (K-2); xûgî (IFb-2/GF); xûkî (K/IFb-2/GF-2/TF); xwîk (BF/Wkt)} {syn: bac; bêş; olam [1]; xer[a]c} [Bw/A/IFb//K/TF//GF//BF/Wkt] <kode>

xûkî خووكى (K/IFb/GF/TF) = tax. See **xûk**.

xûn خــــــــوون (Ba/Z-1/K/IF-2/B/SK/JB1-A/JJ/HH) = blood. See **xwîn**.

xûnav خووناڤ (JB3/IFb) = dew. See **xunav**.

xûndar خـوونـدار (K/B/JJ) = bloody; blood enemy. See **xwîndar**.

xûndin خووندِن (-xûn-) (JB1-A) = to read; to recite; to study. See **xwendin**.

xûndkar خووندكار *m.* **(-ê;-î).** ruler, sovereign, despot, king, monarch: **•Babê Nemrûd *xûndkarê* Ken'aniya bû** (GShA, 226) Nemrud's father was *the ruler of* Canaan. {also: xudkar (FJ-2); xundekar (FJ/CS); xundkar (Kmc); xunkar (A/IFb); xûnkar (K); [khoundkar] خـونـدكـار(JJ); <xunkar خنكار/xundekar خندكار> (HH)} {syn: ĥakim; p'adşa; silt'an} Cf. P xunkār خـنـكـار (<xudāvandigār خـداونـدگـار) --> T hünkâr {xûndkarî} [GShA//JJ//K//A/IFb/HH//Kmc//FJ/CS]

xûndkarî خـوونـدكـارى *f.* **(-ya;-yê).** rule, monarchy, kingship, the throne: **•Hemû milk û mal û *xûndkariya* xo hêla û bi kerekî berê xo da Rûhayê** (GShA, 227) He abandoned all his wealth and possessions, and gave up his *throne* and travelled on a donkey to Ruha [Urfa] **•*Xunkarîya* wî deh ṣala kêşa** (FS) His *rule* lasted for 10 years. {also: xunkarî (A/FS); xûnkarî (K); [xondk'āri] خـونـدكـارى (JJ)} {syn: p'adşatî} [GShA//JJ//K//A/FS] <ĥuk'um; xûndkar>

xûng خوونگ (Dy) = sister. See **xûşk**.

xûnkar خوونكار (K) = ruler, king. See **xûndkar.**

xûnkarî خوونكارى (K) = kingship. See **xûndkarî**.

xûnmij خوونمِژ (K/GF) = bloodthirsty. See **xwînmij**.

xûnşîrin خوونشيرِن (K/B) = amiable. See **xwînşîrîn**.

xûnşîrinî خـــوونـــشـــيـــرِنـــى (K/B) = amiability. See

xwînşîrînî.

xûnşîrintî خــوونــشــيــرِنــتــى (B) = amiability. See **xwînşîrînî.**

xûnşîrîn خوونشيرين (FJ/GF) = amiable. See **xwînşîrîn.**

xûnşîrînî خــوونــشــيــريــنــى (FJ/GF) = amiability. See **xwînşîrînî.**

xûs خووس (FS/JJ) = hoarfrost. See **xûsî.**

xûsar خووسار (GF/HH) = hoarfrost. See **xûsî.**

xûsik خووسِك (IFb) = hoarfrost. See **xûsî.**

xûsî خووسى *f.* **(-ya;-yê).** frost, hoarfrost, rime: **•*Xûsar* a ketî** (Bw) *Frost* has fallen **•Şevê dî *xûsê* qad girtibû** (FS) The night before *frost* had covered [lit. 'taken'] the ground; **-xûsîya serê sibê** (Z-3) early morning hoarfrost. {also: sûxar (Zeb); xusar (IFb); xûs (FS); xûsar (GF); xûsik (IFb-2); xwîsik (IFb-2); xwîsî (Qzl); [khous] خــوس (JJ); <xûsar> خــوســار (HH)} {syn: qeşa; qiřav} [Z-3//IFb//HH/GF/Bw//JJ/FS//Qzl//Zeb] <xunav [1]>

xûşk/xûşk' [JB1-A] خــووشــك *f.* **(-a;-ê).** sister: **•Ez Zîn-xatûnim, qîza mîr Zêvdînim, *xûşka* mîr Sêvdînim, nevîa mîr Etlesim** (FK-kk-1, 262) I'm Lady Zîn, daughter of Mîr Zêvdîn, *sister of* Mîr Sêvdîn, granddaughter of Mîr Atlas **•Gelî bira, hûn ji k'oçka min ḧeta zîndana Memê min têda gere řêke bin'erd çê kin. Çiqas zêř bixazin ezê bidime we, lê t'enê hûn zû bikin, usa jî suřa min, çewa *xûşka* xwe, k'esîřa nevêjin** (Z-1, 61) O brothers, you must make a tunnel from my quarters to the dungeon my Mem is in. I'll give you as much gold as you want, only you must be quick about it, and you must not tell anyone my secret, as if I were your [own] *sister*. {also: xang I (Bg); xohing (JB1-A-2); xong (JB1-A-2); xu[w] (-a;) (Z-3); xuk (-a;) (Z-3); xuşk (AB/IFb/GF); xûng (Dy); xwah (CS-2); xwang (IF-2); xweh I (FJ/CS-2); xwehing (JB1-S-2); xwehişk' (JB1-A-2); xwîşk (K/JB3/GF-2); [khouchk] خــوشــك (JJ); <xuweh> خــــــوه (HH)} [Pok. su̯esor 1051.] 'sister': Skt svásar-; Av x^vaŋhar-; Southern Tati dialects: Chali/Xiaraji/ Ebrahim-abadi x^wāka; Takestani/Eshtehardi xāka; Danesfani xoka; Sagz-abadi xāca (Yar-Shater); P x^vāhar خــواهــر; Sor xuşk خــوشــك; Za wa *f.* (Todd); Hau wałê *f.* (M4); cf. also Lat soror; Rus sestrá сестра; Germ Schwester; Arm k'uyr քոյր [F/A/B/JJ/JB1-S/CS//K/JB3//AB/IFb/GF//HH//FJ//Bg//Dy] <bira I; etik>

xûya خوويا = visible, obvious. See **xuya**.

xûyzî خوويزى (FJ/GF) = spit, saliva. See **xwezî II**.

xûz خــووز *adj.* stooped over, bent over *(of the back)*: **-xwe xûz kirin** (Elk) to stoop, bend down: **•*Xwe xûz ke*!** (Elk) *Bend down* (so you don't bump your head). {syn: xwar[4]} [Elk/K/A/IFb/GF/FJ] <kûz I>

xwah خواه (CS) = sister. See **xûşk**.

xwal خوال (Bx) = maternal uncle. See **xal I**.

xwançe خوانچه (Wkt) = low table. See **xonçe**.

xwanda خــوانــدا (FS) = educated, refined person. See **xuneda**.

xwandegeh خواندهگه (IF) = school. See **xwendegeh**.

xwandin خواندِن (BF/FS) = to read. See **xwendin**.

xwandingeh خواندِنگه (FS) = school. See **xwendegeh**.

xwang خوانگ (IFb) = sister. See **xûşk**.

xwanik خوانِك (Wkt/FS) = low table for making bread. See **xanik**.

xwanî خوانى (GF) = visible, obvious. See **xanê**.

xwar خــوار *adv.* 1) {syn: jêr} down, downward: **-hatin xwarê** (Zeb) to dismount, get down, get out of *(vehicle)* {syn: peya bûn}: **•Ez *dê hême xwarê*** (Zeb) I *will get out* [of the car]; 2) [*adj.*] low, base; 3) {also: xwehr (Bw/TF)} crooked: **-xwaro-maro** (Ba2/K/A)/**xwar û xûr** (Mzg/Srk)/**xwar û xudir** (Mzg)/**xar û xudur** (IFb) crooked; 4) {syn: xûz} bent over, stooped (ZF): **-xwar bûn** (A/B/GF/ZF)/**xwarî *ft-î* bûn** (Epl/Ardû) to bend over stg., stoop down over {syn: xwe xûz kirin}: **•Li vir *xwarî* benê potînên xwe *dibe*, vedike, ji lingên xwe derdixe** (Epl 13) Here he *bends down over* his shoelaces, undoes them, and takes [the shoes] off his feet **•Yek zûzûka *xwarî* tiştekî *dibe* û wî tiştî dibe li paş qûçeke nêzîk vedişêre** (Ardû 20) One quickly *stoops down* over something, and takes that thing and hides it behind a nearby rock. {also: xar I (K/Z-1/SK); xwehr (TF); [khar] خـــوار (JJ)} {x[w]ar[ay]î} Cf. Sor xwar خـوار; Za war (Todd); Hau war (M4) [Z-1/K/SK/JJ//A/IFb/B/ZF//TF] <xwaro-maro>

xwara خوارا (GF) = gluttonous. See **xure**.

xwara•yî خــوارايــى *f.* **(;•yê).** 1) crookedness; 2) slope, incline. {also: xarayî (B-2); xarî (SK); [khwārī] خوارى (JJ)} [B//SK//JJ] <xwar>

xwarek خوارهك (IF) = food. See **xurek**.

xwarin خـــوارِن *vt.* **(-xw- / -xu- / -xo-** [SK/JB1-A&S/Bw]**).** 1) to eat: **•Were, em nanê xwe t'isî bi şîrê xamberdîra *bixun*** (EP-7) Come, let's eat our stale bread with the milk of three-year-old sheep; **-hev xwarin** = to fight, quarrel, argue: **•Şkyatçîa *hevdu xar*** (EP-7) The litigants are quarreling fiercely [lit. '*have eaten each other up*']; **-nan xwarin** (ZF) to eat, have a meal [lit. 'to eat bread']; **-serê *fk-î* xwarin** (Frq) to nag, pester s.o.; **-sond xwarin** (IFb/ZF) to swear, take an oath: **•Bira *sond xar*, ku tiştek serê Ûsib naê** (Ba) The brothers *swore* that nothing would happen to Joseph; 2) to drink (Ag); 3) to take, get, receive *(stg. unpleasant: a punishment, etc.)*, sustain *(a blow)*: **•Gelo te tu carî dar *xwarine*** (HYma 49) Have you ever *been beaten with* a stick? **•...ji wê şimaqa ku *me xwariye* ji kekê xwe** (pirtukxane. blogspot.com 8.iv.2006) ... from that smack which *we got* from our older brother; 4) [*f.* **(-a;-ê).**] {syn: xurek} food: **•Nan û pîvaz *xwarina* birçîyan e** (AB) Bread and onions are (is) *the food of* the hungry **•Li şera xal û xwarzî; li *xwarina*, mam û brazî** (Bx) For battles, maternal uncle and nephew; for *food*, paternal uncle and nephew [prv. illustrating familial relationships]. {also: xarin (Ba/J/Ag); xwerin (F/K); [khourin خورين/kharin خوارين] (JJ); <xuwarin خوارن (dixwe) (دخوه)> (HH)} [Pok. 1. su̯el(k)- 1045.] 'to eat, drink': O Ir *x^Var- (Tsb 39): Av x^Var- (*pres.* x^Vara-) = 'to enjoy, consume': P xōrdan خوردن; Sor xwardin خواردِن; SoK xwa-, xô-, x^wa(r)-, hwar-/xwârd-, xôrd-, x^wârd-, hwârd- (Fat 357); Za wenã [werdiş] (Todd/Srk); Hau war<u>d</u>ey (wer-) vt. (M4); cf. also Eng swallow [A/JB3/IFb/B/HH/JB1-A/GF/TF/ZF//Ba/J/Ag/JJ/SK/JB1-A//F/K] <azûxe [1]; keritandin; nan>

xwaringeh خوارِنگەه *f.* **(-a;-ê).** 1) {syn: aşxane [3]} dining room; 2) {syn: aşxane [2]; xwarinxane} restaurant: **•9 jin di vê *xwaringeha* kurdewarî de kar dikin** (Rûdaw 7.x.2015) 9 women work in this traditional Kurdish *restaurant*. {also: <xaringe> خارِنگە (Zx)} [Zx//Wlt/IFb/GF/ZF3/Wkt]

xwarinxane خوارِنخانە *f.* **().** restaurant. {also: xwerinxane (F/K); xwerinxanî} {syn: aşxane [2]; xwaringeh} [IFb/GF/TF//F/K]

xwaro-maro خوارۆ مارۆ *adj.* crookèd: **-xwaro-maro bûn** = to twist, wind *(vi.)*, meander: **•Ser sîngê Dûmanlûê cîcîna xulexula cewikêd avê bû, êd ku mînanî mara jorda dişûlikîn, *xwaro-maro dibûn*** (Ba2:1, 202) On the slope of {Mount} Dumanlu here and there was the babbling of brooks (of water), those which crept from above like snakes, and *twisted around*. {also: xaromar (K); xaro maro (IFb); xarovar (Zeb/Dh); [khar ou mar] خوار و مار (JJ)} {syn: ç'ewt; kêř II; xwar û xûr (Mzg/Srk); xwar û xudir (Mzg)} Cf. Sor xuwar-u-xêç خووار و خێچ = 'twisted' [Ba2/A/B/GF//K//JJ//IFb//Zeb/Dh] <xwar>

xwarz خوارز (B) = nephew or niece. See **xwarzî**

xwarza خوارزا (FS) = nephew or niece. See **xwarzî**.

xwarzê خوارزێ (A/TF/ZF3) = nephew or niece. See **xwarzî**.

xwarzêtî خوارزێتی (ZF3) = relationship between a child and his or her mother's brother. See **xwarzîtî**.

xwarzî خوارزی *m.&f.* **(-yê/-ya;).** nephew, niece *(child of one's sister)*: **•Li şera xal û *xwarzî*; li xwarina, mam û brazî** (Bx)/**xwarinê de ap û brazî, şer de xal û *xwarzî*** (IF) For battles, maternal uncle and *nephew*; for food, paternal uncle and nephew *[prv. illustrating familial relationships]*. {also: xarz (B-2); xarza (SK); xarzî I (IF-2); xwarz (B); xwarza (FS); xwarzê (A/TF/ZF3); [kvárzá/xoarzi] خوارزا (JJ); <xuwarzî> خوارزی (HH)} {syn: êgan (Ad)} Cf. P x^Vāharzāde خواهرزاده = 'sister's son or daughter, nephew or niece'; Sor xałoza خاڵۆزا = 'cousin, child of maternal uncle'; Za xalza = 'cousin, son of maternal aunt or uncle' (Todd) & ware-zá (JJ) {xarzî II; xarztî; xwarzîtî} [K/JB3/IFb/HH//SK//B//JJ/FS//A/TF/ZF3] <brazî; t'îza; xal I>

xwarzîtî خوارزیتی *f.* **(;-yê).** "nephewhood," "niecehood," relationship between a child and his or her mother's brother. {also: xarzî II (B); xarztî (B-2); xwarzêtî (ZF3)} [GF//B//ZF3] <xwarzî>

xwastin خواستِن (IFb) = to want; to request. See **xwestin**.

xwazgîn خوازگین *m.&f.* **().** matchmaker *{for traditional arranged marriage}*; woman sent to see a prospective bride; go-between in marriage arrangements {T görücü}. {also: xazginçî (Ag); xazgîn; xwezginî (F); xwezgîn (K); xwezgînî II (B/ZF3); [khazgin خازگين/khozgin خوزگين] (JJ)} [IFb//Ag//F//K//B//JJ]

xwazgînî خوازگینی (IFb/GF) = asking for a girl's hand in marriage. See **xwezgînî I**.

xwazî خوازی (JB1-S) = If only! See **xwezî I**.

xwazok خوازۆك *m.* **().** beggar, mendicant. {also: xazok (Bw); xwazûk (ZF3); xwezok (K); [khwazok] خوازك (JJ)} {syn: gede [2]; p'arsek} [Bw//IFb/JJ/GF/ZF3//K]

xwazûk خوازووك (ZF3) = beggar. See **xwazok**.

xwe خوە *prn.* oneself [myself, yourself, himself,

herself, itself, ourselves, yourselves, themselves] *{reflexive pronoun referring back to logical subject of the sentence or phrase}*: **•Ez *xwe* dibînim** = I see *myself* **•Min birayê *xwe* dît** = I saw *my* brother [lit. 'I saw the brother *of myself*']; **-bi xwe** = [by] oneself, on one's own: **•Ez bawar nakim, ku ewî *bi xwe* fe'm kiribe** (Ba) I don't believe that he understood it *on his own* (=that he could have figured it out on his own); **-ji xwe** = of course; **-ya xwe k'etin** (XF) to grow old: **•Ez û dîya teva îdî *ya xwe k'etine*** (Z-1) Your mother and I *have grown old.* {also: xo (SK/JB1-A&S); xoh (JB1-A-2); xweh II (A-2); xwexa; xwexwe; [khou خـو/khé خـوه] (JJ); <xuwe[h]> خـوه (HH)} Cf. P xōd خـود; Sor xo خـۆ; Za xu (Todd); cf. also Rus sebia себя & svoĭ свой; Lat se & suus [K/A/JB3/IFb/B/JJ/TF//HH//SK/JB1-A&S]

xwecih خوەجِه (IFb) = local. See **xwecihî**.

xwecihî خـوەجِـهـی *m.* **().** 1) {syn: binecî; binelî} local inhabitant, native: •[**Eger *xwecihî* lê bidin û mirovekî Ekradan bikujin, êdî ĥetta qiyametê şeř û şiltax̂êd Ekradan xilas nabin**] (BN, 101) If *the local inhabitants* beat them or kill one of the Kurds' men, the battles and squabbles of the Kurds won't end until Judgement Day •[**Û *xwecihî* jî dibêjin ku her çî zarokêd ku ji jinêd Ekradan biwelidin bê edeb û diz û serkêş dibin**] (BN, 100) And *the locals* say that whatever children are born of Kurdish women are rude and thieves and obstinate; 2) [*adj.*] local: •[**Lewranî mumkin nabitin ku Ekrad jinêd *xwecihî* bistînin**] (BN, 99) Therefore it is not possible for Kurds to take [i.e., marry] *local* women. {also: xwecih (IFb); [khou-djihi] خوجهی (JJ)} Sor xocê خۆجێ/xocêyî خۆجێیی (Hej) [BN/JJ/ZF3//IFb]

xwedan خوەدان (JB1-S) = owner, master. See **xwedî**.

xwe-dane-paş خـــوه دانـــه پـــاش *f.* **(-a;).** reluctance; dissociating o.s. from stg.: **•Sebebekî dî ji esbabêt *xo-dan-e-paşa* Kurdan ji dexaleta dewleta behîye ya urosî eweye, dibêjin dewleta urosî dil-ṣaf e** (SK 56:651) Another of the reasons for the Kurds' *reluctance* to submit to the august Russian government is this: it is said that the Russian government is [too] naïve. {also: xo-dan-e-paş (SK)} [SK//K/XF] <havî[bûn]> See also **-xwe dane paş** under **paş**.

Xwedê خوەدێ *m.* **().** God: **-Xwedê dan** (Bw/Zx) to be born: **•Tu kengî *Xwedê dayî*?** (Bw) When *were you born*? [lit. 'when did God give you?']; **-xwedê hebîna** (L/K)/~ **hebînê** (JB3)/~**hebînî** (LC) for God's sake: **•De *xwedê hebînî* yanê ne ez bim kî kane vî derdî bikşîne?** (LC, 12) *For God's sake*, if not for me, who can stand this trouble?; **-Xwedê kerîm e** (L) God is generous; **-Xwedê ře̊ĥme!** (J) God is merciful; **-Xwedê teala** (L) God the exalted on; **-Xwedê te bihêle** (L) May God keep you [among the living]; **-Xwedê zane** (Dz) I swear by God [lit. 'God knows']. {also: xadê (EP-7); xodê (JB1-A); xuda (SK-2); xudê (SK/JB1-S); [khoudi] خـدی (JJ); <xudê> خـدی (HH)} {syn: elah} Cf. P xudā خـدا; Sor xwa خـوا/[Mukri] xuła خولا [K/A/JB3/IFb/B/GF//EP-7//JB1-A//JJ// HH//SK/JB1-S]

xwedêgiravî خـوەدێ گِـراڤـی *conj.* 1) as if, as though; 2) [*interj.*] {syn: qaşo I} supposedly, allegedly, ostensibly: **•Dibêjin, ku *xwedêgiravî* ew çûye** (B) They say that he has *supposedly* gone **•Gilî dikirin, wekî navê Mistê Kalo dane** [sic] **ser gund bona wê yekê, ku, *xwedê giravî*, cara pêşin ewî mêrikî k'ulfeta xweva hatye wê derê xweřa mal çê kirye ...** (Ba2:1, 202) They say that they gave the village the name of Miste Kalo because *supposedly* this man came there first with his family [and] built a house. {also: xwedîgiravî (TF); [khoudi gherawi] خـدی گـراڤـی (JJ)} = Sor guwaya گوایا [Ba2/K/B//TF//JJ] <maxwene>

xwedênas خـوەدێ نـاس *m.&f.* **().** believer in God; *adj.* God-fearing: **•Ez dizanim ew mirovekî xas û *Xudênase*** (GShA, 230) I know he is a holy and *God-fearing* man. {also: xudênas (GShA)} Cf. P xudāšinās خــداشــنــاس = 'pious, religious, God-knowing'; Sor xwanas خواناس [GShA//K/B/IFb/FJ/GF]

xwedênenas خـوەدێ نـەنـاس *m.&f.* **().** atheist, infidel, unbeliever, non-Muslim: **•Qey tu *xwedênenas* î?** (HYma 48) Are you by any chance *an atheist*? {syn: k'afir} Cf. P xudā'nešinās خــدانــشــنــاس = 'impious, ungodly'; Sor xwanenas خــوانــەنــاس [HYma/K/B/IFb/FJ/GF/CS] <bêol>

xwedî خـــــوەدی *m.* **(-yê;).** owner, master, possessor; *often used without izafeh in indicating a quality which one possesses*, e.g., **xwedîbext** = 'lucky, possessing luck'; *in Hekkari & Iraq the preferred form is* ***xudan***: **•Ev helwest nahêle ku HEP *bibe xwedî* şexsiyet** (Wlt 1:43) This attitude does not allow HEP *to have* a personality of its own **•*Xudanê* kerî jî weto xiyal dikir ko her do hewalêt wî dê harî wî ken** (SK 8:80) *The owner* *of* the donkey thought that his two companions would help him; **-xwedî/xweyî bûn** = to own: **•Ez *bûm xweyê* zêřa jî** (J) I also *own* gold now; **-xwedî kirin** = a) [+ **li**] to look after, take care of s.o. {syn: miqatî bûn} **•Neferê wî *xay kir*** (Z-922) He *looked after* his (=another's) people (=family); b) to feed (an animal): **•Di destpêkê de min ew bi ceh û kayê *xwedî dikir*** (HYma, 11) At first I *fed* him barley and straw; c) [+ **ji**] to protect {syn: parastin}: **•[Ç'îyayê] Dûmanlû Zeřîbxane û gundêd dine nêzîk *ji* baêd şimalêne sar *xwey dikir*** (Ba2:1, 202) [Mount] Dumanlu *protected* Zeribkhaneh and other nearby villages from the cold northern winds **•Kela ... Ç'ala Sînekî ... ji cerdê, *ji* duşmin *xwey kin*** (Ba2) Fortresses ... *protect* Chala Sinek from brigands, from the enemy. {also: xay I (Z-1); xayî; xudan II (SK/JB1-A&S); xwedan (JB1-S-2); xweî (F); xwey (B/Ba2); [khouï خوى/khoudi خدى] (JJ); <xuweyî> خويى (HH)} Cf. Sor xawen خاوەن; Za wêr/wihêr (Todd) {xwedîtî; xweytî; [khouïti خويتى/khouïouti خويوتى] (JJ)} [J//F//K/A/IFb/ GF/TF//Z-1//B/Ba2//JJ//HH//SK/ JB1-A&S] <malxwê; milûk; sermiyan>

xwedîbext خوەدى بەخت (IFb/TF/OK) = honest; lucky. See **xudanbext**.

xwedîgiravî خوەدى گِراڤى (TF) = supposedly. See **xwedêgiravî**.

xwedîpez خوەدى پەز m. (). sheep owner. {also: xwedîyê pêz (BK-2)} [BK]

xwedîtî خوەديتى *f.* **(-ya;-yê).** ownership. {also: xweytî (K/B); [khouïti خويتى/khouïouti خويوتى] (JJ)} [K/ B//IF//JJ] <xwedî>

xwefiroş خوەفِرۆش *m.* **(-ê;).** collaborator; traitor, quisling; mercenary: **•Dewleta tirk ya êrîşker û xayîn û *xwefiroşên* Kurd berpirsiyarên rijandina xwîna gelê me ne!** (Wlt 1:37, 2) The bellicose Turkish state and Kurdish traitors and *collaborators* are responsible for the spilling of our people's blood. {syn: altax; destkîs} [Wlt/K/IFb/ TF/ZF3/Wkt] <xayîn>

xweh I خوەه (FJ/CS) = sister. See **xûşk**.

xweh II خوەه (A) = oneself, -self. See **xwe**.

xwehing خوەهِنگ (JB1-S) = sister. See **xûşk**.

xwehişk' خوەهِشك (JB1-A) = sister. See **xûşk**.

xwehr خوەهر (Bw/TF) = crooked. See **xwar**[3].

xweî خوەئى (F) = owner, master. See **xwedî**.

xwelî خوەلى *f.* **(-ya;-yê).** 1) ash(es): **-xwelî li ser** (IFb) pitiful, poor [lit. 'ashes on the head']. See **xwelîser** I; 2) {syn: ax} dirt, soil, earth, ground: **•*K'ulme xwelî* bavêje t'aê zêřa** (Ba) Throw *a handful of dirt* onto the pan of the scales [which has] the gold **•Zelîxe *k'ulme xalî* davêje t'aê zêřa** (Ba) Zelikha throws *a handful of dirt* onto the pan of the scales [which has] the gold. {also: xalî III; xolî (JB1-A/ SK/OK-2); [kholi] خولى (JJ); <xuwelî> خولى (HH)} Cf. Southern Tati dialects (all *f.*): Chali xōla; Takestani, Eshtehardi, & Xiaraji xola; Sagzabadi xuala = 'ash' (Yar-shater); Sor xoł خۆڵ = 'earth'; Za wel *f.* = 'ash' (Todd) [K/A/JB3/IFb/B//HH/ GF/TF/OK//JJ/JB1-A/SK] <agir; ant'êẍ; bizot; helemor>

xwelîdan خوەليدان (GF) = ashtray. See **xwelîdank**.

xwelîdang خوەليدانگ (TF) = ashtray. See **xwelîdank**.

xwelîdank خوەليدانك *f.* **(-a;-ê).** ashtray: **•Ji xwe *xwelîdank* ji berê de li ser masê heye, ger tunebe jî muheqqeq li ser maseyeke din heye** (LC, 34) There is probably *an ashtray* on the table from before, and even if there isn't, there certainly is one on another table. {also: xolîdank (OK); xwelîdan (GF); xwelîdang (TF); xwelîdenk (Btm); xwelîser II (Hk); xwelîvank (Bw)} {syn: teblîk} [Btm//IFb/ZF3/Wkt/BF/FS//OK//GF//TF//Hk//Bw] <xwelî>

xwelîdenk خوەليدەنك (Btm) = ashtray. See **xwelîdank**.

xwelîreng خوەليرەنگ *adj.* gray/gray, ashen, ash-gray: **•Di terembêleke *xwelîreng* de bû** (HYma 29) He was in a *grey* car. {also: xulîreng (FJ)} {syn: bor I; boz; cûn I; gewr[1]; kew II} < xwelî = 'ash' + řeng = 'color'; cf. Sor xułemêşî خوڵەمێشى [HYma/ZF3//FJ]

xwelîser I خوەليسەر *adj.* miserable, poor, wretched, pitiful: **•Xema *xwelîser* guneh e, dilê min pir pê ve ye** (DBgb, 8) It's a shame about *poor* Khem, my heart goes out to her **•*Xwelîser* bi şev û roj di bin barê axê de ye** (DBgb, 8) *The poor thing* is under the agha's thumb [lit. 'burden'] night and day. {syn: belengaz; bikul; dêran II; malxirab; řeben I; şerpeze} [DBgb/K/A/FJ/GF/ZF3/FS]

xwelîser II خوەليسەر (Hk) = ashtray. See **xwelîdank**.

xwelîvank خوەليڤانك (Bw) = ashtray. See **xwelîdank**.

xwendawar خوەنداوار (DM) = reader. See **xwendevan**.

xwendegah خوەندەگاه (K/JB3) = school. See **xwendegeh**.

xwendegeh خوەندەگەه *f.* **(-a;-ê).** educational institution, school: **•Ew li *xwandingehê* dixwînit** (FS) S/he is studying at/in *school*; **-xwendegeha bilind** (JB3) college; **-xwendegeha destpêkî** (JB3)/~ **pêşîn** (ZF3) elementary school {syn:

dibistana seretayî}; **-xwendegeha destxetan** (JB3) school of arts and crafts; **-xwendegeha navîn** (JB3)/**xwendingeha amadeyî** (ZF3) high school. {also: xandingeh (BF); xwandegeh (IF-2); xwandingeh (FS); xwendegah (K/JB3); xwendingeh (Wkt/ZF3)} {syn: dersxane; mek't'eb; xwendinxane (B)} Cf. P x^{v}āngāh خوانگاه = 'Muslim religious brotherhood' [(neol)Ber/IFb/GF/BF//ZF3/Wkt//K/JB3//FS//BF] <dersxane; dibistan; xwendek'ar; zanîngeh>

xwende خوەندە (ZF3) = educated, refined person. See **xuneda**.

xwendeh خوەندەه (IFb) = educated, refined person. See **xuneda**.

xwendek'ar خوەندەکار *m.&f.* **(-ê/-a;-î/-ê).** student, pupil: **•Vê *xwendekarê* bi nivîskî ji zanîngehê xwesti bû ku fêrên zimanê kurdî bên dayîn** (Bultena Kurdî no 43) This *student* (f.) had asked the university in writing that Kurdish language lessons be offered. {also: xundevan (K); xwendevan (K-2); xwendewar (F); xwenkar (A)} {syn: qutabî; şagird} Sor xwêndkar خوێندکار [(neol)IFb/B/GF/OK/ZF3/Wkt/BF//K//F//A] <dersdar; mamosta; suxte; xwendin>

xwendevan خوەندەڤان *m.* **().** 1) reader, one who reads: **•Em bawer in ku *xwendevanên* Welat vê yekê jixwe baş dizanin** (Wlt 2:100, 2) We believe that *the readers of* [the newspaper] Welat know that very well **•Herwekî *xwendevanên* me dizanin li 8ê Hizêranê şer keti bû erdên Sûriye û Libnanê jî** (H2 9:31, 775) As our *readers* know, on June 8th war also broke out in the lands of Syria and Lebanon; 2) student. See **xwendek'ar**. {also: xwendawar (DM); xwendevar (A/JB3/OK); xwendewar (IFb-2); xwendkar (F); xwendiyar (GF-2); <xewenda> خوندا (HH)} Cf. P x^{v}ānande خواننده = 'reader; singer'; Sor xwêndewar خوێندەوار/xwêner خوێنەر = 'reader' [Ber/H2/K/IFb/ B/GF//A/JB3//DM//F//HH] <xwendin>

xwendevar خوەندەڤار (A/JB3/OK) = reader. See **xwendevan**.

xwendewar خوەندەوار = 1) reader (IFb). See **xwendevan**; 2) student (F). See **xwendek'ar**.

xwendin خوەندِن *vt.* **(-xwîn-** [AB/IFb/Wkt/ZF3/BF] / **-xwen-** / **-xîn-** [JB3] / **-xûn-** [B/EP-8/Ag]). 1) to read: **•Behremî pertûkek *xwand*** (FS) B. *read* a book **•Ez vê pirtûkê *dixwînim*** (FS) I am *reading* this book; 2) to recite: **•Eger hûn ji me re helbestekê *bixwînin* em dê kêfxweş bibin** (ZF3) If you *recite* a poem for us we will be very happy **•Ewî ismê sêrê li xwe *xwend*** (L) He *recited* words of magic to himself (=he cast a spell); 3) to sing *(of birds)*: **•Çima ev kevok *naxwênin*?** (HR 3:194) Why *won't* these doves *sing*? **•Kew li ser zinêr *dixwîne*** (AB) The partridge *sings* on the rock; 4) to study, learn, get an education: **•Gelek zarok û ciwanên nû ji Sûriyê û rojavayê Kurdistanê hatine Swêdê bo cara yekem di dibistanên swêdî de dersên zimanê kurdî *dixwînin*** (sverigesradio.se 7.ix.2017) Many children and young people recently arrived in Sweden from Syria and Western Kurdistan are *studying* Kurdish for the first time in Swedish schools; 5) to pronounce: **•Vî navî çawa *dixwînî*?** (Dh) How do you *pronounce* this name? {also: xandin (M-Zx/Bw); xundin (-xûn-) (SK/M); xûndin (-xûn-) (JB1-A); xwandin (BF/FS); [khandin خواندين/ khoundin خوندين] (JJ); <xuwandin خواندن (dixwîne) (دخوينه)> (HH)} [Pok. su̯en- 1046.] 'to sound, ring': Skt svánati = 'sounds, rings'; O Ir *h^{v}an- (Tsb 42): Av x^{v}ānaṭ.čaxra- = 'one whose wheels squeak'; Mid P xwandan (xwān-) (M3); Oss xon- = 'to call' (o<Ā *before nasal*); P x^{v}āndan خواندن = 'to read, to call, to sing', cf. range of meanings of Heb ḳara קרא = 'to read, to call'; Sor xwêndin [xöndin] خوێندِن/xondin خۆندِن; Za wanenã [wendiş] (Todd); Hau wanay (wan-) *vt.* = 'to study' (M4); cf. also Lat sono, -are = 'to resound' [F/K/A/JB3/IFb/B/JB1-S/GF/TF/OK/M-Gul/M-Shn/ZF3/Wkt//JJ//HH//BF/FS//SK/M//M-Zx/Bw//JB1-A]

xwendingeh خوەندِنگەه (Wkt) = school. See **xwendegeh**.

xwendinxan•e خوەندِنخانە *f.* **(;•ê).** school. {also: xwendinxanî (K)} {syn: mek't'eb; xwendegeh} [B//K] <dersxane; p'ol III>

xwendinxanî خوەندِنخانی (K) = school. See **xwendinxane**.

xwendiyar خوەندِيار (GF) = reader. See **xwendevan**.

xwendî خوەندی (B) = educated, refined person. See **xuneda**.

xwendkar خوەندکار (F) = reader. See **xwendevan** [1].

xwenkar خوەنکار (A) = student. See **xwendek'ar**.

xwere خوەرە (TF) = gluttonous. See **xure**.

xwerin خوەرِن (F/K) = to eat; food. See **xwarin**.

xwerinxane خوەرِنخانە(F/K) = restaurant. See **xwarinxane**.

xwerinxanî خوەرِنخانى = restaurant. See **xwarinxane**.

xwer̄û خـــــوەرِروو *adj.* 1) {syn: p'etî} simple, pure, unadulterated: **•Nivîs fesîh û *xwerû* ne** (Wlt 1:27, 10) The writings are eloquent and *simple* **•Vê dawiyê min cehê *xurrû* didayê** (HYma, 11) Recently I have been giving him *pure* barley; 2) {syn: r̄asteqîne} original, genuine, real, authentic; unique. {also: xurû (GF-2); cf. [khorou] خورو (JJ) = 'sole owner, one without a partner' & [khorou kirin] خورو كرين = 'to simplify'} [Wlt/K/IFb/GF/TF/RF]

xweser خوەسەر *adj.* independent, self-willed: **•HEP'a ku nikare bibe xwediyê şexsiyeteke *xweser*, nikare li hemberî partiyên dijber û saziyên dewletê jî, bibe xwedî rûmet û rêz** (Wlt 1:43, 9) [If] the People's Labor Party cannot have an *independent* identity, it cannot be respected by the opposition parties and the instruments of the state. {also: [khou-ser] خوسر (JJ)} {syn: serxwe} Cf. P xodsar خـودسـر = 'obstinate, stubborn'; Sor xoser خـۆسـەر = 'self-willed, independent' [Wlt/K/IFb/GF/TF/OK//JJ]

xwesî خوەسى (B) = mother-in-law. See **xesû**.

xwestin خـــوەســـتِـــن *vt.* **(-xwaz- / -xaz-** [Dz/Ag] **/ -xwez-** [J/EP-7/K]**).** 1) {syn: viyan [3]} to want, wish; [+ *subj.*] to want to *(do stg.) {in Southern Kurmanji [=Bahdini],* ***xwestin*** *means only 'to request' (#2 below); 'to want' is expressed by* ***viyan****}*: **•Ez *dixazim* her̄ime cem xwedê, bizanibim çika r̄astya wî çewane?** (Dz) I *want to* go to God, to know what his truth is like **•Ez *dixwazim* ez we bizewicînim** (L) I *want to* marry you (pl.) off **•Hêzên kolonyalîst *dixwazin* gelê me zêndî bikin gorê** (Ber) The colonialist forces *want to* bury our people alive **•Tiştê go dilê xwe *dixwest* ji xwe re kirî** (L) He bought himself whatever his heart *desired*; 2) to request, ask for: **•Bêje bavê xwe, bira min *bixweze*** (J) Tell your father *to ask* [my father] for me [in marriage to you] **•Lazim e tu herî qîza hakim ji mi re *bixwazî*** (L) You must go *request* the king's daughter for me; **-ji *fk-ê* deyn xwastin** (IFb) to borrow money from s.o., ask for a loan. {also: xastin (-xaz-) (SK); xest'in (-xaz-) (JB1-A); xwastin (IFb-2); [khastin/khoustin] خـواسـتـن (JJ); <xuwestin> خوسـتـن (dixwaze) (دخوازه)> (HH)} Cf. P x^{v}āstan خــواســتــن (-x^{v}āh-) (خــواه); Sor xuwastin خوواستِن = 'to ask for' [& wîstin ويستين] = 'to want'; SoK twâ-, xwâz-/twâst-, xwâst- etc. (Fat 363); Za wazenã [waştiş] (Todd) = 'to want'; Hau wastey (waz-) *vt.* = 'to request' (M4) [F/K/A/JB3/IFb/B/JB1-S/ GF/TF//HH//JJ/SK//JB1-A]

xwesû خوەسوو (Bx) = mother-in-law. See **xesû**.

xweş خــوەش *adj.* 1) pleasant, nice. *Can also precede noun [T influence], e.g.,* **•*Xweş*** [or, ***xoş***] **mirov e** (Bw) He's a *nice* guy; **•Memo ... bi dengê xweyî *xweş* çend k'ilamêd baş distira** [sic] (Ba2:1, 204) Memo would sing some good songs in his *pleasant* voice; **-lê xweş bûn** (A/SK/OK) to forgive. See **lê xweş bûn**; **-lê xweş hatin** (K/IFb) to please s.o.; to like *(rev. constr.)* {syn: k'êfa *fk-ê* bi *bk-î* hatin}: **•Em ȟerdu hêdî diçûn, carna jî disekinîn ... Eva yeka *li* apê minî Şevav *xweş nedihat*** (Ba2:4, 220) We both went slowly, sometimes even stopped ... This *did not please* my uncle Sh. **•Kirina te li min xweş hat** (K) I like what you did; 2) {syn: baş; çê; qenc; r̄ind; =Sor çak; xas} good, fine, well; 3) tasty, delicious (B/TF); 4) {syn: bilez; zû [2]} fast, quick (Bw): **•Wî zixt li hêstirê da ku *xweş* biçit** (FS) He goaded the mule so that it would speed up [lit. 'go *fast*'] **•*Xoş* neçe!** (Bw) Don't go [so] *fast*! {also: xoş (JB1-A-2/SK/GF-2/Bw-2); [khoch] خــــوش (JJ); <xweş> خــوش (HH)} Cf. P xōš خــوش --> T hoş; Sor xoş خـۆش; Za weş; Hau weş (M4) {xweşî} [K/A/JB3/IFb/B/HH/JB1A&S/GF/TF/OK/RZ/Bw/ZF//JJ/SK]

xweşdivî خــوەشــدِڤــى *adj./pp.* dear, beloved: **•Xuşk û birayên *xweşdivî*** (dengekurdistan.nu 31.xii.2015) *Dear* sisters and brothers! {also: xoşdivî (BF); xoştivî (Zx); xweştivî (Wlt); <xoştewî> خۆشـتـەوى (Hej)} {syn: 'ezîz; hêja I[3]} Sor xoşewîst خـۆشـەويـسـت [Wlt//Zx//Hej//ZF3/Wkt//BF]

xweşik خــــوەشِــــك *adj.* beautiful, lovely, pretty; handsome: **•Roj, ji rojên buharê ne. Lê belê hewaya demê ji me re tê xuyan ku ne ew rojên demsala *xweşik* in** (Wlt 2:59, 13) It the days of spring. But the weather makes it seems as if they are not days of that *lovely* season. {also: xweşîk (TF); xweş-kok (GF); <xuweşkok> خــوشــكــوك (HH)} {syn: bedew; cindî; spehî; şep'al} <dim. of **xweş**> [Çnr/Wlt/A/IFb/OK/ZF3/BF/FS//TF//GF/HH] <delal; şep'al>

xweşikayî خوەشِكايى (TF/ZF3) = beauty. See **xweşikî**.

xweşikî خـــوەشِـــكـــى *f.* **(-ya;-yê).** beauty: **•Mêrik ji *xweşikiya* jinikê hîna wusa devjihev û mitûmat e** (Ardû, 171) The man is agape and astounded by the woman's *beauty*. {also: xweşikayî (TF/ZF3)} {syn: bedewtî; spehîtî} [Ardû/A/Wkt//TF/ZF3]

xweşî خوەشی *f.* **(-ya;-yê).** 1) pleasure, pleasantness: **•Řefîqê dirust ewe ye li *xoşî* û ṯengawîyê řefîq bit, ne li *xoşîyê* bi-tinê** (SK 29:269) A true companion is one who is a companion in *pleasant times* and in difficulty, not just in *pleasant times*; 2) goodness: **-bi zor be, bi xweşî be** (L) willy-nilly, whether one wants to or not [bon gré, mal gré]; 3) health: **•Bimîne di *xweşîyê* da** = Take care/Be well *[farewell greeting]*; **-xweşî û řindî** (IFb) in happiness and health; 4) good spirits, good humor (IFb); 5) prosperity (IFb/TF); 6) nice weather, clear sky (HR/ZF): **•Bû *xoşî*, bû tavîk** (HR 3:64) There was *good weather*, there was sunshine **•Dinya wê bê *xweşî*** (HR 3:61) There will be *nice weather*; 6) orgasm: ***•Xweşiya* min hat ango orgazim bûm** (Wkt) I had an *orgasm* [lit. 'My *pleasure* came']. {also: xoşî (SK/HR-2); [khochi] خوشی (JJ)} [K/A/JB3/IFb/B/GF/TF/OK/ZF//JJ/SK] <xweş>

xweşîk خوەشیك (TF) = beautiful. See **xweşik**.

xwişîn خوشین (Alkan) = to rustle. See **xuşîn**.

xweş-kok خوەشکۆك (GF) = beautiful. See **xweşik**.

xweşmêr خوەشمێر *m.* **(-ê;).** gentleman, man of courage and decency: **•Ewran bi mehan arîkarî dabûn** [sic] **wî çiyayê *xweşmêrê* xwezayê** (MG. Tavê ew dît) For months the clouds helped that mountain, *gentleman* of nature. {also: [khoch-mir] خوشمر (JJ)} {syn: c[iw]amêr} < xweş = 'pleasant' + mêr = 'man' [MG/K/IFb/FJ/GF/CS//JJ]

xweştivî خوەشتِڤی (Wlt) = dear. See **xweşdivî**.

xwexa خوەخا = oneself, -self. See **xwe**.

xwexwe خوەخوە = oneself, -self. See **xwe**.

xwey خوەی (B/Ba2) = owner, master. See **xwedî**.

xweya خوەیا (JB1-S) = visible, obvious. See **xuya**.

xweyan I خوەیان (K/A) = visible, obvious. See **xuya**.

xweyan II خوەیان (-xwey-) (Msr) = to appear, seem. See **xuyan I**.

xweydan خوەیدان (K) = to perspire, sweat. See **xûdan**.

xweyî خوەیی (J) = owner, master. See **xwedî**.

xweytî خوەیتی (K/B) = ownership. See **xwedîtî**.

xweza خوەزا *f.* **(-ya;-yê).** nature: **•Dengê hûrbûna belçimî wek dengê mûzîka *xwezayê* ya herî xweş bû û pê bêhn li *xwezayê* çikîya** (MG. Tavê ew dît) The sound of the crushing leaf was like the sound of *nature's* best melody and with that sound *nature* became breathless/was out of breath. {syn: siruşt; ṯebî'et[1]} [(neol)IFb/OK/Kmc/RZ/CS/ZF/BF]

xwezahî خوەزاهی (Wlt) = natural. See **xwezayî**.

xwezayî خوەزایی *adj.* natural: **•Axaftina bi Kurdî mafê *xwezayî* yê gelê Kurd e** (Wlt 2:103, 8) Speaking in Kurdish is the *natural* right of the Kurdish people **•Wê ew bobelata *xwezayî* di nêzîk de bigihîje gundan jî** (FS: M.Baksî. Xemgînîya Xerzan) That *natural* disaster will soon reach the villages as well. {also: xwezahî (Wlt-2)} [(neol)Wlt/FS/Wkt/ZF3] <xweza>

xwezginî خوەزگِنی (F) = matchmaker; marriage broker, go-between. See **xwazgîn**.

xwezgîn خوەزگین (K) = matchmaker; marriage broker, go-between. See **xwazgîn**.

xwezgînî I خوەزگینی *f.* **(-ya;-yê).** asking for a girl's hand in marriage, betrothal *{done by the family of the prospective groom}*: **•Gavanê gund li ser kursîya zêr a *xwezgînîyê* rûniştî ye** (L) The village cowherd sat on the gold chair, the one [reserved] for *requests of marriage*; **-çûn xwezgînî/xwazgînîyê** (IF) = to (try to) arrange a marriage; **-xwazgînî vegeřandin** (IFb) to cancel or annul a wedding engagement. {also: xazgînî (Z-2); xwazgînî (IFb/GF); [xvīzgīni] خویزگینی (JJ); <xazgînî> خازگینی (HH)} Cf. Sor xuwazbênî خووازبێنی = 'sending intermediary to parents of girl to ask for her in marriage' [L/K/ZF3/Wkt//Z-2//IFb/GF//JJ//HH] <xwazgîn>

xwezgînî II خوەزگینی (B/ZF3) = matchmaker; marriage broker, go-between. See **xwazgîn**.

xwezi خوەزِ = if only! See **xwezî I**.

xwezil خوەزِل (B) = if only! See **xwezî I**.

xwezila خوەزِلا = if only! See **xwezî I**.

xwezî I خوەزی *conj.* if only, would that [+ *past subj.*]: ***•Xazil* ew zû(tirê) bihata** (F) *If only* he had come earlier ***•Xozî* tu jî řojek[ê] li min bûbay e mêwan, da min çak qedrê te girtiba, xizmeta te kiriba, da min çakîya te, minneta te ji-ser xo řa-kiriba** (SK 31:275) *If only* one day you would have been my guest so that I could have honored and served you and rid myself of the debt of gratitude I owe you for your goodness ***•Xwezil* ez bal dîya xwe bûma** (B) *If only* I were at my mother's side ; **-xwezîya/xwezila xwe dayîn/ xwezil li *fk-ê* anîn** (B) to envy s.o. *(wishing the same for o.s.)*: **•Ez *xwezil li* te *tînim*** (B) I *envy* you = ***Xwezî* li te be** (K). {also: xazil (F); xozî (JB1-A/SK); xwazî (JB1-S); xwezi; xwezil (B-2); xwezila; [khouzi] خوزی (JJ); <xuwezî> خوزی

(HH)} Sor xozge خـۆزگـه = 'desire, wish; if only' [K/A/JB3/IFb/B/GF/TF//JB1-A/SK//F//JB1-S//HH//JJ]

xwezî II خـوەزی *f.* **(-ya;).** spit, spittle, saliva: **•Carkê teħl tiştkî teħl <hate> devê wî, û *xuziya xuziya avêt* û li ħerdê dan** (HR-7, #79, 14) Something bitter got in his mouth, and he *spit and spit it out* onto the ground **•Ez nikarim *xwezîya* xwe daqurtînim, ji ber ku gewrîya min dêşe** (Şnx) I can't swallow my *spit*, because my throat hurts **•Ew marê ku hawîdorê wî *hatibû xazkirin*, xwe wek miriyan melisand û di nava *xazikê* de sekinî** (ZZ-7, 239-240) That snake which *got spit upon*, crouched like the dead and stayed [motionless] amid *the spit*. {also: xazik (ZZ-7); xazî (IFb); xuzî (HR-7); xûyzî (FJ-2/GF-2)} {syn: ava dev; girêz; t'if; t'ûk II} [ZZ-7//IFb//A/FJ/GF/Şnx//HR-7]

xwezok خوەزۆك (K) = beggar. See **xwazok**.

xw•ê خـوێ *f.* **(•ya/•eya/•iya;).** salt: **•*Xwêya* xwe dike nav h[e]mî giraran** (BF) She puts her *salt* in all the porridges (i.e., sticks her nose in everyone's business); **-bê xwê** (B) bland, unseasoned, without salt {syn: kelî II}: **•Nanê me *bê xwê* ye** (FS) Our work is not appreciated [lit. 'Our bread is *without salt*': *idiom*]; **-xwê kirin** (FS) to salt: **•Wê goşt *xwê kir*** (FS) She *salted* the meat. {also: xay II (FS-2); xê (SK/OK/Bw); xoy (Kg); [kho] خو (JJ); <xuwê> خـوى (HH)} Cf. P xivā خـوا = 'taste, flavor'; Sor xwê [xö] خوێ= 'salt' [K/A/JB3/IFb/B/GF/TF/FS//Kg//JJ//HH//SK/OK/Bw] <îsot; kelî II>

xwêdan I خـوێـدان (F/Msr) = to perspire, sweat. See **xûdan**.

xwêdang خوێدانگ (K) = salt shaker. See **xwêdank**.

xwêdank خوێدانك *f.* **(-a;-ê).** 1) salt shaker, salt cellar: **•Wî xwê kir di *xwêdankê* da** (FS) He put salt in *the salt shaker*; 2) shepherd's bag, *in which salt is kept for sheep* (HH): **•Wî destê xwe avêt *xw[ê]danka* xwe û kevirek jê derxist û bi berkanî veweşand, li eniya Golyat xist** (Dawud û Golyat: 1 Samuel 17:49) He reached into his *bag*, took out a stone and slung it with his catapult, striking Goliath on the forehead. {also: xwêdang (K); [kho-dan] خودان (JJ); <xuwêdan> خـويـدان (HH)} [Dawud û Golyat//ZF3/BF/FD/FS//K//HH]

xwircik خورِجِك (CCG) = saddlebag. See **xurc**.

xwîdan خويدان (K) = to perspire, sweat. See **xûdan**.

xwîk خويك (BF/Wkt) = tax. See **xûk**.

xwîn خوین *f.* **(-a;-ê).** blood: **•*xûna* teyr** (Ba) the bird's blood; **-xûn *fk-êda* neman** = to be terrified [lit. 'for no blood to remain in s.o.']: **•*Xûn* Memê*da* *nemabû*** (Z-1) Mem was terrified [lit. 'There was *no blood left in* Mem']; **-xûna *fk*-ê şîrine** (XF) S.o. is nice, pleasant, or attractive [lit. 'S.o.'s blood is sweet']. (See also **xwînşîrîn**): **•Keç'ikê, çiqas *xûna te* li ber ç'e'vê min *şêrîne*** (Z-2) Girl, how *lovely you are* in my eyes. {also: xîn (SK-2/Bw/Mzg-2); xûn (Ba/z-1/K/IF-2/B/SK/JB1-A); [khoun] خـــون (JJ); <xûn> خـــون (HH)} O Ir *wahu-nā/nī: Av vohunī; Khwarezmian hwny; Pashto wīna; Shughni group: Shughni/Roshani wixin; Bartangi/Sarikoli waxin; Oroshori waxI/ẹ̄n; Yazghulami x̌ʷan (Morg2); P xūn خـــون; Sor xwên خوێن; Za gûnî/gonî/gwînî *f.* (Mal); Hau winî *f.* (M4). M. Schwartz: The Vedic (Skt) word for blood is **asṛ-g** (*gen.* **asn-as**): hence, the expected Iranian form is *ahr-a-. A homophone of this form exists, with the meaning "malicious; the bad stuff" (cf. Ahriman). By euphemistic reversal, *wahu-, meaning "the good stuff" replaces *ahra- "the bad stuff." See: M. Schwartz. "'Blood' in Sogdian and Old Iranian," in: *Monumentum Georg Morgenstierne II*, Hommages et Opera Minora, vol. 8 (Leiden: E.J. Brill, 1982), pp. [189]-196, esp. 193 ff. [HM/Bx/A/JB3/IFb/JB1-S/GF/Mzg//K/B/JJ/HH/SK/JB1-A/Ba/Z-1//Dh] <betan; t'emar>

xwîndar خـويـنـدار *adj.* 1) bloody; bloodstained; 2) [*m.&f.* **(-ê/;).**] blood enemy, in a blood feud or vendetta, one who murders the relative of another, and is put to death in revenge: **•Serokê Eşîreta Zêbarîyan: Niha kes *xwîndarê* me nîne** (waarmedia.com 24.i.2017) Head of the Zebari tribe: Now no one is our *blood enemy*. {also: xûndar (K-2/B); [khoun-dar] خون دار (JJ)} [Bw/IFb/GF/OK//K/B/JJ] <ħeyf>

xwîngiyan خـويـنـگِـيـان (IFb) = to appear, seem. See **xuyan I**.

xwîngîn خوينگين (-xwîngê) (IFb) = to appear, seem. See **xuyan I**.

xwînî خـــويـــنـــى *m.&f.* **(-yê/ ;).** murderer, killer, assassin: **•Rojekê jineke ingilîzî li ser rê hati bû kuştin. Hakimê çînê ê eskerî, hema *xwînîyê* jinikê girt û bê mehkeme da kuştin** (Rnh 1:12, 19) One day an English woman was killed on the road. The Chinese military judge took *the killer of* the woman and had him executed without a trial. {syn: mêrkuj} [Rnh/A/IFb/GF/OK] <kuştin; xwîn>

xwînmêj خوینمێژ (IFb/GF/FS/BF) = bloodthirsty. See **xwînmij**.

xwînmij خوینمِژ *adj.* 1) bloodthirsty, blood sucking; exploitative, exploiting, parasitic: •**Dagîrkerên *xwînmij*, gelek derd û kul dagirtine serê me** (Wlt 1:35, 4) *Bloodthirsty* invaders have filled our heads with much pain and grief; 2) [*m.*(**-ê;).**] vampire; bloodsucker. {also: xûnmij (K/GF); xwînmêj (IFb/GF-2/FS/BF)} Sor xwênmij [xönmij] خوێنمِژ = 'bloodsucker' [Wlt/ZF3/Wkt//K/GF/FS/BF//IFb]

xwînşêrîn خوینشێرین (A/IFb/CS) = amiable. See **xwînşîrîn**.

xwînşîrîn خوینشیرین *adj.* amiable, charming, lovable, likeable, simpatico, nice: •**Keçikek dev li ken, zarxweş û *xwînşêrîn* e** (SBx, 16) She is a merry, well-spoken and *likable* girl. {also: xûnşîrin (K/B); xûnşîrîn (FJ/GF); xwînşêrîn (A/IFb/CS); [khoun-chirin] خون شیرین (JJ)} {syn: dilovan; mihrivan; r̄iḧsivik} Sor xwênşîrîn خوێنشیرین = 'cute, dainty' [SBx/ZF//A/IFb/CS//FJ/GF/JJ//K/B]

xwînşîrînî خوینشیرینی *f.* **(-ya;-yê).** amiability, charm, lovableness, likeability, niceness. {also: xûnşîrinî (K/B); xûnşîrintî (B-2); xûnşîrînî (FJ/GF)} [ZF//FJ/GF//K/B]

xwîsik خویسِك (IFb) = hoarfrost. See **xûsî**.

xwîsî خویسی (Qzl) = hoarfrost. See **xûsî**.

xwîşk خویشك (K/JB3/GF) = sister. See **xûşk**.

xwîya خویيا (L) = visible, obvious. See **xuya**.

xwîyan خوییان (K) = to appear, seem. See **xuyan I**.

xwurandin خووراندِن (F) = to scratch. See **xurandin**.

xwurîyan خووریان (F) = to itch. See **xurîn I**.

xwuyan خوویان: -hatin xwuyanê (F) = to appear. See **xanê** & **xuyan I**.

Ẍ غ

ẍar I غـــار *m.* **().** gallop(ing): **-ẍar dan** (SK) to make gallop: **•Ez *dê* hespê xo *ẍar dem*, çim e serkanîê ḧetta hung tên** (SK 22:200) I *shall gallop* my horse off to the spring until you come; **-ẍar kirin** = to gallop, run fast. {syn: ç'argav} {also: xar III (IFb); <ẍar> غار (HH)} Sor ẍar غار = 'gallop' [HM/K/HH/SK//IFb]

ẍar II غـــــار *m.* **(-ê;).** large flock or herd *(of sheep)*. {also: xar II (DM)} {syn: col; kerî II; sûrî I} [DM//K] <mî I; pez; şivan>

ẍar III غـــار *f.* **(;-ê).** marble, small glass ball: **•Nerî weke *ẍarîkê* ji serê wî derket ... Kanî vê *ẍarê* bide min ...Herzem jî ew *ẍar* da Xweşka Dinyaê** (L-I, #4, 104, l. 5-10) He saw something like *a marble* fall from his head ... Give me that *marble* ...and Herzem gave *the marble* to World Beauty. {also: xar IV (IFb/TF); <ẍare> غـاره (HH)} {syn: dîndoq; mat I; t'ebel} [L-I/GF//IFb/TF//HH]

ẍela غهلا (JB1-S) = famine; shortage. See **xela**.

ẍelet غهلهت (K) = mistake; wrong. See **xelet**.

ẍelîn غـــهـــليـــن *vi.* **(-ẍel-).** to be disturbed or upset (stomach); to be nauseous: **•Dilê min *ẍelya/diẍele*** (Dêrîk) I am nauseous [lit. 'My heart *was/is disturbed*']. {also: xelan I (IFb)} [Drk/Nsb/Amd//IFb]

ẍemgînî غهمگینی (RF) = sorrow. See **xemgînî**.

ẍemgîr غـــهـــمـــگـــيـــر (Rnh/HH) = sad, troubled. See **xemgîn**.

ẍemgîrî غهمگیری (RF) = sorrow. See **xemgînî**.

ẍemm غهمم (SK) = grief; worry. See **xem**.

ẍerîb غـــــهريـــــب (JJ/HH/JB1-A&S)) = strange[r], foreign[er]. See **xerîb**.

ẍerq غـــهرق *f.* **().** 1) sinking, submersion, drowning: **-ẍerq bûn** (K/IFb/JJ) to sink, [be] drown[ed] *(vi.)*: **•Tofaneke mezin li bazirgan ȓadive, bazirgan t'emam cîda *xerq dive* xulam-xizmetk'arava** (Ba3-3, #26) A great flood engulfs the caravan, and the entire caravan *drowns* on the spot, servants and all; **-ẍerq kirin** (K/IFb) to sink, submerge, drown *(vt.)*: **•Belkî tofanek bazirganê te ȓabe, t'emama *xerq bike*** (Ba3-3, #25) Perhaps a flood will engulf your caravan, [and] *drown* everyone; 2) [*adj.*] immersed, absorbed, soaked (SK). {also: xerq (Ba3-3/IF); [gherq] غـــرق (JJ)} <Ar √γ-r-q غـــرق = 'to drown, sink' [Ba3/IFb//K/JJ/SK] <ȓoda çûn; t[']ofan; xeȓiqîn>

ẍeşîm غهشيم (K/OK/JJ-G) = naive. See **xeşîm**.

ẍeware غـــهواره: **-ẍeware bûn** (FS/SS) to disappear, vanish: **•Ew qasid ji ber çavêt wî *ẍeware bû*** (X. Salih. Hindek serhatiyên Kurdî, 113) That messenger *vanished* before his eyes **•Vê gavê kêrik di destê min da bû, hema *ẍeware bû*** (FS) Just now the knife was in my hand, but it *has vanished*. {also xeware (SS)} {syn: beta vebûn; ȓed bûn; ȓoda çûn; winda bûn} [X.Salih/FS//SS]

ẍeyna غهينا = except. See **xêncî**.

ẍeynî غهينى: -[ji] ẍeynî (JB1-S) = except. See **xêncî**.

ẍeyri غهيرِ: -ji ẍeyri (SK) = except. See **xêncî**.

ẍezeb غهزهب (SK) = anger. See **xezeb**.

ẍezebîn غهزهبين (L) = to be angry. See **ẍezibîn**.

ẍezibîn غـهزبيـن *vi.* **(-ẍezib-).** to be or get angry, mad, annoyed: **•Rojekê li me *biẍezebe*, wê me timama bikuje** (L) If he *gets mad* at us one day, he'll kill us all. {also: xezibîn (JB3/IF); ẍezebîn (L)} {syn: erinîn; k'eribîn; xeyidîn} < Ar γaḍaba غـضـب [L//K//JB3/IFb] <hêrs; xezeb>

ẍezûr غهزوور (Krç) = father-in-law. See **xezûr**.

ẍilç غِـلـچ (IFb) = sharp stick for uprooting plants. See **xilç**.

ẍizal غِزال (HR) = gazelle. See **xezal I**.

ẍîret غيرهت (SK) = zeal. See **xîret**.

ẍulam غـــــــولام (JB1-S/SK/OK) = servant boy. See **xulam**.

ẍulamtî غولامتى (HR) = servitude. See **xulamtî**.

ẍumẍum غـــومـــغـــوم (HR) = murmur; buzzing. See **xumxum I**.

ẍurbet غوربهت *f.* **().** 1) {syn: xerîbstan} foreign land, foreign country, strange land; 2) {syn: koçberî; sirgûn} exile, banishment (K). {also: qurbet (K-2); xulbet (Z-2); xurbet (IFb); <ẍurbet> غربـت (HH)} < Ar γurbah غـربـة --> T gurbet; Sor ẍurbet غـوربـهت = 'absence in foreign land' [HH//Z-2//K//IFb] <k'oçberî; mişextî; p'enaberî; xerîb>

ẍûlam غوولام (L) = servant boy. See **xulam**.

Y ی

ya I يـــــا voc. part. O; hey {*vocative particle used in direct address*}: **•ya bo!** (L/TF) hey, dad! **•ya rebbî** (L) oh, my lord! {also: [ia] يـا (JJ); <ya> يـا (HH)} {syn: gelî; lo} Cf. Ar yā يا [L/K/A/IF/JJ/HH/SK]

ya II يا (IFb/SK) = or. See **yan I**.

Yabanî يابانی (BF/Wkt) = Japanese. See **Japonî**.

yahnî یاهنی (IF) = stew. See **êxnî**.

yalî یالی (Ag) = help. See **arîkarî**.

Yalkuşta یالکوشتا = men's folk dance. See **Yarxişte**.

yan I یان *conj.* or: **•Binêre ka ê were *an* na** (Msr) See if he's coming *or* not; **-yan(ê) ... yan(ê)** (B) either ... or: **•*yan[ê]* em, *yan[ê]* hun** (B) *either* we *or* you; **-yan(ê) jî** = or even: **•Diqewimî, wekî gura mîk-dudu birîndar dikirin *yanê jî* dikuştin** (Ba2) It happened that the wolves wounded a sheep or two, *or even* killed [them]. {also: an (Msr); ya II (IFb-2/SK-2); yane (Ba); yanê I (Z-1/Ba2/B-2); [ia يـا/ian يـان/iané يـانـه] (JJ); <yan يـان/yanxuwe يـانخوه> (HH)} [K/A/B/IFb/JJ/HH/SK/GF//Ba//Z-1/Ba2//Msr]

yan II یان (K) = That is to say. See **ye'nî**.

yane یانه (Ba/JJ) = or. See **yan I**.

yanê I یانی (Z-1/Ba2/B) = or. See **yan I**.

yanê II یانێ (IFb) = That is to say. See **ye'nî**.

yani یانِ (GF) = That is to say. See **ye'nî**.

yanî یـانـی/ya'nî یـاعـنـی (JB1-A&S) = That is to say. See **ye'nî**.

yanzde یـانـزده (JB3/JB1-A&S/GF/M-Ak&Am&Ber&Shn/Rh) = eleven. See **yanzdeh**.

yanzdeh یـــانــــزده *num.* eleven, 11. {also: deh û yek (Ad/Kg/Krç); yanzde (JB3/JB1-A&S/M-Ak&Am&Ber&Shn/Rh); yazde (SK); yazde (M-zx&Gul); yazdeh (A); [ianzdeh یـانـزده/deh ou iek ده و یـك] (JJ); <yazdeh> یـــازده (HH)} Cf. P yāzdah یازده; Sor yanze یـانـزه; Za jandes/desûjew (Todd) [Ba/F/K/B/IFb/JJ/SC//A/HH//JB3/JB1-A&S/GF/M/Rh//Ad/Kg/Krç]

yanzdehem یـــانــزدهـــهـم *adj.* eleventh, 11th. {also: yanzdehemîn (IFb/GF-2); yanzdemîn (IFb-2); yazdehem (A/Wkt/CT/ZF); yazdehemîn (CT-2/ZF-2/Wkt-2); yazdeyem (Wkt-2); yazdeyemîn (Wkt-2)} [GF//IFb//A/Wkt/CT/ZF] <yanzdeh>

yanzdehemîn یـانـزدهـهـمـیـن (IFb/GF) = eleventh. See **yanzdehem**.

yanzdemîn یانزدهمین (IFb) = eleventh. See **yanzdehem**.

yaqût یـــاقــــووت *m.* (). 1) {syn: lal II} ruby: **-aqût û almast** (Z-2)/**alqut û almaz** (Z-2)/**alqut û almas** (Z-2) rubies and diamonds; 2) jacinth *(precious stone)* (K). {also: alqut (Z-2); alqût (Z-2); aqût (Z-2/K); [iaqout] یـــاقـــوت (JJ)} Cf. Ar yāqūt یـاقـوت --> T yakut; Sor yaqût یـاقـووت = 'ruby' [F/IFb/JJ/GF//K/Z-2] <almas>

yar یـار *m.&f.* (; /-ê). 1) {syn: dost; heval; hogir} friend; 2) {syn: dilk'etî} beloved, lover; mate, boyfriend or girlfriend: **•Lazime em *yarekê* jêra bibînin** (FK-eb-1) We must find him *a mate*. {also: [iar] یـار (JJ); <yar> یـار (HH)} Cf. P yār یـار --> T yâr; Sor yar یـــار = 'lover, friend, helper' {yarî I} [FK-1/F/K/A/IFb/B/JJ/HH/SK/JB1-A/GF/TF] <neyar>

yarî I یـــــاری *f.* (). 1) {syn: dostî; hevaltî} friendship, amity; 2) relationship *(between lovers)*, love[r] relationship. {also: [iari] یـاری (JJ); <yarî> یـاری (HH)} Cf. P yārī یـاری = 'friendship' [K/A/IFb/JJ/HH/GF/TF] <yar>

yarî II یــــاری *f.* (**-ya;-yê**). 1) {syn: ḧenek; tewz; tinaz; t'iȓane} joke, verbal game: **•Wî *yariyek* bo me got, em hemî pê kenandin** (Wkt) He told us a *joke*, and made us all laugh; 2) {syn: lîstik; t'iȓane} a game: **•Yarîker gelek pwîte [pûte] bi vê *yariyê* diken, çunkî hindî bêjî ya xweş e** (YK 15) Players take great interest in this *game*, because it is quite delightful; **-yarî kirin** (Bw)/**larî kirin** (M-Ak)/**rarî kirin** (Zx) to play {syn: lîstin}: **•Dê, ȓabe, here jor, bo xo larîya digel bike** (M-Ak #671, 302) Get up and go inside and play with her. {also: larî (M-Ak); rarî (Zx)} Cf. Sor yarî یـــــاری = 'game'; Za yarî = 'joke, anecdote' (Mal) [Msr/A/IFb/HH/JB1-A/OK/ZF3/FS/BF/Wkt//M-Ak//Zx] <ḧenek; lîstik; tinaz>

yarîker یـاریـکـەر *m.&f.* (**-ê/;**). 1) {syn: lîstikvan} player: **•Yarî di navbera 2-20 *yarîkera* da dihête kirin** (YK 9) The game is played with 2 to 20 *players*; 2) {syn: henekvan; qeşmer; qirdik} jokester, jester, comedian: **-mirovê yarîker** (BF) do. Sor yarîker یـاریـکـەر = 'player, member of a team in a game' [YK/RZ/SS/GF/ZF/FS/Wkt] <yarî II>

Yarkişta يارکِشتا = men's folk dance. See **Yarxişte**.

Yarkiştan يارکِشتان = men's folk dance. See **Yarxişte**.

Yarxişte يـارخِـشـتـه **().** *folk dance done by groups of men, in pairs: the geographic distribution includes Bitlis, Malatya, Muş, Siirt, & Van.* {also: Alkuşta; Arkuşta; Halkuşta; Harkoşte; Harkuşta; Yalkuşta; Yarkişta; Yarkiştan} See: Şerif Baykurt. *Türk Halk Oyunları* (Ankara: Halkevleri genel merkezi, 1932), passim & p. 197. [Kp/Ş.Baykurt] <govend>

yax ياخ *f.* **(-a;).** collar: **-yaxa xwe ji *f-kê* xilas kirin** (K) to get rid of {syn: aza bûn}: **•Belki boẍ lêxe bikuje, *yaxa* pîrê *jê xilasbe*** (J) Maybe the bull will strike him and kill him, [so that] the old woman *will be rid of him* (lit. 'the collar of the old woman will be rid of him'). {also: yaxe (IFb/FS); yaxî (-ya;-yê) (B); يخه (JJ) = pocket} {syn: berstû; bestik; girîvan; p'êsîr [2]; pisto} < T yaka; -->Sor yexe يەخە/êxe ئێخە (OM-Mukrî) [J/K//IFb/FS/JJ//B]

yaxe ياخە (IFb/FS) = collar. See **yax**.

yaxî ياخی, f. (-ya;-yê) (B) = collar. See **yax**.

yazde يازده (SK)/yazde ياظده (M-Zx&Gul) = eleven. See **yanzdeh**.

yazdeh يازدەه (A) = eleven. See **yanzdeh**.

yazdehem يـــازدەهـــەم (A/Wkt/CT/ZF) = eleventh. See **yanzdehem**.

yazdehemîn يـازدەهـەمـيـن (CT/ZF/Wkt) = eleventh. See **yanzdehem**.

yazdeyem يازدەيەم (Wkt) = eleventh. See **yanzdehem**.

yazdeyemîn يـــازدەيـــەمـــيـــن (Wkt) = eleventh. See **yanzdehem**.

yazî يـازى *f.* **(-ya;-yê).** destiny, fate: **•Idî *yazya* min eve** (EP-7) So this is my *fate*. {syn: bext; enînivîs; nesîb; qeder II; qismet} < T yazı = 'writing; fate, destiny' [EP-7/F/B]

yazlix يازلِخ = balcony. See **yazliẍ**.

yazlixan يازلِخان (K) = balcony. See **yazliẍ**.

yazliẍ يـــازلِـــغ *f.* **(-a;).** balcony: **•Hakimê bajarê D.ê li ser *yazliẍa* xwe ye** (L) The ruler of the city of D. is on his balcony. {also: yazlix; yazlixan (K)} {syn: palkon; r̄ewaq [4]; telar} < T yazlık = 'summer home' [L//K]

yedek يەدەك (GF) = spare horse. See **êrdek**.

yek يـــەك *num. f.* **(-a;-ê).** 1) one, 1: **-ev yek** = this *(dem. prn.)* {syn: ev hinde}: **•...Şîret li Memê dikirin, wekî Memê destê xwe ji *vê yekê* bik'şîne** (Z-1, 50) They advised Mem to renounce *this* [his plan]; **-ew yek** = that *(dem. prn.)* {syn: ew hind}: **•Lê li bextê gundîa r̄a *ew yek* nediqewimî** (Ba2:1, 203) But luckily for the villagers, *that* did not happen; **-ji bona (or, seba) wê yekê** (K)/**ji vê yekê** (Z-1) for this reason, therefore; **-yek û** .../**êk û** (M) one each *(distributive)*, apiece: **•Jina wî çi kir, gazî çar pênc biçûkeka kir, *êk û* dirhem daê** (M-Ak, #611, 278) What did the wife do but call 4 or 5 children, give them *each* a dirhem **•Wextê çûne dikana wî *êk û* kursî bo da na, *êk û* ça bo xast** (M-Ak, #667, 302) When they went into his shop he set a chair for *each of them*, sent for a (glass of) tea for *each of them*; **-yek-yek/yeko-yeko** (Z-1) one by one: **•Agir p'arxanê min *yeko-yeko* dikoje** (Z-1) The fire is gnawing my ribs *one by one*; **-yek bûn [bi *fk-ê* re]/bûne yek** (SK) to unite *(vi.)*, be united [with]: **•Ev cepha ku, *bi* dijminê Kurdan ên herî mezin ... *re bûye yek*** (Wlt 1:36, 1) This front which *has united with* the Kurds' greatest enemy; **-yek girtin** (IFb/GF) to unite (vi.), be united: **-Welatên Yekgirtî** (VoA) United States; 2) same: ***•Yek* e** (B) It's all *the same*/There is no difference/It doesn't matter: **•Ter̄a *yek* nîne** (Dz) Isn't it all *the same* to you?/What does it matter to you?; 3) {also: **êkûdin**; yekdi (Bx); yekdû (Bx); yekûdin (Bx); yekûdî (Bx); yekûdu (Bx); yekûdû (Bx)} {syn: hev; êk} each other, one another. {also: êk II (JB1-A&S/Bw); yêk (JB1-S/SK-2); [iek] يـــك (JJ); <yek> يـــك (HH)} Av aēva-; Mid P ēk (M3); P yek يك; Sor yek يـــەك; Za jew/ju (Todd/Mal)/jo/jû/yew (Mal); Hau yo [*f.* yuwa] (M4) [F/K/A/JB3/IFb/B/JJ/HH/SK/JB1-A/GF/TF/OK//JB1-S/Bw] See also **êkûdin**.

yekbûyî يـــەكـــبـــوويـــى *adj./pp.* united: **•Me Kurdistanek *yekbûyî*, serxwebûyî û demokratîk divê** (Ber) We need (or, want) a *united*, independent, and democratic Kurdistan; **-Neteweyên Yekbûyî** [=NY] (Wlt) The United Nations; **-T'eşkîleta Miletêd Yekbûyî** [=T'MY] (B) The United Nations, UN {syn: Neteweyên Yekgirtî (VoA)} [Ber/B/IFb/GF/TF] <yek>

yekdi يەكدِ (Bx) = each other, one another. See **yek** [3].

yekdû يـــەكـــدوو (Bx) = each other, one another. See **yek** [3].

yekejimar يەكەژمار (CS) = singular. See **yekhejmar**.

yekejmar يەكەژمار (IFb) = singular. See **yekhejmar**.

yekem يـــەكـــەم *adj.* first. {also: yekemîn (K[s]/JB3/IFb-2/GF-2/TF); êkeyê (JB1-S); êkê (JB1-A)} {syn: 'ewil; pêşîn; sift (Ad)} Cf. Sor yekem[în] يـــەكـــەمـــيـــن [(neol)Ber/A/IFb/GF//K(s)/JB3/TF//JB1-S//JB1-A] <yek>

yekemîn یــەکــەمــیــن (K[s]/JB3/IFb/GF/TF) = first. See **yekem**.

yeketî یەکەتی (A) = unity. See **yekîtî**.

yekhejmar یــەکــهــەژمــار *adj.* singular *(in grammar)* [Ar mufrad مــفــرد, T tekil]: •**navên *yekhejmar*** (CT) *singular* nouns. {also: yekejimar (CS); yekejmar (IFb); yekjimar (FJ/ZF3-2/Wkt-2/FD); yekjmar (GF)} = Sor tak تاك [TF/ZF3/RZ/Wkt/CT//IFb//FJ/FD//GF]

yekîne یــەکــیــنــە *f.* **(-ya;-yê).** 1) unit: •**Ba<u>t</u>man *yekîna* kêşanê ye** (FS) A 'batman' is *a unit of* weight; 2) military unit: •**Hejmara leşkerên mirî û birîndar ên vê *yekîneyê* tam nehatiye zelalkirin** (ANFNews 28.ix.2017) The number of dead and wounded soldiers from that *unit* has not been completely clarified •**Zivistana sala 2000 an *yekîneyên* me nêzîkî hev bûn** (P. Can. Berfa Germ, 48) In the winter of 2000 our *units* were near each other; **-yekîneya leşkerî** (ZF3) military unit. {syn: r̄êz I; selef} [P.Can/GF/ZF3/FD/FS/SS]

yekîtî یــەکــیــتــی *f.* **(-ya;-yê).** unity, oneness; union: •***yekîtiya* zimanê Kurdî** (Wlt 2:100, 2) *the unity of* the Kurdish language; **-Êketiya Nivîserên Kurd** = Union of Kurdish Writers; **-Yekîtiya Nîştimanî ya Kurdistanê** (Wkp) Patriotic Union of Kurdistan [of Iraq/Başûr], PUK. {also: êketî (SS-2); yeketî (A); [ieki] یــکــی (JJ)} Sor yekêtî یەکێتی [Wlt/K/IFb/GF/OK/SS//A//JJ]

yekjimar یــەکــژمــار (FJ/ZF3/Wkt/FD) = singular. See **yekhejmar**.

yekjmar یەکژمار (GF) = singular. See **yekhejmar**.

yekkîte یەککیتە (CS/ZF3) = monosyllabic. See **yekkîteyî**.

yekk'îteyî یەککیتەیی *adj.* monosyllabic, consisting of one syllable: •**di bêjeyên *yekkîteyî* de** (RR 3.2) in *monosyllabic* words. {also: yekkîte (CS/ZF3)} [RR/Wkt//CS/ZF3] <k'îte>

yekser یــەکــســەر *adv.* 1) completely, totally, entirely: •**Borî bimbarek bû ser sûrêr̄a firqas kir *yeksere*** (EP-7) Bor [the horse] was blessed, and jumped *completely* over the wall (or, and *right away* jumped over the wall); 2) at once, right away, immediately; 3) at the same time: •**Tu *yekser* vê xebatê jî bike** (B) *While you're at it*, do that job too. {also: êkser (JB1-S)} Cf. Sor yekser یەکسەر /yeksere یــەکــســەرە = 'directly, without warning' [EP-7/K/B/IFb/GF/TF//JB1-S]

Yekşem یەکشەم *f.* **(-a;-ê).** Sunday: •**Îro roja *yekşemê* ye** (ZF3) Today is *Sunday*. {also: Êkşem; Êkşemb (FS/BF-2); Yekşemb (K/JB3); Yekşemî (G); [iek-chem یــك شــم/iek-chembé یــك شــنــبــە] (JJ)} {syn: Bazar [3] (SC); Le'd} Cf. P yekšanbe یکشنبه; Sor Yekşemû یــەکــشــەمــوو/Yekşem[m]e یــەکــشــەمــمــە; Za Yekşeme *m.* (Todd) [A/IF/ZF3/Wkt/FD/BF/JJ/RZ//K/JB3//G//FS]

Yekşemb یەکشەمب (K/JB3) = Sunday. See **Yekşem**.

Yekşemî یەکشەمی (G) = Sunday. See **Yekşem**.

yekûdin یــەکــوودِن (Bx) = each other, one another. See **yek** [3].

yekûdî یــەکــوودی (Bx) = each other, one another. See **yek** [3].

yekûdu یــەکــوودو (Bx)/yekûdû یــەکــوودوو (Bx) = each other, one another. See **yek** [3].

***yeman** یــەمــان **().** animal disease: •**Şivana k'erê xweî ku '*yeman*' derxistibûn danîne 'erdê** (Dz) The shepherds had laid their donkeys, which had come down with '*yeman*,' on the ground. [Dz]

yemanet یەمانەت, m. (-ê;). (L) = entrusting [of an object] for safekeeping. See **anemetî**.

Yemenî یەمەنی *adj.* Yemeni, Yemenite. [IFb/Wkt/BF/Wkp]

ye'nî یــەعــنــی **.** that is, that means, that is to say, i.e., namely. {also: yan II (K); yanê II (IFb); yani (GF); yanî; ya'nî (JB1-A&S); [iani] یــعــنــی (JJ)} {syn: ango; dêmek} <Ar ya'nī یــعــنــی = 'it means; so-so'; Sor yanî یانی [SK//K//IFb//GF//JJ/JB1-A&S]

yeqîn یــەقــیــن *adj./adv.* 1) certain(ly), doubtless, (for) sure, absolutely: •**Ewê *yêqîm* îro bê** (B) He will *surely* come today; **-yeqîn kirin** (SK)/**êqîn kirin** (JB1-S): = a) to ascertain, be sure; b) to convince, persuade; 2) [f.] certainty, conviction (JB1-A). {also: **êqîn** (EP-7/JB1-S); yêqîm (B); <yeqîn> یقین (HH)} < Ar yaqīn یقین [Z-1/K/IFb/HH/SK//EP-7/JB1-A] See also **êqîn**.

Yewnanî یەونانی *adj.* Greek. {also: Yonanî (BF-2)} Sor Yonanî یۆنانی [IFb/GF/Wkt/ZF3/BF]

Yezîdî یەزیدی (A) = Yezidi. See **Êzîdî**.

yêk ییَك (JB1-S/SK) = one. See **yek**.

yêqîm ییَقیم (B) = certain(ly). See **êqîn** & **yeqîn**.

yêr ییَر *f.* **(-a;-ê).** place: •**ḧemû xortê *yêrê*** (Ba) all the local youths (lit. 'all the youths *of the place*') •***Yêra* me bona ḧeywanetxweykirinê ze'f r̄inde** (B) Our *place* is excellent for raising animals. {syn: cî I; der I; dever I; dews; şûn} < T yer = 'place; ground' [Ba/F/K/B]

Yonanî یۆنانی (BF) = Greek. See **Yewnanî**.

Z ز

z̲abeş ظابەش (Slv) = watermelon. See **zebeş**.

zaboq زابـۆق *f.* **(-a;-ê).** 1) {syn: ca'de; kolan II; kûçe; zikak} narrow street, lane, alley; dead end: **•Mala wan li binê *zaboqê* ye** (FS) Their house is at the end of *the lane*; 2) garbage dump, trash heap, place where garbage is dumped: **•Li nêzîkî berateyên qijakan *zaboqa* kîmyewî heye û bi hezaran qijak xwarinên xwe ji vê *zaboqê* peyda dikin** (rojevakurd.com 3.ii.2011) Near the carcasses of the crows there is a chemical *dump* and thousands of crows get their food from this *dump*; 3) channel carved by water (FS/GF): **•Av di *zaboqê* ra diçit** (FS) Water passes through the *channel*. {also: zabûq (GF-2); zamboq (Msr); zamboqe (FS-2); [zābōq] زابوق (JJ); <zaboq> زابوق (HH)} [Frq/K(s)/IFb/JJ-PS/HH/GF/FS//Msr] <dirb; nabos; r̄ê>

zabûq زابـــــــووق (GF) = street; garbage dump. See **zaboq**.

zad زاد/**z̲ad** ظـاد [JB1-A] *m.* **(-ê;).** 1) {syn: dexl; tene I} grain, cereal: **•Çal tijî *zad* e** (AB) The pit is full of *grain*; 2) {syn: azûxe [1]; xurek; xwarin [3]} food, foodstuffs; provisions, supplies: **•Gazî jina xo kir, "Zû be, doşek û balgan da-nê û *zadekî* xoş ḧazir ke, ko mêwanekî zor 'ezîz bo me hatîye"** (SK 8:82) He called to his wife, "Hurry, set out mattresses and cushions and prepare some good *food*, for a very dear guest has come to us"; **-zad anîn** (IF) to stock up on supplies; 3) harvest; crop (JB3). {also: [zad] زاد (JJ); <zad> زاد (HH)} < Ar zād زاد = 'provisions, supplies'; Sor zad زاد = 'food' [L/Bw/K/A/JB3/IF/JJ/HH/SK//JB1-A]

zaf زاف (Ba2/OK) /za'f زاعف (IS) = much; very. See **ze'f**.

zagon زاگـــۆن *f.* **(-a;-ê).** law: **•*Zagona* Kemal Paşa xira be** (Kp) A pox on K. P.'s *law*; **-zakon derxistin** (B) to pass a law. {also: zagûn (K); zakon (B); zaxon (TF)} {syn: qanûn} <Rus zakon закон = 'law' [Kp/IFb//K//B//TF]

zagûn زاگوون (K) = law. See **zagon**.

zaha زاها (Ag) = dry. See **ziwa**.

zahmet زاهمەت (B) = trouble, inconvenience; difficult. See **zeḧmet**.

zahmetk'êş زاهـمـەتـکـێـش (B) = hard worker; hardworking. See **zeḧmetk'êş**.

zahf زاهف (A) = much; very. See **ze'f**.

zahr زاهر (A) = word; talking. See **zar I**.

zak زاك *m.* **(-ê;).** beestings, colostrum, high-protein milk, fresh milk for babies; **-şîrê zak** (FS) do.: **•Şirînê *şîrê zak* kir firo** (FS) Sh. made the *beestings* into 'firo' [i.e., she boiled it]; **-zakê çêlê** (Zeb) cow beestings. {also: <zak> زاك (Hej)} {syn: firo; firşik II; xelendor I; xîç' I} Sor jek ژەك [Zeb/Hej/FS/Wkt]

zakon زاكۆن (B) = law. See **zagon**.

zalût زالووت (ZF3) = corn, maize. See **lazût**.

zamboq زامـــبـــۆق (Msr) = street; garbage dump. See **zaboq**.

zamboqe زامـبـۆقـە (FS) = street; garbage dump. See **zaboq**.

zan زان (JB1-A/Wkt/FS) = to give birth; to be born. See **zayîn**.

zana زانا (JB3/IFb/SK/JJ/HH/GF) = wise. See **zane**.

zanahî زاناهی (GF) = wisdom. See **zanetî**.

zanatî زاناتی (Wlt/ZF3) = wisdom. See **zanetî**.

zanayî زانایی (A/IFb) = wisdom. See **zanetî**.

zanbûn زانبوون (F) = to know. See **zanibûn** & **zanîn**.

zandar زاندار (F) = wise. See **zane**.

zane زانـە *adj.* 1) learnèd, (well-)educated; wise: **•Şêx û beg û aẍa zor bo ḧalê xo û menfe'etê zatîyê xo *zana* û şeytan in, emma r̄e'îyet zor bêçare û nezan û weḧşî ne** (SK 56:655) The shaikhs and begs and aghas are very *wise* and cunning in looking after their own case and their personal profit, but the peasantry are quite hapless and rude and ignorant; 2) [*m.*] a sage, wise man; scholar (JJ). {also: zana (JB3/IFb-2/SK); zandar (F); zanedar (B); [zana] زانا (JJ); <zana> زانا (HH)} Cf. P dānā دانا = 'wise'; Sor zana زانا = 'learned; scholar'; Za zanaye = 'knowledgeable' (Todd) {zanahî; zanatî; zanayî; zanetî; zaneyî} [Ber/K/A/TF/Msr//JB3/IFb/JJ/HH/SK/GF//F//B] <zanîn>

zanebûn زانەبوون = to know. See **zanibûn** & **zanîn**.

zanedar زانەدار (B) = wise. See **zane**.

zanetî زانـەتـی *f.* **(-ya;-yê).** 1) wisdom; 2) knowledge: **•Gelek caran di *zanatîyê* de min diheyrînin** (Wlt 1:32, 7) Many times they amaze me with [their] *knowledge*. {also: zanahî (GF); zanatî (Wlt/ZF3); zanayî (A-2/IFb/GF-2); zaneyî (TF)} [A//Wlt/ZF3//IFb//GF//TF] <zane>

zaneyî زانەیی (TF) = wisdom. See **zanetî**.

zang زانگ *f.(K)/m.(B)* **(-a/;).** ravine, gorge, canyon, gully; precipice, cliff, crag: **•Sîabendê Silîvî lê nihêřî, ç'êlekê wê xwe daye ber *zangekê*** (EP-4) Siyabendê Silîvî saw that the doe [lit. 'cow'] was standing at the precipice. {syn: dergelî; derteng; geboz; gelî II; zer II} [EP-4/K/B/ZF3] <qeya; zinar>

zanibûn زانِبوون *vt.* **(zani-b-).** to know *{used in the imperative, subjunctive, and past tense}*: **•Ez dixazim heřime cem xwedê, *bizanibim* çika řastya wî çewane?** (Dz) I want to go to God, *to know* what his truth is like **•Jinê jî *zanibû*, wekî Ûsibî ze'f aqile** (Ba) The woman also *knew* that Joseph was [lit. 'is'] very smart **•Wekî tiştek bê serê wî, *zanibin*, ezê we gişka qiřkim** (Ba) If anything happens to him, *know* that I will kill you all. {also: zanbûn (F); zanebûn} [Ba/Dz/K/(B)/(JJ)/(JB1-A&S)//F] See also **zanîn**.

zanist زانِست *f.* **(-a;-ê).** science: **•Li gorî hemûyan folklor *zanistek* e û mijara wê jî lêkolîn û nirxandina berhemên çanda gelêrî ye** (YPA, 14) According to everyone, folklore is *a science*, and its subject is the research and evaluation of works of folk culture **•Û xebitî ji bo belavkirina *zanistî* û xwendin û nivîsandin li nav milet da** (Havîbûn 5 [1999], 74) And he strove to spread *science*, reading, and writing among the people; {also: zanistî (OK/RF/RZ); zanîstî (K[s])} {syn: ulm} Sor zanist زانِست = 'science' (HG/K3) [(neol)YPA/ZF/SS/Wkt//OK/RF/RZ//K(s)] <zanyarî>

zanistî زانِستی *adj.* 1) scientific: **•Folklor hemû cureyan li gorî prensîbên *zanistî* tesnîf dike** (YPA, 12) Folklore classifies all the genres according to *scientific* principles; 2) [*f.*] science (OK/RF/RZ). See **zanist**. {also: zanîstî (K[s])} [(neol)IFb/FJ/GF/TF/SS/Wkt/ZF/OK/RF/RZ]

zaniyarî زانیاری (IFb/OK) = knowledge. See **zanyarî**.

zanîn زانین/**z̲anîn** ظانین [JB1-A] *vt.* **([di]zan-;** *neg.* **nizan-;** *subj. & past tenses formed with* **zanibûn:** *subj.* **bizanibim;** *past* **min zanibû).** 1) to know [Germ wissen; Fr savoir]: **•Çawa *tê zanîn*** (Ber) As *is known* **•Ez *nizanim*** = I *don't know* **•Ez *zanim*, ku ew çûye** (B) I *know* that he went; **-bi filan zimên zanîn** = to know *(a language)*: **•Ne, ez *nizanim* bi 'erebçe** [='erebî] (Ks) No, I *don't know* Arabic **•Keçelok *bi* zarifê teyra *zane*** (L) Kechelok *knows* bird-language; **-dan zanîn** (IF) to inform, tell; 2) to consider, deem, regard, think [often + *bi*]: **•K'ê ku p'akî haj ji şivantîyê t'unebû, hew *zanibû*, ku ew tiştekî çetin nîne** (Ba2:1, 203) Those who were not well acquainted with shepherding *thought* that it was something not very difficult; 3) [*f.* **(-a;-ê).**] {syn: ulm; zanyarî} knowledge; knowing (SK): **•Dibistan kana *zanînê* ye** (AB) School is the source of *knowledge*. {also: [zanin] زانین (JJ); <zanîn زانین (dizane) (دزانه)> (HH)} [Pok. 2. ĝen-, ĝenə-, ĝnē-, ĝnō- 376.] 'to know, recognize': Skt √jñā; O Ir *zan- (Tsb 44): Av zan- (*pres.* zanā-/zān-); OP dan- (*past* a-dānā = 'he knew'; Pashto pé-žānəm (*past* pe-žānd-) = 'to know, be acquainted with'; P dānestan دانستن (-dān-) (دان); Sor zanîn زانین; SoK zânısın (Fat 562); Za zanã [zanayiş] (Todd); Hau zanay (zan-) *vt.* (M4); cf. also Rus znat' знать; Lat [co]gnosco; Gr gi-gnōskō γιγνώσκω [F/K/A/JB3/IFb/B/JJ/HH/SK/JB1-S/GF/TF//JB1-A] <nas kirin; zanibûn>

zanîngeh زانینگەه *f.* **(-a;-ê).** university: **•Li lîse û *zanîngehê* ku tê de, di pêvajoya salekê de min şaxê ekonomiyê bi Îngilîzî xwend, ez hînî Îngilîzî bûm** (Wlt 1:35,16) At the high school and at *the university* where I studied economics for a year, I learned English. {also: *zanistan (IF-2); *zanistgeh (TF); *zanîstgeh (K[s])} {syn: ûnîvêrsîtê; zanko} Cf. Sor zanistga زانِستگا/zanko زانکۆ [(neol)Ber/Wlt/K/A/JB3/IFb/GF//TF//K(s)] <dibistan; mek't'eb; xwendegeh>

zanîstî زانیستی (K[s]) = science. See **zanist**.

zanko زانکۆ *f.* **(-ya;-yê).** university, college: **•Kobanî: Ji seretayî heta *zankoyê* xwendin bi Kurdî ye** (Rûdaw 4.v.2018) Kobani: education in Kurdish from elementary school to *college*. {syn: ûnîvêrsîtê; zanîngeh} Sor zanko زانکۆ [(neol)ZF3/Wkt/BF]

zanyarî زانیاری *f.* **(-ya;).** 1) {syn: ulm; zanîn [2]} knowledge, information: **•Bi pêşveçûna *zanyarîya* xwe ya sîyasî ve** (Ber #7, 9) With the advancement of my political *knowledge* [i.e., my knowledge about politics]; 2) [*adj.*] {syn: zanistî} scientific. {also: zaniyarî (IFb/OK)} Sor zanyarî زانیاری = 'knowledge (HG); information, education (K3)' [(neol)Ber/K(s)/A/GF/RZ//IFb/OK]

zar I زار *m.* **(-ê;).** 1) {syn: bêje; gilî[1]; p'eyiv; pirs[2]; şor; xeber} word; 2) {syn: qise;

xeberdan} talking, speech: **•Dûre jî** ***bi zarekî xweş*** **dûrûdirêj ji min re çêlî jiyana koçeriyê kir** (Lab, 11) Afterward he *articulately* described the nomadic way of life to me in detail; **-hatin zarê** (JB3) to complain {syn: şikyat kirin}; **-zarê** ***fk-ê*** **[ber] nageře** (XF/B) to be unable to bring o.s. to say stg.: ***•Zarê wî nageře*** **ku derheqa wê yekêda bêje bavê xwe** (B) *He can't bring himself* to tell his father; 3) {syn: devok; zarava; ziman} language, dialect: ***•zarê*** **Botanî** (FS) Botani *dialect* ***•Zarê*** **Kurdî şirîn e** (Wkt) The Kurdish *language* is sweet ***•zarê*** **Mukrî** (FS) Mukri *dialect*; 4) {also: zehr (Bw/TF)} imitating, aping: **-zar ve kirin** (XF)/**zehrî [zar] [ve]kirin** (Bw)/ **zehr kirin** (TF) to imitate, ape: **•Ez** ***dê zehrî*** **wî** ***kem*** (Bw) I *will imitate* him. {also: zahr (A); zehr (Bw/TF); [zar] زار (JJ)} Cf. Sor zar زار = 'mouth' [K/IFb/B/JJ/XF/FS//A//Bw/TF] <devkî; zarava>

zar II** زار *adj.* pregnant *{of women only: for animals =* ***avis*}* (Ag). {syn: avis; biĥemil; bitişt; duhala; giran I; ĥemle} [Ag/Wkt]

zar III زار *f.* **(-a;).** die, *pl.* dice. {also: [zar] زار (JJ)} Cf. T zar; Za zar, *pl.* zarî (Todd) [K(s)/IFb/JJ/OK/ZF3/FS/Wkt] <k'ap II>

zař IV زاڕ (B/F) = child. See **zařo**.

zarav زاراڤ (K/B/FJ/SS/Kmc) = talking; dialect. See **zarava**.

zarava زاراڤا *m./f.(Wkt)* **(-yê/-ya;).** 1) {syn: p'eyiv[2]; qise [2]} speech, talking: **•Keçelok bi** ***zarifê*** **teyra zane** (L) Kechelok knows bird-*language*; 2) dialect, variety of a language: **•Kurmancî û Soranî du** ***zaravayên*** **zimanê kurdî ne** (Wkt) Kurmanji and Sorani are two *dialects* of the Kurdish language; **-têkilîya zaravayan** (Ber) mixing of dialects; 3) {syn: cins [3]; zayend} gender *(gram.)* (B): **-zaravê jina** (B) feminine gender; **-zaravê mêra** (B) masculine gender. {also: zarav (K/B/FJ/SS/Kmc); zarave (RZ); zarawa (GF/TF); zarif (L)} [Ber/IFb/ZF/Wkt/CS//RZ/GF/TF//L//K/B/FJ/SS/Kmc] <devok; zar I>

zarave زاراڤە (RZ) = talking; dialect. See **zarava**.

zarawa زاراوا (GF/TF) = talking; dialect. See **zarava**.

zarezar زارەزار *f.* **(-a;-ê).** wailing (in pain), moaning (in pain), lamenting: **•Bû** ***zarezara*** **pezkûviyan** (Nbh 135:29) [Suddenly] there was *the wailing* of mountain goats (or: The mountain goats let out a wail). {also: <zarezar> زارزار (HH)} [Nbh/K/B/A/IFb/FJ/GF/HH/ZF/CS/BF] <zarîn>

zargotin زارگۆتن *f.* **(-a;-ê).** folklore: ***•Zargotina*** **me piř dewlemend e. Miletê me ew** ***zargotin*** **afirandiye, niha jî diafirîne. Ew kaniyeke guř e** (Wlt 2:59, 16) Our *folklore* is very rich. Our people has created this *folklore*, and is still creating it. It is a gushing source. {syn: folklor; kelep'ûr} [Ber/Z/TF/ZF/Wkt]

zarif زارِف (L) = talking; dialect. See **zarava**.

zarîn زارین/**zařîn** زاڕین [FS] *vi.* **(-zar-).** to wail *or* moan (in pain), to lament: **•Zařokê wan gelek** ***zařî*** (FS) Their child *wailed* a lot. {also: <zarîn> زارین (HH)} [Nbh/K/IFb/FJ/GF/TF/HH/ZF/CS/BF] <zarezar>

zařo زاڕۆ/**zaro** زارۆ [JB1-S] *m./f.(B/F)* **(-wê/-yê /; /-ê;** *obl. pl.* **zařa[n]).** child: **•ji dêla** ***zaroka*** **ve** (L) instead of *sons* (or, *children*): **-miqatî zara bûn** (F) to take care of the children; **-zar û zêç** (Ber) women and children. See **zav-zêç**; **-zaro-maro** (Haz) do. {also: zař IV (B-2/F); zařok f. (K-2/ IFb-2/TF)/m. (FS); zarole (IFb-2); zařow; zařu (K/ IFb-2); zařuk f. (K-2); zarû (IFb-2); zarûk (AB); [zarou] زارو (JJ); <z̲aro> ظـارو (HH)} {syn: kuř; law; mindal; t'ifal; zêc; [f. keç'[ik]; qîz]} Cf. Sor zaro زارۆ/zarok زارۆك/zarole زارۆلە (=min[d]ał مِـنـدال); Hau zarołe *m.* (M4) {zarok[t]î; zarotî; zařotî; zařtî; zařutî; zařuyî} [AB/K/JJ//TF//A/JB3/IFb/B/GF/Mzg//HH//F//JB1-S] <zayîn>

zařok زاڕۆك, f.(K/IFb/TF)/m.(FS) = child. See **zařo**.

zarokî زارۆكی (GF/TF) = childhood. See **zarotî**.

zaroktî زارۆكتی (A) = childhood. See **zarotî**.

zarole زارۆلە (IFb) = child. See **zařo**.

zarotî زارۆتی/**zařotî** زاڕۆتی [B] *f.* **(-ya;-yê).** childhood: ***•Zaroktiya*** **wî tê bîra min** (Lab, 41) I remember his *childhood*. {also: zarokî (GF-2/TF); zaroktî (A); zařtî (K-2/B-2/F); zařutî (K); zařuyî (K-2); [zarouti] زاروتی (JJ)} {syn: ç'ûç'iktî; mindaltî (K[s])} [JB3/IFb/GF//B//K/JJ//A//TF//F] <zařo>

zařow زاڕۆو = child. See **zařo**.

zařtî زاڕتی (K/B/F) = childhood. See **zarotî**.

zařu زاڕو (K/IFb) = child. See **zařo**.

zařuk زاڕوك, f. (K) = child. See **zařo**.

zařutî زاڕوتی (K/JJ) = childhood. See **zarotî**.

zařuyî زاڕویی (K) = childhood. See **zarotî**.

zarû زاروو (IF) = child. See **zařo**.

zarûk زارووك (AB) = child. See **zařo**.

zar û zêç زار و زێچ (Ber/GF)/zařûzêç زاڕووزێچ (Wkt) = family. See **zav-zêç**.

zarxoş زارخۆش (IFb) = well-spoken. See **zarxweş**.

zarxweş زارخـــوەش *adj.* well-spoken, pleasant and easy to talk with, whose talk is delightful, articulate: **•Keçikek dev li ken, zarxweş û xwînşêrîn e** (SBx, 16) She is a merry, well-spoken and likeable girl. {also: zarxoş (IFb)} < zar + xweş [SBx/FJ/GF/CS//IFb]

zat زات *m.* **(-ê;-î).** person; noble person, personage: **•Çonko cenabê mîr *zatekî* mezin e, ez o r̄îwî xulam în, dibît pişka *zatê* wî zêdetir bît. Bes lazim e ga bo cenabê mîr bît** (SK 7:71) Since his excellency the chief is a great *person*, while the fox and I are servants, his *personal* portion must be greater. The ox must therefore be for his excellency the chief **•Ew zat ... zatê ko ev reben û gelekên mîna evî sermest kiriye, Ehmedê Xanî ye** (Tof, 8) The person ... who has intoxicated this wretched soul and many others like him is Ahmed-i Khani. {also: [zat] ذات (JJ)} {syn: kes} < Ar ḏāt ذات = 'essence, nature, self, person' *fem. of* _dū ذو = 'possessor of, endowed with'; Sor zat زات = 'personage' [Tof/IFb/SK/JJ]

zav•a زاڤـــا *m.* **(•ayê/•ê; •ê).** 1) groom, bridegroom: **•Bûk li *zavê* pîroz be** (AB) May the bride be blessed to *the groom* [*traditional greeting at weddings*] **•*Zava* çû ser xênî** (AB) *The groom* went up to the roof; 2) son-in-law [pl. sons-in-law]; brother-in-law [pl. brothers-in-law]: *generic term for a man marrying into the family*: **•*Ze'vê* te merîkî wisane** (J) Your *son-in-law* is such a man **•Tu nexebitî, *ze'vê* te nên nade te!** (J) [If] You don't work, your *son-in-law* won't give you any food [lit. 'bread']! {also: zawa (SK); ze'va (J/B); [zawa] زاڤا (JJ); <zava> زاڤا (HH)} [Pok. ĝem(e)- 369.] 'to marry': Skt jā́mātar- = 'son-in-law'; Av zāmātar- = 'son-in-law'; Sgd z'mt'y [zām(a)tē]; Khwarezmian z'mk [zāmak] & z'm'd [zāmād]; Mid P dāmād = 'bridegroom, son-in-law' (M3); Southern Tati dialects: Chali zōmā; Eshtehardi zumā; Danesfani zomā = 'son-in-law' (Yar-Shater); Baluchi zāma; P dāmād دامـــــاد --> T damat; Sor zawa زاوا; Za zama *m.* (Todd); Hau zema m. (M4); cf. also Gr gameō γαμέω = 'I marry'; Rus ziat' зять = 'son-in-law or sister's husband' {zavatî (K/A/IF); ze'vatî (B)} [F/K/A/IFb/JB1-S/GF/TF/SC/BK/Kr/Haz//J/B//SK] <bûk I>

zavatî زاڤـاتـى *f.* **(-ya;-yê).** state of being a groom or son-in-law: **•Par *zavatîya* Behremî bû** (FS) Last year B. became a groom [lit. 'was B.'s *groomhood*']. {also: ze'vatî (B)} [K/A/IF/FS/ZF3//B]

zav û zêç زاڤ و زێچ (IFb) = family. See **zav-zêç**.

zav-zêç زاڤ زێـچ *pl.* **().** women and children, family, dependents {cf. T çoluk çocuk}. {also: zar û zêç (Ber/GF)/zar̄ûzêç (Wkt); zav û zêç (IFb)} {syn: 'eyal; k'ulfet [2]; zaro-maro (Haz)} [Mzg/Srk//IFb//Ber/GF//Wkt] <zêç>

zawa زاوا (SK) = groom; son-in-law. See **zava**.

zaxon زاخۆن (TF) = law. See **zagon**.

zayend زايـەنـد *f./m.(Wkt/BF)* **(-a/-ê;-ê/).** grammatical gender: **-zayenda mê/~mêytî** (K) feminine gender; **-zayenda nêr/~mêrîtî** (K) masculine gender; **-zayenda nêtar** (K) neuter gender. {syn: cins [3]; zarav [3]} *Neologism based on the verb* ***zayîn*** *= 'to give birth' and the present participle [zāyende] of its Persian cognate* zādan زادن/ zā'īdan زائيدن [(neol)K/IFb/GF/OK/Wkt/ZF3/BF]

zayin زاين (BK) = to give birth; to be born. See **zayîn**.

zayîn زايـيـن *vt.* **(-zê-/-za- [K-2]).** 1) {syn: r̄azan [2]; welidandin; welidîn (Ag)} to bear, give birth, of animals only: for human beings = **welidîn/ welidandin/anîn**: **•Bizinek ... ḧolikê ava dike, xwera dike gom, têda *dizê*** (J) A goat ... builds a hut, makes a pen for herself, and *gives birth* in it **•Em dibêjin jinê welidand; kûçik teliqî, mih/ bizin/çêlek *za*** (kulturname-Amîdabad 2.ix.2012) We say that a woman gave birth; a dog had puppies, a sheep/goat/cow *brought forth its young*; 2) to be born; 3) [*f.* **(-a;-ê).**] birth: **-berî zayînê** (Wkt) B.C. [before Christ], B.C.E. [before the Common Era]. {also: zan (JB1-A/Wkt/FS); zayin (BK); [zàin] زاين (JJ); <zan زان (dizê) (دزێ)> (HH)} [Pok. 1. ĝen-/ĝenə-/ĝnē-/ĝnō- 373.] 'to give birth, beget' (with laryngals: ĝenH-/ĝnH-): proto Indo-Ir *źanH ~ *źā: Skt jani- & janáyati = 'engenders, gives birth to'; proto Ir *zan- ~ *zā-; Av zayeite (<*ĝn̥-i̯ó) = 'gives birth' & zīzənti/ *thematic* zīzanənti = 'they give birth'; Mid P zādan (zāy-) = 'to bear (offspring), be born' (M3); P zādan زادن/zā'īdan زائـيـدن; Sor zayîn زايـيـن (-zê-); Za zênā [zayiş] (Srk); Hau zay (z-) *vi.* (M4); cf. also Arm cnil ծնիլ = 'to be born' & cnołk' ծնողք = 'parents'; Lat genesis, genitor, etc.; Mod Gr goneis γονεῖς = 'parents' [K/A/JB3/IFb/GF/TF/Ag/Rh//BK/JJ//HH/JB1-A/Wkt/FS] <avis; dê I; ḧemle; t'eliqîn; welidîn; zêstanî>

zayînî زايـيـنـى *adj.* 1) birth-, natal, relating to birth; 2) relating to the birth of Christ; after Christ, A.D.: **•Mela 'Eliyê Teremaxî ewê li sedsala şazdê**

zayînî **jiyay** (Doskî. Ji pêşengên pexşana Kurdî, 5-6) Mulla Ali Taramakhi, who lived in the 16th century *AD*; **-salnameya** ***zayînî*** (Wkt) *Christian* calendar. [(neol.)Doskî/ZF/BF/Wkt]

zebandin زەبانـدِن *vt.* **(-zebîn-).** to stone to death, pelt with stones. {syn: dan ber beran/keviran; kevir kirin} [FJ/GF/SS/Wkt/ZF3]

zebeş زەبـــەش *m.* **(-ê;).** watermelon, bot. *Citrullus vulgaris*: **•Ez çûme serê dîyarekî, min dî heft beran li pey beranek[î] [*pinê zebeş*]** (L) I went to the top of the hill, I saw seven rams after one another *[rdl.; ans.: watermelon plant]*. {also: cebeş (FS-2); jebeş (Zx); şebeş (Btm/Czr/Grc); zabeş (Slv); zeveş (K/B); [zebech] زبـــش (JJ); <cebeş جبش/jebeş ژبش/zebeş زبش> (HH)} {syn: k'al III; şiftî} Cf. clq Ar of Ḥalab (Aleppo), Syria jabas جـبـس; Za zeveş *f.* (Todd) *For another example of initial ş-/z- alternation see* ***şembelîlk I***. [Bx/F/A/JB3/IFb/JJ/HH/GF/TF/OK/AA/FS//K/B//Btm/Czr/Grc//Zx]

zeblek زەبلەك *f./m.(FS)* **(-a/-ê;).** muscle *(of forearms and shins)*: **-zeblekêt belek** (Ak) calf muscles. {also: zevlek (IFb/GF/Wkt/FS/BF); <zeblek> زەبلەك (Hej)} [Ak/Zeb/OK/RZ/Hej/ZF3//IFb/GF/Wkt/FS/BF]

zebûr زەبـــوور *f.* **(-a;-ê).** Psalm(s); book of psalms, psalter: **•Dawid ... li gorî *Zebûrê* di sedsala 10'an a berî zayînê de jiyaye** (Wkp) According to *the Psalms*, David lived in the 10th century BCE. {also: zembûr (K); [zebour] زبـور (JJ)} <Ar zabūr زبور [A/IF/JJ/ZF3/Wkt//K]

zed•e زەدە *f.* **(•a;•ê).** 1) lesion *(on the organs of a human being, animal, or plant)*; 2) sickness, illness, disease; 3) [*fig.*] problem, lack, weakness, deficiency; harm, something wrong, something the matter: **•Aqûb, tu şikê neve ser gura, *zeda* Ûsiv destê birane** (Ba3-3, #22) Jacob, do not suspect the wolves, whatever *harm* came to Joseph was at the hands of his brothers; **-cîyê *fk-êyî* zede** (XF) weak spot, sensitive spot, Achilles' heel [lit. 's.o.'s place of sickness']; **-zeda mezin** (XF) weak spot. [Ba3/K/B/XF/ZF3]

ze'f زەعـف *adj.* 1) much, many: **•*ze'f* cara** (B) *many* times; **-ze'ftir** = more {syn: bêtir; p'iřtir; zêdetir}; 2) plenty, abundant, many: **•Xwarin *zeĥf* e** (FS) The food is *plentiful*; 3) [*adv.*] very: **•Jinê jî zanibû, wekî Ûsibî *ze'f* aqile** (Ba) The woman also knew that Joseph was [lit. 'is'] *very* smart **•Qîzik *ze'f* belengaz dibe** (J) The girl becomes *very* unhappy. {also: zaf (Ba2/OK-2); za'f (IS); zahf (A); zehf (K/IFb/JB1-S/TF/OK); zeĥf (GF/FS); [zahf زحـف/zaf زاف (JJ); <zeĥf> زحـف (HH)} {syn: gelek; p'iř II; qewî; zor II (Bw)} Cf. Za zahf (Todd) [Bx/JB3/B//K/IFb/JB1-S/TF/OK//A//JJ/HH/GF/FS//Ba2//IS]

zeft زەفـت: **-zeft kirin** (IFb/GF): a) to occupy, seize control of, confiscate; to overpower, overcome: **•Te ez kuştim, tuê vê çolê *zept bikî*** (L) If you kill me, you *will take control of* this desert (or, mountain, according to L) ; b) to control, restrain *(lit. & fig.)*; c) to catch, arrest, detain; d) to enclose, envelop, surround: **•Alavê k'oçk-sera *zevt kiribû*** (Z-1) Flames *had enveloped* the palace; **-zeft bûn** (IFb) to be seized. {also: zept kirin (L); zevt kirin (Z-1/B); zewt/zewt kirin (SK); [zabt kirin] ضبط كرين (JJ)} < Ar ḍabṭ ضبط --> P ẓabṭ ضبط--> T zapt [Z-1/B//F/K/A/IFb/JB1-S//L//JJ//SK]

zehf زەهـف (K/IFb/JB1-S/TF/OK) = much; very. See **ze'f**.

zehmet زەهـمـەت (K/IFb/FJ/GF/JB1-A/ZF/SS/CS) = trouble, inconvenience; difficult. See **zeĥmet**.

zehmetî زەهـمـەتـى (Nbh) = trouble, inconvenience; difficult. See **zeĥmet**.

zehmetk'êş زەهمەتكێش (K/B)/zehmetkêş (IFb/GF/ZF/SS/CS) = hard worker; hardworking. See **zeĥmetk'êş**.

zehn زەهن = saddle. See **zîn I**.

zehr زەهر (Bw/TF) = imitating. See **zar I**[4].

zeĥf زەحف (JJ/HH/GF/FS) = much; very. See **ze'f**.

zeĥmet زەحـمـەت *f./m.(K/B)* **(-a/ ;-ê;).** 1) {syn: îza} trouble, bother, inconvenience, burden: **•Dunya hemî noke muttefiq e li-ser meĥw kirin o kuştina Wîlhelim, çonko sebebê *zeĥmeta* hemî dunyaê ew e** (SK 55:632) The whole world now is in agreement to wipe out Wilhelm and kill him, because he is the cause of *the troubles of* the whole world **•Teyrêt biharê hemî li-dû hewesa xo digeřyên. Wextê xoşî w řaĥetiyê digel me dibin, emma dema ko pîçek nêzîkî tengawî w *zeĥmeta* zistanê bon me li-naw *zeĥmeta* kûstanê bi-tinê dihêlin, dû keyfa xo dikewin, diçin** (SK 29:269) The birds of spring all go about after their own desires. They are with us in pleasant and comfortable times but as soon as it gets a little near the difficulties and *troubles of* winter they leave us behind in *the troubles of* the cold country and go off after their own pleasure; **-zeĥmet kêşan** (SK)/**zehmet k'işandin** (GF/ZF): a) to take trouble: **•Belê madam hingo hinde *zeḧmete kêşaye*, hatine mala min, ewe bo hingo her yêkî cotekî kalikêt Akrê bi mecîdiyekî dê kiřim, deme hingo** (SK 14:139) But since you have *taken so much trouble* and come to my house, I'll buy a pair of Akre sandals each for you for a mejidi and give them to you; b) to have difficulty, suffer hardship: **•Çend salan weto ma, ji destê mirîdêt xo gelek *zeḧmet kêşa*. Paşî mir** (SK 46:451) For several years he stayed that way, [and] *suffered* a great deal at the hands of his disciples. Then he died; 2) [*adj.*] {also: bi zeḧmet (SK-2)} {syn: ç'etin; dijwar} difficult, hard: **•Em neşêyn xo aşkera bikeyn, çonko jîna me li-ser wî qewmê ker e. Eger aşkera bikeyn dê me kujin. Ḧalê me zor *zeḧmet* e ji destê wan san** (SK 60:729) We cannot reveal ourselves, because our life depends on that nation of asses. If we reveal [ourselves] they will kill us. Our situation is very *difficult* because of those dogs **•Ḧeqîqeten *bi-zeḧmet* e, emma eger mumkin bît to bişêy biçîye Rezge lalî Mela Se'îd, ji wî bipirsî** (SK 61:761) It is certainly *difficult*, but if it be possible for you to go to Razga to Mulla Sa'id, ask him [if it can be done]. {also: zahmet (B); zehmet (K/IFb/FJ/GF/JB1-A/ZF/SS/CS); zehmetî (Nbh); [zehmet] زحمت (JJ); <zeḧmet> زحمت (HH)} < Ar √z-ḥ-m زحم = 'to press (of a crowd), put in a strait' (Hava); Iraqi clq. Ar zaḥḥam زحّم = 'to inconvenience, trouble, bother' & zaḥmah زحمة = 'inconvenience, bother, trouble'; P zaḥmat زحمت = 'inconvenience, etc.'; T zahmet = 'inconvenience, etc.'; NENA zâh'mat ܙܚܡܬ/zâh'mat ܙܚܡܬ = 'inconvenience; difficult' (Maclean); Sor zeḧmet زەحمەت = '(n.) trouble, bother; (adj.) difficult, burdensome' [JJ/HH/SK//K/IFb/FJ/GF/JB1-A/ZF/SS/CS//B//Nbh]

zeḧmetk'êş زەحمەتكێش *m.&f.* **(-ê/;).** 1) hard worker, toiler, laborer: **•Z.A.A. ji *zehmetkêş* û xemxwerên edebiyata Kurdî ye** (Nbh 125:11) Z.A.A. is one of the *hard workers* who care deeply [lit. 'and carers'] about Kurdish literature; 2) [*adj.*] hardworking, toiling, industrious; 3) {syn: kovan; ře't II; xemxwer} worried, troubled, concerned; suffering. {also: zahmetk'êş (B); zehmetk'êş (K/B-2)/zehmetkêş (IFb/GF/ZF/SS/CS)} Cf. P zaḥmat'kaš زحمت كش = 'painstaking, hardworking, industrious, assiduous'; Sor zeḧmetkêş زەحمەتكێش = 'toiling, struggling' [Nbh/IFb/GF/ZF/SS/CS//K//B] <řêncber>

zeîf زەئيف (B/ZF3) = weak; thin. See **zeyf**.

zeîfî زەئيفى *f.* **(-ya;-yê).** 1) thinness; 2) {syn: qelsî [1]; sistî [1]} weakness; **•*Zeîfîya* Mislimanan dibe sedemê qewetbûna kafiran** (ku.ilkha.com 12.xii.2017) The *weakness* of Muslims has caused the strengthening of infidels. {also: [zayfi] ضعيفى (JJ)} [B/ZF3/Wkt//JJ] <zeyf>

zelal زەلال *adj.* pure, clear, limpid, transparent; pure of water and horses (JJ): **•ava zelal** (AB) clear water; **-zelal kirin** (BF/ZF3): a) to purify: **•Wî ava şêlî *zelal kir*** (FS) He *purified* the murky water; b) to clarify, elucidate, explain: **•Heger zehmet ne bit waneya me ji me ra *zelal bike*!** (BF) Please *explain* our lesson to us! {also: [zoulal] زلال (JJ); <zelal> زلال (HH)} {syn: beřaq; ≠şêlo} {zelalî} [AB/F/K/A/JB3/IFb/B/HH/GF/TF/Msr/BF//JJ] <p'etî>

zelalî زەلالى *f.* **(-ya;-yê).** purity, clarity, limpidity. [K/IFb/B/GF/TF/ZF3/BF] <zelal>

zelam زەلام (K/BF)/ẕelam ظەلام (JB1-A) = (young) man. See **zilam**.

zelamînî زەلامينى (BF/FS) = manliness. See **zilamtî**.

zelf زەلف (B) = saucer. See **zerf** [2].

zeliqandin زەلِقاندِن *vt.* **(-zeliqîn-).** 1) {syn: nûsandin; pêvekirin; pêvenan} [**bi** ...**-ve**] to adhere, stick, glue, paste [to] *(vt.)*: **•[Meḧmed beg derî ji nişkêva vedike, lakin *xwe bi* derîve *dizeliqîne* û dide pişta derî]** (JR) Mehmed beg opens the door suddenly, but he *clings to* the door, and remains [lit. 'gives (himself)'] behind it; 2) to solder (K). {also: [zeliqandin] زلقاندين (JJ); <zeliqandin زلقاندن (dizeliqîne) (دزلقينه)> (HH)} Cf. Ar laziqa لزق = 'to adhere, cling, stick to' [JR/Ba2/F/K/IFb/JJ/HH/GF]

zelû زەلو = leech. See **zûrî**.

zelûl زەلوول *adj.* 1) {syn: melûl} sad, despondent, grief-stricken; gloomy, despairing, pessimistic: **-zelûl bûn** (ZF) to be in dire straits, be in a bad way: **•Paşiya paşîn ez *bûm zelûlê* serencameke kirêt** (WT, 87) In the end I *fell victim to* an unpleasant outcome; 2) poor, in need, needy (K). {also: <zelûl> زلول (HH)} {zelûlî (K/IF/B/GF)} [K/A/IFb/B/HH/GF/TF/ZF/CS] <p'oşman>

zelûlî زەلوولى *f.* **(-ya;-yê).** 1) {syn: melûlî; xemgînî} sadness, sorrow, grief; gloom: **•Bavê wana divîne wekî kuřê wî wê tên, lê Ûsiv nava wanda t'une, ew nêzîkî wana dive û *bi zelûlî* dipirse, divêje: "Kuřo, Ûsivê min k'anê?"** (Ba3-3, #20) Their father sees that his sons are coming, but Joseph is not among them; he approaches them and *sadly* asks, "Boys, where is my Joseph?"; 2) poverty, need (K). [Ba3/K/IF/B/GF/Wkt] <zelûl>

zelût زەلـــــووت *adj.* 1) {syn: kot I; r̄ût; tazî I} naked, nude: **-rût û zilût** (BZ) stark naked {syn: şilf tazî}; 2) {syn: ḧewês; k'eçel} bald. {also: şelût (RZ-2); zilût (BZ/IFb-2)} Cf. Ar zulṭ زلـــــط = 'nakedness, nudity' [BZ//IFb/FJ/GF/RZ/CS/FS/ZF3]

zelzele زەلزەلە *f.* **(-ya;-yê).** earthquake. {also: zilzile (K); [zelzelé] زلزلە (JJ)} {syn: bîbelerz; 'erdḧejîn; 'erdlerzîn} < Ar zalzalah زلزلة [IF/JJ/ZF3/Wkt//K]

zembelik زەمبەلِك (TF) = icicle. See **şembelîlk**.

zembelîlk زەمبەلیلك (GF) = icicle. See **şembelîlk**.

zembelîş زەمبەلیش (HR) = cushion or bolster. See **zemberîş**.

zemberîş زەمبەریش *f.* **(-a;-ê).** fancy cushion or bolster: **•Xwe pal dane ser *zembelîş* û balgiha û dest pê kir û mesela Gul û Sîmo jêr̄a got** (HR 3:268) They leaned back on *bolsters* and cushions and began to tell him the story of G. & S. {also: zembelîş (HR)} {syn: nazbalîşk} [HR//GF/TF/FJ/Kmc] <balgih; balîf>

zembîl زەمبیل *f.* **(-a;-ê).** wicker basket for carrying sweepings or crushed gypsum (JJ): **•Min *zembîla* giran danî** (K2-Fêrîk) I put down the heavy *basket*. {also: [zambil] زنبیل (JJ)} {syn: 'edil; sebet} Arc zabīlā זבילא = 'basket of palm leaves' (M. Jastrow) & Syr zabīlā ܙܒܝܠܐ/zanbīlā ܙܢܒܝܠܐ = 'basket' (Costaz): Ar/P zanbīl زنبیل = 'basket made of palm leaves'; T zembil; W Arm zampił զամբիղ/E Arm zambyuł զամբյուղ; Sor zemîl زەمیل; Za zembîl (Mal) [K/A/IFb/B/GF/TF/FS//JB1-S/JJ] <mekev>

zembîlfiroş زەمبیلفِرۆش *m.* **(-ê;).** 1) basket seller; 2) *a well-known Kurdish folk poem.* {also: zembîlfroş (B-2)} *For a study of this folk poem see*: Zh.S. Musaèlian. *Zambil'frosh: Kurdskaia poema i eë fol'klornye versii* [Замбильфрош : Курдская поэма и её фольклорные версии = Zambilfrosh (=Basket seller) : a Kurdish poem and its folkloric versions] (Moscow: Nauka, 1983), 178 p. [K/A/IFb/B/ZF3/Wkt]

zembîlfroş زەمبیلفرۆش (B) = basket seller. See **zembîlfiroş**.

zembûr زەمبوور (K) = Psalm(s). See **zebûr**.

zencefîl زەنجەفیل *f.* **(-a;-ê).** ginger, bot. *Zingiber officinale*: **•Eger mirov çaya *zencefîlê* vexwe, nema weke berê dilê mirov diçe xwarinê** (rojname.com 28.ii.2017) If one drinks ginger tea, one doesn't feel like eating anymore. {also: [zendjefil/zengibíl (G.)] زنجفیل (JJ)} Cf. Ar/P zanjabīl زنجبیل & T zencefil & P šangalīl شنگلیل (Mid P šangavīr) < Indian vernacular form *s(š)angavīra, corresponding to Pali singivera, Skt śr̥ṅgavera [= 'of a serpent dragon': śr̥ṅga- = 'horn' + vera] (Laufer, p. 583); Sor zencefîl زەنجەفیل [Hk/IFb/JJ/GF/TF/OK/CB]

zencîr زەنجیر (JB3) = chain. See **zincîr**.

zend زەند *f./m.* **(-a/ ;-ê/).** 1) {syn: bask [3]; meçek} wrist: **-zenda destî** (SK) do.: **•...Lix̌awekî asin dû gez dirêj, gezek pan, bi qeder *zenda destî* stûr bide çêkirin** (SK 33:297) Go and get an iron bridle made, two yards long, a yard wide, and as thick as a man's *wrist*; 2) forearm [*m.*(SK)]; 3) {syn: huçik} {also: zendik} sleeve (K): **•Zendê xwe bişidîne!** (K) Take heart!/Courage! [lit. 'Tighten your sleeves']; 4) [*f.*] {syn: movik [1]} joint (SK). {also: [zänd] زند (JJ); <zend> زند (HH)} Cf. Ar/P zand/zind زند = 'ulna (anat.); forearm' [K/IFb/B/JJ/HH/SK/GF/TF/OK]

zendek زەندەك (IFb/HH) = sleeve; cuff. See **zendik**.

zendik زەندِك *f./m.(ZF3)* **(-a/;-ê/).** 1) {syn: huçik; mil [3]} sleeve; 2) cuff (B). {also: **zend I**; zendek (IFb); zendîk (L); <zendek> زندك (HH)} [L//K/A/JB3/B/TF/OK/ZF3//IFb/HH]

zendîk زەندیك (L) = sleeve; cuff. See **zendik**.

zeng زەنگ *f.* **(-a;-ê).** 1) rust: **-zeng girtin** (K/IFb/B)/ **zingarê lê avêtin** (JB3) to rust; 2) mold, mildew. {also: **jeng** (Haz/IFb/K[s]); zengar (MK2)/zengar̄ (FS); zingar (JB3); [jenk] ژنك (JJ); <zeng> زنگ (HH)} Cf. P zang زنگ; Sor jeng ژەنگ/jêng ژێنگ; Za zincar *m.* (Todd) [F/K/A/B/HH/Ba2//Haz/IFb/K(s)//JJ//MK2//FS//JB3] See also **jeng**.

zengal زەنگال *f.* **(;-ê).** 1) knee-length woolen stockings (S&E); 2) gaiters, leggings, leg covering reaching up to ankle, mid-calf, or knee (K). Cf. P zangāl زنگال/zangār زنگار = 'leggings' [S&E/K/B/Wkt]

zengalor زەنگالۆر (FS) = Adam's apple; trachea. See **zengelûk**.

zengar زەنگار (MK2)/zengar̄ زەنگاڕ (FS) = rust; mildew. See **jeng** & **zeng**.

zengarî زەنگاری/**zengar̄î** زەنگاڕی [FS] *adj.* 1) rusty; 2) rust colored. {also: jengar (IFb); **jengarî** (Haz); jengdar (IFb-2/K-2); jengî (SK); jingar (IFb-2); zenggirtî (K/B); zengirtî (K-2); zingarî (JB1-A);

[jenk ghirtiié] ژنك گـرتـيـه (JJ)} Cf. P zangārī زنگارى = 'rust-colored'; Sor jengar ژەنگار/jengdar ژەنـگـدار = 'rusty' & jengawî ژەنـگـاوى = 'rust-colored' [A//K//IFb//Haz//SK//JB1-A] See also **jengarî**.

zengelok زەنـگـەلـۆك (Bx/A) = Adam's apple; trachea. See **zengelûk**.

zengelor زەنـگـەلـۆر (IFb/TF/ZF3) = Adam's apple; trachea. See **zengelûk**.

zengelork زەنـگـەلـۆرك (Bx/IFb) = Adam's apple; trachea. See **zengelûk**.

zengelûk زەنـگـەلـووك *f.* **(;-ê).** 1) Adam's apple; 2) windpipe, trachea: **•Ba di *zengalorê* r̄a diçit di pişê da** (FS) Wind goes through *the trachea* to the lungs; 3) {syn: sorîçk} gullet, esophagus. {also: zengalor (FS); zengelok (Bx/A); zengelor (IFb/TF/ZF3); zengelork (Bx-2/IFb-2); zengilok (GF); zengilor (Wkt); zengûlek (B); [zenghelouk] زنگلوك (JJ)} [Bx/A//F/K/JJ//IFb/TF/ZF3//Wkt//FS//GF//B]

zenggirtî زەنـگـگِـرتـى (K/B) = rusty. See **jengarî** & **zengarî**.

zengil زەنـگِـل *m./f.(Zeb)* **(-ê/ ; zêngil/-ê).** (little) bell: **•Di nav çinge çinga dengê *zengilkan* re** (SBx, 12) Amid the tinkling *of the bells* [lit. 'of the sound of bells]; **-zengil xistin** (B) to ring the bell. {also: zengul (IFb-2); zingil (SW-#18); [zenghil] زنـگـل (JJ); <zingil> زنـگـل (HH)} Cf. P zang زنـگ ='bell' & zangūle زنـگـولـه = 'little bell (dim.)'; Sor zeng زەنـگ = 'bell' & zengûłe زەنگوولّە = 'tinkle-bell'; Hau zeng m. (M4) [K/A/JB3/IFb/B/JJ/SK/OK/Zeb//HH//Sw-#18]

zengilok زەنـگِـلـۆك (GF) = Adam's apple; trachea. See **zengelûk**.

zengilor زەنـگِـلـۆر (Wkt) = Adam's apple; trachea. See **zengelûk**.

zengirtî زەنگِرتى (K) = rusty. See **jengarî** & **zengarî**.

zengî زەنگى (F) = stirrup. See **zengû**.

zengo زەنگۆ (A/HH) = stirrup. See **zengû**.

zengu زەنگو (IFb) = stirrup. See **zengû**.

zengul زەنگول (IFb) = bell. See **zengil**.

zeng•û زەنـگـوو *f.* **(•îya;•îyê/ûyê).** 1) {syn: r̄ik'êb [1]} stirrup, having a rectangular base with sharp corners used as spurs (according to W&E): **•Eva çend r̄oje *zengîya* ser *zengîya* min duxurînî** (Z-1) For several days now you have been jabbing *the stirrups* into my *stirrup-bone*; **-ḧesp avîtin/dayîn ber zengûya** (B)/**ḧesp zengû kirin** (B) to spur a horse on; 2) stirrup-bone, stapes. {also: zengî (F); zengo (A); zengu (IFb); zengwa (L); [zengou] زنـگـو (JJ); <zengo> زنـگـو (HH)} < T üzengi = 'stirrup': Sor awzengî ئاوزەنگى; Za zengu *m.* (Todd). See: Róna-Tas András. "Did the proto-Altaic people know the stirrup?" *Studia Mongolica*, 13 (1973), 169-171; "The periodization and sources of Chuvash linguistic theory" in: *Chuvash Studies*, Bibliotheca Orientalis Hungarica, 28, Asiatische Forschungen, 79 (Budapest & Wiesbaden, 1982), pp. 120-22; "The periodization of Turkic linguistic history," in: *An Introduction to Turkology* (Szeged, 1991), pp. 21-30, esp. 26-27; Ş. Tekin "Some Thoughts on the Etymology of the Turkish Üzengi 'stirrup'," *Journal of Turkish Studies*, 9 (1985), 237-241. [Z-1/K/B/JJ//F//IFb//A/HH//L]

zengûlek زەنگوولەك (B) = Adam's apple; trachea. See **zengelûk**.

zengwa زەنگوا (L) = stirrup. See **zengû**.

zept kirin زەپـت كِـرِن (L) = to occupy, seize; to control. See **zeft: -zeft kirin**.

zeqir زەقِر (Wkt) = mountain pass. See **zuxir**.

zer I زەر *adj.* 1) {syn: qîç'ik} yellow: **•gula *zer*** (FS) *yellow* rose; 2) pale *(complexion)*; blond(e); 3) {syn: sivik; vebûyî} light (of tea) (Bw). {also: [zer] زر (JJ); <zer> زر (HH)} [Pok. 1. ĝhel-/ĝhelə- : ĝhlē-/ĝhlō-/ĝhlə- 429.] 'to shine; with derivatives referring to colors, to bright materials, probably "yellow metal," and to the bile or gall': Skt hári- = 'yellow, blonde'; Av zari- & zairita- = 'yellow(ish)'; Mid P zard = 'yellow' (M3); P zard زرد; Sor zerd زەرد; Za zerd (Todd); Hau zerd (M4) {zerahî; zeranî; zerawî; zerayî; zerî III; <zerî زرى /zerahî زراهى> (HH)} [F/K/A/JB3/IFb/B/JJ/HH/SK/JB1-A&S/GF/TF/Bw/BF]

zer II زەر/**zer̄** زەڕ [B/Wkt] *f.* **(;-ê).** precipice, abyss, chasm, gulf; ravine, gorge, canyon: **•Box strûyê xwe kire p'êsîra wî, girt, *zerê*da avît** (EP-4) The roebuck [lit. 'bull'] stuck his horns into [Siyabend's] collar, picked him up, and threw him into *the ravine*. {syn: dergelî; derteng; geboz; gelî II; zang} Cf. Sor zerd زەرد = 'steep rugged cliffs, gaunt mountain' [EP-4/K/B/GF/Wkt]

zerahî زەراهـى (K/HH) = yellowness; pallor. See **zerî III**.

zeranî زەرانى (K) = yellowness; pallor. See **zerî III**.

zeranîq زەرانيق (GF) = see saw. See **zirnazîq**.

zerar زەرار (F/IFb/OK) = damage. See **zirar**.

zerawî زەراوى (A) = yellowness; pallor. See **zerî III**.

zerayî زەرايـى (A/IFb) = yellowness; pallor. See **zerî**

III.

zerazeng زەرازەنگ *f.* **(-a;).** crown; crown made of flowers or thorns: •***zerzenga*** **paşayî** (FS) the pasha's *crown*. {also: zerzeng (IFb/GF/FJ/FS)} [Qzl//IFb/GF/FJ/FS] <t'ac>

zerb زەرب (K/B/JJ) = strike, hit; salvo. See **derb**.

zerdel•e زەردەلە (;•ê) (K/A/B/HH/Kmc-2/FS) = apricot. See **zerdelî**.

zerdelî زەردەلی *f.* **(-ya;-yê).** apricot, bot. *Prunus armeniaca*. {also: zerdel•e (;•ê) (K/A/B/Kmc-2/FS); zerdelo (OK-2/AA); zerdelû (IFb-2/JB3/B-2/GF-2); [zerdelé زردله/zerdalou زردالو] (JJ); <zerdele> زردله (HH)} {syn: *hêrûg [2]; mişmiş; qeysî} Cf. P zard ālū زرد آلو = 'apricot', orig. 'yellow plum'; Sor zerdałû زەرداڵوو [Ag//K/A/B/Kmc-2/FS//IFb/JJ/HH/GF/OK//JB3//AA] <alûçe>

zerdelo زەردەلۆ (OK/AA) = apricot. See **zerdelî**.

zerdelû زەردەلوو (IFb/JB3/B/GF) = apricot. See **zerdelî**.

zerek زەرەك (GF/HH) = hepatitis. See **zerik III**.

zerer زەرەر (JB3/SK/OK) = damage. See **zirar**.

zerf زەرف *f.* /**z̤erf** ظەرف *m.* **(;-ê/-î).** 1) envelope: •**... bo neyê zanîn ew gustîrk li nav kîjan *zerfî* de ye** (e-rojname.com 3.vi.2018) ...so that it would not be known which *envelope* the ring was in •**Ji wan kaxezan yekê bala min pir kêşa, lê çi navnîşanek ji bilî ya babê Gulê li ser *zerfî* nebû** (nefel.com 15.x.2007) One of those letters caught my attention, but the only address on *the envelope* was "Gulê's father"; 2) saucer, small plate; 3) {syn: hoker; *nîr I[2]; řengpîşe} adverb. {also: zelf (B); [zarf] ظرف (JJ)} <Ar z̤arf ظرف = 'container; envelope; adverb'-->T zarf; Sor zerf زەرف = 'container, dish, tray, bag, envelope' [F/K/IFb/B/JJ/JB1-A/GF/ZF3/Wkt/FD]

zerg زەرگ *f./m.(FT/FS/Wkt)* **(;-ê/).** spearhead, pointed tip of an arrow or lance: •**Hesavê *zergekî* lêxin serê dilê qîzêye/** (FT) It was as if *a spearhead* pierced the tip of the girl's heart; -**zergê řimê** (FS) do. {also: zerge (GF/FS); [zerk/zerg] زرك (JJ)} {syn: xişt III} <Ar √z-r-q زرق = 'to shoot with a javelin' & mizrāq مزراق = 'javelin'; cf. also Heb zarak̦ זרק = 'to throw'; Sor zerg زەرگ = 'skewer having round head with small chains attached and thrust through the cheeks by dervishes as religious exercise' [FT/K/A/IF/B/JJ/Wkt//GF/FS] <niştir; řim; tîr I>

zerge زەرگە (GF/FS) = spearhead. See **zerg**.

zerhimî زەرهِمی/**zerḧimî** زەرحِمی [Wkt-2] *adj.* pale, pallid, wan: •**Tijda bi germahiyeka di dengê wê û sorahiyeka di rûyê wê yê *zerhimî* de hesiya** (EN) T. sensed a warmth in her voice and a passion [lit. 'redness'] in her *pale* face. {also: zermihî (RZ-2)} [EN/ZF/RZ/Wkt]

zerik I زەرِك *f.* **(;-ê).** 1){syn: cifnî} tureen, large bowl; 2) {syn: mencelok} milk pail: •**Wî *zerkeka* mas̱tî kiřî** (FS) He bought a yoghurt *pail*. [Bw/A/IFb/GF/TF/OK/ZF3/Wkt/FS] <firaq>

zer•ik II زەرك *f.* **(•ka;•[i]kê).** egg yolk: -**zerka hêkê** (Bw/OK) do. {also: [zerik] زرك (JJ); <zerik> زرك (HH)} Cf. P zarde زرده /zardī زردی; Sor zerdêne زەردێنە [Bw/K/IFb/B/JJ/HH/GF/TF/ZF3/Wkt/BT//OK] <hêk; spîlik I>

zerik III زەرِك *f.* **(-a;-ê).** hepatitis, jaundice: •***Zerkîyê*** **ew girtiye** (FS) S/he has come down with *hepatitis* [lit. 'Hepatitis has taken him/her']. {also: zerek (GF-2); zerikî (FS); zerkî (OK); [zerik] زرك (JJ); <zerek> زرك (HH)} {syn: qîç'ikayî} Sor zerdûyî زەردوویی [Ak/K/IFb/JJ/GF/TF/ZF3/Wkt/BT//FS//OK//HH]

zerikî زەرِکی (FS) = hepatitis. See **zerik III**.

zerî I زەری *f.* **(-ya;-yê).** 1) beautiful girl; 'miss'; 2) blonde girl. {also: [zeri] زری (JJ)} [HM/K/A/IFb/B/JJ/GF/FS/ZF3/BF/Wkt] <gewr [2]; jin; keç'; qîz>

zerî II زەری, m. (S&E/K) = armor. See **zirx**.

zerî III زەری *f.* **(-ya;-yê).** 1) {syn: qîç'ikayî} yellowness; pallor: •***Zerîya*** **dêmê wî ne ji nexweşîyê ye** (BF) *The pallor of* his cheeks is not from illness; 2) blondness. {also: zerahî (K); zeranî (K-2); zerawî (A); zerayî (A/IFb-2); <zerî زری/zerahî زراهی> (HH)} [K/IFb/HH/ZF3/BF//A] <zer I>

zerkî زەرکی (OK) = hepatitis. See **zerik III**.

zermihî زەرمِهی (RZ) = pale, wan. See **zerhimî**.

zerp زەرپ (FK-eb-2) = strike, hit; salvo. See **derb**.

zerzaniq زەرزانِق (IFb) = see saw. See **zirnazîq**.

zerzanîq زەرزانیق (GF/HH) = see saw. See **zirnazîq**.

zerzeng زەرزەنگ (IFb/GF/FJ/FS) = crown. See **zerazeng**.

zerzirî زەرزِری (FS) = starling. See **zerzûr**.

zerzîrî زەرزیری (-ya;) (Zx/BF) = starling. See **zerzûr**.

zerzûl زەرزوول (ZF3) = starling. See **zerzûr**.

zerzûr زەرزوور *f.* **().** starling, zool. *Sturnus vulgaris* (a small black bird). {also: zerzirî (FS); zerzîrî (-ya;) (Zx/BF); zerzûl (ZF3-2); zirzûl (ZF3);

<zerzûr> زرزور (HH)} {syn: alik; garanîk; r̄eşêlek} cf. Ar zurzūr زرزور /zurzur زرزر [Zx/BF//FS//A/IFb/HH/GF/TF]

ze'va زهعڤا (J/B) = groom; son-in-law. See **zava**.

ze'vatî زهعڤاتی (B) = state of being a groom. See **zavatî**.

zeveş زهڤهش (K/B) = watermelon. See **zebeş**.

zevî زهڤی *f.* **(-ya;-yê).** field, sown field: **•Çû serê *zevîê*** (J) He went to *the field* **•*Zevî* tijî genim e** (AB) *The field* is full of wheat. {also: zewî (SK); [zevi] ضوی (JJ); <zevî> زڤی (HH)} [Pok. ĝhđem-/ĝhđom-, *gen./abl.* ĝh(đ)-és 414.] 'earth, ground': Skt jmán = '[on the] earth'; Av zā̊ (*acc.* ząm; *loc.* zəmē; *gen.* zəmō) = 'earth, ground'; Mid P zamīg = 'earth' (M3); P zamīn زمین = 'land, earth'; Sor zewî زهوی = 'ground, field'; Za zıme *m.* = 'field' (Mal); Hau zemîn *m.* = 'earth' (M4); cf. also Lat humus = 'earth, soil, ground'; Gr chthōn χθών; Rus zemlia земля = 'earth, ground, land' [J/F/K/A/JB3/IFb/B/HH/GF/TF//JJ//SK] <beyar; hox; k'ewşan; k'irêbe>

zevlek زهڤلهك (IFb/GF/Wkt/FS/BF) = muscle. See **zeblek**.

zevt kirin زهڤت کِرِن (Z-1/B) = to occupy, seize; to control. See **zeft: -zeft kirin**.

zewac زهواج *f.* **(-a;-ê).** marriage: **•Îdî we'dê wî *zewacê* bû** (Z-1) Now it was time for him to *marry* [lit. 'It was his time of *marriage*'] {also: ziwac (Sw); [zevadj] زواج (JJ)} < Ar zawāj زواج. For a description of Kurdish marriage practices see: B. Nikitine. *Les Kurdes: étude sociologique et historique* (Paris: Imprimerie Nationale : Librairie C. Klincksieck, 1956), p. 108 ff. (Azerbaijan); M. Mokri. "Le Mariage chez les Kurdes," in: *Recherches de Kurdologie: Contribution scientifique aux études iraniennes* (Paris: Librairie Klincksieck, 1970), pp. 33-61 (Iranian Kurdistan). [Z-1/K/IFb/B/JJ//Sw] <bûk I; de'wat; mehir; zava; zewicîn>

zewicandin زهوجاندِن *vt.* **(-zewicîn-).** to marry s.o. off: **•Ez dixwazim ez we *bizewicînim*** (L) I want *to marry* you (pl.) *off*; **-kur̄ê xwe zewicandin** (IF) to marry one's son off: **•Ewê *kur̄ê xwe zewicand*** (B) She *married off her son.* {also: [zevidjandin] زوجاندين (JJ)} < Ar zawwaja II زوّج = 'to marry s.o. off'; Za zewjnenã [zewjnayiş] (Srk) [L/K/JB3/IFb/B/JJ/JB1-S] <zewac; zewicîn>

zewicîn زهوجين *vi.* **(-zewic-).** to marry (vi.), get married, be wed: **•Ez *nazewcim*** (J) I *won't marry*; **-di dema xwe de zewicîn** (IF) to get married at the right time. {also: [zevidjin] زوجين (JJ)} {syn: jin anîn/standin (said of man) ; mêr kirin (said of woman) } < Ar zawwaja II زوّج = 'to marry s.o. off'; Za zewjênã [zewjyayiş] (Srk) [J/F/K/JB3/IFb/B/JJ/JB1-S]

zewî زهوی (SK) = field. See **zevî**.

zewt زهوت/ẕewt kirin ظهوت کِرِن (SK) = to occupy, seize; to control. See **zeft: -zeft kirin**.

zexim زهخِم (JB3) = strong, sturdy. See **zexm**.

zeximî زهخِمی (Wkt) = sturdiness. See **zexmî**.

zexîr•e زهخیره *f.* **(•a;•ê).** 1) supply, store, reserve; 2) stores, provisions, stock of foodstuffs *(for a trip, the winter, etc., also mil.)*; 3) arsenal; 4) treasure. {also: zex̄îre (K); [zakhiré/zakira (JJ-G)] ذخیره (JJ); <zexîre> زخیره (HH)} <Ar ḏaxīrah ذخیرة ='treasure; stores, supplies; provisions, food; ammunition' [FK-kk-1/F/A/IFb/B/JJ/HH//K]

zexm I زهخم *adj.* 1) {syn: zîx I} strong, powerful, vigorous, firm, sturdy: **•Cawê malê pir *zexm* e** (AB) Homemade cloth is very *strong*; **-zexm kirin** (ZF/IFb) to strengthen, reinforce, consolidate: **•...jibo ku rewşa xwe di Kurdistanê da *zexm bike*** (Bkp, 29) ...in order *to strengthen* his position in Kurdistan; 2) [*f.*] {syn: birî I; ĥêl; hêz; qedûm [2]; qewat; t'aqet; zor I} strength, force, power. {also: zexim (JB3); zex̄m; [zekhm] ضخم (JJ); <zexm> زخم (HH)} < Ar ḍaxm ضخم = 'huge' {zexm[ay]î} [AB/K/IFb/B/HH/JB1-A/GF/ZF//JB3]

zexm II زهخم (K) = stirrup strap. See **zexmik**.

zexmayî زهخمايی (B/ZF3) = sturdiness. See **zexmî**.

zexme زهخمه (Uzun/GF/FS) = stirrup strap. See **zexmik**.

zexmik زهخمِك *f./m.(FS)* **(-ê/ ;-ê/).** strap on stirrup, joining it to the saddle: **•Zengû, *zexme*, rikêb û hesinê lîwanê hespê mîna tîrêjên tavê diçirûsîn** (M.Uzun. R. Evd. Zeyn., 108) The horse's stirrups, straps, spurs & iron bit sparkled like rays of the sun. {also: zexm II (K); zexme (Uzun/GF-2/FS-2); <zexmik> زخمك (HH)} [Uzun//K//A/IFb/B/FJ/GF/HH/FS]

zexmî زهخمی *f.* **(-ya;-yê).** strength, sturdiness, firmness. {also: zeximî (Wkt); zexmayî (B/ZF3-2)} [B//K/IFb/GF/ZF3//Wkt] <zexm I>

zext I زهخت *f.* **(-a;-ê).** pressure, stress: **•Di dema ser êşê de Vicksê li eniya xwe bidin, wê *zextê* kêm bike û êşê sivik bike** (basnews.com 6.x.2016) During a headache, apply Vicks to your forehead, it will reduce *the pressure* and lessen the pain; **-zext lê kirin** (ZF3) to apply pressure. {syn: ç'ews; fişar; p'est; pêk'utî} < Ar ḍaγṭ ضغط [Bw/TF/Wkt/ZF3]

zext II زهخت (K[s]/A/IFb/HH/GF/FJ/ZF3/FS/Wkt) = nail tip on oxgoad. See **zixt**.

zeẍîre زهغیره (K) = stores, supplies. See **zexîre**.

zeẍm زهغم = strong, sturdy. See **zexm**.

zeyde زهیده (JB3/IFb) = more; too much. See **zêde**.

zeydetir زهیدهتِر (JB3) = more. See **zêde: -zêdetir**.

zeyf زهیف *adj.* 1) {syn: jar I; lawaz; leẍer; narîn; qels I; qoř III; zirav I} lean, thin, slim, skinny: **-zeyf bûn** = to grow thin, lose weight; 2) {syn: lawaz [2]; qels I[1]; sist [1]} weak. {also: zeîf (B/ZF3); [zaïf] ضعیف (JJ)} < Ar ḍa'īf ضعیف --> T zayıf {zeîfî; [zayfi] ضعیفی (JJ)} [K//B/ZF3//JJ]

zeyistan زهیِستان (Wkt) = woman in childbed. See **zêstan**.

zey•î زهیی *f.* **(•îya;•ê).** 1) married daughter or sister: *name given to all female relatives who have married and no longer live in their parents' home* (Haz); *If a married woman goes back to her father's house, she is referred to in this way*: **•Bûk derk'etin ji malê xezûrane,/ berê xwe dane malî bavane,/ ji xořa *çûne zeyane*** (Z-2) The brides left the houses of their fathers-in-law,/ headed for their father's houses,/ went *to visit as married women* **•Ka *zeyîyên* me nehatine dawatê?** (IFb) You mean to say that none of *our married daughters* came to the wedding?; 2) {syn: diş} sister-in-law, sister of one's husband *(from point of view of a married woman)* (IFb/Srk/Mzg) {T görümce}; 3) {syn: bars} bee which leaves its hive and goes to "visit" another hive (Haz/ZZ-7): **-hingivê zeyiya** (ZZ-7) the finest honey, *made by such bees*: **•Ez ê ji delalî mala xwe re bînim / *hunguvê zeyiya*** (ZZ-7, 113) I will bring for the beloved of my household *the finest honey*. {also: zêyî (B/Haz/Mzg)} {zey[î]tî; zêtî} [K/IFb/Srk//Haz/Mzg/B/ZZ/ZF/Wkt/FS/G/FD] <bûk I; diş>

zeyîstan زهییستان (A) = woman in childbed. See **zêstan**.

zeyîstanî زهییستانی (Frq) = childbed, confinement. See **zêstanî**.

zeyîtî زهییتی *f.* **().** custom according to which a married daughter (**zeyî**, qv.) comes to visit her father's household two weeks after her wedding (Haz); visit of a married woman to her relatives: **•Bi rastî bûk bûn û *zeyîtî* hat guherandin** (pen-kurd.org:49 kevok bûn) In truth [customs like] being a bride and *returning to visit one's parents* have changed. {also: zeyî (G); zeytî (K); zêtî (Haz); *zêyîn (Srk: Za?); zihî (GF-2); zî II (GF/FS)} [K/ /Kmc/ZF3/Wkt//Haz//Srk//GF/FS] <zeyî>

zeystan زهیستان = winter. See **zivistan**.

zeyt زهیت *f./m.(Zeb)* **(-a/-ê;-ê/-î).** olive oil: **•*Zeyta* zeytûnên Dêrîkê êdî bû marka** (avestakurd.net 14.vi.2014) *The olive oil of* Dêrîk has become a brandname. {also: <zeyt> زيت (HH)} {syn: řûnê zeyt'ûnê (B)} < Ar zayt زيت; T zeyt [Gaziantep] = 'olive oil' (DS, v. 11, p. 4362); Arm cēt' ձէթ [IFb/HH/GF/TF/OK/Zeb/ZF3/Wkt/BF] <zeyt'ûn>

zeytî زهیتی (K) = visit by a married daughter to her father's house. See **zeyîtî**.

zeyt'ûn زهیتوون *f.* **(-a;-ê).** olive(s): **•Efrînî bi xak û *zeytûna* xwe ve girêdayî ne** (Kurdistan24 13.vii.2018) Afrinis are attached to their land and their *olives*; **-dara zeyt'ûnê** (K) olive tree; **-řûnê zeyt'ûnê** (B)/~ **zêîtûnê** (F) olive oil {syn: zeyt}. {also: zêîtûn (F); zêtûn (JB3/OK-2); [zeĭt زيت/zeĭtoun زيتون] (JJ); <zeytûn> زيتون (HH)} < Ar zaytūn زيتون--> T zeytin; Cf. Arm cēt' ձէթ = 'olive oil' & cit'abduł ձիթապտուղ = 'olive'; Sor zeytûn زهیتوون [K/B//A/IFb/JJ/HH/GF/TF/OK/AA/Kmc-2//F//JB3]

zêc زێج (K) = wife; children. See **zêç**.

zêç زێچ *f.* **().** 1) wife: *usually in compound*: **-zar û zêç** (Ber)/**zav-zêç** (Mzg/Srk)/**zav û zêç** (IFb) women and children, family {syn: zaro-maro (Haz)} {cf. T çoluk çocuk}; 2) children. {also: zêc (K)}. See under **zav-zêç**. [Ber/IFb/GF//K]

zêde زێده *adj./adv.* 1) more; excessive, too much (B/JB1-A): **•ne kêm, ne *zêde*** (B) neither *more* nor less **•Paşa kasikekî** [sic] **çînî bo aw-xarinewa xo hebû, gelek çak bû. ... Hemî xulamêt xo gazî kirin. ... Got e xulaman, "Ḧez dikem yêk ji hingo wê kasikê bişkînît." Hemîyan gotin** [sic], **"{Esteẍfiru-llah,} *ji me zêde ye* em kasika paşa bişkînîn"** (SK 22:198) The Pasha had a very fine china cup from which to drink water. ... He summoned all his henchmen. ... He said to the henchmen, "I want one of you to break this cup." They all said, "God forbid! *It is beyond us [=too much for us]* to break the Pasha's cup"; **-bi ser *ft-î* ve zêde kirin** (Bw)/**lê zêde kirin** (ZF3) to add to; **-zêde kirin** (ZF3) to increase, augment, magnify: **•Wî ava coyê *zêde kir*** (FS) He *increased* the water in the irrigation ditch; 2) very (much); 3) much: -**zêdetir** = more {also: zeydetir (JB3)}. {also: zeyde (JB3/IFb-2); zêdê (JB1-S); [zidé] زيـــده (JJ); <zêde> زيـــده (HH)} Cf. Ar ziyādah زيـادة; Sor ziyad زیـاد {zêdeyî (IFb/B) = excess} [Z-1/K/IFb/B/HH/SK/JB1-A/GF//JB3//JB1-S//JJ]

zêdebar زێدەبار: -**zedebarî ku** (FS) in addition to the fact that: •**Hevbendiya Azad û Behremî baş e, *zêdebarî ku* diçin seredana hevdu** (FS) A. and B.'s friendship/connection was good, *in addition to the fact that* they go to visit one another; -**zêdebarî vê çendê** (Zeb/Dh) in addition, moreover: •**Di çerxên burî da ... xwandin û nivîsîn bi her du zimanan *zêdebarî* zimanê Farsî li Kurdistanê dihate xwandin** (I. Badî. Remezanê Cizîrî di dwîvçûn û twêjandineka dîtir da, 13) In past centuries ... reading and writing was done in both languages *in addition to* the Persian language. {syn: serda[2]} [Zeb/Dh/FS/Badî]

zêdegavî زێدەگاڤی *f.* **(-ya;-yê).** overstepping boundaries, crossing over the line *(of moral, decent behavior)*, excess; violation, abuse: •**Serekwezîrê Tirkîyê yê parêzyar yê nû Mesût Yilmaz soz daye ku ji bo bersinggirtina wan zêdegavîyan pêngavên xurt bihavêjît** (VOA[Hk]) Turkey's new conservative prime minister, Mesut Yilmaz, has promised to take concrete measures to curb abuses. [VoA/BF] <destdirêjî>

zêdehî زێدەهی *f.* **(-ya;-yê).** 1) offspring, descendants, progeny, children: •**Çi *zêdehî* bi dûv vê çêlê neketin** (FS) This cow didn't *produce* any offspring [lit. 'no offspring fell in the track of this cow'] •**Erê ma we çi *zêdehî* nînin?** (FS) Don't you have any *children*?; -**bê zêdehî** (Çîvanoka Gayê Sor) childless: •**Dibêjin du birayêt êk bûn, êk yê dewlemend û kedxuda bû ... lê y[ê] *bê dûndeh û zêdehî* bû** (Bêhnişk, 47) They say there were 2 brothers, one was rich and a village chief ... but he was *childless* •**Min evru re'ya xo ya guhirî û min a gotî ez êdî sultaniyê nakem, em d *bê zêdehî* ne, ma ez dê bo kê sultanîyê kem** (Çîvanoka Gayê Sor, 9) Today I changed my mind and said that I will no longer rule as sultan, we are *without offspring*, for whom will I be sultan?; 2) (Wkt) = abundance, excess. See **zêdeyî**. {syn: dol I; dûndan; zuřet II} [Bêhnîşk/Çîvanoka Gayê Sor/FS/Hej/MJ]

zêde•yî زێدەیی *f.* **(;•yê).** abundance; excess. {also: zêdehî[2] (Wkt)} [IF/B/BF/ZF3//Wkt] <zêde>

zêdê زێدێ (JB1-S) = more; too much. See **zêde**.

zêîtûn زێئیتوون (F) = olive. See **zeyt'ûn II**.

zêmar زێمار *f.* **(-a;-ê).** mourning; sorrow, pain: •***Zêmara* wî hate guhê min** (FS) His *mourning* reached my ear; -**zêmar kirin** (Bw/FS) to mourn {also: [zemár kem] (JJ-G) = 'Je chante un cantique funèbre'} {syn: şîn I} <Arc זמר & Syr ܙܡܪ, √z-m-r = 'to sing (in praise of God), chant, play (musical instrument)' [Bw/OK/ZF3/FS/BF//JJ-G] <lûbandin>

zên I زێن *f.* **(;-ê).** 1) {syn: bîr I} memory; mind; 2) {syn: mêze} glance, look: -**zên dan** (MK/K) to look at {syn: fikirîn II; mêze kirin; nêřîn}. < Ar dihn ذهن = 'mind'; Sor zeyn زەین = 'intelligence' [MK/K/B/IFb/ZF3]

zên II زێن (L) = saddle. See **zîn I**.

zêndî زێندی *adj.* alive; lively: •**Hêzên kolonyalîst dixwazin gelê me *zêndî* bikin gorê** (Ber) The colonialist forces want to bury our people *alive*; -**weşana zindî** (ZF3) live broadcast. {also: zindî I (IFb/GF/TF/ZF3); zîndû (K[s]); [zendé] زنده (JJ); <zindî> زندی (HH)} {syn: jîndar} Cf. P zende زنده; Sor zîndû زیندوو/zînde زینده; Hau zînne (M4) [Ber/K/A//IFb/HH/GF/TF/ZF3//K(s)//JJ] <jîn; saẍ>

zêř زێر *m.* **(-ê;).** 1) gold: •**Kursîk li cem hakim heye, zîv e û yek *zêr* e** (L) There is a chair at the prince's [court], it is silver, and there is a *gold* one; -**gustîlka zêř** (B) golden ring; 2) [*pl.*] gold pieces, gold coins: •**Dibîne k'aşa *zêřa* ji ya Ûsib girantire** (Ba) He sees that the weight of *the gold* is more [lit. 'heavier'] than [that of] Joseph •**Ew *zêřa* hildide xweřa** (Ba) He takes *the gold [pieces]* for himself •**Ew *zêřê* gerdena xwe û guharê xwe jî datîne ser t'aê mêzînê** (Ba) She puts *the gold coins* from her necklace and earrings onto the pan of the scales •**K'ulme xwelî bavêje t'aê *zêřa*** (Ba) Throw a handful of dirt onto the scale *with the gold* •**Sed *zêrê* zer bidin kurê pîrê** (L) Give the old woman's boy one hundred *gold pieces*. {also: [zer/zir] زر (JJ); <zêr> زیر (HH)} [Pok. 1. ĝhel-/ĝhelə- : ĝhlē-/ĝhlō-/ĝhlə- 429.] 'to shine; with derivatives referring to colors, to bright materials, probably "yellow metal," and to the bile or gall': Skt híraṇya-; Av zaranya-; OP daraniya- <Proto IE *ĝhḷ-enio- (Kent §32, §66.II, §88); Mid P zarr = 'gold' (M3); P zarr زرّ; Sor zêř زێڕ; Za zêr (Todd)/zer (Mal) *m.*; Hau zeř *m.* = 'money' (M4) [F/K/(A)/JB3/IFb/B/HH/SK/JB1-A&S/GF/TF/SC//JJ] <zer I; zêřîn; zîv>

zêrandin زێـرانـدِن/**zêřandin** زێـرانـدِن [Ba3] *vt.* **(-zêrîn-/-zêřîn-** [Ba3]**).** to bother, torment, upset, oppress: •**Kuřo, Ûsivê min bînin, / řuĥê min *nezêřînin*, / ç'avê min vênesînin** (Ba3-3, #20) Boys, bring [me] my Joseph,/ *don't torment* my soul,/ don't extinguish my eyes. [Ba3/K/IFb/B/ZF3]

zêrevan زێرەڤان *m.&f.* **(-ê/;).** observer; guard. {also: <zîrevan> زیـــرەڤـــان (Hej)} {syn: *dîdevan; nêřevan} [Zeb/OK/ZF3/FS//Hej]

zêrevanî زێـــرەڤـــانـــی *f.* **(-ya;-yê).** observation, surveillance; guarding: •**Heke jinikekê biçûk nebin ... *dê zêrevanîyê* li jinikeka zayî *ket*, da ku heval biçûkê wê bidizît** (JH, 17) If a woman has no children [=cannot get pregnant] ... she *will keep watch over [or, spy on]* a woman in childbed, in order to steal her placenta •**Îran nabît zordarîyê û *zêrevanîya* paporên erebî li wê deverê *biket*** (Metîn 62[1997]:27) Iran may not bother or *spy on* the Arab steamboats in that region. {syn: ç'avdêrî; *dîdevanî; nêřevanî} =Sor çawdêrî چـاودێـری = 'supervision, attention' [JH/Metîn/Zeb/RF/ZF3/FS]

zêřgeř زێرگەڕ (B/JJ/GF/BF) = goldsmith. See **zêřker**.

zêrhel زێـــرهـــەل (FK-eb-2) = raised platform. See **herzal**.

zêringer زێرنگەر (Wkt) = goldsmith. See **zêřker**.

zêřingir زێرنگِر (FS/BF) = goldsmith. See **zêřker**.

zêřîn زێرین/**zêrîn** زێرین [F/A/IFb/JB1-S/GF/TF] *adj.* golden: •**saeta *zêrîn*** (IFb) *golden* watch. {also: [zärīn] زریـــن (JJ)} Cf. P zarrīn زرّیـــن; Sor zeřî زێڕی/ zêřîn زێرین [K/B/SC//F/A/IFb/JB1-S/GF/TF] <zêř>

zêřinger زێرینگەر (JB1-A/GF/ZF3) = goldsmith. See **zêřker**.

zêrkar زێرکار (F/ZF3) = goldsmith. See **zêřker**.

zêřker زێـــرکـــەر *m.* **(-ê;-î).** 1) goldsmith (JB1-A) [zêřinger]: •**Wan xişrên zêřî ji *zêřingirî* kiřîn** (FS) They bought the golden jewelry from *the goldsmith*; 2) gold merchant (JB1-A) [zêřk'iř]. {also: zêřgeř (B/GF/BF-2); zêringer (Wkt); zêřingir (FS/BF); zêřinger (JB1-A/GF-2/ZF3-2); zêrkar (F/ZF3-2); zêřkir (SC); zêřk'iř (JB1-A-2); [zerghiar زرگار /zérgher زرگر/zeringher زرینگر] (JJ)} OP dāraniyakara- (Kent); P zargar زرگر; Sor zeřenger زێڕەنگەر (W&E)/zêřger زێرگەر (K2) [K/IFb/ZF3//B/JJ/GF//Wkt//JB1-A//FS/BF//F//SC] <zêř; zîvker>

zêřkir زێرکِر (SC)/zêřk'iř زێرکِر (JB1-A) = goldsmith. See **zêřker**.

zêrû زێروو (GF) = leech. See **zûrî**.

zêřzemî زێرزەمی = basement. See **zêřzemîn**.

zêřzemîn زێـــرزەمـــیـــن *f.* **(-a;-ê).** basement, cellar; dungeon: •**Mîrê min, 'emir bike, bira padvala û *zêřzemîna* t'emam valakin û bidne t'emizkirinê** (Ba3-3, #34) My emir, give the order that all the *cellars* and dungeons should be emptied out and [then] have them cleaned. {also: jêrzemîn (ZF3/Wkt); zêřzemî (Ba3-3-2); [zir-zemin] زیـرزمـیـن (JJ)} {syn: padval} <P zīrzamīn زیـرزمـیـن [Ba3//JJ//ZF3/Wkt] <zîndan>

zêstan زێـــســـتـــان *f.* **().** woman after childbirth, in childbed (for 40 days): -**jinka zêstan** (FS) do. {also: zeyistan (Wkt-2); zeyîstan (A); zihistan (Hk)} {zeyîstanî; zêstanî; zihistanî; zîstanî} [GF/FS/Wkt//A//Hk]

zêstanî زێـــســـتـــانـــی *f.* **().** 40 days of childbed, confinement, accouchement, parturition. {also: zeyîstanî (Frq); zihistanî (Hk); zîstanî (Frq-2)} [Qzl/FJ/Wkt//Frq//Hk] <zayîn; zêstan>

zêtî زێـــتـــی (Haz) = visit by a married daughter to her father's house. See **zeyîtî**.

zêtûn زێتوون (JB3/OK) = olive. See **zeyt'ûn II**.

zêw زێـو *f.* **(-a;-ê).** festival, picnic held once a year at a shrine *(sheikh's tomb)*: -**Zêwa êlim** (Wkp) Kurdish summer holiday celebrated near Cizîra Botan; -**roja zêwê** (FS) do. {also: zêwek (GF-2); zêwî (A); cf. also [zivé] ضـیـوه (JJ) = 'hospice for the poor' (<Ar ḍayf ضـیـف = 'guest')} [Mdt/GF/ZF3/FS/Wkt/Wkp//A//JJ]

zêwek زێوەك (GF) = festival. See **zêw**.

zêwî زێوی (A) = festival. See **zêw**.

zêyî زێـیـی (B/Haz/Mzg) = married daughter or sister. See **zeyî**.

*zêyîn زێـیـیـن (Srk: Za?) = visit by a married daughter to her father's house. See **zeyîtî**.

zibara زبـــــارا (A) = communal work situation. See **zibare**.

zibar•e زبـــــارە *f.* **(•a;•ê).** 1) working together as a community: *social institution whereby a group of villagers pools their efforts to complete a task for one member of the group, e.g., building a house or harvesting the crop of each member of the group in turn, similar to American [quilting] bees* [T imece; clq Ar ṣabbeh صـــبّـــة]; "In Sisin, *zebarî* exists in the form of reciprocal and rotational types of communal work for one household each time. For instance, a household which has a labour shortage to finish some chore may specify a day as its *zebarî* and sends a child to all the village households asking them to take part in it. Each household thus is obliged to send one member at least. … The joint work lasts as long as a normal work day and is interrupted by several tea-breaks and at least one big meal (with rice and meat) all of which are provided by the *zebarî*-holding household. … [A] non-participating household would not expect anyone from the *zebarî*-holding household to attend its own *zebarî*. The rule is strictly reciprocal." [from: Lale Yalçın-Heckmann. *Tribe and Kinship among the Kurds* (Frankfurt a.M.: Peter Lang, 1991), p. 171]: **•Gundî bo Behremî çûn *zibarê*** (FS) The villagers went *to help* B. *with his task* **•Îro *zibara* mala Behremî ye** (FS) Today is *the zibare* for B.'s household; 2) corvée: "…various kinds of corvée which the Agha feels entitled to impose on each household; two or three days a year ploughing his land, or reaping and threshing; an occasional day cutting or collecting wood and leaves for firewood or winter fodder, laying bricks for a new house, clearing a canal, or going on an errand to the market town--all, of course, with the [peasants'] own tools or animals" [from: C. J. Edmonds. *Kurds, Turks and Arabs* (London: Oxford University Press, 1957), pp. 224-25]. {also: zibara (A); zibaretî (B); <zibare> زبـــــاره (HH)} {syn: p'alûte} Cf. Arc ṣībūrā צִיבוּרא = 'community, congregation'; = Sor herewez هەرەوەز [Haz/K/IFb/HH/GF/FS/BF/ZF3//A//B] <mitare>

zibaretî زِبــارەتـی (B) = communal work situation. See **zibare**.

zibil زِبـل *f./m.(FS/BF)* **(-a/-ê;-ê/).** 1) {syn: r̄îx; sergîn} dung, manure; {syn: peyîn (JJ); terş I} horse manure: **-ziblê diwara** (FS) horse manure; **-ziblê pezî** (FS) sheep dung; 2) garbage, refuse, rubbish (K). {also: zibîl (B); zivil (IFb-2); [zibil] زبـل (JJ); <zibil> زبل (HH)} Cf. Ar zibl زبل; Sor zibił زِبڵ = 'rubbish' [AB/K/IFb/JJ/HH/GF/FS/ZF3//B] <bişkul/pişkul; ç'êrt; dirg; guhûr; k'erme; keşkûr; peyîn; qelax; r̄îx; sergîn; sergo; sêklot; terş I; zirîç>

zibîl زبیل (B) = dung; garbage. See **zibil**.

zift زِفـــــت *f.* **(;-ê).** tar, pitch: **•Ew ketiye nava *qîr û ziftê*** (ZZ-7, 251) He fell into *tar and pitch*. {also: zivt (ZZ-7-2); [zift] زفـت (JJ); <zift> زفـت (HH)} {syn: qîr I} < Ar zift زفت; Sor zift زِفت [ZZ/K/IFb/FJ/GF/TF/JJ/HH/CS/SS/Wkt]

zih زِه (ZF3) = cow's uterus. See **zî**.

ziha I زِها (Z-1/FS) = dry. See **ziwa**.

ziha II زِها (A/FS) = dragon. See **zîha**.

zihar زِهار (IFb) = dragon. See **zîha**.

zihin زِهِن (L) = saddle. See **zîn I**.

zihistan زِهِســـتـان (Hk) = woman in childbed. See **zêstan**.

zihistanî زِهِستانی (Hk) = childbed, confinement. See **zêstanî**.

zihî زِهـــــی (GF) = visit by a married daughter to her father's house. See **zeyîtî**.

zihniyet زهـنـیـەت *f.* **(-a;-ê).** mentality, mindset: **•Bi derketina rojnameya 'Welat' re qelşeke mezin li dîwarê *vê zihniyeta* zirarker ket** (diyarname.com 18.iii.2009) With the issuing of the newspaper 'Welat', a big crack appeared in the wall of *this* harmful *mindset* **•Bi *vê zihniyetê* meseleya Kurd çareser nabe** (dogruhaber.com.tr 26.iii.2016) With *this mentality* the Kurdish issue will not be solved. < Ar ḏihnīyah ذهنية [='aqlīyah عقلية] --> T zihniyet [diyarname/ZF3]

zihya زِهيا = dry. See **ziwa**.

zik زِك *m.* **(-ê;).** 1) stomach, belly; abdomen: **•Bizina kûvî strûê xwe tûj li *zikê* wî dixe** (J) The wild (nanny) goat drives her horns into his *belly* **•Zikê t'êr haj zikê birçî t'une** (K)/**Zikê t'êr haj ê birçî t'ineye** (Dz-#1632) A full *stomach* doesn't understand a hungry one *[prv.]* **•*Zikê* xizanan tim birçî ye** (AB) The stomachs of the poor are always empty [lit. '*The stomach of* the poor is always hungry']; **-zikekî t'êr, duda birçî** (XF) poor, half-starved, on an empty stomach, in dire straits [lit. 'one full stomach [for every] two hungry']: **•Heşt sal bi *zikekî* têr û pazdeyî birçî min li hucreyên feqehan xwend** (Wlt 2:66, 2) For eight years I studied theology, more dead than alive [lit. 'with one full belly and 15 hungry ones']; 2) [*prep.*] inside, in {syn: nav III}: **•*zikê* ȟewşê** (K) *inside* the courtyard; 3) [*adv.*] inside, in {syn: hindur̄}: **•Ez bernedam *zik*** (Ad) I was not allowed *inside*/They wouldn't let me in. {also: sik II (BK-2/HB-2); [zik] زك (JJ); <zik> زك (HH)} Sor sik سِــك/zig زِگ = 'belly, womb' [F/K/A/JB3/IFb/B/JJ/HH/BK/SK/JB1-S/GF/TF/BF/FS]

zikak زِكـــاك *f.* **(-a;-ê).** street: **•Ji bona vî qasî navê vê *zikakê* bûye *zikaka* fitnê** (H, v. 2, 830 [1941, 9:34]) Hence the name of this *street* became '*Street* of intrigue' **•li *zikaka* û li ewcane** (L-v. 2, Sebrî) in *the streets* and alleys. {also: soqaq (F); [zouqaq] زقــــاق (JJ); <zikak> زكــاك (HH)} {syn: ca‘de; kolan II; kûçe; zaboq} Cf. Ar zuqāq زقــــاق = 'lane, alley' -->T sokak = 'sidestreet' [L-v. 2, Sebrî/K/IFb/HH/ZF3/Wkt//F//JJ] <dirb I; ‘ewc; r̄ê>

zikçûn زكـچــوون *f.* **(;-ê).** diarrhea, dysentery: •***Zikçûnê* ew girtiye** (FS) He has come down with *diarrhea* [lit. 'D. has seized him']. {also: cf. [zik cit (G)/zik čū (Lx)] (JJ); <zikçûn> زك چون (Hej)} {syn: nav IV; navêş} Sor sikçûn سِــكــچـــوون = sikeşore سِكەشۆرە [Bw/JJ/GF/OK/RZ/Hej/ZF3/BF/FS]

zikkêşkî زككێشكى *f.* **().** 1) crawling on one's belly: •**Teker rahişt şaşika xwe û *bi zikkişkê* vegeriya mala xwe** (HYma, 50) T. grabbed his turban and returned home *crawling on his belly*; 2) [*adv.*] on one's belly; prone, face down: •**Zar̄oyê wan *zik kêşkî* diçit** (FS) Their child goes/crawls *on his belly*. {also: zikkişkî (Kmc/GF-2)} {syn: *serdev; *serzik} < zik = 'belly' + k'êşîn/k'işîn 'to pull' [HYma/FJ/GF/FS/ZF3//Kmc] <dever̄û>

zikkişkî زككِشكى (Kmc/GF) = (crawling) on one's belly. See **zikkêşkî.**

zikmakî زِكماكى *adj.* natural, native; innate, inborn, instinctive, congenital: •**Koratîya wî *zikmakî* ye** (FS) His blindness is *congenital*; **-nesaxîyên zikmakî** (FS) congenital diseases; **-zimanê zikmakî** (Ber/Wlt/K[s]) mother tongue, native language: •**Ew mirovên ku *zimanê* wan ê *zikmakî* ji wan tê standin tu mane û rûmetekî jiyanê li ba wan namîne** (Wlt) Life loses its meaning [lit. 'no meaning or respect for life remains'] for those people whose *native language* is taken away from them •***Zimanê zikmakî* û mafên mirovên biyanî di vî warî de** (Ber 5/86, 15) One's *mother tongue* and the rights of foreigners in this regard. {also: [zik-i maki زكــى/ماكى/zikimaki زكيماكى] (JJ); <zikmakî> زكماكى (HH)} Cf. Sor sikmak سِــكـــمــاك = 'congenital, hereditary' <zik = 'belly' + mak = 'mother' [Wlt/Ber/K/A/IFb/HH/GF/FS//JJ]

zikr̄eş زكــرِەش *adj.* 1) *(lit.)* blackbellied: •**Sê bra ne: hersê bra *zikreş* in [dûstan]** (L #13, 232) Three brothers, all three *with black bellies* [or, *spiteful*] *[rdl.: ans.: tripod]*; 2) *(fig.)* spiteful, malicious, malevolent, rancorous, resentful. {also: <zikreş> زكــــــرش (HH)} < zik = 'belly' + r̄eş = 'black' [Hk/Zeb/K/A/IFb/HH/GF/TF]

zikr̄eşî زكـــــــرِەشــــــى *f.* **(-ya;-yê).** spite, malice, malevolence, rancor. [K/A/IFb/GF/TF/FS]

zikt'êr زِكــتێـر *adj.* full, sated, with one's belly full: •**Mîna gayekî *ziktêr* Benîşto ketibû xeweke giran û kûr** (HYma, 33) Like a bull *with a full belly*, B. fell into a heavy and deep slumber. {syn: t'êr I} [HYma/K/GF/FJ]

zil زل *f./m.(FS/BF/Wkt)* **(;-ê/).** reed, bulrush. {also: <zil> زل (HH)} {syn: leven; qamîş; qeram} [Qzl/A/IFb/B/HH/GF/TF/FS/BF/Wkt]

zilam زِلام *m.* **(-ê; zilêm, vî zilamî).** man; fellow, guy, chap, bloke; young fellow: •**Ev *zilamê* ha yan mirovekî zehf eḧmeq e, yan mirovekî zehf mezin e** (Rnh 2:17, 307) This *fellow* is either a very stupid man, or a very great man. {also: zelam (K/BF-2/FS-2); z̲elam (JB1-A); zulam} {syn: kabra; meriv; mêr I; mirov; peya I} Cf. Syrian Ar zalameh زلـمة [*pl.* zlām زلام] = 'man, fellow'; Sor zelam زەلام {zilamî; zilamtî} [L/A/IFb/B/JB1-S/GF/TF/BF//K//JB1-A]

zilamî زِلامى (IFb) = manliness. See **zilamtî.**

zilamtî زِلامـــــتـــــى *f.* **(-ya;).** manhood, manliness, masculinity; humanity: •**Çi *zelamînî* li nik vî kurî nîne!** (BF) There is no *manliness* (or, *humanity*) in this boy! •**Kêm kesa *zelamînîya* wekî ya wî heye** (FS) Few people have the *manliness* (or, *humanity*) that he has. {also: zelamînî (BF/FS); zilamî (IFb-2)} [A/IFb/TF//BF/FS]

zilketk زلـكـتك *f.* **(-a;-ê).** wasp, zool. *Vespida*: •**Paşî ku te xilêf dirust kirin, here, hindek *zirkêtan* bigire** (SK 35:314) After you have made the baskets, go and catch some *wasps*. {also: zirkête (SK/RZ); zirkêtk (IFb/RZ-2/FS/BF); [zerkék (G-sic)/zirkit (Rh)] زركت (JJ)} {syn: moz I; *pîzang} [Bw/Zeb//SK/RZ//IFb/FS/BF] <kur̄îfok; mêş; stêng; şehna zilketka>

ziloq زلوق (ZF/ZZ) = wide-eyed. See **zîq.**

zilpik زلپك (Ak) = pimple. See **zipik.**

zilût زلووت (BZ/IFb) = naked; bald. See **zelût.**

zimag زِماگ (Kmc) = shady side. See **zimank.**

zimak زِماك (ZF3) = shady side. See **zimank.**

ziman زِمــان *m.* **(-ê; zimên/zimîn** [B], **vî zimanî).** 1) tongue: **-p'ê li zimanê hev kirin** (XF/EP-7) to be so crowded, that there's no room for a pin to fall; to be up to one's nose in ... [lit. 'to put [their] feet on one another's tongues']: •**Şikyatçî *p'ê zimanê hev dikin*** (Z-1) We're up to our necks in plaintiffs [lit. 'Plaintiffs *are stepping on each other's tongues*'] [*of people coming to the court to air* *their complaints*]; 2) language: •**Şûrê vî *zimanî* qelem e** (AB) The sword of this *language* is the pen; **-zimanê zikmakî** (Ber/Wlt/K[s]) mother tongue, native language; **-zimanên biyanî** = foreign languages. {also: ezman II (Bw); 'ezman II (SK); zman (JB3/IFb-2); [ziman] زمـــــــان (JJ); <ziman> زمــــان (HH)} Proto IE *źhiźhu'ā-: Skt jihvā *f.* <*ĝhiĝhuH- (*perhaps* *ĝhuH- *with reduplication*) cf. √hva- = 'to call'; proto Ir *hizū- *f.*/hiz(u)u̯ā- *f.*/hiz(u)u̯an- (*acc.* hizu̯ānam) *m.*: O P hizānam (*acc.*); Sgd (ə)zβāk; Mid P h(u)zwān (Pahlavi)/izwān (Manichaean) & uzwān/zuwān (M3); P zabān زبان; Sor ziman زِمان; Za zuwan *m.* (Todd); Hau zûan *m.* (M4); cf. also Lat lingua/ dingua; Rus iazyk язык; Germ Zunge *(no nasal in Indo-Iranian)*. See: E. Benveniste. "Études sur le Vieux-Perse," *Bulletin de la Société de Linguistique de Paris* 47 (1951), 22-23. [F/K/A/IFb/B/ JJ/HH/GF/TF/OK/BK/Msr//Bw//SK//JB3] <r̄êziman>

zimandirêj زمـــانــــدرێـــژ *adj.* 1) {syn: devjihev} talkative, blabbermouth: •**Ya ferĥîto, tu çi ferĥîtekî *ziman dirêj*î** (Z-2, 68) Hey ifreet, what a *big mouthed* ifreet you are!; 2) impudent, insolent, smart-aleck: •**Xelkê wî gundî qewî *'ezman-dirêj* û cablos û bê-şerm in** (SK 12:114) The people of that village are very *impudent* and cunning and shameless. {also: 'ezman-dirêj (SK); zmandrêj (IFb)} Cf. P zabān'darāz زبــــان دراز = 'abusive, insolent'; Sor zimandirêj زمانِدرێژ = 'abusive' [Z-2/ K/A/B/GF/TF//IFb//SK] <geveze; ĥur̄; p'arsûstûr>

zimandirêjî زمانـدرێژی f. **(-ya;-yê).** 1) talkativeness; 2) impudence, insolence: •**Belê cezaê bê-edebî û *'ezman-dirêjîya* hingo ewe ye hingo bişelînim, da çu car dî wan terze bê-edebîyane neken** (SK 13:126) But the punishment for your rudeness and *insolence* is that I should strip [=rob] you, so that you aren't ever so rude again. {also: 'ezman-dirêjî (SK); zmandrêjî (IFb)} Cf. P zabān'darāzī زبــــان درازی = 'abusiveness'; Sor zimandirêjî زمانِدرێژی [SK//K/A/B/GF/TF//IFb]

zimank زمـانـك *f.* **().** the northern side, shady side *(of mountain)*. {also: zimag (Kmc-#7622/ZF3); zimak (ZF3-2)} {syn: dubur; nizar I} [S&E (Azer)//Kmc/ZF3] <nizar I>

zimanzan زمــانــزان *m.&f.* **().** linguist: •**Lê berî lîjne bihêt Îraqê daxaz ji hindek *zimanzan* û xemxur û zanayên Kurdan kir ku rêzimanekê bo zarokên devera Kurdistanê berhevken** (Metîn 77[1998], 50) But before the committee came to Iraq, it asked some Kurdish *linguists* and intellectuals to put together a grammar [book] for children of the region of Kurdistan. {also: zmanzan (IFb)} Cf. P zabān'šinās زبــــان شــنــاس; Sor zimanzan زِمانزان. *The forms **zimannas** and **zimanvan** have also been proposed.* {zimanzanî[nî]} [(neol)Metîn/K/B/ GF/TF/RF/ZF3/Wkt//IFb]

zimanzanî زِمـانــزانـی *f.* **(-ya;-yê).** linguistics. {also: zimanzanînî (K)} Cf. P zabān'šināsī زبـان شـنـاسـی [GF/TF/RF/ZF3/Wkt//K] <zimanzan>

zimanzanînî زِمـــانـــزانـــیـــنـــی (K) = linguistics. See **zimanzanî**.

zinaker زناکەر (GF/JJ) = adulterer. See **zinêk'ar**.

zinar I زنـــار *m./f.(Zeb)* **(-ê/-a; zinêr, vî zinarî/).** cliff, rock, crag; massive rock, boulder; jagged rock (JB3): •**Keç'ik r̄adibe ser *zinêr*** (J) The girl gets up (=climbs) onto *the cliff* •**Wexta mêriv li wan *zinarêd* ter̄ikî dinihêr̄î, 'ecêb dima** (Ba2:1, 203) When one looked at those huge *crags*, one was astounded. {also: nisar (IFb-2); nizar II (K[s]); zindar (Ag); zinnar (BK); [zinar زنـار/nizar نـزار] (JJ); <zinar> زنـــار (HH)} {syn: qeya} [J/K/IFb/B/JJ/ HH/GF/Bw//Ag//BK//K(s)] <çelexte>

zinar II زنار (A/IFb/TF) = shady side. See **nizar I**.

zincîr زنـجـیر *f.* **(-a;-ê).** 1) chain: •**Bi Xwedê wê ez bi *zincîrekê* li ber dêrî girêdam** (ZZ-10, 152) By God, she bound me with *a chain* before the door; 2) {syn: çîdar; qeyd} fetters, manacles, handcuffs. {also: zencîr (JB3); [zendjir] زنـــجـــیـــر (JJ)} Cf. P zanjīr زنجیر --> T zincir; Sor zincîr زنجیر [K/A/IFb/ B/SK/ZF//JB3/JJ]

zindan زنـــــــدان *f./m.(Ba3)* **(-a/ ;-ê/zindên).** 1) {syn: girtîgeh; ĥebs} prison, jail (gaol), dungeon: •[**Memu Alan avêtin *zindanê***] (HM) They threw Memo Alan into *prison*; 2) underground chamber: •**Hatin ser devê *zindîyana* go her ro didîn Qambihistê-rî-gaz jê derdiket. Carkê nerîn go şerîtek pê ve girêdaye bi darekî û berdaye di *zindîyanê* de, hema hindurê *zindîyanê* reş e, tarî ye, binê wê ne xwîya e** (L-I, #4, 104, l. 21-25) They came to the opening of the *under-ground chamber* that they saw Tom Thumb come out of every day. They saw that he tied a rope to a stick and let it down into *the chamber*; inside *the chamber* it's black, it's dark, you can't see its bottom [i.e., how deep it is]. {also: singdan (Z-2); zindiyan (HM); zindîyan (L); zîndan (zîndên) (K/

B/IFb-2); [zindan] زنـــدان (JJ); <zindan> زنـــدان (HH)} Cf. Ar zinzānah زنـــزانـــة; T zindan; Sor zîndan زیندان [HM//L//K/B//A/IFb/JJ/HH/GF//Z-2]

zindar زِندار (Ag) = cliff. See **zinar**.

zindiyan زِندِیان (HM) = prison, dungeon. See **zindan**.

zindî I زِندى (IFb/HH/GF/TF/ZF3) = alive. See **zêndî**.

zindîyan زِنديیان (L) = prison, dungeon. See **zindan**.

zinêk'ar زِنێکار *m.* **().** adulterer: •**Bîst jinên te hene, bandana te ji çire ye, tu *zinêkar* î, jinên te bê mehr in** (RN 3:52, 2) You have twenty wives, who are you to make the call to prayers, you are an *adulterer*, your wives are not properly married [to you]. {also: zinaker (GF); zînakar (IFb/OK); [zina-ker/zenakār (G/PS)] زنـاکـر (JJ)} {syn: tol I; tolaz} [RN/K/A/B//GF/JJ//IFb/OK] <çavlider>

zingar زِنگار (JB3) = rust; mildew. See **jeng** & **zeng**.

zingarî زِنـــگـــارى (JB1-A) = rusty. See **jengarî** & **zengarî**.

zingazing زِنگازِنگ (GF) = jingling. See **zinge-zing**.

zinge-zing [Alkan/K]/**zingezing** [A/B] زِنـگـەزِنـگ *f.* **(-a;-ê).** jingling, tinkling (of metal bells); rattling, clanging: •***zinge-zinga* zengilê keriyên pêz** (Alkan, 71) *the tinkling of* the bell of the sheep flocks. {also: zingazing (GF)} [Alkan/K/A/IFb/B/GF]

zingil زِنگِل (Sw-#18) = bell. See **zengil**.

zingîn زِنگین (F) = rattling, clanking. See **şingîn**.

zinnar زِننار (BK) = cliff. See **zinar**.

zipik زِپِك *f.* **().** pimple: •***Zîpik* li rûyê wê hatine** (FS) She got *pimples* on her face. {also: **pizik**; zilpik (Ak); zipîk (A); zîpik II (GF/FS/BF); <zipik> زپك (HH)} [Ak//Zeb/IFb/HH//A//GF/FS/BF] See also **pizik**.

zipîk زِپیك (A) = pimple. See **zipik**.

ziq زِق (KS/ZF3) = wide-eyed. See **zîq**.

ziqre زِقره (Wkt) = mountain pass. See **zuxir**.

ziqûm زِقووم *f.* **(-a;-ê).** 1) {syn: jale; r̄ûl} oleander; 2) *word used in oaths, curses, etc.* < Ar zaqqūm زقّـــوم = 'infernal tree with bitter fruit'; Sor zeqûm زەقـــــووم = 'name of a tree in hell' [IFb/B/ZF3/Wkt] <sinc>

zirar زِرار *f.* **(-a;-ê).** 1) damage, injury, harm {syn: xesar; zîyan}: •**Çi *zirar* hatye serê Ûsib, ji destê biraye** (Ba) Whatever *harm* has befallen Joseph is at the hands of his brothers •**Ma *zerara* pêz tê de heye an na?** (LM, 11) Is there *harm for* the sheep in it or not? (i.d., Is it bad for the sheep or not?) •**Paşî mar hate pêş, got "*Zerera* min mezintir e"** (SK 1:6) Then the snake came forward and said, "The harm I inflict is greater [lit., My *injury* is greater]"; -**zirar dayîn** (B)/~ **gihandin** (Zeb) to damage, injure, harm, hurt: •**Gundê me da kesekî dil nedikir wîr̄a gulaş bigirta, lê wekî nişkêva yekî dil bikira, ewî ew hildibir̄î jorê û, wekî *zirarê nedê*, fesal dadanî ser piştê** (Ba2:1, 204) In our village no one would dare to wrestle with him, but if suddenly someone were to dare, he would pick that person up and, so as *not to harm him*, carefully put him on his back •**Teyrokê *zirar da* me** (B) The hail *injured* us; 2) [*adj.*] damaging, harmful, injurious: •**Cixare k'işandin *zirar*e** (B) Cigarette smoking is *harmful*. {also: zerar (F/IFb/OK); zerer (JB3/SK/OK-2); [zerer ضــــــــرر/zerar ضــرار] (JJ)} < Ar ḍarār ضــرار --> T zarar [F/IFb/JJ//K/B//JB3/SK/OK]

zirav I زِراڤ *adj.* 1) {syn: jar I; lawaz; leẍer; narîn; qels I; qor̄ III; zeyf; ≠k'ok;≠qelew} thin, slim, slender, lean; 2) soft *(of voices, sounds, etc.)*: •**Dengê dya me *zirav*e** (J) Our mother's voice is *soft*. {also: [ziraw] ظـــــــراڤ (JJ); <zirav> زراڤ (HH)} {zirav[t]î} [Krç/K/A/JB3/IFb/B/HH/JB1-S/GF/TF//JJ] <qîq>

zirav II زِراڤ *m.* **(; zirêv).** 1) bile, gall: -**êşa zirav** (BR) tuberculosis, TB; 2) gall-bladder: -**ziravê *fk-ê* qetîya** (XF) for one's heart to sink to one's boots, to get good and scared [lit. 'one's gall bladder split': see also **ziravqetî**]; 3) courage, pluck (HH). {also: ziravik (IFb); [ziraw] زراڤ (JJ); <zirav> ظـراڤ (HH)} Cf. P zardāb زرداب = 'bile, gall'; Sor ziraw زِراو = 'gall, courage' [F/K/A/B/JJ//IFb//HH] <fater̄eşk; hinav; k'ezeb; p'işik>

ziravik زِراڤِك (IFb) = gall; gall-bladder. See **zirav II**.

ziravî زِراڤـــى *f.* **(-ya;-yê).** 1) thinness, slenderness; 2) softness *(of voices, sounds, etc.)*: •***ziravîya* axaftina wan** (tirşik.net:Keçên kurd 16.xi.2014) *the softness of* their speaking. {also: ziravtî (B-2)} [K/A/JB3/IFb/B/GF/TF/ZF3] <zirav I>

ziravqetî زِراڤقەتى *adj./pp.* scared, frightened, afraid, terrified: •**Rûvî *ziravqetîyayîne*, tirsonekin** (Z-904) Foxes are *scaredy-cats*, they're cowards. {also: ziravqetîyayî (Z-904); [ziraw qetiiaié] زراڤ قطيايه (JJ)} <ziravê fk-ê qetîya = 'one's gall bladder split', i.e., 'one got good and scared' [Z-904/JJ//K/B/ZF3] <zirav II>

ziravqetîyayî زِراڤقەتـيـايـى (Z-904) = frightened. See **ziravqetî** .

ziravtî زِراڤـتـــى (B) = thinness; softness (of sounds) . See **ziravî**.

zirazir زِرازِر (GF/HH) = braying. See **zir̄ezir**.

zir̄bab زِرباب (FS/BF) = stepfather. See **zir̄bav**.

zir̄bav زِرباڤ *m.* **(-ê;-ê [B]).** stepfather. {also: zir̄bab (FS/BF); [zir-bab] ضربـاب (JJ); <z̲irbab> ظـربـاب (HH)} {syn: bavmarî (JB3)} < Ar ḍirr ضـــــرّ = 'polygamy, addition of second wife to one's household' + bav = 'father' [F/K/IFb/B/GF/TF/ZF3//FS/BF/JJ//HH] <dêmar̄î; zir̄bira; zir̄dayîk; zir̄xesû; zir̄xweh>

zir̄bira زِربِرا *m.* **(-yê;).** stepbrother. < Ar ḍirr ضـرّ = 'polygamy, addition of second wife to one's household' + bira = 'brother'; Sor zir̄-bira [K/GF/ZF3/FS/BF] <bavmarî; dêmar̄î; zir̄bav; zir̄dayîk; zir̄xesû; zir̄xweh>

zirç زرچ (GF) = bird droppings. See **zirîç I**.

zirda زِردا (A/IFb) = stepmother. See **zir̄dayîk**.

zirdayik زِردايك (ZF3) = stepmother. See **zir̄dayîk**.

zir̄dayîk زِردايــيــك *f.* **(-a;).** stepmother. {also: zirda (A-2/IFb); zirdayik (ZF3); zir̄dayk (FS/BF); zirdê (ZF3-2)} {syn: dêmar̄î; jinbav} < Ar ḍirr ضـــرّ = 'polygamy, addition of second wife to one's household' + dayîk, variant of dê = 'mother'; Sor zir̄-dak زِرداك/zir̄-dayk زِردايــك [K/A//ZF3//FS/BF//IFb] <bavmarî; -ĥilî I; nevisî; zir̄bav; zir̄bira; zir̄xesû; zir̄xweh>

zir̄dayk زِردايك (FS/BF) = stepmother. See **zir̄dayîk**.

zirdê زردێ (ZF3) = stepmother. See **zir̄dayîk**.

zirehpûş زِرەهـپـووش (GF/FD) = armored vehicle: car, ship, tank. See **zirîpoş**.

zirexpûş زرەخپووش (CS) = armored vehicle: car, ship, tank. See **zirîpoş**.

zir̄ezir زِرەزِر *f.* **(-a;-ê).** bray(ing) of donkeys: •...**yan jî ku *zire zira* kera mê dibihîze** (HYma 11) Or else he hears *the braying of* a female donkey. {also: zirazir (GF); <zirazir> ظـراظـر (HH)} Sor zer̄e زەڕە [HYma/K/B/A/IFb/FJ/CS//GF/HH] <zir̄în>

zirê زری (A/ZF3) = armor. See **zirx**.

zirêç زرێـــــــــــچ *m./f.(JB3)* **(-ê/; /-ê).** lead *(chemical element Pb)*. {also: zirîç II (IFb/ZF3/FS); zrêç, f. (JB3/IFb-2); [ziridji] زريـجـی (JJ); <zirîç> زريـچ (HH)} {syn: qerqeşûn I} Cf. Mid P arzīz = 'tin, lead' (M3); = Sor miz مز & sirb سِرب [Bx//JB3//JJ//HH//IFb/ZF3/FS]

zirgêzer زِرگێزەر (IF) = carrot. See **gizêr**.

zirih زِرِه (HH/ZF3) = armor. See **zirx**.

zirihpûş زرِهپووش (ZF3) = armored vehicle: car, ship, tank. See **zirîpoş**.

zirik زِرك (OK)/zir̄ik زِرِك (Zeb) = lye. See **zir̄k**.

zirî I زری (FS) = leech. See **zûrî**.

zirî II زری (BF/ZF3) = armor. See **zirx**.

zirîç I زريچ *f.* **().** bird droppings. {also: zirç (GF); zîrç (A/ZF3); zîr̄ç' (SC)} {syn: ç'êrt} Cf. Arm cirt (W: jird) ծիրտ; Ar ḏarq ذرق/zarq زرق [IFb/BF//GF//A/ZF3//SC] <gû; r̄îtin; sergîn>

zirîç II زِريچ (IFb/ZF3/FS) = lead (metal). See **zirêç**.

zirîhpoş زِريـهـپـۆش (ZF3) = armored vehicle: car, ship, tank. See **zirîpoş**.

zir̄în زِريــن *vi.* **(-zir̄-/-zirê- [IF]).** 1) to bray *(donkey)*; 2) to bawl, yell, cry out, howl, wail (K). {also: [zerin] زرين (JJ); <z̲irîn ظـريـن (diz̲irî) (دظـرى)> (HH)} Cf. Sor zer̄în زەڕيــن = 'to bray' [K/A/IFb/B/M-Ak/SK/GF/TF//HH//JJ] <k'er III; zir̄ezir>

zirîpoş زريــپــۆش *f.* **(-a;-ê).** 1) armored car: **-erebeya zirihpûş** (ZF3) do.; 2) armor-plated warship; 3) armored tank: •**Amerîka dê 250 *zirîpoşan* bişîne Îraqê** (waarmedia.com 13.xii.2014) America will send 250 *tanks* to Iraq. {also: zirehpûş (GF/FD); zirexpûş (CS); zirihpûş (ZF3); zirîhpoş (ZF3-2); zirîpûş (ZF3-2)} [waarmedia/FJ/BF/GF/FD//ZF3//CS] <zirx>

zirîpûş زريــپــووش (ZF3) = armored vehicle: car, ship, tank. See **zirîpoş**.

zir̄k زِرك/**zirk** زرك *f.* **(-a;-ê).** lye (strong alkaline liquor made from ashes used for making soap or for making raisins out of grapes): **-ava zir̄kê** (FS) lye water: •**Berê xelkî cilik bi *ava zir̄kê* dişûştin** (FS) Formerly people would wash their clothes with *lye water*. {also: zirik (OK); zir̄ik (Zeb)} [Bw//Zeb/FS//OK]

zirkête زِركێتە (SK/RZ) = wasp. See **zilketk**.

zirkêtk زِركێتك (IFb/RZ/FS/BF) = wasp. See **zilketk**.

zirna زِرنـا (TF/BF)/zir̄na زِرنـا (FS) = oboe-like reed instrument. See **zirne**.

zirnabêj زِرنـابێـژ *m.* **(-ê;).** one who plays the zurna. {also: zir̄neçî (K)/zirneçî (OK-2); zirnejen (ZF3-2); zirnevan (A/IFb/GF/AD/ZF3); zur̄neçî (B)} [Bw/OK/BF//K//B//A/IFb/GF/AD/ZF3] <diholkut; zirne>

zirnazîq زِرنازيق/**zir̄nazîq** زِرنازيق [FS] *f.* **(;-ê).** see saw, teeter-totter: •**Zar̄o li *zir̄nazîqê* siyar bûn** (FS) The children got on *the see saw*. {also: zeranîq (GF-2); zerzaniq (IFb); zerzanîq (GF); zirnazoq (Mrd); <zerzanîq> زرزانـيـق (HH)} {syn: qir̄neqos; zîqûzir̄} Sor zerzanîq زەرزانـيـق [Bingöl/Stewr/Dyr/Amûd//Mrd/ZF3//FS//GF/HH//IFb]

zirnazoq زِرنازۆق (Mrd) = see saw. See **zirnazîq**.

zirn•e زِرنـــــــــــە *f.* **(•eya;•ê).** zurna (or zurla), a reed instrument resembling an oboe, which emits a loud, shrill sound; it is accompanied by a drum (*dehol*, qv.); most folk dances are danced to the *zirne* and *dehol* (or def û zirne): •**Miṯrib *zir̄nayê* lê didin** (FS) Roma musicians play *the zurna*; **-def û zirne** = drum and zurna. {also: zirna (TF/BF); zir̄na (FS); zorne (JB1-S); zurna; zur̄ne (B); [zourné] زرنه (JJ); <zirne> ظرنه (HH)} Cf. P surney سرنى, T zurna; Sor zur̄na زوڕنا; Za zirrna f. (Todd) [K/A/IFb/GF/ZF3//TF/BF//FS//JB1-S//B//JJ//HH] <borîzan; dehol; govend; nefîr>

zir̄neçî زِڕنەچى (K)/zirneçî زِرنەچى (OK) = zurna player. See **zirnabêj**.

zirnejen زرنەژەن (ZF3) = zurna player. See **zirnabêj**.

zirnevan زِرنەڤان (A/IFb/GF/AD/ZF3) = zurna player. See **zirnabêj**.

zirt زِرت *f.* **(-a;-ê).** boasting, bragging; bluster, nonsense: •**Zirt<a> ji xo nede!** (HR 3:67) Quit bragging! or, Quit blustering! {also: [zyrt] ضرط (JJ) = 'fart'; <ẓirt> ظرت (HH Cf. Ar ḍarṭ ضرط = 'fart'; Sor zirt زِرت = 'wide open and gleaming (eyes)' [HR/K/A/IFb/FJ/TF/GF/CS/JJ/HH/ZF3]

zirtek زِرتەك *m.* **(-ê;).** 1) boaster, braggart, blowhard; 2) chatterbox, gossip; bullshitter, one full of hot air; 3) {syn: balbas; piştmêr} bodyguard, henchman: **-zirtekêt ax̄ay** (Dh) the agha's bodyguards; 4) {syn: qeşmer; qirdik; şemo} clown: **-zirtekê pehlewên** (Qmş) do. {also: zirtekar (FJ-2); zirto (K/IF-2/BF-2/FD-2); zirtok (K-2/GF-2/FJ-2); zirtole (BF-2); zirtonek (IFb-2/BF-2); <ẓirt ظرت/ẓirtek ظرتك/ ẓirtker ظرتكر> (HH)} [Dh/Qmş/IFb/FJ/GF/TF/HH/BF/ZF3/FD//K] <zirt; zordar>

zirtekar زِرتەكار (FJ) = braggart; gossip; bodyguard; clown. See **zirtek**.

zirto زِرتۆ (K/IF/BF/FD) = braggart; gossip; bodyguard; clown. See **zirtek**.

zirtok زِرتۆك (K/GF/FJ) = braggart; gossip; bodyguard; clown. See **zirtek**.

zirtole زِرتۆلە (BF) = braggart; gossip; bodyguard; clown. See **zirtek**.

zirtonek زِرتۆنەك (IFb/BF) = braggart; gossip; bodyguard; clown. See **zirtek**.

zirx زِرخ *f./m.(FS/Wkt/ZF3)* **(-a/-ê;-ê/-î).** coat of mail, hauberk; armor. {also: zerî II, m. (S&E/K-2); zirê (A/ZF3-2); zirih (ZF3); zirî II (BF/ZF3-2); [ziri زرى /zirkh زرخ] (JJ); <zirih> زره (HH)} {syn: ç'ek; r̄ext} Cf. P zirh زره --> T zırh; Ar zarad زرد & dir' درع [S&E//K/IFb/B/JJ/GF/FD//HH/ZF3//A//BF]

zir̄xesû زِڕخەسوو *f.* **(-ya;).** stepmother-in-law. {also: <ẕirxesû> ظرخسو (HH)} < Ar ḍirr ضرّ = 'polygamy, addition of second wife to one's household' + xesû = 'mother-in-law'; Sor zir̄-xesû زڕخەسوو [A/IFb/FS/BF/ZF3//HH] <bavmarî; dêmar̄î; xesû; zir̄bav; zir̄bira; zir̄dayîk; zir̄xweh>

zir̄xezûr زِڕخەزوور *m.* **().** stepfather-in-law. {also: <ẕirxezûr> ظرخزور (HH)} < Ar ḍirr ضرّ = 'polygamy, addition of second wife to one's household' + xezûr = 'father-in-law'; Sor zir̄-xezûr زڕخەزوور [IFb/BF/ZF3//HH] <bavmarî; dêmar̄î; xesû; zir̄bav; zir̄bira; zir̄dayîk; zir̄xesû; zir̄xweh>

zir̄xuşk زِڕخوشك (FS) = stepsister. See **zir̄xweh**.

zirxwe زِرخوه (GF) = stepsister. See **zir̄xweh**.

zir̄xweh زِڕخوەه *f.* **(-a;).** stepsister. {also: zir̄xuşk (FS); zirxwe (GF); zirxweyîng (GF-2); zirxwîşk (GF-2)} < Ar ḍirr ضرّ = 'polygamy, addition of second wife to one's household' + xweh, variant of xûşk = 'sister'; Sor zir̄-xuşk زڕخوشك [K/BF//GF//FS] <bavmarî; dêmar̄î; xûşk; zir̄bav; zir̄bira; zir̄dayîk>

zirxweyîng زِرخوەيينگ (GF) = stepsister. See **zir̄xweh**.

zirxwîşk زِرخويشك (GF) = stepsister. See **zir̄xweh**.

zirzûl زرزوول (ZF3) = starling. See **zerzûr**.

zistan زِستان (SK) = winter. See **zivistan**.

zivarî زِڤارى *f.* **(;-yê).** poverty, indigence, destitution: •**Îro em di *zivarîyê* de ne, malên me ji destên me hatin[e] standin** (H v. 1, 83-84 [1932, 1:4]) Today we are in *poverty*, our homes have been taken from us [lit. 'from our hands']. {also: zîvarî (IFb/GF/BF/CS)} {syn: feqîrî; sêfîlî; xizanî} [H/K/ZF/Wkt//IFb/GF/BF/CS]

zivêr زِڤێر *adj.* [+ **ji**] sick and tired (of), fed up (with): **-zivêr bûn** (ZF/FS) to be or get sick and tired of, be fed up with {syn: k'erixîn}: •**Ev ga *ji* xwediyê xwe *zivêr bûye*** (ZZ-6, 127) This ox has gotten fed up with his owner. [ZZ/ZF/FS]

zivil زِڤِل (IFb) = dung; garbage. See **zibil**.

ziving زِڤِنگ *f.* **(-a;-ê).** inhabitable cave used as winter quarters; *occurs in several place names, e.g.,* **Zivinga Bohtan**, **Zivinga Babizbinya**, **Zivinga Tamika**: •**Şivanî pez bi şevê bir di *zivingê* ve** (FS) The shepherd took the sheep into the cave at night. {also: zîving (IFb-2); <ziving> زڤنگ (HH)} [Ah/A/IFb/HH/GF/BF/FS] <mix̄are; şkeft>

zivir زِڤِر *adj.* harsh, rough, coarse: •**Ev bere *zivr* e**

(FS) This rock is *rough*. {also: zivr (K/GF); [ziwir] زڤر (JJ); <zivir> زڤر (HH)} {syn: gir I[2]} Cf. P zebr زبر; Sor zibr زبر = 'rough (≠smooth), coarse, harsh' [Bw/A/B/JJ/HH/OK/FS/BF/ZF3//K/GF/Dh/Zeb]

zivir̄andin زڤِراندِن *vt.* **(-zivir̄în-).** 1) {syn: ç'erixandin} to turn *(vt.)*, cause to turn, cause to go around: **•Wî hesp li hawîr meydanê *zivir̄and*** (FS) He *had* the horse *go/take a turn* around the square; 2) {syn: veger̄-andin} to bring back, cause to return; to give back: **•Wî Behrem li nîva rêkê *zivir̄and*** (FS) He *brought* B. *back* half way; 3) to answer *(orally)*; in singing songs while dancing at a wedding, for a second singer (or singers) to answer the main singer by repeating the verse sung by the latter [T çevirmek] (Ag). {also: zîvirandin (GF/TF); [ziwirandin] زڤراندين (JJ); <zivirandin زڤراندن (dizivirîne) (دزڤرينه)> (HH)} [Ag/F/K/JB3/IFb/B/JJ/HH/JB1-A/BF/FS//GF/TF] <zivir̄în>

zivir̄ek زڤِرەك (FS) = whirlpool. See **zivir̄ok**.

zivir̄ik زڤِرك (Zeb) = whirlpool. See **zivir̄ok**.

zivir̄în زڤِرين *vi.* **(-zivir̄- / -zvir̄-).** 1) to turn (around) *(vi.)*, revolve, spin, whirl: **•Derwêş li dor xwe *dizivir̄in*** (Wkt) Dervishes *spin*, or, *whirl* **•Kalê *dizvir̄e* ser milê xwe, divê ...** (Dz) The old man *turns* over his shoulder and says ... ; 2) {syn: fetilîn [1]; vegerîn} to return, come or go back: **•Ew duhu *zivir̄î*** (B) He *came back* yesterday **•Ew ḧeta Qersê çû û *zivir̄î*** (FS) He went as far as Kars and *came back/turned back* **•Êmo ji bêrîyê *zivirî*** (AB) Emo *returned* from the sheepfold **•Piştî 15 salên li Ewropayê, *zivir̄î* Kurdistanê** (Wkt) After 15 years in Europe, s/he *returned to* Kurdistan; **-li xwe zivir̄în** (FS/Wkt) to repent {syn: t'obe kirin}: **•Ew *li xwe zivir̄î*** (FS) S/he *repented* **•Heya ez *li xwe zivirîm*, min hew dît ku zarokên min ji dest min çûn jî** (Wkt) By the time I *repented*, I realized that I had lost my children as well. {also: zîvirîn (KS); [ziwirin] زڤرين (JJ); <zivirîn زڤرين (dizivirî) (دزڤرى)> (HH)} [Pok. II. u̯ert- 1156.] 'to turn': Skt √vṛt [vártate]; Av varət- = 'to turn (vi.)'; Sgd zwart- (< *preverb* uz- = 'up' + wart-); cf. also Lat vertere; Rus vërt- вёрт-/vorot- ворот- [F/K/JB3/IFb/B/JJ/HH/JB1-A&S//KS/GF/TF/ZF3/BF/Wkt]

zivirk زڤِرك, m. (OK) = whirlpool. See **zivir̄ok**.

zivir̄ok زڤِرۆك *f.* **(-a;-ê).** 1) {syn: gerînek; *gêjik (IFb)} whirlpool, vortex, eddy: **•Ew ket di *zivir̄okê* da** (FS) S/he fell into (or, got caught up in) the whirlpool; **-zivir̄oka avê** (Zeb) do.; 2) {syn: mis'ar; vizik I; zîzok} spinning top (child's toy) (Hk/K); 3) spiral (Zeb). {also: zivir̄ek (FS-2); zivir̄ik (Zeb-2); zivirk, m. (OK); zivrok (IFb-2)} [Zeb/Dh/K/IFb/B/FS//OK]

zivistan زِڤِستان/**zivisṯan** زِڤِسطان [FS] *f.* **(-a;-ê).** winter: **•Çîrok, şevên *zivistanê* xweş derbaz dikin** (AB) Tales make *winter* evenings pass nicely **•Li *zivisṯanê* befir û baran dibarin** (FS) In *the winter* it snows and rains ***•Zivistanan* xwe gîro neke, biharan xwe ter neke** (BF) Don't be late *in the winter*, don't get wet in the spring; **-zivistanê** (ZF3) in the winter. {also: zeystan; zistan (SK); [ziwistan] زڤستان (JJ)} [Pok. 2. ĝhei-:ĝhi- 425.] 'winter, snow' & [C. ĝhimo- (<ĝhi-mn-o- ?) 426.]: Skt hima- *n.* = 'frost, ice, snow' & héman = '(in) winter'; Av zəmaka- *m.* = 'winter storm' & [B. ĝh[i]i̯ōm, *gen.* ĝhi[e]mós/ghi̯omós 425.] zaiian- *m.* /zyå *f.* = 'winter'; P zamestān زمستان; Sor zistan زِستان/zemsan زەمسان/zusan زوسان [Sinne]; Za zimistan *m.* (Todd); Hau zimsan *m.* (M4); cf. also Arm jmeṛ ձմեռ; Lat hiems, hiemis *f.*; Gr cheimōn χειμών *m.*; Rus zima zima [F/K/A/JB3/IFb/B/JJ/GF/TF/OK/FS/BF//SK] <berf; çelê; serma; şilop'e>

zivr زڤر (K/GF) = coarse. See **zivir**.

zivrok زڤرۆك (IFb) = whirlpool. See **zivir̄ok**.

zivt زڤت (ZZ-7) = tar, pitch. See **zift**.

ziwa زِوا *adj.* dry *(of living things, e.g., earth, hair, lips, and clothing; whereas **ḧişk** [qv.] is dry of inanimate things)* {≠şil I}: **•cilkên *ziha*** (FS) *dry* clothes **•xwelîya *zuhya*** (B) *dry* earth; **-ziwa bûn** (IFb) to dry up, go or get dry *(vi.)*: **•'Erd *ziwa* dibe** (Qzl) The ground *dries up* **•Ji tîhna qirika min êdî *ziwa bûbû*** (LM, 5) My throat *had gone dry* from thirst **•Lêvên min ji tînan *ziwa bûn*** (AB) My lips *became dry* from thirst **•Por *ziwa* dibe** (Qzl) Hair *gets dry*; **-ziwa kirin** (IFb) to dry, dry up, dry off *(vt.)*: **•Min hinek av li ruyê xwe kir, bi xawlîyê ser çavê xwe *zuha kir* şûn de** (LC, 41) I splashed some water on my face, then *dried* it with a towel afterward. {also: zaha (Ag); ziha I (Z-1/FS); zihya; zîya I (K-2); zuha (GF-2/BF/FS-2); zuhya (B); zuwa (K-2); zwa (A); [zouwa زوڤا/zouva زوا/zouha زها] (JJ)} <proto Ir *zu-ta- (*zaw-) (A&L IV,2 [p.84]): Parth wi-zaw- = 'to fade, wither, droop'; Za zwa (Todd) {ziwayî; zwayî; [zouvài زواى/zouwaï زوڤاى] (JJ)} [AB/K/JB3/IFb/GF/TF//A//BF//B//JJ//Ag//Z-1/FS] <ḧişk>

ziwac زِواج (Sw) = marriage. See **zewac**.

ziwayî زِوایـــــی *f.* **(-ya;-yê).** dryness, aridity, drought: **•Roj bi roj bi zêdebûna bendavan ve ava Erez kêm dibe û deşta Îdirê ber bi *ziwayîyê* diçe** (tirşik.net:Erez 10.vi.2014) With the increase in dams, day by day the water of the Araz River is decreasing and the plain of Îdir [Iğdır] is drying up [lit. 'going towards *dryness*'] ***•Zuhayîya* di herêmê de ya herî xirab e di 60 salan de** (sverigesradio.se 31.8.2011) *Drought* in the region is the worst it has been in 60 years. {also: zuhayî (BF/Wkt); zwayî (A); [zouvài زوای/zouwaï زوڤـای] (JJ)} [A//TF/ZF3//JJ//BF/Wkt] <bêavî; bêbaranî; ḧişkî; ziwa>

zixrik زِخرِك (IFb) = pebble. See **zuẍr**.

zixt زخـت *f./m.(FS)* **().** a nail at the end of an oxgoad: **•Misasa cot, alîyekî wî bizmarek e ku dibêjnê *zixt*, alîyê din hesinekî serî pan--labût** (Qzl) An oxgoad has a nail on one end, called "*zixt*," and the other end has a flat piece of metal--"*labût*"; **-zixt lê xistin** (Qzl)/~ **lê dan** (FS) to goad, prod: **•Wî *zixt li* hêstirê *da* ku xweş biçit** (FS) He *goaded* the mule so that it would speed up [lit. 'go fast']. {also: zext II (K[s]/A/IFb-2/HH/GF-2/FJ-2/ZF3/FS-2/Wkt)} [Qzl/IFb/GF/FJ/FS//K(s)/A/HH/ZF3] <labût; misas>

zixur زِخور (IFb/ZF/Wkt) = mountain pass. See **zuxir**.

ziya زِیا (FJ) = dragon. See **zîha**.

ziyan زِیـــــان (A/JB3/IFb/HH/GF/ZF) = damage. See **zîyan**.

ziyaret زِیـــــــــارەت (IFb/JB1-A/SK/GF) = shrine; pilgrimage. See **zîyaret**.

zî I زی *f.* **(-ya;).** animal's uterus or vagina: **-zîya mihê** (FS) ewe's uterus. {also: zih (ZF3); zîh (A/IFb)} [Qzl/FS//A/IFb//ZF3]

zî II زی (GF/FS) = visit by a married daughter to her father's house. See **zeyîtî**.

zîan زیئان (F) = damage. See **zîyan**.

zîh زیه (A/IFb) = cow's uterus. See **zî**.

zîha زیـهـا *m.* **(-yê;).** dragon, serpent: ***•Zihakî* mara heye, di devê kanîya me de ye** (FS) There is a *serpent* [lit. 'a serpent of snakes'], at the mouth of our spring. {also: êzya (M-Ak); ziha II (A/FS); zihar (IFb); ziya (FJ); zîya II (K/B); [ziia] زیا (JJ)} [Qzl//A/FS//IFb//FJ//K/B/JJ//M-Ak] <mar>

zîl زیـل *m.(K/Frq)/f.(B/ZF/Lwj/FS)* **(-ê/-a; /-ê).** young shoot, bud, sprout (bot.): **•Weke *zîleke* giyayê diheşîne [=giyayêd heşîn e]** (Lwj, #7, 35) like *a shoot of* a plant which has become green: **-zîla pîvazê** (Wkt) onion sprout; **-zîl dan** (A/K/FJ/Kmc/ZF)/~ **dayîn** (B) to sprout (of plants): **•Pîvazan *zîl da*** (ZF3) The onions sprouted. {also: <zîl> زیـــــــل (HH)} {syn: aj; bişkoj; gupik III; terh} [Lwj/K/A/B/IFb/FJ/TF/GF/HH/Frq/FS/ZF3]

zîlik زیـلِـك *f.* **(-a;-ê).** 1) {syn: gilik; tîtilk} clitoris; 2) vagina, particularly internal parts (Msr). {also: <zîlik> زیلك (HH)} [Msr/A/IFb/HH/ZF3/BF/FS] <quz>

zîn I زین *m.* **(-ê;).** saddle: **-zîn kirin** (B/TF) to saddle [up]; **-zînê 'erebî** (B) Arab saddle; **-zînê pişta ç'êlê** (Zeb)/**Zînê li çêlê kirî** (BF) *expression describing two things that clash or do not fit well together* [lit. 'saddle (on) the back of a cow']; **-zînê r̄omê** (B/JB1-A) Turkish saddle. {also: zehn; zên II (L); zihin (L-2); [zin] زیـــــن (JJ); <zîn> زیـــــن (HH)} Mid P zēn (M3); P zīn زین; Sor zîn زین; Za zîn *m.* (Todd) [L//AB/F/K/A/JB3/IFb/B/JJ/HH/(JB1-A)/GF/TF/FS/BF/ZF3/Wkt] <kurtan>

Zîn II زیـــــن *f.* **(-a;-ê).** Zin, the heroine of the Kurdish romance known as Mem û Zîn (or Memê Alan). {also: Zînê} [Z-1/EP-7/HM/A/IF]

zînakar زیناکار (IFb/OK) = adulterer. See **zinêk'ar**.

zîndan زیـنـدان (zîndên) (K/B/IFb) = prison, dungeon. See **zindan**.

zîndû زیندوو (K[s]) = alive. See **zêndî**.

Zînê زیـنـێ = heroine of the romance Mem û Zîn (or Memê Alan). See **Zîn II**.

zînker زیـنـكـەر *m.* **().** saddler, saddlemaker. {also: [zīnčī] زیـنـچـی (JJ)} {syn: ser̄ac} Cf. P zīnkar زینکر; Sor zîndirû زیندِروو [EP-7/A/JB3/IFb/GF/ZF3/Wkt//JJ]

zîpik I زیـــپِـك *f.* **(-a;-ê).** hail (precipitation): **•Ber baranê r̄evîm, bin *zîpikê* ketim** (Dz-#81) I ran from the rain, I landed under *the hail [prv.]* ***•Zîpik* bêtir bihar û havînan dibare** (Wkp) *Hail* falls mostly in the spring and summer; **-zîpikê xudanê** (B) beads of perspiration. {also: [zipik] زیپك (JJ); <zîpik> زیپك (HH)} {syn: gijlok; teyrok} [F/K/A/IFb/B/JJ/HH/GF/Wn/ZF3/Wkt] <baran; berf; savarok>

zîpik II زیپك (GF/FS/BF) = pimple. See **zipik**.

zîq زیـق *adj.* wide-eyed; staring, gazing, wide open *(of eyes)*; intent, fixed, penetrating *(look)*: **•çavên *zîq*** (BF) *wide* eyes; **-çavê xwe zîq kirin** (Kmc)/**zîq lê nêrîn** (FS) to stare at s.o.: **•K. Mistê hema *ziloqbû* û li Meyrê niherî** (ZZ-5, 78) K.M. *stared* at Meyrê **•Wî *zîq li* tirimbêla Azadî *nêrî*** (FS) He *stared straight at* Azad's car **•Ziq li xweha xwe niherî** (KS, 8) He stared straight at his sister.

{also: ziloq (ZF/ZZ); ziq (KS/ZF3-2); zoq (K-2/IFb-2/FJ/GF/FD/Wkt-2); zûq (Wkt-2); zwîq (Wkt-2)} {syn: beloq} Sor zeq زەق = 'staring, gazing, wide open (of eyes)' [KS//K/B/IFb/ZF3/FS/CS]

zîqûzer زیقووزەر (GF) = see saw. See **zîqûziř**.

zîqûziř زیـقـووزِڕ *f.* **(;-ê).** see saw, teeter-totter: •**Ez gelek ħez dikim xwe li *sîq-û-sir* bikim** (Qilaban) I really love to play [or, go up and down] on *the see saw*. {also: [siko-sir] (?); sîq-û-sir (Qilaban)/ sîqûsir (Şnx); zîqûzer (GF-2/FS)} {syn: qiřneqos; zirnazîq} [GF/FJ//FS//Qilaban/Şnx]

zîr زیر (FS) = hill. See **zûr**.

zîrç زیـرچ (A/ZF3)/zîřç' زیـڕچ (SC) = bird droppings. See **zirîç I**.

zîre زیره *f.* **(-ya;-yê).** cumin, bot. *Cuminum cyminum*: •**Erdîmeka niştîman ku bi zozanên bilind û *zîreya* xwe te nasîn** (Berxwedan 73 (1989 Şubat)) A region of the homeland which is known for its high summer pastures and for its *cumin*. Cf. Skt jiraṇa/ jīraṇa; P zīre زيره; Sor zîre زیره [Kmc-3/IFb/GF/TF/OK/ZF3/Wkp]

zîrek زیرەك (IFb) = smart; skillful; dynamic. See **jîr**.

zîro زیرۆ (TF) = leech. See **zûrî**.

zîstanî زیـسـتـانـی (Frq) = childbed, confinement. See **zêstanî**.

zîtik زیتِك (RZ/SS) = kicking (of donkeys). See **tîzik**.

zîtirk زیتِرك (FJ) = kicking (of donkeys). See **tîzik**.

zîtok زیتۆك (CS) = kicking (of donkeys). See **tîzik**.

zîv زیــــــڤ *m.* **(-ê;-î).** silver: •**Kursîk li cem hakim heye, *zîv* e û yek zêr e** (L) There is a chair at the prince's [court], it is *silver*, and there is a gold one •**Rê û rêbazên bidestxistina zêr û *zîvê* ku aboriya welatan tevlihev dike** (parzemin.com 12.vi.2015) The methods of acquiring gold and *silver*, which disturbs the economy of countries. {also: zîw (SK); [ziw] زیـڤ (JJ); <zîv> زیـڤ (HH)} Cf. Mid P asēm (M3) < Gr a-sēmon [argyrion] ασημον [αργυριον] = 'unmarked bullion, uncoined [silver]'; P sīm سيم; Sor zêw زێو/zîw زیو; Za sîm *m.* (Todd); Hau zîw *m.* (M4) [L/F/K/A/JB3/IFb/B/JJ/HH/GF/TF/ZF3/BF/Wkt//SK] <sîme; zêř>

zîvan زیـــڤـــان (Zeb/Hej) = darnel; couch grass. See **zîwan**.

zîvarî زیڤاری (IFb/GF/BF/CS) = poverty. See **zivarî**.

zîvger زیڤگەر (GF)/zîvgeř زیڤگەڕ (B/JJ) = silversmith. See **zîvker**.

zîvgir زیڤگِر (OK) = silversmith. See **zîvker**.

zîving زیڤنگ (IFb) = inhabited cave. See **ziving**.

zîvinker (FS) = silversmith. See **zîvker**.

zîvirandin زیڤِراندِن (GF/TF) = to return, give back. See **ziviřandin**.

zîvirîn زیڤِرین (KS/GF/TF) = to [re]turn. See **ziviřîn**.

zîvker زیـــڤـــکـــەر *m.* **(-ê;-î).** silversmith: •***Zîvkerî* ristikeka zîvî bo Rewşê çêkir** (FS) *The silversmith* made a silver necklace for R. {also: zîvger (GF-2)/zîvgeř (B); zîvgir (OK-2); zîvinker (FS-2); zîvkir (FK-eb-2); [ziw-ger] زیـڤـگـر (JJ); <zîvker> زیـڤـکـر (HH)} [FK-2//K/A/IFb/HH/GF/TF/OK/BF/ZF3/FS//B/JJ]

zîvkir زیڤکِر (FK-eb-2) = silversmith. See **zîvker**.

zîw زیو (SK) = silver. See **zîv**.

zîwan زیـــوان *f.* **(-a;-ê).** *type of weed which grows in wheat and barley fields*: 1) darnel, rye grass, bot. *Lolium temulentum* [T karaçayır, delice]; 2) {syn: firîzî} quack grass, couch grass, bot. *Agropyron repens* [T ayrık otu] (Qzl): •**Hêvî dikim ku genim biçînin û li şûna wî--*zîwana reş* hilînin** (Qzl) I hope they will sow wheat and reap *black couch grass* instead *[a curse]*. {also: zîvan (Zeb); [zivan] زوان (JJ); <zîwan> زیـــوان (HH); <zîvan زیڤان/zîwan زیوان> (Hej)} < Ar zu'ān زؤان; Sor zîwan زیوان [Zeb/Hej//Qzl/K/IFb/B/JJ/HH/GF/TF/OK/AA/G]

zîx I زیـخ *adj.* 1) {syn: 'aqil; aqiljîr; aqilmend; aqiltîj; bi zihn} smart, clever, intelligent, skillful: •**Behrem seydayekê *zîx* e** (FS) B. is a *clever* teacher •**Kovan lawekê *zîxe*, li xandingehê** (BF) K. is a *smart* boy, in school; 2) {syn: aza I[3]; bizirav; camêr; delîr} brave, courageous (K[s]/Hej); 3) {syn: zexm I} tough, sturdy, hale and hearty (IFb). {also: <zîx> زیخ (Hej)} [Zeb/K(s)/IFb/GF/Hej/FS/BF/Wkt]

zîx II زیخ (A) = sand. See **xîz**.

zîya I زییا (K) = dry. See **ziwa**.

zîya II زییا (K/B/JJ) = dragon. See **zîha**.

zîyan زیـــیـــان *f.* **(-a;-ê).** 1) {syn: xesar; zirar} harm, damage, injury: -**ziyan dan/gihandin** (ZF) /**kirin** (IFb) to damage, hurt, harm: •**Ezê usa bikim, wekî *zîanê bidim* mêşê** (Dz) I will act in such a way as *to bring harm to* the forest •**Ne min teřa go, *zîyanê mede* mêşe** (Dz) Didn't I tell you *not to harm* the forest?; -**ziyan gihîştin** (ZF) to be harmed, injured [lit. 'for harm to reach (me, you, etc.)']: •**Temoyê xwelîser heta niha *ti ziyana wî negihîştiye me*** (DBgb, 48) Up till now *we have not been harmed* by poor Temo; 2) loss. {also: ziyan (A-2/JB3/IFb/HH/GF/ZF); zîan (F); [ziian] زیـــان (JJ); <ziyan> زیـان (HH)} Cf. P ziyān زيان; Sor ziyan زِيان [Dz/K/A/B/JJ/TF//F//JB3/IFb/HH/GF/ZF]

zîyaret زيارەت *f./m.(SK[1])* **(-a/ ;-ê/).** 1) shrine, holy place, place of pilgrimage or worship: **•*Zyaretek* bi navê Ardawidê hebû ... li ber wê zyaretê qîzkek dima** (EP-7) There was *a shrine* called Ardawid ... A girl stayed (=lived) at this shrine; 2) visit, pilgrimage (SK): **-ziyaret[a] *fk-ê* kirin** (SK) to make a pilgrimage, pay homage to s.o.; 3) *used in oaths, curses, etc.* {also: ziyaret (IFb/JB1-A/SK/GF); zyaret (EP-7); [ziiaret] زيـــــــارت (JJ); <ziyaret> زيـــارت (HH)} < Ar ziyārah زيـــارة = 'visit'; Sor ziyaret زِيـارەت [EP-7//IFb/JB1-A/HH/SK/GF//K/B/JJ] <mergeh>

zîz I زيـــز *adj. describes various qualities of sound, voice, etc.*: 1) tender, gentle, delicate, sensitive; sad: **•Li bilûra xwe dida û stranine *zîz* û melûl … dileyistin** (Dz-anec #22) He would blow his flute and play *gentle* and sad songs; 2) {syn: ḧişk[3]} shrill, piercing; sharp, harsh (B); 3) shaky, tremulous (A/IFb). {also: [ziz] ضـيـز (JJ); <zîz> زيـــــز (HH)} [Dz/K/A/IFb/B/JJ/HH/SK/GF/ZF3] <deng; dilzîz>

zîz II زيـــــز *adj.* angry, annoyed, disgruntled: **-zîz bûn** (Bw/BF) to go home to mother (of angry married women): **•Dibêjin paşî çend salan carekî** [sic] **Perî Xan *zîz bo*, ji qelatê der-kewt, r̄êka zînî girt ko biçît e mala babê xo** (SK 42:414) They say that once, some years later, Pari Khan *was disgruntled* and left the fort and took the road over the pass to return to her father's home. {syn: sil} Sor zîz زيز [Bw/K(s)/A/IFb/SK/OK/BF/FS]

zîz III زيـــز *adj.* spinning (like a top): **-zîz bûn** (LM/FS/RZ) to spin around like a top, spin on its axis {syn: çerx bûn; zivir̄în}: **•Carê rabû pê û *li dora xwe zîz bû.* Bi *zîzbûnê* re, him le erebana xwe dixist, ji alîkî de jî qesîde digot … Tu dibînî çawa *li dora xwe zîz dibe*, eynî wekî perwanê ye** (LM, 6) So he got up and *spun around.* While *spinning around,* he beat on his tambourine, and likewise he recited a poem … Do you see the way *he's spinning around,* just like a fan **•Mis'ar *zîz bû*** (FS) The top *spun around.* [LM/ZF3/FS/RZ] <zîzikandin>

zîzikandin زيـــزِكـــانــدِن *vt.* **(-zîzikîn-).** to twirl stg., whirl, spin, turn stg. around *(vt.)*: **•*Zîzikand*, ser telya xo *zîzikand*, ser her dih telyê xwe berê xwe *zîzikand*, ḧetta kû berê wî sohr bû weke xwînê** (HR-I 3:69) He *twirled* it, he *twirled* it on his finger, on all ten fingers he *twirled* his stone, until his stone was as red as blood. {syn: zivir̄andin} [HR-I/A/GF/FS] <zîz III>

zîzok زيـــزۆك *f.* **(-a;-ê).** spinning top: **•Sal û demsal wekî *zîzokê* dizîvirin û derbas dibin** (Wkt:Diyarname.com: R. War *Havîn*, vi.2007) The years and seasons pass on, spinning like *a top* **•Zar̄o bi *zîzokê* dileyzit** (FS) The child is playing with *the top.* {syn: mis'ar; vizik I; zivir̄ok} [GF/FS/Wkt]

zman زمان (JB3/IFb) = tongue; language. See **ziman.**

zmandrêj زمـــانــدرێژ (IFb) = talkative; impudent. See **zimandirêj.**

zmandrêjî زمـــــانـــــدرێـــــژى (IFb) = talkativeness; impudence. See **zimandirêjî.**

zo زۆ *m.(K/FS)/f.(B)* **(-yê/;).** 1) {syn: cot} pair, couple *(in counting cattle, etc.)*: **•Eto, bijimêre, pişt re nebêjî Xudo pez temam neanî, şanzdeh *zo* û ferek e** (W.Eşo. Sîber, 46) Count them, E., so that later you won't say that Kh. did not bring all the sheep, sixteen *pairs* and one single (32 + 1 =33 sheep) **•Bîst *zo* û ferek mî** (B) 20 *pairs* and one sheep (= 41 sheep) **•*Zoyê* kewa** (FS) *A pair of* partridges; **-zo bi zo** (K) two by two, in pairs; 2) {syn: cêwî} twin. Cf. Ar zawj زوج = 'couple, pair, spouse' [Mzg/K/B/IFb/ZF3/FS] <fer I>

zol زۆل *f.* **(-a;-ê).** stripe; strip *(lit. & fig.)*; long strip made of hide, thong: **•*zola* goştî** (FS) *strip of* meat. {also: [zūväl] زول (JJ); <zol> زول (HH)} Cf. Sor zoł زۆڵ [EP-7/K/IFb/B/HH/GF/ZF3/FS//JJ]

zom زۆم (GF/FS)/z̲om ظـــۆم (SK) = summer pastures; encampment. See **zome.**

zom•e زۆمـــــــــــە *f.* **(;•ê).** 1) {syn: şênî; war} camp, encampment; nomadic residence; group of tents: **•*Zoma* wan deh mal in** (FS) Their *encampment* is ten houses; 2) {syn: zozan [1]} summer pastures: **•*Zoma* gundê wan li serê çiyayî ye** (FS) *The summer pasture of* their village is on the mountaintop. {also: zom (GF/FS)/z̲om (SK); [zomé] زومـه (JJ)} Sor zome زۆمـە = 'group of tents'; Cf. NA zûmâ ܙܘܡܐ = 'a summer camp' (Maclean). See also W. F. Ainsworth."An Account of a Visit to the Chaldeans … in the Summer of 1840," *Journal of the Royal Geographical Society* 11, (1841), 33. [K/IFb/B/JJ//GF/FS/BF//SK] <'eşîr; kon; war>

zomp زۆمـــپ *m.* **(-ê;-î).** large hammer, mallet: **•Wî ber bi *zompî* şkand** (FS) He broke the rock with *a mallet.* {also: zonp (GF-2); <z̲onp> ظـونـپ (HH); <zomp زۆمـپ/zonp زۆنـپ> (Hej)} {syn: çilmêre

[2]} [Qrj/GF/FJ/Hej/ZF3/FS//HH] <ç'akûç; geřan II; mêk'ut; mirc>

zonp زۆنپ (GF/Hej)/z̲onp ظۆنپ (HH) = mallet. See **zomp**.

zoq زۆق (K-2/IFb/FJ/GF/FD/Wkt) = wide-eyed. See **zîq**.

zor I زۆر *f.* **(-a;-ê).** power, might, force; violence: -**bi darê zorê** (Bx) by force; -**bi zor be, bi xweşî be** (L) willy nilly, whether one wants to or not [bon gré, mal gré]; -**zora dijmin birin** (ZF) to defeat an enemy {syn: alt' kirin}: •**Ne em *zora wan dibin* û ne ew jî karin me bigirin** (L) We *can't defeat them*, nor can they catch us •**Piştî 35'an êdî yeko yeko mirov di nav porê xwe de rastî çend tayên sipî tê … Di destpêkê de yek-du ta bûn, min bi destan hildikişandin, yanê *min zora wan dibir*** (LC, 5) After age 35, one by one one finds some white hairs amid the hair on one's head … At first there were one or two hairs, I pulled them out by hand, i.e., I *was victorious over them* •**Yekê *zora şeşa bir*** (HR-II, 7:29, 6) One *defeated six*. {also: [zor] زور (JJ); <z̲or> ظور (HH)} {syn: birî I; ȟêl; hêz; qedûm [2]; qewat; t'aqet; zexm I [2]} Av zāvar- = 'power, strength, force'; Mid P zōr = 'power, strength' (M3); Sor zor زۆر = 'power'; Za zor = 'difficult' (Todd); Hau zor *m.* = 'force, power' (M4); also cf. T zor = 'difficult' [F/K/A/(JB3)/IFb/B/JJ/SK/GF/TF//HH/ZF] <t'undûtîjî>

zor II زۆر *adv.* 1) very, very much: •**Ew *zor* baş e** (FS) That is *very* good; 2) [*pr. mod.*] many, a lot of: •**Wî *zor* sêv kiřîn** (FS) He bought *a lot of* apples. {syn: gelek; p'iř II; ze'f} Sor zor زۆر [Bw/IFb/SK/OK/FS]

zorbe زۆربە (F/K/JJ) = bully. See **zurbe**.

zordar زۆردار *m.* **(-ê;).** despot, tyrant; dictator; oppressor: •**Li *zordarê* xwe nerî û kenî** (welateme.net:Leyla Qasim) She looked at her oppressor and laughed. Cf. P zūrdār زوردار = 'powerful, strong'; Sor zordar زۆردار = 'oppressive, tyrannous' [K/A/IFb/GF/TF/OK/FS/ZF3/BF/Wkt] <zirtek>

zordarî زۆرداری *f.* **(-ya;-yê).** despotism, tyranny; dictatorship; oppression: •**Kes ji *zordarîya* wî par[a]stî nema** (FS) No one was protected from his *tyranny*. [K/A/IFb/GF/TF/OK/FS/ZF3/BF/Wkt/FS]

zordest زۆردەست *adj.* imperious, commanding, in charge of [+ *ezafeh*]: •**Filan jin *zordesta* zelamê xwe ye** (FS) Such and such a woman is *in charge of* her husband •**hêzên *zordest*** (Ber) the *commanding* powers. {zordestî} [Ber/GF/FS/BF/ZF3/Wkt]

zordestî زۆردەستی *f.* **(-ya;-yê).** 1) power, might, authority, domination: •***Zordestîya* îngilîsan li Kurdistanê di sê dehsalîyên pêşin yên sedsala 19an da** (FB:Dermanê Zimanê Kurdî 11.iii.2016) *The domination of* the English in Kurdistan in the first 3 decades of the 19th century; 2) force, tyranny, oppression, abuse. [Ber/K/IFb/GF/BF/ZF3/Wkt]

zorne زۆرنە (JB1-S) = oboe-like reed instrument. See **zirne**.

zotik زۆتِك/**zot̲ik** زۆطِك [FS] *f.* **(-a;-ê).** anus, ass, backside, rear, butt: •**Piştî çend rojan çavekî min wek *zotka* mirîşkê sor bû** (Wkt:lotikxane.com iv.2009) After a few days one of my eyes turned as red as a chicken's ass. {also: zûtik (IFb-2); [zoutik] زوتك (JJ); <z̲otik> ظوتك (HH)} {syn: pind; poz II (Bw)} [Msr/A/IFb/JJ/ZF3/BF//HH//FS] <qûn>

zoxir زۆخِر (AD) = mountain pass. See **zuxir**.

zozan زۆزان *f./m.(ZF/ZZ)* **(-ê/-a; zozên/-ê).** 1) {syn: zome [3]} summer pasture {Cf. T yaylak}; cold land, such as Bitlis and Mount Mutkan, inhabited in the summer by people of the hot plains: •**Feřaşîn *zozaneka* bi nav û deng e** (FS) Ferashin is a famous *summer pasture*; 2) *woman's name*. {also: [zozan] زوزان (JJ); <zozan> زوزان (HH)} Cf. Mongol zuslan зуслан = 'herdman's summer camp'; Sor zozan زۆزان [J/K/A/JB3/IFb/B/JJ/HH/GF/ZF/FS] <havîn; zome>

zrêç زريچ, f. (JB3/IFb) = lead (metal) . See **zirêç**.

zuha زوها (GF/BF/FS) = dry. See **ziwa**.

zuhayî زوهایی (BF/Wkt) = dryness. See **ziwayî**.

zuhya زوهیا (B) = dry. See **ziwa**.

zulam زولام = (young) man. See **zilam**.

zurat زورات (IFb) = corn, maize. See **zuret I**.

zurbe زوربە *m.* **().** tyrant, bully, strongman, one who gets what he wants by using force: •**Ew *zurbe* hazirin me bikujin, bifetisînin** (Ba2-#2, 210) Those *tyrants* are ready to kill [and] strangle us. {also: zorbe (F/K/FS); [zorbe] زوربه (JJ); <z̲orbe> ظوربه (HH)} T zorba = 'bully, tyrant'; Sor zurbe زوربە = 'strong, powerful; majority' [Ba2/IFb/B//F/K/JJ/FS//HH]

zuret I زورەت *f.* **(;-ê).** corn, maize, bot. *Zea mays*. {also: zurat (IFb)} {syn: garis[ê stanbolî]; genimeşamî; genmok; gilgilê stembolê (Haz); lazût} < Ar d̲urah ذرة; Sor zuřat زوڕات [F/B//IFb]

zuřet II زوڕەت/**zuret II** زورەت [B/IFb] f. **(;-ê).**

offspring, descendants, progeny: **-bê zuřet man** (K) to remain childless, without offspring. {also: zuřiyet (SK); zûryet (B-2)} {syn: dol I; dûndan; zêdehî} <Ar ḏurrīyah ذرّيّة --> T zürriyet [K/IFb/B//SK] <bêzuřet>

zuřîyet زورییەت (SK) = offspring. See **zuřet II**.

zurna زورنا = oboe-like reed instrument. See **zirne**.

zuřne زوڕنە (B) = oboe-like reed instrument. See **zirne**.

zuřneçî زوڕنەچی (B) = zurna player. See **zirnabêj**.

zuwa زووا (K) = dry. See **ziwa**.

zuxir زوخِر *m./f.(AD/Wkt)* **(-ê/ ;).** narrow mountain pass: **•Li bin heman dargivîjê rûnişt û berê xwe da *zuxirê* navçeyê** (M.Dicle. Nara, 15) She sat down under the same hawthorn tree and gazed toward the *pass*. {also: zeqir (Wkt-2); ziqre (Wkt-2); zixur (IFb/ZF/Wkt); zoxir (AD)} [M.Dicle//IFb/ZF/Wkt//AD] <gelî II; neqeb; newal>

zuxre زوخره (GF) = pebble. See **zuẍr**.

zuxur زوخور (RF) = pebble. See **zuẍr**.

zuxurk زوخورك (GF) = pebble. See **zuẍr**.

zuẍr زوغر *m.* **(-ê;).** pebble, little stone; gravel: **•Kû kevir û k'ils, û zuẍrê xwe ḧemû hazir kirin, hê jinû dest bi çêkirna avaîyê dikin** (HR-I 1:30) When they have prepared their stones, limestone, and pebbles, they begin to build the house. {also: zixrik (IFb); zuxre (GF); zuxur (RF); zuxurk (GF-2); zuẍur (FS); zûxur (A); zûxûr (A-2); [zuγúr] زغر (JJ); <ziẍrik> زغرك (HH)} {syn: bixûr; xîç'ik} [HR-I//JJ/FS//GF//RF//A//IFb//HH] <ber III; heste; hêtûn; kevir; k'ils; xîz>

zuẍur زوغور (FS) = pebble. See **zuẍr**.

zû زوو *adj.* 1) {≠dereng} early: **•Azad *zû* hat** (FS) A. came early **•*Zû* binive** (BF) Go to bed *early*!; 2) {syn: bilez; xweş [4]; ≠hêdî} fast, quick, rapid: **•Ew ze'f *zû* xeber dide** (B) He speaks very *quickly*; **-zû-zû** (K/B)/**zûzûka** (B) very quickly; 3) [*adv.*] soon. {also: zûka (IF-2); [zou] زو (JJ); <zû> زو (HH)} Skt √jū/jav- = 'to hurry, be quick'; Av √jav- = do.; Mid P zūd = 'quick(ly)' (M3); P zūd زود = 'early; fast'; Sor zû زوو; Hau zû (M4) {zûkanî (IFb); zûtî (IFb); zûyetî (A); zû-zûtî (K)} [F/K/A/JB3/IFb/B/JJ/HH/SK/JB1-A&S/GF/BF/FS]

zûda زوودا *adj.* for or in a long time, in ages, in a while, for years, since a long time ago: **•Em *zûva* vira dijîn** (B) We've lived here *for a long time* **•Ew *zûda* hevaltîyê dikin** (B) They've been friends *for ages* **•*Zûda* ew li derveyî welat dimîne** (BF) He has been living abroad *for some time* **•*Zû de ye* me hev û du nedîtîye** (IFb) We haven't seen each other *in a while*, or, *in a long time*. {also: ji zûde (GF-2); zûde (IFb/GF/ZF3); zûva (B-2)} {syn: ji mêj ve} [K/B/AD/BF/FS//IFb/GF/ZF3]

zûde زوودە (IFb/GF/ZF3) = for a long time. See **zûda**.

zûkahî زووکاهی (Wkt) = rush, hurry. See **zûyetî**.

zûkanî زووکانی (IFb/ZF3) = rush, hurry. See **zûyetî**.

zûkatî زووکاتی (Wkt/ZF3) = rush, hurry. See **zûyetî**.

zûkayî زووکایی (Wkt/ZF3/FD) = rush, hurry. See **zûyetî**.

zûq زووق (Wkt) = wide-eyed. See **zîq**.

zûr زوور *m.* **(-ê;-î).** hill; hilly terrain: **•Pez li *zûrî* diçerî** (FS) The sheep were grazing on *the hillside* **•Zaxo sê se'ete teqrîben ji Mûsil dûr e ... dormandorê wê jî çya ne, *zûr* in--ewwil *zûr* in, paşî çya ne** (M-Zx #771) Zakho is about three hours from Mosul ... All round it there are mountains, *hills*--first there are *hills*, then mountains. {also: zîr (FS-2)} {syn: banî II; dîyar II; gir II; kuç'[3]; t'op III} [Slv/M-Zx/IFb/OK/FS]

zûrî زووری *f./m.(F/FS)* **(; /-yê).** leech, zool. *Hirudo medicinalis*. {also: tizûrig (IFb-2); zelû; zêrû (GF); zirî I (FS); zîro (GF-2/TF); [dizrouk دزروك/ zouri زوری/zelou زلو/zouloul زلول] (JJ); <zûrî> زوری (HH)} Mid P zalūg (M3); P zalū زلو/zālū زالو; Sor zerû زەروو ; W Arm dᵊzrug/E Arm tᵊzruk տզրուկ [F/K/A/IFb/B/JJ/HH//GF//TF//FS]

zûryet زوورەت (B) = offspring. See **zuřet II**.

zûtik زووتِك (IFb) = anus. See **zotik**.

zûtî زووتی (IF) = rush, hurry. See **zûyetî**.

zûva زووڤا (B) = for a long time. See **zûda**.

zûxur زووخور (A) = pebble. See **zuẍr**.

zûxûr زووخوور (A) = pebble. See **zuẍr**.

zûyetî زوویەتی *f.* **(-ya;).** rush, hurry: **•*Zûkanîya* te çiye?** (IFb) What is your *hurry*? {also: zûkahî (Wkt); zûkanî (IFb/ZF3); zûkatî (Wkt-2/ZF3-2); zûkayî (Wkt-2/ZF3-2/FD); zûtî (IFb); zû-zûtî (K)} [A//IFb/ZF3//Wkt//FD//K] <zû>

zû-zûtî زووزووتی (K) = rush, hurry. See **zûyetî**.

zwa زوا (A) = dry. See **ziwa**.

zwayî زوایی (A) = dryness. See **ziwayî**.

zwîq زویق (Wkt) = wide-eyed. See **zîq**.

zyaret زیارەت (EP-7) = shrine; pilgrimage. See **zîyaret**.

Made in United States
Orlando, FL
13 February 2023

29891941R00252